America's
Top-Rated Cities:
A Statistical Handbook

Volume 2

2021
Twenty-Eighth Edition

America's
Top-Rated Cities:
A Statistical Handbook

Volume 2: Western Region

A UNIVERSAL REFERENCE BOOK

Grey House
Publishing

Cover image: Las Vegas, Nevada

PRESIDENT: Richard Gottlieb
PUBLISHER: Leslie Mackenzie
EDITORIAL DIRECTOR: Laura Mars
SENIOR EDITOR: David Garoogian

RESEARCHER & WRITER: Jael Bridgemahon
PRODUCTION MANAGER: Kristen Hayes
MARKETING DIRECTOR: Jessica Moody

A Universal Reference Book
Grey House Publishing, Inc.
4919 Route 22
Amenia, NY 12501
518.789.8700 • Fax 845.373.6390
www.greyhouse.com
books@greyhouse.com

Twenty-eighth Edition
Printed in the USA

Publisher's Cataloging-in-Publication Data
(Prepared by The Donohue Group, Inc.)

America's top-rated cities. Vol. 2, Western region : a statistical handbook. — 1992-

   v. : ill. ; cm.
   Annual, 1995-
   Irregular, 1992-1993
   ISSN: 1082-7102

1. Cities and towns--Ratings--Western States--Statistics--Periodicals. 2. Cities and towns--Western States--Statistics--Periodicals. 3. Social indicators--Western States--Periodicals. 4. Quality of life--Western States--Statistics--Periodicals. 5. Western States--Social conditions--Statistics--Periodicals. I. Title: America's top rated cities. II. Title: Western region

HT123.5.S6 A44
307.76/0973/05   95644648

4-Volume Set	ISBN: 978-1-64265-821-7
Volume 1	ISBN: 978-1-64265-823-1
Volume 2	**ISBN: 978-1-64265-824-8**
Volume 3	ISBN: 978-1-64265-825-5
Volume 4	ISBN: 978-1-64265-826-2

Albuquerque, New Mexico

Anchorage, Alaska

Boise City, Idaho

Boulder, Colorado

Colorado Springs, Colorado

Fort Collins, Colorado

Denver, Colorado

Greeley, Colorado

Honolulu, Hawaii

Las Vegas, Nevada

Los Angeles, California

Phoenix, Arizona

Portland, Oregon

Provo, Utah

Reno, Nevada

Riverside, California

Appendixes

Appendixes

Introduction

This twenty-eighth edition of *America's Top-Rated Cities* is a concise, statistical, 4-volume work identifying America's top-rated cities with estimated populations of approximately 100,000 or more. It profiles 100 cities that have received high marks for business and living from prominent sources such as *Forbes, Fortune, U.S. News & World Report, The Brookings Institution, U.S. Conference of Mayors, The Wall Street Journal,* and *CNNMoney.*

Each volume covers a different region of the country—Southern, Western, Central, Eastern—and includes a detailed Table of Contents, City Chapters, Appendices, and Maps. Each city chapter incorporates information from hundreds of resources to create the following major sections:
- **Background**—lively narrative of significant, up-to-date news for both businesses and residents. These combine historical facts with current developments, "known-for" annual events, and climate data.
- **Rankings**—fun-to-read, bulleted survey results from over 230 books, magazines, and online articles, ranging from general (Great Places to Live), to specific (Friendliest Cities), and everything in between.
- **Statistical Tables**—87 tables and detailed topics that offer an unparalleled view of each city's Business and Living Environments. They are carefully organized with data that is easy to read and understand.
- **Appendices**—five in all, appearing at the end of each volume. These range from listings of Metropolitan Statistical Areas to Comparative Statistics for all 100 cities.

This new edition of *America's Top-Rated Cities* includes cities that not only surveyed well, but ranked highest using our unique weighting system. We looked at violent crime, property crime, population growth, median household income, housing affordability, poverty, educational attainment, and unemployment. You'll find that we have included several American cities despite less-than-stellar numbers. New York, Los Angeles, and Miami remain world-class cities despite challenges faced by many large urban centers. Part of the criteria, in most cases, is that it be the "primary" city in a given metropolitan area. For example, if the metro area is Raleigh-Cary, NC, we would consider Raleigh, not Cary. This allows for a more equitable core city comparison. In general, the core city of a metro area is defined as having substantial influence on neighboring cities. A final consideration is location—we strive to include as many states in the country as possible.

New to this edition are:
Volume 1 - Memphis, TN
Volume 2 - Riverside, CA
Volume 4 - Cincnnati, OH

Praise for previous editions:

> "...[ATRC] has...proven its worth to a wide audience...from businesspeople and corporations planning to launch, relocate, or expand their operations to market researchers, real estate professionals, urban planners, job-seekers, students...interested in...reliable, attractively presented statistical information about larger U.S. cities."
> —ARBA

> "...For individuals or businesses looking to relocate, this resource conveniently reports rankings from more than 300 sources for the top 100 US cities. Recommended..."
> —Choice

> "...While patrons are becoming increasingly comfortable locating statistical data online, there is still something to be said for the ease associated with such a compendium of otherwise scattered data. A well-organized and appropriate update..."
> —Library Journal

BACKGROUND
Each city begins with an informative Background that combines history with current events. These narratives often reflect changes that have occurred during the past year, and touch on the city's environment, politics, employment, cultural offerings, and climate, and include interesting trivia. For example: Peregrine Falcons were rehabilitated and released into the wild from Boise City's World Center for Birds of Prey; Grand Rapids was the first city to introduce fluoride into its drinking water in 1945; and Thomas Alva Edison discovered the phonograph and the light bulb in the city whose name was changed in 1954 from Raritan Township to Edison in his honor. This year, many backgrounds inclue an interesting fact about how the city is reacting to the COVID-19 pandemic.

RANKINGS

This section has rankings from a possible 233 books, articles, and reports. For easy reference, these Rankings are categorized into 16 topics including Business/Finance, Dating/Romance, and Health/Fitness.

The Rankings are presented in an easy-to-read, bulleted format and include results from both annual surveys and one-shot studies. **Fastest-Growing Economies . . . Best Drivers . . . Most Well-Read . . . Most Wired . . . Healthiest for Women . . . Best for Minority Entrepreneurs . . . Safest . . . Best to Retire . . . Most Polite . . . Best for Moviemakers . . . Most Frugal . . . Best for Bikes . . . Most Cultured . . . Least Stressful . . . Best for Families . . . Most Romantic . . . Most Charitable . . . Best for Telecommuters . . . Best for Singles . . . Nerdiest . . . Fittest . . . Best for Dogs . . . Most Tattooed . . . Best for Wheelchair Users**, and more. A number of these relate specifically to COVID-19.

Sources for these Rankings include both well-known magazines and other media, including *Forbes, Fortune, USA Today, Condé Nast Traveler, Gallup, Kiplinger's Personal Finance, Men's Journal,* and *Travel + Leisure,* as well as *Asthma & Allergy Foundation of America, American Lung Association, League of American Bicyclists, The Advocate, National Civic League, National Alliance to End Homelessness, MovieMaker Magazine, National Insurance Crime Bureau, Center for Digital Government, National Association of Home Builders,* and the *Milken Institute.*

Rankings cover a variety of geographic areas; see Appendix B for full geographic definitions.

STATISTICAL TABLES

Each city chapter includes a possible 87 tables and detailed topics—44 in Business and 43 in Living. Over 90% of statistical data has been updated.

Business Environment includes hard facts and figures on 8 major categories, including Demographics, Income, Economy, Employment, and Taxes. *Living Environment* includes 11 major categories, such as Cost of Living, Housing, Health, Education, Safety, and Climate.

To compile the Statistical Tables, editors have again turned to a wide range of sources, some well known, such as the *U.S. Census Bureau, U.S. Environmental Protection Agency, Bureau of Labor Statistics, Centers for Disease Control and Prevention,* and the *Federal Bureau of Investigation,* plus others like *The Council for Community and Economic Research, Texas A&M Transportation Institute,* and *Federation of Tax Administrators.*

APPENDICES: Data for all cities appear in all volumes.
- **Appendix A**—*Comparative Statistics*
- **Appendix B**—*Metropolitan Area Definitions*
- **Appendix C**—*Government Type and County*
- **Appendix D**—*Chambers of Commerce and Economic Development Organizations*
- **Appendix E**—*State Departments of Labor and Employment*

Material provided by public and private agencies and organizations was supplemented by original research, numerous library sources and Internet sites. *America's Top-Rated Cities, 2021,* is designed for a wide range of readers: private individuals considering relocating a residence or business; professionals considering expanding their businesses or changing careers; corporations considering relocating, opening up additional offices or creating new divisions; government agencies; general and market researchers; real estate consultants; human resource personnel; urban planners; investors; and urban government students.

Customers who purchase the four-volume set receive free online access to *America's Top-Rated Cities* allowing them to download city reports and sort and rank by 50-plus data points.

AMERICA'S TOP-RATED CITIES

STATE

- CBSA: Core Based Statistical Area
- Top Rated City
- East Region
- Central Region
- West Region
- South Region

©Larry Mandelin 2021

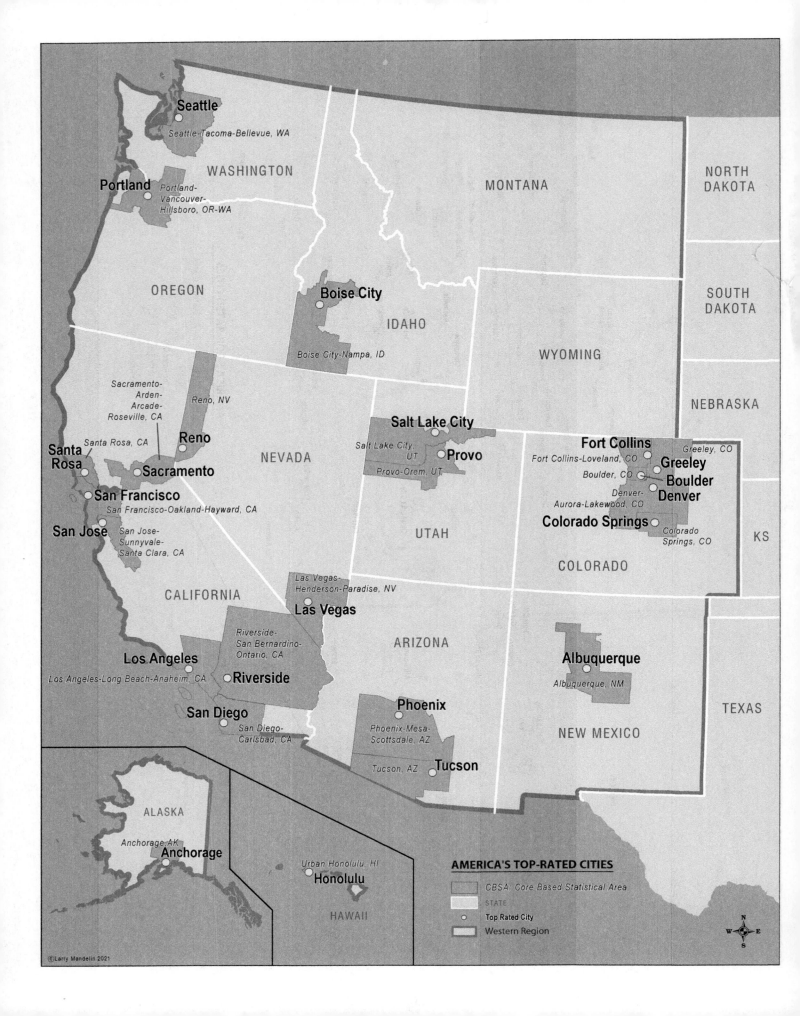

Seattle
Seattle-Tacoma-Bellevue, WA

WASHINGTON

Portland
Portland-Vancouver-Hillsboro, OR-WA

OREGON

MONTANA

NORTH DAKOTA

SOUTH DAKOTA

Boise City
Boise City-Nampa, ID

IDAHO

WYOMING

NEBRASKA

Sacramento-Arden-Arcade-Roseville, CA

Reno, NV

Reno

Santa Rosa, CA

Santa Rosa

NEVADA

Sacramento

Salt Lake City
Salt Lake City, UT

Provo
Provo-Orem, UT

Fort Collins
Fort Collins-Loveland, CO

Greeley, CO

Greeley

Boulder, CO

Boulder

Denver

Denver-Aurora-Lakewood, CO

Colorado Springs
Colorado Springs, CO

KS

San Francisco
San Francisco-Oakland-Hayward, CA

San Jose
San Jose-Sunnyvale-Santa Clara, CA

UTAH

COLORADO

Las Vegas-Henderson-Paradise, NV

CALIFORNIA

Las Vegas

Riverside-San Bernardino-Ontario, CA

Los Angeles
Los Angeles-Long Beach-Anaheim, CA

Riverside

ARIZONA

Albuquerque
Albuquerque, NM

TEXAS

San Diego
San Diego-Carlsbad, CA

Phoenix
Phoenix-Mesa-Scottsdale, AZ

Tucson, AZ **Tucson**

NEW MEXICO

ALASKA

Anchorage, AK

Anchorage

Urban Honolulu, HI

Honolulu

HAWAII

© Larry Mandelin 2021

AMERICA'S TOP-RATED CITIES

CBSA: Core Based Statistical Area

STATE

○ Top Rated City

Western Region

N
W E
S

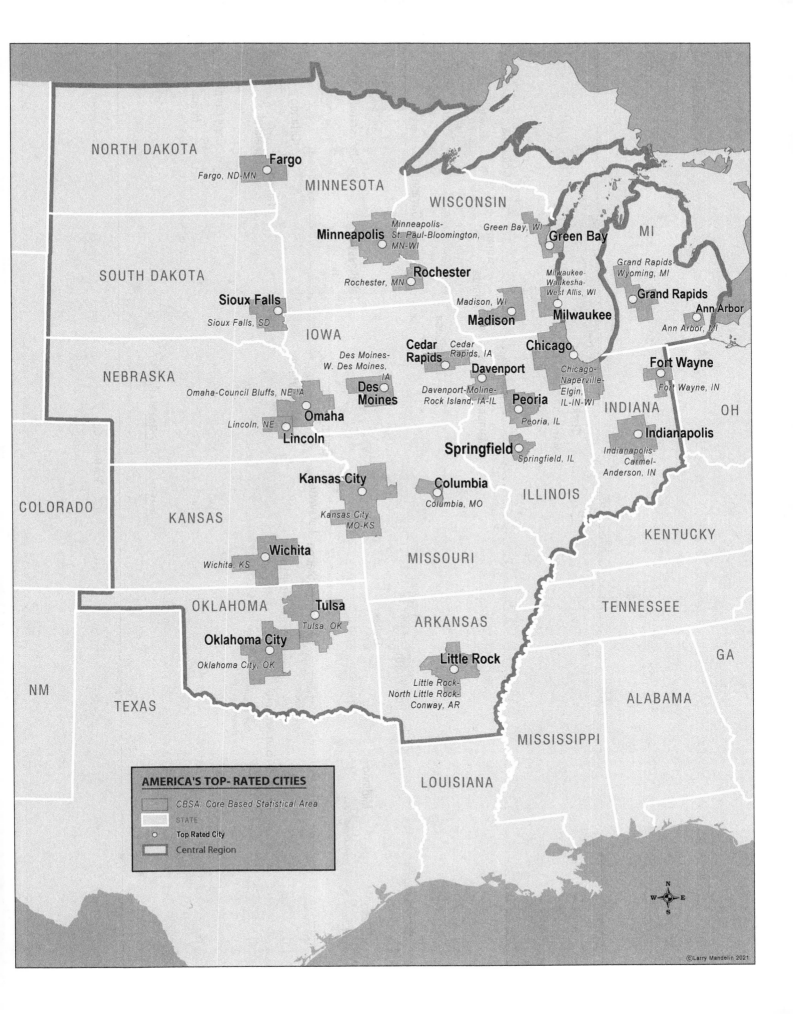

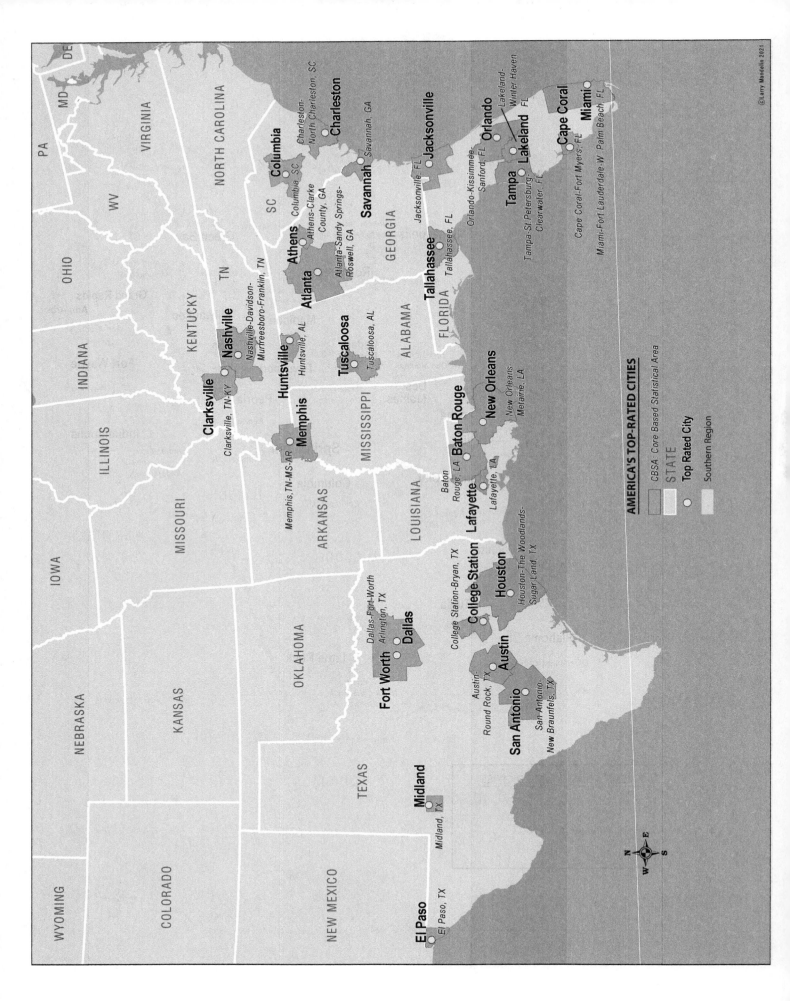

AMERICA'S TOP-RATED CITIES

CBSA: Core Based Statistical Area

STATE

○ Top Rated City

Southern Region

©Larry Mandelin 2021

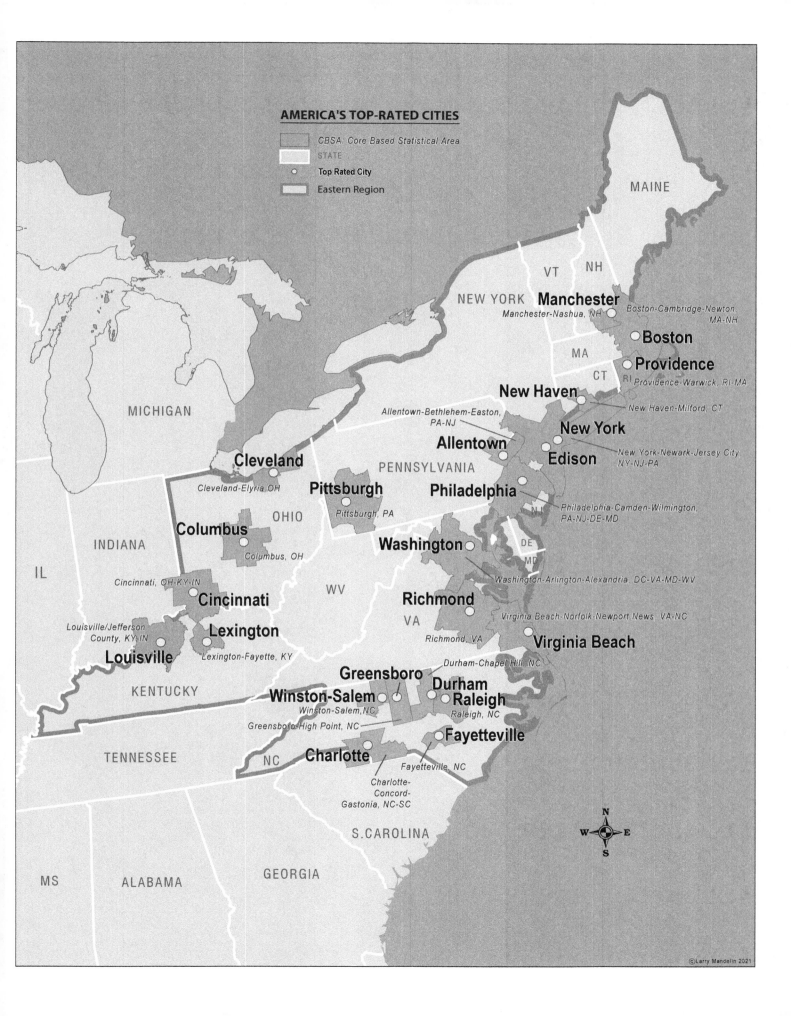

AMERICA'S TOP-RATED CITIES

CBSA: Core Based Statistical Area
STATE
○ Top Rated City
Eastern Region

MAINE

VT   NH

NEW YORK   **Manchester**
Manchester-Nashua, NH   ○   Boston-Cambridge-Newton, MA-NH

○ **Boston**

MA

CT   ○ **Providence**
RI   Providence-Warwick, RI-MA

New Haven ○   New Haven-Milford, CT

Allentown-Bethlehem-Easton,
PA-NJ   **New York**

Cleveland ○   **Allentown** ○   **Edison**   New York-Newark-Jersey City,
NY-NJ-PA

Cleveland-Elyria, OH   PENNSYLVANIA   **Pittsburgh**   **Philadelphia**

MICHIGAN   OHIO   Pittsburgh, PA   NJ   Philadelphia-Camden-Wilmington,
PA-NJ-DE-MD

Columbus ○   DE

INDIANA   Columbus, OH   **Washington** ○   MD
Washington-Arlington-Alexandria, DC-VA-MD-WV

IL   WV   Cincinnati, OH-KY-IN

Cincinnati ○   **Richmond** ○   Virginia Beach-Norfolk-Newport News VA-NC

Louisville/Jefferson
County, KY-IN   **Lexington** ○   VA
Louisville ○   Lexington-Fayette, KY   Richmond, VA   **Virginia Beach**

KENTUCKY   Durham-Chapel Hill, NC

Greensboro ○   **Durham** ○
Winston-Salem ○   **Raleigh** ○

TENNESSEE   Winston-Salem, NC   Raleigh, NC

Greensboro-High Point, NC   **Fayetteville** ○

NC   **Charlotte** ○   Fayetteville, NC

Charlotte-
Concord-
Gastonia, NC-SC

S.CAROLINA   N
W ⊕ E
S

MS   ALABAMA   GEORGIA

©Larry Mandelin 2021

Albuquerque, New Mexico

Background

Pueblo Indians originally inhabited what is now the Albuquerque metropolitan area. In the sixteenth century, Spaniards began arriving from Mexico in search of riches, but it was not until 1706 that they founded the settlement, naming it after the viceroy of New Spain, San Francisco de Alburquerque, a duke whose permission was needed to set up the town. Eventually, the city's name would lose a consonant and become Albuquerque. The city earned the sobriquet "Duke City" because of its namesake.

In the early nineteenth century, Mexico secured her independence from Spanish rule and allowed Americans to enter the province of New Mexico to trade. During the Mexican War of the 1840s, Americans under the command of General Stephen Kearny captured the town, and New Mexico became part of the United States in the Treaty of Guadalupe Hidalgo, ending the war.

During the Civil War, Confederates held the town briefly before surrendering it to a besieging Union army. After the war, the railroad arrived in 1880, bringing with it people and business. In 1891 the town received a city charter. Albuquerque became an important site for tuberculosis sanatoriums during the next few decades because of the healing nature of the dry desert air.

World War II had a great impact on Albuquerque, as Kirtland Air Force Base became an important site for the manufacture of the atomic bomb. Sandia National Laboratories was founded in the city after the war, and was important in defense-related research during the Cold War.

The defense industry is of prime significance to Albuquerque. Institutions once dedicated to defense research are now involved in applying such technology to the private sector, making the city a perfect place for high-tech concerns. In addition to Sandia, the city hosts a branch of the Air Force Research Laboratories and the Los Alamos National Laboratory. Biotech and semiconductor industries also have had a positive impact on the city's economy.

Albuquerque and New Mexico have many programs to assist business. The state has property taxes that are among the lowest in the nation. The city consistently ranks high in business and engineering careers, and generally among best places to live. Additionally, traditional jobs, such as ranching, still have a large presence in the city.

Albuquerque is also a critical transportation center for the American Southwest, with two major interstates that intersect there. Its airport, Albuquerque International Sunport, is served by both major commercial and commuter carriers. The city is home to state-of-the-art manufacturing and shipping facilities and Mesa del Sol, a mixed-used development site connected to the airport by light-rail and a commuter rail line that also serves the region. The New Mexico Rail Runner Express system as well as the Rapid Ride bus service serves Albuquerque's residents. The city also gets high points for its walkability. And as of 2017, there were 291 public parks in the city.

> On Halloween, the city hosted a COVID-safe "Trunk or Treat," with over a dozen vendors delivering candy via contactless methods to families in vehicles.

There are various venues for higher education located in Albuquerque, the most significant of which is the University of New Mexico.

There are popular festive events scheduled throughout the year, including the annual International Albuquerque International Balloon Fiesta and the annual Gathering of Nations Powwow, an international event featuring over 3,000 indigenous Native American dancers and singers representing more than 500 tribes from Canada and the United States. The city is also the setting for recent television shows *In Plain Sight* and *Breaking Bad.* And in 2018, the United Soccer League expanded into New Mexico with its headquarters in Albuquerque.

Albuquerque enjoys a dry, arid climate, with plenty of sunshine, low humidity, and scant rainfall. More than three-fourths of the daylight hours have sunshine, summer and winter. As in all desert climates, temperatures can fluctuate widely between day and night, all year round. Precipitation is meager during the winter, more abundant in summer with afternoon and evening thunderstorms.

Rankings

General Rankings

- For its "Best for Vets: Places to Live 2019" rankings, *Military Times* evaluated 599 cities (83 large, 234 medium, 282 small) and compared the locations across three broad categories: veteran and military culture/services; economic indicators; and livability factors such as health, crime, traffic, and school quality. Albuquerque ranked #14 out of the top 25, in the large city category (population of more than 250,000). Data points more specific to veterans and the military weighed more heavily than others. *rebootcamp.militarytimes.com, "Military Times Best Places to Live 2019," September 10, 2018*

- Albuquerque was selected as one of the best places in the world to "dream of now and go to later" by *National Geographic Travel* editors. The list reflects 25 of the most extraordinary and inspiring destinations that also support National Geographic's tourism goals of cultural engagement, diversity, community benefit, and value. In collaboration with its international editorial teams, the new list reports on the timeless must-see sites for 2021, framed by the five categories of Culture and History, Family, Adventure, Sustainability, and Nature. *www.nationalgeographic.com/travel, "Best of the World, Destinations on the Rise for 2021," November 17, 2020*

- In their seventh annual survey, Livability.com looked at data for more than 1,000 small to mid-sized U.S. cities to determine the rankings for Livability's "Top 100 Best Places to Live" in 2020. Albuquerque ranked #78. Criteria: housing and affordable living; vibrant economy; social and civic engagement; education; demographics; health care options; transportation & infrastructure; and abundant lifestyle amenities. *Livability.com, "Top 100 Best Places to Live 2020" October 2020*

Business/Finance Rankings

- Albuquerque was the #13-ranked city for savers, according to a study by the finance site GOBankingRates, which considered the prospects for people trying to save money. Criteria: average monthly cost of grocery items; median home listing price; median rent; median income; transportation costs; gas prices; and the cost of eating out for an inexpensive and mid-range meal in 100 U.S. cities. *www.gobankingrates.com, "The 20 Best (and Worst) Places to Live If You're Trying to Save Money," August 27, 2019*

- Albuquerque was ranked #13 among 100 U.S. cities for most difficult conditions for savers, according to a study by the finance site GOBankingRates. Criteria: average monthly cost of grocery items; median home listing price; median rent; median income; transportation costs; gas prices; and the cost of eating out for an inexpensive and mid-range meal. *www.gobankingrates.com, "The 20 Best (and Worst) Places to Live If You're Trying to Save Money," August 27, 2019*

- The Brookings Institution ranked the nation's largest cities based on income inequality. Albuquerque was ranked #52 (#1 = greatest inequality). Criteria: the "95/20 ratio," a figure representing the income at which a household earns more than 95 percent of all other households, divided by the income at which a household earns more than only 20 percent of all other households. *Brookings Institution, "Household Income Inequality, Largest Cities of 97 Large U.S. Metro Areas, 2014-2016," February 5, 2018*

- The Brookings Institution ranked the 100 largest metro areas in the U.S. based on income inequality. Albuquerque was ranked #21 (#1 = greatest inequality). Criteria: the "95/20 ratio," a figure representing the income at which a household earns more than 95 percent of all other households, divided by the income at which a household earns more than only 20 percent of all other households. *Brookings Institution, "Household Income Inequality, 100 Largest U.S. Metro Areas, 2014-2016," February 5, 2018*

- The Albuquerque metro area appeared on the Milken Institute "2021 Best Performing Cities" list. Rank: #89 out of 200 large metro areas (population over 250,000). Criteria: job growth; wage and salary growth; high-tech output growth; housing affordability; household broadband access. *Milken Institute, "Best-Performing Cities 2021," February 16, 2021*

- *Forbes* ranked the 200 most populous metro areas to determine the nation's "Best Places for Business and Careers." The Albuquerque metro area was ranked #126. Criteria: costs (business and living); job growth (past and projected); income growth; quality of life; educational attainment (college and high school); projected economic growth; cultural and leisure opportunities; workplace tolerance laws; net migration patterns. *Forbes, "The Best Places for Business and Careers 2019: Seattle Still On Top," October 30, 2019*

Culture/Performing Arts Rankings

- Albuquerque was selected as one of the 25 best cities for moviemakers in North America. COVID-19 has spurred a quest for great film cities that offer more creative space, lower costs, and more great outdoors. NYC & LA were intentionally excluded. Criteria: longstanding reputations as film-friendly communities; efforts to deal with pandemic-specific challenges; and establish appropriate COVID-19 guidelines. The city was ranked #1. *MovieMaker Magazine, "Best Places to Live and Work as a Moviemaker, 2021," January 26, 2021*

Education Rankings

- Personal finance website *WalletHub* analyzed the 150 largest U.S. metropolitan statistical areas to determine where the most educated Americans are putting their degrees to work. Criteria: education levels; percentage of workers with degrees; education quality and attainment gap; public school quality rankings; quality and enrollment of each metro area's universities. Albuquerque was ranked #49 (#1 = most educated city). *www.WalletHub.com, "Most and Least Educated Cities in America," July 20, 2020*

- Albuquerque was selected as one of America's most literate cities. The city ranked #33 out of the 84 largest U.S. cities. Criteria: number of booksellers; library resources; Internet resources; educational attainment; periodical publishing resources; newspaper circulation. *Central Connecticut State University, "America's Most Literate Cities, 2018," February 2019*

Environmental Rankings

- Albuquerque was highlighted as one of the top 98 cleanest metro areas for short-term particle pollution (24-hour PM 2.5) in the U.S. during 2016 through 2018. Monitors in these cities reported no days with unhealthful PM 2.5 levels. *American Lung Association, "State of the Air 2020," April 21, 2020*

Health/Fitness Rankings

- For each of the 100 largest cities in the United States, the American Fitness Index®, published by the American College of Sports Medicine and the Anthem Foundation, evaluated community infrastructure and 33 health behaviors including preventive health, levels of chronic disease conditions, pedestrian safety, air quality, and community resources that support physical activity. Albuquerque ranked #24 for "community fitness." *americanfitnessindex.org, "2020 ACSM American Fitness Index Summary Report," July 14, 2020*

- Albuquerque was identified as a "2021 Spring Allergy Capital." The area ranked #67 out of 100. Three groups of factors were used to identify the most challenging cities for people with allergies during the spring season: annual spring pollen levels; over the counter medicine use; number of board-certified allergy specialists. *Asthma and Allergy Foundation of America, "Spring Allergy Capitals 2021," February 23, 2021*

- Albuquerque was identified as a "2021 Fall Allergy Capital." The area ranked #78 out of 100. Three groups of factors were used to identify the most challenging cities for people with allergies during the fall season: annual fall pollen levels; over the counter medicine use; number of board-certified allergy specialists. *Asthma and Allergy Foundation of America, "Fall Allergy Capitals 2021," February 23, 2021*

- Albuquerque was identified as a "2019 Asthma Capital." The area ranked #27 out of the nation's 100 largest metropolitan areas. Criteria: estimated asthma prevalence; crude death rate from asthma; and ER visits due to asthma. Risk factors analyzed but not factored in the rankings: annual pollen score; annual air quality; public smoking laws; number of board-certified asthma specialists; rescue medication use; controller medication use; uninsured rate; poverty rate. *Asthma and Allergy Foundation of America, "Asthma Capitals 2019: The Most Challenging Places to Live With Asthma," May 7, 2019*

Real Estate Rankings

- *WalletHub* compared the most populated U.S. cities to determine which had the best markets for real estate agents. Albuquerque ranked #170 where demand was high and pay was the best. Criteria: sales per agent; annual median wage for real-estate agents; monthly average starting salary for real estate agents; real estate job density and competition; unemployment rate; home turnover rate; housing-market health index; and other relevant metrics. *www.WalletHub.com, "2019's Best Places to Be a Real Estate Agent," April 24, 2019*

- Albuquerque was ranked #18 in the top 20 out of the 100 largest metro areas in terms of house price appreciation in 2020 (#1 = highest rate). *Federal Housing Finance Agency, House Price Index, 4th Quarter 2020*

- Albuquerque was ranked #136 out of 268 metro areas in terms of housing affordability in 2020 by the National Association of Home Builders (#1 = most affordable). Criteria: the share of homes sold in that area affordable to a family earning the local median income, based on standard mortgage underwriting criteria. *National Association of Home Builders®, NAHB-Wells Fargo Housing Opportunity Index, 4th Quarter 2020*

Safety Rankings

- To identify the most dangerous cities in America, 24/7 Wall Street focused on violent crime categories—murder, non-negligent manslaughter, rape, robbery, and aggravated assault—and property crime as reported in the FBI's 2019 annual Uniform Crime Report. Criteria also included median income from American Community Survey and unemployment figures from Bureau of Labor Statistics. For cities with populations over 100,000, Albuquerque was ranked #10. *247wallst.com, "America's 50 Most Dangerous Cities" November 16, 2020*

- Statistics drawn from the FBI's Uniform Crime Report were used to rank the metropolitan statistical areas where violent crime rose the most between the years 2014–2019. 24/7 Wall Street found that the Albuquerque metro area placed #18 of those with an increase of at least 32.5 percent in violent crime. *247wallst.com, "25 Cities Where Crime Is Soaring," February 18, 2021*

- Allstate ranked the 200 largest cities in America in terms of driver safety. Albuquerque ranked #58. Criteria: internal property damage claims over a two-year period from January 2016 to December 2017. The report helps increase the importance of safety and awareness behind the wheel. *Allstate, "Allstate America's Best Drivers Report, 2019" June 24, 2019*

- Albuquerque was identified as one of the most dangerous cities in America by NeighborhoodScout. The city ranked #21 out of 100 (#1 = most dangerous). Criteria: number of violent crimes per 1,000 residents. The editors evaluated cities with 25,000 or more residents. *NeighborhoodScout.com, "2021 Top 100 Most Dangerous Cities in the U.S.," January 2, 2021*

- The National Insurance Crime Bureau ranked 384 metro areas in the U.S. in terms of per capita rates of vehicle theft. The Albuquerque metro area ranked #2 (#1 = highest rate). Criteria: number of vehicle theft offenses per 100,000 inhabitants in 2019. *National Insurance Crime Bureau, "Hot Spots 2019," July 21, 2020*

Seniors/Retirement Rankings

- From its Best Cities for Successful Aging indexes, the Milken Institute generated rankings for metropolitan areas, weighing data in nine categories—health care, wellness, living arrangements, transportation and convenience, financial characteristics, education, employment, community engagement, and overall livability. The Albuquerque metro area was ranked #87 overall in the large metro area category. *Milken Institute, "Best Cities for Successful Aging, 2017" March 14, 2017*

- Albuquerque was identified as #13 of 20 most popular places to retire in the Southwest region by *Topretirements.com*. The site separated its annual "Best Places to Retire" list by major U.S. regions for 2019. The list reflects the 20 cities that visitors to the website are most interested in for retirement, based on the number of times a city's review was viewed on the website. *Topretirements.com, "20 Most Popular Places to Retire in the Southwest for 2019," October 2, 2019*

Sports/Recreation Rankings

- Albuquerque was chosen as a bicycle friendly community by the League of American Bicyclists. A "Bicycle Friendly Community" welcomes cyclists by providing safe and supportive accommodation for cycling and encouraging people to bike for transportation and recreation. There are five award levels: Diamond; Platinum; Gold; Silver; and Bronze. The community achieved an award level of Silver. *League of American Bicyclists, "Fall 2020 Awards-New & Renewing Bicycle Friendly Communities List," December 16, 2020*

- Albuquerque was chosen as one of America's best cities for bicycling. The city ranked #47 out of 50. Criteria: cycling infrastructure that is safe and friendly for all ages; energy and bike culture. The editors evaluated cities with populations of 100,000 or more. *Bicycling, "The 50 Best Bike Cities in America," October 10, 2018*

Women/Minorities Rankings

- *Women's Health*, together with the site Yelp, identified the 15 "Wellthiest" spots in the U.S. Albuquerque appeared among the top for happiest, healthiest, outdoorsiest and Zen-iest. *Women's Health, "The 15 Wellthiest Cities in the U.S." July 5, 2017*

- Personal finance website *WalletHub* compared more than 180 U.S. cities across two key dimensions, "Hispanic Business-Friendliness" and "Hispanic Purchasing Power," to arrive at the most favorable conditions for Hispanic entrepreneurs. Albuquerque was ranked #39 out of 182. Criteria includes: share of Hispanic-Owned Businesses; Hispanic entrepreneurship rate to median annual income of Hispanics; Small Business-Friendliness score; cost of living; and number of Hispanics with at least a bachelor's degree. *WalletHub.com, "2019's Best Cities for Hispanic Entrepreneurs," May 1, 2019*

Miscellaneous Rankings

- *WalletHub* compared the 150 most populated U.S. cities to determine their operating efficiency. A "Quality of City Services" score was constructed for each city and then divided by the total budget per capita to reveal which were managed the best. Albuquerque ranked #25. Criteria: financial stability; economy; education; safety; health; infrastructure and pollution. *www.WalletHub.com, "2020's Best- & Worst-Run Cities in America," June 29, 2020*

Business Environment

DEMOGRAPHICS

Population Growth

Area	1990 Census	2000 Census	2010 Census	2019* Estimate	Population Growth (%) 1990-2019	Population Growth (%) 2010-2019
City	388,375	448,607	545,852	559,374	44.0	2.5
MSA[1]	599,416	729,649	887,077	912,108	52.2	2.8
U.S.	248,709,873	281,421,906	308,745,538	324,697,795	30.6	5.2

Note: (1) Figures cover the Albuquerque, NM Metropolitan Statistical Area; (*) 2015-2019 5-year estimated population
Source: U.S. Census Bureau, 1990 Census, Census 2000, Census 2010, 2015-2019 American Community Survey 5-Year Estimates

Household Size

Area	Persons in Household (%) One	Two	Three	Four	Five	Six	Seven or More	Average Household Size
City	34.7	33.8	13.9	10.7	4.5	1.5	0.9	2.50
MSA[1]	31.4	35.3	14.4	10.8	5.0	1.9	1.1	2.60
U.S.	27.9	33.9	15.6	12.9	6.0	2.3	1.4	2.60

Note: (1) Figures cover the Albuquerque, NM Metropolitan Statistical Area
Source: U.S. Census Bureau, 2015-2019 American Community Survey 5-Year Estimates

Race

Area	White Alone[2] (%)	Black Alone[2] (%)	Asian Alone[2] (%)	AIAN[3] Alone[2] (%)	NHOPI[4] Alone[2] (%)	Other Race Alone[2] (%)	Two or More Races (%)
City	73.9	3.3	2.9	4.7	0.1	10.6	4.4
MSA[1]	74.9	2.7	2.3	6.0	0.1	10.0	4.0
U.S.	72.5	12.7	5.5	0.8	0.2	4.9	3.3

Note: (1) Figures cover the Albuquerque, NM Metropolitan Statistical Area; (2) Alone is defined as not being in combination with one or more other races; (3) American Indian and Alaska Native; (4) Native Hawaiian and Other Pacific Islander
Source: U.S. Census Bureau, 2015-2019 American Community Survey 5-Year Estimates

Hispanic or Latino Origin

Area	Total (%)	Mexican (%)	Puerto Rican (%)	Cuban (%)	Other (%)
City	49.2	28.0	0.6	0.5	20.2
MSA[1]	49.0	27.7	0.5	0.4	20.4
U.S.	18.0	11.2	1.7	0.7	4.3

Note: Persons of Hispanic or Latino origin can be of any race; (1) Figures cover the Albuquerque, NM Metropolitan Statistical Area
Source: U.S. Census Bureau, 2015-2019 American Community Survey 5-Year Estimates

Ancestry

Area	German	Irish	English	American	Italian	Polish	French[2]	Scottish	Dutch
City	9.0	7.0	6.4	3.8	2.9	1.4	1.7	1.6	0.7
MSA[1]	8.7	6.8	6.4	4.3	2.8	1.3	1.7	1.6	0.7
U.S.	13.3	9.7	7.2	6.2	5.1	2.8	2.3	1.7	1.2

Note: Figures are the percentage of the total population reporting a particular ancestry. The nine most commonly reported ancestries in the U.S. are shown. Figures include multiple ancestries (e.g. if a person reported being Irish and Italian, they were included in both columns); (1) Figures cover the Albuquerque, NM Metropolitan Statistical Area; (2) Excludes Basque
Source: U.S. Census Bureau, 2015-2019 American Community Survey 5-Year Estimates

Foreign-born Population

Area	Percent of Population Born in Any Foreign Country	Asia	Mexico	Europe	Caribbean	Central America[2]	South America	Africa	Canada
City	9.9	2.4	5.3	0.8	0.3	0.2	0.4	0.4	0.1
MSA[1]	8.9	1.8	5.2	0.7	0.3	0.2	0.3	0.3	0.1
U.S.	13.6	4.2	3.5	1.5	1.3	1.1	1.0	0.7	0.2

Note: (1) Figures cover the Albuquerque, NM Metropolitan Statistical Area; (2) Excludes Mexico.
Source: U.S. Census Bureau, 2015-2019 American Community Survey 5-Year Estimates

Marital Status

Area	Never Married	Now Married[2]	Separated	Widowed	Divorced
City	37.7	40.8	1.5	5.6	14.4
MSA[1]	34.9	43.9	1.5	5.8	13.9
U.S.	33.4	48.1	1.9	5.8	10.9

Note: Figures are percentages and cover the population 15 years of age and older; (1) Figures cover the Albuquerque, NM Metropolitan Statistical Area; (2) Excludes separated
Source: U.S. Census Bureau, 2015-2019 American Community Survey 5-Year Estimates

Disability by Age

Area	All Ages	Under 18 Years Old	18 to 64 Years Old	65 Years and Over
City	13.4	4.1	11.7	34.9
MSA[1]	14.3	4.1	12.2	36.6
U.S.	12.6	4.2	10.3	34.5

Note: Figures show percent of the civilian noninstitutionalized population that reported having a disability. Disability status is determined from six types of difficulty: vision, hearing, cognitive, ambulatory, self-care, and independent living. For children under 5 years old, hearing and vision difficulty are used to determine disability status. For children between the ages of 5 and 14, disability status is determined from hearing, vision, cognitive, ambulatory, and self-care difficulties. For people aged 15 years and older, they are considered to have a disability if they have difficulty with any one of the six difficulty types; Note: (1) Figures cover the Albuquerque, NM Metropolitan Statistical Area
Source: U.S. Census Bureau, 2015-2019 American Community Survey 5-Year Estimates

Age

Area	Percent of Population									Median Age
	Under Age 5	Age 5–19	Age 20–34	Age 35–44	Age 45–54	Age 55–64	Age 65–74	Age 75–84	Age 85+	
City	5.9	19.0	22.6	13.0	12.0	12.2	8.8	4.4	1.8	36.6
MSA[1]	5.7	19.2	20.7	12.6	12.4	13.2	9.8	4.7	1.8	38.2
U.S.	6.1	19.1	20.7	12.6	13.0	12.9	9.1	4.6	1.9	38.1

Note: (1) Figures cover the Albuquerque, NM Metropolitan Statistical Area
Source: U.S. Census Bureau, 2015-2019 American Community Survey 5-Year Estimates

Gender

Area	Males	Females	Males per 100 Females
City	272,468	286,906	95.0
MSA[1]	448,642	463,466	96.8
U.S.	159,886,919	164,810,876	97.0

Note: (1) Figures cover the Albuquerque, NM Metropolitan Statistical Area
Source: U.S. Census Bureau, 2015-2019 American Community Survey 5-Year Estimates

Religious Groups by Family

Area	Catholic	Baptist	Non-Den.	Methodist[2]	Lutheran	LDS[3]	Pente-costal	Presby-terian[4]	Muslim[5]	Judaism
MSA[1]	27.2	3.8	4.2	1.5	1.0	2.4	1.5	1.1	0.2	0.3
U.S.	19.1	9.3	4.0	4.0	2.3	2.0	1.9	1.6	0.8	0.7

Note: Figures are the number of adherents as a percentage of the total population; (1) Figures cover the Albuquerque, NM Metropolitan Statistical Area; (2) Methodist/Pietist; (3) Latter Day Saints; (4) Reformed; (5) Figures are estimates
Source: Association of Statisticians of American Religious Bodies, 2010 U.S. Religion Census: Religious Congregations & Membership Study

Religious Groups by Tradition

Area	Catholic	Evangelical Protestant	Mainline Protestant	Other Tradition	Black Protestant	Orthodox
MSA[1]	27.2	11.3	3.3	3.9	0.2	0.2
U.S.	19.1	16.2	7.3	4.3	1.6	0.3

Note: Figures are the number of adherents as a percentage of the total population; (1) Figures cover the Albuquerque, NM Metropolitan Statistical Area
Source: Association of Statisticians of American Religious Bodies, 2010 U.S. Religion Census: Religious Congregations & Membership Study

ECONOMY

Gross Metropolitan Product

Area	2017	2018	2019	2020	Rank[2]
MSA[1]	42.8	44.4	46.3	48.6	68

Note: Figures are in billions of dollars; (1) Figures cover the Albuquerque, NM Metropolitan Statistical Area; (2) Rank is based on 2018 data and ranges from 1 to 381
Source: U.S. Conference of Mayors, U.S. Metro Economies: GMP & Employment 2018-2020, September 2019

Economic Growth

Area	2015-17 (%)	2018 (%)	2019 (%)	2020 (%)	Rank[2]
MSA[1]	0.7	1.4	2.6	2.5	252
U.S.	1.9	2.9	2.3	2.1	–

Note: Figures are real gross metropolitan product (GMP) growth rates and represent average annual percent change; (1) Figures cover the Albuquerque, NM Metropolitan Statistical Area; (2) Rank is based on 2017 2-year average annual percent change and ranges from 1 to 381
Source: U.S. Conference of Mayors, U.S. Metro Economies: GMP & Employment 2018-2020, September 2019

Metropolitan Area Exports

Area	2014	2015	2016	2017	2018	2019	Rank[2]
MSA[1]	1,564.0	1,761.2	999.7	624.2	771.5	1,629.7	114

Note: Figures are in millions of dollars; (1) Figures cover the Albuquerque, NM Metropolitan Statistical Area; (2) Rank is based on 2019 data and ranges from 1 to 386
Source: U.S. Department of Commerce, International Trade Administration, Office of Trade and Economic Analysis, Industry and Analysis, Exports by Metropolitan Area, data extracted March 24, 2021

Building Permits

Area	Single-Family 2018	2019	Pct. Chg.	Multi-Family 2018	2019	Pct. Chg.	Total 2018	2019	Pct. Chg.
City	1,115	906	-18.7	0	188	–	1,115	1,094	-1.9
MSA[1]	2,086	1,872	-10.3	100	276	176.0	2,186	2,148	-1.7
U.S.	855,300	862,100	0.7	473,500	523,900	10.6	1,328,800	1,386,000	4.3

Note: (1) Figures cover the Albuquerque, NM Metropolitan Statistical Area; Figures represent new, privately-owned housing units authorized (unadjusted data); All permit data are based on estimates with imputation
Source: U.S. Census Bureau, Manufacturing, Mining, and Construction Statistics, Building Permits, 2018, 2019

Bankruptcy Filings

Area	Business Filings 2019	2020	% Chg.	Nonbusiness Filings 2019	2020	% Chg.
Bernalillo County	30	33	10.0	1,071	872	-18.6
U.S.	22,780	21,655	-4.9	752,160	522,808	-30.5

Note: Business filings include Chapter 7, Chapter 9, Chapter 11, Chapter 12, Chapter 13, Chapter 15, and Section 304; Nonbusiness filings include Chapter 7, Chapter 11, and Chapter 13
Source: Administrative Office of the U.S. Courts, Business and Nonbusiness Bankruptcy, County Cases Commenced by Chapter of the Bankruptcy Code, During the 12-Month Period Ending December 31, 2019 and Business and Nonbusiness Bankruptcy, County Cases Commenced by Chapter of the Bankruptcy Code, During the 12-Month Period Ending December 31, 2020

Housing Vacancy Rates

Area	Gross Vacancy Rate[2] (%) 2018	2019	2020	Year-Round Vacancy Rate[3] (%) 2018	2019	2020	Rental Vacancy Rate[4] (%) 2018	2019	2020	Homeowner Vacancy Rate[5] (%) 2018	2019	2020
MSA[1]	8.3	7.9	5.1	7.9	7.4	4.9	7.8	6.5	5.4	1.8	1.9	1.4
U.S.	12.3	12.0	10.6	9.7	9.5	8.2	6.9	6.7	6.3	1.5	1.4	1.0

Note: (1) Figures cover the Albuquerque, NM Metropolitan Statistical Area; (2) The percentage of the total housing inventory that is vacant; (3) The percentage of the housing inventory (excluding seasonal units) that is year-round vacant; (4) The percentage of rental inventory that is vacant for rent; (5) The percentage of homeowner inventory that is vacant for sale
Source: U.S. Census Bureau, Housing Vacancies and Homeownership Annual Statistics: 2018, 2019, 2020

INCOME

Income

Area	Per Capita ($)	Median Household ($)	Average Household ($)
City	30,403	52,911	72,265
MSA[1]	29,747	54,072	73,512
U.S.	34,103	62,843	88,607

Note: (1) Figures cover the Albuquerque, NM Metropolitan Statistical Area
Source: U.S. Census Bureau, 2015-2019 American Community Survey 5-Year Estimates

Household Income Distribution

Area	Under $15,000	$15,000 -$24,999	$25,000 -$34,999	$35,000 -$49,999	$50,000 -$74,999	$75,000 -$99,999	$100,000 -$149,999	$150,000 and up
City	13.1	10.8	10.4	13.1	17.7	12.0	13.3	9.4
MSA[1]	12.4	10.7	10.0	13.3	18.0	12.5	13.1	9.8
U.S.	10.3	8.9	8.9	12.3	17.2	12.7	15.1	14.5

Note: (1) Figures cover the Albuquerque, NM Metropolitan Statistical Area
Source: U.S. Census Bureau, 2015-2019 American Community Survey 5-Year Estimates

Poverty Rate

Area	All Ages	Under 18 Years Old	18 to 64 Years Old	65 Years and Over
City	16.9	24.0	16.1	9.5
MSA[1]	16.2	22.6	15.5	10.1
U.S.	13.4	18.5	12.6	9.3

Note: Figures are percentage of people whose income during the past 12 months was below the poverty level;
(1) Figures cover the Albuquerque, NM Metropolitan Statistical Area
Source: U.S. Census Bureau, 2015-2019 American Community Survey 5-Year Estimates

CITY FINANCES

City Government Finances

Component	2017 ($000)	2017 ($ per capita)
Total Revenues	1,133,038	2,026
Total Expenditures	1,032,533	1,847
Debt Outstanding	1,567,121	2,803
Cash and Securities[1]	1,021,824	1,828

Note: (1) Cash and security holdings of a government at the close of its fiscal year,
including those of its dependent agencies, utilities, and liquor stores.
Source: U.S. Census Bureau, State & Local Government Finances 2017

City Government Revenue by Source

Source	2017 ($000)	2017 ($ per capita)	2017 (%)
General Revenue			
From Federal Government	31,366	56	2.8
From State Government	236,271	423	20.9
From Local Governments	2,377	4	0.2
Taxes			
Property	145,853	261	12.9
Sales and Gross Receipts	223,900	400	19.8
Personal Income	0	0	0.0
Corporate Income	0	0	0.0
Motor Vehicle License	0	0	0.0
Other Taxes	16,280	29	1.4
Current Charges	265,880	476	23.5
Liquor Store	0	0	0.0
Utility	153,204	274	13.5
Employee Retirement	0	0	0.0

Source: U.S. Census Bureau, State & Local Government Finances 2017

City Government Expenditures by Function

Function	2017 ($000)	2017 ($ per capita)	2017 (%)
General Direct Expenditures			
Air Transportation	35,681	63	3.5
Corrections	0	0	0.0
Education	0	0	0.0
Employment Security Administration	0	0	0.0
Financial Administration	22,151	39	2.1
Fire Protection	78,917	141	7.6
General Public Buildings	37,002	66	3.6
Governmental Administration, Other	34,409	61	3.3
Health	31,871	57	3.1
Highways	27,886	49	2.7
Hospitals	0	0	0.0
Housing and Community Development	1,896	3	0.2
Interest on General Debt	16,122	28	1.6
Judicial and Legal	5,415	9	0.5
Libraries	15,786	28	1.5
Parking	4,144	7	0.4
Parks and Recreation	104,119	186	10.1
Police Protection	169,422	303	16.4
Public Welfare	28,152	50	2.7
Sewerage	93,521	167	9.1
Solid Waste Management	70,439	126	6.8
Veterans' Services	0	0	0.0
Liquor Store	0	0	0.0
Utility	218,147	390	21.1
Employee Retirement	0	0	0.0

Source: U.S. Census Bureau, State & Local Government Finances 2017

EMPLOYMENT

Labor Force and Employment

Area	Civilian Labor Force			Workers Employed		
	Dec. 2019	Dec. 2020	% Chg.	Dec. 2019	Dec. 2020	% Chg.
City	284,609	280,764	-1.4	273,259	260,057	-4.8
MSA[1]	442,230	434,669	-1.7	423,884	402,897	-5.0
U.S.	164,007,000	160,017,000	-2.4	158,504,000	149,613,000	-5.6

Note: Data is not seasonally adjusted and covers workers 16 years of age and older; (1) Figures cover the Albuquerque, NM Metropolitan Statistical Area
Source: Bureau of Labor Statistics, Local Area Unemployment Statistics

Unemployment Rate

Area	2020											
	Jan.	Feb.	Mar.	Apr.	May	Jun.	Jul.	Aug.	Sep.	Oct.	Nov.	Dec.
City	4.4	4.4	5.5	12.8	9.4	9.1	13.2	11.2	9.5	7.5	6.3	7.4
MSA[1]	4.6	4.6	5.7	12.3	9.1	9.0	13.1	11.1	9.5	7.5	6.4	7.3
U.S.	4.0	3.8	4.5	14.4	13.0	11.2	10.5	8.5	7.7	6.6	6.4	6.5

Note: Data is not seasonally adjusted and covers workers 16 years of age and older; (1) Figures cover the Albuquerque, NM Metropolitan Statistical Area
Source: Bureau of Labor Statistics, Local Area Unemployment Statistics

Average Wages

Occupation	$/Hr.	Occupation	$/Hr.
Accountants and Auditors	33.50	Maintenance and Repair Workers	19.40
Automotive Mechanics	22.00	Marketing Managers	47.10
Bookkeepers	20.10	Network and Computer Systems Admin.	39.30
Carpenters	20.70	Nurses, Licensed Practical	24.30
Cashiers	11.90	Nurses, Registered	36.90
Computer Programmers	38.30	Nursing Assistants	14.70
Computer Systems Analysts	39.90	Office Clerks, General	13.30
Computer User Support Specialists	21.70	Physical Therapists	42.40
Construction Laborers	16.90	Physicians	93.50
Cooks, Restaurant	12.80	Plumbers, Pipefitters and Steamfitters	22.30
Customer Service Representatives	16.20	Police and Sheriff's Patrol Officers	27.80
Dentists	78.00	Postal Service Mail Carriers	25.40
Electricians	23.30	Real Estate Sales Agents	27.90
Engineers, Electrical	58.20	Retail Salespersons	13.70
Fast Food and Counter Workers	10.60	Sales Representatives, Technical/Scientific	53.90
Financial Managers	55.10	Secretaries, Exc. Legal/Medical/Executive	18.00
First-Line Supervisors of Office Workers	27.50	Security Guards	14.00
General and Operations Managers	56.10	Surgeons	117.30
Hairdressers/Cosmetologists	10.80	Teacher Assistants, Exc. Postsecondary*	10.90
Home Health and Personal Care Aides	11.90	Teachers, Secondary School, Exc. Sp. Ed.*	25.70
Janitors and Cleaners	12.40	Telemarketers	n/a
Landscaping/Groundskeeping Workers	14.50	Truck Drivers, Heavy/Tractor-Trailer	20.20
Lawyers	55.30	Truck Drivers, Light/Delivery Services	18.40
Maids and Housekeeping Cleaners	10.80	Waiters and Waitresses	10.00

Note: Wage data covers the Albuquerque, NM Metropolitan Statistical Area; (*) Hourly wages were calculated from annual wage data based on a 40 hour work week; n/a not available.
Source: Bureau of Labor Statistics, Metro Area Occupational Employment & Wage Estimates, May 2020

Employment by Industry

Sector	MSA[1]		U.S.
	Number of Employees	Percent of Total	Percent of Total
Construction, Mining, and Logging	25,400	6.9	5.5
Education and Health Services	64,200	17.3	16.3
Financial Activities	18,200	4.9	6.1
Government	77,800	21.0	15.2
Information	4,900	1.3	1.9
Leisure and Hospitality	32,300	8.7	9.0
Manufacturing	14,300	3.9	8.5
Other Services	10,500	2.8	3.8
Professional and Business Services	61,300	16.5	14.4
Retail Trade	40,600	11.0	10.9
Transportation, Warehousing, and Utilities	10,400	2.8	4.6
Wholesale Trade	10,800	2.9	3.9

Note: Figures are non-farm employment as of December 2020. Figures are not seasonally adjusted and include workers 16 years of age and older; (1) Figures cover the Albuquerque, NM Metropolitan Statistical Area
Source: Bureau of Labor Statistics, Current Employment Statistics, Employment, Hours, and Earnings

Employment by Occupation

Occupation Classification	City (%)	MSA[1] (%)	U.S. (%)
Management, Business, Science, and Arts	41.8	40.0	38.5
Natural Resources, Construction, and Maintenance	7.4	8.9	8.9
Production, Transportation, and Material Moving	7.8	8.6	13.2
Sales and Office	22.9	22.8	21.6
Service	20.2	19.8	17.8

Note: Figures cover employed civilians 16 years of age and older; (1) Figures cover the Albuquerque, NM Metropolitan Statistical Area
Source: U.S. Census Bureau, 2015-2019 American Community Survey 5-Year Estimates

Occupations with Greatest Projected Employment Growth: 2020 – 2022

Occupation[1]	2020 Employment	2022 Projected Employment	Numeric Employment Change	Percent Employment Change
Waiters and Waitresses	12,470	15,720	3,250	26.1
Retail Salespersons	21,590	23,870	2,280	10.6
Cooks, Restaurant	7,120	8,790	1,670	23.5
Teaching Assistants, Except Postsecondary	4,700	6,260	1,560	33.2
Food Servers, Nonrestaurant	1,590	2,820	1,230	77.4
Carpenters	4,830	5,810	980	20.3
Nursing Assistants (SOC 2018)	5,740	6,660	920	16.0
Hairdressers, Hairstylists, and Cosmetologists	1,930	2,730	800	41.5
Medical Secretaries	4,210	4,970	760	18.1
Roustabouts, Oil and Gas	3,700	4,420	720	19.5

Note: Projections cover New Mexico; (1) Sorted by numeric employment change
Source: www.projectionscentral.com, State Occupational Projections, 2020–2022 Short-Term Projections

Fastest-Growing Occupations: 2020 – 2022

Occupation[1]	2020 Employment	2022 Projected Employment	Numeric Employment Change	Percent Employment Change
Fashion Designers	20	70	50	250.0
Gaming and Sports Book Writers and Runners	40	130	90	225.0
New Accounts Clerks	30	90	60	200.0
Conveyor Operators and Tenders	40	110	70	175.0
Ophthalmic Medical Technicians	180	460	280	155.6
Boilermakers	90	220	130	144.4
Multimedia Artists and Animators	150	340	190	126.7
Gaming Service Workers, All Other	60	130	70	116.7
Musicians and Singers	170	360	190	111.8
Baggage Porters and Bellhops	80	160	80	100.0

Note: Projections cover New Mexico; (1) Sorted by percent employment change and excludes occupations with numeric employment change less than 50
Source: www.projectionscentral.com, State Occupational Projections, 2020–2022 Short-Term Projections

TAXES

State Corporate Income Tax Rates

State	Tax Rate (%)	Income Brackets ($)	Num. of Brackets	Financial Institution Tax Rate (%)[a]	Federal Income Tax Ded.
New Mexico	4.8 - 5.9	500,000	2	4.8 - 5.9	No

Note: Tax rates as of January 1, 2021; (a) Rates listed are the corporate income tax rate applied to financial institutions or excise taxes based on income. Some states have other taxes based upon the value of deposits or shares.
Source: Federation of Tax Administrators, State Corporate Income Tax Rates, January 1, 2021

State Individual Income Tax Rates

State	Tax Rate (%)	Income Brackets ($)	Personal Exemptions ($)			Standard Ded. ($)	
			Single	Married	Depend.	Single	Married
New Mexico	1.7 - 5.9	5,500 - 210,000 (q)	(d)	(d)	(d)	12,550	25,100 (d)

Note: Tax rates as of January 1, 2021; Local- and county-level taxes are not included; Federal income tax is not deductible on state income tax returns; (d) These states use the personal exemption/standard deduction amounts provided in the federal Internal Revenue Code; (q) The income brackets reported for New Mexico are for single individuals. For married couples filing jointly, the same tax rates apply to income brackets ranging from $8,000 to $315,000.
Source: Federation of Tax Administrators, State Individual Income Tax Rates, January 1, 2021

Various State Sales and Excise Tax Rates

State	State Sales Tax (%)	Gasoline[1] (¢/gal.)	Cigarette[2] ($/pack)	Spirits[3] ($/gal.)	Wine[4] ($/gal.)	Beer[5] ($/gal.)	Recreational Marijuana (%)
New Mexico	5.125	18.88	2	6.06	1.7	0.41	Not legal

Note: All tax rates as of January 1, 2021; (1) The American Petroleum Institute has developed a methodology for determining the average tax rate on a gallon of fuel. Rates may include any of the following: excise taxes, environmental fees, storage tank fees, other fees or taxes, general sales tax, and local taxes; (2) The federal excise tax of $1.0066 per pack and local taxes are not included; (3) Rates are those applicable to off-premise sales of 40% alcohol by volume (a.b.v.) distilled spirits in 750ml containers. Local excise taxes are excluded; (4) Rates are those applicable to off-premise sales of 11% a.b.v. non-carbonated wine in 750ml containers; (5) Rates are those applicable to off-premise sales of 4.7% a.b.v. beer in 12 ounce containers.
Source: Tax Foundation, 2021 Facts & Figures: How Does Your State Compare?

State Business Tax Climate Index Rankings

State	Overall Rank	Corporate Tax Rank	Individual Income Tax Rank	Sales Tax Rank	Property Tax Rank	Unemployment Insurance Tax Rank
New Mexico	23	9	31	41	1	9

Note: The index is a measure of how each state's tax laws affect economic performance. The lower the rank, the more favorable a state's tax system is for business. States without a given tax are given a ranking of 1. The scores/rankings for the District of Columbia do not affect other states. The 2021 index represents the tax climate as of July 1, 2020.
Source: Tax Foundation, State Business Tax Climate Index 2021

TRANSPORTATION

Means of Transportation to Work

Area	Car/Truck/Van		Public Transportation			Bicycle	Walked	Other Means	Worked at Home
	Drove Alone	Car-pooled	Bus	Subway	Railroad				
City	80.6	9.0	1.8	0.0	0.1	1.1	1.9	1.0	4.4
MSA[1]	80.6	9.6	1.3	0.0	0.2	0.8	1.7	1.1	4.8
U.S.	76.3	9.0	2.4	1.9	0.6	0.5	2.7	1.4	5.2

Note: Figures are percentages and cover workers 16 years of age and older; (1) Figures cover the Albuquerque, NM Metropolitan Statistical Area
Source: U.S. Census Bureau, 2015-2019 American Community Survey 5-Year Estimates

Travel Time to Work

Area	Less Than 10 Minutes	10 to 19 Minutes	20 to 29 Minutes	30 to 44 Minutes	45 to 59 Minutes	60 to 89 Minutes	90 Minutes or More
City	11.1	35.8	28.1	17.7	3.1	2.8	1.4
MSA[1]	10.8	31.6	26.2	20.5	5.7	3.6	1.6
U.S.	12.2	28.4	20.8	20.8	8.3	6.4	2.9

Note: Note: Figures are percentages and include workers 16 years old and over; (1) Figures cover the Albuquerque, NM Metropolitan Statistical Area
Source: U.S. Census Bureau, 2015-2019 American Community Survey 5-Year Estimates

Key Congestion Measures

Measure	1982	1992	2002	2012	2017
Annual Hours of Delay, Total (000)	4,194	8,468	17,730	20,398	23,302
Annual Hours of Delay, Per Auto Commuter	15	24	40	40	44
Annual Congestion Cost, Total (million $)	32	90	241	369	433
Annual Congestion Cost, Per Auto Commuter ($)	194	366	597	761	856

Note: Covers the Albuquerque NM urban area
Source: Texas A&M Transportation Institute, 2019 Urban Mobility Report

Freeway Travel Time Index

Measure	1982	1987	1992	1997	2002	2007	2012	2017
Urban Area Index[1]	1.07	1.08	1.10	1.15	1.18	1.17	1.19	1.20
Urban Area Rank[1,2]	35	44	59	41	37	56	39	39

Note: Freeway Travel Time Index—the ratio of travel time in the peak period to the travel time at free-flow conditions. For example, a value of 1.30 indicates a 20-minute free-flow trip takes 26 minutes in the peak (20 minutes x 1.30 = 26 minutes); (1) Covers the Albuquerque NM urban area; (2) Rank is based on 101 larger urban areas (#1 = highest travel time index)
Source: Texas A&M Transportation Institute, 2019 Urban Mobility Report

Public Transportation

Agency Name / Mode of Transportation	Vehicles Operated in Maximum Service[1]	Annual Unlinked Passenger Trips[2] (in thous.)	Annual Passenger Miles[3] (in thous.)
ABQ Ride			
Bus (directly operated)	131	9,159.7	32,397.9
Demand Response (directly operated)	62	258.8	2,496.4

Note: (1) Number of revenue vehicles operated by the given mode and type of service to meet the annual maximum service requirement. This is the revenue vehicle count during the peak season of the year; on the week and day that maximum service is provided. Vehicles operated in maximum service (VOMS) exclude atypical days and one-time special events; (2) Number of passengers who boarded public transportation vehicles. Passengers are counted each time they board a vehicle no matter how many vehicles they use to travel from their origin to their destination. (3) Sum of the distances ridden by all passengers during the entire fiscal year.
Source: Federal Transit Administration, National Transit Database, 2019

Air Transportation

Airport Name and Code / Type of Service	Passenger Airlines[1]	Passenger Enplanements	Freight Carriers[2]	Freight (lbs)
Albuquerque International (ABQ)				
Domestic service (U.S. carriers - 2020)	24	868,691	10	63,111,288
International service (U.S. carriers - 2019)	1	20	1	37,473

Note: (1) Includes all U.S.-based major, minor and commuter airlines that carried at least one passenger during the year; (2) Includes all U.S.-based airlines and freight carriers that transported at least one pound of freight during the year.
Source: Bureau of Transportation Statistics, The Intermodal Transportation Database, Air Carriers: T-100 Domestic Market (U.S. Carriers), 2020; Bureau of Transportation Statistics, The Intermodal Transportation Database, Air Carriers: T-100 International Market (U.S. Carriers), 2019

BUSINESSES

Major Business Headquarters

Company Name	Industry	Rankings	
		Fortune[1]	Forbes[2]
No companies listed	-	-	-

Note: (1) Companies that produce a 10-K are ranked 1 to 500 based on 2019 revenue; (2) All private companies with at least $2 billion in annual revenue through the end of their most current fiscal year are ranked 1 to 219; companies listed are headquartered in the city; dashes indicate no ranking
Source: Fortune, "Fortune 500," June/July 2020; Forbes, "America's Largest Private Companies," 2020

Fastest-Growing Businesses

According to *Inc.*, Albuquerque is home to one of America's 500 fastest-growing private companies: **RS21** (#485). Criteria: must be an independent, privately-held, for-profit, U.S. corporation, proprietorship or partnership as of December 31, 2019; revenues must be at least $100,000 in 2016 and $2 million in 2019; must have four-year operating/sales history. *Inc., "America's 500 Fastest-Growing Private Companies," 2020*

According to *Initiative for a Competitive Inner City (ICIC)*, Albuquerque is home to four of America's 100 fastest-growing "inner city" companies: **One Community Auto** (#47); **Environment Control of Albuquerque** (#69); **Pooser Corporation (dba Slate Street Cafe)** (#81); **Duran Central Pharmacy** (#98). Criteria for inclusion: company must be headquartered in or have 51 percent or more of its physical operations in an economically distressed urban area; must be an independent, for-profit corporation, partnership or proprietorship; must have 10 or more employees and have a five-year sales history that includes sales of at least $200,000 in the base year and at least $1 million in the current year with no decrease in sales over the two most recent years. Companies were ranked overall by revenue growth over the five-year period between 2015 and 2019. *Initiative for a Competitive Inner City (ICIC), "Inner City 100 Companies," 2020*

Living Environment

COST OF LIVING

Cost of Living Index

Composite Index	Groceries	Housing	Utilities	Trans-portation	Health Care	Misc. Goods/ Services
93.1	97.4	85.8	96.1	88.6	96.2	97.2

Note: The Cost of Living Index measures regional differences in the cost of consumer goods and services, excluding taxes and non-consumer expenditures, for professional and managerial households in the top income quintile. It is based on more than 50,000 prices covering almost 60 different items for which prices are collected three times a year by chambers of commerce, economic development organizations or university applied economic centers in each participating urban area. The numbers shown should be read as a percentage above or below the national average of 100. For example, a value of 115.4 in the groceries column indicates that grocery prices are 15.4% higher than the national average. Small differences in the index numbers should not be interpreted as significant; Figures cover the Albuquerque NM urban area.
Source: The Council for Community and Economic Research, Cost of Living Index, 2020

Grocery Prices

Area[1]	T-Bone Steak ($/pound)	Frying Chicken ($/pound)	Whole Milk ($/half gal.)	Eggs ($/dozen)	Orange Juice ($/64 oz.)	Coffee ($/11.5 oz.)
City[2]	11.18	1.16	2.10	1.41	3.96	4.63
Avg.	11.78	1.39	2.05	1.47	3.57	4.34
Min.	8.03	0.94	1.03	0.74	2.94	3.02
Max.	15.86	2.65	4.31	3.77	5.44	8.69

Note: (1) Values for the local area are compared with the average, minimum and maximum values for all 284 areas in the Cost of Living Index; (2) Figures cover the Albuquerque NM urban area; **T-Bone Steak** (price per pound); **Frying Chicken** (price per pound, whole fryer); **Whole Milk** (half gallon carton); **Eggs** (price per dozen, Grade A, large); **Orange Juice** (64 oz. Tropicana or Florida Natural); **Coffee** (11.5 oz. can, vacuum-packed, Maxwell House, Hills Bros, or Folgers).
Source: The Council for Community and Economic Research, Cost of Living Index, 2020

Housing and Utility Costs

Area[1]	New Home Price ($)	Apartment Rent ($/month)	All Electric ($/month)	Part Electric ($/month)	Other Energy ($/month)	Telephone ($/month)
City[2]	329,645	874	-	114.55	40.75	183.90
Avg.	368,594	1,168	170.86	100.47	65.28	184.30
Min.	190,567	502	91.58	31.42	26.08	169.60
Max.	2,227,806	4,738	470.38	280.31	280.06	206.50

Note: (1) Values for the local area are compared with the average, minimum and maximum values for all 284 areas in the Cost of Living Index; (2) Figures cover the Albuquerque NM urban area; **New Home Price** (2,400 sf living area, 8,000 sf lot, in urban area with full utilities); **Apartment Rent** (950 sf 2 bedroom/1.5 or 2 bath, unfurnished, excluding all utilities except water); **All Electric** (average monthly cost for an all-electric home); **Part Electric** (average monthly cost for a part-electric home); **Other Energy** (average monthly cost for natural gas, fuel oil, coal, wood, and any other forms of energy except electricity); **Telephone** (price includes the base monthly rate plus taxes and fees for three lines of mobile phone service).
Source: The Council for Community and Economic Research, Cost of Living Index, 2020

Health Care, Transportation, and Other Costs

Area[1]	Doctor ($/visit)	Dentist ($/visit)	Optometrist ($/visit)	Gasoline ($/gallon)	Beauty Salon ($/visit)	Men's Shirt ($)
City[2]	106.93	98.97	108.12	1.85	39.81	30.50
Avg.	115.44	99.32	108.10	2.21	39.27	31.37
Min.	36.68	59.00	51.36	1.71	19.00	11.00
Max.	219.00	153.10	250.97	3.46	82.05	58.33

Note: (1) Values for the local area are compared with the average, minimum and maximum values for all 284 areas in the Cost of Living Index; (2) Figures cover the Albuquerque NM urban area; **Doctor** (general practitioners routine exam of an established patient); **Dentist** (adult teeth cleaning and periodic oral examination); **Optometrist** (full vision eye exam for established adult patient); **Gasoline** (one gallon regular unleaded, national brand, including all taxes, cash price at self-service pump if available); **Beauty Salon** (woman's shampoo, trim, and blow-dry); **Men's Shirt** (cotton/polyester dress shirt, pinpoint weave, long sleeves).
Source: The Council for Community and Economic Research, Cost of Living Index, 2020

HOUSING

Homeownership Rate

Area	2012 (%)	2013 (%)	2014 (%)	2015 (%)	2016 (%)	2017 (%)	2018 (%)	2019 (%)	2020 (%)
MSA[1]	62.8	65.9	64.4	64.3	66.9	67.0	67.9	70.0	69.5
U.S.	65.4	65.1	64.5	63.7	63.4	63.9	64.4	64.6	66.6

Note: (1) Figures cover the Albuquerque, NM Metropolitan Statistical Area
Source: U.S. Census Bureau, Housing Vacancies and Homeownership Annual Statistics: 2012-2020

House Price Index (HPI)

Area	National Ranking[2]	Quarterly Change (%)	One-Year Change (%)	Five-Year Change (%)	Since 1991Q1 (%)
MSA[1]	42	2.20	7.86	27.05	163.46
U.S.[3]	–	3.81	10.77	38.99	205.12

Note: The HPI is a weighted repeat sales index. It measures average price changes in repeat sales or refinancings on the same properties. This information is obtained by reviewing repeat mortgage transactions on single-family properties whose mortgages have been purchased or securitized by Fannie Mae or Freddie Mac since January 1975; (1) Figures cover the Albuquerque, NM Metropolitan Statistical Area; (2) Rankings are based on annual percentage change for all metro areas containing at least 15,000 transactions over the last 10 years and ranges from 1 to 253; (3) figures based on a weighted average of Census Division estimates using a seasonally adjusted, purchase-only index; all figures are for the period ending December 31, 2020
Source: Federal Housing Finance Agency, Change in Metropolitan Area House Price Indexes, April 7, 2021

Median Single-Family Home Prices

Area	2018	2019	2020p	Percent Change 2019 to 2020
MSA[1]	205.6	225.0	248.1	10.3
U.S. Average	261.6	274.6	299.9	9.2

Note: Figures are median sales prices of existing single-family homes in thousands of dollars; (p) preliminary; (1) Figures cover the Albuquerque, NM Metropolitan Statistical Area
Source: National Association of Realtors, Median Sales Price of Existing Single-Family Homes for Metropolitan Areas, 4th Quarter 2020

Qualifying Income Based on Median Sales Price of Existing Single-Family Homes

Area	With 5% Down ($)	With 10% Down ($)	With 20% Down ($)
MSA[1]	49,839	47,216	41,970
U.S. Average	59,266	56,147	49,908

Note: Figures are preliminary; Qualifying income is based on a mortgage rate of 2.81%. Monthly principal and interest payment is limited to 25% of income; (1) Figures cover the Albuquerque, NM Metropolitan Statistical Area
Source: National Association of Realtors, Qualifying Income Based on Median Sales Price of Existing Single-Family Homes for Metropolitan Areas, 4th Quarter 2020

Home Value Distribution

Area	Under $50,000	$50,000 -$99,999	$100,000 -$149,999	$150,000 -$199,999	$200,000 -$299,999	$300,000 -$499,999	$500,000 -$999,999	$1,000,000 or more
City	4.5	4.4	16.9	25.1	29.5	15.9	3.3	0.5
MSA[1]	5.8	7.6	16.8	22.7	25.8	15.5	4.8	1.0
U.S.	6.9	12.0	13.3	14.0	19.6	19.3	11.4	3.4

Note: Figures are percentages and cover owner-occupied housing units; (1) Figures cover the Albuquerque, NM Metropolitan Statistical Area
Source: U.S. Census Bureau, 2015-2019 American Community Survey 5-Year Estimates

Year Housing Structure Built

Area	2010 or Later	2000 -2009	1990 -1999	1980 -1989	1970 -1979	1960 -1969	1950 -1959	1940 -1949	Before 1940	Median Year
City	4.3	16.3	15.3	15.5	19.6	10.3	11.5	4.4	2.8	1981
MSA[1]	4.2	17.6	18.2	17.0	18.0	9.2	9.1	3.7	3.0	1984
U.S.	5.2	14.0	13.9	13.4	15.2	10.6	10.3	4.9	12.6	1978

Note: Figures are percentages except for Median Year; Note: (1) Figures cover the Albuquerque, NM Metropolitan Statistical Area
Source: U.S. Census Bureau, 2015-2019 American Community Survey 5-Year Estimates

Gross Monthly Rent

Area	Under $500	$500 -$999	$1,000 -$1,499	$1,500 -$1,999	$2,000 -$2,499	$2,500 -$2,999	$3,000 and up	Median ($)
City	8.1	54.4	29.1	6.5	1.1	0.3	0.4	873
MSA[1]	8.0	52.5	30.1	7.5	1.1	0.3	0.4	892
U.S.	9.4	36.2	30.0	14.0	5.6	2.4	2.4	1,062

Note: Figures are percentages except for Median; Gross rent is the contract rent plus the estimated average monthly cost of utilities (electricity, gas, and water and sewer) and fuels (oil, coal, kerosene, wood, etc.) if these are paid by the renter (or paid for the renter by someone else); (1) Figures cover the Albuquerque, NM Metropolitan Statistical Area
Source: U.S. Census Bureau, 2015-2019 American Community Survey 5-Year Estimates

HEALTH

Health Risk Factors

Category	MSA[1] (%)	U.S. (%)
Adults aged 18–64 who have any kind of health care coverage	86.1	87.3
Adults who reported being in good or better health	80.8	82.4
Adults who have been told they have high blood cholesterol	31.5	33.0
Adults who have been told they have high blood pressure	28.5	32.3
Adults who are current smokers	16.7	17.1
Adults who currently use E-cigarettes	5.3	4.6
Adults who currently use chewing tobacco, snuff, or snus	2.3	4.0
Adults who are heavy drinkers[2]	4.6	6.3
Adults who are binge drinkers[3]	14.2	17.4
Adults who are overweight (BMI 25.0 - 29.9)	37.2	35.3
Adults who are obese (BMI 30.0 - 99.8)	26.8	31.3
Adults who participated in any physical activities in the past month	77.6	74.4
Adults who always or nearly always wears a seat belt	96.5	94.3

Note: (1) Figures cover the Albuquerque, NM Metropolitan Statistical Area; (2) Heavy drinkers are classified as adult men having more than 14 drinks per week and adult women having more than 7 drinks per week; (3) Binge drinkers are classified as males having five or more drinks on one occasion or females having four or more drinks on one occasion
Source: Centers for Disease Control and Prevention, Behaviorial Risk Factor Surveillance System, SMART: Selected Metropolitan Area Risk Trends, 2017

Acute and Chronic Health Conditions

Category	MSA[1] (%)	U.S. (%)
Adults who have ever been told they had a heart attack	3.8	4.2
Adults who have ever been told they have angina or coronary heart disease	2.5	3.9
Adults who have ever been told they had a stroke	2.3	3.0
Adults who have ever been told they have asthma	15.1	14.2
Adults who have ever been told they have arthritis	25.6	24.9
Adults who have ever been told they have diabetes[2]	9.1	10.5
Adults who have ever been told they had skin cancer	6.5	6.2
Adults who have ever been told they had any other types of cancer	6.6	7.1
Adults who have ever been told they have COPD	6.2	6.5
Adults who have ever been told they have kidney disease	3.3	3.0
Adults who have ever been told they have a form of depression	22.0	20.5

Note: (1) Figures cover the Albuquerque, NM Metropolitan Statistical Area; (2) Figures do not include pregnancy-related, borderline, or pre-diabetes
Source: Centers for Disease Control and Prevention, Behaviorial Risk Factor Surveillance System, SMART: Selected Metropolitan Area Risk Trends, 2017

Health Screening and Vaccination Rates

Category	MSA[1] (%)	U.S. (%)
Adults aged 65+ who have had flu shot within the past year	58.9	60.7
Adults aged 65+ who have ever had a pneumonia vaccination	76.5	75.4
Adults who have ever been tested for HIV	39.0	36.1
Adults who have ever had the shingles or zoster vaccine?	36.1	28.9
Adults who have had their blood cholesterol checked within the last five years	82.2	85.9

Note: n/a not available; (1) Figures cover the Albuquerque, NM Metropolitan Statistical Area.
Source: Centers for Disease Control and Prevention, Behaviorial Risk Factor Surveillance System, SMART: Selected Metropolitan Area Risk Trends, 2017

Disability Status

Category	MSA[1] (%)	U.S. (%)
Adults who reported being deaf	6.7	6.7
Are you blind or have serious difficulty seeing, even when wearing glasses?	5.2	4.5
Are you limited in any way in any of your usual activities due of arthritis?	14.3	12.9
Do you have difficulty doing errands alone?	8.0	6.8
Do you have difficulty dressing or bathing?	3.6	3.6
Do you have serious difficulty concentrating/remembering/making decisions?	13.1	10.7
Do you have serious difficulty walking or climbing stairs?	12.8	13.6

Note: (1) Figures cover the Albuquerque, NM Metropolitan Statistical Area.
Source: Centers for Disease Control and Prevention, Behaviorial Risk Factor Surveillance System, SMART: Selected Metropolitan Area Risk Trends, 2017

Mortality Rates for the Top 10 Causes of Death in the U.S.

ICD-10[a] Sub-Chapter	ICD-10[a] Code	Age-Adjusted Mortality Rate[1] per 100,000 population	
		County[2]	U.S.
Malignant neoplasms	C00-C97	135.6	149.2
Ischaemic heart diseases	I20-I25	105.5	90.5
Other forms of heart disease	I30-I51	37.1	52.2
Chronic lower respiratory diseases	J40-J47	41.0	39.6
Other degenerative diseases of the nervous system	G30-G31	31.0	37.6
Cerebrovascular diseases	I60-I69	36.4	37.2
Other external causes of accidental injury	W00-X59	53.8	36.1
Organic, including symptomatic, mental disorders	F01-F09	27.5	29.4
Hypertensive diseases	I10-I15	13.3	24.1
Diabetes mellitus	E10-E14	19.7	21.5

Note: (a) ICD-10 = International Classification of Diseases 10th Revision; (1) Mortality rates are a three-year average covering 2017-2019; (2) Figures cover Bernalillo County.
Source: Centers for Disease Control and Prevention, National Center for Health Statistics. Underlying Cause of Death 1999-2019 on CDC WONDER Online Database

Mortality Rates for Selected Causes of Death

ICD-10[a] Sub-Chapter	ICD-10[a] Code	Age-Adjusted Mortality Rate[1] per 100,000 population	
		County[2]	U.S.
Assault	X85-Y09	12.3	6.0
Diseases of the liver	K70-K76	25.8	14.4
Human immunodeficiency virus (HIV) disease	B20-B24	1.0	1.5
Influenza and pneumonia	J09-J18	11.5	13.8
Intentional self-harm	X60-X84	23.6	14.1
Malnutrition	E40-E46	9.2	2.3
Obesity and other hyperalimentation	E65-E68	2.7	2.1
Renal failure	N17-N19	9.4	12.6
Transport accidents	V01-V99	15.3	12.3
Viral hepatitis	B15-B19	1.8	1.2

Note: (a) ICD-10 = International Classification of Diseases 10th Revision; (1) Mortality rates are a three-year average covering 2017-2019; (2) Figures cover Bernalillo County; Data are suppressed when the data meet the criteria for confidentiality constraints; Mortality rates are flagged as unreliable when the rate would be calculated with a numerator of 20 or less.
Source: Centers for Disease Control and Prevention, National Center for Health Statistics. Underlying Cause of Death 1999-2019 on CDC WONDER Online Database

Health Insurance Coverage

Area	With Health Insurance	With Private Health Insurance	With Public Health Insurance	Without Health Insurance	Population Under Age 19 Without Health Insurance
City	92.1	60.9	43.0	7.9	3.4
MSA[1]	91.7	60.2	44.2	8.3	4.1
U.S.	91.2	67.9	35.1	8.8	5.1

Note: Figures are percentages that cover the civilian noninstitutionalized population; (1) Figures cover the Albuquerque, NM Metropolitan Statistical Area
Source: U.S. Census Bureau, 2015-2019 American Community Survey 5-Year Estimates

Number of Medical Professionals

Area	MDs[3]	DOs[3,4]	Dentists	Podiatrists	Chiropractors	Optometrists
County[1] (number)	3,099	136	592	67	166	115
County[1] (rate[2])	457.1	20.1	87.2	9.9	24.4	16.9
U.S. (rate[2])	282.9	22.7	71.2	6.2	28.1	16.9

35001
Note: Data as of 2019 unless noted; (1) Data covers Bernalillo County; (2) Rate per 100,000 population; (3) Data as of 2018 and includes all active, non-federal physicians; (4) Doctor of Osteopathic Medicine
Source: U.S. Department of Health and Human Services, Health Resources and Services Administration, Bureau of Health Professions, Area Resource File (ARF) 2019-2020

EDUCATION

Public School District Statistics

District Name	Schls	Pupils	Pupil/ Teacher Ratio	Minority Pupils[1] (%)	Free Lunch Eligible[2] (%)	IEP[3] (%)
Albuquerque Public Schools	173	89,788	15.2	79.2	65.3	18.2

Note: Table includes school districts with 2,000 or more students; (1) Percentage of students that are not non-Hispanic white; (2) Percentage of students that are eligible for the free lunch program; (3) Percentage of students that have an Individualized Education Program.
Source: U.S. Department of Education, National Center for Education Statistics, Common Core of Data, Local Education Agency (School District) Universe Survey: School Year 2018-2019; U.S. Department of Education, National Center for Education Statistics, Common Core of Data, Public Elementary/Secondary School Universe Survey: School Year 2018-2019

Best High Schools

According to *U.S. News,* Albuquerque is home to two of the top 500 high schools in the U.S.: **Albuquerque Institute of Math and Science** (#103); **Cottonwood Classical Preparatory School** (#210). Nearly 18,000 public, magnet and charter schools were ranked based on their performance on state assessments and how well they prepare students for college. *U.S. News & World Report, "Best High Schools 2020"*

Highest Level of Education

Area	Less than H.S.	H.S. Diploma	Some College, No Deg.	Associate Degree	Bachelor's Degree	Master's Degree	Prof. School Degree	Doctorate Degree
City	10.3	22.5	23.4	8.5	19.4	10.6	2.7	2.5
MSA[1]	11.4	24.6	23.3	8.5	17.9	9.8	2.3	2.2
U.S.	12.0	27.0	20.4	8.5	19.8	8.8	2.1	1.4

Note: Figures cover persons age 25 and over; (1) Figures cover the Albuquerque, NM Metropolitan Statistical Area
Source: U.S. Census Bureau, 2015-2019 American Community Survey 5-Year Estimates

Educational Attainment by Race

Area	High School Graduate or Higher (%)					Bachelor's Degree or Higher (%)				
	Total	White	Black	Asian	Hisp.[2]	Total	White	Black	Asian	Hisp.[2]
City	89.7	91.1	92.0	85.5	82.5	35.2	38.1	31.2	48.3	21.5
MSA[1]	88.6	90.4	91.0	87.3	81.1	32.2	35.0	30.4	47.8	19.1
U.S.	88.0	89.9	86.0	87.1	68.7	32.1	33.5	21.6	54.3	16.4

Note: Figures shown cover persons 25 years old and over; (1) Figures cover the Albuquerque, NM Metropolitan Statistical Area; (2) People of Hispanic origin can be of any race
Source: U.S. Census Bureau, 2015-2019 American Community Survey 5-Year Estimates

School Enrollment by Grade and Control

Area	Preschool (%)		Kindergarten (%)		Grades 1 - 4 (%)		Grades 5 - 8 (%)		Grades 9 - 12 (%)	
	Public	Private	Public	Private	Public	Private	Public	Private	Public	Private
City	59.3	40.7	87.2	12.8	91.8	8.2	90.0	10.0	92.0	8.0
MSA[1]	64.5	35.5	85.6	14.4	90.1	9.9	89.4	10.6	91.7	8.3
U.S.	59.1	40.9	87.6	12.4	89.5	10.5	89.4	10.6	90.1	9.9

Note: Figures shown cover persons 3 years old and over; (1) Figures cover the Albuquerque, NM Metropolitan Statistical Area
Source: U.S. Census Bureau, 2015-2019 American Community Survey 5-Year Estimates

Higher Education

Four-Year Colleges			Two-Year Colleges			Medical Schools[1]	Law Schools[2]	Voc/ Tech[3]
Public	Private Non-profit	Private For-profit	Public	Private Non-profit	Private For-profit			
1	0	4	2	0	2	1	1	5

Note: Figures cover institutions located within the city limits and include main campuses only; (1) includes schools accredited by the Liaison Committee on Medical Education and the American Osteopathic Association's Commission on Osteopathic College Accreditation; (2) includes ABA-accredited schools, schools with provisional ABA accreditation, and state accredited schools; (3) includes all schools with programs that are less than 2 years.
Source: National Center for Education Statistics, Integrated Postsecondary Education System (IPEDS), 2019-20; Wikipedia, List of Medical Schools in the United States, accessed April 2, 2021; Wikipedia, List of Law Schools in the United States, accessed April 2, 2021

According to *U.S. News & World Report,* the Albuquerque, NM metro area is home to one of the top 200 national universities in the U.S.: **University of New Mexico** (#187 tie). The indicators used to capture academic quality fall into a number of categories: assessment by administrators at peer institutions; retention of students; faculty resources; student selectivity; financial resources; alumni giving; high school counselor ratings of colleges; and graduation rate. *U.S. News & World Report, "America's Best Colleges 2021"*

EMPLOYERS

Major Employers

Company Name	Industry
Central New Mexico Community College	Vocational schools
City of Albuquerque	Municipal government
City of Albuquerque Police Department	Municipal police
Jack Henry & Associates	Computers
Laguna Development Corporation	Grocery stores, independent
Mediplex of Massachusetts	Nursing home, exc skilled & intermediate care facility
Sandia Corporation	Noncommercial research organizations
The Boeing Company	Aircraft
U.S. Fish and Wildlife Service	Fish & wildlife conservation agency, government
United States Department of Energy	Energy development & conservation agency, government
United States Department of the Air Force	Testing laboratories
University of New Mexico	University
University of New Mexico Hospital	General medical & surgical hospitals
USAF	U.S. military
Veterans Health Administration	Administration of veterans' affiars
Veterans Hospital	General medical & surgical hospitals

Note: Companies shown are located within the Albuquerque, NM Metropolitan Statistical Area.
Source: Hoovers.com; Wikipedia

PUBLIC SAFETY

Crime Rate

Area	All Crimes	Violent Crimes				Property Crimes		
		Murder	Rape[3]	Robbery	Aggrav. Assault	Burglary	Larceny -Theft	Motor Vehicle Theft
City	n/a	14.9	86.5	302.4	948.0	n/a	3,672.1	965.4
Suburbs[1]	n/a	2.5	28.6	23.0	502.8	n/a	995.5	214.2
Metro[2]	n/a	10.1	64.0	194.0	775.3	n/a	2,633.7	674.0
U.S.	2,489.3	5.0	42.6	81.6	250.2	340.5	1,549.5	219.9

Note: Figures are crimes per 100,000 population; (1) All areas within the metro area that are located outside the city limits; (2) Figures cover the Albuquerque, NM Metropolitan Statistical Area; (3) All figures shown were reported using the revised Uniform Crime Reporting (UCR) definition of rape.
Source: FBI Uniform Crime Reports, 2019

Hate Crimes

Area	Number of Quarters Reported	Number of Incidents per Bias Motivation					
		Race/Ethnicity/ Ancestry	Religion	Sexual Orientation	Disability	Gender	Gender Identity
City	4	25	7	6	1	0	0
U.S.	4	3,963	1,521	1,195	157	69	198

Source: Federal Bureau of Investigation, Hate Crime Statistics 2019

Identity Theft Consumer Reports

Area	Reports	Reports per 100,000 Population	Rank[2]
MSA[1]	1,830	199	212
U.S.	1,387,615	423	-

Note: (1) Figures cover the Albuquerque, NM Metropolitan Statistical Area; (2) Rank ranges from 1 to 391 where 1 indicates greatest number of identity theft reports per 100,000 population
Source: Federal Trade Commission, Consumer Sentinel Network Data Book 2020

Fraud and Other Consumer Reports

Area	Reports	Reports per 100,000 Population	Rank[2]
MSA[1]	7,868	857	68
U.S.	3,385,133	1,031	-

Note: (1) Figures cover the Albuquerque, NM Metropolitan Statistical Area; (2) Rank ranges from 1 to 391 where 1 indicates greatest number of fraud and other consumer reports per 100,000 population
Source: Federal Trade Commission, Consumer Sentinel Network Data Book 2020

POLITICS

2020 Presidential Election Results

Area	Biden	Trump	Jorgensen	Hawkins	Other
Bernalillo County	61.0	36.6	1.5	0.5	0.4
U.S.	51.3	46.8	1.2	0.3	0.5

Note: Results are percentages and may not add to 100% due to rounding
Source: Dave Leip's Atlas of U.S. Presidential Elections

SPORTS

Professional Sports Teams

Team Name	League	Year Established
No teams are located in the metro area		

Source: Wikipedia, Major Professional Sports Teams of the United States and Canada, April 6, 2021

CLIMATE

Average and Extreme Temperatures

Temperature	Jan	Feb	Mar	Apr	May	Jun	Jul	Aug	Sep	Oct	Nov	Dec	Yr.
Extreme High (°F)	69	76	85	89	98	105	105	101	100	91	77	72	105
Average High (°F)	47	53	61	71	80	90	92	89	83	72	57	48	70
Average Temp. (°F)	35	40	47	56	65	75	79	76	70	58	45	36	57
Average Low (°F)	23	27	33	41	50	59	65	63	56	44	31	24	43
Extreme Low (°F)	-17	-5	8	19	28	40	52	50	37	21	-7	-7	-17

Note: Figures cover the years 1948-1992
Source: National Climatic Data Center, International Station Meteorological Climate Summary, 9/96

Average Precipitation/Snowfall/Humidity

Precip./Humidity	Jan	Feb	Mar	Apr	May	Jun	Jul	Aug	Sep	Oct	Nov	Dec	Yr.
Avg. Precip. (in.)	0.4	0.4	0.5	0.4	0.5	0.5	1.4	1.5	0.9	0.9	0.4	0.5	8.5
Avg. Snowfall (in.)	3	2	2	1	Tr	0	0	0	Tr	Tr	1	3	11
Avg. Rel. Hum. 5am (%)	68	64	55	48	48	45	60	65	61	60	63	68	59
Avg. Rel. Hum. 5pm (%)	41	33	25	20	19	18	27	30	29	29	35	43	29

Note: Figures cover the years 1948-1992; Tr = Trace amounts (<0.05 in. of rain; <0.5 in. of snow)
Source: National Climatic Data Center, International Station Meteorological Climate Summary, 9/96

Weather Conditions

Temperature			Daytime Sky			Precipitation		
10°F & below	32°F & below	90°F & above	Clear	Partly cloudy	Cloudy	0.01 inch or more precip.	0.1 inch or more snow/ice	Thunder-storms
4	114	65	140	160	65	60	9	38

Note: Figures are average number of days per year and cover the years 1948-1992
Source: National Climatic Data Center, International Station Meteorological Climate Summary, 9/96

HAZARDOUS WASTE

Superfund Sites

The Albuquerque, NM metro area is home to three sites on the EPA's Superfund National Priorities List: **AT&SF (Albuquerque)** (final); **Fruit Avenue Plume** (final); **South Valley** (final). There are a total of 1,375 Superfund sites with a status of proposed or final on the list in the U.S. *U.S. Environmental Protection Agency, National Priorities List, April 7, 2021*

AIR QUALITY

Air Quality Trends: Ozone

	1990	1995	2000	2005	2010	2015	2016	2017	2018	2019
MSA[1]	0.072	0.070	0.072	0.073	0.066	0.066	0.065	0.069	0.074	0.067
U.S.	0.088	0.089	0.082	0.080	0.073	0.068	0.069	0.068	0.069	0.065

Note: (1) Data covers the Albuquerque, NM Metropolitan Statistical Area. The values shown are the composite ozone concentration averages among trend sites based on the highest fourth daily maximum 8-hour concentration in parts per million. These trends are based on sites having an adequate record of monitoring data during the trend period. Data from exceptional events are included.
Source: U.S. Environmental Protection Agency, Air Quality Monitoring Information, "Air Quality Trends by City, 1990-2019"

Air Quality Index

Area	Percent of Days when Air Quality was...[2]					AQI Statistics[2]	
	Good	Moderate	Unhealthy for Sensitive Groups	Unhealthy	Very Unhealthy	Maximum	Median
MSA[1]	44.1	54.8	1.1	0.0	0.0	108	53

Note: (1) Data covers the Albuquerque, NM Metropolitan Statistical Area; (2) Based on 365 days with AQI data in 2019. Air Quality Index (AQI) is an index for reporting daily air quality. EPA calculates the AQI for five major air pollutants regulated by the Clean Air Act: ground-level ozone, particle pollution (aka particulate matter), carbon monoxide, sulfur dioxide, and nitrogen dioxide. The AQI runs from 0 to 500. The higher the AQI value, the greater the level of air pollution and the greater the health concern. There are six AQI categories: "Good" AQI is between 0 and 50. Air quality is considered satisfactory; "Moderate" AQI is between 51 and 100. Air quality is acceptable; "Unhealthy for Sensitive Groups" When AQI values are between 101 and 150, members of sensitive groups may experience health effects; "Unhealthy" When AQI values are between 151 and 200 everyone may begin to experience health effects; "Very Unhealthy" AQI values between 201 and 300 trigger a health alert; "Hazardous" AQI values over 300 trigger warnings of emergency conditions (not shown).
Source: U.S. Environmental Protection Agency, Air Quality Index Report, 2019

Air Quality Index Pollutants

Area	Percent of Days when AQI Pollutant was...[2]					
	Carbon Monoxide	Nitrogen Dioxide	Ozone	Sulfur Dioxide	Particulate Matter 2.5	Particulate Matter 10
MSA[1]	0.0	0.0	69.0	0.0	18.1	12.9

Note: (1) Data covers the Albuquerque, NM Metropolitan Statistical Area; (2) Based on 365 days with AQI data in 2019. The Air Quality Index (AQI) is an index for reporting daily air quality. EPA calculates the AQI for five major air pollutants regulated by the Clean Air Act: ground-level ozone, particle pollution (also known as particulate matter), carbon monoxide, sulfur dioxide, and nitrogen dioxide. The AQI runs from 0 to 500. The higher the AQI value, the greater the level of air pollution and the greater the health concern.
Source: U.S. Environmental Protection Agency, Air Quality Index Report, 2019

Maximum Air Pollutant Concentrations: Particulate Matter, Ozone, CO and Lead

	Particulate Matter 10 (ug/m^3)	Particulate Matter 2.5 Wtd AM (ug/m^3)	Particulate Matter 2.5 24-Hr (ug/m^3)	Ozone (ppm)	Carbon Monoxide (ppm)	Lead (ug/m^3)
MSA[1] Level	141	7.7	20	0.069	1	n/a
NAAQS[2]	150	15	35	0.075	9	0.15
Met NAAQS[2]	Yes	Yes	Yes	Yes	Yes	n/a

Note: (1) Data covers the Albuquerque, NM Metropolitan Statistical Area; Data from exceptional events are included; (2) National Ambient Air Quality Standards; ppm = parts per million; ug/m^3 = micrograms per cubic meter; n/a not available.
Concentrations: Particulate Matter 10 (coarse particulate)—highest second maximum 24-hour concentration; Particulate Matter 2.5 Wtd AM (fine particulate)—highest weighted annual mean concentration; Particulate Matter 2.5 24-Hour (fine particulate)—highest 98th percentile 24-hour concentration; Ozone—highest fourth daily maximum 8-hour concentration; Carbon Monoxide—highest second maximum non-overlapping 8-hour concentration; Lead—maximum running 3-month average
Source: U.S. Environmental Protection Agency, Air Quality Monitoring Information, "Air Quality Statistics by City, 2019"

Maximum Air Pollutant Concentrations: Nitrogen Dioxide and Sulfur Dioxide

	Nitrogen Dioxide AM (ppb)	Nitrogen Dioxide 1-Hr (ppb)	Sulfur Dioxide AM (ppb)	Sulfur Dioxide 1-Hr (ppb)	Sulfur Dioxide 24-Hr (ppb)
MSA[1] Level	9	44	n/a	4	n/a
NAAQS[2]	53	100	30	75	140
Met NAAQS[2]	Yes	Yes	n/a	Yes	n/a

Note: (1) Data covers the Albuquerque, NM Metropolitan Statistical Area; Data from exceptional events are included; (2) National Ambient Air Quality Standards; ppm = parts per million; ug/m^3 = micrograms per cubic meter; n/a not available.
Concentrations: Nitrogen Dioxide AM—highest arithmetic mean concentration; Nitrogen Dioxide 1-Hr—highest 98th percentile 1-hour daily maximum concentration; Sulfur Dioxide AM—highest annual mean concentration; Sulfur Dioxide 1-Hr—highest 99th percentile 1-hour daily maximum concentration; Sulfur Dioxide 24-Hr—highest second maximum 24-hour concentration
Source: U.S. Environmental Protection Agency, Air Quality Monitoring Information, "Air Quality Statistics by City, 2019"

Anchorage, Alaska

Background

Anchorage, in south central Alaska, is the state's largest city and a center for the state's communication, transportation, health care, and finance industries. Originally powered by the railroads and the fishing industry, Anchorage's economy has in more recent times been closely tied to petroleum production, which accounts for more than 20 percent of the nation's oil reserves.

This modern city lies in a spectacular natural setting, with the Chugach Mountain Range across its eastern skyline and the waters of the Cook Inlet to the west. The city boasts all the advantages of a dynamic urban center, while its residents enjoy a natural environment that teems with bear, moose, caribou, fox, eagles, wolves, dall sheep, orcas, and beluga whales.

The city was incorporated in 1920, and grew slowly for several decades. During World War II, when airfields and roads were constructed to aid in the war effort, the population expanded dramatically; by 1946, Anchorage was home to more than 40,000 people.

In 1964, the region was hit by the strongest earthquake ever to strike North America. There was extensive damage and some loss of life, but the city was quickly rebuilt; in fact, reconstruction was so prompt, efficient, and successful that many look back on the period with considerable civic pride. Earthquakes are not uncommon to the region, and a moderate 5.7 event occurred in Anchorage in January 2009.

In 1951, Anchorage International Airport, which is now Ted Stevens International Airport (ANC), was completed, and the city became vital to the emerging air transport industry as new routes were created. Ted Stevens International Airport flies more than 560 transcontinental cargo flights each week and is the busiest cargo airport in the country. Elmendorf Air Force Base at the northeast end of town, and Anchorage's pioneering development of bush aviation, which serves the entire interior of Alaska, further testify to the importance of air travel to the city's development. Also located at the airport are Fort Richardson Army Post and Kulis Air National Guard Base that together employ 8,500.

Oil in Alaska was first discovered in 1957, and 17 oil companies subsequently set up headquarters in Anchorage, giving the city a tremendous economic boost. In 1968, the large North Slope field was discovered, Anchorage was again a major beneficiary. With the completion of the Trans-Alaskan Pipeline System in 1977, Anchorage entered into its contemporary period of sustained population growth and dynamic economic development.

Alaska's tourism industry accounts for over 50,000 jobs and an estimated economic impact of more than $80 million in Anchorage alone. Anchorage is also known as a tax-friendly city. The 7-year Anchorage Port Modernization Project was launched in 2017.

The city's cultural amenities include the Anchorage Museum at Rasmuson Center and the Alaska Aviation Heritage Museum, which chronicles the story of Alaska's early and pioneering air transport system. Near the city is the Potter Section House Railway Museum, which pays homage to the state's vital rail industry. The city also boasts the Alaska Center for the Performing Arts and the Alaska Botanical Garden. Delaney Park, also known as the Park Strip, is a venerable and valued recreational resource in the city's business district, and its ongoing improvement looks toward a year-round "Central Park" for Anchorage. The Alaska State Fair has been recognized as one of the Top 100 Events in North America.

The city is an educational center with two universities and many technical, vocational, and private schools. A campus of the University of Alaska has been in Anchorage since 1954, and the city is also home to Alaska Pacific University.

The natural environment of Anchorage is spectacular, and at nearby Portage Glacier, one can watch the glacier "calving," as huge blocks of ice crash into the lake below. Anchorage is also located at one end of the famous annual Iditarod Trail Sled Dog Race.

Because of its long summer days and relatively mild temperatures, Anchorage is called "The City of Lights and Flowers," and is adorned in summer throughout the municipality with open, grassy expanses and flowers. The season brings out a friendly competition among the city's residents, who plant along streets, in parks, private gardens, window boxes, and lobbies.

The weather in Anchorage, contrary to what many believe, is not savagely cold. It is tempered by the city's location on the coast and by the Alaska Mountain Range, which acts as a barrier to very cold air from the north. Snow season lasts from October to May. Summers can bring fog and rain.

Rankings

General Rankings

- For its "Best for Vets: Places to Live 2019" rankings, *Military Times* evaluated 599 cities (83 large, 234 medium, 282 small) and compared the locations across three broad categories: veteran and military culture/services; economic indicators; and livability factors such as health, crime, traffic, and school quality. Anchorage ranked #15 out of the top 25, in the large city category (population of more than 250,000). Data points more specific to veterans and the military weighed more heavily than others. *rebootcamp.militarytimes.com, "Military Times Best Places to Live 2019," September 10, 2018*

- In their seventh annual survey, Livability.com looked at data for more than 1,000 small to mid-sized U.S. cities to determine the rankings for Livability's "Top 100 Best Places to Live" in 2020. Anchorage ranked #31. Criteria: housing and affordable living; vibrant economy; social and civic engagement; education; demographics; health care options; transportation & infrastructure; and abundant lifestyle amenities. *Livability.com, "Top 100 Best Places to Live 2020" October 2020*

Business/Finance Rankings

- For its annual survey of the "Most Expensive U.S. Cities to Live In," Kiplinger applied Cost of Living Index statistics developed by the Council for Community and Economic Research to U.S. Census Bureau population and median household income data for 256 urban areas. Anchorage was among the 20 most expensive in the country. *Kiplinger.com, "The 20 Most Expensive Cities in the U.S.," July 29, 2020*

- The Anchorage metro area appeared on the Milken Institute "2021 Best Performing Cities" list. Rank: #174 out of 200 large metro areas (population over 250,000). Criteria: job growth; wage and salary growth; high-tech output growth; housing affordability; household broadband access. *Milken Institute, "Best-Performing Cities 2021," February 16, 2021*

- *Forbes* ranked the 200 most populous metro areas to determine the nation's "Best Places for Business and Careers." The Anchorage metro area was ranked #185. Criteria: costs (business and living); job growth (past and projected); income growth; quality of life; educational attainment (college and high school); projected economic growth; cultural and leisure opportunities; workplace tolerance laws; net migration patterns. *Forbes, "The Best Places for Business and Careers 2019: Seattle Still On Top," October 30, 2019*

Education Rankings

- Personal finance website *WalletHub* analyzed the 150 largest U.S. metropolitan statistical areas to determine where the most educated Americans are putting their degrees to work. Criteria: education levels; percentage of workers with degrees; education quality and attainment gap; public school quality rankings; quality and enrollment of each metro area's universities. Anchorage was ranked #48 (#1 = most educated city). *www.WalletHub.com, "Most and Least Educated Cities in America," July 20, 2020*

- Anchorage was selected as one of America's most literate cities. The city ranked #52 out of the 84 largest U.S. cities. Criteria: number of booksellers; library resources; Internet resources; educational attainment; periodical publishing resources; newspaper circulation. *Central Connecticut State University, "America's Most Literate Cities, 2018," February 2019*

Environmental Rankings

- Anchorage was highlighted as one of the cleanest metro areas for ozone air pollution in the U.S. during 2016 through 2018. The list represents cities with no monitored ozone air pollution in unhealthful ranges. *American Lung Association, "State of the Air 2020," April 21, 2020*

- Anchorage was highlighted as one of the top 25 cleanest metro areas for year-round particle pollution (Annual PM 2.5) in the U.S. during 2016 through 2018. The area ranked #16. *American Lung Association, "State of the Air 2020," April 21, 2020*

Health/Fitness Rankings

- For each of the 100 largest cities in the United States, the American Fitness Index®, published by the American College of Sports Medicine and the Anthem Foundation, evaluated community infrastructure and 33 health behaviors including preventive health, levels of chronic disease conditions, pedestrian safety, air quality, and community resources that support physical activity. Anchorage ranked #37 for "community fitness." *americanfitnessindex.org, "2020 ACSM American Fitness Index Summary Report," July 14, 2020*

Real Estate Rankings

- *WalletHub* compared the most populated U.S. cities to determine which had the best markets for real estate agents. Anchorage ranked #145 where demand was high and pay was the best. Criteria: sales per agent; annual median wage for real-estate agents; monthly average starting salary for real estate agents; real estate job density and competition; unemployment rate; home turnover rate; housing-market health index; and other relevant metrics. *www.WalletHub.com, "2019's Best Places to Be a Real Estate Agent," April 24, 2019*

- Anchorage was ranked #106 out of 268 metro areas in terms of housing affordability in 2020 by the National Association of Home Builders (#1 = most affordable). Criteria: the share of homes sold in that area affordable to a family earning the local median income, based on standard mortgage underwriting criteria. *National Association of Home Builders®, NAHB-Wells Fargo Housing Opportunity Index, 4th Quarter 2020*

Safety Rankings

- To identify the most dangerous cities in America, 24/7 Wall Street focused on violent crime categories—murder, non-negligent manslaughter, rape, robbery, and aggravated assault—and property crime as reported in the FBI's 2019 annual Uniform Crime Report. Criteria also included median income from American Community Survey and unemployment figures from Bureau of Labor Statistics. For cities with populations over 100,000, Anchorage was ranked #15. *247wallst.com, "America's 50 Most Dangerous Cities" November 16, 2020*

- Statistics drawn from the FBI's Uniform Crime Report were used to rank the metropolitan statistical areas where violent crime rose the most between the years 2014–2019. 24/7 Wall Street found that the Anchorage metro area placed #17 of those with an increase of at least 32.5 percent in violent crime. *247wallst.com, "25 Cities Where Crime Is Soaring," February 18, 2021*

- Allstate ranked the 200 largest cities in America in terms of driver safety. Anchorage ranked #27. Criteria: internal property damage claims over a two-year period from January 2016 to December 2017. The report helps increase the importance of safety and awareness behind the wheel. *Allstate, "Allstate America's Best Drivers Report, 2019" June 24, 2019*

- Anchorage was identified as one of the most dangerous cities in America by NeighborhoodScout. The city ranked #28 out of 100 (#1 = most dangerous). Criteria: number of violent crimes per 1,000 residents. The editors evaluated cities with 25,000 or more residents. *NeighborhoodScout.com, "2021 Top 100 Most Dangerous Cities in the U.S.," January 2, 2021*

- The National Insurance Crime Bureau ranked 384 metro areas in the U.S. in terms of per capita rates of vehicle theft. The Anchorage metro area ranked #23 (#1 = highest rate). Criteria: number of vehicle theft offenses per 100,000 inhabitants in 2019. *National Insurance Crime Bureau, "Hot Spots 2019," July 21, 2020*

Seniors/Retirement Rankings

- From its Best Cities for Successful Aging indexes, the Milken Institute generated rankings for metropolitan areas, weighing data in nine categories—health care, wellness, living arrangements, transportation and convenience, financial characteristics, education, employment, community engagement, and overall livability. The Anchorage metro area was ranked #52 overall in the small metro area category. *Milken Institute, "Best Cities for Successful Aging, 2017" March 14, 2017*

Women/Minorities Rankings

- *Women's Health*, together with the site Yelp, identified the 15 "Wellthiest" spots in the U.S. Anchorage appeared among the top for happiest, healthiest, outdoorsiest and Zen-iest. *Women's Health, "The 15 Wellthiest Cities in the U.S." July 5, 2017*

- Anchorage was selected as one of the gayest cities in America by *The Advocate*. The city ranked #20 out of 25. Criteria, among many: Trans Pride parades/festivals; gay rugby teams; lesbian bars; LGBT centers; theater screenings of "Moonlight"; LGBT-inclusive nondiscrimination ordinances; and gay bowling teams. *The Advocate, "Queerest Cities in America 2017" January 12, 2017*

- Personal finance website *WalletHub* compared more than 180 U.S. cities across two key dimensions, "Hispanic Business-Friendliness" and "Hispanic Purchasing Power," to arrive at the most favorable conditions for Hispanic entrepreneurs. Anchorage was ranked #49 out of 182. Criteria includes: share of Hispanic-Owned Businesses; Hispanic entrepreneurship rate to median annual income of Hispanics; Small Business-Friendliness score; cost of living; and number of Hispanics with at least a bachelor's degree. *WalletHub.com, "2019's Best Cities for Hispanic Entrepreneurs," May 1, 2019*

Miscellaneous Rankings

- *WalletHub* compared the 150 most populated U.S. cities to determine their operating efficiency. A "Quality of City Services" score was constructed for each city and then divided by the total budget per capita to reveal which were managed the best. Anchorage ranked #75. Criteria: financial stability; economy; education; safety; health; infrastructure and pollution. *www.WalletHub.com, "2020's Best- & Worst-Run Cities in America," June 29, 2020*

Business Environment

DEMOGRAPHICS

Population Growth

Area	1990 Census	2000 Census	2010 Census	2019* Estimate	Population Growth (%)	
					1990-2019	2010-2019
City	226,338	260,283	291,826	293,531	29.7	0.6
MSA[1]	266,021	319,605	380,821	398,900	50.0	4.7
U.S.	248,709,873	281,421,906	308,745,538	324,697,795	30.6	5.2

Note: (1) Figures cover the Anchorage, AK Metropolitan Statistical Area; (*) 2015-2019 5-year estimated population
Source: U.S. Census Bureau, 1990 Census, Census 2000, Census 2010, 2015-2019 American Community Survey 5-Year Estimates

Household Size

Area	Persons in Household (%)							Average Household Size
	One	Two	Three	Four	Five	Six	Seven or More	
City	26.3	33.0	16.9	12.5	6.7	2.4	2.1	2.70
MSA[1]	25.5	33.7	16.5	12.7	6.8	2.6	2.2	2.80
U.S.	27.9	33.9	15.6	12.9	6.0	2.3	1.4	2.60

Note: (1) Figures cover the Anchorage, AK Metropolitan Statistical Area
Source: U.S. Census Bureau, 2015-2019 American Community Survey 5-Year Estimates

Race

Area	White Alone[2] (%)	Black Alone[2] (%)	Asian Alone[2] (%)	AIAN[3] Alone[2] (%)	NHOPI[4] Alone[2] (%)	Other Race Alone[2] (%)	Two or More Races (%)
City	62.6	5.6	9.6	7.9	2.4	2.4	9.5
MSA[1]	68.0	4.4	7.5	7.5	1.9	1.8	9.0
U.S.	72.5	12.7	5.5	0.8	0.2	4.9	3.3

Note: (1) Figures cover the Anchorage, AK Metropolitan Statistical Area; (2) Alone is defined as not being in combination with one or more other races; (3) American Indian and Alaska Native; (4) Native Hawaiian and Other Pacific Islander
Source: U.S. Census Bureau, 2015-2019 American Community Survey 5-Year Estimates

Hispanic or Latino Origin

Area	Total (%)	Mexican (%)	Puerto Rican (%)	Cuban (%)	Other (%)
City	9.2	4.8	1.4	0.1	2.8
MSA[1]	8.1	4.2	1.2	0.2	2.4
U.S.	18.0	11.2	1.7	0.7	4.3

Note: Persons of Hispanic or Latino origin can be of any race; (1) Figures cover the Anchorage, AK Metropolitan Statistical Area
Source: U.S. Census Bureau, 2015-2019 American Community Survey 5-Year Estimates

Ancestry

Area	German	Irish	English	American	Italian	Polish	French[2]	Scottish	Dutch
City	14.4	9.7	7.8	3.6	3.0	2.1	2.4	2.6	1.4
MSA[1]	15.3	10.0	7.9	4.1	3.1	2.1	2.7	2.6	1.5
U.S.	13.3	9.7	7.2	6.2	5.1	2.8	2.3	1.7	1.2

Note: Figures are the percentage of the total population reporting a particular ancestry. The nine most commonly reported ancestries in the U.S. are shown. Figures include multiple ancestries (e.g. if a person reported being Irish and Italian, they were included in both columns); (1) Figures cover the Anchorage, AK Metropolitan Statistical Area; (2) Excludes Basque
Source: U.S. Census Bureau, 2015-2019 American Community Survey 5-Year Estimates

Foreign-born Population

Area	Percent of Population Born in								
	Any Foreign Country	Asia	Mexico	Europe	Caribbean	Central America[2]	South America	Africa	Canada
City	10.9	6.2	0.9	1.1	0.5	0.1	0.5	0.6	0.4
MSA[1]	8.9	4.9	0.7	1.1	0.4	0.1	0.4	0.5	0.3
U.S.	13.6	4.2	3.5	1.5	1.3	1.1	1.0	0.7	0.2

Note: (1) Figures cover the Anchorage, AK Metropolitan Statistical Area; (2) Excludes Mexico.
Source: U.S. Census Bureau, 2015-2019 American Community Survey 5-Year Estimates

Marital Status

Area	Never Married	Now Married[2]	Separated	Widowed	Divorced
City	34.5	48.4	1.8	3.6	11.7
MSA[1]	33.9	48.7	1.8	3.7	11.9
U.S.	33.4	48.1	1.9	5.8	10.9

Note: Figures are percentages and cover the population 15 years of age and older; (1) Figures cover the Anchorage, AK Metropolitan Statistical Area; (2) Excludes separated
Source: U.S. Census Bureau, 2015-2019 American Community Survey 5-Year Estimates

Disability by Age

Area	All Ages	Under 18 Years Old	18 to 64 Years Old	65 Years and Over
City	11.4	3.6	10.3	36.3
MSA[1]	11.9	3.7	11.0	36.5
U.S.	12.6	4.2	10.3	34.5

Note: Figures show percent of the civilian noninstitutionalized population that reported having a disability. Disability status is determined from six types of difficulty: vision, hearing, cognitive, ambulatory, self-care, and independent living. For children under 5 years old, hearing and vision difficulty are used to determine disability status. For children between the ages of 5 and 14, disability status is determined from hearing, vision, cognitive, ambulatory, and self-care difficulties. For people aged 15 years and older, they are considered to have a disability if they have difficulty with any one of the six difficulty types; Note: (1) Figures cover the Anchorage, AK Metropolitan Statistical Area
Source: U.S. Census Bureau, 2015-2019 American Community Survey 5-Year Estimates

Age

Area	Under Age 5	Age 5–19	Age 20–34	Age 35–44	Age 45–54	Age 55–64	Age 65–74	Age 75–84	Age 85+	Median Age
City	7.2	19.6	25.4	12.9	12.3	12.2	7.0	2.6	0.9	33.6
MSA[1]	7.2	20.2	24.0	13.0	12.4	12.4	7.2	2.6	0.9	34.0
U.S.	6.1	19.1	20.7	12.6	13.0	12.9	9.1	4.6	1.9	38.1

Note: (1) Figures cover the Anchorage, AK Metropolitan Statistical Area
Source: U.S. Census Bureau, 2015-2019 American Community Survey 5-Year Estimates

Gender

Area	Males	Females	Males per 100 Females
City	149,670	143,861	104.0
MSA[1]	204,508	194,392	105.2
U.S.	159,886,919	164,810,876	97.0

Note: (1) Figures cover the Anchorage, AK Metropolitan Statistical Area
Source: U.S. Census Bureau, 2015-2019 American Community Survey 5-Year Estimates

Religious Groups by Family

Area	Catholic	Baptist	Non-Den.	Methodist[2]	Lutheran	LDS[3]	Pente-costal	Presby-terian[4]	Muslim[5]	Judaism
MSA[1]	6.9	5.0	6.4	1.4	1.9	5.1	1.9	0.7	0.2	0.1
U.S.	19.1	9.3	4.0	4.0	2.3	2.0	1.9	1.6	0.8	0.7

Note: Figures are the number of adherents as a percentage of the total population; (1) Figures cover the Anchorage, AK Metropolitan Statistical Area; (2) Methodist/Pietist; (3) Latter Day Saints; (4) Reformed; (5) Figures are estimates
Source: Association of Statisticians of American Religious Bodies, 2010 U.S. Religion Census: Religious Congregations & Membership Study

Religious Groups by Tradition

Area	Catholic	Evangelical Protestant	Mainline Protestant	Other Tradition	Black Protestant	Orthodox
MSA[1]	6.9	15.7	3.6	6.8	0.3	0.6
U.S.	19.1	16.2	7.3	4.3	1.6	0.3

Note: Figures are the number of adherents as a percentage of the total population; (1) Figures cover the Anchorage, AK Metropolitan Statistical Area
Source: Association of Statisticians of American Religious Bodies, 2010 U.S. Religion Census: Religious Congregations & Membership Study

ECONOMY

Gross Metropolitan Product

Area	2017	2018	2019	2020	Rank[2]
MSA[1]	27.4	28.3	29.3	30.6	102

Note: Figures are in billions of dollars; (1) Figures cover the Anchorage, AK Metropolitan Statistical Area; (2) Rank is based on 2018 data and ranges from 1 to 381
Source: U.S. Conference of Mayors, U.S. Metro Economies: GMP & Employment 2018-2020, September 2019

Economic Growth

Area	2015-17 (%)	2018 (%)	2019 (%)	2020 (%)	Rank[2]
MSA[1]	-1.5	-0.9	2.4	0.6	353
U.S.	1.9	2.9	2.3	2.1	–

Note: Figures are real gross metropolitan product (GMP) growth rates and represent average annual percent change; (1) Figures cover the Anchorage, AK Metropolitan Statistical Area; (2) Rank is based on 2017 2-year average annual percent change and ranges from 1 to 381
Source: U.S. Conference of Mayors, U.S. Metro Economies: GMP & Employment 2018-2020, September 2019

Metropolitan Area Exports

Area	2014	2015	2016	2017	2018	2019	Rank[2]
MSA[1]	571.8	421.9	1,215.4	1,675.9	1,510.8	1,348.0	132

Note: Figures are in millions of dollars; (1) Figures cover the Anchorage, AK Metropolitan Statistical Area; (2) Rank is based on 2019 data and ranges from 1 to 386
Source: U.S. Department of Commerce, International Trade Administration, Office of Trade and Economic Analysis, Industry and Analysis, Exports by Metropolitan Area, data extracted March 24, 2021

Building Permits

Area	Single-Family			Multi-Family			Total		
	2018	2019	Pct. Chg.	2018	2019	Pct. Chg.	2018	2019	Pct. Chg.
City	869	838	-3.6	214	221	3.3	1,083	1,059	-2.2
MSA[1]	938	878	-6.4	321	285	-11.2	1,259	1,163	-7.6
U.S.	855,300	862,100	0.7	473,500	523,900	10.6	1,328,800	1,386,000	4.3

Note: (1) Figures cover the Anchorage, AK Metropolitan Statistical Area; Figures represent new, privately-owned housing units authorized (unadjusted data); All permit data are based on estimates with imputation
Source: U.S. Census Bureau, Manufacturing, Mining, and Construction Statistics, Building Permits, 2018, 2019

Bankruptcy Filings

Area	Business Filings			Nonbusiness Filings		
	2019	2020	% Chg.	2019	2020	% Chg.
Anchorage Borough	17	20	17.6	176	137	-22.2
U.S.	22,780	21,655	-4.9	752,160	522,808	-30.5

Note: Business filings include Chapter 7, Chapter 9, Chapter 11, Chapter 12, Chapter 13, Chapter 15, and Section 304; Nonbusiness filings include Chapter 7, Chapter 11, and Chapter 13
Source: Administrative Office of the U.S. Courts, Business and Nonbusiness Bankruptcy, County Cases Commenced by Chapter of the Bankruptcy Code, During the 12-Month Period Ending December 31, 2019 and Business and Nonbusiness Bankruptcy, County Cases Commenced by Chapter of the Bankruptcy Code, During the 12-Month Period Ending December 31, 2020

Housing Vacancy Rates

Area	Gross Vacancy Rate[2] (%)			Year-Round Vacancy Rate[3] (%)			Rental Vacancy Rate[4] (%)			Homeowner Vacancy Rate[5] (%)		
	2018	2019	2020	2018	2019	2020	2018	2019	2020	2018	2019	2020
MSA[1]	n/a	n/a	n/a	n/a	n/a	n/a	n/a	n/a	n/a	n/a	n/a	n/a
U.S.	12.3	12.0	10.6	9.7	9.5	8.2	6.9	6.7	6.3	1.5	1.4	1.0

Note: (1) Figures cover the Anchorage, AK Metropolitan Statistical Area; (2) The percentage of the total housing inventory that is vacant; (3) The percentage of the housing inventory (excluding seasonal units) that is year-round vacant; (4) The percentage of rental inventory that is vacant for rent; (5) The percentage of homeowner inventory that is vacant for sale; n/a not available
Source: U.S. Census Bureau, Housing Vacancies and Homeownership Annual Statistics: 2018, 2019, 2020

INCOME

Income

Area	Per Capita ($)	Median Household ($)	Average Household ($)
City	41,415	84,928	109,988
MSA[1]	38,725	83,048	105,968
U.S.	34,103	62,843	88,607

Note: (1) Figures cover the Anchorage, AK Metropolitan Statistical Area
Source: U.S. Census Bureau, 2015-2019 American Community Survey 5-Year Estimates

Household Income Distribution

Area	Percent of Households Earning							
	Under $15,000	$15,000 -$24,999	$25,000 -$34,999	$35,000 -$49,999	$50,000 -$74,999	$75,000 -$99,999	$100,000 -$149,999	$150,000 and up
City	5.3	5.1	6.3	9.9	17.4	13.8	20.5	21.6
MSA[1]	6.1	5.6	6.5	9.9	17.2	13.7	20.5	20.5
U.S.	10.3	8.9	8.9	12.3	17.2	12.7	15.1	14.5

Note: (1) Figures cover the Anchorage, AK Metropolitan Statistical Area
Source: U.S. Census Bureau, 2015-2019 American Community Survey 5-Year Estimates

Poverty Rate

Area	All Ages	Under 18 Years Old	18 to 64 Years Old	65 Years and Over
City	9.0	13.1	8.1	5.5
MSA[1]	9.4	12.8	8.6	6.0
U.S.	13.4	18.5	12.6	9.3

Note: Figures are percentage of people whose income during the past 12 months was below the poverty level;
(1) Figures cover the Anchorage, AK Metropolitan Statistical Area
Source: U.S. Census Bureau, 2015-2019 American Community Survey 5-Year Estimates

CITY FINANCES

City Government Finances

Component	2017 ($000)	2017 ($ per capita)
Total Revenues	1,692,559	5,667
Total Expenditures	1,814,180	6,074
Debt Outstanding	1,569,133	5,253
Cash and Securities[1]	996,520	3,336

Note: (1) Cash and security holdings of a government at the close of its fiscal year,
including those of its dependent agencies, utilities, and liquor stores.
Source: U.S. Census Bureau, State & Local Government Finances 2017

City Government Revenue by Source

Source	2017 ($000)	2017 ($ per capita)	2017 (%)
General Revenue			
From Federal Government	38,817	130	2.3
From State Government	581,618	1,947	34.4
From Local Governments	0	0	0.0
Taxes			
Property	528,814	1,770	31.2
Sales and Gross Receipts	53,761	180	3.2
Personal Income	0	0	0.0
Corporate Income	0	0	0.0
Motor Vehicle License	17,395	58	1.0
Other Taxes	9,323	31	0.6
Current Charges	144,994	485	8.6
Liquor Store	0	0	0.0
Utility	232,806	779	13.8
Employee Retirement	27,436	92	1.6

Source: U.S. Census Bureau, State & Local Government Finances 2017

City Government Expenditures by Function

Function	2017 ($000)	2017 ($ per capita)	2017 (%)
General Direct Expenditures			
Air Transportation	11,905	39	0.7
Corrections	0	0	0.0
Education	695,361	2,328	38.3
Employment Security Administration	0	0	0.0
Financial Administration	19,511	65	1.1
Fire Protection	114,612	383	6.3
General Public Buildings	0	0	0.0
Governmental Administration, Other	17,385	58	1.0
Health	21,033	70	1.2
Highways	118,585	397	6.5
Hospitals	0	0	0.0
Housing and Community Development	11,865	39	0.7
Interest on General Debt	28,894	96	1.6
Judicial and Legal	7,633	25	0.4
Libraries	7,990	26	0.4
Parking	0	0	0.0
Parks and Recreation	35,185	117	1.9
Police Protection	132,306	442	7.3
Public Welfare	1,564	5	0.1
Sewerage	45,014	150	2.5
Solid Waste Management	27,439	91	1.5
Veterans' Services	0	0	0.0
Liquor Store	0	0	0.0
Utility	386,931	1,295	21.3
Employee Retirement	31,901	106	1.8

Source: U.S. Census Bureau, State & Local Government Finances 2017

EMPLOYMENT

Labor Force and Employment

Area	Civilian Labor Force			Workers Employed		
	Dec. 2019	Dec. 2020	% Chg.	Dec. 2019	Dec. 2020	% Chg.
City	147,801	150,509	1.8	140,718	142,180	1.0
MSA[1]	195,036	197,957	1.5	184,796	186,758	1.1
U.S.	164,007,000	160,017,000	-2.4	158,504,000	149,613,000	-5.6

Note: Data is not seasonally adjusted and covers workers 16 years of age and older; (1) Figures cover the Anchorage, AK Metropolitan Statistical Area
Source: Bureau of Labor Statistics, Local Area Unemployment Statistics

Unemployment Rate

Area	2020											
	Jan.	Feb.	Mar.	Apr.	May	Jun.	Jul.	Aug.	Sep.	Oct.	Nov.	Dec.
City	5.1	4.5	4.7	13.9	12.3	12.0	10.8	6.5	6.4	5.3	6.0	5.5
MSA[1]	5.7	5.0	5.2	14.3	12.5	12.2	11.0	6.6	6.5	5.3	6.1	5.7
U.S.	4.0	3.8	4.5	14.4	13.0	11.2	10.5	8.5	7.7	6.6	6.4	6.5

Note: Data is not seasonally adjusted and covers workers 16 years of age and older; (1) Figures cover the Anchorage, AK Metropolitan Statistical Area
Source: Bureau of Labor Statistics, Local Area Unemployment Statistics

Average Wages

Occupation	$/Hr.	Occupation	$/Hr.
Accountants and Auditors	39.00	Maintenance and Repair Workers	24.50
Automotive Mechanics	22.70	Marketing Managers	49.00
Bookkeepers	23.60	Network and Computer Systems Admin.	39.60
Carpenters	33.10	Nurses, Licensed Practical	33.70
Cashiers	14.60	Nurses, Registered	45.30
Computer Programmers	44.10	Nursing Assistants	19.50
Computer Systems Analysts	41.50	Office Clerks, General	22.00
Computer User Support Specialists	29.70	Physical Therapists	50.00
Construction Laborers	26.00	Physicians	131.20
Cooks, Restaurant	14.60	Plumbers, Pipefitters and Steamfitters	42.20
Customer Service Representatives	19.50	Police and Sheriff's Patrol Officers	46.40
Dentists	101.00	Postal Service Mail Carriers	25.20
Electricians	33.60	Real Estate Sales Agents	35.70
Engineers, Electrical	54.80	Retail Salespersons	16.70
Fast Food and Counter Workers	12.50	Sales Representatives, Technical/Scientific	41.70
Financial Managers	54.90	Secretaries, Exc. Legal/Medical/Executive	21.30
First-Line Supervisors of Office Workers	32.40	Security Guards	21.50
General and Operations Managers	58.00	Surgeons	n/a
Hairdressers/Cosmetologists	14.30	Teacher Assistants, Exc. Postsecondary*	19.50
Home Health and Personal Care Aides	16.10	Teachers, Secondary School, Exc. Sp. Ed.*	40.20
Janitors and Cleaners	16.50	Telemarketers	n/a
Landscaping/Groundskeeping Workers	17.20	Truck Drivers, Heavy/Tractor-Trailer	28.70
Lawyers	55.20	Truck Drivers, Light/Delivery Services	24.80
Maids and Housekeeping Cleaners	15.10	Waiters and Waitresses	12.40

Note: Wage data covers the Anchorage, AK Metropolitan Statistical Area; (*) Hourly wages were calculated from annual wage data based on a 40 hour work week; n/a not available.
Source: Bureau of Labor Statistics, Metro Area Occupational Employment & Wage Estimates, May 2020

Employment by Industry

Sector	MSA[1]		U.S.
	Number of Employees	Percent of Total	Percent of Total
Construction	9,800	6.1	5.1
Education and Health Services	31,100	19.3	16.3
Financial Activities	7,500	4.6	6.1
Government	33,700	20.9	15.2
Information	3,400	2.1	1.9
Leisure and Hospitality	13,000	8.1	9.0
Manufacturing	1,800	1.1	8.5
Mining and Logging	2,200	1.4	0.4
Other Services	5,600	3.5	3.8
Professional and Business Services	17,700	11.0	14.4
Retail Trade	19,600	12.1	10.9
Transportation, Warehousing, and Utilities	11,200	6.9	4.6
Wholesale Trade	4,800	3.0	3.9

Note: Figures are non-farm employment as of December 2020. Figures are not seasonally adjusted and include workers 16 years of age and older; (1) Figures cover the Anchorage, AK Metropolitan Statistical Area
Source: Bureau of Labor Statistics, Current Employment Statistics, Employment, Hours, and Earnings

Employment by Occupation

Occupation Classification	City (%)	MSA[1] (%)	U.S. (%)
Management, Business, Science, and Arts	41.1	39.4	38.5
Natural Resources, Construction, and Maintenance	8.1	10.1	8.9
Production, Transportation, and Material Moving	11.4	11.4	13.2
Sales and Office	22.0	21.5	21.6
Service	17.4	17.6	17.8

Note: Figures cover employed civilians 16 years of age and older; (1) Figures cover the Anchorage, AK Metropolitan Statistical Area
Source: U.S. Census Bureau, 2015-2019 American Community Survey 5-Year Estimates

Occupations with Greatest Projected Employment Growth: 2020 – 2022

Occupation[1]	2020 Employment	2022 Projected Employment	Numeric Employment Change	Percent Employment Change
Waiters and Waitresses	3,580	4,610	1,030	28.8
Combined Food Preparation and Serving Workers, Including Fast Food	3,790	4,620	830	21.9
Maids and Housekeeping Cleaners	2,640	3,440	800	30.3
Food Preparation Workers	3,200	3,790	590	18.4
Cooks, Restaurant	1,960	2,530	570	29.1
Bartenders	1,150	1,540	390	33.9
Teacher Assistants	3,980	4,330	350	8.8
Counter Attendants, Cafeteria, Food Concession, and Coffee Shop	1,690	2,030	340	20.1
Janitors and Cleaners, Except Maids and Housekeeping Cleaners	5,230	5,570	340	6.5
Dishwashers	1,190	1,520	330	27.7

Note: Projections cover Alaska; (1) Sorted by numeric employment change
Source: www.projectionscentral.com, State Occupational Projections, 2020–2022 Short-Term Projections

Fastest-Growing Occupations: 2020 – 2022

Occupation[1]	2020 Employment	2022 Projected Employment	Numeric Employment Change	Percent Employment Change
Travel Agents	70	130	60	85.7
Concierges	60	110	50	83.3
Tour and Travel Guides	570	870	300	52.6
Hotel, Motel, and Resort Desk Clerks	640	970	330	51.6
Baggage Porters and Bellhops	130	180	50	38.5
Bus Drivers, Transit and Intercity	700	960	260	37.1
Amusement and Recreation Attendants	340	460	120	35.3
Bartenders	1,150	1,540	390	33.9
Lodging Managers	160	210	50	31.3
Ushers, Lobby Attendants, and Ticket Takers	230	300	70	30.4

Note: Projections cover Alaska; (1) Sorted by percent employment change and excludes occupations with numeric employment change less than 50
Source: www.projectionscentral.com, State Occupational Projections, 2020–2022 Short-Term Projections

TAXES

State Corporate Income Tax Rates

State	Tax Rate (%)	Income Brackets ($)	Num. of Brackets	Financial Institution Tax Rate (%)[a]	Federal Income Tax Ded.
Alaska	0 - 9.4	25,000 - 222,000	10	0 - 9.4	No

Note: Tax rates as of January 1, 2021; (a) Rates listed are the corporate income tax rate applied to financial institutions or excise taxes based on income. Some states have other taxes based upon the value of deposits or shares.
Source: Federation of Tax Administrators, State Corporate Income Tax Rates, January 1, 2021

State Individual Income Tax Rates

State	Tax Rate (%)	Income Brackets ($)	Personal Exemptions ($)			Standard Ded. ($)	
			Single	Married	Depend.	Single	Married
Alaska					– No state income tax –		

Note: Tax rates as of January 1, 2021; Local- and county-level taxes are not included
Source: Federation of Tax Administrators, State Individual Income Tax Rates, January 1, 2021

Various State Sales and Excise Tax Rates

State	State Sales Tax (%)	Gasoline[1] (¢/gal.)	Cigarette[2] ($/pack)	Spirits[3] ($/gal.)	Wine[4] ($/gal.)	Beer[5] ($/gal.)	Recreational Marijuana (%)
Alaska	None	13.79	2	12.8	2.5	1.07	(a)

Note: All tax rates as of January 1, 2021; (1) The American Petroleum Institute has developed a methodology for determining the average tax rate on a gallon of fuel. Rates may include any of the following: excise taxes, environmental fees, storage tank fees, other fees or taxes, general sales tax, and local taxes; (2) The federal excise tax of $1.0066 per pack and local taxes are not included; (3) Rates are those applicable to off-premise sales of 40% alcohol by volume (a.b.v.) distilled spirits in 750ml containers. Local excise taxes are excluded; (4) Rates are those applicable to off-premise sales of 11% a.b.v. non-carbonated wine in 750ml containers; (5) Rates are those applicable to off-premise sales of 4.7% a.b.v. beer in 12 ounce containers; (a) $50/oz. mature flowers; $25/oz. immature flowers; $15/oz. trim, $1 per clone
Source: Tax Foundation, 2021 Facts & Figures: How Does Your State Compare?

State Business Tax Climate Index Rankings

State	Overall Rank	Corporate Tax Rank	Individual Income Tax Rank	Sales Tax Rank	Property Tax Rank	Unemployment Insurance Tax Rank
Alaska	3	26	1	5	22	45

Note: The index is a measure of how each state's tax laws affect economic performance. The lower the rank, the more favorable a state's tax system is for business. States without a given tax are given a ranking of 1. The scores/rankings for the District of Columbia do not affect other states. The 2021 index represents the tax climate as of July 1, 2020.
Source: Tax Foundation, State Business Tax Climate Index 2021

TRANSPORTATION

Means of Transportation to Work

Area	Car/Truck/Van Drove Alone	Car-pooled	Public Transportation Bus	Subway	Railroad	Bicycle	Walked	Other Means	Worked at Home
City	76.3	11.8	1.5	0.0	0.0	1.3	2.9	2.3	4.0
MSA[1]	75.7	11.5	1.3	0.0	0.0	1.0	2.7	3.2	4.5
U.S.	76.3	9.0	2.4	1.9	0.6	0.5	2.7	1.4	5.2

Note: Figures are percentages and cover workers 16 years of age and older; (1) Figures cover the Anchorage, AK Metropolitan Statistical Area
Source: U.S. Census Bureau, 2015-2019 American Community Survey 5-Year Estimates

Travel Time to Work

Area	Less Than 10 Minutes	10 to 19 Minutes	20 to 29 Minutes	30 to 44 Minutes	45 to 59 Minutes	60 to 89 Minutes	90 Minutes or More
City	16.3	44.7	23.7	10.4	2.3	1.1	1.5
MSA[1]	15.7	41.0	21.8	10.8	4.3	4.0	2.5
U.S.	12.2	28.4	20.8	20.8	8.3	6.4	2.9

Note: Note: Figures are percentages and include workers 16 years old and over; (1) Figures cover the Anchorage, AK Metropolitan Statistical Area
Source: U.S. Census Bureau, 2015-2019 American Community Survey 5-Year Estimates

Key Congestion Measures

Measure	1982	1992	2002	2012	2017
Annual Hours of Delay, Total (000)	1,172	3,496	6,756	9,177	11,149
Annual Hours of Delay, Per Auto Commuter	9	22	33	40	42
Annual Congestion Cost, Total (million $)	9	37	92	168	209
Annual Congestion Cost, Per Auto Commuter ($)	272	558	840	895	1,054

Note: Covers the Anchorage AK urban area
Source: Texas A&M Transportation Institute, 2019 Urban Mobility Report

Freeway Travel Time Index

Measure	1982	1987	1992	1997	2002	2007	2012	2017
Urban Area Index[1]	1.01	1.05	1.10	1.13	1.17	1.19	1.20	1.22
Urban Area Rank[1,2]	98	79	62	41	41	40	37	33

Note: Freeway Travel Time Index—the ratio of travel time in the peak period to the travel time at free-flow conditions. For example, a value of 1.30 indicates a 20-minute free-flow trip takes 26 minutes in the peak (20 minutes x 1.30 = 26 minutes); (1) Covers the Anchorage AK urban area; (2) Rank is based on 101 larger urban areas (#1 = highest travel time index)
Source: Texas A&M Transportation Institute, 2019 Urban Mobility Report

Public Transportation

Agency Name / Mode of Transportation	Vehicles Operated in Maximum Service[1]	Annual Unlinked Passenger Trips[2] (in thous.)	Annual Passenger Miles[3] (in thous.)
Municipality of Anchorage, dba Public Transportation			
Bus (directly operated)	45	3,251.2	14,819.3
Bus (purchased transportation)	10	158.9	703.1
Demand Response (purchased transportation)	40	131.5	830.6
Vanpool (purchased transportation)	82	208.8	8,524.1

Note: (1) Number of revenue vehicles operated by the given mode and type of service to meet the annual maximum service requirement. This is the revenue vehicle count during the peak season of the year; on the week and day that maximum service is provided. Vehicles operated in maximum service (VOMS) exclude atypical days and one-time special events; (2) Number of passengers who boarded public transportation vehicles. Passengers are counted each time they board a vehicle no matter how many vehicles they use to travel from their origin to their destination. (3) Sum of the distances ridden by all passengers during the entire fiscal year.
Source: Federal Transit Administration, National Transit Database, 2019

Air Transportation

Airport Name and Code / Type of Service	Passenger Airlines[1]	Passenger Enplanements	Freight Carriers[2]	Freight (lbs)
Anchorage International (ANC)				
Domestic service (U.S. carriers - 2020)	21	1,129,573	31	2,492,945,693
International service (U.S. carriers - 2019)	5	779	12	420,978,078

Note: (1) Includes all U.S.-based major, minor and commuter airlines that carried at least one passenger during the year; (2) Includes all U.S.-based airlines and freight carriers that transported at least one pound of freight during the year.
Source: Bureau of Transportation Statistics, The Intermodal Transportation Database, Air Carriers: T-100 Domestic Market (U.S. Carriers), 2020; Bureau of Transportation Statistics, The Intermodal Transportation Database, Air Carriers: T-100 International Market (U.S. Carriers), 2019

BUSINESSES

Major Business Headquarters

Company Name	Industry	Rankings	
		Fortune[1]	Forbes[2]
No companies listed	-	-	-

Note: (1) Companies that produce a 10-K are ranked 1 to 500 based on 2019 revenue; (2) All private companies with at least $2 billion in annual revenue through the end of their most current fiscal year are ranked 1 to 219; companies listed are headquartered in the city; dashes indicate no ranking
Source: Fortune, "Fortune 500," June/July 2020; Forbes, "America's Largest Private Companies," 2020

Fastest-Growing Businesses

According to *Inc.*, Anchorage is home to one of America's 500 fastest-growing private companies: **Arctic Solar Ventures Corporation** (#275). Criteria: must be an independent, privately-held, for-profit, U.S. corporation, proprietorship or partnership as of December 31, 2019; revenues must be at least $100,000 in 2016 and $2 million in 2019; must have four-year operating/sales history. *Inc., "America's 500 Fastest-Growing Private Companies," 2020*

Living Environment

COST OF LIVING

Cost of Living Index

Composite Index	Groceries	Housing	Utilities	Trans- portation	Health Care	Misc. Goods/ Services
124.6	128.5	133.7	127.4	110.9	148.0	115.4

Note: The Cost of Living Index measures regional differences in the cost of consumer goods and services, excluding taxes and non-consumer expenditures, for professional and managerial households in the top income quintile. It is based on more than 50,000 prices covering almost 60 different items for which prices are collected three times a year by chambers of commerce, economic development organizations or university applied economic centers in each participating urban area. The numbers shown should be read as a percentage above or below the national average of 100. For example, a value of 115.4 in the groceries column indicates that grocery prices are 15.4% higher than the national average. Small differences in the index numbers should not be interpreted as significant; Figures cover the Anchorage AK urban area.
Source: The Council for Community and Economic Research, Cost of Living Index, 2020

Grocery Prices

Area[1]	T-Bone Steak ($/pound)	Frying Chicken ($/pound)	Whole Milk ($/half gal.)	Eggs ($/dozen)	Orange Juice ($/64 oz.)	Coffee ($/11.5 oz.)
City[2]	13.95	1.71	2.73	2.19	4.39	5.84
Avg.	11.78	1.39	2.05	1.47	3.57	4.34
Min.	8.03	0.94	1.03	0.74	2.94	3.02
Max.	15.86	2.65	4.31	3.77	5.44	8.69

*Note: (1) Values for the local area are compared with the average, minimum and maximum values for all 284 areas in the Cost of Living Index; (2) Figures cover the Anchorage AK urban area; **T-Bone Steak** (price per pound); **Frying Chicken** (price per pound, whole fryer); **Whole Milk** (half gallon carton); **Eggs** (price per dozen, Grade A, large); **Orange Juice** (64 oz. Tropicana or Florida Natural); **Coffee** (11.5 oz. can, vacuum-packed, Maxwell House, Hills Bros, or Folgers).*
Source: The Council for Community and Economic Research, Cost of Living Index, 2020

Housing and Utility Costs

Area[1]	New Home Price ($)	Apartment Rent ($/month)	All Electric ($/month)	Part Electric ($/month)	Other Energy ($/month)	Telephone ($/month)
City[2]	535,483	1,257	-	111.07	136.23	184.30
Avg.	368,594	1,168	170.86	100.47	65.28	184.30
Min.	190,567	502	91.58	31.42	26.08	169.60
Max.	2,227,806	4,738	470.38	280.31	280.06	206.50

*Note: (1) Values for the local area are compared with the average, minimum and maximum values for all 284 areas in the Cost of Living Index; (2) Figures cover the Anchorage AK urban area; **New Home Price** (2,400 sf living area, 8,000 sf lot, in urban area with full utilities); **Apartment Rent** (950 sf 2 bedroom/1.5 or 2 bath, unfurnished, excluding all utilities except water); **All Electric** (average monthly cost for an all-electric home); **Part Electric** (average monthly cost for a part-electric home); **Other Energy** (average monthly cost for natural gas, fuel oil, coal, wood, and any other forms of energy except electricity); **Telephone** (price includes the base monthly rate plus taxes and fees for three lines of mobile phone service).*
Source: The Council for Community and Economic Research, Cost of Living Index, 2020

Health Care, Transportation, and Other Costs

Area[1]	Doctor ($/visit)	Dentist ($/visit)	Optometrist ($/visit)	Gasoline ($/gallon)	Beauty Salon ($/visit)	Men's Shirt ($)
City[2]	206.08	147.12	219.89	2.59	54.87	16.85
Avg.	115.44	99.32	108.10	2.21	39.27	31.37
Min.	36.68	59.00	51.36	1.71	19.00	11.00
Max.	219.00	153.10	250.97	3.46	82.05	58.33

*Note: (1) Values for the local area are compared with the average, minimum and maximum values for all 284 areas in the Cost of Living Index; (2) Figures cover the Anchorage AK urban area; **Doctor** (general practitioners routine exam of an established patient); **Dentist** (adult teeth cleaning and periodic oral examination); **Optometrist** (full vision eye exam for established adult patient); **Gasoline** (one gallon regular unleaded, national brand, including all taxes, cash price at self-service pump if available); **Beauty Salon** (woman's shampoo, trim, and blow-dry); **Men's Shirt** (cotton/polyester dress shirt, pinpoint weave, long sleeves).*
Source: The Council for Community and Economic Research, Cost of Living Index, 2020

HOUSING

Homeownership Rate

Area	2012 (%)	2013 (%)	2014 (%)	2015 (%)	2016 (%)	2017 (%)	2018 (%)	2019 (%)	2020 (%)
MSA[1]	n/a	n/a	n/a	n/a	n/a	n/a	n/a	n/a	n/a
U.S.	65.4	65.1	64.5	63.7	63.4	63.9	64.4	64.6	66.6

Note: (1) Figures cover the Anchorage, AK Metropolitan Statistical Area; n/a not available
Source: U.S. Census Bureau, Housing Vacancies and Homeownership Annual Statistics: 2012-2020

House Price Index (HPI)

Area	National Ranking[2]	Quarterly Change (%)	One-Year Change (%)	Five-Year Change (%)	Since 1991Q1 (%)
MSA[1]	205	1.39	4.88	9.73	184.56
U.S.[3]	–	3.81	10.77	38.99	205.12

Note: The HPI is a weighted repeat sales index. It measures average price changes in repeat sales or refinancings on the same properties. This information is obtained by reviewing repeat mortgage transactions on single-family properties whose mortgages have been purchased or securitized by Fannie Mae or Freddie Mac since January 1975; (1) Figures cover the Anchorage, AK Metropolitan Statistical Area; (2) Rankings are based on annual percentage change for all metro areas containing at least 15,000 transactions over the last 10 years and ranges from 1 to 253; (3) figures based on a weighted average of Census Division estimates using a seasonally adjusted, purchase-only index; all figures are for the period ending December 31, 2020
Source: Federal Housing Finance Agency, Change in Metropolitan Area House Price Indexes, April 7, 2021

Median Single-Family Home Prices

Area	2018	2019	2020[p]	Percent Change 2019 to 2020
MSA[1]	n/a	n/a	n/a	n/a
U.S. Average	261.6	274.6	299.9	9.2

Note: Figures are median sales prices of existing single-family homes in thousands of dollars; (p) preliminary; n/a not available; (1) Figures cover the Anchorage, AK Metropolitan Statistical Area
Source: National Association of Realtors, Median Sales Price of Existing Single-Family Homes for Metropolitan Areas, 4th Quarter 2020

Qualifying Income Based on Median Sales Price of Existing Single-Family Homes

Area	With 5% Down ($)	With 10% Down ($)	With 20% Down ($)
MSA[1]	n/a	n/a	n/a
U.S. Average	59,266	56,147	49,908

Note: Figures are preliminary; Qualifying income is based on a mortgage rate of 2.81%. Monthly principal and interest payment is limited to 25% of income; n/a not available; (1) Figures cover the Anchorage, AK Metropolitan Statistical Area
Source: National Association of Realtors, Qualifying Income Based on Median Sales Price of Existing Single-Family Homes for Metropolitan Areas, 4th Quarter 2020

Home Value Distribution

Area	Under $50,000	$50,000 -$99,999	$100,000 -$149,999	$150,000 -$199,999	$200,000 -$299,999	$300,000 -$499,999	$500,000 -$999,999	$1,000,000 or more
City	5.3	1.9	4.8	7.0	26.9	40.9	12.2	1.0
MSA[1]	4.9	2.6	5.2	9.3	29.6	37.3	10.3	0.9
U.S.	6.9	12.0	13.3	14.0	19.6	19.3	11.4	3.4

Note: Figures are percentages and cover owner-occupied housing units; (1) Figures cover the Anchorage, AK Metropolitan Statistical Area
Source: U.S. Census Bureau, 2015-2019 American Community Survey 5-Year Estimates

Year Housing Structure Built

Area	2010 or Later	2000 -2009	1990 -1999	1980 -1989	1970 -1979	1960 -1969	1950 -1959	1940 -1949	Before 1940	Median Year
City	3.5	12.2	11.6	26.4	28.2	10.8	6.0	1.0	0.3	1981
MSA[1]	4.5	17.2	13.0	25.7	24.4	9.0	5.0	0.9	0.4	1984
U.S.	5.2	14.0	13.9	13.4	15.2	10.6	10.3	4.9	12.6	1978

Note: Figures are percentages except for Median Year; Note: (1) Figures cover the Anchorage, AK Metropolitan Statistical Area
Source: U.S. Census Bureau, 2015-2019 American Community Survey 5-Year Estimates

Gross Monthly Rent

Area	Under $500	$500 -$999	$1,000 -$1,499	$1,500 -$1,999	$2,000 -$2,499	$2,500 -$2,999	$3,000 and up	Median ($)
City	4.0	21.8	36.9	19.9	11.7	4.1	1.4	1,320
MSA[1]	4.2	23.2	37.1	19.7	10.8	3.7	1.3	1,288
U.S.	9.4	36.2	30.0	14.0	5.6	2.4	2.4	1,062

Note: Figures are percentages except for Median; Gross rent is the contract rent plus the estimated average monthly cost of utilities (electricity, gas, and water and sewer) and fuels (oil, coal, kerosene, wood, etc.) if these are paid by the renter (or paid for the renter by someone else); (1) Figures cover the Anchorage, AK Metropolitan Statistical Area
Source: U.S. Census Bureau, 2015-2019 American Community Survey 5-Year Estimates

HEALTH

Health Risk Factors

Category	MSA[1] (%)	U.S. (%)
Adults aged 18–64 who have any kind of health care coverage	88.2	87.3
Adults who reported being in good or better health	80.9	82.4
Adults who have been told they have high blood cholesterol	32.3	33.0
Adults who have been told they have high blood pressure	32.1	32.3
Adults who are current smokers	19.7	17.1
Adults who currently use E-cigarettes	4.0	4.6
Adults who currently use chewing tobacco, snuff, or snus	5.4	4.0
Adults who are heavy drinkers[2]	8.4	6.3
Adults who are binge drinkers[3]	17.4	17.4
Adults who are overweight (BMI 25.0 - 29.9)	28.1	35.3
Adults who are obese (BMI 30.0 - 99.8)	36.3	31.3
Adults who participated in any physical activities in the past month	81.9	74.4
Adults who always or nearly always wears a seat belt	95.6	94.3

Note: (1) Figures cover the Anchorage, AK Metropolitan Statistical Area; (2) Heavy drinkers are classified as adult men having more than 14 drinks per week and adult women having more than 7 drinks per week; (3) Binge drinkers are classified as males having five or more drinks on one occasion or females having four or more drinks on one occasion
Source: Centers for Disease Control and Prevention, Behaviorial Risk Factor Surveillance System, SMART: Selected Metropolitan Area Risk Trends, 2017

Acute and Chronic Health Conditions

Category	MSA[1] (%)	U.S. (%)
Adults who have ever been told they had a heart attack	3.1	4.2
Adults who have ever been told they have angina or coronary heart disease	3.1	3.9
Adults who have ever been told they had a stroke	1.6	3.0
Adults who have ever been told they have asthma	15.9	14.2
Adults who have ever been told they have arthritis	21.8	24.9
Adults who have ever been told they have diabetes[2]	7.4	10.5
Adults who have ever been told they had skin cancer	3.7	6.2
Adults who have ever been told they had any other types of cancer	7.1	7.1
Adults who have ever been told they have COPD	6.0	6.5
Adults who have ever been told they have kidney disease	2.6	3.0
Adults who have ever been told they have a form of depression	19.6	20.5

Note: (1) Figures cover the Anchorage, AK Metropolitan Statistical Area; (2) Figures do not include pregnancy-related, borderline, or pre-diabetes
Source: Centers for Disease Control and Prevention, Behaviorial Risk Factor Surveillance System, SMART: Selected Metropolitan Area Risk Trends, 2017

Health Screening and Vaccination Rates

Category	MSA[1] (%)	U.S. (%)
Adults aged 65+ who have had flu shot within the past year	53.6	60.7
Adults aged 65+ who have ever had a pneumonia vaccination	72.2	75.4
Adults who have ever been tested for HIV	44.5	36.1
Adults who have ever had the shingles or zoster vaccine?	26.1	28.9
Adults who have had their blood cholesterol checked within the last five years	73.5	85.9

Note: n/a not available; (1) Figures cover the Anchorage, AK Metropolitan Statistical Area.
Source: Centers for Disease Control and Prevention, Behaviorial Risk Factor Surveillance System, SMART: Selected Metropolitan Area Risk Trends, 2017

Disability Status

Category	MSA[1] (%)	U.S. (%)
Adults who reported being deaf	5.0	6.7
Are you blind or have serious difficulty seeing, even when wearing glasses?	3.3	4.5
Are you limited in any way in any of your usual activities due of arthritis?	11.0	12.9
Do you have difficulty doing errands alone?	5.7	6.8
Do you have difficulty dressing or bathing?	2.9	3.6
Do you have serious difficulty concentrating/remembering/making decisions?	10.2	10.7
Do you have serious difficulty walking or climbing stairs?	10.2	13.6

Note: (1) Figures cover the Anchorage, AK Metropolitan Statistical Area.
Source: Centers for Disease Control and Prevention, Behaviorial Risk Factor Surveillance System, SMART: Selected Metropolitan Area Risk Trends, 2017

Mortality Rates for the Top 10 Causes of Death in the U.S.

ICD-10[a] Sub-Chapter	ICD-10[a] Code	Age-Adjusted Mortality Rate[1] per 100,000 population	
		County[2]	U.S.
Malignant neoplasms	C00-C97	140.2	149.2
Ischaemic heart diseases	I20-I25	65.1	90.5
Other forms of heart disease	I30-I51	47.1	52.2
Chronic lower respiratory diseases	J40-J47	30.3	39.6
Other degenerative diseases of the nervous system	G30-G31	37.8	37.6
Cerebrovascular diseases	I60-I69	32.5	37.2
Other external causes of accidental injury	W00-X59	38.8	36.1
Organic, including symptomatic, mental disorders	F01-F09	37.1	29.4
Hypertensive diseases	I10-I15	17.9	24.1
Diabetes mellitus	E10-E14	19.4	21.5

Note: (a) ICD-10 = International Classification of Diseases 10th Revision; (1) Mortality rates are a three-year average covering 2017-2019; (2) Figures cover Anchorage Borough.
Source: Centers for Disease Control and Prevention, National Center for Health Statistics. Underlying Cause of Death 1999-2019 on CDC WONDER Online Database

Mortality Rates for Selected Causes of Death

ICD-10[a] Sub-Chapter	ICD-10[a] Code	Age-Adjusted Mortality Rate[1] per 100,000 population	
		County[2]	U.S.
Assault	X85-Y09	11.3	6.0
Diseases of the liver	K70-K76	19.7	14.4
Human immunodeficiency virus (HIV) disease	B20-B24	Suppressed	1.5
Influenza and pneumonia	J09-J18	9.2	13.8
Intentional self-harm	X60-X84	21.1	14.1
Malnutrition	E40-E46	3.0	2.3
Obesity and other hyperalimentation	E65-E68	2.6	2.1
Renal failure	N17-N19	8.4	12.6
Transport accidents	V01-V99	12.3	12.3
Viral hepatitis	B15-B19	2.3	1.2

Note: (a) ICD-10 = International Classification of Diseases 10th Revision; (1) Mortality rates are a three-year average covering 2017-2019; (2) Figures cover Anchorage Borough; Data are suppressed when the data meet the criteria for confidentiality constraints; Mortality rates are flagged as unreliable when the rate would be calculated with a numerator of 20 or less.
Source: Centers for Disease Control and Prevention, National Center for Health Statistics. Underlying Cause of Death 1999-2019 on CDC WONDER Online Database

Health Insurance Coverage

Area	With Health Insurance	With Private Health Insurance	With Public Health Insurance	Without Health Insurance	Population Under Age 19 Without Health Insurance
City	88.8	70.3	30.4	11.2	8.2
MSA[1]	87.8	68.3	31.3	12.2	9.4
U.S.	91.2	67.9	35.1	8.8	5.1

Note: Figures are percentages that cover the civilian noninstitutionalized population; (1) Figures cover the Anchorage, AK Metropolitan Statistical Area
Source: U.S. Census Bureau, 2015-2019 American Community Survey 5-Year Estimates

Number of Medical Professionals

Area	MDs[3]	DOs[3,4]	Dentists	Podiatrists	Chiropractors	Optometrists
Borough[1] (number)	1,046	134	370	14	182	90
Borough[1] (rate[2])	360.0	46.1	128.5	4.9	63.2	31.3
U.S. (rate[2])	282.9	22.7	71.2	6.2	28.1	16.9

02020
Note: Data as of 2019 unless noted; (1) Data covers Anchorage Borough; (2) Rate per 100,000 population; (3) Data as of 2018 and includes all active, non-federal physicians; (4) Doctor of Osteopathic Medicine
Source: U.S. Department of Health and Human Services, Health Resources and Services Administration, Bureau of Health Professions, Area Resource File (ARF) 2019-2020

EDUCATION

Public School District Statistics

District Name	Schls	Pupils	Pupil/ Teacher Ratio	Minority Pupils[1] (%)	Free Lunch Eligible[2] (%)	IEP[3] (%)
Anchorage School District	100	46,115	17.2	58.5	n/a	15.2

Note: Table includes school districts with 2,000 or more students; (1) Percentage of students that are not non-Hispanic white; (2) Percentage of students that are eligible for the free lunch program; (3) Percentage of students that have an Individualized Education Program.
Source: U.S. Department of Education, National Center for Education Statistics, Common Core of Data, Local Education Agency (School District) Universe Survey: School Year 2018-2019; U.S. Department of Education, National Center for Education Statistics, Common Core of Data, Public Elementary/Secondary School Universe Survey: School Year 2018-2019

Highest Level of Education

Area	Less than H.S.	H.S. Diploma	Some College, No Deg.	Associate Degree	Bachelor's Degree	Master's Degree	Prof. School Degree	Doctorate Degree
City	6.1	23.4	25.4	9.0	22.2	9.5	3.1	1.3
MSA[1]	6.3	26.0	26.2	9.1	20.1	8.5	2.6	1.2
U.S.	12.0	27.0	20.4	8.5	19.8	8.8	2.1	1.4

Note: Figures cover persons age 25 and over; (1) Figures cover the Anchorage, AK Metropolitan Statistical Area
Source: U.S. Census Bureau, 2015-2019 American Community Survey 5-Year Estimates

Educational Attainment by Race

Area	High School Graduate or Higher (%)					Bachelor's Degree or Higher (%)				
	Total	White	Black	Asian	Hisp.[2]	Total	White	Black	Asian	Hisp.[2]
City	93.9	96.5	93.6	84.0	85.3	36.1	43.2	19.6	25.2	22.3
MSA[1]	93.7	95.6	93.5	83.9	86.3	32.3	37.0	19.5	25.0	21.3
U.S.	88.0	89.9	86.0	87.1	68.7	32.1	33.5	21.6	54.3	16.4

Note: Figures shown cover persons 25 years old and over; (1) Figures cover the Anchorage, AK Metropolitan Statistical Area; (2) People of Hispanic origin can be of any race
Source: U.S. Census Bureau, 2015-2019 American Community Survey 5-Year Estimates

School Enrollment by Grade and Control

Area	Preschool (%)		Kindergarten (%)		Grades 1 - 4 (%)		Grades 5 - 8 (%)		Grades 9 - 12 (%)	
	Public	Private	Public	Private	Public	Private	Public	Private	Public	Private
City	56.6	43.4	94.0	6.0	92.3	7.7	92.5	7.5	95.1	4.9
MSA[1]	58.3	41.7	92.4	7.6	90.7	9.3	90.5	9.5	92.8	7.2
U.S.	59.1	40.9	87.6	12.4	89.5	10.5	89.4	10.6	90.1	9.9

Note: Figures shown cover persons 3 years old and over; (1) Figures cover the Anchorage, AK Metropolitan Statistical Area
Source: U.S. Census Bureau, 2015-2019 American Community Survey 5-Year Estimates

Higher Education

Four-Year Colleges			Two-Year Colleges			Medical Schools[1]	Law Schools[2]	Voc/ Tech[3]
Public	Private Non-profit	Private For-profit	Public	Private Non-profit	Private For-profit			
1	1	0	0	0	1	0	0	0

Note: Figures cover institutions located within the city limits and include main campuses only; (1) includes schools accredited by the Liaison Committee on Medical Education and the American Osteopathic Association's Commission on Osteopathic College Accreditation; (2) includes ABA-accredited schools, schools with provisional ABA accreditation, and state accredited schools; (3) includes all schools with programs that are less than 2 years.
Source: National Center for Education Statistics, Integrated Postsecondary Education System (IPEDS), 2019-20; Wikipedia, List of Medical Schools in the United States, accessed April 2, 2021; Wikipedia, List of Law Schools in the United States, accessed April 2, 2021

EMPLOYERS

Major Employers

Company Name	Industry
ASRC Energy Services	Oil & gas field services
AT&T	Telephone communication, except radio
BP Transportation (Alaska)	Crude petroleum production
Bureau of Land Management	Information bureau
Carrs/Safeway	Grocery stores
Federal Aviation Administration	Aircraft regulating agencies
Federal Express Corporation	Air cargo carrier, scheduled
Fred Meyer	Retail
Galen Hospital Alaska	General medical & surgical hospitals
Indian Health Service	General medical & surgical hospitals
Municipality of Anchorage	Mayors' office
Nabors Alaska Drilling	Drilling oil & gas wells
Providence Health Services	Healthcare
U.S. Fish and Wildlife Service	Fish & wildlife conservation agency, government
United States Department of the Air Force	U.S. military
USPHS AK Native Medical Center	General medical & surgical hospitals
Wal-Mart Stores	Retail

Note: Companies shown are located within the Anchorage, AK Metropolitan Statistical Area.
Source: Hoovers.com; Wikipedia

PUBLIC SAFETY

Crime Rate

Area	All Crimes	Violent Crimes				Property Crimes		
		Murder	Rape[3]	Robbery	Aggrav. Assault	Burglary	Larceny -Theft	Motor Vehicle Theft
City	5,505.8	11.1	187.7	215.8	829.9	588.0	3,141.1	532.1
Suburbs[1]	5,634.3	10.9	32.6	92.4	277.1	787.8	3,955.4	478.1
Metro[2]	5,513.6	11.1	178.4	208.4	796.7	600.1	3,190.1	528.8
U.S.	2,489.3	5.0	42.6	81.6	250.2	340.5	1,549.5	219.9

Note: Figures are crimes per 100,000 population; (1) All areas within the metro area that are located outside the city limits; (2) Figures cover the Anchorage, AK Metropolitan Statistical Area; (3) All figures shown were reported using the revised Uniform Crime Reporting (UCR) definition of rape.
Source: FBI Uniform Crime Reports, 2019

Hate Crimes

Area	Number of Quarters Reported	Number of Incidents per Bias Motivation					
		Race/Ethnicity/ Ancestry	Religion	Sexual Orientation	Disability	Gender	Gender Identity
City	4	4	0	2	0	0	0
U.S.	4	3,963	1,521	1,195	157	69	198

Source: Federal Bureau of Investigation, Hate Crime Statistics 2019

Identity Theft Consumer Reports

Area	Reports	Reports per 100,000 Population	Rank[2]
MSA[1]	601	152	292
U.S.	1,387,615	423	-

Note: (1) Figures cover the Anchorage, AK Metropolitan Statistical Area; (2) Rank ranges from 1 to 391 where 1 indicates greatest number of identity theft reports per 100,000 population
Source: Federal Trade Commission, Consumer Sentinel Network Data Book 2020

Fraud and Other Consumer Reports

Area	Reports	Reports per 100,000 Population	Rank[2]
MSA[1]	2,968	749	143
U.S.	3,385,133	1,031	-

Note: (1) Figures cover the Anchorage, AK Metropolitan Statistical Area; (2) Rank ranges from 1 to 391 where 1 indicates greatest number of fraud and other consumer reports per 100,000 population
Source: Federal Trade Commission, Consumer Sentinel Network Data Book 2020

POLITICS

2020 Presidential Election Results

Area	Biden	Trump	Jorgensen	Hawkins	Other
Alaska	42.8	52.8	2.5	0.0	1.9
U.S.	51.3	46.8	1.2	0.3	0.5

Note: Results are percentages and may not add to 100% due to rounding
Source: Dave Leip's Atlas of U.S. Presidential Elections

SPORTS

Professional Sports Teams

Team Name	League	Year Established
No teams are located in the metro area		

Source: Wikipedia, Major Professional Sports Teams of the United States and Canada, April 6, 2021

CLIMATE

Average and Extreme Temperatures

Temperature	Jan	Feb	Mar	Apr	May	Jun	Jul	Aug	Sep	Oct	Nov	Dec	Yr.
Extreme High (°F)	50	48	51	65	77	85	82	82	73	61	53	48	85
Average High (°F)	22	25	33	43	55	62	65	63	55	41	28	22	43
Average Temp. (°F)	15	18	25	36	47	55	59	57	48	35	22	16	36
Average Low (°F)	8	11	17	28	39	47	51	49	41	28	15	10	29
Extreme Low (°F)	-34	-26	-24	-4	17	33	36	31	19	-5	-21	-30	-34

Note: Figures cover the years 1953-1995
Source: National Climatic Data Center, International Station Meteorological Climate Summary, 9/96

Average Precipitation/Snowfall/Humidity

Precip./Humidity	Jan	Feb	Mar	Apr	May	Jun	Jul	Aug	Sep	Oct	Nov	Dec	Yr.
Avg. Precip. (in.)	0.8	0.8	0.7	0.6	0.7	1.0	1.9	2.4	2.7	1.9	1.1	1.1	15.7
Avg. Snowfall (in.)	10	12	10	5	Tr	0	0	0	Tr	8	12	15	71
Avg. Rel. Hum. 6am (%)	74	74	72	75	73	74	80	84	84	78	78	78	77
Avg. Rel. Hum. 3pm (%)	73	67	57	54	50	55	62	64	64	67	74	76	64

Note: Figures cover the years 1953-1995; Tr = Trace amounts (<0.05 in. of rain; <0.5 in. of snow)
Source: National Climatic Data Center, International Station Meteorological Climate Summary, 9/96

Weather Conditions

Temperature			Daytime Sky			Precipitation		
0°F & below	32°F & below	65°F & above	Clear	Partly cloudy	Cloudy	0.01 inch or more precip.	0.1 inch or more snow/ice	Thunder-storms
32	194	41	50	115	200	113	49	2

Note: Figures are average number of days per year and cover the years 1953-1995
Source: National Climatic Data Center, International Station Meteorological Climate Summary, 9/96

HAZARDOUS WASTE

Superfund Sites

The Anchorage, AK metro area is home to two sites on the EPA's Superfund National Priorities List: **Elmendorf Air Force Base** (final); **Fort Richardson (USARMY)** (final). There are a total of 1,375 Superfund sites with a status of proposed or final on the list in the U.S. *U.S. Environmental Protection Agency, National Priorities List, April 7, 2021*

AIR QUALITY

Air Quality Trends: Ozone

	1990	1995	2000	2005	2010	2015	2016	2017	2018	2019
MSA[1]	n/a	n/a	n/a	n/a	n/a	n/a	n/a	n/a	n/a	n/a
U.S.	0.088	0.089	0.082	0.080	0.073	0.068	0.069	0.068	0.069	0.065

Note: (1) Data covers the Anchorage, AK Metropolitan Statistical Area; n/a not available. The values shown are the composite ozone concentration averages among trend sites based on the highest fourth daily maximum 8-hour concentration in parts per million. These trends are based on sites having an adequate record of monitoring data during the trend period. Data from exceptional events are included.
Source: U.S. Environmental Protection Agency, Air Quality Monitoring Information, "Air Quality Trends by City, 1990-2019"

Air Quality Index

Area	Percent of Days when Air Quality was...[2]					AQI Statistics[2]	
	Good	Moderate	Unhealthy for Sensitive Groups	Unhealthy	Very Unhealthy	Maximum	Median
MSA[1]	71.8	24.9	2.2	1.1	0.0	160	31

Note: (1) Data covers the Anchorage, AK Metropolitan Statistical Area; (2) Based on 365 days with AQI data in 2019. Air Quality Index (AQI) is an index for reporting daily air quality. EPA calculates the AQI for five major air pollutants regulated by the Clean Air Act: ground-level ozone, particle pollution (aka particulate matter), carbon monoxide, sulfur dioxide, and nitrogen dioxide. The AQI runs from 0 to 500. The higher the AQI value, the greater the level of air pollution and the greater the health concern. There are six AQI categories: "Good" AQI is between 0 and 50. Air quality is considered satisfactory; "Moderate" AQI is between 51 and 100. Air quality is acceptable; "Unhealthy for Sensitive Groups" When AQI values are between 101 and 150, members of sensitive groups may experience health effects; "Unhealthy" When AQI values are between 151 and 200 everyone may begin to experience health effects; "Very Unhealthy" AQI values between 201 and 300 trigger a health alert; "Hazardous" AQI values over 300 trigger warnings of emergency conditions (not shown).
Source: U.S. Environmental Protection Agency, Air Quality Index Report, 2019

Air Quality Index Pollutants

Area	Percent of Days when AQI Pollutant was...[2]					
	Carbon Monoxide	Nitrogen Dioxide	Ozone	Sulfur Dioxide	Particulate Matter 2.5	Particulate Matter 10
MSA[1]	1.4	0.0	0.0	0.0	69.9	28.8

Note: (1) Data covers the Anchorage, AK Metropolitan Statistical Area; (2) Based on 365 days with AQI data in 2019. The Air Quality Index (AQI) is an index for reporting daily air quality. EPA calculates the AQI for five major air pollutants regulated by the Clean Air Act: ground-level ozone, particle pollution (also known as particulate matter), carbon monoxide, sulfur dioxide, and nitrogen dioxide. The AQI runs from 0 to 500. The higher the AQI value, the greater the level of air pollution and the greater the health concern.
Source: U.S. Environmental Protection Agency, Air Quality Index Report, 2019

Maximum Air Pollutant Concentrations: Particulate Matter, Ozone, CO and Lead

	Particulate Matter 10 (ug/m^3)	Particulate Matter 2.5 Wtd AM (ug/m^3)	Particulate Matter 2.5 24-Hr (ug/m^3)	Ozone (ppm)	Carbon Monoxide (ppm)	Lead (ug/m^3)
MSA[1] Level	148	8.2	42	n/a	2	n/a
NAAQS[2]	150	15	35	0.075	9	0.15
Met NAAQS[2]	Yes	Yes	No	n/a	Yes	n/a

Note: (1) Data covers the Anchorage, AK Metropolitan Statistical Area; Data from exceptional events are included; (2) National Ambient Air Quality Standards; ppm = parts per million; ug/m³ = micrograms per cubic meter; n/a not available.
Concentrations: Particulate Matter 10 (coarse particulate)—highest second maximum 24-hour concentration; Particulate Matter 2.5 Wtd AM (fine particulate)—highest weighted annual mean concentration; Particulate Matter 2.5 24-Hour (fine particulate)—highest 98th percentile 24-hour concentration; Ozone—highest fourth daily maximum 8-hour concentration; Carbon Monoxide—highest second maximum non-overlapping 8-hour concentration; Lead—maximum running 3-month average
Source: U.S. Environmental Protection Agency, Air Quality Monitoring Information, "Air Quality Statistics by City, 2019"

Maximum Air Pollutant Concentrations: Nitrogen Dioxide and Sulfur Dioxide

	Nitrogen Dioxide AM (ppb)	Nitrogen Dioxide 1-Hr (ppb)	Sulfur Dioxide AM (ppb)	Sulfur Dioxide 1-Hr (ppb)	Sulfur Dioxide 24-Hr (ppb)
MSA[1] Level	n/a	n/a	n/a	n/a	n/a
NAAQS[2]	53	100	30	75	140
Met NAAQS[2]	n/a	n/a	n/a	n/a	n/a

Note: (1) Data covers the Anchorage, AK Metropolitan Statistical Area; Data from exceptional events are included; (2) National Ambient Air Quality Standards; ppm = parts per million; ug/m³ = micrograms per cubic meter; n/a not available.
Concentrations: Nitrogen Dioxide AM—highest arithmetic mean concentration; Nitrogen Dioxide 1-Hr—highest 98th percentile 1-hour daily maximum concentration; Sulfur Dioxide AM—highest annual mean concentration; Sulfur Dioxide 1-Hr—highest 99th percentile 1-hour daily maximum concentration; Sulfur Dioxide 24-Hr—highest second maximum 24-hour concentration
Source: U.S. Environmental Protection Agency, Air Quality Monitoring Information, "Air Quality Statistics by City, 2019"

Boise City, Idaho

Background

Boise (boy-see) is the capital and largest city in Idaho, lying along the Boise River adjacent to the foothills of the Rocky Mountains. The city is located southwest of the western slopes of the Rockies, and is the site of a great system of natural warm water springs.

Boise's spectacular natural location is its most popular, and obvious, attraction, and this, coupled with its dynamic economic growth in recent decades, makes Boise an altogether remarkable city. The splendor of its surroundings, together with an average 18-minute drive to work, has allowed the city to combine pleasure and production in an enviable mix.

French-Canadian trappers were familiar with Boise and its environs by 1811, and the name of the city is an Anglicization of the French Les Bois—the trees. The first substantial European settlement dates to 1863 when, in the spring of that year, I.M. Coston built from pegged driftwood a great house that served as a hub for the activities of prospectors, traders, and Native Americans. In the same year, the U.S. Army built Fort Boise, and considerable deposits of gold and silver were discovered in the area. The U.S. Assay Office in Boise, in 1870-71 alone, is said to have valuated more than $75 million in precious metals.

The area is rich in gold rush lore, and six miles above Boise, on the south side of the river, there may even be buried treasure from that era. The eastbound stagecoach from Boise was said to have been waylaid by a robber who, though wounded in the attack by a resourceful passenger, managed to drag off a strongbox filled with $50,000 in gold. The robber died of his wounds and was discovered the next day, but he had apparently buried his loot. No one has ever located it.

The Boise area was subsequently developed for farming, as crops of grains, vegetables, and fruits, replaced the mines as its source of wealth. It became the territorial capital of Idaho in 1864 and the state capital in 1890. Education was served with the opening of a university in 1932, which became Boise State University in 1974 and now enrolls about 20,000 students.

With a large Basque population, the city hosts a Basque festival, Jaialdi , every five years, with the next scheduled for 2025.

The city's natural setting offers a great range of outdoor activities that are pursued energetically by its citizens. Its rivers, mountains, deserts, and lakes offer world-class skiing, hiking, camping, kayaking, river rafting, hunting, and fishing. Bike paths run throughout the city and into Boise's large outdoor trail network, the Boise River Greenbelt. Recreational wilderness exists extensively just outside the city's limits. The Word Center for Birds of Prey is located on the city's southern frontier, and is the site of the Peregrine Falcon's rehabilitation and release into the wild.

Many large regional, national, and international companies are headquartered in Boise, including major call centers for DIRECTV and T-Mobile.

The city produces high- and low-tech products and everything in between: software, computer components, steel and sheet metal products, mobile homes, lumber products, farm machinery, packed meats, and processed foods. Increasingly an advanced technological center, it continues to serve as a trading center for the greater agricultural region.

By virtue of its history and geographical character, the city can be considered a presence on the Pacific Rim. In a more tangible vein, Boise, with ten airlines operating at its airport, is conveniently tied to the wider world.

Boise's Basque community is the largest in the United States and the third largest in the world outside Argentina and the Basque Country in Spain and France. A large Basque festival known as Jaialdi is held once every five years. Boise (along with Valley and Boise Counties) hosted the 2009 Special Olympics World Winter Games. More than 2,500 athletes from over 100 countries participated.

The city is protected by the mountains to the north in such a way that it is largely unbothered by the extreme blizzards that affect eastern Idaho and parts of neighboring states. Boise, and this section of western Idaho generally, is affected by climatic influences from the Pacific Ocean and exhibits an unusually mild climate for this latitude. Summers can be hot, but nights are almost always cool, and sunshine generally prevails.

Rankings

General Rankings

- For its "Best for Vets: Places to Live 2019" rankings, *Military Times* evaluated 599 cities (83 large, 234 medium, 282 small) and compared the locations across three broad categories: veteran and military culture/services; economic indicators; and livability factors such as health, crime, traffic, and school quality. Boise City ranked #13 out of the top 50, in the medium-sized city category (population of 100,000-249,999). Data points more specific to veterans and the military weighed more heavily than others. *rebootcamp.militarytimes.com, "Military Times Best Places to Live 2019," September 10, 2018*

- *US News & World Report* conducted a survey of more than 3,000 people and analyzed the 150 largest metropolitan areas to determine what matters most when selecting the next place to live. Boise City ranked #20 out of the top 25 as having the best combination of desirable factors. Criteria: cost of living; quality of life; net migration; job market; desirability; and other factors. *realestate.usnews.com, "The 25 Best Places to Live in the U.S. in 2020-21," October 13, 2020*

- As part of its *Next Stop* series, *Insider* listed 10 places in the U.S. that were either a classic vacation destination experiencing a renaissance or a new up-and-coming hot spot. That could mean the exploding food scene, experiencing the great outdoors, where cool people are moving to, or not overrun with tourists, according to the website insider.com Boise City is a place to visit in 2020. *Insider, "10 Places in the U.S. You Need to Visit in 2020," December 23, 2019*

- The Boise City metro area was identified as one of America's fastest-growing areas in terms of population and business growth by *MagnifyMoney*. The area ranked #8 out of 35. The 100 most populous metro areas in the U.S. were evaluated on their change from 2011-2016 in the following categories: people and housing; workforce and employment opportunities; growing industry. *www.businessinsider.com, "The 35 Cities in the US with the Biggest Influx of People, the Most Work Opportunities, and the Hottest Business Growth," August 12, 2018*

- The Boise City metro area was identified as one of America's fastest-growing areas in terms of population and economy by *Forbes*. The area ranked #1 out of 25. The 100 most populous metro areas in the U.S. were evaluated on the following criteria: estimated population growth; employment; economic output; wages; home values. *Forbes, "America's Fastest-Growing Cities 2018," February 28, 2018*

- In their seventh annual survey, Livability.com looked at data for more than 1,000 small to mid-sized U.S. cities to determine the rankings for Livability's "Top 100 Best Places to Live" in 2020. Boise City ranked #35. Criteria: housing and affordable living; vibrant economy; social and civic engagement; education; demographics; health care options; transportation & infrastructure; and abundant lifestyle amenities. *Livability.com, "Top 100 Best Places to Live 2020" October 2020*

Business/Finance Rankings

- According to *Business Insider*, the Boise City metro area is a prime place to run a startup or move an existing business to. The area ranked #13. Nearly 190 metro areas were analyzed on overall economic health and investments. Data was based on the 2019 U.S. Census Bureau American Community Survey, the marketing company PitchBook, Bureau of Labor Statistics employment report, and Zillow. Criteria: percentage of change in typical home values and employment rates; quarterly venture capital investment activity; and median household income. *www.businessinsider.com, "The 25 Best Cities to Start a Business-Or Move Your Current One," January 12, 2021*

- The Brookings Institution ranked the nation's largest cities based on income inequality. Boise City was ranked #60 (#1 = greatest inequality). Criteria: the "95/20 ratio," a figure representing the income at which a household earns more than 95 percent of all other households, divided by the income at which a household earns more than only 20 percent of all other households. *Brookings Institution, "Household Income Inequality, Largest Cities of 97 Large U.S. Metro Areas, 2014-2016," February 5, 2018*

- The Brookings Institution ranked the 100 largest metro areas in the U.S. based on income inequality. Boise City was ranked #89 (#1 = greatest inequality). Criteria: the "95/20 ratio," a figure representing the income at which a household earns more than 95 percent of all other households, divided by the income at which a household earns more than only 20 percent of all other households. *Brookings Institution, "Household Income Inequality, 100 Largest U.S. Metro Areas, 2014-2016," February 5, 2018*

- *Forbes* ranked the 100 largest metro areas in the U.S. in terms of the "Best Cities for Young Professionals." The Boise City metro area ranked #20 out of 25. Criteria: median rent of a two-bedroom apartment; job growth and unemployment rate; median salary of college graduates with 5 or less years of work experience; networking opportunities; social outlook; percentage of population 25 years of age and older with college degrees. *Forbes.com, "America's 25 Best Cities for Young Professionals in 2017," May 22, 2017*

- The Boise City metro area appeared on the Milken Institute "2021 Best Performing Cities" list. Rank: #6 out of 200 large metro areas (population over 250,000). Criteria: job growth; wage and salary growth; high-tech output growth; housing affordability; household broadband access. *Milken Institute, "Best-Performing Cities 2021," February 16, 2021*

- *Forbes* ranked the 200 most populous metro areas to determine the nation's "Best Places for Business and Careers." The Boise City metro area was ranked #29. Criteria: costs (business and living); job growth (past and projected); income growth; quality of life; educational attainment (college and high school); projected economic growth; cultural and leisure opportunities; workplace tolerance laws; net migration patterns. *Forbes, "The Best Places for Business and Careers 2019: Seattle Still On Top," October 30, 2019*

Dating/Romance Rankings

- Boise City was ranked #3 out of 25 cities that stood out for inspiring romance and attracting diners on the website OpenTable.com. Criteria: percentage of people who dined out on Valentine's Day in 2018; percentage of romantic restaurants as rated by OpenTable diner reviews; and percentage of tables seated for two. *OpenTable, "25 Most Romantic Cities in America for 2019," February 7, 2019*

Education Rankings

- Personal finance website *WalletHub* analyzed the 150 largest U.S. metropolitan statistical areas to determine where the most educated Americans are putting their degrees to work. Criteria: education levels; percentage of workers with degrees; education quality and attainment gap; public school quality rankings; quality and enrollment of each metro area's universities. Boise City was ranked #55 (#1 = most educated city). *www.WalletHub.com, "Most and Least Educated Cities in America," July 20, 2020*

Food/Drink Rankings

- Boise City was selected as one of America's 10 most vegan-friendly areas. The city was ranked #5. Criteria now includes smaller urban areas, following the migration to smaller cities due to the pandemic. *People for the Ethical Treatment of Animals, "Top 10 Vegan-Friendly Towns and Small Cities of 2020," December 14, 2020*

Health/Fitness Rankings

- For each of the 100 largest cities in the United States, the American Fitness Index®, published by the American College of Sports Medicine and the Anthem Foundation, evaluated community infrastructure and 33 health behaviors including preventive health, levels of chronic disease conditions, pedestrian safety, air quality, and community resources that support physical activity. Boise City ranked #9 for "community fitness." *americanfitnessindex.org, "2020 ACSM American Fitness Index Summary Report," July 14, 2020*

- Boise City was identified as a "2021 Spring Allergy Capital." The area ranked #88 out of 100. Three groups of factors were used to identify the most challenging cities for people with allergies during the spring season: annual spring pollen levels; over the counter medicine use; number of board-certified allergy specialists. *Asthma and Allergy Foundation of America, "Spring Allergy Capitals 2021," February 23, 2021*

- Boise City was identified as a "2021 Fall Allergy Capital." The area ranked #88 out of 100. Three groups of factors were used to identify the most challenging cities for people with allergies during the fall season: annual fall pollen levels; over the counter medicine use; number of board-certified allergy specialists. *Asthma and Allergy Foundation of America, "Fall Allergy Capitals 2021," February 23, 2021*

- Boise City was identified as a "2019 Asthma Capital." The area ranked #55 out of the nation's 100 largest metropolitan areas. Criteria: estimated asthma prevalence; crude death rate from asthma; and ER visits due to asthma. Risk factors analyzed but not factored in the rankings: annual pollen score; annual air quality; public smoking laws; number of board-certified asthma specialists; rescue medication use; controller medication use; uninsured rate; poverty rate. *Asthma and Allergy Foundation of America, "Asthma Capitals 2019: The Most Challenging Places to Live With Asthma," May 7, 2019*

Real Estate Rankings

- *WalletHub* compared the most populated U.S. cities to determine which had the best markets for real estate agents. Boise City ranked #91 where demand was high and pay was the best. Criteria: sales per agent; annual median wage for real-estate agents; monthly average starting salary for real estate agents; real estate job density and competition; unemployment rate; home turnover rate; housing-market health index; and other relevant metrics. *www.WalletHub.com, "2019's Best Places to Be a Real Estate Agent," April 24, 2019*

- The Boise City metro area appeared on Realtor.com's list of hot housing markets to watch in 2021. The area ranked #4. Criteria: healthy existing homes inventory; relative home affordability; local economy/population trends. *Realtor.com®, "Top 10 Housing Markets Positioned for Growth in 2021," December 7, 2020*

- The Boise City metro area was identified as one of the top 15 housing markets to invest in for 2021 by *Forbes*. Criteria: home price appreciation; percentage of home sales within a 2-week time frame; available inventory; number of home sales; and other factors. *Forbes.com, "Top Housing Markets To Watch In 2021," December 15, 2020*

- Boise City was ranked #1 in the top 20 out of the 100 largest metro areas in terms of house price appreciation in 2020 (#1 = highest rate). *Federal Housing Finance Agency, House Price Index, 4th Quarter 2020*

- The Boise City metro area was identified as one of the 20 best housing markets in the U.S. in 2020. The area ranked #7 out of 180 markets. Criteria: year-over-year change of median sales price of existing single-family homes between the 4th quarter of 2019 and the 4th quarter of 2020. *National Association of Realtors®, Median Sales Price of Existing Single-Family Homes for Metropolitan Areas, 4th Quarter 2020*

- Boise City was ranked #235 out of 268 metro areas in terms of housing affordability in 2020 by the National Association of Home Builders (#1 = most affordable). Criteria: the share of homes sold in that area affordable to a family earning the local median income, based on standard mortgage underwriting criteria. *National Association of Home Builders®, NAHB-Wells Fargo Housing Opportunity Index, 4th Quarter 2020*

Safety Rankings

- Allstate ranked the 200 largest cities in America in terms of driver safety. Boise City ranked #2. Criteria: internal property damage claims over a two-year period from January 2016 to December 2017. The report helps increase the importance of safety and awareness behind the wheel. *Allstate, "Allstate America's Best Drivers Report, 2019" June 24, 2019*

- The National Insurance Crime Bureau ranked 384 metro areas in the U.S. in terms of per capita rates of vehicle theft. The Boise City metro area ranked #297 (#1 = highest rate). Criteria: number of vehicle theft offenses per 100,000 inhabitants in 2019. *National Insurance Crime Bureau, "Hot Spots 2019," July 21, 2020*

Seniors/Retirement Rankings

- From its Best Cities for Successful Aging indexes, the Milken Institute generated rankings for metropolitan areas, weighing data in nine categories—health care, wellness, living arrangements, transportation and convenience, financial characteristics, education, employment, community engagement, and overall livability. The Boise City metro area was ranked #34 overall in the large metro area category. *Milken Institute, "Best Cities for Successful Aging, 2017" March 14, 2017*

- Boise City made the 2020 *Forbes* list of "25 Best Places to Retire." Criteria, focused on high-quality retirement living at an affordable price, include: housing/living costs compared to the national average and state taxes; air quality; crime rates; good economic outlook; home price appreciation; risk associated with climate-change; availability of medical care; bikeability; walkability; healthy living. *Forbes.com, "The Best Places to Retire in 2020," August 14, 2020*

- Boise City was identified as #13 of 20 most popular places to retire in the Western region by *Topretirements.com*. The site separated its annual "Best Places to Retire" list by major U.S. regions for 2019. The list reflects the 20 cities that visitors to the website are most interested in for retirement, based on the number of times a city's review was viewed on the website. *Topretirements.com, "20 Best Places to Retire in the West-2019," November 11, 2019*

Sports/Recreation Rankings

- Boise City was chosen as one of America's best cities for bicycling. The city ranked #21 out of 50. Criteria: cycling infrastructure that is safe and friendly for all ages; energy and bike culture. The editors evaluated cities with populations of 100,000 or more. *Bicycling, "The 50 Best Bike Cities in America," October 10, 2018*

Women/Minorities Rankings

- Personal finance website *WalletHub* compared more than 180 U.S. cities across two key dimensions, "Hispanic Business-Friendliness" and "Hispanic Purchasing Power," to arrive at the most favorable conditions for Hispanic entrepreneurs. Boise City was ranked #35 out of 182. Criteria includes: share of Hispanic-Owned Businesses; Hispanic entrepreneurship rate to median annual income of Hispanics; Small Business-Friendliness score; cost of living; and number of Hispanics with at least a bachelor's degree. *WalletHub.com, "2019's Best Cities for Hispanic Entrepreneurs," May 1, 2019*

Miscellaneous Rankings

- *WalletHub* compared the 150 most populated U.S. cities to determine their operating efficiency. A "Quality of City Services" score was constructed for each city and then divided by the total budget per capita to reveal which were managed the best. Boise City ranked #2. Criteria: financial stability; economy; education; safety; health; infrastructure and pollution. *www.WalletHub.com, "2020's Best- & Worst-Run Cities in America," June 29, 2020*

Business Environment

DEMOGRAPHICS

Population Growth

Area	1990 Census	2000 Census	2010 Census	2019* Estimate	Population Growth (%) 1990-2019	Population Growth (%) 2010-2019
City	144,317	185,787	205,671	226,115	56.7	9.9
MSA[1]	319,596	464,840	616,561	710,743	122.4	15.3
U.S.	248,709,873	281,421,906	308,745,538	324,697,795	30.6	5.2

Note: (1) Figures cover the Boise City, ID Metropolitan Statistical Area; (*) 2015-2019 5-year estimated population
Source: U.S. Census Bureau, 1990 Census, Census 2000, Census 2010, 2015-2019 American Community Survey 5-Year Estimates

Household Size

Area	Persons in Household (%) One	Two	Three	Four	Five	Six	Seven or More	Average Household Size
City	34.1	34.1	14.4	10.3	4.7	1.5	0.9	2.40
MSA[1]	27.8	34.4	14.4	12.0	7.0	2.7	1.7	2.70
U.S.	27.9	33.9	15.6	12.9	6.0	2.3	1.4	2.60

Note: (1) Figures cover the Boise City, ID Metropolitan Statistical Area
Source: U.S. Census Bureau, 2015-2019 American Community Survey 5-Year Estimates

Race

Area	White Alone[2] (%)	Black Alone[2] (%)	Asian Alone[2] (%)	AIAN[3] Alone[2] (%)	NHOPI[4] Alone[2] (%)	Other Race Alone[2] (%)	Two or More Races (%)
City	89.3	1.9	2.8	0.5	0.2	1.9	3.4
MSA[1]	88.0	1.0	1.9	0.7	0.2	4.6	3.5
U.S.	72.5	12.7	5.5	0.8	0.2	4.9	3.3

Note: (1) Figures cover the Boise City, ID Metropolitan Statistical Area; (2) Alone is defined as not being in combination with one or more other races; (3) American Indian and Alaska Native; (4) Native Hawaiian and Other Pacific Islander
Source: U.S. Census Bureau, 2015-2019 American Community Survey 5-Year Estimates

Hispanic or Latino Origin

Area	Total (%)	Mexican (%)	Puerto Rican (%)	Cuban (%)	Other (%)
City	9.0	7.2	0.3	0.0	1.5
MSA[1]	13.7	11.6	0.3	0.1	1.6
U.S.	18.0	11.2	1.7	0.7	4.3

Note: Persons of Hispanic or Latino origin can be of any race; (1) Figures cover the Boise City, ID Metropolitan Statistical Area
Source: U.S. Census Bureau, 2015-2019 American Community Survey 5-Year Estimates

Ancestry

Area	German	Irish	English	American	Italian	Polish	French[2]	Scottish	Dutch
City	16.7	11.8	18.5	4.5	3.7	1.7	2.4	3.9	1.7
MSA[1]	16.1	9.6	17.1	5.1	3.4	1.2	2.4	3.2	2.1
U.S.	13.3	9.7	7.2	6.2	5.1	2.8	2.3	1.7	1.2

Note: Figures are the percentage of the total population reporting a particular ancestry. The nine most commonly reported ancestries in the U.S. are shown. Figures include multiple ancestries (e.g. if a person reported being Irish and Italian, they were included in both columns); (1) Figures cover the Boise City, ID Metropolitan Statistical Area; (2) Excludes Basque
Source: U.S. Census Bureau, 2015-2019 American Community Survey 5-Year Estimates

Foreign-born Population

Area	Any Foreign Country	Percent of Population Born in Asia	Mexico	Europe	Caribbean	Central America[2]	South America	Africa	Canada
City	6.4	2.7	1.0	1.4	0.1	0.1	0.3	0.6	0.2
MSA[1]	6.5	1.6	2.7	1.0	0.0	0.2	0.3	0.3	0.3
U.S.	13.6	4.2	3.5	1.5	1.3	1.1	1.0	0.7	0.2

Note: (1) Figures cover the Boise City, ID Metropolitan Statistical Area; (2) Excludes Mexico.
Source: U.S. Census Bureau, 2015-2019 American Community Survey 5-Year Estimates

Marital Status

Area	Never Married	Now Married[2]	Separated	Widowed	Divorced
City	34.1	46.7	0.9	4.5	13.9
MSA[1]	29.6	52.2	1.1	4.5	12.6
U.S.	33.4	48.1	1.9	5.8	10.9

Note: Figures are percentages and cover the population 15 years of age and older; (1) Figures cover the Boise City, ID Metropolitan Statistical Area; (2) Excludes separated
Source: U.S. Census Bureau, 2015-2019 American Community Survey 5-Year Estimates

Disability by Age

Area	All Ages	Under 18 Years Old	18 to 64 Years Old	65 Years and Over
City	10.9	3.3	9.0	31.7
MSA[1]	12.0	4.0	10.5	33.0
U.S.	12.6	4.2	10.3	34.5

Note: Figures show percent of the civilian noninstitutionalized population that reported having a disability. Disability status is determined from six types of difficulty: vision, hearing, cognitive, ambulatory, self-care, and independent living. For children under 5 years old, hearing and vision difficulty are used to determine disability status. For children between the ages of 5 and 14, disability status is determined from hearing, vision, cognitive, ambulatory, and self-care difficulties. For people aged 15 years and older, they are considered to have a disability if they have difficulty with any one of the six difficulty types; Note: (1) Figures cover the Boise City, ID Metropolitan Statistical Area
Source: U.S. Census Bureau, 2015-2019 American Community Survey 5-Year Estimates

Age

Area	Percent of Population									Median Age
	Under Age 5	Age 5–19	Age 20–34	Age 35–44	Age 45–54	Age 55–64	Age 65–74	Age 75–84	Age 85+	
City	5.7	18.9	23.1	14.0	12.3	12.0	8.4	3.7	1.8	36.6
MSA[1]	6.3	21.7	20.0	13.4	12.5	11.8	8.7	4.0	1.4	36.3
U.S.	6.1	19.1	20.7	12.6	13.0	12.9	9.1	4.6	1.9	38.1

Note: (1) Figures cover the Boise City, ID Metropolitan Statistical Area
Source: U.S. Census Bureau, 2015-2019 American Community Survey 5-Year Estimates

Gender

Area	Males	Females	Males per 100 Females
City	112,637	113,478	99.3
MSA[1]	354,905	355,838	99.7
U.S.	159,886,919	164,810,876	97.0

Note: (1) Figures cover the Boise City, ID Metropolitan Statistical Area
Source: U.S. Census Bureau, 2015-2019 American Community Survey 5-Year Estimates

Religious Groups by Family

Area	Catholic	Baptist	Non-Den.	Methodist[2]	Lutheran	LDS[3]	Pentecostal	Presbyterian[4]	Muslim[5]	Judaism
MSA[1]	8.0	2.9	4.2	2.1	1.2	15.9	2.3	0.6	0.1	0.1
U.S.	19.1	9.3	4.0	4.0	2.3	2.0	1.9	1.6	0.8	0.7

Note: Figures are the number of adherents as a percentage of the total population; (1) Figures cover the Boise City, ID Metropolitan Statistical Area; (2) Methodist/Pietist; (3) Latter Day Saints; (4) Reformed; (5) Figures are estimates
Source: Association of Statisticians of American Religious Bodies, 2010 U.S. Religion Census: Religious Congregations & Membership Study

Religious Groups by Tradition

Area	Catholic	Evangelical Protestant	Mainline Protestant	Other Tradition	Black Protestant	Orthodox
MSA[1]	8.0	13.0	4.4	16.7	<0.1	0.1
U.S.	19.1	16.2	7.3	4.3	1.6	0.3

Note: Figures are the number of adherents as a percentage of the total population; (1) Figures cover the Boise City, ID Metropolitan Statistical Area
Source: Association of Statisticians of American Religious Bodies, 2010 U.S. Religion Census: Religious Congregations & Membership Study

ECONOMY

Gross Metropolitan Product

Area	2017	2018	2019	2020	Rank[2]
MSA[1]	33.9	36.5	38.7	40.8	79

Note: Figures are in billions of dollars; (1) Figures cover the Boise City, ID Metropolitan Statistical Area; (2) Rank is based on 2018 data and ranges from 1 to 381
Source: U.S. Conference of Mayors, U.S. Metro Economies: GMP & Employment 2018-2020, September 2019

Economic Growth

Area	2015-17 (%)	2018 (%)	2019 (%)	2020 (%)	Rank[2]
MSA[1]	3.7	5.5	4.1	3.2	45
U.S.	1.9	2.9	2.3	2.1	–

Note: Figures are real gross metropolitan product (GMP) growth rates and represent average annual percent change; (1) Figures cover the Boise City, ID Metropolitan Statistical Area; (2) Rank is based on 2017 2-year average annual percent change and ranges from 1 to 381
Source: U.S. Conference of Mayors, U.S. Metro Economies: GMP & Employment 2018-2020, September 2019

Metropolitan Area Exports

Area	2014	2015	2016	2017	2018	2019	Rank[2]
MSA[1]	3,143.4	2,668.0	3,021.7	2,483.3	2,771.7	2,062.8	101

Note: Figures are in millions of dollars; (1) Figures cover the Boise City, ID Metropolitan Statistical Area; (2) Rank is based on 2019 data and ranges from 1 to 386
Source: U.S. Department of Commerce, International Trade Administration, Office of Trade and Economic Analysis, Industry and Analysis, Exports by Metropolitan Area, data extracted March 24, 2021

Building Permits

Area	Single-Family			Multi-Family			Total		
	2018	2019	Pct. Chg.	2018	2019	Pct. Chg.	2018	2019	Pct. Chg.
City	844	698	-17.3	296	883	198.3	1,140	1,581	38.7
MSA[1]	6,923	7,570	9.3	1,994	3,062	53.6	8,917	10,632	19.2
U.S.	855,300	862,100	0.7	473,500	523,900	10.6	1,328,800	1,386,000	4.3

Note: (1) Figures cover the Boise City, ID Metropolitan Statistical Area; Figures represent new, privately-owned housing units authorized (unadjusted data); All permit data are based on estimates with imputation
Source: U.S. Census Bureau, Manufacturing, Mining, and Construction Statistics, Building Permits, 2018, 2019

Bankruptcy Filings

Area	Business Filings			Nonbusiness Filings		
	2019	2020	% Chg.	2019	2020	% Chg.
Ada County	26	19	-26.9	878	589	-32.9
U.S.	22,780	21,655	-4.9	752,160	522,808	-30.5

Note: Business filings include Chapter 7, Chapter 9, Chapter 11, Chapter 12, Chapter 13, Chapter 15, and Section 304; Nonbusiness filings include Chapter 7, Chapter 11, and Chapter 13
Source: Administrative Office of the U.S. Courts, Business and Nonbusiness Bankruptcy, County Cases Commenced by Chapter of the Bankruptcy Code, During the 12-Month Period Ending December 31, 2019 and Business and Nonbusiness Bankruptcy, County Cases Commenced by Chapter of the Bankruptcy Code, During the 12-Month Period Ending December 31, 2020

Housing Vacancy Rates

Area	Gross Vacancy Rate[2] (%)			Year-Round Vacancy Rate[3] (%)			Rental Vacancy Rate[4] (%)			Homeowner Vacancy Rate[5] (%)		
	2018	2019	2020	2018	2019	2020	2018	2019	2020	2018	2019	2020
MSA[1]	n/a	n/a	n/a	n/a	n/a	n/a	n/a	n/a	n/a	n/a	n/a	n/a
U.S.	12.3	12.0	10.6	9.7	9.5	8.2	6.9	6.7	6.3	1.5	1.4	1.0

Note: (1) Figures cover the Boise City, ID Metropolitan Statistical Area; (2) The percentage of the total housing inventory that is vacant; (3) The percentage of the housing inventory (excluding seasonal units) that is year-round vacant; (4) The percentage of rental inventory that is vacant for rent; (5) The percentage of homeowner inventory that is vacant for sale; n/a not available
Source: U.S. Census Bureau, Housing Vacancies and Homeownership Annual Statistics: 2018, 2019, 2020

INCOME

Income

Area	Per Capita ($)	Median Household ($)	Average Household ($)
City	34,636	60,035	82,424
MSA[1]	30,508	60,568	80,438
U.S.	34,103	62,843	88,607

Note: (1) Figures cover the Boise City, ID Metropolitan Statistical Area
Source: U.S. Census Bureau, 2015-2019 American Community Survey 5-Year Estimates

Household Income Distribution

Area	Percent of Households Earning							
	Under $15,000	$15,000 -$24,999	$25,000 -$34,999	$35,000 -$49,999	$50,000 -$74,999	$75,000 -$99,999	$100,000 -$149,999	$150,000 and up
City	10.2	9.7	9.3	13.2	18.2	12.3	14.8	12.3
MSA[1]	9.5	8.6	9.4	13.5	19.8	13.6	15.2	10.5
U.S.	10.3	8.9	8.9	12.3	17.2	12.7	15.1	14.5

Note: (1) Figures cover the Boise City, ID Metropolitan Statistical Area
Source: U.S. Census Bureau, 2015-2019 American Community Survey 5-Year Estimates

Poverty Rate

Area	All Ages	Under 18 Years Old	18 to 64 Years Old	65 Years and Over
City	13.7	16.2	13.6	10.7
MSA[1]	11.9	13.5	11.8	9.1
U.S.	13.4	18.5	12.6	9.3

Note: Figures are percentage of people whose income during the past 12 months was below the poverty level;
(1) Figures cover the Boise City, ID Metropolitan Statistical Area
Source: U.S. Census Bureau, 2015-2019 American Community Survey 5-Year Estimates

CITY FINANCES

City Government Finances

Component	2017 ($000)	2017 ($ per capita)
Total Revenues	349,840	1,603
Total Expenditures	321,021	1,471
Debt Outstanding	109,334	501
Cash and Securities[1]	150,468	689

Note: (1) Cash and security holdings of a government at the close of its fiscal year,
including those of its dependent agencies, utilities, and liquor stores.
Source: U.S. Census Bureau, State & Local Government Finances 2017

City Government Revenue by Source

Source	2017 ($000)	2017 ($ per capita)	2017 (%)
General Revenue			
From Federal Government	13,589	62	3.9
From State Government	23,894	109	6.8
From Local Governments	0	0	0.0
Taxes			
Property	128,359	588	36.7
Sales and Gross Receipts	8,474	39	2.4
Personal Income	0	0	0.0
Corporate Income	0	0	0.0
Motor Vehicle License	0	0	0.0
Other Taxes	8,866	41	2.5
Current Charges	143,872	659	41.1
Liquor Store	0	0	0.0
Utility	0	0	0.0
Employee Retirement	0	0	0.0

Source: U.S. Census Bureau, State & Local Government Finances 2017

City Government Expenditures by Function

Function	2017 ($000)	2017 ($ per capita)	2017 (%)
General Direct Expenditures			
Air Transportation	33,567	153	10.5
Corrections	0	0	0.0
Education	0	0	0.0
Employment Security Administration	0	0	0.0
Financial Administration	4,836	22	1.5
Fire Protection	47,153	216	14.7
General Public Buildings	5,980	27	1.9
Governmental Administration, Other	8,690	39	2.7
Health	906	4	0.3
Highways	1,898	8	0.6
Hospitals	0	0	0.0
Housing and Community Development	3,271	15	1.0
Interest on General Debt	2,547	11	0.8
Judicial and Legal	5,656	25	1.8
Libraries	11,118	50	3.5
Parking	0	0	0.0
Parks and Recreation	32,044	146	10.0
Police Protection	54,346	249	16.9
Public Welfare	0	0	0.0
Sewerage	59,913	274	18.7
Solid Waste Management	33,292	152	10.4
Veterans' Services	0	0	0.0
Liquor Store	0	0	0.0
Utility	0	0	0.0
Employee Retirement	0	0	0.0

Source: U.S. Census Bureau, State & Local Government Finances 2017

EMPLOYMENT

Labor Force and Employment

Area	Civilian Labor Force			Workers Employed		
	Dec. 2019	Dec. 2020	% Chg.	Dec. 2019	Dec. 2020	% Chg.
City	134,753	133,502	-0.9	131,600	127,739	-2.9
MSA[1]	381,230	377,479	-1.0	371,231	360,351	-2.9
U.S.	164,007,000	160,017,000	-2.4	158,504,000	149,613,000	-5.6

Note: Data is not seasonally adjusted and covers workers 16 years of age and older; (1) Figures cover the Boise City, ID Metropolitan Statistical Area
Source: Bureau of Labor Statistics, Local Area Unemployment Statistics

Unemployment Rate

Area	2020											
	Jan.	Feb.	Mar.	Apr.	May	Jun.	Jul.	Aug.	Sep.	Oct.	Nov.	Dec.
City	2.8	2.4	2.3	12.6	9.6	5.9	5.2	4.0	5.8	5.3	4.8	4.3
MSA[1]	3.2	2.7	2.6	12.3	9.2	5.8	5.2	4.1	6.0	5.4	4.9	4.5
U.S.	4.0	3.8	4.5	14.4	13.0	11.2	10.5	8.5	7.7	6.6	6.4	6.5

Note: Data is not seasonally adjusted and covers workers 16 years of age and older; (1) Figures cover the Boise City, ID Metropolitan Statistical Area
Source: Bureau of Labor Statistics, Local Area Unemployment Statistics

Average Wages

Occupation	$/Hr.	Occupation	$/Hr.
Accountants and Auditors	36.50	Maintenance and Repair Workers	19.30
Automotive Mechanics	21.60	Marketing Managers	64.00
Bookkeepers	20.20	Network and Computer Systems Admin.	39.10
Carpenters	18.40	Nurses, Licensed Practical	23.90
Cashiers	12.60	Nurses, Registered	35.60
Computer Programmers	32.60	Nursing Assistants	14.80
Computer Systems Analysts	45.70	Office Clerks, General	17.50
Computer User Support Specialists	24.00	Physical Therapists	39.50
Construction Laborers	16.80	Physicians	115.70
Cooks, Restaurant	12.70	Plumbers, Pipefitters and Steamfitters	24.20
Customer Service Representatives	16.30	Police and Sheriff's Patrol Officers	30.10
Dentists	105.20	Postal Service Mail Carriers	25.50
Electricians	24.70	Real Estate Sales Agents	19.40
Engineers, Electrical	48.30	Retail Salespersons	15.00
Fast Food and Counter Workers	10.00	Sales Representatives, Technical/Scientific	29.10
Financial Managers	52.80	Secretaries, Exc. Legal/Medical/Executive	17.40
First-Line Supervisors of Office Workers	27.10	Security Guards	13.30
General and Operations Managers	43.70	Surgeons	97.30
Hairdressers/Cosmetologists	15.00	Teacher Assistants, Exc. Postsecondary*	13.30
Home Health and Personal Care Aides	14.10	Teachers, Secondary School, Exc. Sp. Ed.*	24.80
Janitors and Cleaners	13.30	Telemarketers	13.30
Landscaping/Groundskeeping Workers	15.90	Truck Drivers, Heavy/Tractor-Trailer	23.00
Lawyers	54.50	Truck Drivers, Light/Delivery Services	18.30
Maids and Housekeeping Cleaners	11.90	Waiters and Waitresses	12.30

Note: Wage data covers the Boise City, ID Metropolitan Statistical Area; (*) Hourly wages were calculated from annual wage data based on a 40 hour work week; n/a not available.
Source: Bureau of Labor Statistics, Metro Area Occupational Employment & Wage Estimates, May 2020

Employment by Industry

Sector	MSA[1]		U.S.
	Number of Employees	Percent of Total	Percent of Total
Construction, Mining, and Logging	29,200	8.3	5.5
Education and Health Services	50,700	14.4	16.3
Financial Activities	21,300	6.0	6.1
Government	48,000	13.6	15.2
Information	3,600	1.0	1.9
Leisure and Hospitality	32,700	9.3	9.0
Manufacturing	28,700	8.1	8.5
Other Services	12,100	3.4	3.8
Professional and Business Services	53,900	15.3	14.4
Retail Trade	42,100	11.9	10.9
Transportation, Warehousing, and Utilities	13,500	3.8	4.6
Wholesale Trade	16,900	4.8	3.9

Note: Figures are non-farm employment as of December 2020. Figures are not seasonally adjusted and include workers 16 years of age and older; (1) Figures cover the Boise City, ID Metropolitan Statistical Area
Source: Bureau of Labor Statistics, Current Employment Statistics, Employment, Hours, and Earnings

Employment by Occupation

Occupation Classification	City (%)	MSA[1] (%)	U.S. (%)
Management, Business, Science, and Arts	45.3	38.3	38.5
Natural Resources, Construction, and Maintenance	7.0	9.9	8.9
Production, Transportation, and Material Moving	8.6	11.5	13.2
Sales and Office	21.6	23.4	21.6
Service	17.4	16.9	17.8

Note: Figures cover employed civilians 16 years of age and older; (1) Figures cover the Boise City, ID Metropolitan Statistical Area
Source: U.S. Census Bureau, 2015-2019 American Community Survey 5-Year Estimates

Occupations with Greatest Projected Employment Growth: 2020 – 2022

Occupation[1]	2020 Employment	2022 Projected Employment	Numeric Employment Change	Percent Employment Change
Carpenters	11,380	12,540	1,160	10.2
Fast Food and Counter Workers	15,850	16,900	1,050	6.6
Home Health and Personal Care Aides	17,890	18,900	1,010	5.6
Waiters and Waitresses	13,970	14,920	950	6.8
Registered Nurses	15,790	16,620	830	5.3
Office Clerks, General	19,370	20,170	800	4.1
Retail Salespersons	28,310	29,010	700	2.5
Customer Service Representatives	19,040	19,730	690	3.6
Construction Laborers	10,430	11,080	650	6.2
Cooks, Fast Food	8,100	8,670	570	7.0

Note: Projections cover Idaho; (1) Sorted by numeric employment change
Source: www.projectionscentral.com, State Occupational Projections, 2020–2022 Short-Term Projections

Fastest-Growing Occupations: 2020 – 2022

Occupation[1]	2020 Employment	2022 Projected Employment	Numeric Employment Change	Percent Employment Change
Brickmasons and Blockmasons	380	430	50	13.2
Roofers	1,130	1,260	130	11.5
Insulation Workers, Floor, Ceiling, and Wall	450	500	50	11.1
Photographers	740	820	80	10.8
Heating, Air Conditioning, and Refrigeration Mechanics and Installers	2,990	3,300	310	10.4
Cement Masons and Concrete Finishers	2,520	2,780	260	10.3
Drywall and Ceiling Tile Installers	1,550	1,710	160	10.3
Carpenters	11,380	12,540	1,160	10.2
Painters, Construction and Maintenance	3,230	3,560	330	10.2
Plumbers, Pipefitters, and Steamfitters	1,920	2,110	190	9.9

Note: Projections cover Idaho; (1) Sorted by percent employment change and excludes occupations with numeric employment change less than 50
Source: www.projectionscentral.com, State Occupational Projections, 2020–2022 Short-Term Projections

TAXES

State Corporate Income Tax Rates

State	Tax Rate (%)	Income Brackets ($)	Num. of Brackets	Financial Institution Tax Rate (%)[a]	Federal Income Tax Ded.
Idaho	6.925 (g)	Flat rate	1	6.925 (g)	No

Note: Tax rates as of January 1, 2021; (a) Rates listed are the corporate income tax rate applied to financial institutions or excise taxes based on income. Some states have other taxes based upon the value of deposits or shares; (g) Idaho's minimum tax on a corporation is $20. The $10 Permanent Building Fund Tax must be paid by each corporation in a unitary group filing a combined return. Taxpayers with gross sales in Idaho under $100,000, and with no property or payroll in Idaho, may elect to pay 1% on such sales (instead of the tax on net income).
Source: Federation of Tax Administrators, State Corporate Income Tax Rates, January 1, 2021

State Individual Income Tax Rates

State	Tax Rate (%)	Income Brackets ($)	Personal Exemptions ($)			Standard Ded. ($)	
			Single	Married	Depend.	Single	Married
Idaho (a)	1.125 - 6.925	1,568 - 11,760 (b)	(d)	(d)	(d)	12,500	25,100 (d)

Note: Tax rates as of January 1, 2021; Local- and county-level taxes are not included; Federal income tax is not deductible on state income tax returns; (a) 19 states have statutory provision for automatically adjusting to the rate of inflation the dollar values of the income tax brackets, standard deductions, and/or personal exemptions. Michigan indexes the personal exemption only. Oregon does not index the income brackets for $125,000 and over; (b) For joint returns, taxes are twice the tax on half the couple's income; (d) These states use the personal exemption/standard deduction amounts provided in the federal Internal Revenue Code.
Source: Federation of Tax Administrators, State Individual Income Tax Rates, January 1, 2021

Various State Sales and Excise Tax Rates

State	State Sales Tax (%)	Gasoline[1] (¢/gal.)	Cigarette[2] ($/pack)	Spirits[3] ($/gal.)	Wine[4] ($/gal.)	Beer[5] ($/gal.)	Recreational Marijuana (%)
Idaho	6	33	0.57	10.91	0.45	0.15	Not legal

Note: All tax rates as of January 1, 2021; (1) The American Petroleum Institute has developed a methodology for determining the average tax rate on a gallon of fuel. Rates may include any of the following: excise taxes, environmental fees, storage tank fees, other fees or taxes, general sales tax, and local taxes; (2) The federal excise tax of $1.0066 per pack and local taxes are not included; (3) Rates are those applicable to off-premise sales of 40% alcohol by volume (a.b.v.) distilled spirits in 750ml containers. Local excise taxes are excluded; (4) Rates are those applicable to off-premise sales of 11% a.b.v. non-carbonated wine in 750ml containers; (5) Rates are those applicable to off-premise sales of 4.7% a.b.v. beer in 12 ounce containers.
Source: Tax Foundation, 2021 Facts & Figures: How Does Your State Compare?

State Business Tax Climate Index Rankings

State	Overall Rank	Corporate Tax Rank	Individual Income Tax Rank	Sales Tax Rank	Property Tax Rank	Unemployment Insurance Tax Rank
Idaho	20	29	26	9	3	48

Note: The index is a measure of how each state's tax laws affect economic performance. The lower the rank, the more favorable a state's tax system is for business. States without a given tax are given a ranking of 1. The scores/rankings for the District of Columbia do not affect other states. The 2021 index represents the tax climate as of July 1, 2020.
Source: Tax Foundation, State Business Tax Climate Index 2021

TRANSPORTATION

Means of Transportation to Work

Area	Car/Truck/Van		Public Transportation			Bicycle	Walked	Other Means	Worked at Home
	Drove Alone	Car-pooled	Bus	Subway	Railroad				
City	79.6	7.3	0.6	0.0	0.0	2.8	2.5	1.1	6.0
MSA[1]	79.9	8.9	0.3	0.0	0.0	1.2	1.7	1.1	6.8
U.S.	76.3	9.0	2.4	1.9	0.6	0.5	2.7	1.4	5.2

Note: Figures are percentages and cover workers 16 years of age and older; (1) Figures cover the Boise City, ID Metropolitan Statistical Area
Source: U.S. Census Bureau, 2015-2019 American Community Survey 5-Year Estimates

Travel Time to Work

Area	Less Than 10 Minutes	10 to 19 Minutes	20 to 29 Minutes	30 to 44 Minutes	45 to 59 Minutes	60 to 89 Minutes	90 Minutes or More
City	13.7	46.2	25.8	10.4	1.5	1.3	1.1
MSA[1]	12.7	34.6	25.6	18.4	5.1	2.2	1.3
U.S.	12.2	28.4	20.8	20.8	8.3	6.4	2.9

Note: Note: Figures are percentages and include workers 16 years old and over; (1) Figures cover the Boise City, ID Metropolitan Statistical Area
Source: U.S. Census Bureau, 2015-2019 American Community Survey 5-Year Estimates

Key Congestion Measures

Measure	1982	1992	2002	2012	2017
Annual Hours of Delay, Total (000)	489	2,089	6,305	10,196	12,254
Annual Hours of Delay, Per Auto Commuter	5	16	32	36	45
Annual Congestion Cost, Total (million $)	4	22	85	183	227
Annual Congestion Cost, Per Auto Commuter ($)	69	203	477	605	704

Note: Covers the Boise ID urban area
Source: Texas A&M Transportation Institute, 2019 Urban Mobility Report

Freeway Travel Time Index

Measure	1982	1987	1992	1997	2002	2007	2012	2017
Urban Area Index[1]	1.00	1.01	1.05	1.07	1.13	1.16	1.14	1.16
Urban Area Rank[1,2]	101	100	92	94	75	63	79	61

Note: Freeway Travel Time Index—the ratio of travel time in the peak period to the travel time at free-flow conditions. For example, a value of 1.30 indicates a 20-minute free-flow trip takes 26 minutes in the peak (20 minutes x 1.30 = 26 minutes); (1) Covers the Boise ID urban area; (2) Rank is based on 101 larger urban areas (#1 = highest travel time index)
Source: Texas A&M Transportation Institute, 2019 Urban Mobility Report

Public Transportation

Agency Name / Mode of Transportation	Vehicles Operated in Maximum Service[1]	Annual Unlinked Passenger Trips[2] (in thous.)	Annual Passenger Miles[3] (in thous.)
Ada County Highway District, dba ACHD Commuteride			
Vanpool (directly operated)	84	174.5	11,391.0
Boise State University			
Bus (directly operated)	9	224.5	n/a

Note: (1) Number of revenue vehicles operated by the given mode and type of service to meet the annual maximum service requirement. This is the revenue vehicle count during the peak season of the year; on the week and day that maximum service is provided. Vehicles operated in maximum service (VOMS) exclude atypical days and one-time special events; (2) Number of passengers who boarded public transportation vehicles. Passengers are counted each time they board a vehicle no matter how many vehicles they use to travel from their origin to their destination. (3) Sum of the distances ridden by all passengers during the entire fiscal year. Source: Federal Transit Administration, National Transit Database, 2019

Air Transportation

Airport Name and Code / Type of Service	Passenger Airlines[1]	Passenger Enplanements	Freight Carriers[2]	Freight (lbs)
Boise Air Terminal-Gowen Field (BOI)				
Domestic service (U.S. carriers - 2020)	18	991,955	11	44,332,876
International service (U.S. carriers - 2019)	0	0	0	0

Note: (1) Includes all U.S.-based major, minor and commuter airlines that carried at least one passenger during the year; (2) Includes all U.S.-based airlines and freight carriers that transported at least one pound of freight during the year. Source: Bureau of Transportation Statistics, The Intermodal Transportation Database, Air Carriers: T-100 Domestic Market (U.S. Carriers), 2020; Bureau of Transportation Statistics, The Intermodal Transportation Database, Air Carriers: T-100 International Market (U.S. Carriers), 2019

BUSINESSES

Major Business Headquarters

Company Name	Industry	Rankings	
		Fortune[1]	Forbes[2]
Albertsons	Food and Drug Stores	55	-
JR Simplot	Food, Drink & Tobacco	-	71
Micron Technology	Semiconductors and Other Electronic Components	134	-
WinCo Foods	Food Markets	-	53

Note: (1) Companies that produce a 10-K are ranked 1 to 500 based on 2019 revenue; (2) All private companies with at least $2 billion in annual revenue through the end of their most current fiscal year are ranked 1 to 219; companies listed are headquartered in the city; dashes indicate no ranking Source: Fortune, "Fortune 500," June/July 2020; Forbes, "America's Largest Private Companies," 2020

Living Environment

COST OF LIVING

Cost of Living Index

Composite Index	Groceries	Housing	Utilities	Trans-portation	Health Care	Misc. Goods/ Services
99.4	93.5	100.0	83.0	108.9	98.4	103.4

Note: The Cost of Living Index measures regional differences in the cost of consumer goods and services, excluding taxes and non-consumer expenditures, for professional and managerial households in the top income quintile. It is based on more than 50,000 prices covering almost 60 different items for which prices are collected three times a year by chambers of commerce, economic development organizations or university applied economic centers in each participating urban area. The numbers shown should be read as a percentage above or below the national average of 100. For example, a value of 115.4 in the groceries column indicates that grocery prices are 15.4% higher than the national average. Small differences in the index numbers should not be interpreted as significant; Figures cover the Boise ID urban area.
Source: The Council for Community and Economic Research, Cost of Living Index, 2020

Grocery Prices

Area[1]	T-Bone Steak ($/pound)	Frying Chicken ($/pound)	Whole Milk ($/half gal.)	Eggs ($/dozen)	Orange Juice ($/64 oz.)	Coffee ($/11.5 oz.)
City[2]	11.77	1.13	1.37	1.18	3.69	4.46
Avg.	11.78	1.39	2.05	1.47	3.57	4.34
Min.	8.03	0.94	1.03	0.74	2.94	3.02
Max.	15.86	2.65	4.31	3.77	5.44	8.69

*Note: (1) Values for the local area are compared with the average, minimum and maximum values for all 284 areas in the Cost of Living Index; (2) Figures cover the Boise ID urban area; **T-Bone Steak** (price per pound); **Frying Chicken** (price per pound, whole fryer); **Whole Milk** (half gallon carton); **Eggs** (price per dozen, Grade A, large); **Orange Juice** (64 oz. Tropicana or Florida Natural); **Coffee** (11.5 oz. can, vacuum-packed, Maxwell House, Hills Bros, or Folgers).*
Source: The Council for Community and Economic Research, Cost of Living Index, 2020

Housing and Utility Costs

Area[1]	New Home Price ($)	Apartment Rent ($/month)	All Electric ($/month)	Part Electric ($/month)	Other Energy ($/month)	Telephone ($/month)
City[2]	366,858	1,252	-	63.83	62.43	170.20
Avg.	368,594	1,168	170.86	100.47	65.28	184.30
Min.	190,567	502	91.58	31.42	26.08	169.60
Max.	2,227,806	4,738	470.38	280.31	280.06	206.50

*Note: (1) Values for the local area are compared with the average, minimum and maximum values for all 284 areas in the Cost of Living Index; (2) Figures cover the Boise ID urban area; **New Home Price** (2,400 sf living area, 8,000 sf lot, in urban area with full utilities); **Apartment Rent** (950 sf 2 bedroom/1.5 or 2 bath, unfurnished, excluding all utilities except water); **All Electric** (average monthly cost for an all-electric home); **Part Electric** (average monthly cost for a part-electric home); **Other Energy** (average monthly cost for natural gas, fuel oil, coal, wood, and any other forms of energy except electricity); **Telephone** (price includes the base monthly rate plus taxes and fees for three lines of mobile phone service).*
Source: The Council for Community and Economic Research, Cost of Living Index, 2020

Health Care, Transportation, and Other Costs

Area[1]	Doctor ($/visit)	Dentist ($/visit)	Optometrist ($/visit)	Gasoline ($/gallon)	Beauty Salon ($/visit)	Men's Shirt ($)
City[2]	124.87	83.97	133.84	2.37	36.81	42.44
Avg.	115.44	99.32	108.10	2.21	39.27	31.37
Min.	36.68	59.00	51.36	1.71	19.00	11.00
Max.	219.00	153.10	250.97	3.46	82.05	58.33

*Note: (1) Values for the local area are compared with the average, minimum and maximum values for all 284 areas in the Cost of Living Index; (2) Figures cover the Boise ID urban area; **Doctor** (general practitioners routine exam of an established patient); **Dentist** (adult teeth cleaning and periodic oral examination); **Optometrist** (full vision eye exam for established adult patient); **Gasoline** (one gallon regular unleaded, national brand, including all taxes, cash price at self-service pump if available); **Beauty Salon** (woman's shampoo, trim, and blow-dry); **Men's Shirt** (cotton/polyester dress shirt, pinpoint weave, long sleeves).*
Source: The Council for Community and Economic Research, Cost of Living Index, 2020

HOUSING

Homeownership Rate

Area	2012 (%)	2013 (%)	2014 (%)	2015 (%)	2016 (%)	2017 (%)	2018 (%)	2019 (%)	2020 (%)
MSA[1]	n/a	n/a	n/a	n/a	n/a	n/a	n/a	n/a	n/a
U.S.	65.4	65.1	64.5	63.7	63.4	63.9	64.4	64.6	66.6

Note: (1) Figures cover the Boise City, ID Metropolitan Statistical Area; n/a not available
Source: U.S. Census Bureau, Housing Vacancies and Homeownership Annual Statistics: 2012-2020

House Price Index (HPI)

Area	National Ranking[2]	Quarterly Change (%)	One-Year Change (%)	Five-Year Change (%)	Since 1991Q1 (%)
MSA[1]	1	4.90	13.83	78.91	350.41
U.S.[3]	–	3.81	10.77	38.99	205.12

Note: The HPI is a weighted repeat sales index. It measures average price changes in repeat sales or refinancings on the same properties. This information is obtained by reviewing repeat mortgage transactions on single-family properties whose mortgages have been purchased or securitized by Fannie Mae or Freddie Mac since January 1975; (1) Figures cover the Boise City, ID Metropolitan Statistical Area; (2) Rankings are based on annual percentage change for all metro areas containing at least 15,000 transactions over the last 10 years and ranges from 1 to 253; (3) figures based on a weighted average of Census Division estimates using a seasonally adjusted, purchase-only index; all figures are for the period ending December 31, 2020
Source: Federal Housing Finance Agency, Change in Metropolitan Area House Price Indexes, April 7, 2021

Median Single-Family Home Prices

Area	2018	2019	2020p	Percent Change 2019 to 2020
MSA[1]	263.5	294.2	353.9	20.3
U.S. Average	261.6	274.6	299.9	9.2

Note: Figures are median sales prices of existing single-family homes in thousands of dollars; (p) preliminary; (1) Figures cover the Boise City, ID Metropolitan Statistical Area
Source: National Association of Realtors, Median Sales Price of Existing Single-Family Homes for Metropolitan Areas, 4th Quarter 2020

Qualifying Income Based on Median Sales Price of Existing Single-Family Homes

Area	With 5% Down ($)	With 10% Down ($)	With 20% Down ($)
MSA[1]	72,120	68,324	60,733
U.S. Average	59,266	56,147	49,908

Note: Figures are preliminary; Qualifying income is based on a mortgage rate of 2.81%. Monthly principal and interest payment is limited to 25% of income; (1) Figures cover the Boise City, ID Metropolitan Statistical Area
Source: National Association of Realtors, Qualifying Income Based on Median Sales Price of Existing Single-Family Homes for Metropolitan Areas, 4th Quarter 2020

Home Value Distribution

Area	Under $50,000	$50,000 -$99,999	$100,000 -$149,999	$150,000 -$199,999	$200,000 -$299,999	$300,000 -$499,999	$500,000 -$999,999	$1,000,000 or more
City	3.9	1.9	8.6	17.4	31.6	26.6	9.0	1.0
MSA[1]	4.4	4.2	11.1	17.9	28.9	25.3	7.3	1.0
U.S.	6.9	12.0	13.3	14.0	19.6	19.3	11.4	3.4

Note: Figures are percentages and cover owner-occupied housing units; (1) Figures cover the Boise City, ID Metropolitan Statistical Area
Source: U.S. Census Bureau, 2015-2019 American Community Survey 5-Year Estimates

Year Housing Structure Built

Area	2010 or Later	2000 -2009	1990 -1999	1980 -1989	1970 -1979	1960 -1969	1950 -1959	1940 -1949	Before 1940	Median Year
City	6.5	11.9	22.5	15.0	19.2	7.1	7.1	4.4	6.2	1984
MSA[1]	10.5	24.6	21.4	10.3	16.2	4.7	4.4	3.0	4.9	1993
U.S.	5.2	14.0	13.9	13.4	15.2	10.6	10.3	4.9	12.6	1978

Note: Figures are percentages except for Median Year; Note: (1) Figures cover the Boise City, ID Metropolitan Statistical Area
Source: U.S. Census Bureau, 2015-2019 American Community Survey 5-Year Estimates

Gross Monthly Rent

Area	Under $500	$500 -$999	$1,000 -$1,499	$1,500 -$1,999	$2,000 -$2,499	$2,500 -$2,999	$3,000 and up	Median ($)
City	5.6	50.5	34.7	6.9	1.4	0.3	0.7	957
MSA[1]	8.2	47.3	34.8	7.4	1.6	0.4	0.5	958
U.S.	9.4	36.2	30.0	14.0	5.6	2.4	2.4	1,062

Note: Figures are percentages except for Median; Gross rent is the contract rent plus the estimated average monthly cost of utilities (electricity, gas, and water and sewer) and fuels (oil, coal, kerosene, wood, etc.) if these are paid by the renter (or paid for the renter by someone else); (1) Figures cover the Boise City, ID Metropolitan Statistical Area
Source: U.S. Census Bureau, 2015-2019 American Community Survey 5-Year Estimates

HEALTH

Health Risk Factors

Category	MSA[1] (%)	U.S. (%)
Adults aged 18–64 who have any kind of health care coverage	80.9	87.3
Adults who reported being in good or better health	86.2	82.4
Adults who have been told they have high blood cholesterol	30.5	33.0
Adults who have been told they have high blood pressure	29.6	32.3
Adults who are current smokers	12.7	17.1
Adults who currently use E-cigarettes	4.0	4.6
Adults who currently use chewing tobacco, snuff, or snus	3.9	4.0
Adults who are heavy drinkers[2]	7.2	6.3
Adults who are binge drinkers[3]	15.6	17.4
Adults who are overweight (BMI 25.0 - 29.9)	36.1	35.3
Adults who are obese (BMI 30.0 - 99.8)	30.0	31.3
Adults who participated in any physical activities in the past month	78.2	74.4
Adults who always or nearly always wears a seat belt	95.4	94.3

Note: (1) Figures cover the Boise City, ID Metropolitan Statistical Area; (2) Heavy drinkers are classified as adult men having more than 14 drinks per week and adult women having more than 7 drinks per week; (3) Binge drinkers are classified as males having five or more drinks on one occasion or females having four or more drinks on one occasion
Source: Centers for Disease Control and Prevention, Behaviorial Risk Factor Surveillance System, SMART: Selected Metropolitan Area Risk Trends, 2017

Acute and Chronic Health Conditions

Category	MSA[1] (%)	U.S. (%)
Adults who have ever been told they had a heart attack	4.1	4.2
Adults who have ever been told they have angina or coronary heart disease	3.1	3.9
Adults who have ever been told they had a stroke	2.6	3.0
Adults who have ever been told they have asthma	11.4	14.2
Adults who have ever been told they have arthritis	23.0	24.9
Adults who have ever been told they have diabetes[2]	8.6	10.5
Adults who have ever been told they had skin cancer	8.8	6.2
Adults who have ever been told they had any other types of cancer	6.4	7.1
Adults who have ever been told they have COPD	3.8	6.5
Adults who have ever been told they have kidney disease	2.9	3.0
Adults who have ever been told they have a form of depression	20.7	20.5

Note: (1) Figures cover the Boise City, ID Metropolitan Statistical Area; (2) Figures do not include pregnancy-related, borderline, or pre-diabetes
Source: Centers for Disease Control and Prevention, Behaviorial Risk Factor Surveillance System, SMART: Selected Metropolitan Area Risk Trends, 2017

Health Screening and Vaccination Rates

Category	MSA[1] (%)	U.S. (%)
Adults aged 65+ who have had flu shot within the past year	63.0	60.7
Adults aged 65+ who have ever had a pneumonia vaccination	78.9	75.4
Adults who have ever been tested for HIV	28.9	36.1
Adults who have ever had the shingles or zoster vaccine?	30.5	28.9
Adults who have had their blood cholesterol checked within the last five years	79.4	85.9

Note: n/a not available; (1) Figures cover the Boise City, ID Metropolitan Statistical Area.
Source: Centers for Disease Control and Prevention, Behaviorial Risk Factor Surveillance System, SMART: Selected Metropolitan Area Risk Trends, 2017

Disability Status

Category	MSA[1] (%)	U.S. (%)
Adults who reported being deaf	5.9	6.7
Are you blind or have serious difficulty seeing, even when wearing glasses?	2.9	4.5
Are you limited in any way in any of your usual activities due of arthritis?	11.2	12.9
Do you have difficulty doing errands alone?	4.6	6.8
Do you have difficulty dressing or bathing?	2.2	3.6
Do you have serious difficulty concentrating/remembering/making decisions?	8.6	10.7
Do you have serious difficulty walking or climbing stairs?	11.0	13.6

Note: (1) Figures cover the Boise City, ID Metropolitan Statistical Area.
Source: Centers for Disease Control and Prevention, Behaviorial Risk Factor Surveillance System, SMART: Selected Metropolitan Area Risk Trends, 2017

Mortality Rates for the Top 10 Causes of Death in the U.S.

ICD-10[a] Sub-Chapter	ICD-10[a] Code	Age-Adjusted Mortality Rate[1] per 100,000 population	
		County[2]	U.S.
Malignant neoplasms	C00-C97	136.9	149.2
Ischaemic heart diseases	I20-I25	66.9	90.5
Other forms of heart disease	I30-I51	59.8	52.2
Chronic lower respiratory diseases	J40-J47	39.3	39.6
Other degenerative diseases of the nervous system	G30-G31	54.4	37.6
Cerebrovascular diseases	I60-I69	36.2	37.2
Other external causes of accidental injury	W00-X59	30.7	36.1
Organic, including symptomatic, mental disorders	F01-F09	23.6	29.4
Hypertensive diseases	I10-I15	17.5	24.1
Diabetes mellitus	E10-E14	12.2	21.5

Note: (a) ICD-10 = International Classification of Diseases 10th Revision; (1) Mortality rates are a three-year average covering 2017-2019; (2) Figures cover Ada County.
Source: Centers for Disease Control and Prevention, National Center for Health Statistics. Underlying Cause of Death 1999-2019 on CDC WONDER Online Database

Mortality Rates for Selected Causes of Death

ICD-10[a] Sub-Chapter	ICD-10[a] Code	Age-Adjusted Mortality Rate[1] per 100,000 population	
		County[2]	U.S.
Assault	X85-Y09	Unreliable	6.0
Diseases of the liver	K70-K76	11.9	14.4
Human immunodeficiency virus (HIV) disease	B20-B24	Suppressed	1.5
Influenza and pneumonia	J09-J18	9.4	13.8
Intentional self-harm	X60-X84	19.3	14.1
Malnutrition	E40-E46	4.2	2.3
Obesity and other hyperalimentation	E65-E68	1.7	2.1
Renal failure	N17-N19	6.3	12.6
Transport accidents	V01-V99	9.6	12.3
Viral hepatitis	B15-B19	Unreliable	1.2

Note: (a) ICD-10 = International Classification of Diseases 10th Revision; (1) Mortality rates are a three-year average covering 2017-2019; (2) Figures cover Ada County; Data are suppressed when the data meet the criteria for confidentiality constraints; Mortality rates are flagged as unreliable when the rate would be calculated with a numerator of 20 or less.
Source: Centers for Disease Control and Prevention, National Center for Health Statistics. Underlying Cause of Death 1999-2019 on CDC WONDER Online Database

Health Insurance Coverage

Area	With Health Insurance	With Private Health Insurance	With Public Health Insurance	Without Health Insurance	Population Under Age 19 Without Health Insurance
City	91.1	75.8	26.8	8.9	4.4
MSA[1]	89.6	71.7	30.2	10.4	4.8
U.S.	91.2	67.9	35.1	8.8	5.1

Note: Figures are percentages that cover the civilian noninstitutionalized population; (1) Figures cover the Boise City, ID Metropolitan Statistical Area
Source: U.S. Census Bureau, 2015-2019 American Community Survey 5-Year Estimates

Number of Medical Professionals

Area	MDs[3]	DOs[3,4]	Dentists	Podiatrists	Chiropractors	Optometrists
County[1] (number)	1,361	155	390	17	267	94
County[1] (rate[2])	290.3	33.1	81.0	3.5	55.4	19.5
U.S. (rate[2])	282.9	22.7	71.2	6.2	28.1	16.9

16001
Note: Data as of 2019 unless noted; (1) Data covers Ada County; (2) Rate per 100,000 population; (3) Data as of 2018 and includes all active, non-federal physicians; (4) Doctor of Osteopathic Medicine
Source: U.S. Department of Health and Human Services, Health Resources and Services Administration, Bureau of Health Professions, Area Resource File (ARF) 2019-2020

EDUCATION

Public School District Statistics

District Name	Schls	Pupils	Pupil/ Teacher Ratio	Minority Pupils[1] (%)	Free Lunch Eligible[2] (%)	IEP[3] (%)
Boise Independent District	50	26,027	16.9	25.6	25.7	12.3

Note: Table includes school districts with 2,000 or more students; (1) Percentage of students that are not non-Hispanic white; (2) Percentage of students that are eligible for the free lunch program; (3) Percentage of students that have an Individualized Education Program.
Source: U.S. Department of Education, National Center for Education Statistics, Common Core of Data, Local Education Agency (School District) Universe Survey: School Year 2018-2019; U.S. Department of Education, National Center for Education Statistics, Common Core of Data, Public Elementary/Secondary School Universe Survey: School Year 2018-2019

Highest Level of Education

Area	Less than H.S.	H.S. Diploma	Some College, No Deg.	Associate Degree	Bachelor's Degree	Master's Degree	Prof. School Degree	Doctorate Degree
City	4.9	21.4	23.1	9.1	26.8	10.1	2.7	1.9
MSA[1]	8.2	25.8	24.8	9.4	21.3	7.4	1.7	1.3
U.S.	12.0	27.0	20.4	8.5	19.8	8.8	2.1	1.4

Note: Figures cover persons age 25 and over; (1) Figures cover the Boise City, ID Metropolitan Statistical Area
Source: U.S. Census Bureau, 2015-2019 American Community Survey 5-Year Estimates

Educational Attainment by Race

Area	High School Graduate or Higher (%)					Bachelor's Degree or Higher (%)				
	Total	White	Black	Asian	Hisp.[2]	Total	White	Black	Asian	Hisp.[2]
City	95.1	95.7	86.2	89.1	84.2	41.6	41.8	29.9	51.2	22.0
MSA[1]	91.8	93.4	88.7	86.6	67.8	31.7	32.5	27.9	46.7	11.4
U.S.	88.0	89.9	86.0	87.1	68.7	32.1	33.5	21.6	54.3	16.4

Note: Figures shown cover persons 25 years old and over; (1) Figures cover the Boise City, ID Metropolitan Statistical Area; (2) People of Hispanic origin can be of any race
Source: U.S. Census Bureau, 2015-2019 American Community Survey 5-Year Estimates

School Enrollment by Grade and Control

Area	Preschool (%)		Kindergarten (%)		Grades 1 - 4 (%)		Grades 5 - 8 (%)		Grades 9 - 12 (%)	
	Public	Private	Public	Private	Public	Private	Public	Private	Public	Private
City	30.6	69.4	84.8	15.2	90.0	10.0	91.7	8.3	89.1	10.9
MSA[1]	37.7	62.3	86.1	13.9	91.1	8.9	92.8	7.2	90.5	9.5
U.S.	59.1	40.9	87.6	12.4	89.5	10.5	89.4	10.6	90.1	9.9

Note: Figures shown cover persons 3 years old and over; (1) Figures cover the Boise City, ID Metropolitan Statistical Area
Source: U.S. Census Bureau, 2015-2019 American Community Survey 5-Year Estimates

Higher Education

Four-Year Colleges			Two-Year Colleges			Medical Schools[1]	Law Schools[2]	Voc/ Tech[3]
Public	Private Non-profit	Private For-profit	Public	Private Non-profit	Private For-profit			
1	2	0	0	0	2	0	1	4

Note: Figures cover institutions located within the city limits and include main campuses only; (1) includes schools accredited by the Liaison Committee on Medical Education and the American Osteopathic Association's Commission on Osteopathic College Accreditation; (2) includes ABA-accredited schools, schools with provisional ABA accreditation, and state accredited schools; (3) includes all schools with programs that are less than 2 years.
Source: National Center for Education Statistics, Integrated Postsecondary Education System (IPEDS), 2019-20; Wikipedia, List of Medical Schools in the United States, accessed April 2, 2021; Wikipedia, List of Law Schools in the United States, accessed April 2, 2021

EMPLOYERS

Major Employers

Company Name	Industry
Ada County	Administration - local government
Albertsons Companies	Retail grocery
Boise City ISD #1	Education - local government
Boise State University	Education - state government
City of Boise	Municipal government
DirectTV Customer Service	Administrative & waste service
Hewlett-Packard Co.	Manufacturing
Idaho Power Co	Utilities
J R Simplot Co	Manufacturing
McDonalds	Accommodation & food services
Meridian JSD #2	Education - local government
Micron Technology	Manufacturing
Nampa School District #13	Education - local government
St. Alphonsus Regional Medical Center	Health care
St. Lukes Health Systems	Health care
State of Idaho Department of Health	State government
State of Idaho Dept of Corrections	State government
U.S. Postal Service	Transportation & warehousing
U.S. Veterans Administration	Federal government, health care
Wal-Mart Stores	Retail trade
WDS Global	Administrative & waste service
Wells Fargo	Finance & insurance

Note: Companies shown are located within the Boise City, ID Metropolitan Statistical Area.
Source: Hoovers.com; Wikipedia

PUBLIC SAFETY

Crime Rate

Area	All Crimes	Violent Crimes				Property Crimes		
		Murder	Rape[3]	Robbery	Aggrav. Assault	Burglary	Larceny -Theft	Motor Vehicle Theft
City	1,859.8	1.7	70.9	19.0	188.9	203.2	1,276.2	99.9
Suburbs[1]	1,329.9	1.2	52.7	7.5	176.3	201.4	798.8	92.1
Metro[2]	1,493.5	1.3	58.3	11.1	180.2	201.9	946.2	94.5
U.S.	2,489.3	5.0	42.6	81.6	250.2	340.5	1,549.5	219.9

Note: Figures are crimes per 100,000 population; (1) All areas within the metro area that are located outside the city limits; (2) Figures cover the Boise City, ID Metropolitan Statistical Area; (3) All figures shown were reported using the revised Uniform Crime Reporting (UCR) definition of rape.
Source: FBI Uniform Crime Reports, 2019

Hate Crimes

Area	Number of Quarters Reported	Number of Incidents per Bias Motivation					
		Race/Ethnicity/ Ancestry	Religion	Sexual Orientation	Disability	Gender	Gender Identity
City	4	6	0	2	0	0	0
U.S.	4	3,963	1,521	1,195	157	69	198

Source: Federal Bureau of Investigation, Hate Crime Statistics 2019

Identity Theft Consumer Reports

Area	Reports	Reports per 100,000 Population	Rank[2]
MSA[1]	1,196	160	276
U.S.	1,387,615	423	-

Note: (1) Figures cover the Boise City, ID Metropolitan Statistical Area; (2) Rank ranges from 1 to 391 where 1 indicates greatest number of identity theft reports per 100,000 population
Source: Federal Trade Commission, Consumer Sentinel Network Data Book 2020

Fraud and Other Consumer Reports

Area	Reports	Reports per 100,000 Population	Rank[2]
MSA[1]	5,277	704	182
U.S.	3,385,133	1,031	-

Note: (1) Figures cover the Boise City, ID Metropolitan Statistical Area; (2) Rank ranges from 1 to 391 where 1 indicates greatest number of fraud and other consumer reports per 100,000 population
Source: Federal Trade Commission, Consumer Sentinel Network Data Book 2020

POLITICS

2020 Presidential Election Results

Area	Biden	Trump	Jorgensen	Hawkins	Other
Ada County	46.1	50.0	2.0	0.1	1.8
U.S.	51.3	46.8	1.2	0.3	0.5

Note: Results are percentages and may not add to 100% due to rounding
Source: Dave Leip's Atlas of U.S. Presidential Elections

SPORTS

Professional Sports Teams

Team Name	League	Year Established
No teams are located in the metro area		

Source: Wikipedia, Major Professional Sports Teams of the United States and Canada, April 6, 2021

CLIMATE

Average and Extreme Temperatures

Temperature	Jan	Feb	Mar	Apr	May	Jun	Jul	Aug	Sep	Oct	Nov	Dec	Yr.
Extreme High (°F)	63	70	81	92	98	105	111	110	101	94	74	65	111
Average High (°F)	36	44	53	62	71	80	90	88	78	65	48	38	63
Average Temp. (°F)	29	36	42	49	58	66	74	73	63	52	40	31	51
Average Low (°F)	22	27	31	37	44	52	58	57	48	39	30	23	39
Extreme Low (°F)	-17	-15	6	19	22	31	35	34	23	11	-3	-25	-25

Note: Figures cover the years 1948-1995
Source: National Climatic Data Center, International Station Meteorological Climate Summary, 9/96

Average Precipitation/Snowfall/Humidity

Precip./Humidity	Jan	Feb	Mar	Apr	May	Jun	Jul	Aug	Sep	Oct	Nov	Dec	Yr.
Avg. Precip. (in.)	1.4	1.1	1.2	1.2	1.2	0.9	0.3	0.3	0.6	0.7	1.4	1.4	11.8
Avg. Snowfall (in.)	7	4	2	Tr	Tr	0	0	0	Tr	2	6	22	
Avg. Rel. Hum. 7am (%)	81	80	75	69	65	59	48	50	58	67	77	81	68
Avg. Rel. Hum. 4pm (%)	68	58	45	35	34	29	22	23	28	36	55	67	42

Note: Figures cover the years 1948-1995; Tr = Trace amounts (<0.05 in. of rain; <0.5 in. of snow)
Source: National Climatic Data Center, International Station Meteorological Climate Summary, 9/96

Weather Conditions

Temperature			Daytime Sky			Precipitation		
5°F & below	32°F & below	90°F & above	Clear	Partly cloudy	Cloudy	0.01 inch or more precip.	0.1 inch or more snow/ice	Thunder-storms
6	124	45	106	133	126	91	22	14

Note: Figures are average number of days per year and cover the years 1948-1995
Source: National Climatic Data Center, International Station Meteorological Climate Summary, 9/96

HAZARDOUS WASTE

Superfund Sites

The Boise City, ID metro area has no sites on the EPA's Superfund Final National Priorities List. There are a total of 1,375 Superfund sites with a status of proposed or final on the list in the U.S. *U.S. Environmental Protection Agency, National Priorities List, April 7, 2021*

AIR QUALITY

Air Quality Trends: Ozone

	1990	1995	2000	2005	2010	2015	2016	2017	2018	2019
MSA[1]	n/a	n/a	n/a	n/a	n/a	n/a	n/a	n/a	n/a	n/a
U.S.	0.088	0.089	0.082	0.080	0.073	0.068	0.069	0.068	0.069	0.065

Note: (1) Data covers the Boise City, ID Metropolitan Statistical Area; n/a not available. The values shown are the composite ozone concentration averages among trend sites based on the highest fourth daily maximum 8-hour concentration in parts per million. These trends are based on sites having an adequate record of monitoring data during the trend period. Data from exceptional events are included.
Source: U.S. Environmental Protection Agency, Air Quality Monitoring Information, "Air Quality Trends by City, 1990-2019"

Air Quality Index

Area	Percent of Days when Air Quality was...[2]					AQI Statistics[2]	
	Good	Moderate	Unhealthy for Sensitive Groups	Unhealthy	Very Unhealthy	Maximum	Median
MSA[1]	67.9	31.2	0.5	0.3	0.0	165	44

Note: (1) Data covers the Boise City, ID Metropolitan Statistical Area; (2) Based on 365 days with AQI data in 2019. Air Quality Index (AQI) is an index for reporting daily air quality. EPA calculates the AQI for five major air pollutants regulated by the Clean Air Act: ground-level ozone, particle pollution (aka particulate matter), carbon monoxide, sulfur dioxide, and nitrogen dioxide. The AQI runs from 0 to 500. The higher the AQI value, the greater the level of air pollution and the greater the health concern. There are six AQI categories: "Good" AQI is between 0 and 50. Air quality is considered satisfactory; "Moderate" AQI is between 51 and 100. Air quality is acceptable; "Unhealthy for Sensitive Groups" When AQI values are between 101 and 150, members of sensitive groups may experience health effects; "Unhealthy" When AQI values are between 151 and 200 everyone may begin to experience health effects; "Very Unhealthy" AQI values between 201 and 300 trigger a health alert; "Hazardous" AQI values over 300 trigger warnings of emergency conditions (not shown).
Source: U.S. Environmental Protection Agency, Air Quality Index Report, 2019

Air Quality Index Pollutants

Area	Percent of Days when AQI Pollutant was...[2]					
	Carbon Monoxide	Nitrogen Dioxide	Ozone	Sulfur Dioxide	Particulate Matter 2.5	Particulate Matter 10
MSA[1]	0.0	1.1	44.4	0.0	51.0	3.6

Note: (1) Data covers the Boise City, ID Metropolitan Statistical Area; (2) Based on 365 days with AQI data in 2019. The Air Quality Index (AQI) is an index for reporting daily air quality. EPA calculates the AQI for five major air pollutants regulated by the Clean Air Act: ground-level ozone, particle pollution (also known as particulate matter), carbon monoxide, sulfur dioxide, and nitrogen dioxide. The AQI runs from 0 to 500. The higher the AQI value, the greater the level of air pollution and the greater the health concern.
Source: U.S. Environmental Protection Agency, Air Quality Index Report, 2019

Maximum Air Pollutant Concentrations: Particulate Matter, Ozone, CO and Lead

	Particulate Matter 10 (ug/m^3)	Particulate Matter 2.5 Wtd AM (ug/m^3)	Particulate Matter 2.5 24-Hr (ug/m^3)	Ozone (ppm)	Carbon Monoxide (ppm)	Lead (ug/m^3)
MSA[1] Level	83	6.9	25	0.057	1	n/a
NAAQS[2]	150	15	35	0.075	9	0.15
Met NAAQS[2]	Yes	Yes	Yes	Yes	Yes	n/a

Note: (1) Data covers the Boise City, ID Metropolitan Statistical Area; Data from exceptional events are included; (2) National Ambient Air Quality Standards; ppm = parts per million; ug/m^3 = micrograms per cubic meter; n/a not available.
Concentrations: Particulate Matter 10 (coarse particulate)—highest second maximum 24-hour concentration; Particulate Matter 2.5 Wtd AM (fine particulate)—highest weighted annual mean concentration; Particulate Matter 2.5 24-Hour (fine particulate)—highest 98th percentile 24-hour concentration; Ozone—highest fourth daily maximum 8-hour concentration; Carbon Monoxide—highest second maximum non-overlapping 8-hour concentration; Lead—maximum running 3-month average
Source: U.S. Environmental Protection Agency, Air Quality Monitoring Information, "Air Quality Statistics by City, 2019"

Maximum Air Pollutant Concentrations: Nitrogen Dioxide and Sulfur Dioxide

	Nitrogen Dioxide AM (ppb)	Nitrogen Dioxide 1-Hr (ppb)	Sulfur Dioxide AM (ppb)	Sulfur Dioxide 1-Hr (ppb)	Sulfur Dioxide 24-Hr (ppb)
MSA[1] Level	n/a	n/a	n/a	3	n/a
NAAQS[2]	53	100	30	75	140
Met NAAQS[2]	n/a	n/a	n/a	Yes	n/a

Note: (1) Data covers the Boise City, ID Metropolitan Statistical Area; Data from exceptional events are included; (2) National Ambient Air Quality Standards; ppm = parts per million; ug/m^3 = micrograms per cubic meter; n/a not available.
Concentrations: Nitrogen Dioxide AM—highest arithmetic mean concentration; Nitrogen Dioxide 1-Hr—highest 98th percentile 1-hour daily maximum concentration; Sulfur Dioxide AM—highest annual mean concentration; Sulfur Dioxide 1-Hr—highest 99th percentile 1-hour daily maximum concentration; Sulfur Dioxide 24-Hr—highest second maximum 24-hour concentration
Source: U.S. Environmental Protection Agency, Air Quality Monitoring Information, "Air Quality Statistics by City, 2019"

Boulder, Colorado

Background

Boulder lies at the foot of the Rocky Mountains in Boulder County. It is the eighth largest city in Colorado. Tourism is a major industry in Boulder, which offers spectacular views from its elevation of 5,430 feet and many outdoor recreation opportunities in over 31,000 acres of open space.

Boulder Valley originally was home to the Southern Arapahoe tribe. The first white settlement was established by gold miners in 1858 near the entrance to Boulder Canyon at Red Rocks. In 1859, the Boulder City Town Company was formed. The town's first schoolhouse was built in 1860, and in 1874, the University of Colorado opened.

Boulder was incorporated as a town in 1871 and as a city in 1882. By 1890, the railroad provided service from Boulder to Golden, Denver, and the western mining camps. In 1905, amidst a weakening economy, Boulder began promoting tourism to boost its finances. The city raised money to construct a first-class hotel, which was completed in 1908 and named Hotel Boulderado.

Although tourism remained strong until the late 1930s, it had begun to decline by World War II. However, the U.S. Navy's Japanese language school, housed at the city's University of Colorado, proved to be an impressive introduction to the area, and many people later returned to Boulder as students, professionals, and veterans attending the university on the GI Bill. Consequently, Boulder's population grew from 12,958 in 1940 to 20,000 in 1950. To accommodate this huge increase, new public buildings, highways, residential areas, and shopping centers developed, spurring further economic expansion.

Many major tech companies have operations in Boulder, as does NOAA, the National Oceanic and Atmospheric Administration.

Boulder is home to the University of Colorado, which houses a robust research park. Cultural venues in the city include the Boulder Dushanbe Teahouse, a gift to the city from its sister city of Dushanbe in Tajikistan, and the Pearl Street Mall, an open-air walkway that was the city's original downtown and is today rich with restaurants, cafes, bookstores, and street entertainers. Boulder offers many scenic opportunities for outdoor activities, with parks, recreation areas, and hiking trails. The city boasts hundreds of miles of bike trails, lanes and paths as a part of their renowned network of citywide bikeways. Boulder has been recognized by the League of American Bicyclists for being a leading bicyclist-friendly city.

> University of Colorado Boulder researchers developed a scratch-and-sniff COVID-19 test they hypothesized would be cheaper and more effective than the traditional PCR test.

Keeping with Boulder's tradition of outdoor recreation, each Memorial Day, over 50,000 runners, joggers, walkers and wheelers participate in the "Bolder Boulder," a popular race that lures more than 100,000 spectators.

Annual attractions include the Creek Festival in May, Art Fair in July, Fall Festival, and Lights of December Parade. The annual Boulder International Film Festival (BIFF) is held in February, and has created a name for itself in the international film community.

Like the rest of Colorado, Boulder enjoys a cool, dry highland continental climate. In winter, the mountains to the west shield the city from the coldest temperatures. Humidity is generally low. Winter storms moving east from the Pacific drop most of their moisture on the mountains to the west, while summer precipitation comes from scattered thunderstorms.

Rankings

General Rankings

- *US News & World Report* conducted a survey of more than 3,000 people and analyzed the 150 largest metropolitan areas to determine what matters most when selecting the next place to live. Boulder ranked #1 out of the top 25 as having the best combination of desirable factors. Criteria: cost of living; quality of life; net migration; job market; desirability; and other factors. *realestate.usnews.com, "The 25 Best Places to Live in the U.S. in 2020-21," October 13, 2020*

Business/Finance Rankings

- 24/7 Wall Street used metro data from the Bureau of Labor Statistics' Occupational Employment database to identify the cities with the highest percentage of those employed in jobs requiring knowledge in the science, technology, engineering, and math (STEM) fields as well as average wages for STEM jobs. The Boulder metro area was #4. *247wallst.com, "15 Cities with the Most High-Tech Jobs," January 11, 2020*

- The Boulder metro area appeared on the Milken Institute "2021 Best Performing Cities" list. Rank: #44 out of 200 large metro areas (population over 250,000). Criteria: job growth; wage and salary growth; high-tech output growth; housing affordability; household broadband access. *Milken Institute, "Best-Performing Cities 2021," February 16, 2021*

- *Forbes* ranked the 200 most populous metro areas to determine the nation's "Best Places for Business and Careers." The Boulder metro area was ranked #25. Criteria: costs (business and living); job growth (past and projected); income growth; quality of life; educational attainment (college and high school); projected economic growth; cultural and leisure opportunities; workplace tolerance laws; net migration patterns. *Forbes, "The Best Places for Business and Careers 2019: Seattle Still On Top," October 30, 2019*

Environmental Rankings

- Niche compiled a list of the nation's snowiest cities, based on the National Oceanic and Atmospheric Administration's 30-year average snowfall data. Among cities with a population of at least 50,000, Boulder ranked #6. *Niche.com, Top 25 Snowiest Cities in America, December 10, 2018*

Health/Fitness Rankings

- The Sharecare Community Well-Being Index evaluates 10 individual and social health factors in order to measure what matters to Americans in the communities in which they live. The Boulder metro area ranked #6 in the top 10 across all 10 domains. Criteria: access to healthcare, food, and community resources; housng and transportation; economic security; feeling of purpose; physical, financial, social, and community well-being. *www.sharecare.com, "Community Well-Being Index: 2019 Metro Area & County Rankings Report," August 31, 2020*

Real Estate Rankings

- The Boulder metro area was identified as one of the 20 worst housing markets in the U.S. in 2020. The area ranked #178 out of 180 markets. Criteria: year-over-year change of median sales price of existing single-family homes between the 4th quarter of 2019 and the 4th quarter of 2020. *National Association of Realtors®, Median Sales Price of Existing Single-Family Homes for Metropolitan Areas, 4th Quarter 2020*

- The Boulder metro area was identified as one of the 20 least affordable housing markets in the U.S. in 2020. The area ranked #177 out of 183 markets. Criteria: qualification for a mortgage loan with a 10 percent down payment on a typical home. *National Association of Realtors®, Qualifying Income Based on Sales Price of Existing Single-Family Homes for Metropolitan Areas, 2020*

- Boulder was ranked #206 out of 268 metro areas in terms of housing affordability in 2020 by the National Association of Home Builders (#1 = most affordable). Criteria: the share of homes sold in that area affordable to a family earning the local median income, based on standard mortgage underwriting criteria. *National Association of Home Builders®, NAHB-Wells Fargo Housing Opportunity Index, 4th Quarter 2020*

Safety Rankings

- The National Insurance Crime Bureau ranked 384 metro areas in the U.S. in terms of per capita rates of vehicle theft. The Boulder metro area ranked #154 (#1 = highest rate). Criteria: number of vehicle theft offenses per 100,000 inhabitants in 2019. *National Insurance Crime Bureau, "Hot Spots 2019," July 21, 2020*

Seniors/Retirement Rankings

- From its Best Cities for Successful Aging indexes, the Milken Institute generated rankings for metropolitan areas, weighing data in nine categories—health care, wellness, living arrangements, transportation and convenience, financial characteristics, education, employment, community engagement, and overall livability. The Boulder metro area was ranked #11 overall in the small metro area category. *Milken Institute, "Best Cities for Successful Aging, 2017" March 14, 2017*

- Boulder was identified as #11 of 20 most popular places to retire in the Western region by *Topretirements.com*. The site separated its annual "Best Places to Retire" list by major U.S. regions for 2019. The list reflects the 20 cities that visitors to the website are most interested in for retirement, based on the number of times a city's review was viewed on the website. *Topretirements.com, "20 Best Places to Retire in the West-2019," November 11, 2019*

Sports/Recreation Rankings

- Boulder was chosen as one of America's best cities for bicycling. The city ranked #12 out of 50. Criteria: cycling infrastructure that is safe and friendly for all ages; energy and bike culture. The editors evaluated cities with populations of 100,000 or more. *Bicycling, "The 50 Best Bike Cities in America," October 10, 2018*

Women/Minorities Rankings

- *Travel + Leisure* listed the best cities in and around the US for a memorable and fun girls' trip, even on a budget. Whether it is for a special occasion or just to get away, Boulder is sure to have something for all the ladies in your tribe. *Travel + Leisure, "25 Girls' Weekend Getaways That Won't Break the Bank," June 8, 2020*

- *Women's Health*, together with the site Yelp, identified the 15 "Wellthiest" spots in the U.S. Boulder appeared among the top for happiest, healthiest, outdoorsiest and Zen-iest. *Women's Health, "The 15 Wellthiest Cities in the U.S." July 5, 2017*

Business Environment

DEMOGRAPHICS

Population Growth

Area	1990 Census	2000 Census	2010 Census	2019* Estimate	Population Growth (%) 1990-2019	Population Growth (%) 2010-2019
City	87,737	94,673	97,385	106,392	21.3	9.2
MSA[1]	208,898	269,758	294,567	322,510	54.4	9.5
U.S.	248,709,873	281,421,906	308,745,538	324,697,795	30.6	5.2

Note: (1) Figures cover the Boulder, CO Metropolitan Statistical Area; (*) 2015-2019 5-year estimated population
Source: U.S. Census Bureau, 1990 Census, Census 2000, Census 2010, 2015-2019 American Community Survey 5-Year Estimates

Household Size

Area	One	Two	Three	Four	Five	Six	Seven or More	Average Household Size
City	33.8	36.8	14.6	11.0	2.7	0.8	0.4	2.30
MSA[1]	28.7	36.4	15.6	13.0	4.6	1.3	0.4	2.40
U.S.	27.9	33.9	15.6	12.9	6.0	2.3	1.4	2.60

(Persons in Household (%))

Note: (1) Figures cover the Boulder, CO Metropolitan Statistical Area
Source: U.S. Census Bureau, 2015-2019 American Community Survey 5-Year Estimates

Race

Area	White Alone[2] (%)	Black Alone[2] (%)	Asian Alone[2] (%)	AIAN[3] Alone[2] (%)	NHOPI[4] Alone[2] (%)	Other Race Alone[2] (%)	Two or More Races (%)
City	87.4	1.2	5.8	0.2	0.1	1.5	3.8
MSA[1]	89.0	0.9	4.7	0.4	0.1	1.8	3.0
U.S.	72.5	12.7	5.5	0.8	0.2	4.9	3.3

Note: (1) Figures cover the Boulder, CO Metropolitan Statistical Area; (2) Alone is defined as not being in combination with one or more other races; (3) American Indian and Alaska Native; (4) Native Hawaiian and Other Pacific Islander
Source: U.S. Census Bureau, 2015-2019 American Community Survey 5-Year Estimates

Hispanic or Latino Origin

Area	Total (%)	Mexican (%)	Puerto Rican (%)	Cuban (%)	Other (%)
City	9.7	6.0	0.4	0.4	2.9
MSA[1]	13.9	10.4	0.4	0.3	2.8
U.S.	18.0	11.2	1.7	0.7	4.3

Note: Persons of Hispanic or Latino origin can be of any race; (1) Figures cover the Boulder, CO Metropolitan Statistical Area
Source: U.S. Census Bureau, 2015-2019 American Community Survey 5-Year Estimates

Ancestry

Area	German	Irish	English	American	Italian	Polish	French[2]	Scottish	Dutch
City	17.4	12.1	10.5	2.5	6.0	3.5	2.6	3.2	1.3
MSA[1]	18.9	11.5	11.6	3.5	5.4	3.3	2.7	3.3	1.5
U.S.	13.3	9.7	7.2	6.2	5.1	2.8	2.3	1.7	1.2

Note: Figures are the percentage of the total population reporting a particular ancestry. The nine most commonly reported ancestries in the U.S. are shown. Figures include multiple ancestries (e.g. if a person reported being Irish and Italian, they were included in both columns); (1) Figures cover the Boulder, CO Metropolitan Statistical Area; (2) Excludes Basque
Source: U.S. Census Bureau, 2015-2019 American Community Survey 5-Year Estimates

Foreign-born Population

Area	Any Foreign Country	Asia	Mexico	Europe	Caribbean	Central America[2]	South America	Africa	Canada
City	11.0	4.4	1.2	2.8	0.2	0.3	1.0	0.3	0.4
MSA[1]	10.7	3.5	2.8	2.3	0.1	0.3	0.7	0.3	0.5
U.S.	13.6	4.2	3.5	1.5	1.3	1.1	1.0	0.7	0.2

(Percent of Population Born in)

Note: (1) Figures cover the Boulder, CO Metropolitan Statistical Area; (2) Excludes Mexico.
Source: U.S. Census Bureau, 2015-2019 American Community Survey 5-Year Estimates

Marital Status

Area	Never Married	Now Married[2]	Separated	Widowed	Divorced
City	55.6	32.4	0.8	2.6	8.6
MSA[1]	38.1	46.2	1.0	3.7	11.0
U.S.	33.4	48.1	1.9	5.8	10.9

Note: Figures are percentages and cover the population 15 years of age and older; (1) Figures cover the Boulder, CO Metropolitan Statistical Area; (2) Excludes separated
Source: U.S. Census Bureau, 2015-2019 American Community Survey 5-Year Estimates

Disability by Age

Area	All Ages	Under 18 Years Old	18 to 64 Years Old	65 Years and Over
City	6.3	2.8	4.5	23.5
MSA[1]	8.1	3.0	6.1	25.6
U.S.	12.6	4.2	10.3	34.5

Note: Figures show percent of the civilian noninstitutionalized population that reported having a disability. Disability status is determined from six types of difficulty: vision, hearing, cognitive, ambulatory, self-care, and independent living. For children under 5 years old, hearing and vision difficulty are used to determine disability status. For children between the ages of 5 and 14, disability status is determined from hearing, vision, cognitive, ambulatory, and self-care difficulties. For people aged 15 years and older, they are considered to have a disability if they have difficulty with any one of the six difficulty types; Note: (1) Figures cover the Boulder, CO Metropolitan Statistical Area
Source: U.S. Census Bureau, 2015-2019 American Community Survey 5-Year Estimates

Age

Area	Under Age 5	Age 5–19	Age 20–34	Age 35–44	Age 45–54	Age 55–64	Age 65–74	Age 75–84	Age 85+	Median Age
City	2.9	18.7	37.6	10.2	10.4	8.9	6.6	3.0	1.6	28.6
MSA[1]	4.6	19.0	24.3	12.6	13.1	12.7	8.4	3.7	1.6	36.6
U.S.	6.1	19.1	20.7	12.6	13.0	12.9	9.1	4.6	1.9	38.1

Note: (1) Figures cover the Boulder, CO Metropolitan Statistical Area
Source: U.S. Census Bureau, 2015-2019 American Community Survey 5-Year Estimates

Gender

Area	Males	Females	Males per 100 Females
City	55,160	51,232	107.7
MSA[1]	162,211	160,299	101.2
U.S.	159,886,919	164,810,876	97.0

Note: (1) Figures cover the Boulder, CO Metropolitan Statistical Area
Source: U.S. Census Bureau, 2015-2019 American Community Survey 5-Year Estimates

Religious Groups by Family

Area	Catholic	Baptist	Non-Den.	Methodist[2]	Lutheran	LDS[3]	Pentecostal	Presbyterian[4]	Muslim[5]	Judaism
MSA[1]	20.1	2.4	4.8	1.8	3.1	3.0	0.5	2.0	0.1	0.8
U.S.	19.1	9.3	4.0	4.0	2.3	2.0	1.9	1.6	0.8	0.7

Note: Figures are the number of adherents as a percentage of the total population; (1) Figures cover the Boulder, CO Metropolitan Statistical Area; (2) Methodist/Pietist; (3) Latter Day Saints; (4) Reformed; (5) Figures are estimates
Source: Association of Statisticians of American Religious Bodies, 2010 U.S. Religion Census: Religious Congregations & Membership Study

Religious Groups by Tradition

Area	Catholic	Evangelical Protestant	Mainline Protestant	Other Tradition	Black Protestant	Orthodox
MSA[1]	20.1	9.8	6.5	4.9	<0.1	0.2
U.S.	19.1	16.2	7.3	4.3	1.6	0.3

Note: Figures are the number of adherents as a percentage of the total population; (1) Figures cover the Boulder, CO Metropolitan Statistical Area
Source: Association of Statisticians of American Religious Bodies, 2010 U.S. Religion Census: Religious Congregations & Membership Study

ECONOMY

Gross Metropolitan Product

Area	2017	2018	2019	2020	Rank[2]
MSA[1]	25.6	27.2	28.7	29.9	107

Note: Figures are in billions of dollars; (1) Figures cover the Boulder, CO Metropolitan Statistical Area; (2) Rank is based on 2018 data and ranges from 1 to 381
Source: U.S. Conference of Mayors, U.S. Metro Economies: GMP & Employment 2018-2020, September 2019

Economic Growth

Area	2015-17 (%)	2018 (%)	2019 (%)	2020 (%)	Rank[2]
MSA[1]	2.5	4.1	3.9	2.1	98
U.S.	1.9	2.9	2.3	2.1	–

Note: Figures are real gross metropolitan product (GMP) growth rates and represent average annual percent change; (1) Figures cover the Boulder, CO Metropolitan Statistical Area; (2) Rank is based on 2017 2-year average annual percent change and ranges from 1 to 381
Source: U.S. Conference of Mayors, U.S. Metro Economies: GMP & Employment 2018-2020, September 2019

Metropolitan Area Exports

Area	2014	2015	2016	2017	2018	2019	Rank[2]
MSA[1]	1,016.1	1,039.1	956.3	1,012.0	1,044.1	1,014.9	158

Note: Figures are in millions of dollars; (1) Figures cover the Boulder, CO Metropolitan Statistical Area; (2) Rank is based on 2019 data and ranges from 1 to 386
Source: U.S. Department of Commerce, International Trade Administration, Office of Trade and Economic Analysis, Industry and Analysis, Exports by Metropolitan Area, data extracted March 24, 2021

Building Permits

Area	Single-Family			Multi-Family			Total		
	2018	2019	Pct. Chg.	2018	2019	Pct. Chg.	2018	2019	Pct. Chg.
City	80	41	-48.8	667	286	-57.1	747	327	-56.2
MSA[1]	899	742	-17.5	2,055	908	-55.8	2,954	1,650	-44.1
U.S.	855,300	862,100	0.7	473,500	523,900	10.6	1,328,800	1,386,000	4.3

Note: (1) Figures cover the Boulder, CO Metropolitan Statistical Area; Figures represent new, privately-owned housing units authorized (unadjusted data); All permit data are based on estimates with imputation
Source: U.S. Census Bureau, Manufacturing, Mining, and Construction Statistics, Building Permits, 2018, 2019

Bankruptcy Filings

Area	Business Filings			Nonbusiness Filings		
	2019	2020	% Chg.	2019	2020	% Chg.
Boulder County	30	42	40.0	372	286	-23.1
U.S.	22,780	21,655	-4.9	752,160	522,808	-30.5

Note: Business filings include Chapter 7, Chapter 9, Chapter 11, Chapter 12, Chapter 13, Chapter 15, and Section 304; Nonbusiness filings include Chapter 7, Chapter 11, and Chapter 13
Source: Administrative Office of the U.S. Courts, Business and Nonbusiness Bankruptcy, County Cases Commenced by Chapter of the Bankruptcy Code, During the 12-Month Period Ending December 31, 2019 and Business and Nonbusiness Bankruptcy, County Cases Commenced by Chapter of the Bankruptcy Code, During the 12-Month Period Ending December 31, 2020

Housing Vacancy Rates

Area	Gross Vacancy Rate[2] (%)			Year-Round Vacancy Rate[3] (%)			Rental Vacancy Rate[4] (%)			Homeowner Vacancy Rate[5] (%)		
	2018	2019	2020	2018	2019	2020	2018	2019	2020	2018	2019	2020
MSA[1]	n/a	n/a	n/a	n/a	n/a	n/a	n/a	n/a	n/a	n/a	n/a	n/a
U.S.	12.3	12.0	10.6	9.7	9.5	8.2	6.9	6.7	6.3	1.5	1.4	1.0

Note: (1) Figures cover the Boulder, CO Metropolitan Statistical Area; (2) The percentage of the total housing inventory that is vacant; (3) The percentage of the housing inventory (excluding seasonal units) that is year-round vacant; (4) The percentage of rental inventory that is vacant for rent; (5) The percentage of homeowner inventory that is vacant for sale; n/a not available
Source: U.S. Census Bureau, Housing Vacancies and Homeownership Annual Statistics: 2018, 2019, 2020

INCOME

Income

Area	Per Capita ($)	Median Household ($)	Average Household ($)
City	44,942	69,520	109,410
MSA[1]	46,826	83,019	115,966
U.S.	34,103	62,843	88,607

Note: (1) Figures cover the Boulder, CO Metropolitan Statistical Area
Source: U.S. Census Bureau, 2015-2019 American Community Survey 5-Year Estimates

Household Income Distribution

Area	Percent of Households Earning							
	Under $15,000	$15,000 -$24,999	$25,000 -$34,999	$35,000 -$49,999	$50,000 -$74,999	$75,000 -$99,999	$100,000 -$149,999	$150,000 and up
City	13.6	7.5	7.3	10.0	14.3	10.1	13.9	23.4
MSA[1]	8.5	6.0	6.6	10.2	14.5	12.4	17.2	24.5
U.S.	10.3	8.9	8.9	12.3	17.2	12.7	15.1	14.5

Note: (1) Figures cover the Boulder, CO Metropolitan Statistical Area
Source: U.S. Census Bureau, 2015-2019 American Community Survey 5-Year Estimates

Poverty Rate

Area	All Ages	Under 18 Years Old	18 to 64 Years Old	65 Years and Over
City	20.4	6.3	25.2	6.9
MSA[1]	11.7	8.5	13.8	6.3
U.S.	13.4	18.5	12.6	9.3

Note: Figures are percentage of people whose income during the past 12 months was below the poverty level;
(1) Figures cover the Boulder, CO Metropolitan Statistical Area
Source: U.S. Census Bureau, 2015-2019 American Community Survey 5-Year Estimates

CITY FINANCES

City Government Finances

Component	2017 ($000)	2017 ($ per capita)
Total Revenues	386,007	3,596
Total Expenditures	364,986	3,400
Debt Outstanding	125,531	1,169
Cash and Securities[1]	271,999	2,534

Note: (1) Cash and security holdings of a government at the close of its fiscal year,
including those of its dependent agencies, utilities, and liquor stores.
Source: U.S. Census Bureau, State & Local Government Finances 2017

City Government Revenue by Source

Source	2017 ($000)	2017 ($ per capita)	2017 (%)
General Revenue			
From Federal Government	2,707	25	0.7
From State Government	21,940	204	5.7
From Local Governments	4,474	42	1.2
Taxes			
Property	38,834	362	10.1
Sales and Gross Receipts	158,572	1,477	41.1
Personal Income	0	0	0.0
Corporate Income	0	0	0.0
Motor Vehicle License	0	0	0.0
Other Taxes	8,414	78	2.2
Current Charges	37,955	354	9.8
Liquor Store	0	0	0.0
Utility	23,838	222	6.2
Employee Retirement	2,454	23	0.6

Source: U.S. Census Bureau, State & Local Government Finances 2017

City Government Expenditures by Function

Function	2017 ($000)	2017 ($ per capita)	2017 (%)
General Direct Expenditures			
Air Transportation	540	5	0.1
Corrections	0	0	0.0
Education	0	0	0.0
Employment Security Administration	0	0	0.0
Financial Administration	10,268	95	2.8
Fire Protection	26,540	247	7.3
General Public Buildings	5,689	53	1.6
Governmental Administration, Other	23,626	220	6.5
Health	0	0	0.0
Highways	62,767	584	17.2
Hospitals	0	0	0.0
Housing and Community Development	16,404	152	4.5
Interest on General Debt	7,279	67	2.0
Judicial and Legal	4,468	41	1.2
Libraries	13,612	126	3.7
Parking	8,988	83	2.5
Parks and Recreation	58,230	542	16.0
Police Protection	39,895	371	10.9
Public Welfare	0	0	0.0
Sewerage	26,058	242	7.1
Solid Waste Management	1,393	13	0.4
Veterans' Services	0	0	0.0
Liquor Store	0	0	0.0
Utility	16,094	149	4.4
Employee Retirement	2,519	23	0.7

Source: U.S. Census Bureau, State & Local Government Finances 2017

EMPLOYMENT

Labor Force and Employment

Area	Civilian Labor Force			Workers Employed		
	Dec. 2019	Dec. 2020	% Chg.	Dec. 2019	Dec. 2020	% Chg.
City	66,229	64,864	-2.1	65,025	60,677	-6.7
MSA[1]	197,746	194,238	-1.8	193,839	180,878	-6.7
U.S.	164,007,000	160,017,000	-2.4	158,504,000	149,613,000	-5.6

Note: Data is not seasonally adjusted and covers workers 16 years of age and older; (1) Figures cover the Boulder, CO Metropolitan Statistical Area
Source: Bureau of Labor Statistics, Local Area Unemployment Statistics

Unemployment Rate

Area	2020											
	Jan.	Feb.	Mar.	Apr.	May	Jun.	Jul.	Aug.	Sep.	Oct.	Nov.	Dec.
City	2.1	2.4	4.2	9.4	8.1	9.6	6.5	5.4	4.9	4.9	4.7	6.5
MSA[1]	2.4	2.4	4.4	9.7	8.3	9.6	6.7	5.8	5.3	5.2	5.1	6.9
U.S.	4.0	3.8	4.5	14.4	13.0	11.2	10.5	8.5	7.7	6.6	6.4	6.5

Note: Data is not seasonally adjusted and covers workers 16 years of age and older; (1) Figures cover the Boulder, CO Metropolitan Statistical Area
Source: Bureau of Labor Statistics, Local Area Unemployment Statistics

Average Wages

Occupation	$/Hr.	Occupation	$/Hr.
Accountants and Auditors	40.10	Maintenance and Repair Workers	23.40
Automotive Mechanics	24.40	Marketing Managers	85.30
Bookkeepers	22.30	Network and Computer Systems Admin.	45.00
Carpenters	25.30	Nurses, Licensed Practical	26.20
Cashiers	14.10	Nurses, Registered	39.80
Computer Programmers	39.10	Nursing Assistants	17.20
Computer Systems Analysts	48.40	Office Clerks, General	22.70
Computer User Support Specialists	31.00	Physical Therapists	45.00
Construction Laborers	18.50	Physicians	132.80
Cooks, Restaurant	15.60	Plumbers, Pipefitters and Steamfitters	25.80
Customer Service Representatives	20.30	Police and Sheriff's Patrol Officers	40.30
Dentists	107.70	Postal Service Mail Carriers	25.70
Electricians	26.40	Real Estate Sales Agents	29.40
Engineers, Electrical	52.80	Retail Salespersons	16.70
Fast Food and Counter Workers	13.60	Sales Representatives, Technical/Scientific	52.40
Financial Managers	90.40	Secretaries, Exc. Legal/Medical/Executive	20.20
First-Line Supervisors of Office Workers	32.00	Security Guards	16.80
General and Operations Managers	76.40	Surgeons	138.30
Hairdressers/Cosmetologists	20.60	Teacher Assistants, Exc. Postsecondary*	16.60
Home Health and Personal Care Aides	16.10	Teachers, Secondary School, Exc. Sp. Ed.*	33.40
Janitors and Cleaners	17.30	Telemarketers	n/a
Landscaping/Groundskeeping Workers	19.70	Truck Drivers, Heavy/Tractor-Trailer	21.40
Lawyers	n/a	Truck Drivers, Light/Delivery Services	21.10
Maids and Housekeeping Cleaners	14.30	Waiters and Waitresses	15.30

Note: Wage data covers the Boulder, CO Metropolitan Statistical Area; (*) Hourly wages were calculated from annual wage data based on a 40 hour work week; n/a not available.
Source: Bureau of Labor Statistics, Metro Area Occupational Employment & Wage Estimates, May 2020

Employment by Industry

Sector	MSA[1]		U.S.
	Number of Employees	Percent of Total	Percent of Total
Construction, Mining, and Logging	5,600	3.0	5.5
Education and Health Services	24,700	13.3	16.3
Financial Activities	7,200	3.9	6.1
Government	35,100	18.9	15.2
Information	8,400	4.5	1.9
Leisure and Hospitality	12,100	6.5	9.0
Manufacturing	21,000	11.3	8.5
Other Services	5,800	3.1	3.8
Professional and Business Services	39,400	21.2	14.4
Retail Trade	17,700	9.5	10.9
Transportation, Warehousing, and Utilities	2,100	1.1	4.6
Wholesale Trade	6,500	3.5	3.9

Note: Figures are non-farm employment as of December 2020. Figures are not seasonally adjusted and include workers 16 years of age and older; (1) Figures cover the Boulder, CO Metropolitan Statistical Area
Source: Bureau of Labor Statistics, Current Employment Statistics, Employment, Hours, and Earnings

Employment by Occupation

Occupation Classification	City (%)	MSA[1] (%)	U.S. (%)
Management, Business, Science, and Arts	58.2	54.4	38.5
Natural Resources, Construction, and Maintenance	2.7	5.0	8.9
Production, Transportation, and Material Moving	4.7	7.1	13.2
Sales and Office	18.2	18.6	21.6
Service	16.2	14.9	17.8

Note: Figures cover employed civilians 16 years of age and older; (1) Figures cover the Boulder, CO Metropolitan Statistical Area
Source: U.S. Census Bureau, 2015-2019 American Community Survey 5-Year Estimates

Occupations with Greatest Projected Employment Growth: 2020 – 2022

Occupation[1]	2020 Employment	2022 Projected Employment	Numeric Employment Change	Percent Employment Change
Software Developers, Applications	33,470	35,740	2,270	6.8
Personal Care Aides	30,000	31,610	1,610	5.4
Registered Nurses	54,810	56,090	1,280	2.3
Market Research Analysts and Marketing Specialists	21,470	22,380	910	4.2
Business Operations Specialists, All Other	49,470	50,350	880	1.8
Stock Clerks and Order Fillers	37,610	38,390	780	2.1
Computer Occupations, All Other	18,280	18,940	660	3.6
Accountants and Auditors	42,200	42,840	640	1.5
Software Developers, Systems Software	12,390	13,010	620	5.0
Sales Representatives, Wholesale and Manufacturing, Except Technical and Scientific Products	28,620	29,170	550	1.9

Note: Projections cover Colorado; (1) Sorted by numeric employment change
Source: www.projectionscentral.com, State Occupational Projections, 2020–2022 Short-Term Projections

Fastest-Growing Occupations: 2020 – 2022

Occupation[1]	2020 Employment	2022 Projected Employment	Numeric Employment Change	Percent Employment Change
Information Security Analysts	3,860	4,170	310	8.0
Software Developers, Applications	33,470	35,740	2,270	6.8
Statisticians	1,230	1,310	80	6.5
Operations Research Analysts	940	1,000	60	6.4
Veterinary Technologists and Technicians	4,490	4,750	260	5.8
Health Specialties Teachers, Postsecondary	6,160	6,500	340	5.5
Personal Care Aides	30,000	31,610	1,610	5.4
Veterinarians	2,820	2,970	150	5.3
Interpreters and Translators	1,980	2,080	100	5.1
Software Developers, Systems Software	12,390	13,010	620	5.0

Note: Projections cover Colorado; (1) Sorted by percent employment change and excludes occupations with numeric employment change less than 50
Source: www.projectionscentral.com, State Occupational Projections, 2020–2022 Short-Term Projections

TAXES

State Corporate Income Tax Rates

State	Tax Rate (%)	Income Brackets ($)	Num. of Brackets	Financial Institution Tax Rate (%)[a]	Federal Income Tax Ded.
Colorado	4.55	Flat rate	1	4.55	No

Note: Tax rates as of January 1, 2021; (a) Rates listed are the corporate income tax rate applied to financial institutions or excise taxes based on income. Some states have other taxes based upon the value of deposits or shares.
Source: Federation of Tax Administrators, State Corporate Income Tax Rates, January 1, 2021

State Individual Income Tax Rates

State	Tax Rate (%)	Income Brackets ($)	Personal Exemptions ($)			Standard Ded. ($)	
			Single	Married	Depend.	Single	Married
Colorado	4.55	Flat rate	(d)	(d)	(d)	12,550	25,100 (d)

Note: Tax rates as of January 1, 2021; Local- and county-level taxes are not included; Federal income tax is not deductible on state income tax returns; (d) These states use the personal exemption/standard deduction amounts provided in the federal Internal Revenue Code.
Source: Federation of Tax Administrators, State Individual Income Tax Rates, January 1, 2021

Various State Sales and Excise Tax Rates

State	State Sales Tax (%)	Gasoline[1] (¢/gal.)	Cigarette[2] ($/pack)	Spirits[3] ($/gal.)	Wine[4] ($/gal.)	Beer[5] ($/gal.)	Recreational Marijuana (%)
Colorado	2.9	22	1.94	2.28	0.32	0.08	(d)

Note: All tax rates as of January 1, 2021; (1) The American Petroleum Institute has developed a methodology for determining the average tax rate on a gallon of fuel. Rates may include any of the following: excise taxes, environmental fees, storage tank fees, other fees or taxes, general sales tax, and local taxes; (2) The federal excise tax of $1.0066 per pack and local taxes are not included; (3) Rates are those applicable to off-premise sales of 40% alcohol by volume (a.b.v.) distilled spirits in 750ml containers. Local excise taxes are excluded; (4) Rates are those applicable to off-premise sales of 11% a.b.v. non-carbonated wine in 750ml containers; (5) Rates are those applicable to off-premise sales of 4.7% a.b.v. beer in 12 ounce containers; (d) 15% excise tax (levied on wholesale at average market rate); 15% excise tax (retail price)
Source: Tax Foundation, 2021 Facts & Figures: How Does Your State Compare?

State Business Tax Climate Index Rankings

State	Overall Rank	Corporate Tax Rank	Individual Income Tax Rank	Sales Tax Rank	Property Tax Rank	Unemployment Insurance Tax Rank
Colorado	21	10	14	36	32	41

Note: The index is a measure of how each state's tax laws affect economic performance. The lower the rank, the more favorable a state's tax system is for business. States without a given tax are given a ranking of 1. The scores/rankings for the District of Columbia do not affect other states. The 2021 index represents the tax climate as of July 1, 2020.
Source: Tax Foundation, State Business Tax Climate Index 2021

TRANSPORTATION

Means of Transportation to Work

Area	Car/Truck/Van Drove Alone	Car-pooled	Public Transportation Bus	Subway	Railroad	Bicycle	Walked	Other Means	Worked at Home
City	50.8	5.5	7.3	0.0	0.0	9.9	11.1	1.1	14.5
MSA[1]	65.0	7.2	4.7	0.0	0.0	4.2	5.0	1.0	12.8
U.S.	76.3	9.0	2.4	1.9	0.6	0.5	2.7	1.4	5.2

Note: Figures are percentages and cover workers 16 years of age and older; (1) Figures cover the Boulder, CO Metropolitan Statistical Area
Source: U.S. Census Bureau, 2015-2019 American Community Survey 5-Year Estimates

Travel Time to Work

Area	Less Than 10 Minutes	10 to 19 Minutes	20 to 29 Minutes	30 to 44 Minutes	45 to 59 Minutes	60 to 89 Minutes	90 Minutes or More
City	17.6	45.9	16.3	10.3	5.6	3.3	1.0
MSA[1]	13.7	34.4	21.4	17.6	7.0	4.6	1.3
U.S.	12.2	28.4	20.8	20.8	8.3	6.4	2.9

Note: Note: Figures are percentages and include workers 16 years old and over; (1) Figures cover the Boulder, CO Metropolitan Statistical Area
Source: U.S. Census Bureau, 2015-2019 American Community Survey 5-Year Estimates

Key Congestion Measures

Measure	1982	1992	2002	2012	2017
Annual Hours of Delay, Total (000)	421	1,199	2,623	3,602	4,464
Annual Hours of Delay, Per Auto Commuter	8	20	33	39	44
Annual Congestion Cost, Total (million $)	3	13	36	65	83
Annual Congestion Cost, Per Auto Commuter ($)	162	318	542	583	701

Note: Covers the Boulder CO urban area
Source: Texas A&M Transportation Institute, 2019 Urban Mobility Report

Freeway Travel Time Index

Measure	1982	1987	1992	1997	2002	2007	2012	2017
Urban Area Index[1,2]	1.02	1.06	1.10	1.14	1.19	1.21	1.21	1.21
Urban Area Rank[1,2]	90	66	59	47	36	36	34	37

Note: Freeway Travel Time Index—the ratio of travel time in the peak period to the travel time at free-flow conditions. For example, a value of 1.30 indicates a 20-minute free-flow trip takes 26 minutes in the peak (20 minutes x 1.30 = 26 minutes); (1) Covers the Boulder CO urban area; (2) Rank is based on 101 larger urban areas (#1 = highest travel time index)
Source: Texas A&M Transportation Institute, 2019 Urban Mobility Report

Public Transportation

Agency Name / Mode of Transportation	Vehicles Operated in Maximum Service[1]	Annual Unlinked Passenger Trips[2] (in thous.)	Annual Passenger Miles[3] (in thous.)
Community Transit Network			
Bus (directly operated)	483	47,678.2	221,931.3
Bus (purchased transportation)	355	22,053.6	85,104.3
Commuter Rail (purchased transportation)	44	9,711.4	121,331.4
Demand Response (purchased transportation)	441	1,179.0	10,384.1
Light Rail (directly operated)	160	24,585.3	178,266.8

Note: (1) Number of revenue vehicles operated by the given mode and type of service to meet the annual maximum service requirement. This is the revenue vehicle count during the peak season of the year; on the week and day that maximum service is provided. Vehicles operated in maximum service (VOMS) exclude atypical days and one-time special events; (2) Number of passengers who boarded public transportation vehicles. Passengers are counted each time they board a vehicle no matter how many vehicles they use to travel from their origin to their destination. (3) Sum of the distances ridden by all passengers during the entire fiscal year.
Source: Federal Transit Administration, National Transit Database, 2019

Air Transportation

Airport Name and Code / Type of Service	Passenger Airlines[1]	Passenger Enplanements	Freight Carriers[2]	Freight (lbs)
Denver International (40 miles) (DEN)				
Domestic service (U.S. carriers - 2020)	27	15,787,920	18	263,867,762
International service (U.S. carriers - 2019)	7	883,726	3	8,069,938

Note: (1) Includes all U.S.-based major, minor and commuter airlines that carried at least one passenger during the year; (2) Includes all U.S.-based airlines and freight carriers that transported at least one pound of freight during the year.
Source: Bureau of Transportation Statistics, The Intermodal Transportation Database, Air Carriers: T-100 Domestic Market (U.S. Carriers), 2020; Bureau of Transportation Statistics, The Intermodal Transportation Database, Air Carriers: T-100 International Market (U.S. Carriers), 2019

BUSINESSES

Major Business Headquarters

Company Name	Industry	Rankings	
		Fortune[1]	Forbes[2]
No companies listed	-	-	-

Note: (1) Companies that produce a 10-K are ranked 1 to 500 based on 2019 revenue; (2) All private companies with at least $2 billion in annual revenue through the end of their most current fiscal year are ranked 1 to 219; companies listed are headquartered in the city; dashes indicate no ranking
Source: Fortune, "Fortune 500," June/July 2020; Forbes, "America's Largest Private Companies," 2020

Living Environment

COST OF LIVING

Cost of Living Index

Composite Index	Groceries	Housing	Utilities	Trans-portation	Health Care	Misc. Goods/Services
n/a	n/a	n/a	n/a	n/a	n/a	n/a

Note: The Cost of Living Index measures regional differences in the cost of consumer goods and services, excluding taxes and non-consumer expenditures, for professional and managerial households in the top income quintile. It is based on more than 50,000 prices covering almost 60 different items for which prices are collected three times a year by chambers of commerce, economic development organizations or university applied economic centers in each participating urban area. The numbers shown should be read as a percentage above or below the national average of 100. For example, a value of 115.4 in the groceries column indicates that grocery prices are 15.4% higher than the national average. Small differences in the index numbers should not be interpreted as significant; n/a not available.
Source: The Council for Community and Economic Research, Cost of Living Index, 2020

Grocery Prices

Area[1]	T-Bone Steak ($/pound)	Frying Chicken ($/pound)	Whole Milk ($/half gal.)	Eggs ($/dozen)	Orange Juice ($/64 oz.)	Coffee ($/11.5 oz.)
City[2]	n/a	n/a	n/a	n/a	n/a	n/a
Avg.	11.78	1.39	2.05	1.47	3.57	4.34
Min.	8.03	0.94	1.03	0.74	2.94	3.02
Max.	15.86	2.65	4.31	3.77	5.44	8.69

*Note: (1) Values for the local area are compared with the average, minimum and maximum values for all 284 areas in the Cost of Living Index; (2) Figures cover the Boulder CO urban area; n/a not available; **T-Bone Steak** (price per pound); **Frying Chicken** (price per pound, whole fryer); **Whole Milk** (half gallon carton); **Eggs** (price per dozen, Grade A, large); **Orange Juice** (64 oz. Tropicana or Florida Natural); **Coffee** (11.5 oz. can, vacuum-packed, Maxwell House, Hills Bros, or Folgers).*
Source: The Council for Community and Economic Research, Cost of Living Index, 2020

Housing and Utility Costs

Area[1]	New Home Price ($)	Apartment Rent ($/month)	All Electric ($/month)	Part Electric ($/month)	Other Energy ($/month)	Telephone ($/month)
City[2]	n/a	n/a	n/a	n/a	n/a	n/a
Avg.	368,594	1,168	170.86	100.47	65.28	184.30
Min.	190,567	502	91.58	31.42	26.08	169.60
Max.	2,227,806	4,738	470.38	280.31	280.06	206.50

*Note: (1) Values for the local area are compared with the average, minimum and maximum values for all 284 areas in the Cost of Living Index; (2) Figures cover the Boulder CO urban area; n/a not available; **New Home Price** (2,400 sf living area, 8,000 sf lot, in urban area with full utilities); **Apartment Rent** (950 sf 2 bedroom/1.5 or 2 bath, unfurnished, excluding all utilities except water); **All Electric** (average monthly cost for an all-electric home); **Part Electric** (average monthly cost for a part-electric home); **Other Energy** (average monthly cost for natural gas, fuel oil, coal, wood, and any other forms of energy except electricity); **Telephone** (price includes the base monthly rate plus taxes and fees for three lines of mobile phone service).*
Source: The Council for Community and Economic Research, Cost of Living Index, 2020

Health Care, Transportation, and Other Costs

Area[1]	Doctor ($/visit)	Dentist ($/visit)	Optometrist ($/visit)	Gasoline ($/gallon)	Beauty Salon ($/visit)	Men's Shirt ($)
City[2]	n/a	n/a	n/a	n/a	n/a	n/a
Avg.	115.44	99.32	108.10	2.21	39.27	31.37
Min.	36.68	59.00	51.36	1.71	19.00	11.00
Max.	219.00	153.10	250.97	3.46	82.05	58.33

*Note: (1) Values for the local area are compared with the average, minimum and maximum values for all 284 areas in the Cost of Living Index; (2) Figures cover the Boulder CO urban area; n/a not available; **Doctor** (general practitioners routine exam of an established patient); **Dentist** (adult teeth cleaning and periodic oral examination); **Optometrist** (full vision eye exam for established adult patient); **Gasoline** (one gallon regular unleaded, national brand, including all taxes, cash price at self-service pump if available); **Beauty Salon** (woman's shampoo, trim, and blow-dry); **Men's Shirt** (cotton/polyester dress shirt, pinpoint weave, long sleeves).*
Source: The Council for Community and Economic Research, Cost of Living Index, 2020

HOUSING

Homeownership Rate

Area	2012 (%)	2013 (%)	2014 (%)	2015 (%)	2016 (%)	2017 (%)	2018 (%)	2019 (%)	2020 (%)
MSA[1]	n/a	n/a	n/a	n/a	n/a	n/a	n/a	n/a	n/a
U.S.	65.4	65.1	64.5	63.7	63.4	63.9	64.4	64.6	66.6

Note: (1) Figures cover the Boulder, CO Metropolitan Statistical Area; n/a not available
Source: U.S. Census Bureau, Housing Vacancies and Homeownership Annual Statistics: 2012-2020

House Price Index (HPI)

Area	National Ranking[2]	Quarterly Change (%)	One-Year Change (%)	Five-Year Change (%)	Since 1991Q1 (%)
MSA[1]	227	1.79	3.59	36.23	436.16
U.S.[3]	–	3.81	10.77	38.99	205.12

Note: The HPI is a weighted repeat sales index. It measures average price changes in repeat sales or refinancings on the same properties. This information is obtained by reviewing repeat mortgage transactions on single-family properties whose mortgages have been purchased or securitized by Fannie Mae or Freddie Mac since January 1975; (1) Figures cover the Boulder, CO Metropolitan Statistical Area; (2) Rankings are based on annual percentage change for all metro areas containing at least 15,000 transactions over the last 10 years and ranges from 1 to 253; (3) figures based on a weighted average of Census Division estimates using a seasonally adjusted, purchase-only index; all figures are for the period ending December 31, 2020
Source: Federal Housing Finance Agency, Change in Metropolitan Area House Price Indexes, April 7, 2021

Median Single-Family Home Prices

Area	2018	2019	2020[p]	Percent Change 2019 to 2020
MSA[1]	607.4	618.6	645.9	4.4
U.S. Average	261.6	274.6	299.9	9.2

Note: Figures are median sales prices of existing single-family homes in thousands of dollars; (p) preliminary; (1) Figures cover the Boulder, CO Metropolitan Statistical Area
Source: National Association of Realtors, Median Sales Price of Existing Single-Family Homes for Metropolitan Areas, 4th Quarter 2020

Qualifying Income Based on Median Sales Price of Existing Single-Family Homes

Area	With 5% Down ($)	With 10% Down ($)	With 20% Down ($)
MSA[1]	125,080	118,497	105,330
U.S. Average	59,266	56,147	49,908

Note: Figures are preliminary; Qualifying income is based on a mortgage rate of 2.81%. Monthly principal and interest payment is limited to 25% of income; (1) Figures cover the Boulder, CO Metropolitan Statistical Area
Source: National Association of Realtors, Qualifying Income Based on Median Sales Price of Existing Single-Family Homes for Metropolitan Areas, 4th Quarter 2020

Home Value Distribution

Area	Under $50,000	$50,000 -$99,999	$100,000 -$149,999	$150,000 -$199,999	$200,000 -$299,999	$300,000 -$499,999	$500,000 -$999,999	$1,000,000 or more
City	3.8	1.7	1.8	3.3	4.1	13.3	48.9	23.1
MSA[1]	2.9	1.1	1.3	2.9	10.6	31.6	38.3	11.3
U.S.	6.9	12.0	13.3	14.0	19.6	19.3	11.4	3.4

Note: Figures are percentages and cover owner-occupied housing units; (1) Figures cover the Boulder, CO Metropolitan Statistical Area
Source: U.S. Census Bureau, 2015-2019 American Community Survey 5-Year Estimates

Year Housing Structure Built

Area	2010 or Later	2000 -2009	1990 -1999	1980 -1989	1970 -1979	1960 -1969	1950 -1959	1940 -1949	Before 1940	Median Year
City	6.2	7.7	11.2	17.3	21.5	18.3	8.1	2.0	7.6	1976
MSA[1]	6.5	12.1	19.3	17.2	20.8	11.6	4.6	1.5	6.4	1983
U.S.	5.2	14.0	13.9	13.4	15.2	10.6	10.3	4.9	12.6	1978

Note: Figures are percentages except for Median Year; Note: (1) Figures cover the Boulder, CO Metropolitan Statistical Area
Source: U.S. Census Bureau, 2015-2019 American Community Survey 5-Year Estimates

Gross Monthly Rent

Area	Under $500	$500 -$999	$1,000 -$1,499	$1,500 -$1,999	$2,000 -$2,499	$2,500 -$2,999	$3,000 and up	Median ($)
City	2.8	9.4	35.1	25.4	14.8	5.5	6.9	1,554
MSA[1]	4.0	11.7	34.6	27.2	13.3	5.0	4.2	1,495
U.S.	9.4	36.2	30.0	14.0	5.6	2.4	2.4	1,062

Note: Figures are percentages except for Median; Gross rent is the contract rent plus the estimated average monthly cost of utilities (electricity, gas, and water and sewer) and fuels (oil, coal, kerosene, wood, etc.) if these are paid by the renter (or paid for the renter by someone else); (1) Figures cover the Boulder, CO Metropolitan Statistical Area
Source: U.S. Census Bureau, 2015-2019 American Community Survey 5-Year Estimates

HEALTH

Health Risk Factors

Category	MSA[1] (%)	U.S. (%)
Adults aged 18–64 who have any kind of health care coverage	n/a	87.3
Adults who reported being in good or better health	n/a	82.4
Adults who have been told they have high blood cholesterol	n/a	33.0
Adults who have been told they have high blood pressure	n/a	32.3
Adults who are current smokers	n/a	17.1
Adults who currently use E-cigarettes	n/a	4.6
Adults who currently use chewing tobacco, snuff, or snus	n/a	4.0
Adults who are heavy drinkers[2]	n/a	6.3
Adults who are binge drinkers[3]	n/a	17.4
Adults who are overweight (BMI 25.0 - 29.9)	n/a	35.3
Adults who are obese (BMI 30.0 - 99.8)	n/a	31.3
Adults who participated in any physical activities in the past month	n/a	74.4
Adults who always or nearly always wears a seat belt	n/a	94.3

Note: n/a not available; (1) Figures cover the Boulder, CO Metropolitan Statistical Area; (2) Heavy drinkers are classified as adult men having more than 14 drinks per week and adult women having more than 7 drinks per week; (3) Binge drinkers are classified as males having five or more drinks on one occasion or females having four or more drinks on one occasion
Source: Centers for Disease Control and Prevention, Behaviorial Risk Factor Surveillance System, SMART: Selected Metropolitan Area Risk Trends, 2017

Acute and Chronic Health Conditions

Category	MSA[1] (%)	U.S. (%)
Adults who have ever been told they had a heart attack	n/a	4.2
Adults who have ever been told they have angina or coronary heart disease	n/a	3.9
Adults who have ever been told they had a stroke	n/a	3.0
Adults who have ever been told they have asthma	n/a	14.2
Adults who have ever been told they have arthritis	n/a	24.9
Adults who have ever been told they have diabetes[2]	n/a	10.5
Adults who have ever been told they had skin cancer	n/a	6.2
Adults who have ever been told they had any other types of cancer	n/a	7.1
Adults who have ever been told they have COPD	n/a	6.5
Adults who have ever been told they have kidney disease	n/a	3.0
Adults who have ever been told they have a form of depression	n/a	20.5

Note: n/a not available; (1) Figures cover the Boulder, CO Metropolitan Statistical Area; (2) Figures do not include pregnancy-related, borderline, or pre-diabetes
Source: Centers for Disease Control and Prevention, Behaviorial Risk Factor Surveillance System, SMART: Selected Metropolitan Area Risk Trends, 2017

Health Screening and Vaccination Rates

Category	MSA[1] (%)	U.S. (%)
Adults aged 65+ who have had flu shot within the past year	n/a	60.7
Adults aged 65+ who have ever had a pneumonia vaccination	n/a	75.4
Adults who have ever been tested for HIV	n/a	36.1
Adults who have ever had the shingles or zoster vaccine?	n/a	28.9
Adults who have had their blood cholesterol checked within the last five years	n/a	85.9

Note: n/a not available; (1) Figures cover the Boulder, CO Metropolitan Statistical Area.
Source: Centers for Disease Control and Prevention, Behaviorial Risk Factor Surveillance System, SMART: Selected Metropolitan Area Risk Trends, 2017

Disability Status

Category	MSA[1] (%)	U.S. (%)
Adults who reported being deaf	n/a	6.7
Are you blind or have serious difficulty seeing, even when wearing glasses?	n/a	4.5
Are you limited in any way in any of your usual activities due of arthritis?	n/a	12.9
Do you have difficulty doing errands alone?	n/a	6.8
Do you have difficulty dressing or bathing?	n/a	3.6
Do you have serious difficulty concentrating/remembering/making decisions?	n/a	10.7
Do you have serious difficulty walking or climbing stairs?	n/a	13.6

Note: n/a not available; (1) Figures cover the Boulder, CO Metropolitan Statistical Area.
Source: Centers for Disease Control and Prevention, Behaviorial Risk Factor Surveillance System, SMART: Selected Metropolitan Area Risk Trends, 2017

Mortality Rates for the Top 10 Causes of Death in the U.S.

ICD-10[a] Sub-Chapter	ICD-10[a] Code	Age-Adjusted Mortality Rate[1] per 100,000 population	
		County[2]	U.S.
Malignant neoplasms	C00-C97	118.4	149.2
Ischaemic heart diseases	I20-I25	48.0	90.5
Other forms of heart disease	I30-I51	38.1	52.2
Chronic lower respiratory diseases	J40-J47	29.1	39.6
Other degenerative diseases of the nervous system	G30-G31	38.7	37.6
Cerebrovascular diseases	I60-I69	36.7	37.2
Other external causes of accidental injury	W00-X59	35.7	36.1
Organic, including symptomatic, mental disorders	F01-F09	29.3	29.4
Hypertensive diseases	I10-I15	15.2	24.1
Diabetes mellitus	E10-E14	9.0	21.5

Note: (a) ICD-10 = International Classification of Diseases 10th Revision; (1) Mortality rates are a three-year average covering 2017-2019; (2) Figures cover Boulder County.
Source: Centers for Disease Control and Prevention, National Center for Health Statistics. Underlying Cause of Death 1999-2019 on CDC WONDER Online Database

Mortality Rates for Selected Causes of Death

ICD-10[a] Sub-Chapter	ICD-10[a] Code	Age-Adjusted Mortality Rate[1] per 100,000 population	
		County[2]	U.S.
Assault	X85-Y09	Unreliable	6.0
Diseases of the liver	K70-K76	10.3	14.4
Human immunodeficiency virus (HIV) disease	B20-B24	Suppressed	1.5
Influenza and pneumonia	J09-J18	10.3	13.8
Intentional self-harm	X60-X84	17.3	14.1
Malnutrition	E40-E46	6.2	2.3
Obesity and other hyperalimentation	E65-E68	Suppressed	2.1
Renal failure	N17-N19	5.8	12.6
Transport accidents	V01-V99	8.5	12.3
Viral hepatitis	B15-B19	Suppressed	1.2

Note: (a) ICD-10 = International Classification of Diseases 10th Revision; (1) Mortality rates are a three-year average covering 2017-2019; (2) Figures cover Boulder County; Data are suppressed when the data meet the criteria for confidentiality constraints; Mortality rates are flagged as unreliable when the rate would be calculated with a numerator of 20 or less.
Source: Centers for Disease Control and Prevention, National Center for Health Statistics. Underlying Cause of Death 1999-2019 on CDC WONDER Online Database

Health Insurance Coverage

Area	With Health Insurance	With Private Health Insurance	With Public Health Insurance	Without Health Insurance	Population Under Age 19 Without Health Insurance
City	95.9	84.0	20.1	4.1	1.2
MSA[1]	95.4	79.5	25.6	4.6	2.1
U.S.	91.2	67.9	35.1	8.8	5.1

Note: Figures are percentages that cover the civilian noninstitutionalized population; (1) Figures cover the Boulder, CO Metropolitan Statistical Area
Source: U.S. Census Bureau, 2015-2019 American Community Survey 5-Year Estimates

Number of Medical Professionals

Area	MDs[3]	DOs[3,4]	Dentists	Podiatrists	Chiropractors	Optometrists
County[1] (number)	1,142	106	346	20	264	86
County[1] (rate[2])	351.8	32.7	106.1	6.1	80.9	26.4
U.S. (rate[2])	282.9	22.7	71.2	6.2	28.1	16.9

08013
Note: Data as of 2019 unless noted; (1) Data covers Boulder County; (2) Rate per 100,000 population; (3) Data as of 2018 and includes all active, non-federal physicians; (4) Doctor of Osteopathic Medicine
Source: U.S. Department of Health and Human Services, Health Resources and Services Administration, Bureau of Health Professions, Area Resource File (ARF) 2019-2020

EDUCATION

Public School District Statistics

District Name	Schls	Pupils	Pupil/ Teacher Ratio	Minority Pupils[1] (%)	Free Lunch Eligible[2] (%)	IEP[3] (%)
Boulder Valley SD No. Re2	56	31,169	18.1	31.6	17.6	n/a

Note: Table includes school districts with 2,000 or more students; (1) Percentage of students that are not non-Hispanic white; (2) Percentage of students that are eligible for the free lunch program; (3) Percentage of students that have an Individualized Education Program.
Source: U.S. Department of Education, National Center for Education Statistics, Common Core of Data, Local Education Agency (School District) Universe Survey: School Year 2018-2019; U.S. Department of Education, National Center for Education Statistics, Common Core of Data, Public Elementary/Secondary School Universe Survey: School Year 2018-2019

Best High Schools

According to *U.S. News,* Boulder is home to two of the top 500 high schools in the U.S.: **Fairview High School** (#249); **Boulder High School** (#496). Nearly 18,000 public, magnet and charter schools were ranked based on their performance on state assessments and how well they prepare students for college. *U.S. News & World Report, "Best High Schools 2020"*

Highest Level of Education

Area	Less than H.S.	H.S. Diploma	Some College, No Deg.	Associate Degree	Bachelor's Degree	Master's Degree	Prof. School Degree	Doctorate Degree
City	3.1	6.2	11.1	3.6	36.2	24.7	6.4	8.7
MSA[1]	5.0	11.7	15.1	6.1	34.0	18.8	4.1	5.2
U.S.	12.0	27.0	20.4	8.5	19.8	8.8	2.1	1.4

Note: Figures cover persons age 25 and over; (1) Figures cover the Boulder, CO Metropolitan Statistical Area
Source: U.S. Census Bureau, 2015-2019 American Community Survey 5-Year Estimates

Educational Attainment by Race

Area	High School Graduate or Higher (%)					Bachelor's Degree or Higher (%)				
	Total	White	Black	Asian	Hisp.[2]	Total	White	Black	Asian	Hisp.[2]
City	96.9	97.5	92.2	96.1	76.4	76.0	76.9	39.9	80.4	42.1
MSA[1]	95.0	95.8	87.8	93.8	71.6	62.1	62.8	30.5	72.5	26.5
U.S.	88.0	89.9	86.0	87.1	68.7	32.1	33.5	21.6	54.3	16.4

Note: Figures shown cover persons 25 years old and over; (1) Figures cover the Boulder, CO Metropolitan Statistical Area; (2) People of Hispanic origin can be of any race
Source: U.S. Census Bureau, 2015-2019 American Community Survey 5-Year Estimates

School Enrollment by Grade and Control

Area	Preschool (%)		Kindergarten (%)		Grades 1 - 4 (%)		Grades 5 - 8 (%)		Grades 9 - 12 (%)	
	Public	Private	Public	Private	Public	Private	Public	Private	Public	Private
City	44.0	56.0	84.5	15.5	92.5	7.5	93.4	6.6	92.2	7.8
MSA[1]	50.7	49.3	84.7	15.3	90.8	9.2	90.8	9.2	93.9	6.1
U.S.	59.1	40.9	87.6	12.4	89.5	10.5	89.4	10.6	90.1	9.9

Note: Figures shown cover persons 3 years old and over; (1) Figures cover the Boulder, CO Metropolitan Statistical Area
Source: U.S. Census Bureau, 2015-2019 American Community Survey 5-Year Estimates

Higher Education

Four-Year Colleges			Two-Year Colleges			Medical Schools[1]	Law Schools[2]	Voc/ Tech[3]
Public	Private Non-profit	Private For-profit	Public	Private Non-profit	Private For-profit			
1	2	1	0	0	1	0	1	1

Note: Figures cover institutions located within the city limits and include main campuses only; (1) includes schools accredited by the Liaison Committee on Medical Education and the American Osteopathic Association's Commission on Osteopathic College Accreditation; (2) includes ABA-accredited schools, schools with provisional ABA accreditation, and state accredited schools; (3) includes all schools with programs that are less than 2 years.
Source: National Center for Education Statistics, Integrated Postsecondary Education System (IPEDS), 2019-20; Wikipedia, List of Medical Schools in the United States, accessed April 2, 2021; Wikipedia, List of Law Schools in the United States, accessed April 2, 2021

According to *U.S. News & World Report,* the Boulder, CO metro area is home to one of the top 200 national universities in the U.S.: **University of Colorado Boulder** (#103 tie). The indicators used to capture academic quality fall into a number of categories: assessment by administrators at peer institutions; retention of students; faculty resources; student selectivity; financial resources; alumni giving; high school counselor ratings of colleges; and graduation rate. *U.S. News & World Report, "America's Best Colleges 2021"*

According to *U.S. News & World Report,* the Boulder, CO metro area is home to one of the top 100 law schools in the U.S.: **University of Colorado—Boulder** (#48 tie). The rankings are based on a weighted average of 12 measures of quality: peer assessment score; assessment score by law-yers/judges; median LSAT scores; median undergrad GPA; acceptance rate; employment rates for graduates; placement success; bar passage rate; faculty resources; expenditures per student; stu-dent/faculty ratio; and library resources. *U.S. News & World Report, "America's Best Graduate Schools, Law, 2022"*

According to *U.S. News & World Report,* the Boulder, CO metro area is home to one of the top 75 business schools in the U.S.: **University of Colorado—Boulder (Leeds)** (#74 tie). The rankings are based on a weighted average of the following nine measures: quality assessment; peer assessment; re-cruiter assessment; placement success; mean starting salary and bonus; student selectivity; mean GMAT and GRE scores; mean undergraduate GPA; and acceptance rate. *U.S. News & World Report, "America's Best Graduate Schools, Business, 2022"*

EMPLOYERS

Major Employers

Company Name	Industry
Agilent Technologies	Instruments to measure electricity
America's Note Network	Mortgage bankers & loan correspondents
Ball Aerospace & Technologies Corp.	Search & navigation equipment
Ball Corporation	Space research & technology
Corden Pharma Colorado	Pharmaceutical preparations
County of Boulder	County government
Crispin Porter Bogusky	Business services at non-commercial site
Health Carechain	Medical field-related associations
IBM	Magnetic storage devices, computer
Lockheed Martin Corporation	Search & navigation equipment
Micro Motion	Liquid meters
National Oceanic and Atmospheric Admin	Environmental protection agency, government
Natl Inst of Standards & Technology	Commercial physical research
Qualcomm Incorporated	Integrated circuits, semiconductor networks
Staffing Solutions Southwest	Temporary help services
The Regents of the University of Colorado	Noncommercial research organizations
Tyco Healthcare Group	Medical instruments & equipment, blood & bone work
University Corp for Atmospheric Research	Noncommercial research organizations
University of Colorado	Colleges & universities
Wall Street On Demand	Financial services
Whole Foods Market	Grocery stores

Note: Companies shown are located within the Boulder, CO Metropolitan Statistical Area.
Source: Hoovers.com; Wikipedia

PUBLIC SAFETY

Crime Rate

Area	All Crimes	Violent Crimes				Property Crimes		
		Murder	Rape[3]	Robbery	Aggrav. Assault	Burglary	Larceny -Theft	Motor Vehicle Theft
City	3,282.4	0.9	37.8	34.1	183.4	373.2	2,421.7	231.3
Suburbs[1]	2,439.7	0.9	83.1	20.9	175.3	269.8	1,686.5	203.0
Metro[2]	2,717.9	0.9	68.2	25.3	178.0	303.9	1,929.3	212.4
U.S.	2,489.3	5.0	42.6	81.6	250.2	340.5	1,549.5	219.9

Note: Figures are crimes per 100,000 population; (1) All areas within the metro area that are located outside the city limits; (2) Figures cover the Boulder, CO Metropolitan Statistical Area; (3) All figures shown were reported using the revised Uniform Crime Reporting (UCR) definition of rape.
Source: FBI Uniform Crime Reports, 2019

Hate Crimes

Area	Number of Quarters Reported	Number of Incidents per Bias Motivation					
		Race/Ethnicity/ Ancestry	Religion	Sexual Orientation	Disability	Gender	Gender Identity
City	4	4	1	3	0	0	0
U.S.	4	3,963	1,521	1,195	157	69	198

Source: Federal Bureau of Investigation, Hate Crime Statistics 2019

Identity Theft Consumer Reports

Area	Reports	Reports per 100,000 Population	Rank[2]
MSA[1]	1,269	389	79
U.S.	1,387,615	423	-

Note: (1) Figures cover the Boulder, CO Metropolitan Statistical Area; (2) Rank ranges from 1 to 391 where 1 indicates greatest number of identity theft reports per 100,000 population
Source: Federal Trade Commission, Consumer Sentinel Network Data Book 2020

Fraud and Other Consumer Reports

Area	Reports	Reports per 100,000 Population	Rank[2]
MSA[1]	3,074	942	34
U.S.	3,385,133	1,031	-

Note: (1) Figures cover the Boulder, CO Metropolitan Statistical Area; (2) Rank ranges from 1 to 391 where 1 indicates greatest number of fraud and other consumer reports per 100,000 population
Source: Federal Trade Commission, Consumer Sentinel Network Data Book 2020

POLITICS

2020 Presidential Election Results

Area	Biden	Trump	Jorgensen	Hawkins	Other
Boulder County	77.2	20.6	1.2	0.3	0.6
U.S.	51.3	46.8	1.2	0.3	0.5

Note: Results are percentages and may not add to 100% due to rounding
Source: Dave Leip's Atlas of U.S. Presidential Elections

SPORTS

Professional Sports Teams

Team Name	League	Year Established
No teams are located in the metro area		

Source: Wikipedia, Major Professional Sports Teams of the United States and Canada, April 6, 2021

CLIMATE

Average and Extreme Temperatures

Temperature	Jan	Feb	Mar	Apr	May	Jun	Jul	Aug	Sep	Oct	Nov	Dec	Yr.
Extreme High (°F)	73	76	84	90	93	102	103	100	97	89	79	75	103
Average High (°F)	43	47	52	62	71	81	88	86	77	67	52	45	64
Average Temp. (°F)	30	34	39	48	58	67	73	72	63	52	39	32	51
Average Low (°F)	16	20	25	34	44	53	59	57	48	37	25	18	37
Extreme Low (°F)	-25	-25	-10	-2	22	30	43	41	17	3	-8	-25	-25

Note: Figures cover the years 1948-1992
Source: National Climatic Data Center, International Station Meteorological Climate Summary, 9/96

Average Precipitation/Snowfall/Humidity

Precip./Humidity	Jan	Feb	Mar	Apr	May	Jun	Jul	Aug	Sep	Oct	Nov	Dec	Yr.
Avg. Precip. (in.)	0.6	0.6	1.3	1.7	2.5	1.7	1.9	1.5	1.1	1.0	0.9	0.6	15.5
Avg. Snowfall (in.)	9	7	14	9	2	Tr	0	0	2	4	9	8	63
Avg. Rel. Hum. 5am (%)	62	65	67	66	70	68	67	68	66	63	66	63	66
Avg. Rel. Hum. 5pm (%)	49	44	40	35	38	34	34	34	32	34	47	50	39

Note: Figures cover the years 1948-1992; Tr = Trace amounts (<0.05 in. of rain; <0.5 in. of snow)
Source: National Climatic Data Center, International Station Meteorological Climate Summary, 9/96

Weather Conditions

Temperature			Daytime Sky			Precipitation		
10°F & below	32°F & below	90°F & above	Clear	Partly cloudy	Cloudy	0.01 inch or more precip.	0.1 inch or more snow/ice	Thunderstorms
24	155	33	99	177	89	90	38	39

Note: Figures are average number of days per year and cover the years 1948-1992
Source: National Climatic Data Center, International Station Meteorological Climate Summary, 9/96

HAZARDOUS WASTE

Superfund Sites

The Boulder, CO metro area is home to two sites on the EPA's Superfund National Priorities List: **Captain Jack Mill** (final); **Marshall Landfill** (final). There are a total of 1,375 Superfund sites with a status of proposed or final on the list in the U.S. *U.S. Environmental Protection Agency, National Priorities List, April 7, 2021*

AIR QUALITY

Air Quality Trends: Ozone

	1990	1995	2000	2005	2010	2015	2016	2017	2018	2019
MSA[1]	n/a	n/a	n/a	n/a	n/a	n/a	n/a	n/a	n/a	n/a
U.S.	0.088	0.089	0.082	0.080	0.073	0.068	0.069	0.068	0.069	0.065

Note: (1) Data covers the Boulder, CO Metropolitan Statistical Area; n/a not available. The values shown are the composite ozone concentration averages among trend sites based on the highest fourth daily maximum 8-hour concentration in parts per million. These trends are based on sites having an adequate record of monitoring data during the trend period. Data from exceptional events are included.
Source: U.S. Environmental Protection Agency, Air Quality Monitoring Information, "Air Quality Trends by City, 1990-2019"

Air Quality Index

Area	Percent of Days when Air Quality was...[2]					AQI Statistics[2]	
	Good	Moderate	Unhealthy for Sensitive Groups	Unhealthy	Very Unhealthy	Maximum	Median
MSA[1]	62.2	36.4	1.4	0.0	0.0	119	47

Note: (1) Data covers the Boulder, CO Metropolitan Statistical Area; (2) Based on 365 days with AQI data in 2019. Air Quality Index (AQI) is an index for reporting daily air quality. EPA calculates the AQI for five major air pollutants regulated by the Clean Air Act: ground-level ozone, particle pollution (aka particulate matter), carbon monoxide, sulfur dioxide, and nitrogen dioxide. The AQI runs from 0 to 500. The higher the AQI value, the greater the level of air pollution and the greater the health concern. There are six AQI categories: "Good" AQI is between 0 and 50. Air quality is considered satisfactory; "Moderate" AQI is between 51 and 100. Air quality is acceptable; "Unhealthy for Sensitive Groups" When AQI values are between 101 and 150, members of sensitive groups may experience health effects; "Unhealthy" When AQI values are between 151 and 200 everyone may begin to experience health effects; "Very Unhealthy" AQI values between 201 and 300 trigger a health alert; "Hazardous" AQI values over 300 trigger warnings of emergency conditions (not shown).
Source: U.S. Environmental Protection Agency, Air Quality Index Report, 2019

Air Quality Index Pollutants

Area	Percent of Days when AQI Pollutant was...[2]					
	Carbon Monoxide	Nitrogen Dioxide	Ozone	Sulfur Dioxide	Particulate Matter 2.5	Particulate Matter 10
MSA[1]	0.0	0.0	73.7	0.0	26.3	0.0

Note: (1) Data covers the Boulder, CO Metropolitan Statistical Area; (2) Based on 365 days with AQI data in 2019. The Air Quality Index (AQI) is an index for reporting daily air quality. EPA calculates the AQI for five major air pollutants regulated by the Clean Air Act: ground-level ozone, particle pollution (also known as particulate matter), carbon monoxide, sulfur dioxide, and nitrogen dioxide. The AQI runs from 0 to 500. The higher the AQI value, the greater the level of air pollution and the greater the health concern.
Source: U.S. Environmental Protection Agency, Air Quality Index Report, 2019

Maximum Air Pollutant Concentrations: Particulate Matter, Ozone, CO and Lead

	Particulate Matter 10 (ug/m^3)	Particulate Matter 2.5 Wtd AM (ug/m^3)	Particulate Matter 2.5 24-Hr (ug/m^3)	Ozone (ppm)	Carbon Monoxide (ppm)	Lead (ug/m^3)
MSA[1] Level	52	7.4	36	0.069	n/a	n/a
NAAQS[2]	150	15	35	0.075	9	0.15
Met NAAQS[2]	Yes	Yes	No	Yes	n/a	n/a

Note: (1) Data covers the Boulder, CO Metropolitan Statistical Area; Data from exceptional events are included; (2) National Ambient Air Quality Standards; ppm = parts per million; ug/m^3 = micrograms per cubic meter; n/a not available.
Concentrations: Particulate Matter 10 (coarse particulate)—highest second maximum 24-hour concentration; Particulate Matter 2.5 Wtd AM (fine particulate)—highest weighted annual mean concentration; Particulate Matter 2.5 24-Hour (fine particulate)—highest 98th percentile 24-hour concentration; Ozone—highest fourth daily maximum 8-hour concentration; Carbon Monoxide—highest second maximum non-overlapping 8-hour concentration; Lead—maximum running 3-month average
Source: U.S. Environmental Protection Agency, Air Quality Monitoring Information, "Air Quality Statistics by City, 2019"

Maximum Air Pollutant Concentrations: Nitrogen Dioxide and Sulfur Dioxide

	Nitrogen Dioxide AM (ppb)	Nitrogen Dioxide 1-Hr (ppb)	Sulfur Dioxide AM (ppb)	Sulfur Dioxide 1-Hr (ppb)	Sulfur Dioxide 24-Hr (ppb)
MSA[1] Level	n/a	n/a	n/a	n/a	n/a
NAAQS[2]	53	100	30	75	140
Met NAAQS[2]	n/a	n/a	n/a	n/a	n/a

Note: (1) Data covers the Boulder, CO Metropolitan Statistical Area; Data from exceptional events are included; (2) National Ambient Air Quality Standards; ppm = parts per million; ug/m^3 = micrograms per cubic meter; n/a not available.
Concentrations: Nitrogen Dioxide AM—highest arithmetic mean concentration; Nitrogen Dioxide 1-Hr—highest 98th percentile 1-hour daily maximum concentration; Sulfur Dioxide AM—highest annual mean concentration; Sulfur Dioxide 1-Hr—highest 99th percentile 1-hour daily maximum concentration; Sulfur Dioxide 24-Hr—highest second maximum 24-hour concentration
Source: U.S. Environmental Protection Agency, Air Quality Monitoring Information, "Air Quality Statistics by City, 2019"

Colorado Springs, Colorado

Background

Colorado Springs is the seat of El Paso County in central Colorado and sits at the foot of Pike's Peak. A dynamic and growing city, its economy is based on health care, high-tech manufacturing, tourism, and sports, with strong employment links to nearby military installations. With such an economic base and gorgeous surroundings, it is no wonder that Colorado Springs ranks as one of the fastest-growing cities in the country.

In 1806, Lieutenant Zebulon Pike visited the site and the mountain that now bears his name, but true settlement did not begin in earnest until gold was discovered in 1859 and miners flooded into the area.

In 1871, General William Jackson Palmer, a railroad tycoon, purchased the site for $10,000 and began promoting the area as a health and recreation resort. Pike's Peak was already well known as a scenic landmark, and very soon the Garden of the Gods, Seven Falls, Cheyenne Mountain, and Manitou Springs were also widely known as spectacular natural sites. The extraordinary nature of the natural environment has long been celebrated, but perhaps the highest testimonial came from Katherine Lee Bates, who, after a trip to Pike's Peak in 1893, wrote "America the Beautiful."

The planned community of Colorado Springs was incorporated in 1876. As a resort, it was wildly successful, hosting the likes of Oscar Wilde and John D. Rockefeller. It became a special favorite of English visitors, one of whom made the claim that there were two "civilized" places between the Atlantic and the Pacific—Chicago and Colorado Springs.

The English were so enamored of the place, in fact, that it came to be called "Little London," as English visitors settled in the area, introducing golf, cricket, polo, and fox hunting; but since there were no local foxes, an artificial scent was spread out for the hounds, or sometimes a coyote was substituted. Several sumptuous hotels were built during this period, as was an elegantly appointed opera house.

In 1891, gold was again discovered, and the city's population tripled to 35,000 in the following decade. Sufficient gold deposits allowed a lucky few to amass considerable fortunes and build huge houses north of the city. However, not all of the newly minted millionaires were inclined toward conspicuous display; Winfield Scott Stratton, "Midas of the Rockies," bruised emerging aesthetic sensibilities by constructing a crude wooden frame house near the business district.

After the 1890s rush ended, Colorado Springs resumed a more measured pace of growth. During and after World War II, though, the town again saw considerable development as Fort Carson and the Peterson Air Force Base were established, followed by the North American Aerospace Defense Command (NORAD) and the U.S. Air Force Academy in the 1950s. Today NORAD is primarily concerned with the tracking of Intercontinental Ballistic Missiles (ICBM), and celebrated its 61st anniversary in 2019. The city's military connection has contributed in large part to the economic base of the area, and its highly educated and technically skilled workforce. In late 2008, Fort Carson became the home station of the 4th Infantry Division, nearly doubling the population of the base.

Colorado Springs is the site of the headquarters of the United States Olympics Committee, which maintains an important Olympic training center there. The U.S. Olympic and Paralympic Museum opened in 2020.

The city is also home to the World Figure Skating Museum and Hall of Fame, the Pro Rodeo Hall of Fame, and Museum of the American Cowboy. A new Pikes Peak Summit Center is opening in 2021.

The city hosts several institutions of higher learning, including Colorado College (1874), the U.S. Air Force Academy (1954), a campus of the University of Colorado (1965), and Nazarene Bible College (1967). Cultural amenities include the Fine Arts Center and Theatreworks at the University of Colorado.

Although Colorado voters approved Colorado Amendment 64, legalizing retail sales of marijuana for recreational purposes, the Colorado Springs city council voted not to permit retail shops in the city to sell the substance. In 2021, while the number of medical marijuana centers in the city is in the hundreds, there are no recreational cannabis stores.

The region enjoys four seasons, with plenty of sunshine—300 days each year. Rainfall is relatively minimal, but snow can pile up.

Rankings

General Rankings

- For its "Best for Vets: Places to Live 2019" rankings, *Military Times* evaluated 599 cities (83 large, 234 medium, 282 small) and compared the locations across three broad categories: veteran and military culture/services; economic indicators; and livability factors such as health, crime, traffic, and school quality. Colorado Springs ranked #1 out of the top 25, in the large city category (population of more than 250,000). Data points more specific to veterans and the military weighed more heavily than others. *rebootcamp.militarytimes.com, "Military Times Best Places to Live 2019," September 10, 2018*

- *US News & World Report* conducted a survey of more than 3,000 people and analyzed the 150 largest metropolitan areas to determine what matters most when selecting the next place to live. Colorado Springs ranked #4 out of the top 25 as having the best combination of desirable factors. Criteria: cost of living; quality of life; net migration; job market; desirability; and other factors. *realestate.usnews.com, "The 25 Best Places to Live in the U.S. in 2020-21," October 13, 2020*

- The Colorado Springs metro area was identified as one of America's fastest-growing areas in terms of population and business growth by *MagnifyMoney*. The area ranked #23 out of 35. The 100 most populous metro areas in the U.S. were evaluated on their change from 2011-2016 in the following categories: people and housing; workforce and employment opportunities; growing industry. *www.businessinsider.com, "The 35 Cities in the US with the Biggest Influx of People, the Most Work Opportunities, and the Hottest Business Growth," August 12, 2018*

- The Colorado Springs metro area was identified as one of America's fastest-growing areas in terms of population and economy by *Forbes*. The area ranked #18 out of 25. The 100 most populous metro areas in the U.S. were evaluated on the following criteria: estimated population growth; employment; economic output; wages; home values. *Forbes, "America's Fastest-Growing Cities 2018," February 28, 2018*

Business/Finance Rankings

- The Brookings Institution ranked the nation's largest cities based on income inequality. Colorado Springs was ranked #87 (#1 = greatest inequality). Criteria: the "95/20 ratio," a figure representing the income at which a household earns more than 95 percent of all other households, divided by the income at which a household earns more than only 20 percent of all other households. *Brookings Institution, "Household Income Inequality, Largest Cities of 97 Large U.S. Metro Areas, 2014-2016," February 5, 2018*

- The Brookings Institution ranked the 100 largest metro areas in the U.S. based on income inequality. Colorado Springs was ranked #94 (#1 = greatest inequality). Criteria: the "95/20 ratio," a figure representing the income at which a household earns more than 95 percent of all other households, divided by the income at which a household earns more than only 20 percent of all other households. *Brookings Institution, "Household Income Inequality, 100 Largest U.S. Metro Areas, 2014-2016," February 5, 2018*

- The Colorado Springs metro area appeared on the Milken Institute "2021 Best Performing Cities" list. Rank: #17 out of 200 large metro areas (population over 250,000). Criteria: job growth; wage and salary growth; high-tech output growth; housing affordability; household broadband access. *Milken Institute, "Best-Performing Cities 2021," February 16, 2021*

- *Forbes* ranked the 200 most populous metro areas to determine the nation's "Best Places for Business and Careers." The Colorado Springs metro area was ranked #19. Criteria: costs (business and living); job growth (past and projected); income growth; quality of life; educational attainment (college and high school); projected economic growth; cultural and leisure opportunities; workplace tolerance laws; net migration patterns. *Forbes, "The Best Places for Business and Careers 2019: Seattle Still On Top," October 30, 2019*

Education Rankings

- Personal finance website *WalletHub* analyzed the 150 largest U.S. metropolitan statistical areas to determine where the most educated Americans are putting their degrees to work. Criteria: education levels; percentage of workers with degrees; education quality and attainment gap; public school quality rankings; quality and enrollment of each metro area's universities. Colorado Springs was ranked #11 (#1 = most educated city). *www.WalletHub.com, "Most and Least Educated Cities in America," July 20, 2020*

- Colorado Springs was selected as one of America's most literate cities. The city ranked #21 out of the 84 largest U.S. cities. Criteria: number of booksellers; library resources; Internet resources; educational attainment; periodical publishing resources; newspaper circulation. *Central Connecticut State University, "America's Most Literate Cities, 2018," February 2019*

Environmental Rankings

- Colorado Springs was highlighted as one of the top 25 cleanest metro areas for year-round particle pollution (Annual PM 2.5) in the U.S. during 2016 through 2018. The area ranked #22. *American Lung Association, "State of the Air 2020," April 21, 2020*

Health/Fitness Rankings

- For each of the 100 largest cities in the United States, the American Fitness Index®, published by the American College of Sports Medicine and the Anthem Foundation, evaluated community infrastructure and 33 health behaviors including preventive health, levels of chronic disease conditions, pedestrian safety, air quality, and community resources that support physical activity. Colorado Springs ranked #33 for "community fitness." *americanfitnessindex.org, "2020 ACSM American Fitness Index Summary Report," July 14, 2020*

- Colorado Springs was identified as a "2021 Spring Allergy Capital." The area ranked #82 out of 100. Three groups of factors were used to identify the most challenging cities for people with allergies during the spring season: annual spring pollen levels; over the counter medicine use; number of board-certified allergy specialists. *Asthma and Allergy Foundation of America, "Spring Allergy Capitals 2021," February 23, 2021*

- Colorado Springs was identified as a "2021 Fall Allergy Capital." The area ranked #83 out of 100. Three groups of factors were used to identify the most challenging cities for people with allergies during the fall season: annual fall pollen levels; over the counter medicine use; number of board-certified allergy specialists. *Asthma and Allergy Foundation of America, "Fall Allergy Capitals 2021," February 23, 2021*

- Colorado Springs was identified as a "2019 Asthma Capital." The area ranked #75 out of the nation's 100 largest metropolitan areas. Criteria: estimated asthma prevalence; crude death rate from asthma; and ER visits due to asthma. Risk factors analyzed but not factored in the rankings: annual pollen score; annual air quality; public smoking laws; number of board-certified asthma specialists; rescue medication use; controller medication use; uninsured rate; poverty rate. *Asthma and Allergy Foundation of America, "Asthma Capitals 2019: The Most Challenging Places to Live With Asthma," May 7, 2019*

Real Estate Rankings

- *WalletHub* compared the most populated U.S. cities to determine which had the best markets for real estate agents. Colorado Springs ranked #59 where demand was high and pay was the best. Criteria: sales per agent; annual median wage for real-estate agents; monthly average starting salary for real estate agents; real estate job density and competition; unemployment rate; home turnover rate; housing-market health index; and other relevant metrics. *www.WalletHub.com, "2019's Best Places to Be a Real Estate Agent," April 24, 2019*

- The Colorado Springs metro area was identified as one of the nations's 20 hottest housing markets in 2021. Criteria: listing views as an indicator of demand and median days on the market as an indicator of supply. The area ranked #6. *Realtor.com, "January 2021 Top 20 Hottest Housing Markets," February 25, 2021*

- Colorado Springs was ranked #17 in the top 20 out of the 100 largest metro areas in terms of house price appreciation in 2020 (#1 = highest rate). *Federal Housing Finance Agency, House Price Index, 4th Quarter 2020*

- The Colorado Springs metro area was identified as one of the 10 worst condo markets in the U.S. in 2020. The area ranked #54 out of 63 markets. Criteria: year-over-year change of median sales price of existing apartment condo-coop homes between the 4th quarter of 2019 and the 4th quarter of 2020. *National Association of Realtors®, Median Sales Price of Existing Apartment Condo-Coops Homes for Metropolitan Areas, 4th Quarter 2020*

- Colorado Springs was ranked #177 out of 268 metro areas in terms of housing affordability in 2020 by the National Association of Home Builders (#1 = most affordable). Criteria: the share of homes sold in that area affordable to a family earning the local median income, based on standard mortgage underwriting criteria. *National Association of Home Builders®, NAHB-Wells Fargo Housing Opportunity Index, 4th Quarter 2020*

Safety Rankings

- Allstate ranked the 200 largest cities in America in terms of driver safety. Colorado Springs ranked #13. Criteria: internal property damage claims over a two-year period from January 2016 to December 2017. The report helps increase the importance of safety and awareness behind the wheel. *Allstate, "Allstate America's Best Drivers Report, 2019" June 24, 2019*

- The National Insurance Crime Bureau ranked 384 metro areas in the U.S. in terms of per capita rates of vehicle theft. The Colorado Springs metro area ranked #28 (#1 = highest rate). Criteria: number of vehicle theft offenses per 100,000 inhabitants in 2019. *National Insurance Crime Bureau, "Hot Spots 2019," July 21, 2020*

Seniors/Retirement Rankings

- From its Best Cities for Successful Aging indexes, the Milken Institute generated rankings for metropolitan areas, weighing data in nine categories—health care, wellness, living arrangements, transportation and convenience, financial characteristics, education, employment, community engagement, and overall livability. The Colorado Springs metro area was ranked #46 overall in the large metro area category. *Milken Institute, "Best Cities for Successful Aging, 2017" March 14, 2017*

- Colorado Springs was identified as #16 of 20 most popular places to retire in the Western region by *Topretirements.com*. The site separated its annual "Best Places to Retire" list by major U.S. regions for 2019. The list reflects the 20 cities that visitors to the website are most interested in for retirement, based on the number of times a city's review was viewed on the website. *Topretirements.com, "20 Best Places to Retire in the West-2019," November 11, 2019*

Sports/Recreation Rankings

- Colorado Springs was chosen as one of America's best cities for bicycling. The city ranked #28 out of 50. Criteria: cycling infrastructure that is safe and friendly for all ages; energy and bike culture. The editors evaluated cities with populations of 100,000 or more. *Bicycling, "The 50 Best Bike Cities in America," October 10, 2018*

Women/Minorities Rankings

- Personal finance website *WalletHub* compared more than 180 U.S. cities across two key dimensions, "Hispanic Business-Friendliness" and "Hispanic Purchasing Power," to arrive at the most favorable conditions for Hispanic entrepreneurs. Colorado Springs was ranked #93 out of 182. Criteria includes: share of Hispanic-Owned Businesses; Hispanic entrepreneurship rate to median annual income of Hispanics; Small Business-Friendliness score; cost of living; and number of Hispanics with at least a bachelor's degree. *WalletHub.com, "2019's Best Cities for Hispanic Entrepreneurs," May 1, 2019*

Miscellaneous Rankings

- The watchdog site, Charity Navigator, conducted a study of charities in major markets both to analyze statistical differences in their financial, accountability, and transparency practices and to track year-to-year variations in individual philanthropic communities. The Colorado Springs metro area was ranked #28 among the 30 metro markets in the rating category of Overall Score. *www.charitynavigator.org, "2017 Metro Market Study," May 1, 2017*

- *WalletHub* compared the 150 most populated U.S. cities to determine their operating efficiency. A "Quality of City Services" score was constructed for each city and then divided by the total budget per capita to reveal which were managed the best. Colorado Springs ranked #56. Criteria: financial stability; economy; education; safety; health; infrastructure and pollution. *www.WalletHub.com, "2020's Best- & Worst-Run Cities in America," June 29, 2020*

Business Environment

DEMOGRAPHICS

Population Growth

Area	1990 Census	2000 Census	2010 Census	2019* Estimate	Population Growth (%) 1990-2019	Population Growth (%) 2010-2019
City	283,798	360,890	416,427	464,871	63.8	11.6
MSA[1]	409,482	537,484	645,613	723,498	76.7	12.1
U.S.	248,709,873	281,421,906	308,745,538	324,697,795	30.6	5.2

Note: (1) Figures cover the Colorado Springs, CO Metropolitan Statistical Area; (*) 2015-2019 5-year estimated population
Source: U.S. Census Bureau, 1990 Census, Census 2000, Census 2010, 2015-2019 American Community Survey 5-Year Estimates

Household Size

Area	Persons in Household (%) One	Two	Three	Four	Five	Six	Seven or More	Average Household Size
City	28.6	35.2	14.7	12.3	5.9	2.3	1.1	2.50
MSA[1]	25.1	35.5	15.7	13.4	6.6	2.5	1.3	2.60
U.S.	27.9	33.9	15.6	12.9	6.0	2.3	1.4	2.60

Note: (1) Figures cover the Colorado Springs, CO Metropolitan Statistical Area
Source: U.S. Census Bureau, 2015-2019 American Community Survey 5-Year Estimates

Race

Area	White Alone[2] (%)	Black Alone[2] (%)	Asian Alone[2] (%)	AIAN[3] Alone[2] (%)	NHOPI[4] Alone[2] (%)	Other Race Alone[2] (%)	Two or More Races (%)
City	78.5	6.5	2.9	0.8	0.3	5.1	5.9
MSA[1]	80.1	6.2	2.7	0.8	0.4	4.0	5.9
U.S.	72.5	12.7	5.5	0.8	0.2	4.9	3.3

Note: (1) Figures cover the Colorado Springs, CO Metropolitan Statistical Area; (2) Alone is defined as not being in combination with one or more other races; (3) American Indian and Alaska Native; (4) Native Hawaiian and Other Pacific Islander
Source: U.S. Census Bureau, 2015-2019 American Community Survey 5-Year Estimates

Hispanic or Latino Origin

Area	Total (%)	Mexican (%)	Puerto Rican (%)	Cuban (%)	Other (%)
City	17.6	11.3	1.4	0.5	4.5
MSA[1]	16.7	10.3	1.7	0.4	4.4
U.S.	18.0	11.2	1.7	0.7	4.3

Note: Persons of Hispanic or Latino origin can be of any race; (1) Figures cover the Colorado Springs, CO Metropolitan Statistical Area
Source: U.S. Census Bureau, 2015-2019 American Community Survey 5-Year Estimates

Ancestry

Area	German	Irish	English	American	Italian	Polish	French[2]	Scottish	Dutch
City	18.6	11.0	9.7	4.3	4.8	2.3	2.9	2.6	1.5
MSA[1]	18.8	10.9	9.4	4.4	4.9	2.4	2.8	2.7	1.5
U.S.	13.3	9.7	7.2	6.2	5.1	2.8	2.3	1.7	1.2

Note: Figures are the percentage of the total population reporting a particular ancestry. The nine most commonly reported ancestries in the U.S. are shown. Figures include multiple ancestries (e.g. if a person reported being Irish and Italian, they were included in both columns); (1) Figures cover the Colorado Springs, CO Metropolitan Statistical Area; (2) Excludes Basque
Source: U.S. Census Bureau, 2015-2019 American Community Survey 5-Year Estimates

Foreign-born Population

Area	Percent of Population Born in Any Foreign Country	Asia	Mexico	Europe	Caribbean	Central America[2]	South America	Africa	Canada
City	7.5	2.1	2.1	1.5	0.3	0.3	0.3	0.4	0.4
MSA[1]	6.9	1.9	1.8	1.6	0.3	0.3	0.3	0.4	0.3
U.S.	13.6	4.2	3.5	1.5	1.3	1.1	1.0	0.7	0.2

Note: (1) Figures cover the Colorado Springs, CO Metropolitan Statistical Area; (2) Excludes Mexico.
Source: U.S. Census Bureau, 2015-2019 American Community Survey 5-Year Estimates

Marital Status

Area	Never Married	Now Married[2]	Separated	Widowed	Divorced
City	31.2	49.5	1.6	4.6	13.1
MSA[1]	29.5	53.1	1.5	4.2	11.8
U.S.	33.4	48.1	1.9	5.8	10.9

Note: Figures are percentages and cover the population 15 years of age and older; (1) Figures cover the Colorado Springs, CO Metropolitan Statistical Area; (2) Excludes separated
Source: U.S. Census Bureau, 2015-2019 American Community Survey 5-Year Estimates

Disability by Age

Area	All Ages	Under 18 Years Old	18 to 64 Years Old	65 Years and Over
City	13.0	4.6	11.7	33.8
MSA[1]	12.4	4.4	11.4	32.7
U.S.	12.6	4.2	10.3	34.5

Note: Figures show percent of the civilian noninstitutionalized population that reported having a disability. Disability status is determined from six types of difficulty: vision, hearing, cognitive, ambulatory, self-care, and independent living. For children under 5 years old, hearing and vision difficulty are used to determine disability status. For children between the ages of 5 and 14, disability status is determined from hearing, vision, cognitive, ambulatory, and self-care difficulties. For people aged 15 years and older, they are considered to have a disability if they have difficulty with any one of the six difficulty types; Note: (1) Figures cover the Colorado Springs, CO Metropolitan Statistical Area
Source: U.S. Census Bureau, 2015-2019 American Community Survey 5-Year Estimates

Age

Area	Percent of Population									Median Age
	Under Age 5	Age 5–19	Age 20–34	Age 35–44	Age 45–54	Age 55–64	Age 65–74	Age 75–84	Age 85+	
City	6.5	19.3	24.6	12.6	11.9	11.6	8.1	3.8	1.5	34.7
MSA[1]	6.6	20.2	23.6	12.5	12.1	12.1	7.9	3.5	1.3	34.6
U.S.	6.1	19.1	20.7	12.6	13.0	12.9	9.1	4.6	1.9	38.1

Note: (1) Figures cover the Colorado Springs, CO Metropolitan Statistical Area
Source: U.S. Census Bureau, 2015-2019 American Community Survey 5-Year Estimates

Gender

Area	Males	Females	Males per 100 Females
City	232,440	232,431	100.0
MSA[1]	365,383	358,115	102.0
U.S.	159,886,919	164,810,876	97.0

Note: (1) Figures cover the Colorado Springs, CO Metropolitan Statistical Area
Source: U.S. Census Bureau, 2015-2019 American Community Survey 5-Year Estimates

Religious Groups by Family

Area	Catholic	Baptist	Non-Den.	Methodist[2]	Lutheran	LDS[3]	Pentecostal	Presbyterian[4]	Muslim[5]	Judaism
MSA[1]	8.4	4.3	7.4	2.4	2.0	3.0	1.1	2.1	0.1	0.1
U.S.	19.1	9.3	4.0	4.0	2.3	2.0	1.9	1.6	0.8	0.7

Note: Figures are the number of adherents as a percentage of the total population; (1) Figures cover the Colorado Springs, CO Metropolitan Statistical Area; (2) Methodist/Pietist; (3) Latter Day Saints; (4) Reformed; (5) Figures are estimates
Source: Association of Statisticians of American Religious Bodies, 2010 U.S. Religion Census: Religious Congregations & Membership Study

Religious Groups by Tradition

Area	Catholic	Evangelical Protestant	Mainline Protestant	Other Tradition	Black Protestant	Orthodox
MSA[1]	8.4	15.2	5.4	3.7	0.4	0.1
U.S.	19.1	16.2	7.3	4.3	1.6	0.3

Note: Figures are the number of adherents as a percentage of the total population; (1) Figures cover the Colorado Springs, CO Metropolitan Statistical Area
Source: Association of Statisticians of American Religious Bodies, 2010 U.S. Religion Census: Religious Congregations & Membership Study

ECONOMY

Gross Metropolitan Product

Area	2017	2018	2019	2020	Rank[2]
MSA[1]	33.1	34.9	36.6	38.5	84

Note: Figures are in billions of dollars; (1) Figures cover the Colorado Springs, CO Metropolitan Statistical Area; (2) Rank is based on 2018 data and ranges from 1 to 381
Source: U.S. Conference of Mayors, U.S. Metro Economies: GMP & Employment 2018-2020, September 2019

Economic Growth

Area	2015-17 (%)	2018 (%)	2019 (%)	2020 (%)	Rank[2]
MSA[1]	2.9	3.1	3.0	2.8	73
U.S.	1.9	2.9	2.3	2.1	–

Note: Figures are real gross metropolitan product (GMP) growth rates and represent average annual percent change; (1) Figures cover the Colorado Springs, CO Metropolitan Statistical Area; (2) Rank is based on 2017 2-year average annual percent change and ranges from 1 to 381
Source: U.S. Conference of Mayors, U.S. Metro Economies: GMP & Employment 2018-2020, September 2019

Metropolitan Area Exports

Area	2014	2015	2016	2017	2018	2019	Rank[2]
MSA[1]	856.6	832.4	786.9	819.7	850.6	864.2	172

Note: Figures are in millions of dollars; (1) Figures cover the Colorado Springs, CO Metropolitan Statistical Area; (2) Rank is based on 2019 data and ranges from 1 to 386
Source: U.S. Department of Commerce, International Trade Administration, Office of Trade and Economic Analysis, Industry and Analysis, Exports by Metropolitan Area, data extracted March 24, 2021

Building Permits

Area	Single-Family			Multi-Family			Total		
	2018	2019	Pct. Chg.	2018	2019	Pct. Chg.	2018	2019	Pct. Chg.
City	n/a	n/a	n/a	n/a	n/a	n/a	n/a	n/a	n/a
MSA[1]	4,229	4,051	-4.2	1,505	1,457	-3.2	5,734	5,508	-3.9
U.S.	855,300	862,100	0.7	473,500	523,900	10.6	1,328,800	1,386,000	4.3

Note: (1) Figures cover the Colorado Springs, CO Metropolitan Statistical Area; Figures represent new, privately-owned housing units authorized (unadjusted data); All permit data are based on estimates with imputation
Source: U.S. Census Bureau, Manufacturing, Mining, and Construction Statistics, Building Permits, 2018, 2019

Bankruptcy Filings

Area	Business Filings			Nonbusiness Filings		
	2019	2020	% Chg.	2019	2020	% Chg.
El Paso County	39	30	-23.1	1,525	1,154	-24.3
U.S.	22,780	21,655	-4.9	752,160	522,808	-30.5

Note: Business filings include Chapter 7, Chapter 9, Chapter 11, Chapter 12, Chapter 13, Chapter 15, and Section 304; Nonbusiness filings include Chapter 7, Chapter 11, and Chapter 13
Source: Administrative Office of the U.S. Courts, Business and Nonbusiness Bankruptcy, County Cases Commenced by Chapter of the Bankruptcy Code, During the 12-Month Period Ending December 31, 2019 and Business and Nonbusiness Bankruptcy, County Cases Commenced by Chapter of the Bankruptcy Code, During the 12-Month Period Ending December 31, 2020

Housing Vacancy Rates

Area	Gross Vacancy Rate[2] (%)			Year-Round Vacancy Rate[3] (%)			Rental Vacancy Rate[4] (%)			Homeowner Vacancy Rate[5] (%)		
	2018	2019	2020	2018	2019	2020	2018	2019	2020	2018	2019	2020
MSA[1]	n/a	n/a	n/a	n/a	n/a	n/a	n/a	n/a	n/a	n/a	n/a	n/a
U.S.	12.3	12.0	10.6	9.7	9.5	8.2	6.9	6.7	6.3	1.5	1.4	1.0

Note: (1) Figures cover the Colorado Springs, CO Metropolitan Statistical Area; (2) The percentage of the total housing inventory that is vacant; (3) The percentage of the housing inventory (excluding seasonal units) that is year-round vacant; (4) The percentage of rental inventory that is vacant for rent; (5) The percentage of homeowner inventory that is vacant for sale; n/a not available
Source: U.S. Census Bureau, Housing Vacancies and Homeownership Annual Statistics: 2018, 2019, 2020

INCOME

Income

Area	Per Capita ($)	Median Household ($)	Average Household ($)
City	34,076	64,712	84,708
MSA[1]	33,795	68,687	88,185
U.S.	34,103	62,843	88,607

Note: (1) Figures cover the Colorado Springs, CO Metropolitan Statistical Area
Source: U.S. Census Bureau, 2015-2019 American Community Survey 5-Year Estimates

Household Income Distribution

Area	Percent of Households Earning							
	Under $15,000	$15,000 -$24,999	$25,000 -$34,999	$35,000 -$49,999	$50,000 -$74,999	$75,000 -$99,999	$100,000 -$149,999	$150,000 and up
City	8.8	8.3	8.5	12.5	19.0	13.8	16.2	12.8
MSA[1]	7.8	7.4	8.1	12.0	19.0	14.3	17.4	13.9
U.S.	10.3	8.9	8.9	12.3	17.2	12.7	15.1	14.5

Note: (1) Figures cover the Colorado Springs, CO Metropolitan Statistical Area
Source: U.S. Census Bureau, 2015-2019 American Community Survey 5-Year Estimates

Poverty Rate

Area	All Ages	Under 18 Years Old	18 to 64 Years Old	65 Years and Over
City	11.7	15.8	11.1	7.0
MSA[1]	10.0	13.1	9.6	6.3
U.S.	13.4	18.5	12.6	9.3

Note: Figures are percentage of people whose income during the past 12 months was below the poverty level;
(1) Figures cover the Colorado Springs, CO Metropolitan Statistical Area
Source: U.S. Census Bureau, 2015-2019 American Community Survey 5-Year Estimates

CITY FINANCES

City Government Finances

Component	2017 ($000)	2017 ($ per capita)
Total Revenues	1,315,794	2,882
Total Expenditures	1,196,615	2,621
Debt Outstanding	2,481,573	5,435
Cash and Securities[1]	520,076	1,139

Note: (1) Cash and security holdings of a government at the close of its fiscal year,
including those of its dependent agencies, utilities, and liquor stores.
Source: U.S. Census Bureau, State & Local Government Finances 2017

City Government Revenue by Source

Source	2017 ($000)	2017 ($ per capita)	2017 (%)
General Revenue			
From Federal Government	32,875	72	2.5
From State Government	25,725	56	2.0
From Local Governments	979	2	0.1
Taxes			
Property	35,112	77	2.7
Sales and Gross Receipts	291,294	638	22.1
Personal Income	0	0	0.0
Corporate Income	0	0	0.0
Motor Vehicle License	0	0	0.0
Other Taxes	2,281	5	0.2
Current Charges	115,624	253	8.8
Liquor Store	0	0	0.0
Utility	723,895	1,586	55.0
Employee Retirement	0	0	0.0

Source: U.S. Census Bureau, State & Local Government Finances 2017

City Government Expenditures by Function

Function	2017 ($000)	2017 ($ per capita)	2017 (%)
General Direct Expenditures			
Air Transportation	13,636	29	1.1
Corrections	0	0	0.0
Education	0	0	0.0
Employment Security Administration	0	0	0.0
Financial Administration	29,187	63	2.4
Fire Protection	49,268	107	4.1
General Public Buildings	0	0	0.0
Governmental Administration, Other	17,610	38	1.5
Health	1,423	3	0.1
Highways	81,725	179	6.8
Hospitals	0	0	0.0
Housing and Community Development	10,507	23	0.9
Interest on General Debt	20,817	45	1.7
Judicial and Legal	8,215	18	0.7
Libraries	0	0	0.0
Parking	2,645	5	0.2
Parks and Recreation	28,865	63	2.4
Police Protection	92,069	201	7.7
Public Welfare	0	0	0.0
Sewerage	45,530	99	3.8
Solid Waste Management	0	0	0.0
Veterans' Services	0	0	0.0
Liquor Store	0	0	0.0
Utility	716,106	1,568	59.8
Employee Retirement	0	0	0.0

Source: U.S. Census Bureau, State & Local Government Finances 2017

EMPLOYMENT

Labor Force and Employment

Area	Civilian Labor Force			Workers Employed		
	Dec. 2019	Dec. 2020	% Chg.	Dec. 2019	Dec. 2020	% Chg.
City	238,705	245,635	2.9	232,124	223,547	-3.7
MSA[1]	356,603	365,426	2.5	346,681	333,941	-3.7
U.S.	164,007,000	160,017,000	-2.4	158,504,000	149,613,000	-5.6

Note: Data is not seasonally adjusted and covers workers 16 years of age and older; (1) Figures cover the Colorado Springs, CO Metropolitan Statistical Area
Source: Bureau of Labor Statistics, Local Area Unemployment Statistics

Unemployment Rate

Area	2020											
	Jan.	Feb.	Mar.	Apr.	May	Jun.	Jul.	Aug.	Sep.	Oct.	Nov.	Dec.
City	3.3	3.4	6.1	13.0	10.0	10.7	7.1	6.4	6.1	6.1	6.2	9.0
MSA[1]	3.3	3.4	6.2	12.6	9.7	10.5	6.9	6.2	5.9	6.0	6.0	8.6
U.S.	4.0	3.8	4.5	14.4	13.0	11.2	10.5	8.5	7.7	6.6	6.4	6.5

Note: Data is not seasonally adjusted and covers workers 16 years of age and older; (1) Figures cover the Colorado Springs, CO Metropolitan Statistical Area
Source: Bureau of Labor Statistics, Local Area Unemployment Statistics

Average Wages

Occupation	$/Hr.	Occupation	$/Hr.
Accountants and Auditors	36.30	Maintenance and Repair Workers	20.60
Automotive Mechanics	25.50	Marketing Managers	80.70
Bookkeepers	19.90	Network and Computer Systems Admin.	39.90
Carpenters	24.50	Nurses, Licensed Practical	27.50
Cashiers	13.90	Nurses, Registered	36.90
Computer Programmers	34.80	Nursing Assistants	15.90
Computer Systems Analysts	49.80	Office Clerks, General	20.40
Computer User Support Specialists	26.70	Physical Therapists	41.30
Construction Laborers	17.50	Physicians	107.00
Cooks, Restaurant	14.40	Plumbers, Pipefitters and Steamfitters	24.80
Customer Service Representatives	17.20	Police and Sheriff's Patrol Officers	35.00
Dentists	59.70	Postal Service Mail Carriers	25.30
Electricians	24.30	Real Estate Sales Agents	36.10
Engineers, Electrical	52.80	Retail Salespersons	15.80
Fast Food and Counter Workers	12.80	Sales Representatives, Technical/Scientific	51.70
Financial Managers	71.90	Secretaries, Exc. Legal/Medical/Executive	17.70
First-Line Supervisors of Office Workers	28.50	Security Guards	16.30
General and Operations Managers	62.50	Surgeons	138.50
Hairdressers/Cosmetologists	19.90	Teacher Assistants, Exc. Postsecondary*	14.30
Home Health and Personal Care Aides	14.60	Teachers, Secondary School, Exc. Sp. Ed.*	25.10
Janitors and Cleaners	15.00	Telemarketers	16.70
Landscaping/Groundskeeping Workers	15.30	Truck Drivers, Heavy/Tractor-Trailer	23.30
Lawyers	57.70	Truck Drivers, Light/Delivery Services	19.40
Maids and Housekeeping Cleaners	13.70	Waiters and Waitresses	15.20

Note: Wage data covers the Colorado Springs, CO Metropolitan Statistical Area; (*) Hourly wages were calculated from annual wage data based on a 40 hour work week; n/a not available.
Source: Bureau of Labor Statistics, Metro Area Occupational Employment & Wage Estimates, May 2020

Employment by Industry

Sector	MSA[1]		U.S.
	Number of Employees	Percent of Total	Percent of Total
Construction, Mining, and Logging	18,300	6.3	5.5
Education and Health Services	42,600	14.8	16.3
Financial Activities	19,000	6.6	6.1
Government	53,100	18.4	15.2
Information	5,200	1.8	1.9
Leisure and Hospitality	27,400	9.5	9.0
Manufacturing	11,700	4.1	8.5
Other Services	17,200	6.0	3.8
Professional and Business Services	47,900	16.6	14.4
Retail Trade	33,700	11.7	10.9
Transportation, Warehousing, and Utilities	6,400	2.2	4.6
Wholesale Trade	5,900	2.0	3.9

Note: Figures are non-farm employment as of December 2020. Figures are not seasonally adjusted and include workers 16 years of age and older; (1) Figures cover the Colorado Springs, CO Metropolitan Statistical Area
Source: Bureau of Labor Statistics, Current Employment Statistics, Employment, Hours, and Earnings

Employment by Occupation

Occupation Classification	City (%)	MSA[1] (%)	U.S. (%)
Management, Business, Science, and Arts	42.7	41.9	38.5
Natural Resources, Construction, and Maintenance	8.0	8.6	8.9
Production, Transportation, and Material Moving	8.7	9.3	13.2
Sales and Office	22.0	22.0	21.6
Service	18.7	18.2	17.8

Note: Figures cover employed civilians 16 years of age and older; (1) Figures cover the Colorado Springs, CO Metropolitan Statistical Area
Source: U.S. Census Bureau, 2015-2019 American Community Survey 5-Year Estimates

Occupations with Greatest Projected Employment Growth: 2020 – 2022

Occupation[1]	2020 Employment	2022 Projected Employment	Numeric Employment Change	Percent Employment Change
Software Developers, Applications	33,470	35,740	2,270	6.8
Personal Care Aides	30,000	31,610	1,610	5.4
Registered Nurses	54,810	56,090	1,280	2.3
Market Research Analysts and Marketing Specialists	21,470	22,380	910	4.2
Business Operations Specialists, All Other	49,470	50,350	880	1.8
Stock Clerks and Order Fillers	37,610	38,390	780	2.1
Computer Occupations, All Other	18,280	18,940	660	3.6
Accountants and Auditors	42,200	42,840	640	1.5
Software Developers, Systems Software	12,390	13,010	620	5.0
Sales Representatives, Wholesale and Manufacturing, Except Technical and Scientific Products	28,620	29,170	550	1.9

Note: Projections cover Colorado; (1) Sorted by numeric employment change
Source: www.projectionscentral.com, State Occupational Projections, 2020–2022 Short-Term Projections

Fastest-Growing Occupations: 2020 – 2022

Occupation[1]	2020 Employment	2022 Projected Employment	Numeric Employment Change	Percent Employment Change
Information Security Analysts	3,860	4,170	310	8.0
Software Developers, Applications	33,470	35,740	2,270	6.8
Statisticians	1,230	1,310	80	6.5
Operations Research Analysts	940	1,000	60	6.4
Veterinary Technologists and Technicians	4,490	4,750	260	5.8
Health Specialties Teachers, Postsecondary	6,160	6,500	340	5.5
Personal Care Aides	30,000	31,610	1,610	5.4
Veterinarians	2,820	2,970	150	5.3
Interpreters and Translators	1,980	2,080	100	5.1
Software Developers, Systems Software	12,390	13,010	620	5.0

Note: Projections cover Colorado; (1) Sorted by percent employment change and excludes occupations with numeric employment change less than 50
Source: www.projectionscentral.com, State Occupational Projections, 2020–2022 Short-Term Projections

TAXES

State Corporate Income Tax Rates

State	Tax Rate (%)	Income Brackets ($)	Num. of Brackets	Financial Institution Tax Rate (%)[a]	Federal Income Tax Ded.
Colorado	4.55	Flat rate	1	4.55	No

Note: Tax rates as of January 1, 2021; (a) Rates listed are the corporate income tax rate applied to financial institutions or excise taxes based on income. Some states have other taxes based upon the value of deposits or shares.
Source: Federation of Tax Administrators, State Corporate Income Tax Rates, January 1, 2021

State Individual Income Tax Rates

State	Tax Rate (%)	Income Brackets ($)	Personal Exemptions ($)			Standard Ded. ($)	
			Single	Married	Depend.	Single	Married
Colorado	4.55	Flat rate	(d)	(d)	(d)	12,550	25,100 (d)

Note: Tax rates as of January 1, 2021; Local- and county-level taxes are not included; Federal income tax is not deductible on state income tax returns; (d) These states use the personal exemption/standard deduction amounts provided in the federal Internal Revenue Code.
Source: Federation of Tax Administrators, State Individual Income Tax Rates, January 1, 2021

Various State Sales and Excise Tax Rates

State	State Sales Tax (%)	Gasoline[1] (¢/gal.)	Cigarette[2] ($/pack)	Spirits[3] ($/gal.)	Wine[4] ($/gal.)	Beer[5] ($/gal.)	Recreational Marijuana (%)
Colorado	2.9	22	1.94	2.28	0.32	0.08	(d)

Note: All tax rates as of January 1, 2021; (1) The American Petroleum Institute has developed a methodology for determining the average tax rate on a gallon of fuel. Rates may include any of the following: excise taxes, environmental fees, storage tank fees, other fees or taxes, general sales tax, and local taxes; (2) The federal excise tax of $1.0066 per pack and local taxes are not included; (3) Rates are those applicable to off-premise sales of 40% alcohol by volume (a.b.v.) distilled spirits in 750ml containers. Local excise taxes are excluded; (4) Rates are those applicable to off-premise sales of 11% a.b.v. non-carbonated wine in 750ml containers; (5) Rates are those applicable to off-premise sales of 4.7% a.b.v. beer in 12 ounce containers; (d) 15% excise tax (levied on wholesale at average market rate); 15% excise tax (retail price)
Source: Tax Foundation, 2021 Facts & Figures: How Does Your State Compare?

State Business Tax Climate Index Rankings

State	Overall Rank	Corporate Tax Rank	Individual Income Tax Rank	Sales Tax Rank	Property Tax Rank	Unemployment Insurance Tax Rank
Colorado	21	10	14	36	32	41

Note: The index is a measure of how each state's tax laws affect economic performance. The lower the rank, the more favorable a state's tax system is for business. States without a given tax are given a ranking of 1. The scores/rankings for the District of Columbia do not affect other states. The 2021 index represents the tax climate as of July 1, 2020.
Source: Tax Foundation, State Business Tax Climate Index 2021

TRANSPORTATION

Means of Transportation to Work

Area	Car/Truck/Van		Public Transportation			Bicycle	Walked	Other Means	Worked at Home
	Drove Alone	Car-pooled	Bus	Subway	Railroad				
City	77.8	10.9	0.9	0.0	0.0	0.6	1.9	0.9	6.9
MSA[1]	77.0	10.4	0.6	0.0	0.0	0.4	3.4	1.0	7.0
U.S.	76.3	9.0	2.4	1.9	0.6	0.5	2.7	1.4	5.2

Note: Figures are percentages and cover workers 16 years of age and older; (1) Figures cover the Colorado Springs, CO Metropolitan Statistical Area
Source: U.S. Census Bureau, 2015-2019 American Community Survey 5-Year Estimates

Travel Time to Work

Area	Less Than 10 Minutes	10 to 19 Minutes	20 to 29 Minutes	30 to 44 Minutes	45 to 59 Minutes	60 to 89 Minutes	90 Minutes or More
City	11.6	35.9	28.5	15.2	3.5	3.0	2.3
MSA[1]	11.6	32.8	27.2	17.4	5.0	3.7	2.3
U.S.	12.2	28.4	20.8	20.8	8.3	6.4	2.9

Note: Note: Figures are percentages and include workers 16 years old and over; (1) Figures cover the Colorado Springs, CO Metropolitan Statistical Area
Source: U.S. Census Bureau, 2015-2019 American Community Survey 5-Year Estimates

Key Congestion Measures

Measure	1982	1992	2002	2012	2017
Annual Hours of Delay, Total (000)	1,240	5,111	11,613	16,141	17,883
Annual Hours of Delay, Per Auto Commuter	7	23	34	38	43
Annual Congestion Cost, Total (million $)	9	54	157	289	330
Annual Congestion Cost, Per Auto Commuter ($)	122	345	612	666	716

Note: Covers the Colorado Springs CO urban area
Source: Texas A&M Transportation Institute, 2019 Urban Mobility Report

Freeway Travel Time Index

Measure	1982	1987	1992	1997	2002	2007	2012	2017
Urban Area Index[1]	1.03	1.06	1.10	1.14	1.15	1.16	1.15	1.15
Urban Area Rank[1,2]	76	66	59	47	61	63	71	71

Note: Freeway Travel Time Index—the ratio of travel time in the peak period to the travel time at free-flow conditions. For example, a value of 1.30 indicates a 20-minute free-flow trip takes 26 minutes in the peak (20 minutes x 1.30 = 26 minutes); (1) Covers the Colorado Springs CO urban area; (2) Rank is based on 101 larger urban areas (#1 = highest travel time index)
Source: Texas A&M Transportation Institute, 2019 Urban Mobility Report

Public Transportation

Agency Name / Mode of Transportation	Vehicles Operated in Maximum Service[1]	Annual Unlinked Passenger Trips[2] (in thous.)	Annual Passenger Miles[3] (in thous.)
Colorado Springs Transit System			
Bus (purchased transportation)	51	3,214.7	12,067.7
Demand Response (purchased transportation)	42	147.1	1,456.6
Demand Response Taxi (purchased transportation)	14	7.5	38.5
Vanpool (directly operated)	26	42.1	2,499.8

Note: (1) Number of revenue vehicles operated by the given mode and type of service to meet the annual maximum service requirement. This is the revenue vehicle count during the peak season of the year; on the week and day that maximum service is provided. Vehicles operated in maximum service (VOMS) exclude atypical days and one-time special events; (2) Number of passengers who boarded public transportation vehicles. Passengers are counted each time they board a vehicle no matter how many vehicles they use to travel from their origin to their destination. (3) Sum of the distances ridden by all passengers during the entire fiscal year.
Source: Federal Transit Administration, National Transit Database, 2019

Air Transportation

Airport Name and Code / Type of Service	Passenger Airlines[1]	Passenger Enplanements	Freight Carriers[2]	Freight (lbs)
City of Colorado Springs Municipal (COS)				
Domestic service (U.S. carriers - 2020)	17	360,214	5	8,706,842
International service (U.S. carriers - 2019)	2	155	2	140,740

Note: (1) Includes all U.S.-based major, minor and commuter airlines that carried at least one passenger during the year; (2) Includes all U.S.-based airlines and freight carriers that transported at least one pound of freight during the year.
Source: Bureau of Transportation Statistics, The Intermodal Transportation Database, Air Carriers: T-100 Domestic Market (U.S. Carriers), 2020; Bureau of Transportation Statistics, The Intermodal Transportation Database, Air Carriers: T-100 International Market (U.S. Carriers), 2019

BUSINESSES

Major Business Headquarters

Company Name	Industry	Rankings	
		Fortune[1]	Forbes[2]
No companies listed	-	-	-

Note: (1) Companies that produce a 10-K are ranked 1 to 500 based on 2019 revenue; (2) All private companies with at least $2 billion in annual revenue through the end of their most current fiscal year are ranked 1 to 219; companies listed are headquartered in the city; dashes indicate no ranking
Source: Fortune, "Fortune 500," June/July 2020; Forbes, "America's Largest Private Companies," 2020

Fastest-Growing Businesses

According to *Inc.*, Colorado Springs is home to three of America's 500 fastest-growing private companies: **Hemp Depot** (#32); **Quantum Metric** (#124); **Professional Transition Strategies** (#248). Criteria: must be an independent, privately-held, for-profit, U.S. corporation, proprietorship or partnership as of December 31, 2019; revenues must be at least $100,000 in 2016 and $2 million in 2019; must have four-year operating/sales history. *Inc., "America's 500 Fastest-Growing Private Companies," 2020*

According to Deloitte, Colorado Springs is home to one of North America's 500 fastest-growing high-technology companies: **Quantum Metric** (#108). Companies are ranked by percentage growth in revenue over a four-year period. Criteria for inclusion: company must be headquartered within North America; must own proprietary intellectual property or technology that is sold to customers in products that contributes to a significant portion of the company's operating revenue; must have been in business for a minumum of four years with 2016 operating revenues of at least $50,000 USD/CD and 2019 operating revenues of at least $5 million USD/CD. *Deloitte, 2020 Technology Fast 500™*

Living Environment

COST OF LIVING

Cost of Living Index

Composite Index	Groceries	Housing	Utilities	Trans-portation	Health Care	Misc. Goods/ Services
103.6	97.6	106.9	99.0	109.0	104.8	103.0

Note: The Cost of Living Index measures regional differences in the cost of consumer goods and services, excluding taxes and non-consumer expenditures, for professional and managerial households in the top income quintile. It is based on more than 50,000 prices covering almost 60 different items for which prices are collected three times a year by chambers of commerce, economic development organizations or university applied economic centers in each participating urban area. The numbers shown should be read as a percentage above or below the national average of 100. For example, a value of 115.4 in the groceries column indicates that grocery prices are 15.4% higher than the national average. Small differences in the index numbers should not be interpreted as significant; Figures cover the Colorado Springs CO urban area.
Source: The Council for Community and Economic Research, Cost of Living Index, 2020

Grocery Prices

Area[1]	T-Bone Steak ($/pound)	Frying Chicken ($/pound)	Whole Milk ($/half gal.)	Eggs ($/dozen)	Orange Juice ($/64 oz.)	Coffee ($/11.5 oz.)
City[2]	13.95	1.39	1.76	1.27	3.39	4.55
Avg.	11.78	1.39	2.05	1.47	3.57	4.34
Min.	8.03	0.94	1.03	0.74	2.94	3.02
Max.	15.86	2.65	4.31	3.77	5.44	8.69

*Note: (1) Values for the local area are compared with the average, minimum and maximum values for all 284 areas in the Cost of Living Index; (2) Figures cover the Colorado Springs CO urban area; **T-Bone Steak** (price per pound); **Frying Chicken** (price per pound, whole fryer); **Whole Milk** (half gallon carton); **Eggs** (price per dozen, Grade A, large); **Orange Juice** (64 oz. Tropicana or Florida Natural); **Coffee** (11.5 oz. can, vacuum-packed, Maxwell House, Hills Bros, or Folgers).*
Source: The Council for Community and Economic Research, Cost of Living Index, 2020

Housing and Utility Costs

Area[1]	New Home Price ($)	Apartment Rent ($/month)	All Electric ($/month)	Part Electric ($/month)	Other Energy ($/month)	Telephone ($/month)
City[2]	377,643	1,386	-	89.03	76.10	182.20
Avg.	368,594	1,168	170.86	100.47	65.28	184.30
Min.	190,567	502	91.58	31.42	26.08	169.60
Max.	2,227,806	4,738	470.38	280.31	280.06	206.50

*Note: (1) Values for the local area are compared with the average, minimum and maximum values for all 284 areas in the Cost of Living Index; (2) Figures cover the Colorado Springs CO urban area; **New Home Price** (2,400 sf living area, 8,000 sf lot, in urban area with full utilities); **Apartment Rent** (950 sf 2 bedroom/1.5 or 2 bath, unfurnished, excluding all utilities except water); **All Electric** (average monthly cost for an all-electric home); **Part Electric** (average monthly cost for a part-electric home); **Other Energy** (average monthly cost for natural gas, fuel oil, coal, wood, and any other forms of energy except electricity); **Telephone** (price includes the base monthly rate plus taxes and fees for three lines of mobile phone service).*
Source: The Council for Community and Economic Research, Cost of Living Index, 2020

Health Care, Transportation, and Other Costs

Area[1]	Doctor ($/visit)	Dentist ($/visit)	Optometrist ($/visit)	Gasoline ($/gallon)	Beauty Salon ($/visit)	Men's Shirt ($)
City[2]	126.71	105.77	114.08	2.41	42.90	28.17
Avg.	115.44	99.32	108.10	2.21	39.27	31.37
Min.	36.68	59.00	51.36	1.71	19.00	11.00
Max.	219.00	153.10	250.97	3.46	82.05	58.33

*Note: (1) Values for the local area are compared with the average, minimum and maximum values for all 284 areas in the Cost of Living Index; (2) Figures cover the Colorado Springs CO urban area; **Doctor** (general practitioners routine exam of an established patient); **Dentist** (adult teeth cleaning and periodic oral examination); **Optometrist** (full vision eye exam for established adult patient); **Gasoline** (one gallon regular unleaded, national brand, including all taxes, cash price at self-service pump if available); **Beauty Salon** (woman's shampoo, trim, and blow-dry); **Men's Shirt** (cotton/polyester dress shirt, pinpoint weave, long sleeves).*
Source: The Council for Community and Economic Research, Cost of Living Index, 2020

HOUSING

Homeownership Rate

Area	2012 (%)	2013 (%)	2014 (%)	2015 (%)	2016 (%)	2017 (%)	2018 (%)	2019 (%)	2020 (%)
MSA[1]	n/a	n/a	n/a	n/a	n/a	n/a	n/a	n/a	n/a
U.S.	65.4	65.1	64.5	63.7	63.4	63.9	64.4	64.6	66.6

Note: (1) Figures cover the Colorado Springs, CO Metropolitan Statistical Area; n/a not available
Source: U.S. Census Bureau, Housing Vacancies and Homeownership Annual Statistics: 2012-2020

House Price Index (HPI)

Area	National Ranking[2]	Quarterly Change (%)	One-Year Change (%)	Five-Year Change (%)	Since 1991Q1 (%)
MSA[1]	19	3.08	8.89	51.30	301.84
U.S.[3]	–	3.81	10.77	38.99	205.12

Note: The HPI is a weighted repeat sales index. It measures average price changes in repeat sales or refinancings on the same properties. This information is obtained by reviewing repeat mortgage transactions on single-family properties whose mortgages have been purchased or securitized by Fannie Mae or Freddie Mac since January 1975; (1) Figures cover the Colorado Springs, CO Metropolitan Statistical Area; (2) Rankings are based on annual percentage change for all metro areas containing at least 15,000 transactions over the last 10 years and ranges from 1 to 253; (3) figures based on a weighted average of Census Division estimates using a seasonally adjusted, purchase-only index; all figures are for the period ending December 31, 2020
Source: Federal Housing Finance Agency, Change in Metropolitan Area House Price Indexes, April 7, 2021

Median Single-Family Home Prices

Area	2018	2019	2020[p]	Percent Change 2019 to 2020
MSA[1]	312.2	320.5	361.7	12.9
U.S. Average	261.6	274.6	299.9	9.2

Note: Figures are median sales prices of existing single-family homes in thousands of dollars; (p) preliminary; (1) Figures cover the Colorado Springs, CO Metropolitan Statistical Area
Source: National Association of Realtors, Median Sales Price of Existing Single-Family Homes for Metropolitan Areas, 4th Quarter 2020

Qualifying Income Based on Median Sales Price of Existing Single-Family Homes

Area	With 5% Down ($)	With 10% Down ($)	With 20% Down ($)
MSA[1]	70,228	66,532	59,140
U.S. Average	59,266	56,147	49,908

Note: Figures are preliminary; Qualifying income is based on a mortgage rate of 2.81%. Monthly principal and interest payment is limited to 25% of income; (1) Figures cover the Colorado Springs, CO Metropolitan Statistical Area
Source: National Association of Realtors, Qualifying Income Based on Median Sales Price of Existing Single-Family Homes for Metropolitan Areas, 4th Quarter 2020

Home Value Distribution

Area	Under $50,000	$50,000 -$99,999	$100,000 -$149,999	$150,000 -$199,999	$200,000 -$299,999	$300,000 -$499,999	$500,000 -$999,999	$1,000,000 or more
City	3.0	2.1	6.5	14.5	33.6	30.4	8.6	1.2
MSA[1]	3.1	2.0	6.1	14.3	31.7	31.1	10.4	1.2
U.S.	6.9	12.0	13.3	14.0	19.6	19.3	11.4	3.4

Note: Figures are percentages and cover owner-occupied housing units; (1) Figures cover the Colorado Springs, CO Metropolitan Statistical Area
Source: U.S. Census Bureau, 2015-2019 American Community Survey 5-Year Estimates

Year Housing Structure Built

Area	2010 or Later	2000 -2009	1990 -1999	1980 -1989	1970 -1979	1960 -1969	1950 -1959	1940 -1949	Before 1940	Median Year
City	6.5	15.7	15.9	18.6	18.3	10.2	7.1	1.9	5.8	1984
MSA[1]	7.6	18.8	16.9	17.5	17.0	8.9	6.5	1.6	5.2	1986
U.S.	5.2	14.0	13.9	13.4	15.2	10.6	10.3	4.9	12.6	1978

Note: Figures are percentages except for Median Year; Note: (1) Figures cover the Colorado Springs, CO Metropolitan Statistical Area
Source: U.S. Census Bureau, 2015-2019 American Community Survey 5-Year Estimates

Gross Monthly Rent

Area	Under $500	$500 -$999	$1,000 -$1,499	$1,500 -$1,999	$2,000 -$2,499	$2,500 -$2,999	$3,000 and up	Median ($)
City	3.9	34.3	38.3	17.5	3.5	1.8	0.7	1,131
MSA[1]	3.8	31.8	36.9	21.1	4.0	1.8	0.6	1,173
U.S.	9.4	36.2	30.0	14.0	5.6	2.4	2.4	1,062

Note: Figures are percentages except for Median; Gross rent is the contract rent plus the estimated average monthly cost of utilities (electricity, gas, and water and sewer) and fuels (oil, coal, kerosene, wood, etc.) if these are paid by the renter (or paid for the renter by someone else); (1) Figures cover the Colorado Springs, CO Metropolitan Statistical Area
Source: U.S. Census Bureau, 2015-2019 American Community Survey 5-Year Estimates

HEALTH

Health Risk Factors

Category	MSA[1] (%)	U.S. (%)
Adults aged 18–64 who have any kind of health care coverage	89.9	87.3
Adults who reported being in good or better health	85.5	82.4
Adults who have been told they have high blood cholesterol	31.7	33.0
Adults who have been told they have high blood pressure	26.4	32.3
Adults who are current smokers	16.1	17.1
Adults who currently use E-cigarettes	5.9	4.6
Adults who currently use chewing tobacco, snuff, or snus	2.4	4.0
Adults who are heavy drinkers[2]	4.1	6.3
Adults who are binge drinkers[3]	15.6	17.4
Adults who are overweight (BMI 25.0 - 29.9)	37.6	35.3
Adults who are obese (BMI 30.0 - 99.8)	22.8	31.3
Adults who participated in any physical activities in the past month	79.9	74.4
Adults who always or nearly always wears a seat belt	96.5	94.3

Note: (1) Figures cover the Colorado Springs, CO Metropolitan Statistical Area; (2) Heavy drinkers are classified as adult men having more than 14 drinks per week and adult women having more than 7 drinks per week; (3) Binge drinkers are classified as males having five or more drinks on one occasion or females having four or more drinks on one occasion
Source: Centers for Disease Control and Prevention, Behaviorial Risk Factor Surveillance System, SMART: Selected Metropolitan Area Risk Trends, 2017

Acute and Chronic Health Conditions

Category	MSA[1] (%)	U.S. (%)
Adults who have ever been told they had a heart attack	3.5	4.2
Adults who have ever been told they have angina or coronary heart disease	3.1	3.9
Adults who have ever been told they had a stroke	1.8	3.0
Adults who have ever been told they have asthma	15.7	14.2
Adults who have ever been told they have arthritis	21.5	24.9
Adults who have ever been told they have diabetes[2]	6.8	10.5
Adults who have ever been told they had skin cancer	6.8	6.2
Adults who have ever been told they had any other types of cancer	7.3	7.1
Adults who have ever been told they have COPD	4.4	6.5
Adults who have ever been told they have kidney disease	2.1	3.0
Adults who have ever been told they have a form of depression	19.5	20.5

Note: (1) Figures cover the Colorado Springs, CO Metropolitan Statistical Area; (2) Figures do not include pregnancy-related, borderline, or pre-diabetes
Source: Centers for Disease Control and Prevention, Behaviorial Risk Factor Surveillance System, SMART: Selected Metropolitan Area Risk Trends, 2017

Health Screening and Vaccination Rates

Category	MSA[1] (%)	U.S. (%)
Adults aged 65+ who have had flu shot within the past year	68.5	60.7
Adults aged 65+ who have ever had a pneumonia vaccination	83.0	75.4
Adults who have ever been tested for HIV	42.6	36.1
Adults who have ever had the shingles or zoster vaccine?	34.3	28.9
Adults who have had their blood cholesterol checked within the last five years	84.6	85.9

Note: n/a not available; (1) Figures cover the Colorado Springs, CO Metropolitan Statistical Area.
Source: Centers for Disease Control and Prevention, Behaviorial Risk Factor Surveillance System, SMART: Selected Metropolitan Area Risk Trends, 2017

Disability Status

Category	MSA[1] (%)	U.S. (%)
Adults who reported being deaf	4.1	6.7
Are you blind or have serious difficulty seeing, even when wearing glasses?	3.2	4.5
Are you limited in any way in any of your usual activities due of arthritis?	10.9	12.9
Do you have difficulty doing errands alone?	6.2	6.8
Do you have difficulty dressing or bathing?	2.5	3.6
Do you have serious difficulty concentrating/remembering/making decisions?	12.3	10.7
Do you have serious difficulty walking or climbing stairs?	11.0	13.6

Note: (1) Figures cover the Colorado Springs, CO Metropolitan Statistical Area.
Source: Centers for Disease Control and Prevention, Behaviorial Risk Factor Surveillance System, SMART: Selected Metropolitan Area Risk Trends, 2017

Mortality Rates for the Top 10 Causes of Death in the U.S.

ICD-10[a] Sub-Chapter	ICD-10[a] Code	Age-Adjusted Mortality Rate[1] per 100,000 population	
		County[2]	U.S.
Malignant neoplasms	C00-C97	141.4	149.2
Ischaemic heart diseases	I20-I25	69.1	90.5
Other forms of heart disease	I30-I51	41.1	52.2
Chronic lower respiratory diseases	J40-J47	48.8	39.6
Other degenerative diseases of the nervous system	G30-G31	45.4	37.6
Cerebrovascular diseases	I60-I69	39.2	37.2
Other external causes of accidental injury	W00-X59	49.0	36.1
Organic, including symptomatic, mental disorders	F01-F09	28.3	29.4
Hypertensive diseases	I10-I15	29.2	24.1
Diabetes mellitus	E10-E14	19.9	21.5

Note: (a) ICD-10 = International Classification of Diseases 10th Revision; (1) Mortality rates are a three-year average covering 2017-2019; (2) Figures cover El Paso County.
Source: Centers for Disease Control and Prevention, National Center for Health Statistics. Underlying Cause of Death 1999-2019 on CDC WONDER Online Database

Mortality Rates for Selected Causes of Death

ICD-10[a] Sub-Chapter	ICD-10[a] Code	Age-Adjusted Mortality Rate[1] per 100,000 population	
		County[2]	U.S.
Assault	X85-Y09	6.7	6.0
Diseases of the liver	K70-K76	19.2	14.4
Human immunodeficiency virus (HIV) disease	B20-B24	Unreliable	1.5
Influenza and pneumonia	J09-J18	8.5	13.8
Intentional self-harm	X60-X84	26.1	14.1
Malnutrition	E40-E46	3.0	2.3
Obesity and other hyperalimentation	E65-E68	3.1	2.1
Renal failure	N17-N19	10.1	12.6
Transport accidents	V01-V99	15.8	12.3
Viral hepatitis	B15-B19	1.7	1.2

Note: (a) ICD-10 = International Classification of Diseases 10th Revision; (1) Mortality rates are a three-year average covering 2017-2019; (2) Figures cover El Paso County; Data are suppressed when the data meet the criteria for confidentiality constraints; Mortality rates are flagged as unreliable when the rate would be calculated with a numerator of 20 or less.
Source: Centers for Disease Control and Prevention, National Center for Health Statistics. Underlying Cause of Death 1999-2019 on CDC WONDER Online Database

Health Insurance Coverage

Area	With Health Insurance	With Private Health Insurance	With Public Health Insurance	Without Health Insurance	Population Under Age 19 Without Health Insurance
City	92.2	68.7	36.6	7.8	4.2
MSA[1]	92.8	71.1	35.3	7.2	4.1
U.S.	91.2	67.9	35.1	8.8	5.1

Note: Figures are percentages that cover the civilian noninstitutionalized population; (1) Figures cover the Colorado Springs, CO Metropolitan Statistical Area
Source: U.S. Census Bureau, 2015-2019 American Community Survey 5-Year Estimates

Number of Medical Professionals

Area	MDs[3]	DOs[3,4]	Dentists	Podiatrists	Chiropractors	Optometrists
County[1] (number)	1,402	221	753	32	314	177
County[1] (rate[2])	196.9	31.0	104.5	4.4	43.6	24.6
U.S. (rate[2])	282.9	22.7	71.2	6.2	28.1	16.9

08041
Note: Data as of 2019 unless noted; (1) Data covers El Paso County; (2) Rate per 100,000 population; (3) Data as of 2018 and includes all active, non-federal physicians; (4) Doctor of Osteopathic Medicine
Source: U.S. Department of Health and Human Services, Health Resources and Services Administration, Bureau of Health Professions, Area Resource File (ARF) 2019-2020

EDUCATION

Public School District Statistics

District Name	Schls	Pupils	Pupil/ Teacher Ratio	Minority Pupils[1] (%)	Free Lunch Eligible[2] (%)	IEP[3] (%)
Academy School District No. 20	38	26,178	16.6	28.8	8.7	n/a
Cheyenne Mountain SD No. 12	11	5,274	14.6	30.5	10.1	n/a
Colorado Springs SD No. 11	56	26,395	16.4	49.5	48.4	n/a
Harrison School District No. 2	27	11,735	15.4	75.3	61.2	n/a
School District No. 3	16	9,592	16.9	51.8	32.5	n/a

Note: Table includes school districts with 2,000 or more students; (1) Percentage of students that are not non-Hispanic white; (2) Percentage of students that are eligible for the free lunch program; (3) Percentage of students that have an Individualized Education Program.
Source: U.S. Department of Education, National Center for Education Statistics, Common Core of Data, Local Education Agency (School District) Universe Survey: School Year 2018-2019; U.S. Department of Education, National Center for Education Statistics, Common Core of Data, Public Elementary/Secondary School Universe Survey: School Year 2018-2019

Best High Schools

According to *U.S. News,* Colorado Springs is home to one of the top 500 high schools in the U.S.: **The Vanguard School** (#154). Nearly 18,000 public, magnet and charter schools were ranked based on their performance on state assessments and how well they prepare students for college. *U.S. News & World Report, "Best High Schools 2020"*

Highest Level of Education

Area	Less than H.S.	H.S. Diploma	Some College, No Deg.	Associate Degree	Bachelor's Degree	Master's Degree	Prof. School Degree	Doctorate Degree
City	6.1	20.0	23.4	10.6	24.3	12.0	2.0	1.5
MSA[1]	5.6	20.5	24.0	11.3	23.5	11.8	1.8	1.4
U.S.	12.0	27.0	20.4	8.5	19.8	8.8	2.1	1.4

Note: Figures cover persons age 25 and over; (1) Figures cover the Colorado Springs, CO Metropolitan Statistical Area
Source: U.S. Census Bureau, 2015-2019 American Community Survey 5-Year Estimates

Educational Attainment by Race

Area	High School Graduate or Higher (%)					Bachelor's Degree or Higher (%)				
	Total	White	Black	Asian	Hisp.[2]	Total	White	Black	Asian	Hisp.[2]
City	93.9	95.3	94.2	86.3	80.6	39.9	42.7	25.7	48.4	20.9
MSA[1]	94.4	95.5	94.5	87.4	82.7	38.5	40.5	27.2	44.8	20.9
U.S.	88.0	89.9	86.0	87.1	68.7	32.1	33.5	21.6	54.3	16.4

Note: Figures shown cover persons 25 years old and over; (1) Figures cover the Colorado Springs, CO Metropolitan Statistical Area; (2) People of Hispanic origin can be of any race
Source: U.S. Census Bureau, 2015-2019 American Community Survey 5-Year Estimates

School Enrollment by Grade and Control

Area	Preschool (%)		Kindergarten (%)		Grades 1 - 4 (%)		Grades 5 - 8 (%)		Grades 9 - 12 (%)	
	Public	Private	Public	Private	Public	Private	Public	Private	Public	Private
City	57.1	42.9	89.3	10.7	92.5	7.5	92.5	7.5	92.0	8.0
MSA[1]	62.1	37.9	89.5	10.5	92.5	7.5	92.6	7.4	92.2	7.8
U.S.	59.1	40.9	87.6	12.4	89.5	10.5	89.4	10.6	90.1	9.9

Note: Figures shown cover persons 3 years old and over; (1) Figures cover the Colorado Springs, CO Metropolitan Statistical Area
Source: U.S. Census Bureau, 2015-2019 American Community Survey 5-Year Estimates

Higher Education

Four-Year Colleges			Two-Year Colleges			Medical Schools[1]	Law Schools[2]	Voc/ Tech[3]
Public	Private Non-profit	Private For-profit	Public	Private Non-profit	Private For-profit			
2	3	2	0	0	4	0	0	4

Note: Figures cover institutions located within the city limits and include main campuses only; (1) includes schools accredited by the Liaison Committee on Medical Education and the American Osteopathic Association's Commission on Osteopathic College Accreditation; (2) includes ABA-accredited schools, schools with provisional ABA accreditation, and state accredited schools; (3) includes all schools with programs that are less than 2 years.
Source: National Center for Education Statistics, Integrated Postsecondary Education System (IPEDS), 2019-20; Wikipedia, List of Medical Schools in the United States, accessed April 2, 2021; Wikipedia, List of Law Schools in the United States, accessed April 2, 2021

According to *U.S. News & World Report,* the Colorado Springs, CO metro area is home to two of the top 100 liberal arts colleges in the U.S.: **Colorado College** (#25 tie); **United States Air Force Academy** (#28 tie). The indicators used to capture academic quality fall into a number of categories: assessment by administrators at peer institutions; retention of students; faculty resources; student selectivity; financial resources; alumni giving; high school counselor ratings of colleges; and graduation rate. *U.S. News & World Report, "America's Best Colleges 2021"*

EMPLOYERS

Major Employers

Company Name	Industry
Children's Hospital Colorado	Healthcare
Colorado State University	Education
Community Hospital Assn	Healthcare
Denver International Airport	Airports
Exempla St Joseph Hospital	Healthcare
Great-West Funds Inc	Financial services
Great-West Life & Annuity Ins	Insurance
Keystone Resort	Recreation association
Level 3 Communications Inc	Communications
Lockheed Martin Corp	Technology
Lockheed Martin Space Systems	Defense systems & equipment
Memorial Hospital North	Healthcare
Penrose Hospital	Healthcare
Peterson AFB	U.S. military
Poudre Valley Hospital	Healthcare
Schriever Air Force Base	U.S. military
Terumo	Healthcare
University of Boulder	Education
University of Colorado Health	Healthcare
University of Colorado-Boulder	Education
University of Northern Colorado	Education
Verizon Wireless	Wireless communcations
Western Union Co	Payment services

Note: Companies shown are located within the Colorado Springs, CO Metropolitan Statistical Area.
Source: Hoovers.com; Wikipedia

PUBLIC SAFETY

Crime Rate

Area	All Crimes	Violent Crimes				Property Crimes		
		Murder	Rape[3]	Robbery	Aggrav. Assault	Burglary	Larceny -Theft	Motor Vehicle Theft
City	4,251.7	4.8	89.9	101.1	389.2	500.4	2,521.6	644.6
Suburbs[1]	1,634.0	3.7	56.3	25.7	166.4	213.4	951.5	216.8
Metro[2]	3,313.4	4.4	77.8	74.1	309.4	397.5	1,958.8	491.3
U.S.	2,489.3	5.0	42.6	81.6	250.2	340.5	1,549.5	219.9

Note: Figures are crimes per 100,000 population; (1) All areas within the metro area that are located outside the city limits; (2) Figures cover the Colorado Springs, CO Metropolitan Statistical Area; (3) All figures shown were reported using the revised Uniform Crime Reporting (UCR) definition of rape.
Source: FBI Uniform Crime Reports, 2019

Hate Crimes

Area	Number of Quarters Reported	Number of Incidents per Bias Motivation					
		Race/Ethnicity/ Ancestry	Religion	Sexual Orientation	Disability	Gender	Gender Identity
City	4	6	2	4	0	0	0
U.S.	4	3,963	1,521	1,195	157	69	198

Source: Federal Bureau of Investigation, Hate Crime Statistics 2019

Identity Theft Consumer Reports

Area	Reports	Reports per 100,000 Population	Rank[2]
MSA[1]	2,727	366	87
U.S.	1,387,615	423	-

Note: (1) Figures cover the Colorado Springs, CO Metropolitan Statistical Area; (2) Rank ranges from 1 to 391 where 1 indicates greatest number of identity theft reports per 100,000 population
Source: Federal Trade Commission, Consumer Sentinel Network Data Book 2020

Fraud and Other Consumer Reports

Area	Reports	Reports per 100,000 Population	Rank[2]
MSA[1]	7,184	963	27
U.S.	3,385,133	1,031	-

Note: (1) Figures cover the Colorado Springs, CO Metropolitan Statistical Area; (2) Rank ranges from 1 to 391 where 1 indicates greatest number of fraud and other consumer reports per 100,000 population
Source: Federal Trade Commission, Consumer Sentinel Network Data Book 2020

POLITICS

2020 Presidential Election Results

Area	Biden	Trump	Jorgensen	Hawkins	Other
El Paso County	42.7	53.5	2.4	0.3	1.0
U.S.	51.3	46.8	1.2	0.3	0.5

Note: Results are percentages and may not add to 100% due to rounding
Source: Dave Leip's Atlas of U.S. Presidential Elections

SPORTS

Professional Sports Teams

Team Name	League	Year Established
No teams are located in the metro area		

Source: Wikipedia, Major Professional Sports Teams of the United States and Canada, April 6, 2021

CLIMATE

Average and Extreme Temperatures

Temperature	Jan	Feb	Mar	Apr	May	Jun	Jul	Aug	Sep	Oct	Nov	Dec	Yr.
Extreme High (°F)	71	72	78	87	93	99	98	97	94	86	78	75	99
Average High (°F)	41	44	51	61	68	79	85	81	75	63	49	41	62
Average Temp. (°F)	29	32	39	48	55	66	71	69	61	50	37	30	49
Average Low (°F)	17	20	26	34	42	52	57	55	48	36	24	17	36
Extreme Low (°F)	-20	-19	-3	8	22	36	48	39	22	7	-5	-24	-24

Note: Figures cover the years 1948-1993
Source: National Climatic Data Center, International Station Meteorological Climate Summary, 9/96

Average Precipitation/Snowfall/Humidity

Precip./Humidity	Jan	Feb	Mar	Apr	May	Jun	Jul	Aug	Sep	Oct	Nov	Dec	Yr.
Avg. Precip. (in.)	0.3	0.4	1.3	1.3	2.6	2.1	2.6	3.4	1.0	0.9	0.6	0.5	17.0
Avg. Snowfall (in.)	6	6	10	5	2	0	0	0	Tr	3	7	8	48
Avg. Rel. Hum. 5am (%)	57	60	62	62	69	67	66	71	66	59	60	59	63
Avg. Rel. Hum. 5pm (%)	48	43	39	34	39	36	36	43	36	36	45	52	41

Note: Figures cover the years 1948-1993; Tr = Trace amounts (<0.05 in. of rain; <0.5 in. of snow)
Source: National Climatic Data Center, International Station Meteorological Climate Summary, 9/96

Weather Conditions

Temperature			Daytime Sky			Precipitation		
10°F & below	32°F & below	90°F & above	Clear	Partly cloudy	Cloudy	0.01 inch or more precip.	0.1 inch or more snow/ice	Thunder-storms
21	161	18	108	157	100	98	33	49

Note: Figures are average number of days per year and cover the years 1948-1993
Source: National Climatic Data Center, International Station Meteorological Climate Summary, 9/96

HAZARDOUS WASTE

Superfund Sites

The Colorado Springs, CO metro area has no sites on the EPA's Superfund Final National Priorities List. There are a total of 1,375 Superfund sites with a status of proposed or final on the list in the U.S.
U.S. Environmental Protection Agency, National Priorities List, April 7, 2021

AIR QUALITY

Air Quality Trends: Ozone

	1990	1995	2000	2005	2010	2015	2016	2017	2018	2019
MSA[1]	n/a	n/a	n/a	n/a	n/a	n/a	n/a	n/a	n/a	n/a
U.S.	0.088	0.089	0.082	0.080	0.073	0.068	0.069	0.068	0.069	0.065

Note: (1) Data covers the Colorado Springs, CO Metropolitan Statistical Area; n/a not available. The values shown are the composite ozone concentration averages among trend sites based on the highest fourth daily maximum 8-hour concentration in parts per million. These trends are based on sites having an adequate record of monitoring data during the trend period. Data from exceptional events are included.
Source: U.S. Environmental Protection Agency, Air Quality Monitoring Information, "Air Quality Trends by City, 1990-2019"

Air Quality Index

Area	Percent of Days when Air Quality was...[2]					AQI Statistics[2]	
	Good	Moderate	Unhealthy for Sensitive Groups	Unhealthy	Very Unhealthy	Maximum	Median
MSA[1]	71.0	29.0	0.0	0.0	0.0	100	45

Note: (1) Data covers the Colorado Springs, CO Metropolitan Statistical Area; (2) Based on 365 days with AQI data in 2019. Air Quality Index (AQI) is an index for reporting daily air quality. EPA calculates the AQI for five major air pollutants regulated by the Clean Air Act: ground-level ozone, particle pollution (aka particulate matter), carbon monoxide, sulfur dioxide, and nitrogen dioxide. The AQI runs from 0 to 500. The higher the AQI value, the greater the level of air pollution and the greater the health concern. There are six AQI categories: "Good" AQI is between 0 and 50. Air quality is considered satisfactory; "Moderate" AQI is between 51 and 100. Air quality is acceptable; "Unhealthy for Sensitive Groups" When AQI values are between 101 and 150, members of sensitive groups may experience health effects; "Unhealthy" When AQI values are between 151 and 200 everyone may begin to experience health effects; "Very Unhealthy" AQI values between 201 and 300 trigger a health alert; "Hazardous" AQI values over 300 trigger warnings of emergency conditions (not shown).
Source: U.S. Environmental Protection Agency, Air Quality Index Report, 2019

Air Quality Index Pollutants

Area	Percent of Days when AQI Pollutant was...[2]					
	Carbon Monoxide	Nitrogen Dioxide	Ozone	Sulfur Dioxide	Particulate Matter 2.5	Particulate Matter 10
MSA[1]	0.0	0.0	94.5	0.0	4.9	0.5

Note: (1) Data covers the Colorado Springs, CO Metropolitan Statistical Area; (2) Based on 365 days with AQI data in 2019. The Air Quality Index (AQI) is an index for reporting daily air quality. EPA calculates the AQI for five major air pollutants regulated by the Clean Air Act: ground-level ozone, particle pollution (also known as particulate matter), carbon monoxide, sulfur dioxide, and nitrogen dioxide. The AQI runs from 0 to 500. The higher the AQI value, the greater the level of air pollution and the greater the health concern.
Source: U.S. Environmental Protection Agency, Air Quality Index Report, 2019

Maximum Air Pollutant Concentrations: Particulate Matter, Ozone, CO and Lead

	Particulate Matter 10 (ug/m^3)	Particulate Matter 2.5 Wtd AM (ug/m^3)	Particulate Matter 2.5 24-Hr (ug/m^3)	Ozone (ppm)	Carbon Monoxide (ppm)	Lead (ug/m^3)
MSA[1] Level	32	5.0	13	0.065	2	n/a
NAAQS[2]	150	15	35	0.075	9	0.15
Met NAAQS[2]	Yes	Yes	Yes	Yes	Yes	n/a

Note: (1) Data covers the Colorado Springs, CO Metropolitan Statistical Area; Data from exceptional events are included; (2) National Ambient Air Quality Standards; ppm = parts per million; ug/m^3 = micrograms per cubic meter; n/a not available.
Concentrations: Particulate Matter 10 (coarse particulate)—highest second maximum 24-hour concentration; Particulate Matter 2.5 Wtd AM (fine particulate)—highest weighted annual mean concentration; Particulate Matter 2.5 24-Hour (fine particulate)—highest 98th percentile 24-hour concentration; Ozone—highest fourth daily maximum 8-hour concentration; Carbon Monoxide—highest second maximum non-overlapping 8-hour concentration; Lead—maximum running 3-month average
Source: U.S. Environmental Protection Agency, Air Quality Monitoring Information, "Air Quality Statistics by City, 2019"

Maximum Air Pollutant Concentrations: Nitrogen Dioxide and Sulfur Dioxide

	Nitrogen Dioxide AM (ppb)	Nitrogen Dioxide 1-Hr (ppb)	Sulfur Dioxide AM (ppb)	Sulfur Dioxide 1-Hr (ppb)	Sulfur Dioxide 24-Hr (ppb)
MSA[1] Level	n/a	n/a	n/a	10	n/a
NAAQS[2]	53	100	30	75	140
Met NAAQS[2]	n/a	n/a	n/a	Yes	n/a

Note: (1) Data covers the Colorado Springs, CO Metropolitan Statistical Area; Data from exceptional events are included; (2) National Ambient Air Quality Standards; ppm = parts per million; ug/m^3 = micrograms per cubic meter; n/a not available.
Concentrations: Nitrogen Dioxide AM—highest arithmetic mean concentration; Nitrogen Dioxide 1-Hr—highest 98th percentile 1-hour daily maximum concentration; Sulfur Dioxide AM—highest annual mean concentration; Sulfur Dioxide 1-Hr—highest 99th percentile 1-hour daily maximum concentration; Sulfur Dioxide 24-Hr—highest second maximum 24-hour concentration
Source: U.S. Environmental Protection Agency, Air Quality Monitoring Information, "Air Quality Statistics by City, 2019"

Denver, Colorado

Background

From almost anywhere in Denver, you can command a breathtaking view of the 14,000-foot Rocky Mountains. However, the early settlers of Denver were not attracted to the city because of its vistas; they were there in search of gold.

In 1858, there were rumors that gold had been discovered in Cherry Creek, one of the waterways on which Denver stands. Although prospectors came and went without much luck, later it was discovered that there really was gold, and silver as well. By 1867, Denver had been established.

Today Denver, with its sparkling, dramatic skyline of glass and steel towers, bears little resemblance to the dusty frontier village of the nineteenth century. With an excellent location, the "Mile High City" has become a manufacturing, distribution, and transportation center that serves not only the western regions of the United States, but the entire nation. Denver is also home to many companies that are engaged in alternative fuel research and development.

Denver has been the host city of the Democratic National Convention twice: first in 1908 and again in 2008. The city also hosted the international G7 (now G8) summit in 1997. These events bolstered Denver's international reputation both on a political and socioeconomic level.

The massively renovated Colorado Convention Center—now 584,000 square feet—is a magnet for regional and national conferences and shows, and is enhanced by the 5,000-seat Wells Fargo Theatre and new Light Rail Train Station. The renovated historic Denver Union Station operates as a mixed-use retail and multi-modal transportation hub. Another architecturally interesting building is the Jeppesen Terminal at Denver's airport, the largest international hub in the United States. The unique roof is made of heat- and light-reflecting tension fabric. The airport is huge, with 53 square miles and 6 million square feet of public space and 93 gates.

The city is also home to a lively cultural, recreational, and educational scene—concerts at the Boettcher Concert Hall, seasonal drives through the Denver Mountain Park Circle Drive, and skiing and hiking the Rockies just 90 minutes away. Other area attractions include the Denver Museum of Nature and Science, the Colorado History Museum, and the Denver Art Museum, opposite of which is a recently-built condominium complex, Museum Residences. In 2020 one of the city's many neighborhoods changed its name from Stapleton (a KKK member) to Central Park.

The city's public transportation expansion plan, FasTracks, for the Denver-Aurora and Boulder Metropolitan Areas, developed by the Regional Transportation District includes six light rail and diesel commuter rail lines with a combined length of 119 miles.

The city also has its share of offbeat, distinctive places to have fun including the hip Capitol Hill district, which offers small music venues and dank bars that appeal to University of Denver students. Sports fans have the Colorado Avalanche hockey team, the Denver Nuggets basketball team, the Colorado Rockies baseball team, and the Denver Broncos football team. In 2019, the Denver Bandits became part of the Women's National Football League and the first professional women's football team in the state.

In 2005, Denver became the first major city in the U.S. to legalize the private possession of marijuana. In 2012, Colorado Amendment 64 was signed into law by Governor John Hickenlooper and in 2014 Colorado became the first state to allow the sale of marijuana for recreational use. In 2019, Denver became the first U.S. city to decriminalize psilocybin mushrooms.

The Denver Zoo is open year-round and houses nearly 4,000 animals representing 700 species, including the okapi, red-bellied lemur, Amur leopard, black rhino, and Siberian tiger. The zoo continues to implement its master modernization plan of habitats, having recently completed Predator Ridge, home to 14 African species of mammals, birds and reptiles, and an indoor tropical rain forest.

The University of Denver, Community College of Denver, Metropolitan State College, and the University of Colorado at Denver are only a few of the many excellent educational opportunities available in the city.

Denver's invigorating climate matches much of the central Rocky Mountain region, without the frigidly cold mornings of the higher elevations during winter, or the hot afternoons of summer at lower altitudes. Extreme cold and heat are generally short-lived. Low relative humidity, light precipitation, and abundant sunshine characterize Denver's weather. Spring is the cloudiest, wettest, and windiest season, while autumn is the most pleasant. Air pollution remains challenging.

Rankings

General Rankings

- *US News & World Report* conducted a survey of more than 3,000 people and analyzed the 150 largest metropolitan areas to determine what matters most when selecting the next place to live. Denver ranked #2 out of the top 25 as having the best combination of desirable factors. Criteria: cost of living; quality of life; net migration; job market; desirability; and other factors. *realestate.usnews.com, "The 25 Best Places to Live in the U.S. in 2020-21," October 13, 2020*

- The Denver metro area was identified as one of America's fastest-growing areas in terms of population and business growth by *MagnifyMoney*. The area ranked #6 out of 35. The 100 most populous metro areas in the U.S. were evaluated on their change from 2011-2016 in the following categories: people and housing; workforce and employment opportunities; growing industry. *www.businessinsider.com, "The 35 Cities in the US with the Biggest Influx of People, the Most Work Opportunities, and the Hottest Business Growth," August 12, 2018*

- Denver was selected as one of the best places in the world to "dream of now and go to later" by *National Geographic Travel* editors. The list reflects 25 of the most extraordinary and inspiring destinations that also support National Geographic's tourism goals of cultural engagement, diversity, community benefit, and value. In collaboration with its international editorial teams, the new list reports on the timeless must-see sites for 2021, framed by the five categories of Culture and History, Family, Adventure, Sustainability, and Nature. *www.nationalgeographic.com/travel, "Best of the World, Destinations on the Rise for 2021," November 17, 2020*

- Denver was selected as one of the best places to live in America by *Outside Magazine*. Criteria included population, park acreage, neighborhood and resident diversity, new and upcoming things of interest, and opportunities for outdoor adventure. *Outside Magazine, "The 12 Best Places to Live in 2019," July 11, 2019*

Business/Finance Rankings

- 24/7 Wall Street used metro data from the Bureau of Labor Statistics' Occupational Employment database to identify the cities with the highest percentage of those employed in jobs requiring knowledge in the science, technology, engineering, and math (STEM) fields as well as average wages for STEM jobs. The Denver metro area was #15. *247wallst.com, "15 Cities with the Most High-Tech Jobs," January 11, 2020*

- The Brookings Institution ranked the nation's largest cities based on income inequality. Denver was ranked #29 (#1 = greatest inequality). Criteria: the "95/20 ratio," a figure representing the income at which a household earns more than 95 percent of all other households, divided by the income at which a household earns more than only 20 percent of all other households. *Brookings Institution, "Household Income Inequality, Largest Cities of 97 Large U.S. Metro Areas, 2014-2016," February 5, 2018*

- The Brookings Institution ranked the 100 largest metro areas in the U.S. based on income inequality. Denver was ranked #59 (#1 = greatest inequality). Criteria: the "95/20 ratio," a figure representing the income at which a household earns more than 95 percent of all other households, divided by the income at which a household earns more than only 20 percent of all other households. *Brookings Institution, "Household Income Inequality, 100 Largest U.S. Metro Areas, 2014-2016," February 5, 2018*

- *Forbes* ranked the 100 largest metro areas in the U.S. in terms of the "Best Cities for Young Professionals." The Denver metro area ranked #6 out of 25. Criteria: median rent of a two-bedroom apartment; job growth and unemployment rate; median salary of college graduates with 5 or less years of work experience; networking opportunities; social outlook; percentage of population 25 years of age and older with college degrees. *Forbes.com, "America's 25 Best Cities for Young Professionals in 2017," May 22, 2017*

- Payscale.com ranked the 32 largest metro areas in terms of wage growth. The Denver metro area ranked #11. Criteria: private-sector and education professional wage growth between the 4th quarter of 2019 and the 4th quarter of 2020. *PayScale, "Wage Trends by Metro Area-4th Quarter," January 11, 2021*

- The Denver metro area was identified as one of the most debt-ridden places in America by the finance site Credit.com. The metro area was ranked #10. Criteria: residents' average credit card debt as well as median income. *Credit.com, "25 Cities With the Most Credit Card Debt," February 28, 2018*

- Denver was identified as one of the unhappiest cities to work in by CareerBliss.com, an online community for career advancement. The city ranked #1 out of 5. Criteria: an employee's relationship with his or her boss and co-workers; general work environment; compensation; opportunities for advancement; company culture and job reputation; and resources. *Businesswire.com, "CareerBliss Unhappiest Cities to Work 2019," February 12, 2019*

- The Denver metro area appeared on the Milken Institute "2021 Best Performing Cities" list. Rank: #11 out of 200 large metro areas (population over 250,000). Criteria: job growth; wage and salary growth; high-tech output growth; housing affordability; household broadband access. *Milken Institute, "Best-Performing Cities 2021," February 16, 2021*

- *Forbes* ranked the 200 most populous metro areas to determine the nation's "Best Places for Business and Careers." The Denver metro area was ranked #4. Criteria: costs (business and living); job growth (past and projected); income growth; quality of life; educational attainment (college and high school); projected economic growth; cultural and leisure opportunities; workplace tolerance laws; net migration patterns. *Forbes, "The Best Places for Business and Careers 2019: Seattle Still On Top," October 30, 2019*

Dating/Romance Rankings

- *Apartment List* conducted its annual survey of renters for cities that have the best opportunities for dating. More than 11,000 single respondents rated their current city or neighborhood for opportunities to date. Denver ranked #7 out of 86 where single residents were very satisfied or somewhat satisfied, making it among the ten best areas for dating opportunities. Other criteria analyzed included gender and education levels of renters. *Apartment List, "The Best & Worst Metros for Dating 2020," February 4, 2020*

- Denver was selected as one of America's best cities for singles by the readers of *Travel + Leisure* in their annual "America's Favorite Cities" survey. Criteria included good-looking locals, cool shopping, an active bar scene and hipster-magnet coffee bars. *Travel + Leisure, "Best Cities in America for Singles," July 21, 2017*

Education Rankings

- Personal finance website *WalletHub* analyzed the 150 largest U.S. metropolitan statistical areas to determine where the most educated Americans are putting their degrees to work. Criteria: education levels; percentage of workers with degrees; education quality and attainment gap; public school quality rankings; quality and enrollment of each metro area's universities. Denver was ranked #14 (#1 = most educated city). *www.WalletHub.com, "Most and Least Educated Cities in America," July 20, 2020*

- Denver was selected as one of America's most literate cities. The city ranked #8 out of the 84 largest U.S. cities. Criteria: number of booksellers; library resources; Internet resources; educational attainment; periodical publishing resources; newspaper circulation. *Central Connecticut State University, "America's Most Literate Cities, 2018," February 2019*

Environmental Rankings

- Niche compiled a list of the nation's snowiest cities, based on the National Oceanic and Atmospheric Administration's 30-year average snowfall data. Among cities with a population of at least 50,000, Denver ranked #25. *Niche.com, Top 25 Snowiest Cities in America, December 10, 2018*

- The U.S. Environmental Protection Agency (EPA) released a list of U.S. metropolitan areas with the most ENERGY STAR certified buildings in 2019. The Denver metro area was ranked #8 out of 25. *U.S. Environmental Protection Agency, "2020 Energy Star Top Cities," March 2020*

- Denver was highlighted as one of the 25 most ozone-polluted metro areas in the U.S. during 2016 through 2018. The area ranked #10. *American Lung Association, "State of the Air 2020," April 21, 2020*

Food/Drink Rankings

- The U.S. Chamber of Commerce Foundation conducted an in-depth study on local food truck regulations, surveyed 288 food truck owners, and ranked 20 major American cities based on how friendly they are for operating a food truck. The compiled index assessed the following: procedures for obtaining permits and licenses; complying with restrictions; and financial obligations associated with operating a food truck. Denver ranked #2 overall (1 being the best). *www.foodtrucknation.us, "Food Truck Nation," March 20, 2018*

Health/Fitness Rankings

- For each of the 100 largest cities in the United States, the American Fitness Index®, published by the American College of Sports Medicine and the Anthem Foundation, evaluated community infrastructure and 33 health behaviors including preventive health, levels of chronic disease conditions, pedestrian safety, air quality, and community resources that support physical activity. Denver ranked #8 for "community fitness." *americanfitnessindex.org, "2020 ACSM American Fitness Index Summary Report," July 14, 2020*

- The Denver metro area was identified as one of the worst cities for bed bugs in America by pest control company Orkin. The area ranked #20 out of 50 based on the number of bed bug treatments Orkin performed from December 2019 to November 2020. *Orkin, "New Year, New Top City on Orkin's 2021 Bed Bug Cities List: Chicago," February 1, 2021*

- Denver was identified as a "2021 Spring Allergy Capital." The area ranked #91 out of 100. Three groups of factors were used to identify the most challenging cities for people with allergies during the spring season: annual spring pollen levels; over the counter medicine use; number of board-certified allergy specialists. *Asthma and Allergy Foundation of America, "Spring Allergy Capitals 2021," February 23, 2021*

- Denver was identified as a "2021 Fall Allergy Capital." The area ranked #90 out of 100. Three groups of factors were used to identify the most challenging cities for people with allergies during the fall season: annual fall pollen levels; over the counter medicine use; number of board-certified allergy specialists. *Asthma and Allergy Foundation of America, "Fall Allergy Capitals 2021," February 23, 2021*

- Denver was identified as a "2019 Asthma Capital." The area ranked #63 out of the nation's 100 largest metropolitan areas. Criteria: estimated asthma prevalence; crude death rate from asthma; and ER visits due to asthma. Risk factors analyzed but not factored in the rankings: annual pollen score; annual air quality; public smoking laws; number of board-certified asthma specialists; rescue medication use; controller medication use; uninsured rate; poverty rate. *Asthma and Allergy Foundation of America, "Asthma Capitals 2019: The Most Challenging Places to Live With Asthma," May 7, 2019*

Pet Rankings

- Denver appeared on *The Dogington Post* site as one of the top cities for dog lovers, ranking #3 out of 20. The real estate brokerage, Redfin and Rover, the largest pet sitter and dog walker network, compiled a list from over 14,000 U.S. cities to come up with a "Rover Rank." Criteria: highest count of dog walks, the city's Walk Score®, for-sale home listings that mention "dog," number of dog walkers and pet sitters and the hours spent and distance logged. *www.dogingtonpost.com, "The 20 Most Dog-Friendly Cities of 2019," April 4, 2019*

Real Estate Rankings

- FitSmallBusiness looked at 50 of the largest metropolitan areas in the U.S. to determine which metro was the best to start a real estate business. Data was compiled from such sources as: Zillow, Trulia, U.S. Census Bureau, and the Bureau of Labor Statistics. Criteria: location; inventory; annual wages; median sales price of homes; days on the market; median price cut percentage; and other factors that would influence real estate professional growth. The Denver metro area ranked #7. *fitsmallbusiness.com, "The Best Cities to Become a Real Estate Agent in 2018," January 30, 2018*

- *WalletHub* compared the most populated U.S. cities to determine which had the best markets for real estate agents. Denver ranked #6 where demand was high and pay was the best. Criteria: sales per agent; annual median wage for real-estate agents; monthly average starting salary for real estate agents; real estate job density and competition; unemployment rate; home turnover rate; housing-market health index; and other relevant metrics. *www.WalletHub.com, "2019's Best Places to Be a Real Estate Agent," April 24, 2019*

- According to Penske Truck Rental, the Denver metro area was named the #4 moving destination in 2019, based on one-way consumer truck rental reservations made through Penske's website, rental locations, and reservations call center. *gopenske.com/blog, "Penske Truck Rental's 2019 Top Moving Destinations," January 22, 2020*

- The Denver metro area appeared on Realtor.com's list of hot housing markets to watch in 2021. The area ranked #9. Criteria: healthy existing homes inventory; relative home affordability; local economy/population trends. *Realtor.com®, "Top 10 Housing Markets Positioned for Growth in 2021," December 7, 2020*

- The Denver metro area was identified as one of the 20 least affordable housing markets in the U.S. in 2020. The area ranked #170 out of 183 markets. Criteria: qualification for a mortgage loan with a 10 percent down payment on a typical home. *National Association of Realtors®, Qualifying Income Based on Sales Price of Existing Single-Family Homes for Metropolitan Areas, 2020*

- Denver was ranked #195 out of 268 metro areas in terms of housing affordability in 2020 by the National Association of Home Builders (#1 = most affordable). Criteria: the share of homes sold in that area affordable to a family earning the local median income, based on standard mortgage underwriting criteria. *National Association of Home Builders®, NAHB-Wells Fargo Housing Opportunity Index, 4th Quarter 2020*

Safety Rankings

- Allstate ranked the 200 largest cities in America in terms of driver safety. Denver ranked #83. Criteria: internal property damage claims over a two-year period from January 2016 to December 2017. The report helps increase the importance of safety and awareness behind the wheel. *Allstate, "Allstate America's Best Drivers Report, 2019" June 24, 2019*

- The National Insurance Crime Bureau ranked 384 metro areas in the U.S. in terms of per capita rates of vehicle theft. The Denver metro area ranked #19 (#1 = highest rate). Criteria: number of vehicle theft offenses per 100,000 inhabitants in 2019. *National Insurance Crime Bureau, "Hot Spots 2019," July 21, 2020*

Seniors/Retirement Rankings

- From its Best Cities for Successful Aging indexes, the Milken Institute generated rankings for metropolitan areas, weighing data in nine categories—health care, wellness, living arrangements, transportation and convenience, financial characteristics, education, employment, community engagement, and overall livability. The Denver metro area was ranked #12 overall in the large metro area category. *Milken Institute, "Best Cities for Successful Aging, 2017" March 14, 2017*

Sports/Recreation Rankings

- Denver was chosen as one of America's best cities for bicycling. The city ranked #14 out of 50. Criteria: cycling infrastructure that is safe and friendly for all ages; energy and bike culture. The editors evaluated cities with populations of 100,000 or more. *Bicycling, "The 50 Best Bike Cities in America," October 10, 2018*

Women/Minorities Rankings

- The *Houston Chronicle* listed the Denver metro area as #3 in top places for young Latinos to live in the U.S. Research was largely based on housing and occupational data from the largest metropolitan areas performed by *Forbes* and NBC Universo. Criteria: percentage of 18-34 year-olds; Latino college grad rates; and diversity. *blog.chron.com, "The 15 Best Big Cities for Latino Millenials," January 26, 2016*

- Personal finance website *WalletHub* compared more than 180 U.S. cities across two key dimensions, "Hispanic Business-Friendliness" and "Hispanic Purchasing Power," to arrive at the most favorable conditions for Hispanic entrepreneurs. Denver was ranked #41 out of 182. Criteria includes: share of Hispanic-Owned Businesses; Hispanic entrepreneurship rate to median annual income of Hispanics; Small Business-Friendliness score; cost of living; and number of Hispanics with at least a bachelor's degree. *WalletHub.com, "2019's Best Cities for Hispanic Entrepreneurs," May 1, 2019*

Miscellaneous Rankings

- The watchdog site, Charity Navigator, conducted a study of charities in major markets both to analyze statistical differences in their financial, accountability, and transparency practices and to track year-to-year variations in individual philanthropic communities. The Denver metro area was ranked #22 among the 30 metro markets in the rating category of Overall Score. *www.charitynavigator.org, "2017 Metro Market Study," May 1, 2017*

- *WalletHub* compared the 150 most populated U.S. cities to determine their operating efficiency. A "Quality of City Services" score was constructed for each city and then divided by the total budget per capita to reveal which were managed the best. Denver ranked #120. Criteria: financial stability; economy; education; safety; health; infrastructure and pollution. *www.WalletHub.com, "2020's Best- & Worst-Run Cities in America," June 29, 2020*

- Denver was selected as one of "America's Friendliest Cities." The city ranked #20 in the "Friendliest" category. Respondents to an online survey were asked to rate 38 top urban destinations in the United States as to general friendliness, as well as manners, politeness and warm disposition. *Travel + Leisure, "America's Friendliest Cities," October 20, 2017*

- The National Alliance to End Homelessness listed the 25 most populous metro areas with the highest rate of homelessness. The Denver metro area had a high rate of homelessness. Criteria: number of homeless people per 10,000 population in 2016. *National Alliance to End Homelessness, "Homelessness in the 25 Most Populous U.S. Metro Areas," September 1, 2017*

Business Environment

DEMOGRAPHICS

Population Growth

Area	1990 Census	2000 Census	2010 Census	2019* Estimate	Population Growth (%) 1990-2019	Population Growth (%) 2010-2019
City	467,153	554,636	600,158	705,576	51.0	17.6
MSA[1]	1,666,935	2,179,296	2,543,482	2,892,066	73.5	13.7
U.S.	248,709,873	281,421,906	308,745,538	324,697,795	30.6	5.2

Note: (1) Figures cover the Denver-Aurora-Lakewood, CO Metropolitan Statistical Area; (*) 2015-2019 5-year estimated population
Source: U.S. Census Bureau, 1990 Census, Census 2000, Census 2010, 2015-2019 American Community Survey 5-Year Estimates

Household Size

Area	Persons in Household (%) One	Two	Three	Four	Five	Six	Seven or More	Average Household Size
City	38.2	33.0	12.0	9.6	4.3	1.6	1.2	2.30
MSA[1]	28.2	34.3	15.0	13.2	5.7	2.2	1.4	2.60
U.S.	27.9	33.9	15.6	12.9	6.0	2.3	1.4	2.60

Note: (1) Figures cover the Denver-Aurora-Lakewood, CO Metropolitan Statistical Area
Source: U.S. Census Bureau, 2015-2019 American Community Survey 5-Year Estimates

Race

Area	White Alone[2] (%)	Black Alone[2] (%)	Asian Alone[2] (%)	AIAN[3] Alone[2] (%)	NHOPI[4] Alone[2] (%)	Other Race Alone[2] (%)	Two or More Races (%)
City	76.1	9.2	3.7	0.9	0.2	6.1	3.8
MSA[1]	81.0	5.7	4.2	0.8	0.1	4.4	3.7
U.S.	72.5	12.7	5.5	0.8	0.2	4.9	3.3

Note: (1) Figures cover the Denver-Aurora-Lakewood, CO Metropolitan Statistical Area; (2) Alone is defined as not being in combination with one or more other races; (3) American Indian and Alaska Native; (4) Native Hawaiian and Other Pacific Islander
Source: U.S. Census Bureau, 2015-2019 American Community Survey 5-Year Estimates

Hispanic or Latino Origin

Area	Total (%)	Mexican (%)	Puerto Rican (%)	Cuban (%)	Other (%)
City	29.9	23.7	0.6	0.2	5.4
MSA[1]	23.1	17.6	0.6	0.2	4.7
U.S.	18.0	11.2	1.7	0.7	4.3

Note: Persons of Hispanic or Latino origin can be of any race; (1) Figures cover the Denver-Aurora-Lakewood, CO Metropolitan Statistical Area
Source: U.S. Census Bureau, 2015-2019 American Community Survey 5-Year Estimates

Ancestry

Area	German	Irish	English	American	Italian	Polish	French[2]	Scottish	Dutch
City	13.8	9.7	7.8	2.9	4.6	2.7	2.3	2.1	1.4
MSA[1]	17.5	10.7	9.3	3.9	5.0	2.5	2.5	2.4	1.5
U.S.	13.3	9.7	7.2	6.2	5.1	2.4	2.8	2.3	1.2

Note: Figures are the percentage of the total population reporting a particular ancestry. The nine most commonly reported ancestries in the U.S. are shown. Figures include multiple ancestries (e.g. if a person reported being Irish and Italian, they were included in both columns); (1) Figures cover the Denver-Aurora-Lakewood, CO Metropolitan Statistical Area; (2) Excludes Basque
Source: U.S. Census Bureau, 2015-2019 American Community Survey 5-Year Estimates

Foreign-born Population

Area	Percent of Population Born in Any Foreign Country	Asia	Mexico	Europe	Caribbean	Central America[2]	South America	Africa	Canada
City	15.0	3.0	7.3	1.4	0.3	0.8	0.5	1.4	0.3
MSA[1]	12.1	3.3	4.9	1.4	0.2	0.5	0.5	1.0	0.3
U.S.	13.6	4.2	3.5	1.5	1.3	1.1	1.0	0.7	0.2

Note: (1) Figures cover the Denver-Aurora-Lakewood, CO Metropolitan Statistical Area; (2) Excludes Mexico.
Source: U.S. Census Bureau, 2015-2019 American Community Survey 5-Year Estimates

Marital Status

Area	Never Married	Now Married[2]	Separated	Widowed	Divorced
City	42.5	39.5	1.8	4.0	12.2
MSA[1]	33.1	49.6	1.4	4.1	11.8
U.S.	33.4	48.1	1.9	5.8	10.9

Note: Figures are percentages and cover the population 15 years of age and older; (1) Figures cover the Denver-Aurora-Lakewood, CO Metropolitan Statistical Area; (2) Excludes separated
Source: U.S. Census Bureau, 2015-2019 American Community Survey 5-Year Estimates

Disability by Age

Area	All Ages	Under 18 Years Old	18 to 64 Years Old	65 Years and Over
City	9.6	3.5	7.4	33.5
MSA[1]	9.3	3.2	7.4	30.8
U.S.	12.6	4.2	10.3	34.5

Note: Figures show percent of the civilian noninstitutionalized population that reported having a disability. Disability status is determined from six types of difficulty: vision, hearing, cognitive, ambulatory, self-care, and independent living. For children under 5 years old, hearing and vision difficulty are used to determine disability status. For children between the ages of 5 and 14, disability status is determined from hearing, vision, cognitive, ambulatory, and self-care difficulties. For people aged 15 years and older, they are considered to have a disability if they have difficulty with any one of the six difficulty types; Note: (1) Figures cover the Denver-Aurora-Lakewood, CO Metropolitan Statistical Area
Source: U.S. Census Bureau, 2015-2019 American Community Survey 5-Year Estimates

Age

Area	Under Age 5	Age 5–19	Age 20–34	Age 35–44	Age 45–54	Age 55–64	Age 65–74	Age 75–84	Age 85+	Median Age
City	6.1	15.7	29.2	15.9	11.6	10.0	7.0	3.1	1.5	34.5
MSA[1]	6.1	18.9	22.6	14.6	13.2	12.1	7.8	3.3	1.4	36.5
U.S.	6.1	19.1	20.7	12.6	13.0	12.9	9.1	4.6	1.9	38.1

Note: (1) Figures cover the Denver-Aurora-Lakewood, CO Metropolitan Statistical Area
Source: U.S. Census Bureau, 2015-2019 American Community Survey 5-Year Estimates

Gender

Area	Males	Females	Males per 100 Females
City	353,311	352,265	100.3
MSA[1]	1,445,090	1,446,976	99.9
U.S.	159,886,919	164,810,876	97.0

Note: (1) Figures cover the Denver-Aurora-Lakewood, CO Metropolitan Statistical Area
Source: U.S. Census Bureau, 2015-2019 American Community Survey 5-Year Estimates

Religious Groups by Family

Area	Catholic	Baptist	Non-Den.	Methodist[2]	Lutheran	LDS[3]	Pentecostal	Presbyterian[4]	Muslim[5]	Judaism
MSA[1]	16.1	3.0	4.6	1.7	2.1	2.4	1.2	1.6	0.6	0.6
U.S.	19.1	9.3	4.0	4.0	2.3	2.0	1.9	1.6	0.8	0.7

Note: Figures are the number of adherents as a percentage of the total population; (1) Figures cover the Denver-Aurora-Lakewood, CO Metropolitan Statistical Area; (2) Methodist/Pietist; (3) Latter Day Saints; (4) Reformed; (5) Figures are estimates
Source: Association of Statisticians of American Religious Bodies, 2010 U.S. Religion Census: Religious Congregations & Membership Study

Religious Groups by Tradition

Area	Catholic	Evangelical Protestant	Mainline Protestant	Other Tradition	Black Protestant	Orthodox
MSA[1]	16.1	11.1	4.5	4.6	0.4	0.3
U.S.	19.1	16.2	7.3	4.3	1.6	0.3

Note: Figures are the number of adherents as a percentage of the total population; (1) Figures cover the Denver-Aurora-Lakewood, CO Metropolitan Statistical Area
Source: Association of Statisticians of American Religious Bodies, 2010 U.S. Religion Census: Religious Congregations & Membership Study

ECONOMY

Gross Metropolitan Product

Area	2017	2018	2019	2020	Rank[2]
MSA[1]	211.6	225.3	235.8	246.9	18

Note: Figures are in billions of dollars; (1) Figures cover the Denver-Aurora-Lakewood, CO Metropolitan Statistical Area; (2) Rank is based on 2018 data and ranges from 1 to 381
Source: U.S. Conference of Mayors, U.S. Metro Economies: GMP & Employment 2018-2020, September 2019

Economic Growth

Area	2015-17 (%)	2018 (%)	2019 (%)	2020 (%)	Rank[2]
MSA[1]	2.6	3.7	3.0	1.9	89
U.S.	1.9	2.9	2.3	2.1	–

Note: Figures are real gross metropolitan product (GMP) growth rates and represent average annual percent change; (1) Figures cover the Denver-Aurora-Lakewood, CO Metropolitan Statistical Area; (2) Rank is based on 2017 2-year average annual percent change and ranges from 1 to 381
Source: U.S. Conference of Mayors, U.S. Metro Economies: GMP & Employment 2018-2020, September 2019

Metropolitan Area Exports

Area	2014	2015	2016	2017	2018	2019	Rank[2]
MSA[1]	4,958.6	3,909.5	3,649.3	3,954.7	4,544.3	4,555.6	61

Note: Figures are in millions of dollars; (1) Figures cover the Denver-Aurora-Lakewood, CO Metropolitan Statistical Area; (2) Rank is based on 2019 data and ranges from 1 to 386
Source: U.S. Department of Commerce, International Trade Administration, Office of Trade and Economic Analysis, Industry and Analysis, Exports by Metropolitan Area, data extracted March 24, 2021

Building Permits

Area	Single-Family			Multi-Family			Total		
	2018	2019	Pct. Chg.	2018	2019	Pct. Chg.	2018	2019	Pct. Chg.
City	2,428	2,257	-7.0	5,450	5,073	-6.9	7,878	7,330	-7.0
MSA[1]	11,808	11,081	-6.2	9,921	8,227	-17.1	21,729	19,308	-11.1
U.S.	855,300	862,100	0.7	473,500	523,900	10.6	1,328,800	1,386,000	4.3

Note: (1) Figures cover the Denver-Aurora-Lakewood, CO Metropolitan Statistical Area; Figures represent new, privately-owned housing units authorized (unadjusted data); All permit data are based on estimates with imputation
Source: U.S. Census Bureau, Manufacturing, Mining, and Construction Statistics, Building Permits, 2018, 2019

Bankruptcy Filings

Area	Business Filings			Nonbusiness Filings		
	2019	2020	% Chg.	2019	2020	% Chg.
Denver County	68	91	33.8	1,338	1,029	-23.1
U.S.	22,780	21,655	-4.9	752,160	522,808	-30.5

Note: Business filings include Chapter 7, Chapter 9, Chapter 11, Chapter 12, Chapter 13, Chapter 15, and Section 304; Nonbusiness filings include Chapter 7, Chapter 11, and Chapter 13
Source: Administrative Office of the U.S. Courts, Business and Nonbusiness Bankruptcy, County Cases Commenced by Chapter of the Bankruptcy Code, During the 12-Month Period Ending December 31, 2019 and Business and Nonbusiness Bankruptcy, County Cases Commenced by Chapter of the Bankruptcy Code, During the 12-Month Period Ending December 31, 2020

Housing Vacancy Rates

Area	Gross Vacancy Rate[2] (%)			Year-Round Vacancy Rate[3] (%)			Rental Vacancy Rate[4] (%)			Homeowner Vacancy Rate[5] (%)		
	2018	2019	2020	2018	2019	2020	2018	2019	2020	2018	2019	2020
MSA[1]	8.0	7.5	5.8	7.4	7.0	5.1	3.8	4.7	4.8	0.9	1.0	0.5
U.S.	12.3	12.0	10.6	9.7	9.5	8.2	6.9	6.7	6.3	1.5	1.4	1.0

Note: (1) Figures cover the Denver-Aurora-Lakewood, CO Metropolitan Statistical Area; (2) The percentage of the total housing inventory that is vacant; (3) The percentage of the housing inventory (excluding seasonal units) that is year-round vacant; (4) The percentage of rental inventory that is vacant for rent; (5) The percentage of homeowner inventory that is vacant for sale
Source: U.S. Census Bureau, Housing Vacancies and Homeownership Annual Statistics: 2018, 2019, 2020

INCOME

Income

Area	Per Capita ($)	Median Household ($)	Average Household ($)
City	43,770	68,592	99,151
MSA[1]	41,988	79,664	106,322
U.S.	34,103	62,843	88,607

Note: (1) Figures cover the Denver-Aurora-Lakewood, CO Metropolitan Statistical Area
Source: U.S. Census Bureau, 2015-2019 American Community Survey 5-Year Estimates

Household Income Distribution

Area	Percent of Households Earning							
	Under $15,000	$15,000 -$24,999	$25,000 -$34,999	$35,000 -$49,999	$50,000 -$74,999	$75,000 -$99,999	$100,000 -$149,999	$150,000 and up
City	10.0	7.3	7.9	11.3	17.3	12.5	15.7	18.1
MSA[1]	6.7	5.8	6.7	10.8	17.1	13.7	18.9	20.2
U.S.	10.3	8.9	8.9	12.3	17.2	12.7	15.1	14.5

Note: (1) Figures cover the Denver-Aurora-Lakewood, CO Metropolitan Statistical Area
Source: U.S. Census Bureau, 2015-2019 American Community Survey 5-Year Estimates

Poverty Rate

Area	All Ages	Under 18 Years Old	18 to 64 Years Old	65 Years and Over
City	12.9	18.2	11.6	10.9
MSA[1]	8.8	11.4	8.3	6.9
U.S.	13.4	18.5	12.6	9.3

Note: Figures are percentage of people whose income during the past 12 months was below the poverty level;
(1) Figures cover the Denver-Aurora-Lakewood, CO Metropolitan Statistical Area
Source: U.S. Census Bureau, 2015-2019 American Community Survey 5-Year Estimates

CITY FINANCES

City Government Finances

Component	2017 ($000)	2017 ($ per capita)
Total Revenues	3,912,427	5,732
Total Expenditures	3,567,796	5,227
Debt Outstanding	6,263,549	9,177
Cash and Securities[1]	5,937,189	8,699

Note: (1) Cash and security holdings of a government at the close of its fiscal year,
including those of its dependent agencies, utilities, and liquor stores.
Source: U.S. Census Bureau, State & Local Government Finances 2017

City Government Revenue by Source

Source	2017 ($000)	2017 ($ per capita)	2017 (%)
General Revenue			
From Federal Government	4,333	6	0.1
From State Government	252,412	370	6.5
From Local Governments	22,569	33	0.6
Taxes			
Property	408,991	599	10.5
Sales and Gross Receipts	787,635	1,154	20.1
Personal Income	0	0	0.0
Corporate Income	0	0	0.0
Motor Vehicle License	26,787	39	0.7
Other Taxes	111,328	163	2.8
Current Charges	1,431,671	2,098	36.6
Liquor Store	0	0	0.0
Utility	284,454	417	7.3
Employee Retirement	237,113	347	6.1

Source: U.S. Census Bureau, State & Local Government Finances 2017

City Government Expenditures by Function

Function	2017 ($000)	2017 ($ per capita)	2017 (%)
General Direct Expenditures			
Air Transportation	708,202	1,037	19.8
Corrections	132,781	194	3.7
Education	0	0	0.0
Employment Security Administration	0	0	0.0
Financial Administration	73,625	107	2.1
Fire Protection	127,075	186	3.6
General Public Buildings	94,335	138	2.6
Governmental Administration, Other	80,197	117	2.2
Health	61,822	90	1.7
Highways	147,371	215	4.1
Hospitals	0	0	0.0
Housing and Community Development	119,788	175	3.4
Interest on General Debt	247,499	362	6.9
Judicial and Legal	76,278	111	2.1
Libraries	44,818	65	1.3
Parking	19,078	28	0.5
Parks and Recreation	240,424	352	6.7
Police Protection	236,678	346	6.6
Public Welfare	135,733	198	3.8
Sewerage	113,620	166	3.2
Solid Waste Management	12,295	18	0.3
Veterans' Services	0	0	0.0
Liquor Store	0	0	0.0
Utility	337,580	494	9.5
Employee Retirement	227,431	333	6.4

Source: U.S. Census Bureau, State & Local Government Finances 2017

EMPLOYMENT

Labor Force and Employment

Area	Civilian Labor Force			Workers Employed		
	Dec. 2019	Dec. 2020	% Chg.	Dec. 2019	Dec. 2020	% Chg.
City	423,917	436,113	2.9	414,090	395,349	-4.5
MSA[1]	1,688,220	1,720,681	1.9	1,650,053	1,575,283	-4.5
U.S.	164,007,000	160,017,000	-2.4	158,504,000	149,613,000	-5.6

Note: Data is not seasonally adjusted and covers workers 16 years of age and older; (1) Figures cover the Denver-Aurora-Lakewood, CO Metropolitan Statistical Area
Source: Bureau of Labor Statistics, Local Area Unemployment Statistics

Unemployment Rate

Area	2020											
	Jan.	Feb.	Mar.	Apr.	May	Jun.	Jul.	Aug.	Sep.	Oct.	Nov.	Dec.
City	2.8	2.8	5.3	13.4	11.5	12.0	8.8	7.9	7.3	7.3	7.2	9.3
MSA[1]	2.7	2.8	5.2	12.3	10.5	11.1	7.9	7.0	6.5	6.5	6.4	8.5
U.S.	4.0	3.8	4.5	14.4	13.0	11.2	10.5	8.5	7.7	6.6	6.4	6.5

Note: Data is not seasonally adjusted and covers workers 16 years of age and older; (1) Figures cover the Denver-Aurora-Lakewood, CO Metropolitan Statistical Area
Source: Bureau of Labor Statistics, Local Area Unemployment Statistics

Average Wages

Occupation	$/Hr.	Occupation	$/Hr.
Accountants and Auditors	42.60	Maintenance and Repair Workers	21.60
Automotive Mechanics	24.70	Marketing Managers	83.20
Bookkeepers	22.70	Network and Computer Systems Admin.	46.10
Carpenters	25.90	Nurses, Licensed Practical	27.20
Cashiers	14.50	Nurses, Registered	38.10
Computer Programmers	43.50	Nursing Assistants	17.20
Computer Systems Analysts	51.30	Office Clerks, General	22.30
Computer User Support Specialists	30.30	Physical Therapists	42.30
Construction Laborers	19.30	Physicians	119.50
Cooks, Restaurant	15.40	Plumbers, Pipefitters and Steamfitters	29.30
Customer Service Representatives	19.80	Police and Sheriff's Patrol Officers	41.20
Dentists	99.20	Postal Service Mail Carriers	25.30
Electricians	26.90	Real Estate Sales Agents	43.40
Engineers, Electrical	47.80	Retail Salespersons	16.30
Fast Food and Counter Workers	13.30	Sales Representatives, Technical/Scientific	54.00
Financial Managers	85.60	Secretaries, Exc. Legal/Medical/Executive	20.90
First-Line Supervisors of Office Workers	32.50	Security Guards	17.70
General and Operations Managers	74.70	Surgeons	123.00
Hairdressers/Cosmetologists	20.10	Teacher Assistants, Exc. Postsecondary*	15.50
Home Health and Personal Care Aides	14.60	Teachers, Secondary School, Exc. Sp. Ed.*	29.80
Janitors and Cleaners	14.90	Telemarketers	18.70
Landscaping/Groundskeeping Workers	18.10	Truck Drivers, Heavy/Tractor-Trailer	26.50
Lawyers	73.10	Truck Drivers, Light/Delivery Services	20.40
Maids and Housekeeping Cleaners	13.60	Waiters and Waitresses	15.30

Note: Wage data covers the Denver-Aurora-Lakewood, CO Metropolitan Statistical Area; (*) Hourly wages were calculated from annual wage data based on a 40 hour work week; n/a not available.
Source: Bureau of Labor Statistics, Metro Area Occupational Employment & Wage Estimates, May 2020

Employment by Industry

Sector	MSA[1]		U.S.
	Number of Employees	Percent of Total	Percent of Total
Construction, Mining, and Logging	109,200	7.5	5.5
Education and Health Services	186,500	12.8	16.3
Financial Activities	112,800	7.7	6.1
Government	197,500	13.6	15.2
Information	50,300	3.5	1.9
Leisure and Hospitality	107,000	7.3	9.0
Manufacturing	68,700	4.7	8.5
Other Services	54,500	3.7	3.8
Professional and Business Services	275,000	18.9	14.4
Retail Trade	141,400	9.7	10.9
Transportation, Warehousing, and Utilities	80,300	5.5	4.6
Wholesale Trade	72,900	5.0	3.9

Note: Figures are non-farm employment as of December 2020. Figures are not seasonally adjusted and include workers 16 years of age and older; (1) Figures cover the Denver-Aurora-Lakewood, CO Metropolitan Statistical Area
Source: Bureau of Labor Statistics, Current Employment Statistics, Employment, Hours, and Earnings

Employment by Occupation

Occupation Classification	City (%)	MSA[1] (%)	U.S. (%)
Management, Business, Science, and Arts	48.6	44.7	38.5
Natural Resources, Construction, and Maintenance	7.6	8.4	8.9
Production, Transportation, and Material Moving	8.4	9.5	13.2
Sales and Office	19.7	21.9	21.6
Service	15.7	15.5	17.8

Note: Figures cover employed civilians 16 years of age and older; (1) Figures cover the Denver-Aurora-Lakewood, CO Metropolitan Statistical Area
Source: U.S. Census Bureau, 2015-2019 American Community Survey 5-Year Estimates

Occupations with Greatest Projected Employment Growth: 2020 – 2022

Occupation[1]	2020 Employment	2022 Projected Employment	Numeric Employment Change	Percent Employment Change
Software Developers, Applications	33,470	35,740	2,270	6.8
Personal Care Aides	30,000	31,610	1,610	5.4
Registered Nurses	54,810	56,090	1,280	2.3
Market Research Analysts and Marketing Specialists	21,470	22,380	910	4.2
Business Operations Specialists, All Other	49,470	50,350	880	1.8
Stock Clerks and Order Fillers	37,610	38,390	780	2.1
Computer Occupations, All Other	18,280	18,940	660	3.6
Accountants and Auditors	42,200	42,840	640	1.5
Software Developers, Systems Software	12,390	13,010	620	5.0
Sales Representatives, Wholesale and Manufacturing, Except Technical and Scientific Products	28,620	29,170	550	1.9

Note: Projections cover Colorado; (1) Sorted by numeric employment change
Source: www.projectionscentral.com, State Occupational Projections, 2020–2022 Short-Term Projections

Fastest-Growing Occupations: 2020 – 2022

Occupation[1]	2020 Employment	2022 Projected Employment	Numeric Employment Change	Percent Employment Change
Information Security Analysts	3,860	4,170	310	8.0
Software Developers, Applications	33,470	35,740	2,270	6.8
Statisticians	1,230	1,310	80	6.5
Operations Research Analysts	940	1,000	60	6.4
Veterinary Technologists and Technicians	4,490	4,750	260	5.8
Health Specialties Teachers, Postsecondary	6,160	6,500	340	5.5
Personal Care Aides	30,000	31,610	1,610	5.4
Veterinarians	2,820	2,970	150	5.3
Interpreters and Translators	1,980	2,080	100	5.1
Software Developers, Systems Software	12,390	13,010	620	5.0

Note: Projections cover Colorado; (1) Sorted by percent employment change and excludes occupations with numeric employment change less than 50
Source: www.projectionscentral.com, State Occupational Projections, 2020–2022 Short-Term Projections

TAXES

State Corporate Income Tax Rates

State	Tax Rate (%)	Income Brackets ($)	Num. of Brackets	Financial Institution Tax Rate (%)[a]	Federal Income Tax Ded.
Colorado	4.55	Flat rate	1	4.55	No

Note: Tax rates as of January 1, 2021; (a) Rates listed are the corporate income tax rate applied to financial institutions or excise taxes based on income. Some states have other taxes based upon the value of deposits or shares.
Source: Federation of Tax Administrators, State Corporate Income Tax Rates, January 1, 2021

State Individual Income Tax Rates

State	Tax Rate (%)	Income Brackets ($)	Personal Exemptions ($)			Standard Ded. ($)	
			Single	Married	Depend.	Single	Married
Colorado	4.55	Flat rate	(d)	(d)	(d)	12,550	25,100 (d)

Note: Tax rates as of January 1, 2021; Local- and county-level taxes are not included; Federal income tax is not deductible on state income tax returns; (d) These states use the personal exemption/standard deduction amounts provided in the federal Internal Revenue Code.
Source: Federation of Tax Administrators, State Individual Income Tax Rates, January 1, 2021

Various State Sales and Excise Tax Rates

State	State Sales Tax (%)	Gasoline[1] (¢/gal.)	Cigarette[2] ($/pack)	Spirits[3] ($/gal.)	Wine[4] ($/gal.)	Beer[5] ($/gal.)	Recreational Marijuana (%)
Colorado	2.9	22	1.94	2.28	0.32	0.08	(d)

Note: All tax rates as of January 1, 2021; (1) The American Petroleum Institute has developed a methodology for determining the average tax rate on a gallon of fuel. Rates may include any of the following: excise taxes, environmental fees, storage tank fees, other fees or taxes, general sales tax, and local taxes; (2) The federal excise tax of $1.0066 per pack and local taxes are not included; (3) Rates are those applicable to off-premise sales of 40% alcohol by volume (a.b.v.) distilled spirits in 750ml containers. Local excise taxes are excluded; (4) Rates are those applicable to off-premise sales of 11% a.b.v. non-carbonated wine in 750ml containers; (5) Rates are those applicable to off-premise sales of 4.7% a.b.v. beer in 12 ounce containers; (d) 15% excise tax (levied on wholesale at average market rate); 15% excise tax (retail price)
Source: Tax Foundation, 2021 Facts & Figures: How Does Your State Compare?

State Business Tax Climate Index Rankings

State	Overall Rank	Corporate Tax Rank	Individual Income Tax Rank	Sales Tax Rank	Property Tax Rank	Unemployment Insurance Tax Rank
Colorado	21	10	14	36	32	41

Note: The index is a measure of how each state's tax laws affect economic performance. The lower the rank, the more favorable a state's tax system is for business. States without a given tax are given a ranking of 1. The scores/rankings for the District of Columbia do not affect other states. The 2021 index represents the tax climate as of July 1, 2020.
Source: Tax Foundation, State Business Tax Climate Index 2021

TRANSPORTATION

Means of Transportation to Work

Area	Car/Truck/Van		Public Transportation			Bicycle	Walked	Other Means	Worked at Home
	Drove Alone	Car-pooled	Bus	Subway	Railroad				
City	69.1	7.7	4.4	0.9	0.5	2.2	4.7	1.9	8.5
MSA[1]	75.3	8.1	2.8	0.6	0.3	0.8	2.2	1.5	8.4
U.S.	76.3	9.0	2.4	1.9	0.6	0.5	2.7	1.4	5.2

Note: Figures are percentages and cover workers 16 years of age and older; (1) Figures cover the Denver-Aurora-Lakewood, CO Metropolitan Statistical Area
Source: U.S. Census Bureau, 2015-2019 American Community Survey 5-Year Estimates

Travel Time to Work

Area	Less Than 10 Minutes	10 to 19 Minutes	20 to 29 Minutes	30 to 44 Minutes	45 to 59 Minutes	60 to 89 Minutes	90 Minutes or More
City	7.5	28.5	24.6	26.0	8.0	3.9	1.5
MSA[1]	8.0	24.9	23.0	26.3	10.2	5.8	1.8
U.S.	12.2	28.4	20.8	20.8	8.3	6.4	2.9

Note: Note: Figures are percentages and include workers 16 years old and over; (1) Figures cover the Denver-Aurora-Lakewood, CO Metropolitan Statistical Area
Source: U.S. Census Bureau, 2015-2019 American Community Survey 5-Year Estimates

Key Congestion Measures

Measure	1982	1992	2002	2012	2017
Annual Hours of Delay, Total (000)	12,336	23,590	69,178	95,576	107,463
Annual Hours of Delay, Per Auto Commuter	17	24	48	53	61
Annual Congestion Cost, Total (million $)	94	251	937	1,713	1,988
Annual Congestion Cost, Per Auto Commuter ($)	299	393	900	974	1,062

Note: Covers the Denver-Aurora CO urban area
Source: Texas A&M Transportation Institute, 2019 Urban Mobility Report

Freeway Travel Time Index

Measure	1982	1987	1992	1997	2002	2007	2012	2017
Urban Area Index[1]	1.10	1.13	1.15	1.23	1.29	1.31	1.30	1.31
Urban Area Rank[1,2]	19	21	26	15	10	11	16	17

Note: Freeway Travel Time Index—the ratio of travel time in the peak period to the travel time at free-flow conditions. For example, a value of 1.30 indicates a 20-minute free-flow trip takes 26 minutes in the peak (20 minutes x 1.30 = 26 minutes); (1) Covers the Denver-Aurora CO urban area; (2) Rank is based on 101 larger urban areas (#1 = highest travel time index)
Source: Texas A&M Transportation Institute, 2019 Urban Mobility Report

Public Transportation

Agency Name / Mode of Transportation	Vehicles Operated in Maximum Service[1]	Annual Unlinked Passenger Trips[2] (in thous.)	Annual Passenger Miles[3] (in thous.)
Denver Regional Transportation District (RTD)			
Bus (directly operated)	483	47,678.2	221,931.3
Bus (purchased transportation)	355	22,053.6	85,104.3
Commuter Rail (purchased transportation)	44	9,711.4	121,331.4
Demand Response (purchased transportation)	441	1,179.0	10,384.1
Light Rail (directly operated)	160	24,585.3	178,266.8

Note: (1) Number of revenue vehicles operated by the given mode and type of service to meet the annual maximum service requirement. This is the revenue vehicle count during the peak season of the year; on the week and day that maximum service is provided. Vehicles operated in maximum service (VOMS) exclude atypical days and one-time special events; (2) Number of passengers who boarded public transportation vehicles. Passengers are counted each time they board a vehicle no matter how many vehicles they use to travel from their origin to their destination. (3) Sum of the distances ridden by all passengers during the entire fiscal year.
Source: Federal Transit Administration, National Transit Database, 2019

Air Transportation

Airport Name and Code / Type of Service	Passenger Airlines[1]	Passenger Enplanements	Freight Carriers[2]	Freight (lbs)
Denver International (DEN)				
Domestic service (U.S. carriers - 2020)	27	15,787,920	18	263,867,762
International service (U.S. carriers - 2019)	7	883,726	3	8,069,938

Note: (1) Includes all U.S.-based major, minor and commuter airlines that carried at least one passenger during the year; (2) Includes all U.S.-based airlines and freight carriers that transported at least one pound of freight during the year.
Source: Bureau of Transportation Statistics, The Intermodal Transportation Database, Air Carriers: T-100 Domestic Market (U.S. Carriers), 2020; Bureau of Transportation Statistics, The Intermodal Transportation Database, Air Carriers: T-100 International Market (U.S. Carriers), 2019

BUSINESSES

Major Business Headquarters

Company Name	Industry	Rankings	
		Fortune[1]	Forbes[2]
DCP Midstream	Pipelines	413	-
DaVita	Health Care, Medical Facilities	230	-
Leprino Foods	Food, Drink & Tobacco	-	132
Molson Coors Beverage	Beverages	298	-
Optiv Security	Business Services & Supplies	-	182
Ovintiv	Mining, Crude-Oil Production	449	-

Note: (1) Companies that produce a 10-K are ranked 1 to 500 based on 2019 revenue; (2) All private companies with at least $2 billion in annual revenue through the end of their most current fiscal year are ranked 1 to 219; companies listed are headquartered in the city; dashes indicate no ranking
Source: Fortune, "Fortune 500," June/July 2020; Forbes, "America's Largest Private Companies," 2020

Fastest-Growing Businesses

According to *Inc.*, Denver is home to seven of America's 500 fastest-growing private companies: **BrüMate** (#14); **NuLeaf Naturals** (#16); **Guild Education** (#23); **Würk** (#73); **Infinicept** (#95); **Growlink** (#109); **Trustech** (#131). Criteria: must be an independent, privately-held, for-profit, U.S. corporation, proprietorship or partnership as of December 31, 2019; revenues must be at least $100,000 in 2016 and $2 million in 2019; must have four-year operating/sales history. *Inc., "America's 500 Fastest-Growing Private Companies," 2020*

According to Deloitte, Denver is home to two of North America's 500 fastest-growing high-technology companies: **DispatchHealth** (#56); **Mersive Technologies** (#277). Companies are ranked by percentage growth in revenue over a four-year period. Criteria for inclusion: company must be headquartered within North America; must own proprietary intellectual property or technology that is sold to customers in products that contributes to a significant portion of the company's operating revenue; must have been in business for a minumum of four years with 2016 operating revenues of at least $50,000 USD/CD and 2019 operating revenues of at least $5 million USD/CD. *Deloitte, 2020 Technology Fast 500™*

Living Environment

COST OF LIVING

Cost of Living Index

Composite Index	Groceries	Housing	Utilities	Trans- portation	Health Care	Misc. Goods/ Services
113.6	95.0	139.2	79.8	113.3	100.4	111.5

Note: The Cost of Living Index measures regional differences in the cost of consumer goods and services, excluding taxes and non-consumer expenditures, for professional and managerial households in the top income quintile. It is based on more than 50,000 prices covering almost 60 different items for which prices are collected three times a year by chambers of commerce, economic development organizations or university applied economic centers in each participating urban area. The numbers shown should be read as a percentage above or below the national average of 100. For example, a value of 115.4 in the groceries column indicates that grocery prices are 15.4% higher than the national average. Small differences in the index numbers should not be interpreted as significant; Figures cover the Denver CO urban area.
Source: The Council for Community and Economic Research, Cost of Living Index, 2020

Grocery Prices

Area[1]	T-Bone Steak ($/pound)	Frying Chicken ($/pound)	Whole Milk ($/half gal.)	Eggs ($/dozen)	Orange Juice ($/64 oz.)	Coffee ($/11.5 oz.)
City[2]	12.57	1.48	1.76	1.46	3.36	4.17
Avg.	11.78	1.39	2.05	1.47	3.57	4.34
Min.	8.03	0.94	1.03	0.74	2.94	3.02
Max.	15.86	2.65	4.31	3.77	5.44	8.69

*Note: (1) Values for the local area are compared with the average, minimum and maximum values for all 284 areas in the Cost of Living Index; (2) Figures cover the Denver CO urban area; **T-Bone Steak** (price per pound); **Frying Chicken** (price per pound, whole fryer); **Whole Milk** (half gallon carton); **Eggs** (price per dozen, Grade A, large); **Orange Juice** (64 oz. Tropicana or Florida Natural); **Coffee** (11.5 oz. can, vacuum-packed, Maxwell House, Hills Bros, or Folgers).*
Source: The Council for Community and Economic Research, Cost of Living Index, 2020

Housing and Utility Costs

Area[1]	New Home Price ($)	Apartment Rent ($/month)	All Electric ($/month)	Part Electric ($/month)	Other Energy ($/month)	Telephone ($/month)
City[2]	530,852	1,545	-	59.31	46.19	186.50
Avg.	368,594	1,168	170.86	100.47	65.28	184.30
Min.	190,567	502	91.58	31.42	26.08	169.60
Max.	2,227,806	4,738	470.38	280.31	280.06	206.50

*Note: (1) Values for the local area are compared with the average, minimum and maximum values for all 284 areas in the Cost of Living Index; (2) Figures cover the Denver CO urban area; **New Home Price** (2,400 sf living area, 8,000 sf lot, in urban area with full utilities); **Apartment Rent** (950 sf 2 bedroom/1.5 or 2 bath, unfurnished, excluding all utilities except water); **All Electric** (average monthly cost for an all-electric home); **Part Electric** (average monthly cost for a part-electric home); **Other Energy** (average monthly cost for natural gas, fuel oil, coal, wood, and any other forms of energy except electricity); **Telephone** (price includes the base monthly rate plus taxes and fees for three lines of mobile phone service).*
Source: The Council for Community and Economic Research, Cost of Living Index, 2020

Health Care, Transportation, and Other Costs

Area[1]	Doctor ($/visit)	Dentist ($/visit)	Optometrist ($/visit)	Gasoline ($/gallon)	Beauty Salon ($/visit)	Men's Shirt ($)
City[2]	111.77	105.51	104.86	2.49	44.29	30.30
Avg.	115.44	99.32	108.10	2.21	39.27	31.37
Min.	36.68	59.00	51.36	1.71	19.00	11.00
Max.	219.00	153.10	250.97	3.46	82.05	58.33

*Note: (1) Values for the local area are compared with the average, minimum and maximum values for all 284 areas in the Cost of Living Index; (2) Figures cover the Denver CO urban area; **Doctor** (general practitioners routine office visit for an established patient); **Dentist** (adult teeth cleaning and periodic oral examination); **Optometrist** (full vision eye exam for established adult patient); **Gasoline** (one gallon regular unleaded, national brand, including all taxes, cash price at self-service pump if available); **Beauty Salon** (woman's shampoo, trim, and blow-dry); **Men's Shirt** (cotton/polyester dress shirt, pinpoint weave, long sleeves).*
Source: The Council for Community and Economic Research, Cost of Living Index, 2020

HOUSING

Homeownership Rate

Area	2012 (%)	2013 (%)	2014 (%)	2015 (%)	2016 (%)	2017 (%)	2018 (%)	2019 (%)	2020 (%)
MSA[1]	61.8	61.0	61.9	61.6	61.6	59.3	60.1	63.5	62.9
U.S.	65.4	65.1	64.5	63.7	63.4	63.9	64.4	64.6	66.6

Note: (1) Figures cover the Denver-Aurora-Lakewood, CO Metropolitan Statistical Area
Source: U.S. Census Bureau, Housing Vacancies and Homeownership Annual Statistics: 2012-2020

House Price Index (HPI)

Area	National Ranking[2]	Quarterly Change (%)	One-Year Change (%)	Five-Year Change (%)	Since 1991Q1 (%)
MSA[1]	164	1.71	5.57	42.32	404.42
U.S.[3]	–	3.81	10.77	38.99	205.12

Note: The HPI is a weighted repeat sales index. It measures average price changes in repeat sales or refinancings on the same properties. This information is obtained by reviewing repeat mortgage transactions on single-family properties whose mortgages have been purchased or securitized by Fannie Mae or Freddie Mac since January 1975; (1) Figures cover the Denver-Aurora-Lakewood, CO Metropolitan Statistical Area; (2) Rankings are based on annual percentage change for all metro areas containing at least 15,000 transactions over the last 10 years and ranges from 1 to 253; (3) figures based on a weighted average of Census Division estimates using a seasonally adjusted, purchase-only index; all figures are for the period ending December 31, 2020
Source: Federal Housing Finance Agency, Change in Metropolitan Area House Price Indexes, April 7, 2021

Median Single-Family Home Prices

Area	2018	2019	2020p	Percent Change 2019 to 2020
MSA[1]	449.9	462.1	492.7	6.6
U.S. Average	261.6	274.6	299.9	9.2

Note: Figures are median sales prices of existing single-family homes in thousands of dollars; (p) preliminary; (1) Figures cover the Denver-Aurora-Lakewood, CO Metropolitan Statistical Area
Source: National Association of Realtors, Median Sales Price of Existing Single-Family Homes for Metropolitan Areas, 4th Quarter 2020

Qualifying Income Based on Median Sales Price of Existing Single-Family Homes

Area	With 5% Down ($)	With 10% Down ($)	With 20% Down ($)
MSA[1]	96,935	91,833	81,630
U.S. Average	59,266	56,147	49,908

Note: Figures are preliminary; Qualifying income is based on a mortgage rate of 2.81%. Monthly principal and interest payment is limited to 25% of income; (1) Figures cover the Denver-Aurora-Lakewood, CO Metropolitan Statistical Area
Source: National Association of Realtors, Qualifying Income Based on Median Sales Price of Existing Single-Family Homes for Metropolitan Areas, 4th Quarter 2020

Home Value Distribution

Area	Under $50,000	$50,000 -$99,999	$100,000 -$149,999	$150,000 -$199,999	$200,000 -$299,999	$300,000 -$499,999	$500,000 -$999,999	$1,000,000 or more
City	1.3	1.6	3.3	6.8	19.5	34.6	27.3	5.6
MSA[1]	2.2	1.3	2.3	5.3	19.2	42.7	23.3	3.5
U.S.	6.9	12.0	13.3	14.0	19.6	19.3	11.4	3.4

Note: Figures are percentages and cover owner-occupied housing units; (1) Figures cover the Denver-Aurora-Lakewood, CO Metropolitan Statistical Area
Source: U.S. Census Bureau, 2015-2019 American Community Survey 5-Year Estimates

Year Housing Structure Built

Area	2010 or Later	2000 -2009	1990 -1999	1980 -1989	1970 -1979	1960 -1969	1950 -1959	1940 -1949	Before 1940	Median Year
City	9.0	11.3	6.6	7.4	14.2	10.9	15.0	6.6	18.9	1969
MSA[1]	7.4	16.4	15.2	14.2	18.6	9.3	9.2	2.8	6.8	1982
U.S.	5.2	14.0	13.9	13.4	15.2	10.6	10.3	4.9	12.6	1978

Note: Figures are percentages except for Median Year; Note: (1) Figures cover the Denver-Aurora-Lakewood, CO Metropolitan Statistical Area
Source: U.S. Census Bureau, 2015-2019 American Community Survey 5-Year Estimates

Gross Monthly Rent

Area	Under $500	$500 -$999	$1,000 -$1,499	$1,500 -$1,999	$2,000 -$2,499	$2,500 -$2,999	$3,000 and up	Median ($)
City	8.2	18.4	35.8	23.2	9.6	3.2	1.6	1,311
MSA[1]	5.1	16.7	37.2	26.2	10.2	2.9	1.7	1,380
U.S.	9.4	36.2	30.0	14.0	5.6	2.4	2.4	1,062

Note: Figures are percentages except for Median; Gross rent is the contract rent plus the estimated average monthly cost of utilities (electricity, gas, and water and sewer) and fuels (oil, coal, kerosene, wood, etc.) if these are paid by the renter (or paid for the renter by someone else); (1) Figures cover the Denver-Aurora-Lakewood, CO Metropolitan Statistical Area
Source: U.S. Census Bureau, 2015-2019 American Community Survey 5-Year Estimates

HEALTH

Health Risk Factors

Category	MSA[1] (%)	U.S. (%)
Adults aged 18–64 who have any kind of health care coverage	86.7	87.3
Adults who reported being in good or better health	86.5	82.4
Adults who have been told they have high blood cholesterol	30.8	33.0
Adults who have been told they have high blood pressure	25.1	32.3
Adults who are current smokers	13.8	17.1
Adults who currently use E-cigarettes	5.4	4.6
Adults who currently use chewing tobacco, snuff, or snus	3.2	4.0
Adults who are heavy drinkers[2]	7.5	6.3
Adults who are binge drinkers[3]	20.6	17.4
Adults who are overweight (BMI 25.0 - 29.9)	37.3	35.3
Adults who are obese (BMI 30.0 - 99.8)	22.1	31.3
Adults who participated in any physical activities in the past month	80.6	74.4
Adults who always or nearly always wears a seat belt	96.0	94.3

Note: (1) Figures cover the Denver-Aurora-Lakewood, CO Metropolitan Statistical Area; (2) Heavy drinkers are classified as adult men having more than 14 drinks per week and adult women having more than 7 drinks per week; (3) Binge drinkers are classified as males having five or more drinks on one occasion or females having four or more drinks on one occasion
Source: Centers for Disease Control and Prevention, Behaviorial Risk Factor Surveillance System, SMART: Selected Metropolitan Area Risk Trends, 2017

Acute and Chronic Health Conditions

Category	MSA[1] (%)	U.S. (%)
Adults who have ever been told they had a heart attack	2.6	4.2
Adults who have ever been told they have angina or coronary heart disease	2.4	3.9
Adults who have ever been told they had a stroke	2.3	3.0
Adults who have ever been told they have asthma	13.9	14.2
Adults who have ever been told they have arthritis	20.5	24.9
Adults who have ever been told they have diabetes[2]	7.5	10.5
Adults who have ever been told they had skin cancer	6.2	6.2
Adults who have ever been told they had any other types of cancer	5.8	7.1
Adults who have ever been told they have COPD	3.7	6.5
Adults who have ever been told they have kidney disease	2.2	3.0
Adults who have ever been told they have a form of depression	17.6	20.5

Note: (1) Figures cover the Denver-Aurora-Lakewood, CO Metropolitan Statistical Area; (2) Figures do not include pregnancy-related, borderline, or pre-diabetes
Source: Centers for Disease Control and Prevention, Behaviorial Risk Factor Surveillance System, SMART: Selected Metropolitan Area Risk Trends, 2017

Health Screening and Vaccination Rates

Category	MSA[1] (%)	U.S. (%)
Adults aged 65+ who have had flu shot within the past year	67.9	60.7
Adults aged 65+ who have ever had a pneumonia vaccination	84.1	75.4
Adults who have ever been tested for HIV	41.8	36.1
Adults who have ever had the shingles or zoster vaccine?	34.4	28.9
Adults who have had their blood cholesterol checked within the last five years	87.6	85.9

Note: n/a not available; (1) Figures cover the Denver-Aurora-Lakewood, CO Metropolitan Statistical Area.
Source: Centers for Disease Control and Prevention, Behaviorial Risk Factor Surveillance System, SMART: Selected Metropolitan Area Risk Trends, 2017

Disability Status

Category	MSA[1] (%)	U.S. (%)
Adults who reported being deaf	4.2	6.7
Are you blind or have serious difficulty seeing, even when wearing glasses?	2.8	4.5
Are you limited in any way in any of your usual activities due of arthritis?	9.7	12.9
Do you have difficulty doing errands alone?	4.4	6.8
Do you have difficulty dressing or bathing?	2.1	3.6
Do you have serious difficulty concentrating/remembering/making decisions?	8.4	10.7
Do you have serious difficulty walking or climbing stairs?	8.6	13.6

Note: (1) Figures cover the Denver-Aurora-Lakewood, CO Metropolitan Statistical Area.
Source: Centers for Disease Control and Prevention, Behaviorial Risk Factor Surveillance System, SMART: Selected Metropolitan Area Risk Trends, 2017

Mortality Rates for the Top 10 Causes of Death in the U.S.

ICD-10[a] Sub-Chapter	ICD-10[a] Code	Age-Adjusted Mortality Rate[1] per 100,000 population	
		County[2]	U.S.
Malignant neoplasms	C00-C97	134.3	149.2
Ischaemic heart diseases	I20-I25	62.1	90.5
Other forms of heart disease	I30-I51	36.6	52.2
Chronic lower respiratory diseases	J40-J47	42.2	39.6
Other degenerative diseases of the nervous system	G30-G31	33.8	37.6
Cerebrovascular diseases	I60-I69	36.6	37.2
Other external causes of accidental injury	W00-X59	40.4	36.1
Organic, including symptomatic, mental disorders	F01-F09	29.5	29.4
Hypertensive diseases	I10-I15	30.0	24.1
Diabetes mellitus	E10-E14	20.0	21.5

Note: (a) ICD-10 = International Classification of Diseases 10th Revision; (1) Mortality rates are a three-year average covering 2017-2019; (2) Figures cover Denver County.
Source: Centers for Disease Control and Prevention, National Center for Health Statistics. Underlying Cause of Death 1999-2019 on CDC WONDER Online Database

Mortality Rates for Selected Causes of Death

ICD-10[a] Sub-Chapter	ICD-10[a] Code	Age-Adjusted Mortality Rate[1] per 100,000 population	
		County[2]	U.S.
Assault	X85-Y09	6.8	6.0
Diseases of the liver	K70-K76	23.1	14.4
Human immunodeficiency virus (HIV) disease	B20-B24	2.6	1.5
Influenza and pneumonia	J09-J18	10.5	13.8
Intentional self-harm	X60-X84	20.1	14.1
Malnutrition	E40-E46	5.2	2.3
Obesity and other hyperalimentation	E65-E68	2.5	2.1
Renal failure	N17-N19	9.9	12.6
Transport accidents	V01-V99	9.7	12.3
Viral hepatitis	B15-B19	1.9	1.2

Note: (a) ICD-10 = International Classification of Diseases 10th Revision; (1) Mortality rates are a three-year average covering 2017-2019; (2) Figures cover Denver County; Data are suppressed when the data meet the criteria for confidentiality constraints; Mortality rates are flagged as unreliable when the rate would be calculated with a numerator of 20 or less.
Source: Centers for Disease Control and Prevention, National Center for Health Statistics. Underlying Cause of Death 1999-2019 on CDC WONDER Online Database

Health Insurance Coverage

Area	With Health Insurance	With Private Health Insurance	With Public Health Insurance	Without Health Insurance	Population Under Age 19 Without Health Insurance
City	90.7	65.5	33.0	9.3	4.2
MSA[1]	92.6	72.6	29.2	7.4	4.0
U.S.	91.2	67.9	35.1	8.8	5.1

Note: Figures are percentages that cover the civilian noninstitutionalized population; (1) Figures cover the Denver-Aurora-Lakewood, CO Metropolitan Statistical Area
Source: U.S. Census Bureau, 2015-2019 American Community Survey 5-Year Estimates

Number of Medical Professionals

Area	MDs[3]	DOs[3,4]	Dentists	Podiatrists	Chiropractors	Optometrists
County[1] (number)	4,266	234	555	48	263	123
County[1] (rate[2])	595.6	32.7	76.3	6.6	36.2	16.9
U.S. (rate[2])	282.9	22.7	71.2	6.2	28.1	16.9

08031
Note: Data as of 2019 unless noted; (1) Data covers Denver County; (2) Rate per 100,000 population; (3) Data as of 2018 and includes all active, non-federal physicians; (4) Doctor of Osteopathic Medicine
Source: U.S. Department of Health and Human Services, Health Resources and Services Administration, Bureau of Health Professions, Area Resource File (ARF) 2019-2020

Best Hospitals

According to *U.S. News,* the Denver-Aurora-Lakewood, CO metro area is home to three of the best hospitals in the U.S.: **Craig Hospital** (1 adult specialty); **National Jewish Health, Denver-University of Colorado Hospital** (1 adult specialty); **UCHealth University of Colorado Hospital** (9 adult specialties). The hospitals listed were nationally ranked in at least one of 16 adult or 10 pediatric specialties. Only 134 hospitals nationwide were nationally ranked in one or more adult or pediatric specialty; this number increases to 178 counting specialized centers within hospitals. Twenty hospitals in the U.S. made the Honor Roll. The Best Hospitals Honor Roll takes both the national rankings and the procedure and condition ratings into account. Hospitals received points if they were nationally ranked in one of the 16 adult specialties—the higher they ranked, the more points they got—and how many ratings of "high performing" they earned in the 10 procedures and conditions. *U.S. News Online, "America's Best Hospitals 2020-21"*

According to *U.S. News,* the Denver-Aurora-Lakewood, CO metro area is home to one of the best children's hospitals in the U.S.: **Children's Hospital Colorado** (Honor Roll/10 pediatric specialties). The hospital listed was highly ranked in at least one of 10 pediatric specialties. Eighty-eight children's hospitals in the U.S. were nationally ranked in at least one specialty. Hospitals received points for being ranked in a specialty, and the 10 hospitals with the most points across the 10 specialties make up the Honor Roll. *U.S. News Online, "America's Best Children's Hospitals 2020-21"*

EDUCATION

Public School District Statistics

District Name	Schls	Pupils	Pupil/ Teacher Ratio	Minority Pupils[1] (%)	Free Lunch Eligible[2] (%)	IEP[3] (%)
Mapleton School District No. 1	18	8,934	19.8	72.8	43.8	n/a
School District No. 1	206	92,039	15.0	75.2	55.9	n/a
State Charter School Institute	40	18,268	18.3	50.7	26.8	n/a

Note: Table includes school districts with 2,000 or more students; (1) Percentage of students that are not non-Hispanic white; (2) Percentage of students that are eligible for the free lunch program; (3) Percentage of students that have an Individualized Education Program.
Source: U.S. Department of Education, National Center for Education Statistics, Common Core of Data, Local Education Agency (School District) Universe Survey: School Year 2018-2019; U.S. Department of Education, National Center for Education Statistics, Common Core of Data, Public Elementary/Secondary School Universe Survey: School Year 2018-2019

Best High Schools

According to *U.S. News,* Denver is home to six of the top 500 high schools in the U.S.: **D'Evelyn Junior/Senior High School** (#42); **Denver School of the Arts** (#183); **DSST: Stapleton High School** (#233); **KIPP Denver Collegiate High School** (#297); **DSST: Green Valley Ranch High School** (#364); **DSST: Cole High School** (#371). Nearly 18,000 public, magnet and charter schools were ranked based on their performance on state assessments and how well they prepare students for college. *U.S. News & World Report, "Best High Schools 2020"*

Highest Level of Education

Area	Less than H.S.	H.S. Diploma	Some College, No Deg.	Associate Degree	Bachelor's Degree	Master's Degree	Prof. School Degree	Doctorate Degree
City	12.0	16.8	16.5	5.3	30.2	13.1	4.2	2.0
MSA[1]	8.8	19.9	19.8	7.7	27.7	11.8	2.7	1.6
U.S.	12.0	27.0	20.4	8.5	19.8	8.8	2.1	1.4

Note: Figures cover persons age 25 and over; (1) Figures cover the Denver-Aurora-Lakewood, CO Metropolitan Statistical Area
Source: U.S. Census Bureau, 2015-2019 American Community Survey 5-Year Estimates

Educational Attainment by Race

Area	High School Graduate or Higher (%)					Bachelor's Degree or Higher (%)				
	Total	White	Black	Asian	Hisp.[2]	Total	White	Black	Asian	Hisp.[2]
City	88.0	90.3	86.9	83.4	64.7	49.4	54.5	24.7	53.9	15.9
MSA[1]	91.2	92.8	89.8	86.0	71.0	43.8	46.2	27.0	52.1	16.7
U.S.	88.0	89.9	86.0	87.1	68.7	32.1	33.5	21.6	54.3	16.4

Note: Figures shown cover persons 25 years old and over; (1) Figures cover the Denver-Aurora-Lakewood, CO Metropolitan Statistical Area; (2) People of Hispanic origin can be of any race
Source: U.S. Census Bureau, 2015-2019 American Community Survey 5-Year Estimates

School Enrollment by Grade and Control

Area	Preschool (%)		Kindergarten (%)		Grades 1 - 4 (%)		Grades 5 - 8 (%)		Grades 9 - 12 (%)	
	Public	Private	Public	Private	Public	Private	Public	Private	Public	Private
City	64.4	35.6	86.3	13.7	91.4	8.6	91.0	9.0	91.4	8.6
MSA[1]	59.6	40.4	90.1	9.9	92.5	7.5	92.0	8.0	91.9	8.1
U.S.	59.1	40.9	87.6	12.4	89.5	10.5	89.4	10.6	90.1	9.9

Note: Figures shown cover persons 3 years old and over; (1) Figures cover the Denver-Aurora-Lakewood, CO Metropolitan Statistical Area
Source: U.S. Census Bureau, 2015-2019 American Community Survey 5-Year Estimates

Higher Education

Four-Year Colleges			Two-Year Colleges			Medical Schools[1]	Law Schools[2]	Voc/ Tech[3]
Public	Private Non-profit	Private For-profit	Public	Private Non-profit	Private For-profit			
3	4	3	0	1	6	0	1	3

Note: Figures cover institutions located within the city limits and include main campuses only; (1) includes schools accredited by the Liaison Committee on Medical Education and the American Osteopathic Association's Commission on Osteopathic College Accreditation; (2) includes ABA-accredited schools, schools with provisional ABA accreditation, and state accredited schools; (3) includes all schools with programs that are less than 2 years.
Source: National Center for Education Statistics, Integrated Postsecondary Education System (IPEDS), 2019-20; Wikipedia, List of Medical Schools in the United States, accessed April 2, 2021; Wikipedia, List of Law Schools in the United States, accessed April 2, 2021

According to *U.S. News & World Report,* the Denver-Aurora-Lakewood, CO metro area is home to two of the top 200 national universities in the U.S.: **University of Denver** (#80 tie); **Colorado School of Mines** (#88 tie). The indicators used to capture academic quality fall into a number of categories: assessment by administrators at peer institutions; retention of students; faculty resources; student selectivity; financial resources; alumni giving; high school counselor ratings of colleges; and graduation rate. *U.S. News & World Report, "America's Best Colleges 2021"*

According to *U.S. News & World Report,* the Denver-Aurora-Lakewood, CO metro area is home to one of the top 100 law schools in the U.S.: **University of Denver (Sturm)** (#78 tie). The rankings are based on a weighted average of 12 measures of quality: peer assessment score; assessment score by lawyers/judges; median LSAT scores; median undergrad GPA; acceptance rate; employment rates for graduates; placement success; bar passage rate; faculty resources; expenditures per student; student/faculty ratio; and library resources. *U.S. News & World Report, "America's Best Graduate Schools, Law, 2022"*

According to *U.S. News & World Report,* the Denver-Aurora-Lakewood, CO metro area is home to one of the top 75 medical schools for research in the U.S.: **University of Colorado** (#27 tie). The rankings are based on a weighted average of 11 measures of quality: quality assessment; peer assessment score; assessment score by residency directors; research activity; total research activity; average research activity per faculty member; student selectivity; median MCAT total score; median undergraduate GPA; acceptance rate; and faculty resources. *U.S. News & World Report, "America's Best Graduate Schools, Medical, 2022"*

EMPLOYERS

Major Employers

Company Name	Industry
Arvada House Preservation	Apartment building operators
Centura Health Corporation	General medical & surgical hospitals
Colorado Department of Transportation	Regulation, administration of transportation
County of Jefferson	County government
DISH Network Corporation	Cable & other pay television services
Gart Bros Sporting Goods Company	Sporting goods & bicycle shops
HCA Healthone	General medical & surgical hospitals
IBM	Printers, computer
Level 3 Communications	Telephone communication, except radio
Lockheed Martin Corporation	Aircraft & space vehicles
Mormon Church	Mormon church
MWH/Fni Joint Venture	Engineering services
Newmont Gold Company	Gold ores mining
Noodles and Company	Eating places
Strasburg Telephone Company	Telephone communication, except radio
Synergy Services	Payroll accounting service
TW Telecom Holdings	Telephone communication, except radio
Western Union Financial Services	Electronic funds transfer network, including switching

Note: Companies shown are located within the Denver-Aurora-Lakewood, CO Metropolitan Statistical Area.
Source: Hoovers.com; Wikipedia

Best Companies to Work For

VF Corporation, headquartered in Denver, is among the "Top Companies for Executive Women." This list is determined by organizations filling out an in-depth survey that measures female demographics at every level, but with an emphasis on women in senior corporate roles, with profit & loss (P&L) responsibility, and those earning in the top 20 percent of the organization. *Working Mother* defines P&L as having responsibility that involves monitoring the net income after expenses for a department or entire organization, with direct influence on how company resources are allocated. *Working Mother, "Top Companies for Executive Women," 2020+*

PUBLIC SAFETY

Crime Rate

Area	All Crimes	Violent Crimes				Property Crimes		
		Murder	Rape[3]	Robbery	Aggrav. Assault	Burglary	Larceny -Theft	Motor Vehicle Theft
City	4,492.4	9.2	97.8	165.3	476.6	544.2	2,473.0	726.3
Suburbs[1]	n/a	n/a	n/a	n/a	n/a	n/a	n/a	n/a
Metro[2]	n/a	n/a	n/a	n/a	n/a	n/a	n/a	n/a
U.S.	2,489.3	5.0	42.6	81.6	250.2	340.5	1,549.5	219.9

Note: Figures are crimes per 100,000 population; (1) All areas within the metro area that are located outside the city limits; (2) Figures cover the Denver-Aurora-Lakewood, CO Metropolitan Statistical Area; n/a not available; (3) All figures shown were reported using the revised Uniform Crime Reporting (UCR) definition of rape.
Source: FBI Uniform Crime Reports, 2019

Hate Crimes

Area	Number of Quarters Reported	Number of Incidents per Bias Motivation					
		Race/Ethnicity/ Ancestry	Religion	Sexual Orientation	Disability	Gender	Gender Identity
City	4	40	15	26	2	0	2
U.S.	4	3,963	1,521	1,195	157	69	198

Source: Federal Bureau of Investigation, Hate Crime Statistics 2019

Identity Theft Consumer Reports

Area	Reports	Reports per 100,000 Population	Rank[2]
MSA[1]	11,699	394	76
U.S.	1,387,615	423	-

Note: (1) Figures cover the Denver-Aurora-Lakewood, CO Metropolitan Statistical Area; (2) Rank ranges from 1 to 391 where 1 indicates greatest number of identity theft reports per 100,000 population
Source: Federal Trade Commission, Consumer Sentinel Network Data Book 2020

Fraud and Other Consumer Reports

Area	Reports	Reports per 100,000 Population	Rank[2]
MSA[1]	26,615	897	50
U.S.	3,385,133	1,031	-

Note: (1) Figures cover the Denver-Aurora-Lakewood, CO Metropolitan Statistical Area; (2) Rank ranges from 1 to 391 where 1 indicates greatest number of fraud and other consumer reports per 100,000 population
Source: Federal Trade Commission, Consumer Sentinel Network Data Book 2020

POLITICS

2020 Presidential Election Results

Area	Biden	Trump	Jorgensen	Hawkins	Other
Denver County	79.6	18.2	1.2	0.3	0.7
U.S.	51.3	46.8	1.2	0.3	0.5

Note: Results are percentages and may not add to 100% due to rounding
Source: Dave Leip's Atlas of U.S. Presidential Elections

SPORTS

Professional Sports Teams

Team Name	League	Year Established
Colorado Avalanche	National Hockey League (NHL)	1995
Colorado Rapids	Major League Soccer (MLS)	1996
Colorado Rockies	Major League Baseball (MLB)	1993
Denver Broncos	National Football League (NFL)	1960
Denver Nuggets	National Basketball Association (NBA)	1967

Note: Includes teams located in the Denver-Aurora-Lakewood, CO Metropolitan Statistical Area.
Source: Wikipedia, Major Professional Sports Teams of the United States and Canada, April 6, 2021

CLIMATE

Average and Extreme Temperatures

Temperature	Jan	Feb	Mar	Apr	May	Jun	Jul	Aug	Sep	Oct	Nov	Dec	Yr.
Extreme High (°F)	73	76	84	90	93	102	103	100	97	89	79	75	103
Average High (°F)	43	47	52	62	71	81	88	86	77	67	52	45	64
Average Temp. (°F)	30	34	39	48	58	67	73	72	63	52	39	32	51
Average Low (°F)	16	20	25	34	44	53	59	57	48	37	25	18	37
Extreme Low (°F)	-25	-25	-10	-2	22	30	43	41	17	3	-8	-25	-25

Note: Figures cover the years 1948-1992
Source: National Climatic Data Center, International Station Meteorological Climate Summary, 9/96

Average Precipitation/Snowfall/Humidity

Precip./Humidity	Jan	Feb	Mar	Apr	May	Jun	Jul	Aug	Sep	Oct	Nov	Dec	Yr.
Avg. Precip. (in.)	0.6	0.6	1.3	1.7	2.5	1.7	1.9	1.5	1.1	1.0	0.9	0.6	15.5
Avg. Snowfall (in.)	9	7	14	9	2	Tr	0	0	2	4	9	8	63
Avg. Rel. Hum. 5am (%)	62	65	67	66	70	68	67	68	66	63	66	63	66
Avg. Rel. Hum. 5pm (%)	49	44	40	35	38	34	34	34	32	34	47	50	39

Note: Figures cover the years 1948-1992; Tr = Trace amounts (<0.05 in. of rain; <0.5 in. of snow)
Source: National Climatic Data Center, International Station Meteorological Climate Summary, 9/96

Weather Conditions

Temperature			Daytime Sky			Precipitation		
10°F & below	32°F & below	90°F & above	Clear	Partly cloudy	Cloudy	0.01 inch or more precip.	0.1 inch or more snow/ice	Thunder-storms
24	155	33	99	177	89	90	38	39

Note: Figures are average number of days per year and cover the years 1948-1992
Source: National Climatic Data Center, International Station Meteorological Climate Summary, 9/96

HAZARDOUS WASTE

Superfund Sites

The Denver-Aurora-Lakewood, CO metro area is home to nine sites on the EPA's Superfund National Priorities List: **Air Force Plant PJKS** (final); **Broderick Wood Products** (final); **Central City, Clear Creek** (final); **Chemical Sales Co.** (final); **Denver Radium Site** (final); **Lowry Landfill** (final); **Rocky Flats Plant (USDOE)** (final); **Rocky Mountain Arsenal (USARMY)** (final); **Vasquez Boulevard and I-70** (final). There are a total of 1,375 Superfund sites with a status of proposed or final on the list in the U.S. *U.S. Environmental Protection Agency, National Priorities List, April 7, 2021*

AIR QUALITY

Air Quality Trends: Ozone

	1990	1995	2000	2005	2010	2015	2016	2017	2018	2019
MSA[1]	0.077	0.070	0.069	0.072	0.070	0.073	0.071	0.072	0.071	0.068
U.S.	0.088	0.089	0.082	0.080	0.073	0.069	0.069	0.068	0.069	0.065

Note: (1) Data covers the Denver-Aurora-Lakewood, CO Metropolitan Statistical Area. The values shown are the composite ozone concentration averages among trend sites based on the highest fourth daily maximum 8-hour concentration in parts per million. These trends are based on sites having an adequate record of monitoring data during the trend period. Data from exceptional events are included.
Source: U.S. Environmental Protection Agency, Air Quality Monitoring Information, "Air Quality Trends by City, 1990-2019"

Air Quality Index

Area	Percent of Days when Air Quality was...[2]					AQI Statistics[2]	
	Good	Moderate	Unhealthy for Sensitive Groups	Unhealthy	Very Unhealthy	Maximum	Median
MSA[1]	24.9	69.0	5.5	0.5	0.0	154	58

Note: (1) Data covers the Denver-Aurora-Lakewood, CO Metropolitan Statistical Area; (2) Based on 365 days with AQI data in 2019. Air Quality Index (AQI) is an index for reporting daily air quality. EPA calculates the AQI for five major air pollutants regulated by the Clean Air Act: ground-level ozone, particle pollution (aka particulate matter), carbon monoxide, sulfur dioxide, and nitrogen dioxide. The AQI runs from 0 to 500. The higher the AQI value, the greater the level of air pollution and the greater the health concern. There are six AQI categories: "Good" AQI is between 0 and 50. Air quality is considered satisfactory; "Moderate" AQI is between 51 and 100. Air quality is acceptable; "Unhealthy for Sensitive Groups" When AQI values are between 101 and 150, members of sensitive groups may experience health effects; "Unhealthy" When AQI values are between 151 and 200 everyone may begin to experience health effects; "Very Unhealthy" AQI values between 201 and 300 trigger a health alert; "Hazardous" AQI values over 300 trigger warnings of emergency conditions (not shown).
Source: U.S. Environmental Protection Agency, Air Quality Index Report, 2019

Air Quality Index Pollutants

Area	Percent of Days when AQI Pollutant was...[2]					
	Carbon Monoxide	Nitrogen Dioxide	Ozone	Sulfur Dioxide	Particulate Matter 2.5	Particulate Matter 10
MSA[1]	0.0	16.4	57.8	0.3	17.3	8.2

Note: (1) Data covers the Denver-Aurora-Lakewood, CO Metropolitan Statistical Area; (2) Based on 365 days with AQI data in 2019. The Air Quality Index (AQI) is an index for reporting daily air quality. EPA calculates the AQI for five major air pollutants regulated by the Clean Air Act: ground-level ozone, particle pollution (also known as particulate matter), carbon monoxide, sulfur dioxide, and nitrogen dioxide. The AQI runs from 0 to 500. The higher the AQI value, the greater the level of air pollution and the greater the health concern.
Source: U.S. Environmental Protection Agency, Air Quality Index Report, 2019

Maximum Air Pollutant Concentrations: Particulate Matter, Ozone, CO and Lead

	Particulate Matter 10 (ug/m³)	Particulate Matter 2.5 Wtd AM (ug/m³)	Particulate Matter 2.5 24-Hr (ug/m³)	Ozone (ppm)	Carbon Monoxide (ppm)	Lead (ug/m³)
MSA[1] Level	111	10.0	29	0.078	2	n/a
NAAQS[2]	150	15	35	0.075	9	0.15
Met NAAQS[2]	Yes	Yes	Yes	No	Yes	n/a

Note: (1) Data covers the Denver-Aurora-Lakewood, CO Metropolitan Statistical Area; Data from exceptional events are included; (2) National Ambient Air Quality Standards; ppm = parts per million; ug/m³ = micrograms per cubic meter; n/a not available.
Concentrations: Particulate Matter 10 (coarse particulate)—highest second maximum 24-hour concentration; Particulate Matter 2.5 Wtd AM (fine particulate)—highest weighted annual mean concentration; Particulate Matter 2.5 24-Hour (fine particulate)—highest 98th percentile 24-hour concentration; Ozone—highest fourth daily maximum 8-hour concentration; Carbon Monoxide—highest second maximum non-overlapping 8-hour concentration; Lead—maximum running 3-month average
Source: U.S. Environmental Protection Agency, Air Quality Monitoring Information, "Air Quality Statistics by City, 2019"

Maximum Air Pollutant Concentrations: Nitrogen Dioxide and Sulfur Dioxide

	Nitrogen Dioxide AM (ppb)	Nitrogen Dioxide 1-Hr (ppb)	Sulfur Dioxide AM (ppb)	Sulfur Dioxide 1-Hr (ppb)	Sulfur Dioxide 24-Hr (ppb)
MSA[1] Level	27	69	n/a	7	n/a
NAAQS[2]	53	100	30	75	140
Met NAAQS[2]	Yes	Yes	n/a	Yes	n/a

Note: (1) Data covers the Denver-Aurora-Lakewood, CO Metropolitan Statistical Area; Data from exceptional events are included; (2) National Ambient Air Quality Standards; ppm = parts per million; ug/m³ = micrograms per cubic meter; n/a not available.
Concentrations: Nitrogen Dioxide AM—highest arithmetic mean concentration; Nitrogen Dioxide 1-Hr—highest 98th percentile 1-hour daily maximum concentration; Sulfur Dioxide AM—highest annual mean concentration; Sulfur Dioxide 1-Hr—highest 99th percentile 1-hour daily maximum concentration; Sulfur Dioxide 24-Hr—highest second maximum 24-hour concentration
Source: U.S. Environmental Protection Agency, Air Quality Monitoring Information, "Air Quality Statistics by City, 2019"

Fort Collins, Colorado

Background

At 4,985 feet, Fort Collins lies high in the eastern base of the Rocky Mountains' front range along the Cache la Poudre River about one hour from Denver. Although not quite as large as Denver, Fort Collins, home to Colorado State University and its own symphony orchestra, offers virtually everything its citizens need, all within a spectacular landscape.

Fort Collins owes its name to Colonel William Collins of the Civil War era, who was sent with a regiment of Union soldiers to guard farmers and ranchers scattered throughout the valley, and to provide security for the Overland Stage trail. Originally called Camp Collins, the place remained a military reservation until 1866 and was incorporated in 1879.

The early economy of the town depended first on lumber, and then on the raising of livestock and produce, with alfalfa, grain, and sugar beets as the chief crops. Sugar refineries, dairies, and meatpacking plants bolstered the wealth of the town, as did the products of mining and quarrying. Fort Collins is still the commercial center for a rich agricultural region that produces hay, barley, and sugar beets.

Colorado State University, the land grant University of Colorado, was established in Fort Collins in 1879, and offers innumerable cultural, economic, and educational benefits to residents. More than 25,000 students are enrolled at CSU, which is the largest employer in the city. CSU offers a world-class range of undergraduate and graduate programs, and is an internationally recognized center for forestry, agricultural science, veterinary medicine, and civil engineering.

Fort Collins' businesses produce motion-picture film, combustion engines, prefabricated metal buildings, arc welders and rods, cement products, dental hygiene appliances, and miscellaneous plastics. With fabulous scenery, a symphony orchestra, and all the attractions of Denver an hour away, Fort Collins offers an attractive place to live. For outdoor sport enthusiasts, the area is irresistible. The town is only a few hours from Colorado's world-famous ski areas, and cross-country skiing is nearby.

The Fort Collins public school system, within the Poudre School District, is one of the area's largest employers. The latest addition was the city's 32nd elementary school. The city's public library system, Poudre River Public Libraries, operates three branches.

Gateway Natural Area, 15 miles from Fort Collins, offers several recreation opportunities, including a quarter-mile nature trail and a designated boat launch. Lakes are easily accessible for all water sports, and the Cache La Poudre River offers some of the best trout fishing in Colorado. For hunters, the area is a paradise, with ample supplies of antelope, black bear, deer, elk, mountain lion, and small game.

Fort Collins also offers a great range of cultural amenities. The city's Lincoln Center presents year-round performances by a variety of artists. Old Town, a historic downtown shopping district, hosts a number of large festivals each year. Fort Collins Symphony, the Larimer Chorale, Open Stage Theatre, and the Canyon Concert Ballet call Fort Collins their home. The city also cultivates the visual arts, with "Art in Public Places" sponsored by the city, and provides exhibits at the Lincoln Center, Fort Collins Museum, and private galleries.

Transportation in and around the city is convenient. The municipality operates its own bus service, and interstate bus service is available. Residents are served by three nearby airports—Fort Collins/Loveland Airport, Cheyenne Municipal Airport, and Denver International Airport, which is one of the nation's busiest airports.

Fort Collins features four distinct seasons and, though high in the foothills, is buffered from both summer and winter temperature extremes. The most typical day in Fort Collins is warm and dry, and mild nights are the rule. The town enjoys on average more than 300 sunny days per year, and an annual snowfall of 51 inches. Rainfall is far less. Summers are comfortable, while winters are cold.

Rankings

General Rankings

- *US News & World Report* conducted a survey of more than 3,000 people and analyzed the 150 largest metropolitan areas to determine what matters most when selecting the next place to live. Fort Collins ranked #5 out of the top 25 as having the best combination of desirable factors. Criteria: cost of living; quality of life; net migration; job market; desirability; and other factors. *realestate.usnews.com, "The 25 Best Places to Live in the U.S. in 2020-21," October 13, 2020*

- In their seventh annual survey, Livability.com looked at data for more than 1,000 small to mid-sized U.S. cities to determine the rankings for Livability's "Top 100 Best Places to Live" in 2020. Fort Collins ranked #1. Criteria: housing and affordable living; vibrant economy; social and civic engagement; education; demographics; health care options; transportation & infrastructure; and abundant lifestyle amenities. *Livability.com, "Top 100 Best Places to Live 2020" October 2020*

Business/Finance Rankings

- The Fort Collins metro area appeared on the Milken Institute "2021 Best Performing Cities" list. Rank: #12 out of 200 large metro areas (population over 250,000). Criteria: job growth; wage and salary growth; high-tech output growth; housing affordability; household broadband access. *Milken Institute, "Best-Performing Cities 2021," February 16, 2021*

- *Forbes* ranked the 200 most populous metro areas to determine the nation's "Best Places for Business and Careers." The Fort Collins metro area was ranked #27. Criteria: costs (business and living); job growth (past and projected); income growth; quality of life; educational attainment (college and high school); projected economic growth; cultural and leisure opportunities; workplace tolerance laws; net migration patterns. *Forbes, "The Best Places for Business and Careers 2019: Seattle Still On Top," October 30, 2019*

Children/Family Rankings

- Fort Collins was selected as one of the most playful cities in the U.S. by KaBOOM! The organization's Playful City USA initiative honors cities and towns across the nation that have made their communities more playable. Criteria: pledging to integrate play as a solution to challenges in their communities; making it easy for children to get active and balanced play; creating more family-friendly and innovative communities as a result. *KaBOOM! National Campaign for Play, "2017 Playful City USA Communities"*

- Fort Collins was selected as one of the best cities for newlyweds by *Rent.com*. The city ranked #13 of 15. Criteria: cost of living; availability of affordable rental inventory; annual household income; activities and restaurant options; percentage of married couples; concentration of millennials; safety. *Rent.com, "The 15 Best Cities for Newlyweds," December 11, 2018*

Environmental Rankings

- The U.S. Environmental Protection Agency (EPA) released a list of mid-size U.S. metropolitan areas with the most ENERGY STAR certified buildings in 2019. The Fort Collins metro area was ranked #6 out of 10. *U.S. Environmental Protection Agency, "2020 Energy Star Top Cities," March 2020*

- Fort Collins was highlighted as one of the 25 most ozone-polluted metro areas in the U.S. during 2016 through 2018. The area ranked #19. *American Lung Association, "State of the Air 2020," April 21, 2020*

Real Estate Rankings

- The Fort Collins metro area was identified as one of the 20 least affordable housing markets in the U.S. in 2020. The area ranked #163 out of 183 markets. Criteria: qualification for a mortgage loan with a 10 percent down payment on a typical home. *National Association of Realtors®, Qualifying Income Based on Sales Price of Existing Single-Family Homes for Metropolitan Areas, 2020*

- Fort Collins was ranked #145 out of 268 metro areas in terms of housing affordability in 2020 by the National Association of Home Builders (#1 = most affordable). Criteria: the share of homes sold in that area affordable to a family earning the local median income, based on standard mortgage underwriting criteria. *National Association of Home Builders®, NAHB-Wells Fargo Housing Opportunity Index, 4th Quarter 2020*

Safety Rankings

- Allstate ranked the 200 largest cities in America in terms of driver safety. Fort Collins ranked #7. Criteria: internal property damage claims over a two-year period from January 2016 to December 2017. The report helps increase the importance of safety and awareness behind the wheel. *Allstate, "Allstate America's Best Drivers Report, 2019" June 24, 2019*

- The National Insurance Crime Bureau ranked 384 metro areas in the U.S. in terms of per capita rates of vehicle theft. The Fort Collins metro area ranked #246 (#1 = highest rate). Criteria: number of vehicle theft offenses per 100,000 inhabitants in 2019. *National Insurance Crime Bureau, "Hot Spots 2019," July 21, 2020*

Seniors/Retirement Rankings

- From its Best Cities for Successful Aging indexes, the Milken Institute generated rankings for metropolitan areas, weighing data in nine categories—health care, wellness, living arrangements, transportation and convenience, financial characteristics, education, employment, community engagement, and overall livability. The Fort Collins metro area was ranked #88 overall in the small metro area category. *Milken Institute, "Best Cities for Successful Aging, 2017" March 14, 2017*

- Fort Collins was identified as #9 of 20 most popular places to retire in the Western region by *Topretirements.com*. The site separated its annual "Best Places to Retire" list by major U.S. regions for 2019. The list reflects the 20 cities that visitors to the website are most interested in for retirement, based on the number of times a city's review was viewed on the website. *Topretirements.com, "20 Best Places to Retire in the West-2019," November 11, 2019*

Sports/Recreation Rankings

- Fort Collins was chosen as one of America's best cities for bicycling. The city ranked #3 out of 50. Criteria: cycling infrastructure that is safe and friendly for all ages; energy and bike culture. The editors evaluated cities with populations of 100,000 or more. *Bicycling, "The 50 Best Bike Cities in America," October 10, 2018*

Miscellaneous Rankings

- *MoveHub* ranked 446 hipster cities across 20 countries, using its *alternative* Hipster Index and Fort Collins came out as #48 among the top 50. Criteria: population over 150,000; number of vintage boutiques; density of tattoo parlors; vegan places to eat; coffee shops; and density of vinyl record stores. *www.movehub.com, "The Hipster Index: Brighton Pips Portland to Global Top Spot," February 20, 2020*

- Fort Collins was selected as a 2020 Digital Cities Survey winner. The city ranked #6 in the mid-sized city (125,000 to 249,999 population) category. The survey examined and assessed how city governments are utilizing technology to improve transparency, enhance cybersecurity, and respond to the pandemic. Survey questions focused on ten initiatives: cybersecurity, citizen experience, disaster recovery, business intelligence, IT personnel, data governance, collaboration, infrastructure modernization, cloud computing, and mobile applications. *Center for Digital Government, "2020 Digital Cities Survey," November 10, 2020*

Business Environment

DEMOGRAPHICS

Population Growth

Area	1990 Census	2000 Census	2010 Census	2019* Estimate	Population Growth (%) 1990-2019	Population Growth (%) 2010-2019
City	89,555	118,652	143,986	165,609	84.9	15.0
MSA[1]	186,136	251,494	299,630	344,786	85.2	15.1
U.S.	248,709,873	281,421,906	308,745,538	324,697,795	30.6	5.2

Note: (1) Figures cover the Fort Collins, CO Metropolitan Statistical Area; (*) 2015-2019 5-year estimated population
Source: U.S. Census Bureau, 1990 Census, Census 2000, Census 2010, 2015-2019 American Community Survey 5-Year Estimates

Household Size

Area	Persons in Household (%) One	Two	Three	Four	Five	Six	Seven or More	Average Household Size
City	24.7	37.9	17.8	13.9	4.3	1.0	0.4	2.40
MSA[1]	24.3	40.3	15.8	12.3	5.2	1.5	0.6	2.50
U.S.	27.9	33.9	15.6	12.9	6.0	2.3	1.4	2.60

Note: (1) Figures cover the Fort Collins, CO Metropolitan Statistical Area
Source: U.S. Census Bureau, 2015-2019 American Community Survey 5-Year Estimates

Race

Area	White Alone[2] (%)	Black Alone[2] (%)	Asian Alone[2] (%)	AIAN[3] Alone[2] (%)	NHOPI[4] Alone[2] (%)	Other Race Alone[2] (%)	Two or More Races (%)
City	88.3	1.6	3.5	1.0	0.1	1.5	4.0
MSA[1]	91.3	1.0	2.2	0.8	0.1	1.5	3.2
U.S.	72.5	12.7	5.5	0.8	0.2	4.9	3.3

Note: (1) Figures cover the Fort Collins, CO Metropolitan Statistical Area; (2) Alone is defined as not being in combination with one or more other races; (3) American Indian and Alaska Native; (4) Native Hawaiian and Other Pacific Islander
Source: U.S. Census Bureau, 2015-2019 American Community Survey 5-Year Estimates

Hispanic or Latino Origin

Area	Total (%)	Mexican (%)	Puerto Rican (%)	Cuban (%)	Other (%)
City	11.6	8.2	0.4	0.1	3.0
MSA[1]	11.5	8.4	0.3	0.1	2.6
U.S.	18.0	11.2	1.7	0.7	4.3

Note: Persons of Hispanic or Latino origin can be of any race; (1) Figures cover the Fort Collins, CO Metropolitan Statistical Area
Source: U.S. Census Bureau, 2015-2019 American Community Survey 5-Year Estimates

Ancestry

Area	German	Irish	English	American	Italian	Polish	French[2]	Scottish	Dutch
City	22.5	12.7	11.4	3.7	5.3	3.0	3.3	2.9	1.8
MSA[1]	24.3	12.8	12.2	4.4	4.9	2.7	3.4	3.2	2.2
U.S.	13.3	9.7	7.2	6.2	5.1	2.8	2.3	1.7	1.2

Note: Figures are the percentage of the total population reporting a particular ancestry. The nine most commonly reported ancestries in the U.S. are shown. Figures include multiple ancestries (e.g. if a person reported being Irish and Italian, they were included in both columns); (1) Figures cover the Fort Collins, CO Metropolitan Statistical Area; (2) Excludes Basque
Source: U.S. Census Bureau, 2015-2019 American Community Survey 5-Year Estimates

Foreign-born Population

Area	Percent of Population Born in Any Foreign Country	Asia	Mexico	Europe	Caribbean	Central America[2]	South America	Africa	Canada
City	6.8	3.0	1.2	1.4	0.1	0.2	0.4	0.3	0.2
MSA[1]	5.6	1.9	1.3	1.3	0.1	0.2	0.4	0.2	0.2
U.S.	13.6	4.2	3.5	1.5	1.3	1.1	1.0	0.7	0.2

Note: (1) Figures cover the Fort Collins, CO Metropolitan Statistical Area; (2) Excludes Mexico.
Source: U.S. Census Bureau, 2015-2019 American Community Survey 5-Year Estimates

Marital Status

Area	Never Married	Now Married[2]	Separated	Widowed	Divorced
City	46.6	40.6	0.8	3.3	8.7
MSA[1]	34.8	50.1	0.9	4.0	10.2
U.S.	33.4	48.1	1.9	5.8	10.9

Note: Figures are percentages and cover the population 15 years of age and older; (1) Figures cover the Fort Collins, CO Metropolitan Statistical Area; (2) Excludes separated
Source: U.S. Census Bureau, 2015-2019 American Community Survey 5-Year Estimates

Disability by Age

Area	All Ages	Under 18 Years Old	18 to 64 Years Old	65 Years and Over
City	7.9	2.8	6.0	30.0
MSA[1]	9.7	3.1	7.4	28.1
U.S.	12.6	4.2	10.3	34.5

Note: Figures show percent of the civilian noninstitutionalized population that reported having a disability. Disability status is determined from six types of difficulty: vision, hearing, cognitive, ambulatory, self-care, and independent living. For children under 5 years old, hearing and vision difficulty are used to determine disability status. For children between the ages of 5 and 14, disability status is determined from hearing, vision, cognitive, ambulatory, and self-care difficulties. For people aged 15 years and older, they are considered to have a disability if they have difficulty with any one of the six difficulty types; Note: (1) Figures cover the Fort Collins, CO Metropolitan Statistical Area
Source: U.S. Census Bureau, 2015-2019 American Community Survey 5-Year Estimates

Age

Area	Percent of Population									Median Age
	Under Age 5	Age 5–19	Age 20–34	Age 35–44	Age 45–54	Age 55–64	Age 65–74	Age 75–84	Age 85+	
City	5.0	19.5	33.9	11.6	9.7	9.5	6.3	3.0	1.3	29.3
MSA[1]	5.1	18.4	25.2	12.3	11.2	12.6	9.4	4.1	1.7	36.0
U.S.	6.1	19.1	20.7	12.6	13.0	12.9	9.1	4.6	1.9	38.1

Note: (1) Figures cover the Fort Collins, CO Metropolitan Statistical Area
Source: U.S. Census Bureau, 2015-2019 American Community Survey 5-Year Estimates

Gender

Area	Males	Females	Males per 100 Females
City	83,175	82,434	100.9
MSA[1]	172,000	172,786	99.5
U.S.	159,886,919	164,810,876	97.0

Note: (1) Figures cover the Fort Collins, CO Metropolitan Statistical Area
Source: U.S. Census Bureau, 2015-2019 American Community Survey 5-Year Estimates

Religious Groups by Family

Area	Catholic	Baptist	Non-Den.	Methodist[2]	Lutheran	LDS[3]	Pente-costal	Presby-terian[4]	Muslim[5]	Judaism
MSA[1]	11.8	2.2	6.4	4.4	3.5	3.0	4.7	1.9	0.1	<0.1
U.S.	19.1	9.3	4.0	4.0	2.3	2.0	1.9	1.6	0.8	0.7

Note: Figures are the number of adherents as a percentage of the total population; (1) Figures cover the Fort Collins, CO Metropolitan Statistical Area; (2) Methodist/Pietist; (3) Latter Day Saints; (4) Reformed; (5) Figures are estimates
Source: Association of Statisticians of American Religious Bodies, 2010 U.S. Religion Census: Religious Congregations & Membership Study

Religious Groups by Tradition

Area	Catholic	Evangelical Protestant	Mainline Protestant	Other Tradition	Black Protestant	Orthodox
MSA[1]	11.8	18.8	5.9	4.0	<0.1	0.1
U.S.	19.1	16.2	7.3	4.3	1.6	0.3

Note: Figures are the number of adherents as a percentage of the total population; (1) Figures cover the Fort Collins, CO Metropolitan Statistical Area
Source: Association of Statisticians of American Religious Bodies, 2010 U.S. Religion Census: Religious Congregations & Membership Study

ECONOMY

Gross Metropolitan Product

Area	2017	2018	2019	2020	Rank[2]
MSA[1]	17.4	18.4	19.7	20.7	139

Note: Figures are in billions of dollars; (1) Figures cover the Fort Collins, CO Metropolitan Statistical Area; (2) Rank is based on 2018 data and ranges from 1 to 381
Source: U.S. Conference of Mayors, U.S. Metro Economies: GMP & Employment 2018-2020, September 2019

Economic Growth

Area	2015-17 (%)	2018 (%)	2019 (%)	2020 (%)	Rank[2]
MSA[1]	5.3	3.7	4.7	3.1	14
U.S.	1.9	2.9	2.3	2.1	–

Note: Figures are real gross metropolitan product (GMP) growth rates and represent average annual percent change; (1) Figures cover the Fort Collins, CO Metropolitan Statistical Area; (2) Rank is based on 2017 2-year average annual percent change and ranges from 1 to 381
Source: U.S. Conference of Mayors, U.S. Metro Economies: GMP & Employment 2018-2020, September 2019

Metropolitan Area Exports

Area	2014	2015	2016	2017	2018	2019	Rank[2]
MSA[1]	1,037.4	990.7	993.8	1,034.1	1,021.8	1,060.0	152

Note: Figures are in millions of dollars; (1) Figures cover the Fort Collins, CO Metropolitan Statistical Area; (2) Rank is based on 2019 data and ranges from 1 to 386
Source: U.S. Department of Commerce, International Trade Administration, Office of Trade and Economic Analysis, Industry and Analysis, Exports by Metropolitan Area, data extracted March 24, 2021

Building Permits

Area	Single-Family			Multi-Family			Total		
	2018	2019	Pct. Chg.	2018	2019	Pct. Chg.	2018	2019	Pct. Chg.
City	398	316	-20.6	673	632	-6.1	1,071	948	-11.5
MSA[1]	1,679	1,580	-5.9	1,265	910	-28.1	2,944	2,490	-15.4
U.S.	855,300	862,100	0.7	473,500	523,900	10.6	1,328,800	1,386,000	4.3

Note: (1) Figures cover the Fort Collins, CO Metropolitan Statistical Area; Figures represent new, privately-owned housing units authorized (unadjusted data); All permit data are based on estimates with imputation
Source: U.S. Census Bureau, Manufacturing, Mining, and Construction Statistics, Building Permits, 2018, 2019

Bankruptcy Filings

Area	Business Filings			Nonbusiness Filings		
	2019	2020	% Chg.	2019	2020	% Chg.
Larimer County	29	28	-3.4	558	404	-27.6
U.S.	22,780	21,655	-4.9	752,160	522,808	-30.5

Note: Business filings include Chapter 7, Chapter 9, Chapter 11, Chapter 12, Chapter 13, Chapter 15, and Section 304; Nonbusiness filings include Chapter 7, Chapter 11, and Chapter 13
Source: Administrative Office of the U.S. Courts, Business and Nonbusiness Bankruptcy, County Cases Commenced by Chapter of the Bankruptcy Code, During the 12-Month Period Ending December 31, 2019 and Business and Nonbusiness Bankruptcy, County Cases Commenced by Chapter of the Bankruptcy Code, During the 12-Month Period Ending December 31, 2020

Housing Vacancy Rates

Area	Gross Vacancy Rate[2] (%)			Year-Round Vacancy Rate[3] (%)			Rental Vacancy Rate[4] (%)			Homeowner Vacancy Rate[5] (%)		
	2018	2019	2020	2018	2019	2020	2018	2019	2020	2018	2019	2020
MSA[1]	n/a	n/a	n/a	n/a	n/a	n/a	n/a	n/a	n/a	n/a	n/a	n/a
U.S.	12.3	12.0	10.6	9.7	9.5	8.2	6.9	6.7	6.3	1.5	1.4	1.0

Note: (1) Figures cover the Fort Collins, CO Metropolitan Statistical Area; (2) The percentage of the total housing inventory that is vacant; (3) The percentage of the housing inventory (excluding seasonal units) that is year-round vacant; (4) The percentage of rental inventory that is vacant for rent; (5) The percentage of homeowner inventory that is vacant for sale; n/a not available
Source: U.S. Census Bureau, Housing Vacancies and Homeownership Annual Statistics: 2018, 2019, 2020

INCOME

Income

Area	Per Capita ($)	Median Household ($)	Average Household ($)
City	34,482	65,866	87,406
MSA[1]	37,363	71,881	93,301
U.S.	34,103	62,843	88,607

Note: (1) Figures cover the Fort Collins, CO Metropolitan Statistical Area
Source: U.S. Census Bureau, 2015-2019 American Community Survey 5-Year Estimates

Household Income Distribution

Area	Percent of Households Earning							
	Under $15,000	$15,000 -$24,999	$25,000 -$34,999	$35,000 -$49,999	$50,000 -$74,999	$75,000 -$99,999	$100,000 -$149,999	$150,000 and up
City	9.7	8.7	8.0	12.2	17.1	12.9	15.8	15.5
MSA[1]	7.9	7.9	7.3	11.6	17.2	14.1	17.9	16.1
U.S.	10.3	8.9	8.9	12.3	17.2	12.7	15.1	14.5

Note: (1) Figures cover the Fort Collins, CO Metropolitan Statistical Area
Source: U.S. Census Bureau, 2015-2019 American Community Survey 5-Year Estimates

Poverty Rate

Area	All Ages	Under 18 Years Old	18 to 64 Years Old	65 Years and Over
City	16.3	10.3	19.3	7.7
MSA[1]	11.6	9.4	13.5	6.4
U.S.	13.4	18.5	12.6	9.3

Note: Figures are percentage of people whose income during the past 12 months was below the poverty level;
(1) Figures cover the Fort Collins, CO Metropolitan Statistical Area
Source: U.S. Census Bureau, 2015-2019 American Community Survey 5-Year Estimates

CITY FINANCES

City Government Finances

Component	2017 ($000)	2017 ($ per capita)
Total Revenues	484,235	3,004
Total Expenditures	497,852	3,089
Debt Outstanding	143,179	888
Cash and Securities[1]	541,830	3,362

Note: (1) Cash and security holdings of a government at the close of its fiscal year,
including those of its dependent agencies, utilities, and liquor stores.
Source: U.S. Census Bureau, State & Local Government Finances 2017

City Government Revenue by Source

Source	2017 ($000)	2017 ($ per capita)	2017 (%)
General Revenue			
From Federal Government	13,925	86	2.9
From State Government	20,069	125	4.1
From Local Governments	16,576	103	3.4
Taxes			
Property	24,717	153	5.1
Sales and Gross Receipts	146,904	911	30.3
Personal Income	0	0	0.0
Corporate Income	0	0	0.0
Motor Vehicle License	0	0	0.0
Other Taxes	4,735	29	1.0
Current Charges	68,985	428	14.2
Liquor Store	0	0	0.0
Utility	145,948	906	30.1
Employee Retirement	5,298	33	1.1

Source: U.S. Census Bureau, State & Local Government Finances 2017

City Government Expenditures by Function

Function	2017 ($000)	2017 ($ per capita)	2017 (%)
General Direct Expenditures			
Air Transportation	0	0	0.0
Corrections	0	0	0.0
Education	0	0	0.0
Employment Security Administration	0	0	0.0
Financial Administration	36,689	227	7.4
Fire Protection	3,143	19	0.6
General Public Buildings	0	0	0.0
Governmental Administration, Other	0	0	0.0
Health	1,919	11	0.4
Highways	69,220	429	13.9
Hospitals	0	0	0.0
Housing and Community Development	6,285	39	1.3
Interest on General Debt	6,563	40	1.3
Judicial and Legal	0	0	0.0
Libraries	0	0	0.0
Parking	2,574	16	0.5
Parks and Recreation	40,500	251	8.1
Police Protection	43,503	269	8.7
Public Welfare	4,462	27	0.9
Sewerage	14,190	88	2.9
Solid Waste Management	0	0	0.0
Veterans' Services	0	0	0.0
Liquor Store	0	0	0.0
Utility	223,097	1,384	44.8
Employee Retirement	3,538	22	0.7

Source: U.S. Census Bureau, State & Local Government Finances 2017

EMPLOYMENT

Labor Force and Employment

Area	Civilian Labor Force			Workers Employed		
	Dec. 2019	Dec. 2020	% Chg.	Dec. 2019	Dec. 2020	% Chg.
City	103,931	102,364	-1.5	101,963	94,647	-7.2
MSA[1]	209,156	205,612	-1.7	205,003	190,294	-7.2
U.S.	164,007,000	160,017,000	-2.4	158,504,000	149,613,000	-5.6

Note: Data is not seasonally adjusted and covers workers 16 years of age and older; (1) Figures cover the Fort Collins, CO Metropolitan Statistical Area
Source: Bureau of Labor Statistics, Local Area Unemployment Statistics

Unemployment Rate

Area	2020											
	Jan.	Feb.	Mar.	Apr.	May	Jun.	Jul.	Aug.	Sep.	Oct.	Nov.	Dec.
City	2.4	2.5	4.4	11.5	8.7	9.3	6.2	5.5	5.1	5.0	5.0	7.5
MSA[1]	2.5	2.6	4.7	11.1	8.6	9.2	6.2	5.6	5.2	5.1	5.2	7.4
U.S.	4.0	3.8	4.5	14.4	13.0	11.2	10.5	8.5	7.7	6.6	6.4	6.5

Note: Data is not seasonally adjusted and covers workers 16 years of age and older; (1) Figures cover the Fort Collins, CO Metropolitan Statistical Area
Source: Bureau of Labor Statistics, Local Area Unemployment Statistics

Average Wages

Occupation	$/Hr.	Occupation	$/Hr.
Accountants and Auditors	35.90	Maintenance and Repair Workers	21.30
Automotive Mechanics	24.00	Marketing Managers	88.50
Bookkeepers	21.30	Network and Computer Systems Admin.	36.90
Carpenters	23.10	Nurses, Licensed Practical	25.40
Cashiers	14.30	Nurses, Registered	37.00
Computer Programmers	35.40	Nursing Assistants	16.20
Computer Systems Analysts	42.80	Office Clerks, General	20.50
Computer User Support Specialists	28.30	Physical Therapists	38.40
Construction Laborers	18.20	Physicians	114.80
Cooks, Restaurant	14.70	Plumbers, Pipefitters and Steamfitters	26.00
Customer Service Representatives	17.00	Police and Sheriff's Patrol Officers	40.60
Dentists	84.70	Postal Service Mail Carriers	25.00
Electricians	30.00	Real Estate Sales Agents	28.40
Engineers, Electrical	52.40	Retail Salespersons	15.10
Fast Food and Counter Workers	13.50	Sales Representatives, Technical/Scientific	44.50
Financial Managers	72.30	Secretaries, Exc. Legal/Medical/Executive	18.60
First-Line Supervisors of Office Workers	28.30	Security Guards	14.50
General and Operations Managers	58.90	Surgeons	n/a
Hairdressers/Cosmetologists	16.10	Teacher Assistants, Exc. Postsecondary*	14.30
Home Health and Personal Care Aides	15.00	Teachers, Secondary School, Exc. Sp. Ed.*	n/a
Janitors and Cleaners	15.50	Telemarketers	n/a
Landscaping/Groundskeeping Workers	16.80	Truck Drivers, Heavy/Tractor-Trailer	22.10
Lawyers	69.70	Truck Drivers, Light/Delivery Services	18.80
Maids and Housekeeping Cleaners	14.20	Waiters and Waitresses	16.20

Note: Wage data covers the Fort Collins, CO Metropolitan Statistical Area; (*) Hourly wages were calculated from annual wage data based on a 40 hour work week; n/a not available.
Source: Bureau of Labor Statistics, Metro Area Occupational Employment & Wage Estimates, May 2020

Employment by Industry

Sector	MSA[1]		U.S.
	Number of Employees	Percent of Total	Percent of Total
Construction, Mining, and Logging	11,600	7.1	5.5
Education and Health Services	18,500	11.3	16.3
Financial Activities	6,800	4.1	6.1
Government	41,200	25.1	15.2
Information	3,000	1.8	1.9
Leisure and Hospitality	14,600	8.9	9.0
Manufacturing	13,900	8.5	8.5
Other Services	6,300	3.8	3.8
Professional and Business Services	20,100	12.2	14.4
Retail Trade	19,300	11.7	10.9
Transportation, Warehousing, and Utilities	3,900	2.4	4.6
Wholesale Trade	5,200	3.2	3.9

Note: Figures are non-farm employment as of December 2020. Figures are not seasonally adjusted and include workers 16 years of age and older; (1) Figures cover the Fort Collins, CO Metropolitan Statistical Area
Source: Bureau of Labor Statistics, Current Employment Statistics, Employment, Hours, and Earnings

Employment by Occupation

Occupation Classification	City (%)	MSA[1] (%)	U.S. (%)
Management, Business, Science, and Arts	48.3	45.4	38.5
Natural Resources, Construction, and Maintenance	6.2	8.0	8.9
Production, Transportation, and Material Moving	7.7	9.4	13.2
Sales and Office	20.0	20.3	21.6
Service	17.8	16.9	17.8

Note: Figures cover employed civilians 16 years of age and older; (1) Figures cover the Fort Collins, CO Metropolitan Statistical Area
Source: U.S. Census Bureau, 2015-2019 American Community Survey 5-Year Estimates

Occupations with Greatest Projected Employment Growth: 2020 – 2022

Occupation[1]	2020 Employment	2022 Projected Employment	Numeric Employment Change	Percent Employment Change
Software Developers, Applications	33,470	35,740	2,270	6.8
Personal Care Aides	30,000	31,610	1,610	5.4
Registered Nurses	54,810	56,090	1,280	2.3
Market Research Analysts and Marketing Specialists	21,470	22,380	910	4.2
Business Operations Specialists, All Other	49,470	50,350	880	1.8
Stock Clerks and Order Fillers	37,610	38,390	780	2.1
Computer Occupations, All Other	18,280	18,940	660	3.6
Accountants and Auditors	42,200	42,840	640	1.5
Software Developers, Systems Software	12,390	13,010	620	5.0
Sales Representatives, Wholesale and Manufacturing, Except Technical and Scientific Products	28,620	29,170	550	1.9

Note: Projections cover Colorado; (1) Sorted by numeric employment change
Source: www.projectionscentral.com, State Occupational Projections, 2020–2022 Short-Term Projections

Fastest-Growing Occupations: 2020 – 2022

Occupation[1]	2020 Employment	2022 Projected Employment	Numeric Employment Change	Percent Employment Change
Information Security Analysts	3,860	4,170	310	8.0
Software Developers, Applications	33,470	35,740	2,270	6.8
Statisticians	1,230	1,310	80	6.5
Operations Research Analysts	940	1,000	60	6.4
Veterinary Technologists and Technicians	4,490	4,750	260	5.8
Health Specialties Teachers, Postsecondary	6,160	6,500	340	5.5
Personal Care Aides	30,000	31,610	1,610	5.4
Veterinarians	2,820	2,970	150	5.3
Interpreters and Translators	1,980	2,080	100	5.1
Software Developers, Systems Software	12,390	13,010	620	5.0

Note: Projections cover Colorado; (1) Sorted by percent employment change and excludes occupations with numeric employment change less than 50
Source: www.projectionscentral.com, State Occupational Projections, 2020–2022 Short-Term Projections

TAXES

State Corporate Income Tax Rates

State	Tax Rate (%)	Income Brackets ($)	Num. of Brackets	Financial Institution Tax Rate (%)[a]	Federal Income Tax Ded.
Colorado	4.55	Flat rate	1	4.55	No

Note: Tax rates as of January 1, 2021; (a) Rates listed are the corporate income tax rate applied to financial institutions or excise taxes based on income. Some states have other taxes based upon the value of deposits or shares.
Source: Federation of Tax Administrators, State Corporate Income Tax Rates, January 1, 2021

State Individual Income Tax Rates

State	Tax Rate (%)	Income Brackets ($)	Personal Exemptions ($)			Standard Ded. ($)	
			Single	Married	Depend.	Single	Married
Colorado	4.55	Flat rate	(d)	(d)	(d)	12,550	25,100 (d)

Note: Tax rates as of January 1, 2021; Local- and county-level taxes are not included; Federal income tax is not deductible on state income tax returns; (d) These states use the personal exemption/standard deduction amounts provided in the federal Internal Revenue Code.
Source: Federation of Tax Administrators, State Individual Income Tax Rates, January 1, 2021

Various State Sales and Excise Tax Rates

State	State Sales Tax (%)	Gasoline[1] (¢/gal.)	Cigarette[2] ($/pack)	Spirits[3] ($/gal.)	Wine[4] ($/gal.)	Beer[5] ($/gal.)	Recreational Marijuana (%)
Colorado	2.9	22	1.94	2.28	0.32	0.08	(d)

Note: All tax rates as of January 1, 2021; (1) The American Petroleum Institute has developed a methodology for determining the average tax rate on a gallon of fuel. Rates may include any of the following: excise taxes, environmental fees, storage tank fees, other fees or taxes, general sales tax, and local taxes; (2) The federal excise tax of $1.0066 per pack and local taxes are not included; (3) Rates are those applicable to off-premise sales of 40% alcohol by volume (a.b.v.) distilled spirits in 750ml containers. Local excise taxes are excluded; (4) Rates are those applicable to off-premise sales of 11% a.b.v. non-carbonated wine in 750ml containers; (5) Rates are those applicable to off-premise sales of 4.7% a.b.v. beer in 12 ounce containers; (d) 15% excise tax (levied on wholesale at average market rate); 15% excise tax (retail price)
Source: Tax Foundation, 2021 Facts & Figures: How Does Your State Compare?

State Business Tax Climate Index Rankings

State	Overall Rank	Corporate Tax Rank	Individual Income Tax Rank	Sales Tax Rank	Property Tax Rank	Unemployment Insurance Tax Rank
Colorado	21	10	14	36	32	41

Note: The index is a measure of how each state's tax laws affect economic performance. The lower the rank, the more favorable a state's tax system is for business. States without a given tax are given a ranking of 1. The scores/rankings for the District of Columbia do not affect other states. The 2021 index represents the tax climate as of July 1, 2020.
Source: Tax Foundation, State Business Tax Climate Index 2021

TRANSPORTATION

Means of Transportation to Work

Area	Car/Truck/Van Drove Alone	Car/Truck/Van Car-pooled	Public Transportation Bus	Public Transportation Subway	Public Transportation Railroad	Bicycle	Walked	Other Means	Worked at Home
City	71.9	7.2	2.2	0.0	0.0	5.4	4.2	1.0	8.0
MSA[1]	74.9	8.0	1.5	0.0	0.0	3.1	2.7	1.2	8.6
U.S.	76.3	9.0	2.4	1.9	0.6	0.5	2.7	1.4	5.2

Note: Figures are percentages and cover workers 16 years of age and older; (1) Figures cover the Fort Collins, CO Metropolitan Statistical Area
Source: U.S. Census Bureau, 2015-2019 American Community Survey 5-Year Estimates

Travel Time to Work

Area	Less Than 10 Minutes	10 to 19 Minutes	20 to 29 Minutes	30 to 44 Minutes	45 to 59 Minutes	60 to 89 Minutes	90 Minutes or More
City	16.5	42.6	19.9	11.0	5.1	3.5	1.4
MSA[1]	14.5	34.6	22.0	15.6	6.4	5.1	1.9
U.S.	12.2	28.4	20.8	20.8	8.3	6.4	2.9

Note: Note: Figures are percentages and include workers 16 years old and over; (1) Figures cover the Fort Collins, CO Metropolitan Statistical Area
Source: U.S. Census Bureau, 2015-2019 American Community Survey 5-Year Estimates

Key Congestion Measures

Measure	1982	1992	2002	2012	2017
Annual Hours of Delay, Total (000)	n/a	n/a	n/a	n/a	5,968
Annual Hours of Delay, Per Auto Commuter	n/a	n/a	n/a	n/a	21
Annual Congestion Cost, Total (million $)	n/a	n/a	n/a	n/a	121
Annual Congestion Cost, Per Auto Commuter ($)	n/a	n/a	n/a	n/a	420

Note: n/a not available
Source: Texas A&M Transportation Institute, 2019 Urban Mobility Report

Freeway Travel Time Index

Measure	1982	1987	1992	1997	2002	2007	2012	2017
Urban Area Index[1]	n/a	n/a	n/a	n/a	n/a	n/a	n/a	1.10
Urban Area Rank[1,2]	n/a	n/a	n/a	n/a	n/a	n/a	n/a	n/a

Note: Freeway Travel Time Index—the ratio of travel time in the peak period to the travel time at free-flow conditions. For example, a value of 1.30 indicates a 20-minute free-flow trip takes 26 minutes in the peak (20 minutes x 1.30 = 26 minutes); (1) Covers the Fort Collins CO urban area; (2) Rank is based on 101 larger urban areas (#1 = highest travel time index); n/a not available
Source: Texas A&M Transportation Institute, 2019 Urban Mobility Report

Public Transportation

Agency Name / Mode of Transportation	Vehicles Operated in Maximum Service[1]	Annual Unlinked Passenger Trips[2] (in thous.)	Annual Passenger Miles[3] (in thous.)
Transfort			
Bus (directly operated)	32	3,000.7	9,132.5
Bus (purchased transportation)	2	18.8	69.7
Bus Rapid Transit (directly operated)	6	1,445.3	3,619.9
Demand Response (purchased transportation)	2	8.0	83.5
Demand Response Taxi (purchased transportation)	13	30.9	143.5

Note: (1) Number of revenue vehicles operated by the given mode and type of service to meet the annual maximum service requirement. This is the revenue vehicle count during the peak season of the year; on the week and day that maximum service is provided. Vehicles operated in maximum service (VOMS) exclude atypical days and one-time special events; (2) Number of passengers who boarded public transportation vehicles. Passengers are counted each time they board a vehicle no matter how many vehicles they use to travel from their origin to their destination. (3) Sum of the distances ridden by all passengers during the entire fiscal year.
Source: Federal Transit Administration, National Transit Database, 2019

Air Transportation

Airport Name and Code / Type of Service	Passenger Airlines[1]	Passenger Enplanements	Freight Carriers[2]	Freight (lbs)
Denver International (60 miles) (DEN)				
Domestic service (U.S. carriers - 2020)	27	15,787,920	18	263,867,762
International service (U.S. carriers - 2019)	7	883,726	3	8,069,938

Note: (1) Includes all U.S.-based major, minor and commuter airlines that carried at least one passenger during the year; (2) Includes all U.S.-based airlines and freight carriers that transported at least one pound of freight during the year.
Source: Bureau of Transportation Statistics, The Intermodal Transportation Database, Air Carriers: T-100 Domestic Market (U.S. Carriers), 2020; Bureau of Transportation Statistics, The Intermodal Transportation Database, Air Carriers: T-100 International Market (U.S. Carriers), 2019

BUSINESSES

Major Business Headquarters

Company Name	Industry	Rankings	
		Fortune[1]	Forbes[2]
No companies listed	-	-	-

Note: (1) Companies that produce a 10-K are ranked 1 to 500 based on 2019 revenue; (2) All private companies with at least $2 billion in annual revenue through the end of their most current fiscal year are ranked 1 to 219; companies listed are headquartered in the city; dashes indicate no ranking
Source: Fortune, "Fortune 500," June/July 2020; Forbes, "America's Largest Private Companies," 2020

Living Environment

COST OF LIVING

Cost of Living Index

Composite Index	Groceries	Housing	Utilities	Trans-portation	Health Care	Misc. Goods/ Services
n/a	n/a	n/a	n/a	n/a	n/a	n/a

Note: The Cost of Living Index measures regional differences in the cost of consumer goods and services, excluding taxes and non-consumer expenditures, for professional and managerial households in the top income quintile. It is based on more than 50,000 prices covering almost 60 different items for which prices are collected three times a year by chambers of commerce, economic development organizations or university applied economic centers in each participating urban area. The numbers shown should be read as a percentage above or below the national average of 100. For example, a value of 115.4 in the groceries column indicates that grocery prices are 15.4% higher than the national average. Small differences in the index numbers should not be interpreted as significant; n/a not available.
Source: The Council for Community and Economic Research, Cost of Living Index, 2020

Grocery Prices

Area[1]	T-Bone Steak ($/pound)	Frying Chicken ($/pound)	Whole Milk ($/half gal.)	Eggs ($/dozen)	Orange Juice ($/64 oz.)	Coffee ($/11.5 oz.)
City[2]	n/a	n/a	n/a	n/a	n/a	n/a
Avg.	11.78	1.39	2.05	1.47	3.57	4.34
Min.	8.03	0.94	1.03	0.74	2.94	3.02
Max.	15.86	2.65	4.31	3.77	5.44	8.69

Note: (1) Values for the local area are compared with the average, minimum and maximum values for all 284 areas in the Cost of Living Index; (2) Figures cover the Fort Collins CO urban area; n/a not available; T-Bone Steak (price per pound); Frying Chicken (price per pound, whole fryer); Whole Milk (half gallon carton); Eggs (price per dozen, Grade A, large); Orange Juice (64 oz. Tropicana or Florida Natural); Coffee (11.5 oz. can, vacuum-packed, Maxwell House, Hills Bros, or Folgers).
Source: The Council for Community and Economic Research, Cost of Living Index, 2020

Housing and Utility Costs

Area[1]	New Home Price ($)	Apartment Rent ($/month)	All Electric ($/month)	Part Electric ($/month)	Other Energy ($/month)	Telephone ($/month)
City[2]	n/a	n/a	n/a	n/a	n/a	n/a
Avg.	368,594	1,168	170.86	100.47	65.28	184.30
Min.	190,567	502	91.58	31.42	26.08	169.60
Max.	2,227,806	4,738	470.38	280.31	280.06	206.50

Note: (1) Values for the local area are compared with the average, minimum and maximum values for all 284 areas in the Cost of Living Index; (2) Figures cover the Fort Collins CO urban area; n/a not available; New Home Price (2,400 sf living area, 8,000 sf lot, in urban area with full utilities); Apartment Rent (950 sf 2 bedroom/1.5 or 2 bath, unfurnished, excluding all utilities except water); All Electric (average monthly cost for an all-electric home); Part Electric (average monthly cost for a part-electric home); Other Energy (average monthly cost for natural gas, fuel oil, coal, wood, and any other forms of energy except electricity); Telephone (price includes the base monthly rate plus taxes and fees for three lines of mobile phone service).
Source: The Council for Community and Economic Research, Cost of Living Index, 2020

Health Care, Transportation, and Other Costs

Area[1]	Doctor ($/visit)	Dentist ($/visit)	Optometrist ($/visit)	Gasoline ($/gallon)	Beauty Salon ($/visit)	Men's Shirt ($)
City[2]	n/a	n/a	n/a	n/a	n/a	n/a
Avg.	115.44	99.32	108.10	2.21	39.27	31.37
Min.	36.68	59.00	51.36	1.71	19.00	11.00
Max.	219.00	153.10	250.97	3.46	82.05	58.33

Note: (1) Values for the local area are compared with the average, minimum and maximum values for all 284 areas in the Cost of Living Index; (2) Figures cover the Fort Collins CO urban area; n/a not available; Doctor (general practitioners routine exam of an established patient); Dentist (adult teeth cleaning and periodic oral examination); Optometrist (full vision eye exam for established adult patient); Gasoline (one gallon regular unleaded, national brand, including all taxes, cash price at self-service pump if available); Beauty Salon (woman's shampoo, trim, and blow-dry); Men's Shirt (cotton/polyester dress shirt, pinpoint weave, long sleeves).
Source: The Council for Community and Economic Research, Cost of Living Index, 2020

HOUSING

Homeownership Rate

Area	2012 (%)	2013 (%)	2014 (%)	2015 (%)	2016 (%)	2017 (%)	2018 (%)	2019 (%)	2020 (%)
MSA[1]	n/a	n/a	n/a	n/a	n/a	n/a	n/a	n/a	n/a
U.S.	65.4	65.1	64.5	63.7	63.4	63.9	64.4	64.6	66.6

Note: (1) Figures cover the Fort Collins, CO Metropolitan Statistical Area; n/a not available
Source: U.S. Census Bureau, Housing Vacancies and Homeownership Annual Statistics: 2012-2020

House Price Index (HPI)

Area	National Ranking[2]	Quarterly Change (%)	One-Year Change (%)	Five-Year Change (%)	Since 1991Q1 (%)
MSA[1]	217	1.38	4.19	38.15	365.72
U.S.[3]	–	3.81	10.77	38.99	205.12

Note: The HPI is a weighted repeat sales index. It measures average price changes in repeat sales or refinancings on the same properties. This information is obtained by reviewing repeat mortgage transactions on single-family properties whose mortgages have been purchased or securitized by Fannie Mae or Freddie Mac since January 1975; (1) Figures cover the Fort Collins, CO Metropolitan Statistical Area; (2) Rankings are based on annual percentage change for all metro areas containing at least 15,000 transactions over the last 10 years and ranges from 1 to 253; (3) figures based on a weighted average of Census Division estimates using a seasonally adjusted, purchase-only index; all figures are for the period ending December 31, 2020
Source: Federal Housing Finance Agency, Change in Metropolitan Area House Price Indexes, April 7, 2021

Median Single-Family Home Prices

Area	2018	2019	2020[p]	Percent Change 2019 to 2020
MSA[1]	n/a	n/a	n/a	n/a
U.S. Average	261.6	274.6	299.9	9.2

Note: Figures are median sales prices of existing single-family homes in thousands of dollars; (p) preliminary; n/a not available; (1) Figures cover the Fort Collins, CO Metropolitan Statistical Area
Source: National Association of Realtors, Median Sales Price of Existing Single-Family Homes for Metropolitan Areas, 4th Quarter 2020

Qualifying Income Based on Median Sales Price of Existing Single-Family Homes

Area	With 5% Down ($)	With 10% Down ($)	With 20% Down ($)
MSA[1]	86,381	81,835	72,742
U.S. Average	59,266	56,147	49,908

Note: Figures are preliminary; Qualifying income is based on a mortgage rate of 2.81%. Monthly principal and interest payment is limited to 25% of income; (1) Figures cover the Fort Collins, CO Metropolitan Statistical Area
Source: National Association of Realtors, Qualifying Income Based on Median Sales Price of Existing Single-Family Homes for Metropolitan Areas, 4th Quarter 2020

Home Value Distribution

Area	Under $50,000	$50,000 -$99,999	$100,000 -$149,999	$150,000 -$199,999	$200,000 -$299,999	$300,000 -$499,999	$500,000 -$999,999	$1,000,000 or more
City	3.2	1.1	1.5	3.6	19.8	52.8	16.7	1.3
MSA[1]	3.9	1.4	1.6	4.7	20.7	46.4	19.1	2.2
U.S.	6.9	12.0	13.3	14.0	19.6	19.3	11.4	3.4

Note: Figures are percentages and cover owner-occupied housing units; (1) Figures cover the Fort Collins, CO Metropolitan Statistical Area
Source: U.S. Census Bureau, 2015-2019 American Community Survey 5-Year Estimates

Year Housing Structure Built

Area	2010 or Later	2000 -2009	1990 -1999	1980 -1989	1970 -1979	1960 -1969	1950 -1959	1940 -1949	Before 1940	Median Year
City	10.2	17.5	21.3	15.2	18.8	7.1	3.2	1.6	5.2	1989
MSA[1]	10.3	18.8	20.1	13.5	19.1	7.1	3.6	1.7	5.8	1989
U.S.	5.2	14.0	13.9	13.4	15.2	10.6	10.3	4.9	12.6	1978

Note: Figures are percentages except for Median Year; Note: (1) Figures cover the Fort Collins, CO Metropolitan Statistical Area
Source: U.S. Census Bureau, 2015-2019 American Community Survey 5-Year Estimates

Gross Monthly Rent

Area	Under $500	$500 -$999	$1,000 -$1,499	$1,500 -$1,999	$2,000 -$2,499	$2,500 -$2,999	$3,000 and up	Median ($)
City	2.9	20.0	39.7	26.3	9.1	1.4	0.7	1,346
MSA[1]	4.1	23.2	37.4	25.2	7.7	1.7	0.7	1,297
U.S.	9.4	36.2	30.0	14.0	5.6	2.4	2.4	1,062

Note: Figures are percentages except for Median; Gross rent is the contract rent plus the estimated average monthly cost of utilities (electricity, gas, and water and sewer) and fuels (oil, coal, kerosene, wood, etc.) if these are paid by the renter (or paid for the renter by someone else); (1) Figures cover the Fort Collins, CO Metropolitan Statistical Area
Source: U.S. Census Bureau, 2015-2019 American Community Survey 5-Year Estimates

HEALTH

Health Risk Factors

Category	MSA[1] (%)	U.S. (%)
Adults aged 18–64 who have any kind of health care coverage	n/a	87.3
Adults who reported being in good or better health	n/a	82.4
Adults who have been told they have high blood cholesterol	n/a	33.0
Adults who have been told they have high blood pressure	n/a	32.3
Adults who are current smokers	n/a	17.1
Adults who currently use E-cigarettes	n/a	4.6
Adults who currently use chewing tobacco, snuff, or snus	n/a	4.0
Adults who are heavy drinkers[2]	n/a	6.3
Adults who are binge drinkers[3]	n/a	17.4
Adults who are overweight (BMI 25.0 - 29.9)	n/a	35.3
Adults who are obese (BMI 30.0 - 99.8)	n/a	31.3
Adults who participated in any physical activities in the past month	n/a	74.4
Adults who always or nearly always wears a seat belt	n/a	94.3

Note: n/a not available; (1) Figures cover the Fort Collins, CO Metropolitan Statistical Area; (2) Heavy drinkers are classified as adult men having more than 14 drinks per week and adult women having more than 7 drinks per week; (3) Binge drinkers are classified as males having five or more drinks on one occasion or females having four or more drinks on one occasion
Source: Centers for Disease Control and Prevention, Behaviorial Risk Factor Surveillance System, SMART: Selected Metropolitan Area Risk Trends, 2017

Acute and Chronic Health Conditions

Category	MSA[1] (%)	U.S. (%)
Adults who have ever been told they had a heart attack	n/a	4.2
Adults who have ever been told they have angina or coronary heart disease	n/a	3.9
Adults who have ever been told they had a stroke	n/a	3.0
Adults who have ever been told they have asthma	n/a	14.2
Adults who have ever been told they have arthritis	n/a	24.9
Adults who have ever been told they have diabetes[2]	n/a	10.5
Adults who have ever been told they had skin cancer	n/a	6.2
Adults who have ever been told they had any other types of cancer	n/a	7.1
Adults who have ever been told they have COPD	n/a	6.5
Adults who have ever been told they have kidney disease	n/a	3.0
Adults who have ever been told they have a form of depression	n/a	20.5

Note: n/a not available; (1) Figures cover the Fort Collins, CO Metropolitan Statistical Area; (2) Figures do not include pregnancy-related, borderline, or pre-diabetes
Source: Centers for Disease Control and Prevention, Behaviorial Risk Factor Surveillance System, SMART: Selected Metropolitan Area Risk Trends, 2017

Health Screening and Vaccination Rates

Category	MSA[1] (%)	U.S. (%)
Adults aged 65+ who have had flu shot within the past year	n/a	60.7
Adults aged 65+ who have ever had a pneumonia vaccination	n/a	75.4
Adults who have ever been tested for HIV	n/a	36.1
Adults who have ever had the shingles or zoster vaccine?	n/a	28.9
Adults who have had their blood cholesterol checked within the last five years	n/a	85.9

Note: n/a not available; (1) Figures cover the Fort Collins, CO Metropolitan Statistical Area.
Source: Centers for Disease Control and Prevention, Behaviorial Risk Factor Surveillance System, SMART: Selected Metropolitan Area Risk Trends, 2017

Disability Status

Category	MSA[1] (%)	U.S. (%)
Adults who reported being deaf	n/a	6.7
Are you blind or have serious difficulty seeing, even when wearing glasses?	n/a	4.5
Are you limited in any way in any of your usual activities due of arthritis?	n/a	12.9
Do you have difficulty doing errands alone?	n/a	6.8
Do you have difficulty dressing or bathing?	n/a	3.6
Do you have serious difficulty concentrating/remembering/making decisions?	n/a	10.7
Do you have serious difficulty walking or climbing stairs?	n/a	13.6

Note: n/a not available; (1) Figures cover the Fort Collins, CO Metropolitan Statistical Area.
Source: Centers for Disease Control and Prevention, Behaviorial Risk Factor Surveillance System, SMART: Selected Metropolitan Area Risk Trends, 2017

Mortality Rates for the Top 10 Causes of Death in the U.S.

ICD-10[a] Sub-Chapter	ICD-10[a] Code	Age-Adjusted Mortality Rate[1] per 100,000 population	
		County[2]	U.S.
Malignant neoplasms	C00-C97	118.7	149.2
Ischaemic heart diseases	I20-I25	51.7	90.5
Other forms of heart disease	I30-I51	40.8	52.2
Chronic lower respiratory diseases	J40-J47	33.6	39.6
Other degenerative diseases of the nervous system	G30-G31	43.5	37.6
Cerebrovascular diseases	I60-I69	35.6	37.2
Other external causes of accidental injury	W00-X59	30.6	36.1
Organic, including symptomatic, mental disorders	F01-F09	34.5	29.4
Hypertensive diseases	I10-I15	21.2	24.1
Diabetes mellitus	E10-E14	14.3	21.5

Note: (a) ICD-10 = International Classification of Diseases 10th Revision; (1) Mortality rates are a three-year average covering 2017-2019; (2) Figures cover Larimer County.
Source: Centers for Disease Control and Prevention, National Center for Health Statistics. Underlying Cause of Death 1999-2019 on CDC WONDER Online Database

Mortality Rates for Selected Causes of Death

ICD-10[a] Sub-Chapter	ICD-10[a] Code	Age-Adjusted Mortality Rate[1] per 100,000 population	
		County[2]	U.S.
Assault	X85-Y09	1.8	6.0
Diseases of the liver	K70-K76	12.9	14.4
Human immunodeficiency virus (HIV) disease	B20-B24	Suppressed	1.5
Influenza and pneumonia	J09-J18	8.3	13.8
Intentional self-harm	X60-X84	21.6	14.1
Malnutrition	E40-E46	2.6	2.3
Obesity and other hyperalimentation	E65-E68	Unreliable	2.1
Renal failure	N17-N19	7.7	12.6
Transport accidents	V01-V99	11.8	12.3
Viral hepatitis	B15-B19	Suppressed	1.2

Note: (a) ICD-10 = International Classification of Diseases 10th Revision; (1) Mortality rates are a three-year average covering 2017-2019; (2) Figures cover Larimer County; Data are suppressed when the data meet the criteria for confidentiality constraints; Mortality rates are flagged as unreliable when the rate would be calculated with a numerator of 20 or less.
Source: Centers for Disease Control and Prevention, National Center for Health Statistics. Underlying Cause of Death 1999-2019 on CDC WONDER Online Database

Health Insurance Coverage

Area	With Health Insurance	With Private Health Insurance	With Public Health Insurance	Without Health Insurance	Population Under Age 19 Without Health Insurance
City	94.0	78.7	24.3	6.0	5.0
MSA[1]	94.1	76.0	29.1	5.9	4.7
U.S.	91.2	67.9	35.1	8.8	5.1

Note: Figures are percentages that cover the civilian noninstitutionalized population; (1) Figures cover the Fort Collins, CO Metropolitan Statistical Area
Source: U.S. Census Bureau, 2015-2019 American Community Survey 5-Year Estimates

Number of Medical Professionals

Area	MDs[3]	DOs[3,4]	Dentists	Podiatrists	Chiropractors	Optometrists
County[1] (number)	840	105	284	21	198	75
County[1] (rate[2])	239.5	29.9	79.6	5.9	55.5	21.0
U.S. (rate[2])	282.9	22.7	71.2	6.2	28.1	16.9
08069						

Note: Data as of 2019 unless noted; (1) Data covers Larimer County; (2) Rate per 100,000 population; (3) Data as of 2018 and includes all active, non-federal physicians; (4) Doctor of Osteopathic Medicine
Source: U.S. Department of Health and Human Services, Health Resources and Services Administration, Bureau of Health Professions, Area Resource File (ARF) 2019-2020

EDUCATION

Public School District Statistics

District Name	Schls	Pupils	Pupil/ Teacher Ratio	Minority Pupils[1] (%)	Free Lunch Eligible[2] (%)	IEP[3] (%)
Poudre School District R-1	53	30,463	17.1	26.9	24.7	n/a

Note: Table includes school districts with 2,000 or more students; (1) Percentage of students that are not non-Hispanic white; (2) Percentage of students that are eligible for the free lunch program; (3) Percentage of students that have an Individualized Education Program.
Source: U.S. Department of Education, National Center for Education Statistics, Common Core of Data, Local Education Agency (School District) Universe Survey: School Year 2018-2019; U.S. Department of Education, National Center for Education Statistics, Common Core of Data, Public Elementary/Secondary School Universe Survey: School Year 2018-2019

Best High Schools

According to *U.S. News,* Fort Collins is home to one of the top 500 high schools in the U.S.: **Liberty Common Charter School** (#139). Nearly 18,000 public, magnet and charter schools were ranked based on their performance on state assessments and how well they prepare students for college. *U.S. News & World Report, "Best High Schools 2020"*

Highest Level of Education

Area	Less than H.S.	H.S. Diploma	Some College, No Deg.	Associate Degree	Bachelor's Degree	Master's Degree	Prof. School Degree	Doctorate Degree
City	3.5	15.1	17.7	8.3	32.3	16.8	2.4	4.0
MSA[1]	4.1	19.0	20.4	9.2	28.0	13.9	2.1	3.2
U.S.	12.0	27.0	20.4	8.5	19.8	8.8	2.1	1.4

Note: Figures cover persons age 25 and over; (1) Figures cover the Fort Collins, CO Metropolitan Statistical Area
Source: U.S. Census Bureau, 2015-2019 American Community Survey 5-Year Estimates

Educational Attainment by Race

Area	High School Graduate or Higher (%)					Bachelor's Degree or Higher (%)				
	Total	White	Black	Asian	Hisp.[2]	Total	White	Black	Asian	Hisp.[2]
City	96.5	96.9	97.0	93.4	84.3	55.5	55.8	40.2	72.3	34.2
MSA[1]	95.9	96.2	95.7	92.2	83.8	47.3	47.5	37.8	62.7	25.1
U.S.	88.0	89.9	86.0	87.1	68.7	32.1	33.5	21.6	54.3	16.4

Note: Figures shown cover persons 25 years old and over; (1) Figures cover the Fort Collins, CO Metropolitan Statistical Area; (2) People of Hispanic origin can be of any race
Source: U.S. Census Bureau, 2015-2019 American Community Survey 5-Year Estimates

School Enrollment by Grade and Control

Area	Preschool (%)		Kindergarten (%)		Grades 1 - 4 (%)		Grades 5 - 8 (%)		Grades 9 - 12 (%)	
	Public	Private	Public	Private	Public	Private	Public	Private	Public	Private
City	41.9	58.1	91.7	8.3	94.5	5.5	95.1	4.9	94.6	5.4
MSA[1]	52.2	47.8	91.0	9.0	92.3	7.7	91.9	8.1	91.4	8.6
U.S.	59.1	40.9	87.6	12.4	89.5	10.5	89.4	10.6	90.1	9.9

Note: Figures shown cover persons 3 years old and over; (1) Figures cover the Fort Collins, CO Metropolitan Statistical Area
Source: U.S. Census Bureau, 2015-2019 American Community Survey 5-Year Estimates

Higher Education

Four-Year Colleges			Two-Year Colleges			Medical Schools[1]	Law Schools[2]	Voc/ Tech[3]
Public	Private Non-profit	Private For-profit	Public	Private Non-profit	Private For-profit			
1	1	0	0	0	1	0	0	2

Note: Figures cover institutions located within the city limits and include main campuses only; (1) includes schools accredited by the Liaison Committee on Medical Education and the American Osteopathic Association's Commission on Osteopathic College Accreditation; (2) includes ABA-accredited schools, schools with provisional ABA accreditation, and state accredited schools; (3) includes all schools with programs that are less than 2 years.
Source: National Center for Education Statistics, Integrated Postsecondary Education System (IPEDS), 2019-20; Wikipedia, List of Medical Schools in the United States, accessed April 2, 2021; Wikipedia, List of Law Schools in the United States, accessed April 2, 2021

According to *U.S. News & World Report,* the Fort Collins, CO metro area is home to one of the top 200 national universities in the U.S.: **Colorado State University** (#153 tie). The indicators used to capture academic quality fall into a number of categories: assessment by administrators at peer institutions; retention of students; faculty resources; student selectivity; financial resources; alumni giving; high school counselor ratings of colleges; and graduation rate. *U.S. News & World Report, "America's Best Colleges 2021"*

EMPLOYERS

Major Employers

Company Name	Industry
Advanced Energy Industrials	Special industry machinery
Anheuser Busch	Malt beverages
Animal and Plant Health Inspection	Management services
Aramark Corporation	Food/bars
Center Partners	Business services
City of Loveland	Municipal government
Colorado State University	Colleges & universities
Contibeef	Beef cattle feedlots
Deere and Company	Farm machinery/equipment
Hach Company	Analytical instruments
Hewlett-Packard Co.	Electronic computers
Medical Center of the Rockies	General medical & surgical hospitals
Poudre School District	Building cleaning service
Poudre Valley Health Systems	General medical & surgical hospitals
Woodward	Aircraft engines & engine parts

Note: Companies shown are located within the Fort Collins, CO Metropolitan Statistical Area.
Source: Hoovers.com; Wikipedia

PUBLIC SAFETY

Crime Rate

Area	All Crimes	Violent Crimes				Property Crimes		
		Murder	Rape[3]	Robbery	Aggrav. Assault	Burglary	Larceny -Theft	Motor Vehicle Theft
City	2,389.9	0.6	24.0	21.1	171.5	204.8	1,834.5	133.4
Suburbs[1]	1,855.9	1.1	44.9	14.6	189.3	184.4	1,296.7	124.9
Metro[2]	2,112.3	0.8	34.8	17.7	180.7	194.2	1,555.0	129.0
U.S.	2,489.3	5.0	42.6	81.6	250.2	340.5	1,549.5	219.9

Note: Figures are crimes per 100,000 population; (1) All areas within the metro area that are located outside the city limits; (2) Figures cover the Fort Collins, CO Metropolitan Statistical Area; (3) All figures shown were reported using the revised Uniform Crime Reporting (UCR) definition of rape.
Source: FBI Uniform Crime Reports, 2019

Hate Crimes

Area	Number of Quarters Reported	Number of Incidents per Bias Motivation					
		Race/Ethnicity/ Ancestry	Religion	Sexual Orientation	Disability	Gender	Gender Identity
City[1]	4	4	2	1	0	0	0
U.S.	4	3,963	1,521	1,195	157	69	198

Note: (1) Figures include one incident reported with more than one bias motivation.
Source: Federal Bureau of Investigation, Hate Crime Statistics 2019

Identity Theft Consumer Reports

Area	Reports	Reports per 100,000 Population	Rank[2]
MSA[1]	1,432	401	72
U.S.	1,387,615	423	-

Note: (1) Figures cover the Fort Collins, CO Metropolitan Statistical Area; (2) Rank ranges from 1 to 391 where 1 indicates greatest number of identity theft reports per 100,000 population
Source: Federal Trade Commission, Consumer Sentinel Network Data Book 2020

Fraud and Other Consumer Reports

Area	Reports	Reports per 100,000 Population	Rank[2]
MSA[1]	2,763	774	115
U.S.	3,385,133	1,031	-

Note: (1) Figures cover the Fort Collins, CO Metropolitan Statistical Area; (2) Rank ranges from 1 to 391 where 1 indicates greatest number of fraud and other consumer reports per 100,000 population
Source: Federal Trade Commission, Consumer Sentinel Network Data Book 2020

POLITICS

2020 Presidential Election Results

Area	Biden	Trump	Jorgensen	Hawkins	Other
Larimer County	56.2	40.8	1.8	0.3	0.9
U.S.	51.3	46.8	1.2	0.3	0.5

Note: Results are percentages and may not add to 100% due to rounding
Source: Dave Leip's Atlas of U.S. Presidential Elections

SPORTS

Professional Sports Teams

Team Name	League	Year Established

No teams are located in the metro area
Source: Wikipedia, Major Professional Sports Teams of the United States and Canada, April 6, 2021

CLIMATE

Average and Extreme Temperatures

Temperature	Jan	Feb	Mar	Apr	May	Jun	Jul	Aug	Sep	Oct	Nov	Dec	Yr.
Extreme High (°F)	73	76	84	90	93	102	103	100	97	89	79	75	103
Average High (°F)	43	47	52	62	71	81	88	86	77	67	52	45	64
Average Temp. (°F)	30	34	39	48	58	67	73	72	63	52	39	32	51
Average Low (°F)	16	20	25	34	44	53	59	57	48	37	25	18	37
Extreme Low (°F)	-25	-25	-10	-2	22	30	43	41	17	3	-8	-25	-25

Note: Figures cover the years 1948-1992
Source: National Climatic Data Center, International Station Meteorological Climate Summary, 9/96

Average Precipitation/Snowfall/Humidity

Precip./Humidity	Jan	Feb	Mar	Apr	May	Jun	Jul	Aug	Sep	Oct	Nov	Dec	Yr.
Avg. Precip. (in.)	0.6	0.6	1.3	1.7	2.5	1.7	1.9	1.5	1.1	1.0	0.9	0.6	15.5
Avg. Snowfall (in.)	9	7	14	9	2	Tr	0	0	2	4	9	8	63
Avg. Rel. Hum. 5am (%)	62	65	67	66	70	68	67	68	66	63	66	63	66
Avg. Rel. Hum. 5pm (%)	49	44	40	35	38	34	34	34	32	34	47	50	39

Note: Figures cover the years 1948-1992; Tr = Trace amounts (<0.05 in. of rain; <0.5 in. of snow)
Source: National Climatic Data Center, International Station Meteorological Climate Summary, 9/96

Weather Conditions

Temperature			Daytime Sky			Precipitation		
10°F & below	32°F & below	90°F & above	Clear	Partly cloudy	Cloudy	0.01 inch or more precip.	0.1 inch or more snow/ice	Thunder-storms
24	155	33	99	177	89	90	38	39

Note: Figures are average number of days per year and cover the years 1948-1992
Source: National Climatic Data Center, International Station Meteorological Climate Summary, 9/96

HAZARDOUS WASTE

Superfund Sites

The Fort Collins, CO metro area has no sites on the EPA's Superfund Final National Priorities List. There are a total of 1,375 Superfund sites with a status of proposed or final on the list in the U.S. *U.S. Environmental Protection Agency, National Priorities List, April 7, 2021*

AIR QUALITY

Air Quality Trends: Ozone

	1990	1995	2000	2005	2010	2015	2016	2017	2018	2019
MSA[1]	0.066	0.072	0.074	0.076	0.072	0.069	0.070	0.067	0.073	0.065
U.S.	0.088	0.089	0.082	0.080	0.073	0.068	0.069	0.068	0.069	0.065

Note: (1) Data covers the Fort Collins, CO Metropolitan Statistical Area. The values shown are the composite ozone concentration averages among trend sites based on the highest fourth daily maximum 8-hour concentration in parts per million. These trends are based on sites having an adequate record of monitoring data during the trend period. Data from exceptional events are included.
Source: U.S. Environmental Protection Agency, Air Quality Monitoring Information, "Air Quality Trends by City, 1990-2019"

Air Quality Index

Area	Percent of Days when Air Quality was...[2]					AQI Statistics[2]	
	Good	Moderate	Unhealthy for Sensitive Groups	Unhealthy	Very Unhealthy	Maximum	Median
MSA[1]	57.0	41.4	1.6	0.0	0.0	129	48

Note: (1) Data covers the Fort Collins, CO Metropolitan Statistical Area; (2) Based on 365 days with AQI data in 2019. Air Quality Index (AQI) is an index for reporting daily air quality. EPA calculates the AQI for five major air pollutants regulated by the Clean Air Act: ground-level ozone, particle pollution (aka particulate matter), carbon monoxide, sulfur dioxide, and nitrogen dioxide. The AQI runs from 0 to 500. The higher the AQI value, the greater the level of air pollution and the greater the health concern. There are six AQI categories: "Good" AQI is between 0 and 50. Air quality is considered satisfactory; "Moderate" AQI is between 51 and 100. Air quality is acceptable; "Unhealthy for Sensitive Groups" When AQI values are between 101 and 150, members of sensitive groups may experience health effects; "Unhealthy" When AQI values are between 151 and 200 everyone may begin to experience health effects; "Very Unhealthy" AQI values between 201 and 300 trigger a health alert; "Hazardous" AQI values over 300 trigger warnings of emergency conditions (not shown).
Source: U.S. Environmental Protection Agency, Air Quality Index Report, 2019

Air Quality Index Pollutants

Area	Percent of Days when AQI Pollutant was...[2]					
	Carbon Monoxide	Nitrogen Dioxide	Ozone	Sulfur Dioxide	Particulate Matter 2.5	Particulate Matter 10
MSA[1]	0.0	0.0	92.3	0.0	7.7	0.0

Note: (1) Data covers the Fort Collins, CO Metropolitan Statistical Area; (2) Based on 365 days with AQI data in 2019. The Air Quality Index (AQI) is an index for reporting daily air quality. EPA calculates the AQI for five major air pollutants regulated by the Clean Air Act: ground-level ozone, particle pollution (also known as particulate matter), carbon monoxide, sulfur dioxide, and nitrogen dioxide. The AQI runs from 0 to 500. The higher the AQI value, the greater the level of air pollution and the greater the health concern.
Source: U.S. Environmental Protection Agency, Air Quality Index Report, 2019

Maximum Air Pollutant Concentrations: Particulate Matter, Ozone, CO and Lead

	Particulate Matter 10 (ug/m^3)	Particulate Matter 2.5 Wtd AM (ug/m^3)	Particulate Matter 2.5 24-Hr (ug/m^3)	Ozone (ppm)	Carbon Monoxide (ppm)	Lead (ug/m^3)
MSA[1] Level	n/a	6.0	20	0.071	1	n/a
NAAQS[2]	150	15	35	0.075	9	0.15
Met NAAQS[2]	n/a	Yes	Yes	Yes	Yes	n/a

Note: (1) Data covers the Fort Collins, CO Metropolitan Statistical Area; Data from exceptional events are included; (2) National Ambient Air Quality Standards; ppm = parts per million; ug/m³ = micrograms per cubic meter; n/a not available.
Concentrations: Particulate Matter 10 (coarse particulate)—highest second maximum 24-hour concentration; Particulate Matter 2.5 Wtd AM (fine particulate)—highest weighted annual mean concentration; Particulate Matter 2.5 24-Hour (fine particulate)—highest 98th percentile 24-hour concentration; Ozone—highest fourth daily maximum 8-hour concentration; Carbon Monoxide—highest second maximum non-overlapping 8-hour concentration; Lead—maximum running 3-month average
Source: U.S. Environmental Protection Agency, Air Quality Monitoring Information, "Air Quality Statistics by City, 2019"

Maximum Air Pollutant Concentrations: Nitrogen Dioxide and Sulfur Dioxide

	Nitrogen Dioxide AM (ppb)	Nitrogen Dioxide 1-Hr (ppb)	Sulfur Dioxide AM (ppb)	Sulfur Dioxide 1-Hr (ppb)	Sulfur Dioxide 24-Hr (ppb)
MSA[1] Level	n/a	n/a	n/a	n/a	n/a
NAAQS[2]	53	100	30	75	140
Met NAAQS[2]	n/a	n/a	n/a	n/a	n/a

Note: (1) Data covers the Fort Collins, CO Metropolitan Statistical Area; Data from exceptional events are included; (2) National Ambient Air Quality Standards; ppm = parts per million; ug/m³ = micrograms per cubic meter; n/a not available.
Concentrations: Nitrogen Dioxide AM—highest arithmetic mean concentration; Nitrogen Dioxide 1-Hr—highest 98th percentile 1-hour daily maximum concentration; Sulfur Dioxide AM—highest annual mean concentration; Sulfur Dioxide 1-Hr—highest 99th percentile 1-hour daily maximum concentration; Sulfur Dioxide 24-Hr—highest second maximum 24-hour concentration
Source: U.S. Environmental Protection Agency, Air Quality Monitoring Information, "Air Quality Statistics by City, 2019"

Greeley, Colorado

Background

Greeley is a city built on farming and agriculture that does its best to follow modern technologies and trends, making it both stable and friendly, yet bustling and active. It is the most populous municipality in Weld County, Colorado, and is growing in popularity each year.

Greeley is situated in northern Colorado, 49 miles from Denver. To the south of the Greeley/Evans area is the South Platte River; to the north is the Cache la Poudre River.

The city's namesake, Horace Greeley, visited the area in 1859, and was the founder and editor of the *New York Tribune*. The city was first founded as the Union Colony in 1869, the city changed its name in honor of Greeley and incorporated in 1886. The city's population has more than doubled since 1970, and is now over 100,000.

The original incarnation of Greeley was an experimental utopian community built on "temperance, religion, agriculture, education and family values"; Greeley stills treasures many of these aspects today. Greeley's economy relies heavily on farming, energy, and agriculture; its largest employers include meatpacker Swift & Company, wind turbine manufacturer Vestas, and Halliburton Energy Services. A new hospital was opened in Greeley in 2019.

Despite its small town appeal, Greeley is an innovative city for both technology and culture. In 1958 Greeley was the first city to establish a Department of Culture, and the Greeley Creative District is officially state certified. As a sister city to Moriya, Japan, it hosts a number of Japanese students every year for a week-long stay.

Greeley is also a media center for Colorado, recognized as the state's principal city for newspapers, television, and radio. Due to media's influence, Greely's famous sons and daughters include voice actor Dee Bradley Baker, UFC fighter Shane Carwin, and composer Miriam Gideon. Author James A. Michener conceived the idea for his acclaimed 1974 novel *Centennial* during his stay in Greeley at the University of Northern Colorado in 1936-37, which is just one of the multiple colleges and universities in the city.

In 2020, the city expanded its regional bus service to nearby cities.

Its climate is semi-arid, with major variation in temperature due to mountains and lower elevation, especially between day and night. Air quality in Greeley is extremely dry, with the city experiencing less precipitation and fewer thunderstorms than adjacent areas. Extra-tropical cyclones which disrupt the Eastern two-thirds of the United States often originate in Colorado, which means that Greeley does not frequently experience fully developed storm systems.

Rankings

Business/Finance Rankings

▪ The Greeley metro area appeared on the Milken Institute "2021 Best Performing Cities" list. Rank: #43 out of 200 large metro areas (population over 250,000). Criteria: job growth; wage and salary growth; high-tech output growth; housing affordability; household broadband access. *Milken Institute, "Best-Performing Cities 2021," February 16, 2021*

▪ *Forbes* ranked the 200 most populous metro areas to determine the nation's "Best Places for Business and Careers." The Greeley metro area was ranked #52. Criteria: costs (business and living); job growth (past and projected); income growth; quality of life; educational attainment (college and high school); projected economic growth; cultural and leisure opportunities; workplace tolerance laws; net migration patterns. *Forbes, "The Best Places for Business and Careers 2019: Seattle Still On Top," October 30, 2019*

Children/Family Rankings

▪ Greeley was selected as one of the best cities for newlyweds by *Rent.com*. The city ranked #5 of 15. Criteria: cost of living; availability of affordable rental inventory; annual household income; activities and restaurant options; percentage of married couples; concentration of millennials; safety. *Rent.com, "The 15 Best Cities for Newlyweds," December 11, 2018*

Real Estate Rankings

▪ Greeley was ranked #207 out of 268 metro areas in terms of housing affordability in 2020 by the National Association of Home Builders (#1 = most affordable). Criteria: the share of homes sold in that area affordable to a family earning the local median income, based on standard mortgage underwriting criteria. *National Association of Home Builders®, NAHB-Wells Fargo Housing Opportunity Index, 4th Quarter 2020*

Safety Rankings

▪ The National Insurance Crime Bureau ranked 384 metro areas in the U.S. in terms of per capita rates of vehicle theft. The Greeley metro area ranked #136 (#1 = highest rate). Criteria: number of vehicle theft offenses per 100,000 inhabitants in 2019. *National Insurance Crime Bureau, "Hot Spots 2019," July 21, 2020*

Seniors/Retirement Rankings

▪ From its Best Cities for Successful Aging indexes, the Milken Institute generated rankings for metropolitan areas, weighing data in nine categories—health care, wellness, living arrangements, transportation and convenience, financial characteristics, education, employment, community engagement, and overall livability. The Greeley metro area was ranked #170 overall in the small metro area category. *Milken Institute, "Best Cities for Successful Aging, 2017" March 14, 2017*

Business Environment

DEMOGRAPHICS

Population Growth

Area	1990 Census	2000 Census	2010 Census	2019* Estimate	Population Growth (%) 1990-2019	Population Growth (%) 2010-2019
City	60,887	76,930	92,889	105,888	73.9	14.0
MSA[1]	131,816	180,926	252,825	305,345	131.6	20.8
U.S.	248,709,873	281,421,906	308,745,538	324,697,795	30.6	5.2

Note: (1) Figures cover the Greeley, CO Metropolitan Statistical Area; (*) 2015-2019 5-year estimated population
Source: U.S. Census Bureau, 1990 Census, Census 2000, Census 2010, 2015-2019 American Community Survey 5-Year Estimates

Household Size

Area	One	Two	Three	Four	Five	Six	Seven or More	Average Household Size
City	26.1	31.5	16.2	13.3	8.3	3.2	1.4	2.70
MSA[1]	20.6	33.4	16.7	15.7	8.4	3.3	1.8	2.90
U.S.	27.9	33.9	15.6	12.9	6.0	2.3	1.4	2.60

Persons in Household (%)

Note: (1) Figures cover the Greeley, CO Metropolitan Statistical Area
Source: U.S. Census Bureau, 2015-2019 American Community Survey 5-Year Estimates

Race

Area	White Alone[2] (%)	Black Alone[2] (%)	Asian Alone[2] (%)	AIAN[3] Alone[2] (%)	NHOPI[4] Alone[2] (%)	Other Race Alone[2] (%)	Two or More Races (%)
City	88.3	2.4	1.4	1.2	0.2	3.7	2.8
MSA[1]	90.3	1.2	1.6	0.8	0.1	3.0	3.0
U.S.	72.5	12.7	5.5	0.8	0.2	4.9	3.3

Note: (1) Figures cover the Greeley, CO Metropolitan Statistical Area; (2) Alone is defined as not being in combination with one or more other races; (3) American Indian and Alaska Native; (4) Native Hawaiian and Other Pacific Islander
Source: U.S. Census Bureau, 2015-2019 American Community Survey 5-Year Estimates

Hispanic or Latino Origin

Area	Total (%)	Mexican (%)	Puerto Rican (%)	Cuban (%)	Other (%)
City	38.6	31.0	0.6	0.3	6.7
MSA[1]	29.4	24.2	0.4	0.3	4.6
U.S.	18.0	11.2	1.7	0.7	4.3

Note: Persons of Hispanic or Latino origin can be of any race; (1) Figures cover the Greeley, CO Metropolitan Statistical Area
Source: U.S. Census Bureau, 2015-2019 American Community Survey 5-Year Estimates

Ancestry

Area	German	Irish	English	American	Italian	Polish	French[2]	Scottish	Dutch
City	18.4	8.5	6.8	4.2	2.5	1.4	1.6	2.1	1.0
MSA[1]	22.0	9.9	8.7	4.9	3.6	2.1	2.1	1.9	1.4
U.S.	13.3	9.7	7.2	6.2	5.1	2.8	2.3	1.7	1.2

Note: Figures are the percentage of the total population reporting a particular ancestry. The nine most commonly reported ancestries in the U.S. are shown. Figures include multiple ancestries (e.g. if a person reported being Irish and Italian, they were included in both columns); (1) Figures cover the Greeley, CO Metropolitan Statistical Area; (2) Excludes Basque
Source: U.S. Census Bureau, 2015-2019 American Community Survey 5-Year Estimates

Foreign-born Population

Area	Any Foreign Country	Asia	Mexico	Europe	Caribbean	Central America[2]	South America	Africa	Canada
City	11.5	1.0	7.4	0.4	0.2	1.2	0.2	1.1	0.1
MSA[1]	8.7	0.9	5.9	0.4	0.2	0.6	0.2	0.5	0.1
U.S.	13.6	4.2	3.5	1.5	1.3	1.1	1.0	0.7	0.2

Percent of Population Born in

Note: (1) Figures cover the Greeley, CO Metropolitan Statistical Area; (2) Excludes Mexico.
Source: U.S. Census Bureau, 2015-2019 American Community Survey 5-Year Estimates

Marital Status

Area	Never Married	Now Married[2]	Separated	Widowed	Divorced
City	35.8	46.0	1.7	5.1	11.3
MSA[1]	28.2	55.2	1.4	4.5	10.8
U.S.	33.4	48.1	1.9	5.8	10.9

Note: Figures are percentages and cover the population 15 years of age and older; (1) Figures cover the Greeley, CO Metropolitan Statistical Area; (2) Excludes separated
Source: U.S. Census Bureau, 2015-2019 American Community Survey 5-Year Estimates

Disability by Age

Area	All Ages	Under 18 Years Old	18 to 64 Years Old	65 Years and Over
City	11.2	2.3	10.2	36.2
MSA[1]	10.3	3.0	8.9	34.6
U.S.	12.6	4.2	10.3	34.5

Note: Figures show percent of the civilian noninstitutionalized population that reported having a disability. Disability status is determined from six types of difficulty: vision, hearing, cognitive, ambulatory, self-care, and independent living. For children under 5 years old, hearing and vision difficulty are used to determine disability status. For children between the ages of 5 and 14, disability status is determined from hearing, vision, cognitive, ambulatory, and self-care difficulties. For people aged 15 years and older, they are considered to have a disability if they have difficulty with any one of the six difficulty types; Note: (1) Figures cover the Greeley, CO Metropolitan Statistical Area
Source: U.S. Census Bureau, 2015-2019 American Community Survey 5-Year Estimates

Age

Area	Under Age 5	Age 5–19	Age 20–34	Age 35–44	Age 45–54	Age 55–64	Age 65–74	Age 75–84	Age 85+	Median Age
City	6.5	23.6	24.8	12.0	10.9	10.5	6.8	3.4	1.7	31.5
MSA[1]	7.2	22.1	21.5	13.6	12.2	11.5	7.4	3.2	1.2	34.4
U.S.	6.1	19.1	20.7	12.6	13.0	12.9	9.1	4.6	1.9	38.1

Note: (1) Figures cover the Greeley, CO Metropolitan Statistical Area
Source: U.S. Census Bureau, 2015-2019 American Community Survey 5-Year Estimates

Gender

Area	Males	Females	Males per 100 Females
City	52,657	53,231	98.9
MSA[1]	154,294	151,051	102.1
U.S.	159,886,919	164,810,876	97.0

Note: (1) Figures cover the Greeley, CO Metropolitan Statistical Area
Source: U.S. Census Bureau, 2015-2019 American Community Survey 5-Year Estimates

Religious Groups by Family

Area	Catholic	Baptist	Non-Den.	Methodist[2]	Lutheran	LDS[3]	Pentecostal	Presbyterian[4]	Muslim[5]	Judaism
MSA[1]	13.5	1.8	1.5	2.7	2.0	2.0	1.9	1.5	0.1	<0.1
U.S.	19.1	9.3	4.0	4.0	2.3	2.0	1.9	1.6	0.8	0.7

Note: Figures are the number of adherents as a percentage of the total population; (1) Figures cover the Greeley, CO Metropolitan Statistical Area; (2) Methodist/Pietist; (3) Latter Day Saints; (4) Reformed; (5) Figures are estimates
Source: Association of Statisticians of American Religious Bodies, 2010 U.S. Religion Census: Religious Congregations & Membership Study

Religious Groups by Tradition

Area	Catholic	Evangelical Protestant	Mainline Protestant	Other Tradition	Black Protestant	Orthodox
MSA[1]	13.5	9.3	3.9	2.1	<0.1	<0.1
U.S.	19.1	16.2	7.3	4.3	1.6	0.3

Note: Figures are the number of adherents as a percentage of the total population; (1) Figures cover the Greeley, CO Metropolitan Statistical Area
Source: Association of Statisticians of American Religious Bodies, 2010 U.S. Religion Census: Religious Congregations & Membership Study

ECONOMY

Gross Metropolitan Product

Area	2017	2018	2019	2020	Rank[2]
MSA[1]	12.8	13.8	14.7	15.6	178

Note: Figures are in billions of dollars; (1) Figures cover the Greeley, CO Metropolitan Statistical Area; (2) Rank is based on 2018 data and ranges from 1 to 381
Source: U.S. Conference of Mayors, U.S. Metro Economies: GMP & Employment 2018-2020, September 2019

Economic Growth

Area	2015-17 (%)	2018 (%)	2019 (%)	2020 (%)	Rank[2]
MSA[1]	4.1	5.3	4.5	3.9	33
U.S.	1.9	2.9	2.3	2.1	–

Note: Figures are real gross metropolitan product (GMP) growth rates and represent average annual percent change; (1) Figures cover the Greeley, CO Metropolitan Statistical Area; (2) Rank is based on 2017 2-year average annual percent change and ranges from 1 to 381
Source: U.S. Conference of Mayors, U.S. Metro Economies: GMP & Employment 2018-2020, September 2019

Metropolitan Area Exports

Area	2014	2015	2016	2017	2018	2019	Rank[2]
MSA[1]	1,343.6	1,240.1	1,539.6	1,492.8	1,366.5	1,439.2	124

Note: Figures are in millions of dollars; (1) Figures cover the Greeley, CO Metropolitan Statistical Area; (2) Rank is based on 2019 data and ranges from 1 to 386
Source: U.S. Department of Commerce, International Trade Administration, Office of Trade and Economic Analysis, Industry and Analysis, Exports by Metropolitan Area, data extracted March 24, 2021

Building Permits

Area	Single-Family			Multi-Family			Total		
	2018	2019	Pct. Chg.	2018	2019	Pct. Chg.	2018	2019	Pct. Chg.
City	348	170	-51.1	190	697	266.8	538	867	61.2
MSA[1]	3,194	3,335	4.4	913	1,052	15.2	4,107	4,387	6.8
U.S.	855,300	862,100	0.7	473,500	523,900	10.6	1,328,800	1,386,000	4.3

Note: (1) Figures cover the Greeley, CO Metropolitan Statistical Area; Figures represent new, privately-owned housing units authorized (unadjusted data); All permit data are based on estimates with imputation
Source: U.S. Census Bureau, Manufacturing, Mining, and Construction Statistics, Building Permits, 2018, 2019

Bankruptcy Filings

Area	Business Filings			Nonbusiness Filings		
	2019	2020	% Chg.	2019	2020	% Chg.
Weld County	20	21	5.0	691	509	-26.3
U.S.	22,780	21,655	-4.9	752,160	522,808	-30.5

Note: Business filings include Chapter 7, Chapter 9, Chapter 11, Chapter 12, Chapter 13, Chapter 15, and Section 304; Nonbusiness filings include Chapter 7, Chapter 11, and Chapter 13
Source: Administrative Office of the U.S. Courts, Business and Nonbusiness Bankruptcy, County Cases Commenced by Chapter of the Bankruptcy Code, During the 12-Month Period Ending December 31, 2019 and Business and Nonbusiness Bankruptcy, County Cases Commenced by Chapter of the Bankruptcy Code, During the 12-Month Period Ending December 31, 2020

Housing Vacancy Rates

Area	Gross Vacancy Rate[2] (%)			Year-Round Vacancy Rate[3] (%)			Rental Vacancy Rate[4] (%)			Homeowner Vacancy Rate[5] (%)		
	2018	2019	2020	2018	2019	2020	2018	2019	2020	2018	2019	2020
MSA[1]	n/a	n/a	n/a	n/a	n/a	n/a	n/a	n/a	n/a	n/a	n/a	n/a
U.S.	12.3	12.0	10.6	9.7	9.5	8.2	6.9	6.7	6.3	1.5	1.4	1.0

Note: (1) Figures cover the Greeley, CO Metropolitan Statistical Area; (2) The percentage of the total housing inventory that is vacant; (3) The percentage of the housing inventory (excluding seasonal units) that is year-round vacant; (4) The percentage of rental inventory that is vacant for rent; (5) The percentage of homeowner inventory that is vacant for sale; n/a not available
Source: U.S. Census Bureau, Housing Vacancies and Homeownership Annual Statistics: 2018, 2019, 2020

INCOME

Income

Area	Per Capita ($)	Median Household ($)	Average Household ($)
City	26,222	57,586	72,302
MSA[1]	31,793	74,150	89,427
U.S.	34,103	62,843	88,607

Note: (1) Figures cover the Greeley, CO Metropolitan Statistical Area
Source: U.S. Census Bureau, 2015-2019 American Community Survey 5-Year Estimates

Household Income Distribution

Area	Percent of Households Earning							
	Under $15,000	$15,000 -$24,999	$25,000 -$34,999	$35,000 -$49,999	$50,000 -$74,999	$75,000 -$99,999	$100,000 -$149,999	$150,000 and up
City	11.9	9.8	8.3	13.5	18.9	13.7	15.7	8.1
MSA[1]	7.7	6.9	7.2	11.0	17.7	16.3	19.3	13.9
U.S.	10.3	8.9	8.9	12.3	17.2	12.7	15.1	14.5

Note: (1) Figures cover the Greeley, CO Metropolitan Statistical Area
Source: U.S. Census Bureau, 2015-2019 American Community Survey 5-Year Estimates

Poverty Rate

Area	All Ages	Under 18 Years Old	18 to 64 Years Old	65 Years and Over
City	16.2	19.6	16.1	9.3
MSA[1]	10.0	12.0	9.5	8.4
U.S.	13.4	18.5	12.6	9.3

Note: Figures are percentage of people whose income during the past 12 months was below the poverty level;
(1) Figures cover the Greeley, CO Metropolitan Statistical Area
Source: U.S. Census Bureau, 2015-2019 American Community Survey 5-Year Estimates

CITY FINANCES

City Government Finances

Component	2017 ($000)	2017 ($ per capita)
Total Revenues	213,150	2,113
Total Expenditures	206,973	2,052
Debt Outstanding	158,754	1,574
Cash and Securities[1]	208,629	2,068

Note: (1) Cash and security holdings of a government at the close of its fiscal year, including those of its dependent agencies, utilities, and liquor stores.
Source: U.S. Census Bureau, State & Local Government Finances 2017

City Government Revenue by Source

Source	2017 ($000)	2017 ($ per capita)	2017 (%)
General Revenue			
From Federal Government	4,488	44	2.1
From State Government	8,517	84	4.0
From Local Governments	2,865	28	1.3
Taxes			
Property	17,835	177	8.4
Sales and Gross Receipts	74,441	738	34.9
Personal Income	0	0	0.0
Corporate Income	0	0	0.0
Motor Vehicle License	318	3	0.1
Other Taxes	7,361	73	3.5
Current Charges	31,307	310	14.7
Liquor Store	0	0	0.0
Utility	53,970	535	25.3
Employee Retirement	0	0	0.0

Source: U.S. Census Bureau, State & Local Government Finances 2017

City Government Expenditures by Function

Function	2017 ($000)	2017 ($ per capita)	2017 (%)
General Direct Expenditures			
Air Transportation	0	0	0.0
Corrections	0	0	0.0
Education	0	0	0.0
Employment Security Administration	0	0	0.0
Financial Administration	5,302	52	2.6
Fire Protection	14,785	146	7.1
General Public Buildings	8,531	84	4.1
Governmental Administration, Other	17,416	172	8.4
Health	49	< 1	< 0.1
Highways	28,198	279	13.6
Hospitals	0	0	0.0
Housing and Community Development	8,317	82	4.0
Interest on General Debt	2,110	20	1.0
Judicial and Legal	2,278	22	1.1
Libraries	0	0	0.0
Parking	203	2	0.1
Parks and Recreation	20,123	199	9.7
Police Protection	22,289	220	10.8
Public Welfare	0	0	0.0
Sewerage	13,290	131	6.4
Solid Waste Management	215	2	0.1
Veterans' Services	0	0	0.0
Liquor Store	0	0	0.0
Utility	59,570	590	28.8
Employee Retirement	0	0	0.0

Source: U.S. Census Bureau, State & Local Government Finances 2017

EMPLOYMENT

Labor Force and Employment

Area	Civilian Labor Force			Workers Employed		
	Dec. 2019	Dec. 2020	% Chg.	Dec. 2019	Dec. 2020	% Chg.
City	55,458	56,828	2.5	54,063	51,159	-5.4
MSA[1]	172,545	174,099	0.9	168,655	159,598	-5.4
U.S.	164,007,000	160,017,000	-2.4	158,504,000	149,613,000	-5.6

Note: Data is not seasonally adjusted and covers workers 16 years of age and older; (1) Figures cover the Greeley, CO Metropolitan Statistical Area
Source: Bureau of Labor Statistics, Local Area Unemployment Statistics

Unemployment Rate

Area	2020											
	Jan.	Feb.	Mar.	Apr.	May	Jun.	Jul.	Aug.	Sep.	Oct.	Nov.	Dec.
City	3.1	3.2	5.6	10.3	9.3	11.2	8.4	7.9	7.5	7.3	7.7	10.0
MSA[1]	2.7	2.9	5.1	9.9	8.6	10.1	7.3	6.6	6.3	6.2	6.4	8.3
U.S.	4.0	3.8	4.5	14.4	13.0	11.2	10.5	8.5	7.7	6.6	6.4	6.5

Note: Data is not seasonally adjusted and covers workers 16 years of age and older; (1) Figures cover the Greeley, CO Metropolitan Statistical Area
Source: Bureau of Labor Statistics, Local Area Unemployment Statistics

Average Wages

Occupation	$/Hr.	Occupation	$/Hr.
Accountants and Auditors	39.20	Maintenance and Repair Workers	22.40
Automotive Mechanics	25.40	Marketing Managers	72.60
Bookkeepers	20.20	Network and Computer Systems Admin.	35.50
Carpenters	23.00	Nurses, Licensed Practical	29.00
Cashiers	13.80	Nurses, Registered	34.50
Computer Programmers	n/a	Nursing Assistants	15.50
Computer Systems Analysts	58.60	Office Clerks, General	21.20
Computer User Support Specialists	28.60	Physical Therapists	43.70
Construction Laborers	18.30	Physicians	117.70
Cooks, Restaurant	15.10	Plumbers, Pipefitters and Steamfitters	25.40
Customer Service Representatives	16.40	Police and Sheriff's Patrol Officers	36.10
Dentists	80.50	Postal Service Mail Carriers	24.70
Electricians	27.30	Real Estate Sales Agents	n/a
Engineers, Electrical	51.40	Retail Salespersons	17.50
Fast Food and Counter Workers	13.20	Sales Representatives, Technical/Scientific	42.70
Financial Managers	81.30	Secretaries, Exc. Legal/Medical/Executive	18.70
First-Line Supervisors of Office Workers	30.40	Security Guards	16.80
General and Operations Managers	63.00	Surgeons	n/a
Hairdressers/Cosmetologists	16.60	Teacher Assistants, Exc. Postsecondary*	14.60
Home Health and Personal Care Aides	15.20	Teachers, Secondary School, Exc. Sp. Ed.*	25.80
Janitors and Cleaners	15.00	Telemarketers	n/a
Landscaping/Groundskeeping Workers	18.20	Truck Drivers, Heavy/Tractor-Trailer	25.80
Lawyers	51.50	Truck Drivers, Light/Delivery Services	20.10
Maids and Housekeeping Cleaners	13.30	Waiters and Waitresses	12.60

Note: Wage data covers the Greeley, CO Metropolitan Statistical Area; (*) Hourly wages were calculated from annual wage data based on a 40 hour work week; n/a not available.
Source: Bureau of Labor Statistics, Metro Area Occupational Employment & Wage Estimates, May 2020

Employment by Industry

Sector	MSA[1]		U.S.
	Number of Employees	Percent of Total	Percent of Total
Construction, Mining, and Logging	15,600	14.9	5.5
Education and Health Services	10,300	9.9	16.3
Financial Activities	4,400	4.2	6.1
Government	16,600	15.9	15.2
Information	500	0.5	1.9
Leisure and Hospitality	8,500	8.1	9.0
Manufacturing	13,700	13.1	8.5
Other Services	3,600	3.4	3.8
Professional and Business Services	11,200	10.7	14.4
Retail Trade	11,000	10.5	10.9
Transportation, Warehousing, and Utilities	4,800	4.6	4.6
Wholesale Trade	4,200	4.0	3.9

Note: Figures are non-farm employment as of December 2020. Figures are not seasonally adjusted and include workers 16 years of age and older; (1) Figures cover the Greeley, CO Metropolitan Statistical Area
Source: Bureau of Labor Statistics, Current Employment Statistics, Employment, Hours, and Earnings

Employment by Occupation

Occupation Classification	City (%)	MSA[1] (%)	U.S. (%)
Management, Business, Science, and Arts	29.5	34.2	38.5
Natural Resources, Construction, and Maintenance	12.2	13.1	8.9
Production, Transportation, and Material Moving	17.7	15.6	13.2
Sales and Office	22.0	21.1	21.6
Service	18.6	16.0	17.8

Note: Figures cover employed civilians 16 years of age and older; (1) Figures cover the Greeley, CO Metropolitan Statistical Area
Source: U.S. Census Bureau, 2015-2019 American Community Survey 5-Year Estimates

Occupations with Greatest Projected Employment Growth: 2020 – 2022

Occupation[1]	2020 Employment	2022 Projected Employment	Numeric Employment Change	Percent Employment Change
Software Developers, Applications	33,470	35,740	2,270	6.8
Personal Care Aides	30,000	31,610	1,610	5.4
Registered Nurses	54,810	56,090	1,280	2.3
Market Research Analysts and Marketing Specialists	21,470	22,380	910	4.2
Business Operations Specialists, All Other	49,470	50,350	880	1.8
Stock Clerks and Order Fillers	37,610	38,390	780	2.1
Computer Occupations, All Other	18,280	18,940	660	3.6
Accountants and Auditors	42,200	42,840	640	1.5
Software Developers, Systems Software	12,390	13,010	620	5.0
Sales Representatives, Wholesale and Manufacturing, Except Technical and Scientific Products	28,620	29,170	550	1.9

Note: Projections cover Colorado; (1) Sorted by numeric employment change
Source: www.projectionscentral.com, State Occupational Projections, 2020–2022 Short-Term Projections

Fastest-Growing Occupations: 2020 – 2022

Occupation[1]	2020 Employment	2022 Projected Employment	Numeric Employment Change	Percent Employment Change
Information Security Analysts	3,860	4,170	310	8.0
Software Developers, Applications	33,470	35,740	2,270	6.8
Statisticians	1,230	1,310	80	6.5
Operations Research Analysts	940	1,000	60	6.4
Veterinary Technologists and Technicians	4,490	4,750	260	5.8
Health Specialties Teachers, Postsecondary	6,160	6,500	340	5.5
Personal Care Aides	30,000	31,610	1,610	5.4
Veterinarians	2,820	2,970	150	5.3
Interpreters and Translators	1,980	2,080	100	5.1
Software Developers, Systems Software	12,390	13,010	620	5.0

Note: Projections cover Colorado; (1) Sorted by percent employment change and excludes occupations with numeric employment change less than 50
Source: www.projectionscentral.com, State Occupational Projections, 2020–2022 Short-Term Projections

TAXES

State Corporate Income Tax Rates

State	Tax Rate (%)	Income Brackets ($)	Num. of Brackets	Financial Institution Tax Rate (%)[a]	Federal Income Tax Ded.
Colorado	4.55	Flat rate	1	4.55	No

Note: Tax rates as of January 1, 2021; (a) Rates listed are the corporate income tax rate applied to financial institutions or excise taxes based on income. Some states have other taxes based upon the value of deposits or shares.
Source: Federation of Tax Administrators, State Corporate Income Tax Rates, January 1, 2021

State Individual Income Tax Rates

State	Tax Rate (%)	Income Brackets ($)	Personal Exemptions ($)			Standard Ded. ($)	
			Single	Married	Depend.	Single	Married
Colorado	4.55	Flat rate	(d)	(d)	(d)	12,550	25,100 (d)

Note: Tax rates as of January 1, 2021; Local- and county-level taxes are not included; Federal income tax is not deductible on state income tax returns; (d) These states use the personal exemption/standard deduction amounts provided in the federal Internal Revenue Code.
Source: Federation of Tax Administrators, State Individual Income Tax Rates, January 1, 2021

Various State Sales and Excise Tax Rates

State	State Sales Tax (%)	Gasoline[1] (¢/gal.)	Cigarette[2] ($/pack)	Spirits[3] ($/gal.)	Wine[4] ($/gal.)	Beer[5] ($/gal.)	Recreational Marijuana (%)
Colorado	2.9	22	1.94	2.28	0.32	0.08	(d)

Note: All tax rates as of January 1, 2021; (1) The American Petroleum Institute has developed a methodology for determining the average tax rate on a gallon of fuel. Rates may include any of the following: excise taxes, environmental fees, storage tank fees, other fees or taxes, general sales tax, and local taxes; (2) The federal excise tax of $1.0066 per pack and local taxes are not included; (3) Rates are those applicable to off-premise sales of 40% alcohol by volume (a.b.v.) distilled spirits in 750ml containers. Local excise taxes are excluded; (4) Rates are those applicable to off-premise sales of 11% a.b.v. non-carbonated wine in 750ml containers; (5) Rates are those applicable to off-premise sales of 4.7% a.b.v. beer in 12 ounce containers; (d) 15% excise tax (levied on wholesale at average market rate); 15% excise tax (retail price)
Source: Tax Foundation, 2021 Facts & Figures: How Does Your State Compare?

State Business Tax Climate Index Rankings

State	Overall Rank	Corporate Tax Rank	Individual Income Tax Rank	Sales Tax Rank	Property Tax Rank	Unemployment Insurance Tax Rank
Colorado	21	10	14	36	32	41

Note: The index is a measure of how each state's tax laws affect economic performance. The lower the rank, the more favorable a state's tax system is for business. States without a given tax are given a ranking of 1. The scores/rankings for the District of Columbia do not affect other states. The 2021 index represents the tax climate as of July 1, 2020.
Source: Tax Foundation, State Business Tax Climate Index 2021

TRANSPORTATION

Means of Transportation to Work

Area	Car/Truck/Van		Public Transportation			Bicycle	Walked	Other Means	Worked at Home
	Drove Alone	Car-pooled	Bus	Subway	Railroad				
City	79.5	11.3	0.6	0.0	0.0	0.7	2.8	1.2	3.9
MSA[1]	80.4	9.6	0.5	0.0	0.0	0.3	1.9	1.0	6.2
U.S.	76.3	9.0	2.4	1.9	0.6	0.5	2.7	1.4	5.2

Note: Figures are percentages and cover workers 16 years of age and older; (1) Figures cover the Greeley, CO Metropolitan Statistical Area
Source: U.S. Census Bureau, 2015-2019 American Community Survey 5-Year Estimates

Travel Time to Work

Area	Less Than 10 Minutes	10 to 19 Minutes	20 to 29 Minutes	30 to 44 Minutes	45 to 59 Minutes	60 to 89 Minutes	90 Minutes or More
City	16.1	37.4	16.2	14.7	5.9	7.4	2.3
MSA[1]	11.9	27.1	19.2	22.3	9.5	7.5	2.5
U.S.	12.2	28.4	20.8	20.8	8.3	6.4	2.9

Note: Note: Figures are percentages and include workers 16 years old and over; (1) Figures cover the Greeley, CO Metropolitan Statistical Area
Source: U.S. Census Bureau, 2015-2019 American Community Survey 5-Year Estimates

Key Congestion Measures

Measure	1982	1992	2002	2012	2017
Annual Hours of Delay, Total (000)	n/a	n/a	n/a	n/a	2,858
Annual Hours of Delay, Per Auto Commuter	n/a	n/a	n/a	n/a	23
Annual Congestion Cost, Total (million $)	n/a	n/a	n/a	n/a	59
Annual Congestion Cost, Per Auto Commuter ($)	n/a	n/a	n/a	n/a	473

Note: n/a not available
Source: Texas A&M Transportation Institute, 2019 Urban Mobility Report

Freeway Travel Time Index

Measure	1982	1987	1992	1997	2002	2007	2012	2017
Urban Area Index[1]	n/a	n/a	n/a	n/a	n/a	n/a	n/a	1.15
Urban Area Rank[1,2]	n/a	n/a	n/a	n/a	n/a	n/a	n/a	n/a

Note: Freeway Travel Time Index—the ratio of travel time in the peak period to the travel time at free-flow conditions. For example, a value of 1.30 indicates a 20-minute free-flow trip takes 26 minutes in the peak (20 minutes x 1.30 = 26 minutes); (1) Covers the Greeley CO urban area; (2) Rank is based on 101 larger urban areas (#1 = highest travel time index); n/a not available
Source: Texas A&M Transportation Institute, 2019 Urban Mobility Report

Public Transportation

Agency Name / Mode of Transportation	Vehicles Operated in Maximum Service[1]	Annual Unlinked Passenger Trips[2] (in thous.)	Annual Passenger Miles[3] (in thous.)
City of Greeley - Transit Services			
Bus (directly operated)	14	807.8	n/a
Demand Response (directly operated)	7	21.5	n/a

Note: (1) Number of revenue vehicles operated by the given mode and type of service to meet the annual maximum service requirement. This is the revenue vehicle count during the peak season of the year; on the week and day that maximum service is provided. Vehicles operated in maximum service (VOMS) exclude atypical days and one-time special events; (2) Number of passengers who boarded public transportation vehicles. Passengers are counted each time they board a vehicle no matter how many vehicles they use to travel from their origin to their destination. (3) Sum of the distances ridden by all passengers during the entire fiscal year.
Source: Federal Transit Administration, National Transit Database, 2019

Air Transportation

Airport Name and Code / Type of Service	Passenger Airlines[1]	Passenger Enplanements	Freight Carriers[2]	Freight (lbs)
Denver International (55 miles) (DEN)				
Domestic service (U.S. carriers - 2020)	27	15,787,920	18	263,867,762
International service (U.S. carriers - 2019)	7	883,726	3	8,069,938

Note: (1) Includes all U.S.-based major, minor and commuter airlines that carried at least one passenger during the year; (2) Includes all U.S.-based airlines and freight carriers that transported at least one pound of freight during the year.
Source: Bureau of Transportation Statistics, The Intermodal Transportation Database, Air Carriers: T-100 Domestic Market (U.S. Carriers), 2020; Bureau of Transportation Statistics, The Intermodal Transportation Database, Air Carriers: T-100 International Market (U.S. Carriers), 2019

BUSINESSES

Major Business Headquarters

Company Name	Industry	Rankings	
		Fortune[1]	Forbes[2]
Hensel Phelps Construction	Construction	-	74

Note: (1) Companies that produce a 10-K are ranked 1 to 500 based on 2019 revenue; (2) All private companies with at least $2 billion in annual revenue through the end of their most current fiscal year are ranked 1 to 219; companies listed are headquartered in the city; dashes indicate no ranking
Source: Fortune, "Fortune 500," June/July 2020; Forbes, "America's Largest Private Companies," 2020

Living Environment

COST OF LIVING

Cost of Living Index

Composite Index	Groceries	Housing	Utilities	Trans-portation	Health Care	Misc. Goods/ Services
n/a	n/a	n/a	n/a	n/a	n/a	n/a

Note: The Cost of Living Index measures regional differences in the cost of consumer goods and services, excluding taxes and non-consumer expenditures, for professional and managerial households in the top income quintile. It is based on more than 50,000 prices covering almost 60 different items for which prices are collected three times a year by chambers of commerce, economic development organizations or university applied economic centers in each participating urban area. The numbers shown should be read as a percentage above or below the national average of 100. For example, a value of 115.4 in the groceries column indicates that grocery prices are 15.4% higher than the national average. Small differences in the index numbers should not be interpreted as significant; n/a not available.
Source: The Council for Community and Economic Research, Cost of Living Index, 2020

Grocery Prices

Area[1]	T-Bone Steak ($/pound)	Frying Chicken ($/pound)	Whole Milk ($/half gal.)	Eggs ($/dozen)	Orange Juice ($/64 oz.)	Coffee ($/11.5 oz.)
City[2]	n/a	n/a	n/a	n/a	n/a	n/a
Avg.	11.78	1.39	2.05	1.47	3.57	4.34
Min.	8.03	0.94	1.03	0.74	2.94	3.02
Max.	15.86	2.65	4.31	3.77	5.44	8.69

*Note: (1) Values for the local area are compared with the average, minimum and maximum values for all 284 areas in the Cost of Living Index; (2) Figures cover the Greeley CO urban area; n/a not available; **T-Bone Steak** (price per pound); **Frying Chicken** (price per pound, whole fryer); **Whole Milk** (half gallon carton); **Eggs** (price per dozen, Grade A, large); **Orange Juice** (64 oz. Tropicana or Florida Natural); **Coffee** (11.5 oz. can, vacuum-packed, Maxwell House, Hills Bros, or Folgers).*
Source: The Council for Community and Economic Research, Cost of Living Index, 2020

Housing and Utility Costs

Area[1]	New Home Price ($)	Apartment Rent ($/month)	All Electric ($/month)	Part Electric ($/month)	Other Energy ($/month)	Telephone ($/month)
City[2]	n/a	n/a	n/a	n/a	n/a	n/a
Avg.	368,594	1,168	170.86	100.47	65.28	184.30
Min.	190,567	502	91.58	31.42	26.08	169.60
Max.	2,227,806	4,738	470.38	280.31	280.06	206.50

*Note: (1) Values for the local area are compared with the average, minimum and maximum values for all 284 areas in the Cost of Living Index; (2) Figures cover the Greeley CO urban area; n/a not available; **New Home Price** (2,400 sf living area, 8,000 sf lot, in urban area with full utilities); **Apartment Rent** (950 sf 2 bedroom/1.5 or 2 bath, unfurnished, excluding all utilities except water); **All Electric** (average monthly cost for an all-electric home); **Part Electric** (average monthly cost for a part-electric home); **Other Energy** (average monthly cost for natural gas, fuel oil, coal, wood, and any other forms of energy except electricity); **Telephone** (price includes the base monthly rate plus taxes and fees for three lines of mobile phone service).*
Source: The Council for Community and Economic Research, Cost of Living Index, 2020

Health Care, Transportation, and Other Costs

Area[1]	Doctor ($/visit)	Dentist ($/visit)	Optometrist ($/visit)	Gasoline ($/gallon)	Beauty Salon ($/visit)	Men's Shirt ($)
City[2]	n/a	n/a	n/a	n/a	n/a	n/a
Avg.	115.44	99.32	108.10	2.21	39.27	31.37
Min.	36.68	59.00	51.36	1.71	19.00	11.00
Max.	219.00	153.10	250.97	3.46	82.05	58.33

*Note: (1) Values for the local area are compared with the average, minimum and maximum values for all 284 areas in the Cost of Living Index; (2) Figures cover the Greeley CO urban area; n/a not available; **Doctor** (general practitioners routine exam of an established patient); **Dentist** (adult teeth cleaning and periodic oral examination); **Optometrist** (full vision eye exam for established adult patient); **Gasoline** (one gallon regular unleaded, national brand, including all taxes, cash price at self-service pump if available); **Beauty Salon** (woman's shampoo, trim, and blow-dry); **Men's Shirt** (cotton/polyester dress shirt, pinpoint weave, long sleeves).*
Source: The Council for Community and Economic Research, Cost of Living Index, 2020

HOUSING

Homeownership Rate

Area	2012 (%)	2013 (%)	2014 (%)	2015 (%)	2016 (%)	2017 (%)	2018 (%)	2019 (%)	2020 (%)
MSA[1]	n/a	n/a	n/a	n/a	n/a	n/a	n/a	n/a	n/a
U.S.	65.4	65.1	64.5	63.7	63.4	63.9	64.4	64.6	66.6

Note: (1) Figures cover the Greeley, CO Metropolitan Statistical Area; n/a not available
Source: U.S. Census Bureau, Housing Vacancies and Homeownership Annual Statistics: 2012-2020

House Price Index (HPI)

Area	National Ranking[2]	Quarterly Change (%)	One-Year Change (%)	Five-Year Change (%)	Since 1991Q1 (%)
MSA[1]	177	1.80	5.33	46.65	333.63
U.S.[3]	–	3.81	10.77	38.99	205.12

Note: The HPI is a weighted repeat sales index. It measures average price changes in repeat sales or refinancings on the same properties. This information is obtained by reviewing repeat mortgage transactions on single-family properties whose mortgages have been purchased or securitized by Fannie Mae or Freddie Mac since January 1975; (1) Figures cover the Greeley, CO Metropolitan Statistical Area; (2) Rankings are based on annual percentage change for all metro areas containing at least 15,000 transactions over the last 10 years and ranges from 1 to 253; (3) figures based on a weighted average of Census Division estimates using a seasonally adjusted, purchase-only index; all figures are for the period ending December 31, 2020
Source: Federal Housing Finance Agency, Change in Metropolitan Area House Price Indexes, April 7, 2021

Median Single-Family Home Prices

Area	2018	2019	2020[p]	Percent Change 2019 to 2020
MSA[1]	n/a	n/a	n/a	n/a
U.S. Average	261.6	274.6	299.9	9.2

Note: Figures are median sales prices of existing single-family homes in thousands of dollars; (p) preliminary; n/a not available; (1) Figures cover the Greeley, CO Metropolitan Statistical Area
Source: National Association of Realtors, Median Sales Price of Existing Single-Family Homes for Metropolitan Areas, 4th Quarter 2020

Qualifying Income Based on Median Sales Price of Existing Single-Family Homes

Area	With 5% Down ($)	With 10% Down ($)	With 20% Down ($)
MSA[1]	n/a	n/a	n/a
U.S. Average	59,266	56,147	49,908

Note: Figures are preliminary; Qualifying income is based on a mortgage rate of 2.81%. Monthly principal and interest payment is limited to 25% of income; n/a not available; (1) Figures cover the Greeley, CO Metropolitan Statistical Area
Source: National Association of Realtors, Qualifying Income Based on Median Sales Price of Existing Single-Family Homes for Metropolitan Areas, 4th Quarter 2020

Home Value Distribution

Area	Under $50,000	$50,000 -$99,999	$100,000 -$149,999	$150,000 -$199,999	$200,000 -$299,999	$300,000 -$499,999	$500,000 -$999,999	$1,000,000 or more
City	7.1	2.5	7.2	15.2	36.3	27.2	4.3	0.2
MSA[1]	4.6	2.7	4.6	9.7	28.6	36.6	12.0	1.1
U.S.	6.9	12.0	13.3	14.0	19.6	19.3	11.4	3.4

Note: Figures are percentages and cover owner-occupied housing units; (1) Figures cover the Greeley, CO Metropolitan Statistical Area
Source: U.S. Census Bureau, 2015-2019 American Community Survey 5-Year Estimates

Year Housing Structure Built

Area	2010 or Later	2000 -2009	1990 -1999	1980 -1989	1970 -1979	1960 -1969	1950 -1959	1940 -1949	Before 1940	Median Year
City	6.3	19.3	15.7	10.1	21.2	10.3	6.7	2.6	7.8	1982
MSA[1]	10.9	28.6	16.3	7.4	15.2	6.2	4.4	2.4	8.6	1994
U.S.	5.2	14.0	13.9	13.4	15.2	10.6	10.3	4.9	12.6	1978

Note: Figures are percentages except for Median Year; Note: (1) Figures cover the Greeley, CO Metropolitan Statistical Area
Source: U.S. Census Bureau, 2015-2019 American Community Survey 5-Year Estimates

Gross Monthly Rent

Area	Under $500	$500 -$999	$1,000 -$1,499	$1,500 -$1,999	$2,000 -$2,499	$2,500 -$2,999	$3,000 and up	Median ($)
City	9.2	40.3	32.2	14.0	3.2	0.6	0.5	1,007
MSA[1]	7.7	36.4	33.4	16.3	4.0	1.0	1.2	1,085
U.S.	9.4	36.2	30.0	14.0	5.6	2.4	2.4	1,062

Note: Figures are percentages except for Median; Gross rent is the contract rent plus the estimated average monthly cost of utilities (electricity, gas, and water and sewer) and fuels (oil, coal, kerosene, wood, etc.) if these are paid by the renter (or paid for the renter by someone else); (1) Figures cover the Greeley, CO Metropolitan Statistical Area
Source: U.S. Census Bureau, 2015-2019 American Community Survey 5-Year Estimates

HEALTH

Health Risk Factors

Category	MSA[1] (%)	U.S. (%)
Adults aged 18–64 who have any kind of health care coverage	n/a	87.3
Adults who reported being in good or better health	n/a	82.4
Adults who have been told they have high blood cholesterol	n/a	33.0
Adults who have been told they have high blood pressure	n/a	32.3
Adults who are current smokers	n/a	17.1
Adults who currently use E-cigarettes	n/a	4.6
Adults who currently use chewing tobacco, snuff, or snus	n/a	4.0
Adults who are heavy drinkers[2]	n/a	6.3
Adults who are binge drinkers[3]	n/a	17.4
Adults who are overweight (BMI 25.0 - 29.9)	n/a	35.3
Adults who are obese (BMI 30.0 - 99.8)	n/a	31.3
Adults who participated in any physical activities in the past month	n/a	74.4
Adults who always or nearly always wears a seat belt	n/a	94.3

Note: n/a not available; (1) Figures cover the Greeley, CO Metropolitan Statistical Area; (2) Heavy drinkers are classified as adult men having more than 14 drinks per week and adult women having more than 7 drinks per week; (3) Binge drinkers are classified as males having five or more drinks on one occasion or females having four or more drinks on one occasion
Source: Centers for Disease Control and Prevention, Behaviorial Risk Factor Surveillance System, SMART: Selected Metropolitan Area Risk Trends, 2017

Acute and Chronic Health Conditions

Category	MSA[1] (%)	U.S. (%)
Adults who have ever been told they had a heart attack	n/a	4.2
Adults who have ever been told they have angina or coronary heart disease	n/a	3.9
Adults who have ever been told they had a stroke	n/a	3.0
Adults who have ever been told they have asthma	n/a	14.2
Adults who have ever been told they have arthritis	n/a	24.9
Adults who have ever been told they have diabetes[2]	n/a	10.5
Adults who have ever been told they had skin cancer	n/a	6.2
Adults who have ever been told they had any other types of cancer	n/a	7.1
Adults who have ever been told they have COPD	n/a	6.5
Adults who have ever been told they have kidney disease	n/a	3.0
Adults who have ever been told they have a form of depression	n/a	20.5

Note: n/a not available; (1) Figures cover the Greeley, CO Metropolitan Statistical Area; (2) Figures do not include pregnancy-related, borderline, or pre-diabetes
Source: Centers for Disease Control and Prevention, Behaviorial Risk Factor Surveillance System, SMART: Selected Metropolitan Area Risk Trends, 2017

Health Screening and Vaccination Rates

Category	MSA[1] (%)	U.S. (%)
Adults aged 65+ who have had flu shot within the past year	n/a	60.7
Adults aged 65+ who have ever had a pneumonia vaccination	n/a	75.4
Adults who have ever been tested for HIV	n/a	36.1
Adults who have ever had the shingles or zoster vaccine?	n/a	28.9
Adults who have had their blood cholesterol checked within the last five years	n/a	85.9

Note: n/a not available; (1) Figures cover the Greeley, CO Metropolitan Statistical Area.
Source: Centers for Disease Control and Prevention, Behaviorial Risk Factor Surveillance System, SMART: Selected Metropolitan Area Risk Trends, 2017

Disability Status

Category	MSA[1] (%)	U.S. (%)
Adults who reported being deaf	n/a	6.7
Are you blind or have serious difficulty seeing, even when wearing glasses?	n/a	4.5
Are you limited in any way in any of your usual activities due of arthritis?	n/a	12.9
Do you have difficulty doing errands alone?	n/a	6.8
Do you have difficulty dressing or bathing?	n/a	3.6
Do you have serious difficulty concentrating/remembering/making decisions?	n/a	10.7
Do you have serious difficulty walking or climbing stairs?	n/a	13.6

Note: n/a not available; (1) Figures cover the Greeley, CO Metropolitan Statistical Area.
Source: Centers for Disease Control and Prevention, Behaviorial Risk Factor Surveillance System, SMART: Selected Metropolitan Area Risk Trends, 2017

Mortality Rates for the Top 10 Causes of Death in the U.S.

ICD-10[a] Sub-Chapter	ICD-10[a] Code	Age-Adjusted Mortality Rate[1] per 100,000 population	
		County[2]	U.S.
Malignant neoplasms	C00-C97	133.5	149.2
Ischaemic heart diseases	I20-I25	58.1	90.5
Other forms of heart disease	I30-I51	40.9	52.2
Chronic lower respiratory diseases	J40-J47	45.5	39.6
Other degenerative diseases of the nervous system	G30-G31	36.2	37.6
Cerebrovascular diseases	I60-I69	37.1	37.2
Other external causes of accidental injury	W00-X59	38.3	36.1
Organic, including symptomatic, mental disorders	F01-F09	26.6	29.4
Hypertensive diseases	I10-I15	20.0	24.1
Diabetes mellitus	E10-E14	22.3	21.5

Note: (a) ICD-10 = International Classification of Diseases 10th Revision; (1) Mortality rates are a three-year average covering 2017-2019; (2) Figures cover Weld County.
Source: Centers for Disease Control and Prevention, National Center for Health Statistics. Underlying Cause of Death 1999-2019 on CDC WONDER Online Database

Mortality Rates for Selected Causes of Death

ICD-10[a] Sub-Chapter	ICD-10[a] Code	Age-Adjusted Mortality Rate[1] per 100,000 population	
		County[2]	U.S.
Assault	X85-Y09	2.4	6.0
Diseases of the liver	K70-K76	18.4	14.4
Human immunodeficiency virus (HIV) disease	B20-B24	Suppressed	1.5
Influenza and pneumonia	J09-J18	8.9	13.8
Intentional self-harm	X60-X84	19.7	14.1
Malnutrition	E40-E46	2.8	2.3
Obesity and other hyperalimentation	E65-E68	Unreliable	2.1
Renal failure	N17-N19	8.4	12.6
Transport accidents	V01-V99	16.3	12.3
Viral hepatitis	B15-B19	Unreliable	1.2

Note: (a) ICD-10 = International Classification of Diseases 10th Revision; (1) Mortality rates are a three-year average covering 2017-2019; (2) Figures cover Weld County; Data are suppressed when the data meet the criteria for confidentiality constraints; Mortality rates are flagged as unreliable when the rate would be calculated with a numerator of 20 or less.
Source: Centers for Disease Control and Prevention, National Center for Health Statistics. Underlying Cause of Death 1999-2019 on CDC WONDER Online Database

Health Insurance Coverage

Area	With Health Insurance	With Private Health Insurance	With Public Health Insurance	Without Health Insurance	Population Under Age 19 Without Health Insurance
City	91.5	63.7	38.4	8.5	4.3
MSA[1]	92.1	70.1	32.2	7.9	4.6
U.S.	91.2	67.9	35.1	8.8	5.1

Note: Figures are percentages that cover the civilian noninstitutionalized population; (1) Figures cover the Greeley, CO Metropolitan Statistical Area
Source: U.S. Census Bureau, 2015-2019 American Community Survey 5-Year Estimates

Number of Medical Professionals

Area	MDs[3]	DOs[3,4]	Dentists	Podiatrists	Chiropractors	Optometrists
County[1] (number)	409	52	149	9	74	40
County[1] (rate[2])	129.9	16.5	45.9	2.8	22.8	12.3
U.S. (rate[2])	282.9	22.7	71.2	6.2	28.1	16.9

08123
Note: Data as of 2019 unless noted; (1) Data covers Weld County; (2) Rate per 100,000 population; (3) Data as of 2018 and includes all active, non-federal physicians; (4) Doctor of Osteopathic Medicine
Source: U.S. Department of Health and Human Services, Health Resources and Services Administration, Bureau of Health Professions, Area Resource File (ARF) 2019-2020

EDUCATION

Public School District Statistics

District Name	Schls	Pupils	Pupil/ Teacher Ratio	Minority Pupils[1] (%)	Free Lunch Eligible[2] (%)	IEP[3] (%)
Greeleyschool District No. 6	33	22,612	18.2	67.8	51.6	n/a

Note: Table includes school districts with 2,000 or more students; (1) Percentage of students that are not non-Hispanic white; (2) Percentage of students that are eligible for the free lunch program; (3) Percentage of students that have an Individualized Education Program.
Source: U.S. Department of Education, National Center for Education Statistics, Common Core of Data, Local Education Agency (School District) Universe Survey: School Year 2018-2019; U.S. Department of Education, National Center for Education Statistics, Common Core of Data, Public Elementary/Secondary School Universe Survey: School Year 2018-2019

Highest Level of Education

Area	Less than H.S.	H.S. Diploma	Some College, No Deg.	Associate Degree	Bachelor's Degree	Master's Degree	Prof. School Degree	Doctorate Degree
City	15.5	27.2	23.4	9.1	15.4	7.2	1.2	1.0
MSA[1]	11.9	27.3	24.1	9.1	18.6	7.0	1.1	0.9
U.S.	12.0	27.0	20.4	8.5	19.8	8.8	2.1	1.4

Note: Figures cover persons age 25 and over; (1) Figures cover the Greeley, CO Metropolitan Statistical Area
Source: U.S. Census Bureau, 2015-2019 American Community Survey 5-Year Estimates

Educational Attainment by Race

Area	High School Graduate or Higher (%)					Bachelor's Degree or Higher (%)				
	Total	White	Black	Asian	Hisp.[2]	Total	White	Black	Asian	Hisp.[2]
City	84.5	86.2	79.2	80.0	65.6	24.8	25.9	16.6	43.4	8.4
MSA[1]	88.1	89.1	84.2	87.9	66.6	27.5	28.0	27.2	42.4	9.1
U.S.	88.0	89.9	86.0	87.1	68.7	32.1	33.5	21.6	54.3	16.4

Note: Figures shown cover persons 25 years old and over; (1) Figures cover the Greeley, CO Metropolitan Statistical Area; (2) People of Hispanic origin can be of any race
Source: U.S. Census Bureau, 2015-2019 American Community Survey 5-Year Estimates

School Enrollment by Grade and Control

Area	Preschool (%)		Kindergarten (%)		Grades 1 - 4 (%)		Grades 5 - 8 (%)		Grades 9 - 12 (%)	
	Public	Private	Public	Private	Public	Private	Public	Private	Public	Private
City	69.6	30.4	83.6	16.4	91.5	8.5	92.6	7.4	95.3	4.7
MSA[1]	69.7	30.3	89.1	10.9	91.9	8.1	94.0	6.0	93.9	6.1
U.S.	59.1	40.9	87.6	12.4	89.5	10.5	89.4	10.6	90.1	9.9

Note: Figures shown cover persons 3 years old and over; (1) Figures cover the Greeley, CO Metropolitan Statistical Area
Source: U.S. Census Bureau, 2015-2019 American Community Survey 5-Year Estimates

Higher Education

Four-Year Colleges			Two-Year Colleges			Medical Schools[1]	Law Schools[2]	Voc/ Tech[3]
Public	Private Non-profit	Private For-profit	Public	Private Non-profit	Private For-profit			
1	0	0	1	0	0	0	0	1

Note: Figures cover institutions located within the city limits and include main campuses only; (1) includes schools accredited by the Liaison Committee on Medical Education and the American Osteopathic Association's Commission on Osteopathic College Accreditation; (2) includes ABA-accredited schools, schools with provisional ABA accreditation, and state accredited schools; (3) includes all schools with programs that are less than 2 years.
Source: National Center for Education Statistics, Integrated Postsecondary Education System (IPEDS), 2019-20; Wikipedia, List of Medical Schools in the United States, accessed April 2, 2021; Wikipedia, List of Law Schools in the United States, accessed April 2, 2021

EMPLOYERS

Major Employers

Company Name	Industry
A&W Water Services	Energy services
Anadarko Petroleum	Petroleum and natural gas exploration and production
Halliburton Energy Services	Oil field service
JB Swift & Company	Food processing
Noble Energy	Petroleum and natural gas exploration and production
North Colorado Medical Center	Medical center
Select Energy Services	Energy services
State Farm	Insurance
TeleTech	Business process outsourcing
Vestas	Wind turbines

Note: Companies shown are located within the Greeley, CO Metropolitan Statistical Area.
Source: Hoovers.com; Wikipedia

PUBLIC SAFETY

Crime Rate

Area	All Crimes	Violent Crimes				Property Crimes		
		Murder	Rape[3]	Robbery	Aggrav. Assault	Burglary	Larceny -Theft	Motor Vehicle Theft
City	2,680.0	1.8	65.0	61.3	225.2	309.4	1,737.2	280.1
Suburbs[1]	1,419.9	1.4	41.0	12.3	90.5	171.1	940.9	162.6
Metro[2]	1,848.3	1.6	49.2	28.9	136.3	218.1	1,211.6	202.6
U.S.	2,489.3	5.0	42.6	81.6	250.2	340.5	1,549.5	219.9

Note: Figures are crimes per 100,000 population; (1) All areas within the metro area that are located outside the city limits; (2) Figures cover the Greeley, CO Metropolitan Statistical Area; (3) All figures shown were reported using the revised Uniform Crime Reporting (UCR) definition of rape.
Source: FBI Uniform Crime Reports, 2019

Hate Crimes

Area	Number of Quarters Reported	Number of Incidents per Bias Motivation					
		Race/Ethnicity/ Ancestry	Religion	Sexual Orientation	Disability	Gender	Gender Identity
City	4	0	0	0	0	0	0
U.S.	4	3,963	1,521	1,195	157	69	198

Source: Federal Bureau of Investigation, Hate Crime Statistics 2019

Identity Theft Consumer Reports

Area	Reports	Reports per 100,000 Population	Rank[2]
MSA[1]	978	301	118
U.S.	1,387,615	423	-

Note: (1) Figures cover the Greeley, CO Metropolitan Statistical Area; (2) Rank ranges from 1 to 391 where 1 indicates greatest number of identity theft reports per 100,000 population
Source: Federal Trade Commission, Consumer Sentinel Network Data Book 2020

Fraud and Other Consumer Reports

Area	Reports	Reports per 100,000 Population	Rank[2]
MSA[1]	1,959	604	279
U.S.	3,385,133	1,031	-

Note: (1) Figures cover the Greeley, CO Metropolitan Statistical Area; (2) Rank ranges from 1 to 391 where 1 indicates greatest number of fraud and other consumer reports per 100,000 population
Source: Federal Trade Commission, Consumer Sentinel Network Data Book 2020

POLITICS

2020 Presidential Election Results

Area	Biden	Trump	Jorgensen	Hawkins	Other
Weld County	39.6	57.6	1.7	0.2	0.9
U.S.	51.3	46.8	1.2	0.3	0.5

Note: Results are percentages and may not add to 100% due to rounding
Source: Dave Leip's Atlas of U.S. Presidential Elections

SPORTS

Professional Sports Teams

Team Name	League	Year Established

No teams are located in the metro area
Source: Wikipedia, Major Professional Sports Teams of the United States and Canada, April 6, 2021

CLIMATE

Average and Extreme Temperatures

Temperature	Jan	Feb	Mar	Apr	May	Jun	Jul	Aug	Sep	Oct	Nov	Dec	Yr.
Extreme High (°F)	73	76	84	90	93	102	103	100	97	89	79	75	103
Average High (°F)	43	47	52	62	71	81	88	86	77	67	52	45	64
Average Temp. (°F)	30	34	39	48	58	67	73	72	63	52	39	32	51
Average Low (°F)	16	20	25	34	44	53	59	57	48	37	25	18	37
Extreme Low (°F)	-25	-25	-10	-2	22	30	43	41	17	3	-8	-25	-25

Note: Figures cover the years 1948-1992
Source: National Climatic Data Center, International Station Meteorological Climate Summary, 9/96

Average Precipitation/Snowfall/Humidity

Precip./Humidity	Jan	Feb	Mar	Apr	May	Jun	Jul	Aug	Sep	Oct	Nov	Dec	Yr.
Avg. Precip. (in.)	0.6	0.6	1.3	1.7	2.5	1.7	1.9	1.5	1.1	1.0	0.9	0.6	15.5
Avg. Snowfall (in.)	9	7	14	9	2	Tr	0	0	2	4	9	8	63
Avg. Rel. Hum. 5am (%)	62	65	67	66	70	68	67	68	66	63	66	63	66
Avg. Rel. Hum. 5pm (%)	49	44	40	35	38	34	34	34	32	34	47	50	39

Note: Figures cover the years 1948-1992; Tr = Trace amounts (<0.05 in. of rain; <0.5 in. of snow)
Source: National Climatic Data Center, International Station Meteorological Climate Summary, 9/96

Weather Conditions

Temperature			Daytime Sky			Precipitation		
10°F & below	32°F & below	90°F & above	Clear	Partly cloudy	Cloudy	0.01 inch or more precip.	0.1 inch or more snow/ice	Thunder-storms
24	155	33	99	177	89	90	38	39

Note: Figures are average number of days per year and cover the years 1948-1992
Source: National Climatic Data Center, International Station Meteorological Climate Summary, 9/96

HAZARDOUS WASTE

Superfund Sites

The Greeley, CO metro area has no sites on the EPA's Superfund Final National Priorities List. There are a total of 1,375 Superfund sites with a status of proposed or final on the list in the U.S. *U.S. Environmental Protection Agency, National Priorities List, April 7, 2021*

AIR QUALITY

Air Quality Trends: Ozone

	1990	1995	2000	2005	2010	2015	2016	2017	2018	2019
MSA[1]	n/a	n/a	n/a	n/a	n/a	n/a	n/a	n/a	n/a	n/a
U.S.	0.088	0.089	0.082	0.080	0.073	0.068	0.069	0.068	0.069	0.065

Note: (1) Data covers the Greeley, CO Metropolitan Statistical Area; n/a not available. The values shown are the composite ozone concentration averages among trend sites based on the highest fourth daily maximum 8-hour concentration in parts per million. These trends are based on sites having an adequate record of monitoring data during the trend period. Data from exceptional events are included.
Source: U.S. Environmental Protection Agency, Air Quality Monitoring Information, "Air Quality Trends by City, 1990-2019"

Air Quality Index

Area	Percent of Days when Air Quality was...[2]					AQI Statistics[2]	
	Good	Moderate	Unhealthy for Sensitive Groups	Unhealthy	Very Unhealthy	Maximum	Median
MSA[1]	69.0	30.1	0.8	0.0	0.0	125	45

Note: (1) Data covers the Greeley, CO Metropolitan Statistical Area; (2) Based on 365 days with AQI data in 2019. Air Quality Index (AQI) is an index for reporting daily air quality. EPA calculates the AQI for five major air pollutants regulated by the Clean Air Act: ground-level ozone, particle pollution (aka particulate matter), carbon monoxide, sulfur dioxide, and nitrogen dioxide. The AQI runs from 0 to 500. The higher the AQI value, the greater the level of air pollution and the greater the health concern. There are six AQI categories: "Good" AQI is between 0 and 50. Air quality is considered satisfactory; "Moderate" AQI is between 51 and 100. Air quality is acceptable; "Unhealthy for Sensitive Groups" When AQI values are between 101 and 150, members of sensitive groups may experience health effects; "Unhealthy" When AQI values are between 151 and 200 everyone may begin to experience health effects; "Very Unhealthy" AQI values between 201 and 300 trigger a health alert; "Hazardous" AQI values over 300 trigger warnings of emergency conditions (not shown).
Source: U.S. Environmental Protection Agency, Air Quality Index Report, 2019

Air Quality Index Pollutants

Area	Percent of Days when AQI Pollutant was...[2]					
	Carbon Monoxide	Nitrogen Dioxide	Ozone	Sulfur Dioxide	Particulate Matter 2.5	Particulate Matter 10
MSA[1]	0.0	0.0	64.7	0.0	35.3	0.0

Note: (1) Data covers the Greeley, CO Metropolitan Statistical Area; (2) Based on 365 days with AQI data in 2019. The Air Quality Index (AQI) is an index for reporting daily air quality. EPA calculates the AQI for five major air pollutants regulated by the Clean Air Act: ground-level ozone, particle pollution (also known as particulate matter), carbon monoxide, sulfur dioxide, and nitrogen dioxide. The AQI runs from 0 to 500. The higher the AQI value, the greater the level of air pollution and the greater the health concern.
Source: U.S. Environmental Protection Agency, Air Quality Index Report, 2019

Maximum Air Pollutant Concentrations: Particulate Matter, Ozone, CO and Lead

	Particulate Matter 10 (ug/m³)	Particulate Matter 2.5 Wtd AM (ug/m³)	Particulate Matter 2.5 24-Hr (ug/m³)	Ozone (ppm)	Carbon Monoxide (ppm)	Lead (ug/m³)
MSA[1] Level	n/a	9.0	26	0.065	1	n/a
NAAQS[2]	150	15	35	0.075	9	0.15
Met NAAQS[2]	n/a	Yes	Yes	Yes	Yes	n/a

Note: (1) Data covers the Greeley, CO Metropolitan Statistical Area; Data from exceptional events are included; (2) National Ambient Air Quality Standards; ppm = parts per million; ug/m³ = micrograms per cubic meter; n/a not available.
Concentrations: Particulate Matter 10 (coarse particulate)—highest second maximum 24-hour concentration; Particulate Matter 2.5 Wtd AM (fine particulate)—highest weighted annual mean concentration; Particulate Matter 2.5 24-Hour (fine particulate)—highest 98th percentile 24-hour concentration; Ozone—highest fourth daily maximum 8-hour concentration; Carbon Monoxide—highest second maximum non-overlapping 8-hour concentration; Lead—maximum running 3-month average
Source: U.S. Environmental Protection Agency, Air Quality Monitoring Information, "Air Quality Statistics by City, 2019"

Maximum Air Pollutant Concentrations: Nitrogen Dioxide and Sulfur Dioxide

	Nitrogen Dioxide AM (ppb)	Nitrogen Dioxide 1-Hr (ppb)	Sulfur Dioxide AM (ppb)	Sulfur Dioxide 1-Hr (ppb)	Sulfur Dioxide 24-Hr (ppb)
MSA[1] Level	n/a	n/a	n/a	n/a	n/a
NAAQS[2]	53	100	30	75	140
Met NAAQS[2]	n/a	n/a	n/a	n/a	n/a

Note: (1) Data covers the Greeley, CO Metropolitan Statistical Area; Data from exceptional events are included; (2) National Ambient Air Quality Standards; ppm = parts per million; ug/m³ = micrograms per cubic meter; n/a not available.
Concentrations: Nitrogen Dioxide AM—highest arithmetic mean concentration; Nitrogen Dioxide 1-Hr—highest 98th percentile 1-hour daily maximum concentration; Sulfur Dioxide AM—highest annual mean concentration; Sulfur Dioxide 1-Hr—highest 99th percentile 1-hour daily maximum concentration; Sulfur Dioxide 24-Hr—highest second maximum 24-hour concentration
Source: U.S. Environmental Protection Agency, Air Quality Monitoring Information, "Air Quality Statistics by City, 2019"

Honolulu, Hawaii

Background

Honolulu, whose name means "sheltered harbor," is the capital of Hawaii and the seat of Honolulu County. The city sits in one of the most famously attractive areas of the world, on the island of Oahu, home to the extinct volcano Diamond Head, Waikiki Beach, and two mountain ranges, the Koolau and the Waianae. Honolulu is the economic hub of Hawaii, a major seaport and, most importantly, home to a $10 billion tourist industry.

Traditionally home to fishing and horticultural tribal groups, the Hawaiian islands were politically united under the reign of King Kamehameha I, who first moved his triumphant court to Waikiki and subsequently to a site in what is now downtown Honolulu (1804). It was during his time that the port became a center for the sandalwood trade, thus establishing the region as an international presence even before the political interventions of non-Hawaiians.

European activity dates from 1794, when the English sea captain William Brown entered Honolulu, dubbing it Fair Harbor. Two decades later, the first missionaries arrived. American Congregationalists were followed by French Catholics and, later, Mormons and Anglicans. By the end of the nineteenth century, non-Hawaiians owned most of the land. In 1898 Hawaii was annexed by the U.S.

As is true for many strategically located cities, the events of World War II had a profound effect on Honolulu. The Japanese attack on December 7, 1941, forever etched the name of Pearl Harbor into the national memory. During the war, existing military bases were expanded and new bases built, providing considerable economic stimuli. The Vietnam War also had a dramatic effect on Honolulu; by the end of the twentieth century, military families accounted for 10 percent of the population.

Today, the U.S. military employs more than 45,000 throughout the state. Fruit, primarily pineapple, processing and light manufacturing are also important to the economy. Aquaculture, which includes cultivated species of shellfish, finfish and algae, has grown in recent years, as has biotechnology.

Tourism, however, has been the private-sector mainstay of Honolulu's economy, with most of the millions of tourists who visit Hawaii annually coming through its port or airport. Honolulu is a required stop for any holiday ship cruising these waters, and it is also the center for the inter-island air services that ferry tourists to various resort locations.

> Two cruise ships were not allowed to disembark in Honolulu after being turned away by other ports.

The center of Honolulu's downtown district is dominated by the Iolani Palace, once home to Hawaii's original royal family. Nearby are the State Capitol Building and the State Supreme Court Building, known as Ali'iolani Hall. The Aloha Tower Development Corporation continues to modernize the mixed-use space in and around the Aloha Tower Complex along the city's piers.

Construction of the Honolulu High-Capacity Transit Corridor Project, including a new rail line connecting Kapolei in West Oahu to the University of Hawaii at Manoa was completed in 2018.

Honolulu, as it has grown along the southern coast of Oahu, has established a mix of residential zones, with single-family dwellings and relatively small multi-unit buildings. The result is that large parts of what is a major metropolitan area feel like cozy neighborhoods. In fact, Honolulu is governed in part through the device of a Neighborhood Board System, which insures maximal local input with regard to planning decisions and city services.

Cultural amenities include the Bishop Museum, the Honolulu Academy of Arts, and the Contemporary Museum, which together offer world-class collections in Polynesian art and artifacts, Japanese, Chinese, and Korean art, and modern art from the world over. Honolulu also hosts a symphony orchestra, the oldest U.S. symphony orchestra west of the Rocky Mountains, which performs at the Neal S. Blaisdell Center.

Barack Obama, the United States' 44th president, is the first president from Hawaii. Obama was born in Honolulu, causing the city a fair amount of attention during the 2008 presidential election.

Honolulu's weather is subtropical, with temperatures moderated by the surrounding ocean and the trade winds. There are only slight variations in temperature from summer to winter. Rain is moderate, though heavier in summer, when it sometimes comes in the form of quick showers while the sun is shining— known locally as "liquid sunshine."

Rankings

General Rankings

- For its "Best for Vets: Places to Live 2019" rankings, *Military Times* evaluated 599 cities (83 large, 234 medium, 282 small) and compared the locations across three broad categories: veteran and military culture/services; economic indicators; and livability factors such as health, crime, traffic, and school quality. Honolulu ranked #5 out of the top 25, in the large city category (population of more than 250,000). Data points more specific to veterans and the military weighed more heavily than others. *rebootcamp.militarytimes.com, "Military Times Best Places to Live 2019," September 10, 2018*

- The human resources consulting firm Mercer ranked 231 major cities worldwide in terms of overall quality of life. Honolulu ranked #37. Criteria: political, social, economic, and socio-cultural factors; medical and health considerations; schools and education; public services and transportation; recreation; consumer goods; housing; and natural environment. *Mercer, "Mercer 2019 Quality of Living Survey," March 13, 2019*

- Honolulu appeared on *Travel + Leisure's* list of the 15 best cities in the United States. The city was ranked #8. Criteria: sights/landmarks; culture; food; friendliness; shopping; and overall value. *Travel + Leisure, "The World's Best Awards 2020" July 8, 2020*

Business/Finance Rankings

- The Brookings Institution ranked the nation's largest cities based on income inequality. Honolulu was ranked #54 (#1 = greatest inequality). Criteria: the "95/20 ratio," a figure representing the income at which a household earns more than 95 percent of all other households, divided by the income at which a household earns more than only 20 percent of all other households. *Brookings Institution, "Household Income Inequality, Largest Cities of 97 Large U.S. Metro Areas, 2014-2016," February 5, 2018*

- The Brookings Institution ranked the 100 largest metro areas in the U.S. based on income inequality. Honolulu was ranked #79 (#1 = greatest inequality). Criteria: the "95/20 ratio," a figure representing the income at which a household earns more than 95 percent of all other households, divided by the income at which a household earns more than only 20 percent of all other households. *Brookings Institution, "Household Income Inequality, 100 Largest U.S. Metro Areas, 2014-2016," February 5, 2018*

- For its annual survey of the "Most Expensive U.S. Cities to Live In," Kiplinger applied Cost of Living Index statistics developed by the Council for Community and Economic Research to U.S. Census Bureau population and median household income data for 256 urban areas. Honolulu was among the 20 most expensive in the country. *Kiplinger.com, "The 20 Most Expensive Cities in the U.S.," July 29, 2020*

- The Honolulu metro area appeared on the Milken Institute "2021 Best Performing Cities" list. Rank: #196 out of 200 large metro areas (population over 250,000). Criteria: job growth; wage and salary growth; high-tech output growth; housing affordability; household broadband access. *Milken Institute, "Best-Performing Cities 2021," February 16, 2021*

- *Forbes* ranked the 200 most populous metro areas to determine the nation's "Best Places for Business and Careers." The Honolulu metro area was ranked #162. Criteria: costs (business and living); job growth (past and projected); income growth; quality of life; educational attainment (college and high school); projected economic growth; cultural and leisure opportunities; workplace tolerance laws; net migration patterns. *Forbes, "The Best Places for Business and Careers 2019: Seattle Still On Top," October 30, 2019*

- Mercer Human Resources Consulting ranked 209 cities worldwide in terms of cost-of-living. Honolulu ranked #28 (the lower the ranking, the higher the cost-of-living). The survey measured the comparative cost of over 200 items (such as housing, food, clothing, household goods, transportation, and entertainment) in each location. *Mercer, "2020 Cost of Living Survey," June 9, 2020*

Education Rankings

- Personal finance website *WalletHub* analyzed the 150 largest U.S. metropolitan statistical areas to determine where the most educated Americans are putting their degrees to work. Criteria: education levels; percentage of workers with degrees; education quality and attainment gap; public school quality rankings; quality and enrollment of each metro area's universities. Honolulu was ranked #29 (#1 = most educated city). *www.WalletHub.com, "Most and Least Educated Cities in America," July 20, 2020*

- Honolulu was selected as one of America's most literate cities. The city ranked #30 out of the 84 largest U.S. cities. Criteria: number of booksellers; library resources; Internet resources; educational attainment; periodical publishing resources; newspaper circulation. *Central Connecticut State University, "America's Most Literate Cities, 2018," February 2019*

Environmental Rankings

- Honolulu was highlighted as one of the cleanest metro areas for ozone air pollution in the U.S. during 2016 through 2018. The list represents cities with no monitored ozone air pollution in unhealthful ranges. *American Lung Association, "State of the Air 2020," April 21, 2020*

- Honolulu was highlighted as one of the top 25 cleanest metro areas for year-round particle pollution (Annual PM 2.5) in the U.S. during 2016 through 2018. The area ranked #1. *American Lung Association, "State of the Air 2020," April 21, 2020*

- Honolulu was highlighted as one of the top 98 cleanest metro areas for short-term particle pollution (24-hour PM 2.5) in the U.S. during 2016 through 2018. Monitors in these cities reported no days with unhealthful PM 2.5 levels. *American Lung Association, "State of the Air 2020," April 21, 2020*

Health/Fitness Rankings

- For each of the 100 largest cities in the United States, the American Fitness Index®, published by the American College of Sports Medicine and the Anthem Foundation, evaluated community infrastructure and 33 health behaviors including preventive health, levels of chronic disease conditions, pedestrian safety, air quality, and community resources that support physical activity. Honolulu ranked #17 for "community fitness." *americanfitnessindex.org, "2020 ACSM American Fitness Index Summary Report," July 14, 2020*

- The Sharecare Community Well-Being Index evaluates 10 individual and social health factors in order to measure what matters to Americans in the communities in which they live. The Honolulu metro area ranked #7 in the top 10 across all 10 domains. Criteria: access to healthcare, food, and community resources; housng and transportation; economic security; feeling of purpose; physical, financial, social, and community well-being. *www.sharecare.com, "Community Well-Being Index: 2019 Metro Area & County Rankings Report," August 31, 2020*

Real Estate Rankings

- *WalletHub* compared the most populated U.S. cities to determine which had the best markets for real estate agents. Honolulu ranked #69 where demand was high and pay was the best. Criteria: sales per agent; annual median wage for real-estate agents; monthly average starting salary for real estate agents; real estate job density and competition; unemployment rate; home turnover rate; housing-market health index; and other relevant metrics. *www.WalletHub.com, "2019's Best Places to Be a Real Estate Agent," April 24, 2019*

- The Honolulu metro area was identified as one of the 10 worst condo markets in the U.S. in 2020. The area ranked #59 out of 63 markets. Criteria: year-over-year change of median sales price of existing apartment condo-coop homes between the 4th quarter of 2019 and the 4th quarter of 2020. *National Association of Realtors®, Median Sales Price of Existing Apartment Condo-Coops Homes for Metropolitan Areas, 4th Quarter 2020*

- The Honolulu metro area was identified as one of the 20 least affordable housing markets in the U.S. in 2020. The area ranked #180 out of 183 markets. Criteria: qualification for a mortgage loan with a 10 percent down payment on a typical home. *National Association of Realtors®, Qualifying Income Based on Sales Price of Existing Single-Family Homes for Metropolitan Areas, 2020*

- Honolulu was ranked #244 out of 268 metro areas in terms of housing affordability in 2020 by the National Association of Home Builders (#1 = most affordable). Criteria: the share of homes sold in that area affordable to a family earning the local median income, based on standard mortgage underwriting criteria. *National Association of Home Builders®, NAHB-Wells Fargo Housing Opportunity Index, 4th Quarter 2020*

Safety Rankings

- Allstate ranked the 200 largest cities in America in terms of driver safety. Honolulu ranked #94. Criteria: internal property damage claims over a two-year period from January 2016 to December 2017. The report helps increase the importance of safety and awareness behind the wheel. *Allstate, "Allstate America's Best Drivers Report, 2019" June 24, 2019*

- The National Insurance Crime Bureau ranked 384 metro areas in the U.S. in terms of per capita rates of vehicle theft. The Honolulu metro area ranked #92 (#1 = highest rate). Criteria: number of vehicle theft offenses per 100,000 inhabitants in 2019. *National Insurance Crime Bureau, "Hot Spots 2019," July 21, 2020*

Seniors/Retirement Rankings

- From its Best Cities for Successful Aging indexes, the Milken Institute generated rankings for metropolitan areas, weighing data in nine categories—health care, wellness, living arrangements, transportation and convenience, financial characteristics, education, employment, community engagement, and overall livability. The Honolulu metro area was ranked #24 overall in the large metro area category. *Milken Institute, "Best Cities for Successful Aging, 2017" March 14, 2017*

Women/Minorities Rankings

- Personal finance website *WalletHub* compared more than 180 U.S. cities across two key dimensions, "Hispanic Business-Friendliness" and "Hispanic Purchasing Power," to arrive at the most favorable conditions for Hispanic entrepreneurs. Honolulu was ranked #151 out of 182. Criteria includes: share of Hispanic-Owned Businesses; Hispanic entrepreneurship rate to median annual income of Hispanics; Small Business-Friendliness score; cost of living; and number of Hispanics with at least a bachelor's degree. *WalletHub.com, "2019's Best Cities for Hispanic Entrepreneurs," May 1, 2019*

Miscellaneous Rankings

- *MoveHub* ranked 446 hipster cities across 20 countries, using its *alternative* Hipster Index and Honolulu came out as #45 among the top 50. Criteria: population over 150,000; number of vintage boutiques; density of tattoo parlors; vegan places to eat; coffee shops; and density of vinyl record stores. *www.movehub.com, "The Hipster Index: Brighton Pips Portland to Global Top Spot," February 20, 2020*
- Honolulu was selected as one of "America's Friendliest Cities." The city ranked #19 in the "Friendliest" category. Respondents to an online survey were asked to rate 38 top urban destinations in the United States as to general friendliness, as well as manners, politeness and warm disposition. *Travel + Leisure, "America's Friendliest Cities," October 20, 2017*

Business Environment

DEMOGRAPHICS

Population Growth

Area	1990 Census	2000 Census	2010 Census	2019* Estimate	Population Growth (%) 1990-2019	Population Growth (%) 2010-2019
City	376,465	371,657	337,256	348,985	-7.3	3.5
MSA[1]	836,231	876,156	953,207	984,821	17.8	3.3
U.S.	248,709,873	281,421,906	308,745,538	324,697,795	30.6	5.2

Note: (1) Figures cover the Urban Honolulu, HI Metropolitan Statistical Area; (*) 2015-2019 5-year estimated population
Source: U.S. Census Bureau, 1990 Census, Census 2000, Census 2010, 2015-2019 American Community Survey 5-Year Estimates

Household Size

Area	Persons in Household (%) One	Two	Three	Four	Five	Six	Seven or More	Average Household Size
City	33.5	31.3	14.4	10.7	5.1	2.3	2.7	2.60
MSA[1]	24.0	30.5	16.8	13.5	7.3	3.6	4.1	3.00
U.S.	27.9	33.9	15.6	12.9	6.0	2.3	1.4	2.60

Note: (1) Figures cover the Urban Honolulu, HI Metropolitan Statistical Area
Source: U.S. Census Bureau, 2015-2019 American Community Survey 5-Year Estimates

Race

Area	White Alone[2] (%)	Black Alone[2] (%)	Asian Alone[2] (%)	AIAN[3] Alone[2] (%)	NHOPI[4] Alone[2] (%)	Other Race Alone[2] (%)	Two or More Races (%)
City	17.2	2.0	53.2	0.1	8.0	0.9	18.4
MSA[1]	20.9	2.4	42.7	0.2	9.5	1.0	23.2
U.S.	72.5	12.7	5.5	0.8	0.2	4.9	3.3

Note: (1) Figures cover the Urban Honolulu, HI Metropolitan Statistical Area; (2) Alone is defined as not being in combination with one or more other races; (3) American Indian and Alaska Native; (4) Native Hawaiian and Other Pacific Islander
Source: U.S. Census Bureau, 2015-2019 American Community Survey 5-Year Estimates

Hispanic or Latino Origin

Area	Total (%)	Mexican (%)	Puerto Rican (%)	Cuban (%)	Other (%)
City	7.3	2.0	1.8	0.2	3.4
MSA[1]	9.8	2.9	3.1	0.1	3.7
U.S.	18.0	11.2	1.7	0.7	4.3

Note: Persons of Hispanic or Latino origin can be of any race; (1) Figures cover the Urban Honolulu, HI Metropolitan Statistical Area
Source: U.S. Census Bureau, 2015-2019 American Community Survey 5-Year Estimates

Ancestry

Area	German	Irish	English	American	Italian	Polish	French[2]	Scottish	Dutch
City	4.1	3.3	2.8	1.2	1.8	0.7	0.8	0.6	0.3
MSA[1]	5.1	3.8	3.3	1.3	2.0	0.9	1.1	0.9	0.4
U.S.	13.3	9.7	7.2	6.2	5.1	2.8	2.3	1.7	1.2

Note: Figures are the percentage of the total population reporting a particular ancestry. The nine most commonly reported ancestries in the U.S. are shown. Figures include multiple ancestries (e.g. if a person reported being Irish and Italian, they were included in both columns); (1) Figures cover the Urban Honolulu, HI Metropolitan Statistical Area; (2) Excludes Basque
Source: U.S. Census Bureau, 2015-2019 American Community Survey 5-Year Estimates

Foreign-born Population

Area	Percent of Population Born in Any Foreign Country	Asia	Mexico	Europe	Caribbean	Central America[2]	South America	Africa	Canada
City	27.4	23.2	0.1	0.8	0.1	0.1	0.2	0.1	0.2
MSA[1]	19.7	16.1	0.2	0.7	0.1	0.1	0.3	0.1	0.2
U.S.	13.6	4.2	3.5	1.5	1.3	1.1	1.0	0.7	0.2

Note: (1) Figures cover the Urban Honolulu, HI Metropolitan Statistical Area; (2) Excludes Mexico.
Source: U.S. Census Bureau, 2015-2019 American Community Survey 5-Year Estimates

Marital Status

Area	Never Married	Now Married[2]	Separated	Widowed	Divorced
City	36.2	45.8	1.2	6.9	9.9
MSA[1]	33.9	50.1	1.2	6.3	8.6
U.S.	33.4	48.1	1.9	5.8	10.9

Note: Figures are percentages and cover the population 15 years of age and older; (1) Figures cover the Urban Honolulu, HI Metropolitan Statistical Area; (2) Excludes separated
Source: U.S. Census Bureau, 2015-2019 American Community Survey 5-Year Estimates

Disability by Age

Area	All Ages	Under 18 Years Old	18 to 64 Years Old	65 Years and Over
City	11.2	2.6	7.1	31.4
MSA[1]	10.9	2.9	7.4	32.8
U.S.	12.6	4.2	10.3	34.5

Note: Figures show percent of the civilian noninstitutionalized population that reported having a disability. Disability status is determined from six types of difficulty: vision, hearing, cognitive, ambulatory, self-care, and independent living. For children under 5 years old, hearing and vision difficulty are used to determine disability status. For children between the ages of 5 and 14, disability status is determined from hearing, vision, cognitive, ambulatory, and self-care difficulties. For people aged 15 years and older, they are considered to have a disability if they have difficulty with any one of the six difficulty types; Note: (1) Figures cover the Urban Honolulu, HI Metropolitan Statistical Area
Source: U.S. Census Bureau, 2015-2019 American Community Survey 5-Year Estimates

Age

Area	Percent of Population									Median Age
	Under Age 5	Age 5–19	Age 20–34	Age 35–44	Age 45–54	Age 55–64	Age 65–74	Age 75–84	Age 85+	
City	5.2	14.1	22.0	13.0	12.8	12.9	10.5	5.5	3.9	41.5
MSA[1]	6.4	17.0	22.6	12.7	12.1	11.9	9.4	5.0	2.9	37.9
U.S.	6.1	19.1	20.7	12.6	13.0	12.9	9.1	4.6	1.9	38.1

Note: (1) Figures cover the Urban Honolulu, HI Metropolitan Statistical Area
Source: U.S. Census Bureau, 2015-2019 American Community Survey 5-Year Estimates

Gender

Area	Males	Females	Males per 100 Females
City	173,837	175,148	99.3
MSA[1]	496,066	488,755	101.5
U.S.	159,886,919	164,810,876	97.0

Note: (1) Figures cover the Urban Honolulu, HI Metropolitan Statistical Area
Source: U.S. Census Bureau, 2015-2019 American Community Survey 5-Year Estimates

Religious Groups by Family

Area	Catholic	Baptist	Non-Den.	Methodist[2]	Lutheran	LDS[3]	Pente-costal	Presby-terian[4]	Muslim[5]	Judaism
MSA[1]	18.2	1.9	2.2	0.8	0.3	5.1	4.2	1.5	<0.1	0.1
U.S.	19.1	9.3	4.0	4.0	2.3	2.0	1.9	1.6	0.8	0.7

Note: Figures are the number of adherents as a percentage of the total population; (1) Figures cover the Urban Honolulu, HI Metropolitan Statistical Area; (2) Methodist/Pietist; (3) Latter Day Saints; (4) Reformed; (5) Figures are estimates
Source: Association of Statisticians of American Religious Bodies, 2010 U.S. Religion Census: Religious Congregations & Membership Study

Religious Groups by Tradition

Area	Catholic	Evangelical Protestant	Mainline Protestant	Other Tradition	Black Protestant	Orthodox
MSA[1]	18.2	9.7	2.9	8.4	<0.1	<0.1
U.S.	19.1	16.2	7.3	4.3	1.6	0.3

Note: Figures are the number of adherents as a percentage of the total population; (1) Figures cover the Urban Honolulu, HI Metropolitan Statistical Area
Source: Association of Statisticians of American Religious Bodies, 2010 U.S. Religion Census: Religious Congregations & Membership Study

ECONOMY

Gross Metropolitan Product

Area	2017	2018	2019	2020	Rank[2]
MSA[1]	68.2	70.5	73.2	75.5	50

Note: Figures are in billions of dollars; (1) Figures cover the Urban Honolulu, HI Metropolitan Statistical Area; (2) Rank is based on 2018 data and ranges from 1 to 381
Source: U.S. Conference of Mayors, U.S. Metro Economies: GMP & Employment 2018-2020, September 2019

Economic Growth

Area	2015-17 (%)	2018 (%)	2019 (%)	2020 (%)	Rank[2]
MSA[1]	1.6	1.0	1.9	0.9	165
U.S.	1.9	2.9	2.3	2.1	–

Note: Figures are real gross metropolitan product (GMP) growth rates and represent average annual percent change; (1) Figures cover the Urban Honolulu, HI Metropolitan Statistical Area; (2) Rank is based on 2017 2-year average annual percent change and ranges from 1 to 381
Source: U.S. Conference of Mayors, U.S. Metro Economies: GMP & Employment 2018-2020, September 2019

Metropolitan Area Exports

Area	2014	2015	2016	2017	2018	2019	Rank[2]
MSA[1]	765.5	446.4	330.3	393.6	438.9	308.6	250

Note: Figures are in millions of dollars; (1) Figures cover the Urban Honolulu, HI Metropolitan Statistical Area; (2) Rank is based on 2019 data and ranges from 1 to 386
Source: U.S. Department of Commerce, International Trade Administration, Office of Trade and Economic Analysis, Industry and Analysis, Exports by Metropolitan Area, data extracted March 24, 2021

Building Permits

Area	Single-Family			Multi-Family			Total		
	2018	2019	Pct. Chg.	2018	2019	Pct. Chg.	2018	2019	Pct. Chg.
City	n/a	n/a	n/a	n/a	n/a	n/a	n/a	n/a	n/a
MSA[1]	983	912	-7.2	1,427	1,367	-4.2	2,410	2,279	-5.4
U.S.	855,300	862,100	0.7	473,500	523,900	10.6	1,328,800	1,386,000	4.3

Note: (1) Figures cover the Urban Honolulu, HI Metropolitan Statistical Area; Figures represent new, privately-owned housing units authorized (unadjusted data); All permit data are based on estimates with imputation
Source: U.S. Census Bureau, Manufacturing, Mining, and Construction Statistics, Building Permits, 2018, 2019

Bankruptcy Filings

Area	Business Filings			Nonbusiness Filings		
	2019	2020	% Chg.	2019	2020	% Chg.
Honolulu County	35	46	31.4	1,225	1,106	-9.7
U.S.	22,780	21,655	-4.9	752,160	522,808	-30.5

Note: Business filings include Chapter 7, Chapter 9, Chapter 11, Chapter 12, Chapter 13, Chapter 15, and Section 304; Nonbusiness filings include Chapter 7, Chapter 11, and Chapter 13
Source: Administrative Office of the U.S. Courts, Business and Nonbusiness Bankruptcy, County Cases Commenced by Chapter of the Bankruptcy Code, During the 12-Month Period Ending December 31, 2019 and Business and Nonbusiness Bankruptcy, County Cases Commenced by Chapter of the Bankruptcy Code, During the 12-Month Period Ending December 31, 2020

Housing Vacancy Rates

Area	Gross Vacancy Rate[2] (%)			Year-Round Vacancy Rate[3] (%)			Rental Vacancy Rate[4] (%)			Homeowner Vacancy Rate[5] (%)		
	2018	2019	2020	2018	2019	2020	2018	2019	2020	2018	2019	2020
MSA[1]	14.0	11.7	10.0	12.9	10.9	9.6	6.5	5.7	5.5	1.4	1.8	1.0
U.S.	12.3	12.0	10.6	9.7	9.5	8.2	6.9	6.7	6.3	1.5	1.4	1.0

Note: (1) Figures cover the Urban Honolulu, HI Metropolitan Statistical Area; (2) The percentage of the total housing inventory that is vacant; (3) The percentage of the housing inventory (excluding seasonal units) that is year-round vacant; (4) The percentage of rental inventory that is vacant for rent; (5) The percentage of homeowner inventory that is vacant for sale
Source: U.S. Census Bureau, Housing Vacancies and Homeownership Annual Statistics: 2018, 2019, 2020

INCOME

Income

Area	Per Capita ($)	Median Household ($)	Average Household ($)
City	37,834	71,465	97,456
MSA[1]	36,816	85,857	109,304
U.S.	34,103	62,843	88,607

Note: (1) Figures cover the Urban Honolulu, HI Metropolitan Statistical Area
Source: U.S. Census Bureau, 2015-2019 American Community Survey 5-Year Estimates

Household Income Distribution

Area	Percent of Households Earning							
	Under $15,000	$15,000 -$24,999	$25,000 -$34,999	$35,000 -$49,999	$50,000 -$74,999	$75,000 -$99,999	$100,000 -$149,999	$150,000 and up
City	10.1	6.9	6.8	11.8	16.8	12.8	17.0	17.6
MSA[1]	7.1	5.1	5.9	9.6	15.8	13.9	20.2	22.5
U.S.	10.3	8.9	8.9	12.3	17.2	12.7	15.1	14.5

Note: (1) Figures cover the Urban Honolulu, HI Metropolitan Statistical Area
Source: U.S. Census Bureau, 2015-2019 American Community Survey 5-Year Estimates

Poverty Rate

Area	All Ages	Under 18 Years Old	18 to 64 Years Old	65 Years and Over
City	10.6	12.2	10.1	10.9
MSA[1]	8.3	10.1	7.8	7.8
U.S.	13.4	18.5	12.6	9.3

Note: Figures are percentage of people whose income during the past 12 months was below the poverty level;
(1) Figures cover the Urban Honolulu, HI Metropolitan Statistical Area
Source: U.S. Census Bureau, 2015-2019 American Community Survey 5-Year Estimates

CITY FINANCES

City Government Finances

Component	2017 ($000)	2017 ($ per capita)
Total Revenues	3,169,937	3,174
Total Expenditures	3,034,391	3,038
Debt Outstanding	5,300,880	5,308
Cash and Securities[1]	2,625,652	2,629

Note: (1) Cash and security holdings of a government at the close of its fiscal year,
including those of its dependent agencies, utilities, and liquor stores.
Source: U.S. Census Bureau, State & Local Government Finances 2017

City Government Revenue by Source

Source	2017 ($000)	2017 ($ per capita)	2017 (%)
General Revenue			
From Federal Government	255,342	256	8.1
From State Government	161,847	162	5.1
From Local Governments	43	0	0.0
Taxes			
Property	1,099,913	1,101	34.7
Sales and Gross Receipts	356,466	357	11.2
Personal Income	0	0	0.0
Corporate Income	0	0	0.0
Motor Vehicle License	152,344	153	4.8
Other Taxes	30,890	31	1.0
Current Charges	663,402	664	20.9
Liquor Store	0	0	0.0
Utility	285,231	286	9.0
Employee Retirement	0	0	0.0

Source: U.S. Census Bureau, State & Local Government Finances 2017

City Government Expenditures by Function

Function	2017 ($000)	2017 ($ per capita)	2017 (%)
General Direct Expenditures			
Air Transportation	0	0	0.0
Corrections	0	0	0.0
Education	0	0	0.0
Employment Security Administration	0	0	0.0
Financial Administration	48,787	48	1.6
Fire Protection	129,103	129	4.3
General Public Buildings	36,812	36	1.2
Governmental Administration, Other	42,262	42	1.4
Health	42,727	42	1.4
Highways	180,617	180	6.0
Hospitals	0	0	0.0
Housing and Community Development	71,836	71	2.4
Interest on General Debt	202,745	203	6.7
Judicial and Legal	29,291	29	1.0
Libraries	0	0	0.0
Parking	792	< 1	< 0.1
Parks and Recreation	152,847	153	5.0
Police Protection	287,476	287	9.5
Public Welfare	21,317	21	0.7
Sewerage	329,334	329	10.9
Solid Waste Management	194,195	194	6.4
Veterans' Services	0	0	0.0
Liquor Store	0	0	0.0
Utility	1,100,280	1,101	36.3
Employee Retirement	0	0	0.0

Source: U.S. Census Bureau, State & Local Government Finances 2017

EMPLOYMENT

Labor Force and Employment

Area	Civilian Labor Force			Workers Employed		
	Dec. 2019	Dec. 2020	% Chg.	Dec. 2019	Dec. 2020	% Chg.
City	452,859	447,861	-1.1	443,191	411,864	-7.1
MSA[1]	452,859	447,861	-1.1	443,191	411,864	-7.1
U.S.	164,007,000	160,017,000	-2.4	158,504,000	149,613,000	-5.6

Note: Data is not seasonally adjusted and covers workers 16 years of age and older; (1) Figures cover the Urban Honolulu, HI Metropolitan Statistical Area
Source: Bureau of Labor Statistics, Local Area Unemployment Statistics

Unemployment Rate

Area	2020											
	Jan.	Feb.	Mar.	Apr.	May	Jun.	Jul.	Aug.	Sep.	Oct.	Nov.	Dec.
City	2.8	2.5	2.1	20.5	20.8	12.2	11.5	11.0	13.6	12.4	9.1	8.0
MSA[1]	2.8	2.5	2.1	20.5	20.8	12.2	11.5	11.0	13.6	12.4	9.1	8.0
U.S.	4.0	3.8	4.5	14.4	13.0	11.2	10.5	8.5	7.7	6.6	6.4	6.5

Note: Data is not seasonally adjusted and covers workers 16 years of age and older; (1) Figures cover the Urban Honolulu, HI Metropolitan Statistical Area
Source: Bureau of Labor Statistics, Local Area Unemployment Statistics

Average Wages

Occupation	$/Hr.	Occupation	$/Hr.
Accountants and Auditors	31.70	Maintenance and Repair Workers	24.10
Automotive Mechanics	25.70	Marketing Managers	52.10
Bookkeepers	21.40	Network and Computer Systems Admin.	40.40
Carpenters	39.90	Nurses, Licensed Practical	26.10
Cashiers	13.70	Nurses, Registered	51.30
Computer Programmers	39.70	Nursing Assistants	18.50
Computer Systems Analysts	38.50	Office Clerks, General	18.00
Computer User Support Specialists	25.50	Physical Therapists	46.00
Construction Laborers	30.70	Physicians	129.50
Cooks, Restaurant	16.70	Plumbers, Pipefitters and Steamfitters	32.60
Customer Service Representatives	19.20	Police and Sheriff's Patrol Officers	39.30
Dentists	104.00	Postal Service Mail Carriers	26.30
Electricians	38.40	Real Estate Sales Agents	34.80
Engineers, Electrical	43.60	Retail Salespersons	16.90
Fast Food and Counter Workers	13.20	Sales Representatives, Technical/Scientific	42.00
Financial Managers	60.40	Secretaries, Exc. Legal/Medical/Executive	22.10
First-Line Supervisors of Office Workers	29.60	Security Guards	16.80
General and Operations Managers	58.20	Surgeons	125.40
Hairdressers/Cosmetologists	18.80	Teacher Assistants, Exc. Postsecondary*	15.70
Home Health and Personal Care Aides	14.10	Teachers, Secondary School, Exc. Sp. Ed.*	n/a
Janitors and Cleaners	16.40	Telemarketers	12.80
Landscaping/Groundskeeping Workers	19.30	Truck Drivers, Heavy/Tractor-Trailer	25.80
Lawyers	56.10	Truck Drivers, Light/Delivery Services	18.40
Maids and Housekeeping Cleaners	19.90	Waiters and Waitresses	30.10

Note: Wage data covers the Urban Honolulu, HI Metropolitan Statistical Area; (*) Hourly wages were calculated from annual wage data based on a 40 hour work week; n/a not available.
Source: Bureau of Labor Statistics, Metro Area Occupational Employment & Wage Estimates, May 2020

Employment by Industry

Sector	MSA[1]		U.S.
	Number of Employees	Percent of Total	Percent of Total
Construction, Mining, and Logging	26,500	6.5	5.5
Education and Health Services	62,300	15.3	16.3
Financial Activities	21,600	5.3	6.1
Government	91,900	22.5	15.2
Information	5,500	1.3	1.9
Leisure and Hospitality	49,300	12.1	9.0
Manufacturing	8,700	2.1	8.5
Other Services	16,900	4.1	3.8
Professional and Business Services	52,300	12.8	14.4
Retail Trade	39,900	9.8	10.9
Transportation, Warehousing, and Utilities	19,700	4.8	4.6
Wholesale Trade	13,200	3.2	3.9

Note: Figures are non-farm employment as of December 2020. Figures are not seasonally adjusted and include workers 16 years of age and older; (1) Figures cover the Urban Honolulu, HI Metropolitan Statistical Area
Source: Bureau of Labor Statistics, Current Employment Statistics, Employment, Hours, and Earnings

Employment by Occupation

Occupation Classification	City (%)	MSA[1] (%)	U.S. (%)
Management, Business, Science, and Arts	36.9	36.5	38.5
Natural Resources, Construction, and Maintenance	6.5	8.9	8.9
Production, Transportation, and Material Moving	9.0	9.5	13.2
Sales and Office	23.9	23.7	21.6
Service	23.7	21.5	17.8

Note: Figures cover employed civilians 16 years of age and older; (1) Figures cover the Urban Honolulu, HI Metropolitan Statistical Area
Source: U.S. Census Bureau, 2015-2019 American Community Survey 5-Year Estimates

Occupations with Greatest Projected Employment Growth: 2020 – 2022

Occupation[1]	2020 Employment	2022 Projected Employment	Numeric Employment Change	Percent Employment Change
Home Health and Personal Care Aides	9,350	9,630	280	3.0
Medical and Health Services Managers	1,700	1,760	60	3.5
Medical Assistants	4,570	4,620	50	1.1
Solar Photovoltaic Installers	370	410	40	10.8
Nurse Practitioners	450	480	30	6.7
Substance Abuse, Behavioral Disorder, and Mental Health Counselors	810	830	20	2.5
Phlebotomists	880	900	20	2.3
Transportation Security Screeners	1,380	1,400	20	1.4
Social and Community Service Managers	790	800	10	1.3
Information Security Analysts (SOC 2018)	350	360	10	2.9

Note: Projections cover Hawaii; (1) Sorted by numeric employment change
Source: www.projectionscentral.com, State Occupational Projections, 2020–2022 Short-Term Projections

Fastest-Growing Occupations: 2020 – 2022

Occupation[1]	2020 Employment	2022 Projected Employment	Numeric Employment Change	Percent Employment Change
Medical and Health Services Managers	1,700	1,760	60	3.5
Home Health and Personal Care Aides	9,350	9,630	280	3.0
Medical Assistants	4,570	4,620	50	1.1

Note: Projections cover Hawaii; (1) Sorted by percent employment change and excludes occupations with numeric employment change less than 50
Source: www.projectionscentral.com, State Occupational Projections, 2020–2022 Short-Term Projections

TAXES

State Corporate Income Tax Rates

State	Tax Rate (%)	Income Brackets ($)	Num. of Brackets	Financial Institution Tax Rate (%)[a]	Federal Income Tax Ded.
Hawaii	4.4 - 6.4 (f)	25,000 - 100,001	3	7.92 (f)	No

Note: Tax rates as of January 1, 2021; (a) Rates listed are the corporate income tax rate applied to financial institutions or excise taxes based on income. Some states have other taxes based upon the value of deposits or shares; (f) Hawaii taxes capital gains at 4%. Financial institutions pay a franchise tax of 7.92% of taxable income (in lieu of the corporate income tax and general excise taxes).
Source: Federation of Tax Administrators, State Corporate Income Tax Rates, January 1, 2021

State Individual Income Tax Rates

State	Tax Rate (%)	Income Brackets ($)	Personal Exemptions ($)			Standard Ded. ($)	
			Single	Married	Depend.	Single	Married
Hawaii	1.4 - 11.0	2,400 - 200,000 (b)	1,144	2,288	1,144	2,200	4,400

Note: Tax rates as of January 1, 2021; Local- and county-level taxes are not included; Federal income tax is not deductible on state income tax returns; (b) For joint returns, taxes are twice the tax on half the couple's income.
Source: Federation of Tax Administrators, State Individual Income Tax Rates, January 1, 2021

Various State Sales and Excise Tax Rates

State	State Sales Tax (%)	Gasoline[1] (¢/gal.)	Cigarette[2] ($/pack)	Spirits[3] ($/gal.)	Wine[4] ($/gal.)	Beer[5] ($/gal.)	Recreational Marijuana (%)
Hawaii	4	46.84	3.2	5.98	1.38	0.93	Not legal

Note: All tax rates as of January 1, 2021; (1) The American Petroleum Institute has developed a methodology for determining the average tax rate on a gallon of fuel. Rates may include any of the following: excise taxes, environmental fees, storage tank fees, other fees or taxes, general sales tax, and local taxes; (2) The federal excise tax of $1.0066 per pack and local taxes are not included; (3) Rates are those applicable to off-premise sales of 40% alcohol by volume (a.b.v.) distilled spirits in 750ml containers. Local excise taxes are excluded; (4) Rates are those applicable to off-premise sales of 11% a.b.v. non-carbonated wine in 750ml containers; (5) Rates are those applicable to off-premise sales of 4.7% a.b.v. beer in 12 ounce containers.
Source: Tax Foundation, 2021 Facts & Figures: How Does Your State Compare?

State Business Tax Climate Index Rankings

State	Overall Rank	Corporate Tax Rank	Individual Income Tax Rank	Sales Tax Rank	Property Tax Rank	Unemployment Insurance Tax Rank
Hawaii	38	18	47	30	9	25

Note: The index is a measure of how each state's tax laws affect economic performance. The lower the rank, the more favorable a state's tax system is for business. States without a given tax are given a ranking of 1. The scores/rankings for the District of Columbia do not affect other states. The 2021 index represents the tax climate as of July 1, 2020.
Source: Tax Foundation, State Business Tax Climate Index 2021

TRANSPORTATION

Means of Transportation to Work

Area	Drove Alone	Car-pooled	Bus	Subway	Railroad	Bicycle	Walked	Other Means	Worked at Home
City	57.2	13.0	11.6	0.0	0.0	1.6	8.5	4.0	3.9
MSA[1]	64.7	14.2	8.0	0.0	0.0	0.9	5.5	2.7	4.0
U.S.	76.3	9.0	2.4	1.9	0.6	0.5	2.7	1.4	5.2

Note: Figures are percentages and cover workers 16 years of age and older; (1) Figures cover the Urban Honolulu, HI Metropolitan Statistical Area
Source: U.S. Census Bureau, 2015-2019 American Community Survey 5-Year Estimates

Travel Time to Work

Area	Less Than 10 Minutes	10 to 19 Minutes	20 to 29 Minutes	30 to 44 Minutes	45 to 59 Minutes	60 to 89 Minutes	90 Minutes or More
City	7.9	35.3	23.7	22.0	5.5	4.3	1.4
MSA[1]	9.0	24.9	19.6	25.3	9.8	8.5	3.0
U.S.	12.2	28.4	20.8	20.8	8.3	6.4	2.9

Note: Note: Figures are percentages and include workers 16 years old and over; (1) Figures cover the Urban Honolulu, HI Metropolitan Statistical Area
Source: U.S. Census Bureau, 2015-2019 American Community Survey 5-Year Estimates

Key Congestion Measures

Measure	1982	1992	2002	2012	2017
Annual Hours of Delay, Total (000)	6,337	13,566	19,830	29,888	36,378
Annual Hours of Delay, Per Auto Commuter	21	34	45	56	64
Annual Congestion Cost, Total (million $)	50	147	273	549	689
Annual Congestion Cost, Per Auto Commuter ($)	538	791	903	1,065	1,258

Note: Covers the Honolulu HI urban area
Source: Texas A&M Transportation Institute, 2019 Urban Mobility Report

Freeway Travel Time Index

Measure	1982	1987	1992	1997	2002	2007	2012	2017
Urban Area Index[1]	1.15	1.20	1.25	1.30	1.33	1.38	1.38	1.40
Urban Area Rank[1,2]	8	5	4	4	4	3	3	4

Note: Freeway Travel Time Index—the ratio of travel time in the peak period to the travel time at free-flow conditions. For example, a value of 1.30 indicates a 20-minute free-flow trip takes 26 minutes in the peak (20 minutes x 1.30 = 26 minutes); (1) Covers the Honolulu HI urban area; (2) Rank is based on 101 larger urban areas (#1 = highest travel time index)
Source: Texas A&M Transportation Institute, 2019 Urban Mobility Report

Public Transportation

Agency Name / Mode of Transportation	Vehicles Operated in Maximum Service[1]	Annual Unlinked Passenger Trips[2] (in thous.)	Annual Passenger Miles[3] (in thous.)
City and County of Honolulu Dept. of Transportation Services (DTS)			
Bus (purchased transportation)	456	62,554.4	305,290.9
Demand Response (purchased transportation)	230	1,195.4	12,968.5
Demand Response Taxi (purchased transportation)	136	207.6	1,627.4
Vanpool (purchased transportation)	44	108.4	1,817.8

Note: (1) Number of revenue vehicles operated by the given mode and type of service to meet the annual maximum service requirement. This is the revenue vehicle count during the peak season of the year; on the week and day that maximum service is provided. Vehicles operated in maximum service (VOMS) exclude atypical days and one-time special events; (2) Number of passengers who boarded public transportation vehicles. Passengers are counted each time they board a vehicle no matter how many vehicles they use to travel from their origin to their destination. (3) Sum of the distances ridden by all passengers during the entire fiscal year.
Source: Federal Transit Administration, National Transit Database, 2019

Air Transportation

Airport Name and Code / Type of Service	Passenger Airlines[1]	Passenger Enplanements	Freight Carriers[2]	Freight (lbs)
Honolulu International (HNL)				
Domestic service (U.S. carriers - 2020)	14	2,605,898	21	325,214,370
International service (U.S. carriers - 2019)	6	974,216	10	128,230,924

Note: (1) Includes all U.S.-based major, minor and commuter airlines that carried at least one passenger during the year; (2) Includes all U.S.-based airlines and freight carriers that transported at least one pound of freight during the year.
Source: Bureau of Transportation Statistics, The Intermodal Transportation Database, Air Carriers: T-100 Domestic Market (U.S. Carriers), 2020; Bureau of Transportation Statistics, The Intermodal Transportation Database, Air Carriers: T-100 International Market (U.S. Carriers), 2019

BUSINESSES

Major Business Headquarters

Company Name	Industry	Rankings	
		Fortune[1]	Forbes[2]
No companies listed	-	-	-

Note: (1) Companies that produce a 10-K are ranked 1 to 500 based on 2019 revenue; (2) All private companies with at least $2 billion in annual revenue through the end of their most current fiscal year are ranked 1 to 219; companies listed are headquartered in the city; dashes indicate no ranking
Source: Fortune, "Fortune 500," June/July 2020; Forbes, "America's Largest Private Companies," 2020

Fastest-Growing Businesses

According to *Inc.*, Honolulu is home to one of America's 500 fastest-growing private companies: **Blue Planet Energy Systems** (#297). Criteria: must be an independent, privately-held, for-profit, U.S. corporation, proprietorship or partnership as of December 31, 2019; revenues must be at least $100,000 in 2016 and $2 million in 2019; must have four-year operating/sales history. *Inc., "America's 500 Fastest-Growing Private Companies," 2020*

According to *Initiative for a Competitive Inner City (ICIC)*, Honolulu is home to one of America's 100 fastest-growing "inner city" companies: **Hawaiian Pie Company** (#72). Criteria for inclusion: company must be headquartered in or have 51 percent or more of its physical operations in an economically distressed urban area; must be an independent, for-profit corporation, partnership or proprietorship; must have 10 or more employees and have a five-year sales history that includes sales of at least $200,000 in the base year and at least $1 million in the current year with no decrease in sales over the two most recent years. Companies were ranked overall by revenue growth over the five-year period between 2015 and 2019. *Initiative for a Competitive Inner City (ICIC), "Inner City 100 Companies," 2020*

Living Environment

COST OF LIVING

Cost of Living Index

Composite Index	Groceries	Housing	Utilities	Trans-portation	Health Care	Misc. Goods/ Services
199.1	170.9	334.0	201.9	144.6	113.5	127.9

Note: The Cost of Living Index measures regional differences in the cost of consumer goods and services, excluding taxes and non-consumer expenditures, for professional and managerial households in the top income quintile. It is based on more than 50,000 prices covering almost 60 different items for which prices are collected three times a year by chambers of commerce, economic development organizations or university applied economic centers in each participating urban area. The numbers shown should be read as a percentage above or below the national average of 100. For example, a value of 115.4 in the groceries column indicates that grocery prices are 15.4% higher than the national average. Small differences in the index numbers should not be interpreted as significant; Figures cover the Honolulu HI urban area.
Source: The Council for Community and Economic Research, Cost of Living Index, 2020

Grocery Prices

Area[1]	T-Bone Steak ($/pound)	Frying Chicken ($/pound)	Whole Milk ($/half gal.)	Eggs ($/dozen)	Orange Juice ($/64 oz.)	Coffee ($/11.5 oz.)
City[2]	13.84	2.45	4.31	3.77	5.44	8.69
Avg.	11.78	1.39	2.05	1.47	3.57	4.34
Min.	8.03	0.94	1.03	0.74	2.94	3.02
Max.	15.86	2.65	4.31	3.77	5.44	8.69

Note: (1) Values for the local area are compared with the average, minimum and maximum values for all 284 areas in the Cost of Living Index; (2) Figures cover the Honolulu HI urban area; **T-Bone Steak** (price per pound); **Frying Chicken** (price per pound, whole fryer); **Whole Milk** (half gallon carton); **Eggs** (price per dozen, Grade A, large); **Orange Juice** (64 oz. Tropicana or Florida Natural); **Coffee** (11.5 oz. can, vacuum-packed, Maxwell House, Hills Bros, or Folgers).
Source: The Council for Community and Economic Research, Cost of Living Index, 2020

Housing and Utility Costs

Area[1]	New Home Price ($)	Apartment Rent ($/month)	All Electric ($/month)	Part Electric ($/month)	Other Energy ($/month)	Telephone ($/month)
City[2]	1,386,483	3,315	470.38	-	-	178.30
Avg.	368,594	1,168	170.86	100.47	65.28	184.30
Min.	190,567	502	91.58	31.42	26.08	169.60
Max.	2,227,806	4,738	470.38	280.31	280.06	206.50

Note: (1) Values for the local area are compared with the average, minimum and maximum values for all 284 areas in the Cost of Living Index; (2) Figures cover the Honolulu HI urban area; **New Home Price** (2,400 sf living area, 8,000 sf lot, in urban area with full utilities); **Apartment Rent** (950 sf 2 bedroom/1.5 or 2 bath, unfurnished, excluding all utilities except water); **All Electric** (average monthly cost for an all-electric home); **Part Electric** (average monthly cost for a part-electric home); **Other Energy** (average monthly cost for natural gas, fuel oil, coal, wood, and any other forms of energy except electricity); **Telephone** (price includes the base monthly rate plus taxes and fees for three lines of mobile phone service).
Source: The Council for Community and Economic Research, Cost of Living Index, 2020

Health Care, Transportation, and Other Costs

Area[1]	Doctor ($/visit)	Dentist ($/visit)	Optometrist ($/visit)	Gasoline ($/gallon)	Beauty Salon ($/visit)	Men's Shirt ($)
City[2]	145.88	86.68	195.37	3.30	70.00	58.06
Avg.	115.44	99.32	108.10	2.21	39.27	31.37
Min.	36.68	59.00	51.36	1.71	19.00	11.00
Max.	219.00	153.10	250.97	3.46	82.05	58.33

Note: (1) Values for the local area are compared with the average, minimum and maximum values for all 284 areas in the Cost of Living Index; (2) Figures cover the Honolulu HI urban area; **Doctor** (general practitioners routine exam of an established patient); **Dentist** (adult teeth cleaning and periodic oral examination); **Optometrist** (full vision eye exam for established adult patient); **Gasoline** (one gallon regular unleaded, national brand, including all taxes, cash price at self-service pump if available); **Beauty Salon** (woman's shampoo, trim, and blow-dry); **Men's Shirt** (cotton/polyester dress shirt, pinpoint weave, long sleeves).
Source: The Council for Community and Economic Research, Cost of Living Index, 2020

HOUSING

Homeownership Rate

Area	2012 (%)	2013 (%)	2014 (%)	2015 (%)	2016 (%)	2017 (%)	2018 (%)	2019 (%)	2020 (%)
MSA[1]	56.1	57.9	58.2	59.6	57.9	53.8	57.7	59.0	56.9
U.S.	65.4	65.1	64.5	63.7	63.4	63.9	64.4	64.6	66.6

Note: (1) Figures cover the Urban Honolulu, HI Metropolitan Statistical Area
Source: U.S. Census Bureau, Housing Vacancies and Homeownership Annual Statistics: 2012-2020

House Price Index (HPI)

Area	National Ranking[2]	Quarterly Change (%)	One-Year Change (%)	Five-Year Change (%)	Since 1991Q1 (%)
MSA[1]	250	1.23	0.53	16.08	154.83
U.S.[3]	–	3.81	10.77	38.99	205.12

Note: The HPI is a weighted repeat sales index. It measures average price changes in repeat sales or refinancings on the same properties. This information is obtained by reviewing repeat mortgage transactions on single-family properties whose mortgages have been purchased or securitized by Fannie Mae or Freddie Mac since January 1975; (1) Figures cover the Urban Honolulu, HI Metropolitan Statistical Area; (2) Rankings are based on annual percentage change for all metro areas containing at least 15,000 transactions over the last 10 years and ranges from 1 to 253; (3) figures based on a weighted average of Census Division estimates using a seasonally adjusted, purchase-only index; all figures are for the period ending December 31, 2020
Source: Federal Housing Finance Agency, Change in Metropolitan Area House Price Indexes, April 7, 2021

Median Single-Family Home Prices

Area	2018	2019	2020[p]	Percent Change 2019 to 2020
MSA[1]	802.7	802.5	851.5	6.1
U.S. Average	261.6	274.6	299.9	9.2

Note: Figures are median sales prices of existing single-family homes in thousands of dollars; (p) preliminary; (1) Figures cover the Urban Honolulu, HI Metropolitan Statistical Area
Source: National Association of Realtors, Median Sales Price of Existing Single-Family Homes for Metropolitan Areas, 4th Quarter 2020

Qualifying Income Based on Median Sales Price of Existing Single-Family Homes

Area	With 5% Down ($)	With 10% Down ($)	With 20% Down ($)
MSA[1]	170,701	161,717	143,748
U.S. Average	59,266	56,147	49,908

Note: Figures are preliminary; Qualifying income is based on a mortgage rate of 2.81%. Monthly principal and interest payment is limited to 25% of income; (1) Figures cover the Urban Honolulu, HI Metropolitan Statistical Area
Source: National Association of Realtors, Qualifying Income Based on Median Sales Price of Existing Single-Family Homes for Metropolitan Areas, 4th Quarter 2020

Home Value Distribution

Area	Under $50,000	$50,000 -$99,999	$100,000 -$149,999	$150,000 -$199,999	$200,000 -$299,999	$300,000 -$499,999	$500,000 -$999,999	$1,000,000 or more
City	0.8	0.8	0.8	1.4	7.2	22.6	42.5	24.0
MSA[1]	0.7	0.6	0.8	1.0	5.0	19.6	54.6	17.7
U.S.	6.9	12.0	13.3	14.0	19.6	19.3	11.4	3.4

Note: Figures are percentages and cover owner-occupied housing units; (1) Figures cover the Urban Honolulu, HI Metropolitan Statistical Area
Source: U.S. Census Bureau, 2015-2019 American Community Survey 5-Year Estimates

Year Housing Structure Built

Area	2010 or Later	2000 -2009	1990 -1999	1980 -1989	1970 -1979	1960 -1969	1950 -1959	1940 -1949	Before 1940	Median Year
City	4.2	6.9	7.9	9.5	25.3	22.8	12.8	5.5	5.1	1971
MSA[1]	5.1	10.2	11.5	12.2	24.1	18.9	10.7	4.0	3.3	1975
U.S.	5.2	14.0	13.9	13.4	15.2	10.6	10.3	4.9	12.6	1978

Note: Figures are percentages except for Median Year; Note: (1) Figures cover the Urban Honolulu, HI Metropolitan Statistical Area
Source: U.S. Census Bureau, 2015-2019 American Community Survey 5-Year Estimates

Gross Monthly Rent

Area	Under $500	$500 -$999	$1,000 -$1,499	$1,500 -$1,999	$2,000 -$2,499	$2,500 -$2,999	$3,000 and up	Median ($)
City	6.9	13.3	30.4	22.3	11.3	6.7	9.2	1,491
MSA[1]	5.6	10.4	24.1	20.3	14.1	10.0	15.5	1,745
U.S.	9.4	36.2	30.0	14.0	5.6	2.4	2.4	1,062

Note: Figures are percentages except for Median; Gross rent is the contract rent plus the estimated average monthly cost of utilities (electricity, gas, and water and sewer) and fuels (oil, coal, kerosene, wood, etc.) if these are paid by the renter (or paid for the renter by someone else); (1) Figures cover the Urban Honolulu, HI Metropolitan Statistical Area
Source: U.S. Census Bureau, 2015-2019 American Community Survey 5-Year Estimates

HEALTH

Health Risk Factors

Category	MSA[1] (%)	U.S. (%)
Adults aged 18–64 who have any kind of health care coverage	n/a	87.3
Adults who reported being in good or better health	n/a	82.4
Adults who have been told they have high blood cholesterol	n/a	33.0
Adults who have been told they have high blood pressure	n/a	32.3
Adults who are current smokers	n/a	17.1
Adults who currently use E-cigarettes	n/a	4.6
Adults who currently use chewing tobacco, snuff, or snus	n/a	4.0
Adults who are heavy drinkers[2]	n/a	6.3
Adults who are binge drinkers[3]	n/a	17.4
Adults who are overweight (BMI 25.0 - 29.9)	n/a	35.3
Adults who are obese (BMI 30.0 - 99.8)	n/a	31.3
Adults who participated in any physical activities in the past month	n/a	74.4
Adults who always or nearly always wears a seat belt	n/a	94.3

Note: n/a not available; (1) Figures cover the Urban Honolulu, HI Metropolitan Statistical Area; (2) Heavy drinkers are classified as adult men having more than 14 drinks per week and adult women having more than 7 drinks per week; (3) Binge drinkers are classified as males having five or more drinks on one occasion or females having four or more drinks on one occasion
Source: Centers for Disease Control and Prevention, Behaviorial Risk Factor Surveillance System, SMART: Selected Metropolitan Area Risk Trends, 2017

Acute and Chronic Health Conditions

Category	MSA[1] (%)	U.S. (%)
Adults who have ever been told they had a heart attack	n/a	4.2
Adults who have ever been told they have angina or coronary heart disease	n/a	3.9
Adults who have ever been told they had a stroke	n/a	3.0
Adults who have ever been told they have asthma	n/a	14.2
Adults who have ever been told they have arthritis	n/a	24.9
Adults who have ever been told they have diabetes[2]	n/a	10.5
Adults who have ever been told they had skin cancer	n/a	6.2
Adults who have ever been told they had any other types of cancer	n/a	7.1
Adults who have ever been told they have COPD	n/a	6.5
Adults who have ever been told they have kidney disease	n/a	3.0
Adults who have ever been told they have a form of depression	n/a	20.5

Note: n/a not available; (1) Figures cover the Urban Honolulu, HI Metropolitan Statistical Area; (2) Figures do not include pregnancy-related, borderline, or pre-diabetes
Source: Centers for Disease Control and Prevention, Behaviorial Risk Factor Surveillance System, SMART: Selected Metropolitan Area Risk Trends, 2017

Health Screening and Vaccination Rates

Category	MSA[1] (%)	U.S. (%)
Adults aged 65+ who have had flu shot within the past year	n/a	60.7
Adults aged 65+ who have ever had a pneumonia vaccination	n/a	75.4
Adults who have ever been tested for HIV	n/a	36.1
Adults who have ever had the shingles or zoster vaccine?	n/a	28.9
Adults who have had their blood cholesterol checked within the last five years	n/a	85.9

Note: n/a not available; (1) Figures cover the Urban Honolulu, HI Metropolitan Statistical Area.
Source: Centers for Disease Control and Prevention, Behaviorial Risk Factor Surveillance System, SMART: Selected Metropolitan Area Risk Trends, 2017

Disability Status

Category	MSA[1] (%)	U.S. (%)
Adults who reported being deaf	n/a	6.7
Are you blind or have serious difficulty seeing, even when wearing glasses?	n/a	4.5
Are you limited in any way in any of your usual activities due of arthritis?	n/a	12.9
Do you have difficulty doing errands alone?	n/a	6.8
Do you have difficulty dressing or bathing?	n/a	3.6
Do you have serious difficulty concentrating/remembering/making decisions?	n/a	10.7
Do you have serious difficulty walking or climbing stairs?	n/a	13.6

Note: n/a not available; (1) Figures cover the Urban Honolulu, HI Metropolitan Statistical Area.
Source: Centers for Disease Control and Prevention, Behaviorial Risk Factor Surveillance System, SMART: Selected Metropolitan Area Risk Trends, 2017

Mortality Rates for the Top 10 Causes of Death in the U.S.

ICD-10[a] Sub-Chapter	ICD-10[a] Code	Age-Adjusted Mortality Rate[1] per 100,000 population	
		County[2]	U.S.
Malignant neoplasms	C00-C97	123.3	149.2
Ischaemic heart diseases	I20-I25	63.4	90.5
Other forms of heart disease	I30-I51	41.8	52.2
Chronic lower respiratory diseases	J40-J47	16.4	39.6
Other degenerative diseases of the nervous system	G30-G31	20.8	37.6
Cerebrovascular diseases	I60-I69	37.9	37.2
Other external causes of accidental injury	W00-X59	29.4	36.1
Organic, including symptomatic, mental disorders	F01-F09	30.6	29.4
Hypertensive diseases	I10-I15	20.4	24.1
Diabetes mellitus	E10-E14	15.2	21.5

Note: (a) ICD-10 = International Classification of Diseases 10th Revision; (1) Mortality rates are a three-year average covering 2017-2019; (2) Figures cover Honolulu County.
Source: Centers for Disease Control and Prevention, National Center for Health Statistics. Underlying Cause of Death 1999-2019 on CDC WONDER Online Database

Mortality Rates for Selected Causes of Death

ICD-10[a] Sub-Chapter	ICD-10[a] Code	Age-Adjusted Mortality Rate[1] per 100,000 population	
		County[2]	U.S.
Assault	X85-Y09	2.9	6.0
Diseases of the liver	K70-K76	8.4	14.4
Human immunodeficiency virus (HIV) disease	B20-B24	0.7	1.5
Influenza and pneumonia	J09-J18	27.7	13.8
Intentional self-harm	X60-X84	11.3	14.1
Malnutrition	E40-E46	0.7	2.3
Obesity and other hyperalimentation	E65-E68	1.0	2.1
Renal failure	N17-N19	9.8	12.6
Transport accidents	V01-V99	7.0	12.3
Viral hepatitis	B15-B19	0.7	1.2

Note: (a) ICD-10 = International Classification of Diseases 10th Revision; (1) Mortality rates are a three-year average covering 2017-2019; (2) Figures cover Honolulu County; Data are suppressed when the data meet the criteria for confidentiality constraints; Mortality rates are flagged as unreliable when the rate would be calculated with a numerator of 20 or less.
Source: Centers for Disease Control and Prevention, National Center for Health Statistics. Underlying Cause of Death 1999-2019 on CDC WONDER Online Database

Health Insurance Coverage

Area	With Health Insurance	With Private Health Insurance	With Public Health Insurance	Without Health Insurance	Population Under Age 19 Without Health Insurance
City	96.1	77.7	34.5	3.9	2.4
MSA[1]	96.7	80.4	32.2	3.3	2.0
U.S.	91.2	67.9	35.1	8.8	5.1

Note: Figures are percentages that cover the civilian noninstitutionalized population; (1) Figures cover the Urban Honolulu, HI Metropolitan Statistical Area
Source: U.S. Census Bureau, 2015-2019 American Community Survey 5-Year Estimates

Number of Medical Professionals

Area	MDs[3]	DOs[3,4]	Dentists	Podiatrists	Chiropractors	Optometrists
County[1] (number)	3,439	170	985	33	191	237
County[1] (rate[2])	351.0	17.3	101.1	3.4	19.6	24.3
U.S. (rate[2])	282.9	22.7	71.2	6.2	28.1	16.9

15003
Note: Data as of 2019 unless noted; (1) Data covers Honolulu County; (2) Rate per 100,000 population; (3) Data as of 2018 and includes all active, non-federal physicians; (4) Doctor of Osteopathic Medicine
Source: U.S. Department of Health and Human Services, Health Resources and Services Administration, Bureau of Health Professions, Area Resource File (ARF) 2019-2020

EDUCATION

Public School District Statistics

District Name	Schls	Pupils	Pupil/ Teacher Ratio	Minority Pupils[1] (%)	Free Lunch Eligible[2] (%)	IEP[3] (%)
Hawaii Department of Education	292	181,278	14.9	88.0	36.5	10.8

Note: Table includes school districts with 2,000 or more students; (1) Percentage of students that are not non-Hispanic white; (2) Percentage of students that are eligible for the free lunch program; (3) Percentage of students that have an Individualized Education Program.
Source: U.S. Department of Education, National Center for Education Statistics, Common Core of Data, Local Education Agency (School District) Universe Survey: School Year 2018-2019; U.S. Department of Education, National Center for Education Statistics, Common Core of Data, Public Elementary/Secondary School Universe Survey: School Year 2018-2019

Highest Level of Education

Area	Less than H.S.	H.S. Diploma	Some College, No Deg.	Associate Degree	Bachelor's Degree	Master's Degree	Prof. School Degree	Doctorate Degree
City	11.0	23.5	18.3	10.1	23.7	8.3	3.2	2.0
MSA[1]	8.1	25.9	20.3	10.7	22.9	8.1	2.5	1.5
U.S.	12.0	27.0	20.4	8.5	19.8	8.8	2.1	1.4

Note: Figures cover persons age 25 and over; (1) Figures cover the Urban Honolulu, HI Metropolitan Statistical Area
Source: U.S. Census Bureau, 2015-2019 American Community Survey 5-Year Estimates

Educational Attainment by Race

Area	High School Graduate or Higher (%)					Bachelor's Degree or Higher (%)				
	Total	White	Black	Asian	Hisp.[2]	Total	White	Black	Asian	Hisp.[2]
City	89.0	97.6	97.5	85.5	91.9	37.2	53.0	24.5	36.6	27.9
MSA[1]	91.9	97.3	97.0	88.8	93.4	35.0	48.3	29.9	36.1	25.2
U.S.	88.0	89.9	86.0	87.1	68.7	32.1	33.5	21.6	54.3	16.4

Note: Figures shown cover persons 25 years old and over; (1) Figures cover the Urban Honolulu, HI Metropolitan Statistical Area; (2) People of Hispanic origin can be of any race
Source: U.S. Census Bureau, 2015-2019 American Community Survey 5-Year Estimates

School Enrollment by Grade and Control

Area	Preschool (%)		Kindergarten (%)		Grades 1 - 4 (%)		Grades 5 - 8 (%)		Grades 9 - 12 (%)	
	Public	Private	Public	Private	Public	Private	Public	Private	Public	Private
City	34.7	65.3	79.6	20.4	83.3	16.7	73.0	27.0	74.8	25.2
MSA[1]	36.3	63.7	80.0	20.0	85.3	14.7	78.3	21.7	76.8	23.2
U.S.	59.1	40.9	87.6	12.4	89.5	10.5	89.4	10.6	90.1	9.9

Note: Figures shown cover persons 3 years old and over; (1) Figures cover the Urban Honolulu, HI Metropolitan Statistical Area
Source: U.S. Census Bureau, 2015-2019 American Community Survey 5-Year Estimates

Higher Education

Four-Year Colleges			Two-Year Colleges			Medical Schools[1]	Law Schools[2]	Voc/ Tech[3]
Public	Private Non-profit	Private For-profit	Public	Private Non-profit	Private For-profit			
1	4	2	2	0	2	1	1	1

Note: Figures cover institutions located within the city limits and include main campuses only; (1) includes schools accredited by the Liaison Committee on Medical Education and the American Osteopathic Association's Commission on Osteopathic College Accreditation; (2) includes ABA-accredited schools, schools with provisional ABA accreditation, and state accredited schools; (3) includes all schools with programs that are less than 2 years.
Source: National Center for Education Statistics, Integrated Postsecondary Education System (IPEDS), 2019-20; Wikipedia, List of Medical Schools in the United States, accessed April 2, 2021; Wikipedia, List of Law Schools in the United States, accessed April 2, 2021

EMPLOYERS

Major Employers

Company Name	Industry
City and County of Honolulu	Civil service/commission government
First Hawaiin Bank	State commercial banks
Hawaii Dept of Health	Administration of public health programs
Hawaii Dept of Transportation	Administration of transportation
Hawaii Mediacal Services Assoc	Hospital & medical services plans
Hawaii Pacific Health	General medical & surgical hospitals
Hawaiian Telecom	Local & long distance telephone
KYO YA Hotels and Resorts	Hotels & motels
Mormon Church	Misc denominational church
OAHU transit Services	Bus line operations
St. Francis Healthcare Sys of Hawaii	Skilled nursing facility
State of Hawaii	State government
The Boeing Company	Airplanes, fixed or rotary wing
The Queens Medical Center	General medical & surgical hospitals
Trustess of the Estate of Bernice Bishop	Private elementary/secondary schools
University of Hawaii System	Colleges & universities

Note: Companies shown are located within the Urban Honolulu, HI Metropolitan Statistical Area.
Source: Hoovers.com; Wikipedia

PUBLIC SAFETY

Crime Rate

Area	All Crimes	Violent Crimes				Property Crimes		
		Murder	Rape[3]	Robbery	Aggrav. Assault	Burglary	Larceny -Theft	Motor Vehicle Theft
City	3,272.2	2.8	34.9	97.9	135.1	396.3	2,211.7	393.6
Suburbs[1]	n/a	n/a	n/a	n/a	n/a	n/a	n/a	n/a
Metro[2]	n/a	n/a	n/a	n/a	n/a	n/a	n/a	n/a
U.S.	2,489.3	5.0	42.6	81.6	250.2	340.5	1,549.5	219.9

Note: Figures are crimes per 100,000 population; (1) All areas within the metro area that are located outside the city limits; (2) Figures cover the Urban Honolulu, HI Metropolitan Statistical Area; n/a not available; (3) All figures shown were reported using the revised Uniform Crime Reporting (UCR) definition of rape.
Source: FBI Uniform Crime Reports, 2019

Hate Crimes

Area	Number of Quarters Reported	Number of Incidents per Bias Motivation					
		Race/Ethnicity/ Ancestry	Religion	Sexual Orientation	Disability	Gender	Gender Identity
City	4	30	2	9	0	0	0
U.S.	4	3,963	1,521	1,195	157	69	198

Source: Federal Bureau of Investigation, Hate Crime Statistics 2019

Identity Theft Consumer Reports

Area	Reports	Reports per 100,000 Population	Rank[2]
MSA[1]	2,910	299	122
U.S.	1,387,615	423	-

Note: (1) Figures cover the Urban Honolulu, HI Metropolitan Statistical Area; (2) Rank ranges from 1 to 391 where 1 indicates greatest number of identity theft reports per 100,000 population
Source: Federal Trade Commission, Consumer Sentinel Network Data Book 2020

Fraud and Other Consumer Reports

Area	Reports	Reports per 100,000 Population	Rank[2]
MSA[1]	6,565	674	210
U.S.	3,385,133	1,031	-

Note: (1) Figures cover the Urban Honolulu, HI Metropolitan Statistical Area; (2) Rank ranges from 1 to 391 where 1 indicates greatest number of fraud and other consumer reports per 100,000 population
Source: Federal Trade Commission, Consumer Sentinel Network Data Book 2020

POLITICS

2020 Presidential Election Results

Area	Biden	Trump	Jorgensen	Hawkins	Other
Honolulu County	62.5	35.7	0.9	0.6	0.4
U.S.	51.3	46.8	1.2	0.3	0.5

Note: Results are percentages and may not add to 100% due to rounding
Source: Dave Leip's Atlas of U.S. Presidential Elections

SPORTS

Professional Sports Teams

Team Name	League	Year Established
No teams are located in the metro area		

Source: Wikipedia, Major Professional Sports Teams of the United States and Canada, April 6, 2021

CLIMATE

Average and Extreme Temperatures

Temperature	Jan	Feb	Mar	Apr	May	Jun	Jul	Aug	Sep	Oct	Nov	Dec	Yr.
Extreme High (°F)	87	88	89	89	93	92	92	93	94	94	93	89	94
Average High (°F)	80	80	81	82	84	86	87	88	88	86	84	81	84
Average Temp. (°F)	73	73	74	76	77	79	80	81	81	79	77	74	77
Average Low (°F)	66	66	67	69	70	72	73	74	73	72	70	67	70
Extreme Low (°F)	52	53	55	56	60	65	66	67	66	64	57	54	52

Note: Figures cover the years 1949-1990
Source: National Climatic Data Center, International Station Meteorological Climate Summary, 9/96

Average Precipitation/Snowfall/Humidity

Precip./Humidity	Jan	Feb	Mar	Apr	May	Jun	Jul	Aug	Sep	Oct	Nov	Dec	Yr.
Avg. Precip. (in.)	3.7	2.5	2.8	1.4	1.0	0.4	0.5	0.6	0.7	2.0	2.8	3.7	22.4
Avg. Snowfall (in.)	0	0	0	0	0	0	0	0	0	0	0	0	0
Avg. Rel. Hum. 5am (%)	82	80	78	77	76	75	75	75	76	78	79	80	78
Avg. Rel. Hum. 5pm (%)	66	64	62	61	60	58	58	58	60	63	66	66	62

Note: Figures cover the years 1949-1990; Tr = Trace amounts (<0.05 in. of rain; <0.5 in. of snow)
Source: National Climatic Data Center, International Station Meteorological Climate Summary, 9/96

Weather Conditions

Temperature			Daytime Sky			Precipitation		
32°F & below	45°F & below	90°F & above	Clear	Partly cloudy	Cloudy	0.01 inch or more precip.	0.1 inch or more snow/ice	Thunder-storms
0	0	23	25	286	54	98	0	7

Note: Figures are average number of days per year and cover the years 1949-1990
Source: National Climatic Data Center, International Station Meteorological Climate Summary, 9/96

HAZARDOUS WASTE

Superfund Sites

The Urban Honolulu, HI metro area is home to three sites on the EPA's Superfund National Priorities List: **Del Monte Corp. (Oahu Plantation)** (final); **Naval Computer and Telecommunications Area Master Station Eastern Pacific** (final); **Pearl Harbor Naval Complex** (final). There are a total of 1,375 Superfund sites with a status of proposed or final on the list in the U.S. *U.S. Environmental Protection Agency, National Priorities List, April 7, 2021*

AIR QUALITY

Air Quality Trends: Ozone

	1990	1995	2000	2005	2010	2015	2016	2017	2018	2019
MSA[1]	0.034	0.049	0.044	0.042	0.046	0.048	0.047	0.046	0.046	0.053
U.S.	0.088	0.089	0.082	0.080	0.073	0.069	0.068	0.068	0.069	0.065

Note: (1) Data covers the Urban Honolulu, HI Metropolitan Statistical Area. The values shown are the composite ozone concentration averages among trend sites based on the highest fourth daily maximum 8-hour concentration in parts per million. These trends are based on sites having an adequate record of monitoring data during the trend period. Data from exceptional events are included.
Source: U.S. Environmental Protection Agency, Air Quality Monitoring Information, "Air Quality Trends by City, 1990-2019"

Air Quality Index

Area	Percent of Days when Air Quality was...[2]					AQI Statistics[2]	
	Good	Moderate	Unhealthy for Sensitive Groups	Unhealthy	Very Unhealthy	Maximum	Median
MSA[1]	92.9	7.1	0.0	0.0	0.0	94	29

Note: (1) Data covers the Urban Honolulu, HI Metropolitan Statistical Area; (2) Based on 365 days with AQI data in 2019. Air Quality Index (AQI) is an index for reporting daily air quality. EPA calculates the AQI for five major air pollutants regulated by the Clean Air Act: ground-level ozone, particle pollution (aka particulate matter), carbon monoxide, sulfur dioxide, and nitrogen dioxide. The AQI runs from 0 to 500. The higher the AQI value, the greater the level of air pollution and the greater the health concern. There are six AQI categories: "Good" AQI is between 0 and 50. Air quality is considered satisfactory; "Moderate" AQI is between 51 and 100. Air quality is acceptable; "Unhealthy for Sensitive Groups" When AQI values are between 101 and 150, members of sensitive groups may experience health effects; "Unhealthy" When AQI values are between 151 and 200 everyone may begin to experience health effects; "Very Unhealthy" AQI values between 201 and 300 trigger a health alert; "Hazardous" AQI values over 300 trigger warnings of emergency conditions (not shown).
Source: U.S. Environmental Protection Agency, Air Quality Index Report, 2019

Air Quality Index Pollutants

Area	Percent of Days when AQI Pollutant was...[2]					
	Carbon Monoxide	Nitrogen Dioxide	Ozone	Sulfur Dioxide	Particulate Matter 2.5	Particulate Matter 10
MSA[1]	0.3	0.8	71.8	17.8	9.0	0.3

Note: (1) Data covers the Urban Honolulu, HI Metropolitan Statistical Area; (2) Based on 365 days with AQI data in 2019. The Air Quality Index (AQI) is an index for reporting daily air quality. EPA calculates the AQI for five major air pollutants regulated by the Clean Air Act: ground-level ozone, particle pollution (also known as particulate matter), carbon monoxide, sulfur dioxide, and nitrogen dioxide. The AQI runs from 0 to 500. The higher the AQI value, the greater the level of air pollution and the greater the health concern.
Source: U.S. Environmental Protection Agency, Air Quality Index Report, 2019

Maximum Air Pollutant Concentrations: Particulate Matter, Ozone, CO and Lead

	Particulate Matter 10 (ug/m^3)	Particulate Matter 2.5 Wtd AM (ug/m^3)	Particulate Matter 2.5 24-Hr (ug/m^3)	Ozone (ppm)	Carbon Monoxide (ppm)	Lead (ug/m^3)
MSA[1] Level	32	3.9	8	0.053	1	n/a
NAAQS[2]	150	15	35	0.075	9	0.15
Met NAAQS[2]	Yes	Yes	Yes	Yes	Yes	n/a

Note: (1) Data covers the Urban Honolulu, HI Metropolitan Statistical Area; Data from exceptional events are included; (2) National Ambient Air Quality Standards; ppm = parts per million; ug/m³ = micrograms per cubic meter; n/a not available.
Concentrations: Particulate Matter 10 (coarse particulate)—highest second maximum 24-hour concentration; Particulate Matter 2.5 Wtd AM (fine particulate)—highest weighted annual mean concentration; Particulate Matter 2.5 24-Hour (fine particulate)—highest 98th percentile 24-hour concentration; Ozone—highest fourth daily maximum 8-hour concentration; Carbon Monoxide—highest second maximum non-overlapping 8-hour concentration; Lead—maximum running 3-month average
Source: U.S. Environmental Protection Agency, Air Quality Monitoring Information, "Air Quality Statistics by City, 2019"

Maximum Air Pollutant Concentrations: Nitrogen Dioxide and Sulfur Dioxide

	Nitrogen Dioxide AM (ppb)	Nitrogen Dioxide 1-Hr (ppb)	Sulfur Dioxide AM (ppb)	Sulfur Dioxide 1-Hr (ppb)	Sulfur Dioxide 24-Hr (ppb)
MSA[1] Level	4	28	n/a	62	n/a
NAAQS[2]	53	100	30	75	140
Met NAAQS[2]	Yes	Yes	n/a	Yes	n/a

Note: (1) Data covers the Urban Honolulu, HI Metropolitan Statistical Area; Data from exceptional events are included; (2) National Ambient Air Quality Standards; ppm = parts per million; ug/m³ = micrograms per cubic meter; n/a not available.
Concentrations: Nitrogen Dioxide AM—highest arithmetic mean concentration; Nitrogen Dioxide 1-Hr—highest 98th percentile 1-hour daily maximum concentration; Sulfur Dioxide AM—highest annual mean concentration; Sulfur Dioxide 1-Hr—highest 99th percentile 1-hour daily maximum concentration; Sulfur Dioxide 24-Hr—highest second maximum 24-hour concentration
Source: U.S. Environmental Protection Agency, Air Quality Monitoring Information, "Air Quality Statistics by City, 2019"

Las Vegas, Nevada

Background

Upright citizens can accuse Las Vegas of many vices, but not of hypocrisy. Back in 1931, the city officials of this desert town, located 225 miles northeast of Los Angeles, saw gambling to be a growing popular pastime. To capitalize upon that trend, the city simply legalized it. Gambling, combined with spectacular, neon-lit entertainment, lures more than 36.4 million visitors a year to its more than 1,700 casinos and 140,000 hotel rooms.

Before celebrities and tourists flocked to Las Vegas, it was a temporary stopping place for a diverse group of people. In the early 1880s, Las Vegas was a watering hole for those on the trail to California. Areas of the Las Vegas Valley contained artesian wells that supported extensive green meadows, or *vega* in Spanish, hence the name Las Vegas. In 1855 the area was settled by Mormon missionaries, but they left two years later. Finally, in the late 1800s, the land was used for ranching.

In the beginning of the twentieth century, the seeds of the present Las Vegas began to sprout. In 1905 the arrival of the Union Pacific Railroad sprinkled businesses, saloons, and gambling houses along it tracks; the city was formally founded on May 15, 1905. Then, during the Great Depression, men working on the nearby Hoover Dam spent their extra money in the establishments. Finally, gambling was legalized, hydroelectric power from the Hoover Dam lit the city in neon, and hotels began to compete for the brightest stars and the plushest surroundings. Las Vegas was an overnight success, luring many people with get-rich-quick dreams. The dream has thus far endured, and in 2005 the city celebrated its centennial with a suitably festive media blitz, many special events, and the world's largest birthday cake at 130,000 pounds.

Las Vegas is home to the World Series of Poker, which began in Texas in 1969. Winners can pocket close to $10 million.

For the past 25 years, senior citizens have constituted the fastest-growing segment of the Las Vegas population, taking advantage of the dry climate, reasonably priced housing, low property taxes, no sales tax, and plenty of entertainment. Today, the state leads the nation in growth of its senior citizen population, and this is expected to continue. Many programs exist to ensure their comfort and welfare, including quality economic, legal, and medical plans.

The city's World Market Center, a furniture wholesale showroom and marketplace, was built to compete with current furniture market capital of High Point, North Carolina. Megahotels and many smaller projects continue to be developed. Billions have been spent have on hotel and casino construction. At its peak, some 3,000 people moved to the city each month, most of them in construction and casino-related work. The Durango Drive Improvement project has helped to ease traffic congestion with new ramps, a trails system underpass, new auxiliary lanes, and a new traffic signal system.

Since 2012, hundreds of millions of dollars' worth of projects have been completed. They include The Smith Center for the Performing Arts and DISCOVERY Children's Museum, Mob Museum, Neon Museum, City Hall complex and a new Zappos.com corporate headquarters in the old City Hall building.

Las Vegas valley is home to three major professional sports teams: Vegas Golden Knights (NHL); Las Vegas Raiders (NFL); and Las Vegas Aces (WNBA).

One of the more serious problems facing the fast-growing city is its diminishing water supply. Las Vegas uses approximately 350 gallons daily per person, more than any city in the world. The city has raised water rates and encourages conservation by homeowners and businesses through desert landscaping, which can reduce water use by as much as 80 percent.

The city made national headlines in October 2017 when a gunman opened fire on a crowd of concert goers on Las Vegas Boulevard, killing 58 people and injuring 800. This mass shooting, and others in recent years, contributed to the ongoing national debate on gun control.

Las Vegas is located near the center of a broad desert valley, which is almost surrounded by mountains ranging from 2,000 to 10,000 feet. The four seasons are well defined. Summers display desert conditions with extreme high temperatures, but nights are relatively cool due to the closeness of the mountains. For about two weeks almost every summer, warm, moist air predominates, causing higher-than-average humidity and scattered, severe thunderstorms. Winters are generally mild and pleasant with clear skies prevailing. Strong winds, associated with major storms, usually reach the valley from the southwest or through the pass from the northwest. Winds over 50 miles per hour are infrequent but, when they do occur, are the most troublesome of the elements because of the dust and sand they stir up.

Rankings

General Rankings

- The Las Vegas metro area was identified as one of America's fastest-growing areas in terms of population and business growth by *MagnifyMoney*. The area ranked #26 out of 35. The 100 most populous metro areas in the U.S. were evaluated on their change from 2011-2016 in the following categories: people and housing; workforce and employment opportunities; growing industry. *www.businessinsider.com, "The 35 Cities in the US with the Biggest Influx of People, the Most Work Opportunities, and the Hottest Business Growth," August 12, 2018*

- The Las Vegas metro area was identified as one of America's fastest-growing areas in terms of population and economy by *Forbes*. The area ranked #6 out of 25. The 100 most populous metro areas in the U.S. were evaluated on the following criteria: estimated population growth; employment; economic output; wages; home values. *Forbes, "America's Fastest-Growing Cities 2018," February 28, 2018*

Business/Finance Rankings

- According to *Business Insider*, the Las Vegas metro area is a prime place to run a startup or move an existing business to. The area ranked #7. Nearly 190 metro areas were analyzed on overall economic health and investments. Data was based on the 2019 U.S. Census Bureau American Community Survey, the marketing company PitchBook, Bureau of Labor Statistics employment report, and Zillow. Criteria: percentage of change in typical home values and employment rates; quarterly venture capital investment activity; and median household income. *www.businessinsider.com, "The 25 Best Cities to Start a Business-Or Move Your Current One," January 12, 2021*

- The Brookings Institution ranked the nation's largest cities based on income inequality. Las Vegas was ranked #80 (#1 = greatest inequality). Criteria: the "95/20 ratio," a figure representing the income at which a household earns more than 95 percent of all other households, divided by the income at which a household earns more than only 20 percent of all other households. *Brookings Institution, "Household Income Inequality, Largest Cities of 97 Large U.S. Metro Areas, 2014-2016," February 5, 2018*

- The Brookings Institution ranked the 100 largest metro areas in the U.S. based on income inequality. Las Vegas was ranked #86 (#1 = greatest inequality). Criteria: the "95/20 ratio," a figure representing the income at which a household earns more than 95 percent of all other households, divided by the income at which a household earns more than only 20 percent of all other households. *Brookings Institution, "Household Income Inequality, 100 Largest U.S. Metro Areas, 2014-2016," February 5, 2018*

- Las Vegas was identified as one of America's most frugal metro areas by *Coupons.com*. The city ranked #21 out of 25. Criteria: digital coupon usage. *Coupons.com, "America's Most Frugal Cities of 2017," March 22, 2018*

- The Las Vegas metro area appeared on the Milken Institute "2021 Best Performing Cities" list. Rank: #88 out of 200 large metro areas (population over 250,000). Criteria: job growth; wage and salary growth; high-tech output growth; housing affordability; household broadband access. *Milken Institute, "Best-Performing Cities 2021," February 16, 2021*

- *Forbes* ranked the 200 most populous metro areas to determine the nation's "Best Places for Business and Careers." The Las Vegas metro area was ranked #49. Criteria: costs (business and living); job growth (past and projected); income growth; quality of life; educational attainment (college and high school); projected economic growth; cultural and leisure opportunities; workplace tolerance laws; net migration patterns. *Forbes, "The Best Places for Business and Careers 2019: Seattle Still On Top," October 30, 2019*

Culture/Performing Arts Rankings

- Las Vegas was selected as one of "America's Favorite Cities." The city ranked #13 in the "Architecture" category. Respondents to an online survey were asked to rate their favorite place (population over 100,000) in over 65 categories. *Travelandleisure.com, "America's Favorite Cities for Architecture 2016," March 2, 2017*

Dating/Romance Rankings

- Las Vegas was selected as one of America's best cities for singles by the readers of *Travel + Leisure* in their annual "America's Favorite Cities" survey. Criteria included good-looking locals, cool shopping, an active bar scene and hipster-magnet coffee bars. *Travel + Leisure, "Best Cities in America for Singles," July 21, 2017*

- Las Vegas was selected as one of the nation's most romantic cities with 100,000 or more residents by Amazon.com. The city ranked #17 of 20. Criteria: per capita sales of romance novels, relationship books, romantic comedy movies, romantic music, and sexual wellness products. *Amazon.com, "Top 20 Most Romantic Cities in the U.S.," February 1, 2017*

Education Rankings

- Personal finance website *WalletHub* analyzed the 150 largest U.S. metropolitan statistical areas to determine where the most educated Americans are putting their degrees to work. Criteria: education levels; percentage of workers with degrees; education quality and attainment gap; public school quality rankings; quality and enrollment of each metro area's universities. Las Vegas was ranked #120 (#1 = most educated city). *www.WalletHub.com, "Most and Least Educated Cities in America," July 20, 2020*

- Las Vegas was selected as one of America's most literate cities. The city ranked #54 out of the 84 largest U.S. cities. Criteria: number of booksellers; library resources; Internet resources; educational attainment; periodical publishing resources; newspaper circulation. *Central Connecticut State University, "America's Most Literate Cities, 2018," February 2019*

Environmental Rankings

- Las Vegas was highlighted as one of the 25 most ozone-polluted metro areas in the U.S. during 2016 through 2018. The area ranked #9. *American Lung Association, "State of the Air 2020," April 21, 2020*

- Las Vegas was highlighted as one of the 25 metro areas most polluted by short-term particle pollution (24-hour PM 2.5) in the U.S. during 2016 through 2018. The area ranked #25. *American Lung Association, "State of the Air 2020," April 21, 2020*

Food/Drink Rankings

- Las Vegas was identified as one of the cities in America ordering the most vegan food options by GrubHub.com. The city ranked #4 out of 5. Criteria: percentage of vegan, vegetarian and plant-based food orders compared to the overall number of orders. *GrubHub.com, "State of the Plate Report 2020: Top Vegan-Friendly Cities," July 9, 2020*

Health/Fitness Rankings

- For each of the 100 largest cities in the United States, the American Fitness Index®, published by the American College of Sports Medicine and the Anthem Foundation, evaluated community infrastructure and 33 health behaviors including preventive health, levels of chronic disease conditions, pedestrian safety, air quality, and community resources that support physical activity. Las Vegas ranked #88 for "community fitness." *americanfitnessindex.org, "2020 ACSM American Fitness Index Summary Report," July 14, 2020*

- Las Vegas was identified as a "2021 Spring Allergy Capital." The area ranked #9 out of 100. Three groups of factors were used to identify the most challenging cities for people with allergies during the spring season: annual spring pollen levels; over the counter medicine use; number of board-certified allergy specialists. *Asthma and Allergy Foundation of America, "Spring Allergy Capitals 2021," February 23, 2021*

- Las Vegas was identified as a "2021 Fall Allergy Capital." The area ranked #23 out of 100. Three groups of factors were used to identify the most challenging cities for people with allergies during the fall season: annual fall pollen levels; over the counter medicine use; number of board-certified allergy specialists. *Asthma and Allergy Foundation of America, "Fall Allergy Capitals 2021," February 23, 2021*

- Las Vegas was identified as a "2019 Asthma Capital." The area ranked #59 out of the nation's 100 largest metropolitan areas. Criteria: estimated asthma prevalence; crude death rate from asthma; and ER visits due to asthma. Risk factors analyzed but not factored in the rankings: annual pollen score; annual air quality; public smoking laws; number of board-certified asthma specialists; rescue medication use; controller medication use; uninsured rate; poverty rate. *Asthma and Allergy Foundation of America, "Asthma Capitals 2019: The Most Challenging Places to Live With Asthma," May 7, 2019*

Real Estate Rankings

- FitSmallBusiness looked at 50 of the largest metropolitan areas in the U.S. to determine which metro was the best to start a real estate business. Data was compiled from such sources as: Zillow, Trulia, U.S. Census Bureau, and the Bureau of Labor Statistics. Criteria: location; inventory; annual wages; median sales price of homes; days on the market; median price cut percentage; and other factors that would influence real estate professional growth. The Las Vegas metro area ranked #21. *fitsmallbusiness.com, "The Best Cities to Become a Real Estate Agent in 2018," January 30, 2018*

- *WalletHub* compared the most populated U.S. cities to determine which had the best markets for real estate agents. Las Vegas ranked #80 where demand was high and pay was the best. Criteria: sales per agent; annual median wage for real-estate agents; monthly average starting salary for real estate agents; real estate job density and competition; unemployment rate; home turnover rate; housing-market health index; and other relevant metrics. *www.WalletHub.com, "2019's Best Places to Be a Real Estate Agent," April 24, 2019*

- Las Vegas was ranked #194 out of 268 metro areas in terms of housing affordability in 2020 by the National Association of Home Builders (#1 = most affordable). Criteria: the share of homes sold in that area affordable to a family earning the local median income, based on standard mortgage underwriting criteria. *National Association of Home Builders®, NAHB-Wells Fargo Housing Opportunity Index, 4th Quarter 2020*

Safety Rankings

- Allstate ranked the 200 largest cities in America in terms of driver safety. Las Vegas ranked #129. Criteria: internal property damage claims over a two-year period from January 2016 to December 2017. The report helps increase the importance of safety and awareness behind the wheel. *Allstate, "Allstate America's Best Drivers Report, 2019" June 24, 2019*

- The National Insurance Crime Bureau ranked 384 metro areas in the U.S. in terms of per capita rates of vehicle theft. The Las Vegas metro area ranked #30 (#1 = highest rate). Criteria: number of vehicle theft offenses per 100,000 inhabitants in 2019. *National Insurance Crime Bureau, "Hot Spots 2019," July 21, 2020*

Seniors/Retirement Rankings

- From its Best Cities for Successful Aging indexes, the Milken Institute generated rankings for metropolitan areas, weighing data in nine categories—health care, wellness, living arrangements, transportation and convenience, financial characteristics, education, employment, community engagement, and overall livability. The Las Vegas metro area was ranked #77 overall in the large metro area category. *Milken Institute, "Best Cities for Successful Aging, 2017" March 14, 2017*

Women/Minorities Rankings

- *Travel + Leisure* listed the best cities in and around the US for a memorable and fun girls' trip, even on a budget. Whether it is for a special occasion or just to get away, Las Vegas is sure to have something for all the ladies in your tribe. *Travel + Leisure, "25 Girls' Weekend Getaways That Won't Break the Bank," June 8, 2020*

- The *Houston Chronicle* listed the Las Vegas metro area as #15 in top places for young Latinos to live in the U.S. Research was largely based on housing and occupational data from the largest metropolitan areas performed by *Forbes* and NBC Universo. Criteria: percentage of 18-34 year-olds; Latino college grad rates; and diversity. *blog.chron.com, "The 15 Best Big Cities for Latino Millenials," January 26, 2016*

- Personal finance website *WalletHub* compared more than 180 U.S. cities across two key dimensions, "Hispanic Business-Friendliness" and "Hispanic Purchasing Power," to arrive at the most favorable conditions for Hispanic entrepreneurs. Las Vegas was ranked #78 out of 182. Criteria includes: share of Hispanic-Owned Businesses; Hispanic entrepreneurship rate to median annual income of Hispanics; Small Business-Friendliness score; cost of living; and number of Hispanics with at least a bachelor's degree. *WalletHub.com, "2019's Best Cities for Hispanic Entrepreneurs," May 1, 2019*

Miscellaneous Rankings

- *MoveHub* ranked 446 hipster cities across 20 countries, using its *alternative* Hipster Index and Las Vegas came out as #19 among the top 50. Criteria: population over 150,000; number of vintage boutiques; density of tattoo parlors; vegan places to eat; coffee shops; and density of vinyl record stores. *www.movehub.com, "The Hipster Index: Brighton Pips Portland to Global Top Spot," February 20, 2020*

- Las Vegas was selected as a 2020 Digital Cities Survey winner. The city ranked #9 in the large city (500,000 or more population) category. The survey examined and assessed how city governments are utilizing technology to improve transparency, enhance cybersecurity, and respond to the pandemic. Survey questions focused on ten initiatives: cybersecurity, citizen experience, disaster recovery, business intelligence, IT personnel, data governance, collaboration, infrastructure modernization, cloud computing, and mobile applications. *Center for Digital Government, "2020 Digital Cities Survey," November 10, 2020*

- *WalletHub* compared the 150 most populated U.S. cities to determine their operating efficiency. A "Quality of City Services" score was constructed for each city and then divided by the total budget per capita to reveal which were managed the best. Las Vegas ranked #46. Criteria: financial stability; economy; education; safety; health; infrastructure and pollution. *www.WalletHub.com, "2020's Best-& Worst-Run Cities in America," June 29, 2020*

Business Environment

DEMOGRAPHICS

Population Growth

Area	1990 Census	2000 Census	2010 Census	2019* Estimate	Population Growth (%) 1990-2019	Population Growth (%) 2010-2019
City	261,374	478,434	583,756	634,773	142.9	8.7
MSA[1]	741,459	1,375,765	1,951,269	2,182,004	194.3	11.8
U.S.	248,709,873	281,421,906	308,745,538	324,697,795	30.6	5.2

Note: (1) Figures cover the Las Vegas-Henderson-Paradise, NV Metropolitan Statistical Area; (*) 2015-2019 5-year estimated population
Source: U.S. Census Bureau, 1990 Census, Census 2000, Census 2010, 2015-2019 American Community Survey 5-Year Estimates

Household Size

Area	Persons in Household (%) One	Two	Three	Four	Five	Six	Seven or More	Average Household Size
City	30.6	31.7	15.4	11.6	6.3	2.8	1.7	2.70
MSA[1]	28.5	32.8	15.3	12.3	6.5	2.7	1.8	2.80
U.S.	27.9	33.9	15.6	12.9	6.0	2.3	1.4	2.60

Note: (1) Figures cover the Las Vegas-Henderson-Paradise, NV Metropolitan Statistical Area
Source: U.S. Census Bureau, 2015-2019 American Community Survey 5-Year Estimates

Race

Area	White Alone[2] (%)	Black Alone[2] (%)	Asian Alone[2] (%)	AIAN[3] Alone[2] (%)	NHOPI[4] Alone[2] (%)	Other Race Alone[2] (%)	Two or More Races (%)
City	61.9	12.2	6.9	0.9	0.8	12.1	5.2
MSA[1]	60.2	11.7	9.7	0.9	0.8	11.5	5.4
U.S.	72.5	12.7	5.5	0.8	0.2	4.9	3.3

Note: (1) Figures cover the Las Vegas-Henderson-Paradise, NV Metropolitan Statistical Area; (2) Alone is defined as not being in combination with one or more other races; (3) American Indian and Alaska Native; (4) Native Hawaiian and Other Pacific Islander
Source: U.S. Census Bureau, 2015-2019 American Community Survey 5-Year Estimates

Hispanic or Latino Origin

Area	Total (%)	Mexican (%)	Puerto Rican (%)	Cuban (%)	Other (%)
City	33.1	24.7	1.2	1.3	5.9
MSA[1]	31.1	23.1	1.1	1.4	5.6
U.S.	18.0	11.2	1.7	0.7	4.3

Note: Persons of Hispanic or Latino origin can be of any race; (1) Figures cover the Las Vegas-Henderson-Paradise, NV Metropolitan Statistical Area
Source: U.S. Census Bureau, 2015-2019 American Community Survey 5-Year Estimates

Ancestry

Area	German	Irish	English	American	Italian	Polish	French[2]	Scottish	Dutch
City	8.9	7.7	5.6	3.4	5.3	2.1	1.8	1.3	0.8
MSA[1]	8.7	7.2	5.6	3.4	5.0	1.9	1.7	1.2	0.7
U.S.	13.3	9.7	7.2	6.2	5.1	2.8	2.3	1.7	1.2

Note: Figures are the percentage of the total population reporting a particular ancestry. The nine most commonly reported ancestries in the U.S. are shown. Figures include multiple ancestries (e.g. if a person reported being Irish and Italian, they were included in both columns); (1) Figures cover the Las Vegas-Henderson-Paradise, NV Metropolitan Statistical Area; (2) Excludes Basque
Source: U.S. Census Bureau, 2015-2019 American Community Survey 5-Year Estimates

Foreign-born Population

Area	Percent of Population Born in — Any Foreign Country	Asia	Mexico	Europe	Caribbean	Central America[2]	South America	Africa	Canada
City	21.0	5.3	9.2	1.6	1.1	2.3	0.8	0.4	0.4
MSA[1]	22.2	7.2	8.2	1.6	1.1	2.0	0.9	0.8	0.4
U.S.	13.6	4.2	3.5	1.5	1.3	1.1	1.0	0.7	0.2

Note: (1) Figures cover the Las Vegas-Henderson-Paradise, NV Metropolitan Statistical Area; (2) Excludes Mexico.
Source: U.S. Census Bureau, 2015-2019 American Community Survey 5-Year Estimates

Marital Status

Area	Never Married	Now Married[2]	Separated	Widowed	Divorced
City	34.9	43.3	2.3	5.5	14.1
MSA[1]	34.7	43.9	2.3	5.2	13.9
U.S.	33.4	48.1	1.9	5.8	10.9

Note: Figures are percentages and cover the population 15 years of age and older; (1) Figures cover the Las Vegas-Henderson-Paradise, NV Metropolitan Statistical Area; (2) Excludes separated
Source: U.S. Census Bureau, 2015-2019 American Community Survey 5-Year Estimates

Disability by Age

Area	All Ages	Under 18 Years Old	18 to 64 Years Old	65 Years and Over
City	12.9	3.7	10.8	36.3
MSA[1]	12.1	3.8	9.9	34.8
U.S.	12.6	4.2	10.3	34.5

Note: Figures show percent of the civilian noninstitutionalized population that reported having a disability. Disability status is determined from six types of difficulty: vision, hearing, cognitive, ambulatory, self-care, and independent living. For children under 5 years old, hearing and vision difficulty are used to determine disability status. For children between the ages of 5 and 14, disability status is determined from hearing, vision, cognitive, ambulatory, and self-care difficulties. For people aged 15 years and older, they are considered to have a disability if they have difficulty with any one of the six difficulty types; Note: (1) Figures cover the Las Vegas-Henderson-Paradise, NV Metropolitan Statistical Area
Source: U.S. Census Bureau, 2015-2019 American Community Survey 5-Year Estimates

Age

Area	Percent of Population									Median Age
	Under Age 5	Age 5–19	Age 20–34	Age 35–44	Age 45–54	Age 55–64	Age 65–74	Age 75–84	Age 85+	
City	6.4	19.5	20.2	13.3	13.4	12.1	9.1	4.3	1.5	37.8
MSA[1]	6.3	19.3	21.1	13.8	13.3	11.7	8.9	4.2	1.3	37.3
U.S.	6.1	19.1	20.7	12.6	13.0	12.9	9.1	4.6	1.9	38.1

Note: (1) Figures cover the Las Vegas-Henderson-Paradise, NV Metropolitan Statistical Area
Source: U.S. Census Bureau, 2015-2019 American Community Survey 5-Year Estimates

Gender

Area	Males	Females	Males per 100 Females
City	316,556	318,217	99.5
MSA[1]	1,089,228	1,092,776	99.7
U.S.	159,886,919	164,810,876	97.0

Note: (1) Figures cover the Las Vegas-Henderson-Paradise, NV Metropolitan Statistical Area
Source: U.S. Census Bureau, 2015-2019 American Community Survey 5-Year Estimates

Religious Groups by Family

Area	Catholic	Baptist	Non-Den.	Methodist[2]	Lutheran	LDS[3]	Pente-costal	Presby-terian[4]	Muslim[5]	Judaism
MSA[1]	18.1	3.0	3.1	0.4	0.7	6.4	1.5	0.2	0.1	0.3
U.S.	19.1	9.3	4.0	4.0	2.3	2.0	1.9	1.6	0.8	0.7

Note: Figures are the number of adherents as a percentage of the total population; (1) Figures cover the Las Vegas-Henderson-Paradise, NV Metropolitan Statistical Area; (2) Methodist/Pietist; (3) Latter Day Saints; (4) Reformed; (5) Figures are estimates
Source: Association of Statisticians of American Religious Bodies, 2010 U.S. Religion Census: Religious Congregations & Membership Study

Religious Groups by Tradition

Area	Catholic	Evangelical Protestant	Mainline Protestant	Other Tradition	Black Protestant	Orthodox
MSA[1]	18.1	7.7	1.4	7.6	0.4	0.4
U.S.	19.1	16.2	7.3	4.3	1.6	0.3

Note: Figures are the number of adherents as a percentage of the total population; (1) Figures cover the Las Vegas-Henderson-Paradise, NV Metropolitan Statistical Area
Source: Association of Statisticians of American Religious Bodies, 2010 U.S. Religion Census: Religious Congregations & Membership Study

ECONOMY

Gross Metropolitan Product

Area	2017	2018	2019	2020	Rank[2]
MSA[1]	112.8	119.1	124.1	130.3	36

Note: Figures are in billions of dollars; (1) Figures cover the Las Vegas-Henderson-Paradise, NV Metropolitan Statistical Area; (2) Rank is based on 2018 data and ranges from 1 to 381
Source: U.S. Conference of Mayors, U.S. Metro Economies: GMP & Employment 2018-2020, September 2019

Economic Growth

Area	2015-17 (%)	2018 (%)	2019 (%)	2020 (%)	Rank[2]
MSA[1]	1.5	3.1	2.3	2.7	182
U.S.	1.9	2.9	2.3	2.1	–

Note: Figures are real gross metropolitan product (GMP) growth rates and represent average annual percent change; (1) Figures cover the Las Vegas-Henderson-Paradise, NV Metropolitan Statistical Area; (2) Rank is based on 2017 2-year average annual percent change and ranges from 1 to 381
Source: U.S. Conference of Mayors, U.S. Metro Economies: GMP & Employment 2018-2020, September 2019

Metropolitan Area Exports

Area	2014	2015	2016	2017	2018	2019	Rank[2]
MSA[1]	2,509.7	2,916.2	2,312.3	2,710.6	2,240.6	2,430.8	90

Note: Figures are in millions of dollars; (1) Figures cover the Las Vegas-Henderson-Paradise, NV Metropolitan Statistical Area; (2) Rank is based on 2019 data and ranges from 1 to 386
Source: U.S. Department of Commerce, International Trade Administration, Office of Trade and Economic Analysis, Industry and Analysis, Exports by Metropolitan Area, data extracted March 24, 2021

Building Permits

Area	Single-Family			Multi-Family			Total		
	2018	2019	Pct. Chg.	2018	2019	Pct. Chg.	2018	2019	Pct. Chg.
City	1,794	1,885	5.1	179	780	335.8	1,973	2,665	35.1
MSA[1]	9,721	10,042	3.3	2,323	3,861	66.2	12,044	13,903	15.4
U.S.	855,300	862,100	0.7	473,500	523,900	10.6	1,328,800	1,386,000	4.3

Note: (1) Figures cover the Las Vegas-Henderson-Paradise, NV Metropolitan Statistical Area; Figures represent new, privately-owned housing units authorized (unadjusted data); All permit data are based on estimates with imputation
Source: U.S. Census Bureau, Manufacturing, Mining, and Construction Statistics, Building Permits, 2018, 2019

Bankruptcy Filings

Area	Business Filings			Nonbusiness Filings		
	2019	2020	% Chg.	2019	2020	% Chg.
Clark County	228	204	-10.5	8,184	6,529	-20.2
U.S.	22,780	21,655	-4.9	752,160	522,808	-30.5

Note: Business filings include Chapter 7, Chapter 9, Chapter 11, Chapter 12, Chapter 13, Chapter 15, and Section 304; Nonbusiness filings include Chapter 7, Chapter 11, and Chapter 13
Source: Administrative Office of the U.S. Courts, Business and Nonbusiness Bankruptcy, County Cases Commenced by Chapter of the Bankruptcy Code, During the 12-Month Period Ending December 31, 2019 and Business and Nonbusiness Bankruptcy, County Cases Commenced by Chapter of the Bankruptcy Code, During the 12-Month Period Ending December 31, 2020

Housing Vacancy Rates

Area	Gross Vacancy Rate[2] (%)			Year-Round Vacancy Rate[3] (%)			Rental Vacancy Rate[4] (%)			Homeowner Vacancy Rate[5] (%)		
	2018	2019	2020	2018	2019	2020	2018	2019	2020	2018	2019	2020
MSA[1]	11.4	10.2	7.8	10.4	9.5	7.1	6.8	5.5	5.0	0.9	2.0	1.1
U.S.	12.3	12.0	10.6	9.7	9.5	8.2	6.9	6.7	6.3	1.5	1.4	1.0

Note: (1) Figures cover the Las Vegas-Henderson-Paradise, NV Metropolitan Statistical Area; (2) The percentage of the total housing inventory that is vacant; (3) The percentage of the housing inventory (excluding seasonal units) that is year-round vacant; (4) The percentage of rental inventory that is vacant for rent; (5) The percentage of homeowner inventory that is vacant for sale
Source: U.S. Census Bureau, Housing Vacancies and Homeownership Annual Statistics: 2018, 2019, 2020

INCOME

Income

Area	Per Capita ($)	Median Household ($)	Average Household ($)
City	30,761	56,354	79,657
MSA[1]	30,704	59,340	80,762
U.S.	34,103	62,843	88,607

Note: (1) Figures cover the Las Vegas-Henderson-Paradise, NV Metropolitan Statistical Area
Source: U.S. Census Bureau, 2015-2019 American Community Survey 5-Year Estimates

Household Income Distribution

Area	Percent of Households Earning							
	Under $15,000	$15,000 -$24,999	$25,000 -$34,999	$35,000 -$49,999	$50,000 -$74,999	$75,000 -$99,999	$100,000 -$149,999	$150,000 and up
City	11.8	9.5	9.7	13.8	17.5	13.0	14.0	10.7
MSA[1]	10.2	8.8	9.7	13.9	18.6	13.5	14.5	11.0
U.S.	10.3	8.9	8.9	12.3	17.2	12.7	15.1	14.5

Note: (1) Figures cover the Las Vegas-Henderson-Paradise, NV Metropolitan Statistical Area
Source: U.S. Census Bureau, 2015-2019 American Community Survey 5-Year Estimates

Poverty Rate

Area	All Ages	Under 18 Years Old	18 to 64 Years Old	65 Years and Over
City	15.3	21.3	14.1	10.6
MSA[1]	13.7	19.3	12.6	9.2
U.S.	13.4	18.5	12.6	9.3

Note: Figures are percentage of people whose income during the past 12 months was below the poverty level;
(1) Figures cover the Las Vegas-Henderson-Paradise, NV Metropolitan Statistical Area
Source: U.S. Census Bureau, 2015-2019 American Community Survey 5-Year Estimates

CITY FINANCES

City Government Finances

Component	2017 ($000)	2017 ($ per capita)
Total Revenues	851,665	1,365
Total Expenditures	796,547	1,277
Debt Outstanding	797,520	1,279
Cash and Securities[1]	752,353	1,206

Note: (1) Cash and security holdings of a government at the close of its fiscal year,
including those of its dependent agencies, utilities, and liquor stores.
Source: U.S. Census Bureau, State & Local Government Finances 2017

City Government Revenue by Source

Source	2017 ($000)	2017 ($ per capita)	2017 (%)
General Revenue			
From Federal Government	24,297	39	2.9
From State Government	296,381	475	34.8
From Local Governments	79,097	127	9.3
Taxes			
Property	114,519	184	13.4
Sales and Gross Receipts	66,119	106	7.8
Personal Income	0	0	0.0
Corporate Income	0	0	0.0
Motor Vehicle License	0	0	0.0
Other Taxes	44,044	71	5.2
Current Charges	156,472	251	18.4
Liquor Store	0	0	0.0
Utility	87	0	0.0
Employee Retirement	0	0	0.0

Source: U.S. Census Bureau, State & Local Government Finances 2017

City Government Expenditures by Function

Function	2017 ($000)	2017 ($ per capita)	2017 (%)
General Direct Expenditures			
Air Transportation	0	0	0.0
Corrections	62,596	100	7.9
Education	0	0	0.0
Employment Security Administration	0	0	0.0
Financial Administration	8,638	13	1.1
Fire Protection	138,896	222	17.4
General Public Buildings	26,883	43	3.4
Governmental Administration, Other	31,660	50	4.0
Health	4,251	6	0.5
Highways	96,005	153	12.1
Hospitals	0	0	0.0
Housing and Community Development	17,144	27	2.2
Interest on General Debt	34,146	54	4.3
Judicial and Legal	31,702	50	4.0
Libraries	0	0	0.0
Parking	7,936	12	1.0
Parks and Recreation	62,896	100	7.9
Police Protection	10,840	17	1.4
Public Welfare	8	< 1	< 0.1
Sewerage	55,940	89	7.0
Solid Waste Management	5,460	8	0.7
Veterans' Services	0	0	0.0
Liquor Store	0	0	0.0
Utility	0	0	0.0
Employee Retirement	0	0	0.0

Source: U.S. Census Bureau, State & Local Government Finances 2017

EMPLOYMENT

Labor Force and Employment

Area	Civilian Labor Force			Workers Employed		
	Dec. 2019	Dec. 2020	% Chg.	Dec. 2019	Dec. 2020	% Chg.
City	316,225	301,287	-4.7	305,003	270,332	-11.4
MSA[1]	1,136,500	1,084,944	-4.5	1,096,609	971,954	-11.4
U.S.	164,007,000	160,017,000	-2.4	158,504,000	149,613,000	-5.6

Note: Data is not seasonally adjusted and covers workers 16 years of age and older; (1) Figures cover the Las Vegas-Henderson-Paradise, NV Metropolitan Statistical Area
Source: Bureau of Labor Statistics, Local Area Unemployment Statistics

Unemployment Rate

Area	2020											
	Jan.	Feb.	Mar.	Apr.	May	Jun.	Jul.	Aug.	Sep.	Oct.	Nov.	Dec.
City	4.0	3.9	7.3	32.1	27.1	16.7	15.8	14.9	13.9	13.5	11.7	10.3
MSA[1]	3.9	3.9	7.2	34.0	28.8	17.8	16.6	15.6	14.6	13.7	11.8	10.4
U.S.	4.0	3.8	4.5	14.4	13.0	11.2	10.5	8.5	7.7	6.6	6.4	6.5

Note: Data is not seasonally adjusted and covers workers 16 years of age and older; (1) Figures cover the Las Vegas-Henderson-Paradise, NV Metropolitan Statistical Area
Source: Bureau of Labor Statistics, Local Area Unemployment Statistics

Average Wages

Occupation	$/Hr.	Occupation	$/Hr.
Accountants and Auditors	33.30	Maintenance and Repair Workers	22.80
Automotive Mechanics	21.00	Marketing Managers	65.60
Bookkeepers	20.40	Network and Computer Systems Admin.	42.10
Carpenters	29.30	Nurses, Licensed Practical	28.50
Cashiers	12.00	Nurses, Registered	44.60
Computer Programmers	42.00	Nursing Assistants	16.80
Computer Systems Analysts	43.60	Office Clerks, General	18.30
Computer User Support Specialists	24.90	Physical Therapists	54.40
Construction Laborers	18.00	Physicians	112.40
Cooks, Restaurant	15.80	Plumbers, Pipefitters and Steamfitters	29.50
Customer Service Representatives	17.00	Police and Sheriff's Patrol Officers	38.00
Dentists	98.50	Postal Service Mail Carriers	25.70
Electricians	33.90	Real Estate Sales Agents	33.50
Engineers, Electrical	40.80	Retail Salespersons	14.30
Fast Food and Counter Workers	11.00	Sales Representatives, Technical/Scientific	55.80
Financial Managers	57.60	Secretaries, Exc. Legal/Medical/Executive	19.30
First-Line Supervisors of Office Workers	26.00	Security Guards	15.70
General and Operations Managers	62.10	Surgeons	n/a
Hairdressers/Cosmetologists	10.30	Teacher Assistants, Exc. Postsecondary*	15.80
Home Health and Personal Care Aides	12.50	Teachers, Secondary School, Exc. Sp. Ed.*	28.10
Janitors and Cleaners	15.20	Telemarketers	12.80
Landscaping/Groundskeeping Workers	15.40	Truck Drivers, Heavy/Tractor-Trailer	23.40
Lawyers	63.40	Truck Drivers, Light/Delivery Services	17.60
Maids and Housekeeping Cleaners	15.90	Waiters and Waitresses	13.20

Note: Wage data covers the Las Vegas-Henderson-Paradise, NV Metropolitan Statistical Area; (*) Hourly wages were calculated from annual wage data based on a 40 hour work week; n/a not available.
Source: Bureau of Labor Statistics, Metro Area Occupational Employment & Wage Estimates, May 2020

Employment by Industry

Sector	MSA[1]		U.S.
	Number of Employees	Percent of Total	Percent of Total
Construction	63,500	7.0	5.1
Education and Health Services	104,300	11.4	16.3
Financial Activities	53,000	5.8	6.1
Government	102,600	11.3	15.2
Information	9,400	1.0	1.9
Leisure and Hospitality	195,500	21.4	9.0
Manufacturing	24,000	2.6	8.5
Mining and Logging	400	<0.1	0.4
Other Services	27,000	3.0	3.8
Professional and Business Services	131,200	14.4	14.4
Retail Trade	113,600	12.5	10.9
Transportation, Warehousing, and Utilities	63,800	7.0	4.6
Wholesale Trade	23,200	2.5	3.9

Note: Figures are non-farm employment as of December 2020. Figures are not seasonally adjusted and include workers 16 years of age and older; (1) Figures cover the Las Vegas-Henderson-Paradise, NV Metropolitan Statistical Area
Source: Bureau of Labor Statistics, Current Employment Statistics, Employment, Hours, and Earnings

Employment by Occupation

Occupation Classification	City (%)	MSA[1] (%)	U.S. (%)
Management, Business, Science, and Arts	29.8	28.7	38.5
Natural Resources, Construction, and Maintenance	9.0	8.2	8.9
Production, Transportation, and Material Moving	10.5	11.2	13.2
Sales and Office	23.8	23.8	21.6
Service	27.0	28.1	17.8

Note: Figures cover employed civilians 16 years of age and older; (1) Figures cover the Las Vegas-Henderson-Paradise, NV Metropolitan Statistical Area
Source: U.S. Census Bureau, 2015-2019 American Community Survey 5-Year Estimates

Occupations with Greatest Projected Employment Growth: 2020 – 2022

Occupation[1]	2020 Employment	2022 Projected Employment	Numeric Employment Change	Percent Employment Change
Waiters and Waitresses	20,720	32,720	12,000	57.9
Combined Food Preparation and Serving Workers, Including Fast Food	25,450	36,790	11,340	44.6
Gaming Dealers	10,070	18,250	8,180	81.2
Maids and Housekeeping Cleaners	15,980	23,820	7,840	49.1
Cooks, Restaurant	12,590	20,120	7,530	59.8
Retail Salespersons	34,680	42,100	7,420	21.4
Janitors and Cleaners, Except Maids and Housekeeping Cleaners	21,230	28,560	7,330	34.5
Laborers and Freight, Stock, and Material Movers, Hand	36,120	41,930	5,810	16.1
Security Guards	15,710	20,810	5,100	32.5
Bartenders	8,290	13,260	4,970	60.0

Note: Projections cover Nevada; (1) Sorted by numeric employment change
Source: www.projectionscentral.com, State Occupational Projections, 2020–2022 Short-Term Projections

Fastest-Growing Occupations: 2020 – 2022

Occupation[1]	2020 Employment	2022 Projected Employment	Numeric Employment Change	Percent Employment Change
Bus Drivers, Transit and Intercity	940	2,270	1,330	141.5
Athletes and Sports Competitors	50	100	50	100.0
Entertainment Attendants and Related Workers, All Other	150	280	130	86.7
Gaming Service Workers, All Other	1,510	2,760	1,250	82.8
Gaming Surveillance Officers and Gaming Investigators	390	710	320	82.1
Gaming Cage Workers	1,320	2,400	1,080	81.8
Gaming Dealers	10,070	18,250	8,180	81.2
Gaming and Sports Book Writers and Runners	820	1,480	660	80.5
Baggage Porters and Bellhops	1,040	1,860	820	78.8
Agents and Business Managers of Artists, Performers, and Athletes	140	250	110	78.6

Note: Projections cover Nevada; (1) Sorted by percent employment change and excludes occupations with numeric employment change less than 50
Source: www.projectionscentral.com, State Occupational Projections, 2020–2022 Short-Term Projections

TAXES

State Corporate Income Tax Rates

State	Tax Rate (%)	Income Brackets ($)	Num. of Brackets	Financial Institution Tax Rate (%)[a]	Federal Income Tax Ded.
Nevada	None	–		–	–

Note: Tax rates as of January 1, 2021; (a) Rates listed are the corporate income tax rate applied to financial institutions or excise taxes based on income. Some states have other taxes based upon the value of deposits or shares.
Source: Federation of Tax Administrators, State Corporate Income Tax Rates, January 1, 2021

State Individual Income Tax Rates

State	Tax Rate (%)	Income Brackets ($)	Personal Exemptions ($)			Standard Ded. ($)	
			Single	Married	Depend.	Single	Married
Nevada				– No state income tax –			

Note: Tax rates as of January 1, 2021; Local- and county-level taxes are not included
Source: Federation of Tax Administrators, State Individual Income Tax Rates, January 1, 2021

Various State Sales and Excise Tax Rates

State	State Sales Tax (%)	Gasoline[1] (¢/gal.)	Cigarette[2] ($/pack)	Spirits[3] ($/gal.)	Wine[4] ($/gal.)	Beer[5] ($/gal.)	Recreational Marijuana (%)
Nevada	6.85	50.48	1.8	3.6	0.7	0.16	(j)

Note: All tax rates as of January 1, 2021; (1) The American Petroleum Institute has developed a methodology for determining the average tax rate on a gallon of fuel. Rates may include any of the following: excise taxes, environmental fees, storage tank fees, other fees or taxes, general sales tax, and local taxes; (2) The federal excise tax of $1.0066 per pack and local taxes are not included; (3) Rates are those applicable to off-premise sales of 40% alcohol by volume (a.b.v.) distilled spirits in 750ml containers. Local excise taxes are excluded; (4) Rates are those applicable to off-premise sales of 11% a.b.v. non-carbonated wine in 750ml containers; (5) Rates are those applicable to off-premise sales of 4.7% a.b.v. beer in 12 ounce containers; (j) 15% excise tax (fair market value at wholesale); 10% excise tax (retail price)
Source: Tax Foundation, 2021 Facts & Figures: How Does Your State Compare?

State Business Tax Climate Index Rankings

State	Overall Rank	Corporate Tax Rank	Individual Income Tax Rank	Sales Tax Rank	Property Tax Rank	Unemployment Insurance Tax Rank
Nevada	7	25	5	44	5	47

Note: The index is a measure of how each state's tax laws affect economic performance. The lower the rank, the more favorable a state's tax system is for business. States without a given tax are given a ranking of 1. The scores/rankings for the District of Columbia do not affect other states. The 2021 index represents the tax climate as of July 1, 2020.
Source: Tax Foundation, State Business Tax Climate Index 2021

TRANSPORTATION

Means of Transportation to Work

Area	Car/Truck/Van Drove Alone	Car/Truck/Van Car-pooled	Public Transportation Bus	Public Transportation Subway	Public Transportation Railroad	Bicycle	Walked	Other Means	Worked at Home
City	78.0	9.8	3.4	0.0	0.0	0.2	1.5	2.8	4.2
MSA[1]	78.8	9.8	3.3	0.0	0.0	0.3	1.5	2.2	4.2
U.S.	76.3	9.0	2.4	1.9	0.6	0.5	2.7	1.4	5.2

Note: Figures are percentages and cover workers 16 years of age and older; (1) Figures cover the Las Vegas-Henderson-Paradise, NV Metropolitan Statistical Area
Source: U.S. Census Bureau, 2015-2019 American Community Survey 5-Year Estimates

Travel Time to Work

Area	Less Than 10 Minutes	10 to 19 Minutes	20 to 29 Minutes	30 to 44 Minutes	45 to 59 Minutes	60 to 89 Minutes	90 Minutes or More
City	6.9	23.9	29.3	28.7	6.4	2.7	2.0
MSA[1]	7.4	27.5	29.0	26.1	5.4	2.7	1.9
U.S.	12.2	28.4	20.8	20.8	8.3	6.4	2.9

Note: Note: Figures are percentages and include workers 16 years old and over; (1) Figures cover the Las Vegas-Henderson-Paradise, NV Metropolitan Statistical Area
Source: U.S. Census Bureau, 2015-2019 American Community Survey 5-Year Estimates

Key Congestion Measures

Measure	1982	1992	2002	2012	2017
Annual Hours of Delay, Total (000)	2,900	15,864	41,594	57,732	67,761
Annual Hours of Delay, Per Auto Commuter	12	32	43	46	51
Annual Congestion Cost, Total (million $)	22	169	566	1,037	1,258
Annual Congestion Cost, Per Auto Commuter ($)	90	336	687	747	851

Note: Covers the Las Vegas-Henderson NV urban area
Source: Texas A&M Transportation Institute, 2019 Urban Mobility Report

Freeway Travel Time Index

Measure	1982	1987	1992	1997	2002	2007	2012	2017
Urban Area Index[1]	1.07	1.13	1.20	1.23	1.26	1.29	1.25	1.26
Urban Area Rank[1,2]	35	21	15	15	18	15	23	23

Note: Freeway Travel Time Index—the ratio of travel time in the peak period to the travel time at free-flow conditions. For example, a value of 1.30 indicates a 20-minute free-flow trip takes 26 minutes in the peak (20 minutes x 1.30 = 26 minutes); (1) Covers the Las Vegas-Henderson NV urban area; (2) Rank is based on 101 larger urban areas (#1 = highest travel time index)
Source: Texas A&M Transportation Institute, 2019 Urban Mobility Report

Public Transportation

Agency Name / Mode of Transportation	Vehicles Operated in Maximum Service[1]	Annual Unlinked Passenger Trips[2] (in thous.)	Annual Passenger Miles[3] (in thous.)
Regional Transportation Commission of Southern Nevada (RTC)			
Bus (purchased transportation)	336	64,473.6	249,356.5
Demand Response (purchased transportation)	371	1,347.6	14,494.1

Note: (1) Number of revenue vehicles operated by the given mode and type of service to meet the annual maximum service requirement. This is the revenue vehicle count during the peak season of the year; on the week and day that maximum service is provided. Vehicles operated in maximum service (VOMS) exclude atypical days and one-time special events; (2) Number of passengers who boarded public transportation vehicles. Passengers are counted each time they board a vehicle no matter how many vehicles they use to travel from their origin to their destination. (3) Sum of the distances ridden by all passengers during the entire fiscal year.
Source: Federal Transit Administration, National Transit Database, 2019

Air Transportation

Airport Name and Code / Type of Service	Passenger Airlines[1]	Passenger Enplanements	Freight Carriers[2]	Freight (lbs)
McCarran International (LAS)				
Domestic service (U.S. carriers - 2020)	25	10,216,654	16	109,420,410
International service (U.S. carriers - 2019)	7	22,481	3	625,318

Note: (1) Includes all U.S.-based major, minor and commuter airlines that carried at least one passenger during the year; (2) Includes all U.S.-based airlines and freight carriers that transported at least one pound of freight during the year.
Source: Bureau of Transportation Statistics, The Intermodal Transportation Database, Air Carriers: T-100 Domestic Market (U.S. Carriers), 2020; Bureau of Transportation Statistics, The Intermodal Transportation Database, Air Carriers: T-100 International Market (U.S. Carriers), 2019

BUSINESSES

Major Business Headquarters

Company Name	Industry	Rankings	
		Fortune[1]	Forbes[2]
Caesars Holdings	Hotels, Casinos, Resorts	363	-
Las Vegas Sands	Hotels, Casinos, Resorts	235	-
MGM Resorts International	Hotels, Casinos, Resorts	249	-
Wynn Resorts	Hotels, Casinos, Resorts	454	-

Note: (1) Companies that produce a 10-K are ranked 1 to 500 based on 2019 revenue; (2) All private companies with at least $2 billion in annual revenue through the end of their most current fiscal year are ranked 1 to 219; companies listed are headquartered in the city; dashes indicate no ranking
Source: Fortune, "Fortune 500," June/July 2020; Forbes, "America's Largest Private Companies," 2020

Fastest-Growing Businesses

According to *Inc.*, Las Vegas is home to six of America's 500 fastest-growing private companies: **POP Fit Clothing** (#53); **Hyperion Partners** (#143); **Langis** (#213); **Safe Life Defense** (#282); **Foodie Fit** (#340); **Ascent Multifamily Accounting** (#374). Criteria: must be an independent, privately-held, for-profit, U.S. corporation, proprietorship or partnership as of December 31, 2019; revenues must be at least $100,000 in 2016 and $2 million in 2019; must have four-year operating/sales history. *Inc., "America's 500 Fastest-Growing Private Companies," 2020*

Living Environment

COST OF LIVING

Cost of Living Index

Composite Index	Groceries	Housing	Utilities	Trans-portation	Health Care	Misc. Goods/Services
104.9	104.4	110.2	99.2	107.9	95.0	103.0

Note: The Cost of Living Index measures regional differences in the cost of consumer goods and services, excluding taxes and non-consumer expenditures, for professional and managerial households in the top income quintile. It is based on more than 50,000 prices covering almost 60 different items for which prices are collected three times a year by chambers of commerce, economic development organizations or university applied economic centers in each participating urban area. The numbers shown should be read as a percentage above or below the national average of 100. For example, a value of 115.4 in the groceries column indicates that grocery prices are 15.4% higher than the national average. Small differences in the index numbers should not be interpreted as significant; Figures cover the Las Vegas NV urban area.
Source: The Council for Community and Economic Research, Cost of Living Index, 2020

Grocery Prices

Area[1]	T-Bone Steak ($/pound)	Frying Chicken ($/pound)	Whole Milk ($/half gal.)	Eggs ($/dozen)	Orange Juice ($/64 oz.)	Coffee ($/11.5 oz.)
City[2]	10.89	1.35	2.46	2.07	3.99	4.69
Avg.	11.78	1.39	2.05	1.47	3.57	4.34
Min.	8.03	0.94	1.03	0.74	2.94	3.02
Max.	15.86	2.65	4.31	3.77	5.44	8.69

Note: (1) Values for the local area are compared with the average, minimum and maximum values for all 284 areas in the Cost of Living Index; (2) Figures cover the Las Vegas NV urban area; **T-Bone Steak** (price per pound); **Frying Chicken** (price per pound, whole fryer); **Whole Milk** (half gallon carton); **Eggs** (price per dozen, Grade A, large); **Orange Juice** (64 oz. Tropicana or Florida Natural); **Coffee** (11.5 oz. can, vacuum-packed, Maxwell House, Hills Bros, or Folgers).
Source: The Council for Community and Economic Research, Cost of Living Index, 2020

Housing and Utility Costs

Area[1]	New Home Price ($)	Apartment Rent ($/month)	All Electric ($/month)	Part Electric ($/month)	Other Energy ($/month)	Telephone ($/month)
City[2]	412,949	1,205	-	120.44	50.07	175.30
Avg.	368,594	1,168	170.86	100.47	65.28	184.30
Min.	190,567	502	91.58	31.42	26.08	169.60
Max.	2,227,806	4,738	470.38	280.31	280.06	206.50

Note: (1) Values for the local area are compared with the average, minimum and maximum values for all 284 areas in the Cost of Living Index; (2) Figures cover the Las Vegas NV urban area; **New Home Price** (2,400 sf living area, 8,000 sf lot, in urban area with full utilities); **Apartment Rent** (950 sf 2 bedroom/1.5 or 2 bath, unfurnished, excluding all utilities except water); **All Electric** (average monthly cost for an all-electric home); **Part Electric** (average monthly cost for a part-electric home); **Other Energy** (average monthly cost for natural gas, fuel oil, coal, wood, and any other forms of energy except electricity); **Telephone** (price includes the base monthly rate plus taxes and fees for three lines of mobile phone service).
Source: The Council for Community and Economic Research, Cost of Living Index, 2020

Health Care, Transportation, and Other Costs

Area[1]	Doctor ($/visit)	Dentist ($/visit)	Optometrist ($/visit)	Gasoline ($/gallon)	Beauty Salon ($/visit)	Men's Shirt ($)
City[2]	106.13	96.98	105.92	2.36	46.67	29.07
Avg.	115.44	99.32	108.10	2.21	39.27	31.37
Min.	36.68	59.00	51.36	1.71	19.00	11.00
Max.	219.00	153.10	250.97	3.46	82.05	58.33

Note: (1) Values for the local area are compared with the average, minimum and maximum values for all 284 areas in the Cost of Living Index; (2) Figures cover the Las Vegas NV urban area; **Doctor** (general practitioners routine exam of an established patient); **Dentist** (adult teeth cleaning and periodic oral examination); **Optometrist** (full vision eye exam for established adult patient); **Gasoline** (one gallon regular unleaded, national brand, including all taxes, cash price at self-service pump if available); **Beauty Salon** (woman's shampoo, trim, and blow-dry); **Men's Shirt** (cotton/polyester dress shirt, pinpoint weave, long sleeves).
Source: The Council for Community and Economic Research, Cost of Living Index, 2020

HOUSING

Homeownership Rate

Area	2012 (%)	2013 (%)	2014 (%)	2015 (%)	2016 (%)	2017 (%)	2018 (%)	2019 (%)	2020 (%)
MSA[1]	52.6	52.8	53.2	52.1	51.3	54.4	58.1	56.0	57.3
U.S.	65.4	65.1	64.5	63.7	63.4	63.9	64.4	64.6	66.6

Note: (1) Figures cover the Las Vegas-Henderson-Paradise, NV Metropolitan Statistical Area
Source: U.S. Census Bureau, Housing Vacancies and Homeownership Annual Statistics: 2012-2020

House Price Index (HPI)

Area	National Ranking[2]	Quarterly Change (%)	One-Year Change (%)	Five-Year Change (%)	Since 1991Q1 (%)
MSA[1]	171	1.70	5.46	50.47	163.25
U.S.[3]	–	3.81	10.77	38.99	205.12

Note: The HPI is a weighted repeat sales index. It measures average price changes in repeat sales or refinancings on the same properties. This information is obtained by reviewing repeat mortgage transactions on single-family properties whose mortgages have been purchased or securitized by Fannie Mae or Freddie Mac since January 1975; (1) Figures cover the Las Vegas-Henderson-Paradise, NV Metropolitan Statistical Area; (2) Rankings are based on annual percentage change for all metro areas containing at least 15,000 transactions over the last 10 years and ranges from 1 to 253; (3) figures based on a weighted average of Census Division estimates using a seasonally adjusted, purchase-only index; all figures are for the period ending December 31, 2020
Source: Federal Housing Finance Agency, Change in Metropolitan Area House Price Indexes, April 7, 2021

Median Single-Family Home Prices

Area	2018	2019	2020[p]	Percent Change 2019 to 2020
MSA[1]	288.8	306.0	331.0	8.2
U.S. Average	261.6	274.6	299.9	9.2

Note: Figures are median sales prices of existing single-family homes in thousands of dollars; (p) preliminary; (1) Figures cover the Las Vegas-Henderson-Paradise, NV Metropolitan Statistical Area
Source: National Association of Realtors, Median Sales Price of Existing Single-Family Homes for Metropolitan Areas, 4th Quarter 2020

Qualifying Income Based on Median Sales Price of Existing Single-Family Homes

Area	With 5% Down ($)	With 10% Down ($)	With 20% Down ($)
MSA[1]	64,970	61,551	54,712
U.S. Average	59,266	56,147	49,908

Note: Figures are preliminary; Qualifying income is based on a mortgage rate of 2.81%. Monthly principal and interest payment is limited to 25% of income; (1) Figures cover the Las Vegas-Henderson-Paradise, NV Metropolitan Statistical Area
Source: National Association of Realtors, Qualifying Income Based on Median Sales Price of Existing Single-Family Homes for Metropolitan Areas, 4th Quarter 2020

Home Value Distribution

Area	Under $50,000	$50,000 -$99,999	$100,000 -$149,999	$150,000 -$199,999	$200,000 -$299,999	$300,000 -$499,999	$500,000 -$999,999	$1,000,000 or more
City	2.4	4.3	8.7	15.4	31.4	27.3	8.6	1.9
MSA[1]	3.5	4.3	8.0	14.1	31.6	28.6	8.2	1.7
U.S.	6.9	12.0	13.3	14.0	19.6	19.3	11.4	3.4

Note: Figures are percentages and cover owner-occupied housing units; (1) Figures cover the Las Vegas-Henderson-Paradise, NV Metropolitan Statistical Area
Source: U.S. Census Bureau, 2015-2019 American Community Survey 5-Year Estimates

Year Housing Structure Built

Area	2010 or Later	2000 -2009	1990 -1999	1980 -1989	1970 -1979	1960 -1969	1950 -1959	1940 -1949	Before 1940	Median Year
City	5.2	23.0	32.0	16.6	9.9	7.4	4.2	1.3	0.5	1993
MSA[1]	7.2	30.1	29.1	14.6	10.6	5.1	2.2	0.7	0.4	1996
U.S.	5.2	14.0	13.9	13.4	15.2	10.6	10.3	4.9	12.6	1978

Note: Figures are percentages except for Median Year; Note: (1) Figures cover the Las Vegas-Henderson-Paradise, NV Metropolitan Statistical Area
Source: U.S. Census Bureau, 2015-2019 American Community Survey 5-Year Estimates

Gross Monthly Rent

Area	Under $500	$500 -$999	$1,000 -$1,499	$1,500 -$1,999	$2,000 -$2,499	$2,500 -$2,999	$3,000 and up	Median ($)
City	4.7	35.4	41.8	13.8	2.9	0.8	0.6	1,102
MSA[1]	2.8	34.4	42.1	15.9	3.5	0.8	0.6	1,132
U.S.	9.4	36.2	30.0	14.0	5.6	2.4	2.4	1,062

Note: Figures are percentages except for Median; Gross rent is the contract rent plus the estimated average monthly cost of utilities (electricity, gas, and water and sewer) and fuels (oil, coal, kerosene, wood, etc.) if these are paid by the renter (or paid for the renter by someone else); (1) Figures cover the Las Vegas-Henderson-Paradise, NV Metropolitan Statistical Area
Source: U.S. Census Bureau, 2015-2019 American Community Survey 5-Year Estimates

HEALTH

Health Risk Factors

Category	MSA[1] (%)	U.S. (%)
Adults aged 18–64 who have any kind of health care coverage	n/a	87.3
Adults who reported being in good or better health	n/a	82.4
Adults who have been told they have high blood cholesterol	n/a	33.0
Adults who have been told they have high blood pressure	n/a	32.3
Adults who are current smokers	n/a	17.1
Adults who currently use E-cigarettes	n/a	4.6
Adults who currently use chewing tobacco, snuff, or snus	n/a	4.0
Adults who are heavy drinkers[2]	n/a	6.3
Adults who are binge drinkers[3]	n/a	17.4
Adults who are overweight (BMI 25.0 - 29.9)	n/a	35.3
Adults who are obese (BMI 30.0 - 99.8)	n/a	31.3
Adults who participated in any physical activities in the past month	n/a	74.4
Adults who always or nearly always wears a seat belt	n/a	94.3

Note: n/a not available; (1) Figures cover the Las Vegas-Henderson-Paradise, NV Metropolitan Statistical Area; (2) Heavy drinkers are classified as adult men having more than 14 drinks per week and adult women having more than 7 drinks per week; (3) Binge drinkers are classified as males having five or more drinks on one occasion or females having four or more drinks on one occasion
Source: Centers for Disease Control and Prevention, Behavioral Risk Factor Surveillance System, SMART: Selected Metropolitan Area Risk Trends, 2017

Acute and Chronic Health Conditions

Category	MSA[1] (%)	U.S. (%)
Adults who have ever been told they had a heart attack	n/a	4.2
Adults who have ever been told they have angina or coronary heart disease	n/a	3.9
Adults who have ever been told they had a stroke	n/a	3.0
Adults who have ever been told they have asthma	n/a	14.2
Adults who have ever been told they have arthritis	n/a	24.9
Adults who have ever been told they have diabetes[2]	n/a	10.5
Adults who have ever been told they had skin cancer	n/a	6.2
Adults who have ever been told they had any other types of cancer	n/a	7.1
Adults who have ever been told they have COPD	n/a	6.5
Adults who have ever been told they have kidney disease	n/a	3.0
Adults who have ever been told they have a form of depression	n/a	20.5

Note: n/a not available; (1) Figures cover the Las Vegas-Henderson-Paradise, NV Metropolitan Statistical Area; (2) Figures do not include pregnancy-related, borderline, or pre-diabetes
Source: Centers for Disease Control and Prevention, Behaviorial Risk Factor Surveillance System, SMART: Selected Metropolitan Area Risk Trends, 2017

Health Screening and Vaccination Rates

Category	MSA[1] (%)	U.S. (%)
Adults aged 65+ who have had flu shot within the past year	n/a	60.7
Adults aged 65+ who have ever had a pneumonia vaccination	n/a	75.4
Adults who have ever been tested for HIV	n/a	36.1
Adults who have ever had the shingles or zoster vaccine?	n/a	28.9
Adults who have had their blood cholesterol checked within the last five years	n/a	85.9

Note: n/a not available; (1) Figures cover the Las Vegas-Henderson-Paradise, NV Metropolitan Statistical Area.
Source: Centers for Disease Control and Prevention, Behaviorial Risk Factor Surveillance System, SMART: Selected Metropolitan Area Risk Trends, 2017

Disability Status

Category	MSA[1] (%)	U.S. (%)
Adults who reported being deaf	n/a	6.7
Are you blind or have serious difficulty seeing, even when wearing glasses?	n/a	4.5
Are you limited in any way in any of your usual activities due of arthritis?	n/a	12.9
Do you have difficulty doing errands alone?	n/a	6.8
Do you have difficulty dressing or bathing?	n/a	3.6
Do you have serious difficulty concentrating/remembering/making decisions?	n/a	10.7
Do you have serious difficulty walking or climbing stairs?	n/a	13.6

Note: n/a not available; (1) Figures cover the Las Vegas-Henderson-Paradise, NV Metropolitan Statistical Area.
Source: Centers for Disease Control and Prevention, Behaviorial Risk Factor Surveillance System, SMART: Selected Metropolitan Area Risk Trends, 2017

Mortality Rates for the Top 10 Causes of Death in the U.S.

ICD-10[a] Sub-Chapter	ICD-10[a] Code	Age-Adjusted Mortality Rate[1] per 100,000 population	
		County[2]	U.S.
Malignant neoplasms	C00-C97	152.4	149.2
Ischaemic heart diseases	I20-I25	102.8	90.5
Other forms of heart disease	I30-I51	68.2	52.2
Chronic lower respiratory diseases	J40-J47	46.7	39.6
Other degenerative diseases of the nervous system	G30-G31	41.3	37.6
Cerebrovascular diseases	I60-I69	35.8	37.2
Other external causes of accidental injury	W00-X59	32.2	36.1
Organic, including symptomatic, mental disorders	F01-F09	20.7	29.4
Hypertensive diseases	I10-I15	36.0	24.1
Diabetes mellitus	E10-E14	19.3	21.5

Note: (a) ICD-10 = International Classification of Diseases 10th Revision; (1) Mortality rates are a three-year average covering 2017-2019; (2) Figures cover Clark County.
Source: Centers for Disease Control and Prevention, National Center for Health Statistics. Underlying Cause of Death 1999-2019 on CDC WONDER Online Database

Mortality Rates for Selected Causes of Death

ICD-10[a] Sub-Chapter	ICD-10[a] Code	Age-Adjusted Mortality Rate[1] per 100,000 population	
		County[2]	U.S.
Assault	X85-Y09	7.6	6.0
Diseases of the liver	K70-K76	14.8	14.4
Human immunodeficiency virus (HIV) disease	B20-B24	2.0	1.5
Influenza and pneumonia	J09-J18	16.1	13.8
Intentional self-harm	X60-X84	19.0	14.1
Malnutrition	E40-E46	2.5	2.3
Obesity and other hyperalimentation	E65-E68	1.7	2.1
Renal failure	N17-N19	8.1	12.6
Transport accidents	V01-V99	10.1	12.3
Viral hepatitis	B15-B19	1.6	1.2

Note: (a) ICD-10 = International Classification of Diseases 10th Revision; (1) Mortality rates are a three-year average covering 2017-2019; (2) Figures cover Clark County; Data are suppressed when the data meet the criteria for confidentiality constraints; Mortality rates are flagged as unreliable when the rate would be calculated with a numerator of 20 or less.
Source: Centers for Disease Control and Prevention, National Center for Health Statistics. Underlying Cause of Death 1999-2019 on CDC WONDER Online Database

Health Insurance Coverage

Area	With Health Insurance	With Private Health Insurance	With Public Health Insurance	Without Health Insurance	Population Under Age 19 Without Health Insurance
City	87.7	61.6	36.0	12.3	7.2
MSA[1]	88.3	64.2	33.7	11.7	7.4
U.S.	91.2	67.9	35.1	8.8	5.1

Note: Figures are percentages that cover the civilian noninstitutionalized population; (1) Figures cover the Las Vegas-Henderson-Paradise, NV Metropolitan Statistical Area
Source: U.S. Census Bureau, 2015-2019 American Community Survey 5-Year Estimates

Number of Medical Professionals

Area	MDs[3]	DOs[3,4]	Dentists	Podiatrists	Chiropractors	Optometrists
County[1] (number)	3,949	775	1,443	98	444	297
County[1] (rate[2])	177.4	34.8	63.7	4.3	19.6	13.1
U.S. (rate[2])	282.9	22.7	71.2	6.2	28.1	16.9

32003
Note: Data as of 2019 unless noted; (1) Data covers Clark County; (2) Rate per 100,000 population; (3) Data as of 2018 and includes all active, non-federal physicians; (4) Doctor of Osteopathic Medicine
Source: U.S. Department of Health and Human Services, Health Resources and Services Administration, Bureau of Health Professions, Area Resource File (ARF) 2019-2020

EDUCATION

Public School District Statistics

District Name	Schls	Pupils	Pupil/ Teacher Ratio	Minority Pupils[1] (%)	Free Lunch Eligible[2] (%)	IEP[3] (%)
Clark County School District	374	330,225	22.2	75.8	63.2	12.1

Note: Table includes school districts with 2,000 or more students; (1) Percentage of students that are not non-Hispanic white; (2) Percentage of students that are eligible for the free lunch program; (3) Percentage of students that have an Individualized Education Program.
Source: U.S. Department of Education, National Center for Education Statistics, Common Core of Data, Local Education Agency (School District) Universe Survey: School Year 2018-2019; U.S. Department of Education, National Center for Education Statistics, Common Core of Data, Public Elementary/Secondary School Universe Survey: School Year 2018-2019

Best High Schools

According to *U.S. News*, Las Vegas is home to one of the top 500 high schools in the U.S.: **Advanced Technologies Academy** (#152). Nearly 18,000 public, magnet and charter schools were ranked based on their performance on state assessments and how well they prepare students for college. *U.S. News & World Report, "Best High Schools 2020"*

Highest Level of Education

Area	Less than H.S.	H.S. Diploma	Some College, No Deg.	Associate Degree	Bachelor's Degree	Master's Degree	Prof. School Degree	Doctorate Degree
City	15.2	27.6	24.6	8.0	16.0	5.9	1.9	0.8
MSA[1]	13.9	28.5	25.1	8.1	16.2	5.8	1.6	0.8
U.S.	12.0	27.0	20.4	8.5	19.8	8.8	2.1	1.4

Note: Figures cover persons age 25 and over; (1) Figures cover the Las Vegas-Henderson-Paradise, NV Metropolitan Statistical Area
Source: U.S. Census Bureau, 2015-2019 American Community Survey 5-Year Estimates

Educational Attainment by Race

Area	High School Graduate or Higher (%)					Bachelor's Degree or Higher (%)				
	Total	White	Black	Asian	Hisp.[2]	Total	White	Black	Asian	Hisp.[2]
City	84.8	87.5	89.2	91.1	63.5	24.6	26.9	18.2	40.7	9.9
MSA[1]	86.1	88.3	89.7	90.4	66.8	24.5	25.9	17.8	38.8	10.5
U.S.	88.0	89.9	86.0	87.1	68.7	32.1	33.5	21.6	54.3	16.4

Note: Figures shown cover persons 25 years old and over; (1) Figures cover the Las Vegas-Henderson-Paradise, NV Metropolitan Statistical Area; (2) People of Hispanic origin can be of any race
Source: U.S. Census Bureau, 2015-2019 American Community Survey 5-Year Estimates

School Enrollment by Grade and Control

Area	Preschool (%)		Kindergarten (%)		Grades 1 - 4 (%)		Grades 5 - 8 (%)		Grades 9 - 12 (%)	
	Public	Private	Public	Private	Public	Private	Public	Private	Public	Private
City	65.7	34.3	88.6	11.4	91.3	8.7	91.7	8.3	93.0	7.0
MSA[1]	61.7	38.3	89.8	10.2	92.5	7.5	92.9	7.1	93.4	6.6
U.S.	59.1	40.9	87.6	12.4	89.5	10.5	89.4	10.6	90.1	9.9

Note: Figures shown cover persons 3 years old and over; (1) Figures cover the Las Vegas-Henderson-Paradise, NV Metropolitan Statistical Area
Source: U.S. Census Bureau, 2015-2019 American Community Survey 5-Year Estimates

Higher Education

Four-Year Colleges			Two-Year Colleges			Medical Schools[1]	Law Schools[2]	Voc/ Tech[3]
Public	Private Non-profit	Private For-profit	Public	Private Non-profit	Private For-profit			
2	1	3	0	0	7	1	1	9

Note: Figures cover institutions located within the city limits and include main campuses only; (1) includes schools accredited by the Liaison Committee on Medical Education and the American Osteopathic Association's Commission on Osteopathic College Accreditation; (2) includes ABA-accredited schools, schools with provisional ABA accreditation, and state accredited schools; (3) includes all schools with programs that are less than 2 years.
Source: National Center for Education Statistics, Integrated Postsecondary Education System (IPEDS), 2019-20; Wikipedia, List of Medical Schools in the United States, accessed April 2, 2021; Wikipedia, List of Law Schools in the United States, accessed April 2, 2021

According to *U.S. News & World Report*, the Las Vegas-Henderson-Paradise, NV metro area is home to one of the top 100 law schools in the U.S.: **University of Nevada—Las Vegas** (#60 tie). The rankings are based on a weighted average of 12 measures of quality: peer assessment score; assessment score by lawyers/judges; median LSAT scores; median undergrad GPA; acceptance rate; employment rates for graduates; placement success; bar passage rate; faculty resources; expenditures per student; student/faculty ratio; and library resources. *U.S. News & World Report, "America's Best Graduate Schools, Law, 2022"*

EMPLOYERS

Major Employers

Company Name	Industry
American Casino & Entertainment	Hospitality
Blackstone Group	Hospitality
Boyd Gaming Corporation	Hospitality
Caesars Entertainment	Hospitality
Cannery Casino Resorts	Hospitality
City of Henderson	Municipal government
City of Las Vegas	Municipal government
Clark County	County government
Clark County School District	K-12 public education
Dignity Health	Health care
Landry's	Hospitality
Las Vegas Metropolitan Police Department	Police protection
Las Vegas Sands Corporation	Hospitality
MGM Resorts International	Hospitality
Nellis & Creech AFB	National security
Southwest Airlines	Air transportation, scheduled
Stations Casinos	Hospitality
Sunrise Health System	Health care
University Medical Center	Health care
University of Nevada Las Vegas	Higher education
Valley Health System	Health care
Wynn Resorts	Hospitality
Yellow Checker Star Transportation	Taxi/limo service

Note: Companies shown are located within the Las Vegas-Henderson-Paradise, NV Metropolitan Statistical Area.
Source: Hoovers.com; Wikipedia

PUBLIC SAFETY

Crime Rate

Area	All Crimes	Violent Crimes				Property Crimes		
		Murder	Rape[3]	Robbery	Aggrav. Assault	Burglary	Larceny -Theft	Motor Vehicle Theft
City	3,302.8	5.0	86.3	127.1	312.8	638.7	1,694.3	438.6
Suburbs[1]	2,501.4	4.6	36.8	114.4	354.9	390.7	1,310.3	289.7
Metro[2]	3,089.8	4.9	73.2	123.7	324.0	572.8	1,592.2	399.1
U.S.	2,489.3	5.0	42.6	81.6	250.2	340.5	1,549.5	219.9

Note: Figures are crimes per 100,000 population; (1) All areas within the metro area that are located outside the city limits; (2) Figures cover the Las Vegas-Henderson-Paradise, NV Metropolitan Statistical Area; (3) All figures shown were reported using the revised Uniform Crime Reporting (UCR) definition of rape.
Source: FBI Uniform Crime Reports, 2019

Hate Crimes

Area	Number of Quarters Reported	Number of Incidents per Bias Motivation					
		Race/Ethnicity/ Ancestry	Religion	Sexual Orientation	Disability	Gender	Gender Identity
City	4	11	5	4	1	0	1
U.S.	4	3,963	1,521	1,195	157	69	198

Source: Federal Bureau of Investigation, Hate Crime Statistics 2019

Identity Theft Consumer Reports

Area	Reports	Reports per 100,000 Population	Rank[2]
MSA[1]	18,206	803	21
U.S.	1,387,615	423	-

Note: (1) Figures cover the Las Vegas-Henderson-Paradise, NV Metropolitan Statistical Area; (2) Rank ranges from 1 to 391 where 1 indicates greatest number of identity theft reports per 100,000 population
Source: Federal Trade Commission, Consumer Sentinel Network Data Book 2020

Fraud and Other Consumer Reports

Area	Reports	Reports per 100,000 Population	Rank[2]
MSA[1]	27,721	1,223	8
U.S.	3,385,133	1,031	-

Note: (1) Figures cover the Las Vegas-Henderson-Paradise, NV Metropolitan Statistical Area; (2) Rank ranges from 1 to 391 where 1 indicates greatest number of fraud and other consumer reports per 100,000 population
Source: Federal Trade Commission, Consumer Sentinel Network Data Book 2020

POLITICS

2020 Presidential Election Results

Area	Biden	Trump	Jorgensen	Hawkins	Other
Clark County	53.7	44.3	0.9	0.0	1.1
U.S.	51.3	46.8	1.2	0.3	0.5

Note: Results are percentages and may not add to 100% due to rounding
Source: Dave Leip's Atlas of U.S. Presidential Elections

SPORTS

Professional Sports Teams

Team Name	League	Year Established
Las Vegas Raiders	National Football League (NFL)	2020
Vegas Golden Nights	National Hockey League (NHL)	2017

Note: Includes teams located in the Las Vegas-Henderson-Paradise, NV Metropolitan Statistical Area.
Source: Wikipedia, Major Professional Sports Teams of the United States and Canada, April 6, 2021

CLIMATE

Average and Extreme Temperatures

Temperature	Jan	Feb	Mar	Apr	May	Jun	Jul	Aug	Sep	Oct	Nov	Dec	Yr.
Extreme High (°F)	77	87	91	99	109	115	116	116	113	103	87	77	116
Average High (°F)	56	62	69	78	88	99	104	102	94	81	66	57	80
Average Temp. (°F)	45	50	56	65	74	84	90	88	80	68	54	46	67
Average Low (°F)	33	38	43	51	60	69	76	74	66	54	41	34	53
Extreme Low (°F)	8	16	23	31	40	49	60	56	43	26	21	11	8

Note: Figures cover the years 1948-1990
Source: National Climatic Data Center, International Station Meteorological Climate Summary, 9/96

Average Precipitation/Snowfall/Humidity

Precip./Humidity	Jan	Feb	Mar	Apr	May	Jun	Jul	Aug	Sep	Oct	Nov	Dec	Yr.
Avg. Precip. (in.)	0.5	0.4	0.4	0.2	0.2	0.1	0.4	0.5	0.3	0.2	0.4	0.3	4.0
Avg. Snowfall (in.)	1	Tr	Tr	Tr	0	0	0	0	0	0	Tr	Tr	1
Avg. Rel. Hum. 7am (%)	59	52	41	31	26	20	26	31	30	36	47	56	38
Avg. Rel. Hum. 4pm (%)	32	25	20	15	13	10	14	16	16	18	26	31	20

Note: Figures cover the years 1948-1990; Tr = Trace amounts (<0.05 in. of rain; <0.5 in. of snow)
Source: National Climatic Data Center, International Station Meteorological Climate Summary, 9/96

Weather Conditions

Temperature			Daytime Sky			Precipitation		
10°F & below	32°F & below	90°F & above	Clear	Partly cloudy	Cloudy	0.01 inch or more precip.	0.1 inch or more snow/ice	Thunder-storms
< 1	37	134	185	132	48	27	2	13

Note: Figures are average number of days per year and cover the years 1948-1990
Source: National Climatic Data Center, International Station Meteorological Climate Summary, 9/96

HAZARDOUS WASTE

Superfund Sites

The Las Vegas-Henderson-Paradise, NV metro area has no sites on the EPA's Superfund Final National Priorities List. There are a total of 1,375 Superfund sites with a status of proposed or final on the list in the U.S. *U.S. Environmental Protection Agency, National Priorities List, April 7, 2021*

AIR QUALITY

Air Quality Trends: Ozone

	1990	1995	2000	2005	2010	2015	2016	2017	2018	2019
MSA[1]	n/a	n/a	n/a	n/a	n/a	n/a	n/a	n/a	n/a	n/a
U.S.	0.088	0.089	0.082	0.080	0.073	0.068	0.069	0.068	0.069	0.065

Note: (1) Data covers the Las Vegas-Henderson-Paradise, NV Metropolitan Statistical Area; n/a not available. The values shown are the composite ozone concentration averages among trend sites based on the highest fourth daily maximum 8-hour concentration in parts per million. These trends are based on sites having an adequate record of monitoring data during the trend period. Data from exceptional events are included.
Source: U.S. Environmental Protection Agency, Air Quality Monitoring Information, "Air Quality Trends by City, 1990-2019"

Air Quality Index

Area	Percent of Days when Air Quality was...[2]					AQI Statistics[2]	
	Good	Moderate	Unhealthy for Sensitive Groups	Unhealthy	Very Unhealthy	Maximum	Median
MSA[1]	42.2	56.4	1.4	0.0	0.0	122	54

Note: (1) Data covers the Las Vegas-Henderson-Paradise, NV Metropolitan Statistical Area; (2) Based on 365 days with AQI data in 2019. Air Quality Index (AQI) is an index for reporting daily air quality. EPA calculates the AQI for five major air pollutants regulated by the Clean Air Act: ground-level ozone, particle pollution (aka particulate matter), carbon monoxide, sulfur dioxide, and nitrogen dioxide. The AQI runs from 0 to 500. The higher the AQI value, the greater the level of air pollution and the greater the health concern. There are six AQI categories: "Good" AQI is between 0 and 50. Air quality is considered satisfactory; "Moderate" AQI is between 51 and 100. Air quality is acceptable; "Unhealthy for Sensitive Groups" When AQI values are between 101 and 150, members of sensitive groups may experience health effects; "Unhealthy" When AQI values are between 151 and 200 everyone may begin to experience health effects; "Very Unhealthy" AQI values between 201 and 300 trigger a health alert; "Hazardous" AQI values over 300 trigger warnings of emergency conditions (not shown).
Source: U.S. Environmental Protection Agency, Air Quality Index Report, 2019

Air Quality Index Pollutants

Area	Percent of Days when AQI Pollutant was...[2]					
	Carbon Monoxide	Nitrogen Dioxide	Ozone	Sulfur Dioxide	Particulate Matter 2.5	Particulate Matter 10
MSA[1]	0.3	5.5	69.0	0.0	23.0	2.2

Note: (1) Data covers the Las Vegas-Henderson-Paradise, NV Metropolitan Statistical Area; (2) Based on 365 days with AQI data in 2019. The Air Quality Index (AQI) is an index for reporting daily air quality. EPA calculates the AQI for five major air pollutants regulated by the Clean Air Act: ground-level ozone, particle pollution (also known as particulate matter), carbon monoxide, sulfur dioxide, and nitrogen dioxide. The AQI runs from 0 to 500. The higher the AQI value, the greater the level of air pollution and the greater the health concern.
Source: U.S. Environmental Protection Agency, Air Quality Index Report, 2019

Maximum Air Pollutant Concentrations: Particulate Matter, Ozone, CO and Lead

	Particulate Matter 10 (ug/m^3)	Particulate Matter 2.5 Wtd AM (ug/m^3)	Particulate Matter 2.5 24-Hr (ug/m^3)	Ozone (ppm)	Carbon Monoxide (ppm)	Lead (ug/m^3)
MSA[1] Level	104	8.0	26	0.070	2	n/a
NAAQS[2]	150	15	35	0.075	9	0.15
Met NAAQS[2]	Yes	Yes	Yes	Yes	Yes	n/a

Note: (1) Data covers the Las Vegas-Henderson-Paradise, NV Metropolitan Statistical Area; Data from exceptional events are included; (2) National Ambient Air Quality Standards; ppm = parts per million; ug/m^3 = micrograms per cubic meter; n/a not available.
Concentrations: Particulate Matter 10 (coarse particulate)—highest second maximum 24-hour concentration; Particulate Matter 2.5 Wtd AM (fine particulate)—highest weighted annual mean concentration; Particulate Matter 2.5 24-Hour (fine particulate)—highest 98th percentile 24-hour concentration; Ozone—highest fourth daily maximum 8-hour concentration; Carbon Monoxide—highest second maximum non-overlapping 8-hour concentration; Lead—maximum running 3-month average
Source: U.S. Environmental Protection Agency, Air Quality Monitoring Information, "Air Quality Statistics by City, 2019"

Maximum Air Pollutant Concentrations: Nitrogen Dioxide and Sulfur Dioxide

	Nitrogen Dioxide AM (ppb)	Nitrogen Dioxide 1-Hr (ppb)	Sulfur Dioxide AM (ppb)	Sulfur Dioxide 1-Hr (ppb)	Sulfur Dioxide 24-Hr (ppb)
MSA[1] Level	24	58	n/a	5	n/a
NAAQS[2]	53	100	30	75	140
Met NAAQS[2]	Yes	Yes	n/a	Yes	n/a

Note: (1) Data covers the Las Vegas-Henderson-Paradise, NV Metropolitan Statistical Area; Data from exceptional events are included; (2) National Ambient Air Quality Standards; ppm = parts per million; ug/m^3 = micrograms per cubic meter; n/a not available.
Concentrations: Nitrogen Dioxide AM—highest arithmetic mean concentration; Nitrogen Dioxide 1-Hr—highest 98th percentile 1-hour daily maximum concentration; Sulfur Dioxide AM—highest annual mean concentration; Sulfur Dioxide 1-Hr—highest 99th percentile 1-hour daily maximum concentration; Sulfur Dioxide 24-Hr—highest second maximum 24-hour concentration
Source: U.S. Environmental Protection Agency, Air Quality Monitoring Information, "Air Quality Statistics by City, 2019"

Los Angeles, California

Background

There is as much to say about Los Angeles as there are municipalities under its jurisdiction. The city is immense, and in the words of one of its residents, "If you want a life in LA, you need a car."

Los Angeles acquired its many neighborhoods and communities such as Hollywood, Glendale, Burbank, and Alhambra when those cities wanted to share in the water piped into Los Angeles from the Owens River. To obtain it, the cities were required to join the Los Angeles municipal system. Due to those annexations, Los Angeles is now one of the largest U.S. cities in both acreage and population. It is also one of the most racially diverse.

The city's communities are connected through a complex system of freeways which gives Los Angeles its reputation as a congested, car-oriented culture, where people have to schedule their days around the three-hour rush hour.

Despite these challenges, Los Angeles is a city with a diversified economy and an average of 325 days of sunshine a year. What was founded in 1781 as a sleepy pueblo of 44 people, with chickens roaming the footpaths, is now a city leading the nation in commerce, transportation, finance, and, especially, entertainment—with a majority of all motion pictures made in the United States still produced in the Los Angeles area, and headquarters of such major studios as MGM and Universal located in "municipalities" unto themselves.

Playa Vista, the first new community to be established on the Westside of Los Angeles in more than 50 years, is home to Electronic Arts, the world's leading video game publisher. Lincoln Properties built office buildings totaling more than 820,000 square feet in the eastern portion of Playa Vista community known as "The Campus at Playa Vista." The National Basketball Association Clippers has a training facility at the Campus, which is also home to a basketball-themed public park, a fitting way to celebrate the 2011 NBA champion Lakers.

> Jimmy Kimmel hosted the 72nd *Primetime Emmy Awards* from a nearly empty Staples Center as viewers—and the nominees—tuned in from home.

The arts are center-stage in Los Angeles. Home of the Getty Center and Museum, an architectural masterpiece designed by Richard Meier and built on a commanding hill, is a dramatic venue for visual arts and other events. The Los Angeles Opera, under the direction of Placido Domingo, offers a lively season of operas as well as recitals by such luminaries as Cecilia Bartoli and Renee Fleming. The Los Angeles Philharmonic now performs in the Walt Disney Concert Hall, designed by Frank Gehry, famous as the architect of the Guggenheim Museum at Bilbao.

The downtown's first modern industrial park, The Los Angeles World Trade Center, is a 20-acre project that is downtown's only foreign trade zone.

Los Angeles has hosted the Olympic and Paralympic Games twice, and will again in 2028. Los Angeles will be the third city after London and Paris to host the Olympic Games three times. Major league baseball's Los Angeles Dodgers won the World Series in 2020, ending a 32-year drought. Super Bowl LVI will be played at the newly built SoFi Stadium in neighboring Inglewood in 2022.

Inland and up foothill slopes, both high and low temperatures become more extreme and the average relative humidity drops. Relative humidity is frequently high near the coast, but may be quite low along the foothills. Most rain falls November through March, while the summers are very dry. Destructive flash floods occasionally develop in and below some mountain canyons. Snow is often visible on the nearby mountains in the winter, but is extremely rare in the coastal basin. Thunderstorms are infrequent.

The climate of Los Angeles is normally pleasant and mild throughout the year, with unusual differences in temperature, humidity, cloudiness, fog, rain, and sunshine over fairly short distances in the metro area. Low clouds are common at night and in the morning along the coast during spring and summer. Near the foothills, clouds form later in the day and clear earlier. Annual percentages of fog and cloudiness are greatest near the ocean. Sunshine totals are highest on the inland side of the city.

At times, high concentrations of air pollution affect the Los Angeles coastal basin and adjacent areas, when lack of air movement combines with an atmospheric inversion. In the fall and winter, the Santa Ana winds pick up considerable amounts of dust and can blow strongly in the northern and eastern sections of the city and in outlying areas in the north and east, increasing the threat of wild fires in the region, several of which got very close to the city in recent years.

Rankings

General Rankings

- Los Angeles was selected as one of the best places to live in America by *Outside Magazine*. Criteria included population, park acreage, neighborhood and resident diversity, new and upcoming things of interest, and opportunities for outdoor adventure. *Outside Magazine, "The 12 Best Places to Live in 2019," July 11, 2019*

- The human resources consulting firm Mercer ranked 231 major cities worldwide in terms of overall quality of life. Los Angeles ranked #66. Criteria: political, social, economic, and socio-cultural factors; medical and health considerations; schools and education; public services and transportation; recreation; consumer goods; housing; and natural environment. *Mercer, "Mercer 2019 Quality of Living Survey," March 13, 2019*

Business/Finance Rankings

- The Brookings Institution ranked the nation's largest cities based on income inequality. Los Angeles was ranked #15 (#1 = greatest inequality). Criteria: the "95/20 ratio," a figure representing the income at which a household earns more than 95 percent of all other households, divided by the income at which a household earns more than only 20 percent of all other households. *Brookings Institution, "Household Income Inequality, Largest Cities of 97 Large U.S. Metro Areas, 2014-2016," February 5, 2018*

- The Brookings Institution ranked the 100 largest metro areas in the U.S. based on income inequality. Los Angeles was ranked #4 (#1 = greatest inequality). Criteria: the "95/20 ratio," a figure representing the income at which a household earns more than 95 percent of all other households, divided by the income at which a household earns more than only 20 percent of all other households. *Brookings Institution, "Household Income Inequality, 100 Largest U.S. Metro Areas, 2014-2016," February 5, 2018*

- Payscale.com ranked the 32 largest metro areas in terms of wage growth. The Los Angeles metro area ranked #1. Criteria: private-sector and education professional wage growth between the 4th quarter of 2019 and the 4th quarter of 2020. *PayScale, "Wage Trends by Metro Area-4th Quarter," January 11, 2021*

- The Los Angeles metro area was identified as one of the most debt-ridden places in America by the finance site Credit.com. The metro area was ranked #13. Criteria: residents' average credit card debt as well as median income. *Credit.com, "25 Cities With the Most Credit Card Debt," February 28, 2018*

- For its annual survey of the "Most Expensive U.S. Cities to Live In," Kiplinger applied Cost of Living Index statistics developed by the Council for Community and Economic Research to U.S. Census Bureau population and median household income data for 256 urban areas. Los Angeles was among the 20 most expensive in the country. *Kiplinger.com, "The 20 Most Expensive Cities in the U.S.," July 29, 2020*

- The Los Angeles metro area appeared on the Milken Institute "2021 Best Performing Cities" list. Rank: #93 out of 200 large metro areas (population over 250,000). Criteria: job growth; wage and salary growth; high-tech output growth; housing affordability; household broadband access. *Milken Institute, "Best-Performing Cities 2021," February 16, 2021*

- *Forbes* ranked the 200 most populous metro areas to determine the nation's "Best Places for Business and Careers." The Los Angeles metro area was ranked #113. Criteria: costs (business and living); job growth (past and projected); income growth; quality of life; educational attainment (college and high school); projected economic growth; cultural and leisure opportunities; workplace tolerance laws; net migration patterns. *Forbes, "The Best Places for Business and Careers 2019: Seattle Still On Top," October 30, 2019*

- Mercer Human Resources Consulting ranked 209 cities worldwide in terms of cost-of-living. Los Angeles ranked #17 (the lower the ranking, the higher the cost-of-living). The survey measured the comparative cost of over 200 items (such as housing, food, clothing, household goods, transportation, and entertainment) in each location. *Mercer, "2020 Cost of Living Survey," June 9, 2020*

Education Rankings

- Personal finance website *WalletHub* analyzed the 150 largest U.S. metropolitan statistical areas to determine where the most educated Americans are putting their degrees to work. Criteria: education levels; percentage of workers with degrees; education quality and attainment gap; public school quality rankings; quality and enrollment of each metro area's universities. Los Angeles was ranked #92 (#1 = most educated city). *www.WalletHub.com, "Most and Least Educated Cities in America," July 20, 2020*

- Los Angeles was selected as one of America's most literate cities. The city ranked #62 out of the 84 largest U.S. cities. Criteria: number of booksellers; library resources; Internet resources; educational attainment; periodical publishing resources; newspaper circulation. *Central Connecticut State University, "America's Most Literate Cities, 2018," February 2019*

Environmental Rankings

- The U.S. Environmental Protection Agency (EPA) released a list of U.S. metropolitan areas with the most ENERGY STAR certified buildings in 2019. The Los Angeles metro area was ranked #1 out of 25. *U.S. Environmental Protection Agency, "2020 Energy Star Top Cities," March 2020*

- Los Angeles was highlighted as one of the 25 most ozone-polluted metro areas in the U.S. during 2016 through 2018. The area ranked #1. *American Lung Association, "State of the Air 2020," April 21, 2020*

- Los Angeles was highlighted as one of the 25 metro areas most polluted by year-round particle pollution (Annual PM 2.5) in the U.S. during 2016 through 2018. The area ranked #4. *American Lung Association, "State of the Air 2020," April 21, 2020*

- Los Angeles was highlighted as one of the 25 metro areas most polluted by short-term particle pollution (24-hour PM 2.5) in the U.S. during 2016 through 2018. The area ranked #6. *American Lung Association, "State of the Air 2020," April 21, 2020*

Food/Drink Rankings

- The U.S. Chamber of Commerce Foundation conducted an in-depth study on local food truck regulations, surveyed 288 food truck owners, and ranked 20 major American cities based on how friendly they are for operating a food truck. The compiled index assessed the following: procedures for obtaining permits and licenses; complying with restrictions; and financial obligations associated with operating a food truck. Los Angeles ranked #8 overall (1 being the best). *www.foodtrucknation.us, "Food Truck Nation," March 20, 2018*

- Los Angeles was identified as one of the cities in America ordering the most vegan food options by GrubHub.com. The city ranked #2 out of 5. Criteria: percentage of vegan, vegetarian and plant-based food orders compared to the overall number of orders. *GrubHub.com, "State of the Plate Report 2020: Top Vegan-Friendly Cities," July 9, 2020*

- Dodger stadium was selected as one of PETA's "Top 10 Vegan-Friendly Ballparks" for 2019. The park ranked #7. *People for the Ethical Treatment of Animals, "Top 10 Vegan-Friendly Ballparks," May 23, 2019*

Health/Fitness Rankings

- For each of the 100 largest cities in the United States, the American Fitness Index®, published by the American College of Sports Medicine and the Anthem Foundation, evaluated community infrastructure and 33 health behaviors including preventive health, levels of chronic disease conditions, pedestrian safety, air quality, and community resources that support physical activity. Los Angeles ranked #44 for "community fitness." *americanfitnessindex.org, "2020 ACSM American Fitness Index Summary Report," July 14, 2020*

- The Los Angeles metro area was identified as one of the worst cities for bed bugs in America by pest control company Orkin. The area ranked #9 out of 50 based on the number of bed bug treatments Orkin performed from December 2019 to November 2020. *Orkin, "New Year, New Top City on Orkin's 2021 Bed Bug Cities List: Chicago," February 1, 2021*

- Los Angeles was identified as a "2021 Spring Allergy Capital." The area ranked #56 out of 100. Three groups of factors were used to identify the most challenging cities for people with allergies during the spring season: annual spring pollen levels; over the counter medicine use; number of board-certified allergy specialists. *Asthma and Allergy Foundation of America, "Spring Allergy Capitals 2021," February 23, 2021*

- Los Angeles was identified as a "2021 Fall Allergy Capital." The area ranked #57 out of 100. Three groups of factors were used to identify the most challenging cities for people with allergies during the fall season: annual fall pollen levels; over the counter medicine use; number of board-certified allergy specialists. *Asthma and Allergy Foundation of America, "Fall Allergy Capitals 2021," February 23, 2021*

- Los Angeles was identified as a "2019 Asthma Capital." The area ranked #90 out of the nation's 100 largest metropolitan areas. Criteria: estimated asthma prevalence; crude death rate from asthma; and ER visits due to asthma. Risk factors analyzed but not factored in the rankings: annual pollen score; annual air quality; public smoking laws; number of board-certified asthma specialists; rescue medication use; controller medication use; uninsured rate; poverty rate. *Asthma and Allergy Foundation of America, "Asthma Capitals 2019: The Most Challenging Places to Live With Asthma," May 7, 2019*

Pet Rankings

- Los Angeles appeared on *The Dogington Post* site as one of the top cities for dog lovers, ranking #7 out of 20. The real estate brokerage, Redfin and Rover, the largest pet sitter and dog walker network, compiled a list from over 14,000 U.S. cities to come up with a "Rover Rank." Criteria: highest count of dog walks, the city's Walk Score®, for-sale home listings that mention "dog," number of dog walkers and pet sitters and the hours spent and distance logged. *www.dogingtonpost.com, "The 20 Most Dog-Friendly Cities of 2019," April 4, 2019*

Real Estate Rankings

- FitSmallBusiness looked at 50 of the largest metropolitan areas in the U.S. to determine which metro was the best to start a real estate business. Data was compiled from such sources as: Zillow, Trulia, U.S. Census Bureau, and the Bureau of Labor Statistics. Criteria: location; inventory; annual wages; median sales price of homes; days on the market; median price cut percentage; and other factors that would influence real estate professional growth. The Los Angeles metro area ranked #1. *fitsmallbusiness.com, "The Best Cities to Become a Real Estate Agent in 2018," January 30, 2018*

- *WalletHub* compared the most populated U.S. cities to determine which had the best markets for real estate agents. Los Angeles ranked #30 where demand was high and pay was the best. Criteria: sales per agent; annual median wage for real-estate agents; monthly average starting salary for real estate agents; real estate job density and competition; unemployment rate; home turnover rate; housing-market health index; and other relevant metrics. *www.WalletHub.com, "2019's Best Places to Be a Real Estate Agent," April 24, 2019*

- The Los Angeles metro area was identified as one of the 20 least affordable housing markets in the U.S. in 2020. The area ranked #178 out of 183 markets. Criteria: qualification for a mortgage loan with a 10 percent down payment on a typical home. *National Association of Realtors®, Qualifying Income Based on Sales Price of Existing Single-Family Homes for Metropolitan Areas, 2020*

- Los Angeles was ranked #268 out of 268 metro areas in terms of housing affordability in 2020 by the National Association of Home Builders (#1 = most affordable). Criteria: the share of homes sold in that area affordable to a family earning the local median income, based on standard mortgage underwriting criteria. *National Association of Home Builders®, NAHB-Wells Fargo Housing Opportunity Index, 4th Quarter 2020*

Safety Rankings

- Allstate ranked the 200 largest cities in America in terms of driver safety. Los Angeles ranked #195. Criteria: internal property damage claims over a two-year period from January 2016 to December 2017. The report helps increase the importance of safety and awareness behind the wheel. *Allstate, "Allstate America's Best Drivers Report, 2019" June 24, 2019*

- The National Insurance Crime Bureau ranked 384 metro areas in the U.S. in terms of per capita rates of vehicle theft. The Los Angeles metro area ranked #45 (#1 = highest rate). Criteria: number of vehicle theft offenses per 100,000 inhabitants in 2019. *National Insurance Crime Bureau, "Hot Spots 2019," July 21, 2020*

Seniors/Retirement Rankings

- From its Best Cities for Successful Aging indexes, the Milken Institute generated rankings for metropolitan areas, weighing data in nine categories—health care, wellness, living arrangements, transportation and convenience, financial characteristics, education, employment, community engagement, and overall livability. The Los Angeles metro area was ranked #56 overall in the large metro area category. *Milken Institute, "Best Cities for Successful Aging, 2017" March 14, 2017*

Transportation Rankings

- Los Angeles was identified as one of the most congested metro areas in the U.S. The area ranked #1 out of 10. Criteria: yearly delay per auto commuter in hours. *Texas A&M Transportation Institute, "2019 Urban Mobility Report," December 2019*

- According to the INRIX "2019 Global Traffic Scorecard," Los Angeles was identified as one of the most congested metro areas in the U.S. The area ranked #6 out of 10. Criteria: average annual time spent in traffic and average cost of congestion per motorist. *Inrix.com, "Congestion Costs Each American Nearly 100 hours, $1,400 A Year," March 9, 2020*

Women/Minorities Rankings

- The *Houston Chronicle* listed the Los Angeles metro area as #6 in top places for young Latinos to live in the U.S. Research was largely based on housing and occupational data from the largest metropolitan areas performed by *Forbes* and NBC Universo. Criteria: percentage of 18-34 year-olds; Latino college grad rates; and diversity. *blog.chron.com, "The 15 Best Big Cities for Latino Millenials," January 26, 2016*

- Personal finance website *WalletHub* compared more than 180 U.S. cities across two key dimensions, "Hispanic Business-Friendliness" and "Hispanic Purchasing Power," to arrive at the most favorable conditions for Hispanic entrepreneurs. Los Angeles was ranked #123 out of 182. Criteria includes: share of Hispanic-Owned Businesses; Hispanic entrepreneurship rate to median annual income of Hispanics; Small Business-Friendliness score; cost of living; and number of Hispanics with at least a bachelor's degree. *WalletHub.com, "2019's Best Cities for Hispanic Entrepreneurs," May 1, 2019*

Miscellaneous Rankings

- Los Angeles was selected as a 2020 Digital Cities Survey winner. The city ranked #2 in the large city (500,000 or more population) category. The survey examined and assessed how city governments are utilizing technology to improve transparency, enhance cybersecurity, and respond to the pandemic. Survey questions focused on ten initiatives: cybersecurity, citizen experience, disaster recovery, business intelligence, IT personnel, data governance, collaboration, infrastructure modernization, cloud computing, and mobile applications. *Center for Digital Government, "2020 Digital Cities Survey," November 10, 2020*

- The watchdog site, Charity Navigator, conducted a study of charities in major markets both to analyze statistical differences in their financial, accountability, and transparency practices and to track year-to-year variations in individual philanthropic communities. The Los Angeles metro area was ranked #14 among the 30 metro markets in the rating category of Overall Score. *www.charitynavigator.org, "2017 Metro Market Study," May 1, 2017*

- *WalletHub* compared the 150 most populated U.S. cities to determine their operating efficiency. A "Quality of City Services" score was constructed for each city and then divided by the total budget per capita to reveal which were managed the best. Los Angeles ranked #134. Criteria: financial stability; economy; education; safety; health; infrastructure and pollution. *www.WalletHub.com, "2020's Best- & Worst-Run Cities in America," June 29, 2020*

- The National Alliance to End Homelessness listed the 25 most populous metro areas with the highest rate of homelessness. The Los Angeles metro area had a high rate of homelessness. Criteria: number of homeless people per 10,000 population in 2016. *National Alliance to End Homelessness, "Homelessness in the 25 Most Populous U.S. Metro Areas," September 1, 2017*

Business Environment

DEMOGRAPHICS

Population Growth

Area	1990 Census	2000 Census	2010 Census	2019* Estimate	Population Growth (%) 1990-2019	Population Growth (%) 2010-2019
City	3,487,671	3,694,820	3,792,621	3,966,936	13.7	4.6
MSA[1]	11,273,720	12,365,627	12,828,837	13,249,614	17.5	3.3
U.S.	248,709,873	281,421,906	308,745,538	324,697,795	30.6	5.2

Note: (1) Figures cover the Los Angeles-Long Beach-Anaheim, CA Metropolitan Statistical Area;
(*) 2015-2019 5-year estimated population
Source: U.S. Census Bureau, 1990 Census, Census 2000, Census 2010, 2015-2019 American Community Survey 5-Year Estimates

Household Size

Area	One	Two	Three	Four	Five	Six	Seven or More	Average Household Size
City	30.3	28.9	15.4	13.1	6.8	3.0	2.6	2.80
MSA[1]	24.6	28.7	17.1	15.4	8.0	3.4	2.8	3.00
U.S.	27.9	33.9	15.6	12.9	6.0	2.3	1.4	2.60

Note: (1) Figures cover the Los Angeles-Long Beach-Anaheim, CA Metropolitan Statistical Area
Source: U.S. Census Bureau, 2015-2019 American Community Survey 5-Year Estimates

Race

Area	White Alone[2] (%)	Black Alone[2] (%)	Asian Alone[2] (%)	AIAN[3] Alone[2] (%)	NHOPI[4] Alone[2] (%)	Other Race Alone[2] (%)	Two or More Races (%)
City	52.1	8.9	11.6	0.7	0.2	22.8	3.8
MSA[1]	53.6	6.6	16.0	0.7	0.3	18.8	4.0
U.S.	72.5	12.7	5.5	0.8	0.2	4.9	3.3

Note: (1) Figures cover the Los Angeles-Long Beach-Anaheim, CA Metropolitan Statistical Area; (2) Alone is defined as not being in combination with one or more other races; (3) American Indian and Alaska Native; (4) Native Hawaiian and Other Pacific Islander
Source: U.S. Census Bureau, 2015-2019 American Community Survey 5-Year Estimates

Hispanic or Latino Origin

Area	Total (%)	Mexican (%)	Puerto Rican (%)	Cuban (%)	Other (%)
City	48.5	32.2	0.4	0.4	15.4
MSA[1]	45.0	35.0	0.4	0.4	9.3
U.S.	18.0	11.2	1.7	0.7	4.3

Note: Persons of Hispanic or Latino origin can be of any race; (1) Figures cover the Los Angeles-Long Beach-Anaheim, CA Metropolitan Statistical Area
Source: U.S. Census Bureau, 2015-2019 American Community Survey 5-Year Estimates

Ancestry

Area	German	Irish	English	American	Italian	Polish	French[2]	Scottish	Dutch
City	3.9	3.5	2.8	3.6	2.6	1.4	1.1	0.7	0.4
MSA[1]	5.2	4.2	3.8	3.6	2.9	1.2	1.2	0.9	0.6
U.S.	13.3	9.7	7.2	6.2	5.1	2.8	2.3	1.7	1.2

Note: Figures are the percentage of the total population reporting a particular ancestry. The nine most commonly reported ancestries in the U.S. are shown. Figures include multiple ancestries (e.g. if a person reported being Irish and Italian, they were included in both columns); (1) Figures cover the Los Angeles-Long Beach-Anaheim, CA Metropolitan Statistical Area; (2) Excludes Basque
Source: U.S. Census Bureau, 2015-2019 American Community Survey 5-Year Estimates

Foreign-born Population

Area	Any Foreign Country	Asia	Mexico	Europe	Caribbean	Central America[2]	South America	Africa	Canada
City	36.9	11.0	12.5	2.4	0.3	8.4	1.1	0.7	0.4
MSA[1]	33.1	12.8	12.1	1.7	0.3	4.3	0.9	0.6	0.3
U.S.	13.6	4.2	3.5	1.5	1.3	1.1	1.0	0.7	0.2

Note: (1) Figures cover the Los Angeles-Long Beach-Anaheim, CA Metropolitan Statistical Area; (2) Excludes Mexico.
Source: U.S. Census Bureau, 2015-2019 American Community Survey 5-Year Estimates

Marital Status

Area	Never Married	Now Married[2]	Separated	Widowed	Divorced
City	45.8	38.8	2.6	4.6	8.2
MSA[1]	39.9	44.7	2.1	4.9	8.4
U.S.	33.4	48.1	1.9	5.8	10.9

Note: Figures are percentages and cover the population 15 years of age and older; (1) Figures cover the Los Angeles-Long Beach-Anaheim, CA Metropolitan Statistical Area; (2) Excludes separated
Source: U.S. Census Bureau, 2015-2019 American Community Survey 5-Year Estimates

Disability by Age

Area	All Ages	Under 18 Years Old	18 to 64 Years Old	65 Years and Over
City	10.1	3.1	7.3	37.3
MSA[1]	9.6	3.0	6.8	33.9
U.S.	12.6	4.2	10.3	34.5

Note: Figures show percent of the civilian noninstitutionalized population that reported having a disability. Disability status is determined from six types of difficulty: vision, hearing, cognitive, ambulatory, self-care, and independent living. For children under 5 years old, hearing and vision difficulty are used to determine disability status. For children between the ages of 5 and 14, disability status is determined from hearing, vision, cognitive, ambulatory, and self-care difficulties. For people aged 15 years and older, they are considered to have a disability if they have difficulty with any one of the six difficulty types; Note: (1) Figures cover the Los Angeles-Long Beach-Anaheim, CA Metropolitan Statistical Area
Source: U.S. Census Bureau, 2015-2019 American Community Survey 5-Year Estimates

Age

Area	Under Age 5	Age 5–19	Age 20–34	Age 35–44	Age 45–54	Age 55–64	Age 65–74	Age 75–84	Age 85+	Median Age
City	5.9	17.5	25.7	14.3	13.2	11.0	7.0	3.6	1.7	35.6
MSA[1]	6.0	18.6	22.7	13.5	13.6	12.0	7.7	4.0	1.9	36.8
U.S.	6.1	19.1	20.7	12.6	13.0	12.9	9.1	4.6	1.9	38.1

Note: (1) Figures cover the Los Angeles-Long Beach-Anaheim, CA Metropolitan Statistical Area
Source: U.S. Census Bureau, 2015-2019 American Community Survey 5-Year Estimates

Gender

Area	Males	Females	Males per 100 Females
City	1,964,984	2,001,952	98.2
MSA[1]	6,533,214	6,716,400	97.3
U.S.	159,886,919	164,810,876	97.0

Note: (1) Figures cover the Los Angeles-Long Beach-Anaheim, CA Metropolitan Statistical Area
Source: U.S. Census Bureau, 2015-2019 American Community Survey 5-Year Estimates

Religious Groups by Family

Area	Catholic	Baptist	Non-Den.	Methodist[2]	Lutheran	LDS[3]	Pentecostal	Presbyterian[4]	Muslim[5]	Judaism
MSA[1]	33.8	2.8	3.6	1.1	0.7	1.7	1.8	0.9	0.7	1.0
U.S.	19.1	9.3	4.0	4.0	2.3	2.0	1.9	1.6	0.8	0.7

Note: Figures are the number of adherents as a percentage of the total population; (1) Figures cover the Los Angeles-Long Beach-Anaheim, CA Metropolitan Statistical Area; (2) Methodist/Pietist; (3) Latter Day Saints; (4) Reformed; (5) Figures are estimates
Source: Association of Statisticians of American Religious Bodies, 2010 U.S. Religion Census: Religious Congregations & Membership Study

Religious Groups by Tradition

Area	Catholic	Evangelical Protestant	Mainline Protestant	Other Tradition	Black Protestant	Orthodox
MSA[1]	33.8	9.0	2.4	4.6	0.9	0.6
U.S.	19.1	16.2	7.3	4.3	1.6	0.3

Note: Figures are the number of adherents as a percentage of the total population; (1) Figures cover the Los Angeles-Long Beach-Anaheim, CA Metropolitan Statistical Area
Source: Association of Statisticians of American Religious Bodies, 2010 U.S. Religion Census: Religious Congregations & Membership Study

ECONOMY

Gross Metropolitan Product

Area	2017	2018	2019	2020	Rank[2]
MSA[1]	1,067.7	1,125.5	1,164.2	1,207.3	2

Note: Figures are in billions of dollars; (1) Figures cover the Los Angeles-Long Beach-Anaheim, CA Metropolitan Statistical Area; (2) Rank is based on 2018 data and ranges from 1 to 381
Source: U.S. Conference of Mayors, U.S. Metro Economies: GMP & Employment 2018-2020, September 2019

Economic Growth

Area	2015-17 (%)	2018 (%)	2019 (%)	2020 (%)	Rank[2]
MSA[1]	2.3	3.5	1.8	1.6	110
U.S.	1.9	2.9	2.3	2.1	–

Note: Figures are real gross metropolitan product (GMP) growth rates and represent average annual percent change; (1) Figures cover the Los Angeles-Long Beach-Anaheim, CA Metropolitan Statistical Area; (2) Rank is based on 2017 2-year average annual percent change and ranges from 1 to 381
Source: U.S. Conference of Mayors, U.S. Metro Economies: GMP & Employment 2018-2020, September 2019

Metropolitan Area Exports

Area	2014	2015	2016	2017	2018	2019	Rank[2]
MSA[1]	75,471.2	61,758.7	61,245.7	63,752.9	64,814.6	61,041.1	3

Note: Figures are in millions of dollars; (1) Figures cover the Los Angeles-Long Beach-Anaheim, CA Metropolitan Statistical Area; (2) Rank is based on 2019 data and ranges from 1 to 386
Source: U.S. Department of Commerce, International Trade Administration, Office of Trade and Economic Analysis, Industry and Analysis, Exports by Metropolitan Area, data extracted March 24, 2021

Building Permits

Area	Single-Family			Multi-Family			Total		
	2018	2019	Pct. Chg.	2018	2019	Pct. Chg.	2018	2019	Pct. Chg.
City	2,636	2,647	0.4	13,663	11,740	-14.1	16,299	14,387	-11.7
MSA[1]	10,042	9,306	-7.3	19,482	21,248	9.1	29,524	30,554	3.5
U.S.	855,300	862,100	0.7	473,500	523,900	10.6	1,328,800	1,386,000	4.3

Note: (1) Figures cover the Los Angeles-Long Beach-Anaheim, CA Metropolitan Statistical Area; Figures represent new, privately-owned housing units authorized (unadjusted data); All permit data are based on estimates with imputation
Source: U.S. Census Bureau, Manufacturing, Mining, and Construction Statistics, Building Permits, 2018, 2019

Bankruptcy Filings

Area	Business Filings			Nonbusiness Filings		
	2019	2020	% Chg.	2019	2020	% Chg.
Los Angeles County	882	857	-2.8	18,304	13,323	-27.2
U.S.	22,780	21,655	-4.9	752,160	522,808	-30.5

Note: Business filings include Chapter 7, Chapter 9, Chapter 11, Chapter 12, Chapter 13, Chapter 15, and Section 304; Nonbusiness filings include Chapter 7, Chapter 11, and Chapter 13
Source: Administrative Office of the U.S. Courts, Business and Nonbusiness Bankruptcy, County Cases Commenced by Chapter of the Bankruptcy Code, During the 12-Month Period Ending December 31, 2019 and Business and Nonbusiness Bankruptcy, County Cases Commenced by Chapter of the Bankruptcy Code, During the 12-Month Period Ending December 31, 2020

Housing Vacancy Rates

Area	Gross Vacancy Rate[2] (%)			Year-Round Vacancy Rate[3] (%)			Rental Vacancy Rate[4] (%)			Homeowner Vacancy Rate[5] (%)		
	2018	2019	2020	2018	2019	2020	2018	2019	2020	2018	2019	2020
MSA[1]	6.6	6.3	5.5	6.2	5.8	4.8	4.0	4.0	3.6	1.2	1.1	0.6
U.S.	12.3	12.0	10.6	9.7	9.5	8.2	6.9	6.7	6.3	1.5	1.4	1.0

Note: (1) Figures cover the Los Angeles-Long Beach-Anaheim, CA Metropolitan Statistical Area; (2) The percentage of the total housing inventory that is vacant; (3) The percentage of the housing inventory (excluding seasonal units) that is year-round vacant; (4) The percentage of rental inventory that is vacant for rent; (5) The percentage of homeowner inventory that is vacant for sale
Source: U.S. Census Bureau, Housing Vacancies and Homeownership Annual Statistics: 2018, 2019, 2020

INCOME

Income

Area	Per Capita ($)	Median Household ($)	Average Household ($)
City	35,261	62,142	96,416
MSA[1]	35,916	72,998	104,698
U.S.	34,103	62,843	88,607

Note: (1) Figures cover the Los Angeles-Long Beach-Anaheim, CA Metropolitan Statistical Area
Source: U.S. Census Bureau, 2015-2019 American Community Survey 5-Year Estimates

Household Income Distribution

Area	Percent of Households Earning							
	Under $15,000	$15,000 -$24,999	$25,000 -$34,999	$35,000 -$49,999	$50,000 -$74,999	$75,000 -$99,999	$100,000 -$149,999	$150,000 and up
City	12.4	9.3	8.7	11.5	15.4	11.4	14.4	16.9
MSA[1]	9.6	7.7	7.6	10.6	15.6	12.4	16.5	20.1
U.S.	10.3	8.9	8.9	12.3	17.2	12.7	15.1	14.5

Note: (1) Figures cover the Los Angeles-Long Beach-Anaheim, CA Metropolitan Statistical Area
Source: U.S. Census Bureau, 2015-2019 American Community Survey 5-Year Estimates

Poverty Rate

Area	All Ages	Under 18 Years Old	18 to 64 Years Old	65 Years and Over
City	18.0	25.7	16.0	15.6
MSA[1]	13.9	19.2	12.5	12.2
U.S.	13.4	18.5	12.6	9.3

Note: Figures are percentage of people whose income during the past 12 months was below the poverty level;
(1) Figures cover the Los Angeles-Long Beach-Anaheim, CA Metropolitan Statistical Area
Source: U.S. Census Bureau, 2015-2019 American Community Survey 5-Year Estimates

CITY FINANCES

City Government Finances

Component	2017 ($000)	2017 ($ per capita)
Total Revenues	21,221,767	5,343
Total Expenditures	17,033,533	4,289
Debt Outstanding	27,626,947	6,956
Cash and Securities[1]	57,128,972	14,383

Note: (1) Cash and security holdings of a government at the close of its fiscal year,
including those of its dependent agencies, utilities, and liquor stores.
Source: U.S. Census Bureau, State & Local Government Finances 2017

City Government Revenue by Source

Source	2017 ($000)	2017 ($ per capita)	2017 (%)
General Revenue			
From Federal Government	422,999	106	2.0
From State Government	300,051	76	1.4
From Local Governments	407,977	103	1.9
Taxes			
Property	1,947,556	490	9.2
Sales and Gross Receipts	1,811,900	456	8.5
Personal Income	0	0	0.0
Corporate Income	0	0	0.0
Motor Vehicle License	0	0	0.0
Other Taxes	949,257	239	4.5
Current Charges	4,192,579	1,056	19.8
Liquor Store	0	0	0.0
Utility	4,550,794	1,146	21.4
Employee Retirement	5,845,735	1,472	27.5

Source: U.S. Census Bureau, State & Local Government Finances 2017

City Government Expenditures by Function

Function	2017 ($000)	2017 ($ per capita)	2017 (%)
General Direct Expenditures			
Air Transportation	1,784,839	449	10.5
Corrections	0	0	0.0
Education	0	0	0.0
Employment Security Administration	0	0	0.0
Financial Administration	174,846	44	1.0
Fire Protection	486,166	122	2.9
General Public Buildings	0	0	0.0
Governmental Administration, Other	99,080	24	0.6
Health	367,507	92	2.2
Highways	546,845	137	3.2
Hospitals	0	0	0.0
Housing and Community Development	243,125	61	1.4
Interest on General Debt	538,313	135	3.2
Judicial and Legal	93,251	23	0.5
Libraries	170,330	42	1.0
Parking	36,301	9	0.2
Parks and Recreation	458,012	115	2.7
Police Protection	2,194,127	552	12.9
Public Welfare	0	0	0.0
Sewerage	661,982	166	3.9
Solid Waste Management	506,492	127	3.0
Veterans' Services	0	0	0.0
Liquor Store	0	0	0.0
Utility	5,111,687	1,287	30.0
Employee Retirement	2,303,616	580	13.5

Source: U.S. Census Bureau, State & Local Government Finances 2017

EMPLOYMENT

Labor Force and Employment

Area	Civilian Labor Force			Workers Employed		
	Dec. 2019	Dec. 2020	% Chg.	Dec. 2019	Dec. 2020	% Chg.
City	2,095,690	1,987,043	-5.2	2,011,531	1,777,290	-11.6
MD[1]	5,171,306	4,867,991	-5.9	4,946,895	4,270,635	-13.7
U.S.	164,007,000	160,017,000	-2.4	158,504,000	149,613,000	-5.6

Note: Data is not seasonally adjusted and covers workers 16 years of age and older; (1) Figures cover the Los Angeles-Long Beach-Glendale, CA Metropolitan Division
Source: Bureau of Labor Statistics, Local Area Unemployment Statistics

Unemployment Rate

Area	2020											
	Jan.	Feb.	Mar.	Apr.	May	Jun.	Jul.	Aug.	Sep.	Oct.	Nov.	Dec.
City	4.5	4.6	6.6	20.7	21.0	20.0	18.8	17.1	15.5	11.8	10.6	10.6
MD[1]	4.9	4.7	5.6	18.2	18.8	17.9	18.2	17.5	13.2	12.0	11.9	12.3
U.S.	4.0	3.8	4.5	14.4	13.0	11.2	10.5	8.5	7.7	6.6	6.4	6.5

Note: Data is not seasonally adjusted and covers workers 16 years of age and older; (1) Figures cover the Los Angeles-Long Beach-Glendale, CA Metropolitan Division
Source: Bureau of Labor Statistics, Local Area Unemployment Statistics

Average Wages

Occupation	$/Hr.	Occupation	$/Hr.
Accountants and Auditors	40.20	Maintenance and Repair Workers	22.80
Automotive Mechanics	25.80	Marketing Managers	77.30
Bookkeepers	24.20	Network and Computer Systems Admin.	46.70
Carpenters	32.40	Nurses, Licensed Practical	29.90
Cashiers	14.80	Nurses, Registered	54.40
Computer Programmers	47.40	Nursing Assistants	18.30
Computer Systems Analysts	53.50	Office Clerks, General	19.90
Computer User Support Specialists	29.60	Physical Therapists	50.80
Construction Laborers	23.20	Physicians	111.70
Cooks, Restaurant	16.00	Plumbers, Pipefitters and Steamfitters	29.00
Customer Service Representatives	20.30	Police and Sheriff's Patrol Officers	53.20
Dentists	65.90	Postal Service Mail Carriers	26.80
Electricians	37.30	Real Estate Sales Agents	29.50
Engineers, Electrical	58.90	Retail Salespersons	17.10
Fast Food and Counter Workers	14.40	Sales Representatives, Technical/Scientific	49.20
Financial Managers	76.00	Secretaries, Exc. Legal/Medical/Executive	22.30
First-Line Supervisors of Office Workers	31.00	Security Guards	16.50
General and Operations Managers	67.90	Surgeons	89.20
Hairdressers/Cosmetologists	18.20	Teacher Assistants, Exc. Postsecondary*	18.30
Home Health and Personal Care Aides	14.90	Teachers, Secondary School, Exc. Sp. Ed.*	41.90
Janitors and Cleaners	17.50	Telemarketers	15.90
Landscaping/Groundskeeping Workers	19.00	Truck Drivers, Heavy/Tractor-Trailer	24.10
Lawyers	86.60	Truck Drivers, Light/Delivery Services	21.40
Maids and Housekeeping Cleaners	16.20	Waiters and Waitresses	16.10

Note: Wage data covers the Los Angeles-Long Beach-Anaheim, CA Metropolitan Statistical Area; (*) Hourly wages were calculated from annual wage data based on a 40 hour work week; n/a not available.
Source: Bureau of Labor Statistics, Metro Area Occupational Employment & Wage Estimates, May 2020

Employment by Industry

Sector	MD[1]		U.S.
	Number of Employees	Percent of Total	Percent of Total
Construction	144,800	3.5	5.1
Education and Health Services	825,900	20.1	16.3
Financial Activities	210,000	5.1	6.1
Government	550,700	13.4	15.2
Information	178,300	4.3	1.9
Leisure and Hospitality	351,300	8.6	9.0
Manufacturing	306,900	7.5	8.5
Mining and Logging	1,600	<0.1	0.4
Other Services	115,000	2.8	3.8
Professional and Business Services	594,500	14.5	14.4
Retail Trade	400,300	9.8	10.9
Transportation, Warehousing, and Utilities	223,700	5.5	4.6
Wholesale Trade	199,100	4.9	3.9

Note: Figures are non-farm employment as of December 2020. Figures are not seasonally adjusted and include workers 16 years of age and older; (1) Figures cover the Los Angeles-Long Beach-Glendale, CA Metropolitan Division
Source: Bureau of Labor Statistics, Current Employment Statistics, Employment, Hours, and Earnings

Employment by Occupation

Occupation Classification	City (%)	MSA[1] (%)	U.S. (%)
Management, Business, Science, and Arts	38.7	38.8	38.5
Natural Resources, Construction, and Maintenance	7.6	7.3	8.9
Production, Transportation, and Material Moving	12.4	12.9	13.2
Sales and Office	20.5	22.4	21.6
Service	20.7	18.5	17.8

Note: Figures cover employed civilians 16 years of age and older; (1) Figures cover the Los Angeles-Long Beach-Anaheim, CA Metropolitan Statistical Area
Source: U.S. Census Bureau, 2015-2019 American Community Survey 5-Year Estimates

Occupations with Greatest Projected Employment Growth: 2020 – 2022

Occupation[1]	2020 Employment	2022 Projected Employment	Numeric Employment Change	Percent Employment Change
Retail Salespersons	317,300	401,300	84,000	26.5
Laborers and Freight, Stock, and Material Movers, Hand	348,700	411,100	62,400	17.9
Waiters and Waitresses	182,500	242,800	60,300	33.0
Combined Food Preparation and Serving Workers, Including Fast Food	183,800	237,200	53,400	29.1
Cashiers	358,500	407,300	48,800	13.6
Cooks, Restaurant	113,200	156,500	43,300	38.3
Personal Care Aides	409,600	447,900	38,300	9.4
Farmworkers and Laborers, Crop, Nursery, and Greenhouse	242,000	269,700	27,700	11.4
Fast Food and Counter Workers	94,000	120,200	26,200	27.9
General and Operations Managers	242,700	268,300	25,600	10.5

Note: Projections cover California; (1) Sorted by numeric employment change
Source: www.projectionscentral.com, State Occupational Projections, 2020–2022 Short-Term Projections

Fastest-Growing Occupations: 2020 – 2022

Occupation[1]	2020 Employment	2022 Projected Employment	Numeric Employment Change	Percent Employment Change
Manicurists and Pedicurists	7,800	21,300	13,500	173.1
Hairdressers, Hairstylists, and Cosmetologists	22,700	44,600	21,900	96.5
Massage Therapists	8,800	17,100	8,300	94.3
Skincare Specialists	5,500	9,100	3,600	65.5
Dental Hygienists	9,200	14,700	5,500	59.8
Dental Hygienists (SOC 2018)	5,300	8,400	3,100	58.5
Dental Assistants	36,300	56,300	20,000	55.1
Dentists, General	12,600	19,000	6,400	50.8
Parking Lot Attendants	14,300	20,400	6,100	42.7
Lodging Managers	3,300	4,600	1,300	39.4

Note: Projections cover California; (1) Sorted by percent employment change and excludes occupations with numeric employment change less than 50
Source: www.projectionscentral.com, State Occupational Projections, 2020–2022 Short-Term Projections

TAXES

State Corporate Income Tax Rates

State	Tax Rate (%)	Income Brackets ($)	Num. of Brackets	Financial Institution Tax Rate (%)[a]	Federal Income Tax Ded.
California	8.84 (b)	Flat rate	1	10.84 (b)	No

Note: Tax rates as of January 1, 2021; (a) Rates listed are the corporate income tax rate applied to financial institutions or excise taxes based on income. Some states have other taxes based upon the value of deposits or shares; (b) Minimum tax is $800 in California, $250 in District of Columbia, $50 in Arizona and North Dakota (banks), $400 ($100 banks) in Rhode Island, $200 per location in South Dakota (banks), $100 in Utah, $300 in Vermont.
Source: Federation of Tax Administrators, State Corporate Income Tax Rates, January 1, 2021

State Individual Income Tax Rates

State	Tax Rate (%)	Income Brackets ($)	Personal Exemptions ($)			Standard Ded. ($)	
			Single	Married	Depend.	Single	Married
California (a)	1.0 - 12.3 (g)	8,932 - 599,012 (b)	124	248 (c)	383 (c)	4,601	9,202 (a)

Note: Tax rates as of January 1, 2021; Local- and county-level taxes are not included; Federal income tax is not deductible on state income tax returns; (a) 19 states have statutory provision for automatically adjusting to the rate of inflation the dollar values of the income tax brackets, standard deductions, and/or personal exemptions. Michigan indexes the personal exemption only. Oregon does not index the income brackets for $125,000 and over; (b) For joint returns, taxes are twice the tax on half the couple's income; (c) The personal exemption takes the form of a tax credit instead of a deduction; (g) California imposes an additional 1% tax on taxable income over $1 million, making the maximum rate 13.3% over $1 million.
Source: Federation of Tax Administrators, State Individual Income Tax Rates, January 1, 2021

Various State Sales and Excise Tax Rates

State	State Sales Tax (%)	Gasoline[1] (¢/gal.)	Cigarette[2] ($/pack)	Spirits[3] ($/gal.)	Wine[4] ($/gal.)	Beer[5] ($/gal.)	Recreational Marijuana (%)
California	7.25	63.05	2.87	3.3	0.2	0.2	(c)

Note: All tax rates as of January 1, 2021; (1) The American Petroleum Institute has developed a methodology for determining the average tax rate on a gallon of fuel. Rates may include any of the following: excise taxes, environmental fees, storage tank fees, other fees or taxes, general sales tax, and local taxes; (2) The federal excise tax of $1.0066 per pack and local taxes are not included; (3) Rates are those applicable to off-premise sales of 40% alcohol by volume (a.b.v.) distilled spirits in 750ml containers. Local excise taxes are excluded; (4) Rates are those applicable to off-premise sales of 11% a.b.v. non-carbonated wine in 750ml containers; (5) Rates are those applicable to off-premise sales of 4.7% a.b.v. beer in 12 ounce containers; (c) 15% excise tax (levied on wholesale at average market rate); $9.65/oz. flowers & $2.87/oz. leaves cultivation tax; $1.35/oz fresh cannabis plant
Source: Tax Foundation, 2021 Facts & Figures: How Does Your State Compare?

State Business Tax Climate Index Rankings

State	Overall Rank	Corporate Tax Rank	Individual Income Tax Rank	Sales Tax Rank	Property Tax Rank	Unemployment Insurance Tax Rank
California	49	28	49	45	14	21

Note: The index is a measure of how each state's tax laws affect economic performance. The lower the rank, the more favorable a state's tax system is for business. States without a given tax are given a ranking of 1. The scores/rankings for the District of Columbia do not affect other states. The 2021 index represents the tax climate as of July 1, 2020.
Source: Tax Foundation, State Business Tax Climate Index 2021

TRANSPORTATION

Means of Transportation to Work

Area	Car/Truck/Van		Public Transportation			Bicycle	Walked	Other Means	Worked at Home
	Drove Alone	Car-pooled	Bus	Subway	Railroad				
City	69.6	8.8	7.8	0.9	0.2	1.0	3.4	2.0	6.3
MSA[1]	75.1	9.5	4.1	0.4	0.3	0.7	2.5	1.6	5.8
U.S.	76.3	9.0	2.4	1.9	0.6	0.5	2.7	1.4	5.2

Note: Figures are percentages and cover workers 16 years of age and older; (1) Figures cover the Los Angeles-Long Beach-Anaheim, CA Metropolitan Statistical Area
Source: U.S. Census Bureau, 2015-2019 American Community Survey 5-Year Estimates

Travel Time to Work

Area	Less Than 10 Minutes	10 to 19 Minutes	20 to 29 Minutes	30 to 44 Minutes	45 to 59 Minutes	60 to 89 Minutes	90 Minutes or More
City	5.9	21.8	19.0	28.3	10.8	10.5	3.8
MSA[1]	6.9	24.4	19.5	25.4	10.2	9.8	3.7
U.S.	12.2	28.4	20.8	20.8	8.3	6.4	2.9

Note: Note: Figures are percentages and include workers 16 years old and over; (1) Figures cover the Los Angeles-Long Beach-Anaheim, CA Metropolitan Statistical Area
Source: U.S. Census Bureau, 2015-2019 American Community Survey 5-Year Estimates

Key Congestion Measures

Measure	1982	1992	2002	2012	2017
Annual Hours of Delay, Total (000)	304,098	510,543	706,816	859,180	971,478
Annual Hours of Delay, Per Auto Commuter	60	72	88	103	119
Annual Congestion Cost, Total (million $)	2,236	5,326	9,459	15,071	17,784
Annual Congestion Cost, Per Auto Commuter ($)	1,823	2,105	2,272	2,165	2,442

Note: Covers the Los Angeles-Long Beach-Anaheim CA urban area
Source: Texas A&M Transportation Institute, 2019 Urban Mobility Report

Freeway Travel Time Index

Measure	1982	1987	1992	1997	2002	2007	2012	2017
Urban Area Index[1]	1.27	1.32	1.35	1.39	1.41	1.47	1.47	1.51
Urban Area Rank[1,2]	1	1	1	1	1	1	1	1

Note: Freeway Travel Time Index—the ratio of travel time in the peak period to the travel time at free-flow conditions. For example, a value of 1.30 indicates a 20-minute free-flow trip takes 26 minutes in the peak (20 minutes x 1.30 = 26 minutes); (1) Covers the Los Angeles-Long Beach-Anaheim CA urban area; (2) Rank is based on 101 larger urban areas (#1 = highest travel time index)
Source: Texas A&M Transportation Institute, 2019 Urban Mobility Report

Public Transportation

Agency Name / Mode of Transportation	Vehicles Operated in Maximum Service[1]	Annual Unlinked Passenger Trips[2] (in thous.)	Annual Passenger Miles[3] (in thous.)
Los Angeles Co. Metro Transportation Authority (LACMTA)			
Bus (directly operated)	1,784	254,580.2	1,044,644.8
Bus (purchased transportation)	134	12,307.5	59,202.6
Bus Rapid Transit (directly operated)	26	6,860.1	45,206.0
Heavy Rail (directly operated)	68	43,074.3	207,664.9
Light Rail (directly operated)	198	59,655.4	462,756.2
Vanpool (purchased transportation)	1,259	3,240.7	142,563.8
City of Los Angeles Department of Transportation (LADOT)			
Bus (purchased transportation)	173	17,467.1	30,643.6
Commuter Bus (purchased transportation)	99	1,563.1	27,575.1
Demand Response (purchased transportation)	89	198.3	948.5
Demand Response Taxi (purchased transportation)	9	64.2	129.7

Note: (1) Number of revenue vehicles operated by the given mode and type of service to meet the annual maximum service requirement. This is the revenue vehicle count during the peak season of the year; on the week and day that maximum service is provided. Vehicles operated in maximum service (VOMS) exclude atypical days and one-time special events; (2) Number of passengers who boarded public transportation vehicles. Passengers are counted each time they board a vehicle no matter how many vehicles they use to travel from their origin to their destination. (3) Sum of the distances ridden by all passengers during the entire fiscal year.
Source: Federal Transit Administration, National Transit Database, 2019

Air Transportation

Airport Name and Code / Type of Service	Passenger Airlines[1]	Passenger Enplanements	Freight Carriers[2]	Freight (lbs)
Los Angeles International (LAX)				
Domestic service (U.S. carriers - 2020)	29	10,938,700	24	898,565,404
International service (U.S. carriers - 2019)	13	2,913,191	10	234,413,489

Note: (1) Includes all U.S.-based major, minor and commuter airlines that carried at least one passenger during the year; (2) Includes all U.S.-based airlines and freight carriers that transported at least one pound of freight during the year.
Source: Bureau of Transportation Statistics, The Intermodal Transportation Database, Air Carriers: T-100 Domestic Market (U.S. Carriers), 2020; Bureau of Transportation Statistics, The Intermodal Transportation Database, Air Carriers: T-100 International Market (U.S. Carriers), 2019

BUSINESSES

Major Business Headquarters

Company Name	Industry	Rankings	
		Fortune[1]	Forbes[2]
AECOM	Engineering, Construction	163	-
CBRE Group	Real Estate	128	-
Capital Group Companies	Diversified Financials	-	54
Gibson, Dunn & Crutcher	Law	-	214
Reliance Steel & Aluminum	Metals	291	-
The Wonderful Company	Multicompany	-	88

Note: (1) Companies that produce a 10-K are ranked 1 to 500 based on 2019 revenue; (2) All private companies with at least $2 billion in annual revenue through the end of their most current fiscal year are ranked 1 to 219; companies listed are headquartered in the city; dashes indicate no ranking
Source: Fortune, "Fortune 500," June/July 2020; Forbes, "America's Largest Private Companies," 2020

Fastest-Growing Businesses

According to *Inc.*, Los Angeles is home to nine of America's 500 fastest-growing private companies: **Create Music Group** (#2); **CannaSafe** (#13); **Villaway** (#42); **Yedi Houseware Appliances** (#105); **Nova Legal Funding** (#234); **SoLa Impact** (#247); **Artkive** (#272); **PaymentCloud** (#295); **BrillMedia.co** (#370). Criteria: must be an independent, privately-held, for-profit, U.S. corporation, proprietorship or partnership as of December 31, 2019; revenues must be at least $100,000 in 2016 and $2 million in 2019; must have four-year operating/sales history. *Inc., "America's 500 Fastest-Growing Private Companies," 2020*

According to *Fortune*, Los Angeles is home to one of the 100 fastest-growing companies in the world: **Preferred Bank** (#98). Companies were ranked by their revenue growth rate; their EPS growth rate; and their three-year annualized total return to investors for the period ending June 30, 2020. Criteria for inclusion: a company, foreign or domestic, must trade on a major U.S. stock exchange; must file quarterly reports with the SEC; must have a minimum market capitalization of $250 million; must have a stock price of at least $5 on June 30, 2020; must have been trading continuously since June 30, 2017; must have revenue and net income for the four quarters ended on or before April 30, 2020, of at least $50 million and $10 million, respectively; and must have posted a compound annual growth in revenue and earnings per share of at least 15% annually over the three years ending on or before April 30, 2020. Real estate investment trusts, limited-liability companies, limited parterships, business development companies, closed-end investment firms, companies about to be acquired, and companies that lost money in the quarter ending April 30, 2020 were excluded. *Fortune, "100 Fastest-Growing Companies," 2020*

According to *Initiative for a Competitive Inner City (ICIC)*, Los Angeles is home to one of America's 100 fastest-growing "inner city" companies: **Giroux Glass** (#73). Criteria for inclusion: company must be headquartered in or have 51 percent or more of its physical operations in an economically distressed urban area; must be an independent, for-profit corporation, partnership or proprietorship; must have 10 or more employees and have a five-year sales history that includes sales of at least $200,000 in the base year and at least $1 million in the current year with no decrease in sales over the two most recent years. Companies were ranked overall by revenue growth over the five-year period between 2015 and 2019. *Initiative for a Competitive Inner City (ICIC), "Inner City 100 Companies," 2020*

According to Deloitte, Los Angeles is home to six of North America's 500 fastest-growing high-technology companies: **FloQast** (#95); **Heal** (#114); **HopSkipDrive** (#132); **MediaAlpha** (#381); **Gimbal** (#448); **ringDNA** (#455). Companies are ranked by percentage growth in revenue over a four-year period. Criteria for inclusion: company must be headquartered within North America; must own proprietary intellectual property or technology that is sold to customers in products that contributes to a significant portion of the company's operating revenue; must have been in business for a minumum of four years with 2016 operating revenues of at least $50,000 USD/CD and 2019 operating revenues of at least $5 million USD/CD. *Deloitte, 2020 Technology Fast 500*™

Minority Business Opportunity

Los Angeles is home to one company which is on the *Black Enterprise* Industrial/Service list (100 largest companies based on gross sales): **The Client Base Funding Group** (#57). Criteria: operational in previous calendar year; at least 51% black-owned and manufactures/owns the product it sells or provides industrial or consumer services. Brokerages, real estate firms and firms that provide professional services are not eligible. *Black Enterprise, B.E. 100s, 2019*

Los Angeles is home to one company which is on the *Black Enterprise* Bank list (15 largest banks based on total assets, capital, deposits and loans, including mortgage-backed securities for the calendar year): **Broadway Financial Corp. (Broadway Federal Bank)** (#6). Only commercial banks or savings and loans that are classified by the Federal Reserve as black institutions and have been fully operational for the previous calendar year were considered. *Black Enterprise, B.E. 100s, 2019*

Living Environment

COST OF LIVING

Cost of Living Index

Composite Index	Groceries	Housing	Utilities	Trans-portation	Health Care	Misc. Goods/ Services
148.0	113.9	230.0	107.7	134.7	110.5	115.7

Note: The Cost of Living Index measures regional differences in the cost of consumer goods and services, excluding taxes and non-consumer expenditures, for professional and managerial households in the top income quintile. It is based on more than 50,000 prices covering almost 60 different items for which prices are collected three times a year by chambers of commerce, economic development organizations or university applied economic centers in each participating urban area. The numbers shown should be read as a percentage above or below the national average of 100. For example, a value of 115.4 in the groceries column indicates that grocery prices are 15.4% higher than the national average. Small differences in the index numbers should not be interpreted as significant; Figures cover the Los Angeles-Long Beach CA urban area.
Source: The Council for Community and Economic Research, Cost of Living Index, 2020

Grocery Prices

Area[1]	T-Bone Steak ($/pound)	Frying Chicken ($/pound)	Whole Milk ($/half gal.)	Eggs ($/dozen)	Orange Juice ($/64 oz.)	Coffee ($/11.5 oz.)
City[2]	12.32	1.72	2.19	2.88	4.09	4.90
Avg.	11.78	1.39	2.05	1.47	3.57	4.34
Min.	8.03	0.94	1.03	0.74	2.94	3.02
Max.	15.86	2.65	4.31	3.77	5.44	8.69

*Note: (1) Values for the local area are compared with the average, minimum and maximum values for all 284 areas in the Cost of Living Index; (2) Figures cover the Los Angeles-Long Beach CA urban area; **T-Bone Steak** (price per pound); **Frying Chicken** (price per pound, whole fryer); **Whole Milk** (half gallon carton); **Eggs** (price per dozen, Grade A, large); **Orange Juice** (64 oz. Tropicana or Florida Natural); **Coffee** (11.5 oz. can, vacuum-packed, Maxwell House, Hills Bros, or Folgers).*
Source: The Council for Community and Economic Research, Cost of Living Index, 2020

Housing and Utility Costs

Area[1]	New Home Price ($)	Apartment Rent ($/month)	All Electric ($/month)	Part Electric ($/month)	Other Energy ($/month)	Telephone ($/month)
City[2]	841,834	2,775	-	122.73	62.94	189.50
Avg.	368,594	1,168	170.86	100.47	65.28	184.30
Min.	190,567	502	91.58	31.42	26.08	169.60
Max.	2,227,806	4,738	470.38	280.31	280.06	206.50

*Note: (1) Values for the local area are compared with the average, minimum and maximum values for all 284 areas in the Cost of Living Index; (2) Figures cover the Los Angeles-Long Beach CA urban area; **New Home Price** (2,400 sf living area, 8,000 sf lot, in urban area with full utilities); **Apartment Rent** (950 sf 2 bedroom/1.5 or 2 bath, unfurnished, excluding all utilities except water); **All Electric** (average monthly cost for an all-electric home); **Part Electric** (average monthly cost for a part-electric home); **Other Energy** (average monthly cost for natural gas, fuel oil, coal, wood, and any other forms of energy except electricity); **Telephone** (price includes the base monthly rate plus taxes and fees for three lines of mobile phone service).*
Source: The Council for Community and Economic Research, Cost of Living Index, 2020

Health Care, Transportation, and Other Costs

Area[1]	Doctor ($/visit)	Dentist ($/visit)	Optometrist ($/visit)	Gasoline ($/gallon)	Beauty Salon ($/visit)	Men's Shirt ($)
City[2]	125.00	110.78	125.58	3.31	76.50	32.87
Avg.	115.44	99.32	108.10	2.21	39.27	31.37
Min.	36.68	59.00	51.36	1.71	19.00	11.00
Max.	219.00	153.10	250.97	3.46	82.05	58.33

*Note: (1) Values for the local area are compared with the average, minimum and maximum values for all 284 areas in the Cost of Living Index; (2) Figures cover the Los Angeles-Long Beach CA urban area; **Doctor** (general practitioners routine exam of an established patient); **Dentist** (adult teeth cleaning and periodic oral examination); **Optometrist** (full vision eye exam for established adult patient); **Gasoline** (one gallon regular unleaded, national brand, including all taxes, cash price at self-service pump if available); **Beauty Salon** (woman's shampoo, trim, and blow-dry); **Men's Shirt** (cotton/polyester dress shirt, pinpoint weave, long sleeves).*
Source: The Council for Community and Economic Research, Cost of Living Index, 2020

HOUSING

Homeownership Rate

Area	2012 (%)	2013 (%)	2014 (%)	2015 (%)	2016 (%)	2017 (%)	2018 (%)	2019 (%)	2020 (%)
MSA[1]	49.9	48.7	49.0	49.1	47.1	49.1	49.5	48.2	48.5
U.S.	65.4	65.1	64.5	63.7	63.4	63.9	64.4	64.6	66.6

Note: (1) Figures cover the Los Angeles-Long Beach-Anaheim, CA Metropolitan Statistical Area
Source: U.S. Census Bureau, Housing Vacancies and Homeownership Annual Statistics: 2012-2020

House Price Index (HPI)

Area	National Ranking[2]	Quarterly Change (%)	One-Year Change (%)	Five-Year Change (%)	Since 1991Q1 (%)
MD[1]	193	1.98	5.13	31.04	214.04
U.S.[3]	–	3.81	10.77	38.99	205.12

Note: The HPI is a weighted repeat sales index. It measures average price changes in repeat sales or refinancings on the same properties. This information is obtained by reviewing repeat mortgage transactions on single-family properties whose mortgages have been purchased or securitized by Fannie Mae or Freddie Mac since January 1975; (1) Figures cover the Los Angeles-Long Beach-Glendale, CA Metropolitan Division; (2) Rankings are based on annual percentage change for all metro areas containing at least 15,000 transactions over the last 10 years and ranges from 1 to 253; (3) figures based on a weighted average of Census Division estimates using a seasonally adjusted, purchase-only index; all figures are for the period ending December 31, 2020
Source: Federal Housing Finance Agency, Change in Metropolitan Area House Price Indexes, April 7, 2021

Median Single-Family Home Prices

Area	2018	2019	2020[p]	Percent Change 2019 to 2020
MD[1]	590.8	611.2	662.3	8.4
U.S. Average	261.6	274.6	299.9	9.2

Note: Figures are median sales prices of existing single-family homes in thousands of dollars; (p) preliminary; (1) Figures cover the Los Angeles-Long Beach-Glendale, CA Metropolitan Division
Source: National Association of Realtors, Median Sales Price of Existing Single-Family Homes for Metropolitan Areas, 4th Quarter 2020

Qualifying Income Based on Median Sales Price of Existing Single-Family Homes

Area	With 5% Down ($)	With 10% Down ($)	With 20% Down ($)
MD[1]	130,262	123,406	109,694
U.S. Average	59,266	56,147	49,908

Note: Figures are preliminary; Qualifying income is based on a mortgage rate of 2.81%. Monthly principal and interest payment is limited to 25% of income; (1) Figures cover the Los Angeles-Long Beach-Glendale, CA Metropolitan Division
Source: National Association of Realtors, Qualifying Income Based on Median Sales Price of Existing Single-Family Homes for Metropolitan Areas, 4th Quarter 2020

Home Value Distribution

Area	Under $50,000	$50,000 -$99,999	$100,000 -$149,999	$150,000 -$199,999	$200,000 -$299,999	$300,000 -$499,999	$500,000 -$999,999	$1,000,000 or more
City	1.2	0.8	0.7	0.8	4.8	25.2	44.5	22.1
MSA[1]	1.9	1.4	0.9	1.2	4.9	25.2	47.5	17.0
U.S.	6.9	12.0	13.3	14.0	19.6	19.3	11.4	3.4

Note: Figures are percentages and cover owner-occupied housing units; (1) Figures cover the Los Angeles-Long Beach-Anaheim, CA Metropolitan Statistical Area
Source: U.S. Census Bureau, 2015-2019 American Community Survey 5-Year Estimates

Year Housing Structure Built

Area	2010 or Later	2000 -2009	1990 -1999	1980 -1989	1970 -1979	1960 -1969	1950 -1959	1940 -1949	Before 1940	Median Year
City	3.2	5.6	5.7	10.2	13.7	14.1	17.4	9.8	20.3	1962
MSA[1]	2.9	6.1	7.6	12.3	16.1	15.9	18.7	8.4	11.9	1967
U.S.	5.2	14.0	13.9	13.4	15.2	10.6	10.3	4.9	12.6	1978

Note: Figures are percentages except for Median Year; Note: (1) Figures cover the Los Angeles-Long Beach-Anaheim, CA Metropolitan Statistical Area
Source: U.S. Census Bureau, 2015-2019 American Community Survey 5-Year Estimates

Gross Monthly Rent

Area	Under $500	$500 -$999	$1,000 -$1,499	$1,500 -$1,999	$2,000 -$2,499	$2,500 -$2,999	$3,000 and up	Median ($)
City	5.3	15.7	32.0	22.6	12.4	6.1	5.9	1,450
MSA[1]	4.2	12.7	30.8	25.7	14.0	6.7	5.9	1,545
U.S.	9.4	36.2	30.0	14.0	5.6	2.4	2.4	1,062

Note: Figures are percentages except for Median; Gross rent is the contract rent plus the estimated average monthly cost of utilities (electricity, gas, and water and sewer) and fuels (oil, coal, kerosene, wood, etc.) if these are paid by the renter (or paid for the renter by someone else); (1) Figures cover the Los Angeles-Long Beach-Anaheim, CA Metropolitan Statistical Area
Source: U.S. Census Bureau, 2015-2019 American Community Survey 5-Year Estimates

HEALTH

Health Risk Factors

Category	MSA[1] (%)	U.S. (%)
Adults aged 18–64 who have any kind of health care coverage	86.6	87.3
Adults who reported being in good or better health	82.2	82.4
Adults who have been told they have high blood cholesterol	31.1	33.0
Adults who have been told they have high blood pressure	26.0	32.3
Adults who are current smokers	11.7	17.1
Adults who currently use E-cigarettes	2.4	4.6
Adults who currently use chewing tobacco, snuff, or snus	1.2	4.0
Adults who are heavy drinkers[2]	5.2	6.3
Adults who are binge drinkers[3]	16.8	17.4
Adults who are overweight (BMI 25.0 - 29.9)	35.7	35.3
Adults who are obese (BMI 30.0 - 99.8)	24.0	31.3
Adults who participated in any physical activities in the past month	80.8	74.4
Adults who always or nearly always wears a seat belt	97.0	94.3

Note: (1) Figures cover the Los Angeles-Long Beach-Anaheim, CA Metropolitan Statistical Area; (2) Heavy drinkers are classified as adult men having more than 14 drinks per week and adult women having more than 7 drinks per week; (3) Binge drinkers are classified as males having five or more drinks on one occasion or females having four or more drinks on one occasion
Source: Centers for Disease Control and Prevention, Behaviorial Risk Factor Surveillance System, SMART: Selected Metropolitan Area Risk Trends, 2017

Acute and Chronic Health Conditions

Category	MSA[1] (%)	U.S. (%)
Adults who have ever been told they had a heart attack	3.2	4.2
Adults who have ever been told they have angina or coronary heart disease	2.7	3.9
Adults who have ever been told they had a stroke	1.7	3.0
Adults who have ever been told they have asthma	12.6	14.2
Adults who have ever been told they have arthritis	17.3	24.9
Adults who have ever been told they have diabetes[2]	10.1	10.5
Adults who have ever been told they had skin cancer	5.7	6.2
Adults who have ever been told they had any other types of cancer	5.0	7.1
Adults who have ever been told they have COPD	3.4	6.5
Adults who have ever been told they have kidney disease	3.2	3.0
Adults who have ever been told they have a form of depression	16.2	20.5

Note: (1) Figures cover the Los Angeles-Long Beach-Anaheim, CA Metropolitan Statistical Area; (2) Figures do not include pregnancy-related, borderline, or pre-diabetes
Source: Centers for Disease Control and Prevention, Behaviorial Risk Factor Surveillance System, SMART: Selected Metropolitan Area Risk Trends, 2017

Health Screening and Vaccination Rates

Category	MSA[1] (%)	U.S. (%)
Adults aged 65+ who have had flu shot within the past year	59.6	60.7
Adults aged 65+ who have ever had a pneumonia vaccination	79.3	75.4
Adults who have ever been tested for HIV	43.8	36.1
Adults who have ever had the shingles or zoster vaccine?	29.5	28.9
Adults who have had their blood cholesterol checked within the last five years	89.0	85.9

Note: n/a not available; (1) Figures cover the Los Angeles-Long Beach-Anaheim, CA Metropolitan Statistical Area.
Source: Centers for Disease Control and Prevention, Behaviorial Risk Factor Surveillance System, SMART: Selected Metropolitan Area Risk Trends, 2017

Disability Status

Category	MSA[1] (%)	U.S. (%)
Adults who reported being deaf	4.3	6.7
Are you blind or have serious difficulty seeing, even when wearing glasses?	4.8	4.5
Are you limited in any way in any of your usual activities due of arthritis?	9.0	12.9
Do you have difficulty doing errands alone?	5.1	6.8
Do you have difficulty dressing or bathing?	3.8	3.6
Do you have serious difficulty concentrating/remembering/making decisions?	9.9	10.7
Do you have serious difficulty walking or climbing stairs?	10.7	13.6

Note: (1) Figures cover the Los Angeles-Long Beach-Anaheim, CA Metropolitan Statistical Area.
Source: Centers for Disease Control and Prevention, Behaviorial Risk Factor Surveillance System, SMART: Selected Metropolitan Area Risk Trends, 2017

Mortality Rates for the Top 10 Causes of Death in the U.S.

ICD-10[a] Sub-Chapter	ICD-10[a] Code	Age-Adjusted Mortality Rate[1] per 100,000 population	
		County[2]	U.S.
Malignant neoplasms	C00-C97	132.7	149.2
Ischaemic heart diseases	I20-I25	99.4	90.5
Other forms of heart disease	I30-I51	33.4	52.2
Chronic lower respiratory diseases	J40-J47	27.5	39.6
Other degenerative diseases of the nervous system	G30-G31	39.2	37.6
Cerebrovascular diseases	I60-I69	33.9	37.2
Other external causes of accidental injury	W00-X59	16.6	36.1
Organic, including symptomatic, mental disorders	F01-F09	9.7	29.4
Hypertensive diseases	I10-I15	25.6	24.1
Diabetes mellitus	E10-E14	25.2	21.5

Note: (a) ICD-10 = International Classification of Diseases 10th Revision; (1) Mortality rates are a three-year average covering 2017-2019; (2) Figures cover Los Angeles County.
Source: Centers for Disease Control and Prevention, National Center for Health Statistics. Underlying Cause of Death 1999-2019 on CDC WONDER Online Database

Mortality Rates for Selected Causes of Death

ICD-10[a] Sub-Chapter	ICD-10[a] Code	Age-Adjusted Mortality Rate[1] per 100,000 population	
		County[2]	U.S.
Assault	X85-Y09	5.5	6.0
Diseases of the liver	K70-K76	14.6	14.4
Human immunodeficiency virus (HIV) disease	B20-B24	1.8	1.5
Influenza and pneumonia	J09-J18	17.8	13.8
Intentional self-harm	X60-X84	8.4	14.1
Malnutrition	E40-E46	0.8	2.3
Obesity and other hyperalimentation	E65-E68	1.7	2.1
Renal failure	N17-N19	11.9	12.6
Transport accidents	V01-V99	8.7	12.3
Viral hepatitis	B15-B19	1.4	1.2

Note: (a) ICD-10 = International Classification of Diseases 10th Revision; (1) Mortality rates are a three-year average covering 2017-2019; (2) Figures cover Los Angeles County; Data are suppressed when the data meet the criteria for confidentiality constraints; Mortality rates are flagged as unreliable when the rate would be calculated with a numerator of 20 or less.
Source: Centers for Disease Control and Prevention, National Center for Health Statistics. Underlying Cause of Death 1999-2019 on CDC WONDER Online Database

Health Insurance Coverage

Area	With Health Insurance	With Private Health Insurance	With Public Health Insurance	Without Health Insurance	Population Under Age 19 Without Health Insurance
City	88.6	54.4	40.5	11.4	4.2
MSA[1]	90.9	60.6	37.4	9.1	3.8
U.S.	91.2	67.9	35.1	8.8	5.1

Note: Figures are percentages that cover the civilian noninstitutionalized population; (1) Figures cover the Los Angeles-Long Beach-Anaheim, CA Metropolitan Statistical Area
Source: U.S. Census Bureau, 2015-2019 American Community Survey 5-Year Estimates

Number of Medical Professionals

Area	MDs[3]	DOs[3,4]	Dentists	Podiatrists	Chiropractors	Optometrists
County[1] (number)	30,460	1,359	8,999	638	3,017	1,881
County[1] (rate[2])	302.4	13.5	89.6	6.4	30.1	18.7
U.S. (rate[2])	282.9	22.7	71.2	6.2	28.1	16.9
06037						

Note: Data as of 2019 unless noted; (1) Data covers Los Angeles County; (2) Rate per 100,000 population; (3) Data as of 2018 and includes all active, non-federal physicians; (4) Doctor of Osteopathic Medicine
Source: U.S. Department of Health and Human Services, Health Resources and Services Administration, Bureau of Health Professions, Area Resource File (ARF) 2019-2020

Best Hospitals

According to *U.S. News,* the Los Angeles-Long Beach-Glendale, CA metro area is home to 10 of the best hospitals in the U.S.: **Cedars-Sinai Medical Center** (Honor Roll/12 adult specialties); **City of Hope Comprehensive Cancer Center** (1 adult specialty); **Kaiser Permanente Los Angeles Medical Center** (1 adult specialty); **Keck Medical Center of USC** (Honor Roll/11 adult specialties); **MemorialCare Long Beach Medical Center** (1 adult specialty); **Santa Monica-UCLA Medical Center and Orthopedic Hospital** (1 adult specialty); **Stein and Doheny Eye Institutes, UCLA Medical Center** (15 adult specialties and 7 pediatric specialties); **UCLA Medical Center** (Honor Roll/15 adult specialties and 7 pediatric specialties); **USC Norris Cancer Hospital-Keck Medical**

Center of USC (1 adult specialty); USC Roski Eye Institute (11 adult specialties). The hospitals listed were nationally ranked in at least one of 16 adult or 10 pediatric specialties. Only 134 hospitals nationwide were nationally ranked in one or more adult or pediatric specialty; this number increases to 178 counting specialized centers within hospitals. Twenty hospitals in the U.S. made the Honor Roll. The Best Hospitals Honor Roll takes both the national rankings and the procedure and condition ratings into account. Hospitals received points if they were nationally ranked in one of the 16 adult specialties—the higher they ranked, the more points they got—and how many ratings of "high performing" they earned in the 10 procedures and conditions. *U.S. News Online, "America's Best Hospitals 2020-21"*

According to *U.S. News,* the Los Angeles-Long Beach-Glendale, CA metro area is home to three of the best children's hospitals in the U.S.: **Children's Hospital Los Angeles** (Honor Roll/10 pediatric specialties); **MemorialCare Miller Children's & Women's Hospital Long Beach** (1 pediatric specialty); **UCLA Mattel Children's Hospital** (7 pediatric specialties). The hospitals listed were highly ranked in at least one of 10 pediatric specialties. Eighty-eight children's hospitals in the U.S. were nationally ranked in at least one specialty. Hospitals received points for being ranked in a specialty, and the 10 hospitals with the most points across the 10 specialties make up the Honor Roll. *U.S. News Online, "America's Best Children's Hospitals 2020-21"*

EDUCATION

Public School District Statistics

District Name	Schls	Pupils	Pupil/ Teacher Ratio	Minority Pupils[1] (%)	Free Lunch Eligible[2] (%)	IEP[3] (%)
Los Angeles Unified	785	495,255	22.5	89.1	73.4	14.6

Note: Table includes school districts with 2,000 or more students; (1) Percentage of students that are not non-Hispanic white; (2) Percentage of students that are eligible for the free lunch program; (3) Percentage of students that have an Individualized Education Program.
Source: U.S. Department of Education, National Center for Education Statistics, Common Core of Data, Local Education Agency (School District) Universe Survey: School Year 2018-2019; U.S. Department of Education, National Center for Education Statistics, Common Core of Data, Public Elementary/Secondary School Universe Survey: School Year 2018-2019

Best High Schools

According to *U.S. News,* Los Angeles is home to seven of the top 500 high schools in the U.S.: **Harbor Teacher Preparation Academy** (#79); **Los Angeles Center for Enriched Studies** (#167); **Downtown Business High** (#193); **Alliance Ted K. Tajima High School** (#324); **Alliance Marc and Eva Stern Math and Science** (#361); **Francisco Bravo Medical Magnet High** (#388); **Sherman Oaks Center for Enriched Studies** (#495). Nearly 18,000 public, magnet and charter schools were ranked based on their performance on state assessments and how well they prepare students for college. *U.S. News & World Report, "Best High Schools 2020"*

Highest Level of Education

Area	Less than H.S.	H.S. Diploma	Some College, No Deg.	Associate Degree	Bachelor's Degree	Master's Degree	Prof. School Degree	Doctorate Degree
City	22.5	19.2	17.6	6.2	22.6	7.6	2.8	1.4
MSA[1]	19.3	19.8	19.2	7.2	22.4	8.2	2.5	1.4
U.S.	12.0	27.0	20.4	8.5	19.8	8.8	2.1	1.4

Note: Figures cover persons age 25 and over; (1) Figures cover the Los Angeles-Long Beach-Anaheim, CA Metropolitan Statistical Area
Source: U.S. Census Bureau, 2015-2019 American Community Survey 5-Year Estimates

Educational Attainment by Race

Area	High School Graduate or Higher (%)					Bachelor's Degree or Higher (%)				
	Total	White	Black	Asian	Hisp.[2]	Total	White	Black	Asian	Hisp.[2]
City	77.5	80.9	88.7	90.3	56.3	34.4	39.8	26.5	54.9	12.3
MSA[1]	80.7	83.2	89.9	88.2	62.2	34.5	36.6	27.3	53.4	13.3
U.S.	88.0	89.9	86.0	87.1	68.7	32.1	33.5	21.6	54.3	16.4

Note: Figures shown cover persons 25 years old and over; (1) Figures cover the Los Angeles-Long Beach-Anaheim, CA Metropolitan Statistical Area; (2) People of Hispanic origin can be of any race
Source: U.S. Census Bureau, 2015-2019 American Community Survey 5-Year Estimates

School Enrollment by Grade and Control

Area	Preschool (%)		Kindergarten (%)		Grades 1 - 4 (%)		Grades 5 - 8 (%)		Grades 9 - 12 (%)	
	Public	Private	Public	Private	Public	Private	Public	Private	Public	Private
City	60.2	39.8	88.1	11.9	89.0	11.0	88.6	11.4	88.8	11.2
MSA[1]	58.5	41.5	88.4	11.6	90.8	9.2	91.0	9.0	91.4	8.6
U.S.	59.1	40.9	87.6	12.4	89.5	10.5	89.4	10.6	90.1	9.9

Note: Figures shown cover persons 3 years old and over; (1) Figures cover the Los Angeles-Long
Beach-Anaheim, CA Metropolitan Statistical Area
Source: U.S. Census Bureau, 2015-2019 American Community Survey 5-Year Estimates

Higher Education

Four-Year Colleges			Two-Year Colleges			Medical Schools[1]	Law Schools[2]	Voc/ Tech[3]
Public	Private Non-profit	Private For-profit	Public	Private Non-profit	Private For-profit			
2	20	10	6	4	10	2	5	20

Note: Figures cover institutions located within the city limits and include main campuses only; (1) includes
schools accredited by the Liaison Committee on Medical Education and the American Osteopathic
Association's Commission on Osteopathic College Accreditation; (2) includes ABA-accredited schools, schools
with provisional ABA accreditation, and state accredited schools; (3) includes all schools with programs that
are less than 2 years.
Source: National Center for Education Statistics, Integrated Postsecondary Education System (IPEDS),
2019-20; Wikipedia, List of Medical Schools in the United States, accessed April 2, 2021; Wikipedia, List of
Law Schools in the United States, accessed April 2, 2021

According to U.S. News & World Report, the Los Angeles-Long Beach-Glendale, CA metro division
is home to six of the top 200 national universities in the U.S.: **California Institute of Technology** (#9
tie); **University of California—Los Angeles** (#20); **University of Southern California** (#24 tie);
Pepperdine University (#49 tie); **Loyola Marymount University** (#66 tie); **Biola University** (#187
tie). The indicators used to capture academic quality fall into a number of categories: assessment by
administrators at peer institutions; retention of students; faculty resources; student selectivity; financial resources; alumni giving; high school counselor ratings of colleges; and graduation rate. U.S.
News & World Report, "America's Best Colleges 2021"

According to U.S. News & World Report, the Los Angeles-Long Beach-Glendale, CA metro division
is home to six of the top 100 liberal arts colleges in the U.S.: **Pomona College** (#4 tie); **Claremont
McKenna College** (#6 tie); **Harvey Mudd College** (#25 tie); **Scripps College** (#28 tie); **Pitzer College** (#36 tie); **Occidental College** (#40 tie). The indicators used to capture academic quality fall into
a number of categories: assessment by administrators at peer institutions; retention of students; faculty resources; student selectivity; financial resources; alumni giving; high school counselor ratings of
colleges; and graduation rate. U.S. News & World Report, "America's Best Colleges 2021"

According to U.S. News & World Report, the Los Angeles-Long Beach-Glendale, CA metro division
is home to four of the top 100 law schools in the U.S.: **University of California—Los Angeles**
(#14); **University of Southern California (Gould)** (#19); **Pepperdine University Caruso** (#46 tie);
Loyola Marymount University (#72 tie). The rankings are based on a weighted average of 12 measures of quality: peer assessment score; assessment score by lawyers/judges; median LSAT scores;
median undergrad GPA; acceptance rate; employment rates for graduates; placement success; bar passage rate; faculty resources; expenditures per student; student/faculty ratio; and library resources. U.S.
News & World Report, "America's Best Graduate Schools, Law, 2022"

According to U.S. News & World Report, the Los Angeles-Long Beach-Glendale, CA metro division
is home to two of the top 75 medical schools for research in the U.S.: **University of California—Los
Angeles (Geffen)** (#21); **University of Southern California (Keck)** (#29). The rankings are based
on a weighted average of 11 measures of quality: quality assessment; peer assessment score; assessment score by residency directors; research activity; total research activity; average research activity
per faculty member; student selectivity; median MCAT total score; median undergraduate GPA; acceptance rate; and faculty resources. U.S. News & World Report, "America's Best Graduate Schools,
Medical, 2022"

According to U.S. News & World Report, the Los Angeles-Long Beach-Glendale, CA metro division
is home to three of the top 75 business schools in the U.S.: **University of Southern California (Marshall)** (#16 tie); **University of California—Los Angeles (Anderson)** (#18); **Pepperdine University
(Graziadio)** (#68 tie). The rankings are based on a weighted average of the following nine measures:
quality assessment; peer assessment; recruiter assessment; placement success; mean starting salary
and bonus; student selectivity; mean GMAT and GRE scores; mean undergraduate GPA; and acceptance rate. U.S. News & World Report, "America's Best Graduate Schools, Business, 2022"

EMPLOYERS

Major Employers

Company Name	Industry
City of Los Angeles	Municipal government
County of Los Angeles	County government
Decton	Employment agencies
Disney Enterprises	Motion picture production & distribution
Disney Worldwide Services	Telecommunication equipment repair, excl telephones
Electronic Arts	Home entertainment computer software
King Holding Corporation	Bolts, nuts, rivets, & washers
Securitas Security Services USA	Security guard service
Team-One Employment Specialists	Employment agencies
The Boeing Company	Aircraft
The Walt Disney Company	Television broadcasting stations
UCLA Health System	Home health care services
UCLA Medical Group	Medical centers
University of California, Irvine	University
University of Southern California	Colleges & universities
Veterans Health Administration	Administration of veterans' affairs
Warner Bros. Entertainment	Motion picture production & distribution

Note: Companies shown are located within the Los Angeles-Long Beach-Anaheim, CA Metropolitan Statistical Area.
Source: Hoovers.com; Wikipedia

Best Companies to Work For

Farmers Insurance, headquartered in Los Angeles, is among "The 100 Best Companies to Work For." To pick the best companies, *Fortune* partnered with the Great Place to Work Institute. Two-thirds of a company's score is based on the results of the Institute's Trust Index survey, which is sent to a random sample of employees from each company. The questions related to attitudes about management's credibility, job satisfaction, and camaraderie. The other third of the scoring is based on the company's responses to the Institute's Culture Audit, which includes detailed questions about pay and benefit programs, and a series of open-ended questions about hiring practices, internal communication, training, recognition programs, and diversity efforts. Any company that is at least five years old with more than 1,000 U.S. employees is eligible. *Fortune, "The 100 Best Companies to Work For," 2020*

Korn Ferry, headquartered in Los Angeles, is among the "100 Best Companies for Working Mothers." Criteria: paid time off and leaves; workforce profile; benefits; women's issues and advancement; flexible work; company culture and work life programs. *Working Mother, "100 Best Companies for Working Mothers," 2020*

Cedars-Sinai, headquartered in Los Angeles, is among the "100 Best Places to Work in IT." To qualify, companies had to be U.S.-based organizations or be non-U.S.-based employers that met the following criteria: have a minimum of 300 total employees at a U.S. headquarters and a minimum of 30 IT employees in the U.S., with at least 50% of their IT employees based in the U.S. The best places to work were selected based on compensation, benefits, work/life balance, employee morale, and satisfaction with training and development programs. In addition, *InsiderPro* and *Computerworld* looked at retention efforts, programs for recognizing and rewarding outstanding performances, and benefits such as flextime, elder care and child care, and reimbursement for college tuition and the cost of pursuing technology certifications. *InsiderPro and Computerworld, "100 Best Places to Work in IT," 2020*

Korn Ferry, headquartered in Los Angeles, is among the "Top Companies for Executive Women." This list is determined by organizations filling out an in-depth survey that measures female demographics at every level, but with an emphasis on women in senior corporate roles, with profit & loss (P&L) responsibility, and those earning in the top 20 percent of the organization. *Working Mother* defines P&L as having responsibility that involves monitoring the net income after expenses for a department or entire organization, with direct influence on how company resources are allocated. *Working Mother, "Top Companies for Executive Women," 2020+*

Korn Ferry, headquartered in Los Angeles, is among the "Best Companies for Dads." *Working Mother's* newest list recognizes the growing importance companies place on giving dads time off and support for their families. Rankings are determined by measuring gender-neutral or paternity leave offered, as well as actual time taken, phase-back policies, child- and dependent-care benefits, and corporate support groups for men and dads. *Working Mother, "Best Companies for Dads," 2020*

PUBLIC SAFETY

Crime Rate

Area	All Crimes	Violent Crimes				Property Crimes		
		Murder	Rape[3]	Robbery	Aggrav. Assault	Burglary	Larceny -Theft	Motor Vehicle Theft
City	3,115.5	6.4	56.6	240.4	428.7	343.9	1,649.9	389.5
Suburbs[1]	2,574.0	4.1	31.4	148.3	263.3	400.2	1,366.0	360.7
Metro[2]	2,790.2	5.1	41.5	185.0	329.4	377.7	1,479.4	372.2
U.S.	2,489.3	5.0	42.6	81.6	250.2	340.5	1,549.5	219.9

Note: Figures are crimes per 100,000 population; (1) All areas within the metro area that are located outside the city limits; (2) Figures cover the Los Angeles-Long Beach-Glendale, CA Metropolitan Division; (3) All figures shown were reported using the revised Uniform Crime Reporting (UCR) definition of rape.
Source: FBI Uniform Crime Reports, 2019

Hate Crimes

Area	Number of Quarters Reported	Number of Incidents per Bias Motivation					
		Race/Ethnicity/ Ancestry	Religion	Sexual Orientation	Disability	Gender	Gender Identity
City[1]	4	118	81	70	2	0	14
U.S.	4	3,963	1,521	1,195	157	69	198

Note: (1) Figures include one incident reported with more than one bias motivation.
Source: Federal Bureau of Investigation, Hate Crime Statistics 2019

Identity Theft Consumer Reports

Area	Reports	Reports per 100,000 Population	Rank[2]
MSA[1]	75,066	568	45
U.S.	1,387,615	423	-

Note: (1) Figures cover the Los Angeles-Long Beach-Anaheim, CA Metropolitan Statistical Area; (2) Rank ranges from 1 to 391 where 1 indicates greatest number of identity theft reports per 100,000 population
Source: Federal Trade Commission, Consumer Sentinel Network Data Book 2020

Fraud and Other Consumer Reports

Area	Reports	Reports per 100,000 Population	Rank[2]
MSA[1]	112,088	848	75
U.S.	3,385,133	1,031	-

Note: (1) Figures cover the Los Angeles-Long Beach-Anaheim, CA Metropolitan Statistical Area; (2) Rank ranges from 1 to 391 where 1 indicates greatest number of fraud and other consumer reports per 100,000 population
Source: Federal Trade Commission, Consumer Sentinel Network Data Book 2020

POLITICS

2020 Presidential Election Results

Area	Biden	Trump	Jorgensen	Hawkins	Other
Los Angeles County	71.0	26.9	0.8	0.5	0.8
U.S.	51.3	46.8	1.2	0.3	0.5

Note: Results are percentages and may not add to 100% due to rounding
Source: Dave Leip's Atlas of U.S. Presidential Elections

SPORTS

Professional Sports Teams

Team Name	League	Year Established
Anaheim Ducks	National Hockey League (NHL)	1993
C.D. Chivas USA	Major League Soccer (MLS)	2004
Los Angeles Angels of Anaheim	Major League Baseball (MLB)	1961
Los Angeles Chargers	National Football League (NFL)	2017
Los Angeles Clippers	National Basketball Association (NBA)	1984
Los Angeles Dodgers	Major League Baseball (MLB)	1958
Los Angeles FC	Major League Soccer (MLS)	2018
Los Angeles Galaxy	Major League Soccer (MLS)	1996
Los Angeles Kings	National Hockey League (NHL)	1967
Los Angeles Lakers	National Basketball Association (NBA)	1960
Los Angeles Rams	National Football League (NFL)	2016

Note: Includes teams located in the Los Angeles-Long Beach-Anaheim, CA Metropolitan Statistical Area.
Source: Wikipedia, Major Professional Sports Teams of the United States and Canada, April 6, 2021

CLIMATE

Average and Extreme Temperatures

Temperature	Jan	Feb	Mar	Apr	May	Jun	Jul	Aug	Sep	Oct	Nov	Dec	Yr.
Extreme High (°F)	88	92	95	102	97	104	97	98	110	106	101	94	110
Average High (°F)	65	66	65	67	69	72	75	76	76	74	71	66	70
Average Temp. (°F)	56	57	58	60	63	66	69	70	70	67	62	57	63
Average Low (°F)	47	49	50	53	56	59	63	64	63	59	52	48	55
Extreme Low (°F)	27	34	37	43	45	48	52	51	47	43	38	32	27

Note: Figures cover the years 1947-1990
Source: National Climatic Data Center, International Station Meteorological Climate Summary, 9/96

Average Precipitation/Snowfall/Humidity

Precip./Humidity	Jan	Feb	Mar	Apr	May	Jun	Jul	Aug	Sep	Oct	Nov	Dec	Yr.
Avg. Precip. (in.)	2.6	2.3	1.8	0.8	0.1	Tr	Tr	0.1	0.2	0.3	1.5	1.5	11.3
Avg. Snowfall (in.)	Tr	0	0	0	0	0	0	0	0	0	0	0	Tr
Avg. Rel. Hum. 7am (%)	69	72	76	76	77	80	80	81	80	76	69	67	75
Avg. Rel. Hum. 4pm (%)	60	62	64	64	66	67	67	68	67	66	61	60	64

Note: Figures cover the years 1947-1990; Tr = Trace amounts (<0.05 in. of rain; <0.5 in. of snow)
Source: National Climatic Data Center, International Station Meteorological Climate Summary, 9/96

Weather Conditions

Temperature			Daytime Sky			Precipitation		
10°F & below	32°F & below	90°F & above	Clear	Partly cloudy	Cloudy	0.01 inch or more precip.	0.1 inch or more snow/ice	Thunder-storms
0	< 1	5	131	125	109	34	0	1

Note: Figures are average number of days per year and cover the years 1947-1990
Source: National Climatic Data Center, International Station Meteorological Climate Summary, 9/96

HAZARDOUS WASTE

Superfund Sites

The Los Angeles-Long Beach-Glendale, CA metro division is home to 17 sites on the EPA's Superfund National Priorities List: **Cooper Drum Co.** (final); **Del Amo** (final); **Jervis B. Webb Co.** (final); **Jet Propulsion Laboratory (NASA)** (final); **Montrose Chemical Corp.** (final); **Omega Chemical Corporation** (final); **Operating Industries, Inc., Landfill** (final); **Pemaco Maywood** (final); **San Fernando Valley (Area 1)** (final); **San Fernando Valley (Area 2)** (final); **San Fernando Valley (Area 4)** (final); **San Gabriel Valley (Area 1)** (final); **San Gabriel Valley (Area 2)** (final); **San Gabriel Valley (Area 3)** (final); **San Gabriel Valley (Area 4)** (final); **Southern Avenue Industrial Area** (final); **Waste Disposal, Inc.** (final). There are a total of 1,375 Superfund sites with a status of proposed or final on the list in the U.S. *U.S. Environmental Protection Agency, National Priorities List, April 7, 2021*

AIR QUALITY

Air Quality Trends: Ozone

	1990	1995	2000	2005	2010	2015	2016	2017	2018	2019
MSA[1]	0.134	0.114	0.091	0.085	0.076	0.083	0.083	0.093	0.084	0.080
U.S.	0.088	0.089	0.082	0.080	0.073	0.068	0.069	0.068	0.069	0.065

Note: (1) Data covers the Los Angeles-Long Beach-Anaheim, CA Metropolitan Statistical Area. The values shown are the composite ozone concentration averages among trend sites based on the highest fourth daily maximum 8-hour concentration in parts per million. These trends are based on sites having an adequate record of monitoring data during the trend period. Data from exceptional events are included.
Source: U.S. Environmental Protection Agency, Air Quality Monitoring Information, "Air Quality Trends by City, 1990-2019"

Air Quality Index

Area	Percent of Days when Air Quality was...[2]					AQI Statistics[2]	
	Good	Moderate	Unhealthy for Sensitive Groups	Unhealthy	Very Unhealthy	Maximum	Median
MSA[1]	18.1	57.0	17.0	7.7	0.3	201	72

Note: (1) Data covers the Los Angeles-Long Beach-Anaheim, CA Metropolitan Statistical Area; (2) Based on 365 days with AQI data in 2019. Air Quality Index (AQI) is an index for reporting daily air quality. EPA calculates the AQI for five major air pollutants regulated by the Clean Air Act: ground-level ozone, particle pollution (aka particulate matter), carbon monoxide, sulfur dioxide, and nitrogen dioxide. The AQI runs from 0 to 500. The higher the AQI value, the greater the level of air pollution and the greater the health concern. There are six AQI categories: "Good" AQI is between 0 and 50. Air quality is considered satisfactory; "Moderate" AQI is between 51 and 100. Air quality is acceptable; "Unhealthy for Sensitive Groups" When AQI values are between 101 and 150, members of sensitive groups may experience health effects; "Unhealthy" When AQI values are between 151 and 200 everyone may begin to experience health effects; "Very Unhealthy" AQI values between 201 and 300 trigger a health alert; "Hazardous" AQI values over 300 trigger warnings of emergency conditions (not shown).
Source: U.S. Environmental Protection Agency, Air Quality Index Report, 2019

Air Quality Index Pollutants

Area	Percent of Days when AQI Pollutant was...[2]					
	Carbon Monoxide	Nitrogen Dioxide	Ozone	Sulfur Dioxide	Particulate Matter 2.5	Particulate Matter 10
MSA[1]	0.0	9.0	56.2	0.0	32.3	2.5

Note: (1) Data covers the Los Angeles-Long Beach-Anaheim, CA Metropolitan Statistical Area; (2) Based on 365 days with AQI data in 2019. The Air Quality Index (AQI) is an index for reporting daily air quality. EPA calculates the AQI for five major air pollutants regulated by the Clean Air Act: ground-level ozone, particle pollution (also known as particulate matter), carbon monoxide, sulfur dioxide, and nitrogen dioxide. The AQI runs from 0 to 500. The higher the AQI value, the greater the level of air pollution and the greater the health concern.
Source: U.S. Environmental Protection Agency, Air Quality Index Report, 2019

Maximum Air Pollutant Concentrations: Particulate Matter, Ozone, CO and Lead

	Particulate Matter 10 (ug/m^3)	Particulate Matter 2.5 Wtd AM (ug/m^3)	Particulate Matter 2.5 24-Hr (ug/m^3)	Ozone (ppm)	Carbon Monoxide (ppm)	Lead (ug/m^3)
MSA[1] Level	159	11.0	28	0.101	3	0.02
NAAQS[2]	150	15	35	0.075	9	0.15
Met NAAQS[2]	No	Yes	Yes	No	Yes	Yes

Note: (1) Data covers the Los Angeles-Long Beach-Anaheim, CA Metropolitan Statistical Area; Data from exceptional events are included; (2) National Ambient Air Quality Standards; ppm = parts per million; ug/m^3 = micrograms per cubic meter; n/a not available.
Concentrations: Particulate Matter 10 (coarse particulate)—highest second maximum 24-hour concentration; Particulate Matter 2.5 Wtd AM (fine particulate)—highest weighted annual mean concentration; Particulate Matter 2.5 24-Hour (fine particulate)—highest 98th percentile 24-hour concentration; Ozone—highest fourth daily maximum 8-hour concentration; Carbon Monoxide—highest second maximum non-overlapping 8-hour concentration; Lead—maximum running 3-month average
Source: U.S. Environmental Protection Agency, Air Quality Monitoring Information, "Air Quality Statistics by City, 2019"

Maximum Air Pollutant Concentrations: Nitrogen Dioxide and Sulfur Dioxide

	Nitrogen Dioxide AM (ppb)	Nitrogen Dioxide 1-Hr (ppb)	Sulfur Dioxide AM (ppb)	Sulfur Dioxide 1-Hr (ppb)	Sulfur Dioxide 24-Hr (ppb)
MSA[1] Level	23	78	n/a	8	n/a
NAAQS[2]	53	100	30	75	140
Met NAAQS[2]	Yes	Yes	n/a	Yes	n/a

Note: (1) Data covers the Los Angeles-Long Beach-Anaheim, CA Metropolitan Statistical Area; Data from exceptional events are included; (2) National Ambient Air Quality Standards; ppm = parts per million; ug/m^3 = micrograms per cubic meter; n/a not available.
Concentrations: Nitrogen Dioxide AM—highest arithmetic mean concentration; Nitrogen Dioxide 1-Hr—highest 98th percentile 1-hour daily maximum concentration; Sulfur Dioxide AM—highest annual mean concentration; Sulfur Dioxide 1-Hr—highest 99th percentile 1-hour daily maximum concentration; Sulfur Dioxide 24-Hr—highest second maximum 24-hour concentration
Source: U.S. Environmental Protection Agency, Air Quality Monitoring Information, "Air Quality Statistics by City, 2019"

Phoenix, Arizona

Background

Phoenix, the arid "Valley of the Sun," and the capital of Arizona, was named by the English soldier and prospector, "Lord Darell" Duppa for the mythical bird of ancient Greek/Phoenician lore. According to the legend, the Phoenix was a beautiful bird that destroyed itself with its own flames. When nothing remained but embers, it would rise again from the ashes, more awesome and beautiful than before. Like the romantic tale, Duppa hoped that his city of Phoenix would rise again from the mysteriously abandoned Hohokam village.

Many might agree that Phoenix fulfilled Duppa's wish. Within 15 years after its second founding in 1867, Phoenix had grown to be an important supply point for the mining districts of north-central Arizona, as well as an important trading site for farmers, cattlemen, and prospectors.

Around this time, Phoenix entered its Wild West phase, complete with stagecoaches, saloons, gambling houses, soldiers, cowboys, miners, and the pungent air of outlawry. Two public hangings near the end of the 1800s set a dramatic example, and helped turn the tide.

Today, Phoenix is just as exciting as ever, but more law-abiding, and many continue to be attracted to Phoenix's natural beauty. Despite occasional sprawling suburbs and shopping malls, the sophisticated blend of Spanish, Native American, and cowboy culture is obvious in the city's architecture, arts, and crafts. Downtown Phoenix underwent a major renaissance in the 1990s with the completion of a history museum, expanded art museum, new central library, Arizona Science Center, and a renovated concert hall. Today it also features the 20,000 square foot Musical Instrument Museum featuring musical instruments from around the world. More than 300 arts and entertainment venues are located in the Phoenix region, as well as five professional sports teams. Phoenix Concept 2000 split the city into 15 urban villages, each with its own height and density permits, further shaping the city's free-market development culture.

Phoenix is the country's fifth-largest city, with more than one million people, while the Phoenix metro area population has grown to nearly four million. This increase in population continues to make Phoenix an attractive location for companies that are expanding in the fields of electronics and communications. Renewable energy, biomedicine, advanced business services, manufacturing and distribution, aerospace and aviation, and emerging technologies from start-ups are key industries in the region, as are insurance, healthcare, and technology.

The Valley Metro Rail light rail eco-friendly transit system continues expanding toward its goal of 60-miles by 2034.

Phoenix is home to several professional sports franchises. The Phoenix Suns of the NBA and the Phoenix Mercury of the WNBA both play at Talking Stick Resort Arena. The Mercury have won the WNBA championships three times: in 2007, 2009, and 2014. The Arizona Diamondbacks of Major League Baseball play their home games in Chase Field, the second-highest stadium in the country, and defeated the New York Yankees in 2001 to claim the World Series title. The Arizona Cardinals are the oldest continuously run professional football franchise in the nation, though they originated in Chicago. They play at the University of Phoenix Stadium in Glendale, which hosted Super Bowl XLII in 2008 and Super Bowl XLIX in 2015.

In 1981, Phoenix resident Sandra Day O'Connor broke the gender barrier on the U.S. Supreme Court when she was sworn in as the first female justice. The influx of refugees over the decades has resulted in 43 languages being spoken in local schools.

Temperatures in Phoenix are mild in winter and very hot in summer. However, with the low humidity, the summer heat is somewhat more bearable than one might expect. Rainfall is slight and comes in two seasons. In winter rain comes on winds from the Pacific, ending by April. In summer, especially during July and August, there are severe thunderstorms from the southeast.

Rankings

General Rankings

- For its "Best for Vets: Places to Live 2019" rankings, *Military Times* evaluated 599 cities (83 large, 234 medium, 282 small) and compared the locations across three broad categories: veteran and military culture/services; economic indicators; and livability factors such as health, crime, traffic, and school quality. Phoenix ranked #21 out of the top 25, in the large city category (population of more than 250,000). Data points more specific to veterans and the military weighed more heavily than others. *rebootcamp.militarytimes.com, "Military Times Best Places to Live 2019," September 10, 2018*

- The Phoenix metro area was identified as one of America's fastest-growing areas in terms of population and business growth by *MagnifyMoney*. The area ranked #28 out of 35. The 100 most populous metro areas in the U.S. were evaluated on their change from 2011-2016 in the following categories: people and housing; workforce and employment opportunities; growing industry. *www.businessinsider.com, "The 35 Cities in the US with the Biggest Influx of People, the Most Work Opportunities, and the Hottest Business Growth," August 12, 2018*

- The Phoenix metro area was identified as one of America's fastest-growing areas in terms of population and economy by *Forbes*. The area ranked #11 out of 25. The 100 most populous metro areas in the U.S. were evaluated on the following criteria: estimated population growth; employment; economic output; wages; home values. *Forbes, "America's Fastest-Growing Cities 2018," February 28, 2018*

Business/Finance Rankings

- The Brookings Institution ranked the nation's largest cities based on income inequality. Phoenix was ranked #62 (#1 = greatest inequality). Criteria: the "95/20 ratio," a figure representing the income at which a household earns more than 95 percent of all other households, divided by the income at which a household earns more than only 20 percent of all other households. *Brookings Institution, "Household Income Inequality, Largest Cities of 97 Large U.S. Metro Areas, 2014-2016," February 5, 2018*

- The Brookings Institution ranked the 100 largest metro areas in the U.S. based on income inequality. Phoenix was ranked #61 (#1 = greatest inequality). Criteria: the "95/20 ratio," a figure representing the income at which a household earns more than 95 percent of all other households, divided by the income at which a household earns more than only 20 percent of all other households. *Brookings Institution, "Household Income Inequality, 100 Largest U.S. Metro Areas, 2014-2016," February 5, 2018*

- *Forbes* ranked the 100 largest metro areas in the U.S. in terms of the "Best Cities for Young Professionals." The Phoenix metro area ranked #16 out of 25. Criteria: median rent of a two-bedroom apartment; job growth and unemployment rate; median salary of college graduates with 5 or less years of work experience; networking opportunities; social outlook; percentage of population 25 years of age and older with college degrees. *Forbes.com, "America's 25 Best Cities for Young Professionals in 2017," May 22, 2017*

- Payscale.com ranked the 32 largest metro areas in terms of wage growth. The Phoenix metro area ranked #14. Criteria: private-sector and education professional wage growth between the 4th quarter of 2019 and the 4th quarter of 2020. *PayScale, "Wage Trends by Metro Area-4th Quarter," January 11, 2021*

- The Phoenix metro area was identified as one of the most debt-ridden places in America by the finance site Credit.com. The metro area was ranked #17. Criteria: residents' average credit card debt as well as median income. *Credit.com, "25 Cities With the Most Credit Card Debt," February 28, 2018*

- Phoenix was identified as one of America's most frugal metro areas by *Coupons.com*. The city ranked #16 out of 25. Criteria: digital coupon usage. *Coupons.com, "America's Most Frugal Cities of 2017," March 22, 2018*

- Phoenix was cited as one of America's top metros for new and expanded facility projects in 2020. The area ranked #6 in the large metro area category (population over 1 million). *Site Selection, "Top Metros of 2020," March 2021*

- Phoenix was identified as one of the happiest cities to work in by CareerBliss.com, an online community for career advancement. The city ranked #4 out of 10. Criteria: an employee's relationship with his or her boss and co-workers; daily tasks; general work environment; compensation; opportunities for advancement; company culture and job reputation; and resources. *Businesswire.com, "CareerBliss Happiest Cities to Work 2019," February 12, 2019*

- The Phoenix metro area appeared on the Milken Institute "2021 Best Performing Cities" list. Rank: #7 out of 200 large metro areas (population over 250,000). Criteria: job growth; wage and salary growth; high-tech output growth; housing affordability; household broadband access. *Milken Institute, "Best-Performing Cities 2021," February 16, 2021*

- *Forbes* ranked the 200 most populous metro areas to determine the nation's "Best Places for Business and Careers." The Phoenix metro area was ranked #26. Criteria: costs (business and living); job growth (past and projected); income growth; quality of life; educational attainment (college and high school); projected economic growth; cultural and leisure opportunities; workplace tolerance laws; net migration patterns. *Forbes, "The Best Places for Business and Careers 2019: Seattle Still On Top," October 30, 2019*

Education Rankings

- Personal finance website *WalletHub* analyzed the 150 largest U.S. metropolitan statistical areas to determine where the most educated Americans are putting their degrees to work. Criteria: education levels; percentage of workers with degrees; education quality and attainment gap; public school quality rankings; quality and enrollment of each metro area's universities. Phoenix was ranked #80 (#1 = most educated city). *www.WalletHub.com, "Most and Least Educated Cities in America," July 20, 2020*

- Phoenix was selected as one of America's most literate cities. The city ranked #74 out of the 84 largest U.S. cities. Criteria: number of booksellers; library resources; Internet resources; educational attainment; periodical publishing resources; newspaper circulation. *Central Connecticut State University, "America's Most Literate Cities, 2018," February 2019*

Environmental Rankings

- Sperling's BestPlaces assessed the 50 largest metropolitan areas of the United States for the likelihood of dangerously extreme weather events or earthquakes. In general the Southeast and South-Central regions have the highest risk of weather extremes and earthquakes, while the Pacific Northwest enjoys the lowest risk. Of the most risky metropolitan areas, the Phoenix metro area was ranked #9. *www.bestplaces.net, "Avoid Natural Disasters: BestPlaces Reveals The Top 10 Safest Places to Live," October 25, 2017*

- The U.S. Environmental Protection Agency (EPA) released a list of U.S. metropolitan areas with the most ENERGY STAR certified buildings in 2019. The Phoenix metro area was ranked #16 out of 25. *U.S. Environmental Protection Agency, "2020 Energy Star Top Cities," March 2020*

- The U.S. Conference of Mayors and Walmart Stores sponsor the Mayors' Climate Protection Awards Program which recognize mayors for outstanding and innovative practices that mayors are taking to increase energy efficiency in their cities, reduce carbon emissions and expand renewable energy. Phoenix received an Honorable Mention in the large city category. *U.S. Conference of Mayors, "2020 Mayors' Climate Protection Awards," December 18, 2020*

- Phoenix was highlighted as one of the 25 most ozone-polluted metro areas in the U.S. during 2016 through 2018. The area ranked #7. *American Lung Association, "State of the Air 2020," April 21, 2020*

- Phoenix was highlighted as one of the 25 metro areas most polluted by year-round particle pollution (Annual PM 2.5) in the U.S. during 2016 through 2018. The area ranked #7. *American Lung Association, "State of the Air 2020," April 21, 2020*

- Phoenix was highlighted as one of the 25 metro areas most polluted by short-term particle pollution (24-hour PM 2.5) in the U.S. during 2016 through 2018. The area ranked #10. *American Lung Association, "State of the Air 2020," April 21, 2020*

Food/Drink Rankings

- The U.S. Chamber of Commerce Foundation conducted an in-depth study on local food truck regulations, surveyed 288 food truck owners, and ranked 20 major American cities based on how friendly they are for operating a food truck. The compiled index assessed the following: procedures for obtaining permits and licenses; complying with restrictions; and financial obligations associated with operating a food truck. Phoenix ranked #14 overall (1 being the best). *www.foodtrucknation.us, "Food Truck Nation," March 20, 2018*

- Chase Field was selected as one of PETA's "Top 10 Vegan-Friendly Ballparks" for 2019. The park ranked #10. *People for the Ethical Treatment of Animals, "Top 10 Vegan-Friendly Ballparks," May 23, 2019*

Health/Fitness Rankings

- For each of the 100 largest cities in the United States, the American Fitness Index®, published by the American College of Sports Medicine and the Anthem Foundation, evaluated community infrastructure and 33 health behaviors including preventive health, levels of chronic disease conditions, pedestrian safety, air quality, and community resources that support physical activity. Phoenix ranked #71 for "community fitness." *americanfitnessindex.org, "2020 ACSM American Fitness Index Summary Report," July 14, 2020*

- The Phoenix metro area was identified as one of the worst cities for bed bugs in America by pest control company Orkin. The area ranked #42 out of 50 based on the number of bed bug treatments Orkin performed from December 2019 to November 2020. *Orkin, "New Year, New Top City on Orkin's 2021 Bed Bug Cities List: Chicago," February 1, 2021*

- Phoenix was identified as a "2021 Spring Allergy Capital." The area ranked #68 out of 100. Three groups of factors were used to identify the most challenging cities for people with allergies during the spring season: annual spring pollen levels; over the counter medicine use; number of board-certified allergy specialists. *Asthma and Allergy Foundation of America, "Spring Allergy Capitals 2021," February 23, 2021*

- Phoenix was identified as a "2021 Fall Allergy Capital." The area ranked #77 out of 100. Three groups of factors were used to identify the most challenging cities for people with allergies during the fall season: annual fall pollen levels; over the counter medicine use; number of board-certified allergy specialists. *Asthma and Allergy Foundation of America, "Fall Allergy Capitals 2021," February 23, 2021*

- Phoenix was identified as a "2019 Asthma Capital." The area ranked #40 out of the nation's 100 largest metropolitan areas. Criteria: estimated asthma prevalence; crude death rate from asthma; and ER visits due to asthma. Risk factors analyzed but not factored in the rankings: annual pollen score; annual air quality; public smoking laws; number of board-certified asthma specialists; rescue medication use; controller medication use; uninsured rate; poverty rate. *Asthma and Allergy Foundation of America, "Asthma Capitals 2019: The Most Challenging Places to Live With Asthma," May 7, 2019*

Real Estate Rankings

- FitSmallBusiness looked at 50 of the largest metropolitan areas in the U.S. to determine which metro was the best to start a real estate business. Data was compiled from such sources as: Zillow, Trulia, U.S. Census Bureau, and the Bureau of Labor Statistics. Criteria: location; inventory; annual wages; median sales price of homes; days on the market; median price cut percentage; and other factors that would influence real estate professional growth. The Phoenix metro area ranked #16. *fitsmallbusiness.com, "The Best Cities to Become a Real Estate Agent in 2018," January 30, 2018*

- *WalletHub* compared the most populated U.S. cities to determine which had the best markets for real estate agents. Phoenix ranked #10 where demand was high and pay was the best. Criteria: sales per agent; annual median wage for real-estate agents; monthly average starting salary for real estate agents; real estate job density and competition; unemployment rate; home turnover rate; housing-market health index; and other relevant metrics. *www.WalletHub.com, "2019's Best Places to Be a Real Estate Agent," April 24, 2019*

- According to Penske Truck Rental, the Phoenix metro area was named the #1 moving destination in 2019, based on one-way consumer truck rental reservations made through Penske's website, rental locations, and reservations call center. *gopenske.com/blog, "Penske Truck Rental's 2019 Top Moving Destinations," January 22, 2020*

- The Phoenix metro area appeared on Realtor.com's list of hot housing markets to watch in 2021. The area ranked #6. Criteria: healthy existing homes inventory; relative home affordability; local economy/population trends. *Realtor.com®, "Top 10 Housing Markets Positioned for Growth in 2021," December 7, 2020*

- Phoenix was ranked #4 in the top 20 out of the 100 largest metro areas in terms of house price appreciation in 2020 (#1 = highest rate). *Federal Housing Finance Agency, House Price Index, 4th Quarter 2020*

- Phoenix was ranked #176 out of 268 metro areas in terms of housing affordability in 2020 by the National Association of Home Builders (#1 = most affordable). Criteria: the share of homes sold in that area affordable to a family earning the local median income, based on standard mortgage underwriting criteria. *National Association of Home Builders®, NAHB-Wells Fargo Housing Opportunity Index, 4th Quarter 2020*

Safety Rankings

- Allstate ranked the 200 largest cities in America in terms of driver safety. Phoenix ranked #84. Criteria: internal property damage claims over a two-year period from January 2016 to December 2017. The report helps increase the importance of safety and awareness behind the wheel. *Allstate, "Allstate America's Best Drivers Report, 2019" June 24, 2019*

- The National Insurance Crime Bureau ranked 384 metro areas in the U.S. in terms of per capita rates of vehicle theft. The Phoenix metro area ranked #97 (#1 = highest rate). Criteria: number of vehicle theft offenses per 100,000 inhabitants in 2019. *National Insurance Crime Bureau, "Hot Spots 2019," July 21, 2020*

Seniors/Retirement Rankings

- From its Best Cities for Successful Aging indexes, the Milken Institute generated rankings for metropolitan areas, weighing data in nine categories—health care, wellness, living arrangements, transportation and convenience, financial characteristics, education, employment, community engagement, and overall livability. The Phoenix metro area was ranked #88 overall in the large metro area category. *Milken Institute, "Best Cities for Successful Aging, 2017" March 14, 2017*

Women/Minorities Rankings

- The *Houston Chronicle* listed the Phoenix metro area as #5 in top places for young Latinos to live in the U.S. Research was largely based on housing and occupational data from the largest metropolitan areas performed by *Forbes* and NBC Universo. Criteria: percentage of 18-34 year-olds; Latino college grad rates; and diversity. *blog.chron.com, "The 15 Best Big Cities for Latino Millenials," January 26, 2016*

- *Women's Health*, together with the site Yelp, identified the 15 "Wellthiest" spots in the U.S. Phoenix appeared among the top for happiest, healthiest, outdoorsiest and Zen-iest. *Women's Health, "The 15 Wellthiest Cities in the U.S." July 5, 2017*

- Personal finance website *WalletHub* compared more than 180 U.S. cities across two key dimensions, "Hispanic Business-Friendliness" and "Hispanic Purchasing Power," to arrive at the most favorable conditions for Hispanic entrepreneurs. Phoenix was ranked #77 out of 182. Criteria includes: share of Hispanic-Owned Businesses; Hispanic entrepreneurship rate to median annual income of Hispanics; Small Business-Friendliness score; cost of living; and number of Hispanics with at least a bachelor's degree. *WalletHub.com, "2019's Best Cities for Hispanic Entrepreneurs," May 1, 2019*

Miscellaneous Rankings

- Phoenix was selected as a 2020 Digital Cities Survey winner. The city ranked #4 in the large city (500,000 or more population) category. The survey examined and assessed how city governments are utilizing technology to improve transparency, enhance cybersecurity, and respond to the pandemic. Survey questions focused on ten initiatives: cybersecurity, citizen experience, disaster recovery, business intelligence, IT personnel, data governance, collaboration, infrastructure modernization, cloud computing, and mobile applications. *Center for Digital Government, "2020 Digital Cities Survey," November 10, 2020*

- The watchdog site, Charity Navigator, conducted a study of charities in major markets both to analyze statistical differences in their financial, accountability, and transparency practices and to track year-to-year variations in individual philanthropic communities. The Phoenix metro area was ranked #12 among the 30 metro markets in the rating category of Overall Score. *www.charitynavigator.org, "2017 Metro Market Study," May 1, 2017*

- *WalletHub* compared the 150 most populated U.S. cities to determine their operating efficiency. A "Quality of City Services" score was constructed for each city and then divided by the total budget per capita to reveal which were managed the best. Phoenix ranked #34. Criteria: financial stability; economy; education; safety; health; infrastructure and pollution. *www.WalletHub.com, "2020's Best- & Worst-Run Cities in America," June 29, 2020*

- The National Alliance to End Homelessness listed the 25 most populous metro areas with the highest rate of homelessness. The Phoenix metro area had a high rate of homelessness. Criteria: number of homeless people per 10,000 population in 2016. *National Alliance to End Homelessness, "Homelessness in the 25 Most Populous U.S. Metro Areas," September 1, 2017*

Business Environment

DEMOGRAPHICS

Population Growth

Area	1990 Census	2000 Census	2010 Census	2019* Estimate	Population Growth (%) 1990-2019	Population Growth (%) 2010-2019
City	989,873	1,321,045	1,445,632	1,633,017	65.0	13.0
MSA[1]	2,238,480	3,251,876	4,192,887	4,761,603	112.7	13.6
U.S.	248,709,873	281,421,906	308,745,538	324,697,795	30.6	5.2

Note: (1) Figures cover the Phoenix-Mesa-Scottsdale, AZ Metropolitan Statistical Area; (*) 2015-2019 5-year estimated population
Source: U.S. Census Bureau, 1990 Census, Census 2000, Census 2010, 2015-2019 American Community Survey 5-Year Estimates

Household Size

Area	Persons in Household (%) One	Two	Three	Four	Five	Six	Seven or More	Average Household Size
City	27.9	30.1	15.2	13.0	7.3	3.8	2.7	2.90
MSA[1]	26.5	34.4	14.4	12.7	6.7	3.0	2.2	2.80
U.S.	27.9	33.9	15.6	12.9	6.0	2.3	1.4	2.60

Note: (1) Figures cover the Phoenix-Mesa-Scottsdale, AZ Metropolitan Statistical Area
Source: U.S. Census Bureau, 2015-2019 American Community Survey 5-Year Estimates

Race

Area	White Alone[2] (%)	Black Alone[2] (%)	Asian Alone[2] (%)	AIAN[3] Alone[2] (%)	NHOPI[4] Alone[2] (%)	Other Race Alone[2] (%)	Two or More Races (%)
City	72.9	7.1	3.8	2.1	0.2	10.0	3.9
MSA[1]	77.8	5.5	4.0	2.3	0.2	6.5	3.7
U.S.	72.5	12.7	5.5	0.8	0.2	4.9	3.3

Note: (1) Figures cover the Phoenix-Mesa-Scottsdale, AZ Metropolitan Statistical Area; (2) Alone is defined as not being in combination with one or more other races; (3) American Indian and Alaska Native; (4) Native Hawaiian and Other Pacific Islander
Source: U.S. Census Bureau, 2015-2019 American Community Survey 5-Year Estimates

Hispanic or Latino Origin

Area	Total (%)	Mexican (%)	Puerto Rican (%)	Cuban (%)	Other (%)
City	42.6	38.3	0.7	0.3	3.3
MSA[1]	30.9	27.1	0.7	0.3	2.8
U.S.	18.0	11.2	1.7	0.7	4.3

Note: Persons of Hispanic or Latino origin can be of any race; (1) Figures cover the Phoenix-Mesa-Scottsdale, AZ Metropolitan Statistical Area
Source: U.S. Census Bureau, 2015-2019 American Community Survey 5-Year Estimates

Ancestry

Area	German	Irish	English	American	Italian	Polish	French[2]	Scottish	Dutch
City	9.9	7.1	5.5	3.0	3.8	2.0	1.7	1.3	0.9
MSA[1]	12.5	8.3	7.7	3.9	4.4	2.4	2.1	1.6	1.1
U.S.	13.3	9.7	7.2	6.2	5.1	2.8	2.3	1.7	1.2

Note: Figures are the percentage of the total population reporting a particular ancestry. The nine most commonly reported ancestries in the U.S. are shown. Figures include multiple ancestries (e.g. if a person reported being Irish and Italian, they were included in both columns); (1) Figures cover the Phoenix-Mesa-Scottsdale, AZ Metropolitan Statistical Area; (2) Excludes Basque
Source: U.S. Census Bureau, 2015-2019 American Community Survey 5-Year Estimates

Foreign-born Population

Area	Any Foreign Country	Percent of Population Born in Asia	Mexico	Europe	Caribbean	Central America[2]	South America	Africa	Canada
City	19.4	3.4	11.9	1.3	0.3	0.9	0.4	0.8	0.4
MSA[1]	14.3	3.4	7.2	1.3	0.3	0.6	0.3	0.5	0.6
U.S.	13.6	4.2	3.5	1.5	1.3	1.1	1.0	0.7	0.2

Note: (1) Figures cover the Phoenix-Mesa-Scottsdale, AZ Metropolitan Statistical Area; (2) Excludes Mexico.
Source: U.S. Census Bureau, 2015-2019 American Community Survey 5-Year Estimates

Marital Status

Area	Never Married	Now Married[2]	Separated	Widowed	Divorced
City	39.2	42.1	2.0	4.3	12.4
MSA[1]	34.0	47.2	1.6	5.1	12.1
U.S.	33.4	48.1	1.9	5.8	10.9

Note: Figures are percentages and cover the population 15 years of age and older; (1) Figures cover the Phoenix-Mesa-Scottsdale, AZ Metropolitan Statistical Area; (2) Excludes separated
Source: U.S. Census Bureau, 2015-2019 American Community Survey 5-Year Estimates

Disability by Age

Area	All Ages	Under 18 Years Old	18 to 64 Years Old	65 Years and Over
City	10.7	3.9	9.5	34.7
MSA[1]	11.5	3.7	9.3	32.6
U.S.	12.6	4.2	10.3	34.5

Note: Figures show percent of the civilian noninstitutionalized population that reported having a disability. Disability status is determined from six types of difficulty: vision, hearing, cognitive, ambulatory, self-care, and independent living. For children under 5 years old, hearing and vision difficulty are used to determine disability status. For children between the ages of 5 and 14, disability status is determined from hearing, vision, cognitive, ambulatory, and self-care difficulties. For people aged 15 years and older, they are considered to have a disability if they have difficulty with any one of the six difficulty types; Note: (1) Figures cover the Phoenix-Mesa-Scottsdale, AZ Metropolitan Statistical Area
Source: U.S. Census Bureau, 2015-2019 American Community Survey 5-Year Estimates

Age

Area	Percent of Population									Median Age
	Under Age 5	Age 5–19	Age 20–34	Age 35–44	Age 45–54	Age 55–64	Age 65–74	Age 75–84	Age 85+	
City	7.2	21.6	23.2	13.8	12.8	10.9	6.5	2.9	1.2	33.8
MSA[1]	6.4	20.3	21.0	13.1	12.5	11.4	8.9	4.6	1.7	36.7
U.S.	6.1	19.1	20.7	12.6	13.0	12.9	9.1	4.6	1.9	38.1

Note: (1) Figures cover the Phoenix-Mesa-Scottsdale, AZ Metropolitan Statistical Area
Source: U.S. Census Bureau, 2015-2019 American Community Survey 5-Year Estimates

Gender

Area	Males	Females	Males per 100 Females
City	813,775	819,242	99.3
MSA[1]	2,366,181	2,395,422	98.8
U.S.	159,886,919	164,810,876	97.0

Note: (1) Figures cover the Phoenix-Mesa-Scottsdale, AZ Metropolitan Statistical Area
Source: U.S. Census Bureau, 2015-2019 American Community Survey 5-Year Estimates

Religious Groups by Family

Area	Catholic	Baptist	Non-Den.	Methodist[2]	Lutheran	LDS[3]	Pente-costal	Presby-terian[4]	Muslim[5]	Judaism
MSA[1]	13.4	3.5	5.2	1.0	1.6	6.1	2.9	0.6	0.2	0.3
U.S.	19.1	9.3	4.0	4.0	2.3	2.0	1.9	1.6	0.8	0.7

Note: Figures are the number of adherents as a percentage of the total population; (1) Figures cover the Phoenix-Mesa-Scottsdale, AZ Metropolitan Statistical Area; (2) Methodist/Pietist; (3) Latter Day Saints; (4) Reformed; (5) Figures are estimates
Source: Association of Statisticians of American Religious Bodies, 2010 U.S. Religion Census: Religious Congregations & Membership Study

Religious Groups by Tradition

Area	Catholic	Evangelical Protestant	Mainline Protestant	Other Tradition	Black Protestant	Orthodox
MSA[1]	13.4	13.2	2.6	7.8	0.2	0.3
U.S.	19.1	16.2	7.3	4.3	1.6	0.3

Note: Figures are the number of adherents as a percentage of the total population; (1) Figures cover the Phoenix-Mesa-Scottsdale, AZ Metropolitan Statistical Area
Source: Association of Statisticians of American Religious Bodies, 2010 U.S. Religion Census: Religious Congregations & Membership Study

ECONOMY

Gross Metropolitan Product

Area	2017	2018	2019	2020	Rank[2]
MSA[1]	248.0	264.9	280.3	294.0	16

Note: Figures are in billions of dollars; (1) Figures cover the Phoenix-Mesa-Scottsdale, AZ Metropolitan Statistical Area; (2) Rank is based on 2018 data and ranges from 1 to 381
Source: U.S. Conference of Mayors, U.S. Metro Economies: GMP & Employment 2018-2020, September 2019

Economic Growth

Area	2015-17 (%)	2018 (%)	2019 (%)	2020 (%)	Rank[2]
MSA[1]	3.3	4.5	4.0	2.7	54
U.S.	1.9	2.9	2.3	2.1	–

Note: Figures are real gross metropolitan product (GMP) growth rates and represent average annual percent change; (1) Figures cover the Phoenix-Mesa-Scottsdale, AZ Metropolitan Statistical Area; (2) Rank is based on 2017 2-year average annual percent change and ranges from 1 to 381
Source: U.S. Conference of Mayors, U.S. Metro Economies: GMP & Employment 2018-2020, September 2019

Metropolitan Area Exports

Area	2014	2015	2016	2017	2018	2019	Rank[2]
MSA[1]	12,764.4	13,821.5	12,838.2	13,223.1	13,614.9	15,136.6	24

Note: Figures are in millions of dollars; (1) Figures cover the Phoenix-Mesa-Scottsdale, AZ Metropolitan Statistical Area; (2) Rank is based on 2019 data and ranges from 1 to 386
Source: U.S. Department of Commerce, International Trade Administration, Office of Trade and Economic Analysis, Industry and Analysis, Exports by Metropolitan Area, data extracted March 24, 2021

Building Permits

Area	Single-Family 2018	2019	Pct. Chg.	Multi-Family 2018	2019	Pct. Chg.	Total 2018	2019	Pct. Chg.
City	3,732	4,175	11.9	3,530	5,723	62.1	7,262	9,898	36.3
MSA[1]	23,526	25,026	6.4	7,817	10,847	38.8	31,343	35,873	14.5
U.S.	855,300	862,100	0.7	473,500	523,900	10.6	1,328,800	1,386,000	4.3

Note: (1) Figures cover the Phoenix-Mesa-Scottsdale, AZ Metropolitan Statistical Area; Figures represent new, privately-owned housing units authorized (unadjusted data); All permit data are based on estimates with imputation
Source: U.S. Census Bureau, Manufacturing, Mining, and Construction Statistics, Building Permits, 2018, 2019

Bankruptcy Filings

Area	Business Filings 2019	2020	% Chg.	Nonbusiness Filings 2019	2020	% Chg.
Maricopa County	344	261	-24.1	11,095	8,954	-19.3
U.S.	22,780	21,655	-4.9	752,160	522,808	-30.5

Note: Business filings include Chapter 7, Chapter 9, Chapter 11, Chapter 12, Chapter 13, Chapter 15, and Section 304; Nonbusiness filings include Chapter 7, Chapter 11, and Chapter 13
Source: Administrative Office of the U.S. Courts, Business and Nonbusiness Bankruptcy, County Cases Commenced by Chapter of the Bankruptcy Code, During the 12-Month Period Ending December 31, 2019 and Business and Nonbusiness Bankruptcy, County Cases Commenced by Chapter of the Bankruptcy Code, During the 12-Month Period Ending December 31, 2020

Housing Vacancy Rates

Area	Gross Vacancy Rate[2] (%) 2018	2019	2020	Year-Round Vacancy Rate[3] (%) 2018	2019	2020	Rental Vacancy Rate[4] (%) 2018	2019	2020	Homeowner Vacancy Rate[5] (%) 2018	2019	2020
MSA[1]	12.6	10.3	8.9	7.8	6.2	5.3	6.2	5.0	4.9	1.4	1.0	0.7
U.S.	12.3	12.0	10.6	9.7	9.5	8.2	6.9	6.7	6.3	1.5	1.4	1.0

Note: (1) Figures cover the Phoenix-Mesa-Scottsdale, AZ Metropolitan Statistical Area; (2) The percentage of the total housing inventory that is vacant; (3) The percentage of the housing inventory (excluding seasonal units) that is year-round vacant; (4) The percentage of rental inventory that is vacant for rent; (5) The percentage of homeowner inventory that is vacant for sale
Source: U.S. Census Bureau, Housing Vacancies and Homeownership Annual Statistics: 2018, 2019, 2020

INCOME

Income

Area	Per Capita ($)	Median Household ($)	Average Household ($)
City	29,343	57,459	80,631
MSA[1]	32,522	63,883	87,543
U.S.	34,103	62,843	88,607

Note: (1) Figures cover the Phoenix-Mesa-Scottsdale, AZ Metropolitan Statistical Area
Source: U.S. Census Bureau, 2015-2019 American Community Survey 5-Year Estimates

Household Income Distribution

Area	Under $15,000	$15,000 -$24,999	$25,000 -$34,999	$35,000 -$49,999	$50,000 -$74,999	$75,000 -$99,999	$100,000 -$149,999	$150,000 and up
City	10.4	9.3	9.5	14.3	18.5	12.6	13.6	11.9
MSA[1]	8.9	8.0	8.8	13.0	18.5	13.4	15.7	13.7
U.S.	10.3	8.9	8.9	12.3	17.2	12.7	15.1	14.5

Note: (1) Figures cover the Phoenix-Mesa-Scottsdale, AZ Metropolitan Statistical Area
Source: U.S. Census Bureau, 2015-2019 American Community Survey 5-Year Estimates

Poverty Rate

Area	All Ages	Under 18 Years Old	18 to 64 Years Old	65 Years and Over
City	18.0	26.6	15.6	10.8
MSA[1]	13.7	19.6	12.8	8.2
U.S.	13.4	18.5	12.6	9.3

Note: Figures are percentage of people whose income during the past 12 months was below the poverty level;
(1) Figures cover the Phoenix-Mesa-Scottsdale, AZ Metropolitan Statistical Area
Source: U.S. Census Bureau, 2015-2019 American Community Survey 5-Year Estimates

CITY FINANCES

City Government Finances

Component	2017 ($000)	2017 ($ per capita)
Total Revenues	4,028,523	2,577
Total Expenditures	3,201,786	2,048
Debt Outstanding	7,724,365	4,942
Cash and Securities[1]	7,484,717	4,789

Note: (1) Cash and security holdings of a government at the close of its fiscal year,
including those of its dependent agencies, utilities, and liquor stores.
Source: U.S. Census Bureau, State & Local Government Finances 2017

City Government Revenue by Source

Source	2017 ($000)	2017 ($ per capita)	2017 (%)
General Revenue			
From Federal Government	198,778	127	4.9
From State Government	678,446	434	16.8
From Local Governments	23,397	15	0.6
Taxes			
Property	327,885	210	8.1
Sales and Gross Receipts	837,370	536	20.8
Personal Income	0	0	0.0
Corporate Income	0	0	0.0
Motor Vehicle License	0	0	0.0
Other Taxes	88,073	56	2.2
Current Charges	896,551	574	22.3
Liquor Store	0	0	0.0
Utility	458,689	293	11.4
Employee Retirement	315,074	202	7.8

Source: U.S. Census Bureau, State & Local Government Finances 2017

City Government Expenditures by Function

Function	2017 ($000)	2017 ($ per capita)	2017 (%)
General Direct Expenditures			
Air Transportation	389,267	249	12.2
Corrections	0	0	0.0
Education	30,504	19	1.0
Employment Security Administration	0	0	0.0
Financial Administration	36,775	23	1.1
Fire Protection	310,018	198	9.7
General Public Buildings	7,910	5	0.2
Governmental Administration, Other	16,709	10	0.5
Health	0	0	0.0
Highways	91,064	58	2.8
Hospitals	0	0	0.0
Housing and Community Development	135,310	86	4.2
Interest on General Debt	289,075	184	9.0
Judicial and Legal	42,511	27	1.3
Libraries	32,455	20	1.0
Parking	1,715	1	0.1
Parks and Recreation	161,555	103	5.0
Police Protection	453,426	290	14.2
Public Welfare	127	< 1	< 0.1
Sewerage	161,131	103	5.0
Solid Waste Management	130,918	83	4.1
Veterans' Services	0	0	0.0
Liquor Store	0	0	0.0
Utility	555,742	355	17.4
Employee Retirement	223,779	143	7.0

Source: U.S. Census Bureau, State & Local Government Finances 2017

EMPLOYMENT

Labor Force and Employment

Area	Civilian Labor Force			Workers Employed		
	Dec. 2019	Dec. 2020	% Chg.	Dec. 2019	Dec. 2020	% Chg.
City	885,177	887,360	0.2	853,111	820,050	-3.9
MSA[1]	2,548,680	2,536,430	-0.5	2,456,125	2,361,237	-3.9
U.S.	164,007,000	160,017,000	-2.4	158,504,000	149,613,000	-5.6

Note: Data is not seasonally adjusted and covers workers 16 years of age and older; (1) Figures cover the Phoenix-Mesa-Scottsdale, AZ Metropolitan Statistical Area
Source: Bureau of Labor Statistics, Local Area Unemployment Statistics

Unemployment Rate

Area	2020											
	Jan.	Feb.	Mar.	Apr.	May	Jun.	Jul.	Aug.	Sep.	Oct.	Nov.	Dec.
City	4.0	3.9	5.5	12.9	8.8	10.5	11.3	6.5	6.9	8.4	8.2	7.6
MSA[1]	4.0	3.8	5.4	12.5	8.3	9.8	10.4	5.9	6.2	7.4	7.4	6.9
U.S.	4.0	3.8	4.5	14.4	13.0	11.2	10.5	8.5	7.7	6.6	6.4	6.5

Note: Data is not seasonally adjusted and covers workers 16 years of age and older; (1) Figures cover the Phoenix-Mesa-Scottsdale, AZ Metropolitan Statistical Area
Source: Bureau of Labor Statistics, Local Area Unemployment Statistics

Average Wages

Occupation	$/Hr.	Occupation	$/Hr.
Accountants and Auditors	36.30	Maintenance and Repair Workers	20.60
Automotive Mechanics	22.20	Marketing Managers	64.50
Bookkeepers	21.60	Network and Computer Systems Admin.	42.10
Carpenters	23.50	Nurses, Licensed Practical	27.20
Cashiers	13.40	Nurses, Registered	39.10
Computer Programmers	44.20	Nursing Assistants	16.60
Computer Systems Analysts	44.60	Office Clerks, General	20.30
Computer User Support Specialists	25.80	Physical Therapists	44.20
Construction Laborers	19.60	Physicians	117.40
Cooks, Restaurant	14.50	Plumbers, Pipefitters and Steamfitters	25.90
Customer Service Representatives	18.20	Police and Sheriff's Patrol Officers	34.90
Dentists	97.80	Postal Service Mail Carriers	26.10
Electricians	23.90	Real Estate Sales Agents	25.90
Engineers, Electrical	48.60	Retail Salespersons	15.30
Fast Food and Counter Workers	13.10	Sales Representatives, Technical/Scientific	45.70
Financial Managers	64.60	Secretaries, Exc. Legal/Medical/Executive	18.90
First-Line Supervisors of Office Workers	29.30	Security Guards	15.30
General and Operations Managers	58.10	Surgeons	n/a
Hairdressers/Cosmetologists	16.70	Teacher Assistants, Exc. Postsecondary*	13.70
Home Health and Personal Care Aides	13.30	Teachers, Secondary School, Exc. Sp. Ed.*	27.20
Janitors and Cleaners	14.70	Telemarketers	16.20
Landscaping/Groundskeeping Workers	14.90	Truck Drivers, Heavy/Tractor-Trailer	23.90
Lawyers	68.90	Truck Drivers, Light/Delivery Services	19.30
Maids and Housekeeping Cleaners	13.30	Waiters and Waitresses	19.00

Note: Wage data covers the Phoenix-Mesa-Scottsdale, AZ Metropolitan Statistical Area; (*) Hourly wages were calculated from annual wage data based on a 40 hour work week; n/a not available.
Source: Bureau of Labor Statistics, Metro Area Occupational Employment & Wage Estimates, May 2020

Employment by Industry

Sector	MSA[1]		U.S.
	Number of Employees	Percent of Total	Percent of Total
Construction	133,500	6.2	5.1
Education and Health Services	346,300	16.0	16.3
Financial Activities	205,900	9.5	6.1
Government	242,700	11.2	15.2
Information	36,700	1.7	1.9
Leisure and Hospitality	194,100	9.0	9.0
Manufacturing	133,900	6.2	8.5
Mining and Logging	2,800	0.1	0.4
Other Services	67,000	3.1	3.8
Professional and Business Services	364,900	16.8	14.4
Retail Trade	245,400	11.3	10.9
Transportation, Warehousing, and Utilities	115,100	5.3	4.6
Wholesale Trade	80,300	3.7	3.9

Note: Figures are non-farm employment as of December 2020. Figures are not seasonally adjusted and include workers 16 years of age and older; (1) Figures cover the Phoenix-Mesa-Scottsdale, AZ Metropolitan Statistical Area
Source: Bureau of Labor Statistics, Current Employment Statistics, Employment, Hours, and Earnings

Employment by Occupation

Occupation Classification	City (%)	MSA[1] (%)	U.S. (%)
Management, Business, Science, and Arts	34.5	37.8	38.5
Natural Resources, Construction, and Maintenance	9.6	8.5	8.9
Production, Transportation, and Material Moving	12.4	11.1	13.2
Sales and Office	23.9	24.6	21.6
Service	19.6	18.0	17.8

Note: Figures cover employed civilians 16 years of age and older; (1) Figures cover the Phoenix-Mesa-Scottsdale, AZ Metropolitan Statistical Area
Source: U.S. Census Bureau, 2015-2019 American Community Survey 5-Year Estimates

Occupations with Greatest Projected Employment Growth: 2020 – 2022

Occupation[1]	2020 Employment	2022 Projected Employment	Numeric Employment Change	Percent Employment Change
Retail Salespersons	76,020	89,930	13,910	18.3
Laborers and Freight, Stock, and Material Movers, Hand	50,760	62,050	11,290	22.2
Fast Food and Counter Workers	48,850	60,130	11,280	23.1
Stockers and Order Fillers	50,880	60,680	9,800	19.3
Waiters and Waitresses	38,790	48,430	9,640	24.9
Customer Service Representatives	101,690	111,140	9,450	9.3
Home Health and Personal Care Aides	67,820	76,780	8,960	13.2
Cooks, Restaurant	24,250	31,080	6,830	28.2
General and Operations Managers	53,800	59,930	6,130	11.4
Cashiers	59,640	65,200	5,560	9.3

Note: Projections cover Arizona; (1) Sorted by numeric employment change
Source: www.projectionscentral.com, State Occupational Projections, 2020–2022 Short-Term Projections

Fastest-Growing Occupations: 2020 – 2022

Occupation[1]	2020 Employment	2022 Projected Employment	Numeric Employment Change	Percent Employment Change
Models	270	420	150	55.6
Athletes and Sports Competitors	390	560	170	43.6
Conveyor Operators and Tenders	230	320	90	39.1
Aircraft Cargo Handling Supervisors (SOC 2018)	220	300	80	36.4
Hotel, Motel, and Resort Desk Clerks	3,880	5,210	1,330	34.3
Ushers, Lobby Attendants, and Ticket Takers	1,640	2,180	540	32.9
Locker Room, Coatroom, and Dressing Room Attendants	250	330	80	32.0
Funeral Attendants	220	290	70	31.8
Set and Exhibit Designers	160	210	50	31.3
Lodging Managers	880	1,150	270	30.7

Note: Projections cover Arizona; (1) Sorted by percent employment change and excludes occupations with numeric employment change less than 50
Source: www.projectionscentral.com, State Occupational Projections, 2020–2022 Short-Term Projections

TAXES

State Corporate Income Tax Rates

State	Tax Rate (%)	Income Brackets ($)	Num. of Brackets	Financial Institution Tax Rate (%)[a]	Federal Income Tax Ded.
Arizona	4.9 (b)	Flat rate	1	4.9 (b)	No

Note: Tax rates as of January 1, 2021; (a) Rates listed are the corporate income tax rate applied to financial institutions or excise taxes based on income. Some states have other taxes based upon the value of deposits or shares; (b) Minimum tax is $800 in California, $250 in District of Columbia, $50 in Arizona and North Dakota (banks), $400 ($100 banks) in Rhode Island, $200 per location in South Dakota (banks), $100 in Utah, $300 in Vermont.
Source: Federation of Tax Administrators, State Corporate Income Tax Rates, January 1, 2021

State Individual Income Tax Rates

State	Tax Rate (%)	Income Brackets ($)	Personal Exemptions ($)			Standard Ded. ($)	
			Single	Married	Depend.	Single	Married
Arizona (a)	2.59 - 8.0 (aa)	27,272 - 163,633 (b)	–	–	100 (c)	12,400	24,800

Note: Tax rates as of January 1, 2021; Local- and county-level taxes are not included; Federal income tax is not deductible on state income tax returns; (a) 19 states have statutory provision for automatically adjusting to the rate of inflation the dollar values of the income tax brackets, standard deductions, and/or personal exemptions. Michigan indexes the personal exemption only. Oregon does not index the income brackets for $125,000 and over; (b) For joint returns, taxes are twice the tax on half the couple's income; (c) The personal exemption takes the form of a tax credit instead of a deduction; (aa) Proposition 208, approved in November 2020, created an additional bracket on Arizona income above $250,000 ($500,000 joint). It is currently being litigated.
Source: Federation of Tax Administrators, State Individual Income Tax Rates, January 1, 2021

Various State Sales and Excise Tax Rates

State	State Sales Tax (%)	Gasoline[1] (¢/gal.)	Cigarette[2] ($/pack)	Spirits[3] ($/gal.)	Wine[4] ($/gal.)	Beer[5] ($/gal.)	Recreational Marijuana (%)
Arizona	5.6	19	2	3	0.84	0.16	(b)

Note: All tax rates as of January 1, 2021; (1) The American Petroleum Institute has developed a methodology for determining the average tax rate on a gallon of fuel. Rates may include any of the following: excise taxes, environmental fees, storage tank fees, other fees or taxes, general sales tax, and local taxes; (2) The federal excise tax of $1.0066 per pack and local taxes are not included; (3) Rates are those applicable to off-premise sales of 40% alcohol by volume (a.b.v.) distilled spirits in 750ml containers. Local excise taxes are excluded; (4) Rates are those applicable to off-premise sales of 11% a.b.v. non-carbonated wine in 750ml containers; (5) Rates are those applicable to off-premise sales of 4.7% a.b.v. beer in 12 ounce containers; (b) 16% excise tax (retail price)
Source: Tax Foundation, 2021 Facts & Figures: How Does Your State Compare?

State Business Tax Climate Index Rankings

State	Overall Rank	Corporate Tax Rank	Individual Income Tax Rank	Sales Tax Rank	Property Tax Rank	Unemployment Insurance Tax Rank
Arizona	24	22	17	40	11	8

Note: The index is a measure of how each state's tax laws affect economic performance. The lower the rank, the more favorable a state's tax system is for business. States without a given tax are given a ranking of 1. The scores/rankings for the District of Columbia do not affect other states. The 2021 index represents the tax climate as of July 1, 2020.
Source: Tax Foundation, State Business Tax Climate Index 2021

TRANSPORTATION

Means of Transportation to Work

Area	Car/Truck/Van		Public Transportation			Bicycle	Walked	Other Means	Worked at Home
	Drove Alone	Car-pooled	Bus	Subway	Railroad				
City	74.6	12.6	2.7	0.1	0.1	0.6	1.6	1.9	5.9
MSA[1]	76.1	11.1	1.7	0.1	0.0	0.8	1.5	1.8	7.0
U.S.	76.3	9.0	2.4	1.9	0.6	0.5	2.7	1.4	5.2

Note: Figures are percentages and cover workers 16 years of age and older; (1) Figures cover the Phoenix-Mesa-Scottsdale, AZ Metropolitan Statistical Area
Source: U.S. Census Bureau, 2015-2019 American Community Survey 5-Year Estimates

Travel Time to Work

Area	Less Than 10 Minutes	10 to 19 Minutes	20 to 29 Minutes	30 to 44 Minutes	45 to 59 Minutes	60 to 89 Minutes	90 Minutes or More
City	8.8	26.7	25.5	24.9	7.5	4.7	1.9
MSA[1]	9.9	26.2	23.7	23.7	9.0	5.7	1.9
U.S.	12.2	28.4	20.8	20.8	8.3	6.4	2.9

Note: Note: Figures are percentages and include workers 16 years old and over; (1) Figures cover the Phoenix-Mesa-Scottsdale, AZ Metropolitan Statistical Area
Source: U.S. Census Bureau, 2015-2019 American Community Survey 5-Year Estimates

Key Congestion Measures

Measure	1982	1992	2002	2012	2017
Annual Hours of Delay, Total (000)	27,117	47,584	97,832	145,564	163,247
Annual Hours of Delay, Per Auto Commuter	36	41	46	53	62
Annual Congestion Cost, Total (million $)	206	506	1,329	2,614	3,013
Annual Congestion Cost, Per Auto Commuter ($)	405	489	784	914	994

Note: Covers the Phoenix-Mesa AZ urban area
Source: Texas A&M Transportation Institute, 2019 Urban Mobility Report

Freeway Travel Time Index

Measure	1982	1987	1992	1997	2002	2007	2012	2017
Urban Area Index[1]	1.18	1.20	1.21	1.23	1.27	1.30	1.28	1.27
Urban Area Rank[1,2]	5	5	11	15	14	13	20	22

Note: Freeway Travel Time Index—the ratio of travel time in the peak period to the travel time at free-flow conditions. For example, a value of 1.30 indicates a 20-minute free-flow trip takes 26 minutes in the peak (20 minutes x 1.30 = 26 minutes); (1) Covers the Phoenix-Mesa AZ urban area; (2) Rank is based on 101 larger urban areas (#1 = highest travel time index)
Source: Texas A&M Transportation Institute, 2019 Urban Mobility Report

Public Transportation

Agency Name / Mode of Transportation	Vehicles Operated in Maximum Service[1]	Annual Unlinked Passenger Trips[2] (in thous.)	Annual Passenger Miles[3] (in thous.)
City of Phoenix Public Transit Dept. (Valley Metro)			
Bus (purchased transportation)	419	40,696.3	142,767.3
Demand Response (purchased transportation)	110	346.3	3,140.7

Note: (1) Number of revenue vehicles operated by the given mode and type of service to meet the annual maximum service requirement. This is the revenue vehicle count during the peak season of the year; on the week and day that maximum service is provided. Vehicles operated in maximum service (VOMS) exclude atypical days and one-time special events; (2) Number of passengers who boarded public transportation vehicles. Passengers are counted each time they board a vehicle no matter how many vehicles they use to travel from their origin to their destination. (3) Sum of the distances ridden by all passengers during the entire fiscal year.
Source: Federal Transit Administration, National Transit Database, 2019

Air Transportation

Airport Name and Code / Type of Service	Passenger Airlines[1]	Passenger Enplanements	Freight Carriers[2]	Freight (lbs)
Phoenix Sky Harbor International (PHX)				
Domestic service (U.S. carriers - 2020)	26	10,150,354	19	394,159,967
International service (U.S. carriers - 2019)	7	513,765	6	3,561,119

Note: (1) Includes all U.S.-based major, minor and commuter airlines that carried at least one passenger during the year; (2) Includes all U.S.-based airlines and freight carriers that transported at least one pound of freight during the year.
Source: Bureau of Transportation Statistics, The Intermodal Transportation Database, Air Carriers: T-100 Domestic Market (U.S. Carriers), 2020; Bureau of Transportation Statistics, The Intermodal Transportation Database, Air Carriers: T-100 International Market (U.S. Carriers), 2019

BUSINESSES

Major Business Headquarters

Company Name	Industry	Rankings	
		Fortune[1]	Forbes[2]
Avnet	Wholesalers, Electronics and Office Equipment	169	-
Freeport-McMoRan	Mining, Crude-Oil Production	221	-
Petsmart	Retailing	-	59
Republic Services	Waste Management	305	-
Shamrock Foods	Food, Drink & Tobacco	-	154

Note: (1) Companies that produce a 10-K are ranked 1 to 500 based on 2019 revenue; (2) All private companies with at least $2 billion in annual revenue through the end of their most current fiscal year are ranked 1 to 219; companies listed are headquartered in the city; dashes indicate no ranking
Source: Fortune, "Fortune 500," June/July 2020; Forbes, "America's Largest Private Companies," 2020

Fastest-Growing Businesses

According to *Inc.*, Phoenix is home to two of America's 500 fastest-growing private companies: **Freestar** (#36); **Handwrytten** (#148). Criteria: must be an independent, privately-held, for-profit, U.S. corporation, proprietorship or partnership as of December 31, 2019; revenues must be at least $100,000 in 2016 and $2 million in 2019; must have four-year operating/sales history. *Inc., "America's 500 Fastest-Growing Private Companies," 2020*

According to *Fortune*, Phoenix is home to one of the 100 fastest-growing companies in the world: **Knight-Swift Transportation Holdings** (#56). Companies were ranked by their revenue growth rate; their EPS growth rate; and their three-year annualized total return to investors for the period ending June 30, 2020. Criteria for inclusion: a company, foreign or domestic, must trade on a major U.S. stock exchange; must file quarterly reports with the SEC; must have a minimum market capitalization of $250 million; must have a stock price of at least $5 on June 30, 2020; must have been trading continuously since June 30, 2017; must have revenue and net income for the four quarters ended on or before April 30, 2020, of at least $50 million and $10 million, respectively; and must have posted a compound annual growth in revenue and earnings per share of at least 15% annually over the three years ending on or before April 30, 2020. Real estate investment trusts, limited-liability companies, limited parterships, business development companies, closed-end investment firms, companies about to be acquired, and companies that lost money in the quarter ending April 30, 2020 were excluded. *Fortune, "100 Fastest-Growing Companies," 2020*

According to Deloitte, Phoenix is home to two of North America's 500 fastest-growing high-technology companies: **Freestar** (#31); **Iota Communications, Inc.** (#103). Companies are ranked by percentage growth in revenue over a four-year period. Criteria for inclusion: company must be headquartered within North America; must own proprietary intellectual property or technology that is sold to customers in products that contributes to a significant portion of the company's operating revenue; must have been in business for a minumum of four years with 2016 operating revenues of at least $50,000 USD/CD and 2019 operating revenues of at least $5 million USD/CD. *Deloitte, 2020 Technology Fast 500*[TM]

Living Environment

COST OF LIVING

Cost of Living Index

Composite Index	Groceries	Housing	Utilities	Trans-portation	Health Care	Misc. Goods/ Services
102.4	98.7	111.9	106.5	106.1	89.9	96.1

Note: The Cost of Living Index measures regional differences in the cost of consumer goods and services, excluding taxes and non-consumer expenditures, for professional and managerial households in the top income quintile. It is based on more than 50,000 prices covering almost 60 different items for which prices are collected three times a year by chambers of commerce, economic development organizations or university applied economic centers in each participating urban area. The numbers shown should be read as a percentage above or below the national average of 100. For example, a value of 115.4 in the groceries column indicates that grocery prices are 15.4% higher than the national average. Small differences in the index numbers should not be interpreted as significant; Figures cover the Phoenix AZ urban area.
Source: The Council for Community and Economic Research, Cost of Living Index, 2020

Grocery Prices

Area[1]	T-Bone Steak ($/pound)	Frying Chicken ($/pound)	Whole Milk ($/half gal.)	Eggs ($/dozen)	Orange Juice ($/64 oz.)	Coffee ($/11.5 oz.)
City[2]	13.58	1.68	1.63	1.80	3.71	4.84
Avg.	11.78	1.39	2.05	1.47	3.57	4.34
Min.	8.03	0.94	1.03	0.74	2.94	3.02
Max.	15.86	2.65	4.31	3.77	5.44	8.69

*Note: (1) Values for the local area are compared with the average, minimum and maximum values for all 284 areas in the Cost of Living Index; (2) Figures cover the Phoenix AZ urban area; **T-Bone Steak** (price per pound); **Frying Chicken** (price per pound, whole fryer); **Whole Milk** (half gallon carton); **Eggs** (price per dozen, Grade A, large); **Orange Juice** (64 oz. Tropicana or Florida Natural); **Coffee** (11.5 oz. can, vacuum-packed, Maxwell House, Hills Bros, or Folgers).*
Source: The Council for Community and Economic Research, Cost of Living Index, 2020

Housing and Utility Costs

Area[1]	New Home Price ($)	Apartment Rent ($/month)	All Electric ($/month)	Part Electric ($/month)	Other Energy ($/month)	Telephone ($/month)
City[2]	362,970	1,639	189.67	-	-	178.50
Avg.	368,594	1,168	170.86	100.47	65.28	184.30
Min.	190,567	502	91.58	31.42	26.08	169.60
Max.	2,227,806	4,738	470.38	280.31	280.06	206.50

*Note: (1) Values for the local area are compared with the average, minimum and maximum values for all 284 areas in the Cost of Living Index; (2) Figures cover the Phoenix AZ urban area; **New Home Price** (2,400 sf living area, 8,000 sf lot, in urban area with full utilities); **Apartment Rent** (950 sf 2 bedroom/1.5 or 2 bath, unfurnished, excluding all utilities except water); **All Electric** (average monthly cost for an all-electric home); **Part Electric** (average monthly cost for a part-electric home); **Other Energy** (average monthly cost for natural gas, fuel oil, coal, wood, and any other forms of energy except electricity); **Telephone** (price includes the base monthly rate plus taxes and fees for three lines of mobile phone service).*
Source: The Council for Community and Economic Research, Cost of Living Index, 2020

Health Care, Transportation, and Other Costs

Area[1]	Doctor ($/visit)	Dentist ($/visit)	Optometrist ($/visit)	Gasoline ($/gallon)	Beauty Salon ($/visit)	Men's Shirt ($)
City[2]	96.33	89.83	96.17	2.49	41.67	27.57
Avg.	115.44	99.32	108.10	2.21	39.27	31.37
Min.	36.68	59.00	51.36	1.71	19.00	11.00
Max.	219.00	153.10	250.97	3.46	82.05	58.33

*Note: (1) Values for the local area are compared with the average, minimum and maximum values for all 284 areas in the Cost of Living Index; (2) Figures cover the Phoenix AZ urban area; **Doctor** (general practitioners routine exam of an established patient); **Dentist** (adult teeth cleaning and periodic oral examination); **Optometrist** (full vision eye exam for established adult patient); **Gasoline** (one gallon regular unleaded, national brand, including all taxes, cash price at self-service pump if available); **Beauty Salon** (woman's shampoo, trim, and blow-dry); **Men's Shirt** (cotton/polyester dress shirt, pinpoint weave, long sleeves).*
Source: The Council for Community and Economic Research, Cost of Living Index, 2020

HOUSING

Homeownership Rate

Area	2012 (%)	2013 (%)	2014 (%)	2015 (%)	2016 (%)	2017 (%)	2018 (%)	2019 (%)	2020 (%)
MSA[1]	63.1	62.2	61.9	61.0	62.6	64.0	65.3	65.9	67.9
U.S.	65.4	65.1	64.5	63.7	63.4	63.9	64.4	64.6	66.6

Note: (1) Figures cover the Phoenix-Mesa-Scottsdale, AZ Metropolitan Statistical Area
Source: U.S. Census Bureau, Housing Vacancies and Homeownership Annual Statistics: 2012-2020

House Price Index (HPI)

Area	National Ranking[2]	Quarterly Change (%)	One-Year Change (%)	Five-Year Change (%)	Since 1991Q1 (%)
MSA[1]	7	3.44	10.26	47.39	283.82
U.S.[3]	–	3.81	10.77	38.99	205.12

Note: The HPI is a weighted repeat sales index. It measures average price changes in repeat sales or refinancings on the same properties. This information is obtained by reviewing repeat mortgage transactions on single-family properties whose mortgages have been purchased or securitized by Fannie Mae or Freddie Mac since January 1975; (1) Figures cover the Phoenix-Mesa-Scottsdale, AZ Metropolitan Statistical Area; (2) Rankings are based on annual percentage change for all metro areas containing at least 15,000 transactions over the last 10 years and ranges from 1 to 253; (3) figures based on a weighted average of Census Division estimates using a seasonally adjusted, purchase-only index; all figures are for the period ending December 31, 2020
Source: Federal Housing Finance Agency, Change in Metropolitan Area House Price Indexes, April 7, 2021

Median Single-Family Home Prices

Area	2018	2019	2020[p]	Percent Change 2019 to 2020
MSA[1]	269.8	287.1	333.0	16.0
U.S. Average	261.6	274.6	299.9	9.2

Note: Figures are median sales prices of existing single-family homes in thousands of dollars; (p) preliminary; (1) Figures cover the Phoenix-Mesa-Scottsdale, AZ Metropolitan Statistical Area
Source: National Association of Realtors, Median Sales Price of Existing Single-Family Homes for Metropolitan Areas, 4th Quarter 2020

Qualifying Income Based on Median Sales Price of Existing Single-Family Homes

Area	With 5% Down ($)	With 10% Down ($)	With 20% Down ($)
MSA[1]	67,089	63,558	56,496
U.S. Average	59,266	56,147	49,908

Note: Figures are preliminary; Qualifying income is based on a mortgage rate of 2.81%. Monthly principal and interest payment is limited to 25% of income; (1) Figures cover the Phoenix-Mesa-Scottsdale, AZ Metropolitan Statistical Area
Source: National Association of Realtors, Qualifying Income Based on Median Sales Price of Existing Single-Family Homes for Metropolitan Areas, 4th Quarter 2020

Home Value Distribution

Area	Under $50,000	$50,000 -$99,999	$100,000 -$149,999	$150,000 -$199,999	$200,000 -$299,999	$300,000 -$499,999	$500,000 -$999,999	$1,000,000 or more
City	4.3	6.3	11.0	17.7	26.4	23.0	9.6	1.7
MSA[1]	5.5	5.2	8.7	15.2	28.2	25.2	9.8	2.2
U.S.	6.9	12.0	13.3	14.0	19.6	19.3	11.4	3.4

Note: Figures are percentages and cover owner-occupied housing units; (1) Figures cover the Phoenix-Mesa-Scottsdale, AZ Metropolitan Statistical Area
Source: U.S. Census Bureau, 2015-2019 American Community Survey 5-Year Estimates

Year Housing Structure Built

Area	2010 or Later	2000 -2009	1990 -1999	1980 -1989	1970 -1979	1960 -1969	1950 -1959	1940 -1949	Before 1940	Median Year
City	4.3	16.7	16.3	17.1	19.6	11.7	10.1	2.5	1.8	1983
MSA[1]	6.6	25.4	20.3	17.2	16.1	7.3	5.1	1.2	0.9	1991
U.S.	5.2	14.0	13.9	13.4	15.2	10.6	10.3	4.9	12.6	1978

Note: Figures are percentages except for Median Year; Note: (1) Figures cover the Phoenix-Mesa-Scottsdale, AZ Metropolitan Statistical Area
Source: U.S. Census Bureau, 2015-2019 American Community Survey 5-Year Estimates

Gross Monthly Rent

Area	Under $500	$500 -$999	$1,000 -$1,499	$1,500 -$1,999	$2,000 -$2,499	$2,500 -$2,999	$3,000 and up	Median ($)
City	4.5	40.2	40.2	11.5	2.4	0.6	0.5	1,053
MSA[1]	3.6	34.4	40.9	15.4	3.6	1.1	1.1	1,124
U.S.	9.4	36.2	30.0	14.0	5.6	2.4	2.4	1,062

Note: Figures are percentages except for Median; Gross rent is the contract rent plus the estimated average monthly cost of utilities (electricity, gas, and water and sewer) and fuels (oil, coal, kerosene, wood, etc.) if these are paid by the renter (or paid for the renter by someone else); (1) Figures cover the Phoenix-Mesa-Scottsdale, AZ Metropolitan Statistical Area
Source: U.S. Census Bureau, 2015-2019 American Community Survey 5-Year Estimates

HEALTH

Health Risk Factors

Category	MSA[1] (%)	U.S. (%)
Adults aged 18–64 who have any kind of health care coverage	83.8	87.3
Adults who reported being in good or better health	81.5	82.4
Adults who have been told they have high blood cholesterol	32.3	33.0
Adults who have been told they have high blood pressure	29.2	32.3
Adults who are current smokers	14.8	17.1
Adults who currently use E-cigarettes	5.2	4.6
Adults who currently use chewing tobacco, snuff, or snus	2.5	4.0
Adults who are heavy drinkers[2]	5.7	6.3
Adults who are binge drinkers[3]	16.0	17.4
Adults who are overweight (BMI 25.0 - 29.9)	35.3	35.3
Adults who are obese (BMI 30.0 - 99.8)	29.4	31.3
Adults who participated in any physical activities in the past month	75.3	74.4
Adults who always or nearly always wears a seat belt	94.7	94.3

Note: (1) Figures cover the Phoenix-Mesa-Scottsdale, AZ Metropolitan Statistical Area; (2) Heavy drinkers are classified as adult men having more than 14 drinks per week and adult women having more than 7 drinks per week; (3) Binge drinkers are classified as males having five or more drinks on one occasion or females having four or more drinks on one occasion
Source: Centers for Disease Control and Prevention, Behaviorial Risk Factor Surveillance System, SMART: Selected Metropolitan Area Risk Trends, 2017

Acute and Chronic Health Conditions

Category	MSA[1] (%)	U.S. (%)
Adults who have ever been told they had a heart attack	3.6	4.2
Adults who have ever been told they have angina or coronary heart disease	3.4	3.9
Adults who have ever been told they had a stroke	2.8	3.0
Adults who have ever been told they have asthma	16.0	14.2
Adults who have ever been told they have arthritis	23.4	24.9
Adults who have ever been told they have diabetes[2]	10.2	10.5
Adults who have ever been told they had skin cancer	7.7	6.2
Adults who have ever been told they had any other types of cancer	6.9	7.1
Adults who have ever been told they have COPD	5.9	6.5
Adults who have ever been told they have kidney disease	4.0	3.0
Adults who have ever been told they have a form of depression	18.5	20.5

Note: (1) Figures cover the Phoenix-Mesa-Scottsdale, AZ Metropolitan Statistical Area; (2) Figures do not include pregnancy-related, borderline, or pre-diabetes
Source: Centers for Disease Control and Prevention, Behaviorial Risk Factor Surveillance System, SMART: Selected Metropolitan Area Risk Trends, 2017

Health Screening and Vaccination Rates

Category	MSA[1] (%)	U.S. (%)
Adults aged 65+ who have had flu shot within the past year	56.6	60.7
Adults aged 65+ who have ever had a pneumonia vaccination	77.1	75.4
Adults who have ever been tested for HIV	35.9	36.1
Adults who have ever had the shingles or zoster vaccine?	28.7	28.9
Adults who have had their blood cholesterol checked within the last five years	85.4	85.9

Note: n/a not available; (1) Figures cover the Phoenix-Mesa-Scottsdale, AZ Metropolitan Statistical Area.
Source: Centers for Disease Control and Prevention, Behaviorial Risk Factor Surveillance System, SMART: Selected Metropolitan Area Risk Trends, 2017

Disability Status

Category	MSA[1] (%)	U.S. (%)
Adults who reported being deaf	6.4	6.7
Are you blind or have serious difficulty seeing, even when wearing glasses?	4.4	4.5
Are you limited in any way in any of your usual activities due of arthritis?	12.8	12.9
Do you have difficulty doing errands alone?	6.5	6.8
Do you have difficulty dressing or bathing?	3.2	3.6
Do you have serious difficulty concentrating/remembering/making decisions?	10.3	10.7
Do you have serious difficulty walking or climbing stairs?	12.9	13.6

Note: (1) Figures cover the Phoenix-Mesa-Scottsdale, AZ Metropolitan Statistical Area.
Source: Centers for Disease Control and Prevention, Behaviorial Risk Factor Surveillance System, SMART: Selected Metropolitan Area Risk Trends, 2017

Mortality Rates for the Top 10 Causes of Death in the U.S.

ICD-10[a] Sub-Chapter	ICD-10[a] Code	Age-Adjusted Mortality Rate[1] per 100,000 population	
		County[2]	U.S.
Malignant neoplasms	C00-C97	130.2	149.2
Ischaemic heart diseases	I20-I25	78.4	90.5
Other forms of heart disease	I30-I51	33.2	52.2
Chronic lower respiratory diseases	J40-J47	37.9	39.6
Other degenerative diseases of the nervous system	G30-G31	48.9	37.6
Cerebrovascular diseases	I60-I69	30.4	37.2
Other external causes of accidental injury	W00-X59	41.8	36.1
Organic, including symptomatic, mental disorders	F01-F09	14.4	29.4
Hypertensive diseases	I10-I15	30.3	24.1
Diabetes mellitus	E10-E14	22.2	21.5

Note: (a) ICD-10 = International Classification of Diseases 10th Revision; (1) Mortality rates are a three-year average covering 2017-2019; (2) Figures cover Maricopa County.
Source: Centers for Disease Control and Prevention, National Center for Health Statistics. Underlying Cause of Death 1999-2019 on CDC WONDER Online Database

Mortality Rates for Selected Causes of Death

ICD-10[a] Sub-Chapter	ICD-10[a] Code	Age-Adjusted Mortality Rate[1] per 100,000 population	
		County[2]	U.S.
Assault	X85-Y09	5.9	6.0
Diseases of the liver	K70-K76	14.7	14.4
Human immunodeficiency virus (HIV) disease	B20-B24	1.1	1.5
Influenza and pneumonia	J09-J18	10.1	13.8
Intentional self-harm	X60-X84	15.7	14.1
Malnutrition	E40-E46	2.1	2.3
Obesity and other hyperalimentation	E65-E68	2.2	2.1
Renal failure	N17-N19	5.6	12.6
Transport accidents	V01-V99	12.0	12.3
Viral hepatitis	B15-B19	1.5	1.2

Note: (a) ICD-10 = International Classification of Diseases 10th Revision; (1) Mortality rates are a three-year average covering 2017-2019; (2) Figures cover Maricopa County; Data are suppressed when the data meet the criteria for confidentiality constraints; Mortality rates are flagged as unreliable when the rate would be calculated with a numerator of 20 or less.
Source: Centers for Disease Control and Prevention, National Center for Health Statistics. Underlying Cause of Death 1999-2019 on CDC WONDER Online Database

Health Insurance Coverage

Area	With Health Insurance	With Private Health Insurance	With Public Health Insurance	Without Health Insurance	Population Under Age 19 Without Health Insurance
City	85.9	57.2	36.0	14.1	9.5
MSA[1]	89.5	65.4	34.9	10.5	8.2
U.S.	91.2	67.9	35.1	8.8	5.1

Note: Figures are percentages that cover the civilian noninstitutionalized population; (1) Figures cover the Phoenix-Mesa-Scottsdale, AZ Metropolitan Statistical Area
Source: U.S. Census Bureau, 2015-2019 American Community Survey 5-Year Estimates

Number of Medical Professionals

Area	MDs[3]	DOs[3,4]	Dentists	Podiatrists	Chiropractors	Optometrists
County[1] (number)	10,813	1,379	3,060	297	1,487	693
County[1] (rate[2])	245.6	31.3	68.2	6.6	33.2	15.5
U.S. (rate[2])	282.9	22.7	71.2	6.2	28.1	16.9

04013
Note: Data as of 2019 unless noted; (1) Data covers Maricopa County; (2) Rate per 100,000 population; (3) Data as of 2018 and includes all active, non-federal physicians; (4) Doctor of Osteopathic Medicine
Source: U.S. Department of Health and Human Services, Health Resources and Services Administration, Bureau of Health Professions, Area Resource File (ARF) 2019-2020

Best Hospitals

According to *U.S. News,* the Phoenix-Mesa-Scottsdale, AZ metro area is home to two of the best hospitals in the U.S.: **Barrow Neurological Institute** (1 adult specialty); **Mayo Clinic-Phoenix** (Honor Roll/11 adult specialties). The hospitals listed were nationally ranked in at least one of 16 adult or 10 pediatric specialties. Only 134 hospitals nationwide were nationally ranked in one or more adult or pediatric specialty; this number increases to 178 counting specialized centers within hospitals. Twenty hospitals in the U.S. made the Honor Roll. The Best Hospitals Honor Roll takes both the national rankings and the procedure and condition ratings into account. Hospitals received points if they were nationally ranked in one of the 16 adult specialties—the higher they ranked, the more points they got—and how many ratings of "high performing" they earned in the 10 procedures and conditions. *U.S. News Online, "America's Best Hospitals 2020-21"*

According to *U.S. News,* the Phoenix-Mesa-Scottsdale, AZ metro area is home to one of the best children's hospitals in the U.S.: **Phoenix Children's Hospital** (10 pediatric specialties). The hospital listed was highly ranked in at least one of 10 pediatric specialties. Eighty-eight children's hospitals in the U.S. were nationally ranked in at least one specialty. Hospitals received points for being ranked in a specialty, and the 10 hospitals with the most points across the 10 specialties make up the Honor Roll. *U.S. News Online, "America's Best Children's Hospitals 2020-21"*

EDUCATION

Public School District Statistics

District Name	Schls	Pupils	Pupil/ Teacher Ratio	Minority Pupils[1] (%)	Free Lunch Eligible[2] (%)	IEP[3] (%)
Alhambra Elementary District	14	12,551	21.5	94.8	83.4	10.7
Balsz Elementary District	5	2,341	18.8	92.9	87.1	14.1
Cartwright Elementary District	21	16,034	19.2	96.8	80.5	10.6
Creighton Elementary District	10	5,940	17.5	93.5	83.2	12.1
Deer Valley Unified District	39	34,544	18.7	32.1	21.3	12.2
Fowler Elementary District	7	4,555	20.0	93.7	71.5	10.4
Isaac Elementary District	12	6,542	21.1	98.7	75.5	12.4
Madison Elementary District	8	6,009	20.2	54.5	27.0	8.1
Osborn Elementary District	6	2,870	18.5	89.3	68.0	15.9
Paradise Valley Unified District	46	31,105	17.7	43.9	27.7	14.7
Pendergast Elementary District	13	9,435	19.5	89.4	54.4	13.0
Phoenix Elementary District	14	6,540	18.8	94.0	70.4	13.0
Phoenix Union High SD	18	27,573	18.2	95.4	75.2	11.4
Portable Practical Ed. Prep.	2	5,129	n/a	48.5	n/a	15.4
Roosevelt Elementary District	19	8,982	19.4	97.1	81.8	14.3

Note: Table includes school districts with 2,000 or more students; (1) Percentage of students that are not non-Hispanic white; (2) Percentage of students that are eligible for the free lunch program; (3) Percentage of students that have an Individualized Education Program.
Source: U.S. Department of Education, National Center for Education Statistics, Common Core of Data, Local Education Agency (School District) Universe Survey: School Year 2018-2019; U.S. Department of Education, National Center for Education Statistics, Common Core of Data, Public Elementary/Secondary School Universe Survey: School Year 2018-2019

Best High Schools

According to *U.S. News,* Phoenix is home to four of the top 500 high schools in the U.S.: **BASIS Phoenix** (#56); **BASIS Ahwatukee** (#67); **Arizona School for the Arts** (#278); **Phoenix Union Bioscience High School** (#339). Nearly 18,000 public, magnet and charter schools were ranked based on their performance on state assessments and how well they prepare students for college. *U.S. News & World Report, "Best High Schools 2020"*

Highest Level of Education

Area	Less than H.S.	H.S. Diploma	Some College, No Deg.	Associate Degree	Bachelor's Degree	Master's Degree	Prof. School Degree	Doctorate Degree
City	18.1	23.6	22.0	7.7	18.3	7.3	2.0	1.0
MSA[1]	12.5	23.0	24.4	8.6	20.0	8.3	1.9	1.2
U.S.	12.0	27.0	20.4	8.5	19.8	8.8	2.1	1.4

Note: Figures cover persons age 25 and over; (1) Figures cover the Phoenix-Mesa-Scottsdale, AZ Metropolitan Statistical Area
Source: U.S. Census Bureau, 2015-2019 American Community Survey 5-Year Estimates

Educational Attainment by Race

Area	High School Graduate or Higher (%)					Bachelor's Degree or Higher (%)				
	Total	White	Black	Asian	Hisp.[2]	Total	White	Black	Asian	Hisp.[2]
City	81.9	84.0	87.5	84.9	62.1	28.6	30.2	21.8	57.4	10.3
MSA[1]	87.5	89.1	90.1	88.6	68.5	31.5	32.3	25.7	58.9	13.1
U.S.	88.0	89.9	86.0	87.1	68.7	32.1	33.5	21.6	54.3	16.4

Note: Figures shown cover persons 25 years old and over; (1) Figures cover the Phoenix-Mesa-Scottsdale, AZ Metropolitan Statistical Area; (2) People of Hispanic origin can be of any race
Source: U.S. Census Bureau, 2015-2019 American Community Survey 5-Year Estimates

School Enrollment by Grade and Control

Area	Preschool (%)		Kindergarten (%)		Grades 1 - 4 (%)		Grades 5 - 8 (%)		Grades 9 - 12 (%)	
	Public	Private	Public	Private	Public	Private	Public	Private	Public	Private
City	62.7	37.3	90.0	10.0	92.9	7.1	92.4	7.6	93.1	6.9
MSA[1]	60.3	39.7	89.4	10.6	92.0	8.0	92.5	7.5	92.9	7.1
U.S.	59.1	40.9	87.6	12.4	89.5	10.5	89.4	10.6	90.1	9.9

Note: Figures shown cover persons 3 years old and over; (1) Figures cover the Phoenix-Mesa-Scottsdale, AZ Metropolitan Statistical Area
Source: U.S. Census Bureau, 2015-2019 American Community Survey 5-Year Estimates

Higher Education

Four-Year Colleges			Two-Year Colleges			Medical Schools[1]	Law Schools[2]	Voc/ Tech[3]
Public	Private Non-profit	Private For-profit	Public	Private Non-profit	Private For-profit			
1	2	7	4	0	5	1	1	10

Note: Figures cover institutions located within the city limits and include main campuses only; (1) includes schools accredited by the Liaison Committee on Medical Education and the American Osteopathic Association's Commission on Osteopathic College Accreditation; (2) includes ABA-accredited schools, schools with provisional ABA accreditation, and state accredited schools; (3) includes all schools with programs that are less than 2 years.
Source: National Center for Education Statistics, Integrated Postsecondary Education System (IPEDS), 2019-20; Wikipedia, List of Medical Schools in the United States, accessed April 2, 2021; Wikipedia, List of Law Schools in the United States, accessed April 2, 2021

According to *U.S. News & World Report,* the Phoenix-Mesa-Scottsdale, AZ metro area is home to one of the top 200 national universities in the U.S.: **Arizona State University—Tempe** (#103 tie). The indicators used to capture academic quality fall into a number of categories: assessment by administrators at peer institutions; retention of students; faculty resources; student selectivity; financial resources; alumni giving; high school counselor ratings of colleges; and graduation rate. *U.S. News & World Report, "America's Best Colleges 2021"*

According to *U.S. News & World Report,* the Phoenix-Mesa-Scottsdale, AZ metro area is home to one of the top 100 law schools in the U.S.: **Arizona State University (O'Connor)** (#25 tie). The rankings are based on a weighted average of 12 measures of quality: peer assessment score; assessment score by lawyers/judges; median LSAT scores; median undergrad GPA; acceptance rate; employment rates for graduates; placement success; bar passage rate; faculty resources; expenditures per student; student/faculty ratio; and library resources. *U.S. News & World Report, "America's Best Graduate Schools, Law, 2022"*

According to *U.S. News & World Report,* the Phoenix-Mesa-Scottsdale, AZ metro area is home to one of the top 75 business schools in the U.S.: **Arizona State University (W.P. Carey)** (#30). The rankings are based on a weighted average of the following nine measures: quality assessment; peer assessment; recruiter assessment; placement success; mean starting salary and bonus; student selectivity; mean GMAT and GRE scores; mean undergraduate GPA; and acceptance rate. *U.S. News & World Report, "America's Best Graduate Schools, Business, 2022"*

EMPLOYERS

Major Employers

Company Name	Industry
Arizona Dept of Transportation	Regulation, administration of transportation
Arizona State University	University
Avnet	Electronic parts & equipment, nec
Carter & Burgess	Engineering services
Chase Bankcard Services	State commercial banks
City of Mesa	Municipal government
City of Phoenix	Municipal government
General Dynamics C4 Systems	Communications equipment, nec
Grand Canyon Education	Colleges & universities
Honeywell International	Aircraft engines & engine parts
Lockheed Martin Corporation	Search & navigation equipment
Paramount Building Solutions	Janitorial service, contract basis
Salt River Pima-Maricopa Indian Community	Casino resort
Scottsdale Healthcare Osborn Med Ctr	General medical & surgical hospitals
Swift Transportation Company	Trucking, except local
The Boeing Company	Helicopters
Veterans Health Administration	General medical & surgical hospitals

Note: Companies shown are located within the Phoenix-Mesa-Scottsdale, AZ Metropolitan Statistical Area.
Source: Hoovers.com; Wikipedia

Best Companies to Work For

Banner Health, headquartered in Phoenix, is among the "100 Best Places to Work in IT." To qualify, companies had to be U.S.-based organizations or be non-U.S.-based employers that met the following criteria: have a minimum of 300 total employees at a U.S. headquarters and a minimum of 30 IT employees in the U.S., with at least 50% of their IT employees based in the U.S. The best places to work were selected based on compensation, benefits, work/life balance, employee morale, and satisfaction with training and development programs. In addition, *InsiderPro* and *Computerworld* looked at retention efforts, programs for recognizing and rewarding outstanding performances, and benefits such as flextime, elder care and child care, and reimbursement for college tuition and the cost of pursuing technology certifications. *InsiderPro and Computerworld, "100 Best Places to Work in IT," 2020*

PUBLIC SAFETY

Crime Rate

Area	All Crimes	Violent Crimes				Property Crimes		
		Murder	Rape[3]	Robbery	Aggrav. Assault	Burglary	Larceny -Theft	Motor Vehicle Theft
City	4,013.5	7.8	67.4	189.3	434.4	560.8	2,334.7	419.0
Suburbs[1]	n/a	2.9	40.6	49.3	192.6	n/a	1,530.6	165.3
Metro[2]	n/a	4.6	49.8	97.1	275.1	n/a	1,804.9	251.9
U.S.	2,489.3	5.0	42.6	81.6	250.2	340.5	1,549.5	219.9

Note: Figures are crimes per 100,000 population; (1) All areas within the metro area that are located outside the city limits; (2) Figures cover the Phoenix-Mesa-Scottsdale, AZ Metropolitan Statistical Area; (3) All figures shown were reported using the revised Uniform Crime Reporting (UCR) definition of rape.
Source: FBI Uniform Crime Reports, 2019

Hate Crimes

Area	Number of Quarters Reported	Number of Incidents per Bias Motivation					
		Race/Ethnicity/ Ancestry	Religion	Sexual Orientation	Disability	Gender	Gender Identity
City[1]	4	111	20	23	0	2	3
U.S.	4	3,963	1,521	1,195	157	69	198

Note: (1) Figures include one incident reported with more than one bias motivation.
Source: Federal Bureau of Investigation, Hate Crime Statistics 2019

Identity Theft Consumer Reports

Area	Reports	Reports per 100,000 Population	Rank[2]
MSA[1]	21,122	427	67
U.S.	1,387,615	423	-

Note: (1) Figures cover the Phoenix-Mesa-Scottsdale, AZ Metropolitan Statistical Area; (2) Rank ranges from 1 to 391 where 1 indicates greatest number of identity theft reports per 100,000 population
Source: Federal Trade Commission, Consumer Sentinel Network Data Book 2020

Fraud and Other Consumer Reports

Area	Reports	Reports per 100,000 Population	Rank[2]
MSA[1]	43,965	889	54
U.S.	3,385,133	1,031	-

Note: (1) Figures cover the Phoenix-Mesa-Scottsdale, AZ Metropolitan Statistical Area; (2) Rank ranges from 1 to 391 where 1 indicates greatest number of fraud and other consumer reports per 100,000 population
Source: Federal Trade Commission, Consumer Sentinel Network Data Book 2020

POLITICS

2020 Presidential Election Results

Area	Biden	Trump	Jorgensen	Hawkins	Other
Maricopa County	50.1	48.0	1.5	0.0	0.3
U.S.	51.3	46.8	1.2	0.3	0.5

Note: Results are percentages and may not add to 100% due to rounding
Source: Dave Leip's Atlas of U.S. Presidential Elections

SPORTS

Professional Sports Teams

Team Name	League	Year Established
Arizona Cardinals	National Football League (NFL)	1988
Arizona Diamondbacks	Major League Baseball (MLB)	1998
Phoenix Coyotes	National Hockey League (NHL)	1996
Phoenix Suns	National Basketball Association (NBA)	1968

Note: Includes teams located in the Phoenix-Mesa-Scottsdale, AZ Metropolitan Statistical Area.
Source: Wikipedia, Major Professional Sports Teams of the United States and Canada, April 6, 2021

CLIMATE

Average and Extreme Temperatures

Temperature	Jan	Feb	Mar	Apr	May	Jun	Jul	Aug	Sep	Oct	Nov	Dec	Yr.
Extreme High (°F)	88	92	100	105	113	122	118	116	118	107	93	88	122
Average High (°F)	66	70	75	84	93	103	105	103	99	88	75	67	86
Average Temp. (°F)	53	57	62	70	78	88	93	91	85	74	62	54	72
Average Low (°F)	40	44	48	55	63	72	80	78	72	60	48	41	59
Extreme Low (°F)	17	22	25	37	40	51	66	61	47	34	27	22	17

Note: Figures cover the years 1948-1990
Source: National Climatic Data Center, International Station Meteorological Climate Summary, 9/96

Average Precipitation/Snowfall/Humidity

Precip./Humidity	Jan	Feb	Mar	Apr	May	Jun	Jul	Aug	Sep	Oct	Nov	Dec	Yr.
Avg. Precip. (in.)	0.7	0.6	0.8	0.3	0.1	0.1	0.8	1.0	0.7	0.6	0.6	0.9	7.3
Avg. Snowfall (in.)	Tr	Tr	0	0	0	0	0	0	0	0	0	Tr	Tr
Avg. Rel. Hum. 5am (%)	68	63	56	45	37	33	47	53	50	53	59	66	53
Avg. Rel. Hum. 5pm (%)	34	28	24	17	14	12	21	24	23	24	28	34	24

Note: Figures cover the years 1948-1990; Tr = Trace amounts (<0.05 in. of rain; <0.5 in. of snow)
Source: National Climatic Data Center, International Station Meteorological Climate Summary, 9/96

Weather Conditions

Temperature			Daytime Sky			Precipitation		
10°F & below	32°F & below	90°F & above	Clear	Partly cloudy	Cloudy	0.01 inch or more precip.	0.1 inch or more snow/ice	Thunder-storms
0	10	167	186	125	54	37	< 1	23

Note: Figures are average number of days per year and cover the years 1948-1990
Source: National Climatic Data Center, International Station Meteorological Climate Summary, 9/96

HAZARDOUS WASTE

Superfund Sites

The Phoenix-Mesa-Scottsdale, AZ metro area is home to five sites on the EPA's Superfund National Priorities List: **Hassayampa Landfill** (final); **Indian Bend Wash Area** (final); **Motorola, Inc. (52nd Street Plant)** (final); **Phoenix-Goodyear Airport Area** (final); **Williams Air Force Base** (final). There are a total of 1,375 Superfund sites with a status of proposed or final on the list in the U.S. *U.S. Environmental Protection Agency, National Priorities List, April 7, 2021*

AIR QUALITY

Air Quality Trends: Ozone

	1990	1995	2000	2005	2010	2015	2016	2017	2018	2019
MSA[1]	0.080	0.087	0.082	0.077	0.076	0.072	0.071	0.075	0.074	0.071
U.S.	0.088	0.089	0.082	0.080	0.073	0.068	0.069	0.068	0.069	0.065

Note: (1) Data covers the Phoenix-Mesa-Scottsdale, AZ Metropolitan Statistical Area. The values shown are the composite ozone concentration averages among trend sites based on the highest fourth daily maximum 8-hour concentration in parts per million. These trends are based on sites having an adequate record of monitoring data during the trend period. Data from exceptional events are included.
Source: U.S. Environmental Protection Agency, Air Quality Monitoring Information, "Air Quality Trends by City, 1990-2019"

Air Quality Index

Area	Percent of Days when Air Quality was...[2]					AQI Statistics[2]	
	Good	Moderate	Unhealthy for Sensitive Groups	Unhealthy	Very Unhealthy	Maximum	Median
MSA[1]	13.7	71.5	11.5	0.5	0.8	886	74

Note: (1) Data covers the Phoenix-Mesa-Scottsdale, AZ Metropolitan Statistical Area; (2) Based on 365 days with AQI data in 2019. Air Quality Index (AQI) is an index for reporting daily air quality. EPA calculates the AQI for five major air pollutants regulated by the Clean Air Act: ground-level ozone, particle pollution (aka particulate matter), carbon monoxide, sulfur dioxide, and nitrogen dioxide. The AQI runs from 0 to 500. The higher the AQI value, the greater the level of air pollution and the greater the health concern. There are six AQI categories: "Good" AQI is between 0 and 50. Air quality is considered satisfactory; "Moderate" AQI is between 51 and 100. Air quality is acceptable; "Unhealthy for Sensitive Groups" When AQI values are between 101 and 150, members of sensitive groups may experience health effects; "Unhealthy" When AQI values are between 151 and 200 everyone may begin to experience health effects; "Very Unhealthy" AQI values between 201 and 300 trigger a health alert; "Hazardous" AQI values over 300 trigger warnings of emergency conditions (not shown).
Source: U.S. Environmental Protection Agency, Air Quality Index Report, 2019

Air Quality Index Pollutants

Area	Percent of Days when AQI Pollutant was...[2]					
	Carbon Monoxide	Nitrogen Dioxide	Ozone	Sulfur Dioxide	Particulate Matter 2.5	Particulate Matter 10
MSA[1]	0.0	0.8	46.3	0.0	19.7	33.2

Note: (1) Data covers the Phoenix-Mesa-Scottsdale, AZ Metropolitan Statistical Area; (2) Based on 365 days with AQI data in 2019. The Air Quality Index (AQI) is an index for reporting daily air quality. EPA calculates the AQI for five major air pollutants regulated by the Clean Air Act: ground-level ozone, particle pollution (also known as particulate matter), carbon monoxide, sulfur dioxide, and nitrogen dioxide. The AQI runs from 0 to 500. The higher the AQI value, the greater the level of air pollution and the greater the health concern.
Source: U.S. Environmental Protection Agency, Air Quality Index Report, 2019

Maximum Air Pollutant Concentrations: Particulate Matter, Ozone, CO and Lead

	Particulate Matter 10 (ug/m^3)	Particulate Matter 2.5 Wtd AM (ug/m^3)	Particulate Matter 2.5 24-Hr (ug/m^3)	Ozone (ppm)	Carbon Monoxide (ppm)	Lead (ug/m^3)
MSA[1] Level	990	10.9	30	0.076	2	0.05
NAAQS[2]	150	15	35	0.075	9	0.15
Met NAAQS[2]	No	Yes	Yes	No	Yes	Yes

Note: (1) Data covers the Phoenix-Mesa-Scottsdale, AZ Metropolitan Statistical Area; Data from exceptional events are included; (2) National Ambient Air Quality Standards; ppm = parts per million; ug/m^3 = micrograms per cubic meter; n/a not available.
Concentrations: Particulate Matter 10 (coarse particulate)—highest second maximum 24-hour concentration; Particulate Matter 2.5 Wtd AM (fine particulate)—highest weighted annual mean concentration; Particulate Matter 2.5 24-Hour (fine particulate)—highest 98th percentile 24-hour concentration; Ozone—highest fourth daily maximum 8-hour concentration; Carbon Monoxide—highest second maximum non-overlapping 8-hour concentration; Lead—maximum running 3-month average
Source: U.S. Environmental Protection Agency, Air Quality Monitoring Information, "Air Quality Statistics by City, 2019"

Maximum Air Pollutant Concentrations: Nitrogen Dioxide and Sulfur Dioxide

	Nitrogen Dioxide AM (ppb)	Nitrogen Dioxide 1-Hr (ppb)	Sulfur Dioxide AM (ppb)	Sulfur Dioxide 1-Hr (ppb)	Sulfur Dioxide 24-Hr (ppb)
MSA[1] Level	25	52	n/a	5	n/a
NAAQS[2]	53	100	30	75	140
Met NAAQS[2]	Yes	Yes	n/a	Yes	n/a

Note: (1) Data covers the Phoenix-Mesa-Scottsdale, AZ Metropolitan Statistical Area; Data from exceptional events are included; (2) National Ambient Air Quality Standards; ppm = parts per million; ug/m^3 = micrograms per cubic meter; n/a not available.
Concentrations: Nitrogen Dioxide AM—highest arithmetic mean concentration; Nitrogen Dioxide 1-Hr—highest 98th percentile 1-hour daily maximum concentration; Sulfur Dioxide AM—highest annual mean concentration; Sulfur Dioxide 1-Hr—highest 99th percentile 1-hour daily maximum concentration; Sulfur Dioxide 24-Hr—highest second maximum 24-hour concentration
Source: U.S. Environmental Protection Agency, Air Quality Monitoring Information, "Air Quality Statistics by City, 2019"

Portland, Oregon

Background

Portland is the kind of city that inspires civic pride and the desire to preserve. It offers magnificent views of the Cascade Mountains, a mild climate, and an attractive combination of historical brick structures and contemporary architecture.

Nature is the undisputed queen of Portland and embodied in Portlandia, the city's statue of an earth mother kneeling among her animal children. The number of activities, such as fishing, skiing, and hunting, as well as the number of outdoor zoological gardens, attest to the mindset of the typical Portlander.

Portland is a major industrial and commercial center that boasts clean air and water within its city limits, as many of the factories use the electricity generated by mountain rivers; thus, little soot or smoke is belched out. The largest employers in the city are in the health services and Oregon State University.

The city is a major cultural center, with art museums such as the Portland Art Museum and the Oregon Museum of Science and Industry, and educational institutions including Reed College and the University of Portland. In 2001, Portland's PGE Park sports stadium had a multi-million dollar facelift, with a field level bar and grill and pavilion suites, all state-of-the-art and seismic code compliant.

The Portland area's metro region includes 24 cities and parts of three counties. Established in the late 1970s, it is the nation's first and only elected regional government. It attempts to control growth by using its authority over land use, transportation, and the environment. This experiment in urban planning is designed to protect farms, forests, and open space. Portland today has a downtown area that caters to pedestrians and includes a heavily used city park. Visible from the air is a clear line against sprawl—with cities on one side and open spaces on the other.

> A new study conducted in Portland finds COVID-19 antibodies in the breastmilk of vaccinated mothers.

Portland is Oregon's biggest city, and is a shining example of effective sprawl control, a "role model for twenty-first century urban development." And the city's well-organized mass-transit system makes living there all the more enjoyable, with the Portland Streetcar recently added miles of track.

In 2000, the Portland Art Museum completed its "Program for the Millennium," a multi-stage expansion program that brought total exhibition space to 240,000 square feet. In 2005, restoration of the North Building, a former Masonic Temple, was completed. While preserving the historical integrity, the restoration provides space for the Portland Art Museum's Center for Modern and Contemporary Art.

The Portland metropolitan area had a significant LGBTQ population throughout the late 20th and early 21st century. In 2015, it had the second highest percentage of LGBTQ residents in the United States, at 5.4 percent, second only to San Francisco. The city held its first pride festival in 1975 on the Portland State University campus.

Many films have been shot in Portland, from independents to big-budget productions. The city has been featured in various television programs, most notably the comedy series *Portlandia,* which ran 2011 to 2018. Shot on location in Portland, it lovingly satirized the city as a hub of liberal politics, organic food, alternative lifestyles, and anti-establishment attitudes.

Portland has a very definite winter rainfall climate, with the most rain falling October through May in relatively mild temperatures. Summer produces pleasant, mild temperatures with very little precipitation. Fall and spring are transitional. Fall and early winter bring the most frequent fog. Destructive storms are infrequent, with thunderstorms occurring once a month through the spring and summer.

Rankings

General Rankings

- *US News & World Report* conducted a survey of more than 3,000 people and analyzed the 150 largest metropolitan areas to determine what matters most when selecting the next place to live. Portland ranked #9 out of the top 25 as having the best combination of desirable factors. Criteria: cost of living; quality of life; net migration; job market; desirability; and other factors. *realestate.usnews.com, "The 25 Best Places to Live in the U.S. in 2020-21," October 13, 2020*

- The Portland metro area was identified as one of America's fastest-growing areas in terms of population and business growth by *MagnifyMoney*. The area ranked #21 out of 35. The 100 most populous metro areas in the U.S. were evaluated on their change from 2011-2016 in the following categories: people and housing; workforce and employment opportunities; growing industry. *www.businessinsider.com, "The 35 Cities in the US with the Biggest Influx of People, the Most Work Opportunities, and the Hottest Business Growth," August 12, 2018*

- The Portland metro area was identified as one of America's fastest-growing areas in terms of population and economy by *Forbes*. The area ranked #17 out of 25. The 100 most populous metro areas in the U.S. were evaluated on the following criteria: estimated population growth; employment; economic output; wages; home values. *Forbes, "America's Fastest-Growing Cities 2018," February 28, 2018*

- In its eighth annual survey, *Travel + Leisure* readers nominated their favorite small cities and towns in America—those with 100,000 or fewer residents—voting on numerous attractive features in categories including culture, food and drink, quality of life, style, and people. After 50,000 votes, Portland was ranked #17 among the proposed favorites. *www.travelandleisure.com, "America's Favorite Cities," October 20, 2017*

Business/Finance Rankings

- The Brookings Institution ranked the nation's largest cities based on income inequality. Portland was ranked #48 (#1 = greatest inequality). Criteria: the "95/20 ratio," a figure representing the income at which a household earns more than 95 percent of all other households, divided by the income at which a household earns more than only 20 percent of all other households. *Brookings Institution, "Household Income Inequality, Largest Cities of 97 Large U.S. Metro Areas, 2014-2016," February 5, 2018*

- The Brookings Institution ranked the 100 largest metro areas in the U.S. based on income inequality. Portland was ranked #83 (#1 = greatest inequality). Criteria: the "95/20 ratio," a figure representing the income at which a household earns more than 95 percent of all other households, divided by the income at which a household earns more than only 20 percent of all other households. *Brookings Institution, "Household Income Inequality, 100 Largest U.S. Metro Areas, 2014-2016," February 5, 2018*

- *Forbes* ranked the 100 largest metro areas in the U.S. in terms of the "Best Cities for Young Professionals." The Portland metro area ranked #23 out of 25. Criteria: median rent of a two-bedroom apartment; job growth and unemployment rate; median salary of college graduates with 5 or less years of work experience; networking opportunities; social outlook; percentage of population 25 years of age and older with college degrees. *Forbes.com, "America's 25 Best Cities for Young Professionals in 2017," May 22, 2017*

- Payscale.com ranked the 32 largest metro areas in terms of wage growth. The Portland metro area ranked #3. Criteria: private-sector and education professional wage growth between the 4th quarter of 2019 and the 4th quarter of 2020. *PayScale, "Wage Trends by Metro Area-4th Quarter," January 11, 2021*

- The Portland metro area was identified as one of the most debt-ridden places in America by the finance site Credit.com. The metro area was ranked #21. Criteria: residents' average credit card debt as well as median income. *Credit.com, "25 Cities With the Most Credit Card Debt," February 28, 2018*

- For its annual survey of the "Most Expensive U.S. Cities to Live In," Kiplinger applied Cost of Living Index statistics developed by the Council for Community and Economic Research to U.S. Census Bureau population and median household income data for 256 urban areas. Portland was among the 20 most expensive in the country. *Kiplinger.com, "The 20 Most Expensive Cities in the U.S.," July 29, 2020*

- The Portland metro area appeared on the Milken Institute "2021 Best Performing Cities" list. Rank: #38 out of 200 large metro areas (population over 250,000). Criteria: job growth; wage and salary growth; high-tech output growth; housing affordability; household broadband access. *Milken Institute, "Best-Performing Cities 2021," February 16, 2021*

- *Forbes* ranked the 200 most populous metro areas to determine the nation's "Best Places for Business and Careers." The Portland metro area was ranked #5. Criteria: costs (business and living); job growth (past and projected); income growth; quality of life; educational attainment (college and high school); projected economic growth; cultural and leisure opportunities; workplace tolerance laws; net migration patterns. *Forbes, "The Best Places for Business and Careers 2019: Seattle Still On Top," October 30, 2019*

- Mercer Human Resources Consulting ranked 209 cities worldwide in terms of cost-of-living. Portland ranked #92 (the lower the ranking, the higher the cost-of-living). The survey measured the comparative cost of over 200 items (such as housing, food, clothing, household goods, transportation, and entertainment) in each location. *Mercer, "2020 Cost of Living Survey," June 9, 2020*

Culture/Performing Arts Rankings

- Portland was selected as one of the 25 best cities for moviemakers in North America. COVID-19 has spurred a quest for great film cities that offer more creative space, lower costs, and more great outdoors. NYC & LA were intentionally excluded. Criteria: longstanding reputations as film-friendly communities; efforts to deal with pandemic-specific challenges; and establish appropriate COVID-19 guidelines. The city was ranked #19. *MovieMaker Magazine, "Best Places to Live and Work as a Moviemaker, 2021," January 26, 2021*

Dating/Romance Rankings

- Portland was selected as one of the nation's most romantic cities with 100,000 or more residents by Amazon.com. The city ranked #18 of 20. Criteria: per capita sales of romance novels, relationship books, romantic comedy movies, romantic music, and sexual wellness products. *Amazon.com, "Top 20 Most Romantic Cities in the U.S.," February 1, 2017*

Education Rankings

- Personal finance website *WalletHub* analyzed the 150 largest U.S. metropolitan statistical areas to determine where the most educated Americans are putting their degrees to work. Criteria: education levels; percentage of workers with degrees; education quality and attainment gap; public school quality rankings; quality and enrollment of each metro area's universities. Portland was ranked #18 (#1 = most educated city). *www.WalletHub.com, "Most and Least Educated Cities in America," July 20, 2020*

- Portland was selected as one of America's most literate cities. The city ranked #5 out of the 84 largest U.S. cities. Criteria: number of booksellers; library resources; Internet resources; educational attainment; periodical publishing resources; newspaper circulation. *Central Connecticut State University, "America's Most Literate Cities, 2018," February 2019*

Environmental Rankings

- Sperling's BestPlaces assessed the 50 largest metropolitan areas of the United States for the likelihood of dangerously extreme weather events or earthquakes. In general the Southeast and South-Central regions have the highest risk of weather extremes and earthquakes, while the Pacific Northwest enjoys the lowest risk. Of the least risky metropolitan areas, the Portland metro area was ranked #1. *www.bestplaces.net, "Avoid Natural Disasters: BestPlaces Reveals The Top 10 Safest Places to Live," October 25, 2017*

- The U.S. Environmental Protection Agency (EPA) released a list of U.S. metropolitan areas with the most ENERGY STAR certified buildings in 2019. The Portland metro area was ranked #25 out of 25. *U.S. Environmental Protection Agency, "2020 Energy Star Top Cities," March 2020*

- Portland was highlighted as one of the 25 metro areas most polluted by short-term particle pollution (24-hour PM 2.5) in the U.S. during 2016 through 2018. The area ranked #24. *American Lung Association, "State of the Air 2020," April 21, 2020*

Food/Drink Rankings

- The U.S. Chamber of Commerce Foundation conducted an in-depth study on local food truck regulations, surveyed 288 food truck owners, and ranked 20 major American cities based on how friendly they are for operating a food truck. The compiled index assessed the following: procedures for obtaining permits and licenses; complying with restrictions; and financial obligations associated with operating a food truck. Portland ranked #1 overall (1 being the best). *www.foodtrucknation.us, "Food Truck Nation," March 20, 2018*

- Portland was identified as one of the cities in America ordering the most vegan food options by GrubHub.com. The city ranked #3 out of 5. Criteria: percentage of vegan, vegetarian and plant-based food orders compared to the overall number of orders. *GrubHub.com, "State of the Plate Report 2020: Top Vegan-Friendly Cities," July 9, 2020*

Health/Fitness Rankings

- For each of the 100 largest cities in the United States, the American Fitness Index®, published by the American College of Sports Medicine and the Anthem Foundation, evaluated community infrastructure and 33 health behaviors including preventive health, levels of chronic disease conditions, pedestrian safety, air quality, and community resources that support physical activity. Portland ranked #16 for "community fitness." *americanfitnessindex.org, "2020 ACSM American Fitness Index Summary Report," July 14, 2020*

- Portland was identified as a "2021 Spring Allergy Capital." The area ranked #89 out of 100. Three groups of factors were used to identify the most challenging cities for people with allergies during the spring season: annual spring pollen levels; over the counter medicine use; number of board-certified allergy specialists. *Asthma and Allergy Foundation of America, "Spring Allergy Capitals 2021," February 23, 2021*

- Portland was identified as a "2021 Fall Allergy Capital." The area ranked #94 out of 100. Three groups of factors were used to identify the most challenging cities for people with allergies during the fall season: annual fall pollen levels; over the counter medicine use; number of board-certified allergy specialists. *Asthma and Allergy Foundation of America, "Fall Allergy Capitals 2021," February 23, 2021*

- Portland was identified as a "2019 Asthma Capital." The area ranked #72 out of the nation's 100 largest metropolitan areas. Criteria: estimated asthma prevalence; crude death rate from asthma; and ER visits due to asthma. Risk factors analyzed but not factored in the rankings: annual pollen score; annual air quality; public smoking laws; number of board-certified asthma specialists; rescue medication use; controller medication use; uninsured rate; poverty rate. *Asthma and Allergy Foundation of America, "Asthma Capitals 2019: The Most Challenging Places to Live With Asthma," May 7, 2019*

Pet Rankings

- Portland appeared on *The Dogington Post* site as one of the top cities for dog lovers, ranking #6 out of 20. The real estate brokerage, Redfin and Rover, the largest pet sitter and dog walker network, compiled a list from over 14,000 U.S. cities to come up with a "Rover Rank." Criteria: highest count of dog walks, the city's Walk Score®, for-sale home listings that mention "dog," number of dog walkers and pet sitters and the hours spent and distance logged. *www.dogingtonpost.com, "The 20 Most Dog-Friendly Cities of 2019," April 4, 2019*

Real Estate Rankings

- FitSmallBusiness looked at 50 of the largest metropolitan areas in the U.S. to determine which metro was the best to start a real estate business. Data was compiled from such sources as: Zillow, Trulia, U.S. Census Bureau, and the Bureau of Labor Statistics. Criteria: location; inventory; annual wages; median sales price of homes; days on the market; median price cut percentage; and other factors that would influence real estate professional growth. The Portland metro area ranked #24. *fitsmallbusiness.com, "The Best Cities to Become a Real Estate Agent in 2018," January 30, 2018*

- *WalletHub* compared the most populated U.S. cities to determine which had the best markets for real estate agents. Portland ranked #17 where demand was high and pay was the best. Criteria: sales per agent; annual median wage for real-estate agents; monthly average starting salary for real estate agents; real estate job density and competition; unemployment rate; home turnover rate; housing-market health index; and other relevant metrics. *www.WalletHub.com, "2019's Best Places to Be a Real Estate Agent," April 24, 2019*

- The Portland metro area was identified as one of the 20 least affordable housing markets in the U.S. in 2020. The area ranked #164 out of 183 markets. Criteria: qualification for a mortgage loan with a 10 percent down payment on a typical home. *National Association of Realtors®, Qualifying Income Based on Sales Price of Existing Single-Family Homes for Metropolitan Areas, 2020*

- Portland was ranked #226 out of 268 metro areas in terms of housing affordability in 2020 by the National Association of Home Builders (#1 = most affordable). Criteria: the share of homes sold in that area affordable to a family earning the local median income, based on standard mortgage underwriting criteria. *National Association of Home Builders®, NAHB-Wells Fargo Housing Opportunity Index, 4th Quarter 2020*

Safety Rankings

- Allstate ranked the 200 largest cities in America in terms of driver safety. Portland ranked #181. Criteria: internal property damage claims over a two-year period from January 2016 to December 2017. The report helps increase the importance of safety and awareness behind the wheel. *Allstate, "Allstate America's Best Drivers Report, 2019" June 24, 2019*

- The National Insurance Crime Bureau ranked 384 metro areas in the U.S. in terms of per capita rates of vehicle theft. The Portland metro area ranked #21 (#1 = highest rate). Criteria: number of vehicle theft offenses per 100,000 inhabitants in 2019. *National Insurance Crime Bureau, "Hot Spots 2019," July 21, 2020*

Seniors/Retirement Rankings

- From its Best Cities for Successful Aging indexes, the Milken Institute generated rankings for metropolitan areas, weighing data in nine categories—health care, wellness, living arrangements, transportation and convenience, financial characteristics, education, employment, community engagement, and overall livability. The Portland metro area was ranked #40 overall in the large metro area category. *Milken Institute, "Best Cities for Successful Aging, 2017" March 14, 2017*

Sports/Recreation Rankings

- Portland was chosen as one of America's best cities for bicycling. The city ranked #5 out of 50. Criteria: cycling infrastructure that is safe and friendly for all ages; energy and bike culture. The editors evaluated cities with populations of 100,000 or more. *Bicycling, "The 50 Best Bike Cities in America," October 10, 2018*

Transportation Rankings

- Business Insider presented an AllTransit Performance Score ranking of public transportation in major U.S. cities and towns, with populations over 250,000, in which Portland earned the #13-ranked "Transit Score," awarded for frequency of service, access to jobs, quality and number of stops, and affordability. *www.businessinsider.com, "The 17 Major U.S. Cities with the Best Public Transportation," April 17, 2018*

- According to the INRIX "2019 Global Traffic Scorecard," Portland was identified as one of the most congested metro areas in the U.S. The area ranked #8 out of 10. Criteria: average annual time spent in traffic and average cost of congestion per motorist. *Inrix.com, "Congestion Costs Each American Nearly 100 hours, $1,400 A Year," March 9, 2020*

Women/Minorities Rankings

- *Women's Health*, together with the site Yelp, identified the 15 "Wellthiest" spots in the U.S. Portland appeared among the top for happiest, healthiest, outdoorsiest and Zen-iest. *Women's Health, "The 15 Wellthiest Cities in the U.S." July 5, 2017*

- Personal finance website *WalletHub* compared more than 180 U.S. cities across two key dimensions, "Hispanic Business-Friendliness" and "Hispanic Purchasing Power," to arrive at the most favorable conditions for Hispanic entrepreneurs. Portland was ranked #95 out of 182. Criteria includes: share of Hispanic-Owned Businesses; Hispanic entrepreneurship rate to median annual income of Hispanics; Small Business-Friendliness score; cost of living; and number of Hispanics with at least a bachelor's degree. *WalletHub.com, "2019's Best Cities for Hispanic Entrepreneurs," May 1, 2019*

Miscellaneous Rankings

- While the majority of travel ground to a halt in 2020, plugged-in travel influencers and experts were able to rediscover their local regions. Portland appeared on a *Forbes* list of 15 U.S. cities that provided solace as well as local inspiration. Whether it be quirky things to see and do, delicious take out, outdoor exploring and daytrips, these places are must-see destinations. *Forbes, "Bucket List Travel: The 15 Best U.S. Destinations For 2021," January 1, 2021*

- *MoveHub* ranked 446 hipster cities across 20 countries, using its *alternative* Hipster Index and Portland came out as #2 among the top 50. Criteria: population over 150,000; number of vintage boutiques; density of tattoo parlors; vegan places to eat; coffee shops; and density of vinyl record stores. *www.movehub.com, "The Hipster Index: Brighton Pips Portland to Global Top Spot," February 20, 2020*

- The watchdog site, Charity Navigator, conducted a study of charities in major markets both to analyze statistical differences in their financial, accountability, and transparency practices and to track year-to-year variations in individual philanthropic communities. The Portland metro area was ranked #10 among the 30 metro markets in the rating category of Overall Score. *www.charitynavigator.org, "2017 Metro Market Study," May 1, 2017*

- *WalletHub* compared the 150 most populated U.S. cities to determine their operating efficiency. A "Quality of City Services" score was constructed for each city and then divided by the total budget per capita to reveal which were managed the best. Portland ranked #63. Criteria: financial stability; economy; education; safety; health; infrastructure and pollution. *www.WalletHub.com, "2020's Best- & Worst-Run Cities in America," June 29, 2020*

- The National Alliance to End Homelessness listed the 25 most populous metro areas with the highest rate of homelessness. The Portland metro area had a high rate of homelessness. Criteria: number of homeless people per 10,000 population in 2016. *National Alliance to End Homelessness, "Homelessness in the 25 Most Populous U.S. Metro Areas," September 1, 2017*

Business Environment

DEMOGRAPHICS

Population Growth

Area	1990 Census	2000 Census	2010 Census	2019* Estimate	Population Growth (%)	
					1990-2019	2010-2019
City	485,833	529,121	583,776	645,291	32.8	10.5
MSA[1]	1,523,741	1,927,881	2,226,009	2,445,761	60.5	9.9
U.S.	248,709,873	281,421,906	308,745,538	324,697,795	30.6	5.2

Note: (1) Figures cover the Portland-Vancouver-Hillsboro, OR-WA Metropolitan Statistical Area; (*) 2015-2019 5-year estimated population
Source: U.S. Census Bureau, 1990 Census, Census 2000, Census 2010, 2015-2019 American Community Survey 5-Year Estimates

Household Size

Area	Persons in Household (%)							Average Household Size
	One	Two	Three	Four	Five	Six	Seven or More	
City	34.0	34.9	14.1	10.8	3.8	1.5	0.8	2.30
MSA[1]	26.9	35.5	15.4	13.4	5.4	2.2	1.3	2.60
U.S.	27.9	33.9	15.6	12.9	6.0	2.3	1.4	2.60

Note: (1) Figures cover the Portland-Vancouver-Hillsboro, OR-WA Metropolitan Statistical Area
Source: U.S. Census Bureau, 2015-2019 American Community Survey 5-Year Estimates

Race

Area	White Alone[2] (%)	Black Alone[2] (%)	Asian Alone[2] (%)	AIAN[3] Alone[2] (%)	NHOPI[4] Alone[2] (%)	Other Race Alone[2] (%)	Two or More Races (%)
City	77.4	5.8	8.2	0.8	0.6	1.9	5.3
MSA[1]	81.1	2.8	6.7	0.8	0.5	3.0	5.0
U.S.	72.5	12.7	5.5	0.8	0.2	4.9	3.3

Note: (1) Figures cover the Portland-Vancouver-Hillsboro, OR-WA Metropolitan Statistical Area; (2) Alone is defined as not being in combination with one or more other races; (3) American Indian and Alaska Native; (4) Native Hawaiian and Other Pacific Islander
Source: U.S. Census Bureau, 2015-2019 American Community Survey 5-Year Estimates

Hispanic or Latino Origin

Area	Total (%)	Mexican (%)	Puerto Rican (%)	Cuban (%)	Other (%)
City	9.7	6.8	0.4	0.4	2.1
MSA[1]	12.0	9.2	0.4	0.2	2.2
U.S.	18.0	11.2	1.7	0.7	4.3

Note: Persons of Hispanic or Latino origin can be of any race; (1) Figures cover the Portland-Vancouver-Hillsboro, OR-WA Metropolitan Statistical Area
Source: U.S. Census Bureau, 2015-2019 American Community Survey 5-Year Estimates

Ancestry

Area	German	Irish	English	American	Italian	Polish	French[2]	Scottish	Dutch
City	15.9	11.1	10.5	4.6	4.3	2.3	3.0	2.9	1.9
MSA[1]	17.2	10.4	10.4	4.7	3.9	1.8	2.9	2.9	1.9
U.S.	13.3	9.7	7.2	6.2	5.1	2.8	2.3	1.7	1.2

Note: Figures are the percentage of the total population reporting a particular ancestry. The nine most commonly reported ancestries in the U.S. are shown. Figures include multiple ancestries (e.g. if a person reported being Irish and Italian, they were included in both columns); (1) Figures cover the Portland-Vancouver-Hillsboro, OR-WA Metropolitan Statistical Area; (2) Excludes Basque
Source: U.S. Census Bureau, 2015-2019 American Community Survey 5-Year Estimates

Foreign-born Population

Area	Percent of Population Born in								
	Any Foreign Country	Asia	Mexico	Europe	Caribbean	Central America[2]	South America	Africa	Canada
City	13.5	5.9	2.0	2.7	0.3	0.5	0.3	1.0	0.5
MSA[1]	12.6	5.0	3.1	2.3	0.1	0.5	0.3	0.6	0.4
U.S.	13.6	4.2	3.5	1.5	1.3	1.1	1.0	0.7	0.2

Note: (1) Figures cover the Portland-Vancouver-Hillsboro, OR-WA Metropolitan Statistical Area; (2) Excludes Mexico.
Source: U.S. Census Bureau, 2015-2019 American Community Survey 5-Year Estimates

Marital Status

Area	Never Married	Now Married[2]	Separated	Widowed	Divorced
City	41.3	40.9	1.5	3.8	12.5
MSA[1]	32.1	50.0	1.4	4.5	12.0
U.S.	33.4	48.1	1.9	5.8	10.9

Note: Figures are percentages and cover the population 15 years of age and older; (1) Figures cover the Portland-Vancouver-Hillsboro, OR-WA Metropolitan Statistical Area; (2) Excludes separated
Source: U.S. Census Bureau, 2015-2019 American Community Survey 5-Year Estimates

Disability by Age

Area	All Ages	Under 18 Years Old	18 to 64 Years Old	65 Years and Over
City	12.1	4.1	10.0	35.4
MSA[1]	11.9	3.9	9.7	34.1
U.S.	12.6	4.2	10.3	34.5

Note: Figures show percent of the civilian noninstitutionalized population that reported having a disability. Disability status is determined from six types of difficulty: vision, hearing, cognitive, ambulatory, self-care, and independent living. For children under 5 years old, hearing and vision difficulty are used to determine disability status. For children between the ages of 5 and 14, disability status is determined from hearing, vision, cognitive, ambulatory, and self-care difficulties. For people aged 15 years and older, they are considered to have a disability if they have difficulty with any one of the six difficulty types; Note: (1) Figures cover the Portland-Vancouver-Hillsboro, OR-WA Metropolitan Statistical Area
Source: U.S. Census Bureau, 2015-2019 American Community Survey 5-Year Estimates

Age

Area	Percent of Population									Median Age
	Under Age 5	Age 5–19	Age 20–34	Age 35–44	Age 45–54	Age 55–64	Age 65–74	Age 75–84	Age 85+	
City	5.3	14.6	25.9	17.1	13.1	11.3	8.0	3.3	1.5	37.1
MSA[1]	5.7	18.1	21.3	14.7	13.3	12.5	9.0	3.8	1.7	38.1
U.S.	6.1	19.1	20.7	12.6	13.0	12.9	9.1	4.6	1.9	38.1

Note: (1) Figures cover the Portland-Vancouver-Hillsboro, OR-WA Metropolitan Statistical Area
Source: U.S. Census Bureau, 2015-2019 American Community Survey 5-Year Estimates

Gender

Area	Males	Females	Males per 100 Females
City	319,869	325,422	98.3
MSA[1]	1,210,509	1,235,252	98.0
U.S.	159,886,919	164,810,876	97.0

Note: (1) Figures cover the Portland-Vancouver-Hillsboro, OR-WA Metropolitan Statistical Area
Source: U.S. Census Bureau, 2015-2019 American Community Survey 5-Year Estimates

Religious Groups by Family

Area	Catholic	Baptist	Non-Den.	Methodist[2]	Lutheran	LDS[3]	Pente-costal	Presby-terian[4]	Muslim[5]	Judaism
MSA[1]	10.6	2.3	4.5	1.0	1.6	3.8	2.0	1.0	0.1	0.3
U.S.	19.1	9.3	4.0	4.0	2.3	2.0	1.9	1.6	0.8	0.7

Note: Figures are the number of adherents as a percentage of the total population; (1) Figures cover the Portland-Vancouver-Hillsboro, OR-WA Metropolitan Statistical Area; (2) Methodist/Pietist; (3) Latter Day Saints; (4) Reformed; (5) Figures are estimates
Source: Association of Statisticians of American Religious Bodies, 2010 U.S. Religion Census: Religious Congregations & Membership Study

Religious Groups by Tradition

Area	Catholic	Evangelical Protestant	Mainline Protestant	Other Tradition	Black Protestant	Orthodox
MSA[1]	10.6	11.7	3.7	5.2	0.2	0.3
U.S.	19.1	16.2	7.3	4.3	1.6	0.3

Note: Figures are the number of adherents as a percentage of the total population; (1) Figures cover the Portland-Vancouver-Hillsboro, OR-WA Metropolitan Statistical Area
Source: Association of Statisticians of American Religious Bodies, 2010 U.S. Religion Census: Religious Congregations & Membership Study

ECONOMY

Gross Metropolitan Product

Area	2017	2018	2019	2020	Rank[2]
MSA[1]	165.9	175.7	183.8	191.1	21

Note: Figures are in billions of dollars; (1) Figures cover the Portland-Vancouver-Hillsboro, OR-WA Metropolitan Statistical Area; (2) Rank is based on 2018 data and ranges from 1 to 381
Source: U.S. Conference of Mayors, U.S. Metro Economies: GMP & Employment 2018-2020, September 2019

Economic Growth

Area	2015-17 (%)	2018 (%)	2019 (%)	2020 (%)	Rank[2]
MSA[1]	3.9	3.5	2.6	1.6	42
U.S.	1.9	2.9	2.3	2.1	–

Note: Figures are real gross metropolitan product (GMP) growth rates and represent average annual percent change; (1) Figures cover the Portland-Vancouver-Hillsboro, OR-WA Metropolitan Statistical Area; (2) Rank is based on 2017 2-year average annual percent change and ranges from 1 to 381
Source: U.S. Conference of Mayors, U.S. Metro Economies: GMP & Employment 2018-2020, September 2019

Metropolitan Area Exports

Area	2014	2015	2016	2017	2018	2019	Rank[2]
MSA[1]	18,667.2	18,847.8	20,256.8	20,788.8	21,442.9	23,761.9	16

Note: Figures are in millions of dollars; (1) Figures cover the Portland-Vancouver-Hillsboro, OR-WA Metropolitan Statistical Area; (2) Rank is based on 2019 data and ranges from 1 to 386
Source: U.S. Department of Commerce, International Trade Administration, Office of Trade and Economic Analysis, Industry and Analysis, Exports by Metropolitan Area, data extracted March 24, 2021

Building Permits

Area	Single-Family			Multi-Family			Total		
	2018	2019	Pct. Chg.	2018	2019	Pct. Chg.	2018	2019	Pct. Chg.
City	775	703	-9.3	4,873	4,391	-9.9	5,648	5,094	-9.8
MSA[1]	6,869	7,688	11.9	7,311	9,127	24.8	14,180	16,815	18.6
U.S.	855,300	862,100	0.7	473,500	523,900	10.6	1,328,800	1,386,000	4.3

Note: (1) Figures cover the Portland-Vancouver-Hillsboro, OR-WA Metropolitan Statistical Area; Figures represent new, privately-owned housing units authorized (unadjusted data); All permit data are based on estimates with imputation
Source: U.S. Census Bureau, Manufacturing, Mining, and Construction Statistics, Building Permits, 2018, 2019

Bankruptcy Filings

Area	Business Filings			Nonbusiness Filings		
	2019	2020	% Chg.	2019	2020	% Chg.
Multnomah County	62	59	-4.8	1,394	1,147	-17.7
U.S.	22,780	21,655	-4.9	752,160	522,808	-30.5

Note: Business filings include Chapter 7, Chapter 9, Chapter 11, Chapter 12, Chapter 13, Chapter 15, and Section 304; Nonbusiness filings include Chapter 7, Chapter 11, and Chapter 13
Source: Administrative Office of the U.S. Courts, Business and Nonbusiness Bankruptcy, County Cases Commenced by Chapter of the Bankruptcy Code, During the 12-Month Period Ending December 31, 2019 and Business and Nonbusiness Bankruptcy, County Cases Commenced by Chapter of the Bankruptcy Code, During the 12-Month Period Ending December 31, 2020

Housing Vacancy Rates

Area	Gross Vacancy Rate[2] (%)			Year-Round Vacancy Rate[3] (%)			Rental Vacancy Rate[4] (%)			Homeowner Vacancy Rate[5] (%)		
	2018	2019	2020	2018	2019	2020	2018	2019	2020	2018	2019	2020
MSA[1]	6.8	6.6	5.5	6.0	5.6	4.9	3.8	4.4	4.3	1.4	0.9	0.8
U.S.	12.3	12.0	10.6	9.7	9.5	8.2	6.9	6.7	6.3	1.5	1.4	1.0

Note: (1) Figures cover the Portland-Vancouver-Hillsboro, OR-WA Metropolitan Statistical Area; (2) The percentage of the total housing inventory that is vacant; (3) The percentage of the housing inventory (excluding seasonal units) that is year-round vacant; (4) The percentage of rental inventory that is vacant for rent; (5) The percentage of homeowner inventory that is vacant for sale
Source: U.S. Census Bureau, Housing Vacancies and Homeownership Annual Statistics: 2018, 2019, 2020

INCOME

Income

Area	Per Capita ($)	Median Household ($)	Average Household ($)
City	41,310	71,005	95,998
MSA[1]	38,544	74,792	97,930
U.S.	34,103	62,843	88,607

Note: (1) Figures cover the Portland-Vancouver-Hillsboro, OR-WA Metropolitan Statistical Area
Source: U.S. Census Bureau, 2015-2019 American Community Survey 5-Year Estimates

Household Income Distribution

Area	Percent of Households Earning							
	Under $15,000	$15,000 -$24,999	$25,000 -$34,999	$35,000 -$49,999	$50,000 -$74,999	$75,000 -$99,999	$100,000 -$149,999	$150,000 and up
City	10.6	7.2	7.8	10.4	16.4	13.0	16.9	17.7
MSA[1]	7.7	6.7	7.4	11.1	17.3	14.0	18.3	17.6
U.S.	10.3	8.9	8.9	12.3	17.2	12.7	15.1	14.5

Note: (1) Figures cover the Portland-Vancouver-Hillsboro, OR-WA Metropolitan Statistical Area
Source: U.S. Census Bureau, 2015-2019 American Community Survey 5-Year Estimates

Poverty Rate

Area	All Ages	Under 18 Years Old	18 to 64 Years Old	65 Years and Over
City	13.7	15.5	13.9	10.4
MSA[1]	10.6	13.1	10.5	7.7
U.S.	13.4	18.5	12.6	9.3

Note: Figures are percentage of people whose income during the past 12 months was below the poverty level;
(1) Figures cover the Portland-Vancouver-Hillsboro, OR-WA Metropolitan Statistical Area
Source: U.S. Census Bureau, 2015-2019 American Community Survey 5-Year Estimates

CITY FINANCES

City Government Finances

Component	2017 ($000)	2017 ($ per capita)
Total Revenues	1,912,099	3,024
Total Expenditures	1,759,816	2,783
Debt Outstanding	3,150,536	4,983
Cash and Securities[1]	1,542,484	2,439

Note: (1) Cash and security holdings of a government at the close of its fiscal year,
including those of its dependent agencies, utilities, and liquor stores.
Source: U.S. Census Bureau, State & Local Government Finances 2017

City Government Revenue by Source

Source	2017 ($000)	2017 ($ per capita)	2017 (%)
General Revenue			
From Federal Government	15,909	25	0.8
From State Government	84,652	134	4.4
From Local Governments	103,632	164	5.4
Taxes			
Property	533,074	843	27.9
Sales and Gross Receipts	167,669	265	8.8
Personal Income	0	0	0.0
Corporate Income	0	0	0.0
Motor Vehicle License	0	0	0.0
Other Taxes	187,254	296	9.8
Current Charges	577,696	914	30.2
Liquor Store	0	0	0.0
Utility	177,166	280	9.3
Employee Retirement	594	1	0.0

Source: U.S. Census Bureau, State & Local Government Finances 2017

City Government Expenditures by Function

Function	2017 ($000)	2017 ($ per capita)	2017 (%)
General Direct Expenditures			
Air Transportation	0	0	0.0
Corrections	0	0	0.0
Education	0	0	0.0
Employment Security Administration	0	0	0.0
Financial Administration	52,202	82	3.0
Fire Protection	115,792	183	6.6
General Public Buildings	16,316	25	0.9
Governmental Administration, Other	38,447	60	2.2
Health	0	0	0.0
Highways	180,168	284	10.2
Hospitals	0	0	0.0
Housing and Community Development	141,333	223	8.0
Interest on General Debt	114,385	180	6.5
Judicial and Legal	11,861	18	0.7
Libraries	0	0	0.0
Parking	8,508	13	0.5
Parks and Recreation	136,243	215	7.7
Police Protection	205,958	325	11.7
Public Welfare	0	0	0.0
Sewerage	229,464	362	13.0
Solid Waste Management	5,005	7	0.3
Veterans' Services	0	0	0.0
Liquor Store	0	0	0.0
Utility	190,405	301	10.8
Employee Retirement	120,352	190	6.8

Source: U.S. Census Bureau, State & Local Government Finances 2017

EMPLOYMENT

Labor Force and Employment

Area	Civilian Labor Force			Workers Employed		
	Dec. 2019	Dec. 2020	% Chg.	Dec. 2019	Dec. 2020	% Chg.
City	376,061	380,047	1.1	366,666	355,132	-3.1
MSA[1]	1,332,520	1,316,280	-1.2	1,294,803	1,235,940	-4.5
U.S.	164,007,000	160,017,000	-2.4	158,504,000	149,613,000	-5.6

Note: Data is not seasonally adjusted and covers workers 16 years of age and older; (1) Figures cover the Portland-Vancouver-Hillsboro, OR-WA Metropolitan Statistical Area
Source: Bureau of Labor Statistics, Local Area Unemployment Statistics

Unemployment Rate

Area	2020											
	Jan.	Feb.	Mar.	Apr.	May	Jun.	Jul.	Aug.	Sep.	Oct.	Nov.	Dec.
City	3.2	3.2	3.4	16.2	15.9	14.3	13.1	10.7	9.0	7.5	6.4	6.6
MSA[1]	3.4	3.5	3.6	14.2	14.0	11.8	11.2	9.1	7.9	6.6	5.8	6.1
U.S.	4.0	3.8	4.5	14.4	13.0	11.2	10.5	8.5	7.7	6.6	6.4	6.5

Note: Data is not seasonally adjusted and covers workers 16 years of age and older; (1) Figures cover the Portland-Vancouver-Hillsboro, OR-WA Metropolitan Statistical Area
Source: Bureau of Labor Statistics, Local Area Unemployment Statistics

Average Wages

Occupation	$/Hr.	Occupation	$/Hr.
Accountants and Auditors	38.50	Maintenance and Repair Workers	22.40
Automotive Mechanics	24.50	Marketing Managers	65.90
Bookkeepers	22.60	Network and Computer Systems Admin.	43.00
Carpenters	29.10	Nurses, Licensed Practical	27.80
Cashiers	14.70	Nurses, Registered	47.50
Computer Programmers	45.20	Nursing Assistants	18.00
Computer Systems Analysts	48.20	Office Clerks, General	19.70
Computer User Support Specialists	29.20	Physical Therapists	44.10
Construction Laborers	23.10	Physicians	84.10
Cooks, Restaurant	16.00	Plumbers, Pipefitters and Steamfitters	37.80
Customer Service Representatives	20.20	Police and Sheriff's Patrol Officers	39.50
Dentists	107.30	Postal Service Mail Carriers	25.20
Electricians	37.00	Real Estate Sales Agents	27.80
Engineers, Electrical	46.10	Retail Salespersons	16.70
Fast Food and Counter Workers	14.00	Sales Representatives, Technical/Scientific	51.50
Financial Managers	65.30	Secretaries, Exc. Legal/Medical/Executive	22.20
First-Line Supervisors of Office Workers	30.20	Security Guards	16.60
General and Operations Managers	61.20	Surgeons	137.00
Hairdressers/Cosmetologists	16.60	Teacher Assistants, Exc. Postsecondary*	17.40
Home Health and Personal Care Aides	15.30	Teachers, Secondary School, Exc. Sp. Ed.*	39.40
Janitors and Cleaners	16.50	Telemarketers	18.30
Landscaping/Groundskeeping Workers	18.50	Truck Drivers, Heavy/Tractor-Trailer	25.20
Lawyers	68.30	Truck Drivers, Light/Delivery Services	20.10
Maids and Housekeeping Cleaners	15.20	Waiters and Waitresses	15.70

Note: Wage data covers the Portland-Vancouver-Hillsboro, OR-WA Metropolitan Statistical Area; (*) Hourly wages were calculated from annual wage data based on a 40 hour work week; n/a not available.
Source: Bureau of Labor Statistics, Metro Area Occupational Employment & Wage Estimates, May 2020

Employment by Industry

Sector	MSA[1]		U.S.
	Number of Employees	Percent of Total	Percent of Total
Construction	72,200	6.4	5.1
Education and Health Services	179,100	15.8	16.3
Financial Activities	70,800	6.3	6.1
Government	140,700	12.4	15.2
Information	24,800	2.2	1.9
Leisure and Hospitality	71,800	6.3	9.0
Manufacturing	120,800	10.7	8.5
Mining and Logging	1,200	0.1	0.4
Other Services	36,700	3.2	3.8
Professional and Business Services	186,700	16.5	14.4
Retail Trade	118,100	10.4	10.9
Transportation, Warehousing, and Utilities	54,800	4.8	4.6
Wholesale Trade	55,100	4.9	3.9

Note: Figures are non-farm employment as of December 2020. Figures are not seasonally adjusted and include workers 16 years of age and older; (1) Figures cover the Portland-Vancouver-Hillsboro, OR-WA Metropolitan Statistical Area
Source: Bureau of Labor Statistics, Current Employment Statistics, Employment, Hours, and Earnings

Employment by Occupation

Occupation Classification	City (%)	MSA[1] (%)	U.S. (%)
Management, Business, Science, and Arts	50.1	43.2	38.5
Natural Resources, Construction, and Maintenance	4.9	7.6	8.9
Production, Transportation, and Material Moving	9.7	12.1	13.2
Sales and Office	19.0	20.9	21.6
Service	16.3	16.3	17.8

Note: Figures cover employed civilians 16 years of age and older; (1) Figures cover the
Portland-Vancouver-Hillsboro, OR-WA Metropolitan Statistical Area
Source: U.S. Census Bureau, 2015-2019 American Community Survey 5-Year Estimates

Occupations with Greatest Projected Employment Growth: 2020 – 2022

Occupation[1]	2020 Employment	2022 Projected Employment	Numeric Employment Change	Percent Employment Change
Combined Food Preparation and Serving Workers, Including Fast Food	33,130	38,460	5,330	16.1
Waiters and Waitresses	26,970	31,110	4,140	15.4
Cooks, Restaurant	18,020	21,500	3,480	19.3
Retail Salespersons	53,110	56,110	3,000	5.6
Laborers and Freight, Stock, and Material Movers, Hand	28,950	30,650	1,700	5.9
Bartenders	7,110	8,740	1,630	22.9
Cashiers	42,310	43,930	1,620	3.8
First-Line Supervisors of Food Preparation and Serving Workers	10,720	12,330	1,610	15.0
Maids and Housekeeping Cleaners	13,340	14,900	1,560	11.7
Light Truck or Delivery Services Drivers	12,690	14,120	1,430	11.3

Note: Projections cover Oregon; (1) Sorted by numeric employment change
Source: www.projectionscentral.com, State Occupational Projections, 2020–2022 Short-Term Projections

Fastest-Growing Occupations: 2020 – 2022

Occupation[1]	2020 Employment	2022 Projected Employment	Numeric Employment Change	Percent Employment Change
Ushers, Lobby Attendants, and Ticket Takers	520	740	220	42.3
Fine Artists, Including Painters, Sculptors, and Illustrators	350	480	130	37.1
Camera Operators, Television, Video, and Motion Picture	250	340	90	36.0
Multimedia Artists and Animators	1,120	1,480	360	32.1
Film and Video Editors	280	370	90	32.1
Public Address System and Other Announcers	160	210	50	31.3
Travel Agents	450	580	130	28.9
Actors	200	250	50	25.0
Gaming Change Persons and Booth Cashiers	200	250	50	25.0
Gaming Dealers	210	260	50	23.8

Note: Projections cover Oregon; (1) Sorted by percent employment change and excludes occupations with
numeric employment change less than 50
Source: www.projectionscentral.com, State Occupational Projections, 2020–2022 Short-Term Projections

TAXES

State Corporate Income Tax Rates

State	Tax Rate (%)	Income Brackets ($)	Num. of Brackets	Financial Institution Tax Rate (%)[a]	Federal Income Tax Ded.
Oregon	6.6 - 7.6 (u)	1 million	2	6.6 - 7.6 (u)	No

Note: Tax rates as of January 1, 2021; (a) Rates listed are the corporate income tax rate applied to financial
institutions or excise taxes based on income. Some states have other taxes based upon the value of deposits or
shares; (u) Oregon's minimum tax for C corporations depends on the Oregon sales of the filing group. The
minimum tax ranges from $150 for corporations with sales under $500,000, up to $100,000 for companies with
sales of $100 million or above. Oregon also imposes Corporate Activity Tax [CAT] of $250 plus 0.57% of
activity in excess of $1 million.
Source: Federation of Tax Administrators, State Corporate Income Tax Rates, January 1, 2021

State Individual Income Tax Rates

State	Tax Rate (%)	Income Brackets ($)	Personal Exemptions ($) Single	Married	Depend.	Standard Ded. ($) Single	Married
Oregon (a)	4.75 - 9.9	3,650 -125,000 (b)	213	426 (c)	213 (c)	2,350	4,700

Note: Tax rates as of January 1, 2021; Local- and county-level taxes are not included; The deduction for federal income tax is limited to $5,000 for individuals and $10,000 for joint returns in Missouri and Montana, and to $6,500 for all filers in Oregon; (a) 19 states have statutory provision for automatically adjusting to the rate of inflation the dollar values of the income tax brackets, standard deductions, and/or personal exemptions. Michigan indexes the personal exemption only. Oregon does not index the income brackets for $125,000 and over; (b) For joint returns, taxes are twice the tax on half the couple's income; (c) The personal exemption takes the form of a tax credit instead of a deduction
Source: Federation of Tax Administrators, State Individual Income Tax Rates, January 1, 2021

Various State Sales and Excise Tax Rates

State	State Sales Tax (%)	Gasoline[1] (¢/gal.)	Cigarette[2] ($/pack)	Spirits[3] ($/gal.)	Wine[4] ($/gal.)	Beer[5] ($/gal.)	Recreational Marijuana (%)
Oregon	None	38.83	1.33	21.95	0.67	0.08	(l)

Note: All tax rates as of January 1, 2021; (1) The American Petroleum Institute has developed a methodology for determining the average tax rate on a gallon of fuel. Rates may include any of the following: excise taxes, environmental fees, storage tank fees, other fees or taxes, general sales tax, and local taxes; (2) The federal excise tax of $1.0066 per pack and local taxes are not included; (3) Rates are those applicable to off-premise sales of 40% alcohol by volume (a.b.v.) distilled spirits in 750ml containers. Local excise taxes are excluded; (4) Rates are those applicable to off-premise sales of 11% a.b.v. non-carbonated wine in 750ml containers; (5) Rates are those applicable to off-premise sales of 4.7% a.b.v. beer in 12 ounce containers; (l) 17% excise tax (retail price)
Source: Tax Foundation, 2021 Facts & Figures: How Does Your State Compare?

State Business Tax Climate Index Rankings

State	Overall Rank	Corporate Tax Rank	Individual Income Tax Rank	Sales Tax Rank	Property Tax Rank	Unemployment Insurance Tax Rank
Oregon	15	49	38	4	16	36

Note: The index is a measure of how each state's tax laws affect economic performance. The lower the rank, the more favorable a state's tax system is for business. States without a given tax are given a ranking of 1. The scores/rankings for the District of Columbia do not affect other states. The 2021 index represents the tax climate as of July 1, 2020.
Source: Tax Foundation, State Business Tax Climate Index 2021

TRANSPORTATION

Means of Transportation to Work

Area	Car/Truck/Van Drove Alone	Car-pooled	Public Transportation Bus	Subway	Railroad	Bicycle	Walked	Other Means	Worked at Home
City	57.3	8.3	9.9	0.9	0.3	6.0	5.8	3.0	8.5
MSA[1]	70.3	9.1	4.8	0.7	0.2	2.2	3.4	2.0	7.4
U.S.	76.3	9.0	2.4	1.9	0.6	0.5	2.7	1.4	5.2

Note: Figures are percentages and cover workers 16 years of age and older; (1) Figures cover the Portland-Vancouver-Hillsboro, OR-WA Metropolitan Statistical Area
Source: U.S. Census Bureau, 2015-2019 American Community Survey 5-Year Estimates

Travel Time to Work

Area	Less Than 10 Minutes	10 to 19 Minutes	20 to 29 Minutes	30 to 44 Minutes	45 to 59 Minutes	60 to 89 Minutes	90 Minutes or More
City	7.8	26.3	27.0	24.5	7.7	4.9	1.8
MSA[1]	10.2	26.9	22.6	23.1	9.3	5.8	2.1
U.S.	12.2	28.4	20.8	20.8	8.3	6.4	2.9

Note: Note: Figures are percentages and include workers 16 years old and over; (1) Figures cover the Portland-Vancouver-Hillsboro, OR-WA Metropolitan Statistical Area
Source: U.S. Census Bureau, 2015-2019 American Community Survey 5-Year Estimates

Key Congestion Measures

Measure	1982	1992	2002	2012	2017
Annual Hours of Delay, Total (000)	12,104	23,005	49,440	76,716	88,009
Annual Hours of Delay, Per Auto Commuter	20	31	46	55	66
Annual Congestion Cost, Total (million $)	94	247	677	1,403	1,652
Annual Congestion Cost, Per Auto Commuter ($)	403	526	882	1,073	1,193

Note: Covers the Portland OR-WA urban area
Source: Texas A&M Transportation Institute, 2019 Urban Mobility Report

Freeway Travel Time Index

Measure	1982	1987	1992	1997	2002	2007	2012	2017
Urban Area Index[1]	1.13	1.18	1.21	1.27	1.31	1.31	1.35	1.35
Urban Area Rank[1,2]	14	11	11	7	6	11	6	7

Note: Freeway Travel Time Index—the ratio of travel time in the peak period to the travel time at free-flow conditions. For example, a value of 1.30 indicates a 20-minute free-flow trip takes 26 minutes in the peak (20 minutes x 1.30 = 26 minutes); (1) Covers the Portland OR-WA urban area; (2) Rank is based on 101 larger urban areas (#1 = highest travel time index)
Source: Texas A&M Transportation Institute, 2019 Urban Mobility Report

Public Transportation

Agency Name / Mode of Transportation	Vehicles Operated in Maximum Service[1]	Annual Unlinked Passenger Trips[2] (in thous.)	Annual Passenger Miles[3] (in thous.)
Tri-County Metropolitan Transportation District of Oregon (Tri-Met)			
Bus (directly operated)	584	56,429.2	200,008.8
Demand Response (purchased transportation)	219	854.2	7,869.6
Demand Response Taxi (purchased transportation)	50	108.1	1,297.3
Hybrid Rail (purchased transportation)	4	374.0	3,174.0
Light Rail (directly operated)	116	38,867.6	207,967.8
Ride Connection, Inc.			
Bus (directly operated)	7	126.2	387.3
Demand Response (directly operated)	35	90.0	209.1
Demand Response Taxi (purchased transportation)	41	86.0	435.0
City of Portland			
Aerial Tramway (purchased transportation)	2	2,104.4	1,346.8
Streetcar Rail (purchased transportation)	12	4,491.4	5,845.8
Special Mobility Services			
Bus (directly operated)	5	9.6	n/a
Demand Response (directly operated)	1	2.5	n/a

Note: (1) Number of revenue vehicles operated by the given mode and type of service to meet the annual maximum service requirement. This is the revenue vehicle count during the peak season of the year; on the week and day that maximum service is provided. Vehicles operated in maximum service (VOMS) exclude atypical days and one-time special events; (2) Number of passengers who boarded public transportation vehicles. Passengers are counted each time they board a vehicle no matter how many vehicles they use to travel from their origin to their destination. (3) Sum of the distances ridden by all passengers during the entire fiscal year.
Source: Federal Transit Administration, National Transit Database, 2019

Air Transportation

Airport Name and Code / Type of Service	Passenger Airlines[1]	Passenger Enplanements	Freight Carriers[2]	Freight (lbs)
Portland International (PDX)				
Domestic service (U.S. carriers - 2020)	19	3,352,030	19	292,840,478
International service (U.S. carriers - 2019)	6	216,407	5	6,003,643

Note: (1) Includes all U.S.-based major, minor and commuter airlines that carried at least one passenger during the year; (2) Includes all U.S.-based airlines and freight carriers that transported at least one pound of freight during the year.
Source: Bureau of Transportation Statistics, The Intermodal Transportation Database, Air Carriers: T-100 Domestic Market (U.S. Carriers), 2020; Bureau of Transportation Statistics, The Intermodal Transportation Database, Air Carriers: T-100 International Market (U.S. Carriers), 2019

BUSINESSES

Major Business Headquarters

Company Name	Industry	Rankings	
		Fortune[1]	Forbes[2]
Hoffman	Construction	-	205

Note: (1) Companies that produce a 10-K are ranked 1 to 500 based on 2019 revenue; (2) All private companies with at least $2 billion in annual revenue through the end of their most current fiscal year are ranked 1 to 219; companies listed are headquartered in the city; dashes indicate no ranking
Source: Fortune, "Fortune 500," June/July 2020; Forbes, "America's Largest Private Companies," 2020

Fastest-Growing Businesses

According to *Initiative for a Competitive Inner City (ICIC)*, Portland is home to one of America's 100 fastest-growing "inner city" companies: **Tender Loving Empire** (#29). Criteria for inclusion: company must be headquartered in or have 51 percent or more of its physical operations in an economically distressed urban area; must be an independent, for-profit corporation, partnership or proprietorship; must have 10 or more employees and have a five-year sales history that includes sales of at least $200,000 in the base year and at least $1 million in the current year with no decrease in sales over the two most recent years. Companies were ranked overall by revenue growth over the five-year period between 2015 and 2019. *Initiative for a Competitive Inner City (ICIC), "Inner City 100 Companies," 2020*

According to Deloitte, Portland is home to five of North America's 500 fastest-growing high-technology companies: **PayRange** (#83); **Lytics, Inc.** (#91); **CrowdStreet** (#141); **SheerID** (#251); **Smarsh Inc.** (#486). Companies are ranked by percentage growth in revenue over a four-year period. Criteria for inclusion: company must be headquartered within North America; must own proprietary intellectual property or technology that is sold to customers in products that contributes to a significant portion of the company's operating revenue; must have been in business for a minumum of four years with 2016 operating revenues of at least $50,000 USD/CD and 2019 operating revenues of at least $5 million USD/CD. *Deloitte, 2020 Technology Fast 500*[TM]

Living Environment

COST OF LIVING

Cost of Living Index

Composite Index	Groceries	Housing	Utilities	Trans-portation	Health Care	Misc. Goods/ Services
133.9	112.6	182.1	89.0	129.3	116.6	119.7

Note: The Cost of Living Index measures regional differences in the cost of consumer goods and services, excluding taxes and non-consumer expenditures, for professional and managerial households in the top income quintile. It is based on more than 50,000 prices covering almost 60 different items for which prices are collected three times a year by chambers of commerce, economic development organizations or university applied economic centers in each participating urban area. The numbers shown should be read as a percentage above or below the national average of 100. For example, a value of 115.4 in the groceries column indicates that grocery prices are 15.4% higher than the national average. Small differences in the index numbers should not be interpreted as significant; Figures cover the Portland OR urban area.
Source: The Council for Community and Economic Research, Cost of Living Index, 2020

Grocery Prices

Area[1]	T-Bone Steak ($/pound)	Frying Chicken ($/pound)	Whole Milk ($/half gal.)	Eggs ($/dozen)	Orange Juice ($/64 oz.)	Coffee ($/11.5 oz.)
City[2]	11.98	1.58	2.12	2.36	4.10	5.30
Avg.	11.78	1.39	2.05	1.47	3.57	4.34
Min.	8.03	0.94	1.03	0.74	2.94	3.02
Max.	15.86	2.65	4.31	3.77	5.44	8.69

Note: (1) Values for the local area are compared with the average, minimum and maximum values for all 284 areas in the Cost of Living Index; (2) Figures cover the Portland OR urban area; T-Bone Steak (price per pound); Frying Chicken (price per pound, whole fryer); Whole Milk (half gallon carton); Eggs (price per dozen, Grade A, large); Orange Juice (64 oz. Tropicana or Florida Natural); Coffee (11.5 oz. can, vacuum-packed, Maxwell House, Hills Bros, or Folgers).
Source: The Council for Community and Economic Research, Cost of Living Index, 2020

Housing and Utility Costs

Area[1]	New Home Price ($)	Apartment Rent ($/month)	All Electric ($/month)	Part Electric ($/month)	Other Energy ($/month)	Telephone ($/month)
City[2]	623,494	2,459	-	81.22	62.64	170.50
Avg.	368,594	1,168	170.86	100.47	65.28	184.30
Min.	190,567	502	91.58	31.42	26.08	169.60
Max.	2,227,806	4,738	470.38	280.31	280.06	206.50

Note: (1) Values for the local area are compared with the average, minimum and maximum values for all 284 areas in the Cost of Living Index; (2) Figures cover the Portland OR urban area; New Home Price (2,400 sf living area, 8,000 sf lot, in urban area with full utilities); Apartment Rent (950 sf 2 bedroom/1.5 or 2 bath, unfurnished, excluding all utilities except water); All Electric (average monthly cost for an all-electric home); Part Electric (average monthly cost for a part-electric home); Other Energy (average monthly cost for natural gas, fuel oil, coal, wood, and any other forms of energy except electricity); Telephone (price includes the base monthly rate plus taxes and fees for three lines of mobile phone service).
Source: The Council for Community and Economic Research, Cost of Living Index, 2020

Health Care, Transportation, and Other Costs

Area[1]	Doctor ($/visit)	Dentist ($/visit)	Optometrist ($/visit)	Gasoline ($/gallon)	Beauty Salon ($/visit)	Men's Shirt ($)
City[2]	168.67	101.75	146.25	2.78	56.44	41.23
Avg.	115.44	99.32	108.10	2.21	39.27	31.37
Min.	36.68	59.00	51.36	1.71	19.00	11.00
Max.	219.00	153.10	250.97	3.46	82.05	58.33

Note: (1) Values for the local area are compared with the average, minimum and maximum values for all 284 areas in the Cost of Living Index; (2) Figures cover the Portland OR urban area; Doctor (general practitioners routine exam of an established patient); Dentist (adult teeth cleaning and periodic oral examination); Optometrist (full vision eye exam for established adult patient); Gasoline (one gallon regular unleaded, national brand, including all taxes, cash price at self-service pump if available); Beauty Salon (woman's shampoo, trim, and blow-dry); Men's Shirt (cotton/polyester dress shirt, pinpoint weave, long sleeves).
Source: The Council for Community and Economic Research, Cost of Living Index, 2020

HOUSING

Homeownership Rate

Area	2012 (%)	2013 (%)	2014 (%)	2015 (%)	2016 (%)	2017 (%)	2018 (%)	2019 (%)	2020 (%)
MSA[1]	63.9	60.9	59.8	58.9	61.8	61.1	59.2	60.0	62.5
U.S.	65.4	65.1	64.5	63.7	63.4	63.9	64.4	64.6	66.6

Note: (1) Figures cover the Portland-Vancouver-Hillsboro, OR-WA Metropolitan Statistical Area
Source: U.S. Census Bureau, Housing Vacancies and Homeownership Annual Statistics: 2012-2020

House Price Index (HPI)

Area	National Ranking[2]	Quarterly Change (%)	One-Year Change (%)	Five-Year Change (%)	Since 1991Q1 (%)
MSA[1]	127	2.22	6.27	37.96	381.42
U.S.[3]	–	3.81	10.77	38.99	205.12

Note: The HPI is a weighted repeat sales index. It measures average price changes in repeat sales or refinancings on the same properties. This information is obtained by reviewing repeat mortgage transactions on single-family properties whose mortgages have been purchased or securitized by Fannie Mae or Freddie Mac since January 1975; (1) Figures cover the Portland-Vancouver-Hillsboro, OR-WA Metropolitan Statistical Area; (2) Rankings are based on annual percentage change for all metro areas containing at least 15,000 transactions over the last 10 years and ranges from 1 to 253; (3) figures based on a weighted average of Census Division estimates using a seasonally adjusted, purchase-only index; all figures are for the period ending December 31, 2020
Source: Federal Housing Finance Agency, Change in Metropolitan Area House Price Indexes, April 7, 2021

Median Single-Family Home Prices

Area	2018	2019	2020[p]	Percent Change 2019 to 2020
MSA[1]	395.7	409.3	451.0	10.2
U.S. Average	261.6	274.6	299.9	9.2

Note: Figures are median sales prices of existing single-family homes in thousands of dollars; (p) preliminary; (1) Figures cover the Portland-Vancouver-Hillsboro, OR-WA Metropolitan Statistical Area
Source: National Association of Realtors, Median Sales Price of Existing Single-Family Homes for Metropolitan Areas, 4th Quarter 2020

Qualifying Income Based on Median Sales Price of Existing Single-Family Homes

Area	With 5% Down ($)	With 10% Down ($)	With 20% Down ($)
MSA[1]	88,594	83,931	74,606
U.S. Average	59,266	56,147	49,908

Note: Figures are preliminary; Qualifying income is based on a mortgage rate of 2.81%. Monthly principal and interest payment is limited to 25% of income; (1) Figures cover the Portland-Vancouver-Hillsboro, OR-WA Metropolitan Statistical Area
Source: National Association of Realtors, Qualifying Income Based on Median Sales Price of Existing Single-Family Homes for Metropolitan Areas, 4th Quarter 2020

Home Value Distribution

Area	Under $50,000	$50,000 -$99,999	$100,000 -$149,999	$150,000 -$199,999	$200,000 -$299,999	$300,000 -$499,999	$500,000 -$999,999	$1,000,000 or more
City	1.9	0.8	1.5	3.8	16.7	41.6	30.5	3.2
MSA[1]	3.2	1.3	2.1	4.9	21.0	42.8	22.1	2.6
U.S.	6.9	12.0	13.3	14.0	19.6	19.3	11.4	3.4

Note: Figures are percentages and cover owner-occupied housing units; (1) Figures cover the Portland-Vancouver-Hillsboro, OR-WA Metropolitan Statistical Area
Source: U.S. Census Bureau, 2015-2019 American Community Survey 5-Year Estimates

Year Housing Structure Built

Area	2010 or Later	2000 -2009	1990 -1999	1980 -1989	1970 -1979	1960 -1969	1950 -1959	1940 -1949	Before 1940	Median Year
City	5.8	10.5	8.8	6.4	10.7	9.2	12.0	8.2	28.3	1962
MSA[1]	6.3	14.5	18.6	11.3	17.2	8.4	7.1	4.6	11.9	1981
U.S.	5.2	14.0	13.9	13.4	15.2	10.6	10.3	4.9	12.6	1978

Note: Figures are percentages except for Median Year; Note: (1) Figures cover the Portland-Vancouver-Hillsboro, OR-WA Metropolitan Statistical Area
Source: U.S. Census Bureau, 2015-2019 American Community Survey 5-Year Estimates

Gross Monthly Rent

Area	Under $500	$500 -$999	$1,000 -$1,499	$1,500 -$1,999	$2,000 -$2,499	$2,500 -$2,999	$3,000 and up	Median ($)
City	6.5	22.1	38.1	20.9	8.1	2.7	1.6	1,248
MSA[1]	4.8	20.9	42.1	21.8	7.1	1.8	1.4	1,271
U.S.	9.4	36.2	30.0	14.0	5.6	2.4	2.4	1,062

Note: Figures are percentages except for Median; Gross rent is the contract rent plus the estimated average monthly cost of utilities (electricity, gas, and water and sewer) and fuels (oil, coal, kerosene, wood, etc.) if these are paid by the renter (or paid for the renter by someone else); (1) Figures cover the Portland-Vancouver-Hillsboro, OR-WA Metropolitan Statistical Area
Source: U.S. Census Bureau, 2015-2019 American Community Survey 5-Year Estimates

HEALTH

Health Risk Factors

Category	MSA[1] (%)	U.S. (%)
Adults aged 18–64 who have any kind of health care coverage	89.8	87.3
Adults who reported being in good or better health	84.2	82.4
Adults who have been told they have high blood cholesterol	30.0	33.0
Adults who have been told they have high blood pressure	27.6	32.3
Adults who are current smokers	14.6	17.1
Adults who currently use E-cigarettes	4.6	4.6
Adults who currently use chewing tobacco, snuff, or snus	3.0	4.0
Adults who are heavy drinkers[2]	7.5	6.3
Adults who are binge drinkers[3]	16.5	17.4
Adults who are overweight (BMI 25.0 - 29.9)	34.1	35.3
Adults who are obese (BMI 30.0 - 99.8)	27.2	31.3
Adults who participated in any physical activities in the past month	80.5	74.4
Adults who always or nearly always wears a seat belt	97.8	94.3

Note: (1) Figures cover the Portland-Vancouver-Hillsboro, OR-WA Metropolitan Statistical Area; (2) Heavy drinkers are classified as adult men having more than 14 drinks per week and adult women having more than 7 drinks per week; (3) Binge drinkers are classified as males having five or more drinks on one occasion or females having four or more drinks on one occasion
Source: Centers for Disease Control and Prevention, Behaviorial Risk Factor Surveillance System, SMART: Selected Metropolitan Area Risk Trends, 2017

Acute and Chronic Health Conditions

Category	MSA[1] (%)	U.S. (%)
Adults who have ever been told they had a heart attack	3.4	4.2
Adults who have ever been told they have angina or coronary heart disease	3.1	3.9
Adults who have ever been told they had a stroke	2.5	3.0
Adults who have ever been told they have asthma	16.6	14.2
Adults who have ever been told they have arthritis	23.2	24.9
Adults who have ever been told they have diabetes[2]	8.9	10.5
Adults who have ever been told they had skin cancer	6.9	6.2
Adults who have ever been told they had any other types of cancer	7.1	7.1
Adults who have ever been told they have COPD	4.5	6.5
Adults who have ever been told they have kidney disease	2.7	3.0
Adults who have ever been told they have a form of depression	23.1	20.5

Note: (1) Figures cover the Portland-Vancouver-Hillsboro, OR-WA Metropolitan Statistical Area; (2) Figures do not include pregnancy-related, borderline, or pre-diabetes
Source: Centers for Disease Control and Prevention, Behaviorial Risk Factor Surveillance System, SMART: Selected Metropolitan Area Risk Trends, 2017

Health Screening and Vaccination Rates

Category	MSA[1] (%)	U.S. (%)
Adults aged 65+ who have had flu shot within the past year	60.4	60.7
Adults aged 65+ who have ever had a pneumonia vaccination	82.4	75.4
Adults who have ever been tested for HIV	40.6	36.1
Adults who have ever had the shingles or zoster vaccine?	36.4	28.9
Adults who have had their blood cholesterol checked within the last five years	85.0	85.9

Note: n/a not available; (1) Figures cover the Portland-Vancouver-Hillsboro, OR-WA Metropolitan Statistical Area.
Source: Centers for Disease Control and Prevention, Behaviorial Risk Factor Surveillance System, SMART: Selected Metropolitan Area Risk Trends, 2017

Disability Status

Category	MSA[1] (%)	U.S. (%)
Adults who reported being deaf	5.8	6.7
Are you blind or have serious difficulty seeing, even when wearing glasses?	3.2	4.5
Are you limited in any way in any of your usual activities due of arthritis?	12.7	12.9
Do you have difficulty doing errands alone?	6.3	6.8
Do you have difficulty dressing or bathing?	3.2	3.6
Do you have serious difficulty concentrating/remembering/making decisions?	9.3	10.7
Do you have serious difficulty walking or climbing stairs?	10.3	13.6

Note: (1) Figures cover the Portland-Vancouver-Hillsboro, OR-WA Metropolitan Statistical Area.
Source: Centers for Disease Control and Prevention, Behaviorial Risk Factor Surveillance System, SMART: Selected Metropolitan Area Risk Trends, 2017

Mortality Rates for the Top 10 Causes of Death in the U.S.

ICD-10[a] Sub-Chapter	ICD-10[a] Code	Age-Adjusted Mortality Rate[1] per 100,000 population	
		County[2]	U.S.
Malignant neoplasms	C00-C97	148.1	149.2
Ischaemic heart diseases	I20-I25	59.3	90.5
Other forms of heart disease	I30-I51	54.7	52.2
Chronic lower respiratory diseases	J40-J47	33.0	39.6
Other degenerative diseases of the nervous system	G30-G31	44.3	37.6
Cerebrovascular diseases	I60-I69	43.2	37.2
Other external causes of accidental injury	W00-X59	39.1	36.1
Organic, including symptomatic, mental disorders	F01-F09	39.3	29.4
Hypertensive diseases	I10-I15	21.6	24.1
Diabetes mellitus	E10-E14	23.0	21.5

Note: (a) ICD-10 = International Classification of Diseases 10th Revision; (1) Mortality rates are a three-year average covering 2017-2019; (2) Figures cover Multnomah County.
Source: Centers for Disease Control and Prevention, National Center for Health Statistics. Underlying Cause of Death 1999-2019 on CDC WONDER Online Database

Mortality Rates for Selected Causes of Death

ICD-10[a] Sub-Chapter	ICD-10[a] Code	Age-Adjusted Mortality Rate[1] per 100,000 population	
		County[2]	U.S.
Assault	X85-Y09	3.5	6.0
Diseases of the liver	K70-K76	14.4	14.4
Human immunodeficiency virus (HIV) disease	B20-B24	1.3	1.5
Influenza and pneumonia	J09-J18	11.5	13.8
Intentional self-harm	X60-X84	17.3	14.1
Malnutrition	E40-E46	2.7	2.3
Obesity and other hyperalimentation	E65-E68	3.0	2.1
Renal failure	N17-N19	7.4	12.6
Transport accidents	V01-V99	8.2	12.3
Viral hepatitis	B15-B19	2.6	1.2

Note: (a) ICD-10 = International Classification of Diseases 10th Revision; (1) Mortality rates are a three-year average covering 2017-2019; (2) Figures cover Multnomah County; Data are suppressed when the data meet the criteria for confidentiality constraints; Mortality rates are flagged as unreliable when the rate would be calculated with a numerator of 20 or less.
Source: Centers for Disease Control and Prevention, National Center for Health Statistics. Underlying Cause of Death 1999-2019 on CDC WONDER Online Database

Health Insurance Coverage

Area	With Health Insurance	With Private Health Insurance	With Public Health Insurance	Without Health Insurance	Population Under Age 19 Without Health Insurance
City	93.6	71.5	32.0	6.4	2.8
MSA[1]	94.0	73.3	32.6	6.0	2.8
U.S.	91.2	67.9	35.1	8.8	5.1

Note: Figures are percentages that cover the civilian noninstitutionalized population; (1) Figures cover the Portland-Vancouver-Hillsboro, OR-WA Metropolitan Statistical Area
Source: U.S. Census Bureau, 2015-2019 American Community Survey 5-Year Estimates

Number of Medical Professionals

Area	MDs[3]	DOs[3,4]	Dentists	Podiatrists	Chiropractors	Optometrists
County[1] (number)	5,131	251	811	43	607	182
County[1] (rate[2])	634.2	31.0	99.8	5.3	74.7	22.4
U.S. (rate[2])	282.9	22.7	71.2	6.2	28.1	16.9

41051
Note: Data as of 2019 unless noted; (1) Data covers Multnomah County; (2) Rate per 100,000 population; (3) Data as of 2018 and includes all active, non-federal physicians; (4) Doctor of Osteopathic Medicine
Source: U.S. Department of Health and Human Services, Health Resources and Services Administration, Bureau of Health Professions, Area Resource File (ARF) 2019-2020

Best Hospitals

According to *U.S. News,* the Portland-Vancouver-Hillsboro, OR-WA metro area is home to three of the best hospitals in the U.S.: **OHSU Casey Eye Institute** (6 adult specialties and 6 pediatric specialties); **OHSU Hospital** (6 adult specialties and 6 pediatric specialties); **OHSU Hospital-Knight Cardiovascular Institute** (6 adult specialties and 6 pediatric specialties). The hospitals listed were nationally ranked in at least one of 16 adult or 10 pediatric specialties. Only 134 hospitals nationwide were nationally ranked in one or more adult or pediatric specialty; this number increases to 178 counting specialized centers within hospitals. Twenty hospitals in the U.S. made the Honor Roll. The Best Hospitals Honor Roll takes both the national rankings and the procedure and condition ratings into account. Hospitals received points if they were nationally ranked in one of the 16 adult specialties—the higher they ranked, the more points they got—and how many ratings of "high performing" they earned in the 10 procedures and conditions. *U.S. News Online, "America's Best Hospitals 2020-21"*

According to *U.S. News,* the Portland-Vancouver-Hillsboro, OR-WA metro area is home to one of the best children's hospitals in the U.S.: **Doernbecher Children's Hospital at Oregon Health and Science University** (6 pediatric specialties). The hospital listed was highly ranked in at least one of 10 pediatric specialties. Eighty-eight children's hospitals in the U.S. were nationally ranked in at least one specialty. Hospitals received points for being ranked in a specialty, and the 10 hospitals with the most points across the 10 specialties make up the Honor Roll. *U.S. News Online, "America's Best Children's Hospitals 2020-21"*

EDUCATION

Public School District Statistics

District Name	Schls	Pupils	Pupil/ Teacher Ratio	Minority Pupils[1] (%)	Free Lunch Eligible[2] (%)	IEP[3] (%)
Centennial SD 28J	10	6,150	21.2	58.1	55.6	16.5
David Douglas SD 40	14	10,124	19.7	63.0	62.9	13.2
Parkrose SD 3	6	3,123	20.4	66.9	66.6	18.1
Portland SD 1J	87	48,710	17.7	43.4	30.6	16.8
Reynolds SD 7	19	11,122	20.2	68.0	60.4	18.4

Note: Table includes school districts with 2,000 or more students; (1) Percentage of students that are not non-Hispanic white; (2) Percentage of students that are eligible for the free lunch program; (3) Percentage of students that have an Individualized Education Program.
Source: U.S. Department of Education, National Center for Education Statistics, Common Core of Data, Local Education Agency (School District) Universe Survey: School Year 2018-2019; U.S. Department of Education, National Center for Education Statistics, Common Core of Data, Public Elementary/Secondary School Universe Survey: School Year 2018-2019

Best High Schools

According to *U.S. News,* Portland is home to one of the top 500 high schools in the U.S.: **Cleveland High School** (#489). Nearly 18,000 public, magnet and charter schools were ranked based on their performance on state assessments and how well they prepare students for college. *U.S. News & World Report, "Best High Schools 2020"*

Highest Level of Education

Area	Less than H.S.	H.S. Diploma	Some College, No Deg.	Associate Degree	Bachelor's Degree	Master's Degree	Prof. School Degree	Doctorate Degree
City	7.6	15.1	20.3	6.6	30.1	13.8	4.1	2.4
MSA[1]	7.9	19.9	23.6	8.8	24.7	10.5	2.6	1.9
U.S.	12.0	27.0	20.4	8.5	19.8	8.8	2.1	1.4

Note: Figures cover persons age 25 and over; (1) Figures cover the Portland-Vancouver-Hillsboro, OR-WA Metropolitan Statistical Area
Source: U.S. Census Bureau, 2015-2019 American Community Survey 5-Year Estimates

Educational Attainment by Race

Area	High School Graduate or Higher (%)					Bachelor's Degree or Higher (%)				
	Total	White	Black	Asian	Hisp.[2]	Total	White	Black	Asian	Hisp.[2]
City	92.4	94.8	85.9	76.9	76.1	50.4	54.3	23.9	41.2	31.0
MSA[1]	92.1	93.5	88.2	86.7	68.7	39.8	40.3	28.0	52.1	19.5
U.S.	88.0	89.9	86.0	87.1	68.7	32.1	33.5	21.6	54.3	16.4

Note: Figures shown cover persons 25 years old and over; (1) Figures cover the Portland-Vancouver-Hillsboro, OR-WA Metropolitan Statistical Area; (2) People of Hispanic origin can be of any race
Source: U.S. Census Bureau, 2015-2019 American Community Survey 5-Year Estimates

School Enrollment by Grade and Control

Area	Preschool (%)		Kindergarten (%)		Grades 1 - 4 (%)		Grades 5 - 8 (%)		Grades 9 - 12 (%)	
	Public	Private	Public	Private	Public	Private	Public	Private	Public	Private
City	39.4	60.6	84.8	15.2	88.0	12.0	87.1	12.9	85.1	14.9
MSA[1]	42.8	57.2	86.2	13.8	89.0	11.0	89.5	10.5	90.3	9.7
U.S.	59.1	40.9	87.6	12.4	89.5	10.5	89.4	10.6	90.1	9.9

Note: Figures shown cover persons 3 years old and over; (1) Figures cover the Portland-Vancouver-Hillsboro, OR-WA Metropolitan Statistical Area
Source: U.S. Census Bureau, 2015-2019 American Community Survey 5-Year Estimates

Higher Education

Four-Year Colleges			Two-Year Colleges			Medical Schools[1]	Law Schools[2]	Voc/ Tech[3]
Public	Private Non-profit	Private For-profit	Public	Private Non-profit	Private For-profit			
2	15	1	1	1	4	1	1	3

Note: Figures cover institutions located within the city limits and include main campuses only; (1) includes schools accredited by the Liaison Committee on Medical Education and the American Osteopathic Association's Commission on Osteopathic College Accreditation; (2) includes ABA-accredited schools, schools with provisional ABA accreditation, and state accredited schools; (3) includes all schools with programs that are less than 2 years.
Source: National Center for Education Statistics, Integrated Postsecondary Education System (IPEDS), 2019-20; Wikipedia, List of Medical Schools in the United States, accessed April 2, 2021; Wikipedia, List of Law Schools in the United States, accessed April 2, 2021

According to *U.S. News & World Report,* the Portland-Vancouver-Hillsboro, OR-WA metro area is home to one of the top 200 national universities in the U.S.: **Pacific University** (#187 tie). The indicators used to capture academic quality fall into a number of categories: assessment by administrators at peer institutions; retention of students; faculty resources; student selectivity; financial resources; alumni giving; high school counselor ratings of colleges; and graduation rate. *U.S. News & World Report, "America's Best Colleges 2021"*

According to *U.S. News & World Report,* the Portland-Vancouver-Hillsboro, OR-WA metro area is home to two of the top 100 liberal arts colleges in the U.S.: **Reed College** (#63 tie); **Lewis & Clark College** (#76 tie). The indicators used to capture academic quality fall into a number of categories: assessment by administrators at peer institutions; retention of students; faculty resources; student selectivity; financial resources; alumni giving; high school counselor ratings of colleges; and graduation rate. *U.S. News & World Report, "America's Best Colleges 2021"*

According to *U.S. News & World Report,* the Portland-Vancouver-Hillsboro, OR-WA metro area is home to one of the top 100 law schools in the U.S.: **Lewis & Clark College (Northwestern)** (#88 tie). The rankings are based on a weighted average of 12 measures of quality: peer assessment score; assessment score by lawyers/judges; median LSAT scores; median undergrad GPA; acceptance rate; employment rates for graduates; placement success; bar passage rate; faculty resources; expenditures per student; student/faculty ratio; and library resources. *U.S. News & World Report, "America's Best Graduate Schools, Law, 2022"*

According to *U.S. News & World Report,* the Portland-Vancouver-Hillsboro, OR-WA metro area is home to one of the top 75 medical schools for research in the U.S.: **Oregon Health and Science University** (#29 tie). The rankings are based on a weighted average of 11 measures of quality: quality assessment; peer assessment score; assessment score by residency directors; research activity; total research activity; average research activity per faculty member; student selectivity; median MCAT total score; median undergraduate GPA; acceptance rate; and faculty resources. *U.S. News & World Report, "America's Best Graduate Schools, Medical, 2022"*

EMPLOYERS

Major Employers

Company Name	Industry
Children's Creative Learning Center	Child day care services
Clackamas Community College	Community college
Coho Distributing	Liquor
Con-Way Enterprise Services	Accounting, auditing, & bookkeeping
Legacy Emanuel Hospital and Health Center	General medical & surgical hospitals
Nike	Rubber & plastics footwear
Oregon Health & Science University	Colleges & universities
PCC Structurals	Aircraft parts & equipment, nec
Portland Adventist Medical Center	General medical & surgical hospitals
Portland Community College	Community college
Portland State University	Colleges & universities
Providence Health & Services - Oregon	Skilled nursing facility
School Dist 1 Multnomah County	Public elementary & secondary schools
Shilo Management Corp.	Hotels & motels
Southwest Washington Medical Center	General medical & surgical hospitals
Stancorp Mortgage Investors	Life insurance
SW Washington Hospital	General medical & surgical hospitals
Tektronix	Instruments to measure elasticity
The Evergreen Aviation and Space Museum	Museums & art galleries
Veterans Health Administration	Administration of veterans' affairs

Note: Companies shown are located within the Portland-Vancouver-Hillsboro, OR-WA Metropolitan Statistical Area.
Source: Hoovers.com; Wikipedia

Best Companies to Work For

Portland State University, headquartered in Portland, is among the "100 Best Places to Work in IT." To qualify, companies had to be U.S.-based organizations or be non-U.S.-based employers that met the following criteria: have a minimum of 300 total employees at a U.S. headquarters and a minimum of 30 IT employees in the U.S., with at least 50% of their IT employees based in the U.S. The best places to work were selected based on compensation, benefits, work/life balance, employee morale, and satisfaction with training and development programs. In addition, *InsiderPro* and *Computerworld* looked at retention efforts, programs for recognizing and rewarding outstanding performances, and benefits such as flextime, elder care and child care, and reimbursement for college tuition and the cost of pursuing technology certifications. *InsiderPro and Computerworld, "100 Best Places to Work in IT," 2020*

PUBLIC SAFETY

Crime Rate

Area	All Crimes	Violent Crimes				Property Crimes		
		Murder	Rape[3]	Robbery	Aggrav. Assault	Burglary	Larceny -Theft	Motor Vehicle Theft
City	5,748.0	4.4	55.6	147.9	336.8	634.3	3,597.6	971.4
Suburbs[1]	2,077.6	1.6	48.3	37.5	128.0	233.0	1,381.8	247.4
Metro[2]	3,049.5	2.4	50.2	66.7	183.3	339.3	1,968.5	439.1
U.S.	2,489.3	5.0	42.6	81.6	250.2	340.5	1,549.5	219.9

Note: Figures are crimes per 100,000 population; (1) All areas within the metro area that are located outside the city limits; (2) Figures cover the Portland-Vancouver-Hillsboro, OR-WA Metropolitan Statistical Area; (3) All figures shown were reported using the revised Uniform Crime Reporting (UCR) definition of rape.
Source: FBI Uniform Crime Reports, 2019

Hate Crimes

Area	Number of Quarters Reported	Number of Incidents per Bias Motivation					
		Race/Ethnicity/ Ancestry	Religion	Sexual Orientation	Disability	Gender	Gender Identity
City[1]	4	23	4	5	0	1	3
U.S.	4	3,963	1,521	1,195	157	69	198

Note: (1) Figures include one incident reported with more than one bias motivation.
Source: Federal Bureau of Investigation, Hate Crime Statistics 2019

Identity Theft Consumer Reports

Area	Reports	Reports per 100,000 Population	Rank[2]
MSA[1]	6,165	247	164
U.S.	1,387,615	423	-

Note: (1) Figures cover the Portland-Vancouver-Hillsboro, OR-WA Metropolitan Statistical Area; (2) Rank ranges from 1 to 391 where 1 indicates greatest number of identity theft reports per 100,000 population
Source: Federal Trade Commission, Consumer Sentinel Network Data Book 2020

Fraud and Other Consumer Reports

Area	Reports	Reports per 100,000 Population	Rank[2]
MSA[1]	21,526	864	63
U.S.	3,385,133	1,031	-

Note: (1) Figures cover the Portland-Vancouver-Hillsboro, OR-WA Metropolitan Statistical Area; (2) Rank ranges from 1 to 391 where 1 indicates greatest number of fraud and other consumer reports per 100,000 population
Source: Federal Trade Commission, Consumer Sentinel Network Data Book 2020

POLITICS

2020 Presidential Election Results

Area	Biden	Trump	Jorgensen	Hawkins	Other
Multnomah County	79.2	17.9	1.2	0.6	1.0
U.S.	51.3	46.8	1.2	0.3	0.5

Note: Results are percentages and may not add to 100% due to rounding
Source: Dave Leip's Atlas of U.S. Presidential Elections

SPORTS

Professional Sports Teams

Team Name	League	Year Established
Portland Timbers	Major League Soccer (MLS)	2011
Portland Trail Blazers	National Basketball Association (NBA)	1970

Note: Includes teams located in the Portland-Vancouver-Hillsboro, OR-WA Metropolitan Statistical Area.
Source: Wikipedia, Major Professional Sports Teams of the United States and Canada, April 6, 2021

CLIMATE

Average and Extreme Temperatures

Temperature	Jan	Feb	Mar	Apr	May	Jun	Jul	Aug	Sep	Oct	Nov	Dec	Yr.
Extreme High (°F)	65	71	83	93	100	102	107	107	105	92	73	64	107
Average High (°F)	45	50	56	61	68	73	80	79	74	64	53	46	62
Average Temp. (°F)	39	43	48	52	58	63	68	68	63	55	46	41	54
Average Low (°F)	34	36	39	42	48	53	57	57	52	46	40	36	45
Extreme Low (°F)	-2	-3	19	29	29	39	43	44	34	26	13	6	-3

Note: Figures cover the years 1926-1992
Source: National Climatic Data Center, International Station Meteorological Climate Summary, 9/96

Average Precipitation/Snowfall/Humidity

Precip./Humidity	Jan	Feb	Mar	Apr	May	Jun	Jul	Aug	Sep	Oct	Nov	Dec	Yr.
Avg. Precip. (in.)	5.5	4.2	3.8	2.4	2.0	1.5	0.5	0.9	1.7	3.0	5.5	6.6	37.5
Avg. Snowfall (in.)	3	1	1	Tr	Tr	0	0	0	0	0	1	2	7
Avg. Rel. Hum. 7am (%)	85	86	86	84	80	78	77	81	87	90	88	87	84
Avg. Rel. Hum. 4pm (%)	75	67	60	55	53	50	45	45	49	61	74	79	59

Note: Figures cover the years 1926-1992; Tr = Trace amounts (<0.05 in. of rain; <0.5 in. of snow)
Source: National Climatic Data Center, International Station Meteorological Climate Summary, 9/96

Weather Conditions

Temperature			Daytime Sky			Precipitation		
5°F & below	32°F & below	90°F & above	Clear	Partly cloudy	Cloudy	0.01 inch or more precip.	0.1 inch or more snow/ice	Thunder-storms
< 1	37	11	67	116	182	152	4	7

Note: Figures are average number of days per year and cover the years 1926-1992
Source: National Climatic Data Center, International Station Meteorological Climate Summary, 9/96

HAZARDOUS WASTE

Superfund Sites

The Portland-Vancouver-Hillsboro, OR-WA metro area is home to six sites on the EPA's Superfund National Priorities List: **Boomsnub/Airco** (final); **McCormick & Baxter Creosoting Co. (Portland Plant)** (final); **Northwest Pipe & Casing/Hall Process Company** (final); **Portland Harbor** (final); **Reynolds Metals Company** (final); **Taylor Lumber and Treating** (final). There are a total of 1,375 Superfund sites with a status of proposed or final on the list in the U.S. *U.S. Environmental Protection Agency, National Priorities List, April 7, 2021*

AIR QUALITY

Air Quality Trends: Ozone

	1990	1995	2000	2005	2010	2015	2016	2017	2018	2019
MSA[1]	0.081	0.065	0.059	0.059	0.056	0.064	0.057	0.073	0.062	0.058
U.S.	0.088	0.089	0.082	0.080	0.073	0.068	0.069	0.068	0.069	0.065

Note: (1) Data covers the Portland-Vancouver-Hillsboro, OR-WA Metropolitan Statistical Area. The values shown are the composite ozone concentration averages among trend sites based on the highest fourth daily maximum 8-hour concentration in parts per million. These trends are based on sites having an adequate record of monitoring data during the trend period. Data from exceptional events are included.
Source: U.S. Environmental Protection Agency, Air Quality Monitoring Information, "Air Quality Trends by City, 1990-2019"

Air Quality Index

Area	Percent of Days when Air Quality was...[2]					AQI Statistics[2]	
	Good	Moderate	Unhealthy for Sensitive Groups	Unhealthy	Very Unhealthy	Maximum	Median
MSA[1]	78.1	21.1	0.8	0.0	0.0	128	38

Note: (1) Data covers the Portland-Vancouver-Hillsboro, OR-WA Metropolitan Statistical Area; (2) Based on 365 days with AQI data in 2019. Air Quality Index (AQI) is an index for reporting daily air quality. EPA calculates the AQI for five major air pollutants regulated by the Clean Air Act: ground-level ozone, particle pollution (aka particulate matter), carbon monoxide, sulfur dioxide, and nitrogen dioxide. The AQI runs from 0 to 500. The higher the AQI value, the greater the level of air pollution and the greater the health concern. There are six AQI categories: "Good" AQI is between 0 and 50. Air quality is considered satisfactory; "Moderate" AQI is between 51 and 100. Air quality is acceptable; "Unhealthy for Sensitive Groups" When AQI values are between 101 and 150, members of sensitive groups may experience health effects; "Unhealthy" When AQI values are between 151 and 200 everyone may begin to experience health effects; "Very Unhealthy" AQI values between 201 and 300 trigger a health alert; "Hazardous" AQI values over 300 trigger warnings of emergency conditions (not shown).
Source: U.S. Environmental Protection Agency, Air Quality Index Report, 2019

Air Quality Index Pollutants

Area	Carbon Monoxide	Nitrogen Dioxide	Ozone	Sulfur Dioxide	Particulate Matter 2.5	Particulate Matter 10
	Percent of Days when AQI Pollutant was...[2]					
MSA[1]	0.0	2.2	56.4	0.0	41.4	0.0

Note: (1) Data covers the Portland-Vancouver-Hillsboro, OR-WA Metropolitan Statistical Area; (2) Based on 365 days with AQI data in 2019. The Air Quality Index (AQI) is an index for reporting daily air quality. EPA calculates the AQI for five major air pollutants regulated by the Clean Air Act: ground-level ozone, particle pollution (also known as particulate matter), carbon monoxide, sulfur dioxide, and nitrogen dioxide. The AQI runs from 0 to 500. The higher the AQI value, the greater the level of air pollution and the greater the health concern.
Source: U.S. Environmental Protection Agency, Air Quality Index Report, 2019

Maximum Air Pollutant Concentrations: Particulate Matter, Ozone, CO and Lead

	Particulate Matter 10 (ug/m^3)	Particulate Matter 2.5 Wtd AM (ug/m^3)	Particulate Matter 2.5 24-Hr (ug/m^3)	Ozone (ppm)	Carbon Monoxide (ppm)	Lead (ug/m^3)
MSA[1] Level	32	7.0	25	0.065	1	n/a
NAAQS[2]	150	15	35	0.075	9	0.15
Met NAAQS[2]	Yes	Yes	Yes	Yes	Yes	n/a

Note: (1) Data covers the Portland-Vancouver-Hillsboro, OR-WA Metropolitan Statistical Area; Data from exceptional events are included; (2) National Ambient Air Quality Standards; ppm = parts per million; ug/m^3 = micrograms per cubic meter; n/a not available.
Concentrations: Particulate Matter 10 (coarse particulate)—highest second maximum 24-hour concentration; Particulate Matter 2.5 Wtd AM (fine particulate)—highest weighted annual mean concentration; Particulate Matter 2.5 24-Hour (fine particulate)—highest 98th percentile 24-hour concentration; Ozone—highest fourth daily maximum 8-hour concentration; Carbon Monoxide—highest second maximum non-overlapping 8-hour concentration; Lead—maximum running 3-month average
Source: U.S. Environmental Protection Agency, Air Quality Monitoring Information, "Air Quality Statistics by City, 2019"

Maximum Air Pollutant Concentrations: Nitrogen Dioxide and Sulfur Dioxide

	Nitrogen Dioxide AM (ppb)	Nitrogen Dioxide 1-Hr (ppb)	Sulfur Dioxide AM (ppb)	Sulfur Dioxide 1-Hr (ppb)	Sulfur Dioxide 24-Hr (ppb)
MSA[1] Level	11	33	n/a	3	n/a
NAAQS[2]	53	100	30	75	140
Met NAAQS[2]	Yes	Yes	n/a	Yes	n/a

Note: (1) Data covers the Portland-Vancouver-Hillsboro, OR-WA Metropolitan Statistical Area; Data from exceptional events are included; (2) National Ambient Air Quality Standards; ppm = parts per million; ug/m^3 = micrograms per cubic meter; n/a not available.
Concentrations: Nitrogen Dioxide AM—highest arithmetic mean concentration; Nitrogen Dioxide 1-Hr—highest 98th percentile 1-hour daily maximum concentration; Sulfur Dioxide AM—highest annual mean concentration; Sulfur Dioxide 1-Hr—highest 99th percentile 1-hour daily maximum concentration; Sulfur Dioxide 24-Hr—highest second maximum 24-hour concentration
Source: U.S. Environmental Protection Agency, Air Quality Monitoring Information, "Air Quality Statistics by City, 2019"

Provo, Utah

Background

Provo is situated on the Provo River at a site that was, prehistorically, under the waters of Lake Bonneville. Today, Provo enjoys one of the country's highest employment rates, a growing high-tech economy, a low crime rate, and a magnificent natural environment. The seat of Utah County, it lies at the base of the steep Wasatch Mountains, with Provo Peak rising to a height of 11,054 feet just east of the city, making Provo convenient to many of Utah's famed ski areas and to the Uinta National Forest.

Spanish missionaries Francisco Silvestre Velez de Escalante and Francisco Atanasio Dominguez, exploring for a more direct route from present-day New Mexico to California, were probably the first Europeans to view the area. They did not establish a permanent mission, but did note that the area could easily be irrigated and developed into an important agricultural settlement. Etienne Prevot, a Canadian trapper and explorer, likewise visited but did not settle, though he too remarked on the beauty and potential of the site. These early explorers also met with the site's original inhabitants, the Ute Indians, who held an important fish festival on the river every spring.

Permanent European settlement of Provo is strongly linked to Mormon history. In 1849, John S. Higbee, with 30 families in a wagon train, left the larger Salt Lake City community to move north. As they arrived at the site, they confronted a group of Ute, with whom white settlers had already been in some conflict. A short-lived peace agreement gave way to further conflict and a series of battles, after which the Indians agreed to resettlement. Peace ensued, and Provo was subject to long periods of peaceful relations with the Indians, different from many other young Western towns.

Irrigation has been central to Provo's success, and in the very year of Higbee's arrival, two large canals were dug, taking water from the Provo River. Grain mills were constructed to serve the needs of nearby farmers, and important rail links were completed in the 1870s connecting Provo to Salt Lake City and to the Union Pacific System, giving impetus to the region's agricultural and mining industries.

Provo's growth took off, with an electric generating plant built in 1890, and an interurban commuter rail service between Provo and Salt Lake City in 1914. The town had become a major regional industrial center, with ironworks, flourmills, and brickyards. Today, industries include computer hardware and software, food processing, clothing, and electronic equipment.

Provo's industrial dynamism and creativity is reflected in the careers of two of its favorite sons. Dr. Harvey Fletcher, of Bell Laboratories, was the inventor of aids to the deaf and hearing-impaired, and an important early leader of the National Acoustic Association. Philo T. Farnsworth, born in Beaver but raised in Provo, developed the fundamental concepts of television in 1924 at the age of 18.

Provo is home to Farnsworth's alma mater, Brigham Young University (BYU), a private university operated by The Church of Jesus Christ of Latter-day Saints. Founded in 1875 it has earned national respect for everything from its football team and undergraduate liberal arts program to its graduate programs in business and law. Recently rebuilt is The Provo Tabernacle that was destroyed by fire in 2010.

> In a local art contest, students created "their vision of social distancing" and winning pieces were displayed at the Provo City Hall lobby.

In 2001, Provo resident Larry H. Miller donated the Larry H. Miller Field to Brigham Young University, which is currently used as a training and competitive facility by various teams, including the Brigham Young Cougars. In 2009, the city of Provo implemented CITYWATCH, a city-wide emergency notification system. The Utah Valley Convention Center was completed in early 2012.

In July Provo hosts America's Freedom Festival which includes the Stadium of Fire at BYU and is held in LaVell Edwards Stadium, home to BYU's NCAA football team. The popular Independence Day festivities have featured such notable figures as Bob Hope, David Hasselhoff, Reba McEntire, Mandy Moore, Huey Lewis and the News, Toby Keith, Sean Hannity, Fred Willard and Taylor Hicks. More recently, the event included performances by Journey and Olivia Holt, and was hosted by the television personality Montel Williams.

The climate of Provo is semi-arid continental. Summers are generally hot and dry. Winters are cold but not severe. Precipitation is generally light, with most of the rain falling in the spring.

Rankings

General Rankings

- The Provo metro area was identified as one of America's fastest-growing areas in terms of population and business growth by *MagnifyMoney*. The area ranked #2 out of 35. The 100 most populous metro areas in the U.S. were evaluated on their change from 2011-2016 in the following categories: people and housing; workforce and employment opportunities; growing industry. *www.businessinsider.com, "The 35 Cities in the US with the Biggest Influx of People, the Most Work Opportunities, and the Hottest Business Growth," August 12, 2018*

- In their seventh annual survey, Livability.com looked at data for more than 1,000 small to mid-sized U.S. cities to determine the rankings for Livability's "Top 100 Best Places to Live" in 2020. Provo ranked #68. Criteria: housing and affordable living; vibrant economy; social and civic engagement; education; demographics; health care options; transportation & infrastructure; and abundant lifestyle amenities. *Livability.com, "Top 100 Best Places to Live 2020" October 2020*

Business/Finance Rankings

- According to *Business Insider*, the Provo metro area is a prime place to run a startup or move an existing business to. The area ranked #18. Nearly 190 metro areas were analyzed on overall economic health and investments. Data was based on the 2019 U.S. Census Bureau American Community Survey, the marketing company PitchBook, Bureau of Labor Statistics employment report, and Zillow. Criteria: percentage of change in typical home values and employment rates; quarterly venture capital investment activity; and median household income. *www.businessinsider.com, "The 25 Best Cities to Start a Business-Or Move Your Current One," January 12, 2021*

- The Brookings Institution ranked the nation's largest cities based on income inequality. Provo was ranked #63 (#1 = greatest inequality). Criteria: the "95/20 ratio," a figure representing the income at which a household earns more than 95 percent of all other households, divided by the income at which a household earns more than only 20 percent of all other households. *Brookings Institution, "Household Income Inequality, Largest Cities of 97 Large U.S. Metro Areas, 2014-2016," February 5, 2018*

- The Brookings Institution ranked the 100 largest metro areas in the U.S. based on income inequality. Provo was ranked #99 (#1 = greatest inequality). Criteria: the "95/20 ratio," a figure representing the income at which a household earns more than 95 percent of all other households, divided by the income at which a household earns more than only 20 percent of all other households. *Brookings Institution, "Household Income Inequality, 100 Largest U.S. Metro Areas, 2014-2016," February 5, 2018*

- The Provo metro area appeared on the Milken Institute "2021 Best Performing Cities" list. Rank: #1 out of 200 large metro areas (population over 250,000). Criteria: job growth; wage and salary growth; high-tech output growth; housing affordability; household broadband access. *Milken Institute, "Best-Performing Cities 2021," February 16, 2021*

- *Forbes* ranked the 200 most populous metro areas to determine the nation's "Best Places for Business and Careers." The Provo metro area was ranked #6. Criteria: costs (business and living); job growth (past and projected); income growth; quality of life; educational attainment (college and high school); projected economic growth; cultural and leisure opportunities; workplace tolerance laws; net migration patterns. *Forbes, "The Best Places for Business and Careers 2019: Seattle Still On Top," October 30, 2019*

Dating/Romance Rankings

- *Apartment List* conducted its annual survey of renters for cities that have the best opportunities for dating. More than 11,000 single respondents rated their current city or neighborhood for opportunities to date. Provo ranked #1 out of 86 where single residents were very satisfied or somewhat satisfied, making it among the ten best areas for dating opportunities. Other criteria analyzed included gender and education levels of renters. *Apartment List, "The Best & Worst Metros for Dating 2020," February 4, 2020*

Education Rankings

- Personal finance website *WalletHub* analyzed the 150 largest U.S. metropolitan statistical areas to determine where the most educated Americans are putting their degrees to work. Criteria: education levels; percentage of workers with degrees; education quality and attainment gap; public school quality rankings; quality and enrollment of each metro area's universities. Provo was ranked #13 (#1 = most educated city). *www.WalletHub.com, "Most and Least Educated Cities in America," July 20, 2020*

Environmental Rankings

- Niche compiled a list of the nation's snowiest cities, based on the National Oceanic and Atmospheric Administration's 30-year average snowfall data. Among cities with a population of at least 50,000, Provo ranked #20. *Niche.com, Top 25 Snowiest Cities in America, December 10, 2018*

- The U.S. Environmental Protection Agency (EPA) released a list of U.S. metropolitan areas with the most ENERGY STAR certified buildings in 2019. The Provo metro area was ranked #23 out of 25. *U.S. Environmental Protection Agency, "2020 Energy Star Top Cities," March 2020*

- The U.S. Environmental Protection Agency (EPA) released a list of mid-size U.S. metropolitan areas with the most ENERGY STAR certified buildings in 2019. The Provo metro area was ranked #2 out of 10. *U.S. Environmental Protection Agency, "2020 Energy Star Top Cities," March 2020*

Health/Fitness Rankings

- Provo was identified as a "2021 Spring Allergy Capital." The area ranked #99 out of 100. Three groups of factors were used to identify the most challenging cities for people with allergies during the spring season: annual spring pollen levels; over the counter medicine use; number of board-certified allergy specialists. *Asthma and Allergy Foundation of America, "Spring Allergy Capitals 2021," February 23, 2021*

- Provo was identified as a "2021 Fall Allergy Capital." The area ranked #97 out of 100. Three groups of factors were used to identify the most challenging cities for people with allergies during the fall season: annual fall pollen levels; over the counter medicine use; number of board-certified allergy specialists. *Asthma and Allergy Foundation of America, "Fall Allergy Capitals 2021," February 23, 2021*

- Provo was identified as a "2019 Asthma Capital." The area ranked #91 out of the nation's 100 largest metropolitan areas. Criteria: estimated asthma prevalence; crude death rate from asthma; and ER visits due to asthma. Risk factors analyzed but not factored in the rankings: annual pollen score; annual air quality; public smoking laws; number of board-certified asthma specialists; rescue medication use; controller medication use; uninsured rate; poverty rate. *Asthma and Allergy Foundation of America, "Asthma Capitals 2019: The Most Challenging Places to Live With Asthma," May 7, 2019*

Real Estate Rankings

- Provo was ranked #211 out of 268 metro areas in terms of housing affordability in 2020 by the National Association of Home Builders (#1 = most affordable). Criteria: the share of homes sold in that area affordable to a family earning the local median income, based on standard mortgage underwriting criteria. *National Association of Home Builders®, NAHB-Wells Fargo Housing Opportunity Index, 4th Quarter 2020*

Safety Rankings

- To identify the safest cities in America, 24/7 Wall Street focused on violent crime categories—murder, non-negligent manslaughter, rape, robbery, and aggravated assault—and property crime as reported in the FBI's 2018 annual Uniform Crime Report. Criteria also included median income from American Community Survey and unemployment figures from Bureau of Labor Statistics. For cities with populations over 100,000, Provo was ranked #41. *247wallst.com, "America's Safest Cities" January 15, 2020*

- The National Insurance Crime Bureau ranked 384 metro areas in the U.S. in terms of per capita rates of vehicle theft. The Provo metro area ranked #313 (#1 = highest rate). Criteria: number of vehicle theft offenses per 100,000 inhabitants in 2019. *National Insurance Crime Bureau, "Hot Spots 2019," July 21, 2020*

Seniors/Retirement Rankings

- From its Best Cities for Successful Aging indexes, the Milken Institute generated rankings for metropolitan areas, weighing data in nine categories—health care, wellness, living arrangements, transportation and convenience, financial characteristics, education, employment, community engagement, and overall livability. The Provo metro area was ranked #1 overall in the large metro area category. *Milken Institute, "Best Cities for Successful Aging, 2017" March 14, 2017*

Sports/Recreation Rankings

- Provo was chosen as a bicycle friendly community by the League of American Bicyclists. A "Bicycle Friendly Community" welcomes cyclists by providing safe and supportive accommodation for cycling and encouraging people to bike for transportation and recreation. There are five award levels: Diamond; Platinum; Gold; Silver; and Bronze. The community achieved an award level of Silver. *League of American Bicyclists, "Fall 2020 Awards-New & Renewing Bicycle Friendly Communities List," December 16, 2020*

Miscellaneous Rankings

- *WalletHub* compared the 150 most populated U.S. cities to determine their operating efficiency. A "Quality of City Services" score was constructed for each city and then divided by the total budget per capita to reveal which were managed the best. Provo ranked #3. Criteria: financial stability; economy; education; safety; health; infrastructure and pollution. *www.WalletHub.com, "2020's Best- & Worst-Run Cities in America," June 29, 2020*

Business Environment

DEMOGRAPHICS

Population Growth

Area	1990 Census	2000 Census	2010 Census	2019* Estimate	Population Growth (%) 1990-2019	Population Growth (%) 2010-2019
City	87,148	105,166	112,488	116,403	33.6	3.5
MSA[1]	269,407	376,774	526,810	616,791	128.9	17.1
U.S.	248,709,873	281,421,906	308,745,538	324,697,795	30.6	5.2

Note: (1) Figures cover the Provo-Orem, UT Metropolitan Statistical Area; (*) 2015-2019 5-year estimated population
Source: U.S. Census Bureau, 1990 Census, Census 2000, Census 2010, 2015-2019 American Community Survey 5-Year Estimates

Household Size

Area	One	Two	Three	Four	Five	Six	Seven or More	Average Household Size
City	13.3	33.2	18.8	16.1	8.0	7.2	3.4	3.20
MSA[1]	12.0	28.7	15.7	15.6	12.5	9.0	6.5	3.60
U.S.	27.9	33.9	15.6	12.9	6.0	2.3	1.4	2.60

Note: (1) Figures cover the Provo-Orem, UT Metropolitan Statistical Area
Source: U.S. Census Bureau, 2015-2019 American Community Survey 5-Year Estimates

Race

Area	White Alone[2] (%)	Black Alone[2] (%)	Asian Alone[2] (%)	AIAN[3] Alone[2] (%)	NHOPI[4] Alone[2] (%)	Other Race Alone[2] (%)	Two or More Races (%)
City	87.9	0.9	2.7	0.8	1.3	2.2	4.2
MSA[1]	91.7	0.6	1.5	0.5	0.9	1.8	3.1
U.S.	72.5	12.7	5.5	0.8	0.2	4.9	3.3

Note: (1) Figures cover the Provo-Orem, UT Metropolitan Statistical Area; (2) Alone is defined as not being in combination with one or more other races; (3) American Indian and Alaska Native; (4) Native Hawaiian and Other Pacific Islander
Source: U.S. Census Bureau, 2015-2019 American Community Survey 5-Year Estimates

Hispanic or Latino Origin

Area	Total (%)	Mexican (%)	Puerto Rican (%)	Cuban (%)	Other (%)
City	16.7	11.3	0.5	0.1	4.7
MSA[1]	11.7	7.7	0.3	0.1	3.7
U.S.	18.0	11.2	1.7	0.7	4.3

Note: Persons of Hispanic or Latino origin can be of any race; (1) Figures cover the Provo-Orem, UT Metropolitan Statistical Area
Source: U.S. Census Bureau, 2015-2019 American Community Survey 5-Year Estimates

Ancestry

Area	German	Irish	English	American	Italian	Polish	French[2]	Scottish	Dutch
City	10.1	4.1	23.0	3.0	2.0	0.8	1.6	4.8	1.4
MSA[1]	10.5	4.8	26.7	4.7	2.4	0.6	1.9	4.9	1.6
U.S.	13.3	9.7	7.2	6.2	5.1	2.8	2.3	1.7	1.2

Note: Figures are the percentage of the total population reporting a particular ancestry. The nine most commonly reported ancestries in the U.S. are shown. Figures include multiple ancestries (e.g. if a person reported being Irish and Italian, they were included in both columns); (1) Figures cover the Provo-Orem, UT Metropolitan Statistical Area; (2) Excludes Basque
Source: U.S. Census Bureau, 2015-2019 American Community Survey 5-Year Estimates

Foreign-born Population

Area	Any Foreign Country	Asia	Mexico	Europe	Caribbean	Central America[2]	South America	Africa	Canada
City	11.0	2.0	4.4	0.5	0.1	0.6	2.3	0.3	0.4
MSA[1]	7.3	1.1	2.8	0.5	0.1	0.5	1.6	0.2	0.3
U.S.	13.6	4.2	3.5	1.5	1.3	1.1	1.0	0.7	0.2

Note: (1) Figures cover the Provo-Orem, UT Metropolitan Statistical Area; (2) Excludes Mexico.
Source: U.S. Census Bureau, 2015-2019 American Community Survey 5-Year Estimates

Marital Status

Area	Never Married	Now Married[2]	Separated	Widowed	Divorced
City	47.7	44.6	1.1	2.0	4.5
MSA[1]	32.3	58.4	1.0	2.7	5.6
U.S.	33.4	48.1	1.9	5.8	10.9

Note: Figures are percentages and cover the population 15 years of age and older; (1) Figures cover the Provo-Orem, UT Metropolitan Statistical Area; (2) Excludes separated
Source: U.S. Census Bureau, 2015-2019 American Community Survey 5-Year Estimates

Disability by Age

Area	All Ages	Under 18 Years Old	18 to 64 Years Old	65 Years and Over
City	8.2	4.2	6.8	38.3
MSA[1]	7.8	3.3	7.1	32.8
U.S.	12.6	4.2	10.3	34.5

Note: Figures show percent of the civilian noninstitutionalized population that reported having a disability. Disability status is determined from six types of difficulty: vision, hearing, cognitive, ambulatory, self-care, and independent living. For children under 5 years old, hearing and vision difficulty are used to determine disability status. For children between the ages of 5 and 14, disability status is determined from hearing, vision, cognitive, ambulatory, and self-care difficulties. For people aged 15 years and older, they are considered to have a disability if they have difficulty with any one of the six difficulty types; Note: (1) Figures cover the Provo-Orem, UT Metropolitan Statistical Area
Source: U.S. Census Bureau, 2015-2019 American Community Survey 5-Year Estimates

Age

Area				Percent of Population						Median Age
	Under Age 5	Age 5–19	Age 20–34	Age 35–44	Age 45–54	Age 55–64	Age 65–74	Age 75–84	Age 85+	
City	7.1	20.7	47.4	8.3	5.4	5.0	3.1	2.0	0.9	23.6
MSA[1]	9.6	28.3	26.8	12.6	8.4	6.7	4.5	2.3	0.8	24.8
U.S.	6.1	19.1	20.7	12.6	13.0	12.9	9.1	4.6	1.9	38.1

Note: (1) Figures cover the Provo-Orem, UT Metropolitan Statistical Area
Source: U.S. Census Bureau, 2015-2019 American Community Survey 5-Year Estimates

Gender

Area	Males	Females	Males per 100 Females
City	57,489	58,914	97.6
MSA[1]	311,659	305,132	102.1
U.S.	159,886,919	164,810,876	97.0

Note: (1) Figures cover the Provo-Orem, UT Metropolitan Statistical Area
Source: U.S. Census Bureau, 2015-2019 American Community Survey 5-Year Estimates

Religious Groups by Family

Area	Catholic	Baptist	Non-Den.	Methodist[2]	Lutheran	LDS[3]	Pentecostal	Presbyterian[4]	Muslim[5]	Judaism
MSA[1]	1.3	0.1	0.1	0.2	<0.1	88.6	0.1	0.1	<0.1	<0.1
U.S.	19.1	9.3	4.0	4.0	2.3	2.0	1.9	1.6	0.8	0.7

Note: Figures are the number of adherents as a percentage of the total population; (1) Figures cover the Provo-Orem, UT Metropolitan Statistical Area; (2) Methodist/Pietist; (3) Latter Day Saints; (4) Reformed; (5) Figures are estimates
Source: Association of Statisticians of American Religious Bodies, 2010 U.S. Religion Census: Religious Congregations & Membership Study

Religious Groups by Tradition

Area	Catholic	Evangelical Protestant	Mainline Protestant	Other Tradition	Black Protestant	Orthodox
MSA[1]	1.3	0.5	0.1	88.9	<0.1	<0.1
U.S.	19.1	16.2	7.3	4.3	1.6	0.3

Note: Figures are the number of adherents as a percentage of the total population; (1) Figures cover the Provo-Orem, UT Metropolitan Statistical Area
Source: Association of Statisticians of American Religious Bodies, 2010 U.S. Religion Census: Religious Congregations & Membership Study

ECONOMY

Gross Metropolitan Product

Area	2017	2018	2019	2020	Rank[2]
MSA[1]	25.7	27.9	29.5	31.2	104

Note: Figures are in billions of dollars; (1) Figures cover the Provo-Orem, UT Metropolitan Statistical Area; (2) Rank is based on 2018 data and ranges from 1 to 381
Source: U.S. Conference of Mayors, U.S. Metro Economies: GMP & Employment 2018-2020, September 2019

Economic Growth

Area	2015-17 (%)	2018 (%)	2019 (%)	2020 (%)	Rank[2]
MSA[1]	6.6	6.5	4.0	3.7	7
U.S.	1.9	2.9	2.3	2.1	–

Note: Figures are real gross metropolitan product (GMP) growth rates and represent average annual percent change; (1) Figures cover the Provo-Orem, UT Metropolitan Statistical Area; (2) Rank is based on 2017 2-year average annual percent change and ranges from 1 to 381
Source: U.S. Conference of Mayors, U.S. Metro Economies: GMP & Employment 2018-2020, September 2019

Metropolitan Area Exports

Area	2014	2015	2016	2017	2018	2019	Rank[2]
MSA[1]	2,533.4	2,216.4	1,894.8	2,065.3	1,788.1	1,783.7	107

Note: Figures are in millions of dollars; (1) Figures cover the Provo-Orem, UT Metropolitan Statistical Area; (2) Rank is based on 2019 data and ranges from 1 to 386
Source: U.S. Department of Commerce, International Trade Administration, Office of Trade and Economic Analysis, Industry and Analysis, Exports by Metropolitan Area, data extracted March 24, 2021

Building Permits

Area	Single-Family			Multi-Family			Total		
	2018	2019	Pct. Chg.	2018	2019	Pct. Chg.	2018	2019	Pct. Chg.
City	171	174	1.8	286	140	-51.0	457	314	-31.3
MSA[1]	5,516	5,423	-1.7	1,325	1,524	15.0	6,841	6,947	1.5
U.S.	855,300	862,100	0.7	473,500	523,900	10.6	1,328,800	1,386,000	4.3

Note: (1) Figures cover the Provo-Orem, UT Metropolitan Statistical Area; Figures represent new, privately-owned housing units authorized (unadjusted data); All permit data are based on estimates with imputation
Source: U.S. Census Bureau, Manufacturing, Mining, and Construction Statistics, Building Permits, 2018, 2019

Bankruptcy Filings

Area	Business Filings			Nonbusiness Filings		
	2019	2020	% Chg.	2019	2020	% Chg.
Utah County	37	31	-16.2	1,408	1,151	-18.3
U.S.	22,780	21,655	-4.9	752,160	522,808	-30.5

Note: Business filings include Chapter 7, Chapter 9, Chapter 11, Chapter 12, Chapter 13, Chapter 15, and Section 304; Nonbusiness filings include Chapter 7, Chapter 11, and Chapter 13
Source: Administrative Office of the U.S. Courts, Business and Nonbusiness Bankruptcy, County Cases Commenced by Chapter of the Bankruptcy Code, During the 12-Month Period Ending December 31, 2019 and Business and Nonbusiness Bankruptcy, County Cases Commenced by Chapter of the Bankruptcy Code, During the 12-Month Period Ending December 31, 2020

Housing Vacancy Rates

Area	Gross Vacancy Rate[2] (%)			Year-Round Vacancy Rate[3] (%)			Rental Vacancy Rate[4] (%)			Homeowner Vacancy Rate[5] (%)		
	2018	2019	2020	2018	2019	2020	2018	2019	2020	2018	2019	2020
MSA[1]	n/a	n/a	n/a	n/a	n/a	n/a	n/a	n/a	n/a	n/a	n/a	n/a
U.S.	12.3	12.0	10.6	9.7	9.5	8.2	6.9	6.7	6.3	1.5	1.4	1.0

Note: (1) Figures cover the Provo-Orem, UT Metropolitan Statistical Area; (2) The percentage of the total housing inventory that is vacant; (3) The percentage of the housing inventory (excluding seasonal units) that is year-round vacant; (4) The percentage of rental inventory that is vacant for rent; (5) The percentage of homeowner inventory that is vacant for sale; n/a not available
Source: U.S. Census Bureau, Housing Vacancies and Homeownership Annual Statistics: 2018, 2019, 2020

INCOME

Income

Area	Per Capita ($)	Median Household ($)	Average Household ($)
City	20,792	48,888	69,265
MSA[1]	26,153	74,387	93,213
U.S.	34,103	62,843	88,607

Note: (1) Figures cover the Provo-Orem, UT Metropolitan Statistical Area
Source: U.S. Census Bureau, 2015-2019 American Community Survey 5-Year Estimates

Household Income Distribution

Area	Percent of Households Earning							
	Under $15,000	$15,000 -$24,999	$25,000 -$34,999	$35,000 -$49,999	$50,000 -$74,999	$75,000 -$99,999	$100,000 -$149,999	$150,000 and up
City	12.2	12.9	12.3	13.5	18.9	11.8	10.6	7.8
MSA[1]	6.1	6.2	7.5	11.8	18.9	16.1	19.5	14.0
U.S.	10.3	8.9	8.9	12.3	17.2	12.7	15.1	14.5

Note: (1) Figures cover the Provo-Orem, UT Metropolitan Statistical Area
Source: U.S. Census Bureau, 2015-2019 American Community Survey 5-Year Estimates

Poverty Rate

Area	All Ages	Under 18 Years Old	18 to 64 Years Old	65 Years and Over
City	26.3	19.6	30.2	7.9
MSA[1]	10.7	9.5	12.0	5.5
U.S.	13.4	18.5	12.6	9.3

Note: Figures are percentage of people whose income during the past 12 months was below the poverty level;
(1) Figures cover the Provo-Orem, UT Metropolitan Statistical Area
Source: U.S. Census Bureau, 2015-2019 American Community Survey 5-Year Estimates

CITY FINANCES

City Government Finances

Component	2017 ($000)	2017 ($ per capita)
Total Revenues	166,998	1,449
Total Expenditures	163,682	1,420
Debt Outstanding	4,559	40
Cash and Securities[1]	123,957	1,075

Note: (1) Cash and security holdings of a government at the close of its fiscal year,
including those of its dependent agencies, utilities, and liquor stores.
Source: U.S. Census Bureau, State & Local Government Finances 2017

City Government Revenue by Source

Source	2017 ($000)	2017 ($ per capita)	2017 (%)
General Revenue			
From Federal Government	2,849	25	1.7
From State Government	3,152	27	1.9
From Local Governments	147	1	0.1
Taxes			
Property	13,991	121	8.4
Sales and Gross Receipts	22,077	192	13.2
Personal Income	0	0	0.0
Corporate Income	0	0	0.0
Motor Vehicle License	0	0	0.0
Other Taxes	1,702	15	1.0
Current Charges	27,250	236	16.3
Liquor Store	0	0	0.0
Utility	86,018	746	51.5
Employee Retirement	0	0	0.0

Source: U.S. Census Bureau, State & Local Government Finances 2017

City Government Expenditures by Function

Function	2017 ($000)	2017 ($ per capita)	2017 (%)
General Direct Expenditures			
Air Transportation	1,444	12	0.9
Corrections	0	0	0.0
Education	0	0	0.0
Employment Security Administration	0	0	0.0
Financial Administration	950	8	0.6
Fire Protection	9,514	82	5.8
General Public Buildings	99	< 1	< 0.1
Governmental Administration, Other	4,165	36	2.5
Health	437	3	0.3
Highways	5,116	44	3.1
Hospitals	0	0	0.0
Housing and Community Development	5,830	50	3.6
Interest on General Debt	238	2	0.1
Judicial and Legal	2,712	23	1.7
Libraries	3,302	28	2.0
Parking	0	0	0.0
Parks and Recreation	9,515	82	5.8
Police Protection	15,070	130	9.2
Public Welfare	0	0	0.0
Sewerage	11,572	100	7.1
Solid Waste Management	0	0	0.0
Veterans' Services	0	0	0.0
Liquor Store	0	0	0.0
Utility	72,396	628	44.2
Employee Retirement	0	0	0.0

Source: U.S. Census Bureau, State & Local Government Finances 2017

EMPLOYMENT

Labor Force and Employment

Area	Civilian Labor Force			Workers Employed		
	Dec. 2019	Dec. 2020	% Chg.	Dec. 2019	Dec. 2020	% Chg.
City	68,223	69,278	1.5	66,963	67,577	0.9
MSA[1]	319,576	325,243	1.8	313,261	316,139	0.9
U.S.	164,007,000	160,017,000	-2.4	158,504,000	149,613,000	-5.6

Note: Data is not seasonally adjusted and covers workers 16 years of age and older; (1) Figures cover the Provo-Orem, UT Metropolitan Statistical Area
Source: Bureau of Labor Statistics, Local Area Unemployment Statistics

Unemployment Rate

Area	2020											
	Jan.	Feb.	Mar.	Apr.	May	Jun.	Jul.	Aug.	Sep.	Oct.	Nov.	Dec.
City	2.3	2.3	3.2	6.4	5.3	4.0	3.2	3.0	3.3	2.6	2.8	2.5
MSA[1]	2.5	2.5	3.6	7.9	6.2	4.4	3.6	3.4	3.8	3.1	3.3	2.8
U.S.	4.0	3.8	4.5	14.4	11.2	10.5	8.5	7.7	6.6	6.4	6.5	

Note: Data is not seasonally adjusted and covers workers 16 years of age and older; (1) Figures cover the Provo-Orem, UT Metropolitan Statistical Area
Source: Bureau of Labor Statistics, Local Area Unemployment Statistics

Average Wages

Occupation	$/Hr.	Occupation	$/Hr.
Accountants and Auditors	30.20	Maintenance and Repair Workers	20.30
Automotive Mechanics	23.90	Marketing Managers	54.80
Bookkeepers	19.50	Network and Computer Systems Admin.	39.70
Carpenters	21.90	Nurses, Licensed Practical	22.90
Cashiers	12.10	Nurses, Registered	32.50
Computer Programmers	42.50	Nursing Assistants	14.30
Computer Systems Analysts	40.10	Office Clerks, General	17.00
Computer User Support Specialists	26.10	Physical Therapists	44.00
Construction Laborers	16.80	Physicians	101.70
Cooks, Restaurant	13.90	Plumbers, Pipefitters and Steamfitters	26.20
Customer Service Representatives	16.80	Police and Sheriff's Patrol Officers	26.70
Dentists	n/a	Postal Service Mail Carriers	25.20
Electricians	22.40	Real Estate Sales Agents	19.80
Engineers, Electrical	35.80	Retail Salespersons	14.10
Fast Food and Counter Workers	10.50	Sales Representatives, Technical/Scientific	35.30
Financial Managers	59.60	Secretaries, Exc. Legal/Medical/Executive	17.10
First-Line Supervisors of Office Workers	25.60	Security Guards	19.00
General and Operations Managers	41.00	Surgeons	n/a
Hairdressers/Cosmetologists	16.10	Teacher Assistants, Exc. Postsecondary*	13.70
Home Health and Personal Care Aides	13.20	Teachers, Secondary School, Exc. Sp. Ed.*	38.50
Janitors and Cleaners	12.20	Telemarketers	14.10
Landscaping/Groundskeeping Workers	16.10	Truck Drivers, Heavy/Tractor-Trailer	20.40
Lawyers	73.50	Truck Drivers, Light/Delivery Services	18.30
Maids and Housekeeping Cleaners	12.40	Waiters and Waitresses	12.10

Note: Wage data covers the Provo-Orem, UT Metropolitan Statistical Area; (*) Hourly wages were calculated from annual wage data based on a 40 hour work week; n/a not available.
Source: Bureau of Labor Statistics, Metro Area Occupational Employment & Wage Estimates, May 2020

Employment by Industry

Sector	MSA[1]		U.S.
	Number of Employees	Percent of Total	Percent of Total
Construction, Mining, and Logging	26,600	9.5	5.5
Education and Health Services	52,400	18.7	16.3
Financial Activities	12,200	4.4	6.1
Government	33,500	12.0	15.2
Information	13,200	4.7	1.9
Leisure and Hospitality	23,100	8.2	9.0
Manufacturing	20,600	7.4	8.5
Other Services	6,100	2.2	3.8
Professional and Business Services	42,800	15.3	14.4
Retail Trade	37,200	13.3	10.9
Transportation, Warehousing, and Utilities	5,000	1.8	4.6
Wholesale Trade	7,400	2.6	3.9

Note: Figures are non-farm employment as of December 2020. Figures are not seasonally adjusted and include workers 16 years of age and older; (1) Figures cover the Provo-Orem, UT Metropolitan Statistical Area
Source: Bureau of Labor Statistics, Current Employment Statistics, Employment, Hours, and Earnings

Employment by Occupation

Occupation Classification	City (%)	MSA[1] (%)	U.S. (%)
Management, Business, Science, and Arts	42.2	42.1	38.5
Natural Resources, Construction, and Maintenance	5.6	7.7	8.9
Production, Transportation, and Material Moving	8.9	10.5	13.2
Sales and Office	24.6	24.7	21.6
Service	18.8	15.0	17.8

Note: Figures cover employed civilians 16 years of age and older; (1) Figures cover the Provo-Orem, UT Metropolitan Statistical Area
Source: U.S. Census Bureau, 2015-2019 American Community Survey 5-Year Estimates

Occupations with Greatest Projected Employment Growth: 2020 – 2022

Occupation[1]	2020 Employment	2022 Projected Employment	Numeric Employment Change	Percent Employment Change
Fast Food and Counter Workers	42,200	46,310	4,110	9.7
Laborers and Freight, Stock, and Material Movers, Hand	25,360	29,070	3,710	14.6
General and Operations Managers	48,790	52,160	3,370	6.9
Light Truck or Delivery Services Drivers	11,770	14,330	2,560	21.8
Retail Salespersons	46,270	48,780	2,510	5.4
Construction Laborers	19,610	21,610	2,000	10.2
Software Developers and Software Quality Assurance Analysts and Testers	19,350	21,110	1,760	9.1
Waiters and Waitresses	16,290	17,870	1,580	9.7
Home Health and Personal Care Aides	16,180	17,670	1,490	9.2
Office Clerks, General	32,890	34,270	1,380	4.2

Note: Projections cover Utah; (1) Sorted by numeric employment change
Source: www.projectionscentral.com, State Occupational Projections, 2020–2022 Short-Term Projections

Fastest-Growing Occupations: 2020 – 2022

Occupation[1]	2020 Employment	2022 Projected Employment	Numeric Employment Change	Percent Employment Change
Dancers	190	250	60	31.6
Bartenders	2,020	2,480	460	22.8
Light Truck or Delivery Services Drivers	11,770	14,330	2,560	21.8
Hotel, Motel, and Resort Desk Clerks	3,190	3,780	590	18.5
Actors	280	330	50	17.9
Medical Scientists, Except Epidemiologists	1,660	1,950	290	17.5
Statisticians	640	750	110	17.2
Food Servers, Nonrestaurant	1,930	2,260	330	17.1
Lodging Managers	370	430	60	16.2
Couriers and Messengers	950	1,100	150	15.8

Note: Projections cover Utah; (1) Sorted by percent employment change and excludes occupations with numeric employment change less than 50
Source: www.projectionscentral.com, State Occupational Projections, 2020–2022 Short-Term Projections

TAXES

State Corporate Income Tax Rates

State	Tax Rate (%)	Income Brackets ($)	Num. of Brackets	Financial Institution Tax Rate (%)[a]	Federal Income Tax Ded.
Utah	4.95 (b)	Flat rate	–	4.95 (b)	No

Note: Tax rates as of January 1, 2021; (a) Rates listed are the corporate income tax rate applied to financial institutions or excise taxes based on income. Some states have other taxes based upon the value of deposits or shares; (b) Minimum tax is $800 in California, $250 in District of Columbia, $50 in Arizona and North Dakota (banks), $400 ($100 banks) in Rhode Island, $200 per location in South Dakota (banks), $100 in Utah, $300 in Vermont.
Source: Federation of Tax Administrators, State Corporate Income Tax Rates, January 1, 2021

State Individual Income Tax Rates

State	Tax Rate (%)	Income Brackets ($)	Personal Exemptions ($)			Standard Ded. ($)	
			Single	Married	Depend.	Single	Married
Utah	4.95	Flat rate	None	None	None	(u)	(u)

Note: Tax rates as of January 1, 2021; Local- and county-level taxes are not included; Federal income tax is not deductible on state income tax returns; (u) Utah provides a tax credit equal to 6% of the federal personal exemption amounts (and applicable standard deduction).
Source: Federation of Tax Administrators, State Individual Income Tax Rates, January 1, 2021

Various State Sales and Excise Tax Rates

State	State Sales Tax (%)	Gasoline[1] (¢/gal.)	Cigarette[2] ($/pack)	Spirits[3] ($/gal.)	Wine[4] ($/gal.)	Beer[5] ($/gal.)	Recreational Marijuana (%)
Utah	6.1	31.41	1.7	15.92	0.00	0.41	Not legal

Note: All tax rates as of January 1, 2021; (1) The American Petroleum Institute has developed a methodology for determining the average tax rate on a gallon of fuel. Rates may include any of the following: excise taxes, environmental fees, storage tank fees, other fees or taxes, general sales tax, and local taxes; (2) The federal excise tax of $1.0066 per pack and local taxes are not included; (3) Rates are those applicable to off-premise sales of 40% alcohol by volume (a.b.v.) distilled spirits in 750ml containers. Local excise taxes are excluded; (4) Rates are those applicable to off-premise sales of 11% a.b.v. non-carbonated wine in 750ml containers; (5) Rates are those applicable to off-premise sales of 4.7% a.b.v. beer in 12 ounce containers.
Source: Tax Foundation, 2021 Facts & Figures: How Does Your State Compare?

State Business Tax Climate Index Rankings

State	Overall Rank	Corporate Tax Rank	Individual Income Tax Rank	Sales Tax Rank	Property Tax Rank	Unemployment Insurance Tax Rank
Utah	8	14	10	23	7	17

Note: The index is a measure of how each state's tax laws affect economic performance. The lower the rank, the more favorable a state's tax system is for business. States without a given tax are given a ranking of 1. The scores/rankings for the District of Columbia do not affect other states. The 2021 index represents the tax climate as of July 1, 2020.
Source: Tax Foundation, State Business Tax Climate Index 2021

TRANSPORTATION

Means of Transportation to Work

Area	Car/Truck/Van		Public Transportation			Bicycle	Walked	Other Means	Worked at Home
	Drove Alone	Car-pooled	Bus	Subway	Railroad				
City	62.0	11.8	2.6	0.2	1.1	2.4	13.0	1.6	5.3
MSA[1]	73.1	11.4	1.1	0.2	0.9	0.9	4.1	1.2	7.2
U.S.	76.3	9.0	2.4	1.9	0.6	0.5	2.7	1.4	5.2

Note: Figures are percentages and cover workers 16 years of age and older; (1) Figures cover the Provo-Orem, UT Metropolitan Statistical Area
Source: U.S. Census Bureau, 2015-2019 American Community Survey 5-Year Estimates

Travel Time to Work

Area	Less Than 10 Minutes	10 to 19 Minutes	20 to 29 Minutes	30 to 44 Minutes	45 to 59 Minutes	60 to 89 Minutes	90 Minutes or More
City	21.3	45.3	17.3	9.0	2.7	2.9	1.4
MSA[1]	18.0	35.3	20.1	15.5	5.6	3.9	1.6
U.S.	12.2	28.4	20.8	20.8	8.3	6.4	2.9

Note: Note: Figures are percentages and include workers 16 years old and over; (1) Figures cover the Provo-Orem, UT Metropolitan Statistical Area
Source: U.S. Census Bureau, 2015-2019 American Community Survey 5-Year Estimates

Key Congestion Measures

Measure	1982	1992	2002	2012	2017
Annual Hours of Delay, Total (000)	911	2,458	4,724	6,920	8,701
Annual Hours of Delay, Per Auto Commuter	8	14	20	22	25
Annual Congestion Cost, Total (million $)	7	27	65	128	166
Annual Congestion Cost, Per Auto Commuter ($)	112	207	310	356	434

Note: Covers the Provo-Orem UT urban area
Source: Texas A&M Transportation Institute, 2019 Urban Mobility Report

Freeway Travel Time Index

Measure	1982	1987	1992	1997	2002	2007	2012	2017
Urban Area Index[1]	1.04	1.05	1.08	1.09	1.11	1.12	1.11	1.11
Urban Area Rank[1,2]	61	79	76	83	84	90	94	96

Note: Freeway Travel Time Index—the ratio of travel time in the peak period to the travel time at free-flow conditions. For example, a value of 1.30 indicates a 20-minute free-flow trip takes 26 minutes in the peak (20 minutes x 1.30 = 26 minutes); (1) Covers the Provo-Orem UT urban area; (2) Rank is based on 101 larger urban areas (#1 = highest travel time index)
Source: Texas A&M Transportation Institute, 2019 Urban Mobility Report

Public Transportation

Agency Name / Mode of Transportation	Vehicles Operated in Maximum Service[1]	Annual Unlinked Passenger Trips[2] (in thous.)	Annual Passenger Miles[3] (in thous.)
Utah Transit Authority (UT)			
Bus (directly operated)	416	20,175.8	84,702.2
Bus (purchased transportation)	5	74.2	219.0
Commuter Bus (directly operated)	41	549.7	12,128.1
Commuter Rail (directly operated)	50	5,193.9	133,685.5
Demand Response (directly operated)	64	243.1	2,601.4
Demand Response (purchased transportation)	46	145.2	1,822.4
Light Rail (directly operated)	89	17,128.0	83,098.5
Vanpool (directly operated)	430	1,068.4	37,026.6

Note: (1) Number of revenue vehicles operated by the given mode and type of service to meet the annual maximum service requirement. This is the revenue vehicle count during the peak season of the year; on the week and day that maximum service is provided. Vehicles operated in maximum service (VOMS) exclude atypical days and one-time special events; (2) Number of passengers who boarded public transportation vehicles. Passengers are counted each time they board a vehicle no matter how many vehicles they use to travel from their origin to their destination. (3) Sum of the distances ridden by all passengers during the entire fiscal year.
Source: Federal Transit Administration, National Transit Database, 2019

Air Transportation

Airport Name and Code / Type of Service	Passenger Airlines[1]	Passenger Enplanements	Freight Carriers[2]	Freight (lbs)
Salt Lake City International (50 miles) (SLC)				
Domestic service (U.S. carriers - 2020)	21	5,827,005	17	221,351,889
International service (U.S. carriers - 2019)	5	471,947	2	3,443,938

Note: (1) Includes all U.S.-based major, minor and commuter airlines that carried at least one passenger during the year; (2) Includes all U.S.-based airlines and freight carriers that transported at least one pound of freight during the year.
Source: Bureau of Transportation Statistics, The Intermodal Transportation Database, Air Carriers: T-100 Domestic Market (U.S. Carriers), 2020; Bureau of Transportation Statistics, The Intermodal Transportation Database, Air Carriers: T-100 International Market (U.S. Carriers), 2019

BUSINESSES

Major Business Headquarters

Company Name	Industry	Rankings	
		Fortune[1]	Forbes[2]
No companies listed	-	-	-

Note: (1) Companies that produce a 10-K are ranked 1 to 500 based on 2019 revenue; (2) All private companies with at least $2 billion in annual revenue through the end of their most current fiscal year are ranked 1 to 219; companies listed are headquartered in the city; dashes indicate no ranking
Source: Fortune, "Fortune 500," June/July 2020; Forbes, "America's Largest Private Companies," 2020

Fastest-Growing Businesses

According to *Inc.*, Provo is home to two of America's 500 fastest-growing private companies: **Thread Wallets** (#104); **Filevine** (#376). Criteria: must be an independent, privately-held, for-profit, U.S. corporation, proprietorship or partnership as of December 31, 2019; revenues must be at least $100,000 in 2016 and $2 million in 2019; must have four-year operating/sales history. *Inc.*, *"America's 500 Fastest-Growing Private Companies," 2020*

Living Environment

COST OF LIVING

Cost of Living Index

Composite Index	Groceries	Housing	Utilities	Trans-portation	Health Care	Misc. Goods/ Services
97.5	97.2	99.7	87.1	101.1	90.6	98.6

Note: The Cost of Living Index measures regional differences in the cost of consumer goods and services, excluding taxes and non-consumer expenditures, for professional and managerial households in the top income quintile. It is based on more than 50,000 prices covering almost 60 different items for which prices are collected three times a year by chambers of commerce, economic development organizations or university applied economic centers in each participating urban area. The numbers shown should be read as a percentage above or below the national average of 100. For example, a value of 115.4 in the groceries column indicates that grocery prices are 15.4% higher than the national average. Small differences in the index numbers should not be interpreted as significant; Figures cover the Provo-Orem UT urban area.
Source: The Council for Community and Economic Research, Cost of Living Index, 2020

Grocery Prices

Area[1]	T-Bone Steak ($/pound)	Frying Chicken ($/pound)	Whole Milk ($/half gal.)	Eggs ($/dozen)	Orange Juice ($/64 oz.)	Coffee ($/11.5 oz.)
City[2]	11.04	1.66	1.50	1.46	3.65	4.66
Avg.	11.78	1.39	2.05	1.47	3.57	4.34
Min.	8.03	0.94	1.03	0.74	2.94	3.02
Max.	15.86	2.65	4.31	3.77	5.44	8.69

*Note: (1) Values for the local area are compared with the average, minimum and maximum values for all 284 areas in the Cost of Living Index; (2) Figures cover the Provo-Orem UT urban area; **T-Bone Steak** (price per pound); **Frying Chicken** (price per pound, whole fryer); **Whole Milk** (half gallon carton); **Eggs** (price per dozen, Grade A, large); **Orange Juice** (64 oz. Tropicana or Florida Natural); **Coffee** (11.5 oz. can, vacuum-packed, Maxwell House, Hills Bros, or Folgers).*
Source: The Council for Community and Economic Research, Cost of Living Index, 2020

Housing and Utility Costs

Area[1]	New Home Price ($)	Apartment Rent ($/month)	All Electric ($/month)	Part Electric ($/month)	Other Energy ($/month)	Telephone ($/month)
City[2]	382,813	1,129	-	68.02	58.46	187.20
Avg.	368,594	1,168	170.86	100.47	65.28	184.30
Min.	190,567	502	91.58	31.42	26.08	169.60
Max.	2,227,806	4,738	470.38	280.31	280.06	206.50

*Note: (1) Values for the local area are compared with the average, minimum and maximum values for all 284 areas in the Cost of Living Index; (2) Figures cover the Provo-Orem UT urban area; **New Home Price** (2,400 sf living area, 8,000 sf lot, in urban area with full utilities); **Apartment Rent** (950 sf 2 bedroom/1.5 or 2 bath, unfurnished, excluding all utilities except water); **All Electric** (average monthly cost for an all-electric home); **Part Electric** (average monthly cost for a part-electric home); **Other Energy** (average monthly cost for natural gas, fuel oil, coal, wood, and any other forms of energy except electricity); **Telephone** (price includes the base monthly rate plus taxes and fees for three lines of mobile phone service).*
Source: The Council for Community and Economic Research, Cost of Living Index, 2020

Health Care, Transportation, and Other Costs

Area[1]	Doctor ($/visit)	Dentist ($/visit)	Optometrist ($/visit)	Gasoline ($/gallon)	Beauty Salon ($/visit)	Men's Shirt ($)
City[2]	99.81	84.76	97.49	2.39	36.53	24.62
Avg.	115.44	99.32	108.10	2.21	39.27	31.37
Min.	36.68	59.00	51.36	1.71	19.00	11.00
Max.	219.00	153.10	250.97	3.46	82.05	58.33

*Note: (1) Values for the local area are compared with the average, minimum and maximum values for all 284 areas in the Cost of Living Index; (2) Figures cover the Provo-Orem UT urban area; **Doctor** (general practitioners routine exam of an established patient); **Dentist** (adult teeth cleaning and periodic oral examination); **Optometrist** (full vision eye exam for established adult patient); **Gasoline** (one gallon regular unleaded, national brand, including all taxes, cash price at self-service pump if available); **Beauty Salon** (woman's shampoo, trim, and blow-dry); **Men's Shirt** (cotton/polyester dress shirt, pinpoint weave, long sleeves).*
Source: The Council for Community and Economic Research, Cost of Living Index, 2020

HOUSING

Homeownership Rate

Area	2012 (%)	2013 (%)	2014 (%)	2015 (%)	2016 (%)	2017 (%)	2018 (%)	2019 (%)	2020 (%)
MSA[1]	n/a	n/a	n/a	n/a	n/a	n/a	n/a	n/a	n/a
U.S.	65.4	65.1	64.5	63.7	63.4	63.9	64.4	64.6	66.6

Note: (1) Figures cover the Provo-Orem, UT Metropolitan Statistical Area; n/a not available
Source: U.S. Census Bureau, Housing Vacancies and Homeownership Annual Statistics: 2012-2020

House Price Index (HPI)

Area	National Ranking[2]	Quarterly Change (%)	One-Year Change (%)	Five-Year Change (%)	Since 1991Q1 (%)
MSA[1]	23	3.08	8.61	46.91	339.23
U.S.[3]	–	3.81	10.77	38.99	205.12

Note: The HPI is a weighted repeat sales index. It measures average price changes in repeat sales or refinancings on the same properties. This information is obtained by reviewing repeat mortgage transactions on single-family properties whose mortgages have been purchased or securitized by Fannie Mae or Freddie Mac since January 1975; (1) Figures cover the Provo-Orem, UT Metropolitan Statistical Area; (2) Rankings are based on annual percentage change for all metro areas containing at least 15,000 transactions over the last 10 years and ranges from 1 to 253; (3) figures based on a weighted average of Census Division estimates using a seasonally adjusted, purchase-only index; all figures are for the period ending December 31, 2020
Source: Federal Housing Finance Agency, Change in Metropolitan Area House Price Indexes, April 7, 2021

Median Single-Family Home Prices

Area	2018	2019	2020p	Percent Change 2019 to 2020
MSA[1]	n/a	n/a	n/a	n/a
U.S. Average	261.6	274.6	299.9	9.2

Note: Figures are median sales prices of existing single-family homes in thousands of dollars; (p) preliminary; n/a not available; (1) Figures cover the Provo-Orem, UT Metropolitan Statistical Area
Source: National Association of Realtors, Median Sales Price of Existing Single-Family Homes for Metropolitan Areas, 4th Quarter 2020

Qualifying Income Based on Median Sales Price of Existing Single-Family Homes

Area	With 5% Down ($)	With 10% Down ($)	With 20% Down ($)
MSA[1]	n/a	n/a	n/a
U.S. Average	59,266	56,147	49,908

Note: Figures are preliminary; Qualifying income is based on a mortgage rate of 2.81%. Monthly principal and interest payment is limited to 25% of income; n/a not available; (1) Figures cover the Provo-Orem, UT Metropolitan Statistical Area
Source: National Association of Realtors, Qualifying Income Based on Median Sales Price of Existing Single-Family Homes for Metropolitan Areas, 4th Quarter 2020

Home Value Distribution

Area	Under $50,000	$50,000 -$99,999	$100,000 -$149,999	$150,000 -$199,999	$200,000 -$299,999	$300,000 -$499,999	$500,000 -$999,999	$1,000,000 or more
City	3.5	1.2	6.4	13.5	34.5	29.0	9.8	2.2
MSA[1]	2.4	0.9	3.6	10.1	32.2	37.0	12.1	1.7
U.S.	6.9	12.0	13.3	14.0	19.6	19.3	11.4	3.4

Note: Figures are percentages and cover owner-occupied housing units; (1) Figures cover the Provo-Orem, UT Metropolitan Statistical Area
Source: U.S. Census Bureau, 2015-2019 American Community Survey 5-Year Estimates

Year Housing Structure Built

Area	2010 or Later	2000 -2009	1990 -1999	1980 -1989	1970 -1979	1960 -1969	1950 -1959	1940 -1949	Before 1940	Median Year
City	4.6	11.8	21.1	14.3	17.7	10.4	7.6	5.1	7.3	1981
MSA[1]	14.0	25.9	19.2	9.3	13.6	5.0	5.4	3.1	4.6	1995
U.S.	5.2	14.0	13.9	13.4	15.2	10.6	10.3	4.9	12.6	1978

Note: Figures are percentages except for Median Year; Note: (1) Figures cover the Provo-Orem, UT Metropolitan Statistical Area
Source: U.S. Census Bureau, 2015-2019 American Community Survey 5-Year Estimates

Gross Monthly Rent

Area	Under $500	$500 -$999	$1,000 -$1,499	$1,500 -$1,999	$2,000 -$2,499	$2,500 -$2,999	$3,000 and up	Median ($)
City	12.8	49.7	24.3	10.2	2.3	0.5	0.2	877
MSA[1]	6.6	39.1	33.3	15.8	3.7	0.9	0.6	1,054
U.S.	9.4	36.2	30.0	14.0	5.6	2.4	2.4	1,062

Note: Figures are percentages except for Median; Gross rent is the contract rent plus the estimated average monthly cost of utilities (electricity, gas, and water and sewer) and fuels (oil, coal, kerosene, wood, etc.) if these are paid by the renter (or paid for the renter by someone else); (1) Figures cover the Provo-Orem, UT Metropolitan Statistical Area
Source: U.S. Census Bureau, 2015-2019 American Community Survey 5-Year Estimates

HEALTH

Health Risk Factors

Category	MSA[1] (%)	U.S. (%)
Adults aged 18–64 who have any kind of health care coverage	87.5	87.3
Adults who reported being in good or better health	88.1	82.4
Adults who have been told they have high blood cholesterol	25.0	33.0
Adults who have been told they have high blood pressure	18.1	32.3
Adults who are current smokers	4.2	17.1
Adults who currently use E-cigarettes	3.4	4.6
Adults who currently use chewing tobacco, snuff, or snus	1.9	4.0
Adults who are heavy drinkers[2]	1.5	6.3
Adults who are binge drinkers[3]	4.8	17.4
Adults who are overweight (BMI 25.0 - 29.9)	34.2	35.3
Adults who are obese (BMI 30.0 - 99.8)	23.1	31.3
Adults who participated in any physical activities in the past month	80.7	74.4
Adults who always or nearly always wears a seat belt	96.3	94.3

Note: (1) Figures cover the Provo-Orem, UT Metropolitan Statistical Area; (2) Heavy drinkers are classified as adult men having more than 14 drinks per week and adult women having more than 7 drinks per week; (3) Binge drinkers are classified as males having five or more drinks on one occasion or females having four or more drinks on one occasion
Source: Centers for Disease Control and Prevention, Behaviorial Risk Factor Surveillance System, SMART: Selected Metropolitan Area Risk Trends, 2017

Acute and Chronic Health Conditions

Category	MSA[1] (%)	U.S. (%)
Adults who have ever been told they had a heart attack	2.2	4.2
Adults who have ever been told they have angina or coronary heart disease	2.0	3.9
Adults who have ever been told they had a stroke	1.7	3.0
Adults who have ever been told they have asthma	14.6	14.2
Adults who have ever been told they have arthritis	14.3	24.9
Adults who have ever been told they have diabetes[2]	5.7	10.5
Adults who have ever been told they had skin cancer	5.3	6.2
Adults who have ever been told they had any other types of cancer	5.2	7.1
Adults who have ever been told they have COPD	2.2	6.5
Adults who have ever been told they have kidney disease	3.2	3.0
Adults who have ever been told they have a form of depression	20.8	20.5

Note: (1) Figures cover the Provo-Orem, UT Metropolitan Statistical Area; (2) Figures do not include pregnancy-related, borderline, or pre-diabetes
Source: Centers for Disease Control and Prevention, Behaviorial Risk Factor Surveillance System, SMART: Selected Metropolitan Area Risk Trends, 2017

Health Screening and Vaccination Rates

Category	MSA[1] (%)	U.S. (%)
Adults aged 65+ who have had flu shot within the past year	57.2	60.7
Adults aged 65+ who have ever had a pneumonia vaccination	76.4	75.4
Adults who have ever been tested for HIV	16.2	36.1
Adults who have ever had the shingles or zoster vaccine?	26.9	28.9
Adults who have had their blood cholesterol checked within the last five years	77.1	85.9

Note: n/a not available; (1) Figures cover the Provo-Orem, UT Metropolitan Statistical Area.
Source: Centers for Disease Control and Prevention, Behaviorial Risk Factor Surveillance System, SMART: Selected Metropolitan Area Risk Trends, 2017

Disability Status

Category	MSA[1] (%)	U.S. (%)
Adults who reported being deaf	4.6	6.7
Are you blind or have serious difficulty seeing, even when wearing glasses?	2.6	4.5
Are you limited in any way in any of your usual activities due of arthritis?	7.0	12.9
Do you have difficulty doing errands alone?	3.8	6.8
Do you have difficulty dressing or bathing?	1.7	3.6
Do you have serious difficulty concentrating/remembering/making decisions?	9.3	10.7
Do you have serious difficulty walking or climbing stairs?	6.4	13.6

Note: (1) Figures cover the Provo-Orem, UT Metropolitan Statistical Area.
Source: Centers for Disease Control and Prevention, Behaviorial Risk Factor Surveillance System, SMART: Selected Metropolitan Area Risk Trends, 2017

Mortality Rates for the Top 10 Causes of Death in the U.S.

ICD-10[a] Sub-Chapter	ICD-10[a] Code	Age-Adjusted Mortality Rate[1] per 100,000 population	
		County[2]	U.S.
Malignant neoplasms	C00-C97	114.3	149.2
Ischaemic heart diseases	I20-I25	61.7	90.5
Other forms of heart disease	I30-I51	77.2	52.2
Chronic lower respiratory diseases	J40-J47	20.6	39.6
Other degenerative diseases of the nervous system	G30-G31	46.2	37.6
Cerebrovascular diseases	I60-I69	36.9	37.2
Other external causes of accidental injury	W00-X59	32.1	36.1
Organic, including symptomatic, mental disorders	F01-F09	38.5	29.4
Hypertensive diseases	I10-I15	14.1	24.1
Diabetes mellitus	E10-E14	21.6	21.5

Note: (a) ICD-10 = International Classification of Diseases 10th Revision; (1) Mortality rates are a three-year average covering 2017-2019; (2) Figures cover Utah County.
Source: Centers for Disease Control and Prevention, National Center for Health Statistics. Underlying Cause of Death 1999-2019 on CDC WONDER Online Database

Mortality Rates for Selected Causes of Death

ICD-10[a] Sub-Chapter	ICD-10[a] Code	Age-Adjusted Mortality Rate[1] per 100,000 population	
		County[2]	U.S.
Assault	X85-Y09	1.6	6.0
Diseases of the liver	K70-K76	10.3	14.4
Human immunodeficiency virus (HIV) disease	B20-B24	Suppressed	1.5
Influenza and pneumonia	J09-J18	12.7	13.8
Intentional self-harm	X60-X84	17.2	14.1
Malnutrition	E40-E46	8.3	2.3
Obesity and other hyperalimentation	E65-E68	2.0	2.1
Renal failure	N17-N19	18.2	12.6
Transport accidents	V01-V99	6.9	12.3
Viral hepatitis	B15-B19	Suppressed	1.2

Note: (a) ICD-10 = International Classification of Diseases 10th Revision; (1) Mortality rates are a three-year average covering 2017-2019; (2) Figures cover Utah County; Data are suppressed when the data meet the criteria for confidentiality constraints; Mortality rates are flagged as unreliable when the rate would be calculated with a numerator of 20 or less.
Source: Centers for Disease Control and Prevention, National Center for Health Statistics. Underlying Cause of Death 1999-2019 on CDC WONDER Online Database

Health Insurance Coverage

Area	With Health Insurance	With Private Health Insurance	With Public Health Insurance	Without Health Insurance	Population Under Age 19 Without Health Insurance
City	88.8	77.8	17.3	11.2	10.7
MSA[1]	91.9	81.7	17.4	8.1	6.0
U.S.	91.2	67.9	35.1	8.8	5.1

Note: Figures are percentages that cover the civilian noninstitutionalized population; (1) Figures cover the Provo-Orem, UT Metropolitan Statistical Area
Source: U.S. Census Bureau, 2015-2019 American Community Survey 5-Year Estimates

Number of Medical Professionals

Area	MDs[3]	DOs[3,4]	Dentists	Podiatrists	Chiropractors	Optometrists
County[1] (number)	723	118	388	29	162	70
County[1] (rate[2])	116.3	19.0	61.0	4.6	25.5	11.0
U.S. (rate[2])	282.9	22.7	71.2	6.2	28.1	16.9

49049
Note: Data as of 2019 unless noted; (1) Data covers Utah County; (2) Rate per 100,000 population; (3) Data as of 2018 and includes all active, non-federal physicians; (4) Doctor of Osteopathic Medicine
Source: U.S. Department of Health and Human Services, Health Resources and Services Administration, Bureau of Health Professions, Area Resource File (ARF) 2019-2020

EDUCATION

Public School District Statistics

District Name	Schls	Pupils	Pupil/ Teacher Ratio	Minority Pupils[1] (%)	Free Lunch Eligible[2] (%)	IEP[3] (%)
Provo District	23	16,551	24.7	33.7	29.5	11.1

Note: Table includes school districts with 2,000 or more students; (1) Percentage of students that are not non-Hispanic white; (2) Percentage of students that are eligible for the free lunch program; (3) Percentage of students that have an Individualized Education Program.
Source: U.S. Department of Education, National Center for Education Statistics, Common Core of Data, Local Education Agency (School District) Universe Survey: School Year 2018-2019; U.S. Department of Education, National Center for Education Statistics, Common Core of Data, Public Elementary/Secondary School Universe Survey: School Year 2018-2019

Highest Level of Education

Area	Less than H.S.	H.S. Diploma	Some College, No Deg.	Associate Degree	Bachelor's Degree	Master's Degree	Prof. School Degree	Doctorate Degree
City	7.1	14.3	26.5	8.9	29.7	8.9	1.6	2.8
MSA[1]	5.5	16.8	26.7	10.7	27.7	9.2	1.6	1.7
U.S.	12.0	27.0	20.4	8.5	19.8	8.8	2.1	1.4

Note: Figures cover persons age 25 and over; (1) Figures cover the Provo-Orem, UT Metropolitan Statistical Area
Source: U.S. Census Bureau, 2015-2019 American Community Survey 5-Year Estimates

Educational Attainment by Race

Area	High School Graduate or Higher (%)					Bachelor's Degree or Higher (%)				
	Total	White	Black	Asian	Hisp.[2]	Total	White	Black	Asian	Hisp.[2]
City	92.9	93.1	98.0	93.2	75.2	43.1	43.4	27.2	52.9	18.6
MSA[1]	94.5	94.9	97.4	94.6	75.3	40.3	40.6	35.4	58.9	20.2
U.S.	88.0	89.9	86.0	87.1	68.7	32.1	33.5	21.6	54.3	16.4

Note: Figures shown cover persons 25 years old and over; (1) Figures cover the Provo-Orem, UT Metropolitan Statistical Area; (2) People of Hispanic origin can be of any race
Source: U.S. Census Bureau, 2015-2019 American Community Survey 5-Year Estimates

School Enrollment by Grade and Control

Area	Preschool (%)		Kindergarten (%)		Grades 1 - 4 (%)		Grades 5 - 8 (%)		Grades 9 - 12 (%)	
	Public	Private	Public	Private	Public	Private	Public	Private	Public	Private
City	53.8	46.2	95.7	4.3	93.9	6.1	95.8	4.2	88.5	11.5
MSA[1]	53.3	46.7	91.6	8.4	92.9	7.1	94.4	5.6	94.4	5.6
U.S.	59.1	40.9	87.6	12.4	89.5	10.5	89.4	10.6	90.1	9.9

Note: Figures shown cover persons 3 years old and over; (1) Figures cover the Provo-Orem, UT Metropolitan Statistical Area
Source: U.S. Census Bureau, 2015-2019 American Community Survey 5-Year Estimates

Higher Education

Four-Year Colleges			Two-Year Colleges			Medical Schools[1]	Law Schools[2]	Voc/ Tech[3]
Public	Private Non-profit	Private For-profit	Public	Private Non-profit	Private For-profit			
0	1	2	0	0	0	1	1	6

Note: Figures cover institutions located within the city limits and include main campuses only; (1) includes schools accredited by the Liaison Committee on Medical Education and the American Osteopathic Association's Commission on Osteopathic College Accreditation; (2) includes ABA-accredited schools, schools with provisional ABA accreditation, and state accredited schools; (3) includes all schools with programs that are less than 2 years.
Source: National Center for Education Statistics, Integrated Postsecondary Education System (IPEDS), 2019-20; Wikipedia, List of Medical Schools in the United States, accessed April 2, 2021; Wikipedia, List of Law Schools in the United States, accessed April 2, 2021

According to *U.S. News & World Report,* the Provo-Orem, UT metro area is home to one of the top 200 national universities in the U.S.: **Brigham Young University—Provo** (#80 tie). The indicators used to capture academic quality fall into a number of categories: assessment by administrators at peer institutions; retention of students; faculty resources; student selectivity; financial resources; alumni giving; high school counselor ratings of colleges; and graduation rate. *U.S. News & World Report, "America's Best Colleges 2021"*

According to *U.S. News & World Report,* the Provo-Orem, UT metro area is home to one of the top 100 law schools in the U.S.: **Brigham Young University (Clark)** (#29 tie). The rankings are based on a weighted average of 12 measures of quality: peer assessment score; assessment score by lawyers/judges; median LSAT scores; median undergrad GPA; acceptance rate; employment rates for graduates; placement success; bar passage rate; faculty resources; expenditures per student; student/faculty ratio; and library resources. *U.S. News & World Report, "America's Best Graduate Schools, Law, 2022"*

According to *U.S. News & World Report,* the Provo-Orem, UT metro area is home to one of the top 75 business schools in the U.S.: **Brigham Young University (Marriott)** (#31 tie). The rankings are based on a weighted average of the following nine measures: quality assessment; peer assessment; recruiter assessment; placement success; mean starting salary and bonus; student selectivity; mean GMAT and GRE scores; mean undergraduate GPA; and acceptance rate. *U.S. News & World Report, "America's Best Graduate Schools, Business, 2022"*

EMPLOYERS

Major Employers

Company Name	Industry
About Time Technologies	Movements, clock or watch
Ancestry.com	Communication services, nec
Brigham Young University	Colleges & universities
City of Provo	Municipal government
Intermountain Health Care	General medical & surgical hospitals
Morinda Holdings	Bottled & canned soft drinks
Novell	Prepackaged software
Nu Skin Enterprises United States	Drugs, proprietaries, & sundries
Nu Skin International	Toilet preparations
Phone Directories Company	Directories, phone: publish only, not printed on site
RBM Services	Building cleaning service
TPUSA	Telemarketing services
Utah Dept of Human Services	Mental hospital, except for the mentally retarded
Utah Valley University	Colleges & universities
Wal-Mart Stores	Department stores, discount
Wasatch Summit	Management consulting services
Xango	Drugs, proprietaries, & sundries

Note: Companies shown are located within the Provo-Orem, UT Metropolitan Statistical Area.
Source: Hoovers.com; Wikipedia

PUBLIC SAFETY

Crime Rate

Area	All Crimes	Violent Crimes				Property Crimes		
		Murder	Rape[3]	Robbery	Aggrav. Assault	Burglary	Larceny -Theft	Motor Vehicle Theft
City	1,623.0	0.9	37.5	11.1	65.7	139.1	1,259.5	109.2
Suburbs[1]	1,312.0	1.1	30.2	7.2	46.1	131.5	1,018.1	77.8
Metro[2]	1,368.4	1.1	31.6	7.9	49.6	132.9	1,061.8	83.5
U.S.	2,489.3	5.0	42.6	81.6	250.2	340.5	1,549.5	219.9

Note: Figures are crimes per 100,000 population; (1) All areas within the metro area that are located outside the city limits; (2) Figures cover the Provo-Orem, UT Metropolitan Statistical Area; (3) All figures shown were reported using the revised Uniform Crime Reporting (UCR) definition of rape.
Source: FBI Uniform Crime Reports, 2019

Hate Crimes

Area	Number of Quarters Reported	Number of Incidents per Bias Motivation					
		Race/Ethnicity/ Ancestry	Religion	Sexual Orientation	Disability	Gender	Gender Identity
City	4	0	0	0	0	0	0
U.S.	4	3,963	1,521	1,195	157	69	198

Source: Federal Bureau of Investigation, Hate Crime Statistics 2019

Identity Theft Consumer Reports

Area	Reports	Reports per 100,000 Population	Rank[2]
MSA[1]	1,642	253	155
U.S.	1,387,615	423	-

Note: (1) Figures cover the Provo-Orem, UT Metropolitan Statistical Area; (2) Rank ranges from 1 to 391 where 1 indicates greatest number of identity theft reports per 100,000 population
Source: Federal Trade Commission, Consumer Sentinel Network Data Book 2020

Fraud and Other Consumer Reports

Area	Reports	Reports per 100,000 Population	Rank[2]
MSA[1]	3,681	568	320
U.S.	3,385,133	1,031	-

Note: (1) Figures cover the Provo-Orem, UT Metropolitan Statistical Area; (2) Rank ranges from 1 to 391 where 1 indicates greatest number of fraud and other consumer reports per 100,000 population
Source: Federal Trade Commission, Consumer Sentinel Network Data Book 2020

POLITICS

2020 Presidential Election Results

Area	Biden	Trump	Jorgensen	Hawkins	Other
Utah County	26.3	66.7	3.6	0.3	3.1
U.S.	51.3	46.8	1.2	0.3	0.5

Note: Results are percentages and may not add to 100% due to rounding
Source: Dave Leip's Atlas of U.S. Presidential Elections

SPORTS

Professional Sports Teams

Team Name	League	Year Established
No teams are located in the metro area		

Source: Wikipedia, Major Professional Sports Teams of the United States and Canada, April 6, 2021

CLIMATE

Average and Extreme Temperatures

Temperature	Jan	Feb	Mar	Apr	May	Jun	Jul	Aug	Sep	Oct	Nov	Dec	Yr.
Extreme High (°F)	62	69	78	85	93	104	107	104	100	89	75	67	107
Average High (°F)	37	43	52	62	72	83	93	90	80	66	50	38	64
Average Temp. (°F)	28	34	41	50	59	69	78	76	65	53	40	30	52
Average Low (°F)	19	24	31	38	46	54	62	61	51	40	30	22	40
Extreme Low (°F)	-22	-14	2	15	25	35	40	37	27	16	-14	-15	-22

Note: Figures cover the years 1948-1990
Source: National Climatic Data Center, International Station Meteorological Climate Summary, 9/96

Average Precipitation/Snowfall/Humidity

Precip./Humidity	Jan	Feb	Mar	Apr	May	Jun	Jul	Aug	Sep	Oct	Nov	Dec	Yr.
Avg. Precip. (in.)	1.3	1.2	1.8	2.0	1.7	0.9	0.8	0.9	1.1	1.3	1.3	1.4	15.6
Avg. Snowfall (in.)	13	10	11	6	1	Tr	0	0	Tr	2	6	13	63
Avg. Rel. Hum. 5am (%)	79	77	71	67	66	60	53	54	60	68	75	79	67
Avg. Rel. Hum. 5pm (%)	69	59	47	38	33	26	22	23	28	40	59	71	43

Note: Figures cover the years 1948-1990; Tr = Trace amounts (<0.05 in. of rain; <0.5 in. of snow)
Source: National Climatic Data Center, International Station Meteorological Climate Summary, 9/96

Weather Conditions

Temperature			Daytime Sky			Precipitation		
5°F & below	32°F & below	90°F & above	Clear	Partly cloudy	Cloudy	0.01 inch or more precip.	0.1 inch or more snow/ice	Thunder-storms
7	128	56	94	152	119	92	38	38

Note: Figures are average number of days per year and cover the years 1948-1990
Source: National Climatic Data Center, International Station Meteorological Climate Summary, 9/96

HAZARDOUS WASTE

Superfund Sites

The Provo-Orem, UT metro area has no sites on the EPA's Superfund Final National Priorities List. There are a total of 1,375 Superfund sites with a status of proposed or final on the list in the U.S. *U.S. Environmental Protection Agency, National Priorities List, April 7, 2021*

AIR QUALITY

Air Quality Trends: Ozone

	1990	1995	2000	2005	2010	2015	2016	2017	2018	2019
MSA[1]	0.070	0.068	0.083	0.078	0.070	0.073	0.072	0.073	0.073	0.073
U.S.	0.088	0.089	0.082	0.080	0.073	0.068	0.069	0.068	0.069	0.065

Note: (1) Data covers the Provo-Orem, UT Metropolitan Statistical Area. The values shown are the composite ozone concentration averages among trend sites based on the highest fourth daily maximum 8-hour concentration in parts per million. These trends are based on sites having an adequate record of monitoring data during the trend period. Data from exceptional events are included.
Source: U.S. Environmental Protection Agency, Air Quality Monitoring Information, "Air Quality Trends by City, 1990-2019"

Air Quality Index

Area	Percent of Days when Air Quality was...[2]					AQI Statistics[2]	
	Good	Moderate	Unhealthy for Sensitive Groups	Unhealthy	Very Unhealthy	Maximum	Median
MSA[1]	69.3	30.4	0.3	0.0	0.0	107	46

Note: (1) Data covers the Provo-Orem, UT Metropolitan Statistical Area; (2) Based on 365 days with AQI data in 2019. Air Quality Index (AQI) is an index for reporting daily air quality. EPA calculates the AQI for five major air pollutants regulated by the Clean Air Act: ground-level ozone, particle pollution (aka particulate matter), carbon monoxide, sulfur dioxide, and nitrogen dioxide. The AQI runs from 0 to 500. The higher the AQI value, the greater the level of air pollution and the greater the health concern. There are six AQI categories: "Good" AQI is between 0 and 50. Air quality is considered satisfactory; "Moderate" AQI is between 51 and 100. Air quality is acceptable; "Unhealthy for Sensitive Groups" When AQI values are between 101 and 150, members of sensitive groups may experience health effects; "Unhealthy" When AQI values are between 151 and 200 everyone may begin to experience health effects; "Very Unhealthy" AQI values between 201 and 300 trigger a health alert; "Hazardous" AQI values over 300 trigger warnings of emergency conditions (not shown).
Source: U.S. Environmental Protection Agency, Air Quality Index Report, 2019

Air Quality Index Pollutants

Area	Percent of Days when AQI Pollutant was...[2]					
	Carbon Monoxide	Nitrogen Dioxide	Ozone	Sulfur Dioxide	Particulate Matter 2.5	Particulate Matter 10
MSA[1]	0.0	1.9	81.4	0.0	16.2	0.5

Note: (1) Data covers the Provo-Orem, UT Metropolitan Statistical Area; (2) Based on 365 days with AQI data in 2019. The Air Quality Index (AQI) is an index for reporting daily air quality. EPA calculates the AQI for five major air pollutants regulated by the Clean Air Act: ground-level ozone, particle pollution (also known as particulate matter), carbon monoxide, sulfur dioxide, and nitrogen dioxide. The AQI runs from 0 to 500. The higher the AQI value, the greater the level of air pollution and the greater the health concern.
Source: U.S. Environmental Protection Agency, Air Quality Index Report, 2019

Maximum Air Pollutant Concentrations: Particulate Matter, Ozone, CO and Lead

	Particulate Matter 10 (ug/m^3)	Particulate Matter 2.5 Wtd AM (ug/m^3)	Particulate Matter 2.5 24-Hr (ug/m^3)	Ozone (ppm)	Carbon Monoxide (ppm)	Lead (ug/m^3)
MSA[1] Level	53	6.1	21	0.066	1	n/a
NAAQS[2]	150	15	35	0.075	9	0.15
Met NAAQS[2]	Yes	Yes	Yes	Yes	Yes	n/a

Note: (1) Data covers the Provo-Orem, UT Metropolitan Statistical Area; Data from exceptional events are included; (2) National Ambient Air Quality Standards; ppm = parts per million; ug/m^3 = micrograms per cubic meter; n/a not available.
Concentrations: Particulate Matter 10 (coarse particulate)—highest second maximum 24-hour concentration; Particulate Matter 2.5 Wtd AM (fine particulate)—highest weighted annual mean concentration; Particulate Matter 2.5 24-Hour (fine particulate)—highest 98th percentile 24-hour concentration; Ozone—highest fourth daily maximum 8-hour concentration; Carbon Monoxide—highest second maximum non-overlapping 8-hour concentration; Lead—maximum running 3-month average
Source: U.S. Environmental Protection Agency, Air Quality Monitoring Information, "Air Quality Statistics by City, 2019"

Maximum Air Pollutant Concentrations: Nitrogen Dioxide and Sulfur Dioxide

	Nitrogen Dioxide AM (ppb)	Nitrogen Dioxide 1-Hr (ppb)	Sulfur Dioxide AM (ppb)	Sulfur Dioxide 1-Hr (ppb)	Sulfur Dioxide 24-Hr (ppb)
MSA[1] Level	9	42	n/a	n/a	n/a
NAAQS[2]	53	100	30	75	140
Met NAAQS[2]	Yes	Yes	n/a	n/a	n/a

Note: (1) Data covers the Provo-Orem, UT Metropolitan Statistical Area; Data from exceptional events are included; (2) National Ambient Air Quality Standards; ppm = parts per million; ug/m^3 = micrograms per cubic meter; n/a not available.
Concentrations: Nitrogen Dioxide AM—highest arithmetic mean concentration; Nitrogen Dioxide 1-Hr—highest 98th percentile 1-hour daily maximum concentration; Sulfur Dioxide AM—highest annual mean concentration; Sulfur Dioxide 1-Hr—highest 99th percentile 1-hour daily maximum concentration; Sulfur Dioxide 24-Hr—highest second maximum 24-hour concentration
Source: U.S. Environmental Protection Agency, Air Quality Monitoring Information, "Air Quality Statistics by City, 2019"

Reno, Nevada

Background

Dubbed the "Biggest Little City in the World," Reno is known as a mecca for tourists who want to gamble, but it is so much more. Washoes and Paiutes roamed the area before white explorers led by the famed John C. Fremont arrived in the nineteenth century. Due to the Truckee River running through it, the area became a stopping point for people hurrying to California to take advantage of the 1849 gold rush. In 1859, prospectors discovered the Comstock Lode—a massive vein of gold and silver forty miles to the south of the Truckee.

A shrewd entrepreneur by the name of Charles Fuller built a toll bridge across the river for prospectors desperate to reach the lode, as well as a hotel. Floods kept destroying Fuller's bridge, and he sold the land to Myron Lake in 1861, who constructed another bridge around which a settlement grew. Lake turned over to the Central Pacific Railroad several dozen acres of his land, on the condition that half of the transcontinental railroad would run through the area. Here, the town of Reno was founded in 1868 and named after Jesse Lee Reno, a valiant Union officer killed during the Civil War. Reno became an important shipping point for the mines of the Comstock Lode.

By 1900, the lode was in decline and Reno had to look to other commercial ventures. One was the quick divorce—a six weeks' residency requirement was approved by the state legislature in 1931. In a continuing effort to jumpstart the state's economy during the Great Depression, Nevada legalized gambling in 1931. As the number of gambling houses increased in Reno, so did its population.

The Reno Arch (on which is emblazoned the city's nickname) welcomes tourists to an array of glittering casinos and hotels. The tourist and gambling industries are still quite important to the area's commerce but other commercial ventures have been attracted to Reno's business-friendly environment, which includes no corporate or personal income taxes, nor unitary, inventory, or franchise taxes. Urban Outfitters chose Reno for its 462,000 square-foot West Coast fulfillment center, and key industries throughout the Greater Reno-Sparks-Tahoe area include manufacturing; distribution/logistics/

> During a surge in coronavirus cases and a shortage of space, Renown Regional Medical Center turned their parking garage into a COVID-19 unit with 700 beds.

internet fulfillment; back office/business support; financial and intangible assets; clean energy; and aerospace/aviation/defense. Companies with distribution and fulfillment operations in the city include Walmart, PetSmart, Urban Outfitters, and Barnes & Noble.

The University of Nevada at Reno opened its Earthquake Engineering Laboratory in 2014. The lab makes the university's seismic simulation facility the largest in the country and the second-largest in the world. Also in the city is significant meeting space at the Reno-Sparks Convention Center, joined by the Reno Events Center that is part of a multi-million dollar project to increase special event and meeting venues to the downtown area. Reno is home to the National Bowling Stadium and the Reno-Sparks Livestock Events Center, and the Reno Aces play ball under the flag of the MLB-affiliated Pacific Coast League. The city also hosts ArtTown, in which music, visual arts, film, dance, theater and historical tours are highlighted every year in July, for one of the country's largest visual and performing arts festivals.

Skiing and snowboarding are popular winter sports and draw in many tourists. There are 18 ski resorts as close as 11 miles and as far as 98 miles from the Reno-Tahoe International Airport, including Northstar California, Sierra-at-Tahoe, Alpine Meadows, Squaw Valley, Sugar Bowl, Diamond Peak, Heavenly Mountain, and Mount Rose. In 2018, the city changed its flag to a colorful mountain graphic. Other popular winter activities include snowshoeing, ice skating, and snowmobiling. There are many bike paths to ride in the summer time.

Located on a semi-arid plateau to the east of the Sierra Nevada mountains, Reno offers a generally healthy climate with short, hot summers and relatively mild winters. Temperatures can vary widely from day to night. More than half of the city's precipitation falls as a rain-snow mixture during winter. Located at the edge of the Sierra Nevada, snow can pile up but tends to melt within a few days. Reno sees relatively little rain.

Rankings

General Rankings

- Reno was selected as one of the best places to live in America by *Outside Magazine*. Criteria included population, park acreage, neighborhood and resident diversity, new and upcoming things of interest, and opportunities for outdoor adventure. *Outside Magazine, "The 12 Best Places to Live in 2019," July 11, 2019*

- In their seventh annual survey, Livability.com looked at data for more than 1,000 small to mid-sized U.S. cities to determine the rankings for Livability's "Top 100 Best Places to Live" in 2020. Reno ranked #84. Criteria: housing and affordable living; vibrant economy; social and civic engagement; education; demographics; health care options; transportation & infrastructure; and abundant lifestyle amenities. *Livability.com, "Top 100 Best Places to Live 2020" October 2020*

Business/Finance Rankings

- According to *Business Insider*, the Reno metro area is a prime place to run a startup or move an existing business to. The area ranked #8. Nearly 190 metro areas were analyzed on overall economic health and investments. Data was based on the 2019 U.S. Census Bureau American Community Survey, the marketing company PitchBook, Bureau of Labor Statistics employment report, and Zillow. Criteria: percentage of change in typical home values and employment rates; quarterly venture capital investment activity; and median household income. *www.businessinsider.com, "The 25 Best Cities to Start a Business-Or Move Your Current One," January 12, 2021*

- The Reno metro area appeared on the Milken Institute "2021 Best Performing Cities" list. Rank: #18 out of 200 large metro areas (population over 250,000). Criteria: job growth; wage and salary growth; high-tech output growth; housing affordability; household broadband access. *Milken Institute, "Best-Performing Cities 2021," February 16, 2021*

- *Forbes* ranked the 200 most populous metro areas to determine the nation's "Best Places for Business and Careers." The Reno metro area was ranked #11. Criteria: costs (business and living); job growth (past and projected); income growth; quality of life; educational attainment (college and high school); projected economic growth; cultural and leisure opportunities; workplace tolerance laws; net migration patterns. *Forbes, "The Best Places for Business and Careers 2019: Seattle Still On Top," October 30, 2019*

Dating/Romance Rankings

- Reno was ranked #21 out of 25 cities that stood out for inspiring romance and attracting diners on the website OpenTable.com. Criteria: percentage of people who dined out on Valentine's Day in 2018; percentage of romantic restaurants as rated by OpenTable diner reviews; and percentage of tables seated for two. *OpenTable, "25 Most Romantic Cities in America for 2019," February 7, 2019*

Education Rankings

- Personal finance website *WalletHub* analyzed the 150 largest U.S. metropolitan statistical areas to determine where the most educated Americans are putting their degrees to work. Criteria: education levels; percentage of workers with degrees; education quality and attainment gap; public school quality rankings; quality and enrollment of each metro area's universities. Reno was ranked #60 (#1 = most educated city). *www.WalletHub.com, "Most and Least Educated Cities in America," July 20, 2020*

Environmental Rankings

- Reno was highlighted as one of the 25 metro areas most polluted by short-term particle pollution (24-hour PM 2.5) in the U.S. during 2016 through 2018. The area ranked #23. *American Lung Association, "State of the Air 2020," April 21, 2020*

Health/Fitness Rankings

- For each of the 100 largest cities in the United States, the American Fitness Index®, published by the American College of Sports Medicine and the Anthem Foundation, evaluated community infrastructure and 33 health behaviors including preventive health, levels of chronic disease conditions, pedestrian safety, air quality, and community resources that support physical activity. Reno ranked #55 for "community fitness." *americanfitnessindex.org, "2020 ACSM American Fitness Index Summary Report," July 14, 2020*

Real Estate Rankings

- *WalletHub* compared the most populated U.S. cities to determine which had the best markets for real estate agents. Reno ranked #36 where demand was high and pay was the best. Criteria: sales per agent; annual median wage for real-estate agents; monthly average starting salary for real estate agents; real estate job density and competition; unemployment rate; home turnover rate; housing-market health index; and other relevant metrics. *www.WalletHub.com, "2019's Best Places to Be a Real Estate Agent," April 24, 2019*

- The Reno metro area was identified as one of the nations's 20 hottest housing markets in 2021. Criteria: listing views as an indicator of demand and median days on the market as an indicator of supply. The area ranked #8. *Realtor.com, "January 2021 Top 20 Hottest Housing Markets," February 25, 2021*

- The Reno metro area was identified as one of the 10 best condo markets in the U.S. in 2020. The area ranked #4 out of 63 markets. Criteria: year-over-year change of median sales price of existing apartment condo-coop homes between the 4th quarter of 2019 and the 4th quarter of 2020. *National Association of Realtors®, Median Sales Price of Existing Apartment Condo-Coops Homes for Metropolitan Areas, 4th Quarter 2020*

- The Reno metro area was identified as one of the 20 least affordable housing markets in the U.S. in 2020. The area ranked #165 out of 183 markets. Criteria: qualification for a mortgage loan with a 10 percent down payment on a typical home. *National Association of Realtors®, Qualifying Income Based on Sales Price of Existing Single-Family Homes for Metropolitan Areas, 2020*

- Reno was ranked #228 out of 268 metro areas in terms of housing affordability in 2020 by the National Association of Home Builders (#1 = most affordable). Criteria: the share of homes sold in that area affordable to a family earning the local median income, based on standard mortgage underwriting criteria. *National Association of Home Builders®, NAHB-Wells Fargo Housing Opportunity Index, 4th Quarter 2020*

Safety Rankings

- Allstate ranked the 200 largest cities in America in terms of driver safety. Reno ranked #25. Criteria: internal property damage claims over a two-year period from January 2016 to December 2017. The report helps increase the importance of safety and awareness behind the wheel. *Allstate, "Allstate America's Best Drivers Report, 2019" June 24, 2019*

- The National Insurance Crime Bureau ranked 384 metro areas in the U.S. in terms of per capita rates of vehicle theft. The Reno metro area ranked #49 (#1 = highest rate). Criteria: number of vehicle theft offenses per 100,000 inhabitants in 2019. *National Insurance Crime Bureau, "Hot Spots 2019," July 21, 2020*

Seniors/Retirement Rankings

- From its Best Cities for Successful Aging indexes, the Milken Institute generated rankings for metropolitan areas, weighing data in nine categories—health care, wellness, living arrangements, transportation and convenience, financial characteristics, education, employment, community engagement, and overall livability. The Reno metro area was ranked #101 overall in the small metro area category. *Milken Institute, "Best Cities for Successful Aging, 2017" March 14, 2017*

- Reno was identified as #15 of 20 most popular places to retire in the Western region by *Topretirements.com*. The site separated its annual "Best Places to Retire" list by major U.S. regions for 2019. The list reflects the 20 cities that visitors to the website are most interested in for retirement, based on the number of times a city's review was viewed on the website. *Topretirements.com, "20 Best Places to Retire in the West-2019," November 11, 2019*

Women/Minorities Rankings

- Personal finance website *WalletHub* compared more than 180 U.S. cities across two key dimensions, "Hispanic Business-Friendliness" and "Hispanic Purchasing Power," to arrive at the most favorable conditions for Hispanic entrepreneurs. Reno was ranked #102 out of 182. Criteria includes: share of Hispanic-Owned Businesses; Hispanic entrepreneurship rate to median annual income of Hispanics; Small Business-Friendliness score; cost of living; and number of Hispanics with at least a bachelor's degree. *WalletHub.com, "2019's Best Cities for Hispanic Entrepreneurs," May 1, 2019*

Miscellaneous Rankings

- *WalletHub* compared the 150 most populated U.S. cities to determine their operating efficiency. A "Quality of City Services" score was constructed for each city and then divided by the total budget per capita to reveal which were managed the best. Reno ranked #45. Criteria: financial stability; economy; education; safety; health; infrastructure and pollution. *www.WalletHub.com, "2020's Best-& Worst-Run Cities in America," June 29, 2020*

Business Environment

DEMOGRAPHICS

Population Growth

Area	1990 Census	2000 Census	2010 Census	2019* Estimate	Population Growth (%) 1990-2019	Population Growth (%) 2010-2019
City	139,950	180,480	225,221	246,500	76.1	9.4
MSA[1]	257,193	342,885	425,417	460,924	79.2	8.3
U.S.	248,709,873	281,421,906	308,745,538	324,697,795	30.6	5.2

Note: (1) Figures cover the Reno, NV Metropolitan Statistical Area; (*) 2015-2019 5-year estimated population
Source: U.S. Census Bureau, 1990 Census, Census 2000, Census 2010, 2015-2019 American Community Survey 5-Year Estimates

Household Size

Area	One	Two	Three	Four	Five	Six	Seven or More	Average Household Size
City	33.0	33.4	14.6	10.5	5.1	1.9	1.4	2.40
MSA[1]	28.3	35.1	15.6	11.5	5.7	2.4	1.5	2.50
U.S.	27.9	33.9	15.6	12.9	6.0	2.3	1.4	2.60

Persons in Household (%)
Note: (1) Figures cover the Reno, NV Metropolitan Statistical Area
Source: U.S. Census Bureau, 2015-2019 American Community Survey 5-Year Estimates

Race

Area	White Alone[2] (%)	Black Alone[2] (%)	Asian Alone[2] (%)	AIAN[3] Alone[2] (%)	NHOPI[4] Alone[2] (%)	Other Race Alone[2] (%)	Two or More Races (%)
City	75.4	2.8	6.7	1.0	0.8	8.5	4.8
MSA[1]	77.6	2.3	5.3	1.6	0.6	8.1	4.4
U.S.	72.5	12.7	5.5	0.8	0.2	4.9	3.3

Note: (1) Figures cover the Reno, NV Metropolitan Statistical Area; (2) Alone is defined as not being in combination with one or more other races; (3) American Indian and Alaska Native; (4) Native Hawaiian and Other Pacific Islander
Source: U.S. Census Bureau, 2015-2019 American Community Survey 5-Year Estimates

Hispanic or Latino Origin

Area	Total (%)	Mexican (%)	Puerto Rican (%)	Cuban (%)	Other (%)
City	24.7	19.2	0.5	0.3	4.7
MSA[1]	24.3	18.9	0.6	0.3	4.4
U.S.	18.0	11.2	1.7	0.7	4.3

Note: Persons of Hispanic or Latino origin can be of any race; (1) Figures cover the Reno, NV Metropolitan Statistical Area
Source: U.S. Census Bureau, 2015-2019 American Community Survey 5-Year Estimates

Ancestry

Area	German	Irish	English	American	Italian	Polish	French[2]	Scottish	Dutch
City	12.8	10.8	9.1	3.9	6.1	1.7	2.6	2.2	1.1
MSA[1]	13.6	10.9	9.4	3.9	6.5	1.8	2.8	2.2	1.2
U.S.	13.3	9.7	7.2	6.2	5.1	2.8	2.3	1.7	1.2

Note: Figures are the percentage of the total population reporting a particular ancestry. The nine most commonly reported ancestries in the U.S. are shown. Figures include multiple ancestries (e.g. if a person reported being Irish and Italian, they were included in both columns); (1) Figures cover the Reno, NV Metropolitan Statistical Area; (2) Excludes Basque
Source: U.S. Census Bureau, 2015-2019 American Community Survey 5-Year Estimates

Foreign-born Population

Area	Any Foreign Country	Asia	Mexico	Europe	Caribbean	Central America[2]	South America	Africa	Canada
City	15.9	5.3	6.2	1.3	0.2	1.6	0.4	0.3	0.3
MSA[1]	14.0	3.9	6.1	1.1	0.2	1.5	0.4	0.3	0.3
U.S.	13.6	4.2	3.5	1.5	1.3	1.1	1.0	0.7	0.2

Percent of Population Born in
Note: (1) Figures cover the Reno, NV Metropolitan Statistical Area; (2) Excludes Mexico.
Source: U.S. Census Bureau, 2015-2019 American Community Survey 5-Year Estimates

Marital Status

Area	Never Married	Now Married[2]	Separated	Widowed	Divorced
City	35.5	42.5	2.2	4.8	14.9
MSA[1]	30.9	48.6	1.9	4.9	13.7
U.S.	33.4	48.1	1.9	5.8	10.9

Note: Figures are percentages and cover the population 15 years of age and older; (1) Figures cover the Reno, NV Metropolitan Statistical Area; (2) Excludes separated
Source: U.S. Census Bureau, 2015-2019 American Community Survey 5-Year Estimates

Disability by Age

Area	All Ages	Under 18 Years Old	18 to 64 Years Old	65 Years and Over
City	12.2	5.2	10.3	30.7
MSA[1]	12.1	4.7	9.9	30.7
U.S.	12.6	4.2	10.3	34.5

Note: Figures show percent of the civilian noninstitutionalized population that reported having a disability. Disability status is determined from six types of difficulty: vision, hearing, cognitive, ambulatory, self-care, and independent living. For children under 5 years old, hearing and vision difficulty are used to determine disability status. For children between the ages of 5 and 14, disability status is determined from hearing, vision, cognitive, ambulatory, and self-care difficulties. For people aged 15 years and older, they are considered to have a disability if they have difficulty with any one of the six difficulty types; Note: (1) Figures cover the Reno, NV Metropolitan Statistical Area
Source: U.S. Census Bureau, 2015-2019 American Community Survey 5-Year Estimates

Age

Area	Percent of Population									Median Age
	Under Age 5	Age 5–19	Age 20–34	Age 35–44	Age 45–54	Age 55–64	Age 65–74	Age 75–84	Age 85+	
City	6.2	17.8	24.7	12.6	11.7	12.2	9.3	4.1	1.4	35.8
MSA[1]	6.0	18.1	21.5	12.2	12.8	13.2	10.2	4.4	1.4	38.5
U.S.	6.1	19.1	20.7	12.6	13.0	12.9	9.1	4.6	1.9	38.1

Note: (1) Figures cover the Reno, NV Metropolitan Statistical Area
Source: U.S. Census Bureau, 2015-2019 American Community Survey 5-Year Estimates

Gender

Area	Males	Females	Males per 100 Females
City	124,568	121,932	102.2
MSA[1]	232,199	228,725	101.5
U.S.	159,886,919	164,810,876	97.0

Note: (1) Figures cover the Reno, NV Metropolitan Statistical Area
Source: U.S. Census Bureau, 2015-2019 American Community Survey 5-Year Estimates

Religious Groups by Family

Area	Catholic	Baptist	Non-Den.	Methodist[2]	Lutheran	LDS[3]	Pente-costal	Presby-terian[4]	Muslim[5]	Judaism
MSA[1]	14.3	1.5	3.2	0.9	0.8	4.6	2.0	0.4	0.1	0.2
U.S.	19.1	9.3	4.0	4.0	2.3	2.0	1.9	1.6	0.8	0.7

Note: Figures are the number of adherents as a percentage of the total population; (1) Figures cover the Reno, NV Metropolitan Statistical Area; (2) Methodist/Pietist; (3) Latter Day Saints; (4) Reformed; (5) Figures are estimates
Source: Association of Statisticians of American Religious Bodies, 2010 U.S. Religion Census: Religious Congregations & Membership Study

Religious Groups by Tradition

Area	Catholic	Evangelical Protestant	Mainline Protestant	Other Tradition	Black Protestant	Orthodox
MSA[1]	14.3	7.7	1.9	5.1	0.2	0.1
U.S.	19.1	16.2	7.3	4.3	1.6	0.3

Note: Figures are the number of adherents as a percentage of the total population; (1) Figures cover the Reno, NV Metropolitan Statistical Area
Source: Association of Statisticians of American Religious Bodies, 2010 U.S. Religion Census: Religious Congregations & Membership Study

ECONOMY

Gross Metropolitan Product

Area	2017	2018	2019	2020	Rank[2]
MSA[1]	26.8	28.8	30.8	32.3	99

Note: Figures are in billions of dollars; (1) Figures cover the Reno, NV Metropolitan Statistical Area; (2) Rank is based on 2018 data and ranges from 1 to 381
Source: U.S. Conference of Mayors, U.S. Metro Economies: GMP & Employment 2018-2020, September 2019

Economic Growth

Area	2015-17 (%)	2018 (%)	2019 (%)	2020 (%)	Rank[2]
MSA[1]	4.3	5.3	4.9	2.5	27
U.S.	1.9	2.9	2.3	2.1	–

Note: Figures are real gross metropolitan product (GMP) growth rates and represent average annual percent change; (1) Figures cover the Reno, NV Metropolitan Statistical Area; (2) Rank is based on 2017 2-year average annual percent change and ranges from 1 to 381
Source: U.S. Conference of Mayors, U.S. Metro Economies: GMP & Employment 2018-2020, September 2019

Metropolitan Area Exports

Area	2014	2015	2016	2017	2018	2019	Rank[2]
MSA[1]	2,138.9	1,943.3	2,382.1	2,517.3	2,631.7	2,598.3	86

Note: Figures are in millions of dollars; (1) Figures cover the Reno, NV Metropolitan Statistical Area; (2) Rank is based on 2019 data and ranges from 1 to 386
Source: U.S. Department of Commerce, International Trade Administration, Office of Trade and Economic Analysis, Industry and Analysis, Exports by Metropolitan Area, data extracted March 24, 2021

Building Permits

Area	Single-Family			Multi-Family			Total		
	2018	2019	Pct. Chg.	2018	2019	Pct. Chg.	2018	2019	Pct. Chg.
City	1,351	1,176	-13.0	1,883	2,144	13.9	3,234	3,320	2.7
MSA[1]	2,255	2,157	-4.3	2,195	3,106	41.5	4,450	5,263	18.3
U.S.	855,300	862,100	0.7	473,500	523,900	10.6	1,328,800	1,386,000	4.3

Note: (1) Figures cover the Reno, NV Metropolitan Statistical Area; Figures represent new, privately-owned housing units authorized (unadjusted data); All permit data are based on estimates with imputation
Source: U.S. Census Bureau, Manufacturing, Mining, and Construction Statistics, Building Permits, 2018, 2019

Bankruptcy Filings

Area	Business Filings			Nonbusiness Filings		
	2019	2020	% Chg.	2019	2020	% Chg.
Washoe County	34	44	29.4	960	765	-20.3
U.S.	22,780	21,655	-4.9	752,160	522,808	-30.5

Note: Business filings include Chapter 7, Chapter 9, Chapter 11, Chapter 12, Chapter 13, Chapter 15, and Section 304; Nonbusiness filings include Chapter 7, Chapter 11, and Chapter 13
Source: Administrative Office of the U.S. Courts, Business and Nonbusiness Bankruptcy, County Cases Commenced by Chapter of the Bankruptcy Code, During the 12-Month Period Ending December 31, 2019 and Business and Nonbusiness Bankruptcy, County Cases Commenced by Chapter of the Bankruptcy Code, During the 12-Month Period Ending December 31, 2020

Housing Vacancy Rates

Area	Gross Vacancy Rate[2] (%)			Year-Round Vacancy Rate[3] (%)			Rental Vacancy Rate[4] (%)			Homeowner Vacancy Rate[5] (%)		
	2018	2019	2020	2018	2019	2020	2018	2019	2020	2018	2019	2020
MSA[1]	n/a	n/a	n/a	n/a	n/a	n/a	n/a	n/a	n/a	n/a	n/a	n/a
U.S.	12.3	12.0	10.6	9.7	9.5	8.2	6.9	6.7	6.3	1.5	1.4	1.0

Note: (1) Figures cover the Reno, NV Metropolitan Statistical Area; (2) The percentage of the total housing inventory that is vacant; (3) The percentage of the housing inventory (excluding seasonal units) that is year-round vacant; (4) The percentage of rental inventory that is vacant for rent; (5) The percentage of homeowner inventory that is vacant for sale; n/a not available
Source: U.S. Census Bureau, Housing Vacancies and Homeownership Annual Statistics: 2018, 2019, 2020

INCOME

Income

Area	Per Capita ($)	Median Household ($)	Average Household ($)
City	34,475	58,790	81,700
MSA[1]	36,087	64,801	89,057
U.S.	34,103	62,843	88,607

Note: (1) Figures cover the Reno, NV Metropolitan Statistical Area
Source: U.S. Census Bureau, 2015-2019 American Community Survey 5-Year Estimates

Household Income Distribution

Area	Percent of Households Earning							
	Under $15,000	$15,000 -$24,999	$25,000 -$34,999	$35,000 -$49,999	$50,000 -$74,999	$75,000 -$99,999	$100,000 -$149,999	$150,000 and up
City	9.2	9.5	9.5	14.5	18.6	12.7	14.5	11.5
MSA[1]	7.9	8.4	8.5	13.2	18.9	13.8	16.3	13.1
U.S.	10.3	8.9	8.9	12.3	17.2	12.7	15.1	14.5

Note: (1) Figures cover the Reno, NV Metropolitan Statistical Area
Source: U.S. Census Bureau, 2015-2019 American Community Survey 5-Year Estimates

Poverty Rate

Area	All Ages	Under 18 Years Old	18 to 64 Years Old	65 Years and Over
City	13.5	15.8	14.0	8.2
MSA[1]	11.2	14.0	11.2	7.7
U.S.	13.4	18.5	12.6	9.3

Note: Figures are percentage of people whose income during the past 12 months was below the poverty level;
(1) Figures cover the Reno, NV Metropolitan Statistical Area
Source: U.S. Census Bureau, 2015-2019 American Community Survey 5-Year Estimates

CITY FINANCES

City Government Finances

Component	2017 ($000)	2017 ($ per capita)
Total Revenues	392,343	1,625
Total Expenditures	348,525	1,443
Debt Outstanding	621,213	2,573
Cash and Securities[1]	367,828	1,523

Note: (1) Cash and security holdings of a government at the close of its fiscal year,
including those of its dependent agencies, utilities, and liquor stores.
Source: U.S. Census Bureau, State & Local Government Finances 2017

City Government Revenue by Source

Source	2017 ($000)	2017 ($ per capita)	2017 (%)
General Revenue			
From Federal Government	5,528	23	1.4
From State Government	80,118	332	20.4
From Local Governments	4,891	20	1.2
Taxes			
Property	65,039	269	16.6
Sales and Gross Receipts	51,008	211	13.0
Personal Income	0	0	0.0
Corporate Income	0	0	0.0
Motor Vehicle License	0	0	0.0
Other Taxes	30,436	126	7.8
Current Charges	123,806	513	31.6
Liquor Store	0	0	0.0
Utility	0	0	0.0
Employee Retirement	0	0	0.0

Source: U.S. Census Bureau, State & Local Government Finances 2017

City Government Expenditures by Function

Function	2017 ($000)	2017 ($ per capita)	2017 (%)
General Direct Expenditures			
Air Transportation	0	0	0.0
Corrections	0	0	0.0
Education	0	0	0.0
Employment Security Administration	0	0	0.0
Financial Administration	4,754	19	1.4
Fire Protection	46,894	194	13.5
General Public Buildings	0	0	0.0
Governmental Administration, Other	20,285	84	5.8
Health	0	0	0.0
Highways	17,275	71	5.0
Hospitals	0	0	0.0
Housing and Community Development	11,112	46	3.2
Interest on General Debt	15,879	65	4.6
Judicial and Legal	10,674	44	3.1
Libraries	0	0	0.0
Parking	757	3	0.2
Parks and Recreation	11,367	47	3.3
Police Protection	63,498	263	18.2
Public Welfare	0	0	0.0
Sewerage	60,919	252	17.5
Solid Waste Management	0	0	0.0
Veterans' Services	0	0	0.0
Liquor Store	0	0	0.0
Utility	0	0	0.0
Employee Retirement	0	0	0.0

Source: U.S. Census Bureau, State & Local Government Finances 2017

EMPLOYMENT

Labor Force and Employment

Area	Civilian Labor Force			Workers Employed		
	Dec. 2019	Dec. 2020	% Chg.	Dec. 2019	Dec. 2020	% Chg.
City	139,960	134,597	-3.8	136,175	127,830	-6.1
MSA[1]	261,692	251,522	-3.9	254,486	238,896	-6.1
U.S.	164,007,000	160,017,000	-2.4	158,504,000	149,613,000	-5.6

Note: Data is not seasonally adjusted and covers workers 16 years of age and older; (1) Figures cover the
Reno, NV Metropolitan Statistical Area
Source: Bureau of Labor Statistics, Local Area Unemployment Statistics

Unemployment Rate

Area	2020											
	Jan.	Feb.	Mar.	Apr.	May	Jun.	Jul.	Aug.	Sep.	Oct.	Nov.	Dec.
City	3.4	3.2	5.5	20.9	16.9	9.1	8.5	7.6	7.0	6.5	5.7	5.0
MSA[1]	3.4	3.2	5.6	20.4	16.0	8.7	8.2	7.3	6.7	6.3	5.6	5.0
U.S.	4.0	3.8	4.5	14.4	13.0	11.2	10.5	8.5	7.7	6.6	6.4	6.5

Note: Data is not seasonally adjusted and covers workers 16 years of age and older; (1) Figures cover the
Reno, NV Metropolitan Statistical Area
Source: Bureau of Labor Statistics, Local Area Unemployment Statistics

Average Wages

Occupation	$/Hr.	Occupation	$/Hr.
Accountants and Auditors	31.30	Maintenance and Repair Workers	23.30
Automotive Mechanics	25.40	Marketing Managers	55.20
Bookkeepers	21.40	Network and Computer Systems Admin.	41.50
Carpenters	25.20	Nurses, Licensed Practical	30.40
Cashiers	12.10	Nurses, Registered	38.60
Computer Programmers	44.10	Nursing Assistants	15.70
Computer Systems Analysts	43.90	Office Clerks, General	19.50
Computer User Support Specialists	24.90	Physical Therapists	43.30
Construction Laborers	20.60	Physicians	n/a
Cooks, Restaurant	14.80	Plumbers, Pipefitters and Steamfitters	32.90
Customer Service Representatives	17.40	Police and Sheriff's Patrol Officers	n/a
Dentists	99.90	Postal Service Mail Carriers	25.60
Electricians	26.90	Real Estate Sales Agents	18.90
Engineers, Electrical	43.80	Retail Salespersons	16.30
Fast Food and Counter Workers	10.30	Sales Representatives, Technical/Scientific	50.40
Financial Managers	63.60	Secretaries, Exc. Legal/Medical/Executive	20.90
First-Line Supervisors of Office Workers	28.10	Security Guards	18.10
General and Operations Managers	58.60	Surgeons	n/a
Hairdressers/Cosmetologists	14.30	Teacher Assistants, Exc. Postsecondary*	10.40
Home Health and Personal Care Aides	12.00	Teachers, Secondary School, Exc. Sp. Ed.*	25.60
Janitors and Cleaners	14.40	Telemarketers	14.60
Landscaping/Groundskeeping Workers	15.80	Truck Drivers, Heavy/Tractor-Trailer	25.20
Lawyers	59.60	Truck Drivers, Light/Delivery Services	21.40
Maids and Housekeeping Cleaners	14.00	Waiters and Waitresses	11.40

Note: Wage data covers the Reno, NV Metropolitan Statistical Area; (*) Hourly wages were calculated from
annual wage data based on a 40 hour work week; n/a not available.
Source: Bureau of Labor Statistics, Metro Area Occupational Employment & Wage Estimates, May 2020

Employment by Industry

Sector	MSA[1]		U.S.
	Number of Employees	Percent of Total	Percent of Total
Construction	17,600	7.2	5.1
Education and Health Services	28,100	11.5	16.3
Financial Activities	11,100	4.6	6.1
Government	30,400	12.5	15.2
Information	3,000	1.2	1.9
Leisure and Hospitality	30,100	12.4	9.0
Manufacturing	25,200	10.4	8.5
Mining and Logging	500	0.2	0.4
Other Services	5,800	2.4	3.8
Professional and Business Services	35,100	14.4	14.4
Retail Trade	24,100	9.9	10.9
Transportation, Warehousing, and Utilities	22,700	9.3	4.6
Wholesale Trade	9,700	4.0	3.9

Note: Figures are non-farm employment as of December 2020. Figures are not seasonally adjusted and include
workers 16 years of age and older; (1) Figures cover the Reno, NV Metropolitan Statistical Area
Source: Bureau of Labor Statistics, Current Employment Statistics, Employment, Hours, and Earnings

Employment by Occupation

Occupation Classification	City (%)	MSA[1] (%)	U.S. (%)
Management, Business, Science, and Arts	34.8	34.1	38.5
Natural Resources, Construction, and Maintenance	7.6	8.8	8.9
Production, Transportation, and Material Moving	13.8	14.2	13.2
Sales and Office	22.1	22.9	21.6
Service	21.6	20.0	17.8

Note: Figures cover employed civilians 16 years of age and older; (1) Figures cover the Reno, NV Metropolitan Statistical Area
Source: U.S. Census Bureau, 2015-2019 American Community Survey 5-Year Estimates

Occupations with Greatest Projected Employment Growth: 2020 – 2022

Occupation[1]	2020 Employment	2022 Projected Employment	Numeric Employment Change	Percent Employment Change
Waiters and Waitresses	20,720	32,720	12,000	57.9
Combined Food Preparation and Serving Workers, Including Fast Food	25,450	36,790	11,340	44.6
Gaming Dealers	10,070	18,250	8,180	81.2
Maids and Housekeeping Cleaners	15,980	23,820	7,840	49.1
Cooks, Restaurant	12,590	20,120	7,530	59.8
Retail Salespersons	34,680	42,100	7,420	21.4
Janitors and Cleaners, Except Maids and Housekeeping Cleaners	21,230	28,560	7,330	34.5
Laborers and Freight, Stock, and Material Movers, Hand	36,120	41,930	5,810	16.1
Security Guards	15,710	20,810	5,100	32.5
Bartenders	8,290	13,260	4,970	60.0

Note: Projections cover Nevada; (1) Sorted by numeric employment change
Source: www.projectionscentral.com, State Occupational Projections, 2020–2022 Short-Term Projections

Fastest-Growing Occupations: 2020 – 2022

Occupation[1]	2020 Employment	2022 Projected Employment	Numeric Employment Change	Percent Employment Change
Bus Drivers, Transit and Intercity	940	2,270	1,330	141.5
Athletes and Sports Competitors	50	100	50	100.0
Entertainment Attendants and Related Workers, All Other	150	280	130	86.7
Gaming Service Workers, All Other	1,510	2,760	1,250	82.8
Gaming Surveillance Officers and Gaming Investigators	390	710	320	82.1
Gaming Cage Workers	1,320	2,400	1,080	81.8
Gaming Dealers	10,070	18,250	8,180	81.2
Gaming and Sports Book Writers and Runners	820	1,480	660	80.5
Baggage Porters and Bellhops	1,040	1,860	820	78.8
Agents and Business Managers of Artists, Performers, and Athletes	140	250	110	78.6

Note: Projections cover Nevada; (1) Sorted by percent employment change and excludes occupations with numeric employment change less than 50
Source: www.projectionscentral.com, State Occupational Projections, 2020–2022 Short-Term Projections

TAXES

State Corporate Income Tax Rates

State	Tax Rate (%)	Income Brackets ($)	Num. of Brackets	Financial Institution Tax Rate (%)[a]	Federal Income Tax Ded.
Nevada	None	–	–	–	–

Note: Tax rates as of January 1, 2021; (a) Rates listed are the corporate income tax rate applied to financial institutions or excise taxes based on income. Some states have other taxes based upon the value of deposits or shares.
Source: Federation of Tax Administrators, State Corporate Income Tax Rates, January 1, 2021

State Individual Income Tax Rates

State	Tax Rate (%)	Income Brackets ($)	Personal Exemptions ($)			Standard Ded. ($)	
			Single	Married	Depend.	Single	Married
Nevada					– No state income tax –		

Note: Tax rates as of January 1, 2021; Local- and county-level taxes are not included
Source: Federation of Tax Administrators, State Individual Income Tax Rates, January 1, 2021

Various State Sales and Excise Tax Rates

State	State Sales Tax (%)	Gasoline[1] (¢/gal.)	Cigarette[2] ($/pack)	Spirits[3] ($/gal.)	Wine[4] ($/gal.)	Beer[5] ($/gal.)	Recreational Marijuana (%)
Nevada	6.85	50.48	1.8	3.6	0.7	0.16	(j)

Note: All tax rates as of January 1, 2021; (1) The American Petroleum Institute has developed a methodology for determining the average tax rate on a gallon of fuel. Rates may include any of the following: excise taxes, environmental fees, storage tank fees, other fees or taxes, general sales tax, and local taxes; (2) The federal excise tax of $1.0066 per pack and local taxes are not included; (3) Rates are those applicable to off-premise sales of 40% alcohol by volume (a.b.v.) distilled spirits in 750ml containers. Local excise taxes are excluded; (4) Rates are those applicable to off-premise sales of 11% a.b.v. non-carbonated wine in 750ml containers; (5) Rates are those applicable to off-premise sales of 4.7% a.b.v. beer in 12 ounce containers; (j) 15% excise tax (fair market value at wholesale); 10% excise tax (retail price)
Source: Tax Foundation, 2021 Facts & Figures: How Does Your State Compare?

State Business Tax Climate Index Rankings

State	Overall Rank	Corporate Tax Rank	Individual Income Tax Rank	Sales Tax Rank	Property Tax Rank	Unemployment Insurance Tax Rank
Nevada	7	25	5	44	5	47

Note: The index is a measure of how each state's tax laws affect economic performance. The lower the rank, the more favorable a state's tax system is for business. States without a given tax are given a ranking of 1. The scores/rankings for the District of Columbia do not affect other states. The 2021 index represents the tax climate as of July 1, 2020.
Source: Tax Foundation, State Business Tax Climate Index 2021

TRANSPORTATION

Means of Transportation to Work

Area	Car/Truck/Van		Public Transportation			Bicycle	Walked	Other Means	Worked at Home
	Drove Alone	Car-pooled	Bus	Subway	Railroad				
City	75.2	12.6	2.3	0.0	0.0	0.8	3.6	1.1	4.4
MSA[1]	77.2	12.0	1.8	0.0	0.0	0.6	2.6	1.1	4.7
U.S.	76.3	9.0	2.4	1.9	0.6	0.5	2.7	1.4	5.2

Note: Figures are percentages and cover workers 16 years of age and older; (1) Figures cover the Reno, NV Metropolitan Statistical Area
Source: U.S. Census Bureau, 2015-2019 American Community Survey 5-Year Estimates

Travel Time to Work

Area	Less Than 10 Minutes	10 to 19 Minutes	20 to 29 Minutes	30 to 44 Minutes	45 to 59 Minutes	60 to 89 Minutes	90 Minutes or More
City	14.4	43.5	22.1	12.1	3.7	2.7	1.5
MSA[1]	12.1	37.7	25.0	16.6	4.2	2.7	1.7
U.S.	12.2	28.4	20.8	20.8	8.3	6.4	2.9

Note: Note: Figures are percentages and include workers 16 years old and over; (1) Figures cover the Reno, NV Metropolitan Statistical Area
Source: U.S. Census Bureau, 2015-2019 American Community Survey 5-Year Estimates

Key Congestion Measures

Measure	1982	1992	2002	2012	2017
Annual Hours of Delay, Total (000)	n/a	n/a	n/a	n/a	10,955
Annual Hours of Delay, Per Auto Commuter	n/a	n/a	n/a	n/a	26
Annual Congestion Cost, Total (million $)	n/a	n/a	n/a	n/a	226
Annual Congestion Cost, Per Auto Commuter ($)	n/a	n/a	n/a	n/a	541

Note: n/a not available
Source: Texas A&M Transportation Institute, 2019 Urban Mobility Report

Freeway Travel Time Index

Measure	1982	1987	1992	1997	2002	2007	2012	2017
Urban Area Index[1]	n/a	n/a	n/a	n/a	n/a	n/a	n/a	1.13
Urban Area Rank[1,2]	n/a	n/a	n/a	n/a	n/a	n/a	n/a	n/a

Note: Freeway Travel Time Index—the ratio of travel time in the peak period to the travel time at free-flow conditions. For example, a value of 1.30 indicates a 20-minute free-flow trip takes 26 minutes in the peak (20 minutes x 1.30 = 26 minutes); (1) Covers the Reno NV-CA urban area; (2) Rank is based on 101 larger urban areas (#1 = highest travel time index); n/a not available
Source: Texas A&M Transportation Institute, 2019 Urban Mobility Report

Public Transportation

Agency Name / Mode of Transportation	Vehicles Operated in Maximum Service[1]	Annual Unlinked Passenger Trips[2] (in thous.)	Annual Passenger Miles[3] (in thous.)
Regional Transportation Commission of Washoe County (RTC)			
Bus (purchased transportation)	54	7,166.7	21,099.5
Commuter Bus (purchased transportation)	3	30.7	787.4
Demand Response (purchased transportation)	53	217.3	1,742.0
Demand Response Taxi (purchased transportation)	7	9.6	59.9
Vanpool (purchased transportation)	176	439.3	16,123.0

Note: (1) Number of revenue vehicles operated by the given mode and type of service to meet the annual maximum service requirement. This is the revenue vehicle count during the peak season of the year; on the week and day that maximum service is provided. Vehicles operated in maximum service (VOMS) exclude atypical days and one-time special events; (2) Number of passengers who boarded public transportation vehicles. Passengers are counted each time they board a vehicle no matter how many vehicles they use to travel from their origin to their destination. (3) Sum of the distances ridden by all passengers during the entire fiscal year.
Source: Federal Transit Administration, National Transit Database, 2019

Air Transportation

Airport Name and Code / Type of Service	Passenger Airlines[1]	Passenger Enplanements	Freight Carriers[2]	Freight (lbs)
Reno-Tahoe International (RNO)				
Domestic service (U.S. carriers - 2020)	18	961,901	9	89,089,775
International service (U.S. carriers - 2019)	3	496	0	0

Note: (1) Includes all U.S.-based major, minor and commuter airlines that carried at least one passenger during the year; (2) Includes all U.S.-based airlines and freight carriers that transported at least one pound of freight during the year.
Source: Bureau of Transportation Statistics, The Intermodal Transportation Database, Air Carriers: T-100 Domestic Market (U.S. Carriers), 2020; Bureau of Transportation Statistics, The Intermodal Transportation Database, Air Carriers: T-100 International Market (U.S. Carriers), 2019

BUSINESSES

Major Business Headquarters

Company Name	Industry	Rankings	
		Fortune[1]	Forbes[2]
No companies listed	-	-	-

Note: (1) Companies that produce a 10-K are ranked 1 to 500 based on 2019 revenue; (2) All private companies with at least $2 billion in annual revenue through the end of their most current fiscal year are ranked 1 to 219; companies listed are headquartered in the city; dashes indicate no ranking
Source: Fortune, "Fortune 500," June/July 2020; Forbes, "America's Largest Private Companies," 2020

Living Environment

COST OF LIVING

Cost of Living Index

Composite Index	Groceries	Housing	Utilities	Trans-portation	Health Care	Misc. Goods/Services
112.9	112.2	126.9	84.3	128.6	113.3	105.7

Note: The Cost of Living Index measures regional differences in the cost of consumer goods and services, excluding taxes and non-consumer expenditures, for professional and managerial households in the top income quintile. It is based on more than 50,000 prices covering almost 60 different items for which prices are collected three times a year by chambers of commerce, economic development organizations or university applied economic centers in each participating urban area. The numbers shown should be read as a percentage above or below the national average of 100. For example, a value of 115.4 in the groceries column indicates that grocery prices are 15.4% higher than the national average. Small differences in the index numbers should not be interpreted as significant; Figures cover the Reno-Sparks NV urban area.
Source: The Council for Community and Economic Research, Cost of Living Index, 2020

Grocery Prices

Area[1]	T-Bone Steak ($/pound)	Frying Chicken ($/pound)	Whole Milk ($/half gal.)	Eggs ($/dozen)	Orange Juice ($/64 oz.)	Coffee ($/11.5 oz.)
City[2]	12.84	1.58	2.93	2.07	3.36	5.86
Avg.	11.78	1.39	2.05	1.47	3.57	4.34
Min.	8.03	0.94	1.03	0.74	2.94	3.02
Max.	15.86	2.65	4.31	3.77	5.44	8.69

Note: (1) Values for the local area are compared with the average, minimum and maximum values for all 284 areas in the Cost of Living Index; (2) Figures cover the Reno-Sparks NV urban area; **T-Bone Steak** (price per pound); **Frying Chicken** (price per pound, whole fryer); **Whole Milk** (half gallon carton); **Eggs** (price per dozen, Grade A, large); **Orange Juice** (64 oz. Tropicana or Florida Natural); **Coffee** (11.5 oz. can, vacuum-packed, Maxwell House, Hills Bros, or Folgers).
Source: The Council for Community and Economic Research, Cost of Living Index, 2020

Housing and Utility Costs

Area[1]	New Home Price ($)	Apartment Rent ($/month)	All Electric ($/month)	Part Electric ($/month)	Other Energy ($/month)	Telephone ($/month)
City[2]	489,573	1,330	-	82.05	42.67	177.90
Avg.	368,594	1,168	170.86	100.47	65.28	184.30
Min.	190,567	502	91.58	31.42	26.08	169.60
Max.	2,227,806	4,738	470.38	280.31	280.06	206.50

Note: (1) Values for the local area are compared with the average, minimum and maximum values for all 284 areas in the Cost of Living Index; (2) Figures cover the Reno-Sparks NV urban area; **New Home Price** (2,400 sf living area, 8,000 sf lot, in urban area with full utilities); **Apartment Rent** (950 sf 2 bedroom/1.5 or 2 bath, unfurnished, excluding all utilities except water); **All Electric** (average monthly cost for an all-electric home); **Part Electric** (average monthly cost for a part-electric home); **Other Energy** (average monthly cost for natural gas, fuel oil, coal, wood, and any other forms of energy except electricity); **Telephone** (price includes the base monthly rate plus taxes and fees for three lines of mobile phone service).
Source: The Council for Community and Economic Research, Cost of Living Index, 2020

Health Care, Transportation, and Other Costs

Area[1]	Doctor ($/visit)	Dentist ($/visit)	Optometrist ($/visit)	Gasoline ($/gallon)	Beauty Salon ($/visit)	Men's Shirt ($)
City[2]	155.00	114.56	117.17	2.98	40.13	21.17
Avg.	115.44	99.32	108.10	2.21	39.27	31.37
Min.	36.68	59.00	51.36	1.71	19.00	11.00
Max.	219.00	153.10	250.97	3.46	82.05	58.33

Note: (1) Values for the local area are compared with the average, minimum and maximum values for all 284 areas in the Cost of Living Index; (2) Figures cover the Reno-Sparks NV urban area; **Doctor** (general practitioners routine exam of an established patient); **Dentist** (adult teeth cleaning and periodic oral examination); **Optometrist** (full vision eye exam for established adult patient); **Gasoline** (one gallon regular unleaded, national brand, including all taxes, cash price at self-service pump if available); **Beauty Salon** (woman's shampoo, trim, and blow-dry); **Men's Shirt** (cotton/polyester dress shirt, pinpoint weave, long sleeves).
Source: The Council for Community and Economic Research, Cost of Living Index, 2020

HOUSING

Homeownership Rate

Area	2012 (%)	2013 (%)	2014 (%)	2015 (%)	2016 (%)	2017 (%)	2018 (%)	2019 (%)	2020 (%)
MSA[1]	n/a	n/a	n/a	n/a	n/a	n/a	n/a	n/a	n/a
U.S.	65.4	65.1	64.5	63.7	63.4	63.9	64.4	64.6	66.6

Note: (1) Figures cover the Reno, NV Metropolitan Statistical Area; n/a not available
Source: U.S. Census Bureau, Housing Vacancies and Homeownership Annual Statistics: 2012-2020

House Price Index (HPI)

Area	National Ranking[2]	Quarterly Change (%)	One-Year Change (%)	Five-Year Change (%)	Since 1991Q1 (%)
MSA[1]	96	2.61	6.81	48.07	229.64
U.S.[3]	–	3.81	10.77	38.99	205.12

Note: The HPI is a weighted repeat sales index. It measures average price changes in repeat sales or refinancings on the same properties. This information is obtained by reviewing repeat mortgage transactions on single-family properties whose mortgages have been purchased or securitized by Fannie Mae or Freddie Mac since January 1975; (1) Figures cover the Reno, NV Metropolitan Statistical Area; (2) Rankings are based on annual percentage change for all metro areas containing at least 15,000 transactions over the last 10 years and ranges from 1 to 253; (3) figures based on a weighted average of Census Division estimates using a seasonally adjusted, purchase-only index; all figures are for the period ending December 31, 2020
Source: Federal Housing Finance Agency, Change in Metropolitan Area House Price Indexes, April 7, 2021

Median Single-Family Home Prices

Area	2018	2019	2020p	Percent Change 2019 to 2020
MSA[1]	383.1	393.9	440.8	11.9
U.S. Average	261.6	274.6	299.9	9.2

Note: Figures are median sales prices of existing single-family homes in thousands of dollars; (p) preliminary; (1) Figures cover the Reno, NV Metropolitan Statistical Area
Source: National Association of Realtors, Median Sales Price of Existing Single-Family Homes for Metropolitan Areas, 4th Quarter 2020

Qualifying Income Based on Median Sales Price of Existing Single-Family Homes

Area	With 5% Down ($)	With 10% Down ($)	With 20% Down ($)
MSA[1]	88,632	83,967	74,637
U.S. Average	59,266	56,147	49,908

Note: Figures are preliminary; Qualifying income is based on a mortgage rate of 2.81%. Monthly principal and interest payment is limited to 25% of income; (1) Figures cover the Reno, NV Metropolitan Statistical Area
Source: National Association of Realtors, Qualifying Income Based on Median Sales Price of Existing Single-Family Homes for Metropolitan Areas, 4th Quarter 2020

Home Value Distribution

Area	Under $50,000	$50,000 -$99,999	$100,000 -$149,999	$150,000 -$199,999	$200,000 -$299,999	$300,000 -$499,999	$500,000 -$999,999	$1,000,000 or more
City	4.1	2.9	3.7	7.5	22.3	43.2	13.7	2.5
MSA[1]	4.0	2.8	4.2	7.5	23.6	38.4	15.4	4.1
U.S.	6.9	12.0	13.3	14.0	19.6	19.3	11.4	3.4

Note: Figures are percentages and cover owner-occupied housing units; (1) Figures cover the Reno, NV Metropolitan Statistical Area
Source: U.S. Census Bureau, 2015-2019 American Community Survey 5-Year Estimates

Year Housing Structure Built

Area	2010 or Later	2000 -2009	1990 -1999	1980 -1989	1970 -1979	1960 -1969	1950 -1959	1940 -1949	Before 1940	Median Year
City	6.2	19.7	19.2	13.9	18.3	9.5	7.2	3.0	3.0	1987
MSA[1]	5.5	21.1	20.6	15.2	18.9	8.9	5.3	2.2	2.3	1988
U.S.	5.2	14.0	13.9	13.4	15.2	10.6	10.3	4.9	12.6	1978

Note: Figures are percentages except for Median Year; Note: (1) Figures cover the Reno, NV Metropolitan Statistical Area
Source: U.S. Census Bureau, 2015-2019 American Community Survey 5-Year Estimates

Gross Monthly Rent

Area	Under $500	$500 -$999	$1,000 -$1,499	$1,500 -$1,999	$2,000 -$2,499	$2,500 -$2,999	$3,000 and up	Median ($)
City	5.6	42.2	33.7	14.3	3.2	0.5	0.6	1,029
MSA[1]	4.9	39.3	34.7	15.9	3.7	0.8	0.8	1,074
U.S.	9.4	36.2	30.0	14.0	5.6	2.4	2.4	1,062

Note: Figures are percentages except for Median; Gross rent is the contract rent plus the estimated average monthly cost of utilities (electricity, gas, and water and sewer) and fuels (oil, coal, kerosene, wood, etc.) if these are paid by the renter (or paid for the renter by someone else); (1) Figures cover the Reno, NV Metropolitan Statistical Area
Source: U.S. Census Bureau, 2015-2019 American Community Survey 5-Year Estimates

HEALTH

Health Risk Factors

Category	MSA[1] (%)	U.S. (%)
Adults aged 18–64 who have any kind of health care coverage	87.9	87.3
Adults who reported being in good or better health	81.1	82.4
Adults who have been told they have high blood cholesterol	34.9	33.0
Adults who have been told they have high blood pressure	31.1	32.3
Adults who are current smokers	14.7	17.1
Adults who currently use E-cigarettes	6.8	4.6
Adults who currently use chewing tobacco, snuff, or snus	4.2	4.0
Adults who are heavy drinkers[2]	9.2	6.3
Adults who are binge drinkers[3]	20.6	17.4
Adults who are overweight (BMI 25.0 - 29.9)	37.3	35.3
Adults who are obese (BMI 30.0 - 99.8)	24.0	31.3
Adults who participated in any physical activities in the past month	78.5	74.4
Adults who always or nearly always wears a seat belt	95.0	94.3

Note: (1) Figures cover the Reno, NV Metropolitan Statistical Area; (2) Heavy drinkers are classified as adult men having more than 14 drinks per week and adult women having more than 7 drinks per week; (3) Binge drinkers are classified as males having five or more drinks on one occasion or females having four or more drinks on one occasion
Source: Centers for Disease Control and Prevention, Behaviorial Risk Factor Surveillance System, SMART: Selected Metropolitan Area Risk Trends, 2017

Acute and Chronic Health Conditions

Category	MSA[1] (%)	U.S. (%)
Adults who have ever been told they had a heart attack	5.0	4.2
Adults who have ever been told they have angina or coronary heart disease	3.6	3.9
Adults who have ever been told they had a stroke	4.0	3.0
Adults who have ever been told they have asthma	15.2	14.2
Adults who have ever been told they have arthritis	24.6	24.9
Adults who have ever been told they have diabetes[2]	7.7	10.5
Adults who have ever been told they had skin cancer	8.9	6.2
Adults who have ever been told they had any other types of cancer	7.2	7.1
Adults who have ever been told they have COPD	7.2	6.5
Adults who have ever been told they have kidney disease	3.0	3.0
Adults who have ever been told they have a form of depression	19.5	20.5

Note: (1) Figures cover the Reno, NV Metropolitan Statistical Area; (2) Figures do not include pregnancy-related, borderline, or pre-diabetes
Source: Centers for Disease Control and Prevention, Behaviorial Risk Factor Surveillance System, SMART: Selected Metropolitan Area Risk Trends, 2017

Health Screening and Vaccination Rates

Category	MSA[1] (%)	U.S. (%)
Adults aged 65+ who have had flu shot within the past year	56.1	60.7
Adults aged 65+ who have ever had a pneumonia vaccination	80.8	75.4
Adults who have ever been tested for HIV	40.6	36.1
Adults who have ever had the shingles or zoster vaccine?	31.0	28.9
Adults who have had their blood cholesterol checked within the last five years	86.6	85.9

Note: n/a not available; (1) Figures cover the Reno, NV Metropolitan Statistical Area.
Source: Centers for Disease Control and Prevention, Behaviorial Risk Factor Surveillance System, SMART: Selected Metropolitan Area Risk Trends, 2017

Disability Status

Category	MSA[1] (%)	U.S. (%)
Adults who reported being deaf	6.5	6.7
Are you blind or have serious difficulty seeing, even when wearing glasses?	4.4	4.5
Are you limited in any way in any of your usual activities due of arthritis?	12.3	12.9
Do you have difficulty doing errands alone?	6.0	6.8
Do you have difficulty dressing or bathing?	3.2	3.6
Do you have serious difficulty concentrating/remembering/making decisions?	10.8	10.7
Do you have serious difficulty walking or climbing stairs?	11.2	13.6

Note: (1) Figures cover the Reno, NV Metropolitan Statistical Area.
Source: Centers for Disease Control and Prevention, Behaviorial Risk Factor Surveillance System, SMART: Selected Metropolitan Area Risk Trends, 2017

Mortality Rates for the Top 10 Causes of Death in the U.S.

ICD-10[a] Sub-Chapter	ICD-10[a] Code	Age-Adjusted Mortality Rate[1] per 100,000 population	
		County[2]	U.S.
Malignant neoplasms	C00-C97	137.5	149.2
Ischaemic heart diseases	I20-I25	118.6	90.5
Other forms of heart disease	I30-I51	35.7	52.2
Chronic lower respiratory diseases	J40-J47	47.3	39.6
Other degenerative diseases of the nervous system	G30-G31	31.0	37.6
Cerebrovascular diseases	I60-I69	39.0	37.2
Other external causes of accidental injury	W00-X59	45.0	36.1
Organic, including symptomatic, mental disorders	F01-F09	17.2	29.4
Hypertensive diseases	I10-I15	28.5	24.1
Diabetes mellitus	E10-E14	20.6	21.5

Note: (a) ICD-10 = International Classification of Diseases 10th Revision; (1) Mortality rates are a three-year average covering 2017-2019; (2) Figures cover Washoe County.
Source: Centers for Disease Control and Prevention, National Center for Health Statistics. Underlying Cause of Death 1999-2019 on CDC WONDER Online Database

Mortality Rates for Selected Causes of Death

ICD-10[a] Sub-Chapter	ICD-10[a] Code	Age-Adjusted Mortality Rate[1] per 100,000 population	
		County[2]	U.S.
Assault	X85-Y09	4.5	6.0
Diseases of the liver	K70-K76	18.4	14.4
Human immunodeficiency virus (HIV) disease	B20-B24	1.5	1.5
Influenza and pneumonia	J09-J18	15.6	13.8
Intentional self-harm	X60-X84	20.2	14.1
Malnutrition	E40-E46	2.8	2.3
Obesity and other hyperalimentation	E65-E68	2.7	2.1
Renal failure	N17-N19	7.7	12.6
Transport accidents	V01-V99	11.1	12.3
Viral hepatitis	B15-B19	1.2	1.2

Note: (a) ICD-10 = International Classification of Diseases 10th Revision; (1) Mortality rates are a three-year average covering 2017-2019; (2) Figures cover Washoe County; Data are suppressed when the data meet the criteria for confidentiality constraints; Mortality rates are flagged as unreliable when the rate would be calculated with a numerator of 20 or less.
Source: Centers for Disease Control and Prevention, National Center for Health Statistics. Underlying Cause of Death 1999-2019 on CDC WONDER Online Database

Health Insurance Coverage

Area	With Health Insurance	With Private Health Insurance	With Public Health Insurance	Without Health Insurance	Population Under Age 19 Without Health Insurance
City	90.2	68.4	32.1	9.8	8.1
MSA[1]	90.6	69.8	32.2	9.4	7.7
U.S.	91.2	67.9	35.1	8.8	5.1

Note: Figures are percentages that cover the civilian noninstitutionalized population; (1) Figures cover the Reno, NV Metropolitan Statistical Area
Source: U.S. Census Bureau, 2015-2019 American Community Survey 5-Year Estimates

Number of Medical Professionals

Area	MDs[3]	DOs[3,4]	Dentists	Podiatrists	Chiropractors	Optometrists
County[1] (number)	1,367	97	330	19	132	113
County[1] (rate[2])	294.4	20.9	70.0	4.0	28.0	24.0
U.S. (rate[2])	282.9	22.7	71.2	6.2	28.1	16.9

32031
Note: Data as of 2019 unless noted; (1) Data covers Washoe County; (2) Rate per 100,000 population; (3) Data as of 2018 and includes all active, non-federal physicians; (4) Doctor of Osteopathic Medicine
Source: U.S. Department of Health and Human Services, Health Resources and Services Administration, Bureau of Health Professions, Area Resource File (ARF) 2019-2020

EDUCATION

Public School District Statistics

District Name	Schls	Pupils	Pupil/ Teacher Ratio	Minority Pupils[1] (%)	Free Lunch Eligible[2] (%)	IEP[3] (%)
Washoe County School District	109	67,113	18.4	56.2	42.6	13.6

Note: Table includes school districts with 2,000 or more students; (1) Percentage of students that are not non-Hispanic white; (2) Percentage of students that are eligible for the free lunch program; (3) Percentage of students that have an Individualized Education Program.
Source: U.S. Department of Education, National Center for Education Statistics, Common Core of Data, Local Education Agency (School District) Universe Survey: School Year 2018-2019; U.S. Department of Education, National Center for Education Statistics, Common Core of Data, Public Elementary/Secondary School Universe Survey: School Year 2018-2019

Highest Level of Education

Area	Less than H.S.	H.S. Diploma	Some College, No Deg.	Associate Degree	Bachelor's Degree	Master's Degree	Prof. School Degree	Doctorate Degree
City	11.0	22.2	25.0	8.2	20.6	8.4	2.3	2.3
MSA[1]	11.3	23.6	25.7	8.6	19.2	7.8	2.1	1.8
U.S.	12.0	27.0	20.4	8.5	19.8	8.8	2.1	1.4

Note: Figures cover persons age 25 and over; (1) Figures cover the Reno, NV Metropolitan Statistical Area
Source: U.S. Census Bureau, 2015-2019 American Community Survey 5-Year Estimates

Educational Attainment by Race

Area	High School Graduate or Higher (%)					Bachelor's Degree or Higher (%)				
	Total	White	Black	Asian	Hisp.[2]	Total	White	Black	Asian	Hisp.[2]
City	89.0	91.4	91.3	91.6	64.6	33.5	35.3	21.2	48.1	12.5
MSA[1]	88.7	91.0	90.3	91.8	63.3	30.8	32.5	21.7	45.4	11.0
U.S.	88.0	89.9	86.0	87.1	68.7	32.1	33.5	21.6	54.3	16.4

Note: Figures shown cover persons 25 years old and over; (1) Figures cover the Reno, NV Metropolitan Statistical Area; (2) People of Hispanic origin can be of any race
Source: U.S. Census Bureau, 2015-2019 American Community Survey 5-Year Estimates

School Enrollment by Grade and Control

Area	Preschool (%)		Kindergarten (%)		Grades 1 - 4 (%)		Grades 5 - 8 (%)		Grades 9 - 12 (%)	
	Public	Private	Public	Private	Public	Private	Public	Private	Public	Private
City	60.7	39.3	86.1	13.9	94.1	5.9	93.2	6.8	94.0	6.0
MSA[1]	58.2	41.8	85.6	14.4	92.7	7.3	92.9	7.1	93.2	6.8
U.S.	59.1	40.9	87.6	12.4	89.5	10.5	89.4	10.6	90.1	9.9

Note: Figures shown cover persons 3 years old and over; (1) Figures cover the Reno, NV Metropolitan Statistical Area
Source: U.S. Census Bureau, 2015-2019 American Community Survey 5-Year Estimates

Higher Education

Four-Year Colleges			Two-Year Colleges			Medical Schools[1]	Law Schools[2]	Voc/ Tech[3]
Public	Private Non-profit	Private For-profit	Public	Private Non-profit	Private For-profit			
2	0	0	0	0	1	1	0	3

Note: Figures cover institutions located within the city limits and include main campuses only; (1) includes schools accredited by the Liaison Committee on Medical Education and the American Osteopathic Association's Commission on Osteopathic College Accreditation; (2) includes ABA-accredited schools, schools with provisional ABA accreditation, and state accredited schools; (3) includes all schools with programs that are less than 2 years.
Source: National Center for Education Statistics, Integrated Postsecondary Education System (IPEDS), 2019-20; Wikipedia, List of Medical Schools in the United States, accessed April 2, 2021; Wikipedia, List of Law Schools in the United States, accessed April 2, 2021

EMPLOYERS

Major Employers

Company Name	Industry
Atlantis Casino Resort	Casino hotels
Bellagio	Casino hotels
Circus Circus Casinos - Reno	Casino hotels
City of Reno	Municipal government
Desert Palace	Casino hotels
Eldorado Hotel & Casino	Casino hotels
Grand Sierra Resort & Casino	Casino hotels
Harrahs Reno	Casino hotels
IGT	All other miscellaneous manufacturing
Integrity Staffing Solutions	Temporary help services
Mandalay Corp	Casino hotels
Peppermill Hotel Casino - Reno	Casino hotels
Renown Regional Medical Center	General medical & surgical hospitals
Saint Marys	General medical & surgical hospitals
Sierra Nevada Healthcare System	General medical & surgical hospitals
Silver Legacy Resort Casino	Casino hotels
Sparks Nugget	Casino hotels
Truckee Meadows Community Coll	Junior colleges
United Parcel Service	Package delivery services
University of Nevada-Reno	Colleges & universities
Washoe County Comptroller	Executive & legislative offices combined
Washoe County School District	Elementary & secondary schools
West Business Solutions	Telemarketing bureaus

Note: Companies shown are located within the Reno, NV Metropolitan Statistical Area.
Source: Hoovers.com; Wikipedia

PUBLIC SAFETY

Crime Rate

Area	All Crimes	Violent Crimes				Property Crimes		
		Murder	Rape[3]	Robbery	Aggrav. Assault	Burglary	Larceny -Theft	Motor Vehicle Theft
City	2,658.9	4.7	70.0	121.1	362.1	323.2	1,314.3	463.5
Suburbs[1]	1,965.3	1.4	55.1	47.4	262.9	331.5	1,041.2	225.8
Metro[2]	2,336.2	3.2	63.1	86.8	315.9	327.1	1,187.2	352.9
U.S.	2,489.3	5.0	42.6	81.6	250.2	340.5	1,549.5	219.9

Note: Figures are crimes per 100,000 population; (1) All areas within the metro area that are located outside the city limits; (2) Figures cover the Reno, NV Metropolitan Statistical Area; (3) All figures shown were reported using the revised Uniform Crime Reporting (UCR) definition of rape.
Source: FBI Uniform Crime Reports, 2019

Hate Crimes

Area	Number of Quarters Reported	Number of Incidents per Bias Motivation					
		Race/Ethnicity/ Ancestry	Religion	Sexual Orientation	Disability	Gender	Gender Identity
City	4	3	1	0	0	0	0
U.S.	4	3,963	1,521	1,195	157	69	198

Source: Federal Bureau of Investigation, Hate Crime Statistics 2019

Identity Theft Consumer Reports

Area	Reports	Reports per 100,000 Population	Rank[2]
MSA[1]	2,895	609	35
U.S.	1,387,615	423	-

Note: (1) Figures cover the Reno, NV Metropolitan Statistical Area; (2) Rank ranges from 1 to 391 where 1 indicates greatest number of identity theft reports per 100,000 population
Source: Federal Trade Commission, Consumer Sentinel Network Data Book 2020

Fraud and Other Consumer Reports

Area	Reports	Reports per 100,000 Population	Rank[2]
MSA[1]	4,349	914	45
U.S.	3,385,133	1,031	-

Note: (1) Figures cover the Reno, NV Metropolitan Statistical Area; (2) Rank ranges from 1 to 391 where 1 indicates greatest number of fraud and other consumer reports per 100,000 population
Source: Federal Trade Commission, Consumer Sentinel Network Data Book 2020

POLITICS

2020 Presidential Election Results

Area	Biden	Trump	Jorgensen	Hawkins	Other
Washoe County	50.8	46.3	1.4	0.0	1.5
U.S.	51.3	46.8	1.2	0.3	0.5

Note: Results are percentages and may not add to 100% due to rounding
Source: Dave Leip's Atlas of U.S. Presidential Elections

SPORTS

Professional Sports Teams

Team Name	League	Year Established
No teams are located in the metro area		

Source: Wikipedia, Major Professional Sports Teams of the United States and Canada, April 6, 2021

CLIMATE

Average and Extreme Temperatures

Temperature	Jan	Feb	Mar	Apr	May	Jun	Jul	Aug	Sep	Oct	Nov	Dec	Yr.
Extreme High (°F)	70	75	83	89	96	103	104	105	101	91	77	70	105
Average High (°F)	45	51	56	64	73	82	91	89	81	70	55	46	67
Average Temp. (°F)	32	38	41	48	56	63	70	68	61	51	40	33	50
Average Low (°F)	19	23	26	31	38	44	49	47	40	32	25	20	33
Extreme Low (°F)	-16	-16	0	13	18	25	33	24	20	8	1	-16	-16

Note: Figures cover the years 1949-1992
Source: National Climatic Data Center, International Station Meteorological Climate Summary, 9/96

Average Precipitation/Snowfall/Humidity

Precip./Humidity	Jan	Feb	Mar	Apr	May	Jun	Jul	Aug	Sep	Oct	Nov	Dec	Yr.
Avg. Precip. (in.)	1.0	0.9	0.7	0.4	0.7	0.4	0.3	0.2	0.3	0.4	0.8	1.0	7.2
Avg. Snowfall (in.)	6	5	4	1	1	Tr	0	0	Tr	Tr	2	4	24
Avg. Rel. Hum. 7am (%)	79	77	71	61	55	51	49	55	64	72	78	80	66
Avg. Rel. Hum. 4pm (%)	51	41	34	27	26	22	19	19	22	27	41	51	32

Note: Figures cover the years 1949-1992; Tr = Trace amounts (<0.05 in. of rain; <0.5 in. of snow)
Source: National Climatic Data Center, International Station Meteorological Climate Summary, 9/96

Weather Conditions

Temperature			Daytime Sky			Precipitation		
10°F & below	32°F & below	90°F & above	Clear	Partly cloudy	Cloudy	0.01 inch or more precip.	0.1 inch or more snow/ice	Thunder-storms
14	178	50	143	139	83	50	17	14

Note: Figures are average number of days per year and cover the years 1949-1992
Source: National Climatic Data Center, International Station Meteorological Climate Summary, 9/96

HAZARDOUS WASTE

Superfund Sites

The Reno, NV metro area has no sites on the EPA's Superfund Final National Priorities List. There are a total of 1,375 Superfund sites with a status of proposed or final on the list in the U.S. *U.S. Environmental Protection Agency, National Priorities List, April 7, 2021*

AIR QUALITY

Air Quality Trends: Ozone

	1990	1995	2000	2005	2010	2015	2016	2017	2018	2019
MSA[1]	0.074	0.069	0.067	0.069	0.068	0.071	0.070	0.068	0.077	0.063
U.S.	0.088	0.089	0.082	0.080	0.073	0.068	0.069	0.068	0.069	0.065

Note: (1) Data covers the Reno, NV Metropolitan Statistical Area. The values shown are the composite ozone concentration averages among trend sites based on the highest fourth daily maximum 8-hour concentration in parts per million. These trends are based on sites having an adequate record of monitoring data during the trend period. Data from exceptional events are included.
Source: U.S. Environmental Protection Agency, Air Quality Monitoring Information, "Air Quality Trends by City, 1990-2019"

Air Quality Index

Area	Percent of Days when Air Quality was...[2]					AQI Statistics[2]	
	Good	Moderate	Unhealthy for Sensitive Groups	Unhealthy	Very Unhealthy	Maximum	Median
MSA[1]	66.8	33.2	0.0	0.0	0.0	97	46

Note: (1) Data covers the Reno, NV Metropolitan Statistical Area; (2) Based on 365 days with AQI data in 2019. Air Quality Index (AQI) is an index for reporting daily air quality. EPA calculates the AQI for five major air pollutants regulated by the Clean Air Act: ground-level ozone, particle pollution (aka particulate matter), carbon monoxide, sulfur dioxide, and nitrogen dioxide. The AQI runs from 0 to 500. The higher the AQI value, the greater the level of air pollution and the greater the health concern. There are six AQI categories: "Good" AQI is between 0 and 50. Air quality is considered satisfactory; "Moderate" AQI is between 51 and 100. Air quality is acceptable; "Unhealthy for Sensitive Groups" When AQI values are between 101 and 150, members of sensitive groups may experience health effects; "Unhealthy" When AQI values are between 151 and 200 everyone may begin to experience health effects; "Very Unhealthy" AQI values between 201 and 300 trigger a health alert; "Hazardous" AQI values over 300 trigger warnings of emergency conditions (not shown).
Source: U.S. Environmental Protection Agency, Air Quality Index Report, 2019

Air Quality Index Pollutants

Area	Percent of Days when AQI Pollutant was...[2]					
	Carbon Monoxide	Nitrogen Dioxide	Ozone	Sulfur Dioxide	Particulate Matter 2.5	Particulate Matter 10
MSA[1]	0.0	1.1	80.5	0.0	17.0	1.4

Note: (1) Data covers the Reno, NV Metropolitan Statistical Area; (2) Based on 365 days with AQI data in 2019. The Air Quality Index (AQI) is an index for reporting daily air quality. EPA calculates the AQI for five major air pollutants regulated by the Clean Air Act: ground-level ozone, particle pollution (also known as particulate matter), carbon monoxide, sulfur dioxide, and nitrogen dioxide. The AQI runs from 0 to 500. The higher the AQI value, the greater the level of air pollution and the greater the health concern.
Source: U.S. Environmental Protection Agency, Air Quality Index Report, 2019

Maximum Air Pollutant Concentrations: Particulate Matter, Ozone, CO and Lead

	Particulate Matter 10 (ug/m^3)	Particulate Matter 2.5 Wtd AM (ug/m^3)	Particulate Matter 2.5 24-Hr (ug/m^3)	Ozone (ppm)	Carbon Monoxide (ppm)	Lead (ug/m^3)
MSA[1] Level	78	6.0	16	0.066	2	n/a
NAAQS[2]	150	15	35	0.075	9	0.15
Met NAAQS[2]	Yes	Yes	Yes	Yes	Yes	n/a

Note: (1) Data covers the Reno, NV Metropolitan Statistical Area; Data from exceptional events are included; (2) National Ambient Air Quality Standards; ppm = parts per million; ug/m^3 = micrograms per cubic meter; n/a not available.
Concentrations: Particulate Matter 10 (coarse particulate)—highest second maximum 24-hour concentration; Particulate Matter 2.5 Wtd AM (fine particulate)—highest weighted annual mean concentration; Particulate Matter 2.5 24-Hour (fine particulate)—highest 98th percentile 24-hour concentration; Ozone—highest fourth daily maximum 8-hour concentration; Carbon Monoxide—highest second maximum non-overlapping 8-hour concentration; Lead—maximum running 3-month average
Source: U.S. Environmental Protection Agency, Air Quality Monitoring Information, "Air Quality Statistics by City, 2019"

Maximum Air Pollutant Concentrations: Nitrogen Dioxide and Sulfur Dioxide

	Nitrogen Dioxide AM (ppb)	Nitrogen Dioxide 1-Hr (ppb)	Sulfur Dioxide AM (ppb)	Sulfur Dioxide 1-Hr (ppb)	Sulfur Dioxide 24-Hr (ppb)
MSA[1] Level	11	46	n/a	3	n/a
NAAQS[2]	53	100	30	75	140
Met NAAQS[2]	Yes	Yes	n/a	Yes	n/a

Note: (1) Data covers the Reno, NV Metropolitan Statistical Area; Data from exceptional events are included; (2) National Ambient Air Quality Standards; ppm = parts per million; ug/m^3 = micrograms per cubic meter; n/a not available.
Concentrations: Nitrogen Dioxide AM—highest arithmetic mean concentration; Nitrogen Dioxide 1-Hr—highest 98th percentile 1-hour daily maximum concentration; Sulfur Dioxide AM—highest annual mean concentration; Sulfur Dioxide 1-Hr—highest 99th percentile 1-hour daily maximum concentration; Sulfur Dioxide 24-Hr—highest second maximum 24-hour concentration
Source: U.S. Environmental Protection Agency, Air Quality Monitoring Information, "Air Quality Statistics by City, 2019"

Riverside, California

Background

The city of Riverside is located in southern California in Riverside County. It is approximately 100 miles north of San Diego, on the banks of the Santa Ana River. The city is known for its agriculture and is considered by many to be the birthplace of the California citrus industry.

John W. North, a well-known pioneer from Tennessee who also founded the city of Northfield in Minnesota, founded Riverside in 1870. He wanted Riverside to be a place of culture and education, and had the support of investors from both Canada and England. The city was named for its location along the Santa Ana River. In 1871, a local woman named Eliza Tibbets received two Brazilian navel orange trees from a friend at the U.S. Department of Agriculture in Washington, D.C. Seemingly insignificant at the time, the trees thrived in the southern California climate, and the rest is history. By 1882, more than half a million citrus trees were planted in California, half of them in Riverside alone. Developments in irrigation and transportation, such as refrigerated railroad cars, also helped the industry to prosper.

The city's prosperity at the turn of the century led to the construction of the luxury hotels and resorts that made Riverside a popular destination for celebrities and wealthy tourists. Glenwood Tavern, which later became the Mission Inn, was built, modeled after the area's Spanish Mission, and was once famous as the choice of movie stars and U.S. Presidents. Today, the historic property is the upscale Mission Inn Hotel & Spa.

Over the years, Riverside has always had relatively high populations of immigrants, especially from Mexico, China, Japan and Korea. Many came to the city to work the citrus harvest. In the days of Riverside's peak citrus production, immigrant communities sprung up along the railroad tracks on the outskirts of town, but today few remain. One of the city's most famous immigrants was Japanese-born Jukichi Harada. Harada owned a restaurant in Riverside and, in 1915, purchased a home in the name of his American-born children so they would be eligible to attend the public schools. A group of residents protested that he had violated the California Alien Land Law of 1913, which prohibited non-citizens from owning land. The case eventually was heard by the California Supreme Court, which ruled in Harada's favor. The Harada house is now a National Historic Landmark and is owned by the Metropolitan Museum of Riverside.

The middle of the twentieth century saw the citrus industry partially give way to new commercial development. Urban shopping centers, industrial parks and residential communities have replaced many original orange groves. In 2014, the city received state approval to sell or develop significant local properties as part of a Long-Range Property Management Plan affecting more than 80 parcels of land worth an estimated $5.9 million. Among the properties is the Stalder Building at a key intersection, the Imperial Hardware building on the Main Street Mall, as well as property in the Five Points area where road improvements have paved the way for retail development. Another property could be used to expand the Eastside Medical Clinic.

Riverside is now world headquarters of Bourns, Inc. and Luminex Software Inc. Two Metrolink commuter rail stations, the Riverside Transit Agency's bus service, and the Riverside Municipal Airport serve the city. The city is home to four institutions of higher learning: University of California Riverside, California Baptist University, La Sierra University and Riverside Community College. The University of California Riverside is also home to the UCR Botanic Gardens, which boasts three of the city's original orange trees and is a major tourist attraction. Other visitor hot spots include the Mission Inn and the Fox Theater, which hosted the first showing of *Gone With the Wind*. The heavily attended Riverside International Film Festival regularly anticipates five days of independent movies, and continued to be popular during its online-only COVID-19 event in 2020.

Riverside has a warm, dry climate that is appreciated by residents and citrus growers alike. Although summer days are generally very hot, relatively low humidity prevents high temperatures from feeling oppressive. Evening temperatures are generally milder and often accompanied by a cool breeze. The city records most of its annual rainfall between September and April.

Rankings

Business/Finance Rankings

- The Brookings Institution ranked the nation's largest cities based on income inequality. Riverside was ranked #89 (#1 = greatest inequality). Criteria: the "95/20 ratio," a figure representing the income at which a household earns more than 95 percent of all other households, divided by the income at which a household earns more than only 20 percent of all other households. *Brookings Institution, "Household Income Inequality, Largest Cities of 97 Large U.S. Metro Areas, 2014-2016," February 5, 2018*

- The Brookings Institution ranked the 100 largest metro areas in the U.S. based on income inequality. Riverside was ranked #68 (#1 = greatest inequality). Criteria: the "95/20 ratio," a figure representing the income at which a household earns more than 95 percent of all other households, divided by the income at which a household earns more than only 20 percent of all other households. *Brookings Institution, "Household Income Inequality, 100 Largest U.S. Metro Areas, 2014-2016," February 5, 2018*

- The Riverside metro area was identified as one of the most debt-ridden places in America by the finance site Credit.com. The metro area was ranked #25. Criteria: residents' average credit card debt as well as median income. *Credit.com, "25 Cities With the Most Credit Card Debt," February 28, 2018*

- The Riverside metro area appeared on the Milken Institute "2021 Best Performing Cities" list. Rank: #36 out of 200 large metro areas (population over 250,000). Criteria: job growth; wage and salary growth; high-tech output growth; housing affordability; household broadband access. *Milken Institute, "Best-Performing Cities 2021," February 16, 2021*

- *Forbes* ranked the 200 most populous metro areas to determine the nation's "Best Places for Business and Careers." The Riverside metro area was ranked #72. Criteria: costs (business and living); job growth (past and projected); income growth; quality of life; educational attainment (college and high school); projected economic growth; cultural and leisure opportunities; workplace tolerance laws; net migration patterns. *Forbes, "The Best Places for Business and Careers 2019: Seattle Still On Top," October 30, 2019*

Children/Family Rankings

- Riverside was selected as one of the most playful cities in the U.S. by KaBOOM! The organization's Playful City USA initiative honors cities and towns across the nation that have made their communities more playable. Criteria: pledging to integrate play as a solution to challenges in their communities; making it easy for children to get active and balanced play; creating more family-friendly and innovative communities as a result. *KaBOOM! National Campaign for Play, "2017 Playful City USA Communities"*

Education Rankings

- Personal finance website *WalletHub* analyzed the 150 largest U.S. metropolitan statistical areas to determine where the most educated Americans are putting their degrees to work. Criteria: education levels; percentage of workers with degrees; education quality and attainment gap; public school quality rankings; quality and enrollment of each metro area's universities. Riverside was ranked #137 (#1 = most educated city). *www.WalletHub.com, "Most and Least Educated Cities in America," July 20, 2020*

- Riverside was selected as one of America's most literate cities. The city ranked #61 out of the 84 largest U.S. cities. Criteria: number of booksellers; library resources; Internet resources; educational attainment; periodical publishing resources; newspaper circulation. *Central Connecticut State University, "America's Most Literate Cities, 2018," February 2019*

Environmental Rankings

- The U.S. Environmental Protection Agency (EPA) released a list of U.S. metropolitan areas with the most ENERGY STAR certified buildings in 2019. The Riverside metro area was ranked #18 out of 25. *U.S. Environmental Protection Agency, "2020 Energy Star Top Cities," March 2020*

Health/Fitness Rankings

- For each of the 100 largest cities in the United States, the American Fitness Index®, published by the American College of Sports Medicine and the Anthem Foundation, evaluated community infrastructure and 33 health behaviors including preventive health, levels of chronic disease conditions, pedestrian safety, air quality, and community resources that support physical activity. Riverside ranked #59 for "community fitness." *americanfitnessindex.org, "2020 ACSM American Fitness Index Summary Report," July 14, 2020*

- Riverside was identified as a "2021 Spring Allergy Capital." The area ranked #13 out of 100. Three groups of factors were used to identify the most challenging cities for people with allergies during the spring season: annual spring pollen levels; over the counter medicine use; number of board-certified allergy specialists. *Asthma and Allergy Foundation of America, "Spring Allergy Capitals 2021," February 23, 2021*

- Riverside was identified as a "2021 Fall Allergy Capital." The area ranked #16 out of 100. Three groups of factors were used to identify the most challenging cities for people with allergies during the fall season: annual fall pollen levels; over the counter medicine use; number of board-certified allergy specialists. *Asthma and Allergy Foundation of America, "Fall Allergy Capitals 2021," February 23, 2021*

- Riverside was identified as a "2019 Asthma Capital." The area ranked #82 out of the nation's 100 largest metropolitan areas. Criteria: estimated asthma prevalence; crude death rate from asthma; and ER visits due to asthma. Risk factors analyzed but not factored in the rankings: annual pollen score; annual air quality; public smoking laws; number of board-certified asthma specialists; rescue medication use; controller medication use; uninsured rate; poverty rate. *Asthma and Allergy Foundation of America, "Asthma Capitals 2019: The Most Challenging Places to Live With Asthma," May 7, 2019*

Real Estate Rankings

- FitSmallBusiness looked at 50 of the largest metropolitan areas in the U.S. to determine which metro was the best to start a real estate business. Data was compiled from such sources as: Zillow, Trulia, U.S. Census Bureau, and the Bureau of Labor Statistics. Criteria: location; inventory; annual wages; median sales price of homes; days on the market; median price cut percentage; and other factors that would influence real estate professional growth. The Riverside metro area ranked #10. *fitsmallbusiness.com, "The Best Cities to Become a Real Estate Agent in 2018," January 30, 2018*

- *WalletHub* compared the most populated U.S. cities to determine which had the best markets for real estate agents. Riverside ranked #53 where demand was high and pay was the best. Criteria: sales per agent; annual median wage for real-estate agents; monthly average starting salary for real estate agents; real estate job density and competition; unemployment rate; home turnover rate; housing-market health index; and other relevant metrics. *www.WalletHub.com, "2019's Best Places to Be a Real Estate Agent," April 24, 2019*

- The Riverside metro area appeared on Realtor.com's list of hot housing markets to watch in 2021. The area ranked #10. Criteria: healthy existing homes inventory; relative home affordability; local economy/population trends. *Realtor.com®, "Top 10 Housing Markets Positioned for Growth in 2021," December 7, 2020*

- Riverside was ranked #12 in the top 20 out of the 100 largest metro areas in terms of house price appreciation in 2020 (#1 = highest rate). *Federal Housing Finance Agency, House Price Index, 4th Quarter 2020*

- Riverside was ranked #249 out of 268 metro areas in terms of housing affordability in 2020 by the National Association of Home Builders (#1 = most affordable). Criteria: the share of homes sold in that area affordable to a family earning the local median income, based on standard mortgage underwriting criteria. *National Association of Home Builders®, NAHB-Wells Fargo Housing Opportunity Index, 4th Quarter 2020*

- The nation's largest metro areas were analyzed in terms of the percentage of households entering some stage of foreclosure in 2020. The Riverside metro area ranked #10 out of 10 (#1 = highest foreclosure rate). *ATTOM Data Solutions, "2020 Year-End U.S. Foreclosure Market Report™," January 14, 2021*

Safety Rankings

- Allstate ranked the 200 largest cities in America in terms of driver safety. Riverside ranked #134. Criteria: internal property damage claims over a two-year period from January 2016 to December 2017. The report helps increase the importance of safety and awareness behind the wheel. *Allstate, "Allstate America's Best Drivers Report, 2019" June 24, 2019*

- The National Insurance Crime Bureau ranked 384 metro areas in the U.S. in terms of per capita rates of vehicle theft. The Riverside metro area ranked #18 (#1 = highest rate). Criteria: number of vehicle theft offenses per 100,000 inhabitants in 2019. *National Insurance Crime Bureau, "Hot Spots 2019," July 21, 2020*

Seniors/Retirement Rankings

■ From its Best Cities for Successful Aging indexes, the Milken Institute generated rankings for metropolitan areas, weighing data in nine categories—health care, wellness, living arrangements, transportation and convenience, financial characteristics, education, employment, community engagement, and overall livability. The Riverside metro area was ranked #100 overall in the large metro area category. *Milken Institute, "Best Cities for Successful Aging, 2017" March 14, 2017*

Women/Minorities Rankings

■ Personal finance website *WalletHub* compared more than 180 U.S. cities across two key dimensions, "Hispanic Business-Friendliness" and "Hispanic Purchasing Power," to arrive at the most favorable conditions for Hispanic entrepreneurs. Riverside was ranked #74 out of 182. Criteria includes: share of Hispanic-Owned Businesses; Hispanic entrepreneurship rate to median annual income of Hispanics; Small Business-Friendliness score; cost of living; and number of Hispanics with at least a bachelor's degree. *WalletHub.com, "2019's Best Cities for Hispanic Entrepreneurs," May 1, 2019*

Miscellaneous Rankings

■ Riverside was selected as a 2020 Digital Cities Survey winner. The city ranked #6 in the large city (250,000 to 499,999 population) category. The survey examined and assessed how city governments are utilizing technology to improve transparency, enhance cybersecurity, and respond to the pandemic. Survey questions focused on ten initiatives: cybersecurity, citizen experience, disaster recovery, business intelligence, IT personnel, data governance, collaboration, infrastructure modernization, cloud computing, and mobile applications. *Center for Digital Government, "2020 Digital Cities Survey," November 10, 2020*

■ *WalletHub* compared the 150 most populated U.S. cities to determine their operating efficiency. A "Quality of City Services" score was constructed for each city and then divided by the total budget per capita to reveal which were managed the best. Riverside ranked #129. Criteria: financial stability; economy; education; safety; health; infrastructure and pollution. *www.WalletHub.com, "2020's Best- & Worst-Run Cities in America," June 29, 2020*

■ The National Alliance to End Homelessness listed the 25 most populous metro areas with the highest rate of homelessness. The Riverside metro area had a high rate of homelessness. Criteria: number of homeless people per 10,000 population in 2016. *National Alliance to End Homelessness, "Homelessness in the 25 Most Populous U.S. Metro Areas," September 1, 2017*

Business Environment

DEMOGRAPHICS

Population Growth

Area	1990 Census	2000 Census	2010 Census	2019* Estimate	Population Growth (%) 1990-2019	Population Growth (%) 2010-2019
City	226,232	255,166	303,871	326,414	44.3	7.4
MSA[1]	2,588,793	3,254,821	4,224,851	4,560,470	76.2	7.9
U.S.	248,709,873	281,421,906	308,745,538	324,697,795	30.6	5.2

*Note: (1) Figures cover the Riverside-San Bernardino-Ontario, CA Metropolitan Statistical Area;
(*) 2015-2019 5-year estimated population
Source: U.S. Census Bureau, 1990 Census, Census 2000, Census 2010, 2015-2019 American Community
Survey 5-Year Estimates*

Household Size

Area	One	Two	Three	Four	Five	Six	Seven or More	Average Household Size
City	20.4	27.6	17.7	15.6	10.2	4.7	3.9	3.40
MSA[1]	20.4	28.3	16.3	16.1	10.2	4.9	3.7	3.30
U.S.	27.9	33.9	15.6	12.9	6.0	2.3	1.4	2.60

*Note: (1) Figures cover the Riverside-San Bernardino-Ontario, CA Metropolitan Statistical Area
Source: U.S. Census Bureau, 2015-2019 American Community Survey 5-Year Estimates*

Race

Area	White Alone[2] (%)	Black Alone[2] (%)	Asian Alone[2] (%)	AIAN[3] Alone[2] (%)	NHOPI[4] Alone[2] (%)	Other Race Alone[2] (%)	Two or More Races (%)
City	58.3	6.2	7.6	0.8	0.3	22.0	4.9
MSA[1]	60.5	7.4	6.8	0.8	0.3	19.5	4.7
U.S.	72.5	12.7	5.5	0.8	0.2	4.9	3.3

*Note: (1) Figures cover the Riverside-San Bernardino-Ontario, CA Metropolitan Statistical Area; (2) Alone is
defined as not being in combination with one or more other races; (3) American Indian and Alaska Native; (4)
Native Hawaiian and Other Pacific Islander
Source: U.S. Census Bureau, 2015-2019 American Community Survey 5-Year Estimates*

Hispanic or Latino Origin

Area	Total (%)	Mexican (%)	Puerto Rican (%)	Cuban (%)	Other (%)
City	53.7	47.1	0.8	0.2	5.6
MSA[1]	51.0	44.4	0.8	0.3	5.5
U.S.	18.0	11.2	1.7	0.7	4.3

*Note: Persons of Hispanic or Latino origin can be of any race; (1) Figures cover the Riverside-San
Bernardino-Ontario, CA Metropolitan Statistical Area
Source: U.S. Census Bureau, 2015-2019 American Community Survey 5-Year Estimates*

Ancestry

Area	German	Irish	English	American	Italian	Polish	French[2]	Scottish	Dutch
City	5.9	4.6	4.1	3.1	2.9	0.9	1.6	1.0	0.8
MSA[1]	7.1	5.6	4.5	2.9	3.0	0.9	1.6	1.0	0.9
U.S.	13.3	9.7	7.2	6.2	5.1	2.8	2.3	1.7	1.2

*Note: Figures are the percentage of the total population reporting a particular ancestry. The nine most
commonly reported ancestries in the U.S. are shown. Figures include multiple ancestries (e.g. if a person
reported being Irish and Italian, they were included in both columns); (1) Figures cover the Riverside-San
Bernardino-Ontario, CA Metropolitan Statistical Area; (2) Excludes Basque
Source: U.S. Census Bureau, 2015-2019 American Community Survey 5-Year Estimates*

Foreign-born Population

Area	Any Foreign Country	Asia	Mexico	Europe	Caribbean	Central America[2]	South America	Africa	Canada
City	22.6	5.1	13.2	0.9	0.2	2.0	0.6	0.3	0.2
MSA[1]	21.3	4.9	12.3	0.8	0.2	1.7	0.6	0.4	0.3
U.S.	13.6	4.2	3.5	1.5	1.3	1.1	1.0	0.7	0.2

*Note: (1) Figures cover the Riverside-San Bernardino-Ontario, CA Metropolitan Statistical Area; (2) Excludes
Mexico.
Source: U.S. Census Bureau, 2015-2019 American Community Survey 5-Year Estimates*

Marital Status

Area	Never Married	Now Married[2]	Separated	Widowed	Divorced
City	43.1	40.8	2.4	4.7	9.0
MSA[1]	36.0	47.0	2.3	5.1	9.6
U.S.	33.4	48.1	1.9	5.8	10.9

Note: Figures are percentages and cover the population 15 years of age and older; (1) Figures cover the Riverside-San Bernardino-Ontario, CA Metropolitan Statistical Area; (2) Excludes separated
Source: U.S. Census Bureau, 2015-2019 American Community Survey 5-Year Estimates

Disability by Age

Area	All Ages	Under 18 Years Old	18 to 64 Years Old	65 Years and Over
City	11.2	3.9	9.1	40.7
MSA[1]	11.3	3.6	9.1	37.5
U.S.	12.6	4.2	10.3	34.5

Note: Figures show percent of the civilian noninstitutionalized population that reported having a disability. Disability status is determined from six types of difficulty: vision, hearing, cognitive, ambulatory, self-care, and independent living. For children under 5 years old, hearing and vision difficulty are used to determine disability status. For children between the ages of 5 and 14, disability status is determined from hearing, vision, cognitive, ambulatory, and self-care difficulties. For people aged 15 years and older, they are considered to have a disability if they have difficulty with any one of the six difficulty types; Note: (1) Figures cover the Riverside-San Bernardino-Ontario, CA Metropolitan Statistical Area
Source: U.S. Census Bureau, 2015-2019 American Community Survey 5-Year Estimates

Age

Area	Percent of Population									Median Age
	Under Age 5	Age 5–19	Age 20–34	Age 35–44	Age 45–54	Age 55–64	Age 65–74	Age 75–84	Age 85+	
City	6.2	22.3	26.5	12.4	12.0	10.0	6.3	3.1	1.3	31.6
MSA[1]	6.8	22.1	21.8	12.8	12.5	11.2	7.5	3.8	1.4	34.5
U.S.	6.1	19.1	20.7	12.6	13.0	12.9	9.1	4.6	1.9	38.1

Note: (1) Figures cover the Riverside-San Bernardino-Ontario, CA Metropolitan Statistical Area
Source: U.S. Census Bureau, 2015-2019 American Community Survey 5-Year Estimates

Gender

Area	Males	Females	Males per 100 Females
City	162,664	163,750	99.3
MSA[1]	2,270,726	2,289,744	99.2
U.S.	159,886,919	164,810,876	97.0

Note: (1) Figures cover the Riverside-San Bernardino-Ontario, CA Metropolitan Statistical Area
Source: U.S. Census Bureau, 2015-2019 American Community Survey 5-Year Estimates

Religious Groups by Family

Area	Catholic	Baptist	Non-Den.	Methodist[2]	Lutheran	LDS[3]	Pente-costal	Presby-terian[4]	Muslim[5]	Judaism
MSA[1]	24.8	2.6	5.5	0.6	0.5	2.5	1.6	0.6	0.6	0.1
U.S.	19.1	9.3	4.0	4.0	2.3	2.0	1.9	1.6	0.8	0.7

Note: Figures are the number of adherents as a percentage of the total population; (1) Figures cover the Riverside-San Bernardino-Ontario, CA Metropolitan Statistical Area; (2) Methodist/Pietist; (3) Latter Day Saints; (4) Reformed; (5) Figures are estimates
Source: Association of Statisticians of American Religious Bodies, 2010 U.S. Religion Census: Religious Congregations & Membership Study

Religious Groups by Tradition

Area	Catholic	Evangelical Protestant	Mainline Protestant	Other Tradition	Black Protestant	Orthodox
MSA[1]	24.8	11.5	1.3	3.7	0.8	0.2
U.S.	19.1	16.2	7.3	4.3	1.6	0.3

Note: Figures are the number of adherents as a percentage of the total population; (1) Figures cover the Riverside-San Bernardino-Ontario, CA Metropolitan Statistical Area
Source: Association of Statisticians of American Religious Bodies, 2010 U.S. Religion Census: Religious Congregations & Membership Study

ECONOMY

Gross Metropolitan Product

Area	2017	2018	2019	2020	Rank[2]
MSA[1]	161.6	171.0	178.3	186.9	22

Note: Figures are in billions of dollars; (1) Figures cover the Riverside-San Bernardino-Ontario, CA Metropolitan Statistical Area; (2) Rank is based on 2018 data and ranges from 1 to 381
Source: U.S. Conference of Mayors, U.S. Metro Economies: GMP & Employment 2018-2020, September 2019

Economic Growth

Area	2015-17 (%)	2018 (%)	2019 (%)	2020 (%)	Rank[2]
MSA[1]	3.0	3.4	2.3	2.6	65
U.S.	1.9	2.9	2.3	2.1	–

Note: Figures are real gross metropolitan product (GMP) growth rates and represent average annual percent change; (1) Figures cover the Riverside-San Bernardino-Ontario, CA Metropolitan Statistical Area; (2) Rank is based on 2017 2-year average annual percent change and ranges from 1 to 381
Source: U.S. Conference of Mayors, U.S. Metro Economies: GMP & Employment 2018-2020, September 2019

Metropolitan Area Exports

Area	2014	2015	2016	2017	2018	2019	Rank[2]
MSA[1]	9,134.8	8,970.0	10,211.6	8,782.3	9,745.7	9,737.6	37

Note: Figures are in millions of dollars; (1) Figures cover the Riverside-San Bernardino-Ontario, CA Metropolitan Statistical Area; (2) Rank is based on 2019 data and ranges from 1 to 386
Source: U.S. Department of Commerce, International Trade Administration, Office of Trade and Economic Analysis, Industry and Analysis, Exports by Metropolitan Area, data extracted March 24, 2021

Building Permits

Area	Single-Family			Multi-Family			Total		
	2018	2019	Pct. Chg.	2018	2019	Pct. Chg.	2018	2019	Pct. Chg.
City	171	170	-0.6	503	509	1.2	674	679	0.7
MSA[1]	11,591	11,147	-3.8	3,218	3,452	7.3	14,809	14,599	-1.4
U.S.	855,300	862,100	0.7	473,500	523,900	10.6	1,328,800	1,386,000	4.3

Note: (1) Figures cover the Riverside-San Bernardino-Ontario, CA Metropolitan Statistical Area; Figures represent new, privately-owned housing units authorized (unadjusted data); All permit data are based on estimates with imputation
Source: U.S. Census Bureau, Manufacturing, Mining, and Construction Statistics, Building Permits, 2018, 2019

Bankruptcy Filings

Area	Business Filings			Nonbusiness Filings		
	2019	2020	% Chg.	2019	2020	% Chg.
Riverside County	165	145	-12.1	6,195	4,455	-28.1
U.S.	22,780	21,655	-4.9	752,160	522,808	-30.5

Note: Business filings include Chapter 7, Chapter 9, Chapter 11, Chapter 12, Chapter 13, Chapter 15, and Section 304; Nonbusiness filings include Chapter 7, Chapter 11, and Chapter 13
Source: Administrative Office of the U.S. Courts, Business and Nonbusiness Bankruptcy, County Cases Commenced by Chapter of the Bankruptcy Code, During the 12-Month Period Ending December 31, 2019 and Business and Nonbusiness Bankruptcy, County Cases Commenced by Chapter of the Bankruptcy Code, During the 12-Month Period Ending December 31, 2020

Housing Vacancy Rates

Area	Gross Vacancy Rate[2] (%)			Year-Round Vacancy Rate[3] (%)			Rental Vacancy Rate[4] (%)			Homeowner Vacancy Rate[5] (%)		
	2018	2019	2020	2018	2019	2020	2018	2019	2020	2018	2019	2020
MSA[1]	15.1	14.9	11.8	9.1	9.6	7.5	5.1	4.5	4.4	1.6	1.7	0.8
U.S.	12.3	12.0	10.6	9.7	9.5	8.2	6.9	6.7	6.3	1.5	1.4	1.0

Note: (1) Figures cover the Riverside-San Bernardino-Ontario, CA Metropolitan Statistical Area; (2) The percentage of the total housing inventory that is vacant; (3) The percentage of the housing inventory (excluding seasonal units) that is year-round vacant; (4) The percentage of rental inventory that is vacant for rent; (5) The percentage of homeowner inventory that is vacant for sale
Source: U.S. Census Bureau, Housing Vacancies and Homeownership Annual Statistics: 2018, 2019, 2020

INCOME

Income

Area	Per Capita ($)	Median Household ($)	Average Household ($)
City	26,028	69,045	85,486
MSA[1]	27,003	65,121	85,373
U.S.	34,103	62,843	88,607

Note: (1) Figures cover the Riverside-San Bernardino-Ontario, CA Metropolitan Statistical Area
Source: U.S. Census Bureau, 2015-2019 American Community Survey 5-Year Estimates

Household Income Distribution

Area	Percent of Households Earning							
	Under $15,000	$15,000 -$24,999	$25,000 -$34,999	$35,000 -$49,999	$50,000 -$74,999	$75,000 -$99,999	$100,000 -$149,999	$150,000 and up
City	9.0	7.6	8.3	11.4	17.8	14.8	17.6	13.6
MSA[1]	9.4	8.5	8.8	11.9	17.6	13.5	16.5	13.8
U.S.	10.3	8.9	8.9	12.3	17.2	12.7	15.1	14.5

Note: (1) Figures cover the Riverside-San Bernardino-Ontario, CA Metropolitan Statistical Area
Source: U.S. Census Bureau, 2015-2019 American Community Survey 5-Year Estimates

Poverty Rate

Area	All Ages	Under 18 Years Old	18 to 64 Years Old	65 Years and Over
City	13.9	17.9	13.0	10.5
MSA[1]	14.8	20.5	13.2	10.7
U.S.	13.4	18.5	12.6	9.3

Note: Figures are percentage of people whose income during the past 12 months was below the poverty level;
(1) Figures cover the Riverside-San Bernardino-Ontario, CA Metropolitan Statistical Area
Source: U.S. Census Bureau, 2015-2019 American Community Survey 5-Year Estimates

CITY FINANCES

City Government Finances

Component	2017 ($000)	2017 ($ per capita)
Total Revenues	880,935	2,732
Total Expenditures	790,855	2,453
Debt Outstanding	1,790,261	5,553
Cash and Securities[1]	854,533	2,650

Note: (1) Cash and security holdings of a government at the close of its fiscal year,
including those of its dependent agencies, utilities, and liquor stores.
Source: U.S. Census Bureau, State & Local Government Finances 2017

City Government Revenue by Source

Source	2017 ($000)	2017 ($ per capita)	2017 (%)
General Revenue			
From Federal Government	9,633	30	1.1
From State Government	32,076	99	3.6
From Local Governments	5,272	16	0.6
Taxes			
Property	85,904	266	9.8
Sales and Gross Receipts	120,973	375	13.7
Personal Income	0	0	0.0
Corporate Income	0	0	0.0
Motor Vehicle License	0	0	0.0
Other Taxes	17,466	54	2.0
Current Charges	125,312	389	14.2
Liquor Store	0	0	0.0
Utility	429,412	1,332	48.7
Employee Retirement	0	0	0.0

Source: U.S. Census Bureau, State & Local Government Finances 2017

City Government Expenditures by Function

Function	2017 ($000)	2017 ($ per capita)	2017 (%)
General Direct Expenditures			
Air Transportation	1,282	4	0.2
Corrections	0	0	0.0
Education	0	0	0.0
Employment Security Administration	0	0	0.0
Financial Administration	13,289	41	1.7
Fire Protection	47,816	148	6.0
General Public Buildings	0	0	0.0
Governmental Administration, Other	42,219	130	5.3
Health	4,667	14	0.6
Highways	15,696	48	2.0
Hospitals	0	0	0.0
Housing and Community Development	5,289	16	0.7
Interest on General Debt	47,786	148	6.0
Judicial and Legal	0	0	0.0
Libraries	5,738	17	0.7
Parking	3,677	11	0.5
Parks and Recreation	27,367	84	3.5
Police Protection	95,506	296	12.1
Public Welfare	0	0	0.0
Sewerage	58,553	181	7.4
Solid Waste Management	20,502	63	2.6
Veterans' Services	0	0	0.0
Liquor Store	0	0	0.0
Utility	386,573	1,199	48.9
Employee Retirement	0	0	0.0

Source: U.S. Census Bureau, State & Local Government Finances 2017

EMPLOYMENT

Labor Force and Employment

Area	Civilian Labor Force			Workers Employed		
	Dec. 2019	Dec. 2020	% Chg.	Dec. 2019	Dec. 2020	% Chg.
City	156,209	155,456	-0.5	151,257	142,354	-5.9
MSA[1]	2,087,383	2,086,402	0.0	2,014,602	1,896,009	-5.9
U.S.	164,007,000	160,017,000	-2.4	158,504,000	149,613,000	-5.6

Note: Data is not seasonally adjusted and covers workers 16 years of age and older; (1) Figures cover the Riverside-San Bernardino-Ontario, CA Metropolitan Statistical Area
Source: Bureau of Labor Statistics, Local Area Unemployment Statistics

Unemployment Rate

Area	2020											
	Jan.	Feb.	Mar.	Apr.	May	Jun.	Jul.	Aug.	Sep.	Oct.	Nov.	Dec.
City	3.9	3.8	4.8	13.5	13.6	13.4	12.6	9.7	9.4	8.2	7.4	8.4
MSA[1]	4.1	4.0	5.2	14.7	15.1	14.3	13.4	10.5	10.2	8.7	7.9	9.1
U.S.	4.0	3.8	4.5	14.4	13.0	11.2	10.5	8.5	7.7	6.6	6.4	6.5

Note: Data is not seasonally adjusted and covers workers 16 years of age and older; (1) Figures cover the Riverside-San Bernardino-Ontario, CA Metropolitan Statistical Area
Source: Bureau of Labor Statistics, Local Area Unemployment Statistics

Average Wages

Occupation	$/Hr.	Occupation	$/Hr.
Accountants and Auditors	36.20	Maintenance and Repair Workers	22.90
Automotive Mechanics	24.00	Marketing Managers	62.80
Bookkeepers	22.40	Network and Computer Systems Admin.	43.30
Carpenters	26.60	Nurses, Licensed Practical	29.90
Cashiers	14.90	Nurses, Registered	52.80
Computer Programmers	43.60	Nursing Assistants	17.70
Computer Systems Analysts	43.30	Office Clerks, General	18.80
Computer User Support Specialists	29.70	Physical Therapists	49.90
Construction Laborers	24.30	Physicians	101.90
Cooks, Restaurant	15.10	Plumbers, Pipefitters and Steamfitters	28.90
Customer Service Representatives	19.70	Police and Sheriff's Patrol Officers	50.50
Dentists	84.80	Postal Service Mail Carriers	26.10
Electricians	26.50	Real Estate Sales Agents	n/a
Engineers, Electrical	48.20	Retail Salespersons	16.20
Fast Food and Counter Workers	14.70	Sales Representatives, Technical/Scientific	47.50
Financial Managers	62.40	Secretaries, Exc. Legal/Medical/Executive	21.10
First-Line Supervisors of Office Workers	29.70	Security Guards	16.40
General and Operations Managers	57.30	Surgeons	116.40
Hairdressers/Cosmetologists	15.60	Teacher Assistants, Exc. Postsecondary*	18.00
Home Health and Personal Care Aides	14.70	Teachers, Secondary School, Exc. Sp. Ed.*	41.60
Janitors and Cleaners	18.40	Telemarketers	15.30
Landscaping/Groundskeeping Workers	16.80	Truck Drivers, Heavy/Tractor-Trailer	25.60
Lawyers	79.40	Truck Drivers, Light/Delivery Services	22.30
Maids and Housekeeping Cleaners	15.70	Waiters and Waitresses	14.20

Note: Wage data covers the Riverside-San Bernardino-Ontario, CA Metropolitan Statistical Area; (*) Hourly wages were calculated from annual wage data based on a 40 hour work week; n/a not available.
Source: Bureau of Labor Statistics, Metro Area Occupational Employment & Wage Estimates, May 2020

Employment by Industry

Sector	MSA[1]		U.S.
	Number of Employees	Percent of Total	Percent of Total
Construction	109,500	7.2	5.1
Education and Health Services	252,200	16.7	16.3
Financial Activities	43,400	2.9	6.1
Government	245,200	16.2	15.2
Information	8,800	0.6	1.9
Leisure and Hospitality	126,900	8.4	9.0
Manufacturing	90,900	6.0	8.5
Mining and Logging	1,200	0.1	0.4
Other Services	36,600	2.4	3.8
Professional and Business Services	158,300	10.5	14.4
Retail Trade	179,800	11.9	10.9
Transportation, Warehousing, and Utilities	196,300	13.0	4.6
Wholesale Trade	64,100	4.2	3.9

Note: Figures are non-farm employment as of December 2020. Figures are not seasonally adjusted and include workers 16 years of age and older; (1) Figures cover the Riverside-San Bernardino-Ontario, CA Metropolitan Statistical Area
Source: Bureau of Labor Statistics, Current Employment Statistics, Employment, Hours, and Earnings

Employment by Occupation

Occupation Classification	City (%)	MSA[1] (%)	U.S. (%)
Management, Business, Science, and Arts	29.1	29.9	38.5
Natural Resources, Construction, and Maintenance	10.0	10.8	8.9
Production, Transportation, and Material Moving	17.8	16.7	13.2
Sales and Office	22.9	22.9	21.6
Service	20.2	19.8	17.8

Note: Figures cover employed civilians 16 years of age and older; (1) Figures cover the Riverside-San Bernardino-Ontario, CA Metropolitan Statistical Area
Source: U.S. Census Bureau, 2015-2019 American Community Survey 5-Year Estimates

Occupations with Greatest Projected Employment Growth: 2020 – 2022

Occupation[1]	2020 Employment	2022 Projected Employment	Numeric Employment Change	Percent Employment Change
Retail Salespersons	317,300	401,300	84,000	26.5
Laborers and Freight, Stock, and Material Movers, Hand	348,700	411,100	62,400	17.9
Waiters and Waitresses	182,500	242,800	60,300	33.0
Combined Food Preparation and Serving Workers, Including Fast Food	183,800	237,200	53,400	29.1
Cashiers	358,500	407,300	48,800	13.6
Cooks, Restaurant	113,200	156,500	43,300	38.3
Personal Care Aides	409,600	447,900	38,300	9.4
Farmworkers and Laborers, Crop, Nursery, and Greenhouse	242,000	269,700	27,700	11.4
Fast Food and Counter Workers	94,000	120,200	26,200	27.9
General and Operations Managers	242,700	268,300	25,600	10.5

Note: Projections cover California; (1) Sorted by numeric employment change
Source: www.projectionscentral.com, State Occupational Projections, 2020–2022 Short-Term Projections

Fastest-Growing Occupations: 2020 – 2022

Occupation[1]	2020 Employment	2022 Projected Employment	Numeric Employment Change	Percent Employment Change
Manicurists and Pedicurists	7,800	21,300	13,500	173.1
Hairdressers, Hairstylists, and Cosmetologists	22,700	44,600	21,900	96.5
Massage Therapists	8,800	17,100	8,300	94.3
Skincare Specialists	5,500	9,100	3,600	65.5
Dental Hygienists	9,200	14,700	5,500	59.8
Dental Hygienists (SOC 2018)	5,300	8,400	3,100	58.5
Dental Assistants	36,300	56,300	20,000	55.1
Dentists, General	12,600	19,000	6,400	50.8
Parking Lot Attendants	14,300	20,400	6,100	42.7
Lodging Managers	3,300	4,600	1,300	39.4

Note: Projections cover California; (1) Sorted by percent employment change and excludes occupations with numeric employment change less than 50
Source: www.projectionscentral.com, State Occupational Projections, 2020–2022 Short-Term Projections

TAXES

State Corporate Income Tax Rates

State	Tax Rate (%)	Income Brackets ($)	Num. of Brackets	Financial Institution Tax Rate (%)[a]	Federal Income Tax Ded.
California	8.84 (b)	Flat rate	1	10.84 (b)	No

Note: Tax rates as of January 1, 2021; (a) Rates listed are the corporate income tax rate applied to financial institutions or excise taxes based on income. Some states have other taxes based upon the value of deposits or shares; (b) Minimum tax is $800 in California, $250 in District of Columbia, $50 in Arizona and North Dakota (banks), $400 ($100 banks) in Rhode Island, $200 per location in South Dakota (banks), $100 in Utah, $300 in Vermont.
Source: Federation of Tax Administrators, State Corporate Income Tax Rates, January 1, 2021

State Individual Income Tax Rates

State	Tax Rate (%)	Income Brackets ($)	Personal Exemptions ($) Single	Married	Depend.	Standard Ded. ($) Single	Married
California (a)	1.0 - 12.3 (g)	8,932 - 599,012 (b)	124	248 (c)	383 (c)	4,601	9,202 (a)

Note: Tax rates as of January 1, 2021; Local- and county-level taxes are not included; Federal income tax is not deductible on state income tax returns; (a) 19 states have statutory provision for automatically adjusting to the rate of inflation the dollar values of the income tax brackets, standard deductions, and/or personal exemptions. Michigan indexes the personal exemption only. Oregon does not index the income brackets for $125,000 and over; (b) For joint returns, taxes are twice the tax on half the couple's income; (c) The personal exemption takes the form of a tax credit instead of a deduction; (g) California imposes an additional 1% tax on taxable income over $1 million, making the maximum rate 13.3% over $1 million.
Source: Federation of Tax Administrators, State Individual Income Tax Rates, January 1, 2021

Various State Sales and Excise Tax Rates

State	State Sales Tax (%)	Gasoline[1] (¢/gal.)	Cigarette[2] ($/pack)	Spirits[3] ($/gal.)	Wine[4] ($/gal.)	Beer[5] ($/gal.)	Recreational Marijuana (%)
California	7.25	63.05	2.87	3.3	0.2	0.2	(c)

Note: All tax rates as of January 1, 2021; (1) The American Petroleum Institute has developed a methodology for determining the average tax rate on a gallon of fuel. Rates may include any of the following: excise taxes, environmental fees, storage tank fees, other fees or taxes, general sales tax, and local taxes; (2) The federal excise tax of $1.0066 per pack and local taxes are not included; (3) Rates are those applicable to off-premise sales of 40% alcohol by volume (a.b.v.) distilled spirits in 750ml containers. Local excise taxes are excluded; (4) Rates are those applicable to off-premise sales of 11% a.b.v. non-carbonated wine in 750ml containers; (5) Rates are those applicable to off-premise sales of 4.7% a.b.v. beer in 12 ounce containers; (c) 15% excise tax (levied on wholesale at average market rate); $9.65/oz. flowers & $2.87/oz. leaves cultivation tax; $1.35/oz fresh cannabis plant
Source: Tax Foundation, 2021 Facts & Figures: How Does Your State Compare?

State Business Tax Climate Index Rankings

State	Overall Rank	Corporate Tax Rank	Individual Income Tax Rank	Sales Tax Rank	Property Tax Rank	Unemployment Insurance Tax Rank
California	49	28	49	45	14	21

Note: The index is a measure of how each state's tax laws affect economic performance. The lower the rank, the more favorable a state's tax system is for business. States without a given tax are given a ranking of 1. The scores/rankings for the District of Columbia do not affect other states. The 2021 index represents the tax climate as of July 1, 2020.
Source: Tax Foundation, State Business Tax Climate Index 2021

TRANSPORTATION

Means of Transportation to Work

Area	Car/Truck/Van Drove Alone	Car-pooled	Public Transportation Bus	Subway	Railroad	Bicycle	Walked	Other Means	Worked at Home
City	76.4	12.6	1.7	0.0	0.7	0.7	2.6	1.1	4.2
MSA[1]	78.9	11.5	0.9	0.1	0.4	0.3	1.5	1.3	5.3
U.S.	76.3	9.0	2.4	1.9	0.6	0.5	2.7	1.4	5.2

Note: Figures are percentages and cover workers 16 years of age and older; (1) Figures cover the Riverside-San Bernardino-Ontario, CA Metropolitan Statistical Area
Source: U.S. Census Bureau, 2015-2019 American Community Survey 5-Year Estimates

Travel Time to Work

Area	Less Than 10 Minutes	10 to 19 Minutes	20 to 29 Minutes	30 to 44 Minutes	45 to 59 Minutes	60 to 89 Minutes	90 Minutes or More
City	8.9	26.2	19.9	21.7	7.6	9.4	6.4
MSA[1]	9.4	26.2	18.6	19.7	8.5	10.4	7.2
U.S.	12.2	28.4	20.8	20.8	8.3	6.4	2.9

Note: Note: Figures are percentages and include workers 16 years old and over; (1) Figures cover the Riverside-San Bernardino-Ontario, CA Metropolitan Statistical Area
Source: U.S. Census Bureau, 2015-2019 American Community Survey 5-Year Estimates

Key Congestion Measures

Measure	1982	1992	2002	2012	2017
Annual Hours of Delay, Total (000)	12,496	32,801	62,702	94,868	107,411
Annual Hours of Delay, Per Auto Commuter	19	33	49	59	70
Annual Congestion Cost, Total (million $)	92	342	839	1,664	1,965
Annual Congestion Cost, Per Auto Commuter ($)	335	606	903	1,070	1,175

Note: Covers the Riverside-San Bernardino CA urban area
Source: Texas A&M Transportation Institute, 2019 Urban Mobility Report

Freeway Travel Time Index

Measure	1982	1987	1992	1997	2002	2007	2012	2017
Urban Area Index[1]	1.10	1.14	1.18	1.22	1.27	1.32	1.31	1.34
Urban Area Rank[1,2]	19	19	18	22	14	9	13	11

Note: Freeway Travel Time Index—the ratio of travel time in the peak period to the travel time at free-flow conditions. For example, a value of 1.30 indicates a 20-minute free-flow trip takes 26 minutes in the peak (20 minutes x 1.30 = 26 minutes); (1) Covers the Riverside-San Bernardino CA urban area; (2) Rank is based on 101 larger urban areas (#1 = highest travel time index)
Source: Texas A&M Transportation Institute, 2019 Urban Mobility Report

Public Transportation

Agency Name / Mode of Transportation	Vehicles Operated in Maximum Service[1]	Annual Unlinked Passenger Trips[2] (in thous.)	Annual Passenger Miles[3] (in thous.)
City of Riverside Special Transportation (City of Riverside)			
Demand Response (directly operated)	25	139.9	1,173.1
Riverside Transit Agency (RTA)			
Bus (directly operated)	99	6,502.7	41,241.2
Bus (purchased transportation)	51	1,390.9	12,526.0
Commuter Bus (directly operated)	20	323.0	9,699.3
Commuter Bus (purchased transportation)	16	75.0	2,138.1
Demand Response (purchased transportation)	101	393.7	3,411.6
Demand Response Taxi (purchased transportation)	16	12.4	177.2

Note: (1) Number of revenue vehicles operated by the given mode and type of service to meet the annual maximum service requirement. This is the revenue vehicle count during the peak season of the year; on the week and day that maximum service is provided. Vehicles operated in maximum service (VOMS) exclude atypical days and one-time special events; (2) Number of passengers who boarded public transportation vehicles. Passengers are counted each time they board a vehicle no matter how many vehicles they use to travel from their origin to their destination. (3) Sum of the distances ridden by all passengers during the entire fiscal year.
Source: Federal Transit Administration, National Transit Database, 2019

Air Transportation

Airport Name and Code / Type of Service	Passenger Airlines[1]	Passenger Enplanements	Freight Carriers[2]	Freight (lbs)
Ontario International (ONT)				
Domestic service (U.S. carriers - 2020)	16	1,194,605	18	991,208,668
International service (U.S. carriers - 2019)	1	13	2	17,356,895

Note: (1) Includes all U.S.-based major, minor and commuter airlines that carried at least one passenger during the year; (2) Includes all U.S.-based airlines and freight carriers that transported at least one pound of freight during the year.
Source: Bureau of Transportation Statistics, The Intermodal Transportation Database, Air Carriers: T-100 Domestic Market (U.S. Carriers), 2020; Bureau of Transportation Statistics, The Intermodal Transportation Database, Air Carriers: T-100 International Market (U.S. Carriers), 2019

BUSINESSES

Major Business Headquarters

Company Name	Industry	Rankings	
		Fortune[1]	Forbes[2]
No companies listed	-	-	-

Note: (1) Companies that produce a 10-K are ranked 1 to 500 based on 2019 revenue; (2) All private companies with at least $2 billion in annual revenue through the end of their most current fiscal year are ranked 1 to 219; companies listed are headquartered in the city; dashes indicate no ranking
Source: Fortune, "Fortune 500," June/July 2020; Forbes, "America's Largest Private Companies," 2020

Fastest-Growing Businesses

According to *Initiative for a Competitive Inner City (ICIC)*, Riverside is home to one of America's 100 fastest-growing "inner city" companies: **Crystal Pacific Window & Door Systems** (#75). Criteria for inclusion: company must be headquartered in or have 51 percent or more of its physical operations in an economically distressed urban area; must be an independent, for-profit corporation, partnership or proprietorship; must have 10 or more employees and have a five-year sales history that includes sales of at least $200,000 in the base year and at least $1 million in the current year with no decrease in sales over the two most recent years. Companies were ranked overall by revenue growth over the five-year period between 2015 and 2019. *Initiative for a Competitive Inner City (ICIC), "Inner City 100 Companies," 2020*

Living Environment

COST OF LIVING

Cost of Living Index

Composite Index	Groceries	Housing	Utilities	Trans-portation	Health Care	Misc. Goods/ Services
n/a	n/a	n/a	n/a	n/a	n/a	n/a

Note: The Cost of Living Index measures regional differences in the cost of consumer goods and services, excluding taxes and non-consumer expenditures, for professional and managerial households in the top income quintile. It is based on more than 50,000 prices covering almost 60 different items for which prices are collected three times a year by chambers of commerce, economic development organizations or university applied economic centers in each participating urban area. The numbers shown should be read as a percentage above or below the national average of 100. For example, a value of 115.4 in the groceries column indicates that grocery prices are 15.4% higher than the national average. Small differences in the index numbers should not be interpreted as significant; n/a not available.
Source: The Council for Community and Economic Research, Cost of Living Index, 2020

Grocery Prices

Area[1]	T-Bone Steak ($/pound)	Frying Chicken ($/pound)	Whole Milk ($/half gal.)	Eggs ($/dozen)	Orange Juice ($/64 oz.)	Coffee ($/11.5 oz.)
City[2]	n/a	n/a	n/a	n/a	n/a	n/a
Avg.	11.78	1.39	2.05	1.47	3.57	4.34
Min.	8.03	0.94	1.03	0.74	2.94	3.02
Max.	15.86	2.65	4.31	3.77	5.44	8.69

Note: (1) Values for the local area are compared with the average, minimum and maximum values for all 284 areas in the Cost of Living Index; (2) Figures cover the Riverside CA urban area; n/a not available; T-Bone Steak (price per pound); Frying Chicken (price per pound, whole fryer); Whole Milk (half gallon carton); Eggs (price per dozen, Grade A, large); Orange Juice (64 oz. Tropicana or Florida Natural); Coffee (11.5 oz. can, vacuum-packed, Maxwell House, Hills Bros, or Folgers).
Source: The Council for Community and Economic Research, Cost of Living Index, 2020

Housing and Utility Costs

Area[1]	New Home Price ($)	Apartment Rent ($/month)	All Electric ($/month)	Part Electric ($/month)	Other Energy ($/month)	Telephone ($/month)
City[2]	n/a	n/a	n/a	n/a	n/a	n/a
Avg.	368,594	1,168	170.86	100.47	65.28	184.30
Min.	190,567	502	91.58	31.42	26.08	169.60
Max.	2,227,806	4,738	470.38	280.31	280.06	206.50

Note: (1) Values for the local area are compared with the average, minimum and maximum values for all 284 areas in the Cost of Living Index; (2) Figures cover the Riverside CA urban area; n/a not available; New Home Price (2,400 sf living area, 8,000 sf lot, in urban area with full utilities); Apartment Rent (950 sf 2 bedroom/1.5 or 2 bath, unfurnished, excluding all utilities except water); All Electric (average monthly cost for an all-electric home); Part Electric (average monthly cost for a part-electric home); Other Energy (average monthly cost for natural gas, fuel oil, coal, wood, and any other forms of energy except electricity); Telephone (price includes the base monthly rate plus taxes and fees for three lines of mobile phone service).
Source: The Council for Community and Economic Research, Cost of Living Index, 2020

Health Care, Transportation, and Other Costs

Area[1]	Doctor ($/visit)	Dentist ($/visit)	Optometrist ($/visit)	Gasoline ($/gallon)	Beauty Salon ($/visit)	Men's Shirt ($)
City[2]	n/a	n/a	n/a	n/a	n/a	n/a
Avg.	115.44	99.32	108.10	2.21	39.27	31.37
Min.	36.68	59.00	51.36	1.71	19.00	11.00
Max.	219.00	153.10	250.97	3.46	82.05	58.33

Note: (1) Values for the local area are compared with the average, minimum and maximum values for all 284 areas in the Cost of Living Index; (2) Figures cover the Riverside CA urban area; n/a not available; Doctor (general practitioners routine exam of an established patient); Dentist (adult teeth cleaning and periodic oral examination); Optometrist (full vision eye exam for established adult patient); Gasoline (one gallon regular unleaded, national brand, including all taxes, cash price at self-service pump if available); Beauty Salon (woman's shampoo, trim, and blow-dry); Men's Shirt (cotton/polyester dress shirt, pinpoint weave, long sleeves).
Source: The Council for Community and Economic Research, Cost of Living Index, 2020

HOUSING

Homeownership Rate

Area	2012 (%)	2013 (%)	2014 (%)	2015 (%)	2016 (%)	2017 (%)	2018 (%)	2019 (%)	2020 (%)
MSA[1]	58.2	56.3	56.8	61.1	62.9	59.9	62.3	64.4	65.8
U.S.	65.4	65.1	64.5	63.7	63.4	63.9	64.4	64.6	66.6

Note: (1) Figures cover the Riverside-San Bernardino-Ontario, CA Metropolitan Statistical Area
Source: U.S. Census Bureau, Housing Vacancies and Homeownership Annual Statistics: 2012-2020

House Price Index (HPI)

Area	National Ranking[2]	Quarterly Change (%)	One-Year Change (%)	Five-Year Change (%)	Since 1991Q1 (%)
MSA[1]	86	2.74	7.03	34.65	169.25
U.S.[3]	–	3.81	10.77	38.99	205.12

Note: The HPI is a weighted repeat sales index. It measures average price changes in repeat sales or refinancings on the same properties. This information is obtained by reviewing repeat mortgage transactions on single-family properties whose mortgages have been purchased or securitized by Fannie Mae or Freddie Mac since January 1975; (1) Figures cover the Riverside-San Bernardino-Ontario, CA Metropolitan Statistical Area; (2) Rankings are based on annual percentage change for all metro areas containing at least 15,000 transactions over the last 10 years and ranges from 1 to 253; (3) figures based on a weighted average of Census Division estimates using a seasonally adjusted, purchase-only index; all figures are for the period ending December 31, 2020
Source: Federal Housing Finance Agency, Change in Metropolitan Area House Price Indexes, April 7, 2021

Median Single-Family Home Prices

Area	2018	2019	2020[p]	Percent Change 2019 to 2020
MSA[1]	360.0	378.5	422.6	11.7
U.S. Average	261.6	274.6	299.9	9.2

Note: Figures are median sales prices of existing single-family homes in thousands of dollars; (p) preliminary; (1) Figures cover the Riverside-San Bernardino-Ontario, CA Metropolitan Statistical Area
Source: National Association of Realtors, Median Sales Price of Existing Single-Family Homes for Metropolitan Areas, 4th Quarter 2020

Qualifying Income Based on Median Sales Price of Existing Single-Family Homes

Area	With 5% Down ($)	With 10% Down ($)	With 20% Down ($)
MSA[1]	85,114	80,634	71,675
U.S. Average	59,266	56,147	49,908

Note: Figures are preliminary; Qualifying income is based on a mortgage rate of 2.81%. Monthly principal and interest payment is limited to 25% of income; (1) Figures cover the Riverside-San Bernardino-Ontario, CA Metropolitan Statistical Area
Source: National Association of Realtors, Qualifying Income Based on Median Sales Price of Existing Single-Family Homes for Metropolitan Areas, 4th Quarter 2020

Home Value Distribution

Area	Under $50,000	$50,000 -$99,999	$100,000 -$149,999	$150,000 -$199,999	$200,000 -$299,999	$300,000 -$499,999	$500,000 -$999,999	$1,000,000 or more
City	2.9	1.6	1.7	3.4	17.5	55.6	15.4	1.9
MSA[1]	4.9	3.4	4.1	6.8	21.0	40.8	17.0	2.0
U.S.	6.9	12.0	13.3	14.0	19.6	19.3	11.4	3.4

Note: Figures are percentages and cover owner-occupied housing units; (1) Figures cover the Riverside-San Bernardino-Ontario, CA Metropolitan Statistical Area
Source: U.S. Census Bureau, 2015-2019 American Community Survey 5-Year Estimates

Year Housing Structure Built

Area	2010 or Later	2000 -2009	1990 -1999	1980 -1989	1970 -1979	1960 -1969	1950 -1959	1940 -1949	Before 1940	Median Year
City	2.8	11.5	10.6	16.4	18.4	12.1	16.0	5.0	7.2	1975
MSA[1]	4.2	20.5	14.6	21.9	15.7	8.9	8.5	2.8	2.8	1985
U.S.	5.2	14.0	13.9	13.4	15.2	10.6	10.3	4.9	12.6	1978

Note: Figures are percentages except for Median Year; Note: (1) Figures cover the Riverside-San Bernardino-Ontario, CA Metropolitan Statistical Area
Source: U.S. Census Bureau, 2015-2019 American Community Survey 5-Year Estimates

Gross Monthly Rent

Area	Under $500	$500 -$999	$1,000 -$1,499	$1,500 -$1,999	$2,000 -$2,499	$2,500 -$2,999	$3,000 and up	Median ($)
City	3.4	16.0	39.3	28.9	9.9	1.8	0.7	1,378
MSA[1]	4.2	22.6	34.7	23.5	9.9	3.7	1.5	1,326
U.S.	9.4	36.2	30.0	14.0	5.6	2.4	2.4	1,062

Note: Figures are percentages except for Median; Gross rent is the contract rent plus the estimated average monthly cost of utilities (electricity, gas, and water and sewer) and fuels (oil, coal, kerosene, wood, etc.) if these are paid by the renter (or paid for the renter by someone else); (1) Figures cover the Riverside-San Bernardino-Ontario, CA Metropolitan Statistical Area
Source: U.S. Census Bureau, 2015-2019 American Community Survey 5-Year Estimates

HEALTH

Health Risk Factors

Category	MSA[1] (%)	U.S. (%)
Adults aged 18–64 who have any kind of health care coverage	86.4	87.3
Adults who reported being in good or better health	80.3	82.4
Adults who have been told they have high blood cholesterol	32.8	33.0
Adults who have been told they have high blood pressure	32.6	32.3
Adults who are current smokers	11.1	17.1
Adults who currently use E-cigarettes	4.2	4.6
Adults who currently use chewing tobacco, snuff, or snus	0.7	4.0
Adults who are heavy drinkers[2]	7.4	6.3
Adults who are binge drinkers[3]	19.3	17.4
Adults who are overweight (BMI 25.0 - 29.9)	36.0	35.3
Adults who are obese (BMI 30.0 - 99.8)	31.8	31.3
Adults who participated in any physical activities in the past month	74.3	74.4
Adults who always or nearly always wears a seat belt	98.6	94.3

Note: (1) Figures cover the Riverside-San Bernardino-Ontario, CA Metropolitan Statistical Area; (2) Heavy drinkers are classified as adult men having more than 14 drinks per week and adult women having more than 7 drinks per week; (3) Binge drinkers are classified as males having five or more drinks on one occasion or females having four or more drinks on one occasion
Source: Centers for Disease Control and Prevention, Behaviorial Risk Factor Surveillance System, SMART: Selected Metropolitan Area Risk Trends, 2017

Acute and Chronic Health Conditions

Category	MSA[1] (%)	U.S. (%)
Adults who have ever been told they had a heart attack	3.7	4.2
Adults who have ever been told they have angina or coronary heart disease	2.9	3.9
Adults who have ever been told they had a stroke	2.8	3.0
Adults who have ever been told they have asthma	12.3	14.2
Adults who have ever been told they have arthritis	22.6	24.9
Adults who have ever been told they have diabetes[2]	13.7	10.5
Adults who have ever been told they had skin cancer	4.6	6.2
Adults who have ever been told they had any other types of cancer	5.8	7.1
Adults who have ever been told they have COPD	6.6	6.5
Adults who have ever been told they have kidney disease	3.4	3.0
Adults who have ever been told they have a form of depression	18.7	20.5

Note: (1) Figures cover the Riverside-San Bernardino-Ontario, CA Metropolitan Statistical Area; (2) Figures do not include pregnancy-related, borderline, or pre-diabetes
Source: Centers for Disease Control and Prevention, Behaviorial Risk Factor Surveillance System, SMART: Selected Metropolitan Area Risk Trends, 2017

Health Screening and Vaccination Rates

Category	MSA[1] (%)	U.S. (%)
Adults aged 65+ who have had flu shot within the past year	55.2	60.7
Adults aged 65+ who have ever had a pneumonia vaccination	72.4	75.4
Adults who have ever been tested for HIV	41.8	36.1
Adults who have ever had the shingles or zoster vaccine?	22.6	28.9
Adults who have had their blood cholesterol checked within the last five years	89.0	85.9

Note: n/a not available; (1) Figures cover the Riverside-San Bernardino-Ontario, CA Metropolitan Statistical Area.
Source: Centers for Disease Control and Prevention, Behaviorial Risk Factor Surveillance System, SMART: Selected Metropolitan Area Risk Trends, 2017

Disability Status

Category	MSA[1] (%)	U.S. (%)
Adults who reported being deaf	6.5	6.7
Are you blind or have serious difficulty seeing, even when wearing glasses?	5.5	4.5
Are you limited in any way in any of your usual activities due of arthritis?	13.3	12.9
Do you have difficulty doing errands alone?	6.8	6.8
Do you have difficulty dressing or bathing?	3.3	3.6
Do you have serious difficulty concentrating/remembering/making decisions?	11.9	10.7
Do you have serious difficulty walking or climbing stairs?	11.3	13.6

Note: (1) Figures cover the Riverside-San Bernardino-Ontario, CA Metropolitan Statistical Area.
Source: Centers for Disease Control and Prevention, Behaviorial Risk Factor Surveillance System, SMART: Selected Metropolitan Area Risk Trends, 2017

Mortality Rates for the Top 10 Causes of Death in the U.S.

ICD-10[a] Sub-Chapter	ICD-10[a] Code	Age-Adjusted Mortality Rate[1] per 100,000 population	
		County[2]	U.S.
Malignant neoplasms	C00-C97	138.3	149.2
Ischaemic heart diseases	I20-I25	106.9	90.5
Other forms of heart disease	I30-I51	41.8	52.2
Chronic lower respiratory diseases	J40-J47	39.3	39.6
Other degenerative diseases of the nervous system	G30-G31	42.8	37.6
Cerebrovascular diseases	I60-I69	35.7	37.2
Other external causes of accidental injury	W00-X59	26.0	36.1
Organic, including symptomatic, mental disorders	F01-F09	8.7	29.4
Hypertensive diseases	I10-I15	31.9	24.1
Diabetes mellitus	E10-E14	18.3	21.5

Note: (a) ICD-10 = International Classification of Diseases 10th Revision; (1) Mortality rates are a three-year average covering 2017-2019; (2) Figures cover Riverside County.
Source: Centers for Disease Control and Prevention, National Center for Health Statistics. Underlying Cause of Death 1999-2019 on CDC WONDER Online Database

Mortality Rates for Selected Causes of Death

ICD-10[a] Sub-Chapter	ICD-10[a] Code	Age-Adjusted Mortality Rate[1] per 100,000 population	
		County[2]	U.S.
Assault	X85-Y09	4.6	6.0
Diseases of the liver	K70-K76	15.4	14.4
Human immunodeficiency virus (HIV) disease	B20-B24	1.8	1.5
Influenza and pneumonia	J09-J18	12.8	13.8
Intentional self-harm	X60-X84	12.0	14.1
Malnutrition	E40-E46	0.9	2.3
Obesity and other hyperalimentation	E65-E68	1.7	2.1
Renal failure	N17-N19	9.5	12.6
Transport accidents	V01-V99	13.4	12.3
Viral hepatitis	B15-B19	1.4	1.2

Note: (a) ICD-10 = International Classification of Diseases 10th Revision; (1) Mortality rates are a three-year average covering 2017-2019; (2) Figures cover Riverside County; Data are suppressed when the data meet the criteria for confidentiality constraints; Mortality rates are flagged as unreliable when the rate would be calculated with a numerator of 20 or less.
Source: Centers for Disease Control and Prevention, National Center for Health Statistics. Underlying Cause of Death 1999-2019 on CDC WONDER Online Database

Health Insurance Coverage

Area	With Health Insurance	With Private Health Insurance	With Public Health Insurance	Without Health Insurance	Population Under Age 19 Without Health Insurance
City	90.6	58.9	38.2	9.4	3.6
MSA[1]	91.4	57.5	42.0	8.6	3.9
U.S.	91.2	67.9	35.1	8.8	5.1

Note: Figures are percentages that cover the civilian noninstitutionalized population; (1) Figures cover the Riverside-San Bernardino-Ontario, CA Metropolitan Statistical Area
Source: U.S. Census Bureau, 2015-2019 American Community Survey 5-Year Estimates

Number of Medical Professionals

Area	MDs[3]	DOs[3,4]	Dentists	Podiatrists	Chiropractors	Optometrists
County[1] (number)	3,125	373	1,295	64	402	317
County[1] (rate[2])	127.8	15.3	52.4	2.6	16.3	12.8
U.S. (rate[2])	282.9	22.7	71.2	6.2	28.1	16.9

06065
Note: Data as of 2019 unless noted; (1) Data covers Riverside County; (2) Rate per 100,000 population; (3) Data as of 2018 and includes all active, non-federal physicians; (4) Doctor of Osteopathic Medicine
Source: U.S. Department of Health and Human Services, Health Resources and Services Administration, Bureau of Health Professions, Area Resource File (ARF) 2019-2020

EDUCATION

Public School District Statistics

District Name	Schls	Pupils	Pupil/ Teacher Ratio	Minority Pupils[1] (%)	Free Lunch Eligible[2] (%)	IEP[3] (%)
Riverside County Office of Education	5	1,613	12.6	86.2	81.2	1.9
Riverside Unified	49	40,708	24.2	79.3	55.4	12.8

Note: Table includes school districts with 2,000 or more students; (1) Percentage of students that are not non-Hispanic white; (2) Percentage of students that are eligible for the free lunch program; (3) Percentage of students that have an Individualized Education Program.
Source: U.S. Department of Education, National Center for Education Statistics, Common Core of Data, Local Education Agency (School District) Universe Survey: School Year 2018-2019; U.S. Department of Education, National Center for Education Statistics, Common Core of Data, Public Elementary/Secondary School Universe Survey: School Year 2018-2019

Highest Level of Education

Area	Less than H.S.	H.S. Diploma	Some College, No Deg.	Associate Degree	Bachelor's Degree	Master's Degree	Prof. School Degree	Doctorate Degree
City	19.4	26.3	23.7	7.7	13.5	6.4	1.4	1.7
MSA[1]	18.9	26.6	24.6	8.2	13.9	5.6	1.3	0.9
U.S.	12.0	27.0	20.4	8.5	19.8	8.8	2.1	1.4

Note: Figures cover persons age 25 and over; (1) Figures cover the Riverside-San Bernardino-Ontario, CA Metropolitan Statistical Area
Source: U.S. Census Bureau, 2015-2019 American Community Survey 5-Year Estimates

Educational Attainment by Race

Area	High School Graduate or Higher (%)					Bachelor's Degree or Higher (%)				
	Total	White	Black	Asian	Hisp.[2]	Total	White	Black	Asian	Hisp.[2]
City	80.6	83.5	92.0	87.2	68.5	23.0	23.8	26.5	47.8	11.8
MSA[1]	81.1	83.7	89.6	90.4	67.4	21.7	22.0	23.8	48.6	10.7
U.S.	88.0	89.9	86.0	87.1	68.7	32.1	33.5	21.6	54.3	16.4

Note: Figures shown cover persons 25 years old and over; (1) Figures cover the Riverside-San Bernardino-Ontario, CA Metropolitan Statistical Area; (2) People of Hispanic origin can be of any race
Source: U.S. Census Bureau, 2015-2019 American Community Survey 5-Year Estimates

School Enrollment by Grade and Control

Area	Preschool (%)		Kindergarten (%)		Grades 1 - 4 (%)		Grades 5 - 8 (%)		Grades 9 - 12 (%)	
	Public	Private	Public	Private	Public	Private	Public	Private	Public	Private
City	66.0	34.0	90.5	9.5	94.0	6.0	93.6	6.4	95.0	5.0
MSA[1]	68.6	31.4	91.8	8.2	94.4	5.6	94.2	5.8	94.9	5.1
U.S.	59.1	40.9	87.6	12.4	89.5	10.5	89.4	10.6	90.1	9.9

Note: Figures shown cover persons 3 years old and over; (1) Figures cover the Riverside-San Bernardino-Ontario, CA Metropolitan Statistical Area
Source: U.S. Census Bureau, 2015-2019 American Community Survey 5-Year Estimates

Higher Education

Four-Year Colleges			Two-Year Colleges			Medical Schools[1]	Law Schools[2]	Voc/ Tech[3]
Public	Private Non-profit	Private For-profit	Public	Private Non-profit	Private For-profit			
1	2	1	1	0	4	1	0	3

Note: Figures cover institutions located within the city limits and include main campuses only; (1) includes schools accredited by the Liaison Committee on Medical Education and the American Osteopathic Association's Commission on Osteopathic College Accreditation; (2) includes ABA-accredited schools, schools with provisional ABA accreditation, and state accredited schools; (3) includes all schools with programs that are less than 2 years.
Source: National Center for Education Statistics, Integrated Postsecondary Education System (IPEDS), 2019-20; Wikipedia, List of Medical Schools in the United States, accessed April 2, 2021; Wikipedia, List of Law Schools in the United States, accessed April 2, 2021

According to *U.S. News & World Report,* the Riverside-San Bernardino-Ontario, CA metro area is home to one of the top 200 national universities in the U.S.: **University of California—Riverside** (#88 tie). The indicators used to capture academic quality fall into a number of categories: assessment by administrators at peer institutions; retention of students; faculty resources; student selectivity; financial resources; alumni giving; high school counselor ratings of colleges; and graduation rate. *U.S. News & World Report, "America's Best Colleges 2021"*

EMPLOYERS

Major Employers

Company Name	Industry
Agua Caliente Band of Cahuilla Indians	Casino resort
Amazon	E-Commerce
Cal Baptist University	University
City of Riverside	Municipal government
Corona-Norco Unified School District	School district
County of Riverside	County government
Desert Sands Unified School District	School district
Eisenhower Medical Center	Hospital
Hemet Unified School District	School district
Jurupa Unified School District	School district
JW Marriott Desert Springs Resort & Spa	Resort
Kaiser Permanente Riverside Medical Ctr	Hospital
Lake Elsinore Unified School District	School district
March Air Reserve Base	Military reserve base
Moreno Valley Unified School District	School district
Morongo Casino	Resort
Murrieta Valley Unified School District	School district
Palm Springs Unified School District	School district
Pechanga Resort & Casino	Casino resort
Riverside Community College District	Community college
Riverside Community Hospital	Hospital
Riverside Unified School District	School district
Ross Dress For Less	Department stores, discount
Stater Bros	Retail grocery
Temecula Valley Unified School District	School district
University of California	Riverside
Walmart	Department stores, discount

Note: Companies shown are located within the Riverside-San Bernardino-Ontario, CA Metropolitan Statistical Area.
Source: Hoovers.com; Wikipedia

PUBLIC SAFETY

Crime Rate

Area	All Crimes	Violent Crimes				Property Crimes		
		Murder	Rape[3]	Robbery	Aggrav. Assault	Burglary	Larceny -Theft	Motor Vehicle Theft
City	3,443.6	5.1	41.7	142.8	316.3	390.7	2,099.6	447.4
Suburbs[1]	2,643.4	5.8	29.0	111.1	273.8	441.1	1,367.7	414.9
Metro[2]	2,700.9	5.7	29.9	113.4	276.9	437.5	1,420.4	417.2
U.S.	2,489.3	5.0	42.6	81.6	250.2	340.5	1,549.5	219.9

Note: Figures are crimes per 100,000 population; (1) All areas within the metro area that are located outside the city limits; (2) Figures cover the Riverside-San Bernardino-Ontario, CA Metropolitan Statistical Area; (3) All figures shown were reported using the revised Uniform Crime Reporting (UCR) definition of rape.
Source: FBI Uniform Crime Reports, 2019

Hate Crimes

Area	Number of Quarters Reported	Number of Incidents per Bias Motivation					
		Race/Ethnicity/ Ancestry	Religion	Sexual Orientation	Disability	Gender	Gender Identity
City	4	10	1	4	0	0	0
U.S.	4	3,963	1,521	1,195	157	69	198

Source: Federal Bureau of Investigation, Hate Crime Statistics 2019

Identity Theft Consumer Reports

Area	Reports	Reports per 100,000 Population	Rank[2]
MSA[1]	15,709	338	100
U.S.	1,387,615	423	-

Note: (1) Figures cover the Riverside-San Bernardino-Ontario, CA Metropolitan Statistical Area; (2) Rank ranges from 1 to 391 where 1 indicates greatest number of identity theft reports per 100,000 population
Source: Federal Trade Commission, Consumer Sentinel Network Data Book 2020

Fraud and Other Consumer Reports

Area	Reports	Reports per 100,000 Population	Rank[2]
MSA[1]	32,669	702	184
U.S.	3,385,133	1,031	-

Note: (1) Figures cover the Riverside-San Bernardino-Ontario, CA Metropolitan Statistical Area; (2) Rank ranges from 1 to 391 where 1 indicates greatest number of fraud and other consumer reports per 100,000 population
Source: Federal Trade Commission, Consumer Sentinel Network Data Book 2020

POLITICS

2020 Presidential Election Results

Area	Biden	Trump	Jorgensen	Hawkins	Other
Riverside County	53.0	45.0	1.0	0.3	0.6
U.S.	51.3	46.8	1.2	0.3	0.5

Note: Results are percentages and may not add to 100% due to rounding
Source: Dave Leip's Atlas of U.S. Presidential Elections

SPORTS

Professional Sports Teams

Team Name	League	Year Established

No teams are located in the metro area
Source: Wikipedia, Major Professional Sports Teams of the United States and Canada, April 6, 2021

CLIMATE

Average and Extreme Temperatures

Temperature	Jan	Feb	Mar	Apr	May	Jun	Jul	Aug	Sep	Oct	Nov	Dec	Yr.
Extreme High (°F)	90	89	97	110	107	114	114	114	112	110	95	99	114
Average High (°F)	66	68	68	75	79	86	92	92	89	83	73	67	78
Average Temp. (°F)	54	57	58	63	67	73	78	78	76	70	61	55	66
Average Low (°F)	42	45	47	50	55	59	63	64	62	56	47	42	53
Extreme Low (°F)	25	29	30	35	38	43	52	51	47	40	31	24	24

Note: Figures cover the years 1973-1993
Source: National Climatic Data Center, International Station Meteorological Climate Summary, 9/96

Average Precipitation/Snowfall/Humidity

Precip./Humidity	Jan	Feb	Mar	Apr	May	Jun	Jul	Aug	Sep	Oct	Nov	Dec	Yr.
Avg. Precip. (in.)	n/a	n/a	n/a	n/a	n/a	n/a	n/a	n/a	n/a	n/a	n/a	n/a	n/a
Avg. Snowfall (in.)	n/a	n/a	n/a	n/a	n/a	n/a	n/a	n/a	n/a	n/a	n/a	n/a	n/a
Avg. Rel. Hum. 6am (%)	45	44	50	42	44	39	35	36	38	37	36	39	40
Avg. Rel. Hum. 3pm (%)	74	75	79	75	77	76	73	72	71	73	69	70	74

Note: Figures cover the years 1973-1993
Source: National Climatic Data Center, International Station Meteorological Climate Summary, 9/96

Weather Conditions

Temperature			Daytime Sky			Precipitation		
10°F & below	32°F & below	90°F & above	Clear	Partly cloudy	Cloudy	0.01 inch or more precip.	0.1 inch or more snow/ice	Thunderstorms
0	4	82	124	178	63	n/a	n/a	5

Note: Figures are average number of days per year and cover the years 1973-1993
Source: National Climatic Data Center, International Station Meteorological Climate Summary, 9/96

HAZARDOUS WASTE

Superfund Sites

The Riverside-San Bernardino-Ontario, CA metro area is home to eight sites on the EPA's Superfund National Priorities List: **Alark Hard Chrome** (final); **Barstow Marine Corps Logistics Base** (final); **George Air Force Base** (final); **March Air Force Base** (final); **Newmark Ground Water Contamination** (final); **Norton Air Force Base (Landfill #2)** (final); **Rockets, Fireworks, and Flares Site** (final); **Stringfellow** (final). There are a total of 1,375 Superfund sites with a status of proposed or final on the list in the U.S. *U.S. Environmental Protection Agency, National Priorities List, April 7, 2021*

AIR QUALITY

Air Quality Trends: Ozone

	1990	1995	2000	2005	2010	2015	2016	2017	2018	2019
MSA[1]	0.146	0.129	0.104	0.102	0.093	0.094	0.096	0.099	0.097	0.091
U.S.	0.088	0.089	0.082	0.080	0.073	0.069	0.068	0.069	0.069	0.065

Note: (1) Data covers the Riverside-San Bernardino-Ontario, CA Metropolitan Statistical Area. The values shown are the composite ozone concentration averages among trend sites based on the highest fourth daily maximum 8-hour concentration in parts per million. These trends are based on sites having an adequate record of monitoring data during the trend period. Data from exceptional events are included.
Source: U.S. Environmental Protection Agency, Air Quality Monitoring Information, "Air Quality Trends by City, 1990-2019"

Air Quality Index

Area	Percent of Days when Air Quality was...[2]					AQI Statistics[2]	
	Good	Moderate	Unhealthy for Sensitive Groups	Unhealthy	Very Unhealthy	Maximum	Median
MSA[1]	11.5	48.8	21.6	15.9	2.2	213	89

Note: (1) Data covers the Riverside-San Bernardino-Ontario, CA Metropolitan Statistical Area; (2) Based on 365 days with AQI data in 2019. Air Quality Index (AQI) is an index for reporting daily air quality. EPA calculates the AQI for five major air pollutants regulated by the Clean Air Act: ground-level ozone, particle pollution (aka particulate matter), carbon monoxide, sulfur dioxide, and nitrogen dioxide. The AQI runs from 0 to 500. The higher the AQI value, the greater the level of air pollution and the greater the health concern. There are six AQI categories: "Good" AQI is between 0 and 50. Air quality is considered satisfactory; "Moderate" AQI is between 51 and 100. Air quality is acceptable; "Unhealthy for Sensitive Groups" When AQI values are between 101 and 150, members of sensitive groups may experience health effects; "Unhealthy" When AQI values are between 151 and 200 everyone may begin to experience health effects; "Very Unhealthy" AQI values between 201 and 300 trigger a health alert; "Hazardous" AQI values over 300 trigger warnings of emergency conditions (not shown).
Source: U.S. Environmental Protection Agency, Air Quality Index Report, 2019

Air Quality Index Pollutants

Area	Percent of Days when AQI Pollutant was...[2]					
	Carbon Monoxide	Nitrogen Dioxide	Ozone	Sulfur Dioxide	Particulate Matter 2.5	Particulate Matter 10
MSA[1]	0.0	3.0	62.5	0.0	24.4	10.1

Note: (1) Data covers the Riverside-San Bernardino-Ontario, CA Metropolitan Statistical Area; (2) Based on 365 days with AQI data in 2019. The Air Quality Index (AQI) is an index for reporting daily air quality. EPA calculates the AQI for five major air pollutants regulated by the Clean Air Act: ground-level ozone, particle pollution (also known as particulate matter), carbon monoxide, sulfur dioxide, and nitrogen dioxide. The AQI runs from 0 to 500. The higher the AQI value, the greater the level of air pollution and the greater the health concern.
Source: U.S. Environmental Protection Agency, Air Quality Index Report, 2019

Maximum Air Pollutant Concentrations: Particulate Matter, Ozone, CO and Lead

	Particulate Matter 10 (ug/m^3)	Particulate Matter 2.5 Wtd AM (ug/m^3)	Particulate Matter 2.5 24-Hr (ug/m^3)	Ozone (ppm)	Carbon Monoxide (ppm)	Lead (ug/m^3)
MSA[1] Level	243	12.8	36	0.106	1	0.01
NAAQS[2]	150	15	35	0.075	9	0.15
Met NAAQS[2]	No	Yes	No	No	Yes	Yes

Note: (1) Data covers the Riverside-San Bernardino-Ontario, CA Metropolitan Statistical Area; Data from exceptional events are included; (2) National Ambient Air Quality Standards; ppm = parts per million; ug/m^3 = micrograms per cubic meter; n/a not available.
Concentrations: Particulate Matter 10 (coarse particulate)—highest second maximum 24-hour concentration; Particulate Matter 2.5 Wtd AM (fine particulate)—highest weighted annual mean concentration; Particulate Matter 2.5 24-Hour (fine particulate)—highest 98th percentile 24-hour concentration; Ozone—highest fourth daily maximum 8-hour concentration; Carbon Monoxide—highest second maximum non-overlapping 8-hour concentration; Lead—maximum running 3-month average
Source: U.S. Environmental Protection Agency, Air Quality Monitoring Information, "Air Quality Statistics by City, 2019"

Maximum Air Pollutant Concentrations: Nitrogen Dioxide and Sulfur Dioxide

	Nitrogen Dioxide AM (ppb)	Nitrogen Dioxide 1-Hr (ppb)	Sulfur Dioxide AM (ppb)	Sulfur Dioxide 1-Hr (ppb)	Sulfur Dioxide 24-Hr (ppb)
MSA[1] Level	29	74	n/a	7	n/a
NAAQS[2]	53	100	30	75	140
Met NAAQS[2]	Yes	Yes	n/a	Yes	n/a

Note: (1) Data covers the Riverside-San Bernardino-Ontario, CA Metropolitan Statistical Area; Data from exceptional events are included; (2) National Ambient Air Quality Standards; ppm = parts per million; ug/m³ = micrograms per cubic meter; n/a not available.
Concentrations: Nitrogen Dioxide AM—highest arithmetic mean concentration; Nitrogen Dioxide 1-Hr—highest 98th percentile 1-hour daily maximum concentration; Sulfur Dioxide AM—highest annual mean concentration; Sulfur Dioxide 1-Hr—highest 99th percentile 1-hour daily maximum concentration; Sulfur Dioxide 24-Hr—highest second maximum 24-hour concentration
Source: U.S. Environmental Protection Agency, Air Quality Monitoring Information, "Air Quality Statistics by City, 2019"

Sacramento, California

Background

Sacramento is the capital of California and the seat of Sacramento County. It was named after the Sacramento River which derived its name from the word referring to the Catholic Holy Eucharist. It lies at the juncture of the Sacramento and American rivers.

A Swiss soldier, Captain John Augustus Sutter, settled Sacramento in 1839, when he received permission from the Mexican government to establish a new colony which became known as New Helvetia. The 50,000-acre land grant included a wide swath of the rich and fertile valley between the two rivers, and Sutter's ranch, trading post, and agricultural projects were soon productive and profitable. When, in 1846, American troops occupied the area, Sutter was well-positioned to take advantage, and his trade soon extended well up the northern coast.

In 1848, one of Sutter's employees, a carpenter named James W. Marshall, discovered gold at what became known as "Sutter's Mill" in the settlement of Coloma. The discovery brought an onslaught of prospectors and the beginning of the California Gold Rush. The prospectors overwhelmed New Helvetia resources and the havoc that followed destroyed the economic foundation of the town. The newcomers overran Sutter's land and claimed it as their own. Sutter tried to expand his business to include mining supplies, but was only meagerly rewarded. He then ceded land along the Sacramento River to his son, who founded the town that became the city we know today.

Sacramento was a natural center for miners' needs, including housing, food, banking, transportation and necessary mining equipment. One of Sacramento's most famous entrepreneurs is Levi Strauss who sold the ultimate mining pants known as "Levi's." Sacramento's economy was booming, but it was plagued by floods, as well as fire and a cholera epidemic. The flooding that is endemic to the area has since been well controlled by dam projects, which also now supply electricity to a wide area. In 1854, the city managed to fight off a daunting list of competitors, and Sacramento became California's capital.

On April 3, 1860, the legendary Pony Express carried mail from Sacramento to St. Joseph, Missouri. This team of riders relayed the mail on horseback and established a new record time. A ten day journey of nearly 1800 miles, it proved unprofitable but nonetheless caught the attention of the federal government and helped launch of our current postal system.

In the years since, the city has grown rapidly, increasing from 30,000 people in 1900 to over 100,000 in 1940 and passing the 400,000 mark in 2000. As befitting a state capital, government (state, county, and local) is the largest employer in the city. Other notable companies located in the area include Sutter Health, Blue Diamond Growers, Aerojet, Rocketdyne, and the McClatchey Company.

Sutter's Fort State Historical Monument features a restoration of John Sutter's original ranch and trading post, and a designated Old Sacramento Historical Area preserves many buildings from the gold rush period and thereafter. At the city's Crocker Art Museum, visitors can view an extensive collection of works by Michelangelo, Rembrandt, and Leonardo da Vinci. In October 2010, the Crocker completed a 100,000-ft. expansion that more than tripled its size.

> The Golden 1 Center require fans show proof of vaccination or a negative COVID-19 test before being able to attend a Sacramento Kings game.

The Wells Fargo Museum is a monument to the history of the Pony Express and the era of the gold rush. Housed in the original bank building that managed the Pony Express, it features staff dressed in period attire who conduct tours. The museum displays include tools, gold nuggets, documents, and other artifacts relevant to the Pony Express and the miners of the gold rush era.

The Woodland Opera House opened in 1896 in nearby Woodland, California, and is today on the National Register of Historic Places. When motion pictures became the preferred means of entertainment, the opera house suffered financial difficulties and closed in 1913. The boarded up building was dormant until 1971 when it was saved from demolition by Yolo County Historic Society who gave it to the state in 1980. The building underwent a total renovation in 1982, and is now a major entertainment venue.

Since 1985, Sacramento has hosted NBA basketball when the Kings relocated from Kansas City. In addition, the city fields a professional soccer team, the Sacramento Republic FC of the USL Championship League, and a minor league baseball team, the River Cats, who are the AAA affiliate of the San Francisco Giants. Golden1 Center sports arena opened in 2016.

Sacramento has a mild climate with abundant sunshine. A nearly cloud-free sky prevails throughout the summer months, which are usually dry, with warm to hot afternoons and mostly mild nights.

Rankings

General Rankings

- In their seventh annual survey, Livability.com looked at data for more than 1,000 small to mid-sized U.S. cities to determine the rankings for Livability's "Top 100 Best Places to Live" in 2020. Sacramento ranked #63. Criteria: housing and affordable living; vibrant economy; social and civic engagement; education; demographics; health care options; transportation & infrastructure; and abundant lifestyle amenities. *Livability.com, "Top 100 Best Places to Live 2020" October 2020*

Business/Finance Rankings

- The Brookings Institution ranked the nation's largest cities based on income inequality. Sacramento was ranked #71 (#1 = greatest inequality). Criteria: the "95/20 ratio," a figure representing the income at which a household earns more than 95 percent of all other households, divided by the income at which a household earns more than only 20 percent of all other households. *Brookings Institution, "Household Income Inequality, Largest Cities of 97 Large U.S. Metro Areas, 2014-2016," February 5, 2018*

- The Brookings Institution ranked the 100 largest metro areas in the U.S. based on income inequality. Sacramento was ranked #33 (#1 = greatest inequality). Criteria: the "95/20 ratio," a figure representing the income at which a household earns more than 95 percent of all other households, divided by the income at which a household earns more than only 20 percent of all other households. *Brookings Institution, "Household Income Inequality, 100 Largest U.S. Metro Areas, 2014-2016," February 5, 2018*

- The Sacramento metro area appeared on the Milken Institute "2021 Best Performing Cities" list. Rank: #47 out of 200 large metro areas (population over 250,000). Criteria: job growth; wage and salary growth; high-tech output growth; housing affordability; household broadband access. *Milken Institute, "Best-Performing Cities 2021," February 16, 2021*

- *Forbes* ranked the 200 most populous metro areas to determine the nation's "Best Places for Business and Careers." The Sacramento metro area was ranked #56. Criteria: costs (business and living); job growth (past and projected); income growth; quality of life; educational attainment (college and high school); projected economic growth; cultural and leisure opportunities; workplace tolerance laws; net migration patterns. *Forbes, "The Best Places for Business and Careers 2019: Seattle Still On Top," October 30, 2019*

Education Rankings

- Personal finance website *WalletHub* analyzed the 150 largest U.S. metropolitan statistical areas to determine where the most educated Americans are putting their degrees to work. Criteria: education levels; percentage of workers with degrees; education quality and attainment gap; public school quality rankings; quality and enrollment of each metro area's universities. Sacramento was ranked #50 (#1 = most educated city). *www.WalletHub.com, "Most and Least Educated Cities in America," July 20, 2020*

- Sacramento was selected as one of America's most literate cities. The city ranked #42 out of the 84 largest U.S. cities. Criteria: number of booksellers; library resources; Internet resources; educational attainment; periodical publishing resources; newspaper circulation. *Central Connecticut State University, "America's Most Literate Cities, 2018," February 2019*

Environmental Rankings

- Sperling's BestPlaces assessed the 50 largest metropolitan areas of the United States for the likelihood of dangerously extreme weather events or earthquakes. In general the Southeast and South-Central regions have the highest risk of weather extremes and earthquakes, while the Pacific Northwest enjoys the lowest risk. Of the least risky metropolitan areas, the Sacramento metro area was ranked #3. *www.bestplaces.net, "Avoid Natural Disasters: BestPlaces Reveals The Top 10 Safest Places to Live," October 25, 2017*

- The U.S. Environmental Protection Agency (EPA) released a list of U.S. metropolitan areas with the most ENERGY STAR certified buildings in 2019. The Sacramento metro area was ranked #22 out of 25. *U.S. Environmental Protection Agency, "2020 Energy Star Top Cities," March 2020*

- Sacramento was highlighted as one of the 25 most ozone-polluted metro areas in the U.S. during 2016 through 2018. The area ranked #5. *American Lung Association, "State of the Air 2020," April 21, 2020*

- Sacramento was highlighted as one of the 25 metro areas most polluted by year-round particle pollution (Annual PM 2.5) in the U.S. during 2016 through 2018. The area ranked #16. *American Lung Association, "State of the Air 2020," April 21, 2020*

- Sacramento was highlighted as one of the 25 metro areas most polluted by short-term particle pollution (24-hour PM 2.5) in the U.S. during 2016 through 2018. The area ranked #11. *American Lung Association, "State of the Air 2020," April 21, 2020*

Health/Fitness Rankings

- For each of the 100 largest cities in the United States, the American Fitness Index®, published by the American College of Sports Medicine and the Anthem Foundation, evaluated community infrastructure and 33 health behaviors including preventive health, levels of chronic disease conditions, pedestrian safety, air quality, and community resources that support physical activity. Sacramento ranked #20 for "community fitness." *americanfitnessindex.org, "2020 ACSM American Fitness Index Summary Report," July 14, 2020*

- Sacramento was identified as a "2021 Spring Allergy Capital." The area ranked #85 out of 100. Three groups of factors were used to identify the most challenging cities for people with allergies during the spring season: annual spring pollen levels; over the counter medicine use; number of board-certified allergy specialists. *Asthma and Allergy Foundation of America, "Spring Allergy Capitals 2021," February 23, 2021*

- Sacramento was identified as a "2021 Fall Allergy Capital." The area ranked #93 out of 100. Three groups of factors were used to identify the most challenging cities for people with allergies during the fall season: annual fall pollen levels; over the counter medicine use; number of board-certified allergy specialists. *Asthma and Allergy Foundation of America, "Fall Allergy Capitals 2021," February 23, 2021*

- Sacramento was identified as a "2019 Asthma Capital." The area ranked #49 out of the nation's 100 largest metropolitan areas. Criteria: estimated asthma prevalence; crude death rate from asthma; and ER visits due to asthma. Risk factors analyzed but not factored in the rankings: annual pollen score; annual air quality; public smoking laws; number of board-certified asthma specialists; rescue medication use; controller medication use; uninsured rate; poverty rate. *Asthma and Allergy Foundation of America, "Asthma Capitals 2019: The Most Challenging Places to Live With Asthma," May 7, 2019*

Real Estate Rankings

- FitSmallBusiness looked at 50 of the largest metropolitan areas in the U.S. to determine which metro was the best to start a real estate business. Data was compiled from such sources as: Zillow, Trulia, U.S. Census Bureau, and the Bureau of Labor Statistics. Criteria: location; inventory; annual wages; median sales price of homes; days on the market; median price cut percentage; and other factors that would influence real estate professional growth. The Sacramento metro area ranked #25. *fitsmallbusiness.com, "The Best Cities to Become a Real Estate Agent in 2018," January 30, 2018*

- *WalletHub* compared the most populated U.S. cities to determine which had the best markets for real estate agents. Sacramento ranked #46 where demand was high and pay was the best. Criteria: sales per agent; annual median wage for real-estate agents; monthly average starting salary for real estate agents; real estate job density and competition; unemployment rate; home turnover rate; housing-market health index; and other relevant metrics. *www.WalletHub.com, "2019's Best Places to Be a Real Estate Agent," April 24, 2019*

- The Sacramento metro area appeared on Realtor.com's list of hot housing markets to watch in 2021. The area ranked #1. Criteria: healthy existing homes inventory; relative home affordability; local economy/population trends. *Realtor.com®, "Top 10 Housing Markets Positioned for Growth in 2021," December 7, 2020*

- The Sacramento metro area was identified as one of the nations's 20 hottest housing markets in 2021. Criteria: listing views as an indicator of demand and median days on the market as an indicator of supply. The area ranked #10. *Realtor.com, "January 2021 Top 20 Hottest Housing Markets," February 25, 2021*

- The Sacramento metro area was identified as one of the top 15 housing markets to invest in for 2021 by *Forbes*. Criteria: home price appreciation; percentage of home sales within a 2-week time frame; available inventory; number of home sales; and other factors. *Forbes.com, "Top Housing Markets To Watch In 2021," December 15, 2020*

- Sacramento was ranked #247 out of 268 metro areas in terms of housing affordability in 2020 by the National Association of Home Builders (#1 = most affordable). Criteria: the share of homes sold in that area affordable to a family earning the local median income, based on standard mortgage underwriting criteria. *National Association of Home Builders®, NAHB-Wells Fargo Housing Opportunity Index, 4th Quarter 2020*

Safety Rankings

■ Allstate ranked the 200 largest cities in America in terms of driver safety. Sacramento ranked #163. Criteria: internal property damage claims over a two-year period from January 2016 to December 2017. The report helps increase the importance of safety and awareness behind the wheel. *Allstate, "Allstate America's Best Drivers Report, 2019" June 24, 2019*

■ The National Insurance Crime Bureau ranked 384 metro areas in the U.S. in terms of per capita rates of vehicle theft. The Sacramento metro area ranked #48 (#1 = highest rate). Criteria: number of vehicle theft offenses per 100,000 inhabitants in 2019. *National Insurance Crime Bureau, "Hot Spots 2019," July 21, 2020*

Seniors/Retirement Rankings

■ From its Best Cities for Successful Aging indexes, the Milken Institute generated rankings for metropolitan areas, weighing data in nine categories—health care, wellness, living arrangements, transportation and convenience, financial characteristics, education, employment, community engagement, and overall livability. The Sacramento metro area was ranked #82 overall in the large metro area category. *Milken Institute, "Best Cities for Successful Aging, 2017" March 14, 2017*

Sports/Recreation Rankings

■ Sacramento was chosen as one of America's best cities for bicycling. The city ranked #32 out of 50. Criteria: cycling infrastructure that is safe and friendly for all ages; energy and bike culture. The editors evaluated cities with populations of 100,000 or more. *Bicycling, "The 50 Best Bike Cities in America," October 10, 2018*

Women/Minorities Rankings

■ Personal finance website *WalletHub* compared more than 180 U.S. cities across two key dimensions, "Hispanic Business-Friendliness" and "Hispanic Purchasing Power," to arrive at the most favorable conditions for Hispanic entrepreneurs. Sacramento was ranked #125 out of 182. Criteria includes: share of Hispanic-Owned Businesses; Hispanic entrepreneurship rate to median annual income of Hispanics; Small Business-Friendliness score; cost of living; and number of Hispanics with at least a bachelor's degree. *WalletHub.com, "2019's Best Cities for Hispanic Entrepreneurs," May 1, 2019*

Miscellaneous Rankings

■ *MoveHub* ranked 446 hipster cities across 20 countries, using its *alternative* Hipster Index and Sacramento came out as #35 among the top 50. Criteria: population over 150,000; number of vintage boutiques; density of tattoo parlors; vegan places to eat; coffee shops; and density of vinyl record stores. *www.movehub.com, "The Hipster Index: Brighton Pips Portland to Global Top Spot," February 20, 2020*

■ *WalletHub* compared the 150 most populated U.S. cities to determine their operating efficiency. A "Quality of City Services" score was constructed for each city and then divided by the total budget per capita to reveal which were managed the best. Sacramento ranked #124. Criteria: financial stability; economy; education; safety; health; infrastructure and pollution. *www.WalletHub.com, "2020's Best- & Worst-Run Cities in America," June 29, 2020*

Business Environment

DEMOGRAPHICS

Population Growth

Area	1990 Census	2000 Census	2010 Census	2019* Estimate	Population Growth (%) 1990-2019	Population Growth (%) 2010-2019
City	368,923	407,018	466,488	500,930	35.8	7.4
MSA[1]	1,481,126	1,796,857	2,149,127	2,315,980	56.4	7.8
U.S.	248,709,873	281,421,906	308,745,538	324,697,795	30.6	5.2

Note: (1) Figures cover the Sacramento—Arden-Arcade—Roseville, CA Metropolitan Statistical Area;
(*) 2015-2019 5-year estimated population
Source: U.S. Census Bureau, 1990 Census, Census 2000, Census 2010, 2015-2019 American Community Survey 5-Year Estimates

Household Size

Area	One	Two	Three	Four	Five	Six	Seven or More	Average Household Size
City	30.9	30.8	14.8	12.2	6.0	3.0	2.3	2.70
MSA[1]	25.3	33.2	15.9	14.4	6.6	2.8	1.7	2.70
U.S.	27.9	33.9	15.6	12.9	6.0	2.3	1.4	2.60

Note: (1) Figures cover the Sacramento—Arden-Arcade—Roseville, CA Metropolitan Statistical Area
Source: U.S. Census Bureau, 2015-2019 American Community Survey 5-Year Estimates

Race

Area	White Alone[2] (%)	Black Alone[2] (%)	Asian Alone[2] (%)	AIAN[3] Alone[2] (%)	NHOPI[4] Alone[2] (%)	Other Race Alone[2] (%)	Two or More Races (%)
City	46.3	13.2	18.9	0.7	1.7	11.7	7.4
MSA[1]	65.0	7.1	13.3	0.6	0.9	6.5	6.6
U.S.	72.5	12.7	5.5	0.8	0.2	4.9	3.3

Note: (1) Figures cover the Sacramento—Arden-Arcade—Roseville, CA Metropolitan Statistical Area; (2) Alone is defined as not being in combination with one or more other races; (3) American Indian and Alaska Native; (4) Native Hawaiian and Other Pacific Islander
Source: U.S. Census Bureau, 2015-2019 American Community Survey 5-Year Estimates

Hispanic or Latino Origin

Area	Total (%)	Mexican (%)	Puerto Rican (%)	Cuban (%)	Other (%)
City	28.9	24.6	0.7	0.2	3.3
MSA[1]	21.6	17.7	0.7	0.2	3.1
U.S.	18.0	11.2	1.7	0.7	4.3

Note: Persons of Hispanic or Latino origin can be of any race; (1) Figures cover the Sacramento—Arden-Arcade—Roseville, CA Metropolitan Statistical Area
Source: U.S. Census Bureau, 2015-2019 American Community Survey 5-Year Estimates

Ancestry

Area	German	Irish	English	American	Italian	Polish	French[2]	Scottish	Dutch
City	6.7	6.1	4.5	1.7	3.5	0.9	1.5	1.2	0.8
MSA[1]	10.6	8.1	7.5	2.8	4.8	1.3	2.1	1.7	1.1
U.S.	13.3	9.7	7.2	6.2	5.1	2.8	2.3	1.7	1.2

Note: Figures are the percentage of the total population reporting a particular ancestry. The nine most commonly reported ancestries in the U.S. are shown. Figures include multiple ancestries (e.g. if a person reported being Irish and Italian, they were included in both columns); (1) Figures cover the Sacramento—Arden-Arcade—Roseville, CA Metropolitan Statistical Area; (2) Excludes Basque
Source: U.S. Census Bureau, 2015-2019 American Community Survey 5-Year Estimates

Foreign-born Population

Area	Any Foreign Country	Asia	Mexico	Europe	Caribbean	Central America[2]	South America	Africa	Canada
City	22.2	10.7	6.9	1.5	0.1	0.8	0.2	0.6	0.2
MSA[1]	18.6	8.8	4.7	2.7	0.1	0.6	0.3	0.5	0.3
U.S.	13.6	4.2	3.5	1.5	1.3	1.1	1.0	0.7	0.2

Note: (1) Figures cover the Sacramento—Arden-Arcade—Roseville, CA Metropolitan Statistical Area; (2) Excludes Mexico.
Source: U.S. Census Bureau, 2015-2019 American Community Survey 5-Year Estimates

Marital Status

Area	Never Married	Now Married[2]	Separated	Widowed	Divorced
City	40.2	41.0	2.4	5.1	11.4
MSA[1]	33.5	48.2	2.1	5.2	10.9
U.S.	33.4	48.1	1.9	5.8	10.9

Note: Figures are percentages and cover the population 15 years of age and older; (1) Figures cover the Sacramento—Arden-Arcade—Roseville, CA Metropolitan Statistical Area; (2) Excludes separated
Source: U.S. Census Bureau, 2015-2019 American Community Survey 5-Year Estimates

Disability by Age

Area	All Ages	Under 18 Years Old	18 to 64 Years Old	65 Years and Over
City	11.6	3.2	9.3	38.0
MSA[1]	11.5	3.4	9.0	34.8
U.S.	12.6	4.2	10.3	34.5

Note: Figures show percent of the civilian noninstitutionalized population that reported having a disability. Disability status is determined from six types of difficulty: vision, hearing, cognitive, ambulatory, self-care, and independent living. For children under 5 years old, hearing and vision difficulty are used to determine disability status. For children between the ages of 5 and 14, disability status is determined from hearing, vision, cognitive, ambulatory, and self-care difficulties. For people aged 15 years and older, they are considered to have a disability if they have difficulty with any one of the six difficulty types; Note: (1) Figures cover the Sacramento—Arden-Arcade—Roseville, CA Metropolitan Statistical Area
Source: U.S. Census Bureau, 2015-2019 American Community Survey 5-Year Estimates

Age

Area	Under Age 5	Age 5–19	Age 20–34	Age 35–44	Age 45–54	Age 55–64	Age 65–74	Age 75–84	Age 85+	Median Age
					Percent of Population					
City	6.6	18.8	25.4	13.5	11.6	11.1	7.8	3.5	1.8	34.5
MSA[1]	6.1	19.6	21.0	12.8	12.8	12.6	8.8	4.3	1.9	37.4
U.S.	6.1	19.1	20.7	12.6	13.0	12.9	9.1	4.6	1.9	38.1

Note: (1) Figures cover the Sacramento—Arden-Arcade—Roseville, CA Metropolitan Statistical Area
Source: U.S. Census Bureau, 2015-2019 American Community Survey 5-Year Estimates

Gender

Area	Males	Females	Males per 100 Females
City	245,188	255,742	95.9
MSA[1]	1,132,519	1,183,461	95.7
U.S.	159,886,919	164,810,876	97.0

Note: (1) Figures cover the Sacramento—Arden-Arcade—Roseville, CA Metropolitan Statistical Area
Source: U.S. Census Bureau, 2015-2019 American Community Survey 5-Year Estimates

Religious Groups by Family

Area	Catholic	Baptist	Non-Den.	Methodist[2]	Lutheran	LDS[3]	Pentecostal	Presbyterian[4]	Muslim[5]	Judaism
MSA[1]	16.2	3.2	4.0	1.8	0.8	3.4	2.0	0.8	0.8	0.3
U.S.	19.1	9.3	4.0	4.0	2.3	2.0	1.9	1.6	0.8	0.7

Note: Figures are the number of adherents as a percentage of the total population; (1) Figures cover the Sacramento—Arden-Arcade—Roseville, CA Metropolitan Statistical Area; (2) Methodist/Pietist; (3) Latter Day Saints; (4) Reformed; (5) Figures are estimates
Source: Association of Statisticians of American Religious Bodies, 2010 U.S. Religion Census: Religious Congregations & Membership Study

Religious Groups by Tradition

Area	Catholic	Evangelical Protestant	Mainline Protestant	Other Tradition	Black Protestant	Orthodox
MSA[1]	16.2	11.4	2.2	5.8	0.6	0.3
U.S.	19.1	16.2	7.3	4.3	1.6	0.3

Note: Figures are the number of adherents as a percentage of the total population; (1) Figures cover the Sacramento—Arden-Arcade—Roseville, CA Metropolitan Statistical Area
Source: Association of Statisticians of American Religious Bodies, 2010 U.S. Religion Census: Religious Congregations & Membership Study

ECONOMY

Gross Metropolitan Product

Area	2017	2018	2019	2020	Rank[2]
MSA[1]	129.3	137.0	144.3	151.5	34

Note: Figures are in billions of dollars; (1) Figures cover the Sacramento—Arden-Arcade—Roseville, CA Metropolitan Statistical Area; (2) Rank is based on 2018 data and ranges from 1 to 381
Source: U.S. Conference of Mayors, U.S. Metro Economies: GMP & Employment 2018-2020, September 2019

Economic Growth

Area	2015-17 (%)	2018 (%)	2019 (%)	2020 (%)	Rank[2]
MSA[1]	2.6	3.6	3.4	2.7	90
U.S.	1.9	2.9	2.3	2.1	–

Note: Figures are real gross metropolitan product (GMP) growth rates and represent average annual percent change; (1) Figures cover the Sacramento—Arden-Arcade—Roseville, CA Metropolitan Statistical Area; (2) Rank is based on 2017 2-year average annual percent change and ranges from 1 to 381
Source: U.S. Conference of Mayors, U.S. Metro Economies: GMP & Employment 2018-2020, September 2019

Metropolitan Area Exports

Area	2014	2015	2016	2017	2018	2019	Rank[2]
MSA[1]	7,143.9	8,101.2	7,032.1	6,552.6	6,222.8	5,449.2	53

Note: Figures are in millions of dollars; (1) Figures cover the Sacramento—Arden-Arcade—Roseville, CA Metropolitan Statistical Area; (2) Rank is based on 2019 data and ranges from 1 to 386
Source: U.S. Department of Commerce, International Trade Administration, Office of Trade and Economic Analysis, Industry and Analysis, Exports by Metropolitan Area, data extracted March 24, 2021

Building Permits

Area	Single-Family			Multi-Family			Total		
	2018	2019	Pct. Chg.	2018	2019	Pct. Chg.	2018	2019	Pct. Chg.
City	1,610	1,538	-4.5	714	1,463	104.9	2,324	3,001	29.1
MSA[1]	6,393	7,184	12.4	1,480	2,247	51.8	7,873	9,431	19.8
U.S.	855,300	862,100	0.7	473,500	523,900	10.6	1,328,800	1,386,000	4.3

Note: (1) Figures cover the Sacramento—Arden-Arcade—Roseville, CA Metropolitan Statistical Area; Figures represent new, privately-owned housing units authorized (unadjusted data); All permit data are based on estimates with imputation
Source: U.S. Census Bureau, Manufacturing, Mining, and Construction Statistics, Building Permits, 2018, 2019

Bankruptcy Filings

Area	Business Filings			Nonbusiness Filings		
	2019	2020	% Chg.	2019	2020	% Chg.
Sacramento County	95	124	30.5	3,208	2,300	-28.3
U.S.	22,780	21,655	-4.9	752,160	522,808	-30.5

Note: Business filings include Chapter 7, Chapter 9, Chapter 11, Chapter 12, Chapter 13, Chapter 15, and Section 304; Nonbusiness filings include Chapter 7, Chapter 11, and Chapter 13
Source: Administrative Office of the U.S. Courts, Business and Nonbusiness Bankruptcy, County Cases Commenced by Chapter of the Bankruptcy Code, During the 12-Month Period Ending December 31, 2019 and Business and Nonbusiness Bankruptcy, County Cases Commenced by Chapter of the Bankruptcy Code, During the 12-Month Period Ending December 31, 2020

Housing Vacancy Rates

Area	Gross Vacancy Rate[2] (%)			Year-Round Vacancy Rate[3] (%)			Rental Vacancy Rate[4] (%)			Homeowner Vacancy Rate[5] (%)		
	2018	2019	2020	2018	2019	2020	2018	2019	2020	2018	2019	2020
MSA[1]	8.6	7.8	6.1	7.9	7.1	5.8	5.1	4.2	4.2	1.5	0.8	1.0
U.S.	12.3	12.0	10.6	9.7	9.5	8.2	6.9	6.7	6.3	1.5	1.4	1.0

Note: (1) Figures cover the Sacramento—Arden-Arcade—Roseville, CA Metropolitan Statistical Area; (2) The percentage of the total housing inventory that is vacant; (3) The percentage of the housing inventory (excluding seasonal units) that is year-round vacant; (4) The percentage of rental inventory that is vacant for rent; (5) The percentage of homeowner inventory that is vacant for sale
Source: U.S. Census Bureau, Housing Vacancies and Homeownership Annual Statistics: 2018, 2019, 2020

INCOME

Income

Area	Per Capita ($)	Median Household ($)	Average Household ($)
City	31,956	62,335	83,189
MSA[1]	35,563	72,280	96,023
U.S.	34,103	62,843	88,607

Note: (1) Figures cover the Sacramento—Arden-Arcade—Roseville, CA Metropolitan Statistical Area
Source: U.S. Census Bureau, 2015-2019 American Community Survey 5-Year Estimates

Household Income Distribution

Area	Percent of Households Earning							
	Under $15,000	$15,000 -$24,999	$25,000 -$34,999	$35,000 -$49,999	$50,000 -$74,999	$75,000 -$99,999	$100,000 -$149,999	$150,000 and up
City	11.3	9.0	8.7	11.7	17.3	13.1	15.6	13.3
MSA[1]	9.1	7.6	7.7	10.6	16.6	13.1	17.4	17.9
U.S.	10.3	8.9	8.9	12.3	17.2	12.7	15.1	14.5

Note: (1) Figures cover the Sacramento—Arden-Arcade—Roseville, CA Metropolitan Statistical Area
Source: U.S. Census Bureau, 2015-2019 American Community Survey 5-Year Estimates

Poverty Rate

Area	All Ages	Under 18 Years Old	18 to 64 Years Old	65 Years and Over
City	16.6	21.9	15.5	12.3
MSA[1]	13.4	16.8	13.2	8.9
U.S.	13.4	18.5	12.6	9.3

Note: Figures are percentage of people whose income during the past 12 months was below the poverty level;
(1) Figures cover the Sacramento—Arden-Arcade—Roseville, CA Metropolitan Statistical Area
Source: U.S. Census Bureau, 2015-2019 American Community Survey 5-Year Estimates

CITY FINANCES

City Government Finances

Component	2017 ($000)	2017 ($ per capita)
Total Revenues	1,141,874	2,327
Total Expenditures	910,769	1,856
Debt Outstanding	2,283,136	4,653
Cash and Securities[1]	1,469,112	2,994

Note: (1) Cash and security holdings of a government at the close of its fiscal year,
including those of its dependent agencies, utilities, and liquor stores.
Source: U.S. Census Bureau, State & Local Government Finances 2017

City Government Revenue by Source

Source	2017 ($000)	2017 ($ per capita)	2017 (%)
General Revenue			
From Federal Government	24,769	50	2.2
From State Government	27,625	56	2.4
From Local Governments	6,630	14	0.6
Taxes			
Property	179,514	366	15.7
Sales and Gross Receipts	221,978	452	19.4
Personal Income	0	0	0.0
Corporate Income	0	0	0.0
Motor Vehicle License	0	0	0.0
Other Taxes	55,644	113	4.9
Current Charges	363,604	741	31.8
Liquor Store	0	0	0.0
Utility	108,868	222	9.5
Employee Retirement	10,596	22	0.9

Source: U.S. Census Bureau, State & Local Government Finances 2017

City Government Expenditures by Function

Function	2017 ($000)	2017 ($ per capita)	2017 (%)
General Direct Expenditures			
Air Transportation	0	0	0.0
Corrections	0	0	0.0
Education	0	0	0.0
Employment Security Administration	0	0	0.0
Financial Administration	6,520	13	0.7
Fire Protection	113,618	231	12.5
General Public Buildings	0	0	0.0
Governmental Administration, Other	98,228	200	10.8
Health	19,768	40	2.2
Highways	26,129	53	2.9
Hospitals	0	0	0.0
Housing and Community Development	26,461	53	2.9
Interest on General Debt	90,117	183	9.9
Judicial and Legal	0	0	0.0
Libraries	14,903	30	1.6
Parking	18,152	37	2.0
Parks and Recreation	61,095	124	6.7
Police Protection	159,856	325	17.6
Public Welfare	5,658	11	0.6
Sewerage	58,334	118	6.4
Solid Waste Management	49,770	101	5.5
Veterans' Services	0	0	0.0
Liquor Store	0	0	0.0
Utility	101,992	207	11.2
Employee Retirement	32,733	66	3.6

Source: U.S. Census Bureau, State & Local Government Finances 2017

EMPLOYMENT

Labor Force and Employment

Area	Civilian Labor Force			Workers Employed		
	Dec. 2019	Dec. 2020	% Chg.	Dec. 2019	Dec. 2020	% Chg.
City	237,846	239,336	0.6	230,186	217,425	-5.5
MSA[1]	1,104,616	1,096,884	-0.7	1,069,620	1,010,465	-5.5
U.S.	164,007,000	160,017,000	-2.4	158,504,000	149,613,000	-5.6

Note: Data is not seasonally adjusted and covers workers 16 years of age and older; (1) Figures cover the Sacramento—Arden-Arcade—Roseville, CA Metropolitan Statistical Area
Source: Bureau of Labor Statistics, Local Area Unemployment Statistics

Unemployment Rate

Area	2020											
	Jan.	Feb.	Mar.	Apr.	May	Jun.	Jul.	Aug.	Sep.	Oct.	Nov.	Dec.
City	4.0	3.8	4.9	14.5	14.5	14.0	13.1	10.4	10.2	8.7	8.0	9.2
MSA[1]	3.9	3.8	4.8	14.0	13.7	12.8	11.6	9.0	8.7	7.3	6.7	7.9
U.S.	4.0	3.8	4.5	14.4	13.0	11.2	10.5	8.5	7.7	6.6	6.4	6.5

Note: Data is not seasonally adjusted and covers workers 16 years of age and older; (1) Figures cover the Sacramento—Arden-Arcade—Roseville, CA Metropolitan Statistical Area
Source: Bureau of Labor Statistics, Local Area Unemployment Statistics

Average Wages

Occupation	$/Hr.	Occupation	$/Hr.
Accountants and Auditors	40.30	Maintenance and Repair Workers	22.60
Automotive Mechanics	26.50	Marketing Managers	73.60
Bookkeepers	22.60	Network and Computer Systems Admin.	45.60
Carpenters	28.10	Nurses, Licensed Practical	31.20
Cashiers	15.50	Nurses, Registered	64.60
Computer Programmers	39.10	Nursing Assistants	20.20
Computer Systems Analysts	50.30	Office Clerks, General	19.90
Computer User Support Specialists	41.50	Physical Therapists	53.60
Construction Laborers	24.50	Physicians	125.20
Cooks, Restaurant	15.20	Plumbers, Pipefitters and Steamfitters	30.80
Customer Service Representatives	21.10	Police and Sheriff's Patrol Officers	48.20
Dentists	93.40	Postal Service Mail Carriers	26.10
Electricians	30.10	Real Estate Sales Agents	40.50
Engineers, Electrical	52.10	Retail Salespersons	16.20
Fast Food and Counter Workers	14.20	Sales Representatives, Technical/Scientific	49.20
Financial Managers	65.80	Secretaries, Exc. Legal/Medical/Executive	21.10
First-Line Supervisors of Office Workers	31.40	Security Guards	17.10
General and Operations Managers	59.60	Surgeons	n/a
Hairdressers/Cosmetologists	16.80	Teacher Assistants, Exc. Postsecondary*	17.40
Home Health and Personal Care Aides	14.20	Teachers, Secondary School, Exc. Sp. Ed.*	39.20
Janitors and Cleaners	17.90	Telemarketers	15.60
Landscaping/Groundskeeping Workers	19.90	Truck Drivers, Heavy/Tractor-Trailer	25.90
Lawyers	73.60	Truck Drivers, Light/Delivery Services	20.00
Maids and Housekeeping Cleaners	18.60	Waiters and Waitresses	16.20

Note: Wage data covers the Sacramento—Arden-Arcade—Roseville, CA Metropolitan Statistical Area;
(*) Hourly wages were calculated from annual wage data based on a 40 hour work week; n/a not available.
Source: Bureau of Labor Statistics, Metro Area Occupational Employment & Wage Estimates, May 2020

Employment by Industry

Sector	MSA[1]		U.S.
	Number of Employees	Percent of Total	Percent of Total
Construction	73,400	7.5	5.1
Education and Health Services	160,200	16.4	16.3
Financial Activities	51,900	5.3	6.1
Government	234,100	24.0	15.2
Information	9,800	1.0	1.9
Leisure and Hospitality	78,200	8.0	9.0
Manufacturing	35,200	3.6	8.5
Mining and Logging	600	0.1	0.4
Other Services	27,900	2.9	3.8
Professional and Business Services	134,900	13.8	14.4
Retail Trade	102,300	10.5	10.9
Transportation, Warehousing, and Utilities	39,900	4.1	4.6
Wholesale Trade	26,300	2.7	3.9

Note: Figures are non-farm employment as of December 2020. Figures are not seasonally adjusted and include workers 16 years of age and older; (1) Figures cover the Sacramento—Arden-Arcade—Roseville, CA Metropolitan Statistical Area
Source: Bureau of Labor Statistics, Current Employment Statistics, Employment, Hours, and Earnings

Employment by Occupation

Occupation Classification	City (%)	MSA[1] (%)	U.S. (%)
Management, Business, Science, and Arts	40.2	41.0	38.5
Natural Resources, Construction, and Maintenance	7.3	7.9	8.9
Production, Transportation, and Material Moving	11.3	10.1	13.2
Sales and Office	21.6	22.3	21.6
Service	19.6	18.7	17.8

Note: Figures cover employed civilians 16 years of age and older; (1) Figures cover the Sacramento—Arden-Arcade—Roseville, CA Metropolitan Statistical Area
Source: U.S. Census Bureau, 2015-2019 American Community Survey 5-Year Estimates

Occupations with Greatest Projected Employment Growth: 2020 – 2022

Occupation[1]	2020 Employment	2022 Projected Employment	Numeric Employment Change	Percent Employment Change
Retail Salespersons	317,300	401,300	84,000	26.5
Laborers and Freight, Stock, and Material Movers, Hand	348,700	411,100	62,400	17.9
Waiters and Waitresses	182,500	242,800	60,300	33.0
Combined Food Preparation and Serving Workers, Including Fast Food	183,800	237,200	53,400	29.1
Cashiers	358,500	407,300	48,800	13.6
Cooks, Restaurant	113,200	156,500	43,300	38.3
Personal Care Aides	409,600	447,900	38,300	9.4
Farmworkers and Laborers, Crop, Nursery, and Greenhouse	242,000	269,700	27,700	11.4
Fast Food and Counter Workers	94,000	120,200	26,200	27.9
General and Operations Managers	242,700	268,300	25,600	10.5

Note: Projections cover California; (1) Sorted by numeric employment change
Source: www.projectionscentral.com, State Occupational Projections, 2020–2022 Short-Term Projections

Fastest-Growing Occupations: 2020 – 2022

Occupation[1]	2020 Employment	2022 Projected Employment	Numeric Employment Change	Percent Employment Change
Manicurists and Pedicurists	7,800	21,300	13,500	173.1
Hairdressers, Hairstylists, and Cosmetologists	22,700	44,600	21,900	96.5
Massage Therapists	8,800	17,100	8,300	94.3
Skincare Specialists	5,500	9,100	3,600	65.5
Dental Hygienists	9,200	14,700	5,500	59.8
Dental Hygienists (SOC 2018)	5,300	8,400	3,100	58.5
Dental Assistants	36,300	56,300	20,000	55.1
Dentists, General	12,600	19,000	6,400	50.8
Parking Lot Attendants	14,300	20,400	6,100	42.7
Lodging Managers	3,300	4,600	1,300	39.4

Note: Projections cover California; (1) Sorted by percent employment change and excludes occupations with numeric employment change less than 50
Source: www.projectionscentral.com, State Occupational Projections, 2020–2022 Short-Term Projections

TAXES

State Corporate Income Tax Rates

State	Tax Rate (%)	Income Brackets ($)	Num. of Brackets	Financial Institution Tax Rate (%)[a]	Federal Income Tax Ded.
California	8.84 (b)	Flat rate	1	10.84 (b)	No

Note: Tax rates as of January 1, 2021; (a) Rates listed are the corporate income tax rate applied to financial institutions or excise taxes based on income. Some states have other taxes based upon the value of deposits or shares; (b) Minimum tax is $800 in California, $250 in District of Columbia, $50 in Arizona and North Dakota (banks), $400 ($100 banks) in Rhode Island, $200 per location in South Dakota (banks), $100 in Utah, $300 in Vermont.
Source: Federation of Tax Administrators, State Corporate Income Tax Rates, January 1, 2021

State Individual Income Tax Rates

State	Tax Rate (%)	Income Brackets ($)	Personal Exemptions ($)			Standard Ded. ($)	
			Single	Married	Depend.	Single	Married
California (a)	1.0 - 12.3 (g)	8,932 - 599,012 (b)	124	248 (c)	383 (c)	4,601	9,202 (a)

Note: Tax rates as of January 1, 2021; Local- and county-level taxes are not included; Federal income tax is not deductible on state income tax returns; (a) 19 states have statutory provision for automatically adjusting to the rate of inflation the dollar values of the income tax brackets, standard deductions, and/or personal exemptions. Michigan indexes the personal exemption only. Oregon does not index the income brackets for $125,000 and over; (b) For joint returns, taxes are twice the tax on half the couple's income; (c) The personal exemption takes the form of a tax credit instead of a deduction; (g) California imposes an additional 1% tax on taxable income over $1 million, making the maximum rate 13.3% over $1 million.
Source: Federation of Tax Administrators, State Individual Income Tax Rates, January 1, 2021

Various State Sales and Excise Tax Rates

State	State Sales Tax (%)	Gasoline[1] (¢/gal.)	Cigarette[2] ($/pack)	Spirits[3] ($/gal.)	Wine[4] ($/gal.)	Beer[5] ($/gal.)	Recreational Marijuana (%)
California	7.25	63.05	2.87	3.3	0.2	0.2	(c)

Note: All tax rates as of January 1, 2021; (1) The American Petroleum Institute has developed a methodology for determining the average tax rate on a gallon of fuel. Rates may include any of the following: excise taxes, environmental fees, storage tank fees, other fees or taxes, general sales tax, and local taxes; (2) The federal excise tax of $1.0066 per pack and local taxes are not included; (3) Rates are those applicable to off-premise sales of 40% alcohol by volume (a.b.v.) distilled spirits in 750ml containers. Local excise taxes are excluded; (4) Rates are those applicable to off-premise sales of 11% a.b.v. non-carbonated wine in 750ml containers; (5) Rates are those applicable to off-premise sales of 4.7% a.b.v. beer in 12 ounce containers; (c) 15% excise tax (levied on wholesale at average market rate); $9.65/oz. flowers & $2.87/oz. leaves cultivation tax; $1.35/oz fresh cannabis plant
Source: Tax Foundation, 2021 Facts & Figures: How Does Your State Compare?

State Business Tax Climate Index Rankings

State	Overall Rank	Corporate Tax Rank	Individual Income Tax Rank	Sales Tax Rank	Property Tax Rank	Unemployment Insurance Tax Rank
California	49	28	49	45	14	21

Note: The index is a measure of how each state's tax laws affect economic performance. The lower the rank, the more favorable a state's tax system is for business. States without a given tax are given a ranking of 1. The scores/rankings for the District of Columbia do not affect other states. The 2021 index represents the tax climate as of July 1, 2020.
Source: Tax Foundation, State Business Tax Climate Index 2021

TRANSPORTATION

Means of Transportation to Work

Area	Car/Truck/Van		Public Transportation			Bicycle	Walked	Other Means	Worked at Home
	Drove Alone	Car-pooled	Bus	Subway	Railroad				
City	74.4	10.4	2.0	0.2	0.4	1.9	2.8	2.2	5.6
MSA[1]	76.8	9.4	1.6	0.2	0.2	1.4	1.8	1.5	7.1
U.S.	76.3	9.0	2.4	1.9	0.6	0.5	2.7	1.4	5.2

Note: Figures are percentages and cover workers 16 years of age and older; (1) Figures cover the Sacramento—Arden-Arcade—Roseville, CA Metropolitan Statistical Area
Source: U.S. Census Bureau, 2015-2019 American Community Survey 5-Year Estimates

Travel Time to Work

Area	Less Than 10 Minutes	10 to 19 Minutes	20 to 29 Minutes	30 to 44 Minutes	45 to 59 Minutes	60 to 89 Minutes	90 Minutes or More
City	8.0	31.2	25.1	22.5	5.9	4.0	3.3
MSA[1]	9.9	28.2	22.3	23.0	8.1	4.9	3.5
U.S.	12.2	28.4	20.8	20.8	8.3	6.4	2.9

Note: Note: Figures are percentages and include workers 16 years old and over; (1) Figures cover the Sacramento—Arden-Arcade—Roseville, CA Metropolitan Statistical Area
Source: U.S. Census Bureau, 2015-2019 American Community Survey 5-Year Estimates

Key Congestion Measures

Measure	1982	1992	2002	2012	2017
Annual Hours of Delay, Total (000)	8,248	22,087	46,920	65,626	76,437
Annual Hours of Delay, Per Auto Commuter	16	28	40	50	59
Annual Congestion Cost, Total (million $)	62	234	637	1,181	1,423
Annual Congestion Cost, Per Auto Commuter ($)	271	498	825	904	1,022

Note: Covers the Sacramento CA urban area
Source: Texas A&M Transportation Institute, 2019 Urban Mobility Report

Freeway Travel Time Index

Measure	1982	1987	1992	1997	2002	2007	2012	2017
Urban Area Index[1]	1.08	1.11	1.15	1.18	1.21	1.24	1.25	1.28
Urban Area Rank[1,2]	28	29	26	28	31	29	23	21

Note: Freeway Travel Time Index—the ratio of travel time in the peak period to the travel time at free-flow conditions. For example, a value of 1.30 indicates a 20-minute free-flow trip takes 26 minutes in the peak (20 minutes x 1.30 = 26 minutes); (1) Covers the Sacramento CA urban area; (2) Rank is based on 101 larger urban areas (#1 = highest travel time index)
Source: Texas A&M Transportation Institute, 2019 Urban Mobility Report

Public Transportation

Agency Name / Mode of Transportation	Vehicles Operated in Maximum Service[1]	Annual Unlinked Passenger Trips[2] (in thous.)	Annual Passenger Miles[3] (in thous.)
Sacramento Regional Transit District (Sacramento RT)			
Bus (directly operated)	161	9,909.7	35,021.2
Demand Response (directly operated)	28	98.6	360.7
Light Rail (directly operated)	69	9,980.9	63,439.9

Note: (1) Number of revenue vehicles operated by the given mode and type of service to meet the annual maximum service requirement. This is the revenue vehicle count during the peak season of the year; on the week and day that maximum service is provided. Vehicles operated in maximum service (VOMS) exclude atypical days and one-time special events; (2) Number of passengers who boarded public transportation vehicles. Passengers are counted each time they board a vehicle no matter how many vehicles they use to travel from their origin to their destination. (3) Sum of the distances ridden by all passengers during the entire fiscal year.
Source: Federal Transit Administration, National Transit Database, 2019

Air Transportation

Airport Name and Code / Type of Service	Passenger Airlines[1]	Passenger Enplanements	Freight Carriers[2]	Freight (lbs)
Sacramento International (SMF)				
Domestic service (U.S. carriers - 2020)	21	2,619,508	12	143,618,083
International service (U.S. carriers - 2019)	3	14,986	1	216,300

Note: (1) Includes all U.S.-based major, minor and commuter airlines that carried at least one passenger during the year; (2) Includes all U.S.-based airlines and freight carriers that transported at least one pound of freight during the year.
Source: Bureau of Transportation Statistics, The Intermodal Transportation Database, Air Carriers: T-100 Domestic Market (U.S. Carriers), 2020; Bureau of Transportation Statistics, The Intermodal Transportation Database, Air Carriers: T-100 International Market (U.S. Carriers), 2019

BUSINESSES

Major Business Headquarters

Company Name	Industry	Rankings	
		Fortune[1]	Forbes[2]
No companies listed	-	-	-

Note: (1) Companies that produce a 10-K are ranked 1 to 500 based on 2019 revenue; (2) All private companies with at least $2 billion in annual revenue through the end of their most current fiscal year are ranked 1 to 219; companies listed are headquartered in the city; dashes indicate no ranking
Source: Fortune, "Fortune 500," June/July 2020; Forbes, "America's Largest Private Companies," 2020

Fastest-Growing Businesses

According to *Inc.*, Sacramento is home to one of America's 500 fastest-growing private companies: **TransAmerica Express Logistics** (#180). Criteria: must be an independent, privately-held, for-profit, U.S. corporation, proprietorship or partnership as of December 31, 2019; revenues must be at least $100,000 in 2016 and $2 million in 2019; must have four-year operating/sales history. *Inc., "America's 500 Fastest-Growing Private Companies," 2020*

Living Environment

COST OF LIVING

Cost of Living Index

Composite Index	Groceries	Housing	Utilities	Trans-portation	Health Care	Misc. Goods/ Services
123.1	108.0	141.6	109.3	133.3	121.5	115.7

Note: The Cost of Living Index measures regional differences in the cost of consumer goods and services, excluding taxes and non-consumer expenditures, for professional and managerial households in the top income quintile. It is based on more than 50,000 prices covering almost 60 different items for which prices are collected three times a year by chambers of commerce, economic development organizations or university applied economic centers in each participating urban area. The numbers shown should be read as a percentage above or below the national average of 100. For example, a value of 115.4 in the groceries column indicates that grocery prices are 15.4% higher than the national average. Small differences in the index numbers should not be interpreted as significant; Figures cover the Sacramento CA urban area.
Source: The Council for Community and Economic Research, Cost of Living Index, 2020

Grocery Prices

Area[1]	T-Bone Steak ($/pound)	Frying Chicken ($/pound)	Whole Milk ($/half gal.)	Eggs ($/dozen)	Orange Juice ($/64 oz.)	Coffee ($/11.5 oz.)
City[2]	10.84	1.31	2.66	2.50	4.16	5.46
Avg.	11.78	1.39	2.05	1.47	3.57	4.34
Min.	8.03	0.94	1.03	0.74	2.94	3.02
Max.	15.86	2.65	4.31	3.77	5.44	8.69

*Note: (1) Values for the local area are compared with the average, minimum and maximum values for all 284 areas in the Cost of Living Index; (2) Figures cover the Sacramento CA urban area; **T-Bone Steak** (price per pound); **Frying Chicken** (price per pound, whole fryer); **Whole Milk** (half gallon carton); **Eggs** (price per dozen, Grade A, large); **Orange Juice** (64 oz. Tropicana or Florida Natural); **Coffee** (11.5 oz. can, vacuum-packed, Maxwell House, Hills Bros, or Folgers).*
Source: The Council for Community and Economic Research, Cost of Living Index, 2020

Housing and Utility Costs

Area[1]	New Home Price ($)	Apartment Rent ($/month)	All Electric ($/month)	Part Electric ($/month)	Other Energy ($/month)	Telephone ($/month)
City[2]	484,470	1,948	-	145.58	46.79	186.50
Avg.	368,594	1,168	170.86	100.47	65.28	184.30
Min.	190,567	502	91.58	31.42	26.08	169.60
Max.	2,227,806	4,738	470.38	280.31	280.06	206.50

*Note: (1) Values for the local area are compared with the average, minimum and maximum values for all 284 areas in the Cost of Living Index; (2) Figures cover the Sacramento CA urban area; **New Home Price** (2,400 sf living area, 8,000 sf lot, in urban area with full utilities); **Apartment Rent** (950 sf 2 bedroom/1.5 or 2 bath, unfurnished, excluding all utilities except water); **All Electric** (average monthly cost for an all-electric home); **Part Electric** (average monthly cost for a part-electric home); **Other Energy** (average monthly cost for natural gas, fuel oil, coal, wood, and any other forms of energy except electricity); **Telephone** (price includes the base monthly rate plus taxes and fees for three lines of mobile phone service).*
Source: The Council for Community and Economic Research, Cost of Living Index, 2020

Health Care, Transportation, and Other Costs

Area[1]	Doctor ($/visit)	Dentist ($/visit)	Optometrist ($/visit)	Gasoline ($/gallon)	Beauty Salon ($/visit)	Men's Shirt ($)
City[2]	194.75	94.80	148.50	3.24	62.28	24.56
Avg.	115.44	99.32	108.10	2.21	39.27	31.37
Min.	36.68	59.00	51.36	1.71	19.00	11.00
Max.	219.00	153.10	250.97	3.46	82.05	58.33

*Note: (1) Values for the local area are compared with the average, minimum and maximum values for all 284 areas in the Cost of Living Index; (2) Figures cover the Sacramento CA urban area; **Doctor** (general practitioners routine exam of an established patient); **Dentist** (adult teeth cleaning and periodic oral examination); **Optometrist** (full vision eye exam for established adult patient); **Gasoline** (one gallon regular unleaded, national brand, including all taxes, cash price at self-service pump if available); **Beauty Salon** (woman's shampoo, trim, and blow-dry); **Men's Shirt** (cotton/polyester dress shirt, pinpoint weave, long sleeves).*
Source: The Council for Community and Economic Research, Cost of Living Index, 2020

HOUSING

Homeownership Rate

Area	2012 (%)	2013 (%)	2014 (%)	2015 (%)	2016 (%)	2017 (%)	2018 (%)	2019 (%)	2020 (%)
MSA[1]	58.6	60.4	60.1	60.8	60.5	60.1	64.1	61.6	63.4
U.S.	65.4	65.1	64.5	63.7	63.4	63.9	64.4	64.6	66.6

Note: (1) Figures cover the Sacramento—Arden-Arcade—Roseville, CA Metropolitan Statistical Area
Source: U.S. Census Bureau, Housing Vacancies and Homeownership Annual Statistics: 2012-2020

House Price Index (HPI)

Area	National Ranking[2]	Quarterly Change (%)	One-Year Change (%)	Five-Year Change (%)	Since 1991Q1 (%)
MSA[1]	93	2.73	6.92	37.42	166.72
U.S.[3]	–	3.81	10.77	38.99	205.12

Note: The HPI is a weighted repeat sales index. It measures average price changes in repeat sales or refinancings on the same properties. This information is obtained by reviewing repeat mortgage transactions on single-family properties whose mortgages have been purchased or securitized by Fannie Mae or Freddie Mac since January 1975; (1) Figures cover the Sacramento—Roseville—Arden-Arcade, CA Metropolitan Statistical Area; (2) Rankings are based on annual percentage change for all metro areas containing at least 15,000 transactions over the last 10 years and ranges from 1 to 253; (3) figures based on a weighted average of Census Division estimates using a seasonally adjusted, purchase-only index; all figures are for the period ending December 31, 2020
Source: Federal Housing Finance Agency, Change in Metropolitan Area House Price Indexes, April 7, 2021

Median Single-Family Home Prices

Area	2018	2019	2020[p]	Percent Change 2019 to 2020
MSA[1]	365.0	380.0	421.0	10.8
U.S. Average	261.6	274.6	299.9	9.2

Note: Figures are median sales prices of existing single-family homes in thousands of dollars; (p) preliminary; (1) Figures cover the Sacramento—Arden-Arcade—Roseville, CA Metropolitan Statistical Area
Source: National Association of Realtors, Median Sales Price of Existing Single-Family Homes for Metropolitan Areas, 4th Quarter 2020

Qualifying Income Based on Median Sales Price of Existing Single-Family Homes

Area	With 5% Down ($)	With 10% Down ($)	With 20% Down ($)
MSA[1]	83,412	79,022	70,241
U.S. Average	59,266	56,147	49,908

Note: Figures are preliminary; Qualifying income is based on a mortgage rate of 2.81%. Monthly principal and interest payment is limited to 25% of income; (1) Figures cover the Sacramento—Arden-Arcade—Roseville, CA Metropolitan Statistical Area
Source: National Association of Realtors, Qualifying Income Based on Median Sales Price of Existing Single-Family Homes for Metropolitan Areas, 4th Quarter 2020

Home Value Distribution

Area	Under $50,000	$50,000 -$99,999	$100,000 -$149,999	$150,000 -$199,999	$200,000 -$299,999	$300,000 -$499,999	$500,000 -$999,999	$1,000,000 or more
City	2.5	2.0	3.5	7.2	26.0	39.6	17.2	2.0
MSA[1]	2.8	1.7	2.2	4.5	17.7	42.3	25.8	3.0
U.S.	6.9	12.0	13.3	14.0	19.6	19.3	11.4	3.4

Note: Figures are percentages and cover owner-occupied housing units; (1) Figures cover the Sacramento—Arden-Arcade—Roseville, CA Metropolitan Statistical Area
Source: U.S. Census Bureau, 2015-2019 American Community Survey 5-Year Estimates

Year Housing Structure Built

Area	2010 or Later	2000 -2009	1990 -1999	1980 -1989	1970 -1979	1960 -1969	1950 -1959	1940 -1949	Before 1940	Median Year
City	2.3	15.7	8.9	15.7	14.6	11.7	12.4	7.9	10.9	1975
MSA[1]	3.5	17.6	15.1	16.6	18.3	10.9	10.0	3.7	4.2	1982
U.S.	5.2	14.0	13.9	13.4	15.2	10.6	10.3	4.9	12.6	1978

Note: Figures are percentages except for Median Year; Note: (1) Figures cover the Sacramento—Arden-Arcade—Roseville, CA Metropolitan Statistical Area
Source: U.S. Census Bureau, 2015-2019 American Community Survey 5-Year Estimates

Gross Monthly Rent

Area	Under $500	$500 -$999	$1,000 -$1,499	$1,500 -$1,999	$2,000 -$2,499	$2,500 -$2,999	$3,000 and up	Median ($)
City	5.9	24.1	38.5	23.4	6.1	1.4	0.6	1,263
MSA[1]	4.6	22.7	37.5	23.2	8.1	2.4	1.4	1,290
U.S.	9.4	36.2	30.0	14.0	5.6	2.4	2.4	1,062

Note: Figures are percentages except for Median; Gross rent is the contract rent plus the estimated average monthly cost of utilities (electricity, gas, and water and sewer) and fuels (oil, coal, kerosene, wood, etc.) if these are paid by the renter (or paid for the renter by someone else); (1) Figures cover the Sacramento—Arden-Arcade—Roseville, CA Metropolitan Statistical Area
Source: U.S. Census Bureau, 2015-2019 American Community Survey 5-Year Estimates

HEALTH

Health Risk Factors

Category	MSA[1] (%)	U.S. (%)
Adults aged 18–64 who have any kind of health care coverage	90.8	87.3
Adults who reported being in good or better health	85.0	82.4
Adults who have been told they have high blood cholesterol	29.6	33.0
Adults who have been told they have high blood pressure	30.7	32.3
Adults who are current smokers	9.5	17.1
Adults who currently use E-cigarettes	3.3	4.6
Adults who currently use chewing tobacco, snuff, or snus	1.5	4.0
Adults who are heavy drinkers[2]	6.6	6.3
Adults who are binge drinkers[3]	17.6	17.4
Adults who are overweight (BMI 25.0 - 29.9)	36.3	35.3
Adults who are obese (BMI 30.0 - 99.8)	27.9	31.3
Adults who participated in any physical activities in the past month	83.6	74.4
Adults who always or nearly always wears a seat belt	98.5	94.3

Note: (1) Figures cover the Sacramento—Roseville—Arden-Arcade, CA Metropolitan Statistical Area; (2) Heavy drinkers are classified as adult men having more than 14 drinks per week and adult women having more than 7 drinks per week; (3) Binge drinkers are classified as males having five or more drinks on one occasion or females having four or more drinks on one occasion
Source: Centers for Disease Control and Prevention, Behaviorial Risk Factor Surveillance System, SMART: Selected Metropolitan Area Risk Trends, 2017

Acute and Chronic Health Conditions

Category	MSA[1] (%)	U.S. (%)
Adults who have ever been told they had a heart attack	2.5	4.2
Adults who have ever been told they have angina or coronary heart disease	2.0	3.9
Adults who have ever been told they had a stroke	3.1	3.0
Adults who have ever been told they have asthma	19.4	14.2
Adults who have ever been told they have arthritis	21.6	24.9
Adults who have ever been told they have diabetes[2]	10.2	10.5
Adults who have ever been told they had skin cancer	6.2	6.2
Adults who have ever been told they had any other types of cancer	6.9	7.1
Adults who have ever been told they have COPD	5.9	6.5
Adults who have ever been told they have kidney disease	3.5	3.0
Adults who have ever been told they have a form of depression	19.7	20.5

Note: (1) Figures cover the Sacramento—Roseville—Arden-Arcade, CA Metropolitan Statistical Area; (2) Figures do not include pregnancy-related, borderline, or pre-diabetes
Source: Centers for Disease Control and Prevention, Behaviorial Risk Factor Surveillance System, SMART: Selected Metropolitan Area Risk Trends, 2017

Health Screening and Vaccination Rates

Category	MSA[1] (%)	U.S. (%)
Adults aged 65+ who have had flu shot within the past year	69.8	60.7
Adults aged 65+ who have ever had a pneumonia vaccination	87.2	75.4
Adults who have ever been tested for HIV	44.3	36.1
Adults who have ever had the shingles or zoster vaccine?	45.4	28.9
Adults who have had their blood cholesterol checked within the last five years	87.2	85.9

Note: n/a not available; (1) Figures cover the Sacramento—Roseville—Arden-Arcade, CA Metropolitan Statistical Area.
Source: Centers for Disease Control and Prevention, Behaviorial Risk Factor Surveillance System, SMART: Selected Metropolitan Area Risk Trends, 2017

Disability Status

Category	MSA[1] (%)	U.S. (%)
Adults who reported being deaf	6.1	6.7
Are you blind or have serious difficulty seeing, even when wearing glasses?	3.9	4.5
Are you limited in any way in any of your usual activities due of arthritis?	12.0	12.9
Do you have difficulty doing errands alone?	5.9	6.8
Do you have difficulty dressing or bathing?	3.9	3.6
Do you have serious difficulty concentrating/remembering/making decisions?	9.7	10.7
Do you have serious difficulty walking or climbing stairs?	12.9	13.6

Note: (1) Figures cover the Sacramento—Roseville—Arden-Arcade, CA Metropolitan Statistical Area.
Source: Centers for Disease Control and Prevention, Behaviorial Risk Factor Surveillance System, SMART: Selected Metropolitan Area Risk Trends, 2017

Mortality Rates for the Top 10 Causes of Death in the U.S.

ICD-10[a] Sub-Chapter	ICD-10[a] Code	Age-Adjusted Mortality Rate[1] per 100,000 population	
		County[2]	U.S.
Malignant neoplasms	C00-C97	150.5	149.2
Ischaemic heart diseases	I20-I25	89.3	90.5
Other forms of heart disease	I30-I51	42.3	52.2
Chronic lower respiratory diseases	J40-J47	36.8	39.6
Other degenerative diseases of the nervous system	G30-G31	51.6	37.6
Cerebrovascular diseases	I60-I69	43.1	37.2
Other external causes of accidental injury	W00-X59	28.2	36.1
Organic, including symptomatic, mental disorders	F01-F09	22.7	29.4
Hypertensive diseases	I10-I15	29.4	24.1
Diabetes mellitus	E10-E14	28.2	21.5

Note: (a) ICD-10 = International Classification of Diseases 10th Revision; (1) Mortality rates are a three-year average covering 2017-2019; (2) Figures cover Sacramento County.
Source: Centers for Disease Control and Prevention, National Center for Health Statistics. Underlying Cause of Death 1999-2019 on CDC WONDER Online Database

Mortality Rates for Selected Causes of Death

ICD-10[a] Sub-Chapter	ICD-10[a] Code	Age-Adjusted Mortality Rate[1] per 100,000 population	
		County[2]	U.S.
Assault	X85-Y09	5.5	6.0
Diseases of the liver	K70-K76	14.6	14.4
Human immunodeficiency virus (HIV) disease	B20-B24	1.7	1.5
Influenza and pneumonia	J09-J18	14.6	13.8
Intentional self-harm	X60-X84	12.9	14.1
Malnutrition	E40-E46	2.5	2.3
Obesity and other hyperalimentation	E65-E68	2.6	2.1
Renal failure	N17-N19	3.3	12.6
Transport accidents	V01-V99	12.5	12.3
Viral hepatitis	B15-B19	3.1	1.2

Note: (a) ICD-10 = International Classification of Diseases 10th Revision; (1) Mortality rates are a three-year average covering 2017-2019; (2) Figures cover Sacramento County; Data are suppressed when the data meet the criteria for confidentiality constraints; Mortality rates are flagged as unreliable when the rate would be calculated with a numerator of 20 or less.
Source: Centers for Disease Control and Prevention, National Center for Health Statistics. Underlying Cause of Death 1999-2019 on CDC WONDER Online Database

Health Insurance Coverage

Area	With Health Insurance	With Private Health Insurance	With Public Health Insurance	Without Health Insurance	Population Under Age 19 Without Health Insurance
City	94.2	62.2	42.1	5.8	2.2
MSA[1]	94.9	69.3	38.2	5.1	2.5
U.S.	91.2	67.9	35.1	8.8	5.1

Note: Figures are percentages that cover the civilian noninstitutionalized population; (1) Figures cover the Sacramento—Arden-Arcade—Roseville, CA Metropolitan Statistical Area
Source: U.S. Census Bureau, 2015-2019 American Community Survey 5-Year Estimates

Number of Medical Professionals

Area	MDs[3]	DOs[3,4]	Dentists	Podiatrists	Chiropractors	Optometrists
County[1] (number)	4,855	241	1,216	72	341	281
County[1] (rate[2])	315.5	15.7	78.3	4.6	22.0	18.1
U.S. (rate[2])	282.9	22.7	71.2	6.2	28.1	16.9

06067
Note: Data as of 2019 unless noted; (1) Data covers Sacramento County; (2) Rate per 100,000 population; (3) Data as of 2018 and includes all active, non-federal physicians; (4) Doctor of Osteopathic Medicine
Source: U.S. Department of Health and Human Services, Health Resources and Services Administration, Bureau of Health Professions, Area Resource File (ARF) 2019-2020

Best Hospitals

According to *U.S. News*, the Sacramento—Arden-Arcade—Roseville, CA metro area is home to one of the best hospitals in the U.S.: **UC Davis Medical Center** (9 adult specialties and 4 pediatric specialties). The hospital listed was nationally ranked in at least one of 16 adult or 10 pediatric specialties. Only 134 hospitals nationwide were nationally ranked in one or more adult or pediatric specialty; this number increases to 178 counting specialized centers within hospitals. Twenty hospitals in the U.S. made the Honor Roll. The Best Hospitals Honor Roll takes both the national rankings and the procedure and condition ratings into account. Hospitals received points if they were nationally ranked in one of the 16 adult specialties—the higher they ranked, the more points they got—and how many ratings of "high performing" they earned in the 10 procedures and conditions. *U.S. News Online, "America's Best Hospitals 2020-21"*

According to *U.S. News,* the Sacramento—Arden-Arcade—Roseville, CA metro area is home to one of the best children's hospitals in the U.S.: **UC Davis Children's Hospital/Shriners Hospitals for Children-Northern California** (4 pediatric specialties). The hospital listed was highly ranked in at least one of 10 pediatric specialties. Eighty-eight children's hospitals in the U.S. were nationally ranked in at least one specialty. Hospitals received points for being ranked in a specialty, and the 10 hospitals with the most points across the 10 specialties make up the Honor Roll. *U.S. News Online, "America's Best Children's Hospitals 2020-21"*

EDUCATION

Public School District Statistics

District Name	Schls	Pupils	Pupil/ Teacher Ratio	Minority Pupils[1] (%)	Free Lunch Eligible[2] (%)	IEP[3] (%)
Natomas Unified	19	13,457	21.8	83.9	53.1	13.3
Robla Elementary	6	2,047	23.5	86.2	75.8	11.9
Sacramento City Unified	73	42,506	22.7	82.4	61.2	15.2

Note: Table includes school districts with 2,000 or more students; (1) Percentage of students that are not non-Hispanic white; (2) Percentage of students that are eligible for the free lunch program; (3) Percentage of students that have an Individualized Education Program.
Source: U.S. Department of Education, National Center for Education Statistics, Common Core of Data, Local Education Agency (School District) Universe Survey: School Year 2018-2019; U.S. Department of Education, National Center for Education Statistics, Common Core of Data, Public Elementary/Secondary School Universe Survey: School Year 2018-2019

Best High Schools

According to *U.S. News,* Sacramento is home to one of the top 500 high schools in the U.S.: **West Campus High School** (#164). Nearly 18,000 public, magnet and charter schools were ranked based on their performance on state assessments and how well they prepare students for college. *U.S. News & World Report, "Best High Schools 2020"*

Highest Level of Education

Area	Less than H.S.	H.S. Diploma	Some College, No Deg.	Associate Degree	Bachelor's Degree	Master's Degree	Prof. School Degree	Doctorate Degree
City	14.7	21.3	22.4	8.5	21.2	7.7	2.9	1.3
MSA[1]	10.7	21.2	24.7	9.9	21.8	7.8	2.6	1.4
U.S.	12.0	27.0	20.4	8.5	19.8	8.8	2.1	1.4

Note: Figures cover persons age 25 and over; (1) Figures cover the Sacramento—Arden-Arcade—Roseville, CA Metropolitan Statistical Area
Source: U.S. Census Bureau, 2015-2019 American Community Survey 5-Year Estimates

Educational Attainment by Race

Area	High School Graduate or Higher (%)					Bachelor's Degree or Higher (%)				
	Total	White	Black	Asian	Hisp.[2]	Total	White	Black	Asian	Hisp.[2]
City	85.3	89.2	90.1	79.7	73.0	33.1	39.6	21.0	37.4	17.7
MSA[1]	89.3	92.0	90.4	84.3	74.1	33.5	34.8	23.0	44.1	17.9
U.S.	88.0	89.9	86.0	87.1	68.7	32.1	33.5	21.6	54.3	16.4

Note: Figures shown cover persons 25 years old and over; (1) Figures cover the Sacramento—Arden-Arcade—Roseville, CA Metropolitan Statistical Area; (2) People of Hispanic origin can be of any race
Source: U.S. Census Bureau, 2015-2019 American Community Survey 5-Year Estimates

School Enrollment by Grade and Control

Area	Preschool (%)		Kindergarten (%)		Grades 1 - 4 (%)		Grades 5 - 8 (%)		Grades 9 - 12 (%)	
	Public	Private	Public	Private	Public	Private	Public	Private	Public	Private
City	68.9	31.1	92.8	7.2	93.2	6.8	92.9	7.1	92.6	7.4
MSA[1]	62.3	37.7	90.7	9.3	92.4	7.6	92.5	7.5	93.1	6.9
U.S.	59.1	40.9	87.6	12.4	89.5	10.5	89.4	10.6	90.1	9.9

Note: Figures shown cover persons 3 years old and over; (1) Figures cover the Sacramento—Arden-Arcade—Roseville, CA Metropolitan Statistical Area
Source: U.S. Census Bureau, 2015-2019 American Community Survey 5-Year Estimates

Higher Education

Four-Year Colleges			Two-Year Colleges			Medical Schools[1]	Law Schools[2]	Voc/ Tech[3]
Public	Private Non-profit	Private For-profit	Public	Private Non-profit	Private For-profit			
1	1	1	4	0	5	1	3	8

Note: Figures cover institutions located within the city limits and include main campuses only; (1) includes schools accredited by the Liaison Committee on Medical Education and the American Osteopathic Association's Commission on Osteopathic College Accreditation; (2) includes ABA-accredited schools, schools with provisional ABA accreditation, and state accredited schools; (3) includes all schools with programs that are less than 2 years.
Source: National Center for Education Statistics, Integrated Postsecondary Education System (IPEDS), 2019-20; Wikipedia, List of Medical Schools in the United States, accessed April 2, 2021; Wikipedia, List of Law Schools in the United States, accessed April 2, 2021

According to *U.S. News & World Report*, the Sacramento—Arden-Arcade—Roseville, CA metro area is home to one of the top 200 national universities in the U.S.: **University of California—Davis** (#39 tie). The indicators used to capture academic quality fall into a number of categories: assessment by administrators at peer institutions; retention of students; faculty resources; student selectivity; financial resources; alumni giving; high school counselor ratings of colleges; and graduation rate. *U.S. News & World Report, "America's Best Colleges 2021"*

According to *U.S. News & World Report*, the Sacramento—Arden-Arcade—Roseville, CA metro area is home to one of the top 100 law schools in the U.S.: **University of California—Davis** (#35 tie). The rankings are based on a weighted average of 12 measures of quality: peer assessment score; assessment score by lawyers/judges; median LSAT scores; median undergrad GPA; acceptance rate; employment rates for graduates; placement success; bar passage rate; faculty resources; expenditures per student; student/faculty ratio; and library resources. *U.S. News & World Report, "America's Best Graduate Schools, Law, 2022"*

According to *U.S. News & World Report*, the Sacramento—Arden-Arcade—Roseville, CA metro area is home to one of the top 75 medical schools for research in the U.S.: **University of California—Davis** (#48 tie). The rankings are based on a weighted average of 11 measures of quality: quality assessment; peer assessment score; assessment score by residency directors; research activity; total research activity; average research activity per faculty member; student selectivity; median MCAT total score; median undergraduate GPA; acceptance rate; and faculty resources. *U.S. News & World Report, "America's Best Graduate Schools, Medical, 2022"*

According to *U.S. News & World Report*, the Sacramento—Arden-Arcade—Roseville, CA metro area is home to one of the top 75 business schools in the U.S.: **University of California—Davis** (#53 tie). The rankings are based on a weighted average of the following nine measures: quality assessment; peer assessment; recruiter assessment; placement success; mean starting salary and bonus; student selectivity; mean GMAT and GRE scores; mean undergraduate GPA; and acceptance rate. *U.S. News & World Report, "America's Best Graduate Schools, Business, 2022"*

EMPLOYERS

Major Employers

Company Name	Industry
Aerojet Rocketdyne	Aerospace industries, mfg
Agreeya Solutions	Information technology services
Ampac Fine Chemicals	Electronic equipment & supplies, mfg
Apple Distribution Center	Distribution centers, wholesale
California Department of Corrections	State govt-correctional institutions
California Prison Ind Auth	Government offices-state
California State Univercity-Sacramento	Schools-universities & colleges academic
Department of Transportation	Government offices-state
Disabled American Veterans	Veterans' & military organizations
Division of Fiscal Services	Services nec
Employment Development Dept	Government offices-state
Environmental Protection Agency	State government-environmental programs
Intel Corp	Semiconductor devices, mfg
Kaiser Permanente South	Hospitals
L A Care Health Plan	Health plans
Mercy General Hospital	Hospitals
Mercy San Juan Medical Center	Hospitals
Sacramento Municipal Utility	Electric contractors
Securitas Security Services USA	Security guard & patrol services
SMUD	Electric companies
State Compensation Insurance Fund	Insurance
Sutter Medical Center-Sacramento	Hospitals
United Loan Corp	Real estate
Water Resource Dept	Government offices-state

Note: Companies shown are located within the Sacramento—Arden-Arcade—Roseville, CA Metropolitan Statistical Area.
Source: Hoovers.com; Wikipedia

PUBLIC SAFETY

Crime Rate

Area	All Crimes	Violent Crimes				Property Crimes		
		Murder	Rape[3]	Robbery	Aggrav. Assault	Burglary	Larceny -Theft	Motor Vehicle Theft
City	3,809.2	6.6	24.7	202.2	393.6	582.4	2,071.1	528.7
Suburbs[1]	2,195.0	3.4	28.3	73.9	172.0	335.6	1,366.4	215.3
Metro[2]	2,548.0	4.1	27.5	102.0	220.5	389.6	1,520.5	283.8
U.S.	2,489.3	5.0	42.6	81.6	250.2	340.5	1,549.5	219.9

Note: Figures are crimes per 100,000 population; (1) All areas within the metro area that are located outside the city limits; (2) Figures cover the Sacramento—Arden-Arcade—Roseville, CA Metropolitan Statistical Area; (3) All figures shown were reported using the revised Uniform Crime Reporting (UCR) definition of rape.
Source: FBI Uniform Crime Reports, 2019

Hate Crimes

Area	Number of Quarters Reported	Number of Incidents per Bias Motivation					
		Race/Ethnicity/ Ancestry	Religion	Sexual Orientation	Disability	Gender	Gender Identity
City	4	1	1	1	1	0	2
U.S.	4	3,963	1,521	1,195	157	69	198

Source: Federal Bureau of Investigation, Hate Crime Statistics 2019

Identity Theft Consumer Reports

Area	Reports	Reports per 100,000 Population	Rank[2]
MSA[1]	7,073	299	120
U.S.	1,387,615	423	-

Note: (1) Figures cover the Sacramento—Arden-Arcade—Roseville, CA Metropolitan Statistical Area; (2) Rank ranges from 1 to 391 where 1 indicates greatest number of identity theft reports per 100,000 population
Source: Federal Trade Commission, Consumer Sentinel Network Data Book 2020

Fraud and Other Consumer Reports

Area	Reports	Reports per 100,000 Population	Rank[2]
MSA[1]	19,795	837	81
U.S.	3,385,133	1,031	-

Note: (1) Figures cover the Sacramento—Arden-Arcade—Roseville, CA Metropolitan Statistical Area; (2) Rank ranges from 1 to 391 where 1 indicates greatest number of fraud and other consumer reports per 100,000 population
Source: Federal Trade Commission, Consumer Sentinel Network Data Book 2020

POLITICS

2020 Presidential Election Results

Area	Biden	Trump	Jorgensen	Hawkins	Other
Sacramento County	61.4	36.1	1.4	0.5	0.7
U.S.	51.3	46.8	1.2	0.3	0.5

Note: Results are percentages and may not add to 100% due to rounding
Source: Dave Leip's Atlas of U.S. Presidential Elections

SPORTS

Professional Sports Teams

Team Name	League	Year Established
Sacramento Kings	National Basketball Association (NBA)	1985
Sacramento Republic FC	Major League Soccer (MLS)	2023

Note: Includes teams located in the Sacramento—Arden-Arcade—Roseville, CA Metropolitan Statistical Area.
Source: Wikipedia, Major Professional Sports Teams of the United States and Canada, April 6, 2021

CLIMATE

Average and Extreme Temperatures

Temperature	Jan	Feb	Mar	Apr	May	Jun	Jul	Aug	Sep	Oct	Nov	Dec	Yr.
Extreme High (°F)	70	76	88	93	105	115	114	109	108	101	87	72	115
Average High (°F)	53	60	64	71	80	87	93	91	87	78	63	53	73
Average Temp. (°F)	45	51	54	59	65	72	76	75	72	64	53	46	61
Average Low (°F)	38	41	43	46	50	55	58	58	56	50	43	38	48
Extreme Low (°F)	20	23	26	32	34	41	48	48	43	35	26	18	18

Note: Figures cover the years 1947-1990
Source: National Climatic Data Center, International Station Meteorological Climate Summary, 9/96

Average Precipitation/Snowfall/Humidity

Precip./Humidity	Jan	Feb	Mar	Apr	May	Jun	Jul	Aug	Sep	Oct	Nov	Dec	Yr.
Avg. Precip. (in.)	3.6	2.8	2.4	1.3	0.4	0.1	Tr	0.1	0.3	1.0	2.4	2.8	17.3
Avg. Snowfall (in.)	Tr	Tr	Tr	Tr	0	0	0	0	0	0	0	Tr	Tr
Avg. Rel. Hum. 7am (%)	90	88	84	78	71	67	68	73	75	80	87	90	79
Avg. Rel. Hum. 4pm (%)	70	59	51	43	36	31	28	29	31	39	57	70	45

Note: Figures cover the years 1947-1990; Tr = Trace amounts (<0.05 in. of rain; <0.5 in. of snow)
Source: National Climatic Data Center, International Station Meteorological Climate Summary, 9/96

Weather Conditions

Temperature			Daytime Sky			Precipitation		
10°F & below	32°F & below	90°F & above	Clear	Partly cloudy	Cloudy	0.01 inch or more precip.	0.1 inch or more snow/ice	Thunder-storms
0	21	73	175	111	79	58	< 1	2

Note: Figures are average number of days per year and cover the years 1947-1990
Source: National Climatic Data Center, International Station Meteorological Climate Summary, 9/96

HAZARDOUS WASTE

Superfund Sites

The Sacramento—Arden-Arcade—Roseville, CA metro area is home to five sites on the EPA's Superfund National Priorities List: **Aerojet General Corp.** (final); **Frontier Fertilizer** (final); **Mather Air Force Base (AC&W Disposal Site)** (final); **McClellan Air Force Base (Ground Water Contamination)** (final); **Sacramento Army Depot** (final). There are a total of 1,375 Superfund sites with a status of proposed or final on the list in the U.S. *U.S. Environmental Protection Agency, National Priorities List, April 7, 2021*

AIR QUALITY

Air Quality Trends: Ozone

	1990	1995	2000	2005	2010	2015	2016	2017	2018	2019
MSA[1]	0.088	0.093	0.087	0.087	0.074	0.074	0.077	0.073	0.079	0.068
U.S.	0.088	0.089	0.082	0.080	0.073	0.068	0.069	0.068	0.069	0.065

Note: (1) Data covers the Sacramento—Arden-Arcade—Roseville, CA Metropolitan Statistical Area. The values shown are the composite ozone concentration averages among trend sites based on the highest fourth daily maximum 8-hour concentration in parts per million. These trends are based on sites having an adequate record of monitoring data during the trend period. Data from exceptional events are included.
Source: U.S. Environmental Protection Agency, Air Quality Monitoring Information, "Air Quality Trends by City, 1990-2019"

Air Quality Index

Area	Percent of Days when Air Quality was...[2]					AQI Statistics[2]	
	Good	Moderate	Unhealthy for Sensitive Groups	Unhealthy	Very Unhealthy	Maximum	Median
MSA[1]	47.1	47.1	5.8	0.0	0.0	140	52

Note: (1) Data covers the Sacramento—Arden-Arcade—Roseville, CA Metropolitan Statistical Area; (2) Based on 365 days with AQI data in 2019. Air Quality Index (AQI) is an index for reporting daily air quality. EPA calculates the AQI for five major air pollutants regulated by the Clean Air Act: ground-level ozone, particle pollution (aka particulate matter), carbon monoxide, sulfur dioxide, and nitrogen dioxide. The AQI runs from 0 to 500. The higher the AQI value, the greater the level of air pollution and the greater the health concern. There are six AQI categories: "Good" AQI is between 0 and 50. Air quality is considered satisfactory; "Moderate" AQI is between 51 and 100. Air quality is acceptable; "Unhealthy for Sensitive Groups" When AQI values are between 101 and 150, members of sensitive groups may experience health effects; "Unhealthy" When AQI values are between 151 and 200 everyone may begin to experience health effects; "Very Unhealthy" AQI values between 201 and 300 trigger a health alert; "Hazardous" AQI values over 300 trigger warnings of emergency conditions (not shown).
Source: U.S. Environmental Protection Agency, Air Quality Index Report, 2019

Air Quality Index Pollutants

Area	Percent of Days when AQI Pollutant was...[2]					
	Carbon Monoxide	Nitrogen Dioxide	Ozone	Sulfur Dioxide	Particulate Matter 2.5	Particulate Matter 10
MSA[1]	0.0	0.3	71.0	0.0	27.1	1.6

Note: (1) Data covers the Sacramento—Arden-Arcade—Roseville, CA Metropolitan Statistical Area; (2) Based on 365 days with AQI data in 2019. The Air Quality Index (AQI) is an index for reporting daily air quality. EPA calculates the AQI for five major air pollutants regulated by the Clean Air Act: ground-level ozone, particle pollution (also known as particulate matter), carbon monoxide, sulfur dioxide, and nitrogen dioxide. The AQI runs from 0 to 500. The higher the AQI value, the greater the level of air pollution and the greater the health concern.
Source: U.S. Environmental Protection Agency, Air Quality Index Report, 2019

Maximum Air Pollutant Concentrations: Particulate Matter, Ozone, CO and Lead

	Particulate Matter 10 (ug/m^3)	Particulate Matter 2.5 Wtd AM (ug/m^3)	Particulate Matter 2.5 24-Hr (ug/m^3)	Ozone (ppm)	Carbon Monoxide (ppm)	Lead (ug/m^3)
MSA[1] Level	90	8.4	30	0.079	1	n/a
NAAQS[2]	150	15	35	0.075	9	0.15
Met NAAQS[2]	Yes	Yes	Yes	No	Yes	n/a

Note: (1) Data covers the Sacramento—Arden-Arcade—Roseville, CA Metropolitan Statistical Area; Data from exceptional events are included; (2) National Ambient Air Quality Standards; ppm = parts per million; ug/m^3 = micrograms per cubic meter; n/a not available.
Concentrations: Particulate Matter 10 (coarse particulate)—highest second maximum 24-hour concentration; Particulate Matter 2.5 Wtd AM (fine particulate)—highest weighted annual mean concentration; Particulate Matter 2.5 24-Hour (fine particulate)—highest 98th percentile 24-hour concentration; Ozone—highest fourth daily maximum 8-hour concentration; Carbon Monoxide—highest second maximum non-overlapping 8-hour concentration; Lead—maximum running 3-month average
Source: U.S. Environmental Protection Agency, Air Quality Monitoring Information, "Air Quality Statistics by City, 2019"

Maximum Air Pollutant Concentrations: Nitrogen Dioxide and Sulfur Dioxide

	Nitrogen Dioxide AM (ppb)	Nitrogen Dioxide 1-Hr (ppb)	Sulfur Dioxide AM (ppb)	Sulfur Dioxide 1-Hr (ppb)	Sulfur Dioxide 24-Hr (ppb)
MSA[1] Level	12	55	n/a	3	n/a
NAAQS[2]	53	100	30	75	140
Met NAAQS[2]	Yes	Yes	n/a	Yes	n/a

Note: (1) Data covers the Sacramento—Arden-Arcade—Roseville, CA Metropolitan Statistical Area; Data from exceptional events are included; (2) National Ambient Air Quality Standards; ppm = parts per million; ug/m^3 = micrograms per cubic meter; n/a not available.
Concentrations: Nitrogen Dioxide AM—highest arithmetic mean concentration; Nitrogen Dioxide 1-Hr—highest 98th percentile 1-hour daily maximum concentration; Sulfur Dioxide AM—highest annual mean concentration; Sulfur Dioxide 1-Hr—highest 99th percentile 1-hour daily maximum concentration; Sulfur Dioxide 24-Hr—highest second maximum 24-hour concentration
Source: U.S. Environmental Protection Agency, Air Quality Monitoring Information, "Air Quality Statistics by City, 2019"

Maximum Air Pollutant Concentrations: Particulate Matter, Ozone, CO and Lead

	Particulate Matter 10 (µg/m³)	Particulate Matter 2.5 Wtd AM (µg/m³)	Particulate Matter 2.5 24-Hr (µg/m³)	Ozone (ppm)	Carbon Monoxide (ppm)	Lead (µg/m³)
MSA Level	90	8.4	30	0.079	1	n/a
NAAQS	150	15	35	0.075	9	0.15
Met NAAQS?	Yes	Yes	Yes	No	Yes	n/a

Note: (1) Data covers the Sacramento—Roseville—Arden-Arcade, CA Metropolitan Statistical Area. Data were exceptional events are not included. (2) National Ambient Air Quality Standards. ppm = parts per million; ppb = micrograms per cubic meter, n/a = not available.

Concentrations: Particulate Matter 10 (coarse particulates) – highest second maximum 24-hour concentration. Particulate Matter 2.5 Wtd AM (fine particulates) – highest weighted annual mean concentration. Particulate Matter 2.5 24-Hour (fine particulates) – highest 98th percentile 24-hour concentration. Ozone – highest fourth daily maximum 8-hour concentration. Carbon Monoxide – highest second maximum non-overlapping 8-hour concentration. Lead – maximum running 3-month average.

Source: U.S. Environmental Protection Agency, Air Quality Monitoring Information, "Air Quality Statistics by City, 2019."

Maximum Air Pollutant Concentrations: Nitrogen Dioxide and Sulfur Dioxide

	Nitrogen Dioxide AM (ppb)	Nitrogen Dioxide 1-Hr (ppb)	Sulfur Dioxide AM (ppb)	Sulfur Dioxide 1-Hr (ppb)	Sulfur Dioxide 24-Hr (ppb)
MSA Level	12	53	n.a.	3	n/a
NAAQS	53	100	75	30	140
Met NAAQS?	Yes	Yes	n.a.	Yes	n/a

Note: (1) Data covers the Sacramento—Roseville—Arden-Arcade, CA Metropolitan Statistical Area. Data from exceptional events are not included. (2) National Ambient Air Quality Standards. ppm = parts per million; ppb = micrograms per cubic meter, n/a = not available.

Concentrations: Nitrogen Dioxide AM – highest arithmetic mean concentration. Nitrogen Dioxide 1-Hr – highest 98th percentile 1-hour daily maximum concentration. Sulfur Dioxide AM – highest annual mean concentration. Sulfur Dioxide 1-Hr – highest 99th percentile 1-hour daily maximum concentration. Sulfur Dioxide 24-Hr – highest second maximum 24-hour concentration.

Source: U.S. Environmental Protection Agency, Air Quality Monitoring Information, "Air Quality Statistics by City, 2019."

Salt Lake City, Utah

Background

Salt Lake City, Utah's largest city and state capital, is known for its Mormon, or Church of Jesus Christ of Latter-day Saints, origins. The city was founded by Brigham Young on July 24, 1847, as a place of refuge from mainstream ostracism for the Mormon's polygamous lifestyle.

Brigham Young led his people to a "land that nobody wanted," so they could exercise their form of worship in peace. Two scouts, Orson Pratt and Erastus Snow located the site for Brigham Young, who declared: "This is the place." The site that was to be called Salt Lake City was breathtaking. The area was bordered on the east and southwest by the dramatic peaks of the Wasatch Range, and on the northwest by the Great Salt Lake.

The land was too dry and hard for farming, but Mormon industry diverted the flow of mountain streams to irrigate the land, and the valley turned into a prosperous agricultural region. A little more than 10 years after its incorporation as a city, the U.S. government was still suspicious of its Mormon residents. Fort Douglas was erected in 1862, manned by federal troops to keep an eye on the Mormons and their polygamous practices. In 1869, the completion of the Transcontinental Railroad brought mining, industry, and other non-Mormon interests to Salt Lake City. As for polygamy, the Mormon Church made it illegal in 1890.

While mining played a major role in the early development of Salt Lake City, major industry sectors now include construction, trade, transportation, communications, finance, insurance, and real estate. The University of Utah Research Park occupies 320 acres adjacent to campus, and houses 53 companies and 82 academic departments where 9,700 people are employed.

Major efforts to revitalize the downtown area have been continuous. The $1 billion City Creek Center, with residences, offices, and a mall, recently opened and occupies 20 acres. The Salt Lake City Redevelopment Agency renovated retail space that is part of the Utah Theater, a former 1918 vaudeville theater on Main Street. The new $116 million, 2,500-seat Utah Performing Arts Center opened in 2016, boosting downtown economy.

The Utah Pride Festival is an LGBTQ festival which is held in June each year. Since 1983, it has grown dramatically to a three-day festival with attendance over 20,000. Sponsored by the Utah Pride Center, it is one of the largest festivals in the country and includes hundreds of vendors, food, music stars, a 5k run, a dyke and trans march, as well as an interfaith service by the Utah Pride Interfaith Coalition.

Salt Lake City International Airport is home to Delta Airlines' fifth-largest hub. A terminal redevelopment plan is underway, with a new terminal and facilities projected to open in 2022.

Salt Lake City, in 2010, was designated as a Silver-level Bicycle Friendly Community by the League of American Bicyclists, placing the city in the top 18 bicycling cities in the U.S. with a population of at least 100,000. Many streets in the city have bike lanes, and the city has published a bicycle map.

The NBA's Utah Jazz plays at the EnergySolutions Arena. The city is also home to Real Salt Lake of Major League Soccer.

The nearby mountain ranges and the Great Salt Lake greatly influence climatic conditions. Temperatures are

> When Hogle Zoo was shut down for 50 days straight, the zookeepers brought an exercise video to the Great Apes Building and did a full-on Zumba workout in front of the primates.

moderated by the lake in winter, and storm activity is enhanced by both the lake and the mountains. Salt Lake City normally has a semi-arid continental climate with four well-defined seasons. Summers are hot and dry, while winters are cold, but generally not severe. Mountains to the north and east act as a barrier to frequent invasions of cold air. Heavy fog can develop when there is a temperature inversion in winter and may persist for several days at a time.

Rankings

General Rankings

- The Salt Lake City metro area was identified as one of America's fastest-growing areas in terms of population and business growth by *MagnifyMoney*. The area ranked #18 out of 35. The 100 most populous metro areas in the U.S. were evaluated on their change from 2011-2016 in the following categories: people and housing; workforce and employment opportunities; growing industry. *www.businessinsider.com, "The 35 Cities in the US with the Biggest Influx of People, the Most Work Opportunities, and the Hottest Business Growth," August 12, 2018*

- The Salt Lake City metro area was identified as one of America's fastest-growing areas in terms of population and economy by *Forbes*. The area ranked #24 out of 25. The 100 most populous metro areas in the U.S. were evaluated on the following criteria: estimated population growth; employment; economic output; wages; home values. *Forbes, "America's Fastest-Growing Cities 2018," February 28, 2018*

- In their seventh annual survey, Livability.com looked at data for more than 1,000 small to mid-sized U.S. cities to determine the rankings for Livability's "Top 100 Best Places to Live" in 2020. Salt Lake City ranked #18. Criteria: housing and affordable living; vibrant economy; social and civic engagement; education; demographics; health care options; transportation & infrastructure; and abundant lifestyle amenities. *Livability.com, "Top 100 Best Places to Live 2020" October 2020*

Business/Finance Rankings

- According to *Business Insider*, the Salt Lake City metro area is a prime place to run a startup or move an existing business to. The area ranked #14. Nearly 190 metro areas were analyzed on overall economic health and investments. Data was based on the 2019 U.S. Census Bureau American Community Survey, the marketing company PitchBook, Bureau of Labor Statistics employment report, and Zillow. Criteria: percentage of change in typical home values and employment rates; quarterly venture capital investment activity; and median household income. *www.businessinsider.com, "The 25 Best Cities to Start a Business-Or Move Your Current One," January 12, 2021*

- The Brookings Institution ranked the nation's largest cities based on income inequality. Salt Lake City was ranked #57 (#1 = greatest inequality). Criteria: the "95/20 ratio," a figure representing the income at which a household earns more than 95 percent of all other households, divided by the income at which a household earns more than only 20 percent of all other households. *Brookings Institution, "Household Income Inequality, Largest Cities of 97 Large U.S. Metro Areas, 2014-2016," February 5, 2018*

- The Brookings Institution ranked the 100 largest metro areas in the U.S. based on income inequality. Salt Lake City was ranked #98 (#1 = greatest inequality). Criteria: the "95/20 ratio," a figure representing the income at which a household earns more than 95 percent of all other households, divided by the income at which a household earns more than only 20 percent of all other households. *Brookings Institution, "Household Income Inequality, 100 Largest U.S. Metro Areas, 2014-2016," February 5, 2018*

- *Forbes* ranked the 100 largest metro areas in the U.S. in terms of the "Best Cities for Young Professionals." The Salt Lake City metro area ranked #3 out of 25. Criteria: median rent of a two-bedroom apartment; job growth and unemployment rate; median salary of college graduates with 5 or less years of work experience; networking opportunities; social outlook; percentage of population 25 years of age and older with college degrees. *Forbes.com, "America's 25 Best Cities for Young Professionals in 2017," May 22, 2017*

- The Salt Lake City metro area appeared on the Milken Institute "2021 Best Performing Cities" list. Rank: #4 out of 200 large metro areas (population over 250,000). Criteria: job growth; wage and salary growth; high-tech output growth; housing affordability; household broadband access. *Milken Institute, "Best-Performing Cities 2021," February 16, 2021*

- *Forbes* ranked the 200 most populous metro areas to determine the nation's "Best Places for Business and Careers." The Salt Lake City metro area was ranked #21. Criteria: costs (business and living); job growth (past and projected); income growth; quality of life; educational attainment (college and high school); projected economic growth; cultural and leisure opportunities; workplace tolerance laws; net migration patterns. *Forbes, "The Best Places for Business and Careers 2019: Seattle Still On Top," October 30, 2019*

Dating/Romance Rankings

■ Salt Lake City was ranked #22 out of 25 cities that stood out for inspiring romance and attracting diners on the website OpenTable.com. Criteria: percentage of people who dined out on Valentine's Day in 2018; percentage of romantic restaurants as rated by OpenTable diner reviews; and percentage of tables seated for two. *OpenTable, "25 Most Romantic Cities in America for 2019," February 7, 2019*

■ Salt Lake City was selected as one of the nation's most romantic cities with 100,000 or more residents by Amazon.com. The city ranked #5 of 20. Criteria: per capita sales of romance novels, relationship books, romantic comedy movies, romantic music, and sexual wellness products. *Amazon.com, "Top 20 Most Romantic Cities in the U.S.," February 1, 2017*

Education Rankings

■ Personal finance website *WalletHub* analyzed the 150 largest U.S. metropolitan statistical areas to determine where the most educated Americans are putting their degrees to work. Criteria: education levels; percentage of workers with degrees; education quality and attainment gap; public school quality rankings; quality and enrollment of each metro area's universities. Salt Lake City was ranked #40 (#1 = most educated city). *www.WalletHub.com, "Most and Least Educated Cities in America," July 20, 2020*

Environmental Rankings

■ Sperling's BestPlaces assessed the 50 largest metropolitan areas of the United States for the likelihood of dangerously extreme weather events or earthquakes. In general the Southeast and South-Central regions have the highest risk of weather extremes and earthquakes, while the Pacific Northwest enjoys the lowest risk. Of the least risky metropolitan areas, the Salt Lake City metro area was ranked #2. *www.bestplaces.net, "Avoid Natural Disasters: BestPlaces Reveals The Top 10 Safest Places to Live," October 25, 2017*

■ The U.S. Environmental Protection Agency (EPA) released a list of mid-size U.S. metropolitan areas with the most ENERGY STAR certified buildings in 2019. The Salt Lake City metro area was ranked #9 out of 10. *U.S. Environmental Protection Agency, "2020 Energy Star Top Cities," March 2020*

■ Salt Lake City was highlighted as one of the 25 most ozone-polluted metro areas in the U.S. during 2016 through 2018. The area ranked #11. *American Lung Association, "State of the Air 2020," April 21, 2020*

■ Salt Lake City was highlighted as one of the 25 metro areas most polluted by short-term particle pollution (24-hour PM 2.5) in the U.S. during 2016 through 2018. The area ranked #7. *American Lung Association, "State of the Air 2020," April 21, 2020*

Health/Fitness Rankings

■ Trulia analyzed the 100 largest U.S. metro areas to identify the nation's best cities for weight loss, based on the percentage of adults who bike or walk to work, sporting goods stores, grocery stores, access to outdoor activities, weight-loss centers, gyms, and average space reserved for parks. Salt Lake City ranked #1. *Trulia.com, "Where to Live to Get in Shape in the New Year," January 4, 2018*

■ Salt Lake City was identified as a "2021 Spring Allergy Capital." The area ranked #96 out of 100. Three groups of factors were used to identify the most challenging cities for people with allergies during the spring season: annual spring pollen levels; over the counter medicine use; number of board-certified allergy specialists. *Asthma and Allergy Foundation of America, "Spring Allergy Capitals 2021," February 23, 2021*

■ Salt Lake City was identified as a "2021 Fall Allergy Capital." The area ranked #95 out of 100. Three groups of factors were used to identify the most challenging cities for people with allergies during the fall season: annual fall pollen levels; over the counter medicine use; number of board-certified allergy specialists. *Asthma and Allergy Foundation of America, "Fall Allergy Capitals 2021," February 23, 2021*

■ Salt Lake City was identified as a "2019 Asthma Capital." The area ranked #69 out of the nation's 100 largest metropolitan areas. Criteria: estimated asthma prevalence; crude death rate from asthma; and ER visits due to asthma. Risk factors analyzed but not factored in the rankings: annual pollen score; annual air quality; public smoking laws; number of board-certified asthma specialists; rescue medication use; controller medication use; uninsured rate; poverty rate. *Asthma and Allergy Foundation of America, "Asthma Capitals 2019: The Most Challenging Places to Live With Asthma," May 7, 2019*

Real Estate Rankings

- FitSmallBusiness looked at 50 of the largest metropolitan areas in the U.S. to determine which metro was the best to start a real estate business. Data was compiled from such sources as: Zillow, Trulia, U.S. Census Bureau, and the Bureau of Labor Statistics. Criteria: location; inventory; annual wages; median sales price of homes; days on the market; median price cut percentage; and other factors that would influence real estate professional growth. The Salt Lake City metro area ranked #36. *fitsmallbusiness.com, "The Best Cities to Become a Real Estate Agent in 2018," January 30, 2018*

- *WalletHub* compared the most populated U.S. cities to determine which had the best markets for real estate agents. Salt Lake City ranked #81 where demand was high and pay was the best. Criteria: sales per agent; annual median wage for real-estate agents; monthly average starting salary for real estate agents; real estate job density and competition; unemployment rate; home turnover rate; housing-market health index; and other relevant metrics. *www.WalletHub.com, "2019's Best Places to Be a Real Estate Agent," April 24, 2019*

- Salt Lake City was ranked #3 in the top 20 out of the 100 largest metro areas in terms of house price appreciation in 2020 (#1 = highest rate). *Federal Housing Finance Agency, House Price Index, 4th Quarter 2020*

- Salt Lake City was ranked #182 out of 268 metro areas in terms of housing affordability in 2020 by the National Association of Home Builders (#1 = most affordable). Criteria: the share of homes sold in that area affordable to a family earning the local median income, based on standard mortgage underwriting criteria. *National Association of Home Builders®, NAHB-Wells Fargo Housing Opportunity Index, 4th Quarter 2020*

Safety Rankings

- Allstate ranked the 200 largest cities in America in terms of driver safety. Salt Lake City ranked #67. Criteria: internal property damage claims over a two-year period from January 2016 to December 2017. The report helps increase the importance of safety and awareness behind the wheel. *Allstate, "Allstate America's Best Drivers Report, 2019" June 24, 2019*

- The National Insurance Crime Bureau ranked 384 metro areas in the U.S. in terms of per capita rates of vehicle theft. The Salt Lake City metro area ranked #50 (#1 = highest rate). Criteria: number of vehicle theft offenses per 100,000 inhabitants in 2019. *National Insurance Crime Bureau, "Hot Spots 2019," July 21, 2020*

Seniors/Retirement Rankings

- From its Best Cities for Successful Aging indexes, the Milken Institute generated rankings for metropolitan areas, weighing data in nine categories—health care, wellness, living arrangements, transportation and convenience, financial characteristics, education, employment, community engagement, and overall livability. The Salt Lake City metro area was ranked #4 overall in the large metro area category. *Milken Institute, "Best Cities for Successful Aging, 2017" March 14, 2017*

Sports/Recreation Rankings

- Salt Lake City was chosen as one of America's best cities for bicycling. The city ranked #16 out of 50. Criteria: cycling infrastructure that is safe and friendly for all ages; energy and bike culture. The editors evaluated cities with populations of 100,000 or more. *Bicycling, "The 50 Best Bike Cities in America," October 10, 2018*

Women/Minorities Rankings

- Personal finance website *WalletHub* compared more than 180 U.S. cities across two key dimensions, "Hispanic Business-Friendliness" and "Hispanic Purchasing Power," to arrive at the most favorable conditions for Hispanic entrepreneurs. Salt Lake City was ranked #55 out of 182. Criteria includes: share of Hispanic-Owned Businesses; Hispanic entrepreneurship rate to median annual income of Hispanics; Small Business-Friendliness score; cost of living; and number of Hispanics with at least a bachelor's degree. *WalletHub.com, "2019's Best Cities for Hispanic Entrepreneurs," May 1, 2019*

Miscellaneous Rankings

- *MoveHub* ranked 446 hipster cities across 20 countries, using its *alternative* Hipster Index and Salt Lake City came out as #3 among the top 50. Criteria: population over 150,000; number of vintage boutiques; density of tattoo parlors; vegan places to eat; coffee shops; and density of vinyl record stores. *www.movehub.com, "The Hipster Index: Brighton Pips Portland to Global Top Spot," February 20, 2020*

- *WalletHub* compared the 150 most populated U.S. cities to determine their operating efficiency. A "Quality of City Services" score was constructed for each city and then divided by the total budget per capita to reveal which were managed the best. Salt Lake City ranked #27. Criteria: financial stability; economy; education; safety; health; infrastructure and pollution. *www.WalletHub.com, "2020's Best- & Worst-Run Cities in America," June 29, 2020*

Business Environment

DEMOGRAPHICS

Population Growth

Area	1990 Census	2000 Census	2010 Census	2019* Estimate	Population Growth (%) 1990-2019	Population Growth (%) 2010-2019
City	159,796	181,743	186,440	197,756	23.8	6.1
MSA[1]	768,075	968,858	1,124,197	1,201,043	56.4	6.8
U.S.	248,709,873	281,421,906	308,745,538	324,697,795	30.6	5.2

Note: (1) Figures cover the Salt Lake City, UT Metropolitan Statistical Area; (*) 2015-2019 5-year estimated population
Source: U.S. Census Bureau, 1990 Census, Census 2000, Census 2010, 2015-2019 American Community Survey 5-Year Estimates

Household Size

Area	One	Two	Three	Four	Five	Six	Seven or More	Average Household Size
City	36.2	32.2	13.5	10.0	4.2	2.1	1.8	2.40
MSA[1]	22.4	30.5	15.9	14.4	8.6	4.9	3.2	3.00
U.S.	27.9	33.9	15.6	12.9	6.0	2.3	1.4	2.60

Note: (1) Figures cover the Salt Lake City, UT Metropolitan Statistical Area
Source: U.S. Census Bureau, 2015-2019 American Community Survey 5-Year Estimates

Race

Area	White Alone[2] (%)	Black Alone[2] (%)	Asian Alone[2] (%)	AIAN[3] Alone[2] (%)	NHOPI[4] Alone[2] (%)	Other Race Alone[2] (%)	Two or More Races (%)
City	72.8	2.6	5.4	1.5	1.6	12.7	3.3
MSA[1]	79.7	1.8	3.9	0.8	1.4	9.0	3.4
U.S.	72.5	12.7	5.5	0.8	0.2	4.9	3.3

Note: (1) Figures cover the Salt Lake City, UT Metropolitan Statistical Area; (2) Alone is defined as not being in combination with one or more other races; (3) American Indian and Alaska Native; (4) Native Hawaiian and Other Pacific Islander
Source: U.S. Census Bureau, 2015-2019 American Community Survey 5-Year Estimates

Hispanic or Latino Origin

Area	Total (%)	Mexican (%)	Puerto Rican (%)	Cuban (%)	Other (%)
City	21.8	16.9	0.3	0.4	4.2
MSA[1]	18.0	13.3	0.5	0.1	4.1
U.S.	18.0	11.2	1.7	0.7	4.3

Note: Persons of Hispanic or Latino origin can be of any race; (1) Figures cover the Salt Lake City, UT Metropolitan Statistical Area
Source: U.S. Census Bureau, 2015-2019 American Community Survey 5-Year Estimates

Ancestry

Area	German	Irish	English	American	Italian	Polish	French[2]	Scottish	Dutch
City	10.4	6.7	14.9	3.3	3.3	1.5	2.0	3.3	1.9
MSA[1]	10.0	5.6	20.0	4.3	2.9	0.9	1.8	3.9	2.0
U.S.	13.3	9.7	7.2	6.2	5.1	2.8	2.3	1.7	1.2

Note: Figures are the percentage of the total population reporting a particular ancestry. The nine most commonly reported ancestries in the U.S. are shown. Figures include multiple ancestries (e.g. if a person reported being Irish and Italian, they were included in both columns); (1) Figures cover the Salt Lake City, UT Metropolitan Statistical Area; (2) Excludes Basque
Source: U.S. Census Bureau, 2015-2019 American Community Survey 5-Year Estimates

Foreign-born Population

Area	Any Foreign Country	Asia	Mexico	Europe	Caribbean	Central America[2]	South America	Africa	Canada
City	17.1	4.6	6.4	2.0	0.3	0.6	1.3	1.0	0.4
MSA[1]	12.4	3.1	4.6	1.2	0.1	0.6	1.4	0.6	0.3
U.S.	13.6	4.2	3.5	1.5	1.3	1.1	1.0	0.7	0.2

Note: (1) Figures cover the Salt Lake City, UT Metropolitan Statistical Area; (2) Excludes Mexico.
Source: U.S. Census Bureau, 2015-2019 American Community Survey 5-Year Estimates

Marital Status

Area	Never Married	Now Married[2]	Separated	Widowed	Divorced
City	42.4	41.4	1.5	3.9	10.8
MSA[1]	32.1	52.1	1.7	3.8	10.3
U.S.	33.4	48.1	1.9	5.8	10.9

Note: Figures are percentages and cover the population 15 years of age and older; (1) Figures cover the Salt Lake City, UT Metropolitan Statistical Area; (2) Excludes separated
Source: U.S. Census Bureau, 2015-2019 American Community Survey 5-Year Estimates

Disability by Age

Area	All Ages	Under 18 Years Old	18 to 64 Years Old	65 Years and Over
City	10.8	3.2	9.1	35.7
MSA[1]	9.4	3.5	8.3	32.4
U.S.	12.6	4.2	10.3	34.5

Note: Figures show percent of the civilian noninstitutionalized population that reported having a disability. Disability status is determined from six types of difficulty: vision, hearing, cognitive, ambulatory, self-care, and independent living. For children under 5 years old, hearing and vision difficulty are used to determine disability status. For children between the ages of 5 and 14, disability status is determined from hearing, vision, cognitive, ambulatory, and self-care difficulties. For people aged 15 years and older, they are considered to have a disability if they have difficulty with any one of the six difficulty types; Note: (1) Figures cover the Salt Lake City, UT Metropolitan Statistical Area
Source: U.S. Census Bureau, 2015-2019 American Community Survey 5-Year Estimates

Age

Area	Percent of Population									Median Age
	Under Age 5	Age 5–19	Age 20–34	Age 35–44	Age 45–54	Age 55–64	Age 65–74	Age 75–84	Age 85+	
City	6.2	17.1	31.6	13.8	10.1	10.2	6.6	3.2	1.3	32.3
MSA[1]	7.6	22.6	23.3	14.6	11.2	10.1	6.4	3.0	1.1	32.7
U.S.	6.1	19.1	20.7	12.6	13.0	12.9	9.1	4.6	1.9	38.1

Note: (1) Figures cover the Salt Lake City, UT Metropolitan Statistical Area
Source: U.S. Census Bureau, 2015-2019 American Community Survey 5-Year Estimates

Gender

Area	Males	Females	Males per 100 Females
City	100,748	97,008	103.9
MSA[1]	603,034	598,009	100.8
U.S.	159,886,919	164,810,876	97.0

Note: (1) Figures cover the Salt Lake City, UT Metropolitan Statistical Area
Source: U.S. Census Bureau, 2015-2019 American Community Survey 5-Year Estimates

Religious Groups by Family

Area	Catholic	Baptist	Non-Den.	Methodist[2]	Lutheran	LDS[3]	Pentecostal	Presbyterian[4]	Muslim[5]	Judaism
MSA[1]	8.9	0.8	0.5	0.5	0.5	58.9	0.7	0.4	0.4	0.1
U.S.	19.1	9.3	4.0	4.0	2.3	2.0	1.9	1.6	0.8	0.7

Note: Figures are the number of adherents as a percentage of the total population; (1) Figures cover the Salt Lake City, UT Metropolitan Statistical Area; (2) Methodist/Pietist; (3) Latter Day Saints; (4) Reformed; (5) Figures are estimates
Source: Association of Statisticians of American Religious Bodies, 2010 U.S. Religion Census: Religious Congregations & Membership Study

Religious Groups by Tradition

Area	Catholic	Evangelical Protestant	Mainline Protestant	Other Tradition	Black Protestant	Orthodox
MSA[1]	8.9	2.6	1.3	60.1	0.1	0.5
U.S.	19.1	16.2	7.3	4.3	1.6	0.3

Note: Figures are the number of adherents as a percentage of the total population; (1) Figures cover the Salt Lake City, UT Metropolitan Statistical Area
Source: Association of Statisticians of American Religious Bodies, 2010 U.S. Religion Census: Religious Congregations & Membership Study

ECONOMY

Gross Metropolitan Product

Area	2017	2018	2019	2020	Rank[2]
MSA[1]	87.9	93.6	97.8	102.5	41

Note: Figures are in billions of dollars; (1) Figures cover the Salt Lake City, UT Metropolitan Statistical Area; (2) Rank is based on 2018 data and ranges from 1 to 381
Source: U.S. Conference of Mayors, U.S. Metro Economies: GMP & Employment 2018-2020, September 2019

Economic Growth

Area	2015-17 (%)	2018 (%)	2019 (%)	2020 (%)	Rank[2]
MSA[1]	2.3	3.7	2.6	2.7	114
U.S.	1.9	2.9	2.3	2.1	–

Note: Figures are real gross metropolitan product (GMP) growth rates and represent average annual percent change; (1) Figures cover the Salt Lake City, UT Metropolitan Statistical Area; (2) Rank is based on 2017 2-year average annual percent change and ranges from 1 to 381
Source: U.S. Conference of Mayors, U.S. Metro Economies: GMP & Employment 2018-2020, September 2019

Metropolitan Area Exports

Area	2014	2015	2016	2017	2018	2019	Rank[2]
MSA[1]	8,361.5	10,380.5	8,653.7	7,916.9	9,748.6	13,273.9	29

Note: Figures are in millions of dollars; (1) Figures cover the Salt Lake City, UT Metropolitan Statistical Area; (2) Rank is based on 2019 data and ranges from 1 to 386
Source: U.S. Department of Commerce, International Trade Administration, Office of Trade and Economic Analysis, Industry and Analysis, Exports by Metropolitan Area, data extracted March 24, 2021

Building Permits

Area	Single-Family			Multi-Family			Total		
	2018	2019	Pct. Chg.	2018	2019	Pct. Chg.	2018	2019	Pct. Chg.
City	109	127	16.5	793	3,359	323.6	902	3,486	286.5
MSA[1]	5,391	4,760	-11.7	3,359	5,920	76.2	8,750	10,680	22.1
U.S.	855,300	862,100	0.7	473,500	523,900	10.6	1,328,800	1,386,000	4.3

Note: (1) Figures cover the Salt Lake City, UT Metropolitan Statistical Area; Figures represent new, privately-owned housing units authorized (unadjusted data); All permit data are based on estimates with imputation
Source: U.S. Census Bureau, Manufacturing, Mining, and Construction Statistics, Building Permits, 2018, 2019

Bankruptcy Filings

Area	Business Filings			Nonbusiness Filings		
	2019	2020	% Chg.	2019	2020	% Chg.
Salt Lake County	56	60	7.1	4,109	3,232	-21.3
U.S.	22,780	21,655	-4.9	752,160	522,808	-30.5

Note: Business filings include Chapter 7, Chapter 9, Chapter 11, Chapter 12, Chapter 13, Chapter 15, and Section 304; Nonbusiness filings include Chapter 7, Chapter 11, and Chapter 13
Source: Administrative Office of the U.S. Courts, Business and Nonbusiness Bankruptcy, County Cases Commenced by Chapter of the Bankruptcy Code, During the 12-Month Period Ending December 31, 2019 and Business and Nonbusiness Bankruptcy, County Cases Commenced by Chapter of the Bankruptcy Code, During the 12-Month Period Ending December 31, 2020

Housing Vacancy Rates

Area	Gross Vacancy Rate[2] (%)			Year-Round Vacancy Rate[3] (%)			Rental Vacancy Rate[4] (%)			Homeowner Vacancy Rate[5] (%)		
	2018	2019	2020	2018	2019	2020	2018	2019	2020	2018	2019	2020
MSA[1]	5.0	4.8	5.7	4.7	4.8	5.6	6.1	5.0	6.2	0.5	0.8	0.3
U.S.	12.3	12.0	10.6	9.7	9.5	8.2	6.9	6.7	6.3	1.5	1.4	1.0

Note: (1) Figures cover the Salt Lake City, UT Metropolitan Statistical Area; (2) The percentage of the total housing inventory that is vacant; (3) The percentage of the housing inventory (excluding seasonal units) that is year-round vacant; (4) The percentage of rental inventory that is vacant for rent; (5) The percentage of homeowner inventory that is vacant for sale
Source: U.S. Census Bureau, Housing Vacancies and Homeownership Annual Statistics: 2018, 2019, 2020

INCOME

Income

Area	Per Capita ($)	Median Household ($)	Average Household ($)
City	36,779	60,676	88,127
MSA[1]	32,829	74,842	96,196
U.S.	34,103	62,843	88,607

Note: (1) Figures cover the Salt Lake City, UT Metropolitan Statistical Area
Source: U.S. Census Bureau, 2015-2019 American Community Survey 5-Year Estimates

Household Income Distribution

Area	Percent of Households Earning							
	Under $15,000	$15,000 -$24,999	$25,000 -$34,999	$35,000 -$49,999	$50,000 -$74,999	$75,000 -$99,999	$100,000 -$149,999	$150,000 and up
City	12.0	8.5	9.1	12.4	17.6	12.5	14.3	13.7
MSA[1]	6.5	5.9	7.2	11.4	19.1	15.2	19.2	15.5
U.S.	10.3	8.9	8.9	12.3	17.2	12.7	15.1	14.5

Note: (1) Figures cover the Salt Lake City, UT Metropolitan Statistical Area
Source: U.S. Census Bureau, 2015-2019 American Community Survey 5-Year Estimates

Poverty Rate

Area	All Ages	Under 18 Years Old	18 to 64 Years Old	65 Years and Over
City	16.6	20.4	16.4	10.9
MSA[1]	9.0	10.7	8.6	6.7
U.S.	13.4	18.5	12.6	9.3

Note: Figures are percentage of people whose income during the past 12 months was below the poverty level;
(1) Figures cover the Salt Lake City, UT Metropolitan Statistical Area
Source: U.S. Census Bureau, 2015-2019 American Community Survey 5-Year Estimates

CITY FINANCES

City Government Finances

Component	2017 ($000)	2017 ($ per capita)
Total Revenues	779,816	4,047
Total Expenditures	843,243	4,377
Debt Outstanding	1,677,225	8,705
Cash and Securities[1]	1,837,516	9,537

Note: (1) Cash and security holdings of a government at the close of its fiscal year,
including those of its dependent agencies, utilities, and liquor stores.
Source: U.S. Census Bureau, State & Local Government Finances 2017

City Government Revenue by Source

Source	2017 ($000)	2017 ($ per capita)	2017 (%)
General Revenue			
From Federal Government	4,240	22	0.5
From State Government	1,883	10	0.2
From Local Governments	10,424	54	1.3
Taxes			
Property	169,941	882	21.8
Sales and Gross Receipts	79,268	411	10.2
Personal Income	0	0	0.0
Corporate Income	0	0	0.0
Motor Vehicle License	0	0	0.0
Other Taxes	15,146	79	1.9
Current Charges	335,412	1,741	43.0
Liquor Store	0	0	0.0
Utility	140,058	727	18.0
Employee Retirement	0	0	0.0

Source: U.S. Census Bureau, State & Local Government Finances 2017

City Government Expenditures by Function

Function	2017 ($000)	2017 ($ per capita)	2017 (%)
General Direct Expenditures			
Air Transportation	377,731	1,960	44.8
Corrections	0	0	0.0
Education	1,002	5	0.1
Employment Security Administration	0	0	0.0
Financial Administration	6,666	34	0.8
Fire Protection	36,319	188	4.3
General Public Buildings	10,160	52	1.2
Governmental Administration, Other	15,166	78	1.8
Health	5,781	30	0.7
Highways	18,030	93	2.1
Hospitals	0	0	0.0
Housing and Community Development	22,728	118	2.7
Interest on General Debt	12,998	67	1.5
Judicial and Legal	12,848	66	1.5
Libraries	21,004	109	2.5
Parking	2	< 1	< 0.1
Parks and Recreation	38,914	202	4.6
Police Protection	97,713	507	11.6
Public Welfare	0	0	0.0
Sewerage	18,962	98	2.2
Solid Waste Management	201	1	0.0
Veterans' Services	0	0	0.0
Liquor Store	0	0	0.0
Utility	66,702	346	7.9
Employee Retirement	0	0	0.0

Source: U.S. Census Bureau, State & Local Government Finances 2017

EMPLOYMENT

Labor Force and Employment

Area	Civilian Labor Force			Workers Employed		
	Dec. 2019	Dec. 2020	% Chg.	Dec. 2019	Dec. 2020	% Chg.
City	117,922	119,415	1.3	115,531	115,159	-0.3
MSA[1]	679,607	687,168	1.1	665,544	663,455	-0.3
U.S.	164,007,000	160,017,000	-2.4	158,504,000	149,613,000	-5.6

Note: Data is not seasonally adjusted and covers workers 16 years of age and older; (1) Figures cover the Salt Lake City, UT Metropolitan Statistical Area
Source: Bureau of Labor Statistics, Local Area Unemployment Statistics

Unemployment Rate

Area	2020											
	Jan.	Feb.	Mar.	Apr.	May	Jun.	Jul.	Aug.	Sep.	Oct.	Nov.	Dec.
City	2.6	2.6	4.1	12.8	10.9	7.4	6.1	5.3	5.4	4.2	4.2	3.6
MSA[1]	2.6	2.7	4.0	11.2	9.4	6.4	5.3	4.7	5.2	4.1	4.2	3.5
U.S.	4.0	3.8	4.5	14.4	13.0	11.2	10.5	8.5	7.7	6.6	6.4	6.5

Note: Data is not seasonally adjusted and covers workers 16 years of age and older; (1) Figures cover the Salt Lake City, UT Metropolitan Statistical Area
Source: Bureau of Labor Statistics, Local Area Unemployment Statistics

Average Wages

Occupation	$/Hr.	Occupation	$/Hr.
Accountants and Auditors	33.90	Maintenance and Repair Workers	20.90
Automotive Mechanics	21.60	Marketing Managers	62.50
Bookkeepers	20.00	Network and Computer Systems Admin.	39.60
Carpenters	22.60	Nurses, Licensed Practical	25.60
Cashiers	12.10	Nurses, Registered	34.90
Computer Programmers	41.50	Nursing Assistants	15.30
Computer Systems Analysts	37.30	Office Clerks, General	17.50
Computer User Support Specialists	26.10	Physical Therapists	39.40
Construction Laborers	18.30	Physicians	120.00
Cooks, Restaurant	13.10	Plumbers, Pipefitters and Steamfitters	26.90
Customer Service Representatives	18.60	Police and Sheriff's Patrol Officers	30.10
Dentists	60.10	Postal Service Mail Carriers	25.60
Electricians	26.90	Real Estate Sales Agents	n/a
Engineers, Electrical	48.00	Retail Salespersons	15.80
Fast Food and Counter Workers	10.10	Sales Representatives, Technical/Scientific	45.10
Financial Managers	56.60	Secretaries, Exc. Legal/Medical/Executive	19.50
First-Line Supervisors of Office Workers	27.70	Security Guards	17.40
General and Operations Managers	44.40	Surgeons	120.80
Hairdressers/Cosmetologists	16.40	Teacher Assistants, Exc. Postsecondary*	13.40
Home Health and Personal Care Aides	14.70	Teachers, Secondary School, Exc. Sp. Ed.*	29.90
Janitors and Cleaners	12.50	Telemarketers	12.50
Landscaping/Groundskeeping Workers	16.90	Truck Drivers, Heavy/Tractor-Trailer	24.60
Lawyers	72.70	Truck Drivers, Light/Delivery Services	20.00
Maids and Housekeeping Cleaners	12.40	Waiters and Waitresses	10.60

Note: Wage data covers the Salt Lake City, UT Metropolitan Statistical Area; (*) Hourly wages were calculated from annual wage data based on a 40 hour work week; n/a not available.
Source: Bureau of Labor Statistics, Metro Area Occupational Employment & Wage Estimates, May 2020

Employment by Industry

Sector	MSA[1]		U.S.
	Number of Employees	Percent of Total	Percent of Total
Construction, Mining, and Logging	50,100	6.6	5.5
Education and Health Services	88,400	11.6	16.3
Financial Activities	63,000	8.3	6.1
Government	107,400	14.2	15.2
Information	20,700	2.7	1.9
Leisure and Hospitality	56,900	7.5	9.0
Manufacturing	59,400	7.8	8.5
Other Services	21,100	2.8	3.8
Professional and Business Services	133,200	17.5	14.4
Retail Trade	79,600	10.5	10.9
Transportation, Warehousing, and Utilities	45,500	6.0	4.6
Wholesale Trade	33,700	4.4	3.9

Note: Figures are non-farm employment as of December 2020. Figures are not seasonally adjusted and include workers 16 years of age and older; (1) Figures cover the Salt Lake City, UT Metropolitan Statistical Area
Source: Bureau of Labor Statistics, Current Employment Statistics, Employment, Hours, and Earnings

Employment by Occupation

Occupation Classification	City (%)	MSA[1] (%)	U.S. (%)
Management, Business, Science, and Arts	46.5	39.8	38.5
Natural Resources, Construction, and Maintenance	6.4	8.3	8.9
Production, Transportation, and Material Moving	11.4	13.3	13.2
Sales and Office	19.3	24.2	21.6
Service	16.4	14.5	17.8

Note: Figures cover employed civilians 16 years of age and older; (1) Figures cover the Salt Lake City, UT Metropolitan Statistical Area
Source: U.S. Census Bureau, 2015-2019 American Community Survey 5-Year Estimates

Occupations with Greatest Projected Employment Growth: 2020 – 2022

Occupation[1]	2020 Employment	2022 Projected Employment	Numeric Employment Change	Percent Employment Change
Fast Food and Counter Workers	42,200	46,310	4,110	9.7
Laborers and Freight, Stock, and Material Movers, Hand	25,360	29,070	3,710	14.6
General and Operations Managers	48,790	52,160	3,370	6.9
Light Truck or Delivery Services Drivers	11,770	14,330	2,560	21.8
Retail Salespersons	46,270	48,780	2,510	5.4
Construction Laborers	19,610	21,610	2,000	10.2
Software Developers and Software Quality Assurance Analysts and Testers	19,350	21,110	1,760	9.1
Waiters and Waitresses	16,290	17,870	1,580	9.7
Home Health and Personal Care Aides	16,180	17,670	1,490	9.2
Office Clerks, General	32,890	34,270	1,380	4.2

Note: Projections cover Utah; (1) Sorted by numeric employment change
Source: www.projectionscentral.com, State Occupational Projections, 2020–2022 Short-Term Projections

Fastest-Growing Occupations: 2020 – 2022

Occupation[1]	2020 Employment	2022 Projected Employment	Numeric Employment Change	Percent Employment Change
Dancers	190	250	60	31.6
Bartenders	2,020	2,480	460	22.8
Light Truck or Delivery Services Drivers	11,770	14,330	2,560	21.8
Hotel, Motel, and Resort Desk Clerks	3,190	3,780	590	18.5
Actors	280	330	50	17.9
Medical Scientists, Except Epidemiologists	1,660	1,950	290	17.5
Statisticians	640	750	110	17.2
Food Servers, Nonrestaurant	1,930	2,260	330	17.1
Lodging Managers	370	430	60	16.2
Couriers and Messengers	950	1,100	150	15.8

Note: Projections cover Utah; (1) Sorted by percent employment change and excludes occupations with numeric employment change less than 50
Source: www.projectionscentral.com, State Occupational Projections, 2020–2022 Short-Term Projections

TAXES

State Corporate Income Tax Rates

State	Tax Rate (%)	Income Brackets ($)	Num. of Brackets	Financial Institution Tax Rate (%)[a]	Federal Income Tax Ded.
Utah	4.95 (b)	Flat rate	–	4.95 (b)	No

Note: Tax rates as of January 1, 2021; (a) Rates listed are the corporate income tax rate applied to financial institutions or excise taxes based on income. Some states have other taxes based upon the value of deposits or shares; (b) Minimum tax is $800 in California, $250 in District of Columbia, $50 in Arizona and North Dakota (banks), $400 ($100 banks) in Rhode Island, $200 per location in South Dakota (banks), $100 in Utah, $300 in Vermont.
Source: Federation of Tax Administrators, State Corporate Income Tax Rates, January 1, 2021

State Individual Income Tax Rates

State	Tax Rate (%)	Income Brackets ($)	Personal Exemptions ($)			Standard Ded. ($)	
			Single	Married	Depend.	Single	Married
Utah	4.95	Flat rate	None	None	None	(u)	(u)

Note: Tax rates as of January 1, 2021; Local- and county-level taxes are not included; Federal income tax is not deductible on state income tax returns; (u) Utah provides a tax credit equal to 6% of the federal personal exemption amounts (and applicable standard deduction).
Source: Federation of Tax Administrators, State Individual Income Tax Rates, January 1, 2021

Various State Sales and Excise Tax Rates

State	State Sales Tax (%)	Gasoline[1] (¢/gal.)	Cigarette[2] ($/pack)	Spirits[3] ($/gal.)	Wine[4] ($/gal.)	Beer[5] ($/gal.)	Recreational Marijuana (%)
Utah	6.1	31.41	1.7	15.92	0.00	0.41	Not legal

Note: All tax rates as of January 1, 2021; (1) The American Petroleum Institute has developed a methodology for determining the average tax rate on a gallon of fuel. Rates may include any of the following: excise taxes, environmental fees, storage tank fees, other fees or taxes, general sales tax, and local taxes; (2) The federal excise tax of $1.0066 per pack and local taxes are not included; (3) Rates are those applicable to off-premise sales of 40% alcohol by volume (a.b.v.) distilled spirits in 750ml containers. Local excise taxes are excluded; (4) Rates are those applicable to off-premise sales of 11% a.b.v. non-carbonated wine in 750ml containers; (5) Rates are those applicable to off-premise sales of 4.7% a.b.v. beer in 12 ounce containers.
Source: Tax Foundation, 2021 Facts & Figures: How Does Your State Compare?

State Business Tax Climate Index Rankings

State	Overall Rank	Corporate Tax Rank	Individual Income Tax Rank	Sales Tax Rank	Property Tax Rank	Unemployment Insurance Tax Rank
Utah	8	14	10	23	7	17

Note: The index is a measure of how each state's tax laws affect economic performance. The lower the rank, the more favorable a state's tax system is for business. States without a given tax are given a ranking of 1. The scores/rankings for the District of Columbia do not affect other states. The 2021 index represents the tax climate as of July 1, 2020.
Source: Tax Foundation, State Business Tax Climate Index 2021

TRANSPORTATION

Means of Transportation to Work

Area	Car/Truck/Van		Public Transportation			Bicycle	Walked	Other Means	Worked at Home
	Drove Alone	Car-pooled	Bus	Subway	Railroad				
City	67.8	10.5	4.8	0.4	0.8	2.5	5.1	2.7	5.5
MSA[1]	75.4	11.1	2.1	0.3	0.5	0.8	2.1	1.5	6.2
U.S.	76.3	9.0	2.4	1.9	0.6	0.5	2.7	1.4	5.2

Note: Figures are percentages and cover workers 16 years of age and older; (1) Figures cover the Salt Lake City, UT Metropolitan Statistical Area
Source: U.S. Census Bureau, 2015-2019 American Community Survey 5-Year Estimates

Travel Time to Work

Area	Less Than 10 Minutes	10 to 19 Minutes	20 to 29 Minutes	30 to 44 Minutes	45 to 59 Minutes	60 to 89 Minutes	90 Minutes or More
City	12.3	45.3	22.8	13.0	3.6	1.9	1.0
MSA[1]	10.5	33.4	27.0	19.6	5.6	2.8	1.1
U.S.	12.2	28.4	20.8	20.8	8.3	6.4	2.9

Note: Note: Figures are percentages and include workers 16 years old and over; (1) Figures cover the Salt Lake City, UT Metropolitan Statistical Area
Source: U.S. Census Bureau, 2015-2019 American Community Survey 5-Year Estimates

Key Congestion Measures

Measure	1982	1992	2002	2012	2017
Annual Hours of Delay, Total (000)	3,305	7,417	18,332	26,183	29,739
Annual Hours of Delay, Per Auto Commuter	9	16	32	41	45
Annual Congestion Cost, Total (million $)	26	80	252	479	560
Annual Congestion Cost, Per Auto Commuter ($)	207	321	618	691	762

Note: Covers the Salt Lake City-West Valley City UT urban area
Source: Texas A&M Transportation Institute, 2019 Urban Mobility Report

Freeway Travel Time Index

Measure	1982	1987	1992	1997	2002	2007	2012	2017
Urban Area Index[1]	1.05	1.07	1.08	1.11	1.16	1.18	1.18	1.18
Urban Area Rank[1,2]	51	55	76	72	54	44	40	45

Note: Freeway Travel Time Index—the ratio of travel time in the peak period to the travel time at free-flow conditions. For example, a value of 1.30 indicates a 20-minute free-flow trip takes 26 minutes in the peak (20 minutes x 1.30 = 26 minutes); (1) Covers the Salt Lake City-West Valley City UT urban area; (2) Rank is based on 101 larger urban areas (#1 = highest travel time index)
Source: Texas A&M Transportation Institute, 2019 Urban Mobility Report

Public Transportation

Agency Name / Mode of Transportation	Vehicles Operated in Maximum Service[1]	Annual Unlinked Passenger Trips[2] (in thous.)	Annual Passenger Miles[3] (in thous.)
Utah Transit Authority (UTA)			
Bus (directly operated)	416	20,175.8	84,702.2
Bus (purchased transportation)	5	74.2	219.0
Commuter Bus (directly operated)	41	549.7	12,128.1
Commuter Rail (directly operated)	50	5,193.9	133,685.5
Demand Response (directly operated)	64	243.1	2,601.4
Demand Response (purchased transportation)	46	145.2	1,822.4
Light Rail (directly operated)	89	17,128.0	83,098.5
Vanpool (directly operated)	430	1,068.4	37,026.6

Note: (1) Number of revenue vehicles operated by the given mode and type of service to meet the annual maximum service requirement. This is the revenue vehicle count during the peak season of the year; on the week and day that maximum service is provided. Vehicles operated in maximum service (VOMS) exclude atypical days and one-time special events; (2) Number of passengers who boarded public transportation vehicles. Passengers are counted each time they board a vehicle no matter how many vehicles they use to travel from their origin to their destination. (3) Sum of the distances ridden by all passengers during the entire fiscal year.
Source: Federal Transit Administration, National Transit Database, 2019

Air Transportation

Airport Name and Code / Type of Service	Passenger Airlines[1]	Passenger Enplanements	Freight Carriers[2]	Freight (lbs)
Salt Lake City International (SLC)				
Domestic service (U.S. carriers - 2020)	21	5,827,005	17	221,351,889
International service (U.S. carriers - 2019)	5	471,947	2	3,443,938

Note: (1) Includes all U.S.-based major, minor and commuter airlines that carried at least one passenger during the year; (2) Includes all U.S.-based airlines and freight carriers that transported at least one pound of freight during the year.
Source: Bureau of Transportation Statistics, The Intermodal Transportation Database, Air Carriers: T-100 Domestic Market (U.S. Carriers), 2020; Bureau of Transportation Statistics, The Intermodal Transportation Database, Air Carriers: T-100 International Market (U.S. Carriers), 2019

BUSINESSES

Major Business Headquarters

Company Name	Industry	Rankings	
		Fortune[1]	Forbes[2]
Huntsman	Chemicals	382	-
Sinclair Oil	Oil & Gas Operations	-	91

Note: (1) Companies that produce a 10-K are ranked 1 to 500 based on 2019 revenue; (2) All private companies with at least $2 billion in annual revenue through the end of their most current fiscal year are ranked 1 to 219; companies listed are headquartered in the city; dashes indicate no ranking
Source: Fortune, "Fortune 500," June/July 2020; Forbes, "America's Largest Private Companies," 2020

Fastest-Growing Businesses

According to *Inc.*, Salt Lake City is home to one of America's 500 fastest-growing private companies: **Pit Viper** (#366). Criteria: must be an independent, privately-held, for-profit, U.S. corporation, proprietorship or partnership as of December 31, 2019; revenues must be at least $100,000 in 2016 and $2 million in 2019; must have four-year operating/sales history. *Inc., "America's 500 Fastest-Growing Private Companies," 2020*

According to *Initiative for a Competitive Inner City (ICIC)*, Salt Lake City is home to two of America's 100 fastest-growing "inner city" companies: **Brand+Aid** (#42); **La Barba Coffee** (#53). Criteria for inclusion: company must be headquartered in or have 51 percent or more of its physical operations in an economically distressed urban area; must be an independent, for-profit corporation, partnership or proprietorship; must have 10 or more employees and have a five-year sales history that includes sales of at least $200,000 in the base year and at least $1 million in the current year with no decrease in sales over the two most recent years. Companies were ranked overall by revenue growth over the five-year period between 2015 and 2019. *Initiative for a Competitive Inner City (ICIC), "Inner City 100 Companies," 2020*

According to Deloitte, Salt Lake City is home to two of North America's 500 fastest-growing high-technology companies: **PolarityTE, Inc.** (#367); **Signs.com** (#470). Companies are ranked by percentage growth in revenue over a four-year period. Criteria for inclusion: company must be headquartered within North America; must own proprietary intellectual property or technology that is sold to customers in products that contributes to a significant portion of the company's operating revenue; must have been in business for a minumum of four years with 2016 operating revenues of at least $50,000 USD/CD and 2019 operating revenues of at least $5 million USD/CD. *Deloitte, 2020 Technology Fast 500*™

Living Environment

COST OF LIVING

Cost of Living Index

Composite Index	Groceries	Housing	Utilities	Trans- portation	Health Care	Misc. Goods/ Services
102.3	99.7	106.7	90.1	113.1	99.5	100.7

Note: The Cost of Living Index measures regional differences in the cost of consumer goods and services, excluding taxes and non-consumer expenditures, for professional and managerial households in the top income quintile. It is based on more than 50,000 prices covering almost 60 different items for which prices are collected three times a year by chambers of commerce, economic development organizations or university applied economic centers in each participating urban area. The numbers shown should be read as a percentage above or below the national average of 100. For example, a value of 115.4 in the groceries column indicates that grocery prices are 15.4% higher than the national average. Small differences in the index numbers should not be interpreted as significant; Figures cover the Salt Lake City UT urban area.
Source: The Council for Community and Economic Research, Cost of Living Index, 2020

Grocery Prices

Area[1]	T-Bone Steak ($/pound)	Frying Chicken ($/pound)	Whole Milk ($/half gal.)	Eggs ($/dozen)	Orange Juice ($/64 oz.)	Coffee ($/11.5 oz.)
City[2]	11.44	1.81	1.73	1.32	3.44	4.51
Avg.	11.78	1.39	2.05	1.47	3.57	4.34
Min.	8.03	0.94	1.03	0.74	2.94	3.02
Max.	15.86	2.65	4.31	3.77	5.44	8.69

Note: (1) Values for the local area are compared with the average, minimum and maximum values for all 284 areas in the Cost of Living Index; (2) Figures cover the Salt Lake City UT urban area; **T-Bone Steak** (price per pound); **Frying Chicken** (price per pound, whole fryer); **Whole Milk** (half gallon carton); **Eggs** (price per dozen, Grade A, large); **Orange Juice** (64 oz. Tropicana or Florida Natural); **Coffee** (11.5 oz. can, vacuum-packed, Maxwell House, Hills Bros, or Folgers).
Source: The Council for Community and Economic Research, Cost of Living Index, 2020

Housing and Utility Costs

Area[1]	New Home Price ($)	Apartment Rent ($/month)	All Electric ($/month)	Part Electric ($/month)	Other Energy ($/month)	Telephone ($/month)
City[2]	401,866	1,164	-	74.91	60.06	187.80
Avg.	368,594	1,168	170.86	100.47	65.28	184.30
Min.	190,567	502	91.58	31.42	26.08	169.60
Max.	2,227,806	4,738	470.38	280.31	280.06	206.50

Note: (1) Values for the local area are compared with the average, minimum and maximum values for all 284 areas in the Cost of Living Index; (2) Figures cover the Salt Lake City UT urban area; **New Home Price** (2,400 sf living area, 8,000 sf lot, in urban area with full utilities); **Apartment Rent** (950 sf 2 bedroom/1.5 or 2 bath, unfurnished, excluding all utilities except water); **All Electric** (average monthly cost for an all-electric home); **Part Electric** (average monthly cost for a part-electric home); **Other Energy** (average monthly cost for natural gas, fuel oil, coal, wood, and any other forms of energy except electricity); **Telephone** (price includes the base monthly rate plus taxes and fees for three lines of mobile phone service).
Source: The Council for Community and Economic Research, Cost of Living Index, 2020

Health Care, Transportation, and Other Costs

Area[1]	Doctor ($/visit)	Dentist ($/visit)	Optometrist ($/visit)	Gasoline ($/gallon)	Beauty Salon ($/visit)	Men's Shirt ($)
City[2]	107.49	101.65	89.78	2.44	34.97	23.53
Avg.	115.44	99.32	108.10	2.21	39.27	31.37
Min.	36.68	59.00	51.36	1.71	19.00	11.00
Max.	219.00	153.10	250.97	3.46	82.05	58.33

Note: (1) Values for the local area are compared with the average, minimum and maximum values for all 284 areas in the Cost of Living Index; (2) Figures cover the Salt Lake City UT urban area; **Doctor** (general practitioners routine exam of an established patient); **Dentist** (adult teeth cleaning and periodic oral examination); **Optometrist** (full vision eye exam for established adult patient); **Gasoline** (one gallon regular unleaded, national brand, including all taxes, cash price at self-service pump if available); **Beauty Salon** (woman's shampoo, trim, and blow-dry); **Men's Shirt** (cotton/polyester dress shirt, pinpoint weave, long sleeves).
Source: The Council for Community and Economic Research, Cost of Living Index, 2020

HOUSING

Homeownership Rate

Area	2012 (%)	2013 (%)	2014 (%)	2015 (%)	2016 (%)	2017 (%)	2018 (%)	2019 (%)	2020 (%)
MSA[1]	66.9	66.8	68.2	69.1	69.2	68.1	69.5	69.2	68.0
U.S.	65.4	65.1	64.5	63.7	63.4	63.9	64.4	64.6	66.6

Note: (1) Figures cover the Salt Lake City, UT Metropolitan Statistical Area
Source: U.S. Census Bureau, Housing Vacancies and Homeownership Annual Statistics: 2012-2020

House Price Index (HPI)

Area	National Ranking[2]	Quarterly Change (%)	One-Year Change (%)	Five-Year Change (%)	Since 1991Q1 (%)
MSA[1]	15	3.24	9.07	50.25	408.84
U.S.[3]	–	3.81	10.77	38.99	205.12

Note: The HPI is a weighted repeat sales index. It measures average price changes in repeat sales or refinancings on the same properties. This information is obtained by reviewing repeat mortgage transactions on single-family properties whose mortgages have been purchased or securitized by Fannie Mae or Freddie Mac since January 1975; (1) Figures cover the Salt Lake City, UT Metropolitan Statistical Area; (2) Rankings are based on annual percentage change for all metro areas containing at least 15,000 transactions over the last 10 years and ranges from 1 to 253; (3) figures based on a weighted average of Census Division estimates using a seasonally adjusted, purchase-only index; all figures are for the period ending December 31, 2020
Source: Federal Housing Finance Agency, Change in Metropolitan Area House Price Indexes, April 7, 2021

Median Single-Family Home Prices

Area	2018	2019	2020p	Percent Change 2019 to 2020
MSA[1]	331.7	355.2	391.0	10.1
U.S. Average	261.6	274.6	299.9	9.2

Note: Figures are median sales prices of existing single-family homes in thousands of dollars; (p) preliminary; (1) Figures cover the Salt Lake City, UT Metropolitan Statistical Area
Source: National Association of Realtors, Median Sales Price of Existing Single-Family Homes for Metropolitan Areas, 4th Quarter 2020

Qualifying Income Based on Median Sales Price of Existing Single-Family Homes

Area	With 5% Down ($)	With 10% Down ($)	With 20% Down ($)
MSA[1]	76,886	72,840	64,746
U.S. Average	59,266	56,147	49,908

Note: Figures are preliminary; Qualifying income is based on a mortgage rate of 2.81%. Monthly principal and interest payment is limited to 25% of income; (1) Figures cover the Salt Lake City, UT Metropolitan Statistical Area
Source: National Association of Realtors, Qualifying Income Based on Median Sales Price of Existing Single-Family Homes for Metropolitan Areas, 4th Quarter 2020

Home Value Distribution

Area	Under $50,000	$50,000 -$99,999	$100,000 -$149,999	$150,000 -$199,999	$200,000 -$299,999	$300,000 -$499,999	$500,000 -$999,999	$1,000,000 or more
City	2.9	1.4	6.7	13.0	23.6	29.7	19.5	3.3
MSA[1]	2.9	1.2	5.2	11.5	29.6	34.2	13.7	1.7
U.S.	6.9	12.0	13.3	14.0	19.6	19.3	11.4	3.4

Note: Figures are percentages and cover owner-occupied housing units; (1) Figures cover the Salt Lake City, UT Metropolitan Statistical Area
Source: U.S. Census Bureau, 2015-2019 American Community Survey 5-Year Estimates

Year Housing Structure Built

Area	2010 or Later	2000 -2009	1990 -1999	1980 -1989	1970 -1979	1960 -1969	1950 -1959	1940 -1949	Before 1940	Median Year
City	5.3	6.6	7.4	7.7	12.1	10.0	13.2	8.7	29.1	1959
MSA[1]	8.9	15.5	15.5	12.6	18.4	8.8	8.7	3.6	8.0	1982
U.S.	5.2	14.0	13.9	13.4	15.2	10.6	10.3	4.9	12.6	1978

Note: Figures are percentages except for Median Year; Note: (1) Figures cover the Salt Lake City, UT Metropolitan Statistical Area
Source: U.S. Census Bureau, 2015-2019 American Community Survey 5-Year Estimates

Gross Monthly Rent

Area	Under $500	$500 -$999	$1,000 -$1,499	$1,500 -$1,999	$2,000 -$2,499	$2,500 -$2,999	$3,000 and up	Median ($)
City	8.9	42.8	31.8	12.5	3.1	0.6	0.4	985
MSA[1]	5.4	33.3	41.2	15.4	3.3	0.8	0.7	1,114
U.S.	9.4	36.2	30.0	14.0	5.6	2.4	2.4	1,062

Note: Figures are percentages except for Median; Gross rent is the contract rent plus the estimated average monthly cost of utilities (electricity, gas, and water and sewer) and fuels (oil, coal, kerosene, wood, etc.) if these are paid by the renter (or paid for the renter by someone else); (1) Figures cover the Salt Lake City, UT Metropolitan Statistical Area
Source: U.S. Census Bureau, 2015-2019 American Community Survey 5-Year Estimates

HEALTH

Health Risk Factors

Category	MSA[1] (%)	U.S. (%)
Adults aged 18–64 who have any kind of health care coverage	85.1	87.3
Adults who reported being in good or better health	85.4	82.4
Adults who have been told they have high blood cholesterol	29.0	33.0
Adults who have been told they have high blood pressure	25.2	32.3
Adults who are current smokers	10.4	17.1
Adults who currently use E-cigarettes	5.7	4.6
Adults who currently use chewing tobacco, snuff, or snus	3.2	4.0
Adults who are heavy drinkers[2]	4.9	6.3
Adults who are binge drinkers[3]	15.7	17.4
Adults who are overweight (BMI 25.0 - 29.9)	34.9	35.3
Adults who are obese (BMI 30.0 - 99.8)	24.9	31.3
Adults who participated in any physical activities in the past month	77.8	74.4
Adults who always or nearly always wears a seat belt	96.6	94.3

Note: (1) Figures cover the Salt Lake City, UT Metropolitan Statistical Area; (2) Heavy drinkers are classified as adult men having more than 14 drinks per week and adult women having more than 7 drinks per week; (3) Binge drinkers are classified as males having five or more drinks on one occasion or females having four or more drinks on one occasion
Source: Centers for Disease Control and Prevention, Behaviorial Risk Factor Surveillance System, SMART: Selected Metropolitan Area Risk Trends, 2017

Acute and Chronic Health Conditions

Category	MSA[1] (%)	U.S. (%)
Adults who have ever been told they had a heart attack	2.7	4.2
Adults who have ever been told they have angina or coronary heart disease	2.4	3.9
Adults who have ever been told they had a stroke	2.1	3.0
Adults who have ever been told they have asthma	14.3	14.2
Adults who have ever been told they have arthritis	18.1	24.9
Adults who have ever been told they have diabetes[2]	7.3	10.5
Adults who have ever been told they had skin cancer	6.7	6.2
Adults who have ever been told they had any other types of cancer	5.8	7.1
Adults who have ever been told they have COPD	4.1	6.5
Adults who have ever been told they have kidney disease	2.9	3.0
Adults who have ever been told they have a form of depression	23.8	20.5

Note: (1) Figures cover the Salt Lake City, UT Metropolitan Statistical Area; (2) Figures do not include pregnancy-related, borderline, or pre-diabetes
Source: Centers for Disease Control and Prevention, Behaviorial Risk Factor Surveillance System, SMART: Selected Metropolitan Area Risk Trends, 2017

Health Screening and Vaccination Rates

Category	MSA[1] (%)	U.S. (%)
Adults aged 65+ who have had flu shot within the past year	61.2	60.7
Adults aged 65+ who have ever had a pneumonia vaccination	76.0	75.4
Adults who have ever been tested for HIV	28.1	36.1
Adults who have ever had the shingles or zoster vaccine?	32.4	28.9
Adults who have had their blood cholesterol checked within the last five years	80.8	85.9

Note: n/a not available; (1) Figures cover the Salt Lake City, UT Metropolitan Statistical Area.
Source: Centers for Disease Control and Prevention, Behaviorial Risk Factor Surveillance System, SMART: Selected Metropolitan Area Risk Trends, 2017

Disability Status

Category	MSA[1] (%)	U.S. (%)
Adults who reported being deaf	5.1	6.7
Are you blind or have serious difficulty seeing, even when wearing glasses?	3.2	4.5
Are you limited in any way in any of your usual activities due of arthritis?	9.0	12.9
Do you have difficulty doing errands alone?	4.8	6.8
Do you have difficulty dressing or bathing?	2.4	3.6
Do you have serious difficulty concentrating/remembering/making decisions?	10.8	10.7
Do you have serious difficulty walking or climbing stairs?	9.0	13.6

Note: (1) Figures cover the Salt Lake City, UT Metropolitan Statistical Area.
Source: Centers for Disease Control and Prevention, Behaviorial Risk Factor Surveillance System, SMART: Selected Metropolitan Area Risk Trends, 2017

Mortality Rates for the Top 10 Causes of Death in the U.S.

ICD-10[a] Sub-Chapter	ICD-10[a] Code	Age-Adjusted Mortality Rate[1] per 100,000 population	
		County[2]	U.S.
Malignant neoplasms	C00-C97	123.5	149.2
Ischaemic heart diseases	I20-I25	62.5	90.5
Other forms of heart disease	I30-I51	65.3	52.2
Chronic lower respiratory diseases	J40-J47	33.6	39.6
Other degenerative diseases of the nervous system	G30-G31	49.8	37.6
Cerebrovascular diseases	I60-I69	37.2	37.2
Other external causes of accidental injury	W00-X59	36.0	36.1
Organic, including symptomatic, mental disorders	F01-F09	31.0	29.4
Hypertensive diseases	I10-I15	17.2	24.1
Diabetes mellitus	E10-E14	24.8	21.5

Note: (a) ICD-10 = International Classification of Diseases 10th Revision; (1) Mortality rates are a three-year average covering 2017-2019; (2) Figures cover Salt Lake County.
Source: Centers for Disease Control and Prevention, National Center for Health Statistics. Underlying Cause of Death 1999-2019 on CDC WONDER Online Database

Mortality Rates for Selected Causes of Death

ICD-10[a] Sub-Chapter	ICD-10[a] Code	Age-Adjusted Mortality Rate[1] per 100,000 population	
		County[2]	U.S.
Assault	X85-Y09	3.1	6.0
Diseases of the liver	K70-K76	13.6	14.4
Human immunodeficiency virus (HIV) disease	B20-B24	0.7	1.5
Influenza and pneumonia	J09-J18	10.3	13.8
Intentional self-harm	X60-X84	22.4	14.1
Malnutrition	E40-E46	8.6	2.3
Obesity and other hyperalimentation	E65-E68	2.4	2.1
Renal failure	N17-N19	11.3	12.6
Transport accidents	V01-V99	8.9	12.3
Viral hepatitis	B15-B19	1.3	1.2

Note: (a) ICD-10 = International Classification of Diseases 10th Revision; (1) Mortality rates are a three-year average covering 2017-2019; (2) Figures cover Salt Lake County; Data are suppressed when the data meet the criteria for confidentiality constraints; Mortality rates are flagged as unreliable when the rate would be calculated with a numerator of 20 or less.
Source: Centers for Disease Control and Prevention, National Center for Health Statistics. Underlying Cause of Death 1999-2019 on CDC WONDER Online Database

Health Insurance Coverage

Area	With Health Insurance	With Private Health Insurance	With Public Health Insurance	Without Health Insurance	Population Under Age 19 Without Health Insurance
City	87.4	72.5	22.1	12.6	11.7
MSA[1]	89.7	77.5	20.1	10.3	8.2
U.S.	91.2	67.9	35.1	8.8	5.1

Note: Figures are percentages that cover the civilian noninstitutionalized population; (1) Figures cover the Salt Lake City, UT Metropolitan Statistical Area
Source: U.S. Census Bureau, 2015-2019 American Community Survey 5-Year Estimates

Number of Medical Professionals

Area	MDs[3]	DOs[3,4]	Dentists	Podiatrists	Chiropractors	Optometrists
County[1] (number)	4,327	197	910	75	315	157
County[1] (rate[2])	376.7	17.1	78.4	6.5	27.1	13.5
U.S. (rate[2])	282.9	22.7	71.2	6.2	28.1	16.9
49035						

Note: Data as of 2019 unless noted; (1) Data covers Salt Lake County; (2) Rate per 100,000 population; (3) Data as of 2018 and includes all active, non-federal physicians; (4) Doctor of Osteopathic Medicine
Source: U.S. Department of Health and Human Services, Health Resources and Services Administration, Bureau of Health Professions, Area Resource File (ARF) 2019-2020

Best Hospitals

According to *U.S. News,* the Salt Lake City, UT metro area is home to three of the best hospitals in the U.S.: **Huntsman Cancer Institute at the University of Utah** (2 adult specialties); **John A. Moran Eye Center, University of Utah Hospitals and Clinics** (2 adult specialties); **University of Utah Hospital** (2 adult specialties). The hospitals listed were nationally ranked in at least one of 16 adult or 10 pediatric specialties. Only 134 hospitals nationwide were nationally ranked in one or more adult or pediatric specialty; this number increases to 178 counting specialized centers within hospitals. Twenty hospitals in the U.S. made the Honor Roll. The Best Hospitals Honor Roll takes both the national rankings and the procedure and condition ratings into account. Hospitals received points if they were nationally ranked in one of the 16 adult specialties—the higher they ranked, the more points they got—and how many ratings of "high performing" they earned in the 10 procedures and conditions. *U.S. News Online, "America's Best Hospitals 2020-21"*

According to *U.S. News,* the Salt Lake City, UT metro area is home to one of the best children's hospitals in the U.S.: **Intermountain Primary Children's Hospital-Shriners Hospitals for Children-Univer** (8 pediatric specialties). The hospital listed was highly ranked in at least one of 10 pediatric specialties. Eighty-eight children's hospitals in the U.S. were nationally ranked in at least one specialty. Hospitals received points for being ranked in a specialty, and the 10 hospitals with the most points across the 10 specialties make up the Honor Roll. *U.S. News Online, "America's Best Children's Hospitals 2020-21"*

EDUCATION

Public School District Statistics

District Name	Schls	Pupils	Pupil/ Teacher Ratio	Minority Pupils[1] (%)	Free Lunch Eligible[2] (%)	IEP[3] (%)
Granite District	92	66,767	23.3	49.7	45.8	11.8
Salt Lake District	42	23,165	20.7	57.1	51.0	12.5

Note: Table includes school districts with 2,000 or more students; (1) Percentage of students that are not non-Hispanic white; (2) Percentage of students that are eligible for the free lunch program; (3) Percentage of students that have an Individualized Education Program.
Source: U.S. Department of Education, National Center for Education Statistics, Common Core of Data, Local Education Agency (School District) Universe Survey: School Year 2018-2019; U.S. Department of Education, National Center for Education Statistics, Common Core of Data, Public Elementary/Secondary School Universe Survey: School Year 2018-2019

Highest Level of Education

Area	Less than H.S.	H.S. Diploma	Some College, No Deg.	Associate Degree	Bachelor's Degree	Master's Degree	Prof. School Degree	Doctorate Degree
City	11.2	17.5	17.7	7.0	25.7	12.5	4.6	3.7
MSA[1]	9.2	23.0	23.9	9.0	22.5	8.7	2.3	1.5
U.S.	12.0	27.0	20.4	8.5	19.8	8.8	2.1	1.4

Note: Figures cover persons age 25 and over; (1) Figures cover the Salt Lake City, UT Metropolitan Statistical Area
Source: U.S. Census Bureau, 2015-2019 American Community Survey 5-Year Estimates

Educational Attainment by Race

Area	High School Graduate or Higher (%)					Bachelor's Degree or Higher (%)				
	Total	White	Black	Asian	Hisp.[2]	Total	White	Black	Asian	Hisp.[2]
City	88.8	94.2	82.2	83.8	62.2	46.5	51.8	26.7	61.5	16.5
MSA[1]	90.8	94.0	85.4	86.8	69.0	35.0	37.2	25.1	51.4	14.3
U.S.	88.0	89.9	86.0	87.1	68.7	32.1	33.5	21.6	54.3	16.4

Note: Figures shown cover persons 25 years old and over; (1) Figures cover the Salt Lake City, UT Metropolitan Statistical Area; (2) People of Hispanic origin can be of any race
Source: U.S. Census Bureau, 2015-2019 American Community Survey 5-Year Estimates

School Enrollment by Grade and Control

Area	Preschool (%)		Kindergarten (%)		Grades 1 - 4 (%)		Grades 5 - 8 (%)		Grades 9 - 12 (%)	
	Public	Private	Public	Private	Public	Private	Public	Private	Public	Private
City	47.7	52.3	88.2	11.8	91.2	8.8	91.0	9.0	92.8	7.2
MSA[1]	54.5	45.5	88.8	11.2	92.6	7.4	93.4	6.6	93.7	6.3
U.S.	59.1	40.9	87.6	12.4	89.5	10.5	89.4	10.6	90.1	9.9

Note: Figures shown cover persons 3 years old and over; (1) Figures cover the Salt Lake City, UT Metropolitan Statistical Area
Source: U.S. Census Bureau, 2015-2019 American Community Survey 5-Year Estimates

Higher Education

Four-Year Colleges			Two-Year Colleges			Medical Schools[1]	Law Schools[2]	Voc/ Tech[3]
Public	Private Non-profit	Private For-profit	Public	Private Non-profit	Private For-profit			
1	4	3	1	1	1	1	1	4

Note: Figures cover institutions located within the city limits and include main campuses only; (1) includes schools accredited by the Liaison Committee on Medical Education and the American Osteopathic Association's Commission on Osteopathic College Accreditation; (2) includes ABA-accredited schools, schools with provisional ABA accreditation, and state accredited schools; (3) includes all schools with programs that are less than 2 years.
Source: National Center for Education Statistics, Integrated Postsecondary Education System (IPEDS), 2019-20; Wikipedia, List of Medical Schools in the United States, accessed April 2, 2021; Wikipedia, List of Law Schools in the United States, accessed April 2, 2021

According to *U.S. News & World Report,* the Salt Lake City, UT metro area is home to one of the top 200 national universities in the U.S.: **University of Utah** (#97 tie). The indicators used to capture academic quality fall into a number of categories: assessment by administrators at peer institutions; retention of students; faculty resources; student selectivity; financial resources; alumni giving; high school counselor ratings of colleges; and graduation rate. *U.S. News & World Report, "America's Best Colleges 2021"*

According to *U.S. News & World Report,* the Salt Lake City, UT metro area is home to one of the top 100 law schools in the U.S.: **University of Utah (Quinney)** (#43 tie). The rankings are based on a weighted average of 12 measures of quality: peer assessment score; assessment score by lawyers/judges; median LSAT scores; median undergrad GPA; acceptance rate; employment rates for graduates; placement success; bar passage rate; faculty resources; expenditures per student; student/faculty ratio; and library resources. *U.S. News & World Report, "America's Best Graduate Schools, Law, 2022"*

According to *U.S. News & World Report,* the Salt Lake City, UT metro area is home to one of the top 75 medical schools for research in the U.S.: **University of Utah** (#41). The rankings are based on a weighted average of 11 measures of quality: quality assessment; peer assessment score; assessment score by residency directors; research activity; total research activity; average research activity per faculty member; student selectivity; median MCAT total score; median undergraduate GPA; acceptance rate; and faculty resources. *U.S. News & World Report, "America's Best Graduate Schools, Medical, 2022"*

According to *U.S. News & World Report,* the Salt Lake City, UT metro area is home to one of the top 75 business schools in the U.S.: **University of Utah (Eccles)** (#44 tie). The rankings are based on a weighted average of the following nine measures: quality assessment; peer assessment; recruiter assessment; placement success; mean starting salary and bonus; student selectivity; mean GMAT and GRE scores; mean undergraduate GPA; and acceptance rate. *U.S. News & World Report, "America's Best Graduate Schools, Business, 2022"*

EMPLOYERS

Major Employers

Company Name	Industry
ACS Commercial Solutions	Data entry service
Alsco	Laundry & garment services, nec
Boart Longyear Company	Test boring for nonmetallic minerals
Church of Jesus Christ of LDS	Mormon church
Comenity Capital Bank	State commercial banks
County of Salt Lake	County government
EnergySolutions	Nonresidential construction, nec
Executive Office of the State of Utah	Executive offices
Granite School District Aid Association	Public elementary & secondary schools
Huntsman Corporation	Plastics materials & resins
Huntsman Holdings	Polystyrene resins
Intermountain Health Care	General medical & surgical hospitals
Jordan School District	Public elementary & secondary schools
Longyear Holdings	Test boring for nonmetallic minerals
Sinclair Oil Corporation	Petroleum refining
Smith's Food & Drug Centers	Grocery stores
Sportsman's Warehouse Holdings	Hunting equipment
State of Utah	State government
The University of Utah	Colleges & universities
TPUSA	Telemarketing services
University of Utah Hospitals & Clinics	General medical & surgical hospitals
Utah Department of Human Services	Administration of social & manpower programs
Zions Bancorporation	Bank holding companies

Note: Companies shown are located within the Salt Lake City, UT Metropolitan Statistical Area.
Source: Hoovers.com; Wikipedia

Best Companies to Work For

Health Catalyst, headquartered in Salt Lake City, is among the "100 Best Places to Work in IT." To qualify, companies had to be U.S.-based organizations or be non-U.S.-based employers that met the following criteria: have a minimum of 300 total employees at a U.S. headquarters and a minimum of 30 IT employees in the U.S., with at least 50% of their IT employees based in the U.S. The best places to work were selected based on compensation, benefits, work/life balance, employee morale, and satisfaction with training and development programs. In addition, *InsiderPro* and *Computerworld* looked at retention efforts, programs for recognizing and rewarding outstanding performances, and benefits such as flextime, elder care and child care, and reimbursement for college tuition and the cost of pursuing technology certifications. *InsiderPro and Computerworld, "100 Best Places to Work in IT," 2020*

PUBLIC SAFETY

Crime Rate

Area	All Crimes	Violent Crimes				Property Crimes		
		Murder	Rape[3]	Robbery	Aggrav. Assault	Burglary	Larceny -Theft	Motor Vehicle Theft
City	6,369.7	6.4	115.6	199.1	391.3	637.3	4,397.7	622.4
Suburbs[1]	3,178.0	2.3	62.6	48.1	186.0	349.3	2,211.9	317.8
Metro[2]	3,700.3	3.0	71.3	72.8	219.5	396.4	2,569.6	367.6
U.S.	2,489.3	5.0	42.6	81.6	250.2	340.5	1,549.5	219.9

Note: Figures are crimes per 100,000 population; (1) All areas within the metro area that are located outside the city limits; (2) Figures cover the Salt Lake City, UT Metropolitan Statistical Area; (3) All figures shown were reported using the revised Uniform Crime Reporting (UCR) definition of rape.
Source: FBI Uniform Crime Reports, 2019

Hate Crimes

Area	Number of Quarters Reported	Number of Incidents per Bias Motivation					
		Race/Ethnicity/ Ancestry	Religion	Sexual Orientation	Disability	Gender	Gender Identity
City	4	1	0	0	0	0	0
U.S.	4	3,963	1,521	1,195	157	69	198

Source: Federal Bureau of Investigation, Hate Crime Statistics 2019

Identity Theft Consumer Reports

Area	Reports	Reports per 100,000 Population	Rank[2]
MSA[1]	4,538	368	84
U.S.	1,387,615	423	-

Note: (1) Figures cover the Salt Lake City, UT Metropolitan Statistical Area; (2) Rank ranges from 1 to 391 where 1 indicates greatest number of identity theft reports per 100,000 population
Source: Federal Trade Commission, Consumer Sentinel Network Data Book 2020

Fraud and Other Consumer Reports

Area	Reports	Reports per 100,000 Population	Rank[2]
MSA[1]	9,864	800	99
U.S.	3,385,133	1,031	-

Note: (1) Figures cover the Salt Lake City, UT Metropolitan Statistical Area; (2) Rank ranges from 1 to 391 where 1 indicates greatest number of fraud and other consumer reports per 100,000 population
Source: Federal Trade Commission, Consumer Sentinel Network Data Book 2020

POLITICS

2020 Presidential Election Results

Area	Biden	Trump	Jorgensen	Hawkins	Other
Salt Lake County	53.0	42.1	2.2	0.4	2.2
U.S.	51.3	46.8	1.2	0.3	0.5

Note: Results are percentages and may not add to 100% due to rounding
Source: Dave Leip's Atlas of U.S. Presidential Elections

SPORTS

Professional Sports Teams

Team Name	League	Year Established
Real Salt Lake	Major League Soccer (MLS)	2005
Utah Jazz	National Basketball Association (NBA)	1979

Note: Includes teams located in the Salt Lake City, UT Metropolitan Statistical Area.
Source: Wikipedia, Major Professional Sports Teams of the United States and Canada, April 6, 2021

CLIMATE

Average and Extreme Temperatures

Temperature	Jan	Feb	Mar	Apr	May	Jun	Jul	Aug	Sep	Oct	Nov	Dec	Yr.
Extreme High (°F)	62	69	78	85	93	104	107	104	100	89	75	67	107
Average High (°F)	37	43	52	62	72	83	93	90	80	66	50	38	64
Average Temp. (°F)	28	34	41	50	59	69	78	76	65	53	40	30	52
Average Low (°F)	19	24	31	38	46	54	62	61	51	40	30	22	40
Extreme Low (°F)	-22	-14	2	15	25	35	40	37	27	16	-14	-15	-22

Note: Figures cover the years 1948-1990
Source: National Climatic Data Center, International Station Meteorological Climate Summary, 9/96

Average Precipitation/Snowfall/Humidity

Precip./Humidity	Jan	Feb	Mar	Apr	May	Jun	Jul	Aug	Sep	Oct	Nov	Dec	Yr.
Avg. Precip. (in.)	1.3	1.2	1.8	2.0	1.7	0.9	0.8	0.9	1.1	1.3	1.3	1.4	15.6
Avg. Snowfall (in.)	13	10	11	6	1	Tr	0	0	Tr	2	6	13	63
Avg. Rel. Hum. 5am (%)	79	77	71	67	66	60	53	54	60	68	75	79	67
Avg. Rel. Hum. 5pm (%)	69	59	47	38	33	26	22	23	28	40	59	71	43

Note: Figures cover the years 1948-1990; Tr = Trace amounts (<0.05 in. of rain; <0.5 in. of snow)
Source: National Climatic Data Center, International Station Meteorological Climate Summary, 9/96

Weather Conditions

Temperature			Daytime Sky			Precipitation		
5°F & below	32°F & below	90°F & above	Clear	Partly cloudy	Cloudy	0.01 inch or more precip.	0.1 inch or more snow/ice	Thunder-storms
7	128	56	94	152	119	92	38	38

Note: Figures are average number of days per year and cover the years 1948-1990
Source: National Climatic Data Center, International Station Meteorological Climate Summary, 9/96

HAZARDOUS WASTE

Superfund Sites

The Salt Lake City, UT metro area is home to nine sites on the EPA's Superfund National Priorities List: **700 South 1600 East Pce Plume** (final); **Jacobs Smelter** (final); **Kennecott (North Zone)** (proposed); **Murray Smelter** (proposed); **Portland Cement (Kiln Dust 2 & 3)** (final); **Tooele Army Depot (North Area)** (final); **US Magnesium** (final); **Utah Power & Light/American Barrel Co.** (final); **Wasatch Chemical Co. (Lot 6)** (final). There are a total of 1,375 Superfund sites with a status of proposed or final on the list in the U.S. *U.S. Environmental Protection Agency, National Priorities List, April 7, 2021*

AIR QUALITY

Air Quality Trends: Ozone

	1990	1995	2000	2005	2010	2015	2016	2017	2018	2019
MSA[1]	n/a	n/a	n/a	n/a	n/a	n/a	n/a	n/a	n/a	n/a
U.S.	0.088	0.089	0.082	0.080	0.073	0.068	0.069	0.068	0.069	0.065

Note: (1) Data covers the Salt Lake City, UT Metropolitan Statistical Area; n/a not available. The values shown are the composite ozone concentration averages among trend sites based on the highest fourth daily maximum 8-hour concentration in parts per million. These trends are based on sites having an adequate record of monitoring data during the trend period. Data from exceptional events are included.
Source: U.S. Environmental Protection Agency, Air Quality Monitoring Information, "Air Quality Trends by City, 1990-2019"

Air Quality Index

Area	Percent of Days when Air Quality was...[2]					AQI Statistics[2]	
	Good	Moderate	Unhealthy for Sensitive Groups	Unhealthy	Very Unhealthy	Maximum	Median
MSA[1]	46.3	49.0	4.7	0.0	0.0	136	51

Note: (1) Data covers the Salt Lake City, UT Metropolitan Statistical Area; (2) Based on 365 days with AQI data in 2019. Air Quality Index (AQI) is an index for reporting daily air quality. EPA calculates the AQI for five major air pollutants regulated by the Clean Air Act: ground-level ozone, particle pollution (aka particulate matter), carbon monoxide, sulfur dioxide, and nitrogen dioxide. The AQI runs from 0 to 500. The higher the AQI value, the greater the level of air pollution and the greater the health concern. There are six AQI categories: "Good" AQI is between 0 and 50. Air quality is considered satisfactory; "Moderate" AQI is between 51 and 100. Air quality is acceptable; "Unhealthy for Sensitive Groups" When AQI values are between 101 and 150, members of sensitive groups may experience health effects; "Unhealthy" When AQI values are between 151 and 200 everyone may begin to experience health effects; "Very Unhealthy" AQI values between 201 and 300 trigger a health alert; "Hazardous" AQI values over 300 trigger warnings of emergency conditions (not shown).
Source: U.S. Environmental Protection Agency, Air Quality Index Report, 2019

Air Quality Index Pollutants

Area	Percent of Days when AQI Pollutant was...[2]					
	Carbon Monoxide	Nitrogen Dioxide	Ozone	Sulfur Dioxide	Particulate Matter 2.5	Particulate Matter 10
MSA[1]	0.0	8.8	67.1	0.0	22.7	1.4

Note: (1) Data covers the Salt Lake City, UT Metropolitan Statistical Area; (2) Based on 365 days with AQI data in 2019. The Air Quality Index (AQI) is an index for reporting daily air quality. EPA calculates the AQI for five major air pollutants regulated by the Clean Air Act: ground-level ozone, particle pollution (also known as particulate matter), carbon monoxide, sulfur dioxide, and nitrogen dioxide. The AQI runs from 0 to 500. The higher the AQI value, the greater the level of air pollution and the greater the health concern.
Source: U.S. Environmental Protection Agency, Air Quality Index Report, 2019

Maximum Air Pollutant Concentrations: Particulate Matter, Ozone, CO and Lead

	Particulate Matter 10 (ug/m^3)	Particulate Matter 2.5 Wtd AM (ug/m^3)	Particulate Matter 2.5 24-Hr (ug/m^3)	Ozone (ppm)	Carbon Monoxide (ppm)	Lead (ug/m^3)
MSA[1] Level	67	9.0	31	0.073	1	n/a
NAAQS[2]	150	15	35	0.075	9	0.15
Met NAAQS[2]	Yes	Yes	Yes	Yes	Yes	n/a

Note: (1) Data covers the Salt Lake City, UT Metropolitan Statistical Area; Data from exceptional events are included; (2) National Ambient Air Quality Standards; ppm = parts per million; ug/m^3 = micrograms per cubic meter; n/a not available.
Concentrations: Particulate Matter 10 (coarse particulate)—highest second maximum 24-hour concentration; Particulate Matter 2.5 Wtd AM (fine particulate)—highest weighted annual mean concentration; Particulate Matter 2.5 24-Hour (fine particulate)—highest 98th percentile 24-hour concentration; Ozone—highest fourth daily maximum 8-hour concentration; Carbon Monoxide—highest second maximum non-overlapping 8-hour concentration; Lead—maximum running 3-month average
Source: U.S. Environmental Protection Agency, Air Quality Monitoring Information, "Air Quality Statistics by City, 2019"

Maximum Air Pollutant Concentrations: Nitrogen Dioxide and Sulfur Dioxide

	Nitrogen Dioxide AM (ppb)	Nitrogen Dioxide 1-Hr (ppb)	Sulfur Dioxide AM (ppb)	Sulfur Dioxide 1-Hr (ppb)	Sulfur Dioxide 24-Hr (ppb)
MSA[1] Level	18	55	n/a	13	n/a
NAAQS[2]	53	100	30	75	140
Met NAAQS[2]	Yes	Yes	n/a	Yes	n/a

Note: (1) Data covers the Salt Lake City, UT Metropolitan Statistical Area; Data from exceptional events are included; (2) National Ambient Air Quality Standards; ppm = parts per million; ug/m^3 = micrograms per cubic meter; n/a not available.
Concentrations: Nitrogen Dioxide AM—highest arithmetic mean concentration; Nitrogen Dioxide 1-Hr—highest 98th percentile 1-hour daily maximum concentration; Sulfur Dioxide AM—highest annual mean concentration; Sulfur Dioxide 1-Hr—highest 99th percentile 1-hour daily maximum concentration; Sulfur Dioxide 24-Hr—highest second maximum 24-hour concentration
Source: U.S. Environmental Protection Agency, Air Quality Monitoring Information, "Air Quality Statistics by City, 2019"

San Diego, California

Background

San Diego is the archetypal southern California City. Located 100 miles south of Los Angeles, near the Mexican border, San Diego is characterized by sunny days, an excellent harbor, a populous citizenry that alludes to its Spanish heritage, and recreational activities based on ideal weather conditions.

San Diego was first claimed in 1542 for Spain by Juan Rodríguez Cabrillo, a Portuguese navigator in the service of the Spanish crown. The site remained uneventful until 1769, when Spanish colonizer, Gaspar de Portola, established the first European settlement in California. Accompanying de Portola was a Franciscan monk named Junipero Serra, who established the Mission Basilica San Diego de Alcala, the first of a chain of missions along the California coast.

After San Diego fell under the U.S. flag during the Mexican War of 1846, the city existed in relative isolation, deferring status and importance to its sister cities in the north, Los Angeles and San Francisco. Even when San Francisco businessman Alonzo Horton bought 1,000 acres of land near the harbor to establish a downtown there, San Diego remained secondary to both these cities, and saw a decrease in population from 40,000 in 1880 to 17,000 at the turn of the century.

World War II repopulated the city, when the Navy moved one of its bases from Pearl Harbor to San Diego. The naval base brought personnel and a number of related industries, such as nuclear and oceanographic research, and aviation development. In celebration of this past, the famed *Midway*, a 1,000-foot World War II aircraft carrier, has undergone a $6.5 million reconstruction and has been moved to Navy Pier, where it opened in 2004 as a floating museum.

Today, San Diego is the second most populous city in California, with plenty of outdoor activities, jobs, fine educational institutions, theaters, and museums. Its downtown redevelopment agency has transformed what was largely an abandoned downtown into a glittering showcase of waterfront skyscrapers, live-work loft developments, five-star hotels, cafes, restaurants, and shops. The once-industrial East Village adjacent to PETCO ballpark is now the new frontier in San Diego's downtown urban renewal.

The western part of the U.S., from Seattle to the Silicon Valley, and from San Diego to Denver, is the center for hot growth industries, including telecommunications, biomedical products, software, and financial services. San Diego also leads the country in biotechnology companies.

The San Diego Convention Center underwent expansion in 2001, increasing exhibit space from 250,000 to 615,000 square feet. The water supply system, always a significant issue in this part of California, has been upgraded and improved in recent years. Expansion of the city's trolley service will be complete in 2021, and San Diego International Airport is on track with renovations to increase service to more than 27 million by 2030.

> Several gorillas test positive for coronavirus at San Diego Zoo Safari Park in what is believed to be the first known cases among such primates.

San Diego is a LGBTQ-friendly city, with the seventh-highest percentage of gay residents in the U.S. Additionally, San Diego State University (SDSU), one of the city's prominent universities, has been named one of the top LGBTQ-friendly campuses in the nation.

Known for its reef break and iconic palm frond shack, Windansea Beach in San Diego has attracted some of the best surfers in the world, such as Buzzy Bent, Pat Curran, Butch Van Artsdalen, Mike Hynson, and Skip Frye. Windansea was the inspiration for the popular "Beach Party" movies in the 1960s. Today, the Windansea Surf Club continues to compete in surf contests and combines elements of charity and community involvement with its competitive heritage. Windansea's surf shack, originally built in 1946, has been rebuilt by surfers numerous times after storms destroyed it. Designated a Historical Landmark in 1998, it remains a symbol of San Diego's surfing heritage and Hawaiian roots.

San Diego summers are cool and winters are warm in comparison with other locations along the same general latitude, due to the Pacific Ocean. A marked feature of the climate is the wide variation in temperature. In nearby valleys, for example, daytime temperatures are much warmer in summer and noticeably cooler on winter nights than in the city proper. As is usual on the Pacific Coast, nighttime and early morning cloudiness is the norm. Considerable fog occurs along the coast, especially during the winter months.

Rankings

General Rankings

- For its "Best for Vets: Places to Live 2019" rankings, *Military Times* evaluated 599 cities (83 large, 234 medium, 282 small) and compared the locations across three broad categories: veteran and military culture/services; economic indicators; and livability factors such as health, crime, traffic, and school quality. San Diego ranked #4 out of the top 25, in the large city category (population of more than 250,000). Data points more specific to veterans and the military weighed more heavily than others. *rebootcamp.militarytimes.com, "Military Times Best Places to Live 2019," September 10, 2018*

- As part of its *Next Stop* series, *Insider* listed 10 places in the U.S. that were either a classic vacation destination experiencing a renaissance or a new up-and-coming hot spot. That could mean the exploding food scene, experiencing the great outdoors, where cool people are moving to, or not overrun with tourists, according to the website insider.com San Diego is a place to visit in 2020. *Insider, "10 Places in the U.S. You Need to Visit in 2020," December 23, 2019*

- In its eighth annual survey, *Travel + Leisure* readers nominated their favorite small cities and towns in America—those with 100,000 or fewer residents—voting on numerous attractive features in categories including culture, food and drink, quality of life, style, and people. After 50,000 votes, San Diego was ranked #15 among the proposed favorites. *www.travelandleisure.com, "America's Favorite Cities," October 20, 2017*

- For its 33rd annual "Readers' Choice Awards" survey, *Condé Nast Traveler* ranked its readers' favorite cities in the U.S. These places brought feelings of comfort in a time of limited travel. The list was broken into large cities and cities under 250,000. San Diego ranked #7 in the big city category. *Condé Nast Traveler, Readers' Choice Awards 2020, "Best Big Cities in the U.S." October 6, 2020*

Business/Finance Rankings

- The Brookings Institution ranked the nation's largest cities based on income inequality. San Diego was ranked #68 (#1 = greatest inequality). Criteria: the "95/20 ratio," a figure representing the income at which a household earns more than 95 percent of all other households, divided by the income at which a household earns more than only 20 percent of all other households. *Brookings Institution, "Household Income Inequality, Largest Cities of 97 Large U.S. Metro Areas, 2014-2016," February 5, 2018*

- The Brookings Institution ranked the 100 largest metro areas in the U.S. based on income inequality. San Diego was ranked #51 (#1 = greatest inequality). Criteria: the "95/20 ratio," a figure representing the income at which a household earns more than 95 percent of all other households, divided by the income at which a household earns more than only 20 percent of all other households. *Brookings Institution, "Household Income Inequality, 100 Largest U.S. Metro Areas, 2014-2016," February 5, 2018*

- *Forbes* ranked the 100 largest metro areas in the U.S. in terms of the "Best Cities for Young Professionals." The San Diego metro area ranked #23 out of 25. Criteria: median rent of a two-bedroom apartment; job growth and unemployment rate; median salary of college graduates with 5 or less years of work experience; networking opportunities; social outlook; percentage of population 25 years of age and older with college degrees. *Forbes.com, "America's 25 Best Cities for Young Professionals in 2017," May 22, 2017*

- Payscale.com ranked the 32 largest metro areas in terms of wage growth. The San Diego metro area ranked #2. Criteria: private-sector and education professional wage growth between the 4th quarter of 2019 and the 4th quarter of 2020. *PayScale, "Wage Trends by Metro Area-4th Quarter," January 11, 2021*

- The San Diego metro area was identified as one of the most debt-ridden places in America by the finance site Credit.com. The metro area was ranked #8. Criteria: residents' average credit card debt as well as median income. *Credit.com, "25 Cities With the Most Credit Card Debt," February 28, 2018*

- For its annual survey of the "Most Expensive U.S. Cities to Live In," Kiplinger applied Cost of Living Index statistics developed by the Council for Community and Economic Research to U.S. Census Bureau population and median household income data for 256 urban areas. San Diego was among the 20 most expensive in the country. *Kiplinger.com, "The 20 Most Expensive Cities in the U.S.," July 29, 2020*

- The San Diego metro area appeared on the Milken Institute "2021 Best Performing Cities" list. Rank: #49 out of 200 large metro areas (population over 250,000). Criteria: job growth; wage and salary growth; high-tech output growth; housing affordability; household broadband access. *Milken Institute, "Best-Performing Cities 2021," February 16, 2021*

- *Forbes* ranked the 200 most populous metro areas to determine the nation's "Best Places for Business and Careers." The San Diego metro area was ranked #45. Criteria: costs (business and living); job growth (past and projected); income growth; quality of life; educational attainment (college and high school); projected economic growth; cultural and leisure opportunities; workplace tolerance laws; net migration patterns. *Forbes, "The Best Places for Business and Careers 2019: Seattle Still On Top," October 30, 2019*

Children/Family Rankings

- San Diego was selected as one of the best cities for newlyweds by *Rent.com*. The city ranked #9 of 15. Criteria: cost of living; availability of affordable rental inventory; annual household income; activities and restaurant options; percentage of married couples; concentration of millennials; safety. *Rent.com, "The 15 Best Cities for Newlyweds," December 11, 2018*

Culture/Performing Arts Rankings

- San Diego was selected as one of the 25 best cities for moviemakers in North America. COVID-19 has spurred a quest for great film cities that offer more creative space, lower costs, and more great outdoors. NYC & LA were intentionally excluded. Criteria: longstanding reputations as film-friendly communities; efforts to deal with pandemic-specific challenges; and establish appropriate COVID-19 guidelines. The city was ranked #17. *MovieMaker Magazine, "Best Places to Live and Work as a Moviemaker, 2021," January 26, 2021*

Dating/Romance Rankings

- San Diego was selected as one of America's best cities for singles by the readers of *Travel + Leisure* in their annual "America's Favorite Cities" survey. Criteria included good-looking locals, cool shopping, an active bar scene and hipster-magnet coffee bars. *Travel + Leisure, "Best Cities in America for Singles," July 21, 2017*

Education Rankings

- Personal finance website *WalletHub* analyzed the 150 largest U.S. metropolitan statistical areas to determine where the most educated Americans are putting their degrees to work. Criteria: education levels; percentage of workers with degrees; education quality and attainment gap; public school quality rankings; quality and enrollment of each metro area's universities. San Diego was ranked #20 (#1 = most educated city). *www.WalletHub.com, "Most and Least Educated Cities in America," July 20, 2020*

- San Diego was selected as one of America's most literate cities. The city ranked #31 out of the 84 largest U.S. cities. Criteria: number of booksellers; library resources; Internet resources; educational attainment; periodical publishing resources; newspaper circulation. *Central Connecticut State University, "America's Most Literate Cities, 2018," February 2019*

Environmental Rankings

- The U.S. Environmental Protection Agency (EPA) released a list of U.S. metropolitan areas with the most ENERGY STAR certified buildings in 2019. The San Diego metro area was ranked #12 out of 25. *U.S. Environmental Protection Agency, "2020 Energy Star Top Cities," March 2020*

- San Diego was highlighted as one of the 25 most ozone-polluted metro areas in the U.S. during 2016 through 2018. The area ranked #6. *American Lung Association, "State of the Air 2020," April 21, 2020*

Health/Fitness Rankings

- For each of the 100 largest cities in the United States, the American Fitness Index®, published by the American College of Sports Medicine and the Anthem Foundation, evaluated community infrastructure and 33 health behaviors including preventive health, levels of chronic disease conditions, pedestrian safety, air quality, and community resources that support physical activity. San Diego ranked #11 for "community fitness." *americanfitnessindex.org, "2020 ACSM American Fitness Index Summary Report," July 14, 2020*

- Trulia analyzed the 100 largest U.S. metro areas to identify the nation's best cities for weight loss, based on the percentage of adults who bike or walk to work, sporting goods stores, grocery stores, access to outdoor activities, weight-loss centers, gyms, and average space reserved for parks. San Diego ranked #9. *Trulia.com, "Where to Live to Get in Shape in the New Year," January 4, 2018*

- San Diego was identified as a "2021 Spring Allergy Capital." The area ranked #90 out of 100. Three groups of factors were used to identify the most challenging cities for people with allergies during the spring season: annual spring pollen levels; over the counter medicine use; number of board-certified allergy specialists. *Asthma and Allergy Foundation of America, "Spring Allergy Capitals 2021," February 23, 2021*

- San Diego was identified as a "2021 Fall Allergy Capital." The area ranked #87 out of 100. Three groups of factors were used to identify the most challenging cities for people with allergies during the fall season: annual fall pollen levels; over the counter medicine use; number of board-certified allergy specialists. *Asthma and Allergy Foundation of America, "Fall Allergy Capitals 2021," February 23, 2021*

- San Diego was identified as a "2019 Asthma Capital." The area ranked #80 out of the nation's 100 largest metropolitan areas. Criteria: estimated asthma prevalence; crude death rate from asthma; and ER visits due to asthma. Risk factors analyzed but not factored in the rankings: annual pollen score; annual air quality; public smoking laws; number of board-certified asthma specialists; rescue medication use; controller medication use; uninsured rate; poverty rate. *Asthma and Allergy Foundation of America, "Asthma Capitals 2019: The Most Challenging Places to Live With Asthma," May 7, 2019*

- The Sharecare Community Well-Being Index evaluates 10 individual and social health factors in order to measure what matters to Americans in the communities in which they live. The San Diego metro area ranked #10 in the top 10 across all 10 domains. Criteria: access to healthcare, food, and community resources; housng and transportation; economic security; feeling of purpose; physical, financial, social, and community well-being. *www.sharecare.com, "Community Well-Being Index: 2019 Metro Area & County Rankings Report," August 31, 2020*

Pet Rankings

- San Diego appeared on *The Dogington Post* site as one of the top cities for dog lovers, ranking #10 out of 20. The real estate brokerage, Redfin and Rover, the largest pet sitter and dog walker network, compiled a list from over 14,000 U.S. cities to come up with a "Rover Rank." Criteria: highest count of dog walks, the city's Walk Score®, for-sale home listings that mention "dog," number of dog walkers and pet sitters and the hours spent and distance logged. *www.dogingtonpost.com, "The 20 Most Dog-Friendly Cities of 2019," April 4, 2019*

Real Estate Rankings

- FitSmallBusiness looked at 50 of the largest metropolitan areas in the U.S. to determine which metro was the best to start a real estate business. Data was compiled from such sources as: Zillow, Trulia, U.S. Census Bureau, and the Bureau of Labor Statistics. Criteria: location; inventory; annual wages; median sales price of homes; days on the market; median price cut percentage; and other factors that would influence real estate professional growth. The San Diego metro area ranked #14. *fitsmallbusiness.com, "The Best Cities to Become a Real Estate Agent in 2018," January 30, 2018*

- *WalletHub* compared the most populated U.S. cities to determine which had the best markets for real estate agents. San Diego ranked #37 where demand was high and pay was the best. Criteria: sales per agent; annual median wage for real-estate agents; monthly average starting salary for real estate agents; real estate job density and competition; unemployment rate; home turnover rate; housing-market health index; and other relevant metrics. *www.WalletHub.com, "2019's Best Places to Be a Real Estate Agent," April 24, 2019*

- San Diego was ranked #11 in the top 20 out of the 100 largest metro areas in terms of house price appreciation in 2020 (#1 = highest rate). *Federal Housing Finance Agency, House Price Index, 4th Quarter 2020*

- The San Diego metro area was identified as one of the 20 least affordable housing markets in the U.S. in 2020. The area ranked #179 out of 183 markets. Criteria: qualification for a mortgage loan with a 10 percent down payment on a typical home. *National Association of Realtors®, Qualifying Income Based on Sales Price of Existing Single-Family Homes for Metropolitan Areas, 2020*

- San Diego was ranked #264 out of 268 metro areas in terms of housing affordability in 2020 by the National Association of Home Builders (#1 = most affordable). Criteria: the share of homes sold in that area affordable to a family earning the local median income, based on standard mortgage underwriting criteria. *National Association of Home Builders®, NAHB-Wells Fargo Housing Opportunity Index, 4th Quarter 2020*

Safety Rankings

- Allstate ranked the 200 largest cities in America in terms of driver safety. San Diego ranked #119. Criteria: internal property damage claims over a two-year period from January 2016 to December 2017. The report helps increase the importance of safety and awareness behind the wheel. *Allstate, "Allstate America's Best Drivers Report, 2019" June 24, 2019*

- The National Insurance Crime Bureau ranked 384 metro areas in the U.S. in terms of per capita rates of vehicle theft. The San Diego metro area ranked #67 (#1 = highest rate). Criteria: number of vehicle theft offenses per 100,000 inhabitants in 2019. *National Insurance Crime Bureau, "Hot Spots 2019," July 21, 2020*

Seniors/Retirement Rankings

- From its Best Cities for Successful Aging indexes, the Milken Institute generated rankings for metropolitan areas, weighing data in nine categories—health care, wellness, living arrangements, transportation and convenience, financial characteristics, education, employment, community engagement, and overall livability. The San Diego metro area was ranked #22 overall in the large metro area category. *Milken Institute, "Best Cities for Successful Aging, 2017" March 14, 2017*

Women/Minorities Rankings

- *Travel + Leisure* listed the best cities in and around the US for a memorable and fun girls' trip, even on a budget. Whether it is for a special occasion or just to get away, San Diego is sure to have something for all the ladies in your tribe. *Travel + Leisure, "25 Girls' Weekend Getaways That Won't Break the Bank," June 8, 2020*

- The *Houston Chronicle* listed the San Diego metro area as #9 in top places for young Latinos to live in the U.S. Research was largely based on housing and occupational data from the largest metropolitan areas performed by *Forbes* and NBC Universo. Criteria: percentage of 18-34 year-olds; Latino college grad rates; and diversity. *blog.chron.com, "The 15 Best Big Cities for Latino Millenials," January 26, 2016*

- Personal finance website *WalletHub* compared more than 180 U.S. cities across two key dimensions, "Hispanic Business-Friendliness" and "Hispanic Purchasing Power," to arrive at the most favorable conditions for Hispanic entrepreneurs. San Diego was ranked #120 out of 182. Criteria includes: share of Hispanic-Owned Businesses; Hispanic entrepreneurship rate to median annual income of Hispanics; Small Business-Friendliness score; cost of living; and number of Hispanics with at least a bachelor's degree. *WalletHub.com, "2019's Best Cities for Hispanic Entrepreneurs," May 1, 2019*

Miscellaneous Rankings

- While the majority of travel ground to a halt in 2020, plugged-in travel influencers and experts were able to rediscover their local regions. San Diego appeared on a *Forbes* list of 15 U.S. cities that provided solace as well as local inspiration. Whether it be quirky things to see and do, delicious take out, outdoor exploring and daytrips, these places are must-see destinations. *Forbes, "Bucket List Travel: The 15 Best U.S. Destinations For 2021," January 1, 2021*

- San Diego was selected as a 2020 Digital Cities Survey winner. The city ranked #3 in the large city (500,000 or more population) category. The survey examined and assessed how city governments are utilizing technology to improve transparency, enhance cybersecurity, and respond to the pandemic. Survey questions focused on ten initiatives: cybersecurity, citizen experience, disaster recovery, business intelligence, IT personnel, data governance, collaboration, infrastructure modernization, cloud computing, and mobile applications. *Center for Digital Government, "2020 Digital Cities Survey," November 10, 2020*

- In its roundup of St. Patrick's Day parades "Gayot" listed the best festivals and parades of all things Irish. The festivities in San Diego as among the best. *www.gayot.com, "Best St. Patrick's Day Parades," March 2020*

- The watchdog site, Charity Navigator, conducted a study of charities in major markets both to analyze statistical differences in their financial, accountability, and transparency practices and to track year-to-year variations in individual philanthropic communities. The San Diego metro area was ranked #1 among the 30 metro markets in the rating category of Overall Score. *www.charitynavigator.org, "2017 Metro Market Study," May 1, 2017*

- *WalletHub* compared the 150 most populated U.S. cities to determine their operating efficiency. A "Quality of City Services" score was constructed for each city and then divided by the total budget per capita to reveal which were managed the best. San Diego ranked #74. Criteria: financial stability; economy; education; safety; health; infrastructure and pollution. *www.WalletHub.com, "2020's Best-& Worst-Run Cities in America," June 29, 2020*

- The National Alliance to End Homelessness listed the 25 most populous metro areas with the highest rate of homelessness. The San Diego metro area had a high rate of homelessness. Criteria: number of homeless people per 10,000 population in 2016. *National Alliance to End Homelessness, "Homelessness in the 25 Most Populous U.S. Metro Areas," September 1, 2017*

Business Environment

DEMOGRAPHICS

Population Growth

Area	1990 Census	2000 Census	2010 Census	2019* Estimate	Population Growth (%) 1990-2019	Population Growth (%) 2010-2019
City	1,111,048	1,223,400	1,307,402	1,409,573	26.9	7.8
MSA[1]	2,498,016	2,813,833	3,095,313	3,316,073	32.7	7.1
U.S.	248,709,873	281,421,906	308,745,538	324,697,795	30.6	5.2

Note: (1) Figures cover the San Diego-Carlsbad, CA Metropolitan Statistical Area; (*) 2015-2019 5-year estimated population
Source: U.S. Census Bureau, 1990 Census, Census 2000, Census 2010, 2015-2019 American Community Survey 5-Year Estimates

Household Size

Area	Persons in Household (%) One	Two	Three	Four	Five	Six	Seven or More	Average Household Size
City	27.5	33.5	16.1	13.1	5.8	2.4	1.6	2.70
MSA[1]	23.9	32.7	16.9	14.7	7.0	2.9	1.9	2.90
U.S.	27.9	33.9	15.6	12.9	6.0	2.3	1.4	2.60

Note: (1) Figures cover the San Diego-Carlsbad, CA Metropolitan Statistical Area
Source: U.S. Census Bureau, 2015-2019 American Community Survey 5-Year Estimates

Race

Area	White Alone[2] (%)	Black Alone[2] (%)	Asian Alone[2] (%)	AIAN[3] Alone[2] (%)	NHOPI[4] Alone[2] (%)	Other Race Alone[2] (%)	Two or More Races (%)
City	65.1	6.4	16.7	0.5	0.4	5.6	5.3
MSA[1]	70.7	5.0	11.9	0.7	0.4	6.0	5.2
U.S.	72.5	12.7	5.5	0.8	0.2	4.9	3.3

Note: (1) Figures cover the San Diego-Carlsbad, CA Metropolitan Statistical Area; (2) Alone is defined as not being in combination with one or more other races; (3) American Indian and Alaska Native; (4) Native Hawaiian and Other Pacific Islander
Source: U.S. Census Bureau, 2015-2019 American Community Survey 5-Year Estimates

Hispanic or Latino Origin

Area	Total (%)	Mexican (%)	Puerto Rican (%)	Cuban (%)	Other (%)
City	30.3	26.6	0.7	0.2	2.8
MSA[1]	33.7	30.0	0.7	0.2	2.8
U.S.	18.0	11.2	1.7	0.7	4.3

Note: Persons of Hispanic or Latino origin can be of any race; (1) Figures cover the San Diego-Carlsbad, CA Metropolitan Statistical Area
Source: U.S. Census Bureau, 2015-2019 American Community Survey 5-Year Estimates

Ancestry

Area	German	Irish	English	American	Italian	Polish	French[2]	Scottish	Dutch
City	8.3	7.0	5.5	2.4	4.1	1.7	1.8	1.4	0.8
MSA[1]	9.3	7.6	6.2	2.7	4.1	1.7	2.0	1.5	1.0
U.S.	13.3	9.7	7.2	6.2	5.1	2.8	2.3	1.7	1.2

Note: Figures are the percentage of the total population reporting a particular ancestry. The nine most commonly reported ancestries in the U.S. are shown. Figures include multiple ancestries (e.g. if a person reported being Irish and Italian, they were included in both columns); (1) Figures cover the San Diego-Carlsbad, CA Metropolitan Statistical Area; (2) Excludes Basque
Source: U.S. Census Bureau, 2015-2019 American Community Survey 5-Year Estimates

Foreign-born Population

Area	Any Foreign Country	Percent of Population Born in Asia	Mexico	Europe	Caribbean	Central America[2]	South America	Africa	Canada
City	26.1	11.9	9.1	2.3	0.2	0.5	0.8	0.9	0.4
MSA[1]	23.4	9.0	10.1	1.8	0.2	0.5	0.6	0.6	0.4
U.S.	13.6	4.2	3.5	1.5	1.3	1.1	1.0	0.7	0.2

Note: (1) Figures cover the San Diego-Carlsbad, CA Metropolitan Statistical Area; (2) Excludes Mexico.
Source: U.S. Census Bureau, 2015-2019 American Community Survey 5-Year Estimates

Marital Status

Area	Never Married	Now Married[2]	Separated	Widowed	Divorced
City	40.0	44.3	1.7	4.1	9.8
MSA[1]	35.9	47.6	1.7	4.7	10.1
U.S.	33.4	48.1	1.9	5.8	10.9

Note: Figures are percentages and cover the population 15 years of age and older; (1) Figures cover the San Diego-Carlsbad, CA Metropolitan Statistical Area; (2) Excludes separated
Source: U.S. Census Bureau, 2015-2019 American Community Survey 5-Year Estimates

Disability by Age

Area	All Ages	Under 18 Years Old	18 to 64 Years Old	65 Years and Over
City	9.2	3.3	6.5	32.4
MSA[1]	9.9	3.2	7.2	32.8
U.S.	12.6	4.2	10.3	34.5

Note: Figures show percent of the civilian noninstitutionalized population that reported having a disability. Disability status is determined from six types of difficulty: vision, hearing, cognitive, ambulatory, self-care, and independent living. For children under 5 years old, hearing and vision difficulty are used to determine disability status. For children between the ages of 5 and 14, disability status is determined from hearing, vision, cognitive, ambulatory, and self-care difficulties. For people aged 15 years and older, they are considered to have a disability if they have difficulty with any one of the six difficulty types; Note: (1) Figures cover the San Diego-Carlsbad, CA Metropolitan Statistical Area
Source: U.S. Census Bureau, 2015-2019 American Community Survey 5-Year Estimates

Age

Area	Percent of Population									Median Age
	Under Age 5	Age 5–19	Age 20–34	Age 35–44	Age 45–54	Age 55–64	Age 65–74	Age 75–84	Age 85+	
City	5.9	16.8	27.4	13.9	12.3	11.0	7.3	3.7	1.6	34.9
MSA[1]	6.3	18.2	24.2	13.3	12.5	11.7	7.9	4.0	1.8	35.8
U.S.	6.1	19.1	20.7	12.6	13.0	12.9	9.1	4.6	1.9	38.1

Note: (1) Figures cover the San Diego-Carlsbad, CA Metropolitan Statistical Area
Source: U.S. Census Bureau, 2015-2019 American Community Survey 5-Year Estimates

Gender

Area	Males	Females	Males per 100 Females
City	711,134	698,439	101.8
MSA[1]	1,669,515	1,646,558	101.4
U.S.	159,886,919	164,810,876	97.0

Note: (1) Figures cover the San Diego-Carlsbad, CA Metropolitan Statistical Area
Source: U.S. Census Bureau, 2015-2019 American Community Survey 5-Year Estimates

Religious Groups by Family

Area	Catholic	Baptist	Non-Den.	Methodist[2]	Lutheran	LDS[3]	Pente-costal	Presby-terian[4]	Muslim[5]	Judaism
MSA[1]	25.9	2.0	4.8	1.1	1.0	2.3	1.0	0.9	0.7	0.5
U.S.	19.1	9.3	4.0	4.0	2.3	2.0	1.9	1.6	0.8	0.7

Note: Figures are the number of adherents as a percentage of the total population; (1) Figures cover the San Diego-Carlsbad, CA Metropolitan Statistical Area; (2) Methodist/Pietist; (3) Latter Day Saints; (4) Reformed; (5) Figures are estimates
Source: Association of Statisticians of American Religious Bodies, 2010 U.S. Religion Census: Religious Congregations & Membership Study

Religious Groups by Tradition

Area	Catholic	Evangelical Protestant	Mainline Protestant	Other Tradition	Black Protestant	Orthodox
MSA[1]	25.9	9.8	2.4	5.2	0.4	0.3
U.S.	19.1	16.2	7.3	4.3	1.6	0.3

Note: Figures are the number of adherents as a percentage of the total population; (1) Figures cover the San Diego-Carlsbad, CA Metropolitan Statistical Area
Source: Association of Statisticians of American Religious Bodies, 2010 U.S. Religion Census: Religious Congregations & Membership Study

ECONOMY

Gross Metropolitan Product

Area	2017	2018	2019	2020	Rank[2]
MSA[1]	237.2	249.4	260.3	272.1	17

Note: Figures are in billions of dollars; (1) Figures cover the San Diego-Carlsbad, CA Metropolitan Statistical Area; (2) Rank is based on 2018 data and ranges from 1 to 381
Source: U.S. Conference of Mayors, U.S. Metro Economies: GMP & Employment 2018-2020, September 2019

Economic Growth

Area	2015-17 (%)	2018 (%)	2019 (%)	2020 (%)	Rank[2]
MSA[1]	3.1	3.0	2.6	2.3	64
U.S.	1.9	2.9	2.3	2.1	–

Note: Figures are real gross metropolitan product (GMP) growth rates and represent average annual percent change; (1) Figures cover the San Diego-Carlsbad, CA Metropolitan Statistical Area; (2) Rank is based on 2017 2-year average annual percent change and ranges from 1 to 381
Source: U.S. Conference of Mayors, U.S. Metro Economies: GMP & Employment 2018-2020, September 2019

Metropolitan Area Exports

Area	2014	2015	2016	2017	2018	2019	Rank[2]
MSA[1]	18,585.7	17,439.7	18,086.6	18,637.1	20,156.8	19,774.1	20

Note: Figures are in millions of dollars; (1) Figures cover the San Diego-Carlsbad, CA Metropolitan Statistical Area; (2) Rank is based on 2019 data and ranges from 1 to 386
Source: U.S. Department of Commerce, International Trade Administration, Office of Trade and Economic Analysis, Industry and Analysis, Exports by Metropolitan Area, data extracted March 24, 2021

Building Permits

Area	Single-Family			Multi-Family			Total		
	2018	2019	Pct. Chg.	2018	2019	Pct. Chg.	2018	2019	Pct. Chg.
City	774	580	-25.1	3,678	3,361	-8.6	4,452	3,941	-11.5
MSA[1]	3,489	3,019	-13.5	6,345	5,197	-18.1	9,834	8,216	-16.5
U.S.	855,300	862,100	0.7	473,500	523,900	10.6	1,328,800	1,386,000	4.3

Note: (1) Figures cover the San Diego-Carlsbad, CA Metropolitan Statistical Area; Figures represent new, privately-owned housing units authorized (unadjusted data); All permit data are based on estimates with imputation
Source: U.S. Census Bureau, Manufacturing, Mining, and Construction Statistics, Building Permits, 2018, 2019

Bankruptcy Filings

Area	Business Filings			Nonbusiness Filings		
	2019	2020	% Chg.	2019	2020	% Chg.
San Diego County	308	269	-12.7	7,366	5,848	-20.6
U.S.	22,780	21,655	-4.9	752,160	522,808	-30.5

Note: Business filings include Chapter 7, Chapter 9, Chapter 11, Chapter 12, Chapter 13, Chapter 15, and Section 304; Nonbusiness filings include Chapter 7, Chapter 11, and Chapter 13
Source: Administrative Office of the U.S. Courts, Business and Nonbusiness Bankruptcy, County Cases Commenced by Chapter of the Bankruptcy Code, During the 12-Month Period Ending December 31, 2019 and Business and Nonbusiness Bankruptcy, County Cases Commenced by Chapter of the Bankruptcy Code, During the 12-Month Period Ending December 31, 2020

Housing Vacancy Rates

Area	Gross Vacancy Rate[2] (%)			Year-Round Vacancy Rate[3] (%)			Rental Vacancy Rate[4] (%)			Homeowner Vacancy Rate[5] (%)		
	2018	2019	2020	2018	2019	2020	2018	2019	2020	2018	2019	2020
MSA[1]	7.6	7.5	6.0	7.4	7.3	5.6	4.5	5.8	3.9	0.7	0.8	0.8
U.S.	12.3	12.0	10.6	9.7	9.5	8.2	6.9	6.7	6.3	1.5	1.4	1.0

Note: (1) Figures cover the San Diego-Carlsbad, CA Metropolitan Statistical Area; (2) The percentage of the total housing inventory that is vacant; (3) The percentage of the housing inventory (excluding seasonal units) that is year-round vacant; (4) The percentage of rental inventory that is vacant for rent; (5) The percentage of homeowner inventory that is vacant for sale
Source: U.S. Census Bureau, Housing Vacancies and Homeownership Annual Statistics: 2018, 2019, 2020

INCOME

Income

Area	Per Capita ($)	Median Household ($)	Average Household ($)
City	41,112	79,673	108,864
MSA[1]	38,073	78,980	106,600
U.S.	34,103	62,843	88,607

Note: (1) Figures cover the San Diego-Carlsbad, CA Metropolitan Statistical Area
Source: U.S. Census Bureau, 2015-2019 American Community Survey 5-Year Estimates

Household Income Distribution

Area	Percent of Households Earning							
	Under $15,000	$15,000 -$24,999	$25,000 -$34,999	$35,000 -$49,999	$50,000 -$74,999	$75,000 -$99,999	$100,000 -$149,999	$150,000 and up
City	8.1	6.6	6.8	10.0	15.9	12.9	17.8	21.8
MSA[1]	7.6	6.7	7.1	10.3	16.1	13.0	18.0	21.1
U.S.	10.3	8.9	8.9	12.3	17.2	12.7	15.1	14.5

Note: (1) Figures cover the San Diego-Carlsbad, CA Metropolitan Statistical Area
Source: U.S. Census Bureau, 2015-2019 American Community Survey 5-Year Estimates

Poverty Rate

Area	All Ages	Under 18 Years Old	18 to 64 Years Old	65 Years and Over
City	12.8	15.7	12.6	9.4
MSA[1]	11.6	14.7	11.1	8.9
U.S.	13.4	18.5	12.6	9.3

Note: Figures are percentage of people whose income during the past 12 months was below the poverty level;
(1) Figures cover the San Diego-Carlsbad, CA Metropolitan Statistical Area
Source: U.S. Census Bureau, 2015-2019 American Community Survey 5-Year Estimates

CITY FINANCES

City Government Finances

Component	2017 ($000)	2017 ($ per capita)
Total Revenues	4,687,498	3,360
Total Expenditures	3,645,189	2,613
Debt Outstanding	2,779,488	1,993
Cash and Securities[1]	11,423,033	8,189

Note: (1) Cash and security holdings of a government at the close of its fiscal year,
including those of its dependent agencies, utilities, and liquor stores.
Source: U.S. Census Bureau, State & Local Government Finances 2017

City Government Revenue by Source

Source	2017 ($000)	2017 ($ per capita)	2017 (%)
General Revenue			
From Federal Government	284,882	204	6.1
From State Government	41,660	30	0.9
From Local Governments	4,432	3	0.1
Taxes			
Property	591,900	424	12.6
Sales and Gross Receipts	755,674	542	16.1
Personal Income	0	0	0.0
Corporate Income	0	0	0.0
Motor Vehicle License	0	0	0.0
Other Taxes	66,827	48	1.4
Current Charges	1,046,127	750	22.3
Liquor Store	0	0	0.0
Utility	489,114	351	10.4
Employee Retirement	1,020,463	732	21.8

Source: U.S. Census Bureau, State & Local Government Finances 2017

City Government Expenditures by Function

Function	2017 ($000)	2017 ($ per capita)	2017 (%)
General Direct Expenditures			
Air Transportation	9,088	6	0.2
Corrections	0	0	0.0
Education	0	0	0.0
Employment Security Administration	0	0	0.0
Financial Administration	39,547	28	1.1
Fire Protection	176,827	126	4.9
General Public Buildings	76,428	54	2.1
Governmental Administration, Other	38,649	27	1.1
Health	40,191	28	1.1
Highways	185,055	132	5.1
Hospitals	0	0	0.0
Housing and Community Development	378,574	271	10.4
Interest on General Debt	163,975	117	4.5
Judicial and Legal	49,634	35	1.4
Libraries	46,536	33	1.3
Parking	3,146	2	0.1
Parks and Recreation	290,259	208	8.0
Police Protection	318,625	228	8.7
Public Welfare	0	0	0.0
Sewerage	416,481	298	11.4
Solid Waste Management	94,547	67	2.6
Veterans' Services	0	0	0.0
Liquor Store	0	0	0.0
Utility	647,569	464	17.8
Employee Retirement	422,398	302	11.6

Source: U.S. Census Bureau, State & Local Government Finances 2017

EMPLOYMENT

Labor Force and Employment

Area	Civilian Labor Force			Workers Employed		
	Dec. 2019	Dec. 2020	% Chg.	Dec. 2019	Dec. 2020	% Chg.
City	724,077	722,739	-0.2	704,952	665,731	-5.6
MSA[1]	1,597,099	1,593,875	-0.2	1,552,857	1,466,461	-5.6
U.S.	164,007,000	160,017,000	-2.4	158,504,000	149,613,000	-5.6

Note: Data is not seasonally adjusted and covers workers 16 years of age and older; (1) Figures cover the San Diego-Carlsbad, CA Metropolitan Statistical Area
Source: Bureau of Labor Statistics, Local Area Unemployment Statistics

Unemployment Rate

Area	2020											
	Jan.	Feb.	Mar.	Apr.	May	Jun.	Jul.	Aug.	Sep.	Oct.	Nov.	Dec.
City	3.2	3.1	4.0	14.7	14.9	13.7	12.2	9.3	8.7	7.1	6.3	7.9
MSA[1]	3.3	3.2	4.2	15.0	15.2	13.8	12.4	9.5	8.9	7.5	6.6	8.0
U.S.	4.0	3.8	4.5	14.4	13.0	11.2	10.5	8.5	7.7	6.6	6.4	6.5

Note: Data is not seasonally adjusted and covers workers 16 years of age and older; (1) Figures cover the San Diego-Carlsbad, CA Metropolitan Statistical Area
Source: Bureau of Labor Statistics, Local Area Unemployment Statistics

Average Wages

Occupation	$/Hr.	Occupation	$/Hr.
Accountants and Auditors	43.00	Maintenance and Repair Workers	22.60
Automotive Mechanics	25.60	Marketing Managers	71.20
Bookkeepers	23.60	Network and Computer Systems Admin.	47.50
Carpenters	28.60	Nurses, Licensed Practical	31.70
Cashiers	14.50	Nurses, Registered	53.70
Computer Programmers	48.40	Nursing Assistants	19.10
Computer Systems Analysts	45.60	Office Clerks, General	19.90
Computer User Support Specialists	29.30	Physical Therapists	47.30
Construction Laborers	23.90	Physicians	115.40
Cooks, Restaurant	15.90	Plumbers, Pipefitters and Steamfitters	30.70
Customer Service Representatives	20.40	Police and Sheriff's Patrol Officers	44.40
Dentists	53.60	Postal Service Mail Carriers	26.30
Electricians	30.20	Real Estate Sales Agents	n/a
Engineers, Electrical	50.10	Retail Salespersons	16.40
Fast Food and Counter Workers	14.40	Sales Representatives, Technical/Scientific	49.10
Financial Managers	74.60	Secretaries, Exc. Legal/Medical/Executive	21.30
First-Line Supervisors of Office Workers	31.30	Security Guards	16.20
General and Operations Managers	69.70	Surgeons	n/a
Hairdressers/Cosmetologists	18.20	Teacher Assistants, Exc. Postsecondary*	17.00
Home Health and Personal Care Aides	14.90	Teachers, Secondary School, Exc. Sp. Ed.*	41.00
Janitors and Cleaners	17.60	Telemarketers	15.10
Landscaping/Groundskeeping Workers	16.40	Truck Drivers, Heavy/Tractor-Trailer	24.70
Lawyers	70.80	Truck Drivers, Light/Delivery Services	24.00
Maids and Housekeeping Cleaners	15.50	Waiters and Waitresses	15.60

Note: Wage data covers the San Diego-Carlsbad, CA Metropolitan Statistical Area; (*) Hourly wages were calculated from annual wage data based on a 40 hour work week; n/a not available.
Source: Bureau of Labor Statistics, Metro Area Occupational Employment & Wage Estimates, May 2020

Employment by Industry

Sector	MSA[1]		U.S.
	Number of Employees	Percent of Total	Percent of Total
Construction	87,800	6.3	5.1
Education and Health Services	211,800	15.2	16.3
Financial Activities	74,000	5.3	6.1
Government	235,900	17.0	15.2
Information	21,900	1.6	1.9
Leisure and Hospitality	130,400	9.4	9.0
Manufacturing	112,900	8.1	8.5
Mining and Logging	300	<0.1	0.4
Other Services	40,600	2.9	3.8
Professional and Business Services	253,400	18.2	14.4
Retail Trade	144,800	10.4	10.9
Transportation, Warehousing, and Utilities	36,300	2.6	4.6
Wholesale Trade	39,400	2.8	3.9

Note: Figures are non-farm employment as of December 2020. Figures are not seasonally adjusted and include workers 16 years of age and older; (1) Figures cover the San Diego-Carlsbad, CA Metropolitan Statistical Area
Source: Bureau of Labor Statistics, Current Employment Statistics, Employment, Hours, and Earnings

Employment by Occupation

Occupation Classification	City (%)	MSA[1] (%)	U.S. (%)
Management, Business, Science, and Arts	47.7	42.2	38.5
Natural Resources, Construction, and Maintenance	5.6	7.6	8.9
Production, Transportation, and Material Moving	8.2	9.5	13.2
Sales and Office	19.8	21.3	21.6
Service	18.8	19.5	17.8

Note: Figures cover employed civilians 16 years of age and older; (1) Figures cover the San Diego-Carlsbad, CA Metropolitan Statistical Area
Source: U.S. Census Bureau, 2015-2019 American Community Survey 5-Year Estimates

Occupations with Greatest Projected Employment Growth: 2020 – 2022

Occupation[1]	2020 Employment	2022 Projected Employment	Numeric Employment Change	Percent Employment Change
Retail Salespersons	317,300	401,300	84,000	26.5
Laborers and Freight, Stock, and Material Movers, Hand	348,700	411,100	62,400	17.9
Waiters and Waitresses	182,500	242,800	60,300	33.0
Combined Food Preparation and Serving Workers, Including Fast Food	183,800	237,200	53,400	29.1
Cashiers	358,500	407,300	48,800	13.6
Cooks, Restaurant	113,200	156,500	43,300	38.3
Personal Care Aides	409,600	447,900	38,300	9.4
Farmworkers and Laborers, Crop, Nursery, and Greenhouse	242,000	269,700	27,700	11.4
Fast Food and Counter Workers	94,000	120,200	26,200	27.9
General and Operations Managers	242,700	268,300	25,600	10.5

Note: Projections cover California; (1) Sorted by numeric employment change
Source: www.projectionscentral.com, State Occupational Projections, 2020–2022 Short-Term Projections

Fastest-Growing Occupations: 2020 – 2022

Occupation[1]	2020 Employment	2022 Projected Employment	Numeric Employment Change	Percent Employment Change
Manicurists and Pedicurists	7,800	21,300	13,500	173.1
Hairdressers, Hairstylists, and Cosmetologists	22,700	44,600	21,900	96.5
Massage Therapists	8,800	17,100	8,300	94.3
Skincare Specialists	5,500	9,100	3,600	65.5
Dental Hygienists	9,200	14,700	5,500	59.8
Dental Hygienists (SOC 2018)	5,300	8,400	3,100	58.5
Dental Assistants	36,300	56,300	20,000	55.1
Dentists, General	12,600	19,000	6,400	50.8
Parking Lot Attendants	14,300	20,400	6,100	42.7
Lodging Managers	3,300	4,600	1,300	39.4

Note: Projections cover California; (1) Sorted by percent employment change and excludes occupations with numeric employment change less than 50
Source: www.projectionscentral.com, State Occupational Projections, 2020–2022 Short-Term Projections

TAXES

State Corporate Income Tax Rates

State	Tax Rate (%)	Income Brackets ($)	Num. of Brackets	Financial Institution Tax Rate (%)[a]	Federal Income Tax Ded.
California	8.84 (b)	Flat rate	1	10.84 (b)	No

Note: Tax rates as of January 1, 2021; (a) Rates listed are the corporate income tax rate applied to financial institutions or excise taxes based on income. Some states have other taxes based upon the value of deposits or shares; (b) Minimum tax is $800 in California, $250 in District of Columbia, $50 in Arizona and North Dakota (banks), $400 ($100 banks) in Rhode Island, $200 per location in South Dakota (banks), $100 in Utah, $300 in Vermont.
Source: Federation of Tax Administrators, State Corporate Income Tax Rates, January 1, 2021

State Individual Income Tax Rates

State	Tax Rate (%)	Income Brackets ($)	Personal Exemptions ($)			Standard Ded. ($)	
			Single	Married	Depend.	Single	Married
California (a)	1.0 - 12.3 (g)	8,932 - 599,012 (b)	124	248 (c)	383 (c)	4,601	9,202 (a)

Note: Tax rates as of January 1, 2021; Local- and county-level taxes are not included; Federal income tax is not deductible on state income tax returns; (a) 19 states have statutory provision for automatically adjusting to the rate of inflation the dollar values of the income tax brackets, standard deductions, and/or personal exemptions. Michigan indexes the personal exemption only. Oregon does not index the income brackets for $125,000 and over; (b) For joint returns, taxes are twice the tax on half the couple's income; (c) The personal exemption takes the form of a tax credit instead of a deduction; (g) California imposes an additional 1% tax on taxable income over $1 million, making the maximum rate 13.3% over $1 million.
Source: Federation of Tax Administrators, State Individual Income Tax Rates, January 1, 2021

Various State Sales and Excise Tax Rates

State	State Sales Tax (%)	Gasoline[1] (¢/gal.)	Cigarette[2] ($/pack)	Spirits[3] ($/gal.)	Wine[4] ($/gal.)	Beer[5] ($/gal.)	Recreational Marijuana (%)
California	7.25	63.05	2.87	3.3	0.2	0.2	(c)

Note: All tax rates as of January 1, 2021; (1) The American Petroleum Institute has developed a methodology for determining the average tax rate on a gallon of fuel. Rates may include any of the following: excise taxes, environmental fees, storage tank fees, other fees or taxes, general sales tax, and local taxes; (2) The federal excise tax of $1.0066 per pack and local taxes are not included; (3) Rates are those applicable to off-premise sales of 40% alcohol by volume (a.b.v.) distilled spirits in 750ml containers. Local excise taxes are excluded; (4) Rates are those applicable to off-premise sales of 11% a.b.v. non-carbonated wine in 750ml containers; (5) Rates are those applicable to off-premise sales of 4.7% a.b.v. beer in 12 ounce containers; (c) 15% excise tax (levied on wholesale at average market rate); $9.65/oz. flowers & $2.87/oz. leaves cultivation tax; $1.35/oz fresh cannabis plant
Source: Tax Foundation, 2021 Facts & Figures: How Does Your State Compare?

State Business Tax Climate Index Rankings

State	Overall Rank	Corporate Tax Rank	Individual Income Tax Rank	Sales Tax Rank	Property Tax Rank	Unemployment Insurance Tax Rank
California	49	28	49	45	14	21

Note: The index is a measure of how each state's tax laws affect economic performance. The lower the rank, the more favorable a state's tax system is for business. States without a given tax are given a ranking of 1. The scores/rankings for the District of Columbia do not affect other states. The 2021 index represents the tax climate as of July 1, 2020.
Source: Tax Foundation, State Business Tax Climate Index 2021

TRANSPORTATION

Means of Transportation to Work

Area	Car/Truck/Van		Public Transportation			Bicycle	Walked	Other Means	Worked at Home
	Drove Alone	Car-pooled	Bus	Subway	Railroad				
City	74.7	8.6	3.6	0.0	0.1	0.8	3.1	1.8	7.2
MSA[1]	76.2	8.6	2.5	0.0	0.2	0.6	2.9	1.9	7.0
U.S.	76.3	9.0	2.4	1.9	0.6	0.5	2.7	1.4	5.2

Note: Figures are percentages and cover workers 16 years of age and older; (1) Figures cover the San Diego-Carlsbad, CA Metropolitan Statistical Area
Source: U.S. Census Bureau, 2015-2019 American Community Survey 5-Year Estimates

Travel Time to Work

Area	Less Than 10 Minutes	10 to 19 Minutes	20 to 29 Minutes	30 to 44 Minutes	45 to 59 Minutes	60 to 89 Minutes	90 Minutes or More
City	7.6	32.1	27.6	21.7	5.7	3.4	1.8
MSA[1]	8.2	28.9	24.3	23.5	7.7	5.1	2.2
U.S.	12.2	28.4	20.8	20.8	8.3	6.4	2.9

Note: Note: Figures are percentages and include workers 16 years old and over; (1) Figures cover the San Diego-Carlsbad, CA Metropolitan Statistical Area
Source: U.S. Census Bureau, 2015-2019 American Community Survey 5-Year Estimates

Key Congestion Measures

Measure	1982	1992	2002	2012	2017
Annual Hours of Delay, Total (000)	18,925	49,840	97,799	126,354	148,503
Annual Hours of Delay, Per Auto Commuter	18	30	44	57	64
Annual Congestion Cost, Total (million $)	138	517	1,300	2,194	2,699
Annual Congestion Cost, Per Auto Commuter ($)	452	818	1,251	1,267	1,444

Note: Covers the San Diego CA urban area
Source: Texas A&M Transportation Institute, 2019 Urban Mobility Report

Freeway Travel Time Index

Measure	1982	1987	1992	1997	2002	2007	2012	2017
Urban Area Index[1]	1.08	1.12	1.14	1.18	1.24	1.29	1.32	1.35
Urban Area Rank[1,2]	28	26	34	28	23	15	11	7

Note: Freeway Travel Time Index—the ratio of travel time in the peak period to the travel time at free-flow conditions. For example, a value of 1.30 indicates a 20-minute free-flow trip takes 26 minutes in the peak (20 minutes x 1.30 = 26 minutes); (1) Covers the San Diego CA urban area; (2) Rank is based on 101 larger urban areas (#1 = highest travel time index)
Source: Texas A&M Transportation Institute, 2019 Urban Mobility Report

Public Transportation

Agency Name / Mode of Transportation	Vehicles Operated in Maximum Service[1]	Annual Unlinked Passenger Trips[2] (in thous.)	Annual Passenger Miles[3] (in thous.)
San Diego Metropolitan Transit System (MTS)			
Bus (directly operated)	222	22,396.8	98,896.4
Bus (purchased transportation)	288	24,809.1	83,844.5
Commuter Bus (purchased transportation)	19	281.2	6,848.7
Demand Response (purchased transportation)	158	507.4	5,663.9
Demand Response Taxi (purchased transportation)	179	69.3	745.7
Light Rail (directly operated)	103	37,293.8	219,453.2
North San Diego County Transit District (NCTD)			
Bus (purchased transportation)	138	6,404.9	27,569.8
Commuter Rail (purchased transportation)	24	1,408.7	37,232.4
Demand Response (purchased transportation)	33	169.1	2,581.9
Hybrid Rail (purchased transportation)	8	2,409.0	20,676.7
San Diego Association of Governments (SANDAG)			
Vanpool (purchased transportation)	689	1,746.5	81,692.1

Note: (1) Number of revenue vehicles operated by the given mode and type of service to meet the annual maximum service requirement. This is the revenue vehicle count during the peak season of the year; on the week and day that maximum service is provided. Vehicles operated in maximum service (VOMS) exclude atypical days and one-time special events; (2) Number of passengers who boarded public transportation vehicles. Passengers are counted each time they board a vehicle no matter how many vehicles they use to travel from their origin to their destination. (3) Sum of the distances ridden by all passengers during the entire fiscal year.
Source: Federal Transit Administration, National Transit Database, 2019

Air Transportation

Airport Name and Code / Type of Service	Passenger Airlines[1]	Passenger Enplanements	Freight Carriers[2]	Freight (lbs)
San Diego International-Lindbergh Field (SAN)				
Domestic service (U.S. carriers - 2020)	21	4,508,721	14	132,406,052
International service (U.S. carriers - 2019)	6	153,793	3	2,274,876

Note: (1) Includes all U.S.-based major, minor and commuter airlines that carried at least one passenger during the year; (2) Includes all U.S.-based airlines and freight carriers that transported at least one pound of freight during the year.
Source: Bureau of Transportation Statistics, The Intermodal Transportation Database, Air Carriers: T-100 Domestic Market (U.S. Carriers), 2020; Bureau of Transportation Statistics, The Intermodal Transportation Database, Air Carriers: T-100 International Market (U.S. Carriers), 2019

BUSINESSES

Major Business Headquarters

Company Name	Industry	Rankings	
		Fortune[1]	Forbes[2]
Petco Animal Supplies	Retailing	-	107
Qualcomm	Network and Other Communications Equipment	126	-
Sempra Energy	Utilities, Gas and Electric	258	-

Note: (1) Companies that produce a 10-K are ranked 1 to 500 based on 2019 revenue; (2) All private companies with at least $2 billion in annual revenue through the end of their most current fiscal year are ranked 1 to 219; companies listed are headquartered in the city; dashes indicate no ranking
Source: Fortune, "Fortune 500," June/July 2020; Forbes, "America's Largest Private Companies," 2020

Fastest-Growing Businesses

According to *Inc.*, San Diego is home to nine of America's 500 fastest-growing private companies: **Shield AI** (#33); **LeadCrunch** (#35); **GoProto** (#57); **Blenders Eyewear** (#224); **Doctible** (#293); **Gateway Genomics** (#296); **Applied Data Finance** (#345); **TDE Capital Inc** (#383); **Agent Elite** (#439). Criteria: must be an independent, privately-held, for-profit, U.S. corporation, proprietorship or partnership as of December 31, 2019; revenues must be at least $100,000 in 2016 and $2 million in 2019; must have four-year operating/sales history. *Inc.*, "America's 500 Fastest-Growing Private Companies," 2020

According to *Initiative for a Competitive Inner City (ICIC)*, San Diego is home to one of America's 100 fastest-growing "inner city" companies: **Cafe Virtuoso** (#76). Criteria for inclusion: company must be headquartered in or have 51 percent or more of its physical operations in an economically distressed urban area; must be an independent, for-profit corporation, partnership or proprietorship; must have 10 or more employees and have a five-year sales history that includes sales of at least $200,000 in the base year and at least $1 million in the current year with no decrease in sales over the two most recent years. Companies were ranked overall by revenue growth over the five-year period between 2015 and 2019. *Initiative for a Competitive Inner City (ICIC), "Inner City 100 Companies," 2020*

According to Deloitte, San Diego is home to 12 of North America's 500 fastest-growing high-technology companies: **Heron Therapeutics, Inc.** (#17); **Neurocrine Biosciences Inc.** (#42); **La Jolla Pharmaceutical Co.** (#48); **Acadia Pharmaceuticals Inc.** (#72); **Arena Pharmaceuticals Inc.** (#153); **Cloudbeds** (#222); **Seismic** (#224); **Regulus Therapeutics Inc.** (#241); **Classy** (#289); **Tandem Diabetes Care Inc.** (#309); **Sorrento Therapeutics, Inc.** (#344); **Quidel Corp** (#490). Companies are ranked by percentage growth in revenue over a four-year period. Criteria for inclusion: company must be headquartered within North America; must own proprietary intellectual property or technology that is sold to customers in products that contributes to a significant portion of the company's operating revenue; must have been in business for a minumum of four years with 2016 operating revenues of at least $50,000 USD/CD and 2019 operating revenues of at least $5 million USD/CD. *Deloitte, 2020 Technology Fast 500*™

Living Environment

COST OF LIVING

Cost of Living Index

Composite Index	Groceries	Housing	Utilities	Trans-portation	Health Care	Misc. Goods/ Services
143.2	114.3	213.0	125.6	136.2	108.5	110.5

Note: The Cost of Living Index measures regional differences in the cost of consumer goods and services, excluding taxes and non-consumer expenditures, for professional and managerial households in the top income quintile. It is based on more than 50,000 prices covering almost 60 different items for which prices are collected three times a year by chambers of commerce, economic development organizations or university applied economic centers in each participating urban area. The numbers shown should be read as a percentage above or below the national average of 100. For example, a value of 115.4 in the groceries column indicates that grocery prices are 15.4% higher than the national average. Small differences in the index numbers should not be interpreted as significant; Figures cover the San Diego CA urban area.
Source: The Council for Community and Economic Research, Cost of Living Index, 2020

Grocery Prices

Area[1]	T-Bone Steak ($/pound)	Frying Chicken ($/pound)	Whole Milk ($/half gal.)	Eggs ($/dozen)	Orange Juice ($/64 oz.)	Coffee ($/11.5 oz.)
City[2]	12.27	1.72	2.19	2.88	4.09	5.21
Avg.	11.78	1.39	2.05	1.47	3.57	4.34
Min.	8.03	0.94	1.03	0.74	2.94	3.02
Max.	15.86	2.65	4.31	3.77	5.44	8.69

Note: (1) Values for the local area are compared with the average, minimum and maximum values for all 284 areas in the Cost of Living Index; (2) Figures cover the San Diego CA urban area; **T-Bone Steak** (price per pound); **Frying Chicken** (price per pound, whole fryer); **Whole Milk** (half gallon carton); **Eggs** (price per dozen, Grade A, large); **Orange Juice** (64 oz. Tropicana or Florida Natural); **Coffee** (11.5 oz. can, vacuum-packed, Maxwell House, Hills Bros, or Folgers).
Source: The Council for Community and Economic Research, Cost of Living Index, 2020

Housing and Utility Costs

Area[1]	New Home Price ($)	Apartment Rent ($/month)	All Electric ($/month)	Part Electric ($/month)	Other Energy ($/month)	Telephone ($/month)
City[2]	797,634	2,351	-	183.35	64.21	176.00
Avg.	368,594	1,168	170.86	100.47	65.28	184.30
Min.	190,567	502	91.58	31.42	26.08	169.60
Max.	2,227,806	4,738	470.38	280.31	280.06	206.50

Note: (1) Values for the local area are compared with the average, minimum and maximum values for all 284 areas in the Cost of Living Index; (2) Figures cover the San Diego CA urban area; **New Home Price** (2,400 sf living area, 8,000 sf lot, in urban area with full utilities); **Apartment Rent** (950 sf 2 bedroom/1.5 or 2 bath, unfurnished, excluding all utilities except water); **All Electric** (average monthly cost for an all-electric home); **Part Electric** (average monthly cost for a part-electric home); **Other Energy** (average monthly cost for natural gas, fuel oil, coal, wood, and any other forms of energy except electricity); **Telephone** (price includes the base monthly rate plus taxes and fees for three lines of mobile phone service).
Source: The Council for Community and Economic Research, Cost of Living Index, 2020

Health Care, Transportation, and Other Costs

Area[1]	Doctor ($/visit)	Dentist ($/visit)	Optometrist ($/visit)	Gasoline ($/gallon)	Beauty Salon ($/visit)	Men's Shirt ($)
City[2]	125.00	107.18	117.65	3.24	64.57	32.48
Avg.	115.44	99.32	108.10	2.21	39.27	31.37
Min.	36.68	59.00	51.36	1.71	19.00	11.00
Max.	219.00	153.10	250.97	3.46	82.05	58.33

Note: (1) Values for the local area are compared with the average, minimum and maximum values for all 284 areas in the Cost of Living Index; (2) Figures cover the San Diego CA urban area; **Doctor** (general practitioners routine exam of an established patient); **Dentist** (adult teeth cleaning and periodic oral examination); **Optometrist** (full vision eye exam for established adult patient); **Gasoline** (one gallon regular unleaded, national brand, including all taxes, cash price at self-service pump if available); **Beauty Salon** (woman's shampoo, trim, and blow-dry); **Men's Shirt** (cotton/polyester dress shirt, pinpoint weave, long sleeves).
Source: The Council for Community and Economic Research, Cost of Living Index, 2020

HOUSING

Homeownership Rate

Area	2012 (%)	2013 (%)	2014 (%)	2015 (%)	2016 (%)	2017 (%)	2018 (%)	2019 (%)	2020 (%)
MSA[1]	55.4	55.0	57.4	51.8	53.3	56.0	56.1	56.7	57.8
U.S.	65.4	65.1	64.5	63.7	63.4	63.9	64.4	64.6	66.6

Note: (1) Figures cover the San Diego-Carlsbad, CA Metropolitan Statistical Area
Source: U.S. Census Bureau, Housing Vacancies and Homeownership Annual Statistics: 2012-2020

House Price Index (HPI)

Area	National Ranking[2]	Quarterly Change (%)	One-Year Change (%)	Five-Year Change (%)	Since 1991Q1 (%)
MSA[1]	141	1.97	6.01	30.38	235.91
U.S.[3]	–	3.81	10.77	38.99	205.12

Note: The HPI is a weighted repeat sales index. It measures average price changes in repeat sales or refinancings on the same properties. This information is obtained by reviewing repeat mortgage transactions on single-family properties whose mortgages have been purchased or securitized by Fannie Mae or Freddie Mac since January 1975; (1) Figures cover the San Diego-Carlsbad, CA Metropolitan Statistical Area; (2) Rankings are based on annual percentage change for all metro areas containing at least 15,000 transactions over the last 10 years and ranges from 1 to 253; (3) figures based on a weighted average of Census Division estimates using a seasonally adjusted, purchase-only index; all figures are for the period ending December 31, 2020
Source: Federal Housing Finance Agency, Change in Metropolitan Area House Price Indexes, April 7, 2021

Median Single-Family Home Prices

Area	2018	2019	2020[p]	Percent Change 2019 to 2020
MSA[1]	634.0	645.0	710.0	10.1
U.S. Average	261.6	274.6	299.9	9.2

Note: Figures are median sales prices of existing single-family homes in thousands of dollars; (p) preliminary; (1) Figures cover the San Diego-Carlsbad, CA Metropolitan Statistical Area
Source: National Association of Realtors, Median Sales Price of Existing Single-Family Homes for Metropolitan Areas, 4th Quarter 2020

Qualifying Income Based on Median Sales Price of Existing Single-Family Homes

Area	With 5% Down ($)	With 10% Down ($)	With 20% Down ($)
MSA[1]	139,965	132,599	117,865
U.S. Average	59,266	56,147	49,908

Note: Figures are preliminary; Qualifying income is based on a mortgage rate of 2.81%. Monthly principal and interest payment is limited to 25% of income; (1) Figures cover the San Diego-Carlsbad, CA Metropolitan Statistical Area
Source: National Association of Realtors, Qualifying Income Based on Median Sales Price of Existing Single-Family Homes for Metropolitan Areas, 4th Quarter 2020

Home Value Distribution

Area	Under $50,000	$50,000 -$99,999	$100,000 -$149,999	$150,000 -$199,999	$200,000 -$299,999	$300,000 -$499,999	$500,000 -$999,999	$1,000,000 or more
City	1.6	1.0	0.8	1.1	5.3	27.4	47.6	15.3
MSA[1]	2.5	1.9	1.4	1.4	5.2	29.3	46.1	12.2
U.S.	6.9	12.0	13.3	14.0	19.6	19.3	11.4	3.4

Note: Figures are percentages and cover owner-occupied housing units; (1) Figures cover the San Diego-Carlsbad, CA Metropolitan Statistical Area
Source: U.S. Census Bureau, 2015-2019 American Community Survey 5-Year Estimates

Year Housing Structure Built

Area	2010 or Later	2000 -2009	1990 -1999	1980 -1989	1970 -1979	1960 -1969	1950 -1959	1940 -1949	Before 1940	Median Year
City	3.9	10.3	11.4	17.7	21.2	12.5	12.1	4.3	6.7	1977
MSA[1]	3.7	12.0	12.5	18.6	22.6	12.2	10.7	3.5	4.2	1979
U.S.	5.2	14.0	13.9	13.4	15.2	10.6	10.3	4.9	12.6	1978

Note: Figures are percentages except for Median Year; Note: (1) Figures cover the San Diego-Carlsbad, CA Metropolitan Statistical Area
Source: U.S. Census Bureau, 2015-2019 American Community Survey 5-Year Estimates

Gross Monthly Rent

Area	Under $500	$500 -$999	$1,000 -$1,499	$1,500 -$1,999	$2,000 -$2,499	$2,500 -$2,999	$3,000 and up	Median ($)
City	3.4	10.2	25.9	26.9	18.7	8.9	6.0	1,695
MSA[1]	3.5	9.9	28.1	27.2	17.0	8.2	6.2	1,658
U.S.	9.4	36.2	30.0	14.0	5.6	2.4	2.4	1,062

Note: Figures are percentages except for Median; Gross rent is the contract rent plus the estimated average monthly cost of utilities (electricity, gas, and water and sewer) and fuels (oil, coal, kerosene, wood, etc.) if these are paid by the renter (or paid for the renter by someone else); (1) Figures cover the San Diego-Carlsbad, CA Metropolitan Statistical Area
Source: U.S. Census Bureau, 2015-2019 American Community Survey 5-Year Estimates

HEALTH

Health Risk Factors

Category	MSA[1] (%)	U.S. (%)
Adults aged 18–64 who have any kind of health care coverage	n/a	87.3
Adults who reported being in good or better health	n/a	82.4
Adults who have been told they have high blood cholesterol	n/a	33.0
Adults who have been told they have high blood pressure	n/a	32.3
Adults who are current smokers	n/a	17.1
Adults who currently use E-cigarettes	n/a	4.6
Adults who currently use chewing tobacco, snuff, or snus	n/a	4.0
Adults who are heavy drinkers[2]	n/a	6.3
Adults who are binge drinkers[3]	n/a	17.4
Adults who are overweight (BMI 25.0 - 29.9)	n/a	35.3
Adults who are obese (BMI 30.0 - 99.8)	n/a	31.3
Adults who participated in any physical activities in the past month	n/a	74.4
Adults who always or nearly always wears a seat belt	n/a	94.3

Note: n/a not available; (1) Figures cover the San Diego-Carlsbad, CA Metropolitan Statistical Area;
(2) Heavy drinkers are classified as adult men having more than 14 drinks per week and adult women having
more than 7 drinks per week; (3) Binge drinkers are classified as males having five or more drinks on one
occasion or females having four or more drinks on one occasion
Source: Centers for Disease Control and Prevention, Behaviorial Risk Factor Surveillance System, SMART:
Selected Metropolitan Area Risk Trends, 2017

Acute and Chronic Health Conditions

Category	MSA[1] (%)	U.S. (%)
Adults who have ever been told they had a heart attack	n/a	4.2
Adults who have ever been told they have angina or coronary heart disease	n/a	3.9
Adults who have ever been told they had a stroke	n/a	3.0
Adults who have ever been told they have asthma	n/a	14.2
Adults who have ever been told they have arthritis	n/a	24.9
Adults who have ever been told they have diabetes[2]	n/a	10.5
Adults who have ever been told they had skin cancer	n/a	6.2
Adults who have ever been told they had any other types of cancer	n/a	7.1
Adults who have ever been told they have COPD	n/a	6.5
Adults who have ever been told they have kidney disease	n/a	3.0
Adults who have ever been told they have a form of depression	n/a	20.5

Note: n/a not available; (1) Figures cover the San Diego-Carlsbad, CA Metropolitan Statistical Area; (2)
Figures do not include pregnancy-related, borderline, or pre-diabetes
Source: Centers for Disease Control and Prevention, Behaviorial Risk Factor Surveillance System, SMART:
Selected Metropolitan Area Risk Trends, 2017

Health Screening and Vaccination Rates

Category	MSA[1] (%)	U.S. (%)
Adults aged 65+ who have had flu shot within the past year	n/a	60.7
Adults aged 65+ who have ever had a pneumonia vaccination	n/a	75.4
Adults who have ever been tested for HIV	n/a	36.1
Adults who have ever had the shingles or zoster vaccine?	n/a	28.9
Adults who have had their blood cholesterol checked within the last five years	n/a	85.9

Note: n/a not available; (1) Figures cover the San Diego-Carlsbad, CA Metropolitan Statistical Area.
Source: Centers for Disease Control and Prevention, Behaviorial Risk Factor Surveillance System, SMART:
Selected Metropolitan Area Risk Trends, 2017

Disability Status

Category	MSA[1] (%)	U.S. (%)
Adults who reported being deaf	n/a	6.7
Are you blind or have serious difficulty seeing, even when wearing glasses?	n/a	4.5
Are you limited in any way in any of your usual activities due of arthritis?	n/a	12.9
Do you have difficulty doing errands alone?	n/a	6.8
Do you have difficulty dressing or bathing?	n/a	3.6
Do you have serious difficulty concentrating/remembering/making decisions?	n/a	10.7
Do you have serious difficulty walking or climbing stairs?	n/a	13.6

Note: n/a not available; (1) Figures cover the San Diego-Carlsbad, CA Metropolitan Statistical Area.
Source: Centers for Disease Control and Prevention, Behaviorial Risk Factor Surveillance System, SMART:
Selected Metropolitan Area Risk Trends, 2017

Mortality Rates for the Top 10 Causes of Death in the U.S.

ICD-10[a] Sub-Chapter	ICD-10[a] Code	Age-Adjusted Mortality Rate[1] per 100,000 population	
		County[2]	U.S.
Malignant neoplasms	C00-C97	136.4	149.2
Ischaemic heart diseases	I20-I25	71.4	90.5
Other forms of heart disease	I30-I51	40.4	52.2
Chronic lower respiratory diseases	J40-J47	27.5	39.6
Other degenerative diseases of the nervous system	G30-G31	44.2	37.6
Cerebrovascular diseases	I60-I69	39.7	37.2
Other external causes of accidental injury	W00-X59	26.3	36.1
Organic, including symptomatic, mental disorders	F01-F09	17.3	29.4
Hypertensive diseases	I10-I15	22.7	24.1
Diabetes mellitus	E10-E14	21.1	21.5

Note: (a) ICD-10 = International Classification of Diseases 10th Revision; (1) Mortality rates are a three-year average covering 2017-2019; (2) Figures cover San Diego County.
Source: Centers for Disease Control and Prevention, National Center for Health Statistics. Underlying Cause of Death 1999-2019 on CDC WONDER Online Database

Mortality Rates for Selected Causes of Death

ICD-10[a] Sub-Chapter	ICD-10[a] Code	Age-Adjusted Mortality Rate[1] per 100,000 population	
		County[2]	U.S.
Assault	X85-Y09	2.4	6.0
Diseases of the liver	K70-K76	11.1	14.4
Human immunodeficiency virus (HIV) disease	B20-B24	1.2	1.5
Influenza and pneumonia	J09-J18	10.2	13.8
Intentional self-harm	X60-X84	12.4	14.1
Malnutrition	E40-E46	2.2	2.3
Obesity and other hyperalimentation	E65-E68	1.6	2.1
Renal failure	N17-N19	2.6	12.6
Transport accidents	V01-V99	8.5	12.3
Viral hepatitis	B15-B19	1.6	1.2

Note: (a) ICD-10 = International Classification of Diseases 10th Revision; (1) Mortality rates are a three-year average covering 2017-2019; (2) Figures cover San Diego County; Data are suppressed when the data meet the criteria for confidentiality constraints; Mortality rates are flagged as unreliable when the rate would be calculated with a numerator of 20 or less.
Source: Centers for Disease Control and Prevention, National Center for Health Statistics. Underlying Cause of Death 1999-2019 on CDC WONDER Online Database

Health Insurance Coverage

Area	With Health Insurance	With Private Health Insurance	With Public Health Insurance	Without Health Insurance	Population Under Age 19 Without Health Insurance
City	92.2	69.7	31.6	7.8	3.6
MSA[1]	92.2	68.4	33.8	7.8	3.8
U.S.	91.2	67.9	35.1	8.8	5.1

Note: Figures are percentages that cover the civilian noninstitutionalized population; (1) Figures cover the San Diego-Carlsbad, CA Metropolitan Statistical Area
Source: U.S. Census Bureau, 2015-2019 American Community Survey 5-Year Estimates

Number of Medical Professionals

Area	MDs[3]	DOs[3,4]	Dentists	Podiatrists	Chiropractors	Optometrists
County[1] (number)	10,864	611	3,036	144	1,147	637
County[1] (rate[2])	325.9	18.3	90.9	4.3	34.4	19.1
U.S. (rate[2])	282.9	22.7	71.2	6.2	28.1	16.9

06073
Note: Data as of 2019 unless noted; (1) Data covers San Diego County; (2) Rate per 100,000 population; (3) Data as of 2018 and includes all active, non-federal physicians; (4) Doctor of Osteopathic Medicine
Source: U.S. Department of Health and Human Services, Health Resources and Services Administration, Bureau of Health Professions, Area Resource File (ARF) 2019-2020

Best Hospitals

According to *U.S. News*, the San Diego-Carlsbad, CA metro area is home to five of the best hospitals in the U.S.: **Scripps La Jolla Hospitals** (7 adult specialties); **UC San Diego Health** (10 adult specialties); **UC San Diego Health-Jacobs Medical Center** (10 adult specialties); **UC San Diego Health-Moores Cancer Center** (10 adult specialties); **UC San Diego Health-Shiley Eye Institute** (10 adult specialties). The hospitals listed were nationally ranked in at least one of 16 adult or 10 pediatric specialties. Only 134 hospitals nationwide were nationally ranked in one or more adult or pediatric specialty; this number increases to 178 counting specialized centers within hospitals. Twenty hospitals in the U.S. made the Honor Roll. The Best Hospitals Honor Roll takes both the national rankings and the procedure and condition ratings into account. Hospitals received points if they were nationally ranked in one of the 16 adult specialties—the higher they ranked, the more points they got—and how many ratings of "high performing" they earned in the 10 procedures and conditions. *U.S. News Online, "America's Best Hospitals 2020-21"*

According to *U.S. News,* the San Diego-Carlsbad, CA metro area is home to one of the best children's hospitals in the U.S.: **Rady Children's Hospital** (10 pediatric specialties). The hospital listed was highly ranked in at least one of 10 pediatric specialties. Eighty-eight children's hospitals in the U.S. were nationally ranked in at least one specialty. Hospitals received points for being ranked in a specialty, and the 10 hospitals with the most points across the 10 specialties make up the Honor Roll. *U.S. News Online, "America's Best Children's Hospitals 2020-21"*

EDUCATION

Public School District Statistics

District Name	Schls	Pupils	Pupil/ Teacher Ratio	Minority Pupils[1] (%)	Free Lunch Eligible[2] (%)	IEP[3] (%)
Del Mar Union Elementary	8	4,263	23.2	52.0	6.7	15.6
Poway Unified	38	36,450	25.3	55.3	15.3	13.2
San Diego Unified	176	103,194	23.5	75.9	47.3	15.3

Note: Table includes school districts with 2,000 or more students; (1) Percentage of students that are not non-Hispanic white; (2) Percentage of students that are eligible for the free lunch program; (3) Percentage of students that have an Individualized Education Program.
Source: U.S. Department of Education, National Center for Education Statistics, Common Core of Data, Local Education Agency (School District) Universe Survey: School Year 2018-2019; U.S. Department of Education, National Center for Education Statistics, Common Core of Data, Public Elementary/Secondary School Universe Survey: School Year 2018-2019

Best High Schools

According to *U.S. News,* San Diego is home to seven of the top 500 high schools in the U.S.: **Preuss School UCSD** (#87); **Canyon Crest Academy** (#157); **Mt. Everest Academy** (#239); **Westview High** (#400); **Del Norte High** (#436); **The O'Farrell Charter** (#447); **La Jolla High** (#491). Nearly 18,000 public, magnet and charter schools were ranked based on their performance on state assessments and how well they prepare students for college. *U.S. News & World Report, "Best High Schools 2020"*

Highest Level of Education

Area	Less than H.S.	H.S. Diploma	Some College, No Deg.	Associate Degree	Bachelor's Degree	Master's Degree	Prof. School Degree	Doctorate Degree
City	11.9	15.1	19.7	7.4	27.0	12.2	3.7	3.0
MSA[1]	12.6	18.2	22.3	8.1	23.8	10.0	2.9	2.1
U.S.	12.0	27.0	20.4	8.5	19.8	8.8	2.1	1.4

Note: Figures cover persons age 25 and over; (1) Figures cover the San Diego-Carlsbad, CA Metropolitan Statistical Area
Source: U.S. Census Bureau, 2015-2019 American Community Survey 5-Year Estimates

Educational Attainment by Race

Area	High School Graduate or Higher (%)					Bachelor's Degree or Higher (%)				
	Total	White	Black	Asian	Hisp.[2]	Total	White	Black	Asian	Hisp.[2]
City	88.1	89.2	91.3	88.7	69.1	45.9	48.1	25.8	53.8	20.4
MSA[1]	87.4	88.2	91.8	89.2	69.8	38.8	39.5	25.9	51.3	17.8
U.S.	88.0	89.9	86.0	87.1	68.7	32.1	33.5	21.6	54.3	16.4

Note: Figures shown cover persons 25 years old and over; (1) Figures cover the San Diego-Carlsbad, CA Metropolitan Statistical Area; (2) People of Hispanic origin can be of any race
Source: U.S. Census Bureau, 2015-2019 American Community Survey 5-Year Estimates

School Enrollment by Grade and Control

Area	Preschool (%)		Kindergarten (%)		Grades 1 - 4 (%)		Grades 5 - 8 (%)		Grades 9 - 12 (%)	
	Public	Private	Public	Private	Public	Private	Public	Private	Public	Private
City	52.5	47.5	92.9	7.1	90.9	9.1	91.2	8.8	91.5	8.5
MSA[1]	54.0	46.0	90.5	9.5	92.1	7.9	92.1	7.9	92.4	7.6
U.S.	59.1	40.9	87.6	12.4	89.5	10.5	89.4	10.6	90.1	9.9

Note: Figures shown cover persons 3 years old and over; (1) Figures cover the San Diego-Carlsbad, CA Metropolitan Statistical Area
Source: U.S. Census Bureau, 2015-2019 American Community Survey 5-Year Estimates

Higher Education

Four-Year Colleges			Two-Year Colleges			Medical Schools[1]	Law Schools[2]	Voc/ Tech[3]
Public	Private Non-profit	Private For-profit	Public	Private Non-profit	Private For-profit			
3	11	10	2	0	5	1	3	5

Note: Figures cover institutions located within the city limits and include main campuses only; (1) includes schools accredited by the Liaison Committee on Medical Education and the American Osteopathic Association's Commission on Osteopathic College Accreditation; (2) includes ABA-accredited schools, schools with provisional ABA accreditation, and state accredited schools; (3) includes all schools with programs that are less than 2 years.
Source: National Center for Education Statistics, Integrated Postsecondary Education System (IPEDS), 2019-20; Wikipedia, List of Medical Schools in the United States, accessed April 2, 2021; Wikipedia, List of Law Schools in the United States, accessed April 2, 2021

According to *U.S. News & World Report,* the San Diego-Carlsbad, CA metro area is home to three of the top 200 national universities in the U.S.: **University of California—San Diego** (#35 tie); **University of San Diego** (#88 tie); **San Diego State University** (#143 tie). The indicators used to capture academic quality fall into a number of categories: assessment by administrators at peer institutions; retention of students; faculty resources; student selectivity; financial resources; alumni giving; high school counselor ratings of colleges; and graduation rate. *U.S. News & World Report, "America's Best Colleges 2021"*

According to *U.S. News & World Report,* the San Diego-Carlsbad, CA metro area is home to one of the top 100 law schools in the U.S.: **University of San Diego** (#86). The rankings are based on a weighted average of 12 measures of quality: peer assessment score; assessment score by lawyers/judges; median LSAT scores; median undergrad GPA; acceptance rate; employment rates for graduates; placement success; bar passage rate; faculty resources; expenditures per student; student/faculty ratio; and library resources. *U.S. News & World Report, "America's Best Graduate Schools, Law, 2022"*

According to *U.S. News & World Report,* the San Diego-Carlsbad, CA metro area is home to one of the top 75 medical schools for research in the U.S.: **University of California—San Diego** (#19 tie). The rankings are based on a weighted average of 11 measures of quality: quality assessment; peer assessment score; assessment score by residency directors; research activity; total research activity; average research activity per faculty member; student selectivity; median MCAT total score; median undergraduate GPA; acceptance rate; and faculty resources. *U.S. News & World Report, "America's Best Graduate Schools, Medical, 2022"*

EMPLOYERS

Major Employers

Company Name	Industry
Barona Resort & Casino	Resort hotels
CA Dept of Forestry and Fire Protection	Fire department, not including volunteer
CA Dept of Housing & Comm Dev	Housing agency, government
City of San Diego	Municipal government
Elite Show Services	Help supply services
Go-Staff	Temporary help services
Kaiser Foundation Hospitals	Trusts, nec
Palomar Community College District	Junior colleges
Qualcomm International	Patent buying, licensing, leasing
Risk Management Strategies	Employee programs administration
San Diego State University	Colleges & universities
Sharp Memorial Hospital	General medical & surgical hospitals
Solar Turbines Incorporated	Turbines & turbine generator sets
U.S. Marine Corps	Marine corps
U.S. Navy	U.S. military
University of California, San Diego	General medical & surgical hospitals
Veterans Health Administration	Administration of veterans' affairs

Note: Companies shown are located within the San Diego-Carlsbad, CA Metropolitan Statistical Area.
Source: Hoovers.com; Wikipedia

Best Companies to Work For

Scripps Health, headquartered in San Diego, is among "The 100 Best Companies to Work For." To pick the best companies, *Fortune* partnered with the Great Place to Work Institute. Two-thirds of a company's score is based on the results of the Institute's Trust Index survey, which is sent to a random sample of employees from each company. The questions related to attitudes about management's credibility, job satisfaction, and camaraderie. The other third of the scoring is based on the company's responses to the Institute's Culture Audit, which includes detailed questions about pay and benefit programs, and a series of open-ended questions about hiring practices, internal communication, training, recognition programs, and diversity efforts. Any company that is at least five years old with more than 1,000 U.S. employees is eligible. *Fortune, "The 100 Best Companies to Work For," 2020*

Sony Electronics, headquartered in San Diego, is among the "100 Best Companies for Working Mothers." Criteria: paid time off and leaves; workforce profile; benefits; women's issues and advancement; flexible work; company culture and work life programs. *Working Mother, "100 Best Companies for Working Mothers,"* 2020

Sharp HealthCare, headquartered in San Diego, is among the "100 Best Places to Work in IT." To qualify, companies had to be U.S.-based organizations or be non-U.S.-based employers that met the following criteria: have a minimum of 300 total employees at a U.S. headquarters and a minimum of 30 IT employees in the U.S., with at least 50% of their IT employees based in the U.S. The best places to work were selected based on compensation, benefits, work/life balance, employee morale, and satisfaction with training and development programs. In addition, *InsiderPro* and *Computerworld* looked at retention efforts, programs for recognizing and rewarding outstanding performances, and benefits such as flextime, elder care and child care, and reimbursement for college tuition and the cost of pursuing technology certifications. *InsiderPro and Computerworld, "100 Best Places to Work in IT,"* 2020

Sony Electronics, headquartered in San Diego, is among the "Best Companies for Dads." *Working Mother's* newest list recognizes the growing importance companies place on giving dads time off and support for their families. Rankings are determined by measuring gender-neutral or paternity leave offered, as well as actual time taken, phase-back policies, child- and dependent-care benefits, and corporate support groups for men and dads. *Working Mother, "Best Companies for Dads,"* 2020

PUBLIC SAFETY

Crime Rate

Area	All Crimes	Violent Crimes				Property Crimes		
		Murder	Rape[3]	Robbery	Aggrav. Assault	Burglary	Larceny -Theft	Motor Vehicle Theft
City	2,244.2	3.5	38.9	93.4	226.0	245.7	1,278.0	358.7
Suburbs[1]	1,801.2	1.9	28.6	81.2	214.0	218.1	1,020.7	236.8
Metro[2]	1,992.1	2.6	33.1	86.4	219.1	230.0	1,131.6	289.3
U.S.	2,489.3	5.0	42.6	81.6	250.2	340.5	1,549.5	219.9

Note: Figures are crimes per 100,000 population; (1) All areas within the metro area that are located outside the city limits; (2) Figures cover the San Diego-Carlsbad, CA Metropolitan Statistical Area; (3) All figures shown were reported using the revised Uniform Crime Reporting (UCR) definition of rape.
Source: FBI Uniform Crime Reports, 2019

Hate Crimes

Area	Number of Quarters Reported	Number of Incidents per Bias Motivation					
		Race/Ethnicity/ Ancestry	Religion	Sexual Orientation	Disability	Gender	Gender Identity
City	4	8	11	9	1	0	1
U.S.	4	3,963	1,521	1,195	157	69	198

Source: Federal Bureau of Investigation, Hate Crime Statistics 2019

Identity Theft Consumer Reports

Area	Reports	Reports per 100,000 Population	Rank[2]
MSA[1]	10,087	302	116
U.S.	1,387,615	423	-

Note: (1) Figures cover the San Diego-Carlsbad, CA Metropolitan Statistical Area; (2) Rank ranges from 1 to 391 where 1 indicates greatest number of identity theft reports per 100,000 population
Source: Federal Trade Commission, Consumer Sentinel Network Data Book 2020

Fraud and Other Consumer Reports

Area	Reports	Reports per 100,000 Population	Rank[2]
MSA[1]	29,357	879	56
U.S.	3,385,133	1,031	-

Note: (1) Figures cover the San Diego-Carlsbad, CA Metropolitan Statistical Area; (2) Rank ranges from 1 to 391 where 1 indicates greatest number of fraud and other consumer reports per 100,000 population
Source: Federal Trade Commission, Consumer Sentinel Network Data Book 2020

POLITICS

2020 Presidential Election Results

Area	Biden	Trump	Jorgensen	Hawkins	Other
San Diego County	60.2	37.5	1.3	0.5	0.5
U.S.	51.3	46.8	1.2	0.3	0.5

Note: Results are percentages and may not add to 100% due to rounding
Source: Dave Leip's Atlas of U.S. Presidential Elections

SPORTS

Professional Sports Teams

Team Name	League	Year Established
San Diego Padres	Major League Baseball (MLB)	1969

Note: Includes teams located in the San Diego-Carlsbad, CA Metropolitan Statistical Area.
Source: Wikipedia, Major Professional Sports Teams of the United States and Canada, April 6, 2021

CLIMATE

Average and Extreme Temperatures

Temperature	Jan	Feb	Mar	Apr	May	Jun	Jul	Aug	Sep	Oct	Nov	Dec	Yr.
Extreme High (°F)	88	88	93	98	96	101	95	98	111	107	97	88	111
Average High (°F)	65	66	66	68	69	72	76	77	77	74	71	66	71
Average Temp. (°F)	57	58	59	62	64	67	71	72	71	67	62	58	64
Average Low (°F)	48	50	52	55	58	61	65	66	65	60	53	49	57
Extreme Low (°F)	29	36	39	44	48	51	55	58	51	43	38	34	29

Note: Figures cover the years 1948-1990
Source: National Climatic Data Center, International Station Meteorological Climate Summary, 9/96

Average Precipitation/Snowfall/Humidity

Precip./Humidity	Jan	Feb	Mar	Apr	May	Jun	Jul	Aug	Sep	Oct	Nov	Dec	Yr.
Avg. Precip. (in.)	1.9	1.4	1.7	0.8	0.2	0.1	Tr	0.1	0.2	0.4	1.2	1.4	9.5
Avg. Snowfall (in.)	Tr	0	0	0	0	0	0	0	0	0	0	Tr	Tr
Avg. Rel. Hum. 7am (%)	70	72	73	72	73	77	79	79	78	74	69	68	74
Avg. Rel. Hum. 4pm (%)	57	58	59	59	63	66	65	66	65	63	60	58	62

Note: Figures cover the years 1948-1990; Tr = Trace amounts (<0.05 in. of rain; <0.5 in. of snow)
Source: National Climatic Data Center, International Station Meteorological Climate Summary, 9/96

Weather Conditions

Temperature			Daytime Sky			Precipitation		
10°F & below	32°F & below	90°F & above	Clear	Partly cloudy	Cloudy	0.01 inch or more precip.	0.1 inch or more snow/ice	Thunder-storms
0	<1	4	115	126	124	40	0	5

Note: Figures are average number of days per year and cover the years 1948-1990
Source: National Climatic Data Center, International Station Meteorological Climate Summary, 9/96

HAZARDOUS WASTE

Superfund Sites

The San Diego-Carlsbad, CA metro area is home to one site on the EPA's Superfund National Priorities List: **Camp Pendleton Marine Corps Base** (final). There are a total of 1,375 Superfund sites with a status of proposed or final on the list in the U.S. *U.S. Environmental Protection Agency, National Priorities List, April 7, 2021*

AIR QUALITY

Air Quality Trends: Ozone

	1990	1995	2000	2005	2010	2015	2016	2017	2018	2019
MSA[1]	0.112	0.093	0.084	0.079	0.075	0.070	0.073	0.077	0.069	0.071
U.S.	0.088	0.089	0.082	0.080	0.073	0.068	0.069	0.068	0.069	0.065

Note: (1) Data covers the San Diego-Carlsbad, CA Metropolitan Statistical Area. The values shown are the composite ozone concentration averages among trend sites based on the highest fourth daily maximum 8-hour concentration in parts per million. These trends are based on sites having an adequate record of monitoring data during the trend period. Data from exceptional events are included.
Source: U.S. Environmental Protection Agency, Air Quality Monitoring Information, "Air Quality Trends by City, 1990-2019"

Air Quality Index

Area	Percent of Days when Air Quality was...[2]					AQI Statistics[2]	
	Good	Moderate	Unhealthy for Sensitive Groups	Unhealthy	Very Unhealthy	Maximum	Median
MSA[1]	23.8	69.3	6.3	0.5	0.0	169	64

Note: (1) Data covers the San Diego-Carlsbad, CA Metropolitan Statistical Area; (2) Based on 365 days with AQI data in 2019. Air Quality Index (AQI) is an index for reporting daily air quality. EPA calculates the AQI for five major air pollutants regulated by the Clean Air Act: ground-level ozone, particle pollution (aka particulate matter), carbon monoxide, sulfur dioxide, and nitrogen dioxide. The AQI runs from 0 to 500. The higher the AQI value, the greater the level of air pollution and the greater the health concern. There are six AQI categories: "Good" AQI is between 0 and 50. Air quality is considered satisfactory; "Moderate" AQI is between 51 and 100. Air quality is acceptable; "Unhealthy for Sensitive Groups" When AQI values are between 101 and 150, members of sensitive groups may experience health effects; "Unhealthy" When AQI values are between 151 and 200 everyone may begin to experience health effects; "Very Unhealthy" AQI values between 201 and 300 trigger a health alert; "Hazardous" AQI values over 300 trigger warnings of emergency conditions (not shown).
Source: U.S. Environmental Protection Agency, Air Quality Index Report, 2019

Air Quality Index Pollutants

Area	\multicolumn{6}{c}{Percent of Days when AQI Pollutant was...[2]}
	Carbon Monoxide	Nitrogen Dioxide	Ozone	Sulfur Dioxide	Particulate Matter 2.5	Particulate Matter 10
MSA[1]	0.0	0.5	48.2	0.0	50.4	0.8

Note: (1) Data covers the San Diego-Carlsbad, CA Metropolitan Statistical Area; (2) Based on 365 days with AQI data in 2019. The Air Quality Index (AQI) is an index for reporting daily air quality. EPA calculates the AQI for five major air pollutants regulated by the Clean Air Act: ground-level ozone, particle pollution (also known as particulate matter), carbon monoxide, sulfur dioxide, and nitrogen dioxide. The AQI runs from 0 to 500. The higher the AQI value, the greater the level of air pollution and the greater the health concern.
Source: U.S. Environmental Protection Agency, Air Quality Index Report, 2019

Maximum Air Pollutant Concentrations: Particulate Matter, Ozone, CO and Lead

	Particulate Matter 10 (ug/m^3)	Particulate Matter 2.5 Wtd AM (ug/m^3)	Particulate Matter 2.5 24-Hr (ug/m^3)	Ozone (ppm)	Carbon Monoxide (ppm)	Lead (ug/m^3)
MSA[1] Level	153	13.7	27	0.076	2	0.02
NAAQS[2]	150	15	35	0.075	9	0.15
Met NAAQS[2]	No	Yes	Yes	No	Yes	Yes

Note: (1) Data covers the San Diego-Carlsbad, CA Metropolitan Statistical Area; Data from exceptional events are included; (2) National Ambient Air Quality Standards; ppm = parts per million; ug/m^3 = micrograms per cubic meter; n/a not available.
Concentrations: Particulate Matter 10 (coarse particulate)—highest second maximum 24-hour concentration; Particulate Matter 2.5 Wtd AM (fine particulate)—highest weighted annual mean concentration; Particulate Matter 2.5 24-Hour (fine particulate)—highest 98th percentile 24-hour concentration; Ozone—highest fourth daily maximum 8-hour concentration; Carbon Monoxide—highest second maximum non-overlapping 8-hour concentration; Lead—maximum running 3-month average
Source: U.S. Environmental Protection Agency, Air Quality Monitoring Information, "Air Quality Statistics by City, 2019"

Maximum Air Pollutant Concentrations: Nitrogen Dioxide and Sulfur Dioxide

	Nitrogen Dioxide AM (ppb)	Nitrogen Dioxide 1-Hr (ppb)	Sulfur Dioxide AM (ppb)	Sulfur Dioxide 1-Hr (ppb)	Sulfur Dioxide 24-Hr (ppb)
MSA[1] Level	14	47	n/a	1	n/a
NAAQS[2]	53	100	30	75	140
Met NAAQS[2]	Yes	Yes	n/a	Yes	n/a

Note: (1) Data covers the San Diego-Carlsbad, CA Metropolitan Statistical Area; Data from exceptional events are included; (2) National Ambient Air Quality Standards; ppm = parts per million; ug/m^3 = micrograms per cubic meter; n/a not available.
Concentrations: Nitrogen Dioxide AM—highest arithmetic mean concentration; Nitrogen Dioxide 1-Hr—highest 98th percentile 1-hour daily maximum concentration; Sulfur Dioxide AM—highest annual mean concentration; Sulfur Dioxide 1-Hr—highest 99th percentile 1-hour daily maximum concentration; Sulfur Dioxide 24-Hr—highest second maximum 24-hour concentration
Source: U.S. Environmental Protection Agency, Air Quality Monitoring Information, "Air Quality Statistics by City, 2019"

San Francisco, California

Background

San Francisco is one of the most beautiful cities in the world. It is blessed with a mild climate, one of the best landlocked harbors in the world, and a strong sense of civic pride shaped by its unique history.

The hilly peninsula known today as San Francisco and its bay was largely ignored by explorers during the sixteenth and seventeenth centuries. Until the 1760s, no European had seen the "Golden Gate," or the narrow strip of water leading into what was to become one of the greatest harbors in the world. However, even after discovery of that prime piece of real estate, San Francisco remained a quiet and pastoral settlement for nearly 90 years.

The discovery of gold in the Sierra Nevada foothills in 1848 changed San Francisco forever. Every hopeful adventurer from around the world docked in San Francisco, aspiring to make his fortune. San Francisco at this time was a rowdy, frontier, gold-prospecting town, with plenty of gambling houses and saloons.

When the supply of gold dwindled, many went back to their native countries, but some stayed and continued to live in the ethnic neighborhoods they had created—neighborhoods that still exist today, such as Chinatown, the Italian District, and the Japan Center.

The charm of San Francisco lies in its cosmopolitan, yet cohesive, flavor. Ever mindful of its citizenry, newspapers in San Francisco range from English, Irish, Spanish, and Swiss to Chinese, Japanese, and Korean, with many community newspapers in between. In addition, the city has long been home to a significant gay community. It was home to the first lesbian-rights organization in the United States, Daughters of Bilitis; the first openly gay person to run for public office in the United States, José Sarria; the first openly gay man to be elected to public office in California, Harvey Milk; the first openly lesbian judge appointed in the U.S., Mary C. Morgan; and the first transgender police commissioner, Theresa Sparks.

The San Francisco Bay Area is one of the major economic regions of the United States, with one of the highest percentages of college-educated adults in the nation, which translates into a high per-capita real income. The Bay Area is also home to 20 percent of California's environmental companies, and leads the state with the largest concentration of biotech companies. A former warehouse district in San Francisco has become the center for nearly 400 multimedia and technology companies. Before the Internet crash in 2000, this industry cluster, combined with the concentration of multimedia activity in the Bay Area, had produced jobs for nearly 60,000 people. In terms of world trade, high-tech exports from the Silicon Valley area accounted for almost one-third of the nation's high-technology exports.

> A 57-year old female resident of Santa Clara County was the earliest known victim of the pandemic in the United States.

AT&T Park, home of the San Francisco Giants major league baseball team, was completed in 2000, and the Giants won the World Series in 2010, 2012, and 2014. The city offers excellent convention facilities with its Moscone Center, where a third building, Moscone West, was completed in 2003, bringing exhibit space to 770,000 square feet. The center was named for Mayor George Moscone, who championed controversial causes and who was murdered in office in 1978, along with gay activist Harvey Milk. The film, *The Times of Harvey Milk* won the 2008 Academy Award for best picture.

The Fine Arts Museums of San Francisco include the de Young, which is the city's oldest museum, and the Legion of Honor, a beautiful Beaux-arts museum that is home to Rodin's *Thinker*. In 2005, the de Young Museum reopened in a new building in Golden Gate Park, replacing an earlier structure damaged by the 1989 earthquake.

Also damaged in that quake was the main facility of the California Academy of Sciences, which oversees the Steinhart Aquarium, the Morrison Planetarium and the Natural History Museum. The California Academy of Sciences, also located in Golden Gate Park was reopened in 2008. Architect Renzo Piano designed the building to be seismically safe, green and sustainable. Dedicated to the study of art and science, the building allows outside views from nearly anywhere inside.

San Francisco is known as the "Air-Conditioned City" with cool pleasant summers and mild winters. It has greater climatic variability than any other urban area of the same size in the country. Sea fogs and associated low stratus clouds are most common in the summertime.

Rankings

General Rankings

- *US News & World Report* conducted a survey of more than 3,000 people and analyzed the 150 largest metropolitan areas to determine what matters most when selecting the next place to live. San Francisco ranked #10 out of the top 25 as having the best combination of desirable factors. Criteria: cost of living; quality of life; net migration; job market; desirability; and other factors. *realestate.usnews.com, "The 25 Best Places to Live in the U.S. in 2020-21," October 13, 2020*

- The San Francisco metro area was identified as one of America's fastest-growing areas in terms of population and business growth by *MagnifyMoney*. The area ranked #22 out of 35. The 100 most populous metro areas in the U.S. were evaluated on their change from 2011-2016 in the following categories: people and housing; workforce and employment opportunities; growing industry. *www.businessinsider.com, "The 35 Cities in the US with the Biggest Influx of People, the Most Work Opportunities, and the Hottest Business Growth," August 12, 2018*

- In its eighth annual survey, *Travel + Leisure* readers nominated their favorite small cities and towns in America—those with 100,000 or fewer residents—voting on numerous attractive features in categories including culture, food and drink, quality of life, style, and people. After 50,000 votes, San Francisco was ranked #5 among the proposed favorites. *www.travelandleisure.com, "America's Favorite Cities," October 20, 2017*

- The human resources consulting firm Mercer ranked 231 major cities worldwide in terms of overall quality of life. San Francisco ranked #34. Criteria: political, social, economic, and socio-cultural factors; medical and health considerations; schools and education; public services and transportation; recreation; consumer goods; housing; and natural environment. *Mercer, "Mercer 2019 Quality of Living Survey," March 13, 2019*

Business/Finance Rankings

- According to *Business Insider*, the San Francisco metro area is a prime place to run a startup or move an existing business to. The area ranked #2. Nearly 190 metro areas were analyzed on overall economic health and investments. Data was based on the 2019 U.S. Census Bureau American Community Survey, the marketing company PitchBook, Bureau of Labor Statistics employment report, and Zillow. Criteria: percentage of change in typical home values and employment rates; quarterly venture capital investment activity; and median household income. *www.businessinsider.com, "The 25 Best Cities to Start a Business-Or Move Your Current One," January 12, 2021*

- The Brookings Institution ranked the nation's largest cities based on income inequality. San Francisco was ranked #6 (#1 = greatest inequality). Criteria: the "95/20 ratio," a figure representing the income at which a household earns more than 95 percent of all other households, divided by the income at which a household earns more than only 20 percent of all other households. *Brookings Institution, "Household Income Inequality, Largest Cities of 97 Large U.S. Metro Areas, 2014-2016," February 5, 2018*

- The Brookings Institution ranked the 100 largest metro areas in the U.S. based on income inequality. San Francisco was ranked #3 (#1 = greatest inequality). Criteria: the "95/20 ratio," a figure representing the income at which a household earns more than 95 percent of all other households, divided by the income at which a household earns more than only 20 percent of all other households. *Brookings Institution, "Household Income Inequality, 100 Largest U.S. Metro Areas, 2014-2016," February 5, 2018*

- *Forbes* ranked the 100 largest metro areas in the U.S. in terms of the "Best Cities for Young Professionals." The San Francisco metro area ranked #4 out of 25. Criteria: median rent of a two-bedroom apartment; job growth and unemployment rate; median salary of college graduates with 5 or less years of work experience; networking opportunities; social outlook; percentage of population 25 years of age and older with college degrees. *Forbes.com, "America's 25 Best Cities for Young Professionals in 2017," May 22, 2017*

- Payscale.com ranked the 32 largest metro areas in terms of wage growth. The San Francisco metro area ranked #15. Criteria: private-sector and education professional wage growth between the 4th quarter of 2019 and the 4th quarter of 2020. *PayScale, "Wage Trends by Metro Area-4th Quarter," January 11, 2021*

- The San Francisco metro area was identified as one of the most debt-ridden places in America by the finance site Credit.com. The metro area was ranked #15. Criteria: residents' average credit card debt as well as median income. *Credit.com, "25 Cities With the Most Credit Card Debt," February 28, 2018*

- For its annual survey of the "Most Expensive U.S. Cities to Live In," Kiplinger applied Cost of Living Index statistics developed by the Council for Community and Economic Research to U.S. Census Bureau population and median household income data for 256 urban areas. San Francisco was among the 20 most expensive in the country. *Kiplinger.com, "The 20 Most Expensive Cities in the U.S.," July 29, 2020*

- San Francisco was identified as one of America's most frugal metro areas by *Coupons.com.* The city ranked #14 out of 25. Criteria: digital coupon usage. *Coupons.com, "America's Most Frugal Cities of 2017," March 22, 2018*

- San Francisco was identified as one of the happiest cities to work in by CareerBliss.com, an online community for career advancement. The city ranked #1 out of 10. Criteria: an employee's relationship with his or her boss and co-workers; daily tasks; general work environment; compensation; opportunities for advancement; company culture and job reputation; and resources. *Businesswire.com, "CareerBliss Happiest Cities to Work 2019," February 12, 2019*

- The San Francisco metro area appeared on the Milken Institute "2021 Best Performing Cities" list. Rank: #24 out of 200 large metro areas (population over 250,000). Criteria: job growth; wage and salary growth; high-tech output growth; housing affordability; household broadband access. *Milken Institute, "Best-Performing Cities 2021," February 16, 2021*

- *Forbes* ranked the 200 most populous metro areas to determine the nation's "Best Places for Business and Careers." The San Francisco metro area was ranked #18. Criteria: costs (business and living); job growth (past and projected); income growth; quality of life; educational attainment (college and high school); projected economic growth; cultural and leisure opportunities; workplace tolerance laws; net migration patterns. *Forbes, "The Best Places for Business and Careers 2019: Seattle Still On Top," October 30, 2019*

- Mercer Human Resources Consulting ranked 209 cities worldwide in terms of cost-of-living. San Francisco ranked #16 (the lower the ranking, the higher the cost-of-living). The survey measured the comparative cost of over 200 items (such as housing, food, clothing, household goods, transportation, and entertainment) in each location. *Mercer, "2020 Cost of Living Survey," June 9, 2020*

Children/Family Rankings

- San Francisco was selected as one of the most playful cities in the U.S. by KaBOOM! The organization's Playful City USA initiative honors cities and towns across the nation that have made their communities more playable. Criteria: pledging to integrate play as a solution to challenges in their communities; making it easy for children to get active and balanced play; creating more family-friendly and innovative communities as a result. *KaBOOM! National Campaign for Play, "2017 Playful City USA Communities"*

Education Rankings

- Personal finance website *WalletHub* analyzed the 150 largest U.S. metropolitan statistical areas to determine where the most educated Americans are putting their degrees to work. Criteria: education levels; percentage of workers with degrees; education quality and attainment gap; public school quality rankings; quality and enrollment of each metro area's universities. San Francisco was ranked #5 (#1 = most educated city). *www.WalletHub.com, "Most and Least Educated Cities in America," July 20, 2020*

- San Francisco was selected as one of America's most literate cities. The city ranked #3 out of the 84 largest U.S. cities. Criteria: number of booksellers; library resources; Internet resources; educational attainment; periodical publishing resources; newspaper circulation. *Central Connecticut State University, "America's Most Literate Cities, 2018," February 2019*

Environmental Rankings

- Sperling's BestPlaces assessed the 50 largest metropolitan areas of the United States for the likelihood of dangerously extreme weather events or earthquakes. In general the Southeast and South-Central regions have the highest risk of weather extremes and earthquakes, while the Pacific Northwest enjoys the lowest risk. Of the least risky metropolitan areas, the San Francisco metro area was ranked #4. *www.bestplaces.net, "Avoid Natural Disasters: BestPlaces Reveals The Top 10 Safest Places to Live," October 25, 2017*

- The U.S. Environmental Protection Agency (EPA) released a list of U.S. metropolitan areas with the most ENERGY STAR certified buildings in 2019. The San Francisco metro area was ranked #3 out of 25. *U.S. Environmental Protection Agency, "2020 Energy Star Top Cities," March 2020*

Food/Drink Rankings

- The U.S. Chamber of Commerce Foundation conducted an in-depth study on local food truck regulations, surveyed 288 food truck owners, and ranked 20 major American cities based on how friendly they are for operating a food truck. The compiled index assessed the following: procedures for obtaining permits and licenses; complying with restrictions; and financial obligations associated with operating a food truck. San Francisco ranked #18 overall (1 being the best). *www.foodtrucknation.us, "Food Truck Nation," March 20, 2018*

- Oracle Park was selected as one of PETA's "Top 10 Vegan-Friendly Ballparks" for 2019. The park ranked #4. *People for the Ethical Treatment of Animals, "Top 10 Vegan-Friendly Ballparks," May 23, 2019*

Health/Fitness Rankings

- The Sharecare Community Well-Being Index evaluates 10 individual and social health factors in order to measure what matters to Americans in the co mmunities in which they live. The San Francisco metro area was one of the five communities where social determinants of health were the highest. Criteria: access to food, healthcare, and community resources; housing and transportation; economic security. The area ranked #0. *www.sharecare.com, "Community Well-Being Index: 2019 Metro Area & County Rankings Report," August 31, 2020*

- For each of the 100 largest cities in the United States, the American Fitness Index®, published by the American College of Sports Medicine and the Anthem Foundation, evaluated community infrastructure and 33 health behaviors including preventive health, levels of chronic disease conditions, pedestrian safety, air quality, and community resources that support physical activity. San Francisco ranked #5 for "community fitness." *americanfitnessindex.org, "2020 ACSM American Fitness Index Summary Report," July 14, 2020*

- San Francisco was identified as one of the 10 most walkable cities in the U.S. by Walk Score. The city ranked #2. Walk Score measures walkability by analyzing hundreds of walking routes to nearby amenities, and also measures pedestrian friendliness by analyzing population density and road metrics such as block length and intersection density. *WalkScore.com, April 13, 2021*

- The San Francisco metro area was identified as one of the worst cities for bed bugs in America by pest control company Orkin. The area ranked #22 out of 50 based on the number of bed bug treatments Orkin performed from December 2019 to November 2020. *Orkin, "New Year, New Top City on Orkin's 2021 Bed Bug Cities List: Chicago," February 1, 2021*

- San Francisco was identified as a "2021 Spring Allergy Capital." The area ranked #86 out of 100. Three groups of factors were used to identify the most challenging cities for people with allergies during the spring season: annual spring pollen levels; over the counter medicine use; number of board-certified allergy specialists. *Asthma and Allergy Foundation of America, "Spring Allergy Capitals 2021," February 23, 2021*

- San Francisco was identified as a "2021 Fall Allergy Capital." The area ranked #92 out of 100. Three groups of factors were used to identify the most challenging cities for people with allergies during the fall season: annual fall pollen levels; over the counter medicine use; number of board-certified allergy specialists. *Asthma and Allergy Foundation of America, "Fall Allergy Capitals 2021," February 23, 2021*

- San Francisco was identified as a "2019 Asthma Capital." The area ranked #73 out of the nation's 100 largest metropolitan areas. Criteria: estimated asthma prevalence; crude death rate from asthma; and ER visits due to asthma. Risk factors analyzed but not factored in the rankings: annual pollen score; annual air quality; public smoking laws; number of board-certified asthma specialists; rescue medication use; controller medication use; uninsured rate; poverty rate. *Asthma and Allergy Foundation of America, "Asthma Capitals 2019: The Most Challenging Places to Live With Asthma," May 7, 2019*

- The Sharecare Community Well-Being Index evaluates 10 individual and social health factors in order to measure what matters to Americans in the communities in which they live. The San Francisco metro area ranked #1 in the top 10 across all 10 domains. Criteria: access to healthcare, food, and community resources; housng and transportation; economic security; feeling of purpose; physical, financial, social, and community well-being. *www.sharecare.com, "Community Well-Being Index: 2019 Metro Area & County Rankings Report," August 31, 2020*

Pet Rankings

- San Francisco appeared on *The Dogington Post* site as one of the top cities for dog lovers, ranking #9 out of 20. The real estate brokerage, Redfin and Rover, the largest pet sitter and dog walker network, compiled a list from over 14,000 U.S. cities to come up with a "Rover Rank." Criteria: highest count of dog walks, the city's Walk Score®, for-sale home listings that mention "dog," number of dog walkers and pet sitters and the hours spent and distance logged. *www.dogingtonpost.com, "The 20 Most Dog-Friendly Cities of 2019," April 4, 2019*

Real Estate Rankings

- FitSmallBusiness looked at 50 of the largest metropolitan areas in the U.S. to determine which metro was the best to start a real estate business. Data was compiled from such sources as: Zillow, Trulia, U.S. Census Bureau, and the Bureau of Labor Statistics. Criteria: location; inventory; annual wages; median sales price of homes; days on the market; median price cut percentage; and other factors that would influence real estate professional growth. The San Francisco metro area ranked #3. *fitsmallbusiness.com, "The Best Cities to Become a Real Estate Agent in 2018," January 30, 2018*

- *WalletHub* compared the most populated U.S. cities to determine which had the best markets for real estate agents. San Francisco ranked #3 where demand was high and pay was the best. Criteria: sales per agent; annual median wage for real-estate agents; monthly average starting salary for real estate agents; real estate job density and competition; unemployment rate; home turnover rate; housing-market health index; and other relevant metrics. *www.WalletHub.com, "2019's Best Places to Be a Real Estate Agent," April 24, 2019*

- The San Francisco metro area was identified as one of the 10 worst condo markets in the U.S. in 2020. The area ranked #63 out of 63 markets. Criteria: year-over-year change of median sales price of existing apartment condo-coop homes between the 4th quarter of 2019 and the 4th quarter of 2020. *National Association of Realtors®, Median Sales Price of Existing Apartment Condo-Coops Homes for Metropolitan Areas, 4th Quarter 2020*

- The San Francisco metro area was identified as one of the 20 least affordable housing markets in the U.S. in 2020. The area ranked #182 out of 183 markets. Criteria: qualification for a mortgage loan with a 10 percent down payment on a typical home. *National Association of Realtors®, Qualifying Income Based on Sales Price of Existing Single-Family Homes for Metropolitan Areas, 2020*

- San Francisco was ranked #267 out of 268 metro areas in terms of housing affordability in 2020 by the National Association of Home Builders (#1 = most affordable). Criteria: the share of homes sold in that area affordable to a family earning the local median income, based on standard mortgage underwriting criteria. *National Association of Home Builders®, NAHB-Wells Fargo Housing Opportunity Index, 4th Quarter 2020*

Safety Rankings

- Allstate ranked the 200 largest cities in America in terms of driver safety. San Francisco ranked #189. Criteria: internal property damage claims over a two-year period from January 2016 to December 2017. The report helps increase the importance of safety and awareness behind the wheel. *Allstate, "Allstate America's Best Drivers Report, 2019" June 24, 2019*

- The National Insurance Crime Bureau ranked 384 metro areas in the U.S. in terms of per capita rates of vehicle theft. The San Francisco metro area ranked #14 (#1 = highest rate). Criteria: number of vehicle theft offenses per 100,000 inhabitants in 2019. *National Insurance Crime Bureau, "Hot Spots 2019," July 21, 2020*

Seniors/Retirement Rankings

- From its Best Cities for Successful Aging indexes, the Milken Institute generated rankings for metropolitan areas, weighing data in nine categories—health care, wellness, living arrangements, transportation and convenience, financial characteristics, education, employment, community engagement, and overall livability. The San Francisco metro area was ranked #11 overall in the large metro area category. *Milken Institute, "Best Cities for Successful Aging, 2017" March 14, 2017*

Sports/Recreation Rankings

- San Francisco was chosen as one of America's best cities for bicycling. The city ranked #2 out of 50. Criteria: cycling infrastructure that is safe and friendly for all ages; energy and bike culture. The editors evaluated cities with populations of 100,000 or more. *Bicycling, "The 50 Best Bike Cities in America," October 10, 2018*

Transportation Rankings

- Business Insider presented an AllTransit Performance Score ranking of public transportation in major U.S. cities and towns, with populations over 250,000, in which San Francisco earned the #1-ranked "Transit Score," awarded for frequency of service, access to jobs, quality and number of stops, and affordability. *www.businessinsider.com, "The 17 Major U.S. Cities with the Best Public Transportation," April 17, 2018*

- The business website 24/7 Wall Street reviewed U.S. Census data to identify the 25 cities where the largest share of households do not own a vehicle. San Francisco held the #10 position. *247wallst.com, "Cities Where No One Wants to Drive," February 15, 2017*

- San Francisco was identified as one of the most congested metro areas in the U.S. The area ranked #2 out of 10. Criteria: yearly delay per auto commuter in hours. *Texas A&M Transportation Institute, "2019 Urban Mobility Report," December 2019*

- According to the INRIX "2019 Global Traffic Scorecard," San Francisco was identified as one of the most congested metro areas in the U.S. The area ranked #7 out of 10. Criteria: average annual time spent in traffic and average cost of congestion per motorist. *Inrix.com, "Congestion Costs Each American Nearly 100 hours, $1,400 A Year," March 9, 2020*

Women/Minorities Rankings

- *24/7 Wall St.* compared median annual earnings for men and women who worked full-time, year-round, female employment in management roles, bachelor's degree attainment among women, female life expectancy, uninsured rates, and preschool enrollment to identify the best cities for women. The U.S. metropolitan area, San Francisco was ranked #4 in pay disparity and other gender gaps. *24/7 Wall St., "The Easiest (and Toughest) Cities to Be a Woman," January 11, 2020*

- San Francisco was selected as one of the gayest cities in America by *The Advocate*. The city ranked #17 out of 25. Criteria, among many: Trans Pride parades/festivals; gay rugby teams; lesbian bars; LGBT centers; theater screenings of "Moonlight"; LGBT-inclusive nondiscrimination ordinances; and gay bowling teams. *The Advocate, "Queerest Cities in America 2017" January 12, 2017*

- Personal finance website *WalletHub* compared more than 180 U.S. cities across two key dimensions, "Hispanic Business-Friendliness" and "Hispanic Purchasing Power," to arrive at the most favorable conditions for Hispanic entrepreneurs. San Francisco was ranked #87 out of 182. Criteria includes: share of Hispanic-Owned Businesses; Hispanic entrepreneurship rate to median annual income of Hispanics; Small Business-Friendliness score; cost of living; and number of Hispanics with at least a bachelor's degree. *WalletHub.com, "2019's Best Cities for Hispanic Entrepreneurs," May 1, 2019*

Miscellaneous Rankings

- *MoveHub* ranked 446 hipster cities across 20 countries, using its *alternative* Hipster Index and San Francisco came out as #15 among the top 50. Criteria: population over 150,000; number of vintage boutiques; density of tattoo parlors; vegan places to eat; coffee shops; and density of vinyl record stores. *www.movehub.com, "The Hipster Index: Brighton Pips Portland to Global Top Spot," February 20, 2020*

- In its roundup of St. Patrick's Day parades "Gayot" listed the best festivals and parades of all things Irish. The festivities in San Francisco as among the best. *www.gayot.com, "Best St. Patrick's Day Parades," March 2020*

- The watchdog site, Charity Navigator, conducted a study of charities in major markets both to analyze statistical differences in their financial, accountability, and transparency practices and to track year-to-year variations in individual philanthropic communities. The San Francisco metro area was ranked #16 among the 30 metro markets in the rating category of Overall Score. *www.charitynavigator.org, "2017 Metro Market Study," May 1, 2017*

- *WalletHub* compared the 150 most populated U.S. cities to determine their operating efficiency. A "Quality of City Services" score was constructed for each city and then divided by the total budget per capita to reveal which were managed the best. San Francisco ranked #149. Criteria: financial stability; economy; education; safety; health; infrastructure and pollution. *www.WalletHub.com, "2020's Best- & Worst-Run Cities in America," June 29, 2020*

- The National Alliance to End Homelessness listed the 25 most populous metro areas with the highest rate of homelessness. The San Francisco metro area had a high rate of homelessness. Criteria: number of homeless people per 10,000 population in 2016. *National Alliance to End Homelessness, "Homelessness in the 25 Most Populous U.S. Metro Areas," September 1, 2017*

Business Environment

DEMOGRAPHICS

Population Growth

Area	1990 Census	2000 Census	2010 Census	2019* Estimate	Population Growth (%) 1990-2019	Population Growth (%) 2010-2019
City	723,959	776,733	805,235	874,961	20.9	8.7
MSA[1]	3,686,592	4,123,740	4,335,391	4,701,332	27.5	8.4
U.S.	248,709,873	281,421,906	308,745,538	324,697,795	30.6	5.2

Note: (1) Figures cover the San Francisco-Oakland-Hayward, CA Metropolitan Statistical Area; (*) 2015-2019 5-year estimated population
Source: U.S. Census Bureau, 1990 Census, Census 2000, Census 2010, 2015-2019 American Community Survey 5-Year Estimates

Household Size

Area	Persons in Household (%) One	Two	Three	Four	Five	Six	Seven or More	Average Household Size
City	35.6	33.7	14.4	9.8	3.8	1.4	1.4	2.40
MSA[1]	26.2	31.9	17.0	14.8	6.1	2.3	1.7	2.70
U.S.	27.9	33.9	15.6	12.9	6.0	2.3	1.4	2.60

Note: (1) Figures cover the San Francisco-Oakland-Hayward, CA Metropolitan Statistical Area
Source: U.S. Census Bureau, 2015-2019 American Community Survey 5-Year Estimates

Race

Area	White Alone[2] (%)	Black Alone[2] (%)	Asian Alone[2] (%)	AIAN[3] Alone[2] (%)	NHOPI[4] Alone[2] (%)	Other Race Alone[2] (%)	Two or More Races (%)
City	46.4	5.2	34.4	0.4	0.4	7.7	5.6
MSA[1]	49.0	7.3	26.1	0.5	0.7	10.2	6.2
U.S.	72.5	12.7	5.5	0.8	0.2	4.9	3.3

Note: (1) Figures cover the San Francisco-Oakland-Hayward, CA Metropolitan Statistical Area; (2) Alone is defined as not being in combination with one or more other races; (3) American Indian and Alaska Native; (4) Native Hawaiian and Other Pacific Islander
Source: U.S. Census Bureau, 2015-2019 American Community Survey 5-Year Estimates

Hispanic or Latino Origin

Area	Total (%)	Mexican (%)	Puerto Rican (%)	Cuban (%)	Other (%)
City	15.2	7.8	0.6	0.3	6.6
MSA[1]	21.8	14.2	0.7	0.2	6.7
U.S.	18.0	11.2	1.7	0.7	4.3

Note: Persons of Hispanic or Latino origin can be of any race; (1) Figures cover the San Francisco-Oakland-Hayward, CA Metropolitan Statistical Area
Source: U.S. Census Bureau, 2015-2019 American Community Survey 5-Year Estimates

Ancestry

Area	German	Irish	English	American	Italian	Polish	French[2]	Scottish	Dutch
City	7.1	7.7	5.1	2.8	4.5	1.8	2.3	1.4	0.8
MSA[1]	7.6	7.2	5.7	2.4	4.7	1.5	1.9	1.5	0.8
U.S.	13.3	9.7	7.2	6.2	5.1	2.8	2.3	1.7	1.2

Note: Figures are the percentage of the total population reporting a particular ancestry. The nine most commonly reported ancestries in the U.S. are shown. Figures include multiple ancestries (e.g. if a person reported being Irish and Italian, they were included in both columns); (1) Figures cover the San Francisco-Oakland-Hayward, CA Metropolitan Statistical Area; (2) Excludes Basque
Source: U.S. Census Bureau, 2015-2019 American Community Survey 5-Year Estimates

Foreign-born Population

Area	Percent of Population Born in Any Foreign Country	Asia	Mexico	Europe	Caribbean	Central America[2]	South America	Africa	Canada
City	34.3	22.2	2.4	4.5	0.2	2.5	1.0	0.5	0.6
MSA[1]	30.7	17.5	4.9	2.9	0.2	2.5	1.0	0.7	0.5
U.S.	13.6	4.2	3.5	1.5	1.3	1.1	1.0	0.7	0.2

Note: (1) Figures cover the San Francisco-Oakland-Hayward, CA Metropolitan Statistical Area; (2) Excludes Mexico.
Source: U.S. Census Bureau, 2015-2019 American Community Survey 5-Year Estimates

Marital Status

Area	Never Married	Now Married[2]	Separated	Widowed	Divorced
City	45.8	40.3	1.3	4.6	7.9
MSA[1]	36.3	48.7	1.5	4.7	8.8
U.S.	33.4	48.1	1.9	5.8	10.9

Note: Figures are percentages and cover the population 15 years of age and older; (1) Figures cover the San Francisco-Oakland-Hayward, CA Metropolitan Statistical Area; (2) Excludes separated
Source: U.S. Census Bureau, 2015-2019 American Community Survey 5-Year Estimates

Disability by Age

Area	All Ages	Under 18 Years Old	18 to 64 Years Old	65 Years and Over
City	10.2	2.3	6.3	35.2
MSA[1]	9.7	2.9	6.8	31.5
U.S.	12.6	4.2	10.3	34.5

Note: Figures show percent of the civilian noninstitutionalized population that reported having a disability. Disability status is determined from six types of difficulty: vision, hearing, cognitive, ambulatory, self-care, and independent living. For children under 5 years old, hearing and vision difficulty are used to determine disability status. For children between the ages of 5 and 14, disability status is determined from hearing, vision, cognitive, ambulatory, and self-care difficulties. For people aged 15 years and older, they are considered to have a disability if they have difficulty with any one of the six difficulty types; Note: (1) Figures cover the San Francisco-Oakland-Hayward, CA Metropolitan Statistical Area
Source: U.S. Census Bureau, 2015-2019 American Community Survey 5-Year Estimates

Age

Area	Percent of Population									Median Age
	Under Age 5	Age 5–19	Age 20–34	Age 35–44	Age 45–54	Age 55–64	Age 65–74	Age 75–84	Age 85+	
City	4.5	10.5	29.0	15.8	13.2	11.6	8.5	4.5	2.5	38.2
MSA[1]	5.5	16.5	22.0	14.5	13.8	12.6	8.7	4.4	2.1	39.0
U.S.	6.1	19.1	20.7	12.6	13.0	12.9	9.1	4.6	1.9	38.1

Note: (1) Figures cover the San Francisco-Oakland-Hayward, CA Metropolitan Statistical Area
Source: U.S. Census Bureau, 2015-2019 American Community Survey 5-Year Estimates

Gender

Area	Males	Females	Males per 100 Females
City	446,286	428,675	104.1
MSA[1]	2,325,587	2,375,745	97.9
U.S.	159,886,919	164,810,876	97.0

Note: (1) Figures cover the San Francisco-Oakland-Hayward, CA Metropolitan Statistical Area
Source: U.S. Census Bureau, 2015-2019 American Community Survey 5-Year Estimates

Religious Groups by Family

Area	Catholic	Baptist	Non-Den.	Methodist[2]	Lutheran	LDS[3]	Pentecostal	Presbyterian[4]	Muslim[5]	Judaism
MSA[1]	20.8	2.5	2.5	2.0	0.6	1.6	1.2	1.1	1.2	0.9
U.S.	19.1	9.3	4.0	4.0	2.3	2.0	1.9	1.6	0.8	0.7

Note: Figures are the number of adherents as a percentage of the total population; (1) Figures cover the San Francisco-Oakland-Hayward, CA Metropolitan Statistical Area; (2) Methodist/Pietist; (3) Latter Day Saints; (4) Reformed; (5) Figures are estimates
Source: Association of Statisticians of American Religious Bodies, 2010 U.S. Religion Census: Religious Congregations & Membership Study

Religious Groups by Tradition

Area	Catholic	Evangelical Protestant	Mainline Protestant	Other Tradition	Black Protestant	Orthodox
MSA[1]	20.8	6.2	3.8	5.2	1.1	0.7
U.S.	19.1	16.2	7.3	4.3	1.6	0.3

Note: Figures are the number of adherents as a percentage of the total population; (1) Figures cover the San Francisco-Oakland-Hayward, CA Metropolitan Statistical Area
Source: Association of Statisticians of American Religious Bodies, 2010 U.S. Religion Census: Religious Congregations & Membership Study

ECONOMY

Gross Metropolitan Product

Area	2017	2018	2019	2020	Rank[2]
MSA[1]	512.2	547.3	578.7	605.5	6

Note: Figures are in billions of dollars; (1) Figures cover the San Francisco-Oakland-Hayward, CA Metropolitan Statistical Area; (2) Rank is based on 2018 data and ranges from 1 to 381
Source: U.S. Conference of Mayors, U.S. Metro Economies: GMP & Employment 2018-2020, September 2019

Economic Growth

Area	2015-17 (%)	2018 (%)	2019 (%)	2020 (%)	Rank[2]
MSA[1]	4.8	5.1	4.3	2.5	18
U.S.	1.9	2.9	2.3	2.1	–

Note: Figures are real gross metropolitan product (GMP) growth rates and represent average annual percent change; (1) Figures cover the San Francisco-Oakland-Hayward, CA Metropolitan Statistical Area; (2) Rank is based on 2017 2-year average annual percent change and ranges from 1 to 381
Source: U.S. Conference of Mayors, U.S. Metro Economies: GMP & Employment 2018-2020, September 2019

Metropolitan Area Exports

Area	2014	2015	2016	2017	2018	2019	Rank[2]
MSA[1]	26,863.7	25,061.1	24,506.3	29,103.8	27,417.0	28,003.8	12

Note: Figures are in millions of dollars; (1) Figures cover the San Francisco-Oakland-Hayward, CA Metropolitan Statistical Area; (2) Rank is based on 2019 data and ranges from 1 to 386
Source: U.S. Department of Commerce, International Trade Administration, Office of Trade and Economic Analysis, Industry and Analysis, Exports by Metropolitan Area, data extracted March 24, 2021

Building Permits

Area	Single-Family			Multi-Family			Total		
	2018	2019	Pct. Chg.	2018	2019	Pct. Chg.	2018	2019	Pct. Chg.
City	28	22	-21.4	5,150	3,178	-38.3	5,178	3,200	-38.2
MSA[1]	4,048	4,076	0.7	13,373	9,805	-26.7	17,421	13,881	-20.3
U.S.	855,300	862,100	0.7	473,500	523,900	10.6	1,328,800	1,386,000	4.3

Note: (1) Figures cover the San Francisco-Oakland-Hayward, CA Metropolitan Statistical Area; Figures represent new, privately-owned housing units authorized (unadjusted data); All permit data are based on estimates with imputation
Source: U.S. Census Bureau, Manufacturing, Mining, and Construction Statistics, Building Permits, 2018, 2019

Bankruptcy Filings

Area	Business Filings			Nonbusiness Filings		
	2019	2020	% Chg.	2019	2020	% Chg.
San Francisco County	58	67	15.5	564	384	-31.9
U.S.	22,780	21,655	-4.9	752,160	522,808	-30.5

Note: Business filings include Chapter 7, Chapter 9, Chapter 11, Chapter 12, Chapter 13, Chapter 15, and Section 304; Nonbusiness filings include Chapter 7, Chapter 11, and Chapter 13
Source: Administrative Office of the U.S. Courts, Business and Nonbusiness Bankruptcy, County Cases Commenced by Chapter of the Bankruptcy Code, During the 12-Month Period Ending December 31, 2019 and Business and Nonbusiness Bankruptcy, County Cases Commenced by Chapter of the Bankruptcy Code, During the 12-Month Period Ending December 31, 2020

Housing Vacancy Rates

Area	Gross Vacancy Rate[2] (%)			Year-Round Vacancy Rate[3] (%)			Rental Vacancy Rate[4] (%)			Homeowner Vacancy Rate[5] (%)		
	2018	2019	2020	2018	2019	2020	2018	2019	2020	2018	2019	2020
MSA[1]	7.5	7.1	6.4	7.4	6.9	6.2	5.4	3.8	5.3	0.9	0.9	0.5
U.S.	12.3	12.0	10.6	9.7	9.5	8.2	6.9	6.7	6.3	1.5	1.4	1.0

Note: (1) Figures cover the San Francisco-Oakland-Hayward, CA Metropolitan Statistical Area; (2) The percentage of the total housing inventory that is vacant; (3) The percentage of the housing inventory (excluding seasonal units) that is year-round vacant; (4) The percentage of rental inventory that is vacant for rent; (5) The percentage of homeowner inventory that is vacant for sale
Source: U.S. Census Bureau, Housing Vacancies and Homeownership Annual Statistics: 2018, 2019, 2020

INCOME

Income

Area	Per Capita ($)	Median Household ($)	Average Household ($)
City	68,883	112,449	160,396
MSA[1]	55,252	106,025	147,703
U.S.	34,103	62,843	88,607

Note: (1) Figures cover the San Francisco-Oakland-Hayward, CA Metropolitan Statistical Area
Source: U.S. Census Bureau, 2015-2019 American Community Survey 5-Year Estimates

Household Income Distribution

Area	Percent of Households Earning							
	Under $15,000	$15,000 -$24,999	$25,000 -$34,999	$35,000 -$49,999	$50,000 -$74,999	$75,000 -$99,999	$100,000 -$149,999	$150,000 and up
City	9.7	5.8	4.9	6.2	9.8	9.0	15.6	38.9
MSA[1]	7.2	5.2	5.2	7.2	11.7	11.0	17.5	35.0
U.S.	10.3	8.9	8.9	12.3	17.2	12.7	15.1	14.5

Note: (1) Figures cover the San Francisco-Oakland-Hayward, CA Metropolitan Statistical Area
Source: U.S. Census Bureau, 2015-2019 American Community Survey 5-Year Estimates

Poverty Rate

Area	All Ages	Under 18 Years Old	18 to 64 Years Old	65 Years and Over
City	10.3	10.0	9.7	13.6
MSA[1]	9.0	10.2	8.7	8.7
U.S.	13.4	18.5	12.6	9.3

Note: Figures are percentage of people whose income during the past 12 months was below the poverty level;
(1) Figures cover the San Francisco-Oakland-Hayward, CA Metropolitan Statistical Area
Source: U.S. Census Bureau, 2015-2019 American Community Survey 5-Year Estimates

CITY FINANCES

City Government Finances

Component	2017 ($000)	2017 ($ per capita)
Total Revenues	13,761,710	15,913
Total Expenditures	14,038,543	16,233
Debt Outstanding	16,803,807	19,431
Cash and Securities[1]	33,441,473	38,669

Note: (1) Cash and security holdings of a government at the close of its fiscal year,
including those of its dependent agencies, utilities, and liquor stores.
Source: U.S. Census Bureau, State & Local Government Finances 2017

City Government Revenue by Source

Source	2017 ($000)	2017 ($ per capita)	2017 (%)
General Revenue			
From Federal Government	528,207	611	3.8
From State Government	1,411,904	1,633	10.3
From Local Governments	1,045,782	1,209	7.6
Taxes			
Property	2,066,926	2,390	15.0
Sales and Gross Receipts	1,000,840	1,157	7.3
Personal Income	0	0	0.0
Corporate Income	0	0	0.0
Motor Vehicle License	4,550	5	0.0
Other Taxes	663,907	768	4.8
Current Charges	2,524,783	2,919	18.3
Liquor Store	0	0	0.0
Utility	735,208	850	5.3
Employee Retirement	3,047,707	3,524	22.1

Source: U.S. Census Bureau, State & Local Government Finances 2017

City Government Expenditures by Function

Function	2017 ($000)	2017 ($ per capita)	2017 (%)
General Direct Expenditures			
Air Transportation	1,106,391	1,279	7.9
Corrections	223,804	258	1.6
Education	0	0	0.0
Employment Security Administration	0	0	0.0
Financial Administration	60,623	70	0.4
Fire Protection	299,915	346	2.1
General Public Buildings	0	0	0.0
Governmental Administration, Other	346,047	400	2.5
Health	1,906,640	2,204	13.6
Highways	107,976	124	0.8
Hospitals	1,179,764	1,364	8.4
Housing and Community Development	413,032	477	2.9
Interest on General Debt	534,757	618	3.8
Judicial and Legal	129,854	150	0.9
Libraries	109,964	127	0.8
Parking	178,974	207	1.3
Parks and Recreation	259,240	299	1.8
Police Protection	524,927	607	3.7
Public Welfare	1,346,679	1,557	9.6
Sewerage	417,837	483	3.0
Solid Waste Management	0	0	0.0
Veterans' Services	0	0	0.0
Liquor Store	0	0	0.0
Utility	2,463,107	2,848	17.5
Employee Retirement	1,278,140	1,477	9.1

Source: U.S. Census Bureau, State & Local Government Finances 2017

EMPLOYMENT

Labor Force and Employment

Area	Civilian Labor Force			Workers Employed		
	Dec. 2019	Dec. 2020	% Chg.	Dec. 2019	Dec. 2020	% Chg.
City	589,286	566,193	-3.9	578,146	529,919	-8.3
MD[1]	1,054,065	1,010,523	-4.1	1,034,791	948,543	-8.3
U.S.	164,007,000	160,017,000	-2.4	158,504,000	149,613,000	-5.6

Note: Data is not seasonally adjusted and covers workers 16 years of age and older; (1) Figures cover the San Francisco-Redwood City-South San Francisco, CA Metropolitan Division
Source: Bureau of Labor Statistics, Local Area Unemployment Statistics

Unemployment Rate

Area	2020											
	Jan.	Feb.	Mar.	Apr.	May	Jun.	Jul.	Aug.	Sep.	Oct.	Nov.	Dec.
City	2.3	2.3	3.1	12.6	12.7	12.5	11.1	8.5	8.3	6.7	5.7	6.4
MD[1]	2.2	2.2	3.0	12.1	12.0	11.8	10.3	7.9	7.7	6.3	5.4	6.1
U.S.	4.0	3.8	4.5	14.4	13.0	11.2	10.5	8.5	7.7	6.6	6.4	6.5

Note: Data is not seasonally adjusted and covers workers 16 years of age and older; (1) Figures cover the San Francisco-Redwood City-South San Francisco, CA Metropolitan Division
Source: Bureau of Labor Statistics, Local Area Unemployment Statistics

Average Wages

Occupation	$/Hr.	Occupation	$/Hr.
Accountants and Auditors	48.60	Maintenance and Repair Workers	28.00
Automotive Mechanics	31.10	Marketing Managers	94.40
Bookkeepers	26.60	Network and Computer Systems Admin.	51.30
Carpenters	36.40	Nurses, Licensed Practical	35.80
Cashiers	16.60	Nurses, Registered	71.70
Computer Programmers	60.30	Nursing Assistants	23.30
Computer Systems Analysts	60.30	Office Clerks, General	23.80
Computer User Support Specialists	37.80	Physical Therapists	49.70
Construction Laborers	28.40	Physicians	90.10
Cooks, Restaurant	19.20	Plumbers, Pipefitters and Steamfitters	51.00
Customer Service Representatives	24.00	Police and Sheriff's Patrol Officers	58.90
Dentists	85.30	Postal Service Mail Carriers	26.60
Electricians	51.30	Real Estate Sales Agents	35.10
Engineers, Electrical	59.00	Retail Salespersons	18.20
Fast Food and Counter Workers	16.40	Sales Representatives, Technical/Scientific	57.00
Financial Managers	92.00	Secretaries, Exc. Legal/Medical/Executive	25.20
First-Line Supervisors of Office Workers	36.40	Security Guards	20.20
General and Operations Managers	78.00	Surgeons	120.50
Hairdressers/Cosmetologists	18.60	Teacher Assistants, Exc. Postsecondary*	19.30
Home Health and Personal Care Aides	16.60	Teachers, Secondary School, Exc. Sp. Ed.*	44.40
Janitors and Cleaners	20.30	Telemarketers	n/a
Landscaping/Groundskeeping Workers	21.70	Truck Drivers, Heavy/Tractor-Trailer	27.80
Lawyers	97.10	Truck Drivers, Light/Delivery Services	25.20
Maids and Housekeeping Cleaners	21.50	Waiters and Waitresses	19.60

Note: Wage data covers the San Francisco-Oakland-Hayward, CA Metropolitan Statistical Area; (*) Hourly wages were calculated from annual wage data based on a 40 hour work week; n/a not available.
Source: Bureau of Labor Statistics, Metro Area Occupational Employment & Wage Estimates, May 2020

Employment by Industry

Sector	MD[1]		U.S.
	Number of Employees	Percent of Total	Percent of Total
Construction	41,100	3.9	5.1
Education and Health Services	142,200	13.5	16.3
Financial Activities	83,000	7.9	6.1
Government	125,500	12.0	15.2
Information	108,300	10.3	1.9
Leisure and Hospitality	69,100	6.6	9.0
Manufacturing	36,400	3.5	8.5
Mining and Logging	100	<0.1	0.4
Other Services	30,700	2.9	3.8
Professional and Business Services	281,600	26.8	14.4
Retail Trade	70,200	6.7	10.9
Transportation, Warehousing, and Utilities	41,600	4.0	4.6
Wholesale Trade	20,100	1.9	3.9

Note: Figures are non-farm employment as of December 2020. Figures are not seasonally adjusted and include workers 16 years of age and older; (1) Figures cover the San Francisco-Redwood City-South San Francisco, CA Metropolitan Division
Source: Bureau of Labor Statistics, Current Employment Statistics, Employment, Hours, and Earnings

Employment by Occupation

Occupation Classification	City (%)	MSA[1] (%)	U.S. (%)
Management, Business, Science, and Arts	57.6	50.6	38.5
Natural Resources, Construction, and Maintenance	3.1	5.8	8.9
Production, Transportation, and Material Moving	5.9	8.3	13.2
Sales and Office	18.0	19.1	21.6
Service	15.4	16.2	17.8

Note: Figures cover employed civilians 16 years of age and older; (1) Figures cover the San Francisco-Oakland-Hayward, CA Metropolitan Statistical Area
Source: U.S. Census Bureau, 2015-2019 American Community Survey 5-Year Estimates

Occupations with Greatest Projected Employment Growth: 2020 – 2022

Occupation[1]	2020 Employment	2022 Projected Employment	Numeric Employment Change	Percent Employment Change
Retail Salespersons	317,300	401,300	84,000	26.5
Laborers and Freight, Stock, and Material Movers, Hand	348,700	411,100	62,400	17.9
Waiters and Waitresses	182,500	242,800	60,300	33.0
Combined Food Preparation and Serving Workers, Including Fast Food	183,800	237,200	53,400	29.1
Cashiers	358,500	407,300	48,800	13.6
Cooks, Restaurant	113,200	156,500	43,300	38.3
Personal Care Aides	409,600	447,900	38,300	9.4
Farmworkers and Laborers, Crop, Nursery, and Greenhouse	242,000	269,700	27,700	11.4
Fast Food and Counter Workers	94,000	120,200	26,200	27.9
General and Operations Managers	242,700	268,300	25,600	10.5

Note: Projections cover California; (1) Sorted by numeric employment change
Source: www.projectionscentral.com, State Occupational Projections, 2020–2022 Short-Term Projections

Fastest-Growing Occupations: 2020 – 2022

Occupation[1]	2020 Employment	2022 Projected Employment	Numeric Employment Change	Percent Employment Change
Manicurists and Pedicurists	7,800	21,300	13,500	173.1
Hairdressers, Hairstylists, and Cosmetologists	22,700	44,600	21,900	96.5
Massage Therapists	8,800	17,100	8,300	94.3
Skincare Specialists	5,500	9,100	3,600	65.5
Dental Hygienists	9,200	14,700	5,500	59.8
Dental Hygienists (SOC 2018)	5,300	8,400	3,100	58.5
Dental Assistants	36,300	56,300	20,000	55.1
Dentists, General	12,600	19,000	6,400	50.8
Parking Lot Attendants	14,300	20,400	6,100	42.7
Lodging Managers	3,300	4,600	1,300	39.4

Note: Projections cover California; (1) Sorted by percent employment change and excludes occupations with numeric employment change less than 50
Source: www.projectionscentral.com, State Occupational Projections, 2020–2022 Short-Term Projections

TAXES

State Corporate Income Tax Rates

State	Tax Rate (%)	Income Brackets ($)	Num. of Brackets	Financial Institution Tax Rate (%)[a]	Federal Income Tax Ded.
California	8.84 (b)	Flat rate	1	10.84 (b)	No

Note: Tax rates as of January 1, 2021; (a) Rates listed are the corporate income tax rate applied to financial institutions or excise taxes based on income. Some states have other taxes based upon the value of deposits or shares; (b) Minimum tax is $800 in California, $250 in District of Columbia, $50 in Arizona and North Dakota (banks), $400 ($100 banks) in Rhode Island, $200 per location in South Dakota (banks), $100 in Utah, $300 in Vermont.
Source: Federation of Tax Administrators, State Corporate Income Tax Rates, January 1, 2021

State Individual Income Tax Rates

State	Tax Rate (%)	Income Brackets ($)	Personal Exemptions ($)			Standard Ded. ($)	
			Single	Married	Depend.	Single	Married
California (a)	1.0 - 12.3 (g)	8,932 - 599,012 (b)	124	248 (c)	383 (c)	4,601	9,202 (a)

Note: Tax rates as of January 1, 2021; Local- and county-level taxes are not included; Federal income tax is not deductible on state income tax returns; (a) 19 states have statutory provision for automatically adjusting to the rate of inflation the dollar values of the income tax brackets, standard deductions, and/or personal exemptions. Michigan indexes the personal exemption only. Oregon does not index the income brackets for $125,000 and over; (b) For joint returns, taxes are twice the tax on half the couple's income; (c) The personal exemption takes the form of a tax credit instead of a deduction; (g) California imposes an additional 1% tax on taxable income over $1 million, making the maximum rate 13.3% over $1 million.
Source: Federation of Tax Administrators, State Individual Income Tax Rates, January 1, 2021

Various State Sales and Excise Tax Rates

State	State Sales Tax (%)	Gasoline[1] (¢/gal.)	Cigarette[2] ($/pack)	Spirits[3] ($/gal.)	Wine[4] ($/gal.)	Beer[5] ($/gal.)	Recreational Marijuana (%)
California	7.25	63.05	2.87	3.3	0.2	0.2	(c)

Note: All tax rates as of January 1, 2021; (1) The American Petroleum Institute has developed a methodology for determining the average tax rate on a gallon of fuel. Rates may include any of the following: excise taxes, environmental fees, storage tank fees, other fees or taxes, general sales tax, and local taxes; (2) The federal excise tax of $1.0066 per pack and local taxes are not included; (3) Rates are those applicable to off-premise sales of 40% alcohol by volume (a.b.v.) distilled spirits in 750ml containers. Local excise taxes are excluded; (4) Rates are those applicable to off-premise sales of 11% a.b.v. non-carbonated wine in 750ml containers; (5) Rates are those applicable to off-premise sales of 4.7% a.b.v. beer in 12 ounce containers; (c) 15% excise tax (levied on wholesale at average market rate); $9.65/oz. flowers & $2.87/oz. leaves cultivation tax; $1.35/oz fresh cannabis plant
Source: Tax Foundation, 2021 Facts & Figures: How Does Your State Compare?

State Business Tax Climate Index Rankings

State	Overall Rank	Corporate Tax Rank	Individual Income Tax Rank	Sales Tax Rank	Property Tax Rank	Unemployment Insurance Tax Rank
California	49	28	49	45	14	21

Note: The index is a measure of how each state's tax laws affect economic performance. The lower the rank, the more favorable a state's tax system is for business. States without a given tax are given a ranking of 1. The scores/rankings for the District of Columbia do not affect other states. The 2021 index represents the tax climate as of July 1, 2020.
Source: Tax Foundation, State Business Tax Climate Index 2021

TRANSPORTATION

Means of Transportation to Work

Area	Car/Truck/Van		Public Transportation			Bicycle	Walked	Other Means	Worked at Home
	Drove Alone	Car-pooled	Bus	Subway	Railroad				
City	32.1	6.9	22.0	8.8	1.7	4.0	11.8	6.1	6.6
MSA[1]	57.6	9.5	7.6	7.6	1.5	1.9	4.7	3.0	6.6
U.S.	76.3	9.0	2.4	1.9	0.6	0.5	2.7	1.4	5.2

Note: Figures are percentages and cover workers 16 years of age and older; (1) Figures cover the San Francisco-Oakland-Hayward, CA Metropolitan Statistical Area
Source: U.S. Census Bureau, 2015-2019 American Community Survey 5-Year Estimates

Travel Time to Work

Area	Less Than 10 Minutes	10 to 19 Minutes	20 to 29 Minutes	30 to 44 Minutes	45 to 59 Minutes	60 to 89 Minutes	90 Minutes or More
City	3.8	18.0	20.5	30.3	12.3	11.2	3.9
MSA[1]	6.4	22.0	17.4	23.7	12.5	12.9	5.1
U.S.	12.2	28.4	20.8	20.8	8.3	6.4	2.9

Note: Note: Figures are percentages and include workers 16 years old and over; (1) Figures cover the San Francisco-Oakland-Hayward, CA Metropolitan Statistical Area
Source: U.S. Census Bureau, 2015-2019 American Community Survey 5-Year Estimates

Key Congestion Measures

Measure	1982	1992	2002	2012	2017
Annual Hours of Delay, Total (000)	91,032	141,739	187,366	227,441	253,838
Annual Hours of Delay, Per Auto Commuter	55	70	81	95	103
Annual Congestion Cost, Total (million $)	684	1,499	2,542	4,084	4,729
Annual Congestion Cost, Per Auto Commuter ($)	2,104	2,254	2,323	2,209	2,393

Note: Covers the San Francisco-Oakland CA urban area
Source: Texas A&M Transportation Institute, 2019 Urban Mobility Report

Freeway Travel Time Index

Measure	1982	1987	1992	1997	2002	2007	2012	2017
Urban Area Index[1]	1.26	1.31	1.33	1.37	1.38	1.41	1.44	1.50
Urban Area Rank[1,2]	2	2	2	2	2	2	2	2

Note: Freeway Travel Time Index—the ratio of travel time in the peak period to the travel time at free-flow conditions. For example, a value of 1.30 indicates a 20-minute free-flow trip takes 26 minutes in the peak (20 minutes x 1.30 = 26 minutes); (1) Covers the San Francisco-Oakland CA urban area; (2) Rank is based on 101 larger urban areas (#1 = highest travel time index)
Source: Texas A&M Transportation Institute, 2019 Urban Mobility Report

Public Transportation

Agency Name / Mode of Transportation	Vehicles Operated in Maximum Service[1]	Annual Unlinked Passenger Trips[2] (in thous.)	Annual Passenger Miles[3] (in thous.)
San Francisco Municipal Railway (MUNI)			
Bus (directly operated)	484	110,803.0	225,220.9
Cable Car (directly operated)	27	5,703.7	7,395.4
Demand Response (purchased transportation)	134	401.2	2,715.0
Light Rail (directly operated)	146	49,795.7	136,469.6
Streetcar Rail (directly operated)	22	7,386.5	10,615.5
Trolleybus (directly operated)	193	49,247.9	68,856.2
San Francisco Bay Area Rapid Transit District (BART)			
Heavy Rail (directly operated)	588	125,105.5	1,756,364.6
Hybrid Rail (directly operated)	14	2,225.1	15,283.3
Monorail and Automated Guideway (purchased transportation)	3	886.5	2,819.1

Note: (1) Number of revenue vehicles operated by the given mode and type of service to meet the annual maximum service requirement. This is the revenue vehicle count during the peak season of the year; on the week and day that maximum service is provided. Vehicles operated in maximum service (VOMS) exclude atypical days and one-time special events; (2) Number of passengers who boarded public transportation vehicles. Passengers are counted each time they board a vehicle no matter how many vehicles they use to travel from their origin to their destination. (3) Sum of the distances ridden by all passengers during the entire fiscal year.
Source: Federal Transit Administration, National Transit Database, 2019

Air Transportation

Airport Name and Code / Type of Service	Passenger Airlines[1]	Passenger Enplanements	Freight Carriers[2]	Freight (lbs)
San Francisco International (SFO)				
Domestic service (U.S. carriers - 2020)	18	6,193,273	13	191,804,266
International service (U.S. carriers - 2019)	6	2,517,926	7	101,399,216

Note: (1) Includes all U.S.-based major, minor and commuter airlines that carried at least one passenger during the year; (2) Includes all U.S.-based airlines and freight carriers that transported at least one pound of freight during the year.
Source: Bureau of Transportation Statistics, The Intermodal Transportation Database, Air Carriers: T-100 Domestic Market (U.S. Carriers), 2020; Bureau of Transportation Statistics, The Intermodal Transportation Database, Air Carriers: T-100 International Market (U.S. Carriers), 2019

BUSINESSES

Major Business Headquarters

Company Name	Industry	Rankings Fortune[1]	Rankings Forbes[2]
AirBnB	Business Services & Supplies	-	90
Charles Schwab	Securities	271	-
Gap	Specialty Retailers, Apparel	199	-
Hathaway Dinwiddie Construction	Construction	-	215
Levi Strauss	Apparel	495	-
McKesson	Wholesalers, Health Care	8	-
PG&E	Utilities, Gas and Electric	189	-
Salesforce	Computer Software	190	-
Swinerton	Construction	-	96
Uber Technologies	Internet Services and Retailing	228	-
Wells Fargo	Commercial Banks	30	-
Wilbur-Ellis	Chemicals	-	151
Williams-Sonoma	Specialty Retailers, Other	489	-

Note: (1) Companies that produce a 10-K are ranked 1 to 500 based on 2019 revenue; (2) All private companies with at least $2 billion in annual revenue through the end of their most current fiscal year are ranked 1 to 219; companies listed are headquartered in the city; dashes indicate no ranking
Source: Fortune, "Fortune 500," June/July 2020; Forbes, "America's Largest Private Companies," 2020

Fastest-Growing Businesses

According to *Inc.*, San Francisco is home to 17 of America's 500 fastest-growing private companies: **Lattice** (#22); **Grove Collaborative** (#51); **Outschool** (#58); **PeopleGrove** (#112); **Embroker** (#115); **Ripple** (#123); **metadata.io** (#233); **GitLab** (#268); **Mystery.org** (#317); **Paubox** (#320); **Wildflower Health** (#361); **Victorious** (#371); **Carta** (#395); **BairesDev** (#428); **Kountable** (#433); **Swiftly** (#453); **Eden** (#478). Criteria: must be an independent, privately-held, for-profit, U.S. corporation, proprietorship or partnership as of December 31, 2019; revenues must be at least $100,000 in 2016 and $2 million in 2019; must have four-year operating/sales history. *Inc., "America's 500 Fastest-Growing Private Companies," 2020*

According to *Initiative for a Competitive Inner City (ICIC)*, San Francisco is home to one of America's 100 fastest-growing "inner city" companies: **SITELAB urban studio** (#31). Criteria for inclusion: company must be headquartered in or have 51 percent or more of its physical operations in an economically distressed urban area; must be an independent, for-profit corporation, partnership or proprietorship; must have 10 or more employees and have a five-year sales history that includes sales of at least $200,000 in the base year and at least $1 million in the current year with no decrease in sales over the two most recent years. Companies were ranked overall by revenue growth over the five-year period between 2015 and 2019. *Initiative for a Competitive Inner City (ICIC), "Inner City 100 Companies," 2020*

According to Deloitte, San Francisco is home to 38 of North America's 500 fastest-growing high-technology companies: **Bolt** (#22); **Samsara** (#24); **Velano Vascular** (#36); **Unison** (#38); **Juniper Square, Inc.** (#54); **Kong Inc.** (#69); **Lyft, Inc.** (#125); **Blueshift** (#139); **Front** (#140); **HomeLight** (#148); **Sysdig** (#159); **Sigmoid** (#160); **GitLab** (#162); **MindTickle** (#165); **Premise Data** (#182); **IGEL** (#183); **Groove** (#191); **Quizlet** (#192); **Innovaccer** (#205); **Lob** (#207); **Amplitude** (#208); **Fountain** (#221); **Segment** (#234); **Slack Technologies, Inc.** (#236); **CircleCI** (#242); **Twilio Inc.** (#327); **Dialpad** (#347); **Pinterest, Inc.** (#348); **PandaDoc** (#354); **Doximity** (#362); **Uber Technologies, Inc.** (#366); **Okta, Inc.** (#369); **Cloudflare, Inc.** (#392); **Anaplan** (#397); **iRhythm Technologies, Inc.** (#398); **SingleStore** (#488); **DocuSign, Inc.** (#489); **Square, Inc.** (#496). Companies are ranked by percentage growth in revenue over a four-year period. Criteria for inclusion: company must be headquartered within North America; must own proprietary intellectual property or technology that is sold to customers in products that contributes to a significant portion of the company's operating revenue; must have been in business for a minumum of four years with 2016 operating revenues of at least $50,000 USD/CD and 2019 operating revenues of at least $5 million USD/CD. *Deloitte, 2020 Technology Fast 500™*

Minority Business Opportunity

San Francisco is home to one company which is on the *Black Enterprise* Industrial/Service list (100 largest companies based on gross sales): **Rocket Lawyer** (#60). Criteria: operational in previous calendar year; at least 51% black-owned and manufactures/owns the product it sells or provides industrial or consumer services. Brokerages, real estate firms and firms that provide professional services are not eligible. *Black Enterprise, B.E. 100s, 2019*

San Francisco is home to one company which is on the *Black Enterprise* Asset Manager list (10 largest asset management firms based on assets under management): **Progress Investment Management Co.** (#5). Criteria: company must have been operational in previous calendar year and be at least 51% black-owned. *Black Enterprise, B.E. 100s, 2019*

Living Environment

COST OF LIVING

Cost of Living Index

Composite Index	Groceries	Housing	Utilities	Trans-portation	Health Care	Misc. Goods/ Services
194.6	130.5	358.8	137.7	148.5	124.9	126.0

Note: The Cost of Living Index measures regional differences in the cost of consumer goods and services, excluding taxes and non-consumer expenditures, for professional and managerial households in the top income quintile. It is based on more than 50,000 prices covering almost 60 different items for which prices are collected three times a year by chambers of commerce, economic development organizations or university applied economic centers in each participating urban area. The numbers shown should be read as a percentage above or below the national average of 100. For example, a value of 115.4 in the groceries column indicates that grocery prices are 15.4% higher than the national average. Small differences in the index numbers should not be interpreted as significant; Figures cover the San Francisco CA urban area.
Source: The Council for Community and Economic Research, Cost of Living Index, 2020

Grocery Prices

Area[1]	T-Bone Steak ($/pound)	Frying Chicken ($/pound)	Whole Milk ($/half gal.)	Eggs ($/dozen)	Orange Juice ($/64 oz.)	Coffee ($/11.5 oz.)
City[2]	14.94	1.80	2.83	3.16	4.26	6.63
Avg.	11.78	1.39	2.05	1.47	3.57	4.34
Min.	8.03	0.94	1.03	0.74	2.94	3.02
Max.	15.86	2.65	4.31	3.77	5.44	8.69

*Note: (1) Values for the local area are compared with the average, minimum and maximum values for all 284 areas in the Cost of Living Index; (2) Figures cover the San Francisco CA urban area; **T-Bone Steak** (price per pound); **Frying Chicken** (price per pound, whole fryer); **Whole Milk** (half gallon carton); **Eggs** (price per dozen, Grade A, large); **Orange Juice** (64 oz. Tropicana or Florida Natural); **Coffee** (11.5 oz. can, vacuum-packed, Maxwell House, Hills Bros, or Folgers).*
Source: The Council for Community and Economic Research, Cost of Living Index, 2020

Housing and Utility Costs

Area[1]	New Home Price ($)	Apartment Rent ($/month)	All Electric ($/month)	Part Electric ($/month)	Other Energy ($/month)	Telephone ($/month)
City[2]	1,362,163	4,098	-	183.22	84.62	198.20
Avg.	368,594	1,168	170.86	100.47	65.28	184.30
Min.	190,567	502	91.58	31.42	26.08	169.60
Max.	2,227,806	4,738	470.38	280.31	280.06	206.50

*Note: (1) Values for the local area are compared with the average, minimum and maximum values for all 284 areas in the Cost of Living Index; (2) Figures cover the San Francisco CA urban area; **New Home Price** (2,400 sf living area, 8,000 sf lot, in urban area with full utilities); **Apartment Rent** (950 sf 2 bedroom/1.5 or 2 bath, unfurnished, excluding all utilities except water); **All Electric** (average monthly cost for an all-electric home); **Part Electric** (average monthly cost for a part-electric home); **Other Energy** (average monthly cost for natural gas, fuel oil, coal, wood, and any other forms of energy except electricity); **Telephone** (price includes the base monthly rate plus taxes and fees for three lines of mobile phone service).*
Source: The Council for Community and Economic Research, Cost of Living Index, 2020

Health Care, Transportation, and Other Costs

Area[1]	Doctor ($/visit)	Dentist ($/visit)	Optometrist ($/visit)	Gasoline ($/gallon)	Beauty Salon ($/visit)	Men's Shirt ($)
City[2]	149.63	132.68	144.57	3.46	82.05	42.08
Avg.	115.44	99.32	108.10	2.21	39.27	31.37
Min.	36.68	59.00	51.36	1.71	19.00	11.00
Max.	219.00	153.10	250.97	3.46	82.05	58.33

*Note: (1) Values for the local area are compared with the average, minimum and maximum values for all 284 areas in the Cost of Living Index; (2) Figures cover the San Francisco CA urban area; **Doctor** (general practitioners routine exam of an established patient); **Dentist** (adult teeth cleaning and periodic oral examination); **Optometrist** (full vision eye exam for established patient); **Gasoline** (one gallon regular unleaded, national brand, including all taxes, cash price at self-service pump if available); **Beauty Salon** (woman's shampoo, trim, and blow-dry); **Men's Shirt** (cotton/polyester dress shirt, pinpoint weave, long sleeves).*
Source: The Council for Community and Economic Research, Cost of Living Index, 2020

HOUSING

Homeownership Rate

Area	2012 (%)	2013 (%)	2014 (%)	2015 (%)	2016 (%)	2017 (%)	2018 (%)	2019 (%)	2020 (%)
MSA[1]	53.2	55.2	54.6	56.3	55.8	55.7	55.6	52.8	53.0
U.S.	65.4	65.1	64.5	63.7	63.4	63.9	64.4	64.6	66.6

Note: (1) Figures cover the San Francisco-Oakland-Hayward, CA Metropolitan Statistical Area
Source: U.S. Census Bureau, Housing Vacancies and Homeownership Annual Statistics: 2012-2020

House Price Index (HPI)

Area	National Ranking[2]	Quarterly Change (%)	One-Year Change (%)	Five-Year Change (%)	Since 1991Q1 (%)
MD[1]	253	-3.20	-6.72	10.12	283.50
U.S.[3]	–	3.81	10.77	38.99	205.12

Note: The HPI is a weighted repeat sales index. It measures average price changes in repeat sales or refinancings on the same properties. This information is obtained by reviewing repeat mortgage transactions on single-family properties whose mortgages have been purchased or securitized by Fannie Mae or Freddie Mac since January 1975; (1) Figures cover the San Francisco-Redwood City-South San Francisco, CA Metropolitan Division; (2) Rankings are based on annual percentage change for all metro areas containing at least 15,000 transactions over the last 10 years and ranges from 1 to 253; (3) figures based on a weighted average of Census Division estimates using a seasonally adjusted, purchase-only index; all figures are for the period ending December 31, 2020
Source: Federal Housing Finance Agency, Change in Metropolitan Area House Price Indexes, April 7, 2021

Median Single-Family Home Prices

Area	2018	2019	2020p	Percent Change 2019 to 2020
MSA[1]	987.5	988.0	1,100.0	11.3
U.S. Average	261.6	274.6	299.9	9.2

Note: Figures are median sales prices of existing single-family homes in thousands of dollars; (p) preliminary; (1) Figures cover the San Francisco-Oakland-Hayward, CA Metropolitan Statistical Area
Source: National Association of Realtors, Median Sales Price of Existing Single-Family Homes for Metropolitan Areas, 4th Quarter 2020

Qualifying Income Based on Median Sales Price of Existing Single-Family Homes

Area	With 5% Down ($)	With 10% Down ($)	With 20% Down ($)
MSA[1]	215,622	204,273	181,576
U.S. Average	59,266	56,147	49,908

Note: Figures are preliminary; Qualifying income is based on a mortgage rate of 2.81%. Monthly principal and interest payment is limited to 25% of income; (1) Figures cover the San Francisco-Oakland-Hayward, CA Metropolitan Statistical Area
Source: National Association of Realtors, Qualifying Income Based on Median Sales Price of Existing Single-Family Homes for Metropolitan Areas, 4th Quarter 2020

Home Value Distribution

Area	Under $50,000	$50,000 -$99,999	$100,000 -$149,999	$150,000 -$199,999	$200,000 -$299,999	$300,000 -$499,999	$500,000 -$999,999	$1,000,000 or more
City	1.1	0.5	0.4	0.3	1.2	3.9	34.9	57.8
MSA[1]	1.2	0.9	0.8	0.8	2.8	13.2	43.9	36.2
U.S.	6.9	12.0	13.3	14.0	19.6	19.3	11.4	3.4

Note: Figures are percentages and cover owner-occupied housing units; (1) Figures cover the San Francisco-Oakland-Hayward, CA Metropolitan Statistical Area
Source: U.S. Census Bureau, 2015-2019 American Community Survey 5-Year Estimates

Year Housing Structure Built

Area	2010 or Later	2000 -2009	1990 -1999	1980 -1989	1970 -1979	1960 -1969	1950 -1959	1940 -1949	Before 1940	Median Year
City	3.7	6.6	4.3	5.3	7.6	8.2	8.4	9.1	46.8	1944
MSA[1]	3.2	7.7	8.2	11.1	14.9	13.4	13.7	7.8	19.9	1966
U.S.	5.2	14.0	13.9	13.4	15.2	10.6	10.3	4.9	12.6	1978

Note: Figures are percentages except for Median Year; Note: (1) Figures cover the San Francisco-Oakland-Hayward, CA Metropolitan Statistical Area
Source: U.S. Census Bureau, 2015-2019 American Community Survey 5-Year Estimates

Gross Monthly Rent

Area	Under $500	$500 -$999	$1,000 -$1,499	$1,500 -$1,999	$2,000 -$2,499	$2,500 -$2,999	$3,000 and up	Median ($)
City	9.3	13.0	15.6	15.3	13.6	11.7	21.4	1,895
MSA[1]	6.0	9.4	17.2	21.4	18.2	11.9	15.8	1,905
U.S.	9.4	36.2	30.0	14.0	5.6	2.4	2.4	1,062

Note: Figures are percentages except for Median; Gross rent is the contract rent plus the estimated average monthly cost of utilities (electricity, gas, and water and sewer) and fuels (oil, coal, kerosene, wood, etc.) if these are paid by the renter (or paid for the renter by someone else); (1) Figures cover the San Francisco-Oakland-Hayward, CA Metropolitan Statistical Area
Source: U.S. Census Bureau, 2015-2019 American Community Survey 5-Year Estimates

HEALTH

Health Risk Factors

Category	MSA[1] (%)	U.S. (%)
Adults aged 18–64 who have any kind of health care coverage	n/a	87.3
Adults who reported being in good or better health	n/a	82.4
Adults who have been told they have high blood cholesterol	n/a	33.0
Adults who have been told they have high blood pressure	n/a	32.3
Adults who are current smokers	n/a	17.1
Adults who currently use E-cigarettes	n/a	4.6
Adults who currently use chewing tobacco, snuff, or snus	n/a	4.0
Adults who are heavy drinkers[2]	n/a	6.3
Adults who are binge drinkers[3]	n/a	17.4
Adults who are overweight (BMI 25.0 - 29.9)	n/a	35.3
Adults who are obese (BMI 30.0 - 99.8)	n/a	31.3
Adults who participated in any physical activities in the past month	n/a	74.4
Adults who always or nearly always wears a seat belt	n/a	94.3

Note: n/a not available; (1) Figures cover the San Francisco-Oakland-Hayward, CA Metropolitan Statistical Area; (2) Heavy drinkers are classified as adult men having more than 14 drinks per week and adult women having more than 7 drinks per week; (3) Binge drinkers are classified as males having five or more drinks on one occasion or females having four or more drinks on one occasion
Source: Centers for Disease Control and Prevention, Behavioral Risk Factor Surveillance System, SMART: Selected Metropolitan Area Risk Trends, 2017

Acute and Chronic Health Conditions

Category	MSA[1] (%)	U.S. (%)
Adults who have ever been told they had a heart attack	n/a	4.2
Adults who have ever been told they have angina or coronary heart disease	n/a	3.9
Adults who have ever been told they had a stroke	n/a	3.0
Adults who have ever been told they have asthma	n/a	14.2
Adults who have ever been told they have arthritis	n/a	24.9
Adults who have ever been told they have diabetes[2]	n/a	10.5
Adults who have ever been told they had skin cancer	n/a	6.2
Adults who have ever been told they had any other types of cancer	n/a	7.1
Adults who have ever been told they have COPD	n/a	6.5
Adults who have ever been told they have kidney disease	n/a	3.0
Adults who have ever been told they have a form of depression	n/a	20.5

Note: n/a not available; (1) Figures cover the San Francisco-Oakland-Hayward, CA Metropolitan Statistical Area; (2) Figures do not include pregnancy-related, borderline, or pre-diabetes
Source: Centers for Disease Control and Prevention, Behaviorial Risk Factor Surveillance System, SMART: Selected Metropolitan Area Risk Trends, 2017

Health Screening and Vaccination Rates

Category	MSA[1] (%)	U.S. (%)
Adults aged 65+ who have had flu shot within the past year	n/a	60.7
Adults aged 65+ who have ever had a pneumonia vaccination	n/a	75.4
Adults who have ever been tested for HIV	n/a	36.1
Adults who have ever had the shingles or zoster vaccine?	n/a	28.9
Adults who have had their blood cholesterol checked within the last five years	n/a	85.9

Note: n/a not available; (1) Figures cover the San Francisco-Oakland-Hayward, CA Metropolitan Statistical Area.
Source: Centers for Disease Control and Prevention, Behavioral Risk Factor Surveillance System, SMART: Selected Metropolitan Area Risk Trends, 2017

Disability Status

Category	MSA[1] (%)	U.S. (%)
Adults who reported being deaf	n/a	6.7
Are you blind or have serious difficulty seeing, even when wearing glasses?	n/a	4.5
Are you limited in any way in any of your usual activities due of arthritis?	n/a	12.9
Do you have difficulty doing errands alone?	n/a	6.8
Do you have difficulty dressing or bathing?	n/a	3.6
Do you have serious difficulty concentrating/remembering/making decisions?	n/a	10.7
Do you have serious difficulty walking or climbing stairs?	n/a	13.6

Note: n/a not available; (1) Figures cover the San Francisco-Oakland-Hayward, CA Metropolitan Statistical Area.
Source: Centers for Disease Control and Prevention, Behavioral Risk Factor Surveillance System, SMART: Selected Metropolitan Area Risk Trends, 2017

Mortality Rates for the Top 10 Causes of Death in the U.S.

ICD-10[a] Sub-Chapter	ICD-10[a] Code	Age-Adjusted Mortality Rate[1] per 100,000 population	
		County[2]	U.S.
Malignant neoplasms	C00-C97	121.9	149.2
Ischaemic heart diseases	I20-I25	56.6	90.5
Other forms of heart disease	I30-I51	31.2	52.2
Chronic lower respiratory diseases	J40-J47	18.3	39.6
Other degenerative diseases of the nervous system	G30-G31	29.7	37.6
Cerebrovascular diseases	I60-I69	33.9	37.2
Other external causes of accidental injury	W00-X59	36.4	36.1
Organic, including symptomatic, mental disorders	F01-F09	15.8	29.4
Hypertensive diseases	I10-I15	24.5	24.1
Diabetes mellitus	E10-E14	12.2	21.5

Note: (a) ICD-10 = International Classification of Diseases 10th Revision; (1) Mortality rates are a three-year average covering 2017-2019; (2) Figures cover San Francisco County.
Source: Centers for Disease Control and Prevention, National Center for Health Statistics. Underlying Cause of Death 1999-2019 on CDC WONDER Online Database

Mortality Rates for Selected Causes of Death

ICD-10[a] Sub-Chapter	ICD-10[a] Code	Age-Adjusted Mortality Rate[1] per 100,000 population	
		County[2]	U.S.
Assault	X85-Y09	4.5	6.0
Diseases of the liver	K70-K76	9.9	14.4
Human immunodeficiency virus (HIV) disease	B20-B24	4.3	1.5
Influenza and pneumonia	J09-J18	10.6	13.8
Intentional self-harm	X60-X84	9.0	14.1
Malnutrition	E40-E46	1.2	2.3
Obesity and other hyperalimentation	E65-E68	0.6	2.1
Renal failure	N17-N19	7.8	12.6
Transport accidents	V01-V99	4.1	12.3
Viral hepatitis	B15-B19	2.2	1.2

Note: (a) ICD-10 = International Classification of Diseases 10th Revision; (1) Mortality rates are a three-year average covering 2017-2019; (2) Figures cover San Francisco County; Data are suppressed when the data meet the criteria for confidentiality constraints; Mortality rates are flagged as unreliable when the rate would be calculated with a numerator of 20 or less.
Source: Centers for Disease Control and Prevention, National Center for Health Statistics. Underlying Cause of Death 1999-2019 on CDC WONDER Online Database

Health Insurance Coverage

Area	With Health Insurance	With Private Health Insurance	With Public Health Insurance	Without Health Insurance	Population Under Age 19 Without Health Insurance
City	96.3	75.7	29.4	3.7	1.5
MSA[1]	95.7	75.5	30.5	4.3	2.1
U.S.	91.2	67.9	35.1	8.8	5.1

Note: Figures are percentages that cover the civilian noninstitutionalized population; (1) Figures cover the San Francisco-Oakland-Hayward, CA Metropolitan Statistical Area
Source: U.S. Census Bureau, 2015-2019 American Community Survey 5-Year Estimates

Number of Medical Professionals

Area	MDs[3]	DOs[3,4]	Dentists	Podiatrists	Chiropractors	Optometrists
County[1] (number)	7,170	120	1,381	92	349	259
County[1] (rate[2])	814.1	13.6	156.7	10.4	39.6	29.4
U.S. (rate[2])	282.9	22.7	71.2	6.2	28.1	16.9

06075
Note: Data as of 2019 unless noted; (1) Data covers San Francisco County; (2) Rate per 100,000 population; (3) Data as of 2018 and includes all active, non-federal physicians; (4) Doctor of Osteopathic Medicine
Source: U.S. Department of Health and Human Services, Health Resources and Services Administration, Bureau of Health Professions, Area Resource File (ARF) 2019-2020

Best Hospitals

According to *U.S. News,* the San Francisco-Redwood City-South San Francisco, CA metro area is home to one of the best hospitals in the U.S.: **UCSF Medical Center** (15 adult specialties and 10 pediatric specialties). The hospital listed was nationally ranked in at least one of 16 adult or 10 pediatric specialties. Only 134 hospitals nationwide were nationally ranked in one or more adult or pediatric specialty; this number increases to 178 counting specialized centers within hospitals. Twenty hospitals in the U.S. made the Honor Roll. The Best Hospitals Honor Roll takes both the national rankings and the procedure and condition ratings into account. Hospitals received points if they were nationally ranked in one of the 16 adult specialties—the higher they ranked, the more points they got—and how many ratings of "high performing" they earned in the 10 procedures and conditions. *U.S. News Online, "America's Best Hospitals 2020-21"*

According to *U.S. News,* the San Francisco-Redwood City-South San Francisco, CA metro area is home to one of the best children's hospitals in the U.S.: **UCSF Benioff Children's Hospitals, San Francisco and Oakland** (10 pediatric specialties). The hospital listed was highly ranked in at least one of 10 pediatric specialties. Eighty-eight children's hospitals in the U.S. were nationally ranked in at least one specialty. Hospitals received points for being ranked in a specialty, and the 10 hospitals with the most points across the 10 specialties make up the Honor Roll. *U.S. News Online, "America's Best Children's Hospitals 2020-21"*

EDUCATION

Public School District Statistics

District Name	Schls	Pupils	Pupil/ Teacher Ratio	Minority Pupils[1] (%)	Free Lunch Eligible[2] (%)	IEP[3] (%)
Five Keys Independence HSD	1	3,417	29.9	90.9	12.6	2.3
San Francisco Unified	114	52,498	16.5	85.3	44.8	13.7

Note: Table includes school districts with 2,000 or more students; (1) Percentage of students that are not non-Hispanic white; (2) Percentage of students that are eligible for the free lunch program; (3) Percentage of students that have an Individualized Education Program.
Source: U.S. Department of Education, National Center for Education Statistics, Common Core of Data, Local Education Agency (School District) Universe Survey: School Year 2018-2019; U.S. Department of Education, National Center for Education Statistics, Common Core of Data, Public Elementary/Secondary School Universe Survey: School Year 2018-2019

Best High Schools

According to *U.S. News,* San Francisco is home to two of the top 500 high schools in the U.S.: **Lowell High School** (#68); **KIPP San Francisco College Preparatory** (#395). Nearly 18,000 public, magnet and charter schools were ranked based on their performance on state assessments and how well they prepare students for college. *U.S. News & World Report, "Best High Schools 2020"*

Highest Level of Education

Area	Less than H.S.	H.S. Diploma	Some College, No Deg.	Associate Degree	Bachelor's Degree	Master's Degree	Prof. School Degree	Doctorate Degree
City	11.5	12.1	13.3	5.0	34.8	15.4	5.0	2.8
MSA[1]	10.9	15.5	17.3	6.6	29.3	13.7	3.8	2.9
U.S.	12.0	27.0	20.4	8.5	19.8	8.8	2.1	1.4

Note: Figures cover persons age 25 and over; (1) Figures cover the San Francisco-Oakland-Hayward, CA Metropolitan Statistical Area
Source: U.S. Census Bureau, 2015-2019 American Community Survey 5-Year Estimates

Educational Attainment by Race

Area	High School Graduate or Higher (%)					Bachelor's Degree or Higher (%)				
	Total	White	Black	Asian	Hisp.[2]	Total	White	Black	Asian	Hisp.[2]
City	88.5	96.7	88.4	79.3	78.9	58.1	73.8	30.5	46.7	34.2
MSA[1]	89.1	93.6	90.7	87.3	71.5	49.7	56.1	28.8	55.4	21.7
U.S.	88.0	89.9	86.0	87.1	68.7	32.1	33.5	21.6	54.3	16.4

Note: Figures shown cover persons 25 years old and over; (1) Figures cover the San Francisco-Oakland-Hayward, CA Metropolitan Statistical Area; (2) People of Hispanic origin can be of any race
Source: U.S. Census Bureau, 2015-2019 American Community Survey 5-Year Estimates

School Enrollment by Grade and Control

Area	Preschool (%)		Kindergarten (%)		Grades 1 - 4 (%)		Grades 5 - 8 (%)		Grades 9 - 12 (%)	
	Public	Private	Public	Private	Public	Private	Public	Private	Public	Private
City	37.5	62.5	73.1	26.9	72.2	27.8	68.1	31.9	75.0	25.0
MSA[1]	41.3	58.7	84.2	15.8	86.3	13.7	85.8	14.2	87.2	12.8
U.S.	59.1	40.9	87.6	12.4	89.5	10.5	89.4	10.6	90.1	9.9

Note: Figures shown cover persons 3 years old and over; (1) Figures cover the San Francisco-Oakland-Hayward, CA Metropolitan Statistical Area
Source: U.S. Census Bureau, 2015-2019 American Community Survey 5-Year Estimates

Higher Education

Four-Year Colleges			Two-Year Colleges			Medical Schools[1]	Law Schools[2]	Voc/ Tech[3]
Public	Private Non-profit	Private For-profit	Public	Private Non-profit	Private For-profit			
3	8	0	1	0	2	1	4	4

Note: Figures cover institutions located within the city limits and include main campuses only; (1) includes schools accredited by the Liaison Committee on Medical Education and the American Osteopathic Association's Commission on Osteopathic College Accreditation; (2) includes ABA-accredited schools, schools with provisional ABA accreditation, and state accredited schools; (3) includes all schools with programs that are less than 2 years.
Source: National Center for Education Statistics, Integrated Postsecondary Education System (IPEDS), 2019-20; Wikipedia, List of Medical Schools in the United States, accessed April 2, 2021; Wikipedia, List of Law Schools in the United States, accessed April 2, 2021

According to *U.S. News & World Report,* the San Francisco-Redwood City-South San Francisco, CA metro division is home to one of the top 200 national universities in the U.S.: **University of San Francisco** (#103 tie). The indicators used to capture academic quality fall into a number of categories: assessment by administrators at peer institutions; retention of students; faculty resources; student selectivity; financial resources; alumni giving; high school counselor ratings of colleges; and graduation rate. *U.S. News & World Report, "America's Best Colleges 2021"*

According to *U.S. News & World Report,* the San Francisco-Redwood City-South San Francisco, CA metro division is home to one of the top 100 law schools in the U.S.: **University of California (Hastings)** (#50 tie). The rankings are based on a weighted average of 12 measures of quality: peer assessment score; assessment score by lawyers/judges; median LSAT scores; median undergrad GPA; acceptance rate; employment rates for graduates; placement success; bar passage rate; faculty resources; expenditures per student; student/faculty ratio; and library resources. *U.S. News & World Report, "America's Best Graduate Schools, Law, 2022"*

According to *U.S. News & World Report,* the San Francisco-Redwood City-South San Francisco, CA metro division is home to one of the top 75 medical schools for research in the U.S.: **University of California—San Francisco** (#4 tie). The rankings are based on a weighted average of 11 measures of quality: quality assessment; peer assessment score; assessment score by residency directors; research activity; total research activity; average research activity per faculty member; student selectivity; median MCAT total score; median undergraduate GPA; acceptance rate; and faculty resources. *U.S. News & World Report, "America's Best Graduate Schools, Medical, 2022"*

EMPLOYERS

Major Employers

Company Name	Industry
All Hallows Preservation	Apartment building operators
AT&T	Telephone communication, except radio
AT&T Services	Telephone communication, except radio
California Pacific Medical Center	General medical & surgical hospitals
City & County of San Francisco	Public welfare administration: nonoperating, govt.
Edy's Grand Ice Cream	Ice cream & other frozen treats
Franklin Templeton Services	Investment advice
Lawrence Livermore National Laboratory	Noncommercial research organizations
Menlo Worldwide Forwarding	Letter delivery, private air
Oracle America	Minicomputers
Oracle Systems Corporation	Prepackaged software
Pacific Gas and Electric Company	Electric & other services combined
PACPIZZA	Pizzeria, chain
San Francisco Community College District	Colleges & universities
University of California, Berkeley	University
Veterans Health Administration	Administration of veterans' affairs
Wells Fargo	National commercial banks

Note: Companies shown are located within the San Francisco-Oakland-Hayward, CA Metropolitan Statistical Area.
Source: Hoovers.com; Wikipedia

Best Companies to Work For

Atlassian; Dropbox; Kimpton Hotels & Restaurants; Orrick; Salesforce, headquartered in San Francisco, are among "The 100 Best Companies to Work For." To pick the best companies, *Fortune* partnered with the Great Place to Work Institute. Two-thirds of a company's score is based on the results of the Institute's Trust Index survey, which is sent to a random sample of employees from each company. The questions related to attitudes about management's credibility, job satisfaction, and camaraderie. The other third of the scoring is based on the company's responses to the Institute's Culture Audit, which includes detailed questions about pay and benefit programs, and a series of open-ended questions about hiring practices, internal communication, training, recognition programs, and diversity efforts. Any company that is at least five years old with more than 1,000 U.S. employees is eligible. *Fortune, "The 100 Best Companies to Work For," 2020*

Federal Reserve Bank of San Francisco, headquartered in San Francisco, is among the "100 Best Companies for Working Mothers." Criteria: paid time off and leaves; workforce profile; benefits; women's issues and advancement; flexible work; company culture and work life programs. *Working Mother, "100 Best Companies for Working Mothers," 2020*

Gap, headquartered in San Francisco, is among the "Top Companies for Executive Women." This list is determined by organizations filling out an in-depth survey that measures female demographics at every level, but with an emphasis on women in senior corporate roles, with profit & loss (P&L) responsibility, and those earning in the top 20 percent of the organization. *Working Mother* defines P&L as having responsibility that involves monitoring the net income after expenses for a department or entire organization, with direct influence on how company resources are allocated. *Working Mother, "Top Companies for Executive Women," 2020+*

Federal Reserve Bank of San Francisco; Uber Technologies, headquartered in San Francisco, are among the "Best Companies for Dads." *Working Mother's* newest list recognizes the growing importance companies place on giving dads time off and support for their families. Rankings are determined by measuring gender-neutral or paternity leave offered, as well as actual time taken, phase-back policies, child- and dependent-care benefits, and corporate support groups for men and dads. *Working Mother, "Best Companies for Dads," 2020*

PUBLIC SAFETY

Crime Rate

Area	All Crimes	Violent Crimes				Property Crimes		
		Murder	Rape[3]	Robbery	Aggrav. Assault	Burglary	Larceny -Theft	Motor Vehicle Theft
City	6,175.2	4.5	36.6	344.8	283.7	524.1	4,501.9	479.6
Suburbs[1]	2,534.2	1.3	42.6	87.1	128.4	294.1	1,778.4	202.3
Metro[2]	4,482.9	3.0	39.4	225.0	211.5	417.2	3,236.0	350.7
U.S.	2,489.3	5.0	42.6	81.6	250.2	340.5	1,549.5	219.9

Note: Figures are crimes per 100,000 population; (1) All areas within the metro area that are located outside the city limits; (2) Figures cover the San Francisco-Redwood City-South San Francisco, CA Metropolitan Division; (3) All figures shown were reported using the revised Uniform Crime Reporting (UCR) definition of rape.
Source: FBI Uniform Crime Reports, 2019

Hate Crimes

Area	Number of Quarters Reported	Number of Incidents per Bias Motivation					
		Race/Ethnicity/ Ancestry	Religion	Sexual Orientation	Disability	Gender	Gender Identity
City	4	35	5	22	0	0	2
U.S.	4	3,963	1,521	1,195	157	69	198

Source: Federal Bureau of Investigation, Hate Crime Statistics 2019

Identity Theft Consumer Reports

Area	Reports	Reports per 100,000 Population	Rank[2]
MSA[1]	13,527	286	130
U.S.	1,387,615	423	-

Note: (1) Figures cover the San Francisco-Oakland-Hayward, CA Metropolitan Statistical Area; (2) Rank ranges from 1 to 391 where 1 indicates greatest number of identity theft reports per 100,000 population
Source: Federal Trade Commission, Consumer Sentinel Network Data Book 2020

Fraud and Other Consumer Reports

Area	Reports	Reports per 100,000 Population	Rank[2]
MSA[1]	39,771	841	79
U.S.	3,385,133	1,031	-

Note: (1) Figures cover the San Francisco-Oakland-Hayward, CA Metropolitan Statistical Area; (2) Rank ranges from 1 to 391 where 1 indicates greatest number of fraud and other consumer reports per 100,000 population
Source: Federal Trade Commission, Consumer Sentinel Network Data Book 2020

POLITICS

2020 Presidential Election Results

Area	Biden	Trump	Jorgensen	Hawkins	Other
San Francisco County	85.3	12.7	0.7	0.6	0.7
U.S.	51.3	46.8	1.2	0.3	0.5

Note: Results are percentages and may not add to 100% due to rounding
Source: Dave Leip's Atlas of U.S. Presidential Elections

SPORTS

Professional Sports Teams

Team Name	League	Year Established
Golden State Warriors	National Basketball Association (NBA)	1962
Oakland Athletics	Major League Baseball (MLB)	1968
San Francisco 49ers	National Football League (NFL)	1946
San Francisco Giants	Major League Baseball (MLB)	1958

Note: Includes teams located in the San Francisco-Oakland-Hayward, CA Metropolitan Statistical Area.
Source: Wikipedia, Major Professional Sports Teams of the United States and Canada, April 6, 2021

CLIMATE

Average and Extreme Temperatures

Temperature	Jan	Feb	Mar	Apr	May	Jun	Jul	Aug	Sep	Oct	Nov	Dec	Yr.
Extreme High (°F)	72	77	85	92	97	106	105	98	103	99	85	75	106
Average High (°F)	56	59	61	64	66	70	71	72	73	70	63	56	65
Average Temp. (°F)	49	52	53	56	58	61	63	63	64	61	55	50	57
Average Low (°F)	42	44	45	47	49	52	53	54	54	51	47	42	49
Extreme Low (°F)	26	30	31	36	39	43	44	45	41	37	31	24	24

Note: Figures cover the years 1948-1990
Source: National Climatic Data Center, International Station Meteorological Climate Summary, 9/96

Average Precipitation/Snowfall/Humidity

Precip./Humidity	Jan	Feb	Mar	Apr	May	Jun	Jul	Aug	Sep	Oct	Nov	Dec	Yr.
Avg. Precip. (in.)	4.3	3.1	2.9	1.4	0.3	0.1	Tr	Tr	0.2	1.0	2.5	3.4	19.3
Avg. Snowfall (in.)	Tr	Tr	Tr	0	0	0	0	0	0	0	0	Tr	Tr
Avg. Rel. Hum. 7am (%)	86	85	82	79	78	77	81	83	83	83	85	86	82
Avg. Rel. Hum. 4pm (%)	67	65	63	61	61	60	60	62	60	60	64	68	63

Note: Figures cover the years 1948-1990; Tr = Trace amounts (<0.05 in. of rain; <0.5 in. of snow)
Source: National Climatic Data Center, International Station Meteorological Climate Summary, 9/96

Weather Conditions

Temperature			Daytime Sky			Precipitation		
10°F & below	32°F & below	90°F & above	Clear	Partly cloudy	Cloudy	0.01 inch or more precip.	0.1 inch or more snow/ice	Thunder-storms
0	6	4	136	130	99	63	< 1	5

Note: Figures are average number of days per year and cover the years 1948-1990
Source: National Climatic Data Center, International Station Meteorological Climate Summary, 9/96

HAZARDOUS WASTE

Superfund Sites

The San Francisco-Redwood City-South San Francisco, CA metro division is home to one site on the EPA's Superfund National Priorities List: **Treasure Island Naval Station-Hunters Point Annex** (final). There are a total of 1,375 Superfund sites with a status of proposed or final on the list in the U.S.
U.S. Environmental Protection Agency, National Priorities List, April 7, 2021

AIR QUALITY

Air Quality Trends: Ozone

	1990	1995	2000	2005	2010	2015	2016	2017	2018	2019
MSA[1]	0.058	0.074	0.057	0.057	0.061	0.062	0.059	0.060	0.053	0.060
U.S.	0.088	0.089	0.082	0.080	0.073	0.068	0.069	0.068	0.069	0.065

Note: (1) Data covers the San Francisco-Oakland-Hayward, CA Metropolitan Statistical Area. The values shown are the composite ozone concentration averages among trend sites based on the highest fourth daily maximum 8-hour concentration in parts per million. These trends are based on sites having an adequate record of monitoring data during the trend period. Data from exceptional events are included.
Source: U.S. Environmental Protection Agency, Air Quality Monitoring Information, "Air Quality Trends by City, 1990-2019"

Air Quality Index

Area	Percent of Days when Air Quality was...[2]					AQI Statistics[2]	
	Good	Moderate	Unhealthy for Sensitive Groups	Unhealthy	Very Unhealthy	Maximum	Median
MSA[1]	69.6	27.9	2.5	0.0	0.0	150	43

Note: (1) Data covers the San Francisco-Oakland-Hayward, CA Metropolitan Statistical Area; (2) Based on 365 days with AQI data in 2019. Air Quality Index (AQI) is an index for reporting daily air quality. EPA calculates the AQI for five major air pollutants regulated by the Clean Air Act: ground-level ozone, particle pollution (aka particulate matter), carbon monoxide, sulfur dioxide, and nitrogen dioxide. The AQI runs from 0 to 500. The higher the AQI value, the greater the level of air pollution and the greater the health concern. There are six AQI categories: "Good" AQI is between 0 and 50. Air quality is considered satisfactory; "Moderate" AQI is between 51 and 100. Air quality is acceptable; "Unhealthy for Sensitive Groups" When AQI values are between 101 and 150, members of sensitive groups may experience health effects; "Unhealthy" When AQI values are between 151 and 200 everyone may begin to experience health effects; "Very Unhealthy" AQI values between 201 and 300 trigger a health alert; "Hazardous" AQI values over 300 trigger warnings of emergency conditions (not shown).
Source: U.S. Environmental Protection Agency, Air Quality Index Report, 2019

Air Quality Index Pollutants

Area	Percent of Days when AQI Pollutant was...[2]					
	Carbon Monoxide	Nitrogen Dioxide	Ozone	Sulfur Dioxide	Particulate Matter 2.5	Particulate Matter 10
MSA[1]	0.0	6.3	52.1	0.0	41.6	0.0

Note: (1) Data covers the San Francisco-Oakland-Hayward, CA Metropolitan Statistical Area; (2) Based on 365 days with AQI data in 2019. The Air Quality Index (AQI) is an index for reporting daily air quality. EPA calculates the AQI for five major air pollutants regulated by the Clean Air Act: ground-level ozone, particle pollution (also known as particulate matter), carbon monoxide, sulfur dioxide, and nitrogen dioxide. The AQI runs from 0 to 500. The higher the AQI value, the greater the level of air pollution and the greater the health concern.
Source: U.S. Environmental Protection Agency, Air Quality Index Report, 2019

Maximum Air Pollutant Concentrations: Particulate Matter, Ozone, CO and Lead

	Particulate Matter 10 (ug/m³)	Particulate Matter 2.5 Wtd AM (ug/m³)	Particulate Matter 2.5 24-Hr (ug/m³)	Ozone (ppm)	Carbon Monoxide (ppm)	Lead (ug/m³)
MSA[1] Level	34	9.4	19	0.072	2	n/a
NAAQS[2]	150	15	35	0.075	9	0.15
Met NAAQS[2]	Yes	Yes	Yes	Yes	Yes	n/a

Note: (1) Data covers the San Francisco-Oakland-Hayward, CA Metropolitan Statistical Area; Data from exceptional events are included; (2) National Ambient Air Quality Standards; ppm = parts per million; ug/m³ = micrograms per cubic meter; n/a not available.
Concentrations: Particulate Matter 10 (coarse particulate)—highest second maximum 24-hour concentration; Particulate Matter 2.5 Wtd AM (fine particulate)—highest weighted annual mean concentration; Particulate Matter 2.5 24-Hour (fine particulate)—highest 98th percentile 24-hour concentration; Ozone—highest fourth daily maximum 8-hour concentration; Carbon Monoxide—highest second maximum non-overlapping 8-hour concentration; Lead—maximum running 3-month average
Source: U.S. Environmental Protection Agency, Air Quality Monitoring Information, "Air Quality Statistics by City, 2019"

Maximum Air Pollutant Concentrations: Nitrogen Dioxide and Sulfur Dioxide

	Nitrogen Dioxide AM (ppb)	Nitrogen Dioxide 1-Hr (ppb)	Sulfur Dioxide AM (ppb)	Sulfur Dioxide 1-Hr (ppb)	Sulfur Dioxide 24-Hr (ppb)
MSA[1] Level	15	48	n/a	15	n/a
NAAQS[2]	53	100	30	75	140
Met NAAQS[2]	Yes	Yes	n/a	Yes	n/a

Note: (1) Data covers the San Francisco-Oakland-Hayward, CA Metropolitan Statistical Area; Data from exceptional events are included; (2) National Ambient Air Quality Standards; ppm = parts per million; ug/m³ = micrograms per cubic meter; n/a not available.
Concentrations: Nitrogen Dioxide AM—highest arithmetic mean concentration; Nitrogen Dioxide 1-Hr—highest 98th percentile 1-hour daily maximum concentration; Sulfur Dioxide AM—highest annual mean concentration; Sulfur Dioxide 1-Hr—highest 99th percentile 1-hour daily maximum concentration; Sulfur Dioxide 24-Hr—highest second maximum 24-hour concentration
Source: U.S. Environmental Protection Agency, Air Quality Monitoring Information, "Air Quality Statistics by City, 2019"

San Jose, California

Background

Like many cities in the valleys of northern California, San Jose is an abundant cornucopia of wine grapes and produce. Situated only seven miles from the southernmost tip of San Francisco Bay, San Jose is flanked by the Santa Cruz Mountains to the west, and the Mount Hamilton arm of the Diablo Range to the east. The Coyote and Guadalupe rivers gently cut through this landscape, carrying water only in the spring.

San Jose was founded on November 29, 1777, by Spanish colonizers, and can rightfully claim to be the oldest civic settlement in California. Like its present-day role, San Jose was established by the Spanish to be a produce and cattle supplier to the nearby communities and presidios of San Francisco and Monterey.

After U.S. troops wrested the territory of California from Mexican rule, San Jose became its state capital. At the same time, the city served as a supply base to gold prospectors.

Today, San Jose retains much of its history. As in the past, it is still a major shipping and processing center for agricultural produce. Also, San Jose produces some of the best table wines in the country. To remind its citizens of its Spanish heritage, a replica of the Mission of Santa Clara stands on the grounds of the University of Santa Clara.

Due to annexation of surrounding communities after World War II, the population of San Jose has increased more than tenfold. With the additional industries of NASA research, and electronic components and motors production to attract people to the area, San Jose rapidly became a family-oriented community of housing developments and shopping malls.

During the 1990s, San Jose was home to more than half of Silicon Valley's leading semiconductor, networking, and telecommunications companies, giving it the nickname "Capital of Silicon Valley." The renovated downtown is headquarters for a number of major developers of computer software.

In the new century, San Jose suffered from the downturn in electronics and computer industries, but the city has developed numerous strategies to lower unemployment numbers and ensure that the city's economic future remains bright. The region has been cited as the happiest place to work in the United States, noting a large concentration of technology jobs that typically offer a high salary and opportunity for growth, in addition to companies providing "fun and innovative work environment."

The HP Pavilion, home of the San Jose Sharks hockey team, is one of the most active venues for non-sporting events in the world.

Public art is an evolving attraction in the city. The city was one of the first to adopt a public art ordinance at 2 percent of capital improvement building project budgets, a commitment that has affected the visual landscape of the city, with a considerable number of public art projects throughout the downtown area, and a growing collection in the newer civic locations in neighborhoods including libraries, parks, and fire stations. Of particular note, the Mineta Airport has incorporated a program of Art & Technology.

San Jose enjoys a Mediterranean, or dry summer subtropical, climate. The rain that does fall comes mostly during the months of November through March. Severe winter storms with gale winds and heavy rain occur occasionally. The summer weather is dominated by night and morning stratus clouds along with sea breezes blowing from the cold waters of the bay. During the winter months fog is common, causing difficult flying conditions.

Rankings

General Rankings

- The San Jose metro area was identified as one of America's fastest-growing areas in terms of population and business growth by *MagnifyMoney*. The area ranked #19 out of 35. The 100 most populous metro areas in the U.S. were evaluated on their change from 2011-2016 in the following categories: people and housing; workforce and employment opportunities; growing industry. *www.businessinsider.com, "The 35 Cities in the US with the Biggest Influx of People, the Most Work Opportunities, and the Hottest Business Growth," August 12, 2018*

Business/Finance Rankings

- According to *Business Insider*, the San Jose metro area is a prime place to run a startup or move an existing business to. The area ranked #1. Nearly 190 metro areas were analyzed on overall economic health and investments. Data was based on the 2019 U.S. Census Bureau American Community Survey, the marketing company PitchBook, Bureau of Labor Statistics employment report, and Zillow. Criteria: percentage of change in typical home values and employment rates; quarterly venture capital investment activity; and median household income. *www.businessinsider.com, "The 25 Best Cities to Start a Business-Or Move Your Current One," January 12, 2021*

- 24/7 Wall Street used metro data from the Bureau of Labor Statistics' Occupational Employment database to identify the cities with the highest percentage of those employed in jobs requiring knowledge in the science, technology, engineering, and math (STEM) fields as well as average wages for STEM jobs. The San Jose metro area was #11. *247wallst.com, "15 Cities with the Most High-Tech Jobs," January 11, 2020*

- Based on metro area social media reviews, the employment opinion group Glassdoor surveyed 50 of the most populous U.S. metro areas and equally weighed cost of living, hiring opportunity, and job satisfaction to compose a list of "25 Best Cities for Jobs." Median pay and home value, and number of active job openings were also factored in. The San Jose metro area was ranked #16 in overall job satisfaction. *www.glassdoor.com, "Best Cities for Jobs," February 25, 2020*

- The Brookings Institution ranked the nation's largest cities based on income inequality. San Jose was ranked #56 (#1 = greatest inequality). Criteria: the "95/20 ratio," a figure representing the income at which a household earns more than 95 percent of all other households, divided by the income at which a household earns more than only 20 percent of all other households. *Brookings Institution, "Household Income Inequality, Largest Cities of 97 Large U.S. Metro Areas, 2014-2016," February 5, 2018*

- The Brookings Institution ranked the 100 largest metro areas in the U.S. based on income inequality. San Jose was ranked #6 (#1 = greatest inequality). Criteria: the "95/20 ratio," a figure representing the income at which a household earns more than 95 percent of all other households, divided by the income at which a household earns more than only 20 percent of all other households. *Brookings Institution, "Household Income Inequality, 100 Largest U.S. Metro Areas, 2014-2016," February 5, 2018*

- *Forbes* ranked the 100 largest metro areas in the U.S. in terms of the "Best Cities for Young Professionals." The San Jose metro area ranked #12 out of 25. Criteria: median rent of a two-bedroom apartment; job growth and unemployment rate; median salary of college graduates with 5 or less years of work experience; networking opportunities; social outlook; percentage of population 25 years of age and older with college degrees. *Forbes.com, "America's 25 Best Cities for Young Professionals in 2017," May 22, 2017*

- Payscale.com ranked the 32 largest metro areas in terms of wage growth. The San Jose metro area ranked #5. Criteria: private-sector and education professional wage growth between the 4th quarter of 2019 and the 4th quarter of 2020. *PayScale, "Wage Trends by Metro Area-4th Quarter," January 11, 2021*

- The San Jose metro area appeared on the Milken Institute "2021 Best Performing Cities" list. Rank: #22 out of 200 large metro areas (population over 250,000). Criteria: job growth; wage and salary growth; high-tech output growth; housing affordability; household broadband access. *Milken Institute, "Best-Performing Cities 2021," February 16, 2021*

- *Forbes* ranked the 200 most populous metro areas to determine the nation's "Best Places for Business and Careers." The San Jose metro area was ranked #42. Criteria: costs (business and living); job growth (past and projected); income growth; quality of life; educational attainment (college and high school); projected economic growth; cultural and leisure opportunities; workplace tolerance laws; net migration patterns. *Forbes, "The Best Places for Business and Careers 2019: Seattle Still On Top," October 30, 2019*

Education Rankings

- Personal finance website *WalletHub* analyzed the 150 largest U.S. metropolitan statistical areas to determine where the most educated Americans are putting their degrees to work. Criteria: education levels; percentage of workers with degrees; education quality and attainment gap; public school quality rankings; quality and enrollment of each metro area's universities. San Jose was ranked #2 (#1 = most educated city). *www.WalletHub.com, "Most and Least Educated Cities in America," July 20, 2020*

- San Jose was selected as one of America's most literate cities. The city ranked #50 out of the 84 largest U.S. cities. Criteria: number of booksellers; library resources; Internet resources; educational attainment; periodical publishing resources; newspaper circulation. *Central Connecticut State University, "America's Most Literate Cities, 2018," February 2019*

Environmental Rankings

- Sperling's BestPlaces assessed the 50 largest metropolitan areas of the United States for the likelihood of dangerously extreme weather events or earthquakes. In general the Southeast and South-Central regions have the highest risk of weather extremes and earthquakes, while the Pacific Northwest enjoys the lowest risk. Of the least risky metropolitan areas, the San Jose metro area was ranked #6. *www.bestplaces.net, "Avoid Natural Disasters: BestPlaces Reveals The Top 10 Safest Places to Live," October 25, 2017*

- The U.S. Environmental Protection Agency (EPA) released a list of U.S. metropolitan areas with the most ENERGY STAR certified buildings in 2019. The San Jose metro area was ranked #14 out of 25. *U.S. Environmental Protection Agency, "2020 Energy Star Top Cities," March 2020*

- The U.S. Environmental Protection Agency (EPA) released a list of mid-size U.S. metropolitan areas with the most ENERGY STAR certified buildings in 2019. The San Jose metro area was ranked #1 out of 10. *U.S. Environmental Protection Agency, "2020 Energy Star Top Cities," March 2020*

- San Jose was highlighted as one of the 25 most ozone-polluted metro areas in the U.S. during 2016 through 2018. The area ranked #8. *American Lung Association, "State of the Air 2020," April 21, 2020*

- San Jose was highlighted as one of the 25 metro areas most polluted by year-round particle pollution (Annual PM 2.5) in the U.S. during 2016 through 2018. The area ranked #5. *American Lung Association, "State of the Air 2020," April 21, 2020*

- San Jose was highlighted as one of the 25 metro areas most polluted by short-term particle pollution (24-hour PM 2.5) in the U.S. during 2016 through 2018. The area ranked #3. *American Lung Association, "State of the Air 2020," April 21, 2020*

Health/Fitness Rankings

- The Sharecare Community Well-Being Index evaluates 10 individual and social health factors in order to measure what matters to Americans in the co mmunities in which they live. The San Jose metro area was one of the five communities where social determinants of health were the highest. Criteria: access to food, healthcare, and community resources; housing and transportation; economic security. The area ranked #0. *www.sharecare.com, "Community Well-Being Index: 2019 Metro Area & County Rankings Report," August 31, 2020*

- For each of the 100 largest cities in the United States, the American Fitness Index®, published by the American College of Sports Medicine and the Anthem Foundation, evaluated community infrastructure and 33 health behaviors including preventive health, levels of chronic disease conditions, pedestrian safety, air quality, and community resources that support physical activity. San Jose ranked #15 for "community fitness." *americanfitnessindex.org, "2020 ACSM American Fitness Index Summary Report," July 14, 2020*

- Trulia analyzed the 100 largest U.S. metro areas to identify the nation's best cities for weight loss, based on the percentage of adults who bike or walk to work, sporting goods stores, grocery stores, access to outdoor activities, weight-loss centers, gyms, and average space reserved for parks. San Jose ranked #10. *Trulia.com, "Where to Live to Get in Shape in the New Year," January 4, 2018*

- San Jose was identified as a "2021 Spring Allergy Capital." The area ranked #95 out of 100. Three groups of factors were used to identify the most challenging cities for people with allergies during the spring season: annual spring pollen levels; over the counter medicine use; number of board-certified allergy specialists. *Asthma and Allergy Foundation of America, "Spring Allergy Capitals 2021," February 23, 2021*

- San Jose was identified as a "2021 Fall Allergy Capital." The area ranked #96 out of 100. Three groups of factors were used to identify the most challenging cities for people with allergies during the fall season: annual fall pollen levels; over the counter medicine use; number of board-certified allergy specialists. *Asthma and Allergy Foundation of America, "Fall Allergy Capitals 2021," February 23, 2021*

- San Jose was identified as a "2019 Asthma Capital." The area ranked #93 out of the nation's 100 largest metropolitan areas. Criteria: estimated asthma prevalence; crude death rate from asthma; and ER visits due to asthma. Risk factors analyzed but not factored in the rankings: annual pollen score; annual air quality; public smoking laws; number of board-certified asthma specialists; rescue medication use; controller medication use; uninsured rate; poverty rate. *Asthma and Allergy Foundation of America, "Asthma Capitals 2019: The Most Challenging Places to Live With Asthma," May 7, 2019*

- The Sharecare Community Well-Being Index evaluates 10 individual and social health factors in order to measure what matters to Americans in the communities in which they live. The San Jose metro area ranked #4 in the top 10 across all 10 domains. Criteria: access to healthcare, food, and community resources; housng and transportation; economic security; feeling of purpose; physical, financial, social, and community well-being. *www.sharecare.com, "Community Well-Being Index: 2019 Metro Area & County Rankings Report," August 31, 2020*

Pet Rankings

- San Jose appeared on *The Dogington Post* site as one of the top cities for dog lovers, ranking #19 out of 20. The real estate brokerage, Redfin and Rover, the largest pet sitter and dog walker network, compiled a list from over 14,000 U.S. cities to come up with a "Rover Rank." Criteria: highest count of dog walks, the city's Walk Score®, for-sale home listings that mention "dog," number of dog walkers and pet sitters and the hours spent and distance logged. *www.dogingtonpost.com, "The 20 Most Dog-Friendly Cities of 2019," April 4, 2019*

Real Estate Rankings

- FitSmallBusiness looked at 50 of the largest metropolitan areas in the U.S. to determine which metro was the best to start a real estate business. Data was compiled from such sources as: Zillow, Trulia, U.S. Census Bureau, and the Bureau of Labor Statistics. Criteria: location; inventory; annual wages; median sales price of homes; days on the market; median price cut percentage; and other factors that would influence real estate professional growth. The San Jose metro area ranked #9. *fitsmallbusiness.com, "The Best Cities to Become a Real Estate Agent in 2018," January 30, 2018*

- *WalletHub* compared the most populated U.S. cities to determine which had the best markets for real estate agents. San Jose ranked #5 where demand was high and pay was the best. Criteria: sales per agent; annual median wage for real-estate agents; monthly average starting salary for real estate agents; real estate job density and competition; unemployment rate; home turnover rate; housing-market health index; and other relevant metrics. *www.WalletHub.com, "2019's Best Places to Be a Real Estate Agent," April 24, 2019*

- The San Jose metro area appeared on Realtor.com's list of hot housing markets to watch in 2021. The area ranked #2. Criteria: healthy existing homes inventory; relative home affordability; local economy/population trends. *Realtor.com®, "Top 10 Housing Markets Positioned for Growth in 2021," December 7, 2020*

- The San Jose metro area was identified as one of the 20 least affordable housing markets in the U.S. in 2020. The area ranked #183 out of 183 markets. Criteria: qualification for a mortgage loan with a 10 percent down payment on a typical home. *National Association of Realtors®, Qualifying Income Based on Sales Price of Existing Single-Family Homes for Metropolitan Areas, 2020*

- San Jose was ranked #259 out of 268 metro areas in terms of housing affordability in 2020 by the National Association of Home Builders (#1 = most affordable). Criteria: the share of homes sold in that area affordable to a family earning the local median income, based on standard mortgage underwriting criteria. *National Association of Home Builders®, NAHB-Wells Fargo Housing Opportunity Index, 4th Quarter 2020*

Safety Rankings

- Allstate ranked the 200 largest cities in America in terms of driver safety. San Jose ranked #170. Criteria: internal property damage claims over a two-year period from January 2016 to December 2017. The report helps increase the importance of safety and awareness behind the wheel. *Allstate, "Allstate America's Best Drivers Report, 2019" June 24, 2019*

- The National Insurance Crime Bureau ranked 384 metro areas in the U.S. in terms of per capita rates of vehicle theft. The San Jose metro area ranked #24 (#1 = highest rate). Criteria: number of vehicle theft offenses per 100,000 inhabitants in 2019. *National Insurance Crime Bureau, "Hot Spots 2019," July 21, 2020*

Seniors/Retirement Rankings

- From its Best Cities for Successful Aging indexes, the Milken Institute generated rankings for metropolitan areas, weighing data in nine categories—health care, wellness, living arrangements, transportation and convenience, financial characteristics, education, employment, community engagement, and overall livability. The San Jose metro area was ranked #10 overall in the large metro area category. *Milken Institute, "Best Cities for Successful Aging, 2017" March 14, 2017*

Sports/Recreation Rankings

- San Jose was chosen as one of America's best cities for bicycling. The city ranked #43 out of 50. Criteria: cycling infrastructure that is safe and friendly for all ages; energy and bike culture. The editors evaluated cities with populations of 100,000 or more. *Bicycling, "The 50 Best Bike Cities in America," October 10, 2018*

Transportation Rankings

- San Jose was identified as one of the most congested metro areas in the U.S. The area ranked #5 out of 10. Criteria: yearly delay per auto commuter in hours. *Texas A&M Transportation Institute, "2019 Urban Mobility Report," December 2019*

Women/Minorities Rankings

- The *Houston Chronicle* listed the San Jose metro area as #12 in top places for young Latinos to live in the U.S. Research was largely based on housing and occupational data from the largest metropolitan areas performed by *Forbes* and NBC Universo. Criteria: percentage of 18-34 year-olds; Latino college grad rates; and diversity. *blog.chron.com, "The 15 Best Big Cities for Latino Millenials," January 26, 2016*

- Personal finance website *WalletHub* compared more than 180 U.S. cities across two key dimensions, "Hispanic Business-Friendliness" and "Hispanic Purchasing Power," to arrive at the most favorable conditions for Hispanic entrepreneurs. San Jose was ranked #103 out of 182. Criteria includes: share of Hispanic-Owned Businesses; Hispanic entrepreneurship rate to median annual income of Hispanics; Small Business-Friendliness score; cost of living; and number of Hispanics with at least a bachelor's degree. *WalletHub.com, "2019's Best Cities for Hispanic Entrepreneurs," May 1, 2019*

Miscellaneous Rankings

- San Jose was selected as a 2020 Digital Cities Survey winner. The city ranked #1 in the large city (500,000 or more population) category. The survey examined and assessed how city governments are utilizing technology to improve transparency, enhance cybersecurity, and respond to the pandemic. Survey questions focused on ten initiatives: cybersecurity, citizen experience, disaster recovery, business intelligence, IT personnel, data governance, collaboration, infrastructure modernization, cloud computing, and mobile applications. *Center for Digital Government, "2020 Digital Cities Survey," November 10, 2020*

- *WalletHub* compared the 150 most populated U.S. cities to determine their operating efficiency. A "Quality of City Services" score was constructed for each city and then divided by the total budget per capita to reveal which were managed the best. San Jose ranked #91. Criteria: financial stability; economy; education; safety; health; infrastructure and pollution. *www.WalletHub.com, "2020's Best- & Worst-Run Cities in America," June 29, 2020*

- The National Alliance to End Homelessness listed the 25 most populous metro areas with the highest rate of homelessness. The San Jose metro area had a high rate of homelessness. Criteria: number of homeless people per 10,000 population in 2016. *National Alliance to End Homelessness, "Homelessness in the 25 Most Populous U.S. Metro Areas," September 1, 2017*

Business Environment

DEMOGRAPHICS

Population Growth

Area	1990 Census	2000 Census	2010 Census	2019* Estimate	Population Growth (%) 1990-2019	2010-2019
City	784,324	894,943	945,942	1,027,690	31.0	8.6
MSA[1]	1,534,280	1,735,819	1,836,911	1,987,846	29.6	8.2
U.S.	248,709,873	281,421,906	308,745,538	324,697,795	30.6	5.2

Note: (1) Figures cover the San Jose-Sunnyvale-Santa Clara, CA Metropolitan Statistical Area; (*) 2015-2019 5-year estimated population
Source: U.S. Census Bureau, 1990 Census, Census 2000, Census 2010, 2015-2019 American Community Survey 5-Year Estimates

Household Size

Area	One	Two	Three	Four	Five	Six	Seven or More	Average Household Size
City	19.4	28.9	18.6	18.0	8.1	3.6	3.4	3.10
MSA[1]	20.2	30.7	18.8	17.7	7.2	3.0	2.4	3.00
U.S.	27.9	33.9	15.6	12.9	6.0	2.3	1.4	2.60

Note: (1) Figures cover the San Jose-Sunnyvale-Santa Clara, CA Metropolitan Statistical Area
Source: U.S. Census Bureau, 2015-2019 American Community Survey 5-Year Estimates

Race

Area	White Alone[2] (%)	Black Alone[2] (%)	Asian Alone[2] (%)	AIAN[3] Alone[2] (%)	NHOPI[4] Alone[2] (%)	Other Race Alone[2] (%)	Two or More Races (%)
City	39.9	3.0	35.9	0.6	0.5	14.8	5.3
MSA[1]	45.6	2.4	35.4	0.5	0.4	10.4	5.2
U.S.	72.5	12.7	5.5	0.8	0.2	4.9	3.3

Note: (1) Figures cover the San Jose-Sunnyvale-Santa Clara, CA Metropolitan Statistical Area; (2) Alone is defined as not being in combination with one or more other races; (3) American Indian and Alaska Native; (4) Native Hawaiian and Other Pacific Islander
Source: U.S. Census Bureau, 2015-2019 American Community Survey 5-Year Estimates

Hispanic or Latino Origin

Area	Total (%)	Mexican (%)	Puerto Rican (%)	Cuban (%)	Other (%)
City	31.6	27.1	0.6	0.1	3.7
MSA[1]	26.5	22.1	0.5	0.1	3.7
U.S.	18.0	11.2	1.7	0.7	4.3

Note: Persons of Hispanic or Latino origin can be of any race; (1) Figures cover the San Jose-Sunnyvale-Santa Clara, CA Metropolitan Statistical Area
Source: U.S. Census Bureau, 2015-2019 American Community Survey 5-Year Estimates

Ancestry

Area	German	Irish	English	American	Italian	Polish	French[2]	Scottish	Dutch
City	5.0	4.0	3.5	1.8	3.3	0.9	1.2	0.8	0.5
MSA[1]	6.1	4.8	4.5	1.9	3.7	1.2	1.5	1.1	0.7
U.S.	13.3	9.7	7.2	6.2	5.1	2.8	2.3	1.7	1.2

Note: Figures are the percentage of the total population reporting a particular ancestry. The nine most commonly reported ancestries in the U.S. are shown. Figures include multiple ancestries (e.g. if a person reported being Irish and Italian, they were included in both columns); (1) Figures cover the San Jose-Sunnyvale-Santa Clara, CA Metropolitan Statistical Area; (2) Excludes Basque
Source: U.S. Census Bureau, 2015-2019 American Community Survey 5-Year Estimates

Foreign-born Population

Area	Any Foreign Country	Asia	Mexico	Europe	Caribbean	Central America[2]	South America	Africa	Canada
City	39.7	25.6	9.0	2.2	0.1	1.0	0.6	0.8	0.4
MSA[1]	38.6	25.4	7.0	3.1	0.1	0.9	0.7	0.7	0.5
U.S.	13.6	4.2	3.5	1.5	1.3	1.1	1.0	0.7	0.2

Note: (1) Figures cover the San Jose-Sunnyvale-Santa Clara, CA Metropolitan Statistical Area; (2) Excludes Mexico.
Source: U.S. Census Bureau, 2015-2019 American Community Survey 5-Year Estimates

Marital Status

Area	Never Married	Now Married[2]	Separated	Widowed	Divorced
City	35.4	51.0	1.6	4.2	7.8
MSA[1]	33.6	53.2	1.4	4.2	7.5
U.S.	33.4	48.1	1.9	5.8	10.9

Note: Figures are percentages and cover the population 15 years of age and older; (1) Figures cover the San Jose-Sunnyvale-Santa Clara, CA Metropolitan Statistical Area; (2) Excludes separated
Source: U.S. Census Bureau, 2015-2019 American Community Survey 5-Year Estimates

Disability by Age

Area	All Ages	Under 18 Years Old	18 to 64 Years Old	65 Years and Over
City	8.6	2.6	6.1	33.1
MSA[1]	8.1	2.4	5.4	31.2
U.S.	12.6	4.2	10.3	34.5

Note: Figures show percent of the civilian noninstitutionalized population that reported having a disability. Disability status is determined from six types of difficulty: vision, hearing, cognitive, ambulatory, self-care, and independent living. For children under 5 years old, hearing and vision difficulty are used to determine disability status. For children between the ages of 5 and 14, disability status is determined from hearing, vision, cognitive, ambulatory, and self-care difficulties. For people aged 15 years and older, they are considered to have a disability if they have difficulty with any one of the six difficulty types; Note: (1) Figures cover the San Jose-Sunnyvale-Santa Clara, CA Metropolitan Statistical Area
Source: U.S. Census Bureau, 2015-2019 American Community Survey 5-Year Estimates

Age

Area	Percent of Population									Median Age
	Under Age 5	Age 5–19	Age 20–34	Age 35–44	Age 45–54	Age 55–64	Age 65–74	Age 75–84	Age 85+	
City	6.1	18.4	22.7	14.4	13.9	11.8	7.3	3.7	1.5	36.7
MSA[1]	6.1	18.6	22.3	14.5	13.8	11.7	7.4	4.0	1.8	37.1
U.S.	6.1	19.1	20.7	12.6	13.0	12.9	9.1	4.6	1.9	38.1

Note: (1) Figures cover the San Jose-Sunnyvale-Santa Clara, CA Metropolitan Statistical Area
Source: U.S. Census Bureau, 2015-2019 American Community Survey 5-Year Estimates

Gender

Area	Males	Females	Males per 100 Females
City	518,708	508,982	101.9
MSA[1]	1,004,573	983,273	102.2
U.S.	159,886,919	164,810,876	97.0

Note: (1) Figures cover the San Jose-Sunnyvale-Santa Clara, CA Metropolitan Statistical Area
Source: U.S. Census Bureau, 2015-2019 American Community Survey 5-Year Estimates

Religious Groups by Family

Area	Catholic	Baptist	Non-Den.	Methodist[2]	Lutheran	LDS[3]	Pente-costal	Presby-terian[4]	Muslim[5]	Judaism
MSA[1]	26.0	1.4	4.3	1.1	0.6	1.4	1.2	0.7	1.0	0.7
U.S.	19.1	9.3	4.0	4.0	2.3	2.0	1.9	1.6	0.8	0.7

Note: Figures are the number of adherents as a percentage of the total population; (1) Figures cover the San Jose-Sunnyvale-Santa Clara, CA Metropolitan Statistical Area; (2) Methodist/Pietist; (3) Latter Day Saints; (4) Reformed; (5) Figures are estimates
Source: Association of Statisticians of American Religious Bodies, 2010 U.S. Religion Census: Religious Congregations & Membership Study

Religious Groups by Tradition

Area	Catholic	Evangelical Protestant	Mainline Protestant	Other Tradition	Black Protestant	Orthodox
MSA[1]	26.0	8.2	2.5	6.9	0.1	0.4
U.S.	19.1	16.2	7.3	4.3	1.6	0.3

Note: Figures are the number of adherents as a percentage of the total population; (1) Figures cover the San Jose-Sunnyvale-Santa Clara, CA Metropolitan Statistical Area
Source: Association of Statisticians of American Religious Bodies, 2010 U.S. Religion Census: Religious Congregations & Membership Study

ECONOMY

Gross Metropolitan Product

Area	2017	2018	2019	2020	Rank[2]
MSA[1]	281.6	303.1	321.2	334.7	13

Note: Figures are in billions of dollars; (1) Figures cover the San Jose-Sunnyvale-Santa Clara, CA Metropolitan Statistical Area; (2) Rank is based on 2018 data and ranges from 1 to 381
Source: U.S. Conference of Mayors, U.S. Metro Economies: GMP & Employment 2018-2020, September 2019

Economic Growth

Area	2015-17 (%)	2018 (%)	2019 (%)	2020 (%)	Rank[2]
MSA[1]	7.0	6.0	4.6	2.2	5
U.S.	1.9	2.9	2.3	2.1	–

Note: Figures are real gross metropolitan product (GMP) growth rates and represent average annual percent change; (1) Figures cover the San Jose-Sunnyvale-Santa Clara, CA Metropolitan Statistical Area; (2) Rank is based on 2017 2-year average annual percent change and ranges from 1 to 381
Source: U.S. Conference of Mayors, U.S. Metro Economies: GMP & Employment 2018-2020, September 2019

Metropolitan Area Exports

Area	2014	2015	2016	2017	2018	2019	Rank[2]
MSA[1]	21,128.8	19,827.2	21,716.8	21,464.7	22,224.2	20,909.4	19

Note: Figures are in millions of dollars; (1) Figures cover the San Jose-Sunnyvale-Santa Clara, CA Metropolitan Statistical Area; (2) Rank is based on 2019 data and ranges from 1 to 386
Source: U.S. Department of Commerce, International Trade Administration, Office of Trade and Economic Analysis, Industry and Analysis, Exports by Metropolitan Area, data extracted March 24, 2021

Building Permits

Area	Single-Family			Multi-Family			Total		
	2018	2019	Pct. Chg.	2018	2019	Pct. Chg.	2018	2019	Pct. Chg.
City	238	514	116.0	2,598	1,831	-29.5	2,836	2,345	-17.3
MSA[1]	2,466	2,603	5.6	6,278	3,627	-42.2	8,744	6,230	-28.8
U.S.	855,300	862,100	0.7	473,500	523,900	10.6	1,328,800	1,386,000	4.3

Note: (1) Figures cover the San Jose-Sunnyvale-Santa Clara, CA Metropolitan Statistical Area; Figures represent new, privately-owned housing units authorized (unadjusted data); All permit data are based on estimates with imputation
Source: U.S. Census Bureau, Manufacturing, Mining, and Construction Statistics, Building Permits, 2018, 2019

Bankruptcy Filings

Area	Business Filings			Nonbusiness Filings		
	2019	2020	% Chg.	2019	2020	% Chg.
Santa Clara County	94	86	-8.5	1,446	1,018	-29.6
U.S.	22,780	21,655	-4.9	752,160	522,808	-30.5

Note: Business filings include Chapter 7, Chapter 9, Chapter 11, Chapter 12, Chapter 13, Chapter 15, and Section 304; Nonbusiness filings include Chapter 7, Chapter 11, and Chapter 13
Source: Administrative Office of the U.S. Courts, Business and Nonbusiness Bankruptcy, County Cases Commenced by Chapter of the Bankruptcy Code, During the 12-Month Period Ending December 31, 2019 and Business and Nonbusiness Bankruptcy, County Cases Commenced by Chapter of the Bankruptcy Code, During the 12-Month Period Ending December 31, 2020

Housing Vacancy Rates

Area	Gross Vacancy Rate[2] (%)			Year-Round Vacancy Rate[3] (%)			Rental Vacancy Rate[4] (%)			Homeowner Vacancy Rate[5] (%)		
	2018	2019	2020	2018	2019	2020	2018	2019	2020	2018	2019	2020
MSA[1]	5.8	5.6	4.7	5.8	5.6	4.7	4.6	3.7	4.4	0.5	0.5	0.0
U.S.	12.3	12.0	10.6	9.7	9.5	8.2	6.9	6.7	6.3	1.5	1.4	1.0

Note: (1) Figures cover the San Jose-Sunnyvale-Santa Clara, CA Metropolitan Statistical Area; (2) The percentage of the total housing inventory that is vacant; (3) The percentage of the housing inventory (excluding seasonal units) that is year-round vacant; (4) The percentage of rental inventory that is vacant for rent; (5) The percentage of homeowner inventory that is vacant for sale
Source: U.S. Census Bureau, Housing Vacancies and Homeownership Annual Statistics: 2018, 2019, 2020

INCOME

Income

Area	Per Capita ($)	Median Household ($)	Average Household ($)
City	46,599	109,593	142,635
MSA[1]	55,547	122,478	163,355
U.S.	34,103	62,843	88,607

Note: (1) Figures cover the San Jose-Sunnyvale-Santa Clara, CA Metropolitan Statistical Area
Source: U.S. Census Bureau, 2015-2019 American Community Survey 5-Year Estimates

Household Income Distribution

Area	Percent of Households Earning							
	Under $15,000	$15,000 -$24,999	$25,000 -$34,999	$35,000 -$49,999	$50,000 -$74,999	$75,000 -$99,999	$100,000 -$149,999	$150,000 and up
City	6.2	4.8	4.9	7.2	12.0	10.7	18.0	36.2
MSA[1]	5.5	4.3	4.5	6.6	10.8	10.0	17.5	40.9
U.S.	10.3	8.9	8.9	12.3	17.2	12.7	15.1	14.5

Note: (1) Figures cover the San Jose-Sunnyvale-Santa Clara, CA Metropolitan Statistical Area
Source: U.S. Census Bureau, 2015-2019 American Community Survey 5-Year Estimates

Poverty Rate

Area	All Ages	Under 18 Years Old	18 to 64 Years Old	65 Years and Over
City	8.7	9.3	8.4	9.5
MSA[1]	7.5	7.9	7.3	8.0
U.S.	13.4	18.5	12.6	9.3

Note: Figures are percentage of people whose income during the past 12 months was below the poverty level;
(1) Figures cover the San Jose-Sunnyvale-Santa Clara, CA Metropolitan Statistical Area
Source: U.S. Census Bureau, 2015-2019 American Community Survey 5-Year Estimates

CITY FINANCES

City Government Finances

Component	2017 ($000)	2017 ($ per capita)
Total Revenues	2,829,081	2,755
Total Expenditures	1,973,323	1,922
Debt Outstanding	4,767,744	4,643
Cash and Securities[1]	8,077,921	7,866

Note: (1) Cash and security holdings of a government at the close of its fiscal year,
including those of its dependent agencies, utilities, and liquor stores.
Source: U.S. Census Bureau, State & Local Government Finances 2017

City Government Revenue by Source

Source	2017 ($000)	2017 ($ per capita)	2017 (%)
General Revenue			
From Federal Government	44,542	43	1.6
From State Government	50,563	49	1.8
From Local Governments	3,391	3	0.1
Taxes			
Property	597,131	581	21.1
Sales and Gross Receipts	423,928	413	15.0
Personal Income	0	0	0.0
Corporate Income	0	0	0.0
Motor Vehicle License	0	0	0.0
Other Taxes	217,517	212	7.7
Current Charges	725,086	706	25.6
Liquor Store	0	0	0.0
Utility	43,620	42	1.5
Employee Retirement	515,029	502	18.2

Source: U.S. Census Bureau, State & Local Government Finances 2017

City Government Expenditures by Function

Function	2017 ($000)	2017 ($ per capita)	2017 (%)
General Direct Expenditures			
Air Transportation	101,208	98	5.1
Corrections	0	0	0.0
Education	0	0	0.0
Employment Security Administration	0	0	0.0
Financial Administration	0	0	0.0
Fire Protection	141,999	138	7.2
General Public Buildings	0	0	0.0
Governmental Administration, Other	101,536	98	5.1
Health	424	< 1	< 0.1
Highways	47,126	45	2.4
Hospitals	0	0	0.0
Housing and Community Development	43,020	41	2.2
Interest on General Debt	230,366	224	11.7
Judicial and Legal	0	0	0.0
Libraries	27,711	27	1.4
Parking	10,328	10	0.5
Parks and Recreation	157,978	153	8.0
Police Protection	244,718	238	12.4
Public Welfare	0	0	0.0
Sewerage	234,010	227	11.9
Solid Waste Management	112,028	109	5.7
Veterans' Services	0	0	0.0
Liquor Store	0	0	0.0
Utility	34,926	34	1.8
Employee Retirement	379,462	369	19.2

Source: U.S. Census Bureau, State & Local Government Finances 2017

EMPLOYMENT

Labor Force and Employment

Area	Civilian Labor Force			Workers Employed		
	Dec. 2019	Dec. 2020	% Chg.	Dec. 2019	Dec. 2020	% Chg.
City	558,215	552,450	-1.0	545,337	515,386	-5.5
MSA[1]	1,090,183	1,071,686	-1.7	1,065,627	1,007,069	-5.5
U.S.	164,007,000	160,017,000	-2.4	158,504,000	149,613,000	-5.6

Note: Data is not seasonally adjusted and covers workers 16 years of age and older; (1) Figures cover the San Jose-Sunnyvale-Santa Clara, CA Metropolitan Statistical Area
Source: Bureau of Labor Statistics, Local Area Unemployment Statistics

Unemployment Rate

Area	2020											
	Jan.	Feb.	Mar.	Apr.	May	Jun.	Jul.	Aug.	Sep.	Oct.	Nov.	Dec.
City	2.8	2.7	3.6	13.8	13.1	12.4	10.9	8.4	8.1	6.5	5.7	6.7
MSA[1]	2.7	2.7	3.5	12.0	11.3	10.8	9.5	7.3	7.0	5.8	5.2	6.0
U.S.	4.0	3.8	4.5	14.4	13.0	11.2	10.5	8.5	7.7	6.6	6.4	6.5

Note: Data is not seasonally adjusted and covers workers 16 years of age and older; (1) Figures cover the San Jose-Sunnyvale-Santa Clara, CA Metropolitan Statistical Area
Source: Bureau of Labor Statistics, Local Area Unemployment Statistics

Average Wages

Occupation	$/Hr.	Occupation	$/Hr.
Accountants and Auditors	49.50	Maintenance and Repair Workers	26.40
Automotive Mechanics	30.50	Marketing Managers	101.50
Bookkeepers	27.30	Network and Computer Systems Admin.	64.60
Carpenters	31.80	Nurses, Licensed Practical	36.50
Cashiers	17.30	Nurses, Registered	70.60
Computer Programmers	54.60	Nursing Assistants	20.20
Computer Systems Analysts	64.40	Office Clerks, General	22.00
Computer User Support Specialists	34.90	Physical Therapists	51.90
Construction Laborers	27.60	Physicians	106.40
Cooks, Restaurant	17.20	Plumbers, Pipefitters and Steamfitters	40.80
Customer Service Representatives	22.90	Police and Sheriff's Patrol Officers	63.00
Dentists	94.60	Postal Service Mail Carriers	26.30
Electricians	41.60	Real Estate Sales Agents	48.70
Engineers, Electrical	72.40	Retail Salespersons	20.80
Fast Food and Counter Workers	16.40	Sales Representatives, Technical/Scientific	69.20
Financial Managers	92.50	Secretaries, Exc. Legal/Medical/Executive	25.00
First-Line Supervisors of Office Workers	34.50	Security Guards	21.20
General and Operations Managers	84.60	Surgeons	124.60
Hairdressers/Cosmetologists	18.20	Teacher Assistants, Exc. Postsecondary*	19.80
Home Health and Personal Care Aides	15.80	Teachers, Secondary School, Exc. Sp. Ed.*	44.50
Janitors and Cleaners	19.40	Telemarketers	16.70
Landscaping/Groundskeeping Workers	22.60	Truck Drivers, Heavy/Tractor-Trailer	27.50
Lawyers	111.40	Truck Drivers, Light/Delivery Services	25.00
Maids and Housekeeping Cleaners	19.50	Waiters and Waitresses	17.30

Note: Wage data covers the San Jose-Sunnyvale-Santa Clara, CA Metropolitan Statistical Area; (*) Hourly wages were calculated from annual wage data based on a 40 hour work week; n/a not available.
Source: Bureau of Labor Statistics, Metro Area Occupational Employment & Wage Estimates, May 2020

Employment by Industry

Sector	MSA[1]		U.S.
	Number of Employees	Percent of Total	Percent of Total
Construction	51,200	4.8	5.1
Education and Health Services	171,000	16.0	16.3
Financial Activities	37,700	3.5	6.1
Government	93,200	8.7	15.2
Information	107,200	10.0	1.9
Leisure and Hospitality	58,600	5.5	9.0
Manufacturing	168,400	15.7	8.5
Mining and Logging	200	<0.1	0.4
Other Services	20,700	1.9	3.8
Professional and Business Services	239,500	22.4	14.4
Retail Trade	77,200	7.2	10.9
Transportation, Warehousing, and Utilities	17,200	1.6	4.6
Wholesale Trade	28,400	2.7	3.9

Note: Figures are non-farm employment as of December 2020. Figures are not seasonally adjusted and include workers 16 years of age and older; (1) Figures cover the San Jose-Sunnyvale-Santa Clara, CA Metropolitan Statistical Area
Source: Bureau of Labor Statistics, Current Employment Statistics, Employment, Hours, and Earnings

Employment by Occupation

Occupation Classification	City (%)	MSA[1] (%)	U.S. (%)
Management, Business, Science, and Arts	46.8	53.5	38.5
Natural Resources, Construction, and Maintenance	7.1	6.3	8.9
Production, Transportation, and Material Moving	10.1	8.4	13.2
Sales and Office	18.3	16.9	21.6
Service	17.6	14.8	17.8

Note: Figures cover employed civilians 16 years of age and older; (1) Figures cover the San Jose-Sunnyvale-Santa Clara, CA Metropolitan Statistical Area
Source: U.S. Census Bureau, 2015-2019 American Community Survey 5-Year Estimates

Occupations with Greatest Projected Employment Growth: 2020 – 2022

Occupation[1]	2020 Employment	2022 Projected Employment	Numeric Employment Change	Percent Employment Change
Retail Salespersons	317,300	401,300	84,000	26.5
Laborers and Freight, Stock, and Material Movers, Hand	348,700	411,100	62,400	17.9
Waiters and Waitresses	182,500	242,800	60,300	33.0
Combined Food Preparation and Serving Workers, Including Fast Food	183,800	237,200	53,400	29.1
Cashiers	358,500	407,300	48,800	13.6
Cooks, Restaurant	113,200	156,500	43,300	38.3
Personal Care Aides	409,600	447,900	38,300	9.4
Farmworkers and Laborers, Crop, Nursery, and Greenhouse	242,000	269,700	27,700	11.4
Fast Food and Counter Workers	94,000	120,200	26,200	27.9
General and Operations Managers	242,700	268,300	25,600	10.5

Note: Projections cover California; (1) Sorted by numeric employment change
Source: www.projectionscentral.com, State Occupational Projections, 2020–2022 Short-Term Projections

Fastest-Growing Occupations: 2020 – 2022

Occupation[1]	2020 Employment	2022 Projected Employment	Numeric Employment Change	Percent Employment Change
Manicurists and Pedicurists	7,800	21,300	13,500	173.1
Hairdressers, Hairstylists, and Cosmetologists	22,700	44,600	21,900	96.5
Massage Therapists	8,800	17,100	8,300	94.3
Skincare Specialists	5,500	9,100	3,600	65.5
Dental Hygienists	9,200	14,700	5,500	59.8
Dental Hygienists (SOC 2018)	5,300	8,400	3,100	58.5
Dental Assistants	36,300	56,300	20,000	55.1
Dentists, General	12,600	19,000	6,400	50.8
Parking Lot Attendants	14,300	20,400	6,100	42.7
Lodging Managers	3,300	4,600	1,300	39.4

Note: Projections cover California; (1) Sorted by percent employment change and excludes occupations with numeric employment change less than 50
Source: www.projectionscentral.com, State Occupational Projections, 2020–2022 Short-Term Projections

TAXES

State Corporate Income Tax Rates

State	Tax Rate (%)	Income Brackets ($)	Num. of Brackets	Financial Institution Tax Rate (%)[a]	Federal Income Tax Ded.
California	8.84 (b)	Flat rate	1	10.84 (b)	No

Note: Tax rates as of January 1, 2021; (a) Rates listed are the corporate income tax rate applied to financial institutions or excise taxes based on income. Some states have other taxes based upon the value of deposits or shares; (b) Minimum tax is $800 in California, $250 in District of Columbia, $50 in Arizona and North Dakota (banks), $400 ($100 banks) in Rhode Island, $200 per location in South Dakota (banks), $100 in Utah, $300 in Vermont.
Source: Federation of Tax Administrators, State Corporate Income Tax Rates, January 1, 2021

State Individual Income Tax Rates

State	Tax Rate (%)	Income Brackets ($)	Personal Exemptions ($)			Standard Ded. ($)	
			Single	Married	Depend.	Single	Married
California (a)	1.0 - 12.3 (g)	8,932 - 599,012 (b)	124	248 (c)	383 (c)	4,601	9,202 (a)

Note: Tax rates as of January 1, 2021; Local- and county-level taxes are not included; Federal income tax is not deductible on state income tax returns; (a) 19 states have statutory provision for automatically adjusting to the rate of inflation the dollar values of the income tax brackets, standard deductions, and/or personal exemptions. Michigan indexes the personal exemption only. Oregon does not index the income brackets for $125,000 and over; (b) For joint returns, taxes are twice the tax on half the couple's income; (c) The personal exemption takes the form of a tax credit instead of a deduction; (g) California imposes an additional 1% tax on taxable income over $1 million, making the maximum rate 13.3% over $1 million.
Source: Federation of Tax Administrators, State Individual Income Tax Rates, January 1, 2021

Various State Sales and Excise Tax Rates

State	State Sales Tax (%)	Gasoline[1] (¢/gal.)	Cigarette[2] ($/pack)	Spirits[3] ($/gal.)	Wine[4] ($/gal.)	Beer[5] ($/gal.)	Recreational Marijuana (%)
California	7.25	63.05	2.87	3.3	0.2	0.2	(c)

Note: All tax rates as of January 1, 2021; (1) The American Petroleum Institute has developed a methodology for determining the average tax rate on a gallon of fuel. Rates may include any of the following: excise taxes, environmental fees, storage tank fees, other fees or taxes, general sales tax, and local taxes; (2) The federal excise tax of $1.0066 per pack and local taxes are not included; (3) Rates are those applicable to off-premise sales of 40% alcohol by volume (a.b.v.) distilled spirits in 750ml containers. Local excise taxes are excluded; (4) Rates are those applicable to off-premise sales of 11% a.b.v. non-carbonated wine in 750ml containers; (5) Rates are those applicable to off-premise sales of 4.7% a.b.v. beer in 12 ounce containers; (c) 15% excise tax (levied on wholesale at average market rate); $9.65/oz. flowers & $2.87/oz. leaves cultivation tax; $1.35/oz fresh cannabis plant
Source: Tax Foundation, 2021 Facts & Figures: How Does Your State Compare?

State Business Tax Climate Index Rankings

State	Overall Rank	Corporate Tax Rank	Individual Income Tax Rank	Sales Tax Rank	Property Tax Rank	Unemployment Insurance Tax Rank
California	49	28	49	45	14	21

Note: The index is a measure of how each state's tax laws affect economic performance. The lower the rank, the more favorable a state's tax system is for business. States without a given tax are given a ranking of 1. The scores/rankings for the District of Columbia do not affect other states. The 2021 index represents the tax climate as of July 1, 2020.
Source: Tax Foundation, State Business Tax Climate Index 2021

TRANSPORTATION

Means of Transportation to Work

Area	Car/Truck/Van		Public Transportation			Bicycle	Walked	Other Means	Worked at Home
	Drove Alone	Car-pooled	Bus	Subway	Railroad				
City	75.8	11.7	2.6	0.3	1.2	0.8	1.8	1.6	4.2
MSA[1]	74.9	10.6	2.4	0.3	1.5	1.7	2.1	1.6	5.0
U.S.	76.3	9.0	2.4	1.9	0.6	0.5	2.7	1.4	5.2

Note: Figures are percentages and cover workers 16 years of age and older; (1) Figures cover the San Jose-Sunnyvale-Santa Clara, CA Metropolitan Statistical Area
Source: U.S. Census Bureau, 2015-2019 American Community Survey 5-Year Estimates

Travel Time to Work

Area	Less Than 10 Minutes	10 to 19 Minutes	20 to 29 Minutes	30 to 44 Minutes	45 to 59 Minutes	60 to 89 Minutes	90 Minutes or More
City	5.1	22.4	22.1	27.7	10.8	8.7	3.1
MSA[1]	6.6	25.0	22.6	25.1	9.6	7.8	3.2
U.S.	12.2	28.4	20.8	20.8	8.3	6.4	2.9

Note: Note: Figures are percentages and include workers 16 years old and over; (1) Figures cover the San Jose-Sunnyvale-Santa Clara, CA Metropolitan Statistical Area
Source: U.S. Census Bureau, 2015-2019 American Community Survey 5-Year Estimates

Key Congestion Measures

Measure	1982	1992	2002	2012	2017
Annual Hours of Delay, Total (000)	15,571	38,783	66,943	105,662	126,774
Annual Hours of Delay, Per Auto Commuter	19	38	52	72	81
Annual Congestion Cost, Total (million $)	117	410	908	1,895	2,355
Annual Congestion Cost, Per Auto Commuter ($)	453	775	1,043	1,290	1,501

Note: Covers the San Jose CA urban area
Source: Texas A&M Transportation Institute, 2019 Urban Mobility Report

Freeway Travel Time Index

Measure	1982	1987	1992	1997	2002	2007	2012	2017
Urban Area Index[1]	1.11	1.18	1.22	1.24	1.30	1.34	1.38	1.45
Urban Area Rank[1,2]	17	11	6	11	9	7	3	3

Note: Freeway Travel Time Index—the ratio of travel time in the peak period to the travel time at free-flow conditions. For example, a value of 1.30 indicates a 20-minute free-flow trip takes 26 minutes in the peak (20 minutes x 1.30 = 26 minutes); (1) Covers the San Jose CA urban area; (2) Rank is based on 101 larger urban areas (#1 = highest travel time index)
Source: Texas A&M Transportation Institute, 2019 Urban Mobility Report

Public Transportation

Agency Name / Mode of Transportation	Vehicles Operated in Maximum Service[1]	Annual Unlinked Passenger Trips[2] (in thous.)	Annual Passenger Miles[3] (in thous.)
Santa Clara Valley Transportation Authority (VTA)			
Bus (directly operated)	382	27,027.7	135,577.6
Bus (purchased transportation)	12	444.4	1,638.5
Demand Response (purchased transportation)	154	431.9	4,843.6
Demand Response Taxi (purchased transportation)	45	91.0	930.5
Light Rail (directly operated)	57	8,437.9	49,376.2

Note: (1) Number of revenue vehicles operated by the given mode and type of service to meet the annual maximum service requirement. This is the revenue vehicle count during the peak season of the year; on the week and day that maximum service is provided. Vehicles operated in maximum service (VOMS) exclude atypical days and one-time special events; (2) Number of passengers who boarded public transportation vehicles. Passengers are counted each time they board a vehicle no matter how many vehicles they use to travel from their origin to their destination. (3) Sum of the distances ridden by all passengers during the entire fiscal year.
Source: Federal Transit Administration, National Transit Database, 2019

Air Transportation

Airport Name and Code / Type of Service	Passenger Airlines[1]	Passenger Enplanements	Freight Carriers[2]	Freight (lbs)
San Jose International (SJC)				
Domestic service (U.S. carriers - 2020)	23	2,134,599	9	43,233,979
International service (U.S. carriers - 2019)	7	108,822	1	78,104

Note: (1) Includes all U.S.-based major, minor and commuter airlines that carried at least one passenger during the year; (2) Includes all U.S.-based airlines and freight carriers that transported at least one pound of freight during the year.
Source: Bureau of Transportation Statistics, The Intermodal Transportation Database, Air Carriers: T-100 Domestic Market (U.S. Carriers), 2020; Bureau of Transportation Statistics, The Intermodal Transportation Database, Air Carriers: T-100 International Market (U.S. Carriers), 2019

BUSINESSES

Major Business Headquarters

Company Name	Industry	Rankings	
		Fortune[1]	Forbes[2]
Adobe	Computer Software	285	-
Broadcom	Semiconductors and Other Electronic Components	138	-
Cisco Systems	Network and Other Communications Equipment	63	-
Ma Labs	Technology Hardware & Equipment	-	217
PayPal Holdings	Financial Data Services	182	-
Sanmina	Semiconductors and Other Electronic Components	385	-
eBay	Internet Services and Retailing	295	-

Note: (1) Companies that produce a 10-K are ranked 1 to 500 based on 2019 revenue; (2) All private companies with at least $2 billion in annual revenue through the end of their most current fiscal year are ranked 1 to 219; companies listed are headquartered in the city; dashes indicate no ranking
Source: Fortune, "Fortune 500," June/July 2020; Forbes, "America's Largest Private Companies," 2020

Fastest-Growing Businesses

According to *Inc.*, San Jose is home to one of America's 500 fastest-growing private companies: **Infolink Technology Solutions** (#490). Criteria: must be an independent, privately-held, for-profit, U.S. corporation, proprietorship or partnership as of December 31, 2019; revenues must be at least $100,000 in 2016 and $2 million in 2019; must have four-year operating/sales history. *Inc., "America's 500 Fastest-Growing Private Companies," 2020*

According to *Fortune*, San Jose is home to two of the 100 fastest-growing companies in the world: **Adobe** (#26); **PayPal Holdings** (#78). Companies were ranked by their revenue growth rate; their EPS growth rate; and their three-year annualized total return to investors for the period ending June 30, 2020. Criteria for inclusion: a company, foreign or domestic, must trade on a major U.S. stock exchange; must file quarterly reports with the SEC; must have a minimum market capitalization of $250 million; must have a stock price of at least $5 on June 30, 2020; must have been trading continuously since June 30, 2017; must have revenue and net income for the four quarters ended on or before April 30, 2020, of at least $50 million and $10 million, respectively; and must have posted a compound annual growth in revenue and earnings per share of at least 15% annually over the three years ending on or before April 30, 2020. Real estate investment trusts, limited-liability companies, limited parterships, business development companies, closed-end investment firms, companies about to be acquired, and companies that lost money in the quarter ending April 30, 2020 were excluded. *Fortune, "100 Fastest-Growing Companies," 2020*

According to Deloitte, San Jose is home to eight of North America's 500 fastest-growing high-technology companies: **Zoom Video Communications, Inc.** (#131); **Ondot Systems** (#227); **Vectra AI** (#262); **Semler Scientific, Inc.** (#303); **Zscaler** (#352); **Edison Software** (#355); **Wrike** (#423); **Roku, Inc.** (#483). Companies are ranked by percentage growth in revenue over a four-year period. Criteria for inclusion: company must be headquartered within North America; must own proprietary intellectual property or technology that is sold to customers in products that contributes to a significant portion of the company's operating revenue; must have been in business for a minumum of four years with 2016 operating revenues of at least $50,000 USD/CD and 2019 operating revenues of at least $5 million USD/CD. *Deloitte, 2020 Technology Fast 500*™

Minority Business Opportunity

San Jose is home to three companies which are on the *Black Enterprise* Industrial/Service list (100 largest companies based on gross sales): **Overland-Tandberg** (#56); **Mosaic Global Transportation** (#94); **Cerulean Global Services** (#99). Criteria: operational in previous calendar year; at least 51% black-owned and manufactures/owns the product it sells or provides industrial or consumer services. Brokerages, real estate firms and firms that provide professional services are not eligible. *Black Enterprise, B.E. 100s, 2019*

Living Environment

COST OF LIVING

Cost of Living Index

Composite Index	Groceries	Housing	Utilities	Trans-portation	Health Care	Misc. Goods/ Services
n/a	n/a	n/a	n/a	n/a	n/a	n/a

Note: The Cost of Living Index measures regional differences in the cost of consumer goods and services, excluding taxes and non-consumer expenditures, for professional and managerial households in the top income quintile. It is based on more than 50,000 prices covering almost 60 different items for which prices are collected three times a year by chambers of commerce, economic development organizations or university applied economic centers in each participating urban area. The numbers shown should be read as a percentage above or below the national average of 100. For example, a value of 115.4 in the groceries column indicates that grocery prices are 15.4% higher than the national average. Small differences in the index numbers should not be interpreted as significant; n/a not available.
Source: The Council for Community and Economic Research, Cost of Living Index, 2020

Grocery Prices

Area[1]	T-Bone Steak ($/pound)	Frying Chicken ($/pound)	Whole Milk ($/half gal.)	Eggs ($/dozen)	Orange Juice ($/64 oz.)	Coffee ($/11.5 oz.)
City[2]	n/a	n/a	n/a	n/a	n/a	n/a
Avg.	11.78	1.39	2.05	1.47	3.57	4.34
Min.	8.03	0.94	1.03	0.74	2.94	3.02
Max.	15.86	2.65	4.31	3.77	5.44	8.69

Note: (1) Values for the local area are compared with the average, minimum and maximum values for all 284 areas in the Cost of Living Index; (2) Figures cover the San Jose CA urban area; n/a not available; **T-Bone Steak** (price per pound); **Frying Chicken** (price per pound, whole fryer); **Whole Milk** (half gallon carton); **Eggs** (price per dozen, Grade A, large); **Orange Juice** (64 oz. Tropicana or Florida Natural); **Coffee** (11.5 oz. can, vacuum-packed, Maxwell House, Hills Bros, or Folgers).
Source: The Council for Community and Economic Research, Cost of Living Index, 2020

Housing and Utility Costs

Area[1]	New Home Price ($)	Apartment Rent ($/month)	All Electric ($/month)	Part Electric ($/month)	Other Energy ($/month)	Telephone ($/month)
City[2]	n/a	n/a	n/a	n/a	n/a	n/a
Avg.	368,594	1,168	170.86	100.47	65.28	184.30
Min.	190,567	502	91.58	31.42	26.08	169.60
Max.	2,227,806	4,738	470.38	280.31	280.06	206.50

Note: (1) Values for the local area are compared with the average, minimum and maximum values for all 284 areas in the Cost of Living Index; (2) Figures cover the San Jose CA urban area; n/a not available; **New Home Price** (2,400 sf living area, 8,000 sf lot, in urban area with full utilities); **Apartment Rent** (950 sf 2 bedroom/1.5 or 2 bath, unfurnished, excluding all utilities except water); **All Electric** (average monthly cost for an all-electric home); **Part Electric** (average monthly cost for a part-electric home); **Other Energy** (average monthly cost for natural gas, fuel oil, coal, wood, and any other forms of energy except electricity); **Telephone** (price includes the base monthly rate plus taxes and fees for three lines of mobile phone service).
Source: The Council for Community and Economic Research, Cost of Living Index, 2020

Health Care, Transportation, and Other Costs

Area[1]	Doctor ($/visit)	Dentist ($/visit)	Optometrist ($/visit)	Gasoline ($/gallon)	Beauty Salon ($/visit)	Men's Shirt ($)
City[2]	n/a	n/a	n/a	n/a	n/a	n/a
Avg.	115.44	99.32	108.10	2.21	39.27	31.37
Min.	36.68	59.00	51.36	1.71	19.00	11.00
Max.	219.00	153.10	250.97	3.46	82.05	58.33

Note: (1) Values for the local area are compared with the average, minimum and maximum values for all 284 areas in the Cost of Living Index; (2) Figures cover the San Jose CA urban area; n/a not available; **Doctor** (general practitioners routine exam of an established patient); **Dentist** (adult teeth cleaning and periodic oral examination); **Optometrist** (full vision eye exam for established adult patient); **Gasoline** (one gallon regular unleaded, national brand, including all taxes, cash price at self-service pump if available); **Beauty Salon** (woman's shampoo, trim, and blow-dry); **Men's Shirt** (cotton/polyester dress shirt, pinpoint weave, long sleeves).
Source: The Council for Community and Economic Research, Cost of Living Index, 2020

HOUSING

Homeownership Rate

Area	2012 (%)	2013 (%)	2014 (%)	2015 (%)	2016 (%)	2017 (%)	2018 (%)	2019 (%)	2020 (%)
MSA[1]	58.6	56.4	56.4	50.7	49.9	50.4	50.4	52.4	52.6
U.S.	65.4	65.1	64.5	63.7	63.4	63.9	64.4	64.6	66.6

Note: (1) Figures cover the San Jose-Sunnyvale-Santa Clara, CA Metropolitan Statistical Area
Source: U.S. Census Bureau, Housing Vacancies and Homeownership Annual Statistics: 2012-2020

House Price Index (HPI)

Area	National Ranking[2]	Quarterly Change (%)	One-Year Change (%)	Five-Year Change (%)	Since 1991Q1 (%)
MSA[1]	251	0.55	0.10	18.04	296.60
U.S.[3]	–	3.81	10.77	38.99	205.12

Note: The HPI is a weighted repeat sales index. It measures average price changes in repeat sales or refinancings on the same properties. This information is obtained by reviewing repeat mortgage transactions on single-family properties whose mortgages have been purchased or securitized by Fannie Mae or Freddie Mac since January 1975; (1) Figures cover the San Jose-Sunnyvale-Santa Clara, CA Metropolitan Statistical Area; (2) Rankings are based on annual percentage change for all metro areas containing at least 15,000 transactions over the last 10 years and ranges from 1 to 253; (3) figures based on a weighted average of Census Division estimates using a seasonally adjusted, purchase-only index; all figures are for the period ending December 31, 2020
Source: Federal Housing Finance Agency, Change in Metropolitan Area House Price Indexes, April 7, 2021

Median Single-Family Home Prices

Area	2018	2019	2020p	Percent Change 2019 to 2020
MSA[1]	1,340.0	1,265.0	1,385.0	9.5
U.S. Average	261.6	274.6	299.9	9.2

Note: Figures are median sales prices of existing single-family homes in thousands of dollars; (p) preliminary; (1) Figures cover the San Jose-Sunnyvale-Santa Clara, CA Metropolitan Statistical Area
Source: National Association of Realtors, Median Sales Price of Existing Single-Family Homes for Metropolitan Areas, 4th Quarter 2020

Qualifying Income Based on Median Sales Price of Existing Single-Family Homes

Area	With 5% Down ($)	With 10% Down ($)	With 20% Down ($)
MSA[1]	264,799	250,862	222,989
U.S. Average	59,266	56,147	49,908

Note: Figures are preliminary; Qualifying income is based on a mortgage rate of 2.81%. Monthly principal and interest payment is limited to 25% of income; (1) Figures cover the San Jose-Sunnyvale-Santa Clara, CA Metropolitan Statistical Area
Source: National Association of Realtors, Qualifying Income Based on Median Sales Price of Existing Single-Family Homes for Metropolitan Areas, 4th Quarter 2020

Home Value Distribution

Area	Under $50,000	$50,000 -$99,999	$100,000 -$149,999	$150,000 -$199,999	$200,000 -$299,999	$300,000 -$499,999	$500,000 -$999,999	$1,000,000 or more
City	1.5	1.4	1.4	0.9	1.9	7.2	50.0	35.6
MSA[1]	1.3	1.0	1.2	0.9	1.8	6.4	40.1	47.3
U.S.	6.9	12.0	13.3	14.0	19.6	19.3	11.4	3.4

Note: Figures are percentages and cover owner-occupied housing units; (1) Figures cover the San Jose-Sunnyvale-Santa Clara, CA Metropolitan Statistical Area
Source: U.S. Census Bureau, 2015-2019 American Community Survey 5-Year Estimates

Year Housing Structure Built

Area	2010 or Later	2000 -2009	1990 -1999	1980 -1989	1970 -1979	1960 -1969	1950 -1959	1940 -1949	Before 1940	Median Year
City	5.2	9.3	10.6	12.9	24.2	18.6	11.0	3.0	5.2	1975
MSA[1]	5.6	9.0	10.6	12.6	21.6	18.0	13.9	3.6	5.1	1974
U.S.	5.2	14.0	13.9	13.4	15.2	10.6	10.3	4.9	12.6	1978

Note: Figures are percentages except for Median Year; Note: (1) Figures cover the San Jose-Sunnyvale-Santa Clara, CA Metropolitan Statistical Area
Source: U.S. Census Bureau, 2015-2019 American Community Survey 5-Year Estimates

Gross Monthly Rent

Area	Under $500	$500 -$999	$1,000 -$1,499	$1,500 -$1,999	$2,000 -$2,499	$2,500 -$2,999	$3,000 and up	Median ($)
City	4.5	6.9	13.6	20.9	19.2	16.2	18.7	2,107
MSA[1]	3.5	5.8	11.6	18.8	20.7	17.2	22.4	2,249
U.S.	9.4	36.2	30.0	14.0	5.6	2.4	2.4	1,062

Note: Figures are percentages except for Median; Gross rent is the contract rent plus the estimated average monthly cost of utilities (electricity, gas, and water and sewer) and fuels (oil, coal, kerosene, wood, etc.) if these are paid by the renter (or paid for the renter by someone else); (1) Figures cover the San Jose-Sunnyvale-Santa Clara, CA Metropolitan Statistical Area
Source: U.S. Census Bureau, 2015-2019 American Community Survey 5-Year Estimates

HEALTH

Health Risk Factors

Category	MSA[1] (%)	U.S. (%)
Adults aged 18–64 who have any kind of health care coverage	n/a	87.3
Adults who reported being in good or better health	n/a	82.4
Adults who have been told they have high blood cholesterol	n/a	33.0
Adults who have been told they have high blood pressure	n/a	32.3
Adults who are current smokers	n/a	17.1
Adults who currently use E-cigarettes	n/a	4.6
Adults who currently use chewing tobacco, snuff, or snus	n/a	4.0
Adults who are heavy drinkers[2]	n/a	6.3
Adults who are binge drinkers[3]	n/a	17.4
Adults who are overweight (BMI 25.0 - 29.9)	n/a	35.3
Adults who are obese (BMI 30.0 - 99.8)	n/a	31.3
Adults who participated in any physical activities in the past month	n/a	74.4
Adults who always or nearly always wears a seat belt	n/a	94.3

Note: n/a not available; (1) Figures cover the San Jose-Sunnyvale-Santa Clara, CA Metropolitan Statistical Area; (2) Heavy drinkers are classified as adult men having more than 14 drinks per week and adult women having more than 7 drinks per week; (3) Binge drinkers are classified as males having five or more drinks on one occasion or females having four or more drinks on one occasion
Source: Centers for Disease Control and Prevention, Behaviorial Risk Factor Surveillance System, SMART: Selected Metropolitan Area Risk Trends, 2017

Acute and Chronic Health Conditions

Category	MSA[1] (%)	U.S. (%)
Adults who have ever been told they had a heart attack	n/a	4.2
Adults who have ever been told they have angina or coronary heart disease	n/a	3.9
Adults who have ever been told they had a stroke	n/a	3.0
Adults who have ever been told they have asthma	n/a	14.2
Adults who have ever been told they have arthritis	n/a	24.9
Adults who have ever been told they have diabetes[2]	n/a	10.5
Adults who have ever been told they had skin cancer	n/a	6.2
Adults who have ever been told they had any other types of cancer	n/a	7.1
Adults who have ever been told they have COPD	n/a	6.5
Adults who have ever been told they have kidney disease	n/a	3.0
Adults who have ever been told they have a form of depression	n/a	20.5

Note: n/a not available; (1) Figures cover the San Jose-Sunnyvale-Santa Clara, CA Metropolitan Statistical Area; (2) Figures do not include pregnancy-related, borderline, or pre-diabetes
Source: Centers for Disease Control and Prevention, Behaviorial Risk Factor Surveillance System, SMART: Selected Metropolitan Area Risk Trends, 2017

Health Screening and Vaccination Rates

Category	MSA[1] (%)	U.S. (%)
Adults aged 65+ who have had flu shot within the past year	n/a	60.7
Adults aged 65+ who have ever had a pneumonia vaccination	n/a	75.4
Adults who have ever been tested for HIV	n/a	36.1
Adults who have ever had the shingles or zoster vaccine?	n/a	28.9
Adults who have had their blood cholesterol checked within the last five years	n/a	85.9

Note: n/a not available; (1) Figures cover the San Jose-Sunnyvale-Santa Clara, CA Metropolitan Statistical Area.
Source: Centers for Disease Control and Prevention, Behaviorial Risk Factor Surveillance System, SMART: Selected Metropolitan Area Risk Trends, 2017

Disability Status

Category	MSA[1] (%)	U.S. (%)
Adults who reported being deaf	n/a	6.7
Are you blind or have serious difficulty seeing, even when wearing glasses?	n/a	4.5
Are you limited in any way in any of your usual activities due of arthritis?	n/a	12.9
Do you have difficulty doing errands alone?	n/a	6.8
Do you have difficulty dressing or bathing?	n/a	3.6
Do you have serious difficulty concentrating/remembering/making decisions?	n/a	10.7
Do you have serious difficulty walking or climbing stairs?	n/a	13.6

Note: n/a not available; (1) Figures cover the San Jose-Sunnyvale-Santa Clara, CA Metropolitan Statistical Area.
Source: Centers for Disease Control and Prevention, Behaviorial Risk Factor Surveillance System, SMART: Selected Metropolitan Area Risk Trends, 2017

Mortality Rates for the Top 10 Causes of Death in the U.S.

ICD-10[a] Sub-Chapter	ICD-10[a] Code	Age-Adjusted Mortality Rate[1] per 100,000 population	
		County[2]	U.S.
Malignant neoplasms	C00-C97	111.8	149.2
Ischaemic heart diseases	I20-I25	52.2	90.5
Other forms of heart disease	I30-I51	22.9	52.2
Chronic lower respiratory diseases	J40-J47	16.7	39.6
Other degenerative diseases of the nervous system	G30-G31	51.3	37.6
Cerebrovascular diseases	I60-I69	30.6	37.2
Other external causes of accidental injury	W00-X59	18.5	36.1
Organic, including symptomatic, mental disorders	F01-F09	3.4	29.4
Hypertensive diseases	I10-I15	36.2	24.1
Diabetes mellitus	E10-E14	21.8	21.5

Note: (a) ICD-10 = International Classification of Diseases 10th Revision; (1) Mortality rates are a three-year average covering 2017-2019; (2) Figures cover Santa Clara County.
Source: Centers for Disease Control and Prevention, National Center for Health Statistics. Underlying Cause of Death 1999-2019 on CDC WONDER Online Database

Mortality Rates for Selected Causes of Death

ICD-10[a] Sub-Chapter	ICD-10[a] Code	Age-Adjusted Mortality Rate[1] per 100,000 population	
		County[2]	U.S.
Assault	X85-Y09	2.1	6.0
Diseases of the liver	K70-K76	8.3	14.4
Human immunodeficiency virus (HIV) disease	B20-B24	0.5	1.5
Influenza and pneumonia	J09-J18	9.9	13.8
Intentional self-harm	X60-X84	7.7	14.1
Malnutrition	E40-E46	0.5	2.3
Obesity and other hyperalimentation	E65-E68	1.5	2.1
Renal failure	N17-N19	3.1	12.6
Transport accidents	V01-V99	6.9	12.3
Viral hepatitis	B15-B19	1.2	1.2

Note: (a) ICD-10 = International Classification of Diseases 10th Revision; (1) Mortality rates are a three-year average covering 2017-2019; (2) Figures cover Santa Clara County; Data are suppressed when the data meet the criteria for confidentiality constraints; Mortality rates are flagged as unreliable when the rate would be calculated with a numerator of 20 or less.
Source: Centers for Disease Control and Prevention, National Center for Health Statistics. Underlying Cause of Death 1999-2019 on CDC WONDER Online Database

Health Insurance Coverage

Area	With Health Insurance	With Private Health Insurance	With Public Health Insurance	Without Health Insurance	Population Under Age 19 Without Health Insurance
City	94.8	72.3	30.4	5.2	2.1
MSA[1]	95.6	76.7	27.4	4.4	1.9
U.S.	91.2	67.9	35.1	8.8	5.1

Note: Figures are percentages that cover the civilian noninstitutionalized population; (1) Figures cover the San Jose-Sunnyvale-Santa Clara, CA Metropolitan Statistical Area
Source: U.S. Census Bureau, 2015-2019 American Community Survey 5-Year Estimates

Number of Medical Professionals

Area	MDs[3]	DOs[3,4]	Dentists	Podiatrists	Chiropractors	Optometrists
County[1] (number)	8,152	210	2,282	132	823	530
County[1] (rate[2])	421.9	10.9	118.4	6.8	42.7	27.5
U.S. (rate[2])	282.9	22.7	71.2	6.2	28.1	16.9
06085						

Note: Data as of 2019 unless noted; (1) Data covers Santa Clara County; (2) Rate per 100,000 population; (3) Data as of 2018 and includes all active, non-federal physicians; (4) Doctor of Osteopathic Medicine
Source: U.S. Department of Health and Human Services, Health Resources and Services Administration, Bureau of Health Professions, Area Resource File (ARF) 2019-2020

Best Hospitals

According to *U.S. News,* the San Jose-Sunnyvale-Santa Clara, CA metro area is home to two of the best hospitals in the U.S.: **Byers Eye Institute, Stanford Health Care** (12 adult specialties); **Stanford Health Care-Stanford Hospital** (Honor Roll/12 adult specialties). The hospitals listed were nationally ranked in at least one of 16 adult or 10 pediatric specialties. Only 134 hospitals nationwide were nationally ranked in one or more adult or pediatric specialty; this number increases to 178 counting specialized centers within hospitals. Twenty hospitals in the U.S. made the Honor Roll. The Best Hospitals Honor Roll takes both the national rankings and the procedure and condition ratings into account. Hospitals received points if they were nationally ranked in one of the 16 adult specialties—the higher they ranked, the more points they got—and how many ratings of "high performing" they earned in the 10 procedures and conditions. *U.S. News Online, "America's Best Hospitals 2020-21"*

According to *U.S. News,* the San Jose-Sunnyvale-Santa Clara, CA metro area is home to one of the best children's hospitals in the U.S.: **Lucile Packard Children's Hospital Stanford** (Honor Roll/10 pediatric specialties). The hospital listed was highly ranked in at least one of 10 pediatric specialties. Eighty-eight children's hospitals in the U.S. were nationally ranked in at least one specialty. Hospitals received points for being ranked in a specialty, and the 10 hospitals with the most points across the 10 specialties make up the Honor Roll. *U.S. News Online, "America's Best Children's Hospitals 2020-21"*

EDUCATION

Public School District Statistics

District Name	Schls	Pupils	Pupil/ Teacher Ratio	Minority Pupils[1] (%)	Free Lunch Eligible[2] (%)	IEP[3] (%)
Alum Rock Union Elementary	25	9,623	22.4	98.3	66.1	13.7
Berryessa Union Elementary	14	6,988	24.2	95.1	25.5	11.0
Cambrian	6	3,471	23.5	58.2	14.0	13.9
Campbell Union High	6	8,271	23.4	61.9	22.0	12.8
East Side Union High	16	22,606	22.6	94.6	37.6	12.0
Evergreen Elementary	18	10,839	26.8	94.4	24.9	9.7
Franklin-Mckinley Elementary	16	7,324	22.9	98.1	64.6	12.7
Moreland	7	4,703	22.8	76.2	24.0	12.1
Mount Pleasant Elementary	5	2,229	23.1	97.0	58.9	16.9
Oak Grove Elementary	18	9,877	24.2	83.2	33.7	13.4
San Jose Unified	42	29,762	23.7	75.6	34.3	12.2
Union Elementary	8	5,883	23.9	57.6	9.2	11.5

Note: Table includes school districts with 2,000 or more students; (1) Percentage of students that are not non-Hispanic white; (2) Percentage of students that are eligible for the free lunch program; (3) Percentage of students that have an Individualized Education Program.
Source: U.S. Department of Education, National Center for Education Statistics, Common Core of Data, Local Education Agency (School District) Universe Survey: School Year 2018-2019; U.S. Department of Education, National Center for Education Statistics, Common Core of Data, Public Elementary/Secondary School Universe Survey: School Year 2018-2019

Best High Schools

According to *U.S. News,* San Jose is home to three of the top 500 high schools in the U.S.: **Lynbrook High** (#98); **University Preparatory Academy Charter** (#120); **KIPP San Jose Collegiate** (#235). Nearly 18,000 public, magnet and charter schools were ranked based on their performance on state assessments and how well they prepare students for college. *U.S. News & World Report, "Best High Schools 2020"*

Highest Level of Education

Area	Less than H.S.	H.S. Diploma	Some College, No Deg.	Associate Degree	Bachelor's Degree	Master's Degree	Prof. School Degree	Doctorate Degree
City	15.4	16.6	16.8	7.5	25.7	13.6	2.0	2.5
MSA[1]	11.9	14.4	15.4	6.9	27.3	17.5	2.7	3.9
U.S.	12.0	27.0	20.4	8.5	19.8	8.8	2.1	1.4

Note: Figures cover persons age 25 and over; (1) Figures cover the San Jose-Sunnyvale-Santa Clara, CA Metropolitan Statistical Area
Source: U.S. Census Bureau, 2015-2019 American Community Survey 5-Year Estimates

Educational Attainment by Race

Area	High School Graduate or Higher (%)					Bachelor's Degree or Higher (%)				
	Total	White	Black	Asian	Hisp.[2]	Total	White	Black	Asian	Hisp.[2]
City	84.6	88.6	91.8	87.0	67.5	43.7	44.2	35.5	55.9	15.9
MSA[1]	88.1	90.4	92.0	90.8	69.3	51.5	49.4	38.2	65.5	17.6
U.S.	88.0	89.9	86.0	87.1	68.7	32.1	33.5	21.6	54.3	16.4

Note: Figures shown cover persons 25 years old and over; (1) Figures cover the San Jose-Sunnyvale-Santa Clara, CA Metropolitan Statistical Area; (2) People of Hispanic origin can be of any race
Source: U.S. Census Bureau, 2015-2019 American Community Survey 5-Year Estimates

School Enrollment by Grade and Control

Area	Preschool (%)		Kindergarten (%)		Grades 1 - 4 (%)		Grades 5 - 8 (%)		Grades 9 - 12 (%)	
	Public	Private	Public	Private	Public	Private	Public	Private	Public	Private
City	41.9	58.1	81.2	18.8	87.0	13.0	87.0	13.0	86.8	13.2
MSA[1]	36.2	63.8	81.2	18.8	85.7	14.3	85.4	14.6	86.2	13.8
U.S.	59.1	40.9	87.6	12.4	89.5	10.5	89.4	10.6	90.1	9.9

Note: Figures shown cover persons 3 years old and over; (1) Figures cover the San Jose-Sunnyvale-Santa Clara, CA Metropolitan Statistical Area
Source: U.S. Census Bureau, 2015-2019 American Community Survey 5-Year Estimates

Higher Education

Four-Year Colleges			Two-Year Colleges			Medical Schools[1]	Law Schools[2]	Voc/ Tech[3]
Public	Private Non-profit	Private For-profit	Public	Private Non-profit	Private For-profit			
1	1	1	2	0	1	0	1	3

Note: Figures cover institutions located within the city limits and include main campuses only; (1) includes schools accredited by the Liaison Committee on Medical Education and the American Osteopathic Association's Commission on Osteopathic College Accreditation; (2) includes ABA-accredited schools, schools with provisional ABA accreditation, and state accredited schools; (3) includes all schools with programs that are less than 2 years.
Source: National Center for Education Statistics, Integrated Postsecondary Education System (IPEDS), 2019-20; Wikipedia, List of Medical Schools in the United States, accessed April 2, 2021; Wikipedia, List of Law Schools in the United States, accessed April 2, 2021

According to U.S. News & World Report, the San Jose-Sunnyvale-Santa Clara, CA metro area is home to two of the top 200 national universities in the U.S.: **Stanford University** (#6 tie); **Santa Clara University** (#53 tie). The indicators used to capture academic quality fall into a number of categories: assessment by administrators at peer institutions; retention of students; faculty resources; student selectivity; financial resources; alumni giving; high school counselor ratings of colleges; and graduation rate. U.S. News & World Report, "America's Best Colleges 2021"

According to U.S. News & World Report, the San Jose-Sunnyvale-Santa Clara, CA metro area is home to one of the top 100 law schools in the U.S.: **Stanford University** (#2). The rankings are based on a weighted average of 12 measures of quality: peer assessment score; assessment score by lawyers/judges; median LSAT scores; median undergrad GPA; acceptance rate; employment rates for graduates; placement success; bar passage rate; faculty resources; expenditures per student; student/faculty ratio; and library resources. U.S. News & World Report, "America's Best Graduate Schools, Law, 2022"

According to U.S. News & World Report, the San Jose-Sunnyvale-Santa Clara, CA metro area is home to one of the top 75 medical schools for research in the U.S.: **Stanford University** (#4 tie). The rankings are based on a weighted average of 11 measures of quality: quality assessment; peer assessment score; assessment score by residency directors; research activity; total research activity; average research activity per faculty member; student selectivity; median MCAT total score; median undergraduate GPA; acceptance rate; and faculty resources. U.S. News & World Report, "America's Best Graduate Schools, Medical, 2022"

According to U.S. News & World Report, the San Jose-Sunnyvale-Santa Clara, CA metro area is home to one of the top 75 business schools in the U.S.: **Stanford University** (#1). The rankings are based on a weighted average of the following nine measures: quality assessment; peer assessment; recruiter assessment; placement success; mean starting salary and bonus; student selectivity; mean GMAT and GRE scores; mean undergraduate GPA; and acceptance rate. U.S. News & World Report, "America's Best Graduate Schools, Business, 2022"

EMPLOYERS

Major Employers

Company Name	Industry
Adobe Systems Inc	Publishers-computer software, mfg
Advanced Micro Devices Inc	Semiconductor devices, mfg
Apple Inc	Computers-electronic-manufacturers
Applied Materials	Semiconductor manufacturing equip, mfg
Bon Appetit-Cafe Adobe	Restaurant management
California's Great America	Amusement & theme parks
Christopher Ranch	Garlic manufacturers
Cisco Systems Inc	Computer peripherals
Ebay	E-commerce
Flextronics	Solar energy equipment-manufacturers
General Motors Advanced Tech	Automobile manufacturing
Hewlett-Packard Co.	Computers-electronic-manufacturers
Intel Corporation	Semiconductor devices, mfg
Kaiser Permanente Medical Ctr	General medical & surgical hospitals
Lockheed Martin Space Systems	Satellite equipment & systems, mfg
Microsoft	Computer software-manufacturers
NASA	Government offices, federal
Net App Inc	Computer storage devices

Note: *Companies shown are located within the San Jose-Sunnyvale-Santa Clara, CA Metropolitan Statistical Area.*
Source: *Hoovers.com; Wikipedia*

Best Companies to Work For

Adobe; Cadence; Cisco; Nutanix, headquartered in San Jose, are among "The 100 Best Companies to Work For." To pick the best companies, *Fortune* partnered with the Great Place to Work Institute. Two-thirds of a company's score is based on the results of the Institute's Trust Index survey, which is sent to a random sample of employees from each company. The questions related to attitudes about management's credibility, job satisfaction, and camaraderie. The other third of the scoring is based on the company's responses to the Institute's Culture Audit, which includes detailed questions about pay and benefit programs, and a series of open-ended questions about hiring practices, internal communication, training, recognition programs, and diversity efforts. Any company that is at least five years old with more than 1,000 U.S. employees is eligible. *Fortune, "The 100 Best Companies to Work For," 2020*

Adobe; Hewlett Packard Enterprise, headquartered in San Jose, are among the "100 Best Companies for Working Mothers." Criteria: paid time off and leaves; workforce profile; benefits; women's issues and advancement; flexible work; company culture and work life programs. *Working Mother, "100 Best Companies for Working Mothers," 2020*

Paypal, headquartered in San Jose, is among the "Best Companies for Multicultural Women." *Working Mother* selected 50 companies based on a detailed application completed by public and private firms based in the United States, excluding government agencies, companies in the human resources field and non-autonomous divisions. Companies supplied data about the hiring, pay, and promotion of multicultural employees. Applications focused on representation of multicultural women, recruitment, retention and advancement programs, and company culture. *Working Mother, "Best Companies for Multicultural Women," 2020*

Align Technology, headquartered in San Jose, is among the "100 Best Places to Work in IT." To qualify, companies had to be U.S.-based organizations or be non-U.S.-based employers that met the following criteria: have a minimum of 300 total employees at a U.S. headquarters and a minimum of 30 IT employees in the U.S., with at least 50% of their IT employees based in the U.S. The best places to work were selected based on compensation, benefits, work/life balance, employee morale, and satisfaction with training and development programs. In addition, *InsiderPro* and *Computerworld* looked at retention efforts, programs for recognizing and rewarding outstanding performances, and benefits such as flextime, elder care and child care, and reimbursement for college tuition and the cost of pursuing technology certifications. *InsiderPro and Computerworld, "100 Best Places to Work in IT," 2020*

Hewlett Packard Enterprise, headquartered in San Jose, is among the "Best Companies for Dads." *Working Mother's* newest list recognizes the growing importance companies place on giving dads time off and support for their families. Rankings are determined by measuring gender-neutral or paternity leave offered, as well as actual time taken, phase-back policies, child- and dependent-care benefits, and corporate support groups for men and dads. *Working Mother, "Best Companies for Dads," 2020*

PUBLIC SAFETY

Crime Rate

Area	All Crimes	Violent Crimes				Property Crimes		
		Murder	Rape[3]	Robbery	Aggrav. Assault	Burglary	Larceny -Theft	Motor Vehicle Theft
City	2,858.0	3.1	64.5	128.7	242.0	395.6	1,435.0	589.0
Suburbs[1]	2,582.6	1.5	27.9	54.6	118.4	291.8	1,875.3	213.0
Metro[2]	2,725.6	2.3	46.9	93.1	182.6	345.7	1,646.7	408.3
U.S.	2,489.3	5.0	42.6	81.6	250.2	340.5	1,549.5	219.9

Note: Figures are crimes per 100,000 population; (1) All areas within the metro area that are located outside the city limits; (2) Figures cover the San Jose-Sunnyvale-Santa Clara, CA Metropolitan Statistical Area; (3) All figures shown were reported using the revised Uniform Crime Reporting (UCR) definition of rape.
Source: FBI Uniform Crime Reports, 2019

Hate Crimes

Area	Number of Quarters Reported	Number of Incidents per Bias Motivation					
		Race/Ethnicity/ Ancestry	Religion	Sexual Orientation	Disability	Gender	Gender Identity
City	4	13	7	10	1	0	2
U.S.	4	3,963	1,521	1,195	157	69	198

Source: Federal Bureau of Investigation, Hate Crime Statistics 2019

Identity Theft Consumer Reports

Area	Reports	Reports per 100,000 Population	Rank[2]
MSA[1]	5,256	264	145
U.S.	1,387,615	423	-

Note: (1) Figures cover the San Jose-Sunnyvale-Santa Clara, CA Metropolitan Statistical Area; (2) Rank ranges from 1 to 391 where 1 indicates greatest number of identity theft reports per 100,000 population
Source: Federal Trade Commission, Consumer Sentinel Network Data Book 2020

Fraud and Other Consumer Reports

Area	Reports	Reports per 100,000 Population	Rank[2]
MSA[1]	15,688	788	110
U.S.	3,385,133	1,031	-

Note: (1) Figures cover the San Jose-Sunnyvale-Santa Clara, CA Metropolitan Statistical Area; (2) Rank ranges from 1 to 391 where 1 indicates greatest number of fraud and other consumer reports per 100,000 population
Source: Federal Trade Commission, Consumer Sentinel Network Data Book 2020

POLITICS

2020 Presidential Election Results

Area	Biden	Trump	Jorgensen	Hawkins	Other
Santa Clara County	72.6	25.2	1.1	0.5	0.6
U.S.	51.3	46.8	1.2	0.3	0.5

Note: Results are percentages and may not add to 100% due to rounding
Source: Dave Leip's Atlas of U.S. Presidential Elections

SPORTS

Professional Sports Teams

Team Name	League	Year Established
San Jose Earthquakes	Major League Soccer (MLS)	1996
San Jose Sharks	National Hockey League (NHL)	1991

Note: Includes teams located in the San Jose-Sunnyvale-Santa Clara, CA Metropolitan Statistical Area.
Source: Wikipedia, Major Professional Sports Teams of the United States and Canada, April 6, 2021

CLIMATE

Average and Extreme Temperatures

Temperature	Jan	Feb	Mar	Apr	May	Jun	Jul	Aug	Sep	Oct	Nov	Dec	Yr.
Extreme High (°F)	76	82	83	95	103	104	105	101	105	100	87	76	105
Average High (°F)	57	61	63	67	70	74	75	75	76	72	65	58	68
Average Temp. (°F)	50	53	55	58	61	65	66	67	66	63	56	50	59
Average Low (°F)	42	45	46	48	51	55	57	58	57	53	47	42	50
Extreme Low (°F)	21	26	30	32	38	43	45	47	41	33	29	23	21

Note: Figures cover the years 1945-1993
Source: National Climatic Data Center, International Station Meteorological Climate Summary, 9/96

Average Precipitation/Snowfall/Humidity

Precip./Humidity	Jan	Feb	Mar	Apr	May	Jun	Jul	Aug	Sep	Oct	Nov	Dec	Yr.
Avg. Precip. (in.)	2.7	2.3	2.2	0.9	0.3	0.1	Tr	Tr	0.2	0.7	1.7	2.3	13.5
Avg. Snowfall (in.)	Tr	Tr	Tr	0	0	0	0	0	0	0	0	Tr	Tr
Avg. Rel. Hum. 7am (%)	82	82	80	76	74	73	77	79	79	79	81	82	79
Avg. Rel. Hum. 4pm (%)	62	59	56	52	53	54	58	58	55	54	59	63	57

Note: Figures cover the years 1945-1993; Tr = Trace amounts (<0.05 in. of rain; <0.5 in. of snow)
Source: National Climatic Data Center, International Station Meteorological Climate Summary, 9/96

Weather Conditions

Temperature			Daytime Sky			Precipitation		
10°F & below	32°F & below	90°F & above	Clear	Partly cloudy	Cloudy	0.01 inch or more precip.	0.1 inch or more snow/ice	Thunder-storms
0	5	5	106	180	79	57	< 1	6

Note: Figures are average number of days per year and cover the years 1945-1993
Source: National Climatic Data Center, International Station Meteorological Climate Summary, 9/96

HAZARDOUS WASTE

Superfund Sites

The San Jose-Sunnyvale-Santa Clara, CA metro area is home to 22 sites on the EPA's Superfund National Priorities List: **Advanced Micro Devices, Inc.** (final); **Advanced Micro Devices, Inc. (Building 915)** (final); **Applied Materials** (final); **CTS Printex, Inc.** (final); **Fairchild Semiconductor Corp. (Mountain View Plant)** (final); **Fairchild Semiconductor Corp. (South San Jose Plant)** (final); **Hewlett-Packard (620-640 Page Mill Road)** (final); **Intel Corp. (Mountain View Plant)** (final); **Intel Magnetics** (final); **Intersil Inc./Siemens Components** (final); **Lorentz Barrel & Drum Co.** (final); **Moffett Field Naval Air Station** (final); **Monolithic Memories** (final); **National Semiconductor Corp.** (final); **New Idria Mercury Mine** (final); **Raytheon Corp.** (final); **South Bay Asbestos Area** (final); **Spectra-Physics, Inc.** (final); **Synertek, Inc. (Building 1)** (final); **Teledyne Semiconductor** (final); **TRW Microwave, Inc (Building 825)** (final); **Westinghouse Electric Corp. (Sunnyvale Plant)** (final). There are a total of 1,375 Superfund sites with a status of proposed or final on the list in the U.S. *U.S. Environmental Protection Agency, National Priorities List, April 7, 2021*

AIR QUALITY

Air Quality Trends: Ozone

	1990	1995	2000	2005	2010	2015	2016	2017	2018	2019
MSA[1]	0.079	0.085	0.070	0.065	0.073	0.067	0.063	0.065	0.061	0.062
U.S.	0.088	0.089	0.082	0.080	0.073	0.068	0.069	0.068	0.069	0.065

Note: (1) Data covers the San Jose-Sunnyvale-Santa Clara, CA Metropolitan Statistical Area. The values shown are the composite ozone concentration averages among trend sites based on the highest fourth daily maximum 8-hour concentration in parts per million. These trends are based on sites having an adequate record of monitoring data during the trend period. Data from exceptional events are included.
Source: U.S. Environmental Protection Agency, Air Quality Monitoring Information, "Air Quality Trends by City, 1990-2019"

Air Quality Index

Area	Percent of Days when Air Quality was...[2]					AQI Statistics[2]	
	Good	Moderate	Unhealthy for Sensitive Groups	Unhealthy	Very Unhealthy	Maximum	Median
MSA[1]	72.1	26.8	1.1	0.0	0.0	136	43

Note: (1) Data covers the San Jose-Sunnyvale-Santa Clara, CA Metropolitan Statistical Area; (2) Based on 365 days with AQI data in 2019. Air Quality Index (AQI) is an index for reporting daily air quality. EPA calculates the AQI for five major air pollutants regulated by the Clean Air Act: ground-level ozone, particle pollution (aka particulate matter), carbon monoxide, sulfur dioxide, and nitrogen dioxide. The AQI runs from 0 to 500. The higher the AQI value, the greater the level of air pollution and the greater the health concern. There are six AQI categories: "Good" AQI is between 0 and 50. Air quality is considered satisfactory; "Moderate" AQI is between 51 and 100. Air quality is acceptable; "Unhealthy for Sensitive Groups" When AQI values are between 101 and 150, members of sensitive groups may experience health effects; "Unhealthy" When AQI values are between 151 and 200 everyone may begin to experience health effects; "Very Unhealthy" AQI values between 201 and 300 trigger a health alert; "Hazardous" AQI values over 300 trigger warnings of emergency conditions (not shown).
Source: U.S. Environmental Protection Agency, Air Quality Index Report, 2019

Air Quality Index Pollutants

Area	Percent of Days when AQI Pollutant was...[2]					
	Carbon Monoxide	Nitrogen Dioxide	Ozone	Sulfur Dioxide	Particulate Matter 2.5	Particulate Matter 10
MSA[1]	0.0	0.5	64.7	0.0	33.7	1.1

Note: (1) Data covers the San Jose-Sunnyvale-Santa Clara, CA Metropolitan Statistical Area; (2) Based on 365 days with AQI data in 2019. The Air Quality Index (AQI) is an index for reporting daily air quality. EPA calculates the AQI for five major air pollutants regulated by the Clean Air Act: ground-level ozone, particle pollution (also known as particulate matter), carbon monoxide, sulfur dioxide, and nitrogen dioxide. The AQI runs from 0 to 500. The higher the AQI value, the greater the level of air pollution and the greater the health concern.
Source: U.S. Environmental Protection Agency, Air Quality Index Report, 2019

Maximum Air Pollutant Concentrations: Particulate Matter, Ozone, CO and Lead

	Particulate Matter 10 (ug/m^3)	Particulate Matter 2.5 Wtd AM (ug/m^3)	Particulate Matter 2.5 24-Hr (ug/m^3)	Ozone (ppm)	Carbon Monoxide (ppm)	Lead (ug/m^3)
MSA[1] Level	75	9.1	21	0.064	2	0.07
NAAQS[2]	150	15	35	0.075	9	0.15
Met NAAQS[2]	Yes	Yes	Yes	Yes	Yes	Yes

Note: (1) Data covers the San Jose-Sunnyvale-Santa Clara, CA Metropolitan Statistical Area; Data from exceptional events are included; (2) National Ambient Air Quality Standards; ppm = parts per million; ug/m^3 = micrograms per cubic meter; n/a not available.
Concentrations: Particulate Matter 10 (coarse particulate)—highest second maximum 24-hour concentration; Particulate Matter 2.5 Wtd AM (fine particulate)—highest weighted annual mean concentration; Particulate Matter 2.5 24-Hour (fine particulate)—highest 98th percentile 24-hour concentration; Ozone—highest fourth daily maximum 8-hour concentration; Carbon Monoxide—highest second maximum non-overlapping 8-hour concentration; Lead—maximum running 3-month average
Source: U.S. Environmental Protection Agency, Air Quality Monitoring Information, "Air Quality Statistics by City, 2019"

Maximum Air Pollutant Concentrations: Nitrogen Dioxide and Sulfur Dioxide

	Nitrogen Dioxide AM (ppb)	Nitrogen Dioxide 1-Hr (ppb)	Sulfur Dioxide AM (ppb)	Sulfur Dioxide 1-Hr (ppb)	Sulfur Dioxide 24-Hr (ppb)
MSA[1] Level	14	52	n/a	2	n/a
NAAQS[2]	53	100	30	75	140
Met NAAQS[2]	Yes	Yes	n/a	Yes	n/a

Note: (1) Data covers the San Jose-Sunnyvale-Santa Clara, CA Metropolitan Statistical Area; Data from exceptional events are included; (2) National Ambient Air Quality Standards; ppm = parts per million; ug/m^3 = micrograms per cubic meter; n/a not available.
Concentrations: Nitrogen Dioxide AM—highest arithmetic mean concentration; Nitrogen Dioxide 1-Hr—highest 98th percentile 1-hour daily maximum concentration; Sulfur Dioxide AM—highest annual mean concentration; Sulfur Dioxide 1-Hr—highest 99th percentile 1-hour daily maximum concentration; Sulfur Dioxide 24-Hr—highest second maximum 24-hour concentration
Source: U.S. Environmental Protection Agency, Air Quality Monitoring Information, "Air Quality Statistics by City, 2019"

Santa Rosa, California

Background

Santa Rosa is located 55 miles north of San Francisco in the county seat of Sonoma County and home to one-third of the county's residents. The city is part of both the San Francisco Bay Area and the region known as California's wine country. The popularity of the vineyards, especially among tourists, has helped the city evolve from a small farming town during the California gold rush to a thriving, modern city known for its climate, location and natural beauty.

During the early days of European exploration, the area that is now Santa Rosa was a homestead for wealthy and prominent families, both under Mexican and Spanish rule. In 1852, the Mexican-American War ended and the territory of California became part of the United States. Also around this time, the California Gold Rush brought large numbers of new settlers to the area. As the gold rush waned, explorers found they could make more money farming than they could digging for gold. The community began to grow, and the city was officially incorporated 1868. That same year, the first railroad line reached the city helping Santa Rosa's population to increase tenfold in just seven years.

During the twentieth century, population began to level off, and Santa Rosa settled into a medium-sized city that affords residents the benefits of living in a larger urban center.

Population began increasing rapidly at the end of the twentieth century, and now the city's *Santa Rosa 2030 Vision* plans for future growth. In November 2017, the city annexed the community of Roseland in its quest for more land.

The city has two Sonoma-Marin Area Rail transit (SMART) stations—one downtown and the other in North Santa Rosa—enhancing pedestrian-friendly neighborhoods.

Downtown Santa Rosa, including the central Old Courthouse Square and historic Railroad Square is an area of shopping, restaurants, nightclubs and theaters. The city's health care facilities include a Kaiser Permanente medical hub, and Sutter Medical Center.

Largely as a result of the city's natural beauty and highly regarded vineyards, Santa Rosa is a popular destination for tourists, and an ideal destination for wine enthusiasts. In addition to wine production, major attractions in Santa Rosa include the Luther Burbank Home and Gardens, the Redwood Empire Ice Arena, the Sonoma County Museum, and the 6th Street Playhouse. The city is also home to the Charles M. Schulz Museum and Research Center, which celebrates the life and work of the Peanuts comic strip and its creator, who lived in Santa Rosa for over 30 years. In 2000, the city renamed its airport "Charles M. Schulz Sonoma County Airport," which is served by Alaska Airlines, with destinations that include San Diego, Los Angeles, Portland and Seattle.

> Facing a homeless crisis mid-pandemic, the city authorized a tent city in Finley Park, with mask and physical-distancing requirements. Good samaritans dropped off food, clothing, and hand sanitizer.

Institutions of higher learning in the city include the University of San Francisco Santa Rosa, Empire College and Santa Rosa Junior College.

The city has the same comfortable northern California climate as other Bay Area cities with hot average temperatures and low humidity, ideal for wine grape production. The majority of the city's precipitation falls during the spring and winter months, when temperatures are generally much cooler. Summer and fall hold potential for wild fires, and the October 2017 firestorm in the region was the most destructive and third deadliest in California history.

Rankings

Business/Finance Rankings

- The Santa Rosa metro area appeared on the Milken Institute "2021 Best Performing Cities" list. Rank: #59 out of 200 large metro areas (population over 250,000). Criteria: job growth; wage and salary growth; high-tech output growth; housing affordability; household broadband access. *Milken Institute, "Best-Performing Cities 2021," February 16, 2021*

- *Forbes* ranked the 200 most populous metro areas to determine the nation's "Best Places for Business and Careers." The Santa Rosa metro area was ranked #110. Criteria: costs (business and living); job growth (past and projected); income growth; quality of life; educational attainment (college and high school); projected economic growth; cultural and leisure opportunities; workplace tolerance laws; net migration patterns. *Forbes, "The Best Places for Business and Careers 2019: Seattle Still On Top," October 30, 2019*

Education Rankings

- Personal finance website *WalletHub* analyzed the 150 largest U.S. metropolitan statistical areas to determine where the most educated Americans are putting their degrees to work. Criteria: education levels; percentage of workers with degrees; education quality and attainment gap; public school quality rankings; quality and enrollment of each metro area's universities. Santa Rosa was ranked #31 (#1 = most educated city). *www.WalletHub.com, "Most and Least Educated Cities in America," July 20, 2020*

Real Estate Rankings

- *WalletHub* compared the most populated U.S. cities to determine which had the best markets for real estate agents. Santa Rosa ranked #11 where demand was high and pay was the best. Criteria: sales per agent; annual median wage for real-estate agents; monthly average starting salary for real estate agents; real estate job density and competition; unemployment rate; home turnover rate; housing-market health index; and other relevant metrics. *www.WalletHub.com, "2019's Best Places to Be a Real Estate Agent," April 24, 2019*

- Santa Rosa was ranked #241 out of 268 metro areas in terms of housing affordability in 2020 by the National Association of Home Builders (#1 = most affordable). Criteria: the share of homes sold in that area affordable to a family earning the local median income, based on standard mortgage underwriting criteria. *National Association of Home Builders®, NAHB-Wells Fargo Housing Opportunity Index, 4th Quarter 2020*

Safety Rankings

- Allstate ranked the 200 largest cities in America in terms of driver safety. Santa Rosa ranked #90. Criteria: internal property damage claims over a two-year period from January 2016 to December 2017. The report helps increase the importance of safety and awareness behind the wheel. *Allstate, "Allstate America's Best Drivers Report, 2019" June 24, 2019*

- The National Insurance Crime Bureau ranked 384 metro areas in the U.S. in terms of per capita rates of vehicle theft. The Santa Rosa metro area ranked #222 (#1 = highest rate). Criteria: number of vehicle theft offenses per 100,000 inhabitants in 2019. *National Insurance Crime Bureau, "Hot Spots 2019," July 21, 2020*

Seniors/Retirement Rankings

- From its Best Cities for Successful Aging indexes, the Milken Institute generated rankings for metropolitan areas, weighing data in nine categories—health care, wellness, living arrangements, transportation and convenience, financial characteristics, education, employment, community engagement, and overall livability. The Santa Rosa metro area was ranked #148 overall in the small metro area category. *Milken Institute, "Best Cities for Successful Aging, 2017" March 14, 2017*

Women/Minorities Rankings

- Personal finance website *WalletHub* compared more than 180 U.S. cities across two key dimensions, "Hispanic Business-Friendliness" and "Hispanic Purchasing Power," to arrive at the most favorable conditions for Hispanic entrepreneurs. Santa Rosa was ranked #114 out of 182. Criteria includes: share of Hispanic-Owned Businesses; Hispanic entrepreneurship rate to median annual income of Hispanics; Small Business-Friendliness score; cost of living; and number of Hispanics with at least a bachelor's degree. *WalletHub.com, "2019's Best Cities for Hispanic Entrepreneurs," May 1, 2019*

Business Environment

DEMOGRAPHICS

Population Growth

Area	1990 Census	2000 Census	2010 Census	2019* Estimate	Population Growth (%) 1990-2019	Population Growth (%) 2010-2019
City	123,297	147,595	167,815	179,701	45.7	7.1
MSA[1]	388,222	458,614	483,878	499,772	28.7	3.3
U.S.	248,709,873	281,421,906	308,745,538	324,697,795	30.6	5.2

Note: (1) Figures cover the Santa Rosa, CA Metropolitan Statistical Area; (*) 2015-2019 5-year estimated population
Source: U.S. Census Bureau, 1990 Census, Census 2000, Census 2010, 2015-2019 American Community Survey 5-Year Estimates

Household Size

Area	Persons in Household (%) One	Two	Three	Four	Five	Six	Seven or More	Average Household Size
City	28.2	32.6	15.4	13.3	6.2	2.3	2.0	2.70
MSA[1]	27.5	34.8	15.5	13.0	5.9	2.0	1.3	2.60
U.S.	27.9	33.9	15.6	12.9	6.0	2.3	1.4	2.60

Note: (1) Figures cover the Santa Rosa, CA Metropolitan Statistical Area
Source: U.S. Census Bureau, 2015-2019 American Community Survey 5-Year Estimates

Race

Area	White Alone[2] (%)	Black Alone[2] (%)	Asian Alone[2] (%)	AIAN[3] Alone[2] (%)	NHOPI[4] Alone[2] (%)	Other Race Alone[2] (%)	Two or More Races (%)
City	66.8	2.6	5.5	1.3	0.6	17.1	6.0
MSA[1]	74.8	1.7	4.1	0.9	0.3	12.9	5.4
U.S.	72.5	12.7	5.5	0.8	0.2	4.9	3.3

Note: (1) Figures cover the Santa Rosa, CA Metropolitan Statistical Area; (2) Alone is defined as not being in combination with one or more other races; (3) American Indian and Alaska Native; (4) Native Hawaiian and Other Pacific Islander
Source: U.S. Census Bureau, 2015-2019 American Community Survey 5-Year Estimates

Hispanic or Latino Origin

Area	Total (%)	Mexican (%)	Puerto Rican (%)	Cuban (%)	Other (%)
City	32.8	28.8	0.4	0.1	3.5
MSA[1]	26.7	22.6	0.4	0.1	3.6
U.S.	18.0	11.2	1.7	0.7	4.3

Note: Persons of Hispanic or Latino origin can be of any race; (1) Figures cover the Santa Rosa, CA Metropolitan Statistical Area
Source: U.S. Census Bureau, 2015-2019 American Community Survey 5-Year Estimates

Ancestry

Area	German	Irish	English	American	Italian	Polish	French[2]	Scottish	Dutch
City	11.4	10.1	8.9	2.8	7.4	1.4	3.0	2.2	1.2
MSA[1]	12.9	12.2	9.8	2.7	8.6	1.8	3.3	2.6	1.4
U.S.	13.3	9.7	7.2	6.2	5.1	2.8	2.3	1.7	1.2

Note: Figures are the percentage of the total population reporting a particular ancestry. The nine most commonly reported ancestries in the U.S. are shown. Figures include multiple ancestries (e.g. if a person reported being Irish and Italian, they were included in both columns); (1) Figures cover the Santa Rosa, CA Metropolitan Statistical Area; (2) Excludes Basque
Source: U.S. Census Bureau, 2015-2019 American Community Survey 5-Year Estimates

Foreign-born Population

Area	Percent of Population Born in Any Foreign Country	Asia	Mexico	Europe	Caribbean	Central America[2]	South America	Africa	Canada
City	20.1	4.0	11.6	1.7	0.0	0.9	0.3	0.8	0.3
MSA[1]	16.4	2.9	9.0	1.9	0.1	0.9	0.5	0.4	0.4
U.S.	13.6	4.2	3.5	1.5	1.3	1.1	1.0	0.7	0.2

Note: (1) Figures cover the Santa Rosa, CA Metropolitan Statistical Area; (2) Excludes Mexico.
Source: U.S. Census Bureau, 2015-2019 American Community Survey 5-Year Estimates

Marital Status

Area	Never Married	Now Married[2]	Separated	Widowed	Divorced
City	34.6	44.5	1.9	5.5	13.5
MSA[1]	32.1	47.8	1.7	5.3	13.1
U.S.	33.4	48.1	1.9	5.8	10.9

Note: Figures are percentages and cover the population 15 years of age and older; (1) Figures cover the Santa Rosa, CA Metropolitan Statistical Area; (2) Excludes separated
Source: U.S. Census Bureau, 2015-2019 American Community Survey 5-Year Estimates

Disability by Age

Area	All Ages	Under 18 Years Old	18 to 64 Years Old	65 Years and Over
City	12.0	4.0	9.9	30.5
MSA[1]	11.9	3.8	9.4	28.5
U.S.	12.6	4.2	10.3	34.5

Note: Figures show percent of the civilian noninstitutionalized population that reported having a disability. Disability status is determined from six types of difficulty: vision, hearing, cognitive, ambulatory, self-care, and independent living. For children under 5 years old, hearing and vision difficulty are used to determine disability status. For children between the ages of 5 and 14, disability status is determined from hearing, vision, cognitive, ambulatory, and self-care difficulties. For people aged 15 years and older, they are considered to have a disability if they have difficulty with any one of the six difficulty types; Note: (1) Figures cover the Santa Rosa, CA Metropolitan Statistical Area
Source: U.S. Census Bureau, 2015-2019 American Community Survey 5-Year Estimates

Age

Area	Percent of Population									Median Age
	Under Age 5	Age 5–19	Age 20–34	Age 35–44	Age 45–54	Age 55–64	Age 65–74	Age 75–84	Age 85+	
City	5.9	17.8	21.2	12.8	12.6	12.9	9.6	4.8	2.3	38.8
MSA[1]	5.0	17.2	18.7	12.4	13.0	14.5	11.6	5.1	2.2	42.1
U.S.	6.1	19.1	20.7	12.6	13.0	12.9	9.1	4.6	1.9	38.1

Note: (1) Figures cover the Santa Rosa, CA Metropolitan Statistical Area
Source: U.S. Census Bureau, 2015-2019 American Community Survey 5-Year Estimates

Gender

Area	Males	Females	Males per 100 Females
City	86,927	92,774	93.7
MSA[1]	244,045	255,727	95.4
U.S.	159,886,919	164,810,876	97.0

Note: (1) Figures cover the Santa Rosa, CA Metropolitan Statistical Area
Source: U.S. Census Bureau, 2015-2019 American Community Survey 5-Year Estimates

Religious Groups by Family

Area	Catholic	Baptist	Non-Den.	Methodist[2]	Lutheran	LDS[3]	Pente-costal	Presby-terian[4]	Muslim[5]	Judaism
MSA[1]	22.3	1.4	1.5	0.9	1.0	1.9	0.7	0.9	0.5	0.4
U.S.	19.1	9.3	4.0	4.0	2.3	2.0	1.9	1.6	0.8	0.7

Note: Figures are the number of adherents as a percentage of the total population; (1) Figures cover the Santa Rosa, CA Metropolitan Statistical Area; (2) Methodist/Pietist; (3) Latter Day Saints; (4) Reformed; (5) Figures are estimates
Source: Association of Statisticians of American Religious Bodies, 2010 U.S. Religion Census: Religious Congregations & Membership Study

Religious Groups by Tradition

Area	Catholic	Evangelical Protestant	Mainline Protestant	Other Tradition	Black Protestant	Orthodox
MSA[1]	22.3	5.3	2.4	4.8	<0.1	0.3
U.S.	19.1	16.2	7.3	4.3	1.6	0.3

Note: Figures are the number of adherents as a percentage of the total population; (1) Figures cover the Santa Rosa, CA Metropolitan Statistical Area
Source: Association of Statisticians of American Religious Bodies, 2010 U.S. Religion Census: Religious Congregations & Membership Study

ECONOMY

Gross Metropolitan Product

Area	2017	2018	2019	2020	Rank[2]
MSA[1]	29.3	30.4	31.4	32.5	91

Note: Figures are in billions of dollars; (1) Figures cover the Santa Rosa, CA Metropolitan Statistical Area; (2) Rank is based on 2018 data and ranges from 1 to 381
Source: U.S. Conference of Mayors, U.S. Metro Economies: GMP & Employment 2018-2020, September 2019

Economic Growth

Area	2015-17 (%)	2018 (%)	2019 (%)	2020 (%)	Rank[2]
MSA[1]	2.5	1.2	1.7	1.1	100
U.S.	1.9	2.9	2.3	2.1	–

Note: Figures are real gross metropolitan product (GMP) growth rates and represent average annual percent change; (1) Figures cover the Santa Rosa, CA Metropolitan Statistical Area; (2) Rank is based on 2017 2-year average annual percent change and ranges from 1 to 381
Source: U.S. Conference of Mayors, U.S. Metro Economies: GMP & Employment 2018-2020, September 2019

Metropolitan Area Exports

Area	2014	2015	2016	2017	2018	2019	Rank[2]
MSA[1]	1,103.7	1,119.8	1,194.3	1,168.2	1,231.7	1,234.5	135

Note: Figures are in millions of dollars; (1) Figures cover the Santa Rosa, CA Metropolitan Statistical Area; (2) Rank is based on 2019 data and ranges from 1 to 386
Source: U.S. Department of Commerce, International Trade Administration, Office of Trade and Economic Analysis, Industry and Analysis, Exports by Metropolitan Area, data extracted March 24, 2021

Building Permits

Area	Single-Family			Multi-Family			Total		
	2018	2019	Pct. Chg.	2018	2019	Pct. Chg.	2018	2019	Pct. Chg.
City	1,632	939	-42.5	69	251	263.8	1,701	1,190	-30.0
MSA[1]	3,169	2,079	-34.4	110	350	218.2	3,279	2,429	-25.9
U.S.	855,300	862,100	0.7	473,500	523,900	10.6	1,328,800	1,386,000	4.3

Note: (1) Figures cover the Santa Rosa, CA Metropolitan Statistical Area; Figures represent new, privately-owned housing units authorized (unadjusted data); All permit data are based on estimates with imputation
Source: U.S. Census Bureau, Manufacturing, Mining, and Construction Statistics, Building Permits, 2018, 2019

Bankruptcy Filings

Area	Business Filings			Nonbusiness Filings		
	2019	2020	% Chg.	2019	2020	% Chg.
Sonoma County	32	29	-9.4	531	388	-26.9
U.S.	22,780	21,655	-4.9	752,160	522,808	-30.5

Note: Business filings include Chapter 7, Chapter 9, Chapter 11, Chapter 12, Chapter 13, Chapter 15, and Section 304; Nonbusiness filings include Chapter 7, Chapter 11, and Chapter 13
Source: Administrative Office of the U.S. Courts, Business and Nonbusiness Bankruptcy, County Cases Commenced by Chapter of the Bankruptcy Code, During the 12-Month Period Ending December 31, 2019 and Business and Nonbusiness Bankruptcy, County Cases Commenced by Chapter of the Bankruptcy Code, During the 12-Month Period Ending December 31, 2020

Housing Vacancy Rates

Area	Gross Vacancy Rate[2] (%)			Year-Round Vacancy Rate[3] (%)			Rental Vacancy Rate[4] (%)			Homeowner Vacancy Rate[5] (%)		
	2018	2019	2020	2018	2019	2020	2018	2019	2020	2018	2019	2020
MSA[1]	n/a	n/a	n/a	n/a	n/a	n/a	n/a	n/a	n/a	n/a	n/a	n/a
U.S.	12.3	12.0	10.6	9.7	9.5	8.2	6.9	6.7	6.3	1.5	1.4	1.0

Note: (1) Figures cover the Santa Rosa, CA Metropolitan Statistical Area; (2) The percentage of the total housing inventory that is vacant; (3) The percentage of the housing inventory (excluding seasonal units) that is year-round vacant; (4) The percentage of rental inventory that is vacant for rent; (5) The percentage of homeowner inventory that is vacant for sale; n/a not available
Source: U.S. Census Bureau, Housing Vacancies and Homeownership Annual Statistics: 2018, 2019, 2020

INCOME

Income

Area	Per Capita ($)	Median Household ($)	Average Household ($)
City	36,935	75,630	96,786
MSA[1]	42,178	81,018	108,169
U.S.	34,103	62,843	88,607

Note: (1) Figures cover the Santa Rosa, CA Metropolitan Statistical Area
Source: U.S. Census Bureau, 2015-2019 American Community Survey 5-Year Estimates

Household Income Distribution

Area	Percent of Households Earning							
	Under $15,000	$15,000 -$24,999	$25,000 -$34,999	$35,000 -$49,999	$50,000 -$74,999	$75,000 -$99,999	$100,000 -$149,999	$150,000 and up
City	7.0	5.9	7.1	11.0	18.4	14.8	18.5	17.3
MSA[1]	6.7	6.0	6.8	10.0	16.6	14.2	18.5	21.1
U.S.	10.3	8.9	8.9	12.3	17.2	12.7	15.1	14.5

Note: (1) Figures cover the Santa Rosa, CA Metropolitan Statistical Area
Source: U.S. Census Bureau, 2015-2019 American Community Survey 5-Year Estimates

Poverty Rate

Area	All Ages	Under 18 Years Old	18 to 64 Years Old	65 Years and Over
City	10.3	13.7	9.8	7.7
MSA[1]	9.2	10.7	9.4	7.0
U.S.	13.4	18.5	12.6	9.3

Note: Figures are percentage of people whose income during the past 12 months was below the poverty level;
(1) Figures cover the Santa Rosa, CA Metropolitan Statistical Area
Source: U.S. Census Bureau, 2015-2019 American Community Survey 5-Year Estimates

CITY FINANCES

City Government Finances

Component	2017 ($000)	2017 ($ per capita)
Total Revenues	347,266	1,985
Total Expenditures	385,271	2,202
Debt Outstanding	404,892	2,314
Cash and Securities[1]	383,792	2,193

Note: (1) Cash and security holdings of a government at the close of its fiscal year,
including those of its dependent agencies, utilities, and liquor stores.
Source: U.S. Census Bureau, State & Local Government Finances 2017

City Government Revenue by Source

Source	2017 ($000)	2017 ($ per capita)	2017 (%)
General Revenue			
From Federal Government	3,425	20	1.0
From State Government	44,554	255	12.8
From Local Governments	8,298	47	2.4
Taxes			
Property	43,191	247	12.4
Sales and Gross Receipts	61,459	351	17.7
Personal Income	0	0	0.0
Corporate Income	0	0	0.0
Motor Vehicle License	0	0	0.0
Other Taxes	12,026	69	3.5
Current Charges	108,322	619	31.2
Liquor Store	0	0	0.0
Utility	44,638	255	12.9
Employee Retirement	0	0	0.0

Source: U.S. Census Bureau, State & Local Government Finances 2017

City Government Expenditures by Function

Function	2017 ($000)	2017 ($ per capita)	2017 (%)
General Direct Expenditures			
Air Transportation	0	0	0.0
Corrections	0	0	0.0
Education	0	0	0.0
Employment Security Administration	0	0	0.0
Financial Administration	9,565	54	2.5
Fire Protection	37,671	215	9.8
General Public Buildings	0	0	0.0
Governmental Administration, Other	32,409	185	8.4
Health	1,684	9	0.4
Highways	33,425	191	8.7
Hospitals	0	0	0.0
Housing and Community Development	11,462	65	3.0
Interest on General Debt	10,759	61	2.8
Judicial and Legal	2,266	13	0.6
Libraries	0	0	0.0
Parking	4,784	27	1.2
Parks and Recreation	19,365	110	5.0
Police Protection	51,946	296	13.5
Public Welfare	0	0	0.0
Sewerage	62,973	359	16.3
Solid Waste Management	0	0	0.0
Veterans' Services	0	0	0.0
Liquor Store	0	0	0.0
Utility	66,902	382	17.4
Employee Retirement	0	0	0.0

Source: U.S. Census Bureau, State & Local Government Finances 2017

EMPLOYMENT

Labor Force and Employment

Area	Civilian Labor Force			Workers Employed		
	Dec. 2019	Dec. 2020	% Chg.	Dec. 2019	Dec. 2020	% Chg.
City	90,456	87,703	-3.0	88,298	81,635	-7.5
MSA[1]	259,689	250,632	-3.5	253,575	234,440	-7.5
U.S.	164,007,000	160,017,000	-2.4	158,504,000	149,613,000	-5.6

Note: Data is not seasonally adjusted and covers workers 16 years of age and older; (1) Figures cover the Santa Rosa, CA Metropolitan Statistical Area
Source: Bureau of Labor Statistics, Local Area Unemployment Statistics

Unemployment Rate

Area	2020											
	Jan.	Feb.	Mar.	Apr.	May	Jun.	Jul.	Aug.	Sep.	Oct.	Nov.	Dec.
City	3.0	2.9	3.8	14.9	13.6	12.2	10.4	8.0	7.7	6.7	6.1	6.9
MSA[1]	2.9	2.8	3.7	14.5	13.0	11.6	10.0	7.5	7.2	6.0	5.5	6.5
U.S.	4.0	3.8	4.5	14.4	13.0	11.2	10.5	8.5	7.7	6.6	6.4	6.5

Note: Data is not seasonally adjusted and covers workers 16 years of age and older; (1) Figures cover the Santa Rosa, CA Metropolitan Statistical Area
Source: Bureau of Labor Statistics, Local Area Unemployment Statistics

Average Wages

Occupation	$/Hr.	Occupation	$/Hr.
Accountants and Auditors	44.30	Maintenance and Repair Workers	25.10
Automotive Mechanics	28.50	Marketing Managers	77.50
Bookkeepers	26.80	Network and Computer Systems Admin.	43.90
Carpenters	35.30	Nurses, Licensed Practical	36.00
Cashiers	15.90	Nurses, Registered	60.00
Computer Programmers	44.90	Nursing Assistants	18.90
Computer Systems Analysts	43.30	Office Clerks, General	21.00
Computer User Support Specialists	28.80	Physical Therapists	52.10
Construction Laborers	25.30	Physicians	110.90
Cooks, Restaurant	17.30	Plumbers, Pipefitters and Steamfitters	36.10
Customer Service Representatives	20.30	Police and Sheriff's Patrol Officers	55.60
Dentists	98.40	Postal Service Mail Carriers	25.10
Electricians	35.20	Real Estate Sales Agents	n/a
Engineers, Electrical	50.50	Retail Salespersons	18.80
Fast Food and Counter Workers	14.40	Sales Representatives, Technical/Scientific	58.80
Financial Managers	69.10	Secretaries, Exc. Legal/Medical/Executive	22.50
First-Line Supervisors of Office Workers	31.20	Security Guards	17.90
General and Operations Managers	61.60	Surgeons	n/a
Hairdressers/Cosmetologists	17.00	Teacher Assistants, Exc. Postsecondary*	17.80
Home Health and Personal Care Aides	16.20	Teachers, Secondary School, Exc. Sp. Ed.*	42.70
Janitors and Cleaners	17.50	Telemarketers	n/a
Landscaping/Groundskeeping Workers	19.20	Truck Drivers, Heavy/Tractor-Trailer	26.90
Lawyers	84.00	Truck Drivers, Light/Delivery Services	23.20
Maids and Housekeeping Cleaners	16.90	Waiters and Waitresses	17.60

Note: Wage data covers the Santa Rosa, CA Metropolitan Statistical Area; (*) Hourly wages were calculated from annual wage data based on a 40 hour work week; n/a not available.
Source: Bureau of Labor Statistics, Metro Area Occupational Employment & Wage Estimates, May 2020

Employment by Industry

Sector	MSA[1]		U.S.
	Number of Employees	Percent of Total	Percent of Total
Construction	15,900	8.6	5.1
Education and Health Services	32,100	17.4	16.3
Financial Activities	7,200	3.9	6.1
Government	26,300	14.3	15.2
Information	2,200	1.2	1.9
Leisure and Hospitality	15,200	8.2	9.0
Manufacturing	21,900	11.9	8.5
Mining and Logging	200	0.1	0.4
Other Services	5,600	3.0	3.8
Professional and Business Services	22,100	12.0	14.4
Retail Trade	23,800	12.9	10.9
Transportation, Warehousing, and Utilities	4,400	2.4	4.6
Wholesale Trade	7,400	4.0	3.9

Note: Figures are non-farm employment as of December 2020. Figures are not seasonally adjusted and include workers 16 years of age and older; (1) Figures cover the Santa Rosa, CA Metropolitan Statistical Area
Source: Bureau of Labor Statistics, Current Employment Statistics, Employment, Hours, and Earnings

Employment by Occupation

Occupation Classification	City (%)	MSA[1] (%)	U.S. (%)
Management, Business, Science, and Arts	35.6	38.2	38.5
Natural Resources, Construction, and Maintenance	10.8	10.4	8.9
Production, Transportation, and Material Moving	11.9	10.3	13.2
Sales and Office	21.6	21.2	21.6
Service	20.0	19.9	17.8

Note: Figures cover employed civilians 16 years of age and older; (1) Figures cover the Santa Rosa, CA Metropolitan Statistical Area
Source: U.S. Census Bureau, 2015-2019 American Community Survey 5-Year Estimates

Occupations with Greatest Projected Employment Growth: 2020 – 2022

Occupation[1]	2020 Employment	2022 Projected Employment	Numeric Employment Change	Percent Employment Change
Retail Salespersons	317,300	401,300	84,000	26.5
Laborers and Freight, Stock, and Material Movers, Hand	348,700	411,100	62,400	17.9
Waiters and Waitresses	182,500	242,800	60,300	33.0
Combined Food Preparation and Serving Workers, Including Fast Food	183,800	237,200	53,400	29.1
Cashiers	358,500	407,300	48,800	13.6
Cooks, Restaurant	113,200	156,500	43,300	38.3
Personal Care Aides	409,600	447,900	38,300	9.4
Farmworkers and Laborers, Crop, Nursery, and Greenhouse	242,000	269,700	27,700	11.4
Fast Food and Counter Workers	94,000	120,200	26,200	27.9
General and Operations Managers	242,700	268,300	25,600	10.5

Note: Projections cover California; (1) Sorted by numeric employment change
Source: www.projectionscentral.com, State Occupational Projections, 2020–2022 Short-Term Projections

Fastest-Growing Occupations: 2020 – 2022

Occupation[1]	2020 Employment	2022 Projected Employment	Numeric Employment Change	Percent Employment Change
Manicurists and Pedicurists	7,800	21,300	13,500	173.1
Hairdressers, Hairstylists, and Cosmetologists	22,700	44,600	21,900	96.5
Massage Therapists	8,800	17,100	8,300	94.3
Skincare Specialists	5,500	9,100	3,600	65.5
Dental Hygienists	9,200	14,700	5,500	59.8
Dental Hygienists (SOC 2018)	5,300	8,400	3,100	58.5
Dental Assistants	36,300	56,300	20,000	55.1
Dentists, General	12,600	19,000	6,400	50.8
Parking Lot Attendants	14,300	20,400	6,100	42.7
Lodging Managers	3,300	4,600	1,300	39.4

Note: Projections cover California; (1) Sorted by percent employment change and excludes occupations with numeric employment change less than 50
Source: www.projectionscentral.com, State Occupational Projections, 2020–2022 Short-Term Projections

TAXES

State Corporate Income Tax Rates

State	Tax Rate (%)	Income Brackets ($)	Num. of Brackets	Financial Institution Tax Rate (%)[a]	Federal Income Tax Ded.
California	8.84 (b)	Flat rate	1	10.84 (b)	No

Note: Tax rates as of January 1, 2021; (a) Rates listed are the corporate income tax rate applied to financial institutions or excise taxes based on income. Some states have other taxes based upon the value of deposits or shares; (b) Minimum tax is $800 in California, $250 in District of Columbia, $50 in Arizona and North Dakota (banks), $400 ($100 banks) in Rhode Island, $200 per location in South Dakota (banks), $100 in Utah, $300 in Vermont.
Source: Federation of Tax Administrators, State Corporate Income Tax Rates, January 1, 2021

State Individual Income Tax Rates

State	Tax Rate (%)	Income Brackets ($)	Personal Exemptions ($)			Standard Ded. ($)	
			Single	Married	Depend.	Single	Married
California (a)	1.0 - 12.3 (g)	8,932 - 599,012 (b)	124	248 (c)	383 (c)	4,601	9,202 (a)

Note: Tax rates as of January 1, 2021; Local- and county-level taxes are not included; Federal income tax is not deductible on state income tax returns; (a) 19 states have statutory provision for automatically adjusting to the rate of inflation the dollar values of the income tax brackets, standard deductions, and/or personal exemptions. Michigan indexes the personal exemption only. Oregon does not index the income brackets for $125,000 and over; (b) For joint returns, taxes are twice the tax on half the couple's income; (c) The personal exemption takes the form of a tax credit instead of a deduction; (g) California imposes an additional 1% tax on taxable income over $1 million, making the maximum rate 13.3% over $1 million.
Source: Federation of Tax Administrators, State Individual Income Tax Rates, January 1, 2021

Various State Sales and Excise Tax Rates

State	State Sales Tax (%)	Gasoline[1] (¢/gal.)	Cigarette[2] ($/pack)	Spirits[3] ($/gal.)	Wine[4] ($/gal.)	Beer[5] ($/gal.)	Recreational Marijuana (%)
California	7.25	63.05	2.87	3.3	0.2	0.2	(c)

Note: All tax rates as of January 1, 2021; (1) The American Petroleum Institute has developed a methodology for determining the average tax rate on a gallon of fuel. Rates may include any of the following: excise taxes, environmental fees, storage tank fees, other fees or taxes, general sales tax, and local taxes; (2) The federal excise tax of $1.0066 per pack and local taxes are not included; (3) Rates are those applicable to off-premise sales of 40% alcohol by volume (a.b.v.) distilled spirits in 750ml containers. Local excise taxes are excluded; (4) Rates are those applicable to off-premise sales of 11% a.b.v. non-carbonated wine in 750ml containers; (5) Rates are those applicable to off-premise sales of 4.7% a.b.v. beer in 12 ounce containers; (c) 15% excise tax (levied on wholesale at average market rate); $9.65/oz. flowers & $2.87/oz. leaves cultivation tax; $1.35/oz fresh cannabis plant
Source: Tax Foundation, 2021 Facts & Figures: How Does Your State Compare?

State Business Tax Climate Index Rankings

State	Overall Rank	Corporate Tax Rank	Individual Income Tax Rank	Sales Tax Rank	Property Tax Rank	Unemployment Insurance Tax Rank
California	49	28	49	45	14	21

Note: The index is a measure of how each state's tax laws affect economic performance. The lower the rank, the more favorable a state's tax system is for business. States without a given tax are given a ranking of 1. The scores/rankings for the District of Columbia do not affect other states. The 2021 index represents the tax climate as of July 1, 2020.
Source: Tax Foundation, State Business Tax Climate Index 2021

TRANSPORTATION

Means of Transportation to Work

Area	Car/Truck/Van		Public Transportation			Bicycle	Walked	Other Means	Worked at Home
	Drove Alone	Car-pooled	Bus	Subway	Railroad				
City	77.9	11.5	1.6	0.0	0.1	1.2	1.7	1.1	4.8
MSA[1]	74.6	11.3	1.6	0.0	0.2	1.0	2.7	1.3	7.4
U.S.	76.3	9.0	2.4	1.9	0.6	0.5	2.7	1.4	5.2

Note: Figures are percentages and cover workers 16 years of age and older; (1) Figures cover the Santa Rosa, CA Metropolitan Statistical Area
Source: U.S. Census Bureau, 2015-2019 American Community Survey 5-Year Estimates

Travel Time to Work

Area	Less Than 10 Minutes	10 to 19 Minutes	20 to 29 Minutes	30 to 44 Minutes	45 to 59 Minutes	60 to 89 Minutes	90 Minutes or More
City	13.8	39.2	21.7	13.6	3.9	4.6	3.2
MSA[1]	15.1	32.2	20.4	16.8	5.8	5.9	3.9
U.S.	12.2	28.4	20.8	20.8	8.3	6.4	2.9

Note: Note: Figures are percentages and include workers 16 years old and over; (1) Figures cover the Santa Rosa, CA Metropolitan Statistical Area
Source: U.S. Census Bureau, 2015-2019 American Community Survey 5-Year Estimates

Key Congestion Measures

Measure	1982	1992	2002	2012	2017
Annual Hours of Delay, Total (000)	n/a	n/a	n/a	n/a	18,599
Annual Hours of Delay, Per Auto Commuter	n/a	n/a	n/a	n/a	53
Annual Congestion Cost, Total (million $)	n/a	n/a	n/a	n/a	383
Annual Congestion Cost, Per Auto Commuter ($)	n/a	n/a	n/a	n/a	1,094

Note: n/a not available
Source: Texas A&M Transportation Institute, 2019 Urban Mobility Report

Freeway Travel Time Index

Measure	1982	1987	1992	1997	2002	2007	2012	2017
Urban Area Index[1]	n/a	n/a	n/a	n/a	n/a	n/a	n/a	1.22
Urban Area Rank[1,2]	n/a	n/a	n/a	n/a	n/a	n/a	n/a	n/a

Note: Freeway Travel Time Index—the ratio of travel time in the peak period to the travel time at free-flow conditions. For example, a value of 1.30 indicates a 20-minute free-flow trip takes 26 minutes in the peak (20 minutes x 1.30 = 26 minutes); (1) Covers the Santa Rosa CA urban area; (2) Rank is based on 101 larger urban areas (#1 = highest travel time index); n/a not available
Source: Texas A&M Transportation Institute, 2019 Urban Mobility Report

Public Transportation

Agency Name / Mode of Transportation	Vehicles Operated in Maximum Service[1]	Annual Unlinked Passenger Trips[2] (in thous.)	Annual Passenger Miles[3] (in thous.)
City of Santa Rosa (Santa Rosa CityBus)			
Bus (directly operated)	24	1,808.2	7,847.8
Bus (purchased transportation)	2	8.9	28.0
Demand Response (purchased transportation)	12	34.9	239.0
Sonoma County Transit			
Bus (purchased transportation)	41	906.9	7,552.3
Demand Response (purchased transportation)	25	58.8	715.2

Note: (1) Number of revenue vehicles operated by the given mode and type of service to meet the annual maximum service requirement. This is the revenue vehicle count during the peak season of the year; on the week and day that maximum service is provided. Vehicles operated in maximum service (VOMS) exclude atypical days and one-time special events; (2) Number of passengers who boarded public transportation vehicles. Passengers are counted each time they board a vehicle no matter how many vehicles they use to travel from their origin to their destination. (3) Sum of the distances ridden by all passengers during the entire fiscal year.
Source: Federal Transit Administration, National Transit Database, 2019

Air Transportation

Airport Name and Code / Type of Service	Passenger Airlines[1]	Passenger Enplanements	Freight Carriers[2]	Freight (lbs)
San Francisco International (SFO)				
Domestic service (U.S. carriers - 2020)	18	6,193,273	13	191,804,266
International service (U.S. carriers - 2019)	6	2,517,926	7	101,399,216

Note: (1) Includes all U.S.-based major, minor and commuter airlines that carried at least one passenger during the year; (2) Includes all U.S.-based airlines and freight carriers that transported at least one pound of freight during the year.
Source: Bureau of Transportation Statistics, The Intermodal Transportation Database, Air Carriers: T-100 Domestic Market (U.S. Carriers), 2020; Bureau of Transportation Statistics, The Intermodal Transportation Database, Air Carriers: T-100 International Market (U.S. Carriers), 2019

BUSINESSES

Major Business Headquarters

Company Name	Industry	Rankings	
		Fortune[1]	Forbes[2]
No companies listed	-	-	-

Note: (1) Companies that produce a 10-K are ranked 1 to 500 based on 2019 revenue; (2) All private companies with at least $2 billion in annual revenue through the end of their most current fiscal year are ranked 1 to 219; companies listed are headquartered in the city; dashes indicate no ranking
Source: Fortune, "Fortune 500," June/July 2020; Forbes, "America's Largest Private Companies," 2020

Living Environment

COST OF LIVING

Cost of Living Index

Composite Index	Groceries	Housing	Utilities	Trans-portation	Health Care	Misc. Goods/ Services
n/a	n/a	n/a	n/a	n/a	n/a	n/a

Note: The Cost of Living Index measures regional differences in the cost of consumer goods and services, excluding taxes and non-consumer expenditures, for professional and managerial households in the top income quintile. It is based on more than 50,000 prices covering almost 60 different items for which prices are collected three times a year by chambers of commerce, economic development organizations or university applied economic centers in each participating urban area. The numbers shown should be read as a percentage above or below the national average of 100. For example, a value of 115.4 in the groceries column indicates that grocery prices are 15.4% higher than the national average. Small differences in the index numbers should not be interpreted as significant; n/a not available.
Source: The Council for Community and Economic Research, Cost of Living Index, 2020

Grocery Prices

Area[1]	T-Bone Steak ($/pound)	Frying Chicken ($/pound)	Whole Milk ($/half gal.)	Eggs ($/dozen)	Orange Juice ($/64 oz.)	Coffee ($/11.5 oz.)
City[2]	n/a	n/a	n/a	n/a	n/a	n/a
Avg.	11.78	1.39	2.05	1.47	3.57	4.34
Min.	8.03	0.94	1.03	0.74	2.94	3.02
Max.	15.86	2.65	4.31	3.77	5.44	8.69

*Note: (1) Values for the local area are compared with the average, minimum and maximum values for all 284 areas in the Cost of Living Index; (2) Figures cover the Santa Rosa CA urban area; n/a not available; **T-Bone Steak** (price per pound); **Frying Chicken** (price per pound, whole fryer); **Whole Milk** (half gallon carton); **Eggs** (price per dozen, Grade A, large); **Orange Juice** (64 oz. Tropicana or Florida Natural); **Coffee** (11.5 oz. can, vacuum-packed, Maxwell House, Hills Bros, or Folgers).*
Source: The Council for Community and Economic Research, Cost of Living Index, 2020

Housing and Utility Costs

Area[1]	New Home Price ($)	Apartment Rent ($/month)	All Electric ($/month)	Part Electric ($/month)	Other Energy ($/month)	Telephone ($/month)
City[2]	n/a	n/a	n/a	n/a	n/a	n/a
Avg.	368,594	1,168	170.86	100.47	65.28	184.30
Min.	190,567	502	91.58	31.42	26.08	169.60
Max.	2,227,806	4,738	470.38	280.31	280.06	206.50

*Note: (1) Values for the local area are compared with the average, minimum and maximum values for all 284 areas in the Cost of Living Index; (2) Figures cover the Santa Rosa CA urban area; n/a not available; **New Home Price** (2,400 sf living area, 8,000 sf lot, in urban area with full utilities); **Apartment Rent** (950 sf 2 bedroom/1.5 or 2 bath, unfurnished, excluding all utilities except water); **All Electric** (average monthly cost for an all-electric home); **Part Electric** (average monthly cost for a part-electric home); **Other Energy** (average monthly cost for natural gas, fuel oil, coal, wood, and any other forms of energy except electricity); **Telephone** (price includes the base monthly rate plus taxes and fees for three lines of mobile phone service).*
Source: The Council for Community and Economic Research, Cost of Living Index, 2020

Health Care, Transportation, and Other Costs

Area[1]	Doctor ($/visit)	Dentist ($/visit)	Optometrist ($/visit)	Gasoline ($/gallon)	Beauty Salon ($/visit)	Men's Shirt ($)
City[2]	n/a	n/a	n/a	n/a	n/a	n/a
Avg.	115.44	99.32	108.10	2.21	39.27	31.37
Min.	36.68	59.00	51.36	1.71	19.00	11.00
Max.	219.00	153.10	250.97	3.46	82.05	58.33

*Note: (1) Values for the local area are compared with the average, minimum and maximum values for all 284 areas in the Cost of Living Index; (2) Figures cover the Santa Rosa CA urban area; n/a not available; **Doctor** (general practitioners routine exam of an established patient); **Dentist** (adult teeth cleaning and periodic oral examination); **Optometrist** (full vision eye exam for established adult patient); **Gasoline** (one gallon regular unleaded, national brand, including all taxes, cash price at self-service pump if available); **Beauty Salon** (woman's shampoo, trim, and blow-dry); **Men's Shirt** (cotton/polyester dress shirt, pinpoint weave, long sleeves).*
Source: The Council for Community and Economic Research, Cost of Living Index, 2020

HOUSING

Homeownership Rate

Area	2012 (%)	2013 (%)	2014 (%)	2015 (%)	2016 (%)	2017 (%)	2018 (%)	2019 (%)	2020 (%)
MSA[1]	n/a	n/a	n/a	n/a	n/a	n/a	n/a	n/a	n/a
U.S.	65.4	65.1	64.5	63.7	63.4	63.9	64.4	64.6	66.6

Note: (1) Figures cover the Santa Rosa, CA Metropolitan Statistical Area; n/a not available
Source: U.S. Census Bureau, Housing Vacancies and Homeownership Annual Statistics: 2012-2020

House Price Index (HPI)

Area	National Ranking[2]	Quarterly Change (%)	One-Year Change (%)	Five-Year Change (%)	Since 1991Q1 (%)
MSA[1]	246	1.59	2.15	26.52	225.13
U.S.[3]	–	3.81	10.77	38.99	205.12

Note: The HPI is a weighted repeat sales index. It measures average price changes in repeat sales or refinancings on the same properties. This information is obtained by reviewing repeat mortgage transactions on single-family properties whose mortgages have been purchased or securitized by Fannie Mae or Freddie Mac since January 1975; (1) Figures cover the Santa Rosa, CA Metropolitan Statistical Area; (2) Rankings are based on annual percentage change for all metro areas containing at least 15,000 transactions over the last 10 years and ranges from 1 to 253; (3) figures based on a weighted average of Census Division estimates using a seasonally adjusted, purchase-only index; all figures are for the period ending December 31, 2020
Source: Federal Housing Finance Agency, Change in Metropolitan Area House Price Indexes, April 7, 2021

Median Single-Family Home Prices

Area	2018	2019	2020[p]	Percent Change 2019 to 2020
MSA[1]	n/a	n/a	n/a	n/a
U.S. Average	261.6	274.6	299.9	9.2

Note: Figures are median sales prices of existing single-family homes in thousands of dollars; (p) preliminary; n/a not available; (1) Figures cover the Santa Rosa, CA Metropolitan Statistical Area
Source: National Association of Realtors, Median Sales Price of Existing Single-Family Homes for Metropolitan Areas, 4th Quarter 2020

Qualifying Income Based on Median Sales Price of Existing Single-Family Homes

Area	With 5% Down ($)	With 10% Down ($)	With 20% Down ($)
MSA[1]	n/a	n/a	n/a
U.S. Average	59,266	56,147	49,908

Note: Figures are preliminary; Qualifying income is based on a mortgage rate of 2.81%. Monthly principal and interest payment is limited to 25% of income; n/a not available; (1) Figures cover the Santa Rosa, CA Metropolitan Statistical Area
Source: National Association of Realtors, Qualifying Income Based on Median Sales Price of Existing Single-Family Homes for Metropolitan Areas, 4th Quarter 2020

Home Value Distribution

Area	Under $50,000	$50,000 -$99,999	$100,000 -$149,999	$150,000 -$199,999	$200,000 -$299,999	$300,000 -$499,999	$500,000 -$999,999	$1,000,000 or more
City	2.7	2.0	1.7	1.5	5.2	30.6	50.0	6.2
MSA[1]	2.6	2.6	1.6	1.2	4.2	22.2	51.9	13.7
U.S.	6.9	12.0	13.3	14.0	19.6	19.3	11.4	3.4

Note: Figures are percentages and cover owner-occupied housing units; (1) Figures cover the Santa Rosa, CA Metropolitan Statistical Area
Source: U.S. Census Bureau, 2015-2019 American Community Survey 5-Year Estimates

Year Housing Structure Built

Area	2010 or Later	2000 -2009	1990 -1999	1980 -1989	1970 -1979	1960 -1969	1950 -1959	1940 -1949	Before 1940	Median Year
City	2.9	12.4	13.0	19.4	21.8	11.8	8.2	4.9	5.6	1979
MSA[1]	2.5	10.6	13.6	18.6	21.0	11.6	8.5	5.0	8.4	1978
U.S.	5.2	14.0	13.9	13.4	15.2	10.6	10.3	4.9	12.6	1978

Note: Figures are percentages except for Median Year; Note: (1) Figures cover the Santa Rosa, CA Metropolitan Statistical Area
Source: U.S. Census Bureau, 2015-2019 American Community Survey 5-Year Estimates

Gross Monthly Rent

Area	Under $500	$500 -$999	$1,000 -$1,499	$1,500 -$1,999	$2,000 -$2,499	$2,500 -$2,999	$3,000 and up	Median ($)
City	5.4	8.4	30.1	27.8	18.2	6.9	3.2	1,609
MSA[1]	5.2	10.6	27.7	27.0	17.3	7.6	4.5	1,621
U.S.	9.4	36.2	30.0	14.0	5.6	2.4	2.4	1,062

Note: Figures are percentages except for Median; Gross rent is the contract rent plus the estimated average monthly cost of utilities (electricity, gas, and water and sewer) and fuels (oil, coal, kerosene, wood, etc.) if these are paid by the renter (or paid for the renter by someone else); (1) Figures cover the Santa Rosa, CA Metropolitan Statistical Area
Source: U.S. Census Bureau, 2015-2019 American Community Survey 5-Year Estimates

HEALTH

Health Risk Factors

Category	MSA[1] (%)	U.S. (%)
Adults aged 18–64 who have any kind of health care coverage	n/a	87.3
Adults who reported being in good or better health	n/a	82.4
Adults who have been told they have high blood cholesterol	n/a	33.0
Adults who have been told they have high blood pressure	n/a	32.3
Adults who are current smokers	n/a	17.1
Adults who currently use E-cigarettes	n/a	4.6
Adults who currently use chewing tobacco, snuff, or snus	n/a	4.0
Adults who are heavy drinkers[2]	n/a	6.3
Adults who are binge drinkers[3]	n/a	17.4
Adults who are overweight (BMI 25.0 - 29.9)	n/a	35.3
Adults who are obese (BMI 30.0 - 99.8)	n/a	31.3
Adults who participated in any physical activities in the past month	n/a	74.4
Adults who always or nearly always wears a seat belt	n/a	94.3

Note: n/a not available; (1) Figures cover the Santa Rosa, CA Metropolitan Statistical Area; (2) Heavy drinkers are classified as adult men having more than 14 drinks per week and adult women having more than 7 drinks per week; (3) Binge drinkers are classified as males having five or more drinks on one occasion or females having four or more drinks on one occasion
Source: Centers for Disease Control and Prevention, Behaviorial Risk Factor Surveillance System, SMART: Selected Metropolitan Area Risk Trends, 2017

Acute and Chronic Health Conditions

Category	MSA[1] (%)	U.S. (%)
Adults who have ever been told they had a heart attack	n/a	4.2
Adults who have ever been told they have angina or coronary heart disease	n/a	3.9
Adults who have ever been told they had a stroke	n/a	3.0
Adults who have ever been told they have asthma	n/a	14.2
Adults who have ever been told they have arthritis	n/a	24.9
Adults who have ever been told they have diabetes[2]	n/a	10.5
Adults who have ever been told they had skin cancer	n/a	6.2
Adults who have ever been told they had any other types of cancer	n/a	7.1
Adults who have ever been told they have COPD	n/a	6.5
Adults who have ever been told they have kidney disease	n/a	3.0
Adults who have ever been told they have a form of depression	n/a	20.5

Note: n/a not available; (1) Figures cover the Santa Rosa, CA Metropolitan Statistical Area; (2) Figures do not include pregnancy-related, borderline, or pre-diabetes
Source: Centers for Disease Control and Prevention, Behaviorial Risk Factor Surveillance System, SMART: Selected Metropolitan Area Risk Trends, 2017

Health Screening and Vaccination Rates

Category	MSA[1] (%)	U.S. (%)
Adults aged 65+ who have had flu shot within the past year	n/a	60.7
Adults aged 65+ who have ever had a pneumonia vaccination	n/a	75.4
Adults who have ever been tested for HIV	n/a	36.1
Adults who have ever had the shingles or zoster vaccine?	n/a	28.9
Adults who have had their blood cholesterol checked within the last five years	n/a	85.9

Note: n/a not available; (1) Figures cover the Santa Rosa, CA Metropolitan Statistical Area.
Source: Centers for Disease Control and Prevention, Behaviorial Risk Factor Surveillance System, SMART: Selected Metropolitan Area Risk Trends, 2017

Disability Status

Category	MSA[1] (%)	U.S. (%)
Adults who reported being deaf	n/a	6.7
Are you blind or have serious difficulty seeing, even when wearing glasses?	n/a	4.5
Are you limited in any way in any of your usual activities due of arthritis?	n/a	12.9
Do you have difficulty doing errands alone?	n/a	6.8
Do you have difficulty dressing or bathing?	n/a	3.6
Do you have serious difficulty concentrating/remembering/making decisions?	n/a	10.7
Do you have serious difficulty walking or climbing stairs?	n/a	13.6

Note: n/a not available; (1) Figures cover the Santa Rosa, CA Metropolitan Statistical Area.
Source: Centers for Disease Control and Prevention, Behaviorial Risk Factor Surveillance System, SMART: Selected Metropolitan Area Risk Trends, 2017

Mortality Rates for the Top 10 Causes of Death in the U.S.

ICD-10[a] Sub-Chapter	ICD-10[a] Code	Age-Adjusted Mortality Rate[1] per 100,000 population	
		County[2]	U.S.
Malignant neoplasms	C00-C97	134.5	149.2
Ischaemic heart diseases	I20-I25	66.2	90.5
Other forms of heart disease	I30-I51	42.7	52.2
Chronic lower respiratory diseases	J40-J47	26.1	39.6
Other degenerative diseases of the nervous system	G30-G31	41.5	37.6
Cerebrovascular diseases	I60-I69	34.8	37.2
Other external causes of accidental injury	W00-X59	27.5	36.1
Organic, including symptomatic, mental disorders	F01-F09	20.4	29.4
Hypertensive diseases	I10-I15	16.9	24.1
Diabetes mellitus	E10-E14	17.3	21.5

Note: (a) ICD-10 = International Classification of Diseases 10th Revision; (1) Mortality rates are a three-year average covering 2017-2019; (2) Figures cover Sonoma County.
Source: Centers for Disease Control and Prevention, National Center for Health Statistics. Underlying Cause of Death 1999-2019 on CDC WONDER Online Database

Mortality Rates for Selected Causes of Death

ICD-10[a] Sub-Chapter	ICD-10[a] Code	Age-Adjusted Mortality Rate[1] per 100,000 population	
		County[2]	U.S.
Assault	X85-Y09	1.9	6.0
Diseases of the liver	K70-K76	9.9	14.4
Human immunodeficiency virus (HIV) disease	B20-B24	1.2	1.5
Influenza and pneumonia	J09-J18	10.0	13.8
Intentional self-harm	X60-X84	13.9	14.1
Malnutrition	E40-E46	1.9	2.3
Obesity and other hyperalimentation	E65-E68	2.0	2.1
Renal failure	N17-N19	4.4	12.6
Transport accidents	V01-V99	9.7	12.3
Viral hepatitis	B15-B19	1.4	1.2

Note: (a) ICD-10 = International Classification of Diseases 10th Revision; (1) Mortality rates are a three-year average covering 2017-2019; (2) Figures cover Sonoma County; Data are suppressed when the data meet the criteria for confidentiality constraints; Mortality rates are flagged as unreliable when the rate would be calculated with a numerator of 20 or less.
Source: Centers for Disease Control and Prevention, National Center for Health Statistics. Underlying Cause of Death 1999-2019 on CDC WONDER Online Database

Health Insurance Coverage

Area	With Health Insurance	With Private Health Insurance	With Public Health Insurance	Without Health Insurance	Population Under Age 19 Without Health Insurance
City	92.4	67.6	37.9	7.6	4.9
MSA[1]	93.9	71.6	36.7	6.1	3.2
U.S.	91.2	67.9	35.1	8.8	5.1

Note: Figures are percentages that cover the civilian noninstitutionalized population; (1) Figures cover the Santa Rosa, CA Metropolitan Statistical Area
Source: U.S. Census Bureau, 2015-2019 American Community Survey 5-Year Estimates

Number of Medical Professionals

Area	MDs[3]	DOs[3,4]	Dentists	Podiatrists	Chiropractors	Optometrists
County[1] (number)	1,394	91	463	33	202	90
County[1] (rate[2])	279.6	18.2	93.7	6.7	40.9	18.2
U.S. (rate[2])	282.9	22.7	71.2	6.2	28.1	16.9

06097
Note: Data as of 2019 unless noted; (1) Data covers Sonoma County; (2) Rate per 100,000 population; (3) Data as of 2018 and includes all active, non-federal physicians; (4) Doctor of Osteopathic Medicine
Source: U.S. Department of Health and Human Services, Health Resources and Services Administration, Bureau of Health Professions, Area Resource File (ARF) 2019-2020

EDUCATION

Public School District Statistics

District Name	Schls	Pupils	Pupil/ Teacher Ratio	Minority Pupils[1] (%)	Free Lunch Eligible[2] (%)	IEP[3] (%)
Rincon Valley Union Elementary	9	3,307	20.7	45.1	29.9	14.3
Santa Rosa Elementary	12	4,876	21.8	73.7	46.6	15.6
Santa Rosa High	12	11,104	22.8	66.2	35.2	16.6

Note: Table includes school districts with 2,000 or more students; (1) Percentage of students that are not non-Hispanic white; (2) Percentage of students that are eligible for the free lunch program; (3) Percentage of students that have an Individualized Education Program.
Source: U.S. Department of Education, National Center for Education Statistics, Common Core of Data, Local Education Agency (School District) Universe Survey: School Year 2018-2019; U.S. Department of Education, National Center for Education Statistics, Common Core of Data, Public Elementary/Secondary School Universe Survey: School Year 2018-2019

Highest Level of Education

Area	Less than H.S.	H.S. Diploma	Some College, No Deg.	Associate Degree	Bachelor's Degree	Master's Degree	Prof. School Degree	Doctorate Degree
City	13.8	19.3	24.5	9.8	20.1	8.0	2.9	1.5
MSA[1]	11.2	18.7	25.0	9.6	22.2	8.6	3.1	1.6
U.S.	12.0	27.0	20.4	8.5	19.8	8.8	2.1	1.4

Note: Figures cover persons age 25 and over; (1) Figures cover the Santa Rosa, CA Metropolitan Statistical Area
Source: U.S. Census Bureau, 2015-2019 American Community Survey 5-Year Estimates

Educational Attainment by Race

Area	High School Graduate or Higher (%)					Bachelor's Degree or Higher (%)				
	Total	White	Black	Asian	Hisp.[2]	Total	White	Black	Asian	Hisp.[2]
City	86.2	91.3	87.6	87.1	62.8	32.6	37.4	30.2	40.2	12.1
MSA[1]	88.8	92.9	89.3	88.9	64.6	35.5	39.3	29.8	44.4	14.1
U.S.	88.0	89.9	86.0	87.1	68.7	32.1	33.5	21.6	54.3	16.4

Note: Figures shown cover persons 25 years old and over; (1) Figures cover the Santa Rosa, CA Metropolitan Statistical Area; (2) People of Hispanic origin can be of any race
Source: U.S. Census Bureau, 2015-2019 American Community Survey 5-Year Estimates

School Enrollment by Grade and Control

Area	Preschool (%)		Kindergarten (%)		Grades 1 - 4 (%)		Grades 5 - 8 (%)		Grades 9 - 12 (%)	
	Public	Private	Public	Private	Public	Private	Public	Private	Public	Private
City	53.6	46.4	94.6	5.4	95.9	4.1	92.5	7.5	92.0	8.0
MSA[1]	48.6	51.4	93.0	7.0	92.8	7.2	90.3	9.7	90.9	9.1
U.S.	59.1	40.9	87.6	12.4	89.5	10.5	89.4	10.6	90.1	9.9

Note: Figures shown cover persons 3 years old and over; (1) Figures cover the Santa Rosa, CA Metropolitan Statistical Area
Source: U.S. Census Bureau, 2015-2019 American Community Survey 5-Year Estimates

Higher Education

Four-Year Colleges			Two-Year Colleges			Medical Schools[1]	Law Schools[2]	Voc/ Tech[3]
Public	Private Non-profit	Private For-profit	Public	Private Non-profit	Private For-profit			
0	0	1	1	0	0	0	1	1

Note: Figures cover institutions located within the city limits and include main campuses only; (1) includes schools accredited by the Liaison Committee on Medical Education and the American Osteopathic Association's Commission on Osteopathic College Accreditation; (2) includes ABA-accredited schools, schools with provisional ABA accreditation, and state accredited schools; (3) includes all schools with programs that are less than 2 years.
Source: National Center for Education Statistics, Integrated Postsecondary Education System (IPEDS), 2019-20; Wikipedia, List of Medical Schools in the United States, accessed April 2, 2021; Wikipedia, List of Law Schools in the United States, accessed April 2, 2021

EMPLOYERS

Major Employers

Company Name	Industry
Amy's Kitchen	Food manufacturing
AT&T	Utility company
Bear Republic Brewing Co.	Brewing company
Empire College	Education
Exchange Bank	Financial services
G&G Supermarket	Grocery stores
Ghilotti Construction Co.	Construction
Graton Resort & Casino	Casino resort
Hansel Auto Group	Auto sales
Hyatt Vineyard Creek Hotel & Spa	Hotels & motels
Jackson Family Wines	Winery
JDSU	Optical communications networks, communications equip
Kaiser Permanente	Healthcare
Keysight Technologies	Test equipment for labratories
Korbel	Korbel
La Tortilla Factory	Grocery stores
Mary's Pizza Shack	Grocery stores
Medtronic	Medical device manufacturer
Redwood Credit Union	Credit union
River Rock Casino	Casino resort
Sonoma Media Investments	Financial services
St. Joseph Health, Sonoma County	Healthcare
Sutter Santa Rosa Regional Hospital	Healthcare

Note: Companies shown are located within the Santa Rosa, CA Metropolitan Statistical Area.
Source: Hoovers.com; Wikipedia

PUBLIC SAFETY

Crime Rate

Area	All Crimes	Violent Crimes				Property Crimes		
		Murder	Rape[3]	Robbery	Aggrav. Assault	Burglary	Larceny -Theft	Motor Vehicle Theft
City	2,097.4	1.7	82.1	70.8	327.2	273.2	1,167.6	174.8
Suburbs[1]	1,577.8	1.9	41.0	36.6	283.0	232.0	903.5	79.7
Metro[2]	1,763.5	1.8	55.7	48.8	298.8	246.8	997.9	113.7
U.S.	2,489.3	5.0	42.6	81.6	250.2	340.5	1,549.5	219.9

Note: Figures are crimes per 100,000 population; (1) All areas within the metro area that are located outside the city limits; (2) Figures cover the Santa Rosa, CA Metropolitan Statistical Area; (3) All figures shown were reported using the revised Uniform Crime Reporting (UCR) definition of rape.
Source: FBI Uniform Crime Reports, 2019

Hate Crimes

Area	Number of Quarters Reported	Number of Incidents per Bias Motivation					
		Race/Ethnicity/ Ancestry	Religion	Sexual Orientation	Disability	Gender	Gender Identity
City	4	2	0	2	0	1	0
U.S.	4	3,963	1,521	1,195	157	69	198

Source: Federal Bureau of Investigation, Hate Crime Statistics 2019

Identity Theft Consumer Reports

Area	Reports	Reports per 100,000 Population	Rank[2]
MSA[1]	847	171	257
U.S.	1,387,615	423	-

Note: (1) Figures cover the Santa Rosa, CA Metropolitan Statistical Area; (2) Rank ranges from 1 to 391 where 1 indicates greatest number of identity theft reports per 100,000 population
Source: Federal Trade Commission, Consumer Sentinel Network Data Book 2020

Fraud and Other Consumer Reports

Area	Reports	Reports per 100,000 Population	Rank[2]
MSA[1]	3,381	684	200
U.S.	3,385,133	1,031	-

Note: (1) Figures cover the Santa Rosa, CA Metropolitan Statistical Area; (2) Rank ranges from 1 to 391 where 1 indicates greatest number of fraud and other consumer reports per 100,000 population
Source: Federal Trade Commission, Consumer Sentinel Network Data Book 2020

POLITICS

2020 Presidential Election Results

Area	Biden	Trump	Jorgensen	Hawkins	Other
Sonoma County	74.5	23.0	1.3	0.6	0.6
U.S.	51.3	46.8	1.2	0.3	0.5

Note: Results are percentages and may not add to 100% due to rounding
Source: Dave Leip's Atlas of U.S. Presidential Elections

SPORTS

Professional Sports Teams

Team Name	League	Year Established
No teams are located in the metro area		

Source: Wikipedia, Major Professional Sports Teams of the United States and Canada, April 6, 2021

CLIMATE

Average and Extreme Temperatures

Temperature	Jan	Feb	Mar	Apr	May	Jun	Jul	Aug	Sep	Oct	Nov	Dec	Yr.
Extreme High (°F)	69	72	83	89	99	102	103	105	109	94	85	73	109
Average High (°F)	56	61	65	69	74	79	81	84	84	75	65	58	71
Average Temp. (°F)	46	50	51	55	60	63	65	66	65	60	52	47	57
Average Low (°F)	35	38	36	41	45	47	49	47	46	44	39	35	42
Extreme Low (°F)	24	26	25	29	32	36	41	40	36	32	28	23	23

Note: Figures cover the years 1948-1990
Source: National Climatic Data Center, International Station Meteorological Climate Summary, 9/96

Average Precipitation/Snowfall/Humidity

Precip./Humidity	Jan	Feb	Mar	Apr	May	Jun	Jul	Aug	Sep	Oct	Nov	Dec	Yr.
Avg. Precip. (in.)	5.6	6.2	4.5	0.7	0.9	0.1	0.0	0.0	0.0	2.3	4.7	4.0	29.0
Avg. Snowfall (in.)	n/a	n/a	n/a	0	0	0	0	0	0	0	n/a	n/a	n/a
Avg. Rel. Hum. (%)	85	74	70	69	68	63	71	68	66	74	81	82	73

Note: Figures cover the years 1948-1990
Source: National Climatic Data Center, International Station Meteorological Climate Summary, 9/96

Weather Conditions

Temperature			Daytime Sky			Precipitation		
0°F & below	32°F & below	90°F & above	Clear	Partly cloudy	Cloudy	0.01 inch or more precip.	0.1 inch or more snow/ice	Thunder-storms
0	43	30	n/a	n/a	n/a	n/a	n/a	2

Note: Figures are average number of days per year and cover the years 1948-1990
Source: National Climatic Data Center, International Station Meteorological Climate Summary, 9/96

HAZARDOUS WASTE

Superfund Sites

The Santa Rosa, CA metro area has no sites on the EPA's Superfund Final National Priorities List. There are a total of 1,375 Superfund sites with a status of proposed or final on the list in the U.S. *U.S. Environmental Protection Agency, National Priorities List, April 7, 2021*

AIR QUALITY

Air Quality Trends: Ozone

	1990	1995	2000	2005	2010	2015	2016	2017	2018	2019
MSA[1]	0.063	0.071	0.061	0.050	0.053	0.059	0.055	0.062	0.055	0.056
U.S.	0.088	0.089	0.082	0.080	0.073	0.068	0.069	0.068	0.069	0.065

Note: (1) Data covers the Santa Rosa, CA Metropolitan Statistical Area. The values shown are the composite ozone concentration averages among trend sites based on the highest fourth daily maximum 8-hour concentration in parts per million. These trends are based on sites having an adequate record of monitoring data during the trend period. Data from exceptional events are included.
Source: U.S. Environmental Protection Agency, Air Quality Monitoring Information, "Air Quality Trends by City, 1990-2019"

Air Quality Index

Area	Percent of Days when Air Quality was...[2]					AQI Statistics[2]	
	Good	Moderate	Unhealthy for Sensitive Groups	Unhealthy	Very Unhealthy	Maximum	Median
MSA[1]	95.3	4.7	0.0	0.0	0.0	87	33

Note: (1) Data covers the Santa Rosa, CA Metropolitan Statistical Area; (2) Based on 365 days with AQI data in 2019. Air Quality Index (AQI) is an index for reporting daily air quality. EPA calculates the AQI for five major air pollutants regulated by the Clean Air Act: ground-level ozone, particle pollution (aka particulate matter), carbon monoxide, sulfur dioxide, and nitrogen dioxide. The AQI runs from 0 to 500. The higher the AQI value, the greater the level of air pollution and the greater the health concern. There are six AQI categories: "Good" AQI is between 0 and 50. Air quality is considered satisfactory; "Moderate" AQI is between 51 and 100. Air quality is acceptable; "Unhealthy for Sensitive Groups" When AQI values are between 101 and 150, members of sensitive groups may experience health effects; "Unhealthy" When AQI values are between 151 and 200 everyone may begin to experience health effects; "Very Unhealthy" AQI values between 201 and 300 trigger a health alert; "Hazardous" AQI values over 300 trigger warnings of emergency conditions (not shown).
Source: U.S. Environmental Protection Agency, Air Quality Index Report, 2019

Air Quality Index Pollutants

Area	Percent of Days when AQI Pollutant was...[2]					
	Carbon Monoxide	Nitrogen Dioxide	Ozone	Sulfur Dioxide	Particulate Matter 2.5	Particulate Matter 10
MSA[1]	0.0	0.8	70.7	0.0	25.8	2.7

Note: (1) Data covers the Santa Rosa, CA Metropolitan Statistical Area; (2) Based on 365 days with AQI data in 2019. The Air Quality Index (AQI) is an index for reporting daily air quality. EPA calculates the AQI for five major air pollutants regulated by the Clean Air Act: ground-level ozone, particle pollution (also known as particulate matter), carbon monoxide, sulfur dioxide, and nitrogen dioxide. The AQI runs from 0 to 500. The higher the AQI value, the greater the level of air pollution and the greater the health concern.
Source: U.S. Environmental Protection Agency, Air Quality Index Report, 2019

Maximum Air Pollutant Concentrations: Particulate Matter, Ozone, CO and Lead

	Particulate Matter 10 (ug/m^3)	Particulate Matter 2.5 Wtd AM (ug/m^3)	Particulate Matter 2.5 24-Hr (ug/m^3)	Ozone (ppm)	Carbon Monoxide (ppm)	Lead (ug/m^3)
MSA[1] Level	73	5.7	14	0.056	1	n/a
NAAQS[2]	150	15	35	0.075	9	0.15
Met NAAQS[2]	Yes	Yes	Yes	Yes	Yes	n/a

Note: (1) Data covers the Santa Rosa, CA Metropolitan Statistical Area; Data from exceptional events are included; (2) National Ambient Air Quality Standards; ppm = parts per million; ug/m^3 = micrograms per cubic meter; n/a not available.
Concentrations: Particulate Matter 10 (coarse particulate)—highest second maximum 24-hour concentration; Particulate Matter 2.5 Wtd AM (fine particulate)—highest weighted annual mean concentration; Particulate Matter 2.5 24-Hour (fine particulate)—highest 98th percentile 24-hour concentration; Ozone—highest fourth daily maximum 8-hour concentration; Carbon Monoxide—highest second maximum non-overlapping 8-hour concentration; Lead—maximum running 3-month average
Source: U.S. Environmental Protection Agency, Air Quality Monitoring Information, "Air Quality Statistics by City, 2019"

Maximum Air Pollutant Concentrations: Nitrogen Dioxide and Sulfur Dioxide

	Nitrogen Dioxide AM (ppb)	Nitrogen Dioxide 1-Hr (ppb)	Sulfur Dioxide AM (ppb)	Sulfur Dioxide 1-Hr (ppb)	Sulfur Dioxide 24-Hr (ppb)
MSA[1] Level	4	28	n/a	n/a	n/a
NAAQS[2]	53	100	30	75	140
Met NAAQS[2]	Yes	Yes	n/a	n/a	n/a

Note: (1) Data covers the Santa Rosa, CA Metropolitan Statistical Area; Data from exceptional events are included; (2) National Ambient Air Quality Standards; ppm = parts per million; ug/m^3 = micrograms per cubic meter; n/a not available.
Concentrations: Nitrogen Dioxide AM—highest arithmetic mean concentration; Nitrogen Dioxide 1-Hr—highest 98th percentile 1-hour daily maximum concentration; Sulfur Dioxide AM—highest annual mean concentration; Sulfur Dioxide 1-Hr—highest 99th percentile 1-hour daily maximum concentration; Sulfur Dioxide 24-Hr—highest second maximum 24-hour concentration
Source: U.S. Environmental Protection Agency, Air Quality Monitoring Information, "Air Quality Statistics by City, 2019"

Seattle, Washington

Background

Believe it or not, the virgin hinterlands and wide curving arch of Elliot Bay in present-day Seattle were once named New York. The city was renamed Seattle in 1853, for the Native American Indian Chief Seattle, two years after its first five families from Illinois had settled into the narrow strip of land between Puget Sound and Lake Washington.

The lush, green forests of the "Emerald City," created by the infamously frequent rains and its many natural waterways, gave birth to Seattle's first major industry—lumber, which also bred a society of bearded, rabble-rousing bachelors. To alleviate that problem, Asa Mercer, president of the Territorial University, which later became the University of Washington, trekked back east and recruited marriageable women, aka "Mercer girls."

Today, the city does not rely on lumber as its major industry, but boasts commercial aircraft production and missile research, importing and exporting, and technology. As the closest U.S. mainland port to Asia, Seattle has become a key trade center for goods such as cars, forest products, electronic equipment, bananas, and petroleum products. The city is home to headquarters of a number of large companies including Amazon.com, Nordstrom, Starbucks, and Expeditors International of Washington.

On the technology front, Seattle continues moving toward becoming the next Silicon Valley. It is predominantly a software town dominated by Microsoft in nearby Redmond. Corbis, the online photo-archive company, is headquartered in the city's historic Pioneer Square, and Amazon's move from Seattle's Beacon Hill to the South Lake Union neighborhood sparked a historic construction boom in 2017.

The Seattle Seaport Terminal Project, comprised of small-and-large-scale projects designed to improve the port's facilities for businesses, passengers, residents, and tourists, has included a major renovation of Terminal 5, construction of a Cruise Ship Terminal improvement, and port facilities improvements. Seattle is the fourth largest container port in North America.

Seattle has undergone a cultural and commercial reemergence of its downtown. Tourists and locals are drawn by luxury hotels, restaurants, a 16-screen movie theater, and other entertainment-oriented businesses, including the first in a nationwide chain of Game Works, computerized playgrounds for adults. Center City Seattle continues to see renovation and development projects, as city planners try to deal with more people living, working and visiting in the city.

> The city approved legislation requiring grocery stores with more than 500 employees to pay an extra $4 an hour in hazard pay during the COVID-19 pandemic.

The arts are a vital part of Seattle life. The world-famous Seattle Opera, now performing in a state-of-the-art hall dedicated in 2003, is well known for its summer presentations of Wagner's *Ring* cycle. The Seattle Philharmonic Orchestra celebrated its 50th anniversary in 2004; its annual Bushnell Concerto Competition features promising new area musicians. The city's jazz scene developed the early careers of Ray Charles and Quincy Jones, and is the birthplace of rocker Jimi Hendrix, the bands Nirvana, Pearl Jam, Soundgarden and Foo Fighters, and the alternative rock movement grunge.

The Seattle Museum constructed in Olympic Sculpture Park turned disused waterfront property into a permanent green space with plantings native to Puget Sound. The Seattle Museum of Flight's remarkable collection—the largest on the West Coast—includes a Concorde, donated by British Airways, and the Boeing 707 used as Air Force One by presidents from Eisenhower to Nixon.

Seattle's professional sports teams are popular and many. Football's Seattle Seahawks are Super Bowl XLVIII champions. Major league rugby team, Seattle Seawolves won back to back championships in 2018 and 2019.

Seattle has a distinctly marine climate. The city's location on Puget Sound and between two mountain ranges ensures a mild climate year round with moderate variations in temperature, and also puts it in a major earthquake zone. Summers are generally sunny and, while winters are rainy, most of the rain falls between October and March.

Rankings

General Rankings

- For its "Best for Vets: Places to Live 2019" rankings, *Military Times* evaluated 599 cities (83 large, 234 medium, 282 small) and compared the locations across three broad categories: veteran and military culture/services; economic indicators; and livability factors such as health, crime, traffic, and school quality. Seattle ranked #7 out of the top 25, in the large city category (population of more than 250,000). Data points more specific to veterans and the military weighed more heavily than others. *rebootcamp.militarytimes.com, "Military Times Best Places to Live 2019," September 10, 2018*

- *US News & World Report* conducted a survey of more than 3,000 people and analyzed the 150 largest metropolitan areas to determine what matters most when selecting the next place to live. Seattle ranked #13 out of the top 25 as having the best combination of desirable factors. Criteria: cost of living; quality of life; net migration; job market; desirability; and other factors. *realestate.usnews.com, "The 25 Best Places to Live in the U.S. in 2020-21," October 13, 2020*

- The Seattle metro area was identified as one of America's fastest-growing areas in terms of population and business growth by *MagnifyMoney*. The area ranked #20 out of 35. The 100 most populous metro areas in the U.S. were evaluated on their change from 2011-2016 in the following categories: people and housing; workforce and employment opportunities; growing industry. *www.businessinsider.com, "The 35 Cities in the US with the Biggest Influx of People, the Most Work Opportunities, and the Hottest Business Growth," August 12, 2018*

- The Seattle metro area was identified as one of America's fastest-growing areas in terms of population and economy by *Forbes*. The area ranked #2 out of 25. The 100 most populous metro areas in the U.S. were evaluated on the following criteria: estimated population growth; employment; economic output; wages; home values. *Forbes, "America's Fastest-Growing Cities 2018," February 28, 2018*

- The human resources consulting firm Mercer ranked 231 major cities worldwide in terms of overall quality of life. Seattle ranked #46. Criteria: political, social, economic, and socio-cultural factors; medical and health considerations; schools and education; public services and transportation; recreation; consumer goods; housing; and natural environment. *Mercer, "Mercer 2019 Quality of Living Survey," March 13, 2019*

Business/Finance Rankings

- According to *Business Insider*, the Seattle metro area is a prime place to run a startup or move an existing business to. The area ranked #5. Nearly 190 metro areas were analyzed on overall economic health and investments. Data was based on the 2019 U.S. Census Bureau American Community Survey, the marketing company PitchBook, Bureau of Labor Statistics employment report, and Zillow. Criteria: percentage of change in typical home values and employment rates; quarterly venture capital investment activity; and median household income. *www.businessinsider.com, "The 25 Best Cities to Start a Business-Or Move Your Current One," January 12, 2021*

- Based on metro area social media reviews, the employment opinion group Glassdoor surveyed 50 of the most populous U.S. metro areas and equally weighed cost of living, hiring opportunity, and job satisfaction to compose a list of "25 Best Cities for Jobs." Median pay and home value, and number of active job openings were also factored in. The Seattle metro area was ranked #23 in overall job satisfaction. *www.glassdoor.com, "Best Cities for Jobs," February 25, 2020*

- The Brookings Institution ranked the nation's largest cities based on income inequality. Seattle was ranked #34 (#1 = greatest inequality). Criteria: the "95/20 ratio," a figure representing the income at which a household earns more than 95 percent of all other households, divided by the income at which a household earns more than only 20 percent of all other households. *Brookings Institution, "Household Income Inequality, Largest Cities of 97 Large U.S. Metro Areas, 2014-2016," February 5, 2018*

- The Brookings Institution ranked the 100 largest metro areas in the U.S. based on income inequality. Seattle was ranked #71 (#1 = greatest inequality). Criteria: the "95/20 ratio," a figure representing the income at which a household earns more than 95 percent of all other households, divided by the income at which a household earns more than only 20 percent of all other households. *Brookings Institution, "Household Income Inequality, 100 Largest U.S. Metro Areas, 2014-2016," February 5, 2018*

- *Forbes* ranked the 100 largest metro areas in the U.S. in terms of the "Best Cities for Young Professionals." The Seattle metro area ranked #1 out of 25. Criteria: median rent of a two-bedroom apartment; job growth and unemployment rate; median salary of college graduates with 5 or less years of work experience; networking opportunities; social outlook; percentage of population 25 years of age and older with college degrees. *Forbes.com, "America's 25 Best Cities for Young Professionals in 2017," May 22, 2017*

- Payscale.com ranked the 32 largest metro areas in terms of wage growth. The Seattle metro area ranked #8. Criteria: private-sector and education professional wage growth between the 4th quarter of 2019 and the 4th quarter of 2020. *PayScale, "Wage Trends by Metro Area-4th Quarter," January 11, 2021*

- The Seattle metro area was identified as one of the most debt-ridden places in America by the finance site Credit.com. The metro area was ranked #9. Criteria: residents' average credit card debt as well as median income. *Credit.com, "25 Cities With the Most Credit Card Debt," February 28, 2018*

- For its annual survey of the "Most Expensive U.S. Cities to Live In," Kiplinger applied Cost of Living Index statistics developed by the Council for Community and Economic Research to U.S. Census Bureau population and median household income data for 256 urban areas. Seattle was among the 20 most expensive in the country. *Kiplinger.com, "The 20 Most Expensive Cities in the U.S.," July 29, 2020*

- The Seattle metro area appeared on the Milken Institute "2021 Best Performing Cities" list. Rank: #13 out of 200 large metro areas (population over 250,000). Criteria: job growth; wage and salary growth; high-tech output growth; housing affordability; household broadband access. *Milken Institute, "Best-Performing Cities 2021," February 16, 2021*

- *Forbes* ranked the 200 most populous metro areas to determine the nation's "Best Places for Business and Careers." The Seattle metro area was ranked #1. Criteria: costs (business and living); job growth (past and projected); income growth; quality of life; educational attainment (college and high school); projected economic growth; cultural and leisure opportunities; workplace tolerance laws; net migration patterns. *Forbes, "The Best Places for Business and Careers 2019: Seattle Still On Top," October 30, 2019*

- Mercer Human Resources Consulting ranked 209 cities worldwide in terms of cost-of-living. Seattle ranked #55 (the lower the ranking, the higher the cost-of-living). The survey measured the comparative cost of over 200 items (such as housing, food, clothing, household goods, transportation, and entertainment) in each location. *Mercer, "2020 Cost of Living Survey," June 9, 2020*

Culture/Performing Arts Rankings

- Seattle was selected as one of the 25 best cities for moviemakers in North America. COVID-19 has spurred a quest for great film cities that offer more creative space, lower costs, and more great outdoors. NYC & LA were intentionally excluded. Criteria: longstanding reputations as film-friendly communities; efforts to deal with pandemic-specific challenges; and establish appropriate COVID-19 guidelines. The city was ranked #23. *MovieMaker Magazine, "Best Places to Live and Work as a Moviemaker, 2021," January 26, 2021*

Dating/Romance Rankings

- Seattle was selected as one of the nation's most romantic cities with 100,000 or more residents by Amazon.com. The city ranked #14 of 20. Criteria: per capita sales of romance novels, relationship books, romantic comedy movies, romantic music, and sexual wellness products. *Amazon.com, "Top 20 Most Romantic Cities in the U.S.," February 1, 2017*

- Seattle was selected as one of the best cities for post grads by *Rent.com*. The city ranked among the top 10. Criteria: jobs per capita; unemployment rate; mean annual income; cost of living; rental inventory. *Rent.com, "Best Cities for College Grads," December 11, 2018*

Education Rankings

- Personal finance website *WalletHub* analyzed the 150 largest U.S. metropolitan statistical areas to determine where the most educated Americans are putting their degrees to work. Criteria: education levels; percentage of workers with degrees; education quality and attainment gap; public school quality rankings; quality and enrollment of each metro area's universities. Seattle was ranked #8 (#1 = most educated city). *www.WalletHub.com, "Most and Least Educated Cities in America," July 20, 2020*

- Seattle was selected as one of America's most literate cities. The city ranked #1 out of the 84 largest U.S. cities. Criteria: number of booksellers; library resources; Internet resources; educational attainment; periodical publishing resources; newspaper circulation. *Central Connecticut State University, "America's Most Literate Cities, 2018," February 2019*

Environmental Rankings

- Sperling's BestPlaces assessed the 50 largest metropolitan areas of the United States for the likelihood of dangerously extreme weather events or earthquakes. In general the Southeast and South-Central regions have the highest risk of weather extremes and earthquakes, while the Pacific Northwest enjoys the lowest risk. Of the least risky metropolitan areas, the Seattle metro area was ranked #5. *www.bestplaces.net, "Avoid Natural Disasters: BestPlaces Reveals The Top 10 Safest Places to Live," October 25, 2017*

- The U.S. Environmental Protection Agency (EPA) released a list of U.S. metropolitan areas with the most ENERGY STAR certified buildings in 2019. The Seattle metro area was ranked #13 out of 25. *U.S. Environmental Protection Agency, "2020 Energy Star Top Cities," March 2020*

- Seattle was highlighted as one of the 25 metro areas most polluted by short-term particle pollution (24-hour PM 2.5) in the U.S. during 2016 through 2018. The area ranked #14. *American Lung Association, "State of the Air 2020," April 21, 2020*

Food/Drink Rankings

- The U.S. Chamber of Commerce Foundation conducted an in-depth study on local food truck regulations, surveyed 288 food truck owners, and ranked 20 major American cities based on how friendly they are for operating a food truck. The compiled index assessed the following: procedures for obtaining permits and licenses; complying with restrictions; and financial obligations associated with operating a food truck. Seattle ranked #17 overall (1 being the best). *www.foodtrucknation.us, "Food Truck Nation," March 20, 2018*

- T-Mobile Park was selected as one of PETA's "Top 10 Vegan-Friendly Ballparks" for 2019. The park ranked #8. *People for the Ethical Treatment of Animals, "Top 10 Vegan-Friendly Ballparks," May 23, 2019*

Health/Fitness Rankings

- For each of the 100 largest cities in the United States, the American Fitness Index®, published by the American College of Sports Medicine and the Anthem Foundation, evaluated community infrastructure and 33 health behaviors including preventive health, levels of chronic disease conditions, pedestrian safety, air quality, and community resources that support physical activity. Seattle ranked #2 for "community fitness." *americanfitnessindex.org, "2020 ACSM American Fitness Index Summary Report," July 14, 2020*

- Seattle was identified as one of the 10 most walkable cities in the U.S. by Walk Score. The city ranked #8. Walk Score measures walkability by analyzing hundreds of walking routes to nearby amenities, and also measures pedestrian friendliness by analyzing population density and road metrics such as block length and intersection density. *WalkScore.com, April 13, 2021*

- The Seattle metro area was identified as one of the worst cities for bed bugs in America by pest control company Orkin. The area ranked #44 out of 50 based on the number of bed bug treatments Orkin performed from December 2019 to November 2020. *Orkin, "New Year, New Top City on Orkin's 2021 Bed Bug Cities List: Chicago," February 1, 2021*

- Seattle was identified as a "2021 Spring Allergy Capital." The area ranked #98 out of 100. Three groups of factors were used to identify the most challenging cities for people with allergies during the spring season: annual spring pollen levels; over the counter medicine use; number of board-certified allergy specialists. *Asthma and Allergy Foundation of America, "Spring Allergy Capitals 2021," February 23, 2021*

- Seattle was identified as a "2021 Fall Allergy Capital." The area ranked #99 out of 100. Three groups of factors were used to identify the most challenging cities for people with allergies during the fall season: annual fall pollen levels; over the counter medicine use; number of board-certified allergy specialists. *Asthma and Allergy Foundation of America, "Fall Allergy Capitals 2021," February 23, 2021*

- Seattle was identified as a "2019 Asthma Capital." The area ranked #64 out of the nation's 100 largest metropolitan areas. Criteria: estimated asthma prevalence; crude death rate from asthma; and ER visits due to asthma. Risk factors analyzed but not factored in the rankings: annual pollen score; annual air quality; public smoking laws; number of board-certified asthma specialists; rescue medication use; controller medication use; uninsured rate; poverty rate. *Asthma and Allergy Foundation of America, "Asthma Capitals 2019: The Most Challenging Places to Live With Asthma," May 7, 2019*

Pet Rankings

- Seattle appeared on *The Dogington Post* site as one of the top cities for dog lovers, ranking #1 out of 20. The real estate brokerage, Redfin and Rover, the largest pet sitter and dog walker network, compiled a list from over 14,000 U.S. cities to come up with a "Rover Rank." Criteria: highest count of dog walks, the city's Walk Score®, for-sale home listings that mention "dog," number of dog walkers and pet sitters and the hours spent and distance logged. *www.dogingtonpost.com, "The 20 Most Dog-Friendly Cities of 2019," April 4, 2019*

Real Estate Rankings

- FitSmallBusiness looked at 50 of the largest metropolitan areas in the U.S. to determine which metro was the best to start a real estate business. Data was compiled from such sources as: Zillow, Trulia, U.S. Census Bureau, and the Bureau of Labor Statistics. Criteria: location; inventory; annual wages; median sales price of homes; days on the market; median price cut percentage; and other factors that would influence real estate professional growth. The Seattle metro area ranked #27. *fitsmallbusiness.com, "The Best Cities to Become a Real Estate Agent in 2018," January 30, 2018*

- *WalletHub* compared the most populated U.S. cities to determine which had the best markets for real estate agents. Seattle ranked #1 where demand was high and pay was the best. Criteria: sales per agent; annual median wage for real-estate agents; monthly average starting salary for real estate agents; real estate job density and competition; unemployment rate; home turnover rate; housing-market health index; and other relevant metrics. *www.WalletHub.com, "2019's Best Places to Be a Real Estate Agent," April 24, 2019*

- According to Penske Truck Rental, the Seattle metro area was named the #7 moving destination in 2019, based on one-way consumer truck rental reservations made through Penske's website, rental locations, and reservations call center. *gopenske.com/blog, "Penske Truck Rental's 2019 Top Moving Destinations," January 22, 2020*

- The Seattle metro area appeared on Realtor.com's list of hot housing markets to watch in 2021. The area ranked #5. Criteria: healthy existing homes inventory; relative home affordability; local economy/population trends. *Realtor.com®, "Top 10 Housing Markets Positioned for Growth in 2021," December 7, 2020*

- The Seattle metro area was identified as one of the top 15 housing markets to invest in for 2021 by *Forbes.* Criteria: home price appreciation; percentage of home sales within a 2-week time frame; available inventory; number of home sales; and other factors. *Forbes.com, "Top Housing Markets To Watch In 2021," December 15, 2020*

- Seattle was ranked #10 in the top 20 out of the 100 largest metro areas in terms of house price appreciation in 2020 (#1 = highest rate). *Federal Housing Finance Agency, House Price Index, 4th Quarter 2020*

- The Seattle metro area was identified as one of the 20 least affordable housing markets in the U.S. in 2020. The area ranked #176 out of 183 markets. Criteria: qualification for a mortgage loan with a 10 percent down payment on a typical home. *National Association of Realtors®, Qualifying Income Based on Sales Price of Existing Single-Family Homes for Metropolitan Areas, 2020*

- Seattle was ranked #238 out of 268 metro areas in terms of housing affordability in 2020 by the National Association of Home Builders (#1 = most affordable). Criteria: the share of homes sold in that area affordable to a family earning the local median income, based on standard mortgage underwriting criteria. *National Association of Home Builders®, NAHB-Wells Fargo Housing Opportunity Index, 4th Quarter 2020*

Safety Rankings

- Allstate ranked the 200 largest cities in America in terms of driver safety. Seattle ranked #155. Criteria: internal property damage claims over a two-year period from January 2016 to December 2017. The report helps increase the importance of safety and awareness behind the wheel. *Allstate, "Allstate America's Best Drivers Report, 2019" June 24, 2019*

- The National Insurance Crime Bureau ranked 384 metro areas in the U.S. in terms of per capita rates of vehicle theft. The Seattle metro area ranked #32 (#1 = highest rate). Criteria: number of vehicle theft offenses per 100,000 inhabitants in 2019. *National Insurance Crime Bureau, "Hot Spots 2019," July 21, 2020*

Seniors/Retirement Rankings

- From its Best Cities for Successful Aging indexes, the Milken Institute generated rankings for metropolitan areas, weighing data in nine categories—health care, wellness, living arrangements, transportation and convenience, financial characteristics, education, employment, community engagement, and overall livability. The Seattle metro area was ranked #35 overall in the large metro area category. *Milken Institute, "Best Cities for Successful Aging, 2017" March 14, 2017*

Sports/Recreation Rankings

- Seattle was chosen as one of America's best cities for bicycling. The city ranked #1 out of 50. Criteria: cycling infrastructure that is safe and friendly for all ages; energy and bike culture. The editors evaluated cities with populations of 100,000 or more. *Bicycling, "The 50 Best Bike Cities in America," October 10, 2018*

Transportation Rankings

- Business Insider presented an AllTransit Performance Score ranking of public transportation in major U.S. cities and towns, with populations over 250,000, in which Seattle earned the #16-ranked "Transit Score," awarded for frequency of service, access to jobs, quality and number of stops, and affordability. *www.businessinsider.com, "The 17 Major U.S. Cities with the Best Public Transportation," April 17, 2018*

- Seattle was identified as one of the most congested metro areas in the U.S. The area ranked #7 out of 10. Criteria: yearly delay per auto commuter in hours. *Texas A&M Transportation Institute, "2019 Urban Mobility Report," December 2019*

Women/Minorities Rankings

- Seattle was selected as one of the gayest cities in America by *The Advocate*. The city ranked #24 out of 25. Criteria, among many: Trans Pride parades/festivals; gay rugby teams; lesbian bars; LGBT centers; theater screenings of "Moonlight"; LGBT-inclusive nondiscrimination ordinances; and gay bowling teams. *The Advocate, "Queerest Cities in America 2017" January 12, 2017*

- Personal finance website *WalletHub* compared more than 180 U.S. cities across two key dimensions, "Hispanic Business-Friendliness" and "Hispanic Purchasing Power," to arrive at the most favorable conditions for Hispanic entrepreneurs. Seattle was ranked #107 out of 182. Criteria includes: share of Hispanic-Owned Businesses; Hispanic entrepreneurship rate to median annual income of Hispanics; Small Business-Friendliness score; cost of living; and number of Hispanics with at least a bachelor's degree. *WalletHub.com, "2019's Best Cities for Hispanic Entrepreneurs," May 1, 2019*

Miscellaneous Rankings

- *MoveHub* ranked 446 hipster cities across 20 countries, using its *alternative* Hipster Index and Seattle came out as #4 among the top 50. Criteria: population over 150,000; number of vintage boutiques; density of tattoo parlors; vegan places to eat; coffee shops; and density of vinyl record stores. *www.movehub.com, "The Hipster Index: Brighton Pips Portland to Global Top Spot," February 20, 2020*

- The watchdog site, Charity Navigator, conducted a study of charities in major markets both to analyze statistical differences in their financial, accountability, and transparency practices and to track year-to-year variations in individual philanthropic communities. The Seattle metro area was ranked #25 among the 30 metro markets in the rating category of Overall Score. *www.charitynavigator.org, "2017 Metro Market Study," May 1, 2017*

- *WalletHub* compared the 150 most populated U.S. cities to determine their operating efficiency. A "Quality of City Services" score was constructed for each city and then divided by the total budget per capita to reveal which were managed the best. Seattle ranked #114. Criteria: financial stability; economy; education; safety; health; infrastructure and pollution. *www.WalletHub.com, "2020's Best- & Worst-Run Cities in America," June 29, 2020*

- The National Alliance to End Homelessness listed the 25 most populous metro areas with the highest rate of homelessness. The Seattle metro area had a high rate of homelessness. Criteria: number of homeless people per 10,000 population in 2016. *National Alliance to End Homelessness, "Homelessness in the 25 Most Populous U.S. Metro Areas," September 1, 2017*

Business Environment

DEMOGRAPHICS

Population Growth

Area	1990 Census	2000 Census	2010 Census	2019* Estimate	Population Growth (%) 1990-2019	2010-2019
City	516,262	563,374	608,660	724,305	40.3	19.0
MSA[1]	2,559,164	3,043,878	3,439,809	3,871,323	51.3	12.5
U.S.	248,709,873	281,421,906	308,745,538	324,697,795	30.6	5.2

Note: (1) Figures cover the Seattle-Tacoma-Bellevue, WA Metropolitan Statistical Area; (*) 2015-2019 5-year estimated population
Source: U.S. Census Bureau, 1990 Census, Census 2000, Census 2010, 2015-2019 American Community Survey 5-Year Estimates

Household Size

Area	One	Two	Three	Four	Five	Six	Seven or More	Average Household Size
City	38.5	35.7	12.5	8.9	2.9	0.8	0.7	2.10
MSA[1]	27.2	34.5	16.0	13.6	5.3	2.0	1.4	2.50
U.S.	27.9	33.9	15.6	12.9	6.0	2.3	1.4	2.60

Note: (1) Figures cover the Seattle-Tacoma-Bellevue, WA Metropolitan Statistical Area
Source: U.S. Census Bureau, 2015-2019 American Community Survey 5-Year Estimates

Race

Area	White Alone[2] (%)	Black Alone[2] (%)	Asian Alone[2] (%)	AIAN[3] Alone[2] (%)	NHOPI[4] Alone[2] (%)	Other Race Alone[2] (%)	Two or More Races (%)
City	67.3	7.3	15.4	0.5	0.3	2.3	6.9
MSA[1]	68.3	5.8	13.6	0.8	0.9	3.7	6.8
U.S.	72.5	12.7	5.5	0.8	0.2	4.9	3.3

Note: (1) Figures cover the Seattle-Tacoma-Bellevue, WA Metropolitan Statistical Area; (2) Alone is defined as not being in combination with one or more other races; (3) American Indian and Alaska Native; (4) Native Hawaiian and Other Pacific Islander
Source: U.S. Census Bureau, 2015-2019 American Community Survey 5-Year Estimates

Hispanic or Latino Origin

Area	Total (%)	Mexican (%)	Puerto Rican (%)	Cuban (%)	Other (%)
City	6.7	3.9	0.4	0.2	2.1
MSA[1]	10.0	7.1	0.6	0.2	2.2
U.S.	18.0	11.2	1.7	0.7	4.3

Note: Persons of Hispanic or Latino origin can be of any race; (1) Figures cover the Seattle-Tacoma-Bellevue, WA Metropolitan Statistical Area
Source: U.S. Census Bureau, 2015-2019 American Community Survey 5-Year Estimates

Ancestry

Area	German	Irish	English	American	Italian	Polish	French[2]	Scottish	Dutch
City	14.8	11.4	10.1	2.3	4.4	2.7	3.0	2.9	1.6
MSA[1]	14.6	9.7	9.3	3.2	3.7	1.9	2.8	2.6	1.5
U.S.	13.3	9.7	7.2	6.2	5.1	2.8	2.3	1.7	1.2

Note: Figures are the percentage of the total population reporting a particular ancestry. The nine most commonly reported ancestries in the U.S. are shown. Figures include multiple ancestries (e.g. if a person reported being Irish and Italian, they were included in both columns); (1) Figures cover the Seattle-Tacoma-Bellevue, WA Metropolitan Statistical Area; (2) Excludes Basque
Source: U.S. Census Bureau, 2015-2019 American Community Survey 5-Year Estimates

Foreign-born Population

Area	Any Foreign Country	Asia	Mexico	Europe	Caribbean	Central America[2]	South America	Africa	Canada
City	18.8	10.6	1.2	2.5	0.1	0.5	0.5	2.1	1.0
MSA[1]	18.7	9.9	2.4	2.6	0.2	0.5	0.5	1.5	0.7
U.S.	13.6	4.2	3.5	1.5	1.3	1.1	1.0	0.7	0.2

Note: (1) Figures cover the Seattle-Tacoma-Bellevue, WA Metropolitan Statistical Area; (2) Excludes Mexico.
Source: U.S. Census Bureau, 2015-2019 American Community Survey 5-Year Estimates

Marital Status

Area	Never Married	Now Married[2]	Separated	Widowed	Divorced
City	44.5	41.1	1.2	3.4	9.9
MSA[1]	32.6	50.8	1.4	4.2	11.0
U.S.	33.4	48.1	1.9	5.8	10.9

Note: Figures are percentages and cover the population 15 years of age and older; (1) Figures cover the Seattle-Tacoma-Bellevue, WA Metropolitan Statistical Area; (2) Excludes separated
Source: U.S. Census Bureau, 2015-2019 American Community Survey 5-Year Estimates

Disability by Age

Area	All Ages	Under 18 Years Old	18 to 64 Years Old	65 Years and Over
City	9.2	2.5	6.9	30.9
MSA[1]	10.8	3.5	8.7	33.4
U.S.	12.6	4.2	10.3	34.5

Note: Figures show percent of the civilian noninstitutionalized population that reported having a disability. Disability status is determined from six types of difficulty: vision, hearing, cognitive, ambulatory, self-care, and independent living. For children under 5 years old, hearing and vision difficulty are used to determine disability status. For children between the ages of 5 and 14, disability status is determined from hearing, vision, cognitive, ambulatory, and self-care difficulties. For people aged 15 years and older, they are considered to have a disability if they have difficulty with any one of the six difficulty types; Note: (1) Figures cover the Seattle-Tacoma-Bellevue, WA Metropolitan Statistical Area
Source: U.S. Census Bureau, 2015-2019 American Community Survey 5-Year Estimates

Age

Area				Percent of Population						Median Age
	Under Age 5	Age 5–19	Age 20–34	Age 35–44	Age 45–54	Age 55–64	Age 65–74	Age 75–84	Age 85+	
City	4.8	12.8	31.8	15.3	12.3	10.7	7.4	3.3	1.8	35.3
MSA[1]	6.1	17.6	23.0	14.3	13.4	12.4	7.9	3.5	1.6	37.0
U.S.	6.1	19.1	20.7	12.6	13.0	12.9	9.1	4.6	1.9	38.1

Note: (1) Figures cover the Seattle-Tacoma-Bellevue, WA Metropolitan Statistical Area
Source: U.S. Census Bureau, 2015-2019 American Community Survey 5-Year Estimates

Gender

Area	Males	Females	Males per 100 Females
City	366,442	357,863	102.4
MSA[1]	1,938,723	1,932,600	100.3
U.S.	159,886,919	164,810,876	97.0

Note: (1) Figures cover the Seattle-Tacoma-Bellevue, WA Metropolitan Statistical Area
Source: U.S. Census Bureau, 2015-2019 American Community Survey 5-Year Estimates

Religious Groups by Family

Area	Catholic	Baptist	Non-Den.	Methodist[2]	Lutheran	LDS[3]	Pente-costal	Presby-terian[4]	Muslim[5]	Judaism
MSA[1]	12.3	2.2	5.0	1.2	2.1	3.3	2.8	1.4	0.5	0.5
U.S.	19.1	9.3	4.0	4.0	2.3	2.0	1.9	1.6	0.8	0.7

Note: Figures are the number of adherents as a percentage of the total population; (1) Figures cover the Seattle-Tacoma-Bellevue, WA Metropolitan Statistical Area; (2) Methodist/Pietist; (3) Latter Day Saints; (4) Reformed; (5) Figures are estimates
Source: Association of Statisticians of American Religious Bodies, 2010 U.S. Religion Census: Religious Congregations & Membership Study

Religious Groups by Tradition

Area	Catholic	Evangelical Protestant	Mainline Protestant	Other Tradition	Black Protestant	Orthodox
MSA[1]	12.3	11.9	4.7	5.9	0.4	0.4
U.S.	19.1	16.2	7.3	4.3	1.6	0.3

Note: Figures are the number of adherents as a percentage of the total population; (1) Figures cover the Seattle-Tacoma-Bellevue, WA Metropolitan Statistical Area
Source: Association of Statisticians of American Religious Bodies, 2010 U.S. Religion Census: Religious Congregations & Membership Study

ECONOMY

Gross Metropolitan Product

Area	2017	2018	2019	2020	Rank[2]
MSA[1]	367.9	397.5	416.9	435.0	11

Note: Figures are in billions of dollars; (1) Figures cover the Seattle-Tacoma-Bellevue, WA Metropolitan Statistical Area; (2) Rank is based on 2018 data and ranges from 1 to 381
Source: U.S. Conference of Mayors, U.S. Metro Economies: GMP & Employment 2018-2020, September 2019

Economic Growth

Area	2015-17 (%)	2018 (%)	2019 (%)	2020 (%)	Rank[2]
MSA[1]	4.3	6.3	3.4	2.4	29
U.S.	1.9	2.9	2.3	2.1	–

Note: Figures are real gross metropolitan product (GMP) growth rates and represent average annual percent change; (1) Figures cover the Seattle-Tacoma-Bellevue, WA Metropolitan Statistical Area; (2) Rank is based on 2017 2-year average annual percent change and ranges from 1 to 381
Source: U.S. Conference of Mayors, U.S. Metro Economies: GMP & Employment 2018-2020, September 2019

Metropolitan Area Exports

Area	2014	2015	2016	2017	2018	2019	Rank[2]
MSA[1]	61,938.4	67,226.4	61,881.0	59,007.0	59,742.9	41,249.0	5

Note: Figures are in millions of dollars; (1) Figures cover the Seattle-Tacoma-Bellevue, WA Metropolitan Statistical Area; (2) Rank is based on 2019 data and ranges from 1 to 386
Source: U.S. Department of Commerce, International Trade Administration, Office of Trade and Economic Analysis, Industry and Analysis, Exports by Metropolitan Area, data extracted March 24, 2021

Building Permits

Area	Single-Family			Multi-Family			Total		
	2018	2019	Pct. Chg.	2018	2019	Pct. Chg.	2018	2019	Pct. Chg.
City	523	507	-3.1	7,395	10,277	39.0	7,918	10,784	36.2
MSA[1]	9,134	8,737	-4.3	19,052	17,862	-6.2	28,186	26,599	-5.6
U.S.	855,300	862,100	0.7	473,500	523,900	10.6	1,328,800	1,386,000	4.3

Note: (1) Figures cover the Seattle-Tacoma-Bellevue, WA Metropolitan Statistical Area; Figures represent new, privately-owned housing units authorized (unadjusted data); All permit data are based on estimates with imputation
Source: U.S. Census Bureau, Manufacturing, Mining, and Construction Statistics, Building Permits, 2018, 2019

Bankruptcy Filings

Area	Business Filings			Nonbusiness Filings		
	2019	2020	% Chg.	2019	2020	% Chg.
King County	115	96	-16.5	2,174	1,516	-30.3
U.S.	22,780	21,655	-4.9	752,160	522,808	-30.5

Note: Business filings include Chapter 7, Chapter 9, Chapter 11, Chapter 12, Chapter 13, Chapter 15, and Section 304; Nonbusiness filings include Chapter 7, Chapter 11, and Chapter 13
Source: Administrative Office of the U.S. Courts, Business and Nonbusiness Bankruptcy, County Cases Commenced by Chapter of the Bankruptcy Code, During the 12-Month Period Ending December 31, 2019 and Business and Nonbusiness Bankruptcy, County Cases Commenced by Chapter of the Bankruptcy Code, During the 12-Month Period Ending December 31, 2020

Housing Vacancy Rates

Area	Gross Vacancy Rate[2] (%)			Year-Round Vacancy Rate[3] (%)			Rental Vacancy Rate[4] (%)			Homeowner Vacancy Rate[5] (%)		
	2018	2019	2020	2018	2019	2020	2018	2019	2020	2018	2019	2020
MSA[1]	5.9	5.5	4.7	5.4	5.2	4.5	4.8	4.4	3.6	0.8	1.0	0.6
U.S.	12.3	12.0	10.6	9.7	9.5	8.2	6.9	6.7	6.3	1.5	1.4	1.0

Note: (1) Figures cover the Seattle-Tacoma-Bellevue, WA Metropolitan Statistical Area; (2) The percentage of the total housing inventory that is vacant; (3) The percentage of the housing inventory (excluding seasonal units) that is year-round vacant; (4) The percentage of rental inventory that is vacant for rent; (5) The percentage of homeowner inventory that is vacant for sale
Source: U.S. Census Bureau, Housing Vacancies and Homeownership Annual Statistics: 2018, 2019, 2020

INCOME

Income

Area	Per Capita ($)	Median Household ($)	Average Household ($)
City	59,835	92,263	128,184
MSA[1]	45,750	86,856	115,653
U.S.	34,103	62,843	88,607

Note: (1) Figures cover the Seattle-Tacoma-Bellevue, WA Metropolitan Statistical Area
Source: U.S. Census Bureau, 2015-2019 American Community Survey 5-Year Estimates

Household Income Distribution

Area	Percent of Households Earning							
	Under $15,000	$15,000 -$24,999	$25,000 -$34,999	$35,000 -$49,999	$50,000 -$74,999	$75,000 -$99,999	$100,000 -$149,999	$150,000 and up
City	8.8	5.3	5.6	8.7	13.5	11.4	18.3	28.4
MSA[1]	6.7	5.4	5.9	9.5	15.7	13.3	19.5	23.9
U.S.	10.3	8.9	8.9	12.3	17.2	12.7	15.1	14.5

Note: (1) Figures cover the Seattle-Tacoma-Bellevue, WA Metropolitan Statistical Area
Source: U.S. Census Bureau, 2015-2019 American Community Survey 5-Year Estimates

Poverty Rate

Area	All Ages	Under 18 Years Old	18 to 64 Years Old	65 Years and Over
City	11.0	10.9	10.9	11.2
MSA[1]	9.0	10.8	8.6	7.8
U.S.	13.4	18.5	12.6	9.3

Note: Figures are percentage of people whose income during the past 12 months was below the poverty level;
(1) Figures cover the Seattle-Tacoma-Bellevue, WA Metropolitan Statistical Area
Source: U.S. Census Bureau, 2015-2019 American Community Survey 5-Year Estimates

CITY FINANCES

City Government Finances

Component	2017 ($000)	2017 ($ per capita)
Total Revenues	4,199,469	6,136
Total Expenditures	4,116,980	6,015
Debt Outstanding	5,049,001	7,377
Cash and Securities[1]	4,252,916	6,214

Note: (1) Cash and security holdings of a government at the close of its fiscal year, including those of its dependent agencies, utilities, and liquor stores.
Source: U.S. Census Bureau, State & Local Government Finances 2017

City Government Revenue by Source

Source	2017 ($000)	2017 ($ per capita)	2017 (%)
General Revenue			
From Federal Government	61,076	89	1.5
From State Government	172,017	251	4.1
From Local Governments	23,223	34	0.6
Taxes			
Property	543,943	795	13.0
Sales and Gross Receipts	624,068	912	14.9
Personal Income	0	0	0.0
Corporate Income	0	0	0.0
Motor Vehicle License	63,396	93	1.5
Other Taxes	201,398	294	4.8
Current Charges	883,577	1,291	21.0
Liquor Store	0	0	0.0
Utility	1,134,864	1,658	27.0
Employee Retirement	272,857	399	6.5

Source: U.S. Census Bureau, State & Local Government Finances 2017

City Government Expenditures by Function

Function	2017 ($000)	2017 ($ per capita)	2017 (%)
General Direct Expenditures			
Air Transportation	0	0	0.0
Corrections	0	0	0.0
Education	47,669	69	1.2
Employment Security Administration	0	0	0.0
Financial Administration	10,139	14	0.2
Fire Protection	191,403	279	4.6
General Public Buildings	0	0	0.0
Governmental Administration, Other	45,158	66	1.1
Health	12,809	18	0.3
Highways	437,302	638	10.6
Hospitals	0	0	0.0
Housing and Community Development	72,186	105	1.8
Interest on General Debt	61,679	90	1.5
Judicial and Legal	57,655	84	1.4
Libraries	73,388	107	1.8
Parking	12,039	17	0.3
Parks and Recreation	254,521	371	6.2
Police Protection	214,965	314	5.2
Public Welfare	103,701	151	2.5
Sewerage	212,916	311	5.2
Solid Waste Management	172,548	252	4.2
Veterans' Services	0	0	0.0
Liquor Store	0	0	0.0
Utility	1,345,210	1,965	32.7
Employee Retirement	185,606	271	4.5

Source: U.S. Census Bureau, State & Local Government Finances 2017

EMPLOYMENT

Labor Force and Employment

Area	Civilian Labor Force			Workers Employed		
	Dec. 2019	Dec. 2020	% Chg.	Dec. 2019	Dec. 2020	% Chg.
City	475,147	468,970	-1.3	464,721	440,258	-5.3
MD[1]	1,724,567	1,722,800	-0.1	1,683,121	1,619,303	-3.8
U.S.	164,007,000	160,017,000	-2.4	158,504,000	149,613,000	-5.6

Note: Data is not seasonally adjusted and covers workers 16 years of age and older; (1) Figures cover the
Seattle-Bellevue-Everett, WA Metropolitan Division
Source: Bureau of Labor Statistics, Local Area Unemployment Statistics

Unemployment Rate

Area	2020											
	Jan.	Feb.	Mar.	Apr.	May	Jun.	Jul.	Aug.	Sep.	Oct.	Nov.	Dec.
City	2.4	2.2	5.3	13.7	13.2	9.0	7.9	6.8	6.5	4.2	3.9	6.1
MD[1]	2.7	2.6	5.3	16.2	12.6	10.7	9.5	7.9	7.4	6.5	6.1	6.0
U.S.	4.0	3.8	4.5	14.4	13.0	11.2	10.5	8.5	7.7	6.6	6.4	6.5

Note: Data is not seasonally adjusted and covers workers 16 years of age and older; (1) Figures cover the
Seattle-Bellevue-Everett, WA Metropolitan Division
Source: Bureau of Labor Statistics, Local Area Unemployment Statistics

Average Wages

Occupation	$/Hr.	Occupation	$/Hr.
Accountants and Auditors	42.20	Maintenance and Repair Workers	24.20
Automotive Mechanics	26.20	Marketing Managers	81.40
Bookkeepers	24.40	Network and Computer Systems Admin.	48.50
Carpenters	33.30	Nurses, Licensed Practical	29.50
Cashiers	16.50	Nurses, Registered	45.70
Computer Programmers	n/a	Nursing Assistants	18.20
Computer Systems Analysts	54.00	Office Clerks, General	22.00
Computer User Support Specialists	30.90	Physical Therapists	44.20
Construction Laborers	27.10	Physicians	121.60
Cooks, Restaurant	17.90	Plumbers, Pipefitters and Steamfitters	39.50
Customer Service Representatives	22.60	Police and Sheriff's Patrol Officers	41.70
Dentists	81.60	Postal Service Mail Carriers	25.90
Electricians	39.80	Real Estate Sales Agents	34.20
Engineers, Electrical	57.70	Retail Salespersons	18.50
Fast Food and Counter Workers	16.00	Sales Representatives, Technical/Scientific	53.30
Financial Managers	76.30	Secretaries, Exc. Legal/Medical/Executive	23.40
First-Line Supervisors of Office Workers	37.00	Security Guards	19.60
General and Operations Managers	73.20	Surgeons	111.00
Hairdressers/Cosmetologists	22.80	Teacher Assistants, Exc. Postsecondary*	19.80
Home Health and Personal Care Aides	16.20	Teachers, Secondary School, Exc. Sp. Ed.*	38.00
Janitors and Cleaners	21.20	Telemarketers	21.40
Landscaping/Groundskeeping Workers	20.10	Truck Drivers, Heavy/Tractor-Trailer	26.90
Lawyers	66.70	Truck Drivers, Light/Delivery Services	22.90
Maids and Housekeeping Cleaners	16.40	Waiters and Waitresses	20.80

Note: Wage data covers the Seattle-Tacoma-Bellevue, WA Metropolitan Statistical Area; (*) Hourly wages were
calculated from annual wage data based on a 40 hour work week; n/a not available.
Source: Bureau of Labor Statistics, Metro Area Occupational Employment & Wage Estimates, May 2020

Employment by Industry

Sector	MD[1]		U.S.
	Number of Employees	Percent of Total	Percent of Total
Construction	104,000	6.3	5.1
Education and Health Services	216,800	13.1	16.3
Financial Activities	86,000	5.2	6.1
Government	202,900	12.3	15.2
Information	134,300	8.1	1.9
Leisure and Hospitality	103,400	6.2	9.0
Manufacturing	142,300	8.6	8.5
Mining and Logging	800	<0.1	0.4
Other Services	57,100	3.4	3.8
Professional and Business Services	271,500	16.4	14.4
Retail Trade	213,000	12.9	10.9
Transportation, Warehousing, and Utilities	57,500	3.5	4.6
Wholesale Trade	65,800	4.0	3.9

Note: Figures are non-farm employment as of December 2020. Figures are not seasonally adjusted and include
workers 16 years of age and older; (1) Figures cover the Seattle-Bellevue-Everett, WA Metropolitan Division
Source: Bureau of Labor Statistics, Current Employment Statistics, Employment, Hours, and Earnings

Employment by Occupation

Occupation Classification	City (%)	MSA[1] (%)	U.S. (%)
Management, Business, Science, and Arts	61.6	46.7	38.5
Natural Resources, Construction, and Maintenance	3.2	7.6	8.9
Production, Transportation, and Material Moving	5.5	10.9	13.2
Sales and Office	16.2	19.3	21.6
Service	13.6	15.6	17.8

Note: Figures cover employed civilians 16 years of age and older; (1) Figures cover the Seattle-Tacoma-Bellevue, WA Metropolitan Statistical Area
Source: U.S. Census Bureau, 2015-2019 American Community Survey 5-Year Estimates

Occupations with Greatest Projected Employment Growth: 2020 – 2022

Occupation[1]	2020 Employment	2022 Projected Employment	Numeric Employment Change	Percent Employment Change
Software Developers and Software Quality Assurance Analysts and Testers	96,700	106,060	9,360	9.7
Retail Salespersons	88,430	93,910	5,480	6.2
Marketing Managers	17,970	21,960	3,990	22.2
Fast Food and Counter Workers	69,980	73,000	3,020	4.3
Computer Occupations, All Other (SOC 2018)	19,880	22,810	2,930	14.7
Office Clerks, General	69,900	72,580	2,680	3.8
Management Analysts	31,700	34,180	2,480	7.8
Personal Service Managers; Entertainment & Recreation Managers, Except Gambling; and Managers, All	35,650	38,100	2,450	6.9
General and Operations Managers	48,470	50,860	2,390	4.9
Registered Nurses	57,970	60,310	2,340	4.0

Note: Projections cover Washington; (1) Sorted by numeric employment change
Source: www.projectionscentral.com, State Occupational Projections, 2020–2022 Short-Term Projections

Fastest-Growing Occupations: 2020 – 2022

Occupation[1]	2020 Employment	2022 Projected Employment	Numeric Employment Change	Percent Employment Change
Gaming Surveillance Officers and Gaming Investigators	270	360	90	33.3
Gaming Dealers	3,530	4,610	1,080	30.6
Gaming Cage Workers	690	890	200	29.0
Gaming Change Persons and Booth Cashiers	530	680	150	28.3
First-Line Supervisors of Gambling Services Workers	400	490	90	22.5
Marketing Managers	17,970	21,960	3,990	22.2
Computer Occupations, All Other (SOC 2018)	19,880	22,810	2,930	14.7
Barbers	2,360	2,700	340	14.4
Manicurists and Pedicurists	5,790	6,610	820	14.2
Tailors, Dressmakers, and Custom Sewers	710	810	100	14.1

Note: Projections cover Washington; (1) Sorted by percent employment change and excludes occupations with numeric employment change less than 50
Source: www.projectionscentral.com, State Occupational Projections, 2020–2022 Short-Term Projections

TAXES

State Corporate Income Tax Rates

State	Tax Rate (%)	Income Brackets ($)	Num. of Brackets	Financial Institution Tax Rate (%)[a]	Federal Income Tax Ded.
Washington	None	–	–	–	–

Note: Tax rates as of January 1, 2021; (a) Rates listed are the corporate income tax rate applied to financial institutions or excise taxes based on income. Some states have other taxes based upon the value of deposits or shares.
Source: Federation of Tax Administrators, State Corporate Income Tax Rates, January 1, 2021

State Individual Income Tax Rates

State	Tax Rate (%)	Income Brackets ($)	Personal Exemptions ($)			Standard Ded. ($)	
			Single	Married	Depend.	Single	Married
Washington				– No state income tax –			

Note: Tax rates as of January 1, 2021; Local- and county-level taxes are not included
Source: Federation of Tax Administrators, State Individual Income Tax Rates, January 1, 2021

Various State Sales and Excise Tax Rates

State	State Sales Tax (%)	Gasoline[1] (¢/gal.)	Cigarette[2] ($/pack)	Spirits[3] ($/gal.)	Wine[4] ($/gal.)	Beer[5] ($/gal.)	Recreational Marijuana (%)
Washington	6.5	49.4	3.025	35.31	0.87	0.26	(o)

Note: All tax rates as of January 1, 2021; (1) The American Petroleum Institute has developed a methodology for determining the average tax rate on a gallon of fuel. Rates may include any of the following: excise taxes, environmental fees, storage tank fees, other fees or taxes, general sales tax, and local taxes; (2) The federal excise tax of $1.0066 per pack and local taxes are not included; (3) Rates are those applicable to off-premise sales of 40% alcohol by volume (a.b.v.) distilled spirits in 750ml containers. Local excise taxes are excluded; (4) Rates are those applicable to off-premise sales of 11% a.b.v. non-carbonated wine in 750ml containers; (5) Rates are those applicable to off-premise sales of 4.7% a.b.v. beer in 12 ounce containers; (o) 37% excise tax (retail price)
Source: Tax Foundation, 2021 Facts & Figures: How Does Your State Compare?

State Business Tax Climate Index Rankings

State	Overall Rank	Corporate Tax Rank	Individual Income Tax Rank	Sales Tax Rank	Property Tax Rank	Unemployment Insurance Tax Rank
Washington	16	40	6	48	18	19

Note: The index is a measure of how each state's tax laws affect economic performance. The lower the rank, the more favorable a state's tax system is for business. States without a given tax are given a ranking of 1. The scores/rankings for the District of Columbia do not affect other states. The 2021 index represents the tax climate as of July 1, 2020.
Source: Tax Foundation, State Business Tax Climate Index 2021

TRANSPORTATION

Means of Transportation to Work

Area	Car/Truck/Van Drove Alone	Car-pooled	Public Transportation Bus	Subway	Railroad	Bicycle	Walked	Other Means	Worked at Home
City	46.5	7.2	20.1	1.3	0.1	3.5	11.3	2.5	7.4
MSA[1]	67.5	10.0	8.7	0.4	0.5	1.1	4.0	1.5	6.2
U.S.	76.3	9.0	2.4	1.9	0.6	0.5	2.7	1.4	5.2

Note: Figures are percentages and cover workers 16 years of age and older; (1) Figures cover the Seattle-Tacoma-Bellevue, WA Metropolitan Statistical Area
Source: U.S. Census Bureau, 2015-2019 American Community Survey 5-Year Estimates

Travel Time to Work

Area	Less Than 10 Minutes	10 to 19 Minutes	20 to 29 Minutes	30 to 44 Minutes	45 to 59 Minutes	60 to 89 Minutes	90 Minutes or More
City	6.7	23.4	24.4	28.6	10.5	5.0	1.5
MSA[1]	7.7	22.2	20.8	25.5	11.4	9.0	3.4
U.S.	12.2	28.4	20.8	20.8	8.3	6.4	2.9

Note: Note: Figures are percentages and include workers 16 years old and over; (1) Figures cover the Seattle-Tacoma-Bellevue, WA Metropolitan Statistical Area
Source: U.S. Census Bureau, 2015-2019 American Community Survey 5-Year Estimates

Key Congestion Measures

Measure	1982	1992	2002	2012	2017
Annual Hours of Delay, Total (000)	31,531	62,542	104,808	148,850	167,384
Annual Hours of Delay, Per Auto Commuter	32	46	58	69	78
Annual Congestion Cost, Total (million $)	237	661	1,417	2,669	3,111
Annual Congestion Cost, Per Auto Commuter ($)	651	888	1,160	1,291	1,408

Note: Covers the Seattle WA urban area
Source: Texas A&M Transportation Institute, 2019 Urban Mobility Report

Freeway Travel Time Index

Measure	1982	1987	1992	1997	2002	2007	2012	2017
Urban Area Index[1]	1.19	1.23	1.28	1.31	1.35	1.37	1.37	1.37
Urban Area Rank[1,2]	4	3	3	3	3	4	5	5

Note: Freeway Travel Time Index—the ratio of travel time in the peak period to the travel time at free-flow conditions. For example, a value of 1.30 indicates a 20-minute free-flow trip takes 26 minutes in the peak (20 minutes x 1.30 = 26 minutes); (1) Covers the Seattle WA urban area; (2) Rank is based on 101 larger urban areas (#1 = highest travel time index)
Source: Texas A&M Transportation Institute, 2019 Urban Mobility Report

Public Transportation

Agency Name / Mode of Transportation	Vehicles Operated in Maximum Service[1]	Annual Unlinked Passenger Trips[2] (in thous.)	Annual Passenger Miles[3] (in thous.)
King County Department of Transportation (KC Metro)			
Bus (directly operated)	986	103,527.5	473,228.3
Bus (purchased transportation)	29	834.7	3,219.6
Demand Response (purchased transportation)	327	887.9	8,887.8
Demand Response Taxi (purchased transportation)	89	177.8	2,398.9
Ferryboat (directly operated)	3	701.6	3,464.1
Streetcar Rail (directly operated)	10	1,863.4	2,027.9
Trolleybus (directly operated)	140	17,373.5	32,207.1
Vanpool (directly operated)	1,649	3,300.2	61,644.5
Central Puget Sound Regional Transit Authority (Sound Transit)			
Commuter Bus (directly operated)	222	13,713.5	193,826.0
Commuter Bus (purchased transportation)	52	3,781.1	61,314.0
Commuter Rail (purchased transportation)	70	4,612.4	116,066.3
Light Rail (directly operated)	54	24,761.7	163,463.7
Streetcar Rail (directly operated)	2	937.0	849.2
Washington State Ferries			
Ferryboat (directly operated)	19	24,255.4	190,973.6
City of Seattle (Seattle Center Monorail)			
Monorail and Automated Guideway (purchased transportation)	8	1,939.2	1,745.3

Note: (1) Number of revenue vehicles operated by the given mode and type of service to meet the annual maximum service requirement. This is the revenue vehicle count during the peak season of the year; on the week and day that maximum service is provided. Vehicles operated in maximum service (VOMS) exclude atypical days and one-time special events; (2) Number of passengers who boarded public transportation vehicles. Passengers are counted each time they board a vehicle no matter how many vehicles they use to travel from their origin to their destination. (3) Sum of the distances ridden by all passengers during the entire fiscal year.
Source: Federal Transit Administration, National Transit Database, 2019

Air Transportation

Airport Name and Code / Type of Service	Passenger Airlines[1]	Passenger Enplanements	Freight Carriers[2]	Freight (lbs)
Seattle-Tacoma International (SEA)				
Domestic service (U.S. carriers - 2020)	18	8,807,018	18	361,727,087
International service (U.S. carriers - 2019)	7	1,279,462	7	26,854,772

Note: (1) Includes all U.S.-based major, minor and commuter airlines that carried at least one passenger during the year; (2) Includes all U.S.-based airlines and freight carriers that transported at least one pound of freight during the year.
Source: Bureau of Transportation Statistics, The Intermodal Transportation Database, Air Carriers: T-100 Domestic Market (U.S. Carriers), 2020; Bureau of Transportation Statistics, The Intermodal Transportation Database, Air Carriers: T-100 International Market (U.S. Carriers), 2019

BUSINESSES

Major Business Headquarters

Company Name	Industry	Rankings	
		Fortune[1]	Forbes[2]
Alaska Air Group	Airlines	360	-
Amazon	Internet Services and Retailing	2	-
Expeditors Intl. of Washington	Transportation and Logistics	389	-
Nordstrom	General Merchandisers	205	-
Saltchuk	Transportation	-	170
Starbucks	Food Services	114	-
Trident Seafoods	Food, Drink & Tobacco	-	172

Note: (1) Companies that produce a 10-K are ranked 1 to 500 based on 2019 revenue; (2) All private companies with at least $2 billion in annual revenue through the end of their most current fiscal year are ranked 1 to 219; companies listed are headquartered in the city; dashes indicate no ranking
Source: Fortune, "Fortune 500," June/July 2020; Forbes, "America's Largest Private Companies," 2020

Fastest-Growing Businesses

According to *Inc.*, Seattle is home to eight of America's 500 fastest-growing private companies: **DefinedCrowd Corporation** (#27); **Perch Partners** (#87); **PNW Components** (#114); **Spees Design Build** (#172); **Seeq Corporation** (#261); **Wild Things Snacks** (#292); **MightyKidz Child Care** (#344); **Outreach** (#468). Criteria: must be an independent, privately-held, for-profit, U.S. corporation, proprietorship or partnership as of December 31, 2019; revenues must be at least $100,000 in 2016 and $2 million in 2019; must have four-year operating/sales history. *Inc., "America's 500 Fastest-Growing Private Companies," 2020*

According to *Fortune*, Seattle is home to one of the 100 fastest-growing companies in the world: **Amazon** (#10). Companies were ranked by their revenue growth rate; their EPS growth rate; and their three-year annualized total return to investors for the period ending June 30, 2020. Criteria for inclusion: a company, foreign or domestic, must trade on a major U.S. stock exchange; must file quarterly reports with the SEC; must have a minimum market capitalization of $250 million; must have a stock price of at least $5 on June 30, 2020; must have been trading continuously since June 30, 2017; must have revenue and net income for the four quarters ended on or before April 30, 2020, of at least $50 million and $10 million, respectively; and must have posted a compound annual growth in revenue and earnings per share of at least 15% annually over the three years ending on or before April 30, 2020. Real estate investment trusts, limited-liability companies, limited parterships, business development companies, closed-end investment firms, companies about to be acquired, and companies that lost money in the quarter ending April 30, 2020 were excluded. *Fortune, "100 Fastest-Growing Companies," 2020*

According to Deloitte, Seattle is home to 16 of North America's 500 fastest-growing high-technology companies: **DefinedCrowd** (#27); **Outreach** (#58); **Seeq** (#76); **Hiya** (#86); **FLEXE** (#87); **Highspot** (#101); **Remitly** (#230); **Zipwhip** (#270); **SirionLabs** (#313); **Lighthouse** (#364); **Adaptive Biotechnologies** (#383); **Discuss.io** (#417); **Zillow Group, Inc.** (#418); **MedBridge** (#468); **Redfin Corporation** (#469); **Apptentive, Inc.** (#484). Companies are ranked by percentage growth in revenue over a four-year period. Criteria for inclusion: company must be headquartered within North America; must own proprietary intellectual property or technology that is sold to customers in products that contributes to a significant portion of the company's operating revenue; must have been in business for a minumum of four years with 2016 operating revenues of at least $50,000 USD/CD and 2019 operating revenues of at least $5 million USD/CD. *Deloitte, 2020 Technology Fast 500*[TM]

Minority Business Opportunity

Seattle is home to one company which is on the *Black Enterprise* Asset Manager list (10 largest asset management firms based on assets under management): **Pugh Capital Management** (#4). Criteria: company must have been operational in previous calendar year and be at least 51% black-owned. *Black Enterprise, B.E. 100s, 2019*

Living Environment

COST OF LIVING

Cost of Living Index

Composite Index	Groceries	Housing	Utilities	Trans-portation	Health Care	Misc. Goods/Services
157.2	127.7	233.8	109.3	141.0	127.8	128.9

Note: The Cost of Living Index measures regional differences in the cost of consumer goods and services, excluding taxes and non-consumer expenditures, for professional and managerial households in the top income quintile. It is based on more than 50,000 prices covering almost 60 different items for which prices are collected three times a year by chambers of commerce, economic development organizations or university applied economic centers in each participating urban area. The numbers shown should be read as a percentage above or below the national average of 100. For example, a value of 115.4 in the groceries column indicates that grocery prices are 15.4% higher than the national average. Small differences in the index numbers should not be interpreted as significant; Figures cover the Seattle WA urban area.
Source: The Council for Community and Economic Research, Cost of Living Index, 2020

Grocery Prices

Area[1]	T-Bone Steak ($/pound)	Frying Chicken ($/pound)	Whole Milk ($/half gal.)	Eggs ($/dozen)	Orange Juice ($/64 oz.)	Coffee ($/11.5 oz.)
City[2]	12.88	2.15	2.50	2.13	4.05	6.00
Avg.	11.78	1.39	2.05	1.47	3.57	4.34
Min.	8.03	0.94	1.03	0.74	2.94	3.02
Max.	15.86	2.65	4.31	3.77	5.44	8.69

Note: (1) Values for the local area are compared with the average, minimum and maximum values for all 284 areas in the Cost of Living Index; (2) Figures cover the Seattle WA urban area; T-Bone Steak (price per pound); Frying Chicken (price per pound, whole fryer); Whole Milk (half gallon carton); Eggs (price per dozen, Grade A, large); Orange Juice (64 oz. Tropicana or Florida Natural); Coffee (11.5 oz. can, vacuum-packed, Maxwell House, Hills Bros, or Folgers).
Source: The Council for Community and Economic Research, Cost of Living Index, 2020

Housing and Utility Costs

Area[1]	New Home Price ($)	Apartment Rent ($/month)	All Electric ($/month)	Part Electric ($/month)	Other Energy ($/month)	Telephone ($/month)
City[2]	854,748	2,680	186.95	-	-	194.20
Avg.	368,594	1,168	170.86	100.47	65.28	184.30
Min.	190,567	502	91.58	31.42	26.08	169.60
Max.	2,227,806	4,738	470.38	280.31	280.06	206.50

Note: (1) Values for the local area are compared with the average, minimum and maximum values for all 284 areas in the Cost of Living Index; (2) Figures cover the Seattle WA urban area; New Home Price (2,400 sf living area, 8,000 sf lot, in urban area with full utilities); Apartment Rent (950 sf 2 bedroom/1.5 or 2 bath, unfurnished, excluding all utilities except water); All Electric (average monthly cost for an all-electric home); Part Electric (average monthly cost for a part-electric home); Other Energy (average monthly cost for natural gas, fuel oil, coal, wood, and any other forms of energy except electricity); Telephone (price includes the base monthly rate plus taxes and fees for three lines of mobile phone service).
Source: The Council for Community and Economic Research, Cost of Living Index, 2020

Health Care, Transportation, and Other Costs

Area[1]	Doctor ($/visit)	Dentist ($/visit)	Optometrist ($/visit)	Gasoline ($/gallon)	Beauty Salon ($/visit)	Men's Shirt ($)
City[2]	136.39	143.77	158.73	3.19	50.33	36.89
Avg.	115.44	99.32	108.10	2.21	39.27	31.37
Min.	36.68	59.00	51.36	1.71	19.00	11.00
Max.	219.00	153.10	250.97	3.46	82.05	58.33

Note: (1) Values for the local area are compared with the average, minimum and maximum values for all 284 areas in the Cost of Living Index; (2) Figures cover the Seattle WA urban area; Doctor (general practitioners routine exam of an established patient); Dentist (adult teeth cleaning and periodic oral examination); Optometrist (full vision eye exam for established adult patient); Gasoline (one gallon regular unleaded, national brand, including all taxes, cash price at self-service pump if available); Beauty Salon (woman's shampoo, trim, and blow-dry); Men's Shirt (cotton/polyester dress shirt, pinpoint weave, long sleeves).
Source: The Council for Community and Economic Research, Cost of Living Index, 2020

HOUSING

Homeownership Rate

Area	2012 (%)	2013 (%)	2014 (%)	2015 (%)	2016 (%)	2017 (%)	2018 (%)	2019 (%)	2020 (%)
MSA[1]	60.4	61.0	61.3	59.5	57.7	59.5	62.5	61.5	59.4
U.S.	65.4	65.1	64.5	63.7	63.4	63.9	64.4	64.6	66.6

Note: (1) Figures cover the Seattle-Tacoma-Bellevue, WA Metropolitan Statistical Area
Source: U.S. Census Bureau, Housing Vacancies and Homeownership Annual Statistics: 2012-2020

House Price Index (HPI)

Area	National Ranking[2]	Quarterly Change (%)	One-Year Change (%)	Five-Year Change (%)	Since 1991Q1 (%)
MD[1]	97	2.16	6.81	48.46	324.48
U.S.[3]	–	3.81	10.77	38.99	205.12

Note: The HPI is a weighted repeat sales index. It measures average price changes in repeat sales or refinancings on the same properties. This information is obtained by reviewing repeat mortgage transactions on single-family properties whose mortgages have been purchased or securitized by Fannie Mae or Freddie Mac since January 1975; (1) Figures cover the Seattle-Bellevue-Everett, WA Metropolitan Division; (2) Rankings are based on annual percentage change for all metro areas containing at least 15,000 transactions over the last 10 years and ranges from 1 to 253; (3) figures based on a weighted average of Census Division estimates using a seasonally adjusted, purchase-only index; all figures are for the period ending December 31, 2020
Source: Federal Housing Finance Agency, Change in Metropolitan Area House Price Indexes, April 7, 2021

Median Single-Family Home Prices

Area	2018	2019	2020[p]	Percent Change 2019 to 2020
MSA[1]	501.4	524.7	596.9	13.8
U.S. Average	261.6	274.6	299.9	9.2

Note: Figures are median sales prices of existing single-family homes in thousands of dollars; (p) preliminary; (1) Figures cover the Seattle-Tacoma-Bellevue, WA Metropolitan Statistical Area
Source: National Association of Realtors, Median Sales Price of Existing Single-Family Homes for Metropolitan Areas, 4th Quarter 2020

Qualifying Income Based on Median Sales Price of Existing Single-Family Homes

Area	With 5% Down ($)	With 10% Down ($)	With 20% Down ($)
MSA[1]	116,266	110,146	97,908
U.S. Average	59,266	56,147	49,908

Note: Figures are preliminary; Qualifying income is based on a mortgage rate of 2.81%. Monthly principal and interest payment is limited to 25% of income; (1) Figures cover the Seattle-Tacoma-Bellevue, WA Metropolitan Statistical Area
Source: National Association of Realtors, Qualifying Income Based on Median Sales Price of Existing Single-Family Homes for Metropolitan Areas, 4th Quarter 2020

Home Value Distribution

Area	Under $50,000	$50,000 -$99,999	$100,000 -$149,999	$150,000 -$199,999	$200,000 -$299,999	$300,000 -$499,999	$500,000 -$999,999	$1,000,000 or more
City	0.6	0.4	0.4	1.0	5.0	22.3	52.5	17.8
MSA[1]	2.5	1.2	2.0	4.2	15.3	34.2	32.0	8.5
U.S.	6.9	12.0	13.3	14.0	19.6	19.3	11.4	3.4

Note: Figures are percentages and cover owner-occupied housing units; (1) Figures cover the Seattle-Tacoma-Bellevue, WA Metropolitan Statistical Area
Source: U.S. Census Bureau, 2015-2019 American Community Survey 5-Year Estimates

Year Housing Structure Built

Area	2010 or Later	2000 -2009	1990 -1999	1980 -1989	1970 -1979	1960 -1969	1950 -1959	1940 -1949	Before 1940	Median Year
City	10.4	13.2	8.3	7.9	8.2	8.7	9.8	8.3	25.2	1968
MSA[1]	7.7	15.2	15.5	14.4	14.2	11.0	7.4	4.4	10.1	1982
U.S.	5.2	14.0	13.9	13.4	15.2	10.6	10.3	4.9	12.6	1978

Note: Figures are percentages except for Median Year; Note: (1) Figures cover the Seattle-Tacoma-Bellevue, WA Metropolitan Statistical Area
Source: U.S. Census Bureau, 2015-2019 American Community Survey 5-Year Estimates

Gross Monthly Rent

Area	Under $500	$500 -$999	$1,000 -$1,499	$1,500 -$1,999	$2,000 -$2,499	$2,500 -$2,999	$3,000 and up	Median ($)
City	6.5	10.0	27.1	28.0	14.9	7.0	6.4	1,614
MSA[1]	5.1	14.0	31.4	27.7	12.8	5.0	4.0	1,492
U.S.	9.4	36.2	30.0	14.0	5.6	2.4	2.4	1,062

Note: Figures are percentages except for Median; Gross rent is the contract rent plus the estimated average monthly cost of utilities (electricity, gas, and water and sewer) and fuels (oil, coal, kerosene, wood, etc.) if these are paid by the renter (or paid for the renter by someone else); (1) Figures cover the Seattle-Tacoma-Bellevue, WA Metropolitan Statistical Area
Source: U.S. Census Bureau, 2015-2019 American Community Survey 5-Year Estimates

HEALTH

Health Risk Factors

Category	MD[1] (%)	U.S. (%)
Adults aged 18–64 who have any kind of health care coverage	89.6	87.3
Adults who reported being in good or better health	86.4	82.4
Adults who have been told they have high blood cholesterol	29.6	33.0
Adults who have been told they have high blood pressure	26.4	32.3
Adults who are current smokers	10.4	17.1
Adults who currently use E-cigarettes	3.2	4.6
Adults who currently use chewing tobacco, snuff, or snus	2.7	4.0
Adults who are heavy drinkers[2]	5.9	6.3
Adults who are binge drinkers[3]	16.5	17.4
Adults who are overweight (BMI 25.0 - 29.9)	33.6	35.3
Adults who are obese (BMI 30.0 - 99.8)	23.2	31.3
Adults who participated in any physical activities in the past month	83.3	74.4
Adults who always or nearly always wears a seat belt	97.6	94.3

Note: (1) Figures cover the Seattle-Bellevue-Everett, WA Metropolitan Division; (2) Heavy drinkers are classified as adult men having more than 14 drinks per week and adult women having more than 7 drinks per week; (3) Binge drinkers are classified as males having five or more drinks on one occasion or females having four or more drinks on one occasion
Source: Centers for Disease Control and Prevention, Behaviorial Risk Factor Surveillance System, SMART: Selected Metropolitan Area Risk Trends, 2017

Acute and Chronic Health Conditions

Category	MD[1] (%)	U.S. (%)
Adults who have ever been told they had a heart attack	2.9	4.2
Adults who have ever been told they have angina or coronary heart disease	2.7	3.9
Adults who have ever been told they had a stroke	2.5	3.0
Adults who have ever been told they have asthma	15.0	14.2
Adults who have ever been told they have arthritis	20.5	24.9
Adults who have ever been told they have diabetes[2]	7.5	10.5
Adults who have ever been told they had skin cancer	6.0	6.2
Adults who have ever been told they had any other types of cancer	6.5	7.1
Adults who have ever been told they have COPD	3.8	6.5
Adults who have ever been told they have kidney disease	2.9	3.0
Adults who have ever been told they have a form of depression	21.6	20.5

Note: (1) Figures cover the Seattle-Bellevue-Everett, WA Metropolitan Division; (2) Figures do not include pregnancy-related, borderline, or pre-diabetes
Source: Centers for Disease Control and Prevention, Behaviorial Risk Factor Surveillance System, SMART: Selected Metropolitan Area Risk Trends, 2017

Health Screening and Vaccination Rates

Category	MD[1] (%)	U.S. (%)
Adults aged 65+ who have had flu shot within the past year	69.2	60.7
Adults aged 65+ who have ever had a pneumonia vaccination	81.5	75.4
Adults who have ever been tested for HIV	41.2	36.1
Adults who have ever had the shingles or zoster vaccine?	36.8	28.9
Adults who have had their blood cholesterol checked within the last five years	87.0	85.9

Note: n/a not available; (1) Figures cover the Seattle-Bellevue-Everett, WA Metropolitan Division.
Source: Centers for Disease Control and Prevention, Behaviorial Risk Factor Surveillance System, SMART: Selected Metropolitan Area Risk Trends, 2017

Disability Status

Category	MD[1] (%)	U.S. (%)
Adults who reported being deaf	4.4	6.7
Are you blind or have serious difficulty seeing, even when wearing glasses?	2.8	4.5
Are you limited in any way in any of your usual activities due of arthritis?	10.1	12.9
Do you have difficulty doing errands alone?	4.3	6.8
Do you have difficulty dressing or bathing?	2.2	3.6
Do you have serious difficulty concentrating/remembering/making decisions?	8.9	10.7
Do you have serious difficulty walking or climbing stairs?	8.2	13.6

Note: (1) Figures cover the Seattle-Bellevue-Everett, WA Metropolitan Division.
Source: Centers for Disease Control and Prevention, Behaviorial Risk Factor Surveillance System, SMART: Selected Metropolitan Area Risk Trends, 2017

Mortality Rates for the Top 10 Causes of Death in the U.S.

ICD-10[a] Sub-Chapter	ICD-10[a] Code	Age-Adjusted Mortality Rate[1] per 100,000 population	
		County[2]	U.S.
Malignant neoplasms	C00-C97	127.0	149.2
Ischaemic heart diseases	I20-I25	67.1	90.5
Other forms of heart disease	I30-I51	29.9	52.2
Chronic lower respiratory diseases	J40-J47	21.6	39.6
Other degenerative diseases of the nervous system	G30-G31	49.8	37.6
Cerebrovascular diseases	I60-I69	29.6	37.2
Other external causes of accidental injury	W00-X59	29.3	36.1
Organic, including symptomatic, mental disorders	F01-F09	19.2	29.4
Hypertensive diseases	I10-I15	21.9	24.1
Diabetes mellitus	E10-E14	17.2	21.5

Note: (a) ICD-10 = International Classification of Diseases 10th Revision; (1) Mortality rates are a three-year average covering 2017-2019; (2) Figures cover King County.
Source: Centers for Disease Control and Prevention, National Center for Health Statistics. Underlying Cause of Death 1999-2019 on CDC WONDER Online Database

Mortality Rates for Selected Causes of Death

ICD-10[a] Sub-Chapter	ICD-10[a] Code	Age-Adjusted Mortality Rate[1] per 100,000 population	
		County[2]	U.S.
Assault	X85-Y09	3.2	6.0
Diseases of the liver	K70-K76	11.8	14.4
Human immunodeficiency virus (HIV) disease	B20-B24	1.0	1.5
Influenza and pneumonia	J09-J18	9.5	13.8
Intentional self-harm	X60-X84	12.8	14.1
Malnutrition	E40-E46	1.5	2.3
Obesity and other hyperalimentation	E65-E68	1.9	2.1
Renal failure	N17-N19	3.9	12.6
Transport accidents	V01-V99	6.2	12.3
Viral hepatitis	B15-B19	1.5	1.2

Note: (a) ICD-10 = International Classification of Diseases 10th Revision; (1) Mortality rates are a three-year average covering 2017-2019; (2) Figures cover King County; Data are suppressed when the data meet the criteria for confidentiality constraints; Mortality rates are flagged as unreliable when the rate would be calculated with a numerator of 20 or less.
Source: Centers for Disease Control and Prevention, National Center for Health Statistics. Underlying Cause of Death 1999-2019 on CDC WONDER Online Database

Health Insurance Coverage

Area	With Health Insurance	With Private Health Insurance	With Public Health Insurance	Without Health Insurance	Population Under Age 19 Without Health Insurance
City	95.8	80.6	24.0	4.2	1.4
MSA[1]	94.4	75.9	29.2	5.6	2.5
U.S.	91.2	67.9	35.1	8.8	5.1

Note: Figures are percentages that cover the civilian noninstitutionalized population; (1) Figures cover the Seattle-Tacoma-Bellevue, WA Metropolitan Statistical Area
Source: U.S. Census Bureau, 2015-2019 American Community Survey 5-Year Estimates

Number of Medical Professionals

Area	MDs[3]	DOs[3,4]	Dentists	Podiatrists	Chiropractors	Optometrists
County[1] (number)	10,908	348	2,471	145	1,053	490
County[1] (rate[2])	489.5	15.6	109.7	6.4	46.7	21.8
U.S. (rate[2])	282.9	22.7	71.2	6.2	28.1	16.9

53033
Note: Data as of 2019 unless noted; (1) Data covers King County; (2) Rate per 100,000 population; (3) Data as of 2018 and includes all active, non-federal physicians; (4) Doctor of Osteopathic Medicine
Source: U.S. Department of Health and Human Services, Health Resources and Services Administration, Bureau of Health Professions, Area Resource File (ARF) 2019-2020

Best Hospitals

According to *U.S. News,* the Seattle-Bellevue-Everett, WA metro area is home to two of the best hospitals in the U.S.: **Seattle Cancer Care Alliance/University of Washington Medical Center** (1 adult specialty); **University of Washington Medical Center** (9 adult specialties). The hospitals listed were nationally ranked in at least one of 16 adult or 10 pediatric specialties. Only 134 hospitals nationwide were nationally ranked in one or more adult or pediatric specialty; this number increases to 178 counting specialized centers within hospitals. Twenty hospitals in the U.S. made the Honor Roll. The Best Hospitals Honor Roll takes both the national rankings and the procedure and condition ratings into account. Hospitals received points if they were nationally ranked in one of the 16 adult specialties—the higher they ranked, the more points they got—and how many ratings of "high performing" they earned in the 10 procedures and conditions. *U.S. News Online, "America's Best Hospitals 2020-21"*

According to *U.S. News,* the Seattle-Bellevue-Everett, WA metro area is home to one of the best children's hospitals in the U.S.: **Seattle Children's Hospital** (10 pediatric specialties). The hospital listed was highly ranked in at least one of 10 pediatric specialties. Eighty-eight children's hospitals in the U.S. were nationally ranked in at least one specialty. Hospitals received points for being ranked in a specialty, and the 10 hospitals with the most points across the 10 specialties make up the Honor Roll. *U.S. News Online, "America's Best Children's Hospitals 2020-21"*

EDUCATION

Public School District Statistics

District Name	Schls	Pupils	Pupil/ Teacher Ratio	Minority Pupils[1] (%)	Free Lunch Eligible[2] (%)	IEP[3] (%)
Seattle Public Schools	108	55,271	16.7	53.2	24.6	13.4

Note: Table includes school districts with 2,000 or more students; (1) Percentage of students that are not non-Hispanic white; (2) Percentage of students that are eligible for the free lunch program; (3) Percentage of students that have an Individualized Education Program.
Source: U.S. Department of Education, National Center for Education Statistics, Common Core of Data, Local Education Agency (School District) Universe Survey: School Year 2018-2019; U.S. Department of Education, National Center for Education Statistics, Common Core of Data, Public Elementary/Secondary School Universe Survey: School Year 2018-2019

Highest Level of Education

Area	Less than H.S.	H.S. Diploma	Some College, No Deg.	Associate Degree	Bachelor's Degree	Master's Degree	Prof. School Degree	Doctorate Degree
City	5.2	9.6	15.0	6.2	36.7	18.1	5.3	3.9
MSA[1]	7.4	19.4	21.0	9.3	26.6	11.7	2.7	2.0
U.S.	12.0	27.0	20.4	8.5	19.8	8.8	2.1	1.4

Note: Figures cover persons age 25 and over; (1) Figures cover the Seattle-Tacoma-Bellevue, WA Metropolitan Statistical Area
Source: U.S. Census Bureau, 2015-2019 American Community Survey 5-Year Estimates

Educational Attainment by Race

Area	High School Graduate or Higher (%)					Bachelor's Degree or Higher (%)				
	Total	White	Black	Asian	Hisp.[2]	Total	White	Black	Asian	Hisp.[2]
City	94.8	97.8	86.8	88.4	83.5	64.0	69.8	29.5	61.5	43.0
MSA[1]	92.6	95.0	89.6	88.8	73.3	43.0	43.8	25.8	56.1	22.4
U.S.	88.0	89.9	86.0	87.1	68.7	32.1	33.5	21.6	54.3	16.4

Note: Figures shown cover persons 25 years old and over; (1) Figures cover the Seattle-Tacoma-Bellevue, WA Metropolitan Statistical Area; (2) People of Hispanic origin can be of any race
Source: U.S. Census Bureau, 2015-2019 American Community Survey 5-Year Estimates

School Enrollment by Grade and Control

Area	Preschool (%)		Kindergarten (%)		Grades 1 - 4 (%)		Grades 5 - 8 (%)		Grades 9 - 12 (%)	
	Public	Private	Public	Private	Public	Private	Public	Private	Public	Private
City	32.6	67.4	79.7	20.3	81.6	18.4	75.9	24.1	79.8	20.2
MSA[1]	41.4	58.6	83.9	16.1	88.3	11.7	88.3	11.7	90.5	9.5
U.S.	59.1	40.9	87.6	12.4	89.5	10.5	89.4	10.6	90.1	9.9

Note: Figures shown cover persons 3 years old and over; (1) Figures cover the Seattle-Tacoma-Bellevue, WA Metropolitan Statistical Area
Source: U.S. Census Bureau, 2015-2019 American Community Survey 5-Year Estimates

Higher Education

Four-Year Colleges			Two-Year Colleges			Medical Schools[1]	Law Schools[2]	Voc/ Tech[3]
Public	Private Non-profit	Private For-profit	Public	Private Non-profit	Private For-profit			
4	6	2	0	1	1	1	2	4

Note: Figures cover institutions located within the city limits and include main campuses only; (1) includes schools accredited by the Liaison Committee on Medical Education and the American Osteopathic Association's Commission on Osteopathic College Accreditation; (2) includes ABA-accredited schools, schools with provisional ABA accreditation, and state accredited schools; (3) includes all schools with programs that are less than 2 years.
Source: National Center for Education Statistics, Integrated Postsecondary Education System (IPEDS), 2019-20; Wikipedia, List of Medical Schools in the United States, accessed April 2, 2021; Wikipedia, List of Law Schools in the United States, accessed April 2, 2021

According to *U.S. News & World Report,* the Seattle-Bellevue-Everett, WA metro division is home to three of the top 200 national universities in the U.S.: **University of Washington** (#58 tie); **Seattle University** (#124 tie); **Seattle Pacific University** (#196 tie). The indicators used to capture academic quality fall into a number of categories: assessment by administrators at peer institutions; retention of students; faculty resources; student selectivity; financial resources; alumni giving; high school counselor ratings of colleges; and graduation rate. *U.S. News & World Report,* "America's Best Colleges 2021"

According to *U.S. News & World Report,* the Seattle-Bellevue-Everett, WA metro division is home to one of the top 100 law schools in the U.S.: **University of Washington** (#45). The rankings are based on a weighted average of 12 measures of quality: peer assessment score; assessment score by lawyers/judges; median LSAT scores; median undergrad GPA; acceptance rate; employment rates for graduates; placement success; bar passage rate; faculty resources; expenditures per student; student/faculty ratio; and library resources. *U.S. News & World Report,* "America's Best Graduate Schools, Law, 2022"

According to *U.S. News & World Report,* the Seattle-Bellevue-Everett, WA metro division is home to one of the top 75 medical schools for research in the U.S.: **University of Washington** (#7 tie). The rankings are based on a weighted average of 11 measures of quality: quality assessment; peer assessment score; assessment score by residency directors; research activity; total research activity; average research activity per faculty member; student selectivity; median MCAT total score; median undergraduate GPA; acceptance rate; and faculty resources. *U.S. News & World Report,* "America's Best Graduate Schools, Medical, 2022"

According to *U.S. News & World Report,* the Seattle-Bellevue-Everett, WA metro division is home to one of the top 75 business schools in the U.S.: **University of Washington (Foster)** (#22). The rankings are based on a weighted average of the following nine measures: quality assessment; peer assessment; recruiter assessment; placement success; mean starting salary and bonus; student selectivity; mean GMAT and GRE scores; mean undergraduate GPA; and acceptance rate. *U.S. News & World Report,* "America's Best Graduate Schools, Business, 2022"

EMPLOYERS

Major Employers

Company Name	Industry
City of Tacoma	Municipal government
Costco Wholesale Corporation	Miscellaneous general merchandise stores
County of Snohomish	County government
Evergreen Healthcare	General medical & surgical hospitals
Harborview Medical Center	General medical & surgical hospitals
King County Public Hospital Dist No. 2	Hospital & health services consultant
Microsoft	Prepackaged software
Prologix Distribution Services	General merchandise, non-durable
R U Corporation	American restaurant
SNC-Lavalin Constructors	Heavy construction, nec
Swedish Health Services	General medical & surgical hospitals
T-Mobile USA	Radio, telephone communication
The Boeing Company	Airplanes, fixed or rotary wing
Tulalip Resort Casino	Casino hotels
United States Department of the Army	Medical centers
University of Washington	Colleges & universities
Virginia Mason Medical Center	General medical & surgical hospitals
Virginia Mason Seattle Main Clinic	Clinic, operated by physicians
Washington Dept of Social & Health Svcs	General medical & surgical hospitals

Note: Companies shown are located within the Seattle-Tacoma-Bellevue, WA Metropolitan Statistical Area.
Source: Hoovers.com; Wikipedia

Best Companies to Work For

Perkins Coie; Slalom, headquartered in Seattle, are among "The 100 Best Companies to Work For." To pick the best companies, *Fortune* partnered with the Great Place to Work Institute. Two-thirds of a company's score is based on the results of the Institute's Trust Index survey, which is sent to a random sample of employees from each company. The questions related to attitudes about management's credibility, job satisfaction, and camaraderie. The other third of the scoring is based on the company's responses to the Institute's Culture Audit, which includes detailed questions about pay and benefit programs, and a series of open-ended questions about hiring practices, internal communication, training, recognition programs, and diversity efforts. Any company that is at least five years old with more than 1,000 U.S. employees is eligible. *Fortune, "The 100 Best Companies to Work For," 2020*

Moss Adams, headquartered in Seattle, is among the "100 Best Companies for Working Mothers." Criteria: paid time off and leaves; workforce profile; benefits; women's issues and advancement; flexible work; company culture and work life programs. *Working Mother, "100 Best Companies for Working Mothers," 2020*

Avanade; ExtraHop, headquartered in Seattle, are among the "100 Best Places to Work in IT." To qualify, companies had to be U.S.-based organizations or be non-U.S.-based employers that met the following criteria: have a minimum of 300 total employees at a U.S. headquarters and a minimum of 30 IT employees in the U.S., with at least 50% of their IT employees based in the U.S. The best places to work were selected based on compensation, benefits, work/life balance, employee morale, and satisfaction with training and development programs. In addition, *InsiderPro* and *Computerworld* looked at retention efforts, programs for recognizing and rewarding outstanding performances, and benefits such as flextime, elder care and child care, and reimbursement for college tuition and the cost of pursuing technology certifications. *InsiderPro and Computerworld, "100 Best Places to Work in IT," 2020*

Moss Adams, headquartered in Seattle, is among the "Top Companies for Executive Women." This list is determined by organizations filling out an in-depth survey that measures female demographics at every level, but with an emphasis on women in senior corporate roles, with profit & loss (P&L) responsibility, and those earning in the top 20 percent of the organization. *Working Mother* defines P&L as having responsibility that involves monitoring the net income after expenses for a department or entire organization, with direct influence on how company resources are allocated. *Working Mother, "Top Companies for Executive Women," 2020+*

Moss Adams, headquartered in Seattle, is among the "Best Companies for Dads." *Working Mother's* newest list recognizes the growing importance companies place on giving dads time off and support for their families. Rankings are determined by measuring gender-neutral or paternity leave offered, as well as actual time taken, phase-back policies, child- and dependent-care benefits, and corporate support groups for men and dads. *Working Mother, "Best Companies for Dads," 2020*

PUBLIC SAFETY

Crime Rate

| Area | All Crimes | Violent Crimes | | | | Property Crimes | | |
		Murder	Rape[3]	Robbery	Aggrav. Assault	Burglary	Larceny -Theft	Motor Vehicle Theft
City	5,081.0	3.7	46.9	175.3	359.6	944.1	3,074.2	477.3
Suburbs[1]	n/a	n/a	n/a	n/a	n/a	n/a	n/a	n/a
Metro[2]	n/a	n/a	n/a	n/a	n/a	n/a	n/a	n/a
U.S.	2,489.3	5.0	42.6	81.6	250.2	340.5	1,549.5	219.9

Note: Figures are crimes per 100,000 population; (1) All areas within the metro area that are located outside the city limits; (2) Figures cover the Seattle-Bellevue-Everett, WA Metropolitan Division; n/a not available; (3) All figures shown were reported using the revised Uniform Crime Reporting (UCR) definition of rape.
Source: FBI Uniform Crime Reports, 2019

Hate Crimes

| Area | Number of Quarters Reported | Number of Incidents per Bias Motivation | | | | | |
		Race/Ethnicity/ Ancestry	Religion	Sexual Orientation	Disability	Gender	Gender Identity
City[1]	4	178	26	80	3	4	13
U.S.	4	3,963	1,521	1,195	157	69	198

Note: (1) Figures include one incident reported with more than one bias motivation.
Source: Federal Bureau of Investigation, Hate Crime Statistics 2019

Identity Theft Consumer Reports

Area	Reports	Reports per 100,000 Population	Rank[2]
MSA[1]	34,968	879	15
U.S.	1,387,615	423	-

Note: (1) Figures cover the Seattle-Tacoma-Bellevue, WA Metropolitan Statistical Area; (2) Rank ranges from 1 to 391 where 1 indicates greatest number of identity theft reports per 100,000 population
Source: Federal Trade Commission, Consumer Sentinel Network Data Book 2020

Fraud and Other Consumer Reports

Area	Reports	Reports per 100,000 Population	Rank[2]
MSA[1]	35,803	900	48
U.S.	3,385,133	1,031	-

Note: (1) Figures cover the Seattle-Tacoma-Bellevue, WA Metropolitan Statistical Area; (2) Rank ranges from 1 to 391 where 1 indicates greatest number of fraud and other consumer reports per 100,000 population
Source: Federal Trade Commission, Consumer Sentinel Network Data Book 2020

POLITICS

2020 Presidential Election Results

Area	Biden	Trump	Jorgensen	Hawkins	Other
King County	75.0	22.2	1.5	0.5	0.8
U.S.	51.3	46.8	1.2	0.3	0.5

Note: Results are percentages and may not add to 100% due to rounding
Source: Dave Leip's Atlas of U.S. Presidential Elections

SPORTS

Professional Sports Teams

Team Name	League	Year Established
Seattle Kraken	National Hockey League (NHL)	2021
Seattle Mariners	Major League Baseball (MLB)	1977
Seattle Seahawks	National Football League (NFL)	1976
Seattle Sounders FC	Major League Soccer (MLS)	2009

Note: Includes teams located in the Seattle-Tacoma-Bellevue, WA Metropolitan Statistical Area.
Source: Wikipedia, Major Professional Sports Teams of the United States and Canada, April 6, 2021

CLIMATE

Average and Extreme Temperatures

Temperature	Jan	Feb	Mar	Apr	May	Jun	Jul	Aug	Sep	Oct	Nov	Dec	Yr.
Extreme High (°F)	64	70	75	85	93	96	98	99	98	89	74	63	99
Average High (°F)	44	48	52	57	64	69	75	74	69	59	50	45	59
Average Temp. (°F)	39	43	45	49	55	61	65	65	60	52	45	41	52
Average Low (°F)	34	36	38	41	46	51	54	55	51	45	39	36	44
Extreme Low (°F)	0	1	11	29	28	38	43	44	35	28	6	6	0

Note: Figures cover the years 1948-1990
Source: National Climatic Data Center, International Station Meteorological Climate Summary, 9/96

Average Precipitation/Snowfall/Humidity

Precip./Humidity	Jan	Feb	Mar	Apr	May	Jun	Jul	Aug	Sep	Oct	Nov	Dec	Yr.
Avg. Precip. (in.)	5.7	4.2	3.7	2.4	1.7	1.4	0.8	1.1	1.9	3.5	5.9	5.9	38.4
Avg. Snowfall (in.)	5	2	1	Tr	Tr	0	0	0	0	Tr	1	3	13
Avg. Rel. Hum. 7am (%)	83	83	84	83	80	79	79	84	87	88	85	85	83
Avg. Rel. Hum. 4pm (%)	76	69	63	57	54	54	49	51	57	68	76	79	63

Note: Figures cover the years 1948-1990; Tr = Trace amounts (<0.05 in. of rain; <0.5 in. of snow)
Source: National Climatic Data Center, International Station Meteorological Climate Summary, 9/96

Weather Conditions

Temperature			Daytime Sky			Precipitation		
5°F & below	32°F & below	90°F & above	Clear	Partly cloudy	Cloudy	0.01 inch or more precip.	0.1 inch or more snow/ice	Thunder-storms
< 1	38	3	57	120	188	157	8	8

Note: Figures are average number of days per year and cover the years 1948-1990
Source: National Climatic Data Center, International Station Meteorological Climate Summary, 9/96

HAZARDOUS WASTE

Superfund Sites

The Seattle-Bellevue-Everett, WA metro division is home to 10 sites on the EPA's Superfund National Priorities List: **Harbor Island (Lead)** (final); **Lockheed West Seattle** (final); **Lower Duwamish Waterway** (final); **Midway Landfill** (final); **Pacific Car & Foundry Co.** (final); **Pacific Sound Resources** (final); **Queen City Farms** (final); **Quendall Terminals** (final); **Seattle Municipal Landfill (Kent Highlands)** (final); **Western Processing Co., Inc.** (final). There are a total of 1,375 Superfund sites with a status of proposed or final on the list in the U.S. *U.S. Environmental Protection Agency, National Priorities List, April 7, 2021*

AIR QUALITY

Air Quality Trends: Ozone

	1990	1995	2000	2005	2010	2015	2016	2017	2018	2019
MSA[1]	0.082	0.062	0.056	0.053	0.053	0.059	0.054	0.076	0.067	0.052
U.S.	0.088	0.089	0.082	0.080	0.073	0.068	0.069	0.068	0.069	0.065

Note: (1) Data covers the Seattle-Tacoma-Bellevue, WA Metropolitan Statistical Area. The values shown are the composite ozone concentration averages among trend sites based on the highest fourth daily maximum 8-hour concentration in parts per million. These trends are based on sites having an adequate record of monitoring data during the trend period. Data from exceptional events are included.
Source: U.S. Environmental Protection Agency, Air Quality Monitoring Information, "Air Quality Trends by City, 1990-2019"

Air Quality Index

Area	Percent of Days when Air Quality was...[2]					AQI Statistics[2]	
	Good	Moderate	Unhealthy for Sensitive Groups	Unhealthy	Very Unhealthy	Maximum	Median
MSA[1]	64.7	34.8	0.5	0.0	0.0	142	45

Note: (1) Data covers the Seattle-Tacoma-Bellevue, WA Metropolitan Statistical Area; (2) Based on 365 days with AQI data in 2019. Air Quality Index (AQI) is an index for reporting daily air quality. EPA calculates the AQI for five major air pollutants regulated by the Clean Air Act: ground-level ozone, particle pollution (aka particulate matter), carbon monoxide, sulfur dioxide, and nitrogen dioxide. The AQI runs from 0 to 500. The higher the AQI value, the greater the level of air pollution and the greater the health concern. There are six AQI categories: "Good" AQI is between 0 and 50. Air quality is considered satisfactory; "Moderate" AQI is between 51 and 100. Air quality is acceptable; "Unhealthy for Sensitive Groups" When AQI values are between 101 and 150, members of sensitive groups may experience health effects; "Unhealthy" When AQI values are between 151 and 200 everyone may begin to experience health effects; "Very Unhealthy" AQI values between 201 and 300 trigger a health alert; "Hazardous" AQI values over 300 trigger warnings of emergency conditions (not shown).
Source: U.S. Environmental Protection Agency, Air Quality Index Report, 2019

Air Quality Index Pollutants

Area	Percent of Days when AQI Pollutant was...[2]					
	Carbon Monoxide	Nitrogen Dioxide	Ozone	Sulfur Dioxide	Particulate Matter 2.5	Particulate Matter 10
MSA[1]	0.0	8.5	43.3	0.0	48.2	0.0

Note: (1) Data covers the Seattle-Tacoma-Bellevue, WA Metropolitan Statistical Area; (2) Based on 365 days with AQI data in 2019. The Air Quality Index (AQI) is an index for reporting daily air quality. EPA calculates the AQI for five major air pollutants regulated by the Clean Air Act: ground-level ozone, particle pollution (also known as particulate matter), carbon monoxide, sulfur dioxide, and nitrogen dioxide. The AQI runs from 0 to 500. The higher the AQI value, the greater the level of air pollution and the greater the health concern.
Source: U.S. Environmental Protection Agency, Air Quality Index Report, 2019

Maximum Air Pollutant Concentrations: Particulate Matter, Ozone, CO and Lead

	Particulate Matter 10 (ug/m^3)	Particulate Matter 2.5 Wtd AM (ug/m^3)	Particulate Matter 2.5 24-Hr (ug/m^3)	Ozone (ppm)	Carbon Monoxide (ppm)	Lead (ug/m^3)
MSA[1] Level	22	8.5	28	0.056	1	n/a
NAAQS[2]	150	15	35	0.075	9	0.15
Met NAAQS[2]	Yes	Yes	Yes	Yes	Yes	n/a

Note: (1) Data covers the Seattle-Tacoma-Bellevue, WA Metropolitan Statistical Area; Data from exceptional events are included; (2) National Ambient Air Quality Standards; ppm = parts per million; ug/m^3 = micrograms per cubic meter; n/a not available.
Concentrations: Particulate Matter 10 (coarse particulate)—highest second maximum 24-hour concentration; Particulate Matter 2.5 Wtd AM (fine particulate)—highest weighted annual mean concentration; Particulate Matter 2.5 24-Hour (fine particulate)—highest 98th percentile 24-hour concentration; Ozone—highest fourth daily maximum 8-hour concentration; Carbon Monoxide—highest second maximum non-overlapping 8-hour concentration; Lead—maximum running 3-month average
Source: U.S. Environmental Protection Agency, Air Quality Monitoring Information, "Air Quality Statistics by City, 2019"

Maximum Air Pollutant Concentrations: Nitrogen Dioxide and Sulfur Dioxide

	Nitrogen Dioxide AM (ppb)	Nitrogen Dioxide 1-Hr (ppb)	Sulfur Dioxide AM (ppb)	Sulfur Dioxide 1-Hr (ppb)	Sulfur Dioxide 24-Hr (ppb)
MSA[1] Level	18	57	n/a	6	n/a
NAAQS[2]	53	100	30	75	140
Met NAAQS[2]	Yes	Yes	n/a	Yes	n/a

Note: (1) Data covers the Seattle-Tacoma-Bellevue, WA Metropolitan Statistical Area; Data from exceptional events are included; (2) National Ambient Air Quality Standards; ppm = parts per million; ug/m^3 = micrograms per cubic meter; n/a not available.
Concentrations: Nitrogen Dioxide AM—highest arithmetic mean concentration; Nitrogen Dioxide 1-Hr—highest 98th percentile 1-hour daily maximum concentration; Sulfur Dioxide AM—highest annual mean concentration; Sulfur Dioxide 1-Hr—highest 99th percentile 1-hour daily maximum concentration; Sulfur Dioxide 24-Hr—highest second maximum 24-hour concentration
Source: U.S. Environmental Protection Agency, Air Quality Monitoring Information, "Air Quality Statistics by City, 2019"

Tucson, Arizona

Background

Tucson lies in a high desert valley that was once the floor of an ancient inland sea. Its name derives from the Papago tribe's term for the ancient settlement, Stukshon, which in Spanish is Tuquison. It is believed that the Spanish Jesuit Eusebio Francesco Kino, who established the San Xavier Mission, was the first European to visit the area in 1700. Spanish prospectors who came after Father Kino were driven out by the native tribes trying to protect their territory.

Tucson came under Mexican jurisdiction in 1821, when Mexico was no longer ruled by Spain. In 1853 Mexico sold the area to the U.S. and soon after, overland stage service from San Antonio was instituted. The Civil War interrupted travel along this route to California. After the war, Tucson continued as a supply and distribution point, first for the army and then for miners. From 1867 to 1877, it was the capital of the territory.

Tucson grew slowly until World War II when it became more industrialized. Today, the city is both an industrial center and a health resort. Aircraft and missile manufacturing, electronics research, tourism, and education are among the city's chief industries. The University of Arizona is the city's largest employer while Raytheon Missile Systems and the Davis-Monthan Air Force Base are other major sources of jobs.

Recreation in Tucson revolves around the breathtaking natural beauty of it surroundings. Its attractions include the Arizona-Sonoran Desert Museum—21 acres of wild desert inhabited by over 300 animal species and 1,200 types of plants—and Kitt Peak National Observatory, crowning a 6,882-foot mountain, where visitors can take advantage of 24 optical telescopes and two radio telescopes, along with exhibits and tours. Saguaro National Park is a 91,000-acre park featuring one of the world's largest saguaro, or tall cactus, stands. Mount Lemmon, over 9,000 feet high, offers hiking, camping, picnicking, and skiing. The Biosphere 2 is located nearby, where eight people attempted to live for two years in its glass-enclosed, airtight environment. The area is now a large-scale laboratory—a research and teaching center under the stewardship of the University of Arizona, and is a popular tourist attraction.

To deal with its ever-present water scarcity, the city embarked on a water harvesting program which saved 52.1 million gallons of water in 2018-2019. Tucson also aims to be carbon-neutral by 2030.

Arizona State Museum features extensive basketry and fiber arts exhibits, celebrating the Southwest United States' ancient fiber-weaving traditions. The unparalleled collections of basketry and pottery have been named National Treasures by the National Endowment for the Humanities. Other notable museums include the University of Arizona Museum of Art, the Arizona-Sonora Desert Museum, and the Pima Air & Space Museum. The city is home to numerous annual events, including the Tucson Gem & Mineral Show, the Tucson Festival of Books, the Tucson Folk Festival, and the All Souls Procession Weekend.

The college scene in Tucson includes the University of Arizona, one of the top research universities in the U.S., with 45,000 national and international students, and Pima Community College, serving 75,000 students on six campuses with occupational and special interest courses. Tucson's sports scene is largely focused on the University of Arizona, with the men's basketball team and the women's softball team representing particularly competitive programs. A 2018 addition to the city was the Indoor Football League expansion team, the Tucson Sugar Skulls, playing in the renovated Tucson Arena.

Nightlife in Tucson abounds with music of all kinds—blues, jazz, country, folk, Latino, and reggae. The diverse restaurant scene, including Japanese, Southwestern, and Italian, is world-renowned.

The region is known for its nearly perfect climate. Surrounded by four mountain ranges, Tucson has much sunshine, dry air, and rich desert vegetation.

Rankings

General Rankings

- Tucson was selected as one of the best places to live in America by *Outside Magazine*. Criteria included population, park acreage, neighborhood and resident diversity, new and upcoming things of interest, and opportunities for outdoor adventure. *Outside Magazine, "The 12 Best Places to Live in 2019," July 11, 2019*

- For its 33rd annual "Readers' Choice Awards" survey, *Condé Nast Traveler* ranked its readers' favorite cities in the U.S. These places brought feelings of comfort in a time of limited travel. The list was broken into large cities and cities under 250,000. Tucson ranked #9 in the big city category. *Condé Nast Traveler, Readers' Choice Awards 2020, "Best Big Cities in the U.S." October 6, 2020*

- In their seventh annual survey, Livability.com looked at data for more than 1,000 small to mid-sized U.S. cities to determine the rankings for Livability's "Top 100 Best Places to Live" in 2020. Tucson ranked #79. Criteria: housing and affordable living; vibrant economy; social and civic engagement; education; demographics; health care options; transportation & infrastructure; and abundant lifestyle amenities. *Livability.com, "Top 100 Best Places to Live 2020" October 2020*

Business/Finance Rankings

- The Brookings Institution ranked the nation's largest cities based on income inequality. Tucson was ranked #58 (#1 = greatest inequality). Criteria: the "95/20 ratio," a figure representing the income at which a household earns more than 95 percent of all other households, divided by the income at which a household earns more than only 20 percent of all other households. *Brookings Institution, "Household Income Inequality, Largest Cities of 97 Large U.S. Metro Areas, 2014-2016," February 5, 2018*

- The Brookings Institution ranked the 100 largest metro areas in the U.S. based on income inequality. Tucson was ranked #24 (#1 = greatest inequality). Criteria: the "95/20 ratio," a figure representing the income at which a household earns more than 95 percent of all other households, divided by the income at which a household earns more than only 20 percent of all other households. *Brookings Institution, "Household Income Inequality, 100 Largest U.S. Metro Areas, 2014-2016," February 5, 2018*

- The Tucson metro area appeared on the Milken Institute "2021 Best Performing Cities" list. Rank: #41 out of 200 large metro areas (population over 250,000). Criteria: job growth; wage and salary growth; high-tech output growth; housing affordability; household broadband access. *Milken Institute, "Best-Performing Cities 2021," February 16, 2021*

- *Forbes* ranked the 200 most populous metro areas to determine the nation's "Best Places for Business and Careers." The Tucson metro area was ranked #107. Criteria: costs (business and living); job growth (past and projected); income growth; quality of life; educational attainment (college and high school); projected economic growth; cultural and leisure opportunities; workplace tolerance laws; net migration patterns. *Forbes, "The Best Places for Business and Careers 2019: Seattle Still On Top," October 30, 2019*

Children/Family Rankings

- Tucson was selected as one of the most playful cities in the U.S. by KaBOOM! The organization's Playful City USA initiative honors cities and towns across the nation that have made their communities more playable. Criteria: pledging to integrate play as a solution to challenges in their communities; making it easy for children to get active and balanced play; creating more family-friendly and innovative communities as a result. *KaBOOM! National Campaign for Play, "2017 Playful City USA Communities"*

Education Rankings

- Personal finance website *WalletHub* analyzed the 150 largest U.S. metropolitan statistical areas to determine where the most educated Americans are putting their degrees to work. Criteria: education levels; percentage of workers with degrees; education quality and attainment gap; public school quality rankings; quality and enrollment of each metro area's universities. Tucson was ranked #63 (#1 = most educated city). *www.WalletHub.com, "Most and Least Educated Cities in America," July 20, 2020*

- Tucson was selected as one of America's most literate cities. The city ranked #56 out of the 84 largest U.S. cities. Criteria: number of booksellers; library resources; Internet resources; educational attainment; periodical publishing resources; newspaper circulation. *Central Connecticut State University, "America's Most Literate Cities, 2018," February 2019*

Environmental Rankings

- The U.S. Conference of Mayors and Walmart Stores sponsor the Mayors' Climate Protection Awards Program which recognize mayors for outstanding and innovative practices that mayors are taking to increase energy efficiency in their cities, reduce carbon emissions and expand renewable energy. Tucson received an Honorable Mention in the large city category. *U.S. Conference of Mayors, "2020 Mayors' Climate Protection Awards," December 18, 2020*

Health/Fitness Rankings

- For each of the 100 largest cities in the United States, the American Fitness Index®, published by the American College of Sports Medicine and the Anthem Foundation, evaluated community infrastructure and 33 health behaviors including preventive health, levels of chronic disease conditions, pedestrian safety, air quality, and community resources that support physical activity. Tucson ranked #58 for "community fitness." *americanfitnessindex.org, "2020 ACSM American Fitness Index Summary Report," July 14, 2020*

- Tucson was identified as a "2021 Spring Allergy Capital." The area ranked #30 out of 100. Three groups of factors were used to identify the most challenging cities for people with allergies during the spring season: annual spring pollen levels; over the counter medicine use; number of board-certified allergy specialists. *Asthma and Allergy Foundation of America, "Spring Allergy Capitals 2021," February 23, 2021*

- Tucson was identified as a "2021 Fall Allergy Capital." The area ranked #49 out of 100. Three groups of factors were used to identify the most challenging cities for people with allergies during the fall season: annual fall pollen levels; over the counter medicine use; number of board-certified allergy specialists. *Asthma and Allergy Foundation of America, "Fall Allergy Capitals 2021," February 23, 2021*

- Tucson was identified as a "2019 Asthma Capital." The area ranked #46 out of the nation's 100 largest metropolitan areas. Criteria: estimated asthma prevalence; crude death rate from asthma; and ER visits due to asthma. Risk factors analyzed but not factored in the rankings: annual pollen score; annual air quality; public smoking laws; number of board-certified asthma specialists; rescue medication use; controller medication use; uninsured rate; poverty rate. *Asthma and Allergy Foundation of America, "Asthma Capitals 2019: The Most Challenging Places to Live With Asthma," May 7, 2019*

Real Estate Rankings

- *WalletHub* compared the most populated U.S. cities to determine which had the best markets for real estate agents. Tucson ranked #138 where demand was high and pay was the best. Criteria: sales per agent; annual median wage for real-estate agents; monthly average starting salary for real estate agents; real estate job density and competition; unemployment rate; home turnover rate; housing-market health index; and other relevant metrics. *www.WalletHub.com, "2019's Best Places to Be a Real Estate Agent," April 24, 2019*

- Tucson was ranked #135 out of 268 metro areas in terms of housing affordability in 2020 by the National Association of Home Builders (#1 = most affordable). Criteria: the share of homes sold in that area affordable to a family earning the local median income, based on standard mortgage underwriting criteria. *National Association of Home Builders®, NAHB-Wells Fargo Housing Opportunity Index, 4th Quarter 2020*

Safety Rankings

- Allstate ranked the 200 largest cities in America in terms of driver safety. Tucson ranked #40. Criteria: internal property damage claims over a two-year period from January 2016 to December 2017. The report helps increase the importance of safety and awareness behind the wheel. *Allstate, "Allstate America's Best Drivers Report, 2019" June 24, 2019*

- The National Insurance Crime Bureau ranked 384 metro areas in the U.S. in terms of per capita rates of vehicle theft. The Tucson metro area ranked #71 (#1 = highest rate). Criteria: number of vehicle theft offenses per 100,000 inhabitants in 2019. *National Insurance Crime Bureau, "Hot Spots 2019," July 21, 2020*

Seniors/Retirement Rankings

- From its Best Cities for Successful Aging indexes, the Milken Institute generated rankings for metropolitan areas, weighing data in nine categories—health care, wellness, living arrangements, transportation and convenience, financial characteristics, education, employment, community engagement, and overall livability. The Tucson metro area was ranked #60 overall in the large metro area category. *Milken Institute, "Best Cities for Successful Aging, 2017" March 14, 2017*

- Tucson was identified as #4 of 20 most popular places to retire in the Southwest region by *Topretirements.com*. The site separated its annual "Best Places to Retire" list by major U.S. regions for 2019. The list reflects the 20 cities that visitors to the website are most interested in for retirement, based on the number of times a city's review was viewed on the website. *Topretirements.com, "20 Most Popular Places to Retire in the Southwest for 2019," October 2, 2019*

Sports/Recreation Rankings

- Tucson was chosen as one of America's best cities for bicycling. The city ranked #24 out of 50. Criteria: cycling infrastructure that is safe and friendly for all ages; energy and bike culture. The editors evaluated cities with populations of 100,000 or more. *Bicycling, "The 50 Best Bike Cities in America," October 10, 2018*

Women/Minorities Rankings

- The *Houston Chronicle* listed the Tucson metro area as #10 in top places for young Latinos to live in the U.S. Research was largely based on housing and occupational data from the largest metropolitan areas performed by *Forbes* and NBC Universo. Criteria: percentage of 18-34 year-olds; Latino college grad rates; and diversity. *blog.chron.com, "The 15 Best Big Cities for Latino Millenials," January 26, 2016*

- Personal finance website *WalletHub* compared more than 180 U.S. cities across two key dimensions, "Hispanic Business-Friendliness" and "Hispanic Purchasing Power," to arrive at the most favorable conditions for Hispanic entrepreneurs. Tucson was ranked #92 out of 182. Criteria includes: share of Hispanic-Owned Businesses; Hispanic entrepreneurship rate to median annual income of Hispanics; Small Business-Friendliness score; cost of living; and number of Hispanics with at least a bachelor's degree. *WalletHub.com, "2019's Best Cities for Hispanic Entrepreneurs," May 1, 2019*

Miscellaneous Rankings

- *WalletHub* compared the 150 most populated U.S. cities to determine their operating efficiency. A "Quality of City Services" score was constructed for each city and then divided by the total budget per capita to reveal which were managed the best. Tucson ranked #38. Criteria: financial stability; economy; education; safety; health; infrastructure and pollution. *www.WalletHub.com, "2020's Best- & Worst-Run Cities in America," June 29, 2020*

Business Environment

DEMOGRAPHICS

Population Growth

Area	1990 Census	2000 Census	2010 Census	2019* Estimate	Population Growth (%) 1990-2019	Population Growth (%) 2010-2019
City	417,942	486,699	520,116	541,482	29.6	4.1
MSA[1]	666,880	843,746	980,263	1,027,207	54.0	4.8
U.S.	248,709,873	281,421,906	308,745,538	324,697,795	30.6	5.2

Note: (1) Figures cover the Tucson, AZ Metropolitan Statistical Area; (*) 2015-2019 5-year estimated population
Source: U.S. Census Bureau, 1990 Census, Census 2000, Census 2010, 2015-2019 American Community Survey 5-Year Estimates

Household Size

Area	Persons in Household (%) One	Two	Three	Four	Five	Six	Seven or More	Average Household Size
City	34.6	31.2	14.8	10.8	5.1	2.0	1.3	2.40
MSA[1]	30.5	35.9	13.8	11.3	5.2	2.0	1.4	2.50
U.S.	27.9	33.9	15.6	12.9	6.0	2.3	1.4	2.60

Note: (1) Figures cover the Tucson, AZ Metropolitan Statistical Area
Source: U.S. Census Bureau, 2015-2019 American Community Survey 5-Year Estimates

Race

Area	White Alone[2] (%)	Black Alone[2] (%)	Asian Alone[2] (%)	AIAN[3] Alone[2] (%)	NHOPI[4] Alone[2] (%)	Other Race Alone[2] (%)	Two or More Races (%)
City	72.1	5.2	3.2	3.7	0.2	10.2	5.4
MSA[1]	76.0	3.6	2.9	3.9	0.2	8.6	4.9
U.S.	72.5	12.7	5.5	0.8	0.2	4.9	3.3

Note: (1) Figures cover the Tucson, AZ Metropolitan Statistical Area; (2) Alone is defined as not being in combination with one or more other races; (3) American Indian and Alaska Native; (4) Native Hawaiian and Other Pacific Islander
Source: U.S. Census Bureau, 2015-2019 American Community Survey 5-Year Estimates

Hispanic or Latino Origin

Area	Total (%)	Mexican (%)	Puerto Rican (%)	Cuban (%)	Other (%)
City	43.6	39.5	0.8	0.2	3.1
MSA[1]	37.2	33.5	0.8	0.2	2.7
U.S.	18.0	11.2	1.7	0.7	4.3

Note: Persons of Hispanic or Latino origin can be of any race; (1) Figures cover the Tucson, AZ Metropolitan Statistical Area
Source: U.S. Census Bureau, 2015-2019 American Community Survey 5-Year Estimates

Ancestry

Area	German	Irish	English	American	Italian	Polish	French[2]	Scottish	Dutch
City	11.0	8.2	6.4	3.0	3.6	1.9	2.0	1.5	0.9
MSA[1]	13.4	9.1	8.2	3.3	4.0	2.3	2.3	1.9	1.1
U.S.	13.3	9.7	7.2	6.2	5.1	2.8	2.3	1.7	1.2

Note: Figures are the percentage of the total population reporting a particular ancestry. The nine most commonly reported ancestries in the U.S. are shown. Figures include multiple ancestries (e.g. if a person reported being Irish and Italian, they were included in both columns); (1) Figures cover the Tucson, AZ Metropolitan Statistical Area; (2) Excludes Basque
Source: U.S. Census Bureau, 2015-2019 American Community Survey 5-Year Estimates

Foreign-born Population

Area	Percent of Population Born in Any Foreign Country	Asia	Mexico	Europe	Caribbean	Central America[2]	South America	Africa	Canada
City	15.3	2.7	9.5	1.0	0.1	0.4	0.3	0.9	0.3
MSA[1]	13.0	2.3	7.6	1.2	0.1	0.3	0.3	0.6	0.4
U.S.	13.6	4.2	3.5	1.5	1.3	1.1	1.0	0.7	0.2

Note: (1) Figures cover the Tucson, AZ Metropolitan Statistical Area; (2) Excludes Mexico.
Source: U.S. Census Bureau, 2015-2019 American Community Survey 5-Year Estimates

Marital Status

Area	Never Married	Now Married[2]	Separated	Widowed	Divorced
City	42.5	36.0	2.2	5.4	14.0
MSA[1]	34.4	45.0	1.8	5.9	12.9
U.S.	33.4	48.1	1.9	5.8	10.9

Note: Figures are percentages and cover the population 15 years of age and older; (1) Figures cover the Tucson, AZ Metropolitan Statistical Area; (2) Excludes separated
Source: U.S. Census Bureau, 2015-2019 American Community Survey 5-Year Estimates

Disability by Age

Area	All Ages	Under 18 Years Old	18 to 64 Years Old	65 Years and Over
City	15.3	5.5	13.2	39.5
MSA[1]	15.3	5.1	12.5	35.1
U.S.	12.6	4.2	10.3	34.5

Note: Figures show percent of the civilian noninstitutionalized population that reported having a disability. Disability status is determined from six types of difficulty: vision, hearing, cognitive, ambulatory, self-care, and independent living. For children under 5 years old, hearing and vision difficulty are used to determine disability status. For children between the ages of 5 and 14, disability status is determined from hearing, vision, cognitive, ambulatory, and self-care difficulties. For people aged 15 years and older, they are considered to have a disability if they have difficulty with any one of the six difficulty types; Note: (1) Figures cover the Tucson, AZ Metropolitan Statistical Area
Source: U.S. Census Bureau, 2015-2019 American Community Survey 5-Year Estimates

Age

Area	Percent of Population									Median Age
	Under Age 5	Age 5–19	Age 20–34	Age 35–44	Age 45–54	Age 55–64	Age 65–74	Age 75–84	Age 85+	
City	6.0	19.1	26.5	11.9	10.9	11.2	8.3	4.2	1.9	33.7
MSA[1]	5.7	18.6	21.5	11.4	11.2	12.6	10.9	6.0	2.2	38.5
U.S.	6.1	19.1	20.7	12.6	13.0	12.9	9.1	4.6	1.9	38.1

Note: (1) Figures cover the Tucson, AZ Metropolitan Statistical Area
Source: U.S. Census Bureau, 2015-2019 American Community Survey 5-Year Estimates

Gender

Area	Males	Females	Males per 100 Females
City	269,403	272,079	99.0
MSA[1]	505,666	521,541	97.0
U.S.	159,886,919	164,810,876	97.0

Note: (1) Figures cover the Tucson, AZ Metropolitan Statistical Area
Source: U.S. Census Bureau, 2015-2019 American Community Survey 5-Year Estimates

Religious Groups by Family

Area	Catholic	Baptist	Non-Den.	Methodist[2]	Lutheran	LDS[3]	Pentecostal	Presbyterian[4]	Muslim[5]	Judaism
MSA[1]	20.8	3.3	3.8	1.4	1.5	3.0	1.6	1.0	<0.1	0.6
U.S.	19.1	9.3	4.0	4.0	2.3	2.0	1.9	1.6	0.8	0.7

Note: Figures are the number of adherents as a percentage of the total population; (1) Figures cover the Tucson, AZ Metropolitan Statistical Area; (2) Methodist/Pietist; (3) Latter Day Saints; (4) Reformed; (5) Figures are estimates
Source: Association of Statisticians of American Religious Bodies, 2010 U.S. Religion Census: Religious Congregations & Membership Study

Religious Groups by Tradition

Area	Catholic	Evangelical Protestant	Mainline Protestant	Other Tradition	Black Protestant	Orthodox
MSA[1]	20.8	10.0	3.8	4.6	0.4	0.2
U.S.	19.1	16.2	7.3	4.3	1.6	0.3

Note: Figures are the number of adherents as a percentage of the total population; (1) Figures cover the Tucson, AZ Metropolitan Statistical Area
Source: Association of Statisticians of American Religious Bodies, 2010 U.S. Religion Census: Religious Congregations & Membership Study

ECONOMY

Gross Metropolitan Product

Area	2017	2018	2019	2020	Rank[2]
MSA[1]	39.9	41.7	43.6	45.5	74

Note: Figures are in billions of dollars; (1) Figures cover the Tucson, AZ Metropolitan Statistical Area; (2) Rank is based on 2018 data and ranges from 1 to 381
Source: U.S. Conference of Mayors, U.S. Metro Economies: GMP & Employment 2018-2020, September 2019

Economic Growth

Area	2015-17 (%)	2018 (%)	2019 (%)	2020 (%)	Rank[2]
MSA[1]	2.0	2.7	2.8	2.0	133
U.S.	1.9	2.9	2.3	2.1	—

Note: Figures are real gross metropolitan product (GMP) growth rates and represent average annual percent change; (1) Figures cover the Tucson, AZ Metropolitan Statistical Area; (2) Rank is based on 2017 2-year average annual percent change and ranges from 1 to 381
Source: U.S. Conference of Mayors, U.S. Metro Economies: GMP & Employment 2018-2020, September 2019

Metropolitan Area Exports

Area	2014	2015	2016	2017	2018	2019	Rank[2]
MSA[1]	2,277.4	2,485.9	2,563.9	2,683.9	2,824.8	2,943.7	81

Note: Figures are in millions of dollars; (1) Figures cover the Tucson, AZ Metropolitan Statistical Area; (2) Rank is based on 2019 data and ranges from 1 to 386
Source: U.S. Department of Commerce, International Trade Administration, Office of Trade and Economic Analysis, Industry and Analysis, Exports by Metropolitan Area, data extracted March 24, 2021

Building Permits

Area	Single-Family			Multi-Family			Total		
	2018	2019	Pct. Chg.	2018	2019	Pct. Chg.	2018	2019	Pct. Chg.
City	680	999	46.9	860	817	-5.0	1,540	1,816	17.9
MSA[1]	3,240	3,490	7.7	1,164	823	-29.3	4,404	4,313	-2.1
U.S.	855,300	862,100	0.7	473,500	523,900	10.6	1,328,800	1,386,000	4.3

Note: (1) Figures cover the Tucson, AZ Metropolitan Statistical Area; Figures represent new, privately-owned housing units authorized (unadjusted data); All permit data are based on estimates with imputation
Source: U.S. Census Bureau, Manufacturing, Mining, and Construction Statistics, Building Permits, 2018, 2019

Bankruptcy Filings

Area	Business Filings			Nonbusiness Filings		
	2019	2020	% Chg.	2019	2020	% Chg.
Pima County	50	32	-36.0	2,438	1,727	-29.2
U.S.	22,780	21,655	-4.9	752,160	522,808	-30.5

Note: Business filings include Chapter 7, Chapter 9, Chapter 11, Chapter 12, Chapter 13, Chapter 15, and Section 304; Nonbusiness filings include Chapter 7, Chapter 11, and Chapter 13
Source: Administrative Office of the U.S. Courts, Business and Nonbusiness Bankruptcy, County Cases Commenced by Chapter of the Bankruptcy Code, During the 12-Month Period Ending December 31, 2019 and Business and Nonbusiness Bankruptcy, County Cases Commenced by Chapter of the Bankruptcy Code, During the 12-Month Period Ending December 31, 2020

Housing Vacancy Rates

Area	Gross Vacancy Rate[2] (%)			Year-Round Vacancy Rate[3] (%)			Rental Vacancy Rate[4] (%)			Homeowner Vacancy Rate[5] (%)		
	2018	2019	2020	2018	2019	2020	2018	2019	2020	2018	2019	2020
MSA[1]	12.5	14.8	12.1	8.1	9.2	7.7	4.4	7.3	8.6	1.8	1.5	0.5
U.S.	12.3	12.0	10.6	9.7	9.5	8.2	6.9	6.7	6.3	1.5	1.4	1.0

Note: (1) Figures cover the Tucson, AZ Metropolitan Statistical Area; (2) The percentage of the total housing inventory that is vacant; (3) The percentage of the housing inventory (excluding seasonal units) that is year-round vacant; (4) The percentage of rental inventory that is vacant for rent; (5) The percentage of homeowner inventory that is vacant for sale
Source: U.S. Census Bureau, Housing Vacancies and Homeownership Annual Statistics: 2018, 2019, 2020

INCOME

Income

Area	Per Capita ($)	Median Household ($)	Average Household ($)
City	23,655	43,425	58,057
MSA[1]	29,707	53,379	73,554
U.S.	34,103	62,843	88,607

Note: (1) Figures cover the Tucson, AZ Metropolitan Statistical Area
Source: U.S. Census Bureau, 2015-2019 American Community Survey 5-Year Estimates

Household Income Distribution

Area	Percent of Households Earning							
	Under $15,000	$15,000 -$24,999	$25,000 -$34,999	$35,000 -$49,999	$50,000 -$74,999	$75,000 -$99,999	$100,000 -$149,999	$150,000 and up
City	15.8	13.2	11.7	15.6	17.9	10.8	9.7	5.3
MSA[1]	12.0	10.6	10.2	14.3	18.2	12.3	12.7	9.6
U.S.	10.3	8.9	8.9	12.3	17.2	12.7	15.1	14.5

Note: (1) Figures cover the Tucson, AZ Metropolitan Statistical Area
Source: U.S. Census Bureau, 2015-2019 American Community Survey 5-Year Estimates

Poverty Rate

Area	All Ages	Under 18 Years Old	18 to 64 Years Old	65 Years and Over
City	22.5	30.5	21.9	13.0
MSA[1]	16.8	23.9	16.9	8.8
U.S.	13.4	18.5	12.6	9.3

Note: Figures are percentage of people whose income during the past 12 months was below the poverty level;
(1) Figures cover the Tucson, AZ Metropolitan Statistical Area
Source: U.S. Census Bureau, 2015-2019 American Community Survey 5-Year Estimates

CITY FINANCES

City Government Finances

Component	2017 ($000)	2017 ($ per capita)
Total Revenues	1,077,765	2,027
Total Expenditures	1,088,396	2,047
Debt Outstanding	1,005,807	1,892
Cash and Securities[1]	1,260,259	2,371

Note: (1) Cash and security holdings of a government at the close of its fiscal year,
including those of its dependent agencies, utilities, and liquor stores.
Source: U.S. Census Bureau, State & Local Government Finances 2017

City Government Revenue by Source

Source	2017 ($000)	2017 ($ per capita)	2017 (%)
General Revenue			
From Federal Government	66,017	124	6.1
From State Government	198,825	374	18.4
From Local Governments	0	0	0.0
Taxes			
Property	50,727	95	4.7
Sales and Gross Receipts	250,986	472	23.3
Personal Income	0	0	0.0
Corporate Income	0	0	0.0
Motor Vehicle License	0	0	0.0
Other Taxes	11,419	21	1.1
Current Charges	153,305	288	14.2
Liquor Store	0	0	0.0
Utility	213,717	402	19.8
Employee Retirement	118,631	223	11.0

Source: U.S. Census Bureau, State & Local Government Finances 2017

City Government Expenditures by Function

Function	2017 ($000)	2017 ($ per capita)	2017 (%)
General Direct Expenditures			
Air Transportation	51,573	97	4.7
Corrections	0	0	0.0
Education	0	0	0.0
Employment Security Administration	0	0	0.0
Financial Administration	22,103	41	2.0
Fire Protection	97,475	183	9.0
General Public Buildings	610	1	0.1
Governmental Administration, Other	21,550	40	2.0
Health	0	0	0.0
Highways	98,247	184	9.0
Hospitals	0	0	0.0
Housing and Community Development	66,112	124	6.1
Interest on General Debt	10,581	19	1.0
Judicial and Legal	27,368	51	2.5
Libraries	0	0	0.0
Parking	5,171	9	0.5
Parks and Recreation	38,756	72	3.6
Police Protection	206,023	387	18.9
Public Welfare	0	0	0.0
Sewerage	0	0	0.0
Solid Waste Management	52,217	98	4.8
Veterans' Services	0	0	0.0
Liquor Store	0	0	0.0
Utility	292,342	549	26.9
Employee Retirement	74,883	140	6.9

Source: U.S. Census Bureau, State & Local Government Finances 2017

EMPLOYMENT

Labor Force and Employment

Area	Civilian Labor Force			Workers Employed		
	Dec. 2019	Dec. 2020	% Chg.	Dec. 2019	Dec. 2020	% Chg.
City	271,283	268,958	-0.9	259,611	246,980	-4.9
MSA[1]	504,172	497,081	-1.4	483,909	460,365	-4.9
U.S.	164,007,000	160,017,000	-2.4	158,504,000	149,613,000	-5.6

Note: Data is not seasonally adjusted and covers workers 16 years of age and older; (1) Figures cover the Tucson, AZ Metropolitan Statistical Area
Source: Bureau of Labor Statistics, Local Area Unemployment Statistics

Unemployment Rate

Area	2020											
	Jan.	Feb.	Mar.	Apr.	May	Jun.	Jul.	Aug.	Sep.	Oct.	Nov.	Dec.
City	4.7	4.4	6.3	13.8	9.2	10.9	11.7	6.6	7.1	8.7	8.6	8.2
MSA[1]	4.5	4.2	6.0	12.8	8.4	9.9	10.6	5.9	6.3	7.8	7.7	7.4
U.S.	4.0	3.8	4.5	14.4	13.0	11.2	10.5	8.5	7.7	6.6	6.4	6.5

Note: Data is not seasonally adjusted and covers workers 16 years of age and older; (1) Figures cover the Tucson, AZ Metropolitan Statistical Area
Source: Bureau of Labor Statistics, Local Area Unemployment Statistics

Average Wages

Occupation	$/Hr.	Occupation	$/Hr.
Accountants and Auditors	34.30	Maintenance and Repair Workers	18.20
Automotive Mechanics	21.60	Marketing Managers	54.40
Bookkeepers	18.90	Network and Computer Systems Admin.	37.60
Carpenters	20.40	Nurses, Licensed Practical	26.50
Cashiers	13.60	Nurses, Registered	36.90
Computer Programmers	42.90	Nursing Assistants	15.70
Computer Systems Analysts	41.80	Office Clerks, General	19.70
Computer User Support Specialists	25.00	Physical Therapists	42.90
Construction Laborers	17.40	Physicians	96.10
Cooks, Restaurant	13.80	Plumbers, Pipefitters and Steamfitters	24.40
Customer Service Representatives	16.80	Police and Sheriff's Patrol Officers	31.20
Dentists	102.10	Postal Service Mail Carriers	26.10
Electricians	25.20	Real Estate Sales Agents	28.30
Engineers, Electrical	44.70	Retail Salespersons	14.90
Fast Food and Counter Workers	12.90	Sales Representatives, Technical/Scientific	41.90
Financial Managers	53.30	Secretaries, Exc. Legal/Medical/Executive	17.70
First-Line Supervisors of Office Workers	25.40	Security Guards	14.50
General and Operations Managers	46.50	Surgeons	n/a
Hairdressers/Cosmetologists	16.70	Teacher Assistants, Exc. Postsecondary*	13.60
Home Health and Personal Care Aides	13.20	Teachers, Secondary School, Exc. Sp. Ed.*	21.20
Janitors and Cleaners	14.70	Telemarketers	14.70
Landscaping/Groundskeeping Workers	14.30	Truck Drivers, Heavy/Tractor-Trailer	23.50
Lawyers	70.80	Truck Drivers, Light/Delivery Services	18.80
Maids and Housekeeping Cleaners	14.80	Waiters and Waitresses	17.10

Note: Wage data covers the Tucson, AZ Metropolitan Statistical Area; (*) Hourly wages were calculated from annual wage data based on a 40 hour work week; n/a not available.
Source: Bureau of Labor Statistics, Metro Area Occupational Employment & Wage Estimates, May 2020

Employment by Industry

Sector	MSA[1]		U.S.
	Number of Employees	Percent of Total	Percent of Total
Construction	18,500	4.9	5.1
Education and Health Services	68,800	18.2	16.3
Financial Activities	17,700	4.7	6.1
Government	75,100	19.8	15.2
Information	5,000	1.3	1.9
Leisure and Hospitality	35,300	9.3	9.0
Manufacturing	27,100	7.2	8.5
Mining and Logging	1,900	0.5	0.4
Other Services	12,800	3.4	3.8
Professional and Business Services	46,300	12.2	14.4
Retail Trade	42,800	11.3	10.9
Transportation, Warehousing, and Utilities	20,500	5.4	4.6
Wholesale Trade	6,800	1.8	3.9

Note: Figures are non-farm employment as of December 2020. Figures are not seasonally adjusted and include workers 16 years of age and older; (1) Figures cover the Tucson, AZ Metropolitan Statistical Area
Source: Bureau of Labor Statistics, Current Employment Statistics, Employment, Hours, and Earnings

Employment by Occupation

Occupation Classification	City (%)	MSA[1] (%)	U.S. (%)
Management, Business, Science, and Arts	33.7	37.0	38.5
Natural Resources, Construction, and Maintenance	9.0	8.7	8.9
Production, Transportation, and Material Moving	10.2	9.5	13.2
Sales and Office	23.6	23.2	21.6
Service	23.5	21.6	17.8

Note: Figures cover employed civilians 16 years of age and older; (1) Figures cover the Tucson, AZ Metropolitan Statistical Area
Source: U.S. Census Bureau, 2015-2019 American Community Survey 5-Year Estimates

Occupations with Greatest Projected Employment Growth: 2020 – 2022

Occupation[1]	2020 Employment	2022 Projected Employment	Numeric Employment Change	Percent Employment Change
Retail Salespersons	76,020	89,930	13,910	18.3
Laborers and Freight, Stock, and Material Movers, Hand	50,760	62,050	11,290	22.2
Fast Food and Counter Workers	48,850	60,130	11,280	23.1
Stockers and Order Fillers	50,880	60,680	9,800	19.3
Waiters and Waitresses	38,790	48,430	9,640	24.9
Customer Service Representatives	101,690	111,140	9,450	9.3
Home Health and Personal Care Aides	67,820	76,780	8,960	13.2
Cooks, Restaurant	24,250	31,080	6,830	28.2
General and Operations Managers	53,800	59,930	6,130	11.4
Cashiers	59,640	65,200	5,560	9.3

Note: Projections cover Arizona; (1) Sorted by numeric employment change
Source: www.projectionscentral.com, State Occupational Projections, 2020–2022 Short-Term Projections

Fastest-Growing Occupations: 2020 – 2022

Occupation[1]	2020 Employment	2022 Projected Employment	Numeric Employment Change	Percent Employment Change
Models	270	420	150	55.6
Athletes and Sports Competitors	390	560	170	43.6
Conveyor Operators and Tenders	230	320	90	39.1
Aircraft Cargo Handling Supervisors (SOC 2018)	220	300	80	36.4
Hotel, Motel, and Resort Desk Clerks	3,880	5,210	1,330	34.3
Ushers, Lobby Attendants, and Ticket Takers	1,640	2,180	540	32.9
Locker Room, Coatroom, and Dressing Room Attendants	250	330	80	32.0
Funeral Attendants	220	290	70	31.8
Set and Exhibit Designers	160	210	50	31.3
Lodging Managers	880	1,150	270	30.7

Note: Projections cover Arizona; (1) Sorted by percent employment change and excludes occupations with numeric employment change less than 50
Source: www.projectionscentral.com, State Occupational Projections, 2020–2022 Short-Term Projections

TAXES

State Corporate Income Tax Rates

State	Tax Rate (%)	Income Brackets ($)	Num. of Brackets	Financial Institution Tax Rate (%)[a]	Federal Income Tax Ded.
Arizona	4.9 (b)	Flat rate	1	4.9 (b)	No

Note: Tax rates as of January 1, 2021; (a) Rates listed are the corporate income tax rate applied to financial institutions or excise taxes based on income. Some states have other taxes based upon the value of deposits or shares; (b) Minimum tax is $800 in California, $250 in District of Columbia, $50 in Arizona and North Dakota (banks), $400 ($100 banks) in Rhode Island, $200 per location in South Dakota (banks), $100 in Utah, $300 in Vermont.
Source: Federation of Tax Administrators, State Corporate Income Tax Rates, January 1, 2021

State Individual Income Tax Rates

State	Tax Rate (%)	Income Brackets ($)	Personal Exemptions ($)			Standard Ded. ($)	
			Single	Married	Depend.	Single	Married
Arizona (a)	2.59 - 8.0 (aa)	27,272 - 163,633 (b)	–	–	100 (c)	12,400	24,800

Note: Tax rates as of January 1, 2021; Local- and county-level taxes are not included; Federal income tax is not deductible on state income tax returns; (a) 19 states have statutory provision for automatically adjusting to the rate of inflation the dollar values of the income tax brackets, standard deductions, and/or personal exemptions. Michigan indexes the personal exemption only. Oregon does not index the income brackets for $125,000 and over; (b) For joint returns, taxes are twice the tax on half the couple's income; (c) The personal exemption takes the form of a tax credit instead of a deduction; (aa) Proposition 208, approved in November 2020, created an additional bracket on Arizona income above $250,000 ($500,000 joint). It is currently being litigated.
Source: Federation of Tax Administrators, State Individual Income Tax Rates, January 1, 2021

Various State Sales and Excise Tax Rates

State	State Sales Tax (%)	Gasoline[1] (¢/gal.)	Cigarette[2] ($/pack)	Spirits[3] ($/gal.)	Wine[4] ($/gal.)	Beer[5] ($/gal.)	Recreational Marijuana (%)
Arizona	5.6	19	2	3	0.84	0.16	(b)

Note: All tax rates as of January 1, 2021; (1) The American Petroleum Institute has developed a methodology for determining the average tax rate on a gallon of fuel. Rates may include any of the following: excise taxes, environmental fees, storage tank fees, other fees or taxes, general sales tax, and local taxes; (2) The federal excise tax of $1.0066 per pack and local taxes are not included; (3) Rates are those applicable to off-premise sales of 40% alcohol by volume (a.b.v.) distilled spirits in 750ml containers. Local excise taxes are excluded; (4) Rates are those applicable to off-premise sales of 11% a.b.v. non-carbonated wine in 750ml containers; (5) Rates are those applicable to off-premise sales of 4.7% a.b.v. beer in 12 ounce containers; (b) 16% excise tax (retail price)
Source: Tax Foundation, 2021 Facts & Figures: How Does Your State Compare?

State Business Tax Climate Index Rankings

State	Overall Rank	Corporate Tax Rank	Individual Income Tax Rank	Sales Tax Rank	Property Tax Rank	Unemployment Insurance Tax Rank
Arizona	24	22	17	40	11	8

Note: The index is a measure of how each state's tax laws affect economic performance. The lower the rank, the more favorable a state's tax system is for business. States without a given tax are given a ranking of 1. The scores/rankings for the District of Columbia do not affect other states. The 2021 index represents the tax climate as of July 1, 2020.
Source: Tax Foundation, State Business Tax Climate Index 2021

TRANSPORTATION

Means of Transportation to Work

Area	Car/Truck/Van		Public Transportation			Bicycle	Walked	Other Means	Worked at Home
	Drove Alone	Car-pooled	Bus	Subway	Railroad				
City	74.5	10.6	3.3	0.0	0.0	2.4	3.1	1.7	4.5
MSA[1]	76.8	10.0	2.2	0.0	0.0	1.5	2.3	1.8	5.4
U.S.	76.3	9.0	2.4	1.9	0.6	0.5	2.7	1.4	5.2

Note: Figures are percentages and cover workers 16 years of age and older; (1) Figures cover the Tucson, AZ Metropolitan Statistical Area
Source: U.S. Census Bureau, 2015-2019 American Community Survey 5-Year Estimates

Travel Time to Work

Area	Less Than 10 Minutes	10 to 19 Minutes	20 to 29 Minutes	30 to 44 Minutes	45 to 59 Minutes	60 to 89 Minutes	90 Minutes or More
City	11.9	34.4	25.0	19.7	4.8	2.5	1.6
MSA[1]	10.7	28.9	24.6	23.6	7.4	3.0	1.9
U.S.	12.2	28.4	20.8	20.8	8.3	6.4	2.9

Note: Note: Figures are percentages and include workers 16 years old and over; (1) Figures cover the Tucson, AZ Metropolitan Statistical Area
Source: U.S. Census Bureau, 2015-2019 American Community Survey 5-Year Estimates

Key Congestion Measures

Measure	1982	1992	2002	2012	2017
Annual Hours of Delay, Total (000)	4,854	11,198	19,242	28,979	32,305
Annual Hours of Delay, Per Auto Commuter	17	31	40	44	52
Annual Congestion Cost, Total (million $)	37	119	261	521	598
Annual Congestion Cost, Per Auto Commuter ($)	280	444	595	702	759

Note: Covers the Tucson AZ urban area
Source: Texas A&M Transportation Institute, 2019 Urban Mobility Report

Freeway Travel Time Index

Measure	1982	1987	1992	1997	2002	2007	2012	2017
Urban Area Index[1]	1.08	1.11	1.15	1.17	1.20	1.22	1.20	1.21
Urban Area Rank[1,2]	28	29	26	32	35	34	37	37

Note: Freeway Travel Time Index—the ratio of travel time in the peak period to the travel time at free-flow conditions. For example, a value of 1.30 indicates a 20-minute free-flow trip takes 26 minutes in the peak (20 minutes x 1.30 = 26 minutes); (1) Covers the Tucson AZ urban area; (2) Rank is based on 101 larger urban areas (#1 = highest travel time index)
Source: Texas A&M Transportation Institute, 2019 Urban Mobility Report

Public Transportation

Agency Name / Mode of Transportation	Vehicles Operated in Maximum Service[1]	Annual Unlinked Passenger Trips[2] (in thous.)	Annual Passenger Miles[3] (in thous.)
City of Tucson (COT)			
Bus (purchased transportation)	202	14,262.8	57,873.1
Demand Response (purchased transportation)	123	543.2	4,715.3
Streetcar Rail (purchased transportation)	6	897.0	1,406.5

Note: (1) Number of revenue vehicles operated by the given mode and type of service to meet the annual maximum service requirement. This is the revenue vehicle count during the peak season of the year; on the week and day that maximum service is provided. Vehicles operated in maximum service (VOMS) exclude atypical days and one-time special events; (2) Number of passengers who boarded public transportation vehicles. Passengers are counted each time they board a vehicle no matter how many vehicles they use to travel from their origin to their destination. (3) Sum of the distances ridden by all passengers during the entire fiscal year.
Source: Federal Transit Administration, National Transit Database, 2019

Air Transportation

Airport Name and Code / Type of Service	Passenger Airlines[1]	Passenger Enplanements	Freight Carriers[2]	Freight (lbs)
Tucson International (TUS)				
Domestic service (U.S. carriers - 2020)	20	823,289	9	30,960,824
International service (U.S. carriers - 2019)	1	157	2	62,762

Note: (1) Includes all U.S.-based major, minor and commuter airlines that carried at least one passenger during the year; (2) Includes all U.S.-based airlines and freight carriers that transported at least one pound of freight during the year.
Source: Bureau of Transportation Statistics, The Intermodal Transportation Database, Air Carriers: T-100 Domestic Market (U.S. Carriers), 2020; Bureau of Transportation Statistics, The Intermodal Transportation Database, Air Carriers: T-100 International Market (U.S. Carriers), 2019

BUSINESSES

Major Business Headquarters

Company Name	Industry	Rankings	
		Fortune[1]	Forbes[2]
No companies listed	-	-	-

Note: (1) Companies that produce a 10-K are ranked 1 to 500 based on 2019 revenue; (2) All private companies with at least $2 billion in annual revenue through the end of their most current fiscal year are ranked 1 to 219; companies listed are headquartered in the city; dashes indicate no ranking
Source: Fortune, "Fortune 500," June/July 2020; Forbes, "America's Largest Private Companies," 2020

Fastest-Growing Businesses

According to Deloitte, Tucson is home to three of North America's 500 fastest-growing high-technology companies: **Accelerate Diagnostics, Inc.** (#47); **AudioEye** (#122); **HTG Molecular Diagnostics, Inc.** (#361). Companies are ranked by percentage growth in revenue over a four-year period. Criteria for inclusion: company must be headquartered within North America; must own proprietary intellectual property or technology that is sold to customers in products that contributes to a significant portion of the company's operating revenue; must have been in business for a minumum of four years with 2016 operating revenues of at least $50,000 USD/CD and 2019 operating revenues of at least $5 million USD/CD. *Deloitte, 2020 Technology Fast 500*[TM]

Living Environment

COST OF LIVING

Cost of Living Index

Composite Index	Groceries	Housing	Utilities	Trans-portation	Health Care	Misc. Goods/ Services
100.1	103.5	94.2	101.3	96.9	101.6	103.6

Note: The Cost of Living Index measures regional differences in the cost of consumer goods and services, excluding taxes and non-consumer expenditures, for professional and managerial households in the top income quintile. It is based on more than 50,000 prices covering almost 60 different items for which prices are collected three times a year by chambers of commerce, economic development organizations or university applied economic centers in each participating urban area. The numbers shown should be read as a percentage above or below the national average of 100. For example, a value of 115.4 in the groceries column indicates that grocery prices are 15.4% higher than the national average. Small differences in the index numbers should not be interpreted as significant; Figures cover the Tucson AZ urban area.
Source: The Council for Community and Economic Research, Cost of Living Index, 2020

Grocery Prices

Area[1]	T-Bone Steak ($/pound)	Frying Chicken ($/pound)	Whole Milk ($/half gal.)	Eggs ($/dozen)	Orange Juice ($/64 oz.)	Coffee ($/11.5 oz.)
City[2]	13.61	1.65	1.59	1.89	3.70	5.03
Avg.	11.78	1.39	2.05	1.47	3.57	4.34
Min.	8.03	0.94	1.03	0.74	2.94	3.02
Max.	15.86	2.65	4.31	3.77	5.44	8.69

*Note: (1) Values for the local area are compared with the average, minimum and maximum values for all 284 areas in the Cost of Living Index; (2) Figures cover the Tucson AZ urban area; **T-Bone Steak** (price per pound); **Frying Chicken** (price per pound, whole fryer); **Whole Milk** (half gallon carton); **Eggs** (price per dozen, Grade A, large); **Orange Juice** (64 oz. Tropicana or Florida Natural); **Coffee** (11.5 oz. can, vacuum-packed, Maxwell House, Hills Bros, or Folgers).*
Source: The Council for Community and Economic Research, Cost of Living Index, 2020

Housing and Utility Costs

Area[1]	New Home Price ($)	Apartment Rent ($/month)	All Electric ($/month)	Part Electric ($/month)	Other Energy ($/month)	Telephone ($/month)
City[2]	372,120	955	-	121.08	48.38	185.50
Avg.	368,594	1,168	170.86	100.47	65.28	184.30
Min.	190,567	502	91.58	31.42	26.08	169.60
Max.	2,227,806	4,738	470.38	280.31	280.06	206.50

*Note: (1) Values for the local area are compared with the average, minimum and maximum values for all 284 areas in the Cost of Living Index; (2) Figures cover the Tucson AZ urban area; **New Home Price** (2,400 sf living area, 8,000 sf lot, in urban area with full utilities); **Apartment Rent** (950 sf 2 bedroom/1.5 or 2 bath, unfurnished, excluding all utilities except water); **All Electric** (average monthly cost for an all-electric home); **Part Electric** (average monthly cost for a part-electric home); **Other Energy** (average monthly cost for natural gas, fuel oil, coal, wood, and any other forms of energy except electricity); **Telephone** (price includes the base monthly rate plus taxes and fees for three lines of mobile phone service).*
Source: The Council for Community and Economic Research, Cost of Living Index, 2020

Health Care, Transportation, and Other Costs

Area[1]	Doctor ($/visit)	Dentist ($/visit)	Optometrist ($/visit)	Gasoline ($/gallon)	Beauty Salon ($/visit)	Men's Shirt ($)
City[2]	138.05	91.20	96.00	2.14	51.51	49.50
Avg.	115.44	99.32	108.10	2.21	39.27	31.37
Min.	36.68	59.00	51.36	1.71	19.00	11.00
Max.	219.00	153.10	250.97	3.46	82.05	58.33

*Note: (1) Values for the local area are compared with the average, minimum and maximum values for all 284 areas in the Cost of Living Index; (2) Figures cover the Tucson AZ urban area; **Doctor** (general practitioners routine exam of an established patient); **Dentist** (adult teeth cleaning and periodic oral examination); **Optometrist** (full vision eye exam for established adult patient); **Gasoline** (one gallon regular unleaded, national brand, including all taxes, cash price at self-service pump if available); **Beauty Salon** (woman's shampoo, trim, and blow-dry); **Men's Shirt** (cotton/polyester dress shirt, pinpoint weave, long sleeves).*
Source: The Council for Community and Economic Research, Cost of Living Index, 2020

HOUSING

Homeownership Rate

Area	2012 (%)	2013 (%)	2014 (%)	2015 (%)	2016 (%)	2017 (%)	2018 (%)	2019 (%)	2020 (%)
MSA[1]	64.9	66.1	66.7	61.4	56.0	60.1	63.8	60.1	67.1
U.S.	65.4	65.1	64.5	63.7	63.4	63.9	64.4	64.6	66.6

Note: (1) Figures cover the Tucson, AZ Metropolitan Statistical Area
Source: U.S. Census Bureau, Housing Vacancies and Homeownership Annual Statistics: 2012-2020

House Price Index (HPI)

Area	National Ranking[2]	Quarterly Change (%)	One-Year Change (%)	Five-Year Change (%)	Since 1991Q1 (%)
MSA[1]	29	2.33	8.30	39.73	202.45
U.S.[3]	–	3.81	10.77	38.99	205.12

Note: The HPI is a weighted repeat sales index. It measures average price changes in repeat sales or refinancings on the same properties. This information is obtained by reviewing repeat mortgage transactions on single-family properties whose mortgages have been purchased or securitized by Fannie Mae or Freddie Mac since January 1975; (1) Figures cover the Tucson, AZ Metropolitan Statistical Area; (2) Rankings are based on annual percentage change for all metro areas containing at least 15,000 transactions over the last 10 years and ranges from 1 to 253; (3) figures based on a weighted average of Census Division estimates using a seasonally adjusted, purchase-only index; all figures are for the period ending December 31, 2020
Source: Federal Housing Finance Agency, Change in Metropolitan Area House Price Indexes, April 7, 2021

Median Single-Family Home Prices

Area	2018	2019	2020p	Percent Change 2019 to 2020
MSA[1]	223.0	238.9	265.1	11.0
U.S. Average	261.6	274.6	299.9	9.2

Note: Figures are median sales prices of existing single-family homes in thousands of dollars; (p) preliminary; (1) Figures cover the Tucson, AZ Metropolitan Statistical Area
Source: National Association of Realtors, Median Sales Price of Existing Single-Family Homes for Metropolitan Areas, 4th Quarter 2020

Qualifying Income Based on Median Sales Price of Existing Single-Family Homes

Area	With 5% Down ($)	With 10% Down ($)	With 20% Down ($)
MSA[1]	52,979	50,190	44,614
U.S. Average	59,266	56,147	49,908

Note: Figures are preliminary; Qualifying income is based on a mortgage rate of 2.81%. Monthly principal and interest payment is limited to 25% of income; (1) Figures cover the Tucson, AZ Metropolitan Statistical Area
Source: National Association of Realtors, Qualifying Income Based on Median Sales Price of Existing Single-Family Homes for Metropolitan Areas, 4th Quarter 2020

Home Value Distribution

Area	Under $50,000	$50,000 -$99,999	$100,000 -$149,999	$150,000 -$199,999	$200,000 -$299,999	$300,000 -$499,999	$500,000 -$999,999	$1,000,000 or more
City	10.6	13.5	22.6	24.6	19.6	6.8	1.9	0.3
MSA[1]	8.4	10.7	16.2	19.9	22.5	15.4	5.8	1.0
U.S.	6.9	12.0	13.3	14.0	19.6	19.3	11.4	3.4

Note: Figures are percentages and cover owner-occupied housing units; (1) Figures cover the Tucson, AZ Metropolitan Statistical Area
Source: U.S. Census Bureau, 2015-2019 American Community Survey 5-Year Estimates

Year Housing Structure Built

Area	2010 or Later	2000 -2009	1990 -1999	1980 -1989	1970 -1979	1960 -1969	1950 -1959	1940 -1949	Before 1940	Median Year
City	2.6	12.6	13.4	16.2	21.4	11.5	14.8	3.9	3.7	1978
MSA[1]	4.5	18.6	17.5	17.8	19.6	8.5	8.9	2.5	2.2	1985
U.S.	5.2	14.0	13.9	13.4	15.2	10.6	10.3	4.9	12.6	1978

Note: Figures are percentages except for Median Year; Note: (1) Figures cover the Tucson, AZ Metropolitan Statistical Area
Source: U.S. Census Bureau, 2015-2019 American Community Survey 5-Year Estimates

Gross Monthly Rent

Area	Under $500	$500 -$999	$1,000 -$1,499	$1,500 -$1,999	$2,000 -$2,499	$2,500 -$2,999	$3,000 and up	Median ($)
City	7.9	57.2	27.6	5.4	1.1	0.4	0.5	846
MSA[1]	7.2	51.4	30.9	7.5	1.6	0.7	0.8	907
U.S.	9.4	36.2	30.0	14.0	5.6	2.4	2.4	1,062

Note: Figures are percentages except for Median; Gross rent is the contract rent plus the estimated average monthly cost of utilities (electricity, gas, and water and sewer) and fuels (oil, coal, kerosene, wood, etc.) if these are paid by the renter (or paid for the renter by someone else); (1) Figures cover the Tucson, AZ Metropolitan Statistical Area
Source: U.S. Census Bureau, 2015-2019 American Community Survey 5-Year Estimates

HEALTH

Health Risk Factors

Category	MSA[1] (%)	U.S. (%)
Adults aged 18–64 who have any kind of health care coverage	n/a	87.3
Adults who reported being in good or better health	n/a	82.4
Adults who have been told they have high blood cholesterol	n/a	33.0
Adults who have been told they have high blood pressure	n/a	32.3
Adults who are current smokers	n/a	17.1
Adults who currently use E-cigarettes	n/a	4.6
Adults who currently use chewing tobacco, snuff, or snus	n/a	4.0
Adults who are heavy drinkers[2]	n/a	6.3
Adults who are binge drinkers[3]	n/a	17.4
Adults who are overweight (BMI 25.0 - 29.9)	n/a	35.3
Adults who are obese (BMI 30.0 - 99.8)	n/a	31.3
Adults who participated in any physical activities in the past month	n/a	74.4
Adults who always or nearly always wears a seat belt	n/a	94.3

Note: n/a not available; (1) Figures cover the Tucson, AZ Metropolitan Statistical Area; (2) Heavy drinkers are classified as adult men having more than 14 drinks per week and adult women having more than 7 drinks per week; (3) Binge drinkers are classified as males having five or more drinks on one occasion or females having four or more drinks on one occasion
Source: Centers for Disease Control and Prevention, Behaviorial Risk Factor Surveillance System, SMART: Selected Metropolitan Area Risk Trends, 2017

Acute and Chronic Health Conditions

Category	MSA[1] (%)	U.S. (%)
Adults who have ever been told they had a heart attack	n/a	4.2
Adults who have ever been told they have angina or coronary heart disease	n/a	3.9
Adults who have ever been told they had a stroke	n/a	3.0
Adults who have ever been told they have asthma	n/a	14.2
Adults who have ever been told they have arthritis	n/a	24.9
Adults who have ever been told they have diabetes[2]	n/a	10.5
Adults who have ever been told they had skin cancer	n/a	6.2
Adults who have ever been told they had any other types of cancer	n/a	7.1
Adults who have ever been told they have COPD	n/a	6.5
Adults who have ever been told they have kidney disease	n/a	3.0
Adults who have ever been told they have a form of depression	n/a	20.5

Note: n/a not available; (1) Figures cover the Tucson, AZ Metropolitan Statistical Area; (2) Figures do not include pregnancy-related, borderline, or pre-diabetes
Source: Centers for Disease Control and Prevention, Behaviorial Risk Factor Surveillance System, SMART: Selected Metropolitan Area Risk Trends, 2017

Health Screening and Vaccination Rates

Category	MSA[1] (%)	U.S. (%)
Adults aged 65+ who have had flu shot within the past year	n/a	60.7
Adults aged 65+ who have ever had a pneumonia vaccination	n/a	75.4
Adults who have ever been tested for HIV	n/a	36.1
Adults who have ever had the shingles or zoster vaccine?	n/a	28.9
Adults who have had their blood cholesterol checked within the last five years	n/a	85.9

Note: n/a not available; (1) Figures cover the Tucson, AZ Metropolitan Statistical Area.
Source: Centers for Disease Control and Prevention, Behaviorial Risk Factor Surveillance System, SMART: Selected Metropolitan Area Risk Trends, 2017

Disability Status

Category	MSA[1] (%)	U.S. (%)
Adults who reported being deaf	n/a	6.7
Are you blind or have serious difficulty seeing, even when wearing glasses?	n/a	4.5
Are you limited in any way in any of your usual activities due of arthritis?	n/a	12.9
Do you have difficulty doing errands alone?	n/a	6.8
Do you have difficulty dressing or bathing?	n/a	3.6
Do you have serious difficulty concentrating/remembering/making decisions?	n/a	10.7
Do you have serious difficulty walking or climbing stairs?	n/a	13.6

Note: n/a not available; (1) Figures cover the Tucson, AZ Metropolitan Statistical Area.
Source: Centers for Disease Control and Prevention, Behaviorial Risk Factor Surveillance System, SMART: Selected Metropolitan Area Risk Trends, 2017

Mortality Rates for the Top 10 Causes of Death in the U.S.

ICD-10[a] Sub-Chapter	ICD-10[a] Code	Age-Adjusted Mortality Rate[1] per 100,000 population	
		County[2]	U.S.
Malignant neoplasms	C00-C97	135.7	149.2
Ischaemic heart diseases	I20-I25	83.9	90.5
Other forms of heart disease	I30-I51	31.2	52.2
Chronic lower respiratory diseases	J40-J47	39.2	39.6
Other degenerative diseases of the nervous system	G30-G31	48.5	37.6
Cerebrovascular diseases	I60-I69	33.2	37.2
Other external causes of accidental injury	W00-X59	43.9	36.1
Organic, including symptomatic, mental disorders	F01-F09	14.2	29.4
Hypertensive diseases	I10-I15	23.9	24.1
Diabetes mellitus	E10-E14	25.5	21.5

Note: (a) ICD-10 = International Classification of Diseases 10th Revision; (1) Mortality rates are a three-year average covering 2017-2019; (2) Figures cover Pima County.
Source: Centers for Disease Control and Prevention, National Center for Health Statistics. Underlying Cause of Death 1999-2019 on CDC WONDER Online Database

Mortality Rates for Selected Causes of Death

ICD-10[a] Sub-Chapter	ICD-10[a] Code	Age-Adjusted Mortality Rate[1] per 100,000 population	
		County[2]	U.S.
Assault	X85-Y09	7.3	6.0
Diseases of the liver	K70-K76	19.4	14.4
Human immunodeficiency virus (HIV) disease	B20-B24	1.1	1.5
Influenza and pneumonia	J09-J18	11.7	13.8
Intentional self-harm	X60-X84	20.5	14.1
Malnutrition	E40-E46	3.8	2.3
Obesity and other hyperalimentation	E65-E68	3.3	2.1
Renal failure	N17-N19	8.2	12.6
Transport accidents	V01-V99	13.4	12.3
Viral hepatitis	B15-B19	2.2	1.2

Note: (a) ICD-10 = International Classification of Diseases 10th Revision; (1) Mortality rates are a three-year average covering 2017-2019; (2) Figures cover Pima County; Data are suppressed when the data meet the criteria for confidentiality constraints; Mortality rates are flagged as unreliable when the rate would be calculated with a numerator of 20 or less.
Source: Centers for Disease Control and Prevention, National Center for Health Statistics. Underlying Cause of Death 1999-2019 on CDC WONDER Online Database

Health Insurance Coverage

Area	With Health Insurance	With Private Health Insurance	With Public Health Insurance	Without Health Insurance	Population Under Age 19 Without Health Insurance
City	88.5	56.5	42.8	11.5	8.1
MSA[1]	90.8	62.2	42.6	9.2	7.1
U.S.	91.2	67.9	35.1	8.8	5.1

Note: Figures are percentages that cover the civilian noninstitutionalized population; (1) Figures cover the Tucson, AZ Metropolitan Statistical Area
Source: U.S. Census Bureau, 2015-2019 American Community Survey 5-Year Estimates

Number of Medical Professionals

Area	MDs[3]	DOs[3,4]	Dentists	Podiatrists	Chiropractors	Optometrists
County[1] (number)	3,751	255	682	57	200	167
County[1] (rate[2])	361.9	24.6	65.1	5.4	19.1	15.9
U.S. (rate[2])	282.9	22.7	71.2	6.2	28.1	16.9

04019
Note: Data as of 2019 unless noted; (1) Data covers Pima County; (2) Rate per 100,000 population; (3) Data as of 2018 and includes all active, non-federal physicians; (4) Doctor of Osteopathic Medicine
Source: U.S. Department of Health and Human Services, Health Resources and Services Administration, Bureau of Health Professions, Area Resource File (ARF) 2019-2020

EDUCATION

Public School District Statistics

District Name	Schls	Pupils	Pupil/ Teacher Ratio	Minority Pupils[1] (%)	Free Lunch Eligible[2] (%)	IEP[3] (%)
Amphitheater Unified District	22	13,658	17.6	55.8	39.8	17.5
Arizona Community Dev. Corp.	3	2,031	n/a	77.0	60.7	10.4
Catalina Foothills Unified District	8	5,427	19.0	41.3	9.0	8.8
Flowing Wells Unified District	11	5,650	19.5	71.8	59.6	15.8
Leman Academy of Excellence	6	3,139	n/a	46.2	n/a	8.0
Sunnyside Unified District	23	16,154	19.9	96.3	72.6	12.0
Tanque Verde Unified District	4	2,103	17.2	26.1	9.0	14.2
Tucson Unified District	88	45,560	17.5	79.8	55.5	14.9

Note: Table includes school districts with 2,000 or more students; (1) Percentage of students that are not non-Hispanic white; (2) Percentage of students that are eligible for the free lunch program; (3) Percentage of students that have an Individualized Education Program.
Source: U.S. Department of Education, National Center for Education Statistics, Common Core of Data, Local Education Agency (School District) Universe Survey: School Year 2018-2019; U.S. Department of Education, National Center for Education Statistics, Common Core of Data, Public Elementary/Secondary School Universe Survey: School Year 2018-2019

Best High Schools

According to *U.S. News,* Tucson is home to two of the top 500 high schools in the U.S.: **University High School (Tucson)** (#22); **BASIS Tucson North** (#48). Nearly 18,000 public, magnet and charter schools were ranked based on their performance on state assessments and how well they prepare students for college. *U.S. News & World Report, "Best High Schools 2020"*

Highest Level of Education

Area	Less than H.S.	H.S. Diploma	Some College, No Deg.	Associate Degree	Bachelor's Degree	Master's Degree	Prof. School Degree	Doctorate Degree
City	15.0	23.6	25.6	8.4	16.5	7.8	1.4	1.6
MSA[1]	11.6	22.2	25.1	8.7	18.7	9.4	2.3	2.0
U.S.	12.0	27.0	20.4	8.5	19.8	8.8	2.1	1.4

Note: Figures cover persons age 25 and over; (1) Figures cover the Tucson, AZ Metropolitan Statistical Area
Source: U.S. Census Bureau, 2015-2019 American Community Survey 5-Year Estimates

Educational Attainment by Race

Area	High School Graduate or Higher (%)					Bachelor's Degree or Higher (%)				
	Total	White	Black	Asian	Hisp.[2]	Total	White	Black	Asian	Hisp.[2]
City	85.0	88.0	84.3	86.7	72.7	27.4	30.1	21.3	48.0	14.0
MSA[1]	88.4	90.9	87.6	88.0	75.8	32.4	35.1	25.6	53.1	16.3
U.S.	88.0	89.9	86.0	87.1	68.7	32.1	33.5	21.6	54.3	16.4

Note: Figures shown cover persons 25 years old and over; (1) Figures cover the Tucson, AZ Metropolitan Statistical Area; (2) People of Hispanic origin can be of any race
Source: U.S. Census Bureau, 2015-2019 American Community Survey 5-Year Estimates

School Enrollment by Grade and Control

Area	Preschool (%)		Kindergarten (%)		Grades 1 - 4 (%)		Grades 5 - 8 (%)		Grades 9 - 12 (%)	
	Public	Private	Public	Private	Public	Private	Public	Private	Public	Private
City	74.0	26.0	85.8	14.2	89.6	10.4	91.3	8.7	92.8	7.2
MSA[1]	65.7	34.3	87.8	12.2	90.4	9.6	90.1	9.9	92.1	7.9
U.S.	59.1	40.9	87.6	12.4	89.5	10.5	89.4	10.6	90.1	9.9

Note: Figures shown cover persons 3 years old and over; (1) Figures cover the Tucson, AZ Metropolitan Statistical Area
Source: U.S. Census Bureau, 2015-2019 American Community Survey 5-Year Estimates

Higher Education

Four-Year Colleges			Two-Year Colleges			Medical Schools[1]	Law Schools[2]	Voc/ Tech[3]
Public	Private Non-profit	Private For-profit	Public	Private Non-profit	Private For-profit			
1	1	3	1	0	1	1	1	8

Note: Figures cover institutions located within the city limits and include main campuses only; (1) includes schools accredited by the Liaison Committee on Medical Education and the American Osteopathic Association's Commission on Osteopathic College Accreditation; (2) includes ABA-accredited schools, schools with provisional ABA accreditation, and state accredited schools; (3) includes all schools with programs that are less than 2 years.
Source: National Center for Education Statistics, Integrated Postsecondary Education System (IPEDS), 2019-20; Wikipedia, List of Medical Schools in the United States, accessed April 2, 2021; Wikipedia, List of Law Schools in the United States, accessed April 2, 2021

According to *U.S. News & World Report,* the Tucson, AZ metro area is home to one of the top 200 national universities in the U.S.: **University of Arizona** (#97 tie). The indicators used to capture academic quality fall into a number of categories: assessment by administrators at peer institutions; retention of students; faculty resources; student selectivity; financial resources; alumni giving; high school counselor ratings of colleges; and graduation rate. *U.S. News & World Report, "America's Best Colleges 2021"*

According to *U.S. News & World Report,* the Tucson, AZ metro area is home to one of the top 100 law schools in the U.S.: **University of Arizona (Rogers)** (#46 tie). The rankings are based on a weighted average of 12 measures of quality: peer assessment score; assessment score by lawyers/judges; median LSAT scores; median undergrad GPA; acceptance rate; employment rates for graduates; placement success; bar passage rate; faculty resources; expenditures per student; student/faculty ratio; and library resources. *U.S. News & World Report, "America's Best Graduate Schools, Law, 2022"*

According to *U.S. News & World Report,* the Tucson, AZ metro area is home to one of the top 75 medical schools for research in the U.S.: **University of Arizona—Tucson** (#70 tie). The rankings are based on a weighted average of 11 measures of quality: quality assessment; peer assessment score; assessment score by residency directors; research activity; total research activity; average research activity per faculty member; student selectivity; median MCAT total score; median undergraduate GPA; acceptance rate; and faculty resources. *U.S. News & World Report, "America's Best Graduate Schools, Medical, 2022"*

According to *U.S. News & World Report,* the Tucson, AZ metro area is home to one of the top 75 business schools in the U.S.: **University of Arizona (Eller)** (#64 tie). The rankings are based on a weighted average of the following nine measures: quality assessment; peer assessment; recruiter assessment; placement success; mean starting salary and bonus; student selectivity; mean GMAT and GRE scores; mean undergraduate GPA; and acceptance rate. *U.S. News & World Report, "America's Best Graduate Schools, Business, 2022"*

EMPLOYERS

Major Employers

Company Name	Industry
Banner University Medical Center Tucson	General medical & surgical hospitals
Davis-Monthan Air Force Base	U.S. military
Freeport-McMoran Copper & Gold	Mining
Pima County	County government
Raytheon Missile Systems	Missile systems
State of Arizona	State government
Tucson Unified School District	School districts
U.S. Customs and Border Protection	Federal government
University of Arizona	Public research university
Wal-Mart Stores	Retail stores

Note: Companies shown are located within the Tucson, AZ Metropolitan Statistical Area.
Source: Hoovers.com; Wikipedia

PUBLIC SAFETY

Crime Rate

Area	All Crimes	Violent Crimes				Property Crimes		
		Murder	Rape[3]	Robbery	Aggrav. Assault	Burglary	Larceny -Theft	Motor Vehicle Theft
City	3,960.4	7.3	96.1	201.5	383.5	455.3	2,406.4	410.3
Suburbs[1]	2,634.2	3.2	25.3	38.5	115.5	349.9	1,905.9	195.9
Metro[2]	3,328.8	5.3	62.4	123.9	255.9	405.1	2,168.0	308.2
U.S.	2,489.3	5.0	42.6	81.6	250.2	340.5	1,549.5	219.9

Note: Figures are crimes per 100,000 population; (1) All areas within the metro area that are located outside the city limits; (2) Figures cover the Tucson, AZ Metropolitan Statistical Area; (3) All figures shown were reported using the revised Uniform Crime Reporting (UCR) definition of rape.
Source: FBI Uniform Crime Reports, 2019

Hate Crimes

Area	Number of Quarters Reported	Number of Incidents per Bias Motivation					
		Race/Ethnicity/ Ancestry	Religion	Sexual Orientation	Disability	Gender	Gender Identity
City	4	6	6	4	0	0	0
U.S.	4	3,963	1,521	1,195	157	69	198

Source: Federal Bureau of Investigation, Hate Crime Statistics 2019

Identity Theft Consumer Reports

Area	Reports	Reports per 100,000 Population	Rank[2]
MSA[1]	3,410	326	109
U.S.	1,387,615	423	-

Note: (1) Figures cover the Tucson, AZ Metropolitan Statistical Area; (2) Rank ranges from 1 to 391 where 1 indicates greatest number of identity theft reports per 100,000 population
Source: Federal Trade Commission, Consumer Sentinel Network Data Book 2020

Fraud and Other Consumer Reports

Area	Reports	Reports per 100,000 Population	Rank[2]
MSA[1]	9,091	868	62
U.S.	3,385,133	1,031	-

Note: (1) Figures cover the Tucson, AZ Metropolitan Statistical Area; (2) Rank ranges from 1 to 391 where 1 indicates greatest number of fraud and other consumer reports per 100,000 population
Source: Federal Trade Commission, Consumer Sentinel Network Data Book 2020

POLITICS

2020 Presidential Election Results

Area	Biden	Trump	Jorgensen	Hawkins	Other
Pima County	58.4	39.8	1.5	0.0	0.3
U.S.	51.3	46.8	1.2	0.3	0.5

Note: Results are percentages and may not add to 100% due to rounding
Source: Dave Leip's Atlas of U.S. Presidential Elections

SPORTS

Professional Sports Teams

Team Name	League	Year Established

No teams are located in the metro area
Source: Wikipedia, Major Professional Sports Teams of the United States and Canada, April 6, 2021

CLIMATE

Average and Extreme Temperatures

Temperature	Jan	Feb	Mar	Apr	May	Jun	Jul	Aug	Sep	Oct	Nov	Dec	Yr.
Extreme High (°F)	87	92	99	104	107	117	114	108	107	101	90	84	117
Average High (°F)	64	68	73	81	89	99	99	96	94	84	73	65	82
Average Temp. (°F)	51	54	59	66	74	84	86	84	81	71	59	52	69
Average Low (°F)	38	40	44	51	58	68	74	72	67	57	45	39	55
Extreme Low (°F)	16	20	20	33	38	47	62	61	44	26	24	16	16

Note: Figures cover the years 1946-1990
Source: National Climatic Data Center, International Station Meteorological Climate Summary, 9/96

Average Precipitation/Snowfall/Humidity

Precip./Humidity	Jan	Feb	Mar	Apr	May	Jun	Jul	Aug	Sep	Oct	Nov	Dec	Yr.
Avg. Precip. (in.)	0.9	0.7	0.7	0.3	0.1	0.2	2.5	2.2	1.4	0.9	0.6	0.9	11.6
Avg. Snowfall (in.)	Tr	Tr	Tr	Tr	0	0	0	0	0	0	Tr	Tr	2
Avg. Rel. Hum. 5am (%)	62	58	52	41	34	32	58	65	55	52	54	61	52
Avg. Rel. Hum. 5pm (%)	31	26	22	16	13	13	29	32	26	24	27	33	24

Note: Figures cover the years 1946-1990; Tr = Trace amounts (<0.05 in. of rain; <0.5 in. of snow)
Source: National Climatic Data Center, International Station Meteorological Climate Summary, 9/96

Weather Conditions

Temperature			Daytime Sky			Precipitation		
10°F & below	32°F & below	90°F & above	Clear	Partly cloudy	Cloudy	0.01 inch or more precip.	0.1 inch or more snow/ice	Thunder-storms
0	18	140	177	119	69	54	2	42

Note: Figures are average number of days per year and cover the years 1946-1990
Source: National Climatic Data Center, International Station Meteorological Climate Summary, 9/96

HAZARDOUS WASTE

Superfund Sites

The Tucson, AZ metro area is home to one site on the EPA's Superfund National Priorities List: **Tucson International Airport Area** (final). There are a total of 1,375 Superfund sites with a status of proposed or final on the list in the U.S. *U.S. Environmental Protection Agency, National Priorities List, April 7, 2021*

AIR QUALITY

Air Quality Trends: Ozone

	1990	1995	2000	2005	2010	2015	2016	2017	2018	2019
MSA[1]	0.073	0.078	0.074	0.075	0.068	0.065	0.065	0.070	0.069	0.065
U.S.	0.088	0.089	0.088	0.080	0.073	0.068	0.069	0.068	0.069	0.065

Note: (1) Data covers the Tucson, AZ Metropolitan Statistical Area. The values shown are the composite ozone concentration averages among trend sites based on the highest fourth daily maximum 8-hour concentration in parts per million. These trends are based on sites having an adequate record of monitoring data during the trend period. Data from exceptional events are included.
Source: U.S. Environmental Protection Agency, Air Quality Monitoring Information, "Air Quality Trends by City, 1990-2019"

Air Quality Index

Area	Percent of Days when Air Quality was...[2]					AQI Statistics[2]	
	Good	Moderate	Unhealthy for Sensitive Groups	Unhealthy	Very Unhealthy	Maximum	Median
MSA[1]	61.6	37.8	0.5	0.0	0.0	103	47

Note: (1) Data covers the Tucson, AZ Metropolitan Statistical Area; (2) Based on 365 days with AQI data in 2019. Air Quality Index (AQI) is an index for reporting daily air quality. EPA calculates the AQI for five major air pollutants regulated by the Clean Air Act: ground-level ozone, particle pollution (aka particulate matter), carbon monoxide, sulfur dioxide, and nitrogen dioxide. The AQI runs from 0 to 500. The higher the AQI value, the greater the level of air pollution and the greater the health concern. There are six AQI categories: "Good" AQI is between 0 and 50. Air quality is considered satisfactory; "Moderate" AQI is between 51 and 100. Air quality is acceptable; "Unhealthy for Sensitive Groups" When AQI values are between 101 and 150, members of sensitive groups may experience health effects; "Unhealthy" When AQI values are between 151 and 200 everyone may begin to experience health effects; "Very Unhealthy" AQI values between 201 and 300 trigger a health alert; "Hazardous" AQI values over 300 trigger warnings of emergency conditions (not shown).
Source: U.S. Environmental Protection Agency, Air Quality Index Report, 2019

Air Quality Index Pollutants

Area	Percent of Days when AQI Pollutant was...[2]					
	Carbon Monoxide	Nitrogen Dioxide	Ozone	Sulfur Dioxide	Particulate Matter 2.5	Particulate Matter 10
MSA[1]	0.0	0.3	71.5	0.0	5.5	22.7

Note: (1) Data covers the Tucson, AZ Metropolitan Statistical Area; (2) Based on 365 days with AQI data in 2019. The Air Quality Index (AQI) is an index for reporting daily air quality. EPA calculates the AQI for five major air pollutants regulated by the Clean Air Act: ground-level ozone, particle pollution (also known as particulate matter), carbon monoxide, sulfur dioxide, and nitrogen dioxide. The AQI runs from 0 to 500. The higher the AQI value, the greater the level of air pollution and the greater the health concern.
Source: U.S. Environmental Protection Agency, Air Quality Index Report, 2019

Maximum Air Pollutant Concentrations: Particulate Matter, Ozone, CO and Lead

	Particulate Matter 10 (ug/m^3)	Particulate Matter 2.5 Wtd AM (ug/m^3)	Particulate Matter 2.5 24-Hr (ug/m^3)	Ozone (ppm)	Carbon Monoxide (ppm)	Lead (ug/m^3)
MSA[1] Level	139	3.8	9	0.065	1	n/a
NAAQS[2]	150	15	35	0.075	9	0.15
Met NAAQS[2]	Yes	Yes	Yes	Yes	Yes	n/a

Note: (1) Data covers the Tucson, AZ Metropolitan Statistical Area; Data from exceptional events are included; (2) National Ambient Air Quality Standards; ppm = parts per million; ug/m^3 = micrograms per cubic meter; n/a not available.
Concentrations: Particulate Matter 10 (coarse particulate)—highest second maximum 24-hour concentration; Particulate Matter 2.5 Wtd AM (fine particulate)—highest weighted annual mean concentration; Particulate Matter 2.5 24-Hour (fine particulate)—highest 98th percentile 24-hour concentration; Ozone—highest fourth daily maximum 8-hour concentration; Carbon Monoxide—highest second maximum non-overlapping 8-hour concentration; Lead—maximum running 3-month average
Source: U.S. Environmental Protection Agency, Air Quality Monitoring Information, "Air Quality Statistics by City, 2019"

Maximum Air Pollutant Concentrations: Nitrogen Dioxide and Sulfur Dioxide

	Nitrogen Dioxide AM (ppb)	Nitrogen Dioxide 1-Hr (ppb)	Sulfur Dioxide AM (ppb)	Sulfur Dioxide 1-Hr (ppb)	Sulfur Dioxide 24-Hr (ppb)
MSA[1] Level	7	30	n/a	1	n/a
NAAQS[2]	53	100	30	75	140
Met NAAQS[2]	Yes	Yes	n/a	Yes	n/a

Note: (1) Data covers the Tucson, AZ Metropolitan Statistical Area; Data from exceptional events are included; (2) National Ambient Air Quality Standards; ppm = parts per million; ug/m^3 = micrograms per cubic meter; n/a not available.
Concentrations: Nitrogen Dioxide AM—highest arithmetic mean concentration; Nitrogen Dioxide 1-Hr—highest 98th percentile 1-hour daily maximum concentration; Sulfur Dioxide AM—highest annual mean concentration; Sulfur Dioxide 1-Hr—highest 99th percentile 1-hour daily maximum concentration; Sulfur Dioxide 24-Hr—highest second maximum 24-hour concentration
Source: U.S. Environmental Protection Agency, Air Quality Monitoring Information, "Air Quality Statistics by City, 2019"

Appendixes

Appendixes

Appendix A: Comparative Statistics

Table of Contents

Population Growth: City

Area	1990 Census	2000 Census	2010 Census	2019* Estimate	Population Growth (%)	
					1990-2019	2010-2019
Albuquerque, NM	388,375	448,607	545,852	559,374	44.0	2.5
Allentown, PA	105,066	106,632	118,032	120,915	15.1	2.4
Anchorage, AK	226,338	260,283	291,826	293,531	29.7	0.6
Ann Arbor, MI	111,018	114,024	113,934	120,735	8.8	6.0
Athens, GA	86,561	100,266	115,452	124,719	44.1	8.0
Atlanta, GA	394,092	416,474	420,003	488,800	24.0	16.4
Austin, TX	499,053	656,562	790,390	950,807	90.5	20.3
Baton Rouge, LA	223,299	227,818	229,493	224,149	0.4	-2.3
Boise City, ID	144,317	185,787	205,671	226,115	56.7	9.9
Boston, MA	574,283	589,141	617,594	684,379	19.2	10.8
Boulder, CO	87,737	94,673	97,385	106,392	21.3	9.2
Cape Coral, FL	75,507	102,286	154,305	183,942	143.6	19.2
Cedar Rapids, IA	110,829	120,758	126,326	132,301	19.4	4.7
Charleston, SC	96,102	96,650	120,083	135,257	40.7	12.6
Charlotte, NC	428,283	540,828	731,424	857,425	100.2	17.2
Chicago, IL	2,783,726	2,896,016	2,695,598	2,709,534	-2.7	0.5
Cincinnati, OH	363,974	331,285	296,943	301,394	-17.2	1.5
Clarksville, TN	78,569	103,455	132,929	152,934	94.6	15.0
Cleveland, OH	505,333	478,403	396,815	385,282	-23.8	-2.9
College Station, TX	53,318	67,890	93,857	113,686	113.2	21.1
Colorado Springs, CO	283,798	360,890	416,427	464,871	63.8	11.6
Columbia, MO	71,069	84,531	108,500	121,230	70.6	11.7
Columbia, SC	115,475	116,278	129,272	133,273	15.4	3.1
Columbus, OH	648,656	711,470	787,033	878,553	35.4	11.6
Dallas, TX	1,006,971	1,188,580	1,197,816	1,330,612	32.1	11.1
Davenport, IA	95,705	98,359	99,685	102,169	6.8	2.5
Denver, CO	467,153	554,636	600,158	705,576	51.0	17.6
Des Moines, IA	193,569	198,682	203,433	215,636	11.4	6.0
Durham, NC	151,737	187,035	228,330	269,702	77.7	18.1
Edison, NJ	88,680	97,687	99,967	100,447	13.3	0.5
El Paso, TX	515,541	563,662	649,121	679,813	31.9	4.7
Fargo, ND	74,372	90,599	105,549	121,889	63.9	15.5
Fayetteville, NC	118,247	121,015	200,564	210,432	78.0	4.9
Fort Collins, CO	89,555	118,652	143,986	165,609	84.9	15.0
Fort Wayne, IN	205,671	205,727	253,691	265,752	29.2	4.8
Fort Worth, TX	448,311	534,694	741,206	874,401	95.0	18.0
Grand Rapids, MI	189,145	197,800	188,040	198,401	4.9	5.5
Greeley, CO	60,887	76,930	92,889	105,888	73.9	14.0
Green Bay, WI	96,466	102,313	104,057	104,777	8.6	0.7
Greensboro, NC	193,389	223,891	269,666	291,303	50.6	8.0
Honolulu, HI	376,465	371,657	337,256	348,985	-7.3	3.5
Houston, TX	1,697,610	1,953,631	2,099,451	2,310,432	36.1	10.0
Huntsville, AL	161,842	158,216	180,105	196,219	21.2	8.9
Indianapolis, IN	730,993	781,870	820,445	864,447	18.3	5.4
Jacksonville, FL	635,221	735,617	821,784	890,467	40.2	8.4
Kansas City, MO	434,967	441,545	459,787	486,404	11.8	5.8
Lafayette, LA	104,735	110,257	120,623	126,666	20.9	5.0
Lakeland, FL	73,375	78,452	97,422	107,922	47.1	10.8
Las Vegas, NV	261,374	478,434	583,756	634,773	142.9	8.7
Lexington, KY	225,366	260,512	295,803	320,601	42.3	8.4
Lincoln, NE	193,629	225,581	258,379	283,839	46.6	9.9
Little Rock, AR	177,519	183,133	193,524	197,958	11.5	2.3
Los Angeles, CA	3,487,671	3,694,820	3,792,621	3,966,936	13.7	4.6
Louisville, KY	269,160	256,231	597,337	617,790	129.5	3.4
Madison, WI	193,451	208,054	233,209	254,977	31.8	9.3

Table continued on following page.

Area	1990 Census	2000 Census	2010 Census	2019* Estimate	Population Growth (%) 1990-2019	Population Growth (%) 2010-2019
Manchester, NH	99,567	107,006	109,565	112,109	12.6	2.3
Memphis, TN	660,536	650,100	646,889	651,932	-1.3	0.8
Miami, FL	358,843	362,470	399,457	454,279	26.6	13.7
Midland, TX	89,358	94,996	111,147	138,549	55.0	24.7
Milwaukee, WI	628,095	596,974	594,833	594,548	-5.3	0.0
Minneapolis, MN	368,383	382,618	382,578	420,324	14.1	9.9
Nashville, TN	488,364	545,524	601,222	663,750	35.9	10.4
New Haven, CT	130,474	123,626	129,779	130,331	-0.1	0.4
New Orleans, LA	496,938	484,674	343,829	390,845	-21.3	13.7
New York, NY	7,322,552	8,008,278	8,175,133	8,419,316	15.0	3.0
Oklahoma City, OK	445,065	506,132	579,999	643,692	44.6	11.0
Omaha, NE	371,972	390,007	408,958	475,862	27.9	16.4
Orlando, FL	161,172	185,951	238,300	280,832	74.2	17.8
Peoria, IL	114,341	112,936	115,007	113,532	-0.7	-1.3
Philadelphia, PA	1,585,577	1,517,550	1,526,006	1,579,075	-0.4	3.5
Phoenix, AZ	989,873	1,321,045	1,445,632	1,633,017	65.0	13.0
Pittsburgh, PA	369,785	334,563	305,704	302,205	-18.3	-1.1
Portland, OR	485,833	529,121	583,776	645,291	32.8	10.5
Providence, RI	160,734	173,618	178,042	179,494	11.7	0.8
Provo, UT	87,148	105,166	112,488	116,403	33.6	3.5
Raleigh, NC	226,841	276,093	403,892	464,485	104.8	15.0
Reno, NV	139,950	180,480	225,221	246,500	76.1	9.4
Richmond, VA	202,783	197,790	204,214	226,622	11.8	11.0
Riverside, CA	226,232	255,166	303,871	326,414	44.3	7.4
Rochester, MN	74,151	85,806	106,769	115,557	55.8	8.2
Sacramento, CA	368,923	407,018	466,488	500,930	35.8	7.4
Salt Lake City, UT	159,796	181,743	186,440	197,756	23.8	6.1
San Antonio, TX	997,258	1,144,646	1,327,407	1,508,083	51.2	13.6
San Diego, CA	1,111,048	1,223,400	1,307,402	1,409,573	26.9	7.8
San Francisco, CA	723,959	776,733	805,235	874,961	20.9	8.7
San Jose, CA	784,324	894,943	945,942	1,027,690	31.0	8.6
Santa Rosa, CA	123,297	147,595	167,815	179,701	45.7	7.1
Savannah, GA	138,038	131,510	136,286	145,403	5.3	6.7
Seattle, WA	516,262	563,374	608,660	724,305	40.3	19.0
Sioux Falls, SD	102,262	123,975	153,888	177,117	73.2	15.1
Springfield, IL	108,997	111,454	116,250	115,888	6.3	-0.3
Tallahassee, FL	128,014	150,624	181,376	191,279	49.4	5.5
Tampa, FL	279,960	303,447	335,709	387,916	38.6	15.6
Tucson, AZ	417,942	486,699	520,116	541,482	29.6	4.1
Tulsa, OK	367,241	393,049	391,906	402,324	9.6	2.7
Tuscaloosa, AL	81,075	77,906	90,468	99,390	22.6	9.9
Virginia Beach, VA	393,069	425,257	437,994	450,201	14.5	2.8
Washington, DC	606,900	572,059	601,723	692,683	14.1	15.1
Wichita, KS	313,693	344,284	382,368	389,877	24.3	2.0
Winston-Salem, NC	168,139	185,776	229,617	244,115	45.2	6.3
U.S.	248,709,873	281,421,906	308,745,538	324,697,795	30.6	5.2

Note: (*) 2014-2019 5-year estimated population
Source: U.S. Census Bureau, 1990 Census, Census 2000, Census 2010, 2015-2019 American Community Survey 5-Year Estimates

Population Growth: Metro Area

Area	1990 Census	2000 Census	2010 Census	2019* Estimate	Population Growth (%) 1990-2019	2010-2019
Albuquerque, NM	599,416	729,649	887,077	912,108	52.2	2.8
Allentown, PA	686,666	740,395	821,173	837,610	22.0	2.0
Anchorage, AK	266,021	319,605	380,821	398,900	50.0	4.7
Ann Arbor, MI	282,937	322,895	344,791	367,000	29.7	6.4
Athens, GA	136,025	166,079	192,541	208,457	53.2	8.3
Atlanta, GA	3,069,411	4,247,981	5,268,860	5,862,424	91.0	11.3
Austin, TX	846,217	1,249,763	1,716,289	2,114,441	149.9	23.2
Baton Rouge, LA	623,853	705,973	802,484	854,318	36.9	6.5
Boise City, ID	319,596	464,840	616,561	710,743	122.4	15.3
Boston, MA	4,133,895	4,391,344	4,552,402	4,832,346	16.9	6.1
Boulder, CO	208,898	269,758	294,567	322,510	54.4	9.5
Cape Coral, FL	335,113	440,888	618,754	737,468	120.1	19.2
Cedar Rapids, IA	210,640	237,230	257,940	270,056	28.2	4.7
Charleston, SC	506,875	549,033	664,607	774,508	52.8	16.5
Charlotte, NC	1,024,331	1,330,448	1,758,038	2,545,560	148.5	44.8
Chicago, IL	8,182,076	9,098,316	9,461,105	9,508,605	16.2	0.5
Cincinnati, OH	1,844,917	2,009,632	2,130,151	2,201,741	19.3	3.4
Clarksville, TN	189,277	232,000	273,949	299,470	58.2	9.3
Cleveland, OH	2,102,219	2,148,143	2,077,240	2,056,898	-2.2	-1.0
College Station, TX	150,998	184,885	228,660	258,029	70.9	12.8
Colorado Springs, CO	409,482	537,484	645,613	723,498	76.7	12.1
Columbia, MO	122,010	145,666	172,786	205,369	68.3	18.9
Columbia, SC	548,325	647,158	767,598	824,278	50.3	7.4
Columbus, OH	1,405,176	1,612,694	1,836,536	2,077,761	47.9	13.1
Dallas, TX	3,989,294	5,161,544	6,371,773	7,320,663	83.5	14.9
Davenport, IA	368,151	376,019	379,690	381,175	3.5	0.4
Denver, CO	1,666,935	2,179,296	2,543,482	2,892,066	73.5	13.7
Des Moines, IA	416,346	481,394	569,633	680,439	63.4	19.5
Durham, NC	344,646	426,493	504,357	626,695	81.8	24.3
Edison, NJ	16,845,992	18,323,002	18,897,109	19,294,236	14.5	2.1
El Paso, TX	591,610	679,622	800,647	840,477	42.1	5.0
Fargo, ND	153,296	174,367	208,777	240,421	56.8	15.2
Fayetteville, NC	297,422	336,609	366,383	519,101	74.5	41.7
Fort Collins, CO	186,136	251,494	299,630	344,786	85.2	15.1
Fort Wayne, IN	354,435	390,156	416,257	406,305	14.6	-2.4
Fort Worth, TX	3,989,294	5,161,544	6,371,773	7,320,663	83.5	14.9
Grand Rapids, MI	645,914	740,482	774,160	1,062,392	64.5	37.2
Greeley, CO	131,816	180,926	252,825	305,345	131.6	20.8
Green Bay, WI	243,698	282,599	306,241	319,401	31.1	4.3
Greensboro, NC	540,257	643,430	723,801	762,063	41.1	5.3
Honolulu, HI	836,231	876,156	953,207	984,821	17.8	3.3
Houston, TX	3,767,335	4,715,407	5,946,800	6,884,138	82.7	15.8
Huntsville, AL	293,047	342,376	417,593	457,003	55.9	9.4
Indianapolis, IN	1,294,217	1,525,104	1,756,241	2,029,472	56.8	15.6
Jacksonville, FL	925,213	1,122,750	1,345,596	1,503,574	62.5	11.7
Kansas City, MO	1,636,528	1,836,038	2,035,334	2,124,518	29.8	4.4
Lafayette, LA	208,740	239,086	273,738	489,914	134.7	79.0
Lakeland, FL	405,382	483,924	602,095	686,218	69.3	14.0
Las Vegas, NV	741,459	1,375,765	1,951,269	2,182,004	194.3	11.8
Lexington, KY	348,428	408,326	472,099	510,647	46.6	8.2
Lincoln, NE	229,091	266,787	302,157	330,329	44.2	9.3
Little Rock, AR	535,034	610,518	699,757	737,015	37.8	5.3
Los Angeles, CA	11,273,720	12,365,627	12,828,837	13,249,614	17.5	3.3
Louisville, KY	1,055,973	1,161,975	1,283,566	1,257,088	19.0	-2.1
Madison, WI	432,323	501,774	568,593	653,725	51.2	15.0

Table continued on following page.

Area	1990 Census	2000 Census	2010 Census	2019* Estimate	Population Growth (%) 1990-2019	Population Growth (%) 2010-2019
Manchester, NH	336,073	380,841	400,721	413,035	22.9	3.1
Memphis, TN	1,067,263	1,205,204	1,316,100	1,339,623	25.5	1.8
Miami, FL	4,056,100	5,007,564	5,564,635	6,090,660	50.2	9.5
Midland, TX	106,611	116,009	136,872	173,816	63.0	27.0
Milwaukee, WI	1,432,149	1,500,741	1,555,908	1,575,223	10.0	1.2
Minneapolis, MN	2,538,834	2,968,806	3,279,833	3,573,609	40.8	9.0
Nashville, TN	1,048,218	1,311,789	1,589,934	1,871,903	78.6	17.7
New Haven, CT	804,219	824,008	862,477	857,513	6.6	-0.6
New Orleans, LA	1,264,391	1,316,510	1,167,764	1,267,777	0.3	8.6
New York, NY	16,845,992	18,323,002	18,897,109	19,294,236	14.5	2.1
Oklahoma City, OK	971,042	1,095,421	1,252,987	1,382,841	42.4	10.4
Omaha, NE	685,797	767,041	865,350	931,779	35.9	7.7
Orlando, FL	1,224,852	1,644,561	2,134,411	2,508,970	104.8	17.5
Peoria, IL	358,552	366,899	379,186	406,883	13.5	7.3
Philadelphia, PA	5,435,470	5,687,147	5,965,343	6,079,130	11.8	1.9
Phoenix, AZ	2,238,480	3,251,876	4,192,887	4,761,603	112.7	13.6
Pittsburgh, PA	2,468,289	2,431,087	2,356,285	2,331,447	-5.5	-1.1
Portland, OR	1,523,741	1,927,881	2,226,009	2,445,761	60.5	9.9
Providence, RI	1,509,789	1,582,997	1,600,852	1,618,268	7.2	1.1
Provo, UT	269,407	376,774	526,810	616,791	128.9	17.1
Raleigh, NC	541,081	797,071	1,130,490	1,332,311	146.2	17.9
Reno, NV	257,193	342,885	425,417	460,924	79.2	8.3
Richmond, VA	949,244	1,096,957	1,258,251	1,269,530	33.7	0.9
Riverside, CA	2,588,793	3,254,821	4,224,851	4,560,470	76.2	7.9
Rochester, MN	141,945	163,618	186,011	217,964	53.6	17.2
Sacramento, CA	1,481,126	1,796,857	2,149,127	2,315,980	56.4	7.8
Salt Lake City, UT	768,075	968,858	1,124,197	1,201,043	56.4	6.8
San Antonio, TX	1,407,745	1,711,703	2,142,508	2,468,193	75.3	15.2
San Diego, CA	2,498,016	2,813,833	3,095,313	3,316,073	32.7	7.1
San Francisco, CA	3,686,592	4,123,740	4,335,391	4,701,332	27.5	8.4
San Jose, CA	1,534,280	1,735,819	1,836,911	1,987,846	29.6	8.2
Santa Rosa, CA	388,222	458,614	483,878	499,772	28.7	3.3
Savannah, GA	258,060	293,000	347,611	386,036	49.6	11.1
Seattle, WA	2,559,164	3,043,878	3,439,809	3,871,323	51.3	12.5
Sioux Falls, SD	153,500	187,093	228,261	259,348	69.0	13.6
Springfield, IL	189,550	201,437	210,170	209,167	10.3	-0.5
Tallahassee, FL	259,096	320,304	367,413	382,197	47.5	4.0
Tampa, FL	2,067,959	2,395,997	2,783,243	3,097,859	49.8	11.3
Tucson, AZ	666,880	843,746	980,263	1,027,207	54.0	4.8
Tulsa, OK	761,019	859,532	937,478	990,544	30.2	5.7
Tuscaloosa, AL	176,123	192,034	219,461	250,681	42.3	14.2
Virginia Beach, VA	1,449,389	1,576,370	1,671,683	1,761,729	21.5	5.4
Washington, DC	4,122,914	4,796,183	5,582,170	6,196,585	50.3	11.0
Wichita, KS	511,111	571,166	623,061	637,690	24.8	2.3
Winston-Salem, NC	361,091	421,961	477,717	666,216	84.5	39.5
U.S.	248,709,873	281,421,906	308,745,538	324,697,795	30.6	5.2

Note: (*) 2014-2019 5-year estimated population; Figures cover the Metropolitan Statistical Area (MSA)—see Appendix B for areas included

Source: U.S. Census Bureau, 1990 Census, Census 2000, Census 2010, 2015-2019 American Community Survey 5-Year Estimates

Household Size: City

City	Persons in Household (%)							Average Household Size
	One	Two	Three	Four	Five	Six	Seven or More	
Albuquerque, NM	34.6	33.7	13.8	10.7	4.5	1.5	0.8	2.47
Allentown, PA	27.6	28.9	15.4	13.8	8.0	3.6	2.3	2.73
Anchorage, AK	26.3	33.0	16.9	12.5	6.6	2.4	2.0	2.69
Ann Arbor, MI	34.6	37.8	11.7	10.4	3.0	1.5	0.8	2.26
Athens, GA	33.4	35.2	14.5	11.2	3.6	1.4	0.4	2.35
Atlanta, GA	46.7	30.7	10.6	7.2	2.9	1.0	0.6	2.19
Austin, TX	34.5	32.7	14.3	11.3	4.4	1.5	0.9	2.44
Baton Rouge, LA	36.1	32.4	15.6	9.0	4.1	1.7	0.9	2.58
Boise City, ID	34.1	34.1	14.3	10.3	4.6	1.4	0.8	2.43
Boston, MA	36.2	32.4	15.4	9.4	3.9	1.6	0.8	2.36
Boulder, CO	33.8	36.8	14.5	10.9	2.7	0.7	0.3	2.27
Cape Coral, FL	23.7	43.0	14.2	12.3	4.4	1.6	0.5	2.81
Cedar Rapids, IA	34.1	33.9	14.0	10.5	4.4	2.2	0.6	2.33
Charleston, SC	35.4	37.8	14.2	9.0	2.4	0.6	0.1	2.31
Charlotte, NC	32.9	32.2	15.5	11.9	4.8	1.5	0.8	2.56
Chicago, IL	37.1	29.7	13.8	10.2	5.1	2.2	1.5	2.48
Cincinnati, OH	44.3	30.1	12.0	7.5	3.5	1.3	0.8	2.10
Clarksville, TN	24.7	30.7	19.6	15.1	5.8	2.3	1.3	2.66
Cleveland, OH	44.4	27.5	13.1	8.0	4.2	1.6	0.9	2.18
College Station, TX	29.7	33.8	16.5	14.1	3.5	1.8	0.4	2.53
Colorado Springs, CO	28.6	35.1	14.6	12.2	5.8	2.2	1.0	2.52
Columbia, MO	32.7	32.8	15.0	12.9	4.7	1.1	0.4	2.33
Columbia, SC	40.6	33.0	12.3	8.9	3.6	0.8	0.5	2.21
Columbus, OH	35.5	32.4	13.9	10.1	4.8	1.8	1.2	2.39
Dallas, TX	35.3	29.1	13.7	11.2	6.2	2.5	1.7	2.56
Davenport, IA	35.3	33.5	13.1	9.7	5.2	1.8	1.0	2.46
Denver, CO	38.2	32.9	12.0	9.5	4.3	1.6	1.2	2.29
Des Moines, IA	34.1	30.5	14.7	11.4	5.3	2.2	1.5	2.45
Durham, NC	33.9	33.5	15.4	10.1	4.4	1.6	0.8	2.36
Edison, NJ	18.9	29.0	21.1	20.3	6.4	2.5	1.5	2.86
El Paso, TX	25.5	28.5	17.7	15.9	7.5	3.2	1.3	2.97
Fargo, ND	36.4	34.0	14.4	8.9	4.2	1.3	0.5	2.14
Fayetteville, NC	35.6	31.3	15.3	10.7	4.2	1.8	0.8	2.42
Fort Collins, CO	24.7	37.9	17.8	13.8	4.3	0.9	0.4	2.44
Fort Wayne, IN	32.1	33.0	14.3	11.2	5.9	2.2	1.0	2.45
Fort Worth, TX	26.1	28.8	16.5	15.1	7.8	3.3	2.1	2.89
Grand Rapids, MI	33.1	31.4	13.8	11.1	5.9	2.5	1.9	2.53
Greeley, CO	26.0	31.4	16.1	13.3	8.2	3.2	1.3	2.72
Green Bay, WI	34.1	32.1	12.7	11.3	6.5	1.5	1.5	2.39
Greensboro, NC	34.2	33.1	15.4	10.2	4.6	1.4	0.7	2.37
Honolulu, HI	33.4	31.3	14.3	10.6	5.1	2.3	2.6	2.60
Houston, TX	32.3	28.9	15.2	12.3	6.6	2.8	1.7	2.65
Huntsville, AL	35.7	34.3	14.5	9.4	4.1	1.2	0.4	2.21
Indianapolis, IN	37.8	31.3	13.2	9.6	4.9	1.9	1.0	2.51
Jacksonville, FL	30.4	33.7	16.6	11.4	5.0	1.7	0.9	2.57
Kansas City, MO	37.0	31.9	12.9	10.0	4.9	1.8	1.1	2.35
Lafayette, LA	35.1	34.5	13.9	9.5	3.9	1.7	1.0	2.40
Lakeland, FL	33.1	37.5	14.3	8.9	3.6	1.6	0.7	2.50
Las Vegas, NV	30.6	31.6	15.3	11.5	6.2	2.7	1.7	2.70
Lexington, KY	31.5	35.0	15.1	11.2	4.6	1.6	0.6	2.37
Lincoln, NE	31.5	34.8	13.9	11.5	5.2	2.0	0.9	2.38
Little Rock, AR	36.6	32.0	14.0	10.1	4.6	1.8	0.7	2.37
Los Angeles, CA	30.2	28.8	15.3	13.0	6.8	2.9	2.5	2.80
Louisville, KY	33.3	32.9	15.3	10.5	4.8	1.8	1.0	2.43

Table continued on following page.

City	Persons in Household (%)							Average Household Size
	One	Two	Three	Four	Five	Six	Seven or More	
Madison, WI	35.3	36.2	13.2	9.8	3.7	1.1	0.4	2.21
Manchester, NH	31.4	34.1	16.5	10.7	4.4	1.6	1.0	2.37
Memphis, TN	37.1	30.3	14.8	9.8	4.2	2.2	1.3	2.53
Miami, FL	37.3	31.0	16.1	8.8	3.9	1.5	0.9	2.51
Midland, TX	26.1	31.2	16.4	14.4	7.3	3.0	1.3	2.90
Milwaukee, WI	36.3	29.3	14.0	10.4	5.7	2.4	1.6	2.51
Minneapolis, MN	40.4	31.2	11.9	9.5	3.5	1.7	1.5	2.28
Nashville, TN	33.9	33.9	15.2	9.6	4.5	1.6	1.0	2.36
New Haven, CT	38.4	27.3	15.4	9.9	5.3	2.3	1.0	2.46
New Orleans, LA	45.9	29.2	12.6	7.8	2.6	1.0	0.6	2.45
New York, NY	32.2	28.4	16.2	12.5	5.9	2.5	2.0	2.60
Oklahoma City, OK	31.1	32.1	14.5	12.2	6.2	2.5	1.1	2.60
Omaha, NE	32.6	32.0	13.5	11.2	6.0	2.7	1.6	2.48
Orlando, FL	33.6	33.1	16.7	9.8	4.0	1.8	0.6	2.48
Peoria, IL	38.2	31.4	13.3	9.1	5.2	1.7	0.9	2.37
Philadelphia, PA	37.5	29.2	14.7	10.4	4.8	1.9	1.3	2.55
Phoenix, AZ	27.9	30.0	15.2	12.9	7.3	3.7	2.7	2.85
Pittsburgh, PA	43.6	32.4	12.8	6.7	2.5	1.1	0.6	2.02
Portland, OR	34.0	34.8	14.1	10.8	3.8	1.4	0.8	2.34
Providence, RI	33.2	29.0	15.6	11.7	7.0	1.7	1.5	2.67
Provo, UT	13.2	33.1	18.8	16.1	7.9	7.1	3.4	3.17
Raleigh, NC	33.0	32.4	15.2	12.4	4.7	1.3	0.6	2.42
Reno, NV	33.0	33.4	14.6	10.5	5.1	1.8	1.4	2.36
Richmond, VA	43.4	32.8	12.0	6.8	2.9	1.2	0.6	2.39
Riverside, CA	20.4	27.5	17.7	15.5	10.1	4.7	3.8	3.43
Rochester, MN	31.0	33.2	14.4	13.0	4.7	1.8	1.5	2.40
Sacramento, CA	30.9	30.7	14.7	12.1	6.0	2.9	2.3	2.66
Salt Lake City, UT	36.1	32.2	13.5	9.9	4.2	2.0	1.7	2.42
San Antonio, TX	29.9	29.5	16.2	12.9	6.7	2.8	1.7	2.96
San Diego, CA	27.5	33.4	16.1	13.1	5.7	2.3	1.5	2.70
San Francisco, CA	35.6	33.6	14.3	9.7	3.7	1.4	1.3	2.36
San Jose, CA	19.4	28.8	18.6	17.9	8.1	3.5	3.4	3.12
Santa Rosa, CA	28.2	32.6	15.3	13.2	6.2	2.3	2.0	2.66
Savannah, GA	33.5	34.0	15.6	9.8	4.3	1.4	1.0	2.55
Seattle, WA	38.5	35.6	12.5	8.8	2.9	0.8	0.6	2.11
Sioux Falls, SD	32.0	34.0	13.0	12.2	5.3	2.0	1.1	2.37
Springfield, IL	38.0	34.0	13.3	8.7	3.1	1.4	1.0	2.20
Tallahassee, FL	35.0	33.0	16.8	10.2	3.6	0.9	0.1	2.33
Tampa, FL	35.7	31.5	15.3	10.8	4.2	1.5	0.6	2.47
Tucson, AZ	34.6	31.2	14.7	10.8	5.1	2.0	1.3	2.42
Tulsa, OK	35.1	32.5	13.6	10.2	5.1	2.1	1.1	2.41
Tuscaloosa, AL	35.4	33.7	15.9	9.9	3.4	1.0	0.4	2.55
Virginia Beach, VA	24.4	34.4	17.5	14.8	5.8	1.9	0.8	2.58
Washington, DC	44.0	31.0	11.7	7.8	3.1	1.2	0.8	2.30
Wichita, KS	33.3	31.3	13.4	11.3	6.5	2.7	1.2	2.51
Winston-Salem, NC	35.7	31.5	15.0	9.4	5.2	1.8	1.1	2.46
U.S.	27.8	33.9	15.5	12.9	5.9	2.2	1.4	2.62

U.S. Census Bureau, 2015-2019 American Community Survey 5-Year Estimates

Household Size: Metro Area

Metro Area	Persons in Household (%)							Average Household Size
	One	Two	Three	Four	Five	Six	Seven or More	
Albuquerque, NM	31.4	35.2	14.4	10.8	5.0	1.9	1.1	2.56
Allentown, PA	26.1	35.4	15.7	13.4	6.0	2.1	1.0	2.54
Anchorage, AK	25.5	33.6	16.4	12.7	6.8	2.6	2.1	2.83
Ann Arbor, MI	29.6	36.9	13.7	12.3	4.5	1.8	1.0	2.45
Athens, GA	28.9	35.3	15.2	13.1	4.8	1.6	0.8	2.50
Atlanta, GA	26.7	31.6	16.9	14.3	6.3	2.4	1.4	2.74
Austin, TX	27.9	33.1	15.5	13.9	6.0	2.1	1.2	2.71
Baton Rouge, LA	28.6	33.8	16.7	12.3	5.6	1.8	0.9	2.69
Boise City, ID	27.8	34.4	14.3	12.0	7.0	2.7	1.6	2.68
Boston, MA	27.7	33.0	16.6	14.3	5.4	1.7	0.9	2.55
Boulder, CO	28.7	36.3	15.5	12.9	4.6	1.2	0.4	2.44
Cape Coral, FL	28.0	44.7	11.5	9.0	4.1	1.6	0.8	2.64
Cedar Rapids, IA	29.6	36.5	13.8	11.9	5.0	2.0	0.8	2.41
Charleston, SC	29.1	35.6	16.5	11.7	4.6	1.5	0.6	2.60
Charlotte, NC	27.1	34.0	16.3	14.0	5.5	1.8	0.9	2.63
Chicago, IL	28.9	31.1	15.6	13.7	6.6	2.4	1.4	2.66
Cincinnati, OH	28.8	34.3	15.1	12.7	5.7	1.9	1.0	2.50
Clarksville, TN	24.9	32.2	18.3	14.2	6.2	2.5	1.2	2.64
Cleveland, OH	34.0	33.8	14.2	10.7	4.5	1.5	0.8	2.34
College Station, TX	28.1	33.9	15.7	13.2	5.1	2.6	1.2	2.61
Colorado Springs, CO	25.0	35.4	15.6	13.4	6.5	2.4	1.3	2.64
Columbia, MO	30.1	34.4	15.1	13.2	4.8	1.3	0.7	2.41
Columbia, SC	29.8	34.3	15.6	12.1	5.2	1.7	0.9	2.53
Columbus, OH	28.5	33.9	15.6	12.9	5.9	1.9	1.0	2.55
Dallas, TX	25.0	30.6	16.8	15.2	7.5	2.9	1.7	2.83
Davenport, IA	31.1	35.7	13.2	11.9	5.3	1.7	0.8	2.42
Denver, CO	28.2	34.3	14.9	13.2	5.7	2.1	1.3	2.57
Des Moines, IA	27.9	34.2	14.6	13.8	6.2	2.1	0.8	2.50
Durham, NC	30.5	35.7	15.4	11.2	4.8	1.3	0.7	2.42
Edison, NJ	28.0	29.4	16.9	14.5	6.5	2.4	1.9	2.70
El Paso, TX	23.8	28.1	17.8	16.5	8.3	3.5	1.6	3.06
Fargo, ND	31.1	35.0	14.5	11.6	5.0	1.5	0.8	2.31
Fayetteville, NC	30.7	31.5	16.0	12.4	5.8	2.2	1.0	2.64
Fort Collins, CO	24.2	40.2	15.7	12.3	5.1	1.5	0.5	2.45
Fort Wayne, IN	28.9	34.3	14.4	12.2	6.3	2.4	1.2	2.52
Fort Worth, TX	25.0	30.6	16.8	15.2	7.5	2.9	1.7	2.83
Grand Rapids, MI	24.8	34.6	14.9	14.3	6.9	2.7	1.4	2.65
Greeley, CO	20.5	33.4	16.7	15.7	8.3	3.2	1.8	2.85
Green Bay, WI	28.3	36.9	14.1	12.2	5.8	1.5	0.9	2.40
Greensboro, NC	29.4	35.0	16.1	11.4	5.0	1.8	1.0	2.48
Honolulu, HI	24.0	30.5	16.7	13.5	7.3	3.5	4.1	3.03
Houston, TX	24.1	29.7	17.1	15.6	8.1	3.1	1.9	2.89
Huntsville, AL	29.4	35.1	15.5	12.2	5.1	1.7	0.6	2.47
Indianapolis, IN	30.1	33.5	14.8	12.8	5.7	1.9	0.9	2.56
Jacksonville, FL	27.1	35.6	16.6	12.4	5.3	1.8	0.8	2.62
Kansas City, MO	29.0	34.1	14.8	12.9	5.8	2.0	1.1	2.52
Lafayette, LA	26.9	34.0	16.7	12.9	6.1	2.1	1.0	2.65
Lakeland, FL	25.2	37.9	15.1	11.6	5.9	2.5	1.4	2.86
Las Vegas, NV	28.5	32.8	15.3	12.3	6.5	2.6	1.7	2.76
Lexington, KY	28.4	35.6	15.9	12.3	5.0	1.7	0.7	2.44
Lincoln, NE	30.1	35.7	13.7	11.9	5.3	2.0	1.0	2.41
Little Rock, AR	29.8	34.2	15.9	11.8	5.2	1.8	0.8	2.55
Los Angeles, CA	24.5	28.6	17.0	15.4	7.9	3.4	2.8	2.99
Louisville, KY	30.3	34.1	15.7	11.7	5.1	1.8	0.9	2.51

Table continued on following page.

Metro Area	Persons in Household (%)							Average Household Size
	One	Two	Three	Four	Five	Six	Seven or More	
Madison, WI	30.1	36.8	14.0	12.1	4.6	1.4	0.7	2.35
Manchester, NH	25.5	36.2	16.4	13.5	5.2	1.9	1.0	2.51
Memphis, TN	29.8	32.5	16.2	12.3	5.3	2.2	1.3	2.64
Miami, FL	28.2	32.6	16.8	13.2	5.8	2.1	1.1	2.82
Midland, TX	26.3	30.8	15.9	14.4	7.8	2.9	1.6	2.93
Milwaukee, WI	31.5	34.3	14.0	11.9	5.2	1.8	0.9	2.45
Minneapolis, MN	27.9	34.1	14.8	13.6	5.8	2.1	1.3	2.56
Nashville, TN	26.0	34.8	16.7	13.3	5.8	2.0	1.0	2.59
New Haven, CT	31.2	33.0	16.1	12.3	4.8	1.7	0.7	2.51
New Orleans, LA	33.4	32.2	15.4	11.5	4.6	1.6	0.9	2.58
New York, NY	28.0	29.4	16.9	14.5	6.5	2.4	1.9	2.70
Oklahoma City, OK	28.2	34.1	15.4	12.6	6.0	2.3	1.1	2.62
Omaha, NE	28.4	33.9	14.3	12.6	6.4	2.7	1.5	2.54
Orlando, FL	24.8	34.2	17.4	13.9	5.9	2.3	1.1	2.83
Peoria, IL	31.3	35.3	14.0	11.0	5.2	2.0	0.8	2.42
Philadelphia, PA	29.1	32.3	16.2	13.5	5.7	1.9	1.0	2.60
Phoenix, AZ	26.4	34.4	14.4	12.6	6.7	3.0	2.2	2.76
Pittsburgh, PA	33.2	35.5	14.3	10.8	4.0	1.3	0.5	2.25
Portland, OR	26.8	35.4	15.3	13.4	5.3	2.2	1.2	2.56
Providence, RI	29.8	33.3	16.6	12.8	5.0	1.5	0.7	2.48
Provo, UT	11.9	28.6	15.6	15.6	12.4	9.0	6.5	3.55
Raleigh, NC	25.0	33.1	17.6	15.3	6.1	1.8	0.8	2.64
Reno, NV	28.2	35.0	15.5	11.4	5.7	2.3	1.5	2.47
Richmond, VA	29.4	34.2	16.0	12.3	5.3	1.8	0.7	2.57
Riverside, CA	20.4	28.3	16.3	16.0	10.1	4.9	3.7	3.28
Rochester, MN	27.2	36.2	14.1	13.5	5.3	2.2	1.2	2.45
Sacramento, CA	25.3	33.2	15.9	14.4	6.6	2.7	1.7	2.74
Salt Lake City, UT	22.4	30.5	15.8	14.3	8.6	4.9	3.2	3.00
San Antonio, TX	26.3	31.2	16.5	13.8	7.1	3.0	1.7	3.00
San Diego, CA	23.8	32.6	16.9	14.7	7.0	2.8	1.9	2.87
San Francisco, CA	26.2	31.9	16.9	14.8	6.1	2.2	1.6	2.71
San Jose, CA	20.1	30.6	18.8	17.7	7.2	2.9	2.4	2.96
Santa Rosa, CA	27.4	34.8	15.4	12.9	5.9	2.0	1.3	2.59
Savannah, GA	28.0	35.9	16.1	12.2	5.0	1.5	0.9	2.62
Seattle, WA	27.1	34.5	16.0	13.5	5.2	2.0	1.3	2.54
Sioux Falls, SD	28.6	35.0	13.6	13.1	6.2	2.1	1.1	2.46
Springfield, IL	32.9	35.7	14.0	10.6	4.2	1.6	0.7	2.30
Tallahassee, FL	30.5	35.2	17.0	11.0	4.2	1.2	0.5	2.43
Tampa, FL	30.8	36.7	14.7	10.8	4.4	1.5	0.8	2.51
Tucson, AZ	30.5	35.8	13.7	11.2	5.1	2.0	1.3	2.46
Tulsa, OK	28.2	34.5	15.2	12.1	5.9	2.4	1.2	2.56
Tuscaloosa, AL	29.4	35.0	16.4	11.5	5.3	1.3	0.8	2.69
Virginia Beach, VA	27.2	34.1	17.3	13.1	5.3	1.8	0.9	2.55
Washington, DC	27.2	30.8	16.5	14.6	6.5	2.6	1.6	2.75
Wichita, KS	29.9	32.8	14.0	11.6	7.0	2.8	1.4	2.56
Winston-Salem, NC	29.5	35.9	15.4	11.3	5.0	1.6	0.9	2.46
U.S.	27.8	33.9	15.5	12.9	5.9	2.2	1.4	2.62

Note: Figures cover the Metropolitan Statistical Area (MSA)—see Appendix B for areas included
Source: U.S. Census Bureau, 2015-2019 American Community Survey 5-Year Estimates

Race: City

City	White Alone[1] (%)	Black Alone[1] (%)	Asian Alone[1] (%)	AIAN[2] Alone[1] (%)	NHOPI[3] Alone[1] (%)	Other Race Alone[1] (%)	Two or More Races (%)
Albuquerque, NM	73.9	3.3	2.9	4.7	0.1	10.6	4.4
Allentown, PA	62.3	14.7	2.9	0.7	0.1	14.7	4.6
Anchorage, AK	62.6	5.6	9.6	7.9	2.4	2.4	9.5
Ann Arbor, MI	71.1	6.8	16.9	0.4	0.1	0.7	4.1
Athens, GA	63.2	28.0	3.9	0.1	0.1	2.1	2.6
Atlanta, GA	40.9	51.0	4.4	0.3	0.0	1.0	2.4
Austin, TX	72.6	7.8	7.6	0.7	0.1	7.8	3.5
Baton Rouge, LA	38.7	54.7	3.5	0.3	0.1	1.5	1.3
Boise City, ID	89.3	1.9	2.8	0.5	0.2	1.9	3.4
Boston, MA	52.8	25.2	9.7	0.3	0.1	6.7	5.3
Boulder, CO	87.4	1.2	5.8	0.2	0.1	1.5	3.8
Cape Coral, FL	89.5	5.2	1.8	0.2	0.0	1.8	1.6
Cedar Rapids, IA	83.9	7.8	2.9	0.3	0.2	1.1	3.8
Charleston, SC	74.1	21.7	1.9	0.1	0.1	0.6	1.5
Charlotte, NC	48.8	35.2	6.5	0.4	0.1	6.1	2.8
Chicago, IL	50.0	29.6	6.6	0.3	0.0	10.6	2.8
Cincinnati, OH	50.7	42.3	2.2	0.1	0.1	0.9	3.7
Clarksville, TN	65.1	24.3	2.5	0.7	0.5	1.8	5.2
Cleveland, OH	40.0	48.8	2.6	0.5	0.1	3.6	4.4
College Station, TX	77.8	7.6	10.1	0.3	0.0	1.5	2.7
Colorado Springs, CO	78.5	6.5	2.9	0.8	0.3	5.1	5.9
Columbia, MO	77.1	10.9	6.2	0.4	0.1	0.9	4.4
Columbia, SC	53.4	39.8	2.7	0.1	0.2	1.0	2.8
Columbus, OH	58.6	29.0	5.8	0.3	0.0	2.1	4.2
Dallas, TX	62.7	24.3	3.4	0.3	0.0	6.9	2.4
Davenport, IA	81.4	11.3	2.3	0.5	0.0	1.0	3.5
Denver, CO	76.1	9.2	3.7	0.9	0.2	6.1	3.8
Des Moines, IA	75.8	11.4	6.2	0.4	0.1	2.3	3.9
Durham, NC	49.2	38.7	5.4	0.3	0.0	3.4	3.2
Edison, NJ	35.3	8.2	48.7	0.3	0.1	4.0	3.5
El Paso, TX	80.1	3.6	1.4	0.6	0.2	11.4	2.7
Fargo, ND	84.6	7.0	3.5	1.2	0.0	0.5	3.1
Fayetteville, NC	44.6	42.1	2.9	1.1	0.4	2.9	6.1
Fort Collins, CO	88.3	1.6	3.5	1.0	0.1	1.5	4.0
Fort Wayne, IN	73.4	15.1	4.7	0.2	0.1	2.1	4.5
Fort Worth, TX	63.8	18.9	4.6	0.5	0.1	9.0	3.2
Grand Rapids, MI	67.2	18.6	2.4	0.4	0.0	5.7	5.6
Greeley, CO	88.3	2.4	1.4	1.2	0.2	3.7	2.8
Green Bay, WI	76.7	4.2	4.2	3.5	0.0	6.0	5.4
Greensboro, NC	47.3	41.4	5.0	0.5	0.1	2.7	3.0
Honolulu, HI	17.2	2.0	53.2	0.1	8.0	0.9	18.4
Houston, TX	57.0	22.6	6.8	0.3	0.1	11.1	2.2
Huntsville, AL	61.3	30.7	2.6	0.4	0.1	2.0	2.8
Indianapolis, IN	60.9	28.6	3.4	0.3	0.0	3.5	3.3
Jacksonville, FL	58.2	31.0	4.8	0.2	0.1	2.1	3.6
Kansas City, MO	60.9	28.2	2.7	0.4	0.2	4.0	3.6
Lafayette, LA	64.0	30.9	2.2	0.3	0.0	0.6	2.1
Lakeland, FL	72.3	20.5	2.2	0.4	0.1	2.8	1.8
Las Vegas, NV	61.9	12.2	6.9	0.9	0.8	12.1	5.2
Lexington, KY	74.9	14.6	3.8	0.2	0.0	2.8	3.8
Lincoln, NE	84.9	4.4	4.6	0.7	0.1	1.5	3.9
Little Rock, AR	50.3	42.0	3.3	0.3	0.1	1.8	2.3
Los Angeles, CA	52.1	8.9	11.6	0.7	0.2	22.8	3.8
Louisville, KY	69.9	23.6	2.7	0.2	0.1	1.0	2.6

Table continued on following page.

City	White Alone[1] (%)	Black Alone[1] (%)	Asian Alone[1] (%)	AIAN[2] Alone[1] (%)	NHOPI[3] Alone[1] (%)	Other Race Alone[1] (%)	Two or More Races (%)
Madison, WI	78.6	7.0	9.0	0.5	0.1	1.4	3.5
Manchester, NH	84.8	6.1	5.1	0.1	0.0	0.9	3.0
Memphis, TN	29.2	64.1	1.7	0.2	0.0	3.3	1.5
Miami, FL	76.1	16.8	1.1	0.2	0.0	4.0	1.7
Midland, TX	80.6	7.8	2.2	0.6	0.1	6.4	2.3
Milwaukee, WI	44.4	38.7	4.3	0.6	0.0	8.0	4.0
Minneapolis, MN	63.6	19.2	5.9	1.4	0.0	5.0	4.8
Nashville, TN	63.5	27.6	3.7	0.2	0.1	2.4	2.6
New Haven, CT	44.4	32.6	5.0	0.4	0.0	13.1	4.4
New Orleans, LA	33.9	59.5	2.9	0.2	0.0	1.5	1.9
New York, NY	42.7	24.3	14.1	0.4	0.1	14.7	3.6
Oklahoma City, OK	67.7	14.3	4.5	2.9	0.1	4.1	6.3
Omaha, NE	77.5	12.3	3.8	0.6	0.0	2.3	3.4
Orlando, FL	61.3	24.5	4.2	0.2	0.0	6.2	3.5
Peoria, IL	60.1	27.1	6.1	0.3	0.0	2.1	4.3
Philadelphia, PA	40.7	42.1	7.2	0.4	0.0	6.5	3.1
Phoenix, AZ	72.9	7.1	3.8	2.1	0.2	10.0	3.9
Pittsburgh, PA	66.8	23.0	5.8	0.2	0.0	0.6	3.5
Portland, OR	77.4	5.8	8.2	0.8	0.6	1.9	5.3
Providence, RI	55.1	16.8	6.0	1.0	0.1	16.3	4.7
Provo, UT	87.9	0.9	2.7	0.8	1.3	2.2	4.2
Raleigh, NC	58.3	29.0	4.6	0.4	0.0	4.8	2.9
Reno, NV	75.4	2.8	6.7	1.0	0.8	8.5	4.8
Richmond, VA	45.5	46.9	2.1	0.4	0.0	1.7	3.4
Riverside, CA	58.3	6.2	7.6	0.8	0.3	22.0	4.9
Rochester, MN	79.4	8.2	7.3	0.5	0.1	1.1	3.4
Sacramento, CA	46.3	13.2	18.9	0.7	1.7	11.7	7.4
Salt Lake City, UT	72.8	2.6	5.4	1.5	1.6	12.7	3.3
San Antonio, TX	80.3	7.0	2.8	0.8	0.1	6.0	3.0
San Diego, CA	65.1	6.4	16.7	0.5	0.4	5.6	5.3
San Francisco, CA	46.4	5.2	34.4	0.4	0.4	7.7	5.6
San Jose, CA	39.9	3.0	35.9	0.6	0.5	14.8	5.3
Santa Rosa, CA	66.8	2.6	5.5	1.3	0.6	17.1	6.0
Savannah, GA	38.9	53.9	2.6	0.3	0.1	1.4	2.8
Seattle, WA	67.3	7.3	15.4	0.5	0.3	2.3	6.9
Sioux Falls, SD	84.5	6.2	2.5	2.1	0.0	1.6	3.2
Springfield, IL	72.9	19.9	3.1	0.1	0.0	0.5	3.5
Tallahassee, FL	56.2	35.0	4.6	0.2	0.0	1.1	2.9
Tampa, FL	65.4	23.6	4.3	0.3	0.1	2.5	3.9
Tucson, AZ	72.1	5.2	3.2	3.7	0.2	10.2	5.4
Tulsa, OK	64.3	15.2	3.4	4.5	0.1	4.9	7.5
Tuscaloosa, AL	51.2	44.0	2.5	0.3	0.1	0.9	1.0
Virginia Beach, VA	66.3	19.0	6.7	0.3	0.1	2.1	5.6
Washington, DC	41.3	46.3	4.0	0.3	0.1	5.0	3.1
Wichita, KS	74.3	10.9	5.1	1.0	0.1	4.2	4.4
Winston-Salem, NC	56.6	34.9	2.5	0.3	0.1	2.8	2.8
U.S.	72.5	12.7	5.5	0.8	0.2	4.9	3.3

Note: (1) Alone is defined as not being in combination with one or more other races; (2) American Indian and Alaska Native; (3) Native Hawaiian and Other Pacific Islander
Source: U.S. Census Bureau, 2015-2019 American Community Survey 5-Year Estimates

Race: Metro Area

Metro Area	White Alone[1] (%)	Black Alone[1] (%)	Asian Alone[1] (%)	AIAN[2] Alone[1] (%)	NHOPI[3] Alone[1] (%)	Other Race Alone[1] (%)	Two or More Races (%)
Albuquerque, NM	74.9	2.7	2.3	6.0	0.1	10.0	4.0
Allentown, PA	84.0	6.0	2.9	0.2	0.0	3.7	3.1
Anchorage, AK	68.0	4.4	7.5	7.5	1.9	1.8	9.0
Ann Arbor, MI	73.6	11.9	9.1	0.4	0.0	0.8	4.2
Athens, GA	72.0	20.6	3.1	0.1	0.1	1.8	2.3
Atlanta, GA	53.4	34.2	5.9	0.4	0.0	3.4	2.7
Austin, TX	76.0	7.3	5.9	0.5	0.1	6.7	3.6
Baton Rouge, LA	59.2	35.3	1.9	0.2	0.0	1.4	1.9
Boise City, ID	88.0	1.0	1.9	0.7	0.2	4.6	3.5
Boston, MA	76.0	8.3	7.9	0.2	0.0	4.2	3.3
Boulder, CO	89.0	0.9	4.7	0.4	0.1	1.8	3.0
Cape Coral, FL	84.4	8.6	1.6	0.2	0.1	3.4	1.8
Cedar Rapids, IA	89.4	4.8	2.0	0.2	0.1	0.7	2.8
Charleston, SC	67.6	25.6	1.8	0.3	0.1	1.9	2.7
Charlotte, NC	66.9	22.8	3.7	0.4	0.1	3.6	2.5
Chicago, IL	65.7	16.6	6.6	0.3	0.0	8.0	2.7
Cincinnati, OH	81.8	12.0	2.6	0.1	0.0	0.9	2.6
Clarksville, TN	72.7	19.1	1.9	0.6	0.4	1.3	4.1
Cleveland, OH	73.4	19.9	2.3	0.2	0.0	1.3	2.9
College Station, TX	77.0	11.5	5.3	0.4	0.1	3.0	2.8
Colorado Springs, CO	80.1	6.2	2.7	0.8	0.4	4.0	5.9
Columbia, MO	82.3	8.6	3.9	0.4	0.1	0.9	3.8
Columbia, SC	59.6	33.4	2.1	0.2	0.1	1.8	2.7
Columbus, OH	75.3	15.5	4.2	0.2	0.0	1.3	3.4
Dallas, TX	68.3	15.8	6.9	0.5	0.1	5.4	3.0
Davenport, IA	85.1	7.6	2.3	0.3	0.0	1.7	3.0
Denver, CO	81.0	5.7	4.2	0.8	0.1	4.4	3.7
Des Moines, IA	86.9	5.2	3.9	0.3	0.1	1.1	2.5
Durham, NC	62.5	26.6	4.5	0.4	0.0	3.0	3.1
Edison, NJ	57.5	17.3	11.2	0.3	0.0	10.5	3.1
El Paso, TX	79.6	3.3	1.2	0.6	0.1	12.4	2.7
Fargo, ND	88.0	5.1	2.5	1.2	0.1	0.6	2.7
Fayetteville, NC	53.8	32.6	2.0	2.0	0.3	4.1	5.3
Fort Collins, CO	91.3	1.0	2.2	0.8	0.1	1.5	3.2
Fort Wayne, IN	80.4	10.6	3.5	0.2	0.0	1.7	3.6
Fort Worth, TX	68.3	15.8	6.9	0.5	0.1	5.4	3.0
Grand Rapids, MI	83.9	6.7	2.6	0.3	0.0	2.9	3.5
Greeley, CO	90.3	1.2	1.6	0.8	0.1	3.0	3.0
Green Bay, WI	87.1	2.1	2.7	2.2	0.0	2.9	3.0
Greensboro, NC	63.0	26.8	3.7	0.5	0.1	3.3	2.6
Honolulu, HI	20.9	2.4	42.7	0.2	9.5	1.0	23.2
Houston, TX	65.0	17.3	7.7	0.4	0.1	7.0	2.5
Huntsville, AL	70.5	22.1	2.4	0.6	0.1	1.5	2.8
Indianapolis, IN	76.6	15.2	3.2	0.2	0.0	2.0	2.7
Jacksonville, FL	69.3	21.5	3.8	0.3	0.1	1.8	3.4
Kansas City, MO	78.3	12.3	2.9	0.4	0.2	2.7	3.3
Lafayette, LA	70.6	24.6	1.7	0.3	0.0	0.8	2.0
Lakeland, FL	77.1	15.3	1.8	0.3	0.0	3.0	2.5
Las Vegas, NV	60.2	11.7	9.7	0.9	0.8	11.5	5.4
Lexington, KY	80.7	11.0	2.7	0.2	0.0	2.3	3.1
Lincoln, NE	86.6	3.8	4.0	0.7	0.1	1.3	3.5
Little Rock, AR	70.3	23.3	1.7	0.4	0.1	1.6	2.5
Los Angeles, CA	53.6	6.6	16.0	0.7	0.3	18.8	4.0
Louisville, KY	79.4	14.8	2.1	0.2	0.0	0.9	2.5

Table continued on following page.

Metro Area	White Alone[1] (%)	Black Alone[1] (%)	Asian Alone[1] (%)	AIAN[2] Alone[1] (%)	NHOPI[3] Alone[1] (%)	Other Race Alone[1] (%)	Two or More Races (%)
Madison, WI	86.0	4.4	5.0	0.3	0.0	1.4	2.8
Manchester, NH	89.4	2.9	4.0	0.1	0.1	0.9	2.5
Memphis, TN	46.3	47.1	2.1	0.2	0.0	2.3	1.9
Miami, FL	70.2	21.2	2.5	0.2	0.0	3.5	2.3
Midland, TX	82.1	6.5	1.9	0.6	0.1	6.4	2.4
Milwaukee, WI	72.5	16.5	3.7	0.4	0.0	3.8	2.9
Minneapolis, MN	78.7	8.5	6.6	0.6	0.0	2.2	3.4
Nashville, TN	77.6	15.3	2.8	0.2	0.0	1.6	2.5
New Haven, CT	73.3	13.5	4.0	0.2	0.0	5.7	3.3
New Orleans, LA	57.3	35.1	2.9	0.4	0.0	2.2	2.0
New York, NY	57.5	17.3	11.2	0.3	0.0	10.5	3.1
Oklahoma City, OK	73.7	10.2	3.2	3.6	0.1	2.8	6.5
Omaha, NE	84.0	7.7	2.9	0.5	0.1	1.9	2.9
Orlando, FL	69.7	16.6	4.3	0.3	0.1	5.7	3.3
Peoria, IL	85.4	8.8	2.3	0.2	0.0	0.8	2.4
Philadelphia, PA	66.6	21.0	5.9	0.2	0.0	3.4	2.8
Phoenix, AZ	77.8	5.5	4.0	2.3	0.2	6.5	3.7
Pittsburgh, PA	86.6	8.1	2.3	0.1	0.0	0.4	2.5
Portland, OR	81.1	2.8	6.7	0.8	0.5	3.0	5.0
Providence, RI	81.7	5.9	3.0	0.4	0.1	5.7	3.2
Provo, UT	91.7	0.6	1.5	0.5	0.9	1.8	3.1
Raleigh, NC	67.2	20.0	5.7	0.4	0.0	3.7	2.9
Reno, NV	77.6	2.3	5.3	1.6	0.6	8.1	4.4
Richmond, VA	61.1	29.7	3.8	0.3	0.1	1.8	3.1
Riverside, CA	60.5	7.4	6.8	0.8	0.3	19.5	4.7
Rochester, MN	87.4	4.5	4.3	0.3	0.1	1.1	2.4
Sacramento, CA	65.0	7.1	13.3	0.6	0.9	6.5	6.6
Salt Lake City, UT	79.7	1.8	3.9	0.8	1.4	9.0	3.4
San Antonio, TX	80.7	6.8	2.5	0.6	0.1	5.9	3.4
San Diego, CA	70.7	5.0	11.9	0.7	0.4	6.0	5.2
San Francisco, CA	49.0	7.3	26.1	0.5	0.7	10.2	6.2
San Jose, CA	45.6	2.4	35.4	0.5	0.4	10.4	5.2
Santa Rosa, CA	74.8	1.7	4.1	0.9	0.3	12.9	5.4
Savannah, GA	59.6	33.3	2.2	0.3	0.1	1.5	3.0
Seattle, WA	68.3	5.8	13.6	0.8	0.9	3.7	6.8
Sioux Falls, SD	88.3	4.5	1.8	1.6	0.0	1.1	2.7
Springfield, IL	82.8	12.1	1.9	0.1	0.1	0.4	2.6
Tallahassee, FL	60.6	32.7	2.7	0.2	0.0	1.3	2.4
Tampa, FL	77.8	12.2	3.4	0.3	0.1	2.9	3.3
Tucson, AZ	76.0	3.6	2.9	3.9	0.2	8.6	4.9
Tulsa, OK	71.2	8.0	2.5	7.3	0.1	2.7	8.2
Tuscaloosa, AL	60.6	35.8	1.4	0.2	0.0	0.8	1.1
Virginia Beach, VA	59.0	30.6	3.8	0.3	0.1	1.8	4.5
Washington, DC	53.5	25.3	10.1	0.3	0.1	6.5	4.2
Wichita, KS	80.9	7.5	3.7	0.9	0.1	2.9	4.0
Winston-Salem, NC	75.8	17.8	1.8	0.4	0.1	2.0	2.2
U.S.	72.5	12.7	5.5	0.8	0.2	4.9	3.3

Note: (1) Figures cover the Metropolitan Statistical Area (MSA)—see Appendix B for areas included; (1) Alone is defined as not being in combination with one or more other races; (2) American Indian and Alaska Native; (3) Native Hawaiian & Other Pacific Islander
Source: U.S. Census Bureau, 2015-2019 American Community Survey 5-Year Estimates

Hispanic Origin: City

City	Hispanic or Latino (%)	Mexican (%)	Puerto Rican (%)	Cuban (%)	Other Hispanic or Latino (%)
Albuquerque, NM	49.2	28.0	0.6	0.5	20.2
Allentown, PA	52.5	1.9	28.8	0.9	20.9
Anchorage, AK	9.2	4.8	1.4	0.1	2.8
Ann Arbor, MI	4.8	2.2	0.4	0.3	1.9
Athens, GA	10.9	6.7	0.7	0.4	3.1
Atlanta, GA	4.3	2.0	0.6	0.3	1.4
Austin, TX	33.9	27.2	0.9	0.7	5.2
Baton Rouge, LA	3.7	1.1	0.3	0.2	2.1
Boise City, ID	9.0	7.2	0.3	0.0	1.5
Boston, MA	19.8	1.2	5.3	0.5	12.9
Boulder, CO	9.7	6.0	0.4	0.4	2.9
Cape Coral, FL	20.9	2.0	5.0	7.8	6.1
Cedar Rapids, IA	4.0	2.8	0.2	0.0	1.0
Charleston, SC	3.2	1.3	0.5	0.2	1.2
Charlotte, NC	14.3	5.3	1.2	0.5	7.3
Chicago, IL	28.8	21.3	3.6	0.3	3.5
Cincinnati, OH	3.8	1.2	0.6	0.1	2.0
Clarksville, TN	11.5	5.2	3.7	0.3	2.3
Cleveland, OH	11.9	1.3	8.5	0.2	1.9
College Station, TX	15.8	11.2	0.3	0.4	3.9
Colorado Springs, CO	17.6	11.3	1.4	0.5	4.5
Columbia, MO	3.6	2.2	0.3	0.1	1.1
Columbia, SC	5.5	2.1	1.3	0.3	1.7
Columbus, OH	6.2	3.2	0.9	0.1	1.9
Dallas, TX	41.8	35.4	0.5	0.3	5.5
Davenport, IA	8.7	7.8	0.3	0.0	0.5
Denver, CO	29.9	23.7	0.6	0.2	5.4
Des Moines, IA	13.6	10.6	0.4	0.1	2.4
Durham, NC	13.8	6.1	1.1	0.2	6.4
Edison, NJ	9.9	1.8	2.5	0.8	4.8
El Paso, TX	81.4	76.9	1.1	0.1	3.2
Fargo, ND	3.0	1.9	0.4	0.0	0.6
Fayetteville, NC	12.4	4.2	4.1	0.4	3.7
Fort Collins, CO	11.6	8.2	0.4	0.1	3.0
Fort Wayne, IN	9.2	6.8	0.5	0.1	1.7
Fort Worth, TX	35.1	30.6	1.1	0.3	3.1
Grand Rapids, MI	16.1	9.5	1.5	0.2	4.8
Greeley, CO	38.6	31.0	0.6	0.3	6.7
Green Bay, WI	15.8	12.5	1.4	0.1	1.8
Greensboro, NC	7.9	4.7	0.7	0.2	2.2
Honolulu, HI	7.3	2.0	1.8	0.2	3.4
Houston, TX	45.0	31.8	0.6	0.8	11.7
Huntsville, AL	6.2	3.8	0.9	0.2	1.4
Indianapolis, IN	10.5	7.1	0.6	0.2	2.6
Jacksonville, FL	10.0	2.0	3.0	1.2	3.7
Kansas City, MO	10.6	8.0	0.4	0.3	1.9
Lafayette, LA	3.6	1.4	0.2	0.2	1.7
Lakeland, FL	16.4	3.5	6.3	2.5	4.0
Las Vegas, NV	33.1	24.7	1.2	1.3	5.9
Lexington, KY	7.2	4.8	0.7	0.2	1.5
Lincoln, NE	7.6	5.5	0.3	0.2	1.6
Little Rock, AR	7.4	4.8	0.3	0.3	2.1
Los Angeles, CA	48.5	32.2	0.4	0.4	15.4
Louisville, KY	5.6	2.0	0.5	1.9	1.2
Madison, WI	7.0	4.1	0.7	0.2	2.0

Table continued on following page.

City	Hispanic or Latino (%)	Mexican (%)	Puerto Rican (%)	Cuban (%)	Other Hispanic or Latino (%)
Manchester, NH	10.4	1.5	4.4	0.1	4.4
Memphis, TN	7.2	5.1	0.3	0.2	1.6
Miami, FL	72.7	1.9	3.4	35.0	32.4
Midland, TX	44.2	40.6	0.5	0.9	2.2
Milwaukee, WI	19.0	13.4	4.4	0.2	1.1
Minneapolis, MN	9.6	5.8	0.5	0.2	3.1
Nashville, TN	10.5	6.2	0.6	0.4	3.4
New Haven, CT	31.2	5.6	17.6	0.3	7.7
New Orleans, LA	5.5	1.3	0.3	0.4	3.5
New York, NY	29.1	4.0	8.1	0.5	16.5
Oklahoma City, OK	19.7	16.6	0.3	0.1	2.8
Omaha, NE	13.9	10.7	0.4	0.1	2.7
Orlando, FL	32.6	1.9	15.6	3.0	12.0
Peoria, IL	6.3	4.6	0.4	0.1	1.1
Philadelphia, PA	14.7	1.3	8.8	0.3	4.3
Phoenix, AZ	42.6	38.3	0.7	0.3	3.3
Pittsburgh, PA	3.2	1.0	0.7	0.2	1.3
Portland, OR	9.7	6.8	0.4	0.4	2.1
Providence, RI	43.3	1.8	9.3	0.3	31.9
Provo, UT	16.7	11.3	0.5	0.1	4.7
Raleigh, NC	11.2	5.1	1.2	0.4	4.5
Reno, NV	24.7	19.2	0.5	0.3	4.7
Richmond, VA	6.9	1.7	0.7	0.2	4.3
Riverside, CA	53.7	47.1	0.8	0.2	5.6
Rochester, MN	5.9	3.7	0.4	0.2	1.6
Sacramento, CA	28.9	24.6	0.7	0.2	3.3
Salt Lake City, UT	21.8	16.9	0.3	0.4	4.2
San Antonio, TX	64.2	56.9	1.3	0.3	5.7
San Diego, CA	30.3	26.6	0.7	0.2	2.8
San Francisco, CA	15.2	7.8	0.6	0.3	6.6
San Jose, CA	31.6	27.1	0.6	0.1	3.7
Santa Rosa, CA	32.8	28.8	0.4	0.1	3.5
Savannah, GA	5.8	2.3	1.5	0.2	1.8
Seattle, WA	6.7	3.9	0.4	0.2	2.1
Sioux Falls, SD	5.5	3.1	0.4	0.1	1.9
Springfield, IL	2.8	1.5	0.5	0.1	0.7
Tallahassee, FL	6.7	1.2	1.4	1.3	2.8
Tampa, FL	26.4	3.1	7.6	8.0	7.7
Tucson, AZ	43.6	39.5	0.8	0.2	3.1
Tulsa, OK	16.5	13.2	0.6	0.2	2.6
Tuscaloosa, AL	3.2	1.6	0.1	0.2	1.4
Virginia Beach, VA	8.2	2.5	2.4	0.3	3.0
Washington, DC	11.0	2.0	0.9	0.4	7.6
Wichita, KS	17.2	14.7	0.4	0.2	1.9
Winston-Salem, NC	15.0	9.9	1.4	0.2	3.5
U.S.	18.0	11.2	1.7	0.7	4.3

Note: Persons of Hispanic or Latino origin can be of any race
Source: U.S. Census Bureau, 2015-2019 American Community Survey 5-Year Estimates

Hispanic Origin: Metro Area

Metro Area	Hispanic or Latino (%)	Mexican (%)	Puerto Rican (%)	Cuban (%)	Other Hispanic or Latino (%)
Albuquerque, NM	49.0	27.7	0.5	0.4	20.4
Allentown, PA	17.0	1.2	9.2	0.3	6.2
Anchorage, AK	8.1	4.2	1.2	0.2	2.4
Ann Arbor, MI	4.7	2.6	0.3	0.2	1.6
Athens, GA	8.6	5.0	0.7	0.3	2.6
Atlanta, GA	10.7	5.6	1.0	0.4	3.6
Austin, TX	32.4	26.8	0.9	0.5	4.3
Baton Rouge, LA	4.0	1.5	0.3	0.2	2.0
Boise City, ID	13.7	11.6	0.3	0.1	1.6
Boston, MA	11.1	0.7	2.9	0.2	7.3
Boulder, CO	13.9	10.4	0.4	0.3	2.8
Cape Coral, FL	21.4	6.0	4.3	4.9	6.2
Cedar Rapids, IA	3.0	2.1	0.1	0.0	0.8
Charleston, SC	5.6	2.7	0.8	0.1	2.0
Charlotte, NC	10.1	4.7	1.0	0.4	4.1
Chicago, IL	22.1	17.3	2.2	0.2	2.4
Cincinnati, OH	3.2	1.5	0.4	0.1	1.2
Clarksville, TN	8.8	4.2	2.7	0.2	1.7
Cleveland, OH	5.8	1.3	3.4	0.1	1.0
College Station, TX	24.9	21.4	0.2	0.2	3.0
Colorado Springs, CO	16.7	10.3	1.7	0.4	4.4
Columbia, MO	3.2	2.1	0.2	0.1	0.8
Columbia, SC	5.5	2.8	1.1	0.2	1.4
Columbus, OH	4.2	2.1	0.7	0.1	1.3
Dallas, TX	28.9	23.9	0.7	0.3	4.0
Davenport, IA	8.7	7.7	0.4	0.1	0.6
Denver, CO	23.1	17.6	0.6	0.2	4.7
Des Moines, IA	7.1	5.4	0.2	0.1	1.4
Durham, NC	11.1	5.7	0.9	0.2	4.3
Edison, NJ	24.6	3.0	6.2	0.8	14.7
El Paso, TX	82.5	78.2	1.0	0.1	3.2
Fargo, ND	3.2	2.2	0.3	0.0	0.7
Fayetteville, NC	12.1	5.3	3.5	0.3	2.9
Fort Collins, CO	11.5	8.4	0.3	0.1	2.6
Fort Wayne, IN	7.0	5.2	0.4	0.1	1.3
Fort Worth, TX	28.9	23.9	0.7	0.3	4.0
Grand Rapids, MI	9.6	6.7	0.8	0.3	1.8
Greeley, CO	29.4	24.2	0.4	0.3	4.6
Green Bay, WI	7.4	5.8	0.7	0.0	0.9
Greensboro, NC	8.4	5.5	0.7	0.2	1.9
Honolulu, HI	9.8	2.9	3.1	0.1	3.7
Houston, TX	37.3	27.8	0.7	0.6	8.3
Huntsville, AL	5.2	3.2	0.7	0.2	1.0
Indianapolis, IN	6.7	4.4	0.5	0.1	1.7
Jacksonville, FL	8.9	1.8	2.8	1.2	3.1
Kansas City, MO	9.0	6.9	0.4	0.2	1.6
Lafayette, LA	4.0	2.1	0.2	0.2	1.5
Lakeland, FL	22.5	7.5	9.3	1.6	4.0
Las Vegas, NV	31.1	23.1	1.1	1.4	5.6
Lexington, KY	6.2	4.2	0.5	0.1	1.3
Lincoln, NE	6.8	4.9	0.3	0.2	1.5
Little Rock, AR	5.3	3.7	0.2	0.1	1.3
Los Angeles, CA	45.0	35.0	0.4	0.4	9.3
Louisville, KY	4.9	2.4	0.4	1.1	1.1
Madison, WI	5.7	3.6	0.5	0.1	1.5

Table continued on following page.

Metro Area	Hispanic or Latino (%)	Mexican (%)	Puerto Rican (%)	Cuban (%)	Other Hispanic or Latino (%)
Manchester, NH	6.8	1.0	2.5	0.2	3.0
Memphis, TN	5.6	4.0	0.2	0.1	1.2
Miami, FL	45.2	2.5	3.9	19.0	19.8
Midland, TX	44.7	41.6	0.5	0.7	1.9
Milwaukee, WI	10.7	7.4	2.3	0.1	0.9
Minneapolis, MN	5.9	3.8	0.3	0.1	1.6
Nashville, TN	7.3	4.4	0.5	0.2	2.2
New Haven, CT	18.1	1.9	10.6	0.4	5.3
New Orleans, LA	8.8	1.9	0.5	0.6	5.9
New York, NY	24.6	3.0	6.2	0.8	14.7
Oklahoma City, OK	13.3	10.9	0.3	0.1	2.0
Omaha, NE	10.4	7.9	0.4	0.1	2.0
Orlando, FL	30.7	2.9	15.2	2.4	10.1
Peoria, IL	3.5	2.5	0.3	0.0	0.6
Philadelphia, PA	9.4	1.9	4.6	0.3	2.7
Phoenix, AZ	30.9	27.1	0.7	0.3	2.8
Pittsburgh, PA	1.8	0.5	0.5	0.1	0.7
Portland, OR	12.0	9.2	0.4	0.2	2.2
Providence, RI	12.9	0.9	4.3	0.2	7.4
Provo, UT	11.7	7.7	0.3	0.1	3.7
Raleigh, NC	10.6	5.5	1.3	0.4	3.4
Reno, NV	24.3	18.9	0.6	0.3	4.4
Richmond, VA	6.3	1.6	1.0	0.2	3.5
Riverside, CA	51.0	44.4	0.8	0.3	5.5
Rochester, MN	4.4	2.9	0.2	0.1	1.2
Sacramento, CA	21.6	17.7	0.7	0.2	3.1
Salt Lake City, UT	18.0	13.3	0.5	0.1	4.1
San Antonio, TX	55.4	48.8	1.3	0.2	5.0
San Diego, CA	33.7	30.0	0.7	0.2	2.8
San Francisco, CA	21.8	14.2	0.7	0.2	6.7
San Jose, CA	26.5	22.1	0.5	0.1	3.7
Santa Rosa, CA	26.7	22.6	0.4	0.1	3.6
Savannah, GA	6.2	2.9	1.2	0.4	1.6
Seattle, WA	10.0	7.1	0.6	0.2	2.2
Sioux Falls, SD	4.3	2.5	0.3	0.1	1.5
Springfield, IL	2.3	1.3	0.4	0.1	0.5
Tallahassee, FL	6.6	1.9	1.3	1.0	2.4
Tampa, FL	19.6	3.8	6.2	4.0	5.6
Tucson, AZ	37.2	33.5	0.8	0.2	2.7
Tulsa, OK	9.9	7.8	0.4	0.1	1.6
Tuscaloosa, AL	3.5	2.2	0.2	0.1	1.0
Virginia Beach, VA	6.7	2.2	2.0	0.3	2.3
Washington, DC	15.8	2.3	1.1	0.3	12.1
Wichita, KS	13.1	11.0	0.4	0.1	1.5
Winston-Salem, NC	10.2	6.7	0.9	0.2	2.5
U.S.	18.0	11.2	1.7	0.7	4.3

Note: Persons of Hispanic or Latino origin can be of any race; Figures cover the Metropolitan Statistical Area (MSA)—see Appendix B for areas included
Source: U.S. Census Bureau, 2015-2019 American Community Survey 5-Year Estimates

Age: City

City	Percent of Population									Median Age
	Under Age 5	Age 5–19	Age 20–34	Age 35–44	Age 45–54	Age 55–64	Age 65–74	Age 75–84	Age 85+	
Albuquerque, NM	5.9	19.0	22.6	13.0	12.0	12.2	8.8	4.4	1.8	36.6
Allentown, PA	7.6	22.8	24.6	11.9	11.3	10.0	6.5	3.3	2.0	31.6
Anchorage, AK	7.2	19.6	25.4	12.9	12.3	12.2	7.0	2.6	0.9	33.6
Ann Arbor, MI	3.7	18.5	40.1	9.5	8.3	8.2	6.8	3.4	1.5	27.5
Athens, GA	5.3	20.8	34.5	11.2	8.8	8.8	6.3	3.2	1.0	28.0
Atlanta, GA	5.4	16.9	30.7	13.8	11.8	9.8	6.8	3.4	1.4	33.3
Austin, TX	6.4	16.7	30.2	16.0	11.9	9.8	5.6	2.3	1.0	33.3
Baton Rouge, LA	6.7	19.6	28.3	10.5	10.1	11.1	8.0	3.9	1.9	31.5
Boise City, ID	5.7	18.9	23.1	14.0	12.3	12.0	8.4	3.7	1.8	36.6
Boston, MA	5.0	15.4	34.8	12.4	10.9	10.1	6.6	3.3	1.6	32.2
Boulder, CO	2.9	18.7	37.6	10.2	10.4	8.9	6.6	3.0	1.6	28.6
Cape Coral, FL	4.4	15.9	15.7	11.4	14.2	15.7	13.2	6.7	2.8	46.7
Cedar Rapids, IA	6.5	18.9	22.8	13.0	11.6	11.9	8.4	4.4	2.4	36.3
Charleston, SC	6.0	14.5	29.8	12.4	10.7	11.9	9.0	3.7	1.9	34.8
Charlotte, NC	6.8	19.4	25.1	14.8	13.1	10.7	6.4	2.8	1.1	34.2
Chicago, IL	6.3	17.0	27.3	14.0	11.9	10.9	7.2	3.7	1.5	34.6
Cincinnati, OH	7.1	19.0	28.3	11.3	10.5	11.6	7.0	3.3	1.9	32.2
Clarksville, TN	9.0	20.6	30.7	13.0	10.0	8.5	5.2	2.1	0.9	29.6
Cleveland, OH	6.3	18.3	23.7	11.5	12.4	13.8	8.0	4.2	1.8	36.3
College Station, TX	5.1	22.9	42.6	9.9	6.8	6.0	4.3	1.9	0.6	23.0
Colorado Springs, CO	6.5	19.3	24.6	12.6	11.9	11.6	8.1	3.8	1.5	34.7
Columbia, MO	5.9	19.0	34.6	11.0	9.5	9.4	6.0	3.2	1.3	28.5
Columbia, SC	5.1	23.2	31.9	10.1	10.1	9.4	6.2	2.8	1.2	28.5
Columbus, OH	7.3	18.2	29.4	12.9	11.3	10.6	6.2	2.7	1.3	32.2
Dallas, TX	7.5	19.9	26.4	13.7	11.8	10.4	6.1	2.9	1.2	32.7
Davenport, IA	6.4	19.2	21.8	12.3	12.3	12.7	8.6	4.1	2.5	36.7
Denver, CO	6.1	15.7	29.2	15.9	11.6	10.0	7.0	3.1	1.5	34.5
Des Moines, IA	6.9	19.7	24.5	13.0	12.0	11.8	7.1	3.3	1.6	34.2
Durham, NC	6.8	18.4	26.7	14.0	11.9	10.7	7.1	3.0	1.4	33.9
Edison, NJ	6.1	18.4	17.9	15.7	14.0	13.1	8.4	4.1	2.3	39.6
El Paso, TX	7.4	22.2	23.2	12.4	11.7	10.6	7.1	3.9	1.7	32.9
Fargo, ND	6.7	17.4	32.0	12.3	9.5	10.1	6.6	3.3	2.0	31.0
Fayetteville, NC	7.7	18.9	30.9	11.0	9.8	10.1	6.7	3.5	1.4	30.0
Fort Collins, CO	5.0	19.5	33.9	11.6	9.7	9.5	6.3	3.0	1.3	29.3
Fort Wayne, IN	7.1	20.6	22.2	12.1	11.7	12.1	8.3	3.8	1.8	35.0
Fort Worth, TX	8.0	22.5	23.3	14.0	12.4	10.1	5.9	2.6	1.2	32.6
Grand Rapids, MI	6.9	18.6	30.3	11.2	10.1	10.8	6.6	3.4	2.1	31.4
Greeley, CO	6.5	23.6	24.8	12.0	10.9	10.5	6.8	3.4	1.7	31.5
Green Bay, WI	7.6	20.3	22.8	12.4	12.3	11.8	7.2	3.7	1.9	34.5
Greensboro, NC	6.0	19.9	24.0	12.5	12.4	11.5	8.0	3.9	1.8	35.1
Honolulu, HI	5.2	14.1	22.0	13.0	12.8	12.9	10.5	5.5	3.9	41.5
Houston, TX	7.6	19.9	25.9	14.0	11.7	10.4	6.3	3.0	1.2	33.0
Huntsville, AL	6.1	17.6	23.8	11.6	12.1	12.7	8.9	5.2	2.1	36.9
Indianapolis, IN	7.3	19.8	24.1	12.8	11.9	11.9	7.2	3.4	1.5	34.2
Jacksonville, FL	6.9	18.3	23.3	12.7	12.8	12.5	8.2	3.8	1.5	35.9
Kansas City, MO	6.8	18.4	24.6	13.2	12.0	12.2	7.5	3.6	1.7	35.1
Lafayette, LA	5.7	18.5	24.4	11.5	11.5	13.5	8.9	4.2	1.7	35.8
Lakeland, FL	4.9	17.8	19.9	11.9	11.4	11.9	11.8	7.2	3.2	41.1
Las Vegas, NV	6.4	19.5	20.2	13.3	13.4	12.1	9.1	4.3	1.5	37.8
Lexington, KY	6.1	18.4	26.0	13.1	11.8	11.5	7.8	3.7	1.5	34.6
Lincoln, NE	6.5	19.9	26.7	12.4	10.5	10.9	7.7	3.6	1.7	32.7
Little Rock, AR	6.7	18.8	22.1	13.5	11.9	12.8	8.4	3.6	2.2	36.7
Los Angeles, CA	5.9	17.5	25.7	14.3	13.2	11.0	7.0	3.6	1.7	35.6
Louisville, KY	6.5	18.5	21.5	12.4	12.8	13.4	8.7	4.3	1.9	37.6

Table continued on following page.

City	Percent of Population									Median Age
	Under Age 5	Age 5–19	Age 20–34	Age 35–44	Age 45–54	Age 55–64	Age 65–74	Age 75–84	Age 85+	
Madison, WI	4.9	16.4	35.5	12.2	9.7	9.7	6.9	3.2	1.5	31.0
Manchester, NH	6.0	15.7	26.6	12.8	13.2	12.4	7.2	3.7	2.3	36.0
Memphis, TN	7.6	19.9	23.7	12.0	11.8	12.0	7.7	3.6	1.5	34.0
Miami, FL	5.9	13.4	23.0	14.6	14.5	11.8	8.5	5.8	2.6	40.1
Midland, TX	8.8	21.0	25.5	13.0	10.8	10.5	5.7	3.1	1.6	31.7
Milwaukee, WI	7.4	21.9	25.6	12.6	11.2	10.7	6.3	2.8	1.4	31.5
Minneapolis, MN	6.5	16.9	32.0	13.8	10.8	10.1	6.3	2.6	1.1	32.3
Nashville, TN	6.8	17.0	27.6	13.8	11.8	11.4	7.1	3.3	1.3	34.2
New Haven, CT	6.3	21.2	29.6	12.6	11.1	8.9	6.4	2.7	1.2	30.8
New Orleans, LA	5.9	16.6	24.6	13.4	12.1	13.3	8.7	3.7	1.7	36.8
New York, NY	6.5	16.5	24.3	13.7	12.7	11.8	8.1	4.4	2.0	36.7
Oklahoma City, OK	7.6	20.6	23.1	13.4	11.5	11.5	7.4	3.5	1.5	34.1
Omaha, NE	7.3	20.4	22.9	12.7	11.9	11.9	7.6	3.6	1.7	34.5
Orlando, FL	6.7	15.9	29.7	15.1	12.1	10.1	6.3	2.7	1.2	33.8
Peoria, IL	7.6	19.5	22.5	12.1	11.3	11.8	8.4	4.4	2.4	35.2
Philadelphia, PA	6.7	18.0	26.2	12.4	11.7	11.6	7.7	4.0	1.8	34.4
Phoenix, AZ	7.2	21.6	23.2	13.8	12.8	10.9	6.5	2.9	1.2	33.8
Pittsburgh, PA	4.7	15.4	33.3	10.6	9.5	11.8	8.1	4.3	2.3	32.9
Portland, OR	5.3	14.6	25.9	17.1	13.1	11.3	8.0	3.3	1.5	37.1
Providence, RI	6.3	21.9	28.3	12.3	10.9	9.4	5.9	3.2	1.7	30.6
Provo, UT	7.1	20.7	47.4	8.3	5.4	5.0	3.1	2.0	0.9	23.6
Raleigh, NC	5.9	18.9	27.5	14.5	12.7	9.9	6.4	2.9	1.3	33.6
Reno, NV	6.2	17.8	24.7	12.6	11.7	12.2	9.3	4.1	1.4	35.8
Richmond, VA	5.9	15.6	30.2	11.8	11.2	12.4	7.7	3.3	1.8	34.0
Riverside, CA	6.2	22.3	26.5	12.4	12.0	10.0	6.3	3.1	1.3	31.6
Rochester, MN	7.2	18.8	22.6	13.1	11.6	11.8	8.0	4.6	2.4	35.7
Sacramento, CA	6.6	18.8	25.4	13.5	11.6	11.1	7.8	3.5	1.8	34.5
Salt Lake City, UT	6.2	17.1	31.6	13.8	10.1	10.2	6.6	3.2	1.3	32.3
San Antonio, TX	6.9	21.0	24.2	13.2	12.0	10.7	7.1	3.5	1.5	33.6
San Diego, CA	5.9	16.8	27.4	13.9	12.3	11.0	7.3	3.7	1.6	34.9
San Francisco, CA	4.5	10.5	29.0	15.8	13.2	11.6	8.5	4.5	2.5	38.2
San Jose, CA	6.1	18.4	22.7	14.4	13.9	11.8	7.3	3.7	1.5	36.7
Santa Rosa, CA	5.9	17.8	21.2	12.8	12.6	12.9	9.6	4.8	2.3	38.8
Savannah, GA	6.4	18.2	29.1	11.6	10.4	11.2	7.7	3.7	1.7	32.6
Seattle, WA	4.8	12.8	31.8	15.3	12.3	10.7	7.4	3.3	1.8	35.3
Sioux Falls, SD	7.5	19.9	23.5	13.3	11.4	11.7	7.6	3.4	1.7	34.4
Springfield, IL	6.1	18.2	20.2	11.6	12.2	14.0	10.0	5.3	2.3	39.4
Tallahassee, FL	4.9	19.2	38.0	10.0	8.8	8.7	6.3	2.8	1.2	26.9
Tampa, FL	6.4	18.5	24.2	13.5	13.4	11.8	7.3	3.5	1.5	35.7
Tucson, AZ	6.0	19.1	26.5	11.9	10.9	11.2	8.3	4.2	1.9	33.7
Tulsa, OK	7.1	20.0	22.8	12.4	11.4	12.3	8.1	4.0	1.9	35.1
Tuscaloosa, AL	5.2	22.9	29.5	10.0	9.9	10.3	6.9	3.9	1.4	29.3
Virginia Beach, VA	6.3	18.2	23.7	13.0	12.7	12.1	8.1	4.0	1.6	36.2
Washington, DC	6.5	14.5	31.0	14.8	11.0	10.1	7.0	3.5	1.6	34.0
Wichita, KS	7.0	20.7	22.4	11.9	11.6	12.5	8.2	3.9	1.8	35.0
Winston-Salem, NC	6.5	20.9	21.8	12.4	12.1	12.0	8.1	4.3	1.7	35.5
U.S.	6.1	19.1	20.7	12.6	13.0	12.9	9.1	4.6	1.9	38.1

Source: U.S. Census Bureau, 2015-2019 American Community Survey 5-Year Estimates

Age: Metro Area

Metro Area	Percent of Population									Median Age
	Under Age 5	Age 5–19	Age 20–34	Age 35–44	Age 45–54	Age 55–64	Age 65–74	Age 75–84	Age 85+	
Albuquerque, NM	5.7	19.2	20.7	12.6	12.4	13.2	9.8	4.7	1.8	38.2
Allentown, PA	5.3	18.7	18.6	11.9	13.8	14.1	9.9	5.2	2.6	41.4
Anchorage, AK	7.2	20.2	24.0	13.0	12.4	12.4	7.2	2.6	0.9	34.0
Ann Arbor, MI	4.9	19.5	27.4	11.5	11.8	11.5	8.2	3.7	1.6	33.6
Athens, GA	5.4	21.1	27.1	12.0	11.0	10.7	7.8	3.8	1.2	32.2
Atlanta, GA	6.4	21.0	20.6	14.0	14.3	11.8	7.5	3.2	1.1	36.4
Austin, TX	6.4	19.7	24.3	15.5	12.9	10.6	6.7	2.7	1.1	34.7
Baton Rouge, LA	6.5	20.1	22.7	12.7	12.2	12.2	8.4	3.9	1.4	35.6
Boise City, ID	6.3	21.7	20.0	13.4	12.5	11.8	8.7	4.0	1.4	36.3
Boston, MA	5.3	17.7	22.2	12.5	13.7	13.2	8.8	4.4	2.1	38.7
Boulder, CO	4.6	19.0	24.3	12.6	13.1	12.7	8.4	3.7	1.6	36.6
Cape Coral, FL	4.7	15.2	15.8	10.3	11.9	14.1	15.5	9.3	3.3	48.5
Cedar Rapids, IA	6.2	19.5	19.6	12.7	12.9	12.9	9.0	4.8	2.3	38.4
Charleston, SC	6.1	18.5	22.1	13.2	12.7	12.8	9.3	3.9	1.5	37.2
Charlotte, NC	6.2	20.2	20.1	13.9	14.2	12.1	8.2	3.8	1.4	37.5
Chicago, IL	6.1	19.4	21.0	13.3	13.3	12.7	8.2	4.1	1.8	37.5
Cincinnati, OH	6.3	20.1	19.9	12.4	13.2	13.4	8.7	4.2	1.9	37.9
Clarksville, TN	8.4	20.8	27.0	12.4	10.8	9.8	6.6	3.2	1.2	31.1
Cleveland, OH	5.6	18.1	18.9	11.6	13.3	14.5	10.1	5.4	2.5	41.3
College Station, TX	6.1	20.9	32.9	11.0	9.5	9.2	6.1	3.0	1.2	27.8
Colorado Springs, CO	6.6	20.2	23.6	12.5	12.1	12.1	7.9	3.5	1.3	34.6
Columbia, MO	5.8	19.4	28.5	11.6	10.7	11.3	7.5	3.7	1.4	32.1
Columbia, SC	5.8	20.2	21.6	12.5	12.7	12.7	8.9	4.1	1.5	36.6
Columbus, OH	6.7	19.8	22.2	13.4	13.0	12.1	7.8	3.6	1.5	36.0
Dallas, TX	7.0	21.8	21.5	14.2	13.4	11.2	6.8	3.1	1.1	34.8
Davenport, IA	6.2	19.3	18.3	12.3	12.5	13.8	10.0	5.3	2.4	39.7
Denver, CO	6.1	18.9	22.6	14.6	13.2	12.1	7.8	3.3	1.4	36.5
Des Moines, IA	7.0	20.5	20.7	13.7	12.8	11.9	7.9	3.9	1.6	36.2
Durham, NC	5.7	18.6	22.3	13.0	13.0	12.6	9.1	4.0	1.7	37.6
Edison, NJ	6.1	17.8	21.2	13.1	13.6	12.8	8.6	4.6	2.2	38.6
El Paso, TX	7.6	22.8	23.3	12.5	11.5	10.4	6.7	3.7	1.5	32.2
Fargo, ND	7.1	19.5	27.4	12.8	10.5	10.7	6.6	3.4	1.9	32.5
Fayetteville, NC	7.7	20.7	25.7	12.5	11.4	10.6	7.0	3.4	1.1	32.3
Fort Collins, CO	5.1	18.4	25.2	12.3	11.2	12.6	9.4	4.1	1.7	36.0
Fort Wayne, IN	7.0	21.1	20.1	12.3	12.4	12.6	8.6	4.1	1.8	36.4
Fort Worth, TX	7.0	21.8	21.5	14.2	13.4	11.2	6.8	3.1	1.1	34.8
Grand Rapids, MI	6.5	20.6	21.8	12.3	12.4	12.5	8.1	4.0	1.9	35.8
Greeley, CO	7.2	22.1	21.5	13.6	12.2	11.5	7.4	3.2	1.2	34.4
Green Bay, WI	6.2	19.7	19.2	12.4	13.4	13.7	9.0	4.6	1.8	38.8
Greensboro, NC	5.8	19.7	19.8	12.1	13.7	13.0	9.3	4.7	1.9	38.8
Honolulu, HI	6.4	17.0	22.6	12.7	12.1	11.9	9.4	5.0	2.9	37.9
Houston, TX	7.3	21.9	21.7	14.2	12.8	11.2	6.8	3.0	1.0	34.3
Huntsville, AL	5.8	19.0	20.3	12.4	14.1	13.5	8.6	4.5	1.6	38.7
Indianapolis, IN	6.7	20.5	20.7	13.2	13.1	12.3	8.0	3.8	1.6	36.5
Jacksonville, FL	6.2	18.5	20.7	12.7	13.3	13.2	9.5	4.3	1.6	38.3
Kansas City, MO	6.5	20.0	20.0	13.2	12.9	12.8	8.5	4.2	1.8	37.4
Lafayette, LA	6.9	20.2	21.3	12.6	12.4	12.9	8.1	4.0	1.6	36.0
Lakeland, FL	5.8	18.8	19.0	11.8	12.1	12.3	11.4	6.7	2.1	40.2
Las Vegas, NV	6.3	19.3	21.1	13.8	13.3	11.7	8.9	4.2	1.3	37.3
Lexington, KY	6.2	19.0	23.2	13.0	12.6	12.1	8.3	4.0	1.5	36.1
Lincoln, NE	6.4	20.4	25.0	12.3	10.9	11.4	8.1	3.8	1.8	33.7
Little Rock, AR	6.4	19.6	21.3	12.9	12.4	12.5	8.9	4.2	1.8	36.9
Los Angeles, CA	6.0	18.6	22.7	13.5	13.6	12.0	7.7	4.0	1.9	36.8
Louisville, KY	6.1	18.7	19.9	12.8	13.3	13.6	9.3	4.4	1.8	39.0

Table continued on following page.

Metro Area	Percent of Population									Median Age
	Under Age 5	Age 5–19	Age 20–34	Age 35–44	Age 45–54	Age 55–64	Age 65–74	Age 75–84	Age 85+	
Madison, WI	5.6	18.2	24.4	13.0	12.3	12.5	8.5	3.8	1.7	36.2
Manchester, NH	5.2	17.8	19.8	12.3	14.9	14.7	9.0	4.3	1.9	40.7
Memphis, TN	6.8	20.7	20.8	12.7	12.9	12.5	8.3	3.8	1.4	36.3
Miami, FL	5.7	17.0	19.4	13.1	14.2	12.8	9.4	5.8	2.7	41.0
Midland, TX	8.8	22.1	24.4	13.1	10.6	10.8	5.8	3.1	1.5	31.7
Milwaukee, WI	6.2	19.6	20.4	12.5	12.8	13.3	8.7	4.3	2.2	37.8
Minneapolis, MN	6.5	19.7	20.7	13.3	13.3	13.0	8.0	3.8	1.7	37.1
Nashville, TN	6.4	19.4	22.1	13.7	13.3	12.3	8.0	3.6	1.3	36.4
New Haven, CT	5.2	18.2	20.2	11.8	13.7	13.8	9.5	4.9	2.6	40.3
New Orleans, LA	6.2	18.3	21.0	12.8	12.8	13.7	9.3	4.3	1.7	38.3
New York, NY	6.1	17.8	21.2	13.1	13.6	12.8	8.6	4.6	2.2	38.6
Oklahoma City, OK	6.8	20.6	22.2	13.0	11.8	12.0	8.1	3.9	1.6	35.2
Omaha, NE	7.2	21.0	20.8	13.2	12.3	12.2	8.0	3.8	1.6	35.7
Orlando, FL	5.9	18.7	22.2	13.7	13.3	11.7	8.5	4.3	1.7	37.2
Peoria, IL	6.3	19.1	18.5	12.3	12.6	13.5	9.9	5.3	2.6	39.9
Philadelphia, PA	5.9	18.6	20.7	12.3	13.4	13.5	8.9	4.6	2.1	38.8
Phoenix, AZ	6.4	20.3	21.0	13.1	12.5	11.4	8.9	4.6	1.7	36.7
Pittsburgh, PA	5.1	16.5	19.2	11.5	13.1	15.2	10.8	5.8	3.0	43.1
Portland, OR	5.7	18.1	21.3	14.7	13.3	12.5	9.0	3.8	1.7	38.1
Providence, RI	5.2	17.9	20.5	11.9	13.9	13.9	9.5	4.8	2.5	40.3
Provo, UT	9.6	28.3	26.8	12.6	8.4	6.7	4.5	2.3	0.8	24.8
Raleigh, NC	6.2	20.8	20.4	14.8	14.5	11.6	7.4	3.2	1.2	36.7
Reno, NV	6.0	18.1	21.5	12.2	12.8	13.2	10.2	4.4	1.4	38.5
Richmond, VA	5.8	18.7	20.7	12.8	13.6	13.5	9.2	4.1	1.8	38.8
Riverside, CA	6.8	22.1	21.8	12.8	12.5	11.2	7.5	3.8	1.4	34.5
Rochester, MN	6.7	19.8	18.9	12.6	12.4	13.4	8.8	5.0	2.3	38.4
Sacramento, CA	6.1	19.6	21.0	12.8	12.8	12.6	8.8	4.3	1.9	37.4
Salt Lake City, UT	7.6	22.6	23.3	14.6	11.2	10.1	6.4	3.0	1.1	32.7
San Antonio, TX	6.9	21.4	22.2	13.3	12.4	11.2	7.6	3.7	1.5	34.7
San Diego, CA	6.3	18.2	24.2	13.3	12.5	11.7	7.9	4.0	1.8	35.8
San Francisco, CA	5.5	16.5	22.0	14.5	13.8	12.6	8.7	4.4	2.1	39.0
San Jose, CA	6.1	18.6	22.3	14.5	13.8	11.7	7.4	4.0	1.8	37.1
Santa Rosa, CA	5.0	17.2	18.7	12.4	13.0	14.5	11.6	5.1	2.2	42.1
Savannah, GA	6.6	19.4	23.2	12.9	12.1	11.9	8.5	4.0	1.5	35.6
Seattle, WA	6.1	17.6	23.0	14.3	13.4	12.4	7.9	3.5	1.6	37.0
Sioux Falls, SD	7.6	20.7	21.4	13.5	11.8	12.0	7.8	3.4	1.8	35.2
Springfield, IL	5.8	19.0	18.4	12.2	13.1	14.2	10.1	5.1	2.1	40.4
Tallahassee, FL	5.2	18.9	27.4	11.5	11.2	11.8	8.7	3.8	1.5	33.8
Tampa, FL	5.4	16.8	18.9	12.4	13.5	13.6	10.9	6.0	2.5	42.1
Tucson, AZ	5.7	18.6	21.5	11.4	11.2	12.6	10.9	6.0	2.2	38.5
Tulsa, OK	6.7	20.5	20.1	12.6	12.4	12.7	8.9	4.5	1.7	37.0
Tuscaloosa, AL	6.0	20.5	24.3	11.8	11.5	12.0	8.4	4.1	1.5	34.4
Virginia Beach, VA	6.3	18.6	23.4	12.3	12.4	12.7	8.5	4.2	1.7	36.3
Washington, DC	6.5	19.0	21.3	14.3	14.0	12.1	7.7	3.6	1.4	37.0
Wichita, KS	6.9	21.3	20.4	12.1	11.8	12.7	8.3	4.3	1.9	36.0
Winston-Salem, NC	5.7	19.4	18.3	11.9	14.1	13.7	9.9	5.3	1.8	40.6
U.S.	6.1	19.1	20.7	12.6	13.0	12.9	9.1	4.6	1.9	38.1

Note: Figures cover the Metropolitan Statistical Area (MSA)—see Appendix B for areas included
Source: U.S. Census Bureau, 2015-2019 American Community Survey 5-Year Estimates

Religious Groups by Family

Area[1]	Catholic	Baptist	Non-Den.	Methodist[2]	Lutheran	LDS[3]	Pente-costal	Presby-terian[4]	Muslim[5]	Judaism
Albuquerque, NM	27.1	3.7	4.2	1.4	0.9	2.3	1.4	1.0	0.2	0.2
Allentown, PA	23.1	0.4	1.9	3.9	7.9	0.3	0.4	6.2	0.6	0.6
Anchorage, AK	6.9	5.0	6.4	1.3	1.9	5.1	1.8	0.6	0.2	0.1
Ann Arbor, MI	12.3	2.2	1.5	3.0	2.8	0.8	1.9	2.9	1.2	0.9
Athens, GA	4.4	16.2	2.2	8.3	0.3	0.8	2.8	2.0	0.3	0.2
Atlanta, GA	7.4	17.4	6.8	7.8	0.5	0.7	2.6	1.8	0.7	0.5
Austin, TX	16.0	10.3	4.5	3.6	1.9	1.1	0.8	1.0	1.2	0.2
Baton Rouge, LA	22.5	18.2	9.6	4.6	0.2	0.7	1.1	0.6	0.2	0.1
Boise City, ID	8.0	2.9	4.1	2.1	1.1	15.8	2.3	0.6	0.1	0.1
Boston, MA	44.3	1.1	1.0	0.9	0.3	0.4	0.6	1.6	0.4	1.4
Boulder, CO	20.1	2.3	4.7	1.7	3.0	2.9	0.4	2.0	0.1	0.7
Cape Coral, FL	16.2	4.9	3.0	2.5	1.1	0.5	4.3	1.4	0.9	0.2
Cedar Rapids, IA	18.8	2.3	3.0	7.3	11.3	0.8	1.8	3.2	0.5	0.1
Charleston, SC	6.1	12.4	7.0	10.0	1.1	0.9	2.0	2.3	0.1	0.3
Charlotte, NC	5.9	17.2	6.7	8.6	1.3	0.7	3.2	4.5	0.2	0.3
Chicago, IL	34.2	3.2	4.4	1.9	3.0	0.3	1.2	1.9	3.2	0.8
Cincinnati, OH	19.0	9.5	3.6	3.8	1.1	0.5	2.2	1.5	0.2	0.5
Clarksville, TN	4.0	30.9	2.2	6.1	0.5	1.5	1.8	1.0	0.1	<0.1
Cleveland, OH	28.8	4.3	3.3	2.8	2.5	0.3	1.1	2.0	0.1	1.4
College Station, TX	11.7	15.6	3.9	4.7	1.5	1.2	0.6	0.9	1.1	<0.1
Colorado Springs, CO	8.3	4.3	7.4	2.4	1.9	3.0	1.0	2.0	<0.1	0.1
Columbia, MO	6.6	14.6	5.4	4.3	1.7	1.3	1.0	2.3	0.3	0.2
Columbia, SC	3.1	18.0	5.2	9.3	3.4	1.0	2.6	3.3	0.1	0.2
Columbus, OH	11.7	5.3	3.5	4.7	2.4	0.7	1.9	2.0	0.8	0.5
Dallas, TX	13.3	18.7	7.7	5.2	0.7	1.1	2.1	0.9	2.4	0.3
Davenport, IA	14.9	4.9	2.7	5.3	8.6	0.8	1.4	2.9	0.9	0.1
Denver, CO	16.0	2.9	4.6	1.7	2.1	2.4	1.2	1.5	0.5	0.6
Des Moines, IA	13.6	4.7	3.3	6.9	8.2	0.9	2.3	2.9	0.3	0.3
Durham, NC	5.0	13.8	5.6	8.1	0.4	0.7	1.3	2.5	0.4	0.5
Edison, NJ	36.9	1.8	1.7	1.3	0.7	0.3	0.8	1.0	2.3	4.7
El Paso, TX	43.2	3.7	4.9	0.8	0.3	1.5	1.4	0.2	<0.1	0.2
Fargo, ND	17.4	0.4	0.4	3.3	32.5	0.6	1.5	1.8	0.1	<0.1
Fayetteville, NC	2.6	14.1	10.4	6.2	0.1	1.4	4.8	2.1	0.1	<0.1
Fort Collins, CO	11.8	2.2	6.3	4.3	3.4	2.9	4.7	1.9	0.1	<0.1
Fort Wayne, IN	14.2	6.0	6.8	5.1	8.5	0.4	1.4	1.6	0.2	0.1
Fort Worth, TX	13.3	18.7	7.7	5.2	0.7	1.1	2.1	0.9	2.4	0.3
Grand Rapids, MI	17.1	1.7	8.3	3.0	2.1	0.5	1.1	9.9	1.0	0.1
Greeley, CO	13.5	1.8	1.5	2.6	2.0	1.9	1.8	1.4	0.1	<0.1
Green Bay, WI	42.0	0.7	3.4	2.2	12.7	0.3	0.6	1.0	0.1	<0.1
Greensboro, NC	2.6	12.8	7.4	9.8	0.6	0.8	2.4	3.1	0.6	0.4
Honolulu, HI	18.2	1.9	2.2	0.8	0.3	5.1	4.1	1.4	<0.1	<0.1
Houston, TX	17.0	16.0	7.2	4.8	1.0	1.1	1.5	0.8	2.6	0.3
Huntsville, AL	3.9	27.6	3.1	7.5	0.7	1.1	1.2	1.7	0.2	0.1
Indianapolis, IN	10.5	10.2	7.1	4.9	1.6	0.7	1.6	1.6	0.2	0.3
Jacksonville, FL	9.8	18.5	7.7	4.5	0.6	1.1	1.9	1.6	0.6	0.4
Kansas City, MO	12.6	13.1	5.2	5.8	2.2	2.4	2.6	1.6	0.3	0.4
Lafayette, LA	47.0	14.7	3.9	2.5	0.2	0.4	2.9	0.1	0.1	<0.1
Lakeland, FL	7.5	13.6	5.0	3.9	0.9	0.7	4.0	1.6	0.4	<0.1
Las Vegas, NV	18.1	2.9	3.0	0.4	0.7	6.3	1.5	0.2	<0.1	0.3
Lexington, KY	6.7	24.9	2.3	5.9	0.4	1.0	2.1	1.3	0.1	0.3
Lincoln, NE	14.7	2.4	1.9	7.1	11.2	1.1	1.4	3.9	0.2	0.1
Little Rock, AR	4.5	25.9	6.0	7.3	0.5	0.9	2.8	0.8	0.1	0.1
Los Angeles, CA	33.8	2.7	3.6	1.0	0.6	1.7	1.7	0.9	0.7	0.9
Louisville, KY	13.6	25.0	1.7	3.7	0.6	0.8	0.9	1.1	0.5	0.4
Madison, WI	21.8	1.1	1.5	3.6	12.7	0.5	0.3	2.1	0.4	0.4

Table continued on following page.

Area[1]	Catholic	Baptist	Non-Den.	Methodist[2]	Lutheran	LDS[3]	Pente-costal	Presby-terian[4]	Muslim[5]	Judaism
Manchester, NH	31.1	1.3	2.3	1.1	0.5	0.6	0.4	2.0	0.3	0.5
Memphis, TN	5.2	30.8	5.4	6.2	0.3	0.6	4.7	2.4	0.3	0.6
Miami, FL	18.5	5.3	4.1	1.2	0.4	0.5	1.7	0.6	0.9	1.5
Midland, TX	22.4	25.2	8.8	4.2	0.6	1.2	1.6	1.8	3.7	<0.1
Milwaukee, WI	24.6	3.1	3.8	1.5	10.7	0.4	1.9	1.5	0.5	0.5
Minneapolis, MN	21.7	2.4	2.9	2.7	14.4	0.6	1.7	1.8	0.4	0.7
Nashville, TN	4.1	25.2	5.8	6.1	0.3	0.7	2.1	2.1	0.3	0.1
New Haven, CT	35.3	1.4	1.9	1.5	0.6	0.3	1.0	2.2	0.5	1.2
New Orleans, LA	31.5	8.4	3.7	2.6	0.8	0.5	2.1	0.5	0.4	0.5
New York, NY	36.9	1.8	1.7	1.3	0.7	0.3	0.8	1.0	2.3	4.7
Oklahoma City, OK	6.3	25.3	7.0	10.6	0.7	1.2	3.1	0.9	0.2	0.1
Omaha, NE	21.6	4.5	1.8	3.9	7.8	1.7	1.2	2.2	0.5	0.4
Orlando, FL	13.2	6.9	5.6	2.9	0.9	0.9	3.2	1.3	1.3	0.2
Peoria, IL	11.4	5.5	5.2	4.9	6.1	0.5	1.5	2.8	5.2	0.1
Philadelphia, PA	33.4	3.9	2.8	2.9	1.8	0.3	0.8	2.1	1.2	1.3
Phoenix, AZ	13.3	3.4	5.1	1.0	1.6	6.1	2.9	0.6	0.1	0.3
Pittsburgh, PA	32.8	2.3	2.8	5.6	3.3	0.3	1.1	4.6	0.3	0.7
Portland, OR	10.5	2.3	4.5	1.0	1.6	3.7	2.0	0.9	0.1	0.3
Providence, RI	47.0	1.4	1.2	0.8	0.5	0.3	0.5	1.0	0.1	0.7
Provo, UT	1.3	<0.1	<0.1	0.1	<0.1	88.5	0.1	<0.1	<0.1	<0.1
Raleigh, NC	9.1	12.1	5.9	6.7	0.9	0.8	2.2	2.2	0.9	0.3
Reno, NV	14.3	1.5	3.1	0.9	0.7	4.6	1.9	0.4	<0.1	0.1
Richmond, VA	5.9	19.9	5.4	6.1	0.6	0.9	1.8	2.1	2.7	0.3
Riverside, CA	24.8	2.6	5.5	0.6	0.5	2.4	1.5	0.6	0.5	<0.1
Rochester, MN	23.3	1.6	4.6	4.8	21.0	1.1	1.2	2.9	0.2	0.2
Sacramento, CA	16.1	3.1	4.0	1.7	0.7	3.3	2.0	0.8	0.8	0.2
Salt Lake City, UT	8.9	0.8	0.5	0.5	0.5	58.9	0.6	0.3	0.4	0.1
San Antonio, TX	28.4	8.5	6.0	3.0	1.6	1.4	1.3	0.7	0.9	0.2
San Diego, CA	25.9	2.0	4.8	1.1	0.9	2.3	1.0	0.9	0.7	0.5
San Francisco, CA	20.7	2.5	2.4	1.9	0.5	1.5	1.2	1.1	1.2	0.8
San Jose, CA	26.0	1.3	4.2	1.0	0.5	1.4	1.1	0.7	1.0	0.6
Santa Rosa, CA	22.2	1.3	1.5	0.9	0.9	1.9	0.6	0.9	0.4	0.4
Savannah, GA	7.0	19.6	6.9	8.9	1.6	0.9	2.3	1.0	0.1	0.8
Seattle, WA	12.3	2.1	5.0	1.2	2.0	3.3	2.8	1.4	0.4	0.4
Sioux Falls, SD	14.9	3.0	1.5	3.8	21.4	0.7	1.0	6.2	0.3	<0.1
Springfield, IL	15.5	11.7	2.7	6.8	5.6	0.7	4.9	2.0	1.5	0.2
Tallahassee, FL	4.8	16.0	6.7	9.1	0.4	1.0	2.1	1.5	0.8	0.3
Tampa, FL	10.8	7.0	3.7	3.4	0.9	0.6	2.1	0.9	1.2	0.4
Tucson, AZ	20.7	3.3	3.7	1.3	1.5	2.9	1.5	1.0	<0.1	0.5
Tulsa, OK	5.8	22.9	7.6	9.2	0.7	1.1	3.3	1.2	0.3	0.2
Tuscaloosa, AL	1.7	32.2	4.5	8.3	<0.1	0.6	1.5	1.3	0.1	<0.1
Virginia Beach, VA	6.4	11.5	6.1	5.2	0.7	0.9	1.9	2.0	2.0	0.3
Washington, DC	14.5	7.3	4.8	4.5	1.2	1.1	1.0	1.3	2.3	1.1
Wichita, KS	14.5	13.4	3.1	7.1	1.7	1.4	1.9	1.6	0.1	<0.1
Winston-Salem, NC	3.5	17.4	9.3	12.4	0.7	0.6	2.5	2.2	0.3	0.1
U.S.	19.1	9.3	4.0	4.0	2.3	2.0	1.9	1.6	0.8	0.7

Note: Figures are the number of adherents as a percentage of the total population; (1) Figures cover the Metropolitan Statistical Area—see Appendix B for areas included; (2) Methodist/Pietist; (3) Latter Day Saints; (4) Reformed; (5) Figures are estimates
Source: Association of Statisticians of American Religious Bodies, 2010 U.S. Religion Census: Religious Congregations & Membership Study

Religious Groups by Tradition

Area	Catholic	Evangelical Protestant	Mainline Protestant	Other Tradition	Black Protestant	Orthodox
Albuquerque, NM	27.1	11.2	3.2	3.9	0.2	0.1
Allentown, PA	23.1	5.3	17.7	3.0	0.1	0.6
Anchorage, AK	6.9	15.6	3.5	6.8	0.3	0.6
Ann Arbor, MI	12.3	7.3	7.5	3.7	1.5	0.2
Athens, GA	4.4	21.1	9.7	1.7	2.4	0.1
Atlanta, GA	7.4	26.0	9.8	2.9	3.1	0.2
Austin, TX	16.0	16.1	6.3	3.9	1.3	0.1
Baton Rouge, LA	22.5	24.8	5.6	1.5	5.1	<0.1
Boise City, ID	8.0	12.9	4.3	16.7	<0.1	<0.1
Boston, MA	44.3	3.2	4.5	3.4	0.1	1.0
Boulder, CO	20.1	9.7	6.4	4.8	<0.1	0.2
Cape Coral, FL	16.2	14.3	4.6	2.0	0.3	0.1
Cedar Rapids, IA	18.8	13.7	17.5	1.9	0.1	0.2
Charleston, SC	6.1	19.6	11.1	1.8	7.3	0.1
Charlotte, NC	5.9	27.5	13.3	1.6	2.7	0.4
Chicago, IL	34.2	9.7	5.1	5.0	2.0	0.9
Cincinnati, OH	19.0	15.5	7.1	1.5	1.1	0.1
Clarksville, TN	4.0	35.3	7.2	1.6	2.4	<0.1
Cleveland, OH	28.8	9.0	7.5	2.6	2.1	0.8
College Station, TX	11.7	20.6	6.6	2.5	0.9	<0.1
Colorado Springs, CO	8.3	15.2	5.3	3.7	0.4	0.1
Columbia, MO	6.6	19.9	10.4	2.3	0.4	0.1
Columbia, SC	3.1	25.5	13.4	2.1	5.4	0.1
Columbus, OH	11.7	11.8	9.5	3.1	1.1	0.2
Dallas, TX	13.3	28.3	6.9	4.7	1.7	0.1
Davenport, IA	14.9	11.3	15.1	2.3	1.5	0.1
Denver, CO	16.0	11.0	4.5	4.6	0.3	0.3
Des Moines, IA	13.6	12.3	16.8	1.8	0.9	0.1
Durham, NC	5.0	19.3	11.7	2.9	3.1	<0.1
Edison, NJ	36.9	3.9	4.1	8.3	1.2	0.9
El Paso, TX	43.2	10.8	1.2	2.0	0.2	<0.1
Fargo, ND	17.4	10.7	30.8	0.8	<0.1	<0.1
Fayetteville, NC	2.6	26.7	7.8	1.7	4.3	0.1
Fort Collins, CO	11.8	18.8	5.9	3.9	<0.1	0.1
Fort Wayne, IN	14.2	24.6	9.1	0.9	2.4	0.2
Fort Worth, TX	13.3	28.3	6.9	4.7	1.7	0.1
Grand Rapids, MI	17.1	20.7	7.5	2.1	1.0	0.2
Greeley, CO	13.5	9.2	3.8	2.1	<0.1	<0.1
Green Bay, WI	42.0	14.1	8.1	0.6	<0.1	<0.1
Greensboro, NC	2.6	23.2	14.0	2.1	2.6	<0.1
Honolulu, HI	18.2	9.6	2.9	8.4	<0.1	<0.1
Houston, TX	17.0	24.9	6.6	4.9	1.3	0.2
Huntsville, AL	3.9	33.3	9.6	1.8	1.8	<0.1
Indianapolis, IN	10.5	18.2	9.6	1.6	1.8	0.2
Jacksonville, FL	9.8	27.1	5.6	2.9	4.2	0.2
Kansas City, MO	12.6	20.5	9.9	3.6	2.6	0.1
Lafayette, LA	47.0	12.7	3.2	0.7	9.2	<0.1
Lakeland, FL	7.5	24.6	5.2	1.4	1.7	<0.1
Las Vegas, NV	18.1	7.7	1.3	7.6	0.4	0.4
Lexington, KY	6.7	28.3	10.2	1.7	2.0	0.1
Lincoln, NE	14.7	14.8	16.2	2.0	0.1	<0.1
Little Rock, AR	4.5	33.9	8.1	1.7	3.4	<0.1
Los Angeles, CA	33.8	9.0	2.3	4.6	0.8	0.6
Louisville, KY	13.6	24.5	7.1	2.0	2.9	<0.1
Madison, WI	21.8	7.2	15.3	2.2	0.1	<0.1

Table continued on following page.

Area	Catholic	Evangelical Protestant	Mainline Protestant	Other Tradition	Black Protestant	Orthodox
Manchester, NH	31.1	5.1	4.4	1.8	<0.1	0.7
Memphis, TN	5.2	29.4	8.3	2.1	13.4	<0.1
Miami, FL	18.5	11.4	2.4	3.5	1.7	0.2
Midland, TX	22.4	35.4	7.2	5.3	1.0	<0.1
Milwaukee, WI	24.6	14.6	7.1	2.3	2.4	0.6
Minneapolis, MN	21.7	12.8	14.5	2.2	0.4	0.2
Nashville, TN	4.1	32.9	8.0	1.7	3.3	0.4
New Haven, CT	35.3	3.8	6.1	2.3	0.7	0.4
New Orleans, LA	31.5	12.7	4.0	2.1	2.9	0.1
New York, NY	36.9	3.9	4.1	8.3	1.2	0.9
Oklahoma City, OK	6.3	39.0	9.8	2.7	1.9	0.1
Omaha, NE	21.6	12.1	10.7	3.2	1.4	0.1
Orlando, FL	13.2	17.8	4.7	3.2	1.2	0.3
Peoria, IL	11.4	18.9	11.1	6.1	0.9	0.1
Philadelphia, PA	33.4	6.3	8.9	3.7	1.7	0.4
Phoenix, AZ	13.3	13.2	2.6	7.8	0.1	0.3
Pittsburgh, PA	32.8	7.3	13.8	2.0	0.8	0.6
Portland, OR	10.5	11.6	3.6	5.2	0.1	0.3
Providence, RI	47.0	2.8	4.7	1.6	<0.1	0.5
Provo, UT	1.3	0.4	<0.1	88.8	<0.1	<0.1
Raleigh, NC	9.1	19.9	10.1	3.2	1.7	0.2
Reno, NV	14.3	7.6	1.9	5.1	0.2	0.1
Richmond, VA	5.9	23.6	13.3	4.5	2.4	0.1
Riverside, CA	24.8	11.4	1.3	3.7	0.8	0.1
Rochester, MN	23.3	18.9	21.0	2.0	<0.1	0.1
Sacramento, CA	16.1	11.3	2.2	5.8	0.5	0.3
Salt Lake City, UT	8.9	2.6	1.2	60.0	0.1	0.4
San Antonio, TX	28.4	16.9	5.0	3.1	0.4	<0.1
San Diego, CA	25.9	9.7	2.4	5.2	0.3	0.2
San Francisco, CA	20.7	6.1	3.8	5.2	1.0	0.6
San Jose, CA	26.0	8.2	2.4	6.8	0.1	0.4
Santa Rosa, CA	22.2	5.3	2.3	4.8	<0.1	0.2
Savannah, GA	7.0	25.0	9.4	2.6	8.5	0.1
Seattle, WA	12.3	11.9	4.6	5.9	0.3	0.4
Sioux Falls, SD	14.9	12.9	28.0	1.2	0.1	0.1
Springfield, IL	15.5	21.4	11.6	3.1	2.1	0.1
Tallahassee, FL	4.8	21.9	6.3	2.9	9.1	0.1
Tampa, FL	10.8	13.6	5.1	3.1	1.1	0.8
Tucson, AZ	20.7	10.0	3.7	4.5	0.4	0.2
Tulsa, OK	5.8	34.6	11.2	2.1	1.5	<0.1
Tuscaloosa, AL	1.7	35.2	6.4	0.9	8.5	<0.1
Virginia Beach, VA	6.4	18.0	9.4	3.9	2.2	0.3
Washington, DC	14.5	12.4	8.7	5.9	2.3	0.6
Wichita, KS	14.5	20.7	11.0	2.4	1.8	0.2
Winston-Salem, NC	3.5	29.1	15.6	1.2	2.2	0.2
U.S.	19.1	16.2	7.3	4.3	1.6	0.3

Note: Figures are the number of adherents as a percentage of the total population; (1) Figures cover the Metropolitan Statistical Area—see Appendix B for areas included
Source: Association of Statisticians of American Religious Bodies, 2010 U.S. Religion Census: Religious Congregations & Membership Study

Ancestry: City

City	German	Irish	English	American	Italian	Polish	French[1]	Scottish	Dutch
Albuquerque, NM	9.0	7.0	6.4	3.8	2.9	1.4	1.7	1.6	0.7
Allentown, PA	10.3	4.9	1.7	2.1	4.4	1.7	0.9	0.5	1.1
Anchorage, AK	14.4	9.7	7.8	3.6	3.0	2.1	2.4	2.6	1.4
Ann Arbor, MI	17.1	9.9	9.5	3.8	4.9	6.0	3.0	2.7	2.3
Athens, GA	8.4	8.2	8.0	4.3	3.0	1.6	1.7	2.7	1.0
Atlanta, GA	6.1	5.6	7.2	5.4	2.6	1.4	1.7	1.8	0.6
Austin, TX	10.4	7.4	7.4	3.1	3.0	1.7	2.3	2.0	0.8
Baton Rouge, LA	5.2	5.0	4.5	5.5	3.3	0.4	6.9	1.3	0.3
Boise City, ID	16.7	11.8	18.5	4.5	3.7	1.7	2.4	3.9	1.7
Boston, MA	4.6	13.4	4.3	2.5	7.7	2.2	1.9	1.2	0.5
Boulder, CO	17.4	12.1	10.5	2.5	6.0	3.5	2.6	3.2	1.3
Cape Coral, FL	14.1	11.5	7.3	15.3	10.4	3.5	2.2	1.6	1.2
Cedar Rapids, IA	30.6	13.8	7.8	4.5	1.9	1.6	2.3	1.6	1.9
Charleston, SC	10.4	9.9	9.9	23.1	4.4	1.9	2.2	2.7	0.7
Charlotte, NC	8.7	7.0	6.6	4.7	3.4	1.6	1.4	1.9	0.7
Chicago, IL	7.3	7.5	2.4	2.0	4.0	5.6	1.0	0.6	0.5
Cincinnati, OH	17.7	10.0	5.3	3.9	3.5	1.7	1.6	1.2	0.8
Clarksville, TN	10.7	8.3	5.6	7.8	3.5	1.5	1.8	1.3	1.1
Cleveland, OH	9.0	8.3	2.6	2.1	4.8	3.8	0.9	0.6	0.5
College Station, TX	16.9	8.9	7.7	3.5	3.5	2.3	3.5	2.3	0.7
Colorado Springs, CO	18.6	11.0	9.7	4.3	4.8	2.3	2.9	2.6	1.5
Columbia, MO	23.9	12.3	8.8	5.6	3.7	2.4	2.5	1.9	1.5
Columbia, SC	9.9	6.9	8.3	5.3	2.9	1.3	2.0	2.2	0.8
Columbus, OH	16.4	10.1	6.1	4.3	4.9	2.2	1.7	1.7	0.9
Dallas, TX	5.1	4.0	4.5	3.8	1.5	0.8	1.2	1.1	0.4
Davenport, IA	28.8	15.3	6.3	4.0	2.3	2.1	1.5	1.5	1.8
Denver, CO	13.8	9.7	7.8	2.9	4.6	2.7	2.3	2.1	1.4
Des Moines, IA	20.3	11.6	6.6	3.6	3.9	1.0	1.8	1.3	2.6
Durham, NC	7.4	5.8	7.0	4.3	2.8	1.7	1.6	1.5	0.6
Edison, NJ	4.9	6.8	1.6	1.7	7.8	4.6	0.8	0.6	0.3
El Paso, TX	3.6	2.3	1.7	2.4	1.2	0.5	0.8	0.4	0.2
Fargo, ND	37.1	8.8	3.9	2.2	1.1	3.1	3.6	1.2	1.1
Fayetteville, NC	8.8	6.9	6.6	3.9	2.8	1.4	1.5	1.8	0.6
Fort Collins, CO	22.5	12.7	11.4	3.7	5.3	3.0	3.3	2.9	1.8
Fort Wayne, IN	24.3	9.5	6.9	5.7	2.4	2.1	3.0	1.5	1.3
Fort Worth, TX	7.4	6.0	5.6	5.0	1.9	0.9	1.5	1.4	0.7
Grand Rapids, MI	15.0	8.7	7.0	2.3	3.0	6.8	2.2	1.6	13.9
Greeley, CO	18.4	8.5	6.8	4.2	2.5	1.4	1.6	2.1	1.0
Green Bay, WI	29.5	9.3	3.8	3.4	2.3	7.9	4.2	0.6	3.0
Greensboro, NC	7.0	5.5	7.3	4.8	2.4	1.1	1.1	1.7	0.7
Honolulu, HI	4.1	3.3	2.8	1.2	1.8	0.7	0.8	0.6	0.3
Houston, TX	4.8	3.6	3.7	4.0	1.5	0.8	1.6	0.9	0.4
Huntsville, AL	8.6	8.8	8.7	11.4	2.4	0.9	1.8	2.0	0.9
Indianapolis, IN	13.5	8.6	5.9	5.9	2.2	1.6	1.5	1.5	1.0
Jacksonville, FL	7.9	7.8	6.0	5.4	3.8	1.5	1.4	1.5	0.8
Kansas City, MO	15.4	10.5	7.0	3.9	3.5	1.4	2.0	1.6	1.1
Lafayette, LA	7.4	5.5	5.7	6.4	3.8	0.4	17.8	1.1	0.5
Lakeland, FL	10.1	8.1	8.7	8.1	4.5	1.8	2.6	1.7	1.4
Las Vegas, NV	8.9	7.7	5.6	3.4	5.3	2.1	1.8	1.3	0.8
Lexington, KY	13.7	11.8	10.8	9.2	2.9	1.7	1.9	2.9	1.1
Lincoln, NE	33.2	11.3	8.0	3.6	2.3	2.5	2.1	1.5	2.0
Little Rock, AR	7.1	6.8	7.5	5.5	1.6	0.9	1.8	1.6	0.5
Los Angeles, CA	3.9	3.5	2.8	3.6	2.6	1.4	1.1	0.7	0.4
Louisville, KY	15.1	11.5	7.8	8.7	2.5	1.0	1.9	1.6	0.9
Madison, WI	31.4	12.4	8.1	2.0	4.1	5.7	2.9	1.5	1.8
Manchester, NH	6.6	19.3	9.0	2.9	8.2	3.9	13.5	3.2	0.5

Table continued on following page.

City	German	Irish	English	American	Italian	Polish	French[1]	Scottish	Dutch
Memphis, TN	3.4	4.2	3.9	3.9	1.6	0.7	1.0	1.0	0.3
Miami, FL	1.5	1.2	0.8	3.3	2.3	0.7	0.9	0.2	0.2
Midland, TX	6.8	6.0	6.7	4.4	1.4	0.6	1.6	1.6	0.7
Milwaukee, WI	16.3	5.6	2.1	1.2	2.7	6.6	1.3	0.5	0.7
Minneapolis, MN	20.9	10.1	5.6	1.8	2.7	4.0	2.5	1.4	1.4
Nashville, TN	8.4	7.9	7.3	8.2	2.4	1.3	1.7	1.9	0.8
New Haven, CT	4.1	6.5	3.2	1.1	7.7	2.1	1.3	0.6	0.5
New Orleans, LA	6.1	5.4	4.1	2.5	3.9	0.9	5.4	1.1	0.4
New York, NY	2.9	4.4	1.6	4.2	6.2	2.4	0.8	0.5	0.3
Oklahoma City, OK	10.6	8.1	6.2	5.9	1.9	0.8	1.5	1.5	0.9
Omaha, NE	25.2	13.1	6.9	3.0	4.1	3.6	2.0	1.3	1.4
Orlando, FL	6.3	5.3	4.5	5.6	4.3	1.6	1.7	1.3	0.5
Peoria, IL	18.3	11.3	6.7	4.7	3.1	1.9	2.1	1.2	1.0
Philadelphia, PA	6.4	10.4	2.6	2.3	7.4	3.3	0.7	0.5	0.3
Phoenix, AZ	9.9	7.1	5.5	3.0	3.8	2.0	1.7	1.3	0.9
Pittsburgh, PA	18.7	14.6	5.1	3.6	12.3	6.9	1.6	1.4	0.6
Portland, OR	15.9	11.1	10.5	4.6	4.3	2.3	3.0	2.9	1.9
Providence, RI	3.2	7.6	3.9	2.9	7.2	1.9	2.9	0.8	0.3
Provo, UT	10.1	4.1	23.0	3.0	2.0	0.8	1.6	4.8	1.4
Raleigh, NC	8.9	7.5	9.0	12.2	4.0	2.2	1.7	2.3	0.6
Reno, NV	12.8	10.8	9.1	3.9	6.1	1.7	2.6	2.2	1.1
Richmond, VA	6.9	6.3	7.4	4.2	3.5	1.3	1.4	2.1	0.5
Riverside, CA	5.9	4.6	4.1	3.1	2.9	0.9	1.6	1.0	0.8
Rochester, MN	29.1	11.3	6.1	3.0	2.0	3.6	2.1	1.3	1.7
Sacramento, CA	6.7	6.1	4.5	1.7	3.5	0.9	1.5	1.2	0.8
Salt Lake City, UT	10.4	6.7	14.9	3.3	3.3	1.5	2.0	3.3	1.9
San Antonio, TX	6.8	4.3	3.6	3.1	1.6	1.0	1.3	0.9	0.4
San Diego, CA	8.3	7.0	5.5	2.4	4.1	1.7	1.8	1.4	0.8
San Francisco, CA	7.1	7.7	5.1	2.8	4.5	1.8	2.3	1.4	0.8
San Jose, CA	5.0	4.0	3.5	1.8	3.3	0.9	1.2	0.8	0.5
Santa Rosa, CA	11.4	10.1	8.9	2.8	7.4	1.4	3.0	2.2	1.2
Savannah, GA	5.5	6.7	4.6	3.6	2.8	1.2	1.6	1.6	0.7
Seattle, WA	14.8	11.4	10.1	2.3	4.4	2.7	3.0	2.9	1.6
Sioux Falls, SD	35.1	11.2	5.3	3.2	1.5	1.7	2.2	1.2	5.6
Springfield, IL	20.1	12.8	9.0	4.8	4.7	2.1	2.3	1.7	1.2
Tallahassee, FL	8.5	8.1	7.8	3.8	3.7	1.8	1.9	2.1	0.7
Tampa, FL	8.7	8.0	6.0	6.2	6.0	2.0	2.0	1.5	0.8
Tucson, AZ	11.0	8.2	6.4	3.0	3.6	1.9	2.0	1.5	0.9
Tulsa, OK	11.0	9.1	7.5	6.2	2.0	0.9	1.9	2.0	1.0
Tuscaloosa, AL	5.8	6.6	5.6	7.3	2.3	0.9	1.2	2.2	0.6
Virginia Beach, VA	11.7	11.0	9.1	9.4	5.6	2.4	2.3	2.3	0.9
Washington, DC	6.9	6.7	5.2	2.3	3.9	2.2	1.5	1.4	0.7
Wichita, KS	19.3	9.5	7.8	5.0	1.7	1.0	2.2	1.6	1.5
Winston-Salem, NC	9.6	6.8	7.8	5.2	2.8	1.1	1.3	2.3	1.0
U.S.	13.3	9.7	7.2	6.2	5.1	2.8	2.3	1.7	1.2

Note: Figures are the percentage of the total population reporting a particular ancestry. The nine most commonly reported ancestries in the U.S. are shown. Figures include multiple ancestries (e.g. if a person reported being Irish and Italian, they were included in both columns); (1) Excludes Basque
Source: U.S. Census Bureau, 2015-2019 American Community Survey 5-Year Estimates

Ancestry: Metro Area

Metro Area	German	Irish	English	American	Italian	Polish	French[1]	Scottish	Dutch
Albuquerque, NM	8.7	6.8	6.4	4.3	2.8	1.3	1.7	1.6	0.7
Allentown, PA	24.3	13.5	5.8	4.5	12.8	5.2	1.6	1.1	2.3
Anchorage, AK	15.3	10.0	7.9	4.1	3.1	2.1	2.7	2.6	1.5
Ann Arbor, MI	19.0	10.7	9.9	6.6	4.7	6.4	3.1	2.6	2.1
Athens, GA	8.6	9.4	9.1	7.9	2.8	1.2	1.6	2.8	0.9
Atlanta, GA	6.6	6.6	7.2	9.2	2.5	1.2	1.4	1.7	0.6
Austin, TX	12.3	7.7	7.9	3.8	2.7	1.6	2.4	2.0	0.8
Baton Rouge, LA	6.8	6.6	5.0	7.8	4.7	0.5	12.3	1.1	0.3
Boise City, ID	16.1	9.6	17.1	5.1	3.4	1.2	2.4	3.2	2.1
Boston, MA	5.9	20.8	9.4	3.5	13.1	3.4	4.5	2.3	0.6
Boulder, CO	18.9	11.5	11.6	3.5	5.4	3.3	2.7	3.3	1.5
Cape Coral, FL	13.5	11.0	8.1	14.3	7.7	3.3	2.3	1.8	1.3
Cedar Rapids, IA	34.2	14.5	8.0	4.7	1.9	1.2	2.4	1.5	2.0
Charleston, SC	9.9	9.7	8.2	13.3	3.7	1.9	2.0	2.5	0.8
Charlotte, NC	11.0	8.4	7.8	9.1	3.9	1.7	1.6	2.3	0.9
Chicago, IL	14.3	10.8	4.2	2.6	6.6	8.8	1.4	0.9	1.2
Cincinnati, OH	27.2	13.8	8.3	7.1	4.2	1.6	1.9	1.8	1.2
Clarksville, TN	11.1	9.0	6.4	9.3	2.8	1.4	1.8	1.6	0.9
Cleveland, OH	18.8	13.4	7.0	3.8	9.8	7.7	1.5	1.5	0.9
College Station, TX	14.0	8.0	6.6	3.9	2.9	2.0	2.5	2.0	0.6
Colorado Springs, CO	18.8	10.9	9.4	4.4	4.9	2.4	2.8	2.7	1.5
Columbia, MO	25.0	11.9	9.0	6.8	3.0	1.7	2.4	2.0	1.5
Columbia, SC	10.0	7.4	7.3	8.5	2.3	1.1	1.7	2.0	0.7
Columbus, OH	21.8	12.6	8.5	6.3	5.4	2.4	1.9	2.1	1.3
Dallas, TX	8.6	6.5	6.7	6.3	2.1	1.1	1.7	1.6	0.7
Davenport, IA	27.7	14.7	7.6	4.2	2.4	2.1	1.8	1.5	2.0
Denver, CO	17.5	10.7	9.3	3.9	5.0	2.5	2.5	2.4	1.5
Des Moines, IA	27.1	13.0	8.4	4.3	3.2	1.3	1.9	1.7	3.8
Durham, NC	8.9	7.4	9.3	6.0	3.1	1.8	1.8	2.3	0.8
Edison, NJ	6.2	9.2	2.7	4.4	12.2	3.8	0.9	0.7	0.6
El Paso, TX	3.4	2.2	1.6	2.3	1.1	0.5	0.8	0.4	0.2
Fargo, ND	37.4	8.2	4.3	2.0	1.1	2.8	3.1	1.2	1.2
Fayetteville, NC	8.7	7.0	6.6	5.6	3.0	1.4	1.5	2.2	0.6
Fort Collins, CO	24.3	12.8	12.2	4.4	4.9	2.7	3.4	3.2	2.2
Fort Wayne, IN	27.0	9.3	7.2	6.9	2.6	2.1	3.3	1.6	1.4
Fort Worth, TX	8.6	6.5	6.7	6.3	2.1	1.1	1.7	1.6	0.7
Grand Rapids, MI	20.0	10.1	8.8	3.7	3.1	6.6	2.9	1.8	18.9
Greeley, CO	22.0	9.9	8.7	4.9	3.6	2.1	2.1	1.9	1.4
Green Bay, WI	36.3	9.7	4.1	3.6	2.2	9.8	4.3	0.7	4.4
Greensboro, NC	8.0	6.6	8.2	8.3	2.3	1.1	1.2	1.9	0.8
Honolulu, HI	5.1	3.8	3.3	1.3	2.0	0.9	1.1	0.9	0.4
Houston, TX	7.8	5.3	5.2	4.3	2.0	1.2	2.1	1.2	0.6
Huntsville, AL	8.9	9.5	9.3	12.2	2.2	1.1	1.8	2.1	1.0
Indianapolis, IN	17.3	10.0	8.0	9.3	2.7	1.9	1.8	1.8	1.4
Jacksonville, FL	10.0	9.6	7.9	7.9	4.6	1.9	1.9	2.0	0.9
Kansas City, MO	20.7	12.3	9.7	5.4	3.3	1.5	2.3	1.9	1.4
Lafayette, LA	6.3	4.2	3.8	9.0	2.4	0.4	18.4	0.7	0.3
Lakeland, FL	8.9	7.4	7.3	13.2	3.6	1.7	2.0	1.5	1.0
Las Vegas, NV	8.7	7.2	5.6	3.4	5.0	1.9	1.7	1.2	0.7
Lexington, KY	13.0	11.8	10.9	13.6	2.6	1.5	1.8	2.7	1.1
Lincoln, NE	34.6	11.1	8.0	3.7	2.2	2.5	2.1	1.4	2.2
Little Rock, AR	9.3	8.8	7.9	7.9	1.5	1.0	1.7	1.9	1.0
Los Angeles, CA	5.2	4.2	3.8	3.6	2.9	1.2	1.2	0.9	0.6
Louisville, KY	17.2	12.4	9.1	10.1	2.4	1.1	2.1	1.9	1.0
Madison, WI	37.1	13.1	8.5	2.8	3.8	5.4	2.8	1.5	1.9
Manchester, NH	8.4	20.8	13.0	3.5	10.0	4.4	12.4	3.4	0.8

Table continued on following page.

Metro Area	German	Irish	English	American	Italian	Polish	French[1]	Scottish	Dutch
Memphis, TN	5.2	6.3	6.0	7.1	2.1	0.7	1.2	1.4	0.5
Miami, FL	4.4	4.3	2.7	6.0	5.0	1.9	1.2	0.6	0.4
Midland, TX	6.9	6.1	6.4	4.5	1.4	0.6	1.6	1.5	0.6
Milwaukee, WI	33.0	9.8	4.3	2.0	4.3	10.8	2.5	0.9	1.3
Minneapolis, MN	29.1	10.9	5.6	3.1	2.6	4.4	3.3	1.3	1.5
Nashville, TN	10.0	9.6	9.2	10.8	2.7	1.4	1.8	2.2	1.0
New Haven, CT	7.9	14.9	6.8	2.7	20.6	6.2	3.5	1.2	0.6
New Orleans, LA	9.7	7.4	4.5	5.0	7.9	0.7	11.7	1.0	0.4
New York, NY	6.2	9.2	2.7	4.4	12.2	3.8	0.9	0.7	0.6
Oklahoma City, OK	12.0	9.1	7.2	7.6	2.0	0.9	1.7	1.7	1.2
Omaha, NE	29.2	13.6	7.9	3.6	3.9	3.7	2.1	1.4	1.7
Orlando, FL	8.2	7.3	6.1	7.6	5.1	1.9	1.9	1.4	0.7
Peoria, IL	27.2	12.4	9.1	6.7	3.9	2.0	2.4	1.8	1.6
Philadelphia, PA	14.6	18.0	7.0	3.2	13.0	5.0	1.4	1.3	0.8
Phoenix, AZ	12.5	8.3	7.7	3.9	4.4	2.4	2.1	1.6	1.1
Pittsburgh, PA	26.1	17.3	8.0	3.7	15.6	8.4	1.8	1.9	1.1
Portland, OR	17.2	10.4	10.4	4.7	3.9	1.8	2.9	2.9	1.9
Providence, RI	4.5	17.6	10.6	3.4	13.6	3.7	9.4	1.6	0.4
Provo, UT	10.5	4.8	26.7	4.7	2.4	0.6	1.9	4.9	1.6
Raleigh, NC	10.3	9.0	10.1	10.3	4.8	2.2	1.9	2.5	0.9
Reno, NV	13.6	10.9	9.4	3.9	6.5	1.8	2.8	2.2	1.2
Richmond, VA	9.2	7.9	10.7	6.7	3.7	1.6	1.6	2.1	0.7
Riverside, CA	7.1	5.6	4.5	2.9	3.0	0.9	1.6	1.0	0.9
Rochester, MN	35.4	11.7	6.2	3.2	1.7	3.3	2.2	1.3	2.0
Sacramento, CA	10.6	8.1	7.5	2.8	4.8	1.3	2.1	1.7	1.1
Salt Lake City, UT	10.0	5.6	20.0	4.3	2.9	0.9	1.8	3.9	2.0
San Antonio, TX	10.1	5.5	5.1	3.5	1.9	1.5	1.7	1.2	0.5
San Diego, CA	9.3	7.6	6.2	2.7	4.1	1.7	2.0	1.5	1.0
San Francisco, CA	7.6	7.2	5.7	2.4	4.7	1.5	1.9	1.5	0.8
San Jose, CA	6.1	4.8	4.5	1.9	3.7	1.2	1.5	1.1	0.7
Santa Rosa, CA	12.9	12.2	9.8	2.7	8.6	1.8	3.3	2.6	1.4
Savannah, GA	9.1	9.7	7.4	7.9	3.3	1.3	1.8	1.8	0.7
Seattle, WA	14.6	9.7	9.3	3.2	3.7	1.9	2.8	2.6	1.5
Sioux Falls, SD	37.2	10.8	5.2	3.8	1.4	1.6	2.1	1.0	6.4
Springfield, IL	23.5	13.6	10.0	5.6	5.0	2.0	2.4	1.9	1.4
Tallahassee, FL	8.4	8.2	8.0	5.2	3.3	1.6	1.9	2.3	0.9
Tampa, FL	12.3	10.8	7.8	8.6	7.5	3.0	2.6	1.8	1.1
Tucson, AZ	13.4	9.1	8.2	3.3	4.0	2.3	2.3	1.9	1.1
Tulsa, OK	12.9	10.5	8.0	6.7	1.9	1.0	2.1	2.0	1.2
Tuscaloosa, AL	5.1	6.5	5.3	11.4	1.6	0.6	1.0	1.8	0.5
Virginia Beach, VA	9.8	8.8	8.7	9.3	4.1	1.8	1.9	1.9	0.8
Washington, DC	9.3	8.3	6.9	4.1	4.3	2.3	1.6	1.6	0.7
Wichita, KS	21.8	9.9	8.1	6.7	1.7	1.0	2.3	1.9	1.6
Winston-Salem, NC	11.7	7.8	9.0	9.8	2.5	1.0	1.3	2.4	1.1
U.S.	13.3	9.7	7.2	6.2	5.1	2.8	2.3	1.7	1.2

Note: Figures are the percentage of the total population reporting a particular ancestry. The nine most commonly reported ancestries in the U.S. are shown. Figures include multiple ancestries (e.g. if a person reported being Irish and Italian, they were included in both columns); Figures cover the Metropolitan Statistical Area—see Appendix B for areas included; (1) Excludes Basque
Source: U.S. Census Bureau, 2015-2019 American Community Survey 5-Year Estimates

Foreign-Born Population: City

City	Any Foreign Country	Percent of Population Born in							
		Asia	Mexico	Europe	Caribbean	Central America[1]	South America	Africa	Canada
Albuquerque, NM	9.9	2.4	5.3	0.8	0.3	0.2	0.4	0.4	0.1
Allentown, PA	19.2	3.6	1.0	0.8	9.0	1.3	2.5	0.8	0.1
Anchorage, AK	10.9	6.2	0.9	1.1	0.5	0.1	0.5	0.6	0.4
Ann Arbor, MI	19.1	12.7	0.4	3.0	0.2	0.1	0.8	0.9	0.9
Athens, GA	10.1	2.9	3.0	0.9	0.4	1.0	1.0	0.7	0.2
Atlanta, GA	7.6	3.2	0.7	1.3	0.6	0.1	0.6	0.7	0.3
Austin, TX	18.8	6.0	7.4	1.3	0.6	1.7	0.6	0.8	0.3
Baton Rouge, LA	5.5	2.8	0.4	0.5	0.2	1.0	0.2	0.3	0.0
Boise City, ID	6.4	2.7	1.0	1.4	0.1	0.1	0.3	0.6	0.2
Boston, MA	28.3	7.6	0.4	3.4	8.2	2.6	2.4	3.1	0.4
Boulder, CO	11.0	4.4	1.2	2.8	0.2	0.3	1.0	0.3	0.4
Cape Coral, FL	15.2	1.4	0.7	2.1	6.8	0.7	2.8	0.1	0.6
Cedar Rapids, IA	6.1	2.7	0.7	0.5	0.1	0.1	0.2	1.5	0.1
Charleston, SC	4.8	1.7	0.6	1.3	0.4	0.1	0.3	0.2	0.2
Charlotte, NC	16.7	5.4	2.6	1.2	1.1	2.8	1.4	1.9	0.2
Chicago, IL	20.6	5.2	8.4	3.5	0.4	0.9	1.1	1.0	0.2
Cincinnati, OH	6.0	1.8	0.3	0.8	0.2	0.9	0.3	1.6	0.2
Clarksville, TN	5.3	1.7	1.1	0.9	0.4	0.4	0.4	0.3	0.1
Cleveland, OH	5.9	2.5	0.3	1.0	0.5	0.4	0.3	0.7	0.1
College Station, TX	13.4	7.9	1.6	1.0	0.1	0.5	1.2	0.9	0.2
Colorado Springs, CO	7.5	2.1	2.1	1.5	0.3	0.3	0.3	0.4	0.4
Columbia, MO	9.1	5.3	0.5	1.3	0.1	0.3	0.3	1.0	0.2
Columbia, SC	5.0	2.1	0.5	0.8	0.3	0.3	0.5	0.4	0.1
Columbus, OH	12.7	5.1	1.2	0.8	0.5	0.5	0.3	4.2	0.1
Dallas, TX	24.8	2.8	15.4	0.7	0.4	2.6	0.6	1.9	0.2
Davenport, IA	4.5	1.6	1.9	0.4	0.3	0.0	0.0	0.2	0.1
Denver, CO	15.0	3.0	7.3	1.4	0.3	0.8	0.5	1.4	0.3
Des Moines, IA	12.5	4.5	3.3	0.9	0.1	1.1	0.2	2.3	0.1
Durham, NC	15.0	4.6	2.8	1.1	0.6	3.2	0.7	1.5	0.4
Edison, NJ	46.9	37.6	1.0	2.8	1.5	0.3	1.7	1.8	0.2
El Paso, TX	23.1	1.1	20.7	0.5	0.1	0.3	0.2	0.2	0.0
Fargo, ND	9.0	3.5	0.1	1.0	0.2	0.1	0.2	3.7	0.2
Fayetteville, NC	7.1	2.3	0.6	1.0	0.9	0.8	0.6	0.6	0.1
Fort Collins, CO	6.8	3.0	1.2	1.4	0.1	0.2	0.4	0.3	0.2
Fort Wayne, IN	8.2	3.9	1.9	0.8	0.1	0.7	0.3	0.4	0.1
Fort Worth, TX	16.8	3.4	9.8	0.6	0.3	0.9	0.5	1.2	0.2
Grand Rapids, MI	10.9	2.3	3.3	1.2	0.6	1.8	0.2	1.3	0.3
Greeley, CO	11.5	1.0	7.4	0.4	0.2	1.2	0.2	1.1	0.1
Green Bay, WI	9.9	2.0	5.9	0.5	0.1	0.6	0.2	0.5	0.0
Greensboro, NC	11.0	3.9	2.0	1.2	0.6	0.6	0.5	2.0	0.2
Honolulu, HI	27.4	23.2	0.1	0.8	0.1	0.1	0.2	0.1	0.2
Houston, TX	29.3	6.0	11.4	1.1	1.1	6.3	1.3	1.9	0.2
Huntsville, AL	6.6	2.3	1.7	0.7	0.4	0.5	0.2	0.6	0.1
Indianapolis, IN	9.7	2.8	3.0	0.5	0.4	0.9	0.3	1.6	0.1
Jacksonville, FL	11.3	4.0	0.6	1.8	2.0	0.8	1.3	0.6	0.2
Kansas City, MO	8.2	2.5	2.3	0.6	0.5	0.6	0.3	1.2	0.1
Lafayette, LA	4.3	1.8	0.5	0.7	0.2	0.4	0.2	0.2	0.1
Lakeland, FL	10.9	1.8	1.3	0.8	4.0	0.5	1.4	0.2	0.9
Las Vegas, NV	21.0	5.3	9.2	1.6	1.1	2.3	0.8	0.4	0.4
Lexington, KY	9.7	3.7	2.4	1.0	0.2	0.5	0.3	1.2	0.2
Lincoln, NE	8.5	4.5	1.3	0.9	0.2	0.4	0.3	0.8	0.1
Little Rock, AR	7.7	2.7	2.3	0.7	0.1	1.0	0.3	0.5	0.1
Los Angeles, CA	36.9	11.0	12.5	2.4	0.3	8.4	1.1	0.7	0.4
Louisville, KY	7.7	2.5	0.7	0.9	1.6	0.4	0.3	1.2	0.1

Table continued on following page.

City	Percent of Population Born in								
	Any Foreign Country	Asia	Mexico	Europe	Caribbean	Central America[1]	South America	Africa	Canada
Madison, WI	12.1	6.7	1.5	1.4	0.2	0.3	0.8	1.0	0.3
Manchester, NH	14.5	5.1	0.5	2.5	1.6	1.2	0.8	1.9	0.8
Memphis, TN	6.2	1.5	2.2	0.3	0.2	0.9	0.2	0.8	0.1
Miami, FL	58.3	1.1	0.9	2.0	32.5	11.9	9.6	0.3	0.2
Midland, TX	14.1	1.8	8.6	0.3	1.2	0.6	0.4	0.8	0.4
Milwaukee, WI	10.0	2.9	4.8	0.8	0.4	0.2	0.2	0.7	0.1
Minneapolis, MN	15.6	4.0	2.4	1.3	0.3	0.4	1.3	5.6	0.3
Nashville, TN	13.3	4.0	3.1	0.9	0.4	1.9	0.3	2.5	0.2
New Haven, CT	17.8	4.6	3.1	1.9	2.5	1.0	2.9	1.2	0.5
New Orleans, LA	5.5	2.0	0.3	0.8	0.3	1.5	0.3	0.2	0.1
New York, NY	36.8	10.9	2.0	5.3	10.2	1.4	4.8	1.7	0.3
Oklahoma City, OK	11.8	3.3	6.0	0.4	0.2	1.0	0.3	0.6	0.1
Omaha, NE	10.7	3.4	3.8	0.6	0.1	1.0	0.3	1.3	0.1
Orlando, FL	22.0	2.9	0.5	1.5	6.9	1.2	8.0	0.6	0.3
Peoria, IL	7.6	4.7	1.2	0.5	0.1	0.2	0.3	0.3	0.1
Philadelphia, PA	14.1	5.5	0.5	2.2	2.7	0.6	0.9	1.6	0.1
Phoenix, AZ	19.4	3.4	11.9	1.3	0.3	0.9	0.4	0.8	0.4
Pittsburgh, PA	9.0	4.8	0.3	1.9	0.3	0.1	0.5	0.8	0.2
Portland, OR	13.5	5.9	2.0	2.7	0.3	0.5	0.3	1.0	0.5
Providence, RI	28.7	4.2	0.6	2.2	12.3	5.0	1.4	2.7	0.2
Provo, UT	11.0	2.0	4.4	0.5	0.1	0.6	2.3	0.3	0.4
Raleigh, NC	13.4	3.9	2.7	1.4	0.9	1.4	0.7	2.1	0.3
Reno, NV	15.9	5.3	6.2	1.3	0.2	1.6	0.4	0.3	0.3
Richmond, VA	7.0	1.5	0.8	0.7	0.4	2.5	0.4	0.6	0.2
Riverside, CA	22.6	5.1	13.2	0.9	0.2	2.0	0.6	0.3	0.2
Rochester, MN	14.1	5.8	1.5	1.6	0.2	0.2	0.5	3.9	0.2
Sacramento, CA	22.2	10.7	6.9	1.5	0.1	0.8	0.2	0.6	0.2
Salt Lake City, UT	17.1	4.6	6.4	2.0	0.3	0.6	1.3	1.0	0.4
San Antonio, TX	14.3	2.6	9.1	0.6	0.2	0.8	0.4	0.3	0.1
San Diego, CA	26.1	11.9	9.1	2.3	0.2	0.5	0.8	0.9	0.4
San Francisco, CA	34.3	22.2	2.4	4.5	0.2	2.5	1.0	0.5	0.6
San Jose, CA	39.7	25.6	9.0	2.2	0.1	1.0	0.6	0.8	0.4
Santa Rosa, CA	20.1	4.0	11.6	1.7	0.0	0.9	0.3	0.8	0.3
Savannah, GA	6.2	2.7	0.7	0.9	0.4	0.4	0.5	0.3	0.1
Seattle, WA	18.8	10.6	1.2	2.5	0.1	0.5	0.5	2.1	1.0
Sioux Falls, SD	8.5	2.3	0.5	0.9	0.1	0.9	0.1	3.5	0.1
Springfield, IL	4.5	2.5	0.4	0.5	0.2	0.1	0.2	0.5	0.1
Tallahassee, FL	8.1	3.6	0.2	0.9	1.0	0.4	0.7	0.9	0.3
Tampa, FL	17.2	3.8	1.1	1.4	6.9	1.1	2.0	0.4	0.4
Tucson, AZ	15.3	2.7	9.5	1.0	0.1	0.4	0.3	0.9	0.3
Tulsa, OK	11.2	2.7	5.6	0.5	0.2	1.0	0.4	0.5	0.1
Tuscaloosa, AL	4.6	2.2	0.5	0.4	0.1	0.9	0.1	0.3	0.1
Virginia Beach, VA	9.4	4.9	0.5	1.6	0.7	0.6	0.5	0.4	0.1
Washington, DC	13.7	3.0	0.6	2.5	1.2	2.6	1.3	2.1	0.3
Wichita, KS	10.2	3.8	4.3	0.5	0.1	0.6	0.2	0.6	0.1
Winston-Salem, NC	9.9	2.1	4.3	0.7	0.4	1.1	0.5	0.6	0.1
U.S.	13.6	4.2	3.5	1.5	1.3	1.1	1.0	0.7	0.2

Note: (1) Excludes Mexico
Source: U.S. Census Bureau, 2015-2019 American Community Survey 5-Year Estimates

Foreign-Born Population: Metro Area

Metro Area	Any Foreign Country	Percent of Population Born in							
		Asia	Mexico	Europe	Caribbean	Central America[1]	South America	Africa	Canada
Albuquerque, NM	8.9	1.8	5.2	0.7	0.3	0.2	0.3	0.3	0.1
Allentown, PA	9.3	2.8	0.4	1.6	2.2	0.6	1.2	0.5	0.1
Anchorage, AK	8.9	4.9	0.7	1.1	0.4	0.1	0.4	0.5	0.3
Ann Arbor, MI	12.5	7.4	0.4	2.1	0.2	0.3	0.5	0.9	0.6
Athens, GA	7.8	2.3	2.1	0.8	0.3	0.9	0.7	0.5	0.1
Atlanta, GA	13.8	4.6	2.6	1.2	1.4	1.1	1.1	1.6	0.2
Austin, TX	15.2	4.5	6.4	1.1	0.4	1.2	0.6	0.7	0.3
Baton Rouge, LA	4.0	1.5	0.7	0.3	0.2	0.9	0.2	0.2	0.1
Boise City, ID	6.5	1.6	2.7	1.0	0.0	0.2	0.3	0.3	0.3
Boston, MA	18.9	6.1	0.2	3.3	3.4	1.6	2.1	1.6	0.5
Boulder, CO	10.7	3.5	2.8	2.3	0.1	0.3	0.7	0.3	0.5
Cape Coral, FL	16.7	1.3	2.5	2.0	5.9	1.8	2.0	0.1	1.1
Cedar Rapids, IA	3.8	1.8	0.5	0.4	0.1	0.1	0.1	0.8	0.1
Charleston, SC	5.4	1.5	1.1	1.0	0.3	0.5	0.5	0.2	0.2
Charlotte, NC	10.1	3.0	2.1	1.1	0.6	1.4	0.9	0.9	0.2
Chicago, IL	17.7	5.2	6.5	3.7	0.3	0.6	0.6	0.6	0.2
Cincinnati, OH	4.8	2.1	0.5	0.7	0.1	0.4	0.2	0.7	0.1
Clarksville, TN	4.1	1.3	0.7	0.7	0.3	0.3	0.3	0.3	0.1
Cleveland, OH	6.0	2.2	0.3	2.2	0.2	0.2	0.2	0.4	0.2
College Station, TX	12.5	4.2	5.5	0.7	0.1	0.5	0.7	0.7	0.1
Colorado Springs, CO	6.9	1.9	1.8	1.6	0.3	0.3	0.3	0.4	0.3
Columbia, MO	6.1	3.3	0.4	1.0	0.1	0.2	0.2	0.6	0.2
Columbia, SC	5.0	1.6	1.1	0.7	0.3	0.5	0.3	0.4	0.1
Columbus, OH	8.2	3.6	0.7	0.8	0.3	0.3	0.2	2.2	0.1
Dallas, TX	18.7	5.3	8.4	0.8	0.3	1.5	0.6	1.5	0.2
Davenport, IA	5.2	1.7	1.9	0.5	0.1	0.1	0.1	0.8	0.1
Denver, CO	12.1	3.3	4.9	1.4	0.2	0.5	0.5	1.0	0.3
Des Moines, IA	7.7	3.0	1.5	1.1	0.1	0.5	0.2	1.2	0.1
Durham, NC	11.7	3.6	2.6	1.4	0.4	2.0	0.5	0.9	0.4
Edison, NJ	29.5	8.7	1.5	4.4	6.9	2.0	4.4	1.4	0.2
El Paso, TX	24.2	1.0	22.0	0.4	0.1	0.3	0.2	0.2	0.0
Fargo, ND	6.7	2.7	0.2	0.8	0.1	0.1	0.2	2.4	0.3
Fayetteville, NC	6.2	1.6	1.4	0.9	0.7	0.8	0.4	0.3	0.1
Fort Collins, CO	5.6	1.9	1.3	1.3	0.1	0.2	0.4	0.2	0.2
Fort Wayne, IN	6.3	3.0	1.4	0.7	0.1	0.5	0.2	0.3	0.1
Fort Worth, TX	18.7	5.3	8.4	0.8	0.3	1.5	0.6	1.5	0.2
Grand Rapids, MI	6.8	2.1	1.8	1.0	0.4	0.6	0.1	0.5	0.2
Greeley, CO	8.7	0.9	5.9	0.4	0.2	0.6	0.2	0.5	0.1
Green Bay, WI	5.1	1.5	2.4	0.5	0.0	0.4	0.1	0.2	0.1
Greensboro, NC	8.8	2.9	2.5	0.8	0.4	0.6	0.4	1.0	0.2
Honolulu, HI	19.7	16.1	0.2	0.7	0.1	0.1	0.3	0.1	0.2
Houston, TX	23.4	6.0	8.9	1.0	0.8	3.6	1.3	1.4	0.3
Huntsville, AL	5.1	1.9	1.2	0.7	0.3	0.4	0.2	0.4	0.2
Indianapolis, IN	7.0	2.6	1.7	0.6	0.2	0.5	0.3	0.9	0.1
Jacksonville, FL	9.3	3.1	0.5	1.7	1.5	0.6	1.1	0.4	0.3
Kansas City, MO	6.9	2.3	2.0	0.6	0.2	0.6	0.3	0.7	0.1
Lafayette, LA	3.3	1.2	0.7	0.3	0.2	0.5	0.1	0.2	0.1
Lakeland, FL	10.0	1.3	2.3	0.9	2.8	0.6	1.4	0.2	0.5
Las Vegas, NV	22.2	7.2	8.2	1.6	1.1	2.0	0.9	0.8	0.4
Lexington, KY	7.5	2.6	2.1	0.9	0.2	0.5	0.2	0.8	0.1
Lincoln, NE	7.5	4.0	1.1	0.8	0.2	0.3	0.3	0.7	0.1
Little Rock, AR	4.3	1.4	1.3	0.5	0.1	0.6	0.2	0.2	0.1
Los Angeles, CA	33.1	12.8	12.1	1.7	0.3	4.3	0.9	0.6	0.3
Louisville, KY	5.9	1.9	0.9	0.7	0.9	0.3	0.2	0.7	0.1

Table continued on following page.

Metro Area	Percent of Population Born in								
	Any Foreign Country	Asia	Mexico	Europe	Caribbean	Central America[1]	South America	Africa	Canada
Madison, WI	7.6	3.6	1.2	1.0	0.1	0.2	0.6	0.6	0.2
Manchester, NH	9.7	3.6	0.4	1.8	1.0	0.5	0.8	0.9	0.8
Memphis, TN	5.3	1.7	1.6	0.4	0.2	0.5	0.2	0.6	0.1
Miami, FL	40.7	2.1	1.1	2.3	21.2	4.2	8.8	0.4	0.5
Midland, TX	13.4	1.6	8.8	0.3	1.0	0.5	0.3	0.6	0.3
Milwaukee, WI	7.4	2.8	2.3	1.3	0.2	0.2	0.2	0.4	0.1
Minneapolis, MN	10.7	4.2	1.3	1.1	0.2	0.4	0.5	2.8	0.2
Nashville, TN	8.3	2.6	2.0	0.7	0.2	1.0	0.3	1.1	0.2
New Haven, CT	12.7	3.3	1.0	2.8	1.9	0.5	1.9	0.9	0.3
New Orleans, LA	7.6	2.1	0.6	0.6	0.7	2.7	0.5	0.3	0.1
New York, NY	29.5	8.7	1.5	4.4	6.9	2.0	4.4	1.4	0.2
Oklahoma City, OK	7.9	2.4	3.5	0.4	0.1	0.6	0.3	0.4	0.1
Omaha, NE	7.4	2.4	2.5	0.6	0.1	0.7	0.2	0.9	0.1
Orlando, FL	18.5	3.0	1.1	1.5	5.7	1.1	5.2	0.6	0.3
Peoria, IL	3.3	1.7	0.6	0.4	0.0	0.1	0.1	0.1	0.1
Philadelphia, PA	11.0	4.5	0.9	1.9	1.3	0.4	0.6	1.1	0.2
Phoenix, AZ	14.3	3.4	7.2	1.3	0.3	0.6	0.3	0.5	0.6
Pittsburgh, PA	3.9	2.0	0.1	1.0	0.1	0.1	0.2	0.3	0.1
Portland, OR	12.6	5.0	3.1	2.3	0.1	0.5	0.3	0.6	0.4
Providence, RI	13.3	2.3	0.2	4.2	2.3	1.4	1.0	1.6	0.2
Provo, UT	7.3	1.1	2.8	0.5	0.1	0.5	1.6	0.2	0.3
Raleigh, NC	12.3	4.4	2.6	1.4	0.6	1.1	0.6	1.2	0.4
Reno, NV	14.0	3.9	6.1	1.1	0.2	1.5	0.4	0.3	0.3
Richmond, VA	7.9	3.2	0.6	1.0	0.4	1.4	0.5	0.6	0.1
Riverside, CA	21.3	4.9	12.3	0.8	0.2	1.7	0.6	0.4	0.3
Rochester, MN	8.5	3.4	1.0	1.1	0.1	0.3	0.3	2.1	0.2
Sacramento, CA	18.6	8.8	4.7	2.7	0.1	0.6	0.3	0.5	0.3
Salt Lake City, UT	12.4	3.1	4.6	1.2	0.1	0.6	1.4	0.6	0.3
San Antonio, TX	11.8	2.2	7.3	0.6	0.2	0.7	0.4	0.3	0.1
San Diego, CA	23.4	9.0	10.1	1.8	0.2	0.5	0.6	0.6	0.4
San Francisco, CA	30.7	17.5	4.9	2.9	0.2	2.5	1.0	0.7	0.5
San Jose, CA	38.6	25.4	7.0	3.1	0.1	0.9	0.7	0.7	0.5
Santa Rosa, CA	16.4	2.9	9.0	1.9	0.1	0.9	0.5	0.4	0.4
Savannah, GA	5.7	2.0	1.1	0.8	0.5	0.4	0.4	0.3	0.2
Seattle, WA	18.7	9.9	2.4	2.6	0.2	0.5	0.5	1.5	0.7
Sioux Falls, SD	6.2	1.6	0.4	0.7	0.1	0.7	0.1	2.4	0.1
Springfield, IL	3.1	1.6	0.3	0.4	0.1	0.1	0.1	0.3	0.1
Tallahassee, FL	6.1	2.2	0.5	0.8	0.9	0.5	0.5	0.6	0.2
Tampa, FL	13.9	2.8	1.3	2.2	3.7	0.8	1.9	0.5	0.6
Tucson, AZ	13.0	2.3	7.6	1.2	0.1	0.3	0.3	0.6	0.4
Tulsa, OK	6.6	1.9	2.9	0.5	0.1	0.5	0.3	0.3	0.1
Tuscaloosa, AL	3.4	1.1	0.9	0.4	0.1	0.6	0.1	0.2	0.1
Virginia Beach, VA	6.5	2.8	0.4	1.1	0.6	0.7	0.4	0.4	0.1
Washington, DC	22.8	8.2	0.8	1.8	1.1	4.9	2.2	3.5	0.2
Wichita, KS	7.4	2.7	3.0	0.4	0.1	0.4	0.2	0.4	0.1
Winston-Salem, NC	6.8	1.4	3.0	0.6	0.2	0.9	0.4	0.3	0.1
U.S.	13.6	4.2	3.5	1.5	1.3	1.1	1.0	0.7	0.2

Note: Figures cover the Metropolitan Statistical Area—see Appendix B for areas included; (1) Excludes Mexico
Source: U.S. Census Bureau, 2015-2019 American Community Survey 5-Year Estimates

Marital Status: City

City	Never Married	Now Married[1]	Separated	Widowed	Divorced
Albuquerque, NM	37.7	40.8	1.5	5.6	14.4
Allentown, PA	47.4	33.2	3.6	5.4	10.4
Anchorage, AK	34.5	48.4	1.8	3.6	11.7
Ann Arbor, MI	56.5	33.8	0.4	2.6	6.6
Athens, GA	54.4	32.2	1.6	3.5	8.2
Atlanta, GA	55.2	27.3	1.9	5.1	10.5
Austin, TX	43.2	40.9	1.7	3.1	11.0
Baton Rouge, LA	50.2	30.4	2.0	6.4	11.0
Boise City, ID	34.1	46.7	0.9	4.5	13.9
Boston, MA	56.0	30.3	2.6	3.9	7.2
Boulder, CO	55.6	32.4	0.8	2.6	8.6
Cape Coral, FL	25.5	52.0	1.5	7.3	13.7
Cedar Rapids, IA	35.2	45.7	1.0	6.0	12.1
Charleston, SC	41.9	41.6	1.5	5.2	9.7
Charlotte, NC	40.7	42.5	2.6	4.0	10.2
Chicago, IL	48.7	35.5	2.3	5.2	8.3
Cincinnati, OH	52.0	28.3	2.4	5.1	12.1
Clarksville, TN	30.2	50.9	2.2	4.0	12.6
Cleveland, OH	51.4	25.1	3.2	6.2	14.1
College Station, TX	59.7	32.4	0.8	2.1	5.0
Colorado Springs, CO	31.2	49.5	1.6	4.6	13.1
Columbia, MO	48.0	39.0	1.2	3.4	8.4
Columbia, SC	55.8	27.8	2.6	4.4	9.4
Columbus, OH	45.0	36.3	2.1	4.3	12.4
Dallas, TX	41.6	40.4	3.2	4.5	10.4
Davenport, IA	36.7	42.6	1.5	6.3	12.9
Denver, CO	42.5	39.5	1.8	4.0	12.2
Des Moines, IA	39.0	40.0	2.0	5.3	13.7
Durham, NC	43.1	39.9	2.5	4.3	10.2
Edison, NJ	25.7	61.0	1.0	6.1	6.2
El Paso, TX	35.3	44.5	3.5	5.8	10.8
Fargo, ND	42.8	42.9	1.1	4.5	8.7
Fayetteville, NC	38.4	40.7	3.6	5.5	11.8
Fort Collins, CO	46.6	40.6	0.8	3.3	8.7
Fort Wayne, IN	35.3	44.4	1.5	5.8	13.0
Fort Worth, TX	35.4	46.3	2.3	4.5	11.4
Grand Rapids, MI	46.2	36.9	1.3	5.1	10.4
Greeley, CO	35.8	46.0	1.7	5.1	11.3
Green Bay, WI	37.9	43.2	1.5	5.1	12.3
Greensboro, NC	42.2	38.4	2.6	5.7	11.0
Honolulu, HI	36.2	45.8	1.2	6.9	9.9
Houston, TX	41.0	41.3	3.2	4.6	9.9
Huntsville, AL	34.9	44.8	2.0	6.0	12.3
Indianapolis, IN	42.9	37.7	1.8	5.1	12.5
Jacksonville, FL	35.5	42.6	2.2	5.6	14.0
Kansas City, MO	39.7	39.9	2.1	5.4	12.9
Lafayette, LA	42.2	38.8	1.7	6.0	11.2
Lakeland, FL	34.9	41.7	2.1	8.2	13.1
Las Vegas, NV	34.9	43.3	2.3	5.5	14.1
Lexington, KY	38.8	43.1	1.7	4.6	11.8
Lincoln, NE	39.0	45.6	1.0	4.4	10.0
Little Rock, AR	37.7	39.9	2.5	6.2	13.7
Los Angeles, CA	45.8	38.8	2.6	4.6	8.2
Louisville, KY	36.3	42.1	2.1	6.1	13.4
Madison, WI	50.2	37.3	0.8	3.3	8.4
Manchester, NH	38.8	39.9	2.0	5.8	13.4

Table continued on following page.

City	Never Married	Now Married[1]	Separated	Widowed	Divorced
Memphis, TN	47.8	31.3	3.7	5.8	11.4
Miami, FL	40.2	36.0	3.7	6.6	13.5
Midland, TX	30.1	51.1	2.1	5.1	11.6
Milwaukee, WI	53.3	30.0	1.9	4.6	10.2
Minneapolis, MN	50.5	34.4	1.6	2.9	10.5
Nashville, TN	40.7	40.8	1.8	4.7	11.9
New Haven, CT	57.8	26.1	1.9	4.3	9.9
New Orleans, LA	49.2	29.4	2.7	5.9	12.8
New York, NY	43.4	40.4	3.0	5.4	7.8
Oklahoma City, OK	33.3	45.8	2.3	5.4	13.2
Omaha, NE	36.4	45.9	1.6	4.8	11.2
Orlando, FL	43.0	36.5	3.1	4.1	13.3
Peoria, IL	40.5	39.9	1.3	6.2	12.1
Philadelphia, PA	50.7	30.6	3.3	6.2	9.3
Phoenix, AZ	39.2	42.1	2.0	4.3	12.4
Pittsburgh, PA	52.4	30.7	1.9	5.8	9.3
Portland, OR	41.3	40.9	1.5	3.8	12.5
Providence, RI	54.4	30.6	2.3	4.2	8.5
Provo, UT	47.7	44.6	1.1	2.0	4.5
Raleigh, NC	42.7	40.3	2.5	3.7	10.8
Reno, NV	35.5	42.5	2.2	4.8	14.9
Richmond, VA	52.7	27.3	3.0	5.4	11.6
Riverside, CA	43.1	40.8	2.4	4.7	9.0
Rochester, MN	32.1	52.3	1.0	5.2	9.4
Sacramento, CA	40.2	41.0	2.4	5.1	11.4
Salt Lake City, UT	42.4	41.4	1.5	3.9	10.8
San Antonio, TX	39.0	40.6	3.1	5.2	12.1
San Diego, CA	40.0	44.3	1.7	4.1	9.8
San Francisco, CA	45.8	40.3	1.3	4.6	7.9
San Jose, CA	35.4	51.0	1.6	4.2	7.8
Santa Rosa, CA	34.6	44.5	1.9	5.5	13.5
Savannah, GA	47.5	31.2	3.0	5.9	12.4
Seattle, WA	44.5	41.1	1.2	3.4	9.9
Sioux Falls, SD	33.6	48.8	1.4	5.0	11.1
Springfield, IL	37.5	40.8	1.5	6.4	13.7
Tallahassee, FL	56.3	29.3	1.3	3.3	9.8
Tampa, FL	40.4	38.4	2.7	5.0	13.6
Tucson, AZ	42.5	36.0	2.2	5.4	14.0
Tulsa, OK	34.5	42.5	2.4	5.9	14.8
Tuscaloosa, AL	53.2	30.8	1.9	4.3	9.9
Virginia Beach, VA	30.4	51.1	2.4	5.0	11.1
Washington, DC	56.4	28.9	2.1	4.1	8.5
Wichita, KS	33.5	45.6	2.0	5.6	13.3
Winston-Salem, NC	40.4	39.9	2.8	5.9	11.1
U.S.	33.4	48.1	1.9	5.8	10.9

Note: Figures are percentages and cover the population 15 years of age and older; (1) Excludes separated
Source: U.S. Census Bureau, 2015-2019 American Community Survey 5-Year Estimates

Marital Status: Metro Area

Metro Area	Never Married	Now Married[1]	Separated	Widowed	Divorced
Albuquerque, NM	34.9	43.9	1.5	5.8	13.9
Allentown, PA	32.3	49.3	2.1	6.4	9.9
Anchorage, AK	33.9	48.7	1.8	3.7	11.9
Ann Arbor, MI	43.0	44.1	0.8	3.7	8.4
Athens, GA	42.7	41.9	1.6	4.7	9.1
Atlanta, GA	35.3	47.4	1.9	4.6	10.8
Austin, TX	36.4	47.4	1.7	3.7	10.8
Baton Rouge, LA	37.2	43.2	2.1	6.1	11.4
Boise City, ID	29.6	52.2	1.1	4.5	12.6
Boston, MA	37.1	47.5	1.5	5.1	8.7
Boulder, CO	38.1	46.2	1.0	3.7	11.0
Cape Coral, FL	26.2	50.8	1.6	8.2	13.2
Cedar Rapids, IA	30.0	52.0	0.9	5.8	11.2
Charleston, SC	34.5	46.9	2.4	5.5	10.7
Charlotte, NC	32.6	49.4	2.4	5.2	10.3
Chicago, IL	37.0	46.9	1.6	5.5	8.9
Cincinnati, OH	32.3	49.0	1.6	5.7	11.3
Clarksville, TN	28.3	52.5	2.0	5.1	12.0
Cleveland, OH	34.9	45.0	1.6	6.6	11.8
College Station, TX	46.3	40.1	1.9	3.8	7.9
Colorado Springs, CO	29.5	53.1	1.5	4.2	11.8
Columbia, MO	40.0	44.6	1.2	4.4	9.7
Columbia, SC	36.6	44.2	2.8	5.7	10.7
Columbus, OH	34.7	47.0	1.7	4.9	11.6
Dallas, TX	32.8	50.3	2.1	4.4	10.5
Davenport, IA	29.9	50.2	1.3	6.6	12.0
Denver, CO	33.1	49.6	1.4	4.1	11.8
Des Moines, IA	29.9	52.1	1.3	5.0	11.8
Durham, NC	36.9	45.4	2.3	5.1	10.2
Edison, NJ	37.8	46.3	2.3	5.7	7.9
El Paso, TX	35.4	45.2	3.5	5.5	10.3
Fargo, ND	36.8	49.6	0.9	4.3	8.3
Fayetteville, NC	33.8	46.1	3.2	5.8	11.2
Fort Collins, CO	34.8	50.1	0.9	4.0	10.2
Fort Wayne, IN	31.5	49.6	1.3	5.7	11.9
Fort Worth, TX	32.8	50.3	2.1	4.4	10.5
Grand Rapids, MI	32.7	51.3	1.0	4.9	10.2
Greeley, CO	28.2	55.2	1.4	4.5	10.8
Green Bay, WI	30.2	53.2	0.9	5.2	10.5
Greensboro, NC	33.6	46.1	2.7	6.3	11.3
Honolulu, HI	33.9	50.1	1.2	6.3	8.6
Houston, TX	33.7	49.8	2.5	4.5	9.6
Huntsville, AL	30.1	50.8	1.7	5.6	11.8
Indianapolis, IN	33.5	47.9	1.4	5.3	11.9
Jacksonville, FL	31.4	47.8	1.9	5.8	13.2
Kansas City, MO	30.5	50.4	1.6	5.4	12.0
Lafayette, LA	34.7	46.2	1.9	6.0	11.3
Lakeland, FL	31.8	46.9	2.1	7.2	12.1
Las Vegas, NV	34.7	43.9	2.3	5.2	13.9
Lexington, KY	34.3	46.5	1.7	5.1	12.3
Lincoln, NE	36.7	48.2	0.9	4.4	9.7
Little Rock, AR	30.7	47.4	2.1	6.3	13.6
Los Angeles, CA	39.9	44.7	2.1	4.9	8.4
Louisville, KY	31.6	47.4	1.9	6.1	13.0
Madison, WI	36.5	48.8	0.8	4.2	9.6
Manchester, NH	30.4	51.3	1.4	5.3	11.6

Table continued on following page.

Metro Area	Never Married	Now Married[1]	Separated	Widowed	Divorced
Memphis, TN	38.4	42.0	2.9	5.7	11.0
Miami, FL	34.6	43.3	2.8	6.4	12.8
Midland, TX	29.2	51.8	2.0	5.0	11.9
Milwaukee, WI	37.0	46.4	1.1	5.5	10.1
Minneapolis, MN	33.2	51.4	1.0	4.3	10.1
Nashville, TN	32.0	50.3	1.6	5.0	11.2
New Haven, CT	37.9	43.6	1.3	6.2	10.9
New Orleans, LA	37.8	41.3	2.3	6.3	12.2
New York, NY	37.8	46.3	2.3	5.7	7.9
Oklahoma City, OK	31.4	48.3	2.0	5.6	12.7
Omaha, NE	31.4	51.6	1.3	4.9	10.7
Orlando, FL	34.8	46.0	2.2	5.2	11.8
Peoria, IL	29.9	50.3	1.1	7.0	11.8
Philadelphia, PA	37.2	45.5	2.1	6.0	9.2
Phoenix, AZ	34.0	47.2	1.6	5.1	12.1
Pittsburgh, PA	31.7	49.4	1.7	7.3	9.9
Portland, OR	32.1	50.0	1.4	4.5	12.0
Providence, RI	36.0	45.2	1.6	6.1	11.0
Provo, UT	32.3	58.4	1.0	2.7	5.6
Raleigh, NC	32.0	51.7	2.3	4.2	9.9
Reno, NV	30.9	48.6	1.9	4.9	13.7
Richmond, VA	34.9	46.0	2.5	5.8	10.9
Riverside, CA	36.0	47.0	2.3	5.1	9.6
Rochester, MN	27.8	56.9	0.8	5.1	9.4
Sacramento, CA	33.5	48.2	2.1	5.2	10.9
Salt Lake City, UT	32.1	52.1	1.7	3.8	10.3
San Antonio, TX	35.1	45.6	2.6	5.2	11.5
San Diego, CA	35.9	47.6	1.7	4.7	10.1
San Francisco, CA	36.3	48.7	1.5	4.7	8.8
San Jose, CA	33.6	53.2	1.4	4.2	7.5
Santa Rosa, CA	32.1	47.8	1.7	5.3	13.1
Savannah, GA	34.9	44.9	2.2	5.8	12.1
Seattle, WA	32.6	50.8	1.4	4.2	11.0
Sioux Falls, SD	30.2	53.1	1.2	5.0	10.5
Springfield, IL	32.1	47.5	1.3	6.1	13.0
Tallahassee, FL	43.9	39.0	1.6	4.6	10.9
Tampa, FL	31.2	45.9	2.1	7.0	13.9
Tucson, AZ	34.4	45.0	1.8	5.9	12.9
Tulsa, OK	28.4	50.3	1.9	6.2	13.2
Tuscaloosa, AL	40.8	41.1	2.1	5.6	10.3
Virginia Beach, VA	33.5	47.3	2.7	5.6	11.0
Washington, DC	36.1	48.9	1.9	4.4	8.8
Wichita, KS	30.0	50.3	1.6	5.9	12.2
Winston-Salem, NC	29.8	49.6	2.5	6.8	11.3
U.S.	33.4	48.1	1.9	5.8	10.9

Note: Figures are percentages and cover the population 15 years of age and older; Figures cover the Metropolitan Statistical Area—see Appendix B for areas included; (1) Excludes separated
Source: U.S. Census Bureau, 2015-2019 American Community Survey 5-Year Estimates

Disability by Age: City

City	All Ages	Under 18 Years Old	18 to 64 Years Old	65 Years and Over
Albuquerque, NM	13.4	4.1	11.7	34.9
Allentown, PA	17.1	9.2	16.9	37.5
Anchorage, AK	11.4	3.6	10.3	36.3
Ann Arbor, MI	7.1	3.0	4.9	25.7
Athens, GA	11.5	6.6	9.4	35.1
Atlanta, GA	11.9	4.7	9.7	36.8
Austin, TX	8.4	3.9	6.9	30.7
Baton Rouge, LA	16.8	8.5	14.6	40.3
Boise City, ID	10.9	3.3	9.0	31.7
Boston, MA	11.9	5.3	8.9	41.0
Boulder, CO	6.3	2.8	4.5	23.5
Cape Coral, FL	12.9	3.4	9.3	29.9
Cedar Rapids, IA	10.6	3.5	8.5	29.7
Charleston, SC	9.9	2.8	7.2	30.6
Charlotte, NC	7.9	2.5	6.5	29.7
Chicago, IL	10.5	2.9	8.3	35.5
Cincinnati, OH	13.3	5.5	11.9	35.8
Clarksville, TN	14.9	4.7	16.1	41.1
Cleveland, OH	20.0	8.6	18.8	44.3
College Station, TX	6.3	3.8	4.9	28.7
Colorado Springs, CO	13.0	4.6	11.7	33.8
Columbia, MO	10.1	2.9	8.0	38.2
Columbia, SC	12.6	5.4	10.8	35.7
Columbus, OH	11.7	5.0	10.5	35.3
Dallas, TX	9.6	3.3	8.1	35.0
Davenport, IA	12.4	4.8	10.3	33.5
Denver, CO	9.6	3.5	7.4	33.5
Des Moines, IA	14.0	5.8	12.7	38.2
Durham, NC	9.1	2.9	7.3	31.9
Edison, NJ	8.2	3.3	5.3	29.0
El Paso, TX	13.7	5.0	11.3	43.4
Fargo, ND	10.0	2.8	7.7	36.5
Fayetteville, NC	17.5	6.7	16.6	44.5
Fort Collins, CO	7.9	2.8	6.0	30.0
Fort Wayne, IN	13.6	5.2	12.6	34.0
Fort Worth, TX	10.2	3.8	9.1	35.9
Grand Rapids, MI	13.2	5.4	12.0	35.8
Greeley, CO	11.2	2.3	10.2	36.2
Green Bay, WI	13.0	6.6	11.6	32.5
Greensboro, NC	10.7	4.3	8.7	30.9
Honolulu, HI	11.2	2.6	7.1	31.4
Houston, TX	9.5	3.2	7.7	35.6
Huntsville, AL	13.7	4.8	11.2	34.7
Indianapolis, IN	13.3	5.1	12.0	37.5
Jacksonville, FL	13.5	5.0	11.5	37.6
Kansas City, MO	12.7	3.9	11.2	36.2
Lafayette, LA	12.4	3.7	10.7	32.7
Lakeland, FL	15.8	4.3	11.8	37.1
Las Vegas, NV	12.9	3.7	10.8	36.3
Lexington, KY	12.4	4.5	10.7	34.3
Lincoln, NE	10.8	4.4	8.6	32.7
Little Rock, AR	13.4	5.8	11.5	35.4
Los Angeles, CA	10.1	3.1	7.3	37.3
Louisville, KY	14.8	4.6	13.4	36.4
Madison, WI	8.0	3.2	6.2	26.3

Table continued on following page.

City	All Ages	Under 18 Years Old	18 to 64 Years Old	65 Years and Over
Manchester, NH	14.1	6.0	11.7	39.8
Memphis, TN	13.5	5.1	12.0	37.8
Miami, FL	11.8	3.9	7.7	36.3
Midland, TX	9.7	2.4	8.2	38.5
Milwaukee, WI	13.0	5.7	11.8	38.8
Minneapolis, MN	11.2	4.7	10.1	32.9
Nashville, TN	11.5	4.0	9.8	35.4
New Haven, CT	10.2	5.2	8.6	31.9
New Orleans, LA	14.2	5.0	12.3	36.4
New York, NY	10.8	3.4	7.9	35.1
Oklahoma City, OK	13.2	4.2	12.0	38.6
Omaha, NE	10.9	3.3	9.7	32.3
Orlando, FL	10.1	5.4	8.2	32.5
Peoria, IL	12.4	3.2	11.0	33.2
Philadelphia, PA	16.7	6.0	15.0	43.2
Phoenix, AZ	10.7	3.9	9.5	34.7
Pittsburgh, PA	13.9	6.9	10.7	36.8
Portland, OR	12.1	4.1	10.0	35.4
Providence, RI	13.3	5.5	12.2	38.5
Provo, UT	8.2	4.2	6.8	38.3
Raleigh, NC	9.0	4.7	6.8	31.6
Reno, NV	12.2	5.2	10.3	30.7
Richmond, VA	15.2	6.7	13.2	38.0
Riverside, CA	11.2	3.9	9.1	40.7
Rochester, MN	10.5	4.7	8.2	30.1
Sacramento, CA	11.6	3.2	9.3	38.0
Salt Lake City, UT	10.8	3.2	9.1	35.7
San Antonio, TX	14.6	5.8	13.2	41.1
San Diego, CA	9.2	3.3	6.5	32.4
San Francisco, CA	10.2	2.3	6.3	35.2
San Jose, CA	8.6	2.6	6.1	33.1
Santa Rosa, CA	12.0	4.0	9.9	30.5
Savannah, GA	15.2	6.1	12.5	43.4
Seattle, WA	9.2	2.5	6.9	30.9
Sioux Falls, SD	10.2	3.3	9.0	30.1
Springfield, IL	14.9	5.8	12.9	33.6
Tallahassee, FL	9.9	4.7	8.2	30.5
Tampa, FL	12.2	3.7	9.9	39.4
Tucson, AZ	15.3	5.5	13.2	39.5
Tulsa, OK	14.5	4.7	13.5	36.2
Tuscaloosa, AL	11.1	2.8	9.5	32.4
Virginia Beach, VA	11.2	3.5	9.4	31.6
Washington, DC	11.7	4.1	9.6	35.3
Wichita, KS	13.7	4.6	12.4	36.3
Winston-Salem, NC	9.8	2.8	8.3	28.6
U.S.	12.6	4.2	10.3	34.5

Note: Figures show percent of the civilian noninstitutionalized population that reported having a disability. Disability status is determined from from six types of difficulty: vision, hearing, cognitive, ambulatory, self-care, and independent living. For children under 5 years old, hearing and vision difficulty are used to determine disability status. For children between the ages of 5 and 14, disability status is determined from hearing, vision, cognitive, ambulatory, and self-care difficulties. For people aged 15 years and older, they are considered to have a disability if they have difficulty with any one of the six difficulty types.
Source: U.S. Census Bureau, 2015-2019 American Community Survey 5-Year Estimates

Disability by Age: Metro Area

Metro Area	All Ages	Under 18 Years Old	18 to 64 Years Old	65 Years and Over
Albuquerque, NM	14.3	4.1	12.2	36.6
Allentown, PA	13.3	5.7	10.8	31.8
Anchorage, AK	11.9	3.7	11.0	36.5
Ann Arbor, MI	9.4	3.7	7.3	27.9
Athens, GA	12.5	6.0	10.1	35.8
Atlanta, GA	10.0	3.5	8.4	32.5
Austin, TX	9.2	3.7	7.6	31.4
Baton Rouge, LA	14.8	6.2	13.0	38.1
Boise City, ID	12.0	4.0	10.5	33.0
Boston, MA	10.6	4.0	7.8	31.3
Boulder, CO	8.1	3.0	6.1	25.6
Cape Coral, FL	13.9	3.8	9.9	28.2
Cedar Rapids, IA	10.4	3.6	8.1	29.8
Charleston, SC	12.2	4.0	10.0	33.9
Charlotte, NC	10.5	3.4	8.7	32.4
Chicago, IL	9.9	3.0	7.7	31.8
Cincinnati, OH	12.4	4.7	10.6	32.7
Clarksville, TN	16.5	5.7	16.6	43.2
Cleveland, OH	14.2	5.2	11.7	33.8
College Station, TX	9.5	4.1	7.3	35.2
Colorado Springs, CO	12.4	4.4	11.4	32.7
Columbia, MO	12.1	4.0	10.0	37.2
Columbia, SC	14.1	4.6	12.2	36.8
Columbus, OH	12.0	4.7	10.3	33.7
Dallas, TX	9.5	3.4	7.9	33.7
Davenport, IA	12.3	4.4	9.6	31.8
Denver, CO	9.3	3.2	7.4	30.8
Des Moines, IA	10.6	4.0	8.9	31.4
Durham, NC	11.4	3.9	9.1	32.3
Edison, NJ	10.0	3.2	7.2	31.6
El Paso, TX	13.8	5.5	11.5	44.6
Fargo, ND	9.5	3.1	7.4	33.9
Fayetteville, NC	16.4	6.0	15.7	43.7
Fort Collins, CO	9.7	3.1	7.4	28.1
Fort Wayne, IN	12.6	4.5	11.3	32.8
Fort Worth, TX	9.5	3.4	7.9	33.7
Grand Rapids, MI	11.4	4.0	9.8	31.7
Greeley, CO	10.3	3.0	8.9	34.6
Green Bay, WI	11.2	4.7	9.1	29.4
Greensboro, NC	12.7	4.5	10.7	32.5
Honolulu, HI	10.9	2.9	7.4	32.8
Houston, TX	9.4	3.3	7.8	34.0
Huntsville, AL	13.7	4.9	11.3	37.7
Indianapolis, IN	12.2	4.5	10.5	35.0
Jacksonville, FL	13.2	4.7	11.0	34.7
Kansas City, MO	12.1	3.9	10.2	34.2
Lafayette, LA	14.5	5.0	12.9	39.1
Lakeland, FL	15.4	5.7	12.4	34.7
Las Vegas, NV	12.1	3.8	9.9	34.8
Lexington, KY	13.5	5.1	11.8	35.5
Lincoln, NE	10.7	4.1	8.4	32.5
Little Rock, AR	15.7	5.9	13.8	39.5
Los Angeles, CA	9.6	3.0	6.8	33.9
Louisville, KY	14.1	4.2	12.4	35.5
Madison, WI	8.9	3.4	6.9	26.9

Table continued on following page.

Metro Area	All Ages	Under 18 Years Old	18 to 64 Years Old	65 Years and Over
Manchester, NH	11.8	4.7	9.5	31.8
Memphis, TN	12.9	4.5	11.2	36.4
Miami, FL	10.9	3.4	7.2	32.1
Midland, TX	9.8	2.3	8.3	39.5
Milwaukee, WI	11.4	4.2	9.1	31.6
Minneapolis, MN	9.9	3.7	8.0	30.0
Nashville, TN	12.0	4.0	10.2	35.2
New Haven, CT	11.6	4.0	8.8	31.5
New Orleans, LA	14.4	5.0	12.3	36.6
New York, NY	10.0	3.2	7.2	31.6
Oklahoma City, OK	13.9	4.3	12.2	39.4
Omaha, NE	11.0	3.5	9.6	32.2
Orlando, FL	12.2	5.1	9.6	34.5
Peoria, IL	12.0	3.4	9.5	32.2
Philadelphia, PA	12.7	4.6	10.5	33.4
Phoenix, AZ	11.5	3.7	9.3	32.6
Pittsburgh, PA	14.5	5.4	11.4	33.8
Portland, OR	11.9	3.9	9.7	34.1
Providence, RI	13.6	5.2	11.2	33.3
Provo, UT	7.8	3.3	7.1	32.8
Raleigh, NC	9.6	3.8	7.7	32.1
Reno, NV	12.1	4.7	9.9	30.7
Richmond, VA	12.6	5.0	10.4	32.6
Riverside, CA	11.3	3.6	9.1	37.5
Rochester, MN	10.2	4.0	7.7	29.4
Sacramento, CA	11.5	3.4	9.0	34.8
Salt Lake City, UT	9.4	3.5	8.3	32.4
San Antonio, TX	14.0	5.3	12.5	39.2
San Diego, CA	9.9	3.2	7.2	32.8
San Francisco, CA	9.7	2.9	6.8	31.5
San Jose, CA	8.1	2.4	5.4	31.2
Santa Rosa, CA	11.9	3.8	9.4	28.5
Savannah, GA	13.7	5.5	11.6	37.0
Seattle, WA	10.8	3.5	8.7	33.4
Sioux Falls, SD	9.9	3.1	8.8	29.7
Springfield, IL	13.7	5.4	11.4	32.9
Tallahassee, FL	12.7	5.9	10.2	33.9
Tampa, FL	14.0	4.4	10.8	34.3
Tucson, AZ	15.3	5.1	12.5	35.1
Tulsa, OK	14.5	4.6	12.9	37.9
Tuscaloosa, AL	14.4	4.0	12.4	40.2
Virginia Beach, VA	13.1	4.7	11.1	34.4
Washington, DC	8.7	3.0	6.7	29.1
Wichita, KS	13.4	4.9	11.7	36.1
Winston-Salem, NC	12.7	3.8	10.2	33.8
U.S.	12.6	4.2	10.3	34.5

Note: Figures show percent of the civilian noninstitutionalized population that reported having a disability. Disability status is determined from from six types of difficulty: vision, hearing, cognitive, ambulatory, self-care, and independent living. For children under 5 years old, hearing and vision difficulty are used to determine disability status. For children between the ages of 5 and 14, disability status is determined from hearing, vision, cognitive, ambulatory, and self-care difficulties. For people aged 15 years and older, they are considered to have a disability if they have difficulty with any one of the six difficulty types; Figures cover the Metropolitan Statistical Area—see Appendix B for areas included
Source: U.S. Census Bureau, 2015-2019 American Community Survey 5-Year Estimates

Male/Female Ratio: City

City	Males	Females	Males per 100 Females
Albuquerque, NM	272,468	286,906	95.0
Allentown, PA	59,101	61,814	95.6
Anchorage, AK	149,670	143,861	104.0
Ann Arbor, MI	60,089	60,646	99.1
Athens, GA	59,357	65,362	90.8
Atlanta, GA	237,192	251,608	94.3
Austin, TX	482,605	468,202	103.1
Baton Rouge, LA	107,345	116,804	91.9
Boise City, ID	112,637	113,478	99.3
Boston, MA	328,503	355,876	92.3
Boulder, CO	55,160	51,232	107.7
Cape Coral, FL	91,158	92,784	98.2
Cedar Rapids, IA	64,863	67,438	96.2
Charleston, SC	63,863	71,394	89.5
Charlotte, NC	412,035	445,390	92.5
Chicago, IL	1,317,791	1,391,743	94.7
Cincinnati, OH	145,900	155,494	93.8
Clarksville, TN	76,399	76,535	99.8
Cleveland, OH	185,274	200,008	92.6
College Station, TX	58,117	55,569	104.6
Colorado Springs, CO	232,440	232,431	100.0
Columbia, MO	58,250	62,980	92.5
Columbia, SC	67,638	65,635	103.1
Columbus, OH	429,868	448,685	95.8
Dallas, TX	657,714	672,898	97.7
Davenport, IA	50,216	51,953	96.7
Denver, CO	353,311	352,265	100.3
Des Moines, IA	106,316	109,320	97.3
Durham, NC	126,897	142,805	88.9
Edison, NJ	50,210	50,237	99.9
El Paso, TX	332,917	346,896	96.0
Fargo, ND	61,988	59,901	103.5
Fayetteville, NC	105,869	104,563	101.2
Fort Collins, CO	83,175	82,434	100.9
Fort Wayne, IN	128,483	137,269	93.6
Fort Worth, TX	428,238	446,163	96.0
Grand Rapids, MI	97,940	100,461	97.5
Greeley, CO	52,657	53,231	98.9
Green Bay, WI	51,929	52,848	98.3
Greensboro, NC	135,572	155,731	87.1
Honolulu, HI	173,837	175,148	99.3
Houston, TX	1,153,417	1,157,015	99.7
Huntsville, AL	94,803	101,416	93.5
Indianapolis, IN	416,893	447,554	93.1
Jacksonville, FL	431,133	459,334	93.9
Kansas City, MO	235,974	250,430	94.2
Lafayette, LA	61,742	64,924	95.1
Lakeland, FL	51,105	56,817	89.9
Las Vegas, NV	316,556	318,217	99.5
Lexington, KY	157,231	163,370	96.2
Lincoln, NE	142,589	141,250	100.9
Little Rock, AR	94,939	103,019	92.2
Los Angeles, CA	1,964,984	2,001,952	98.2
Louisville, KY	299,406	318,384	94.0
Madison, WI	126,190	128,787	98.0

Table continued on following page.

City	Males	Females	Males per 100 Females
Manchester, NH	56,510	55,599	101.6
Memphis, TN	308,460	343,472	89.8
Miami, FL	224,810	229,469	98.0
Midland, TX	70,558	67,991	103.8
Milwaukee, WI	286,081	308,467	92.7
Minneapolis, MN	212,823	207,501	102.6
Nashville, TN	319,844	343,906	93.0
New Haven, CT	61,926	68,405	90.5
New Orleans, LA	185,513	205,332	90.3
New York, NY	4,015,982	4,403,334	91.2
Oklahoma City, OK	316,500	327,192	96.7
Omaha, NE	234,719	241,143	97.3
Orlando, FL	134,785	146,047	92.3
Peoria, IL	54,542	58,990	92.5
Philadelphia, PA	747,479	831,596	89.9
Phoenix, AZ	813,775	819,242	99.3
Pittsburgh, PA	147,776	154,429	95.7
Portland, OR	319,869	325,422	98.3
Providence, RI	86,874	92,620	93.8
Provo, UT	57,489	58,914	97.6
Raleigh, NC	223,942	240,543	93.1
Reno, NV	124,568	121,932	102.2
Richmond, VA	107,430	119,192	90.1
Riverside, CA	162,664	163,750	99.3
Rochester, MN	56,262	59,295	94.9
Sacramento, CA	245,188	255,742	95.9
Salt Lake City, UT	100,748	97,008	103.9
San Antonio, TX	744,596	763,487	97.5
San Diego, CA	711,134	698,439	101.8
San Francisco, CA	446,286	428,675	104.1
San Jose, CA	518,708	508,982	101.9
Santa Rosa, CA	86,927	92,774	93.7
Savannah, GA	69,220	76,183	90.9
Seattle, WA	366,442	357,863	102.4
Sioux Falls, SD	88,410	88,707	99.7
Springfield, IL	54,935	60,953	90.1
Tallahassee, FL	90,053	101,226	89.0
Tampa, FL	188,134	199,782	94.2
Tucson, AZ	269,403	272,079	99.0
Tulsa, OK	195,534	206,790	94.6
Tuscaloosa, AL	47,718	51,672	92.3
Virginia Beach, VA	221,324	228,877	96.7
Washington, DC	328,644	364,039	90.3
Wichita, KS	191,730	198,147	96.8
Winston-Salem, NC	114,592	129,523	88.5
U.S.	159,886,919	164,810,876	97.0

Source: U.S. Census Bureau, 2015-2019 American Community Survey 5-Year Estimates

Male/Female Ratio: Metro Area

Metro Area	Males	Females	Males per 100 Females
Albuquerque, NM	448,642	463,466	96.8
Allentown, PA	411,125	426,485	96.4
Anchorage, AK	204,508	194,392	105.2
Ann Arbor, MI	181,923	185,077	98.3
Athens, GA	100,687	107,770	93.4
Atlanta, GA	2,834,134	3,028,290	93.6
Austin, TX	1,059,553	1,054,888	100.4
Baton Rouge, LA	417,717	436,601	95.7
Boise City, ID	354,905	355,838	99.7
Boston, MA	2,347,899	2,484,447	94.5
Boulder, CO	162,211	160,299	101.2
Cape Coral, FL	361,232	376,236	96.0
Cedar Rapids, IA	133,800	136,256	98.2
Charleston, SC	378,374	396,134	95.5
Charlotte, NC	1,235,495	1,310,065	94.3
Chicago, IL	4,654,160	4,854,445	95.9
Cincinnati, OH	1,079,705	1,122,036	96.2
Clarksville, TN	151,723	147,747	102.7
Cleveland, OH	993,227	1,063,671	93.4
College Station, TX	129,895	128,134	101.4
Colorado Springs, CO	365,383	358,115	102.0
Columbia, MO	100,711	104,658	96.2
Columbia, SC	399,998	424,280	94.3
Columbus, OH	1,022,627	1,055,134	96.9
Dallas, TX	3,601,569	3,719,094	96.8
Davenport, IA	187,831	193,344	97.1
Denver, CO	1,445,090	1,446,976	99.9
Des Moines, IA	336,082	344,357	97.6
Durham, NC	301,581	325,114	92.8
Edison, NJ	9,327,459	9,966,777	93.6
El Paso, TX	413,883	426,594	97.0
Fargo, ND	120,992	119,429	101.3
Fayetteville, NC	257,939	261,162	98.8
Fort Collins, CO	172,000	172,786	99.5
Fort Wayne, IN	198,843	207,462	95.8
Fort Worth, TX	3,601,569	3,719,094	96.8
Grand Rapids, MI	527,777	534,615	98.7
Greeley, CO	154,294	151,051	102.1
Green Bay, WI	159,123	160,278	99.3
Greensboro, NC	364,321	397,742	91.6
Honolulu, HI	496,066	488,755	101.5
Houston, TX	3,417,036	3,467,102	98.6
Huntsville, AL	224,226	232,777	96.3
Indianapolis, IN	991,392	1,038,080	95.5
Jacksonville, FL	733,355	770,219	95.2
Kansas City, MO	1,042,927	1,081,591	96.4
Lafayette, LA	238,957	250,957	95.2
Lakeland, FL	336,279	349,939	96.1
Las Vegas, NV	1,089,228	1,092,776	99.7
Lexington, KY	249,429	261,218	95.5
Lincoln, NE	165,977	164,352	101.0
Little Rock, AR	356,611	380,404	93.7
Los Angeles, CA	6,533,214	6,716,400	97.3
Louisville, KY	613,822	643,266	95.4
Madison, WI	325,952	327,773	99.4

Table continued on following page.

Metro Area	Males	Females	Males per 100 Females
Manchester, NH	205,394	207,641	98.9
Memphis, TN	640,257	699,366	91.5
Miami, FL	2,959,743	3,130,917	94.5
Midland, TX	87,984	85,832	102.5
Milwaukee, WI	767,950	807,273	95.1
Minneapolis, MN	1,771,443	1,802,166	98.3
Nashville, TN	913,820	958,083	95.4
New Haven, CT	413,519	443,994	93.1
New Orleans, LA	612,116	655,661	93.4
New York, NY	9,327,459	9,966,777	93.6
Oklahoma City, OK	682,133	700,708	97.3
Omaha, NE	461,556	470,223	98.2
Orlando, FL	1,226,241	1,282,729	95.6
Peoria, IL	200,311	206,572	97.0
Philadelphia, PA	2,939,397	3,139,733	93.6
Phoenix, AZ	2,366,181	2,395,422	98.8
Pittsburgh, PA	1,135,076	1,196,371	94.9
Portland, OR	1,210,509	1,235,252	98.0
Providence, RI	785,383	832,885	94.3
Provo, UT	311,659	305,132	102.1
Raleigh, NC	649,577	682,734	95.1
Reno, NV	232,199	228,725	101.5
Richmond, VA	613,475	656,055	93.5
Riverside, CA	2,270,726	2,289,744	99.2
Rochester, MN	107,432	110,532	97.2
Sacramento, CA	1,132,519	1,183,461	95.7
Salt Lake City, UT	603,034	598,009	100.8
San Antonio, TX	1,220,720	1,247,473	97.9
San Diego, CA	1,669,515	1,646,558	101.4
San Francisco, CA	2,325,587	2,375,745	97.9
San Jose, CA	1,004,573	983,273	102.2
Santa Rosa, CA	244,045	255,727	95.4
Savannah, GA	187,309	198,727	94.3
Seattle, WA	1,938,723	1,932,600	100.3
Sioux Falls, SD	130,188	129,160	100.8
Springfield, IL	100,527	108,640	92.5
Tallahassee, FL	184,249	197,948	93.1
Tampa, FL	1,502,972	1,594,887	94.2
Tucson, AZ	505,666	521,541	97.0
Tulsa, OK	486,355	504,189	96.5
Tuscaloosa, AL	120,524	130,157	92.6
Virginia Beach, VA	867,843	893,886	97.1
Washington, DC	3,028,975	3,167,610	95.6
Wichita, KS	316,050	321,640	98.3
Winston-Salem, NC	320,092	346,124	92.5
U.S.	159,886,919	164,810,876	97.0

Note: Figures cover the Metropolitan Statistical Area (MSA)—see Appendix B for areas included
Source: U.S. Census Bureau, 2015-2019 American Community Survey 5-Year Estimates

Gross Metropolitan Product

MSA[1]	2017	2018	2019	2020	Rank[2]
Albuquerque, NM	42.8	44.4	46.3	48.6	68
Allentown, PA	43.9	46.2	48.1	49.9	64
Anchorage, AK	27.4	28.3	29.3	30.6	102
Ann Arbor, MI	23.5	24.6	25.5	26.4	112
Athens, GA	10.1	10.5	10.8	11.2	205
Atlanta, GA	391.0	409.9	431.6	452.0	10
Austin, TX	145.1	156.6	164.6	174.0	25
Baton Rouge, LA	53.2	56.3	58.3	61.0	59
Boise City, ID	33.9	36.5	38.7	40.8	79
Boston, MA	449.5	472.7	493.6	515.0	8
Boulder, CO	25.6	27.2	28.7	29.9	107
Cape Coral, FL	28.3	30.0	31.8	33.4	93
Cedar Rapids, IA	17.8	18.4	18.8	19.4	141
Charleston, SC	42.5	44.6	46.7	49.0	67
Charlotte, NC	174.1	185.6	195.5	205.3	20
Chicago, IL	683.3	716.3	743.3	770.7	3
Cincinnati, OH	137.2	143.5	150.7	156.1	29
Clarksville, TN	11.0	11.6	12.2	12.6	194
Cleveland, OH	138.3	145.9	152.3	157.1	28
College Station, TX	9.9	10.6	11.2	11.7	204
Colorado Springs, CO	33.1	34.9	36.6	38.5	84
Columbia, MO	9.2	9.6	9.9	10.3	220
Columbia, SC	41.4	42.3	43.9	45.8	73
Columbus, OH	135.6	142.2	148.6	154.7	32
Dallas, TX	522.3	556.9	586.7	620.6	5
Davenport, IA	19.8	20.7	21.6	22.3	124
Denver, CO	211.6	225.3	235.8	246.9	18
Des Moines, IA	55.0	57.7	60.3	62.8	58
Durham, NC	43.4	45.5	48.0	50.7	65
Edison, NJ	1,765.5	1,851.9	1,932.1	2,007.4	1
El Paso, TX	28.3	29.4	30.5	31.5	97
Fargo, ND	15.3	16.1	16.8	17.5	156
Fayetteville, NC	17.2	17.6	18.1	18.8	149
Fort Collins, CO	17.4	18.4	19.7	20.7	139
Fort Wayne, IN	21.9	22.9	23.9	24.8	117
Fort Worth, TX	522.3	556.9	586.7	620.6	5
Grand Rapids, MI	60.6	63.6	66.2	68.3	54
Greeley, CO	12.8	13.8	14.7	15.6	178
Green Bay, WI	19.4	20.4	21.3	22.1	128
Greensboro, NC	41.5	43.0	44.3	45.7	71
Honolulu, HI	68.2	70.5	73.2	75.5	50
Houston, TX	478.1	513.9	546.1	583.7	7
Huntsville, AL	25.9	27.2	28.4	29.8	106
Indianapolis, IN	140.6	147.0	152.8	159.1	27
Jacksonville, FL	77.6	82.8	86.5	90.6	45
Kansas City, MO	131.8	138.2	144.1	149.7	33
Lafayette, LA	21.4	23.0	24.0	25.4	116
Lakeland, FL	21.4	22.6	23.6	24.6	119
Las Vegas, NV	112.8	119.1	124.1	130.3	36
Lexington, KY	29.7	30.8	31.9	33.0	90
Lincoln, NE	19.7	20.6	21.2	22.0	125
Little Rock, AR	38.5	39.8	41.1	42.7	76
Los Angeles, CA	1,067.7	1,125.5	1,164.2	1,207.3	2
Louisville, KY	75.3	78.1	81.3	83.9	48
Madison, WI	49.5	52.1	54.5	56.5	61
Manchester, NH	28.7	30.0	31.2	32.5	94

Table continued on following page.

MSA[1]	2017	2018	2019	2020	Rank[2]
Memphis, TN	72.9	76.2	79.4	82.2	49
Miami, FL	349.2	369.5	386.7	403.4	12
Midland, TX	27.1	35.0	38.1	44.4	83
Milwaukee, WI	104.6	109.2	112.8	116.2	37
Minneapolis, MN	260.9	273.1	284.6	296.0	14
Nashville, TN	134.3	142.5	149.8	156.5	30
New Haven, CT	46.1	47.8	49.7	51.2	62
New Orleans, LA	76.7	81.0	83.8	87.5	46
New York, NY	1,765.5	1,851.9	1,932.1	2,007.4	1
Oklahoma City, OK	74.2	79.6	83.2	88.3	47
Omaha, NE	63.3	65.9	68.5	71.0	52
Orlando, FL	134.1	142.4	150.7	158.6	31
Peoria, IL	19.2	20.1	20.9	21.6	133
Philadelphia, PA	445.1	465.5	485.8	504.6	9
Phoenix, AZ	248.0	264.9	280.3	294.0	16
Pittsburgh, PA	147.4	156.4	162.8	168.5	26
Portland, OR	165.9	175.7	183.8	191.1	21
Providence, RI	84.0	86.8	89.5	93.0	44
Provo, UT	25.7	27.9	29.5	31.2	104
Raleigh, NC	83.2	88.3	92.8	97.8	42
Reno, NV	26.8	28.8	30.8	32.3	99
Richmond, VA	83.0	87.2	91.0	94.7	43
Riverside, CA	161.6	171.0	178.3	186.9	22
Rochester, MN	12.6	13.2	13.9	14.4	182
Sacramento, CA	129.3	137.0	144.3	151.5	34
Salt Lake City, UT	87.9	93.6	97.8	102.5	41
San Antonio, TX	126.1	134.5	140.1	148.6	35
San Diego, CA	237.2	249.4	260.3	272.1	17
San Francisco, CA	512.2	547.3	578.7	605.5	6
San Jose, CA	281.6	303.1	321.2	334.7	13
Santa Rosa, CA	29.3	30.4	31.4	32.5	91
Savannah, GA	18.8	19.7	20.6	21.2	134
Seattle, WA	367.9	397.5	416.9	435.0	11
Sioux Falls, SD	19.6	20.5	21.5	22.4	127
Springfield, IL	10.3	10.7	11.0	11.4	202
Tallahassee, FL	16.4	17.1	17.9	18.7	152
Tampa, FL	148.2	156.6	164.0	172.0	24
Tucson, AZ	39.9	41.7	43.6	45.5	74
Tulsa, OK	57.2	60.9	63.7	67.4	55
Tuscaloosa, AL	11.8	12.4	13.0	13.4	190
Virginia Beach, VA	95.2	99.3	103.6	107.4	39
Washington, DC	539.6	562.6	585.8	612.1	4
Wichita, KS	34.3	35.7	37.0	38.0	81
Winston-Salem, NC	29.7	31.2	32.5	33.8	88

Note: Figures are in billions of dollars; (1) Metropolitan Statistical Area—see Appendix B for areas included; (2) Rank is based on 2018 data and ranges from 1 to 381.
Source: The U.S. Conference of Mayors, U.S. Metro Economies: GMP & Employment 2018-2020, September 2019

Economic Growth

MSA[1]	2015-17 (%)	2018 (%)	2019 (%)	2020 (%)	Rank[2]
Albuquerque, NM	0.7	1.4	2.6	2.5	252
Allentown, PA	1.2	2.6	2.3	1.6	210
Anchorage, AK	-1.5	-0.9	2.4	0.6	353
Ann Arbor, MI	2.1	2.5	1.9	1.3	123
Athens, GA	6.8	1.5	1.3	1.4	6
Atlanta, GA	3.7	2.8	3.6	2.6	47
Austin, TX	6.3	4.4	3.5	2.6	9
Baton Rouge, LA	1.6	0.8	1.2	2.4	170
Boise City, ID	3.7	5.5	4.1	3.2	45
Boston, MA	2.0	3.0	2.8	2.1	134
Boulder, CO	2.5	4.1	3.9	2.1	98
Cape Coral, FL	2.7	3.7	3.7	3.0	83
Cedar Rapids, IA	-1.6	0.9	0.8	1.0	354
Charleston, SC	5.0	2.4	2.9	2.6	16
Charlotte, NC	3.4	4.2	3.7	2.8	51
Chicago, IL	0.8	2.3	2.0	1.6	247
Cincinnati, OH	2.0	1.7	3.3	1.4	132
Clarksville, TN	-0.6	3.0	3.0	1.6	331
Cleveland, OH	1.7	1.9	2.8	0.9	160
College Station, TX	1.0	3.4	3.3	1.4	224
Colorado Springs, CO	2.9	3.1	3.0	2.8	73
Columbia, MO	0.9	1.6	1.5	1.8	242
Columbia, SC	0.8	-0.1	1.9	2.3	245
Columbus, OH	2.0	2.1	2.6	1.9	130
Dallas, TX	2.7	2.8	3.7	2.7	87
Davenport, IA	-0.2	2.4	2.4	1.2	311
Denver, CO	2.6	3.7	3.0	1.9	89
Des Moines, IA	2.8	1.8	2.7	1.9	78
Durham, NC	-2.0	2.9	3.7	3.5	363
Edison, NJ	1.3	2.6	2.6	1.6	196
El Paso, TX	0.9	1.5	1.6	1.4	244
Fargo, ND	0.4	2.1	2.6	2.0	283
Fayetteville, NC	-1.0	0.0	1.2	1.5	343
Fort Collins, CO	5.3	3.7	4.7	3.1	14
Fort Wayne, IN	1.9	2.5	2.5	1.3	149
Fort Worth, TX	2.7	2.8	3.7	2.7	87
Grand Rapids, MI	1.9	3.4	2.3	1.2	139
Greeley, CO	4.1	5.3	4.5	3.9	33
Green Bay, WI	1.2	3.2	2.6	1.2	203
Greensboro, NC	-0.2	1.5	1.2	1.2	312
Honolulu, HI	1.6	1.0	1.9	0.9	165
Houston, TX	-1.7	2.9	4.6	3.1	360
Huntsville, AL	1.8	3.0	2.5	2.7	155
Indianapolis, IN	2.5	1.9	2.1	2.0	101
Jacksonville, FL	4.1	4.3	2.6	2.5	34
Kansas City, MO	0.6	2.6	2.4	1.7	263
Lafayette, LA	-4.9	2.6	3.0	2.0	380
Lakeland, FL	2.7	3.2	2.5	2.4	82
Las Vegas, NV	1.5	3.1	2.3	2.7	182
Lexington, KY	1.6	1.3	2.0	1.1	167
Lincoln, NE	0.3	2.1	1.3	1.5	287
Little Rock, AR	0.4	0.9	1.6	1.5	286
Los Angeles, CA	2.3	3.5	1.8	1.6	110
Louisville, KY	0.7	1.4	2.3	1.2	254
Madison, WI	2.4	3.2	2.8	1.7	107
Manchester, NH	2.7	2.6	2.3	1.8	84

Table continued on following page.

MSA[1]	2015-17 (%)	2018 (%)	2019 (%)	2020 (%)	Rank[2]
Memphis, TN	0.1	2.3	2.3	1.4	299
Miami, FL	3.2	3.5	2.9	2.1	56
Midland, TX	1.0	13.0	9.2	3.6	231
Milwaukee, WI	0.9	2.1	1.5	0.9	243
Minneapolis, MN	1.9	2.3	2.5	1.9	144
Nashville, TN	4.0	3.9	3.3	2.3	39
New Haven, CT	1.2	1.7	2.1	0.9	204
New Orleans, LA	-0.6	1.2	1.3	2.0	329
New York, NY	1.3	2.6	2.6	1.6	196
Oklahoma City, OK	0.7	2.8	2.9	2.2	259
Omaha, NE	0.6	1.7	2.2	1.5	272
Orlando, FL	2.4	3.8	4.0	3.0	109
Peoria, IL	-4.0	2.5	2.0	1.3	376
Philadelphia, PA	1.4	1.9	2.7	1.7	188
Phoenix, AZ	3.3	4.5	4.0	2.7	54
Pittsburgh, PA	2.0	2.6	2.5	1.3	137
Portland, OR	3.9	3.5	2.6	1.6	42
Providence, RI	0.7	1.0	1.3	1.7	262
Provo, UT	6.6	6.5	4.0	3.7	7
Raleigh, NC	3.1	3.9	3.4	3.3	62
Reno, NV	4.3	5.3	4.9	2.5	27
Richmond, VA	1.5	3.0	2.6	1.8	179
Riverside, CA	3.0	3.4	2.3	2.6	65
Rochester, MN	3.6	2.9	3.1	1.1	48
Sacramento, CA	2.6	3.6	3.4	2.7	90
Salt Lake City, UT	2.3	3.7	2.6	2.7	114
San Antonio, TX	4.2	2.0	2.7	1.7	30
San Diego, CA	3.1	3.0	2.6	2.3	64
San Francisco, CA	4.8	5.1	4.3	2.5	18
San Jose, CA	7.0	6.0	4.6	2.2	5
Santa Rosa, CA	2.5	1.2	1.7	1.1	100
Savannah, GA	2.3	2.7	2.4	1.2	115
Seattle, WA	4.3	6.3	3.4	2.4	29
Sioux Falls, SD	1.2	1.6	3.2	2.2	206
Springfield, IL	-0.8	0.8	1.4	0.9	337
Tallahassee, FL	3.1	2.6	2.8	1.9	61
Tampa, FL	2.7	3.5	2.9	2.6	85
Tucson, AZ	2.0	2.7	2.8	2.0	133
Tulsa, OK	-3.3	1.3	3.1	1.7	373
Tuscaloosa, AL	1.0	2.8	3.4	1.5	227
Virginia Beach, VA	-0.4	2.2	2.5	1.4	323
Washington, DC	2.0	2.3	2.4	2.1	131
Wichita, KS	1.9	1.5	1.8	0.5	141
Winston-Salem, NC	-0.2	2.6	2.6	1.6	314
U.S.	1.9	2.9	2.3	2.1	–

Note: Figures are real gross metropolitan product (GMP) growth rates and represent annual average percent change; (1) Metropolitan Statistical Area—see Appendix B for areas included; (2) Rank is based on 2017 2-year average annual percent change and ranges from 1 to 381
Source: The U.S. Conference of Mayors, U.S. Metro Economies: GMP & Employment 2018-2020, September 2019

Metropolitan Area Exports

Area	2014	2015	2016	2017	2018	2019	Rank[2]
Albuquerque, NM	1,564.0	1,761.2	999.7	624.2	771.5	1,629.7	114
Allentown, PA	3,152.5	3,439.9	3,657.2	3,639.4	3,423.2	3,796.3	66
Anchorage, AK	571.8	421.9	1,215.4	1,675.9	1,510.8	1,348.0	132
Ann Arbor, MI	1,213.6	1,053.0	1,207.9	1,447.4	1,538.7	1,432.7	128
Athens, GA	320.8	327.4	332.1	297.7	378.2	442.1	219
Atlanta, GA	19,870.3	19,163.9	20,480.1	21,748.0	24,091.6	25,800.8	14
Austin, TX	9,400.0	10,094.5	10,682.7	12,451.5	12,929.9	12,509.0	30
Baton Rouge, LA	7,528.3	6,505.4	6,580.5	8,830.3	10,506.1	8,981.2	40
Boise City, ID	3,143.4	2,668.0	3,021.7	2,483.3	2,771.7	2,062.8	101
Boston, MA	23,378.5	21,329.5	21,168.0	23,116.2	24,450.1	23,505.8	17
Boulder, CO	1,016.1	1,039.1	956.3	1,012.0	1,044.1	1,014.9	158
Cape Coral, FL	496.6	487.3	540.3	592.3	668.0	694.9	190
Cedar Rapids, IA	879.0	873.5	945.0	1,071.6	1,025.0	1,028.4	157
Charleston, SC	5,866.7	6,457.5	9,508.1	8,845.2	10,943.2	16,337.9	23
Charlotte, NC	12,885.3	13,985.8	11,944.1	13,122.5	14,083.2	13,892.4	27
Chicago, IL	47,340.1	44,820.9	43,932.7	46,140.2	47,287.8	42,438.8	4
Cincinnati, OH	22,280.7	24,127.0	26,326.2	28,581.8	27,396.3	28,778.3	11
Clarksville, TN	323.7	296.5	376.1	360.2	435.5	341.8	241
Cleveland, OH	10,706.5	9,629.7	8,752.9	8,944.9	9,382.9	8,829.9	41
College Station, TX	129.7	122.5	113.2	145.4	153.0	160.5	313
Colorado Springs, CO	856.6	832.4	786.9	819.7	850.6	864.2	172
Columbia, MO	237.7	214.0	213.7	224.0	238.6	291.4	260
Columbia, SC	2,007.9	2,011.8	2,007.7	2,123.9	2,083.8	2,184.6	97
Columbus, OH	6,245.6	6,201.6	5,675.4	5,962.2	7,529.5	7,296.6	47
Dallas, TX	28,669.4	27,372.9	27,187.8	30,269.1	36,260.9	39,474.0	7
Davenport, IA	6,563.2	5,711.8	4,497.6	5,442.7	6,761.9	6,066.3	51
Denver, CO	4,958.6	3,909.5	3,649.3	3,954.7	4,544.3	4,555.6	61
Des Moines, IA	1,361.8	1,047.8	1,052.2	1,141.2	1,293.7	1,437.8	126
Durham, NC	2,934.0	2,807.2	2,937.4	3,128.4	3,945.8	4,452.9	62
Edison, NJ	105,266.6	95,645.4	89,649.5	93,693.7	97,692.4	87,365.7	2
El Paso, TX	20,079.3	24,560.9	26,452.8	25,814.1	30,052.0	32,749.6	10
Fargo, ND	782.8	543.2	474.5	519.5	553.5	515.0	207
Fayetteville, NC	375.8	256.3	179.8	231.6	260.5	287.8	263
Fort Collins, CO	1,037.4	990.7	993.8	1,034.1	1,021.8	1,060.0	152
Fort Wayne, IN	1,581.1	1,529.0	1,322.2	1,422.8	1,593.3	1,438.5	125
Fort Worth, TX	28,669.4	27,372.9	27,187.8	30,269.1	36,260.9	39,474.0	7
Grand Rapids, MI	5,244.5	5,143.0	5,168.5	5,385.8	5,420.9	5,214.1	55
Greeley, CO	1,343.6	1,240.1	1,539.6	1,492.8	1,366.5	1,439.2	124
Green Bay, WI	988.7	968.1	1,044.0	1,054.8	1,044.3	928.2	167
Greensboro, NC	3,505.5	3,286.1	3,730.4	3,537.9	3,053.5	2,561.8	87
Honolulu, HI	765.5	446.4	330.3	393.6	438.9	308.6	250
Houston, TX	118,966.0	97,054.3	84,105.5	95,760.3	120,714.3	129,656.0	1
Huntsville, AL	1,440.4	1,344.7	1,827.3	1,889.2	1,608.7	1,534.2	122
Indianapolis, IN	9,539.4	9,809.4	9,655.4	10,544.2	11,069.9	11,148.7	33
Jacksonville, FL	2,473.7	2,564.4	2,159.0	2,141.7	2,406.7	2,975.5	79
Kansas City, MO	8,262.9	6,723.2	6,709.8	7,015.0	7,316.9	7,652.6	45
Lafayette, LA	1,532.7	1,165.2	1,335.2	954.8	1,001.7	1,086.2	148
Lakeland, FL	2,151.9	1,318.6	995.5	1,147.2	1,299.8	1,141.5	143
Las Vegas, NV	2,509.7	2,916.2	2,312.3	2,710.6	2,240.6	2,430.8	90
Lexington, KY	2,191.4	2,065.7	2,069.6	2,119.8	2,148.0	2,093.8	100
Lincoln, NE	1,173.9	1,189.3	796.9	860.9	885.6	807.0	177
Little Rock, AR	2,463.5	1,777.5	1,871.0	2,146.1	1,607.4	1,642.5	113
Los Angeles, CA	75,471.2	61,758.7	61,245.7	63,752.9	64,814.6	61,041.1	3
Louisville, KY	8,877.3	8,037.9	7,793.3	8,925.9	8,987.0	9,105.5	39
Madison, WI	2,369.5	2,280.4	2,204.8	2,187.7	2,460.2	2,337.6	93
Manchester, NH	1,575.4	1,556.6	1,465.2	1,714.7	1,651.4	1,587.1	118

Table continued on following page.

Area	2014	2015	2016	2017	2018	2019	Rank[2]
Memphis, TN	11,002.0	11,819.5	11,628.7	11,233.9	12,695.4	13,751.7	28
Miami, FL	37,969.5	33,258.5	32,734.5	34,780.5	35,650.2	35,498.9	8
Midland, TX	122.7	110.1	69.6	69.4	63.6	63.7	357
Milwaukee, WI	8,696.0	7,953.6	7,256.2	7,279.1	7,337.6	6,896.3	49
Minneapolis, MN	21,198.2	19,608.6	18,329.2	19,070.9	20,016.2	18,633.0	22
Nashville, TN	9,620.9	9,353.0	9,460.1	10,164.3	8,723.7	7,940.7	44
New Haven, CT	1,834.5	1,756.3	1,819.8	1,876.3	2,082.3	2,133.8	98
New Orleans, LA	34,881.5	27,023.3	29,518.8	31,648.5	36,570.4	34,109.6	9
New York, NY	105,266.6	95,645.4	89,649.5	93,693.7	97,692.4	87,365.7	2
Oklahoma City, OK	1,622.0	1,353.1	1,260.0	1,278.8	1,489.4	1,434.5	127
Omaha, NE	4,528.5	3,753.4	3,509.7	3,756.2	4,371.6	3,725.7	68
Orlando, FL	3,134.8	3,082.7	3,363.9	3,196.7	3,131.7	3,363.9	73
Peoria, IL	11,234.8	9,826.9	7,260.1	9,403.6	9,683.6	8,151.9	42
Philadelphia, PA	26,321.3	24,236.1	21,359.9	21,689.7	23,663.2	24,721.3	15
Phoenix, AZ	12,764.4	13,821.5	12,838.2	13,223.1	13,614.9	15,136.6	24
Pittsburgh, PA	10,015.8	9,137.1	7,971.0	9,322.7	9,824.2	9,672.9	38
Portland, OR	18,667.2	18,847.8	20,256.8	20,788.8	21,442.9	23,761.9	16
Providence, RI	6,595.1	5,048.8	6,595.7	7,125.4	6,236.6	7,424.8	46
Provo, UT	2,533.4	2,216.4	1,894.8	2,065.3	1,788.1	1,783.7	107
Raleigh, NC	2,713.1	2,553.4	2,620.4	2,865.8	3,193.2	3,546.8	70
Reno, NV	2,138.9	1,943.3	2,382.1	2,517.3	2,631.7	2,598.3	86
Richmond, VA	3,307.0	3,325.9	3,525.7	3,663.7	3,535.0	3,203.2	76
Riverside, CA	9,134.8	8,970.0	10,211.6	8,782.3	9,745.7	9,737.6	37
Rochester, MN	720.5	530.2	398.0	495.3	537.6	390.1	235
Sacramento, CA	7,143.9	8,101.2	7,032.1	6,552.6	6,222.8	5,449.2	53
Salt Lake City, UT	8,361.5	10,380.5	8,653.7	7,916.9	9,748.6	13,273.9	29
San Antonio, TX	25,781.8	15,919.2	5,621.2	9,184.1	11,678.1	11,668.0	32
San Diego, CA	18,585.7	17,439.7	18,086.6	18,637.1	20,156.8	19,774.1	20
San Francisco, CA	26,863.7	25,061.1	24,506.3	29,103.8	27,417.0	28,003.8	12
San Jose, CA	21,128.8	19,827.2	21,716.8	21,464.7	22,224.2	20,909.4	19
Santa Rosa, CA	1,103.7	1,119.8	1,194.3	1,168.2	1,231.7	1,234.5	135
Savannah, GA	5,093.4	5,447.5	4,263.4	4,472.0	5,407.8	4,925.5	58
Seattle, WA	61,938.4	67,226.4	61,881.0	59,007.0	59,742.9	41,249.0	5
Sioux Falls, SD	455.3	375.0	334.3	386.8	400.0	431.5	224
Springfield, IL	94.4	111.7	88.3	107.5	91.2	99.8	338
Tallahassee, FL	174.0	191.2	223.1	241.1	270.8	219.7	291
Tampa, FL	5,817.3	5,660.4	5,702.9	6,256.0	4,966.7	6,219.7	50
Tucson, AZ	2,277.4	2,485.9	2,563.9	2,683.9	2,824.8	2,943.7	81
Tulsa, OK	3,798.5	2,699.7	2,363.0	2,564.7	3,351.7	3,399.2	72
Tuscaloosa, AL	n/a	n/a	n/a	n/a	n/a	n/a	400
Virginia Beach, VA	3,573.2	3,556.4	3,291.1	3,307.2	3,950.6	3,642.4	69
Washington, DC	13,053.6	13,900.4	13,582.4	12,736.1	13,602.7	14,563.8	25
Wichita, KS	4,011.7	3,717.6	3,054.9	3,299.2	3,817.0	3,494.7	71
Winston-Salem, NC	1,441.9	1,267.4	1,234.6	1,131.7	1,107.5	1,209.1	137

Note: Figures are in millions of dollars; (1) Metropolitan Statistical Area—see Appendix B for areas included; (2) Rank is based on 2019 data and ranges from 1 to 386
Source: U.S. Department of Commerce, International Trade Administration, Office of Trade and Economic Analysis, Industry and Analysis, Exports by Metropolitan Area, extracted March 24, 2021

Building Permits: City

City	Single-Family			Multi-Family			Total		
	2018	2019	Pct. Chg.	2018	2019	Pct. Chg.	2018	2019	Pct. Chg.
Albuquerque, NM	1,115	906	-18.7	0	188	–	1,115	1,094	-1.9
Allentown, PA	0	0	0.0	0	0	0.0	0	0	0.0
Anchorage, AK	869	838	-3.6	214	221	3.3	1,083	1,059	-2.2
Ann Arbor, MI	126	96	-23.8	0	0	0.0	126	96	-23.8
Athens, GA	345	517	49.9	261	766	193.5	606	1,283	111.7
Atlanta, GA	1,184	728	-38.5	5,312	2,555	-51.9	6,496	3,283	-49.5
Austin, TX	4,433	4,568	3.0	8,850	10,141	14.6	13,283	14,709	10.7
Baton Rouge, LA	282	354	25.5	58	0	-100.0	340	354	4.1
Boise City, ID	844	698	-17.3	296	883	198.3	1,140	1,581	38.7
Boston, MA	49	37	-24.5	3,553	2,956	-16.8	3,602	2,993	-16.9
Boulder, CO	80	41	-48.8	667	286	-57.1	747	327	-56.2
Cape Coral, FL	2,245	1,878	-16.3	356	810	127.5	2,601	2,688	3.3
Cedar Rapids, IA	147	173	17.7	325	197	-39.4	472	370	-21.6
Charleston, SC	810	828	2.2	354	360	1.7	1,164	1,188	2.1
Charlotte, NC	n/a	n/a	n/a	n/a	n/a	n/a	n/a	n/a	n/a
Chicago, IL	439	410	-6.6	6,010	7,504	24.9	6,449	7,914	22.7
Cincinnati, OH	98	135	37.8	632	992	57.0	730	1,127	54.4
Clarksville, TN	669	1,428	113.5	269	160	-40.5	938	1,588	69.3
Cleveland, OH	114	78	-31.6	34	19	-44.1	148	97	-34.5
College Station, TX	459	398	-13.3	572	219	-61.7	1,031	617	-40.2
Colorado Springs, CO	n/a	n/a	n/a	n/a	n/a	n/a	n/a	n/a	n/a
Columbia, MO	261	338	29.5	2	166	8,200.0	263	504	91.6
Columbia, SC	449	464	3.3	28	10	-64.3	477	474	-0.6
Columbus, OH	555	512	-7.7	3,742	2,258	-39.7	4,297	2,770	-35.5
Dallas, TX	2,009	2,093	4.2	6,038	6,000	-0.6	8,047	8,093	0.6
Davenport, IA	68	122	79.4	0	196	–	68	318	367.6
Denver, CO	2,428	2,257	-7.0	5,450	5,073	-6.9	7,878	7,330	-7.0
Des Moines, IA	180	391	117.2	391	279	-28.6	571	670	17.3
Durham, NC	1,894	1,945	2.7	1,336	1,884	41.0	3,230	3,829	18.5
Edison, NJ	71	55	-22.5	100	175	75.0	171	230	34.5
El Paso, TX	1,588	1,873	17.9	621	413	-33.5	2,209	2,286	3.5
Fargo, ND	313	311	-0.6	897	172	-80.8	1,210	483	-60.1
Fayetteville, NC	241	240	-0.4	0	282	–	241	522	116.6
Fort Collins, CO	398	316	-20.6	673	632	-6.1	1,071	948	-11.5
Fort Wayne, IN	n/a	n/a	n/a	n/a	n/a	n/a	n/a	n/a	n/a
Fort Worth, TX	5,477	5,063	-7.6	3,833	6,276	63.7	9,310	11,339	21.8
Grand Rapids, MI	124	153	23.4	690	183	-73.5	814	336	-58.7
Greeley, CO	348	170	-51.1	190	697	266.8	538	867	61.2
Green Bay, WI	101	63	-37.6	0	0	0.0	101	63	-37.6
Greensboro, NC	597	548	-8.2	249	385	54.6	846	933	10.3
Honolulu, HI	n/a	n/a	n/a	n/a	n/a	n/a	n/a	n/a	n/a
Houston, TX	5,417	5,120	-5.5	7,820	10,343	32.3	13,237	15,463	16.8
Huntsville, AL	1,241	1,436	15.7	71	167	135.2	1,312	1,603	22.2
Indianapolis, IN	1,090	1,153	5.8	1,196	1,229	2.8	2,286	2,382	4.2
Jacksonville, FL	3,780	4,155	9.9	3,223	2,650	-17.8	7,003	6,805	-2.8
Kansas City, MO	813	619	-23.9	1,341	879	-34.5	2,154	1,498	-30.5
Lafayette, LA	n/a	n/a	n/a	n/a	n/a	n/a	n/a	n/a	n/a
Lakeland, FL	435	606	39.3	0	953	–	435	1,559	258.4
Las Vegas, NV	1,794	1,885	5.1	179	780	335.8	1,973	2,665	35.1
Lexington, KY	733	579	-21.0	1,056	804	-23.9	1,789	1,383	-22.7
Lincoln, NE	859	863	0.5	673	864	28.4	1,532	1,727	12.7
Little Rock, AR	325	480	47.7	145	539	271.7	470	1,019	116.8
Los Angeles, CA	2,636	2,647	0.4	13,663	11,740	-14.1	16,299	14,387	-11.7
Louisville, KY	1,183	1,207	2.0	2,080	2,204	6.0	3,263	3,411	4.5

Table continued on following page.

City	Single-Family			Multi-Family			Total		
	2018	2019	Pct. Chg.	2018	2019	Pct. Chg.	2018	2019	Pct. Chg.
Madison, WI	334	426	27.5	1,109	1,232	11.1	1,443	1,658	14.9
Manchester, NH	151	106	-29.8	59	26	-55.9	210	132	-37.1
Memphis, TN	n/a	n/a	n/a	n/a	n/a	n/a	n/a	n/a	n/a
Miami, FL	80	107	33.8	4,545	4,361	-4.0	4,625	4,468	-3.4
Midland, TX	1,222	1,290	5.6	0	0	0.0	1,222	1,290	5.6
Milwaukee, WI	39	15	-61.5	717	178	-75.2	756	193	-74.5
Minneapolis, MN	162	122	-24.7	3,463	4,691	35.5	3,625	4,813	32.8
Nashville, TN	3,560	3,830	7.6	3,268	5,935	81.6	6,828	9,765	43.0
New Haven, CT	4	4	0.0	456	695	52.4	460	699	52.0
New Orleans, LA	524	558	6.5	779	748	-4.0	1,303	1,306	0.2
New York, NY	417	332	-20.4	20,493	26,215	27.9	20,910	26,547	27.0
Oklahoma City, OK	2,955	3,243	9.7	142	128	-9.9	3,097	3,371	8.8
Omaha, NE	1,237	1,179	-4.7	1,650	965	-41.5	2,887	2,144	-25.7
Orlando, FL	790	747	-5.4	2,289	1,887	-17.6	3,079	2,634	-14.5
Peoria, IL	32	33	3.1	0	0	0.0	32	33	3.1
Philadelphia, PA	683	894	30.9	2,556	3,672	43.7	3,239	4,566	41.0
Phoenix, AZ	3,732	4,175	11.9	3,530	5,723	62.1	7,262	9,898	36.3
Pittsburgh, PA	90	78	-13.3	553	582	5.2	643	660	2.6
Portland, OR	775	703	-9.3	4,873	4,391	-9.9	5,648	5,094	-9.8
Providence, RI	1	14	1,300.0	0	183	–	1	197	19,600.0
Provo, UT	171	174	1.8	286	140	-51.0	457	314	-31.3
Raleigh, NC	1,304	380	-70.9	2,907	827	-71.6	4,211	1,207	-71.3
Reno, NV	1,351	1,176	-13.0	1,883	2,144	13.9	3,234	3,320	2.7
Richmond, VA	273	353	29.3	290	887	205.9	563	1,240	120.2
Riverside, CA	171	170	-0.6	503	509	1.2	674	679	0.7
Rochester, MN	347	296	-14.7	1,068	478	-55.2	1,415	774	-45.3
Sacramento, CA	1,610	1,538	-4.5	714	1,463	104.9	2,324	3,001	29.1
Salt Lake City, UT	109	127	16.5	793	3,359	323.6	902	3,486	286.5
San Antonio, TX	3,266	3,890	19.1	2,663	5,306	99.2	5,929	9,196	55.1
San Diego, CA	774	580	-25.1	3,678	3,361	-8.6	4,452	3,941	-11.5
San Francisco, CA	28	22	-21.4	5,150	3,178	-38.3	5,178	3,200	-38.2
San Jose, CA	238	514	116.0	2,598	1,831	-29.5	2,836	2,345	-17.3
Santa Rosa, CA	1,632	939	-42.5	69	251	263.8	1,701	1,190	-30.0
Savannah, GA	399	339	-15.0	0	0	0.0	399	339	-15.0
Seattle, WA	523	507	-3.1	7,395	10,277	39.0	7,918	10,784	36.2
Sioux Falls, SD	1,083	1,013	-6.5	898	643	-28.4	1,981	1,656	-16.4
Springfield, IL	74	57	-23.0	219	112	-48.9	293	169	-42.3
Tallahassee, FL	396	407	2.8	1,128	1,275	13.0	1,524	1,682	10.4
Tampa, FL	1,109	1,159	4.5	679	3,618	432.8	1,788	4,777	167.2
Tucson, AZ	680	999	46.9	860	817	-5.0	1,540	1,816	17.9
Tulsa, OK	471	629	33.5	343	580	69.1	814	1,209	48.5
Tuscaloosa, AL	353	321	-9.1	469	844	80.0	822	1,165	41.7
Virginia Beach, VA	534	667	24.9	245	683	178.8	779	1,350	73.3
Washington, DC	112	168	50.0	4,503	5,777	28.3	4,615	5,945	28.8
Wichita, KS	532	618	16.2	326	364	11.7	858	982	14.5
Winston-Salem, NC	1,251	1,185	-5.3	84	0	-100.0	1,335	1,185	-11.2
U.S.	855,300	862,100	0.7	473,500	523,900	10.6	1,328,800	1,386,000	4.3

Note: Figures represent new, privately-owned housing units authorized (unadjusted data); All permit data are based on estimates with imputation
Source: U.S. Census Bureau, Manufacturing, Mining, and Construction Statistics, Building Permits, 2018, 2019

Building Permits: Metro Area

Metro Area	Single-Family			Multi-Family			Total		
	2018	2019	Pct. Chg.	2018	2019	Pct. Chg.	2018	2019	Pct. Chg.
Albuquerque, NM	2,086	1,872	-10.3	100	276	176.0	2,186	2,148	-1.7
Allentown, PA	1,082	1,078	-0.4	164	267	62.8	1,246	1,345	7.9
Anchorage, AK	938	878	-6.4	321	285	-11.2	1,259	1,163	-7.6
Ann Arbor, MI	652	608	-6.7	153	207	35.3	805	815	1.2
Athens, GA	729	821	12.6	340	770	126.5	1,069	1,591	48.8
Atlanta, GA	26,506	26,261	-0.9	12,935	6,575	-49.2	39,441	32,836	-16.7
Austin, TX	17,030	18,426	8.2	13,005	13,611	4.7	30,035	32,037	6.7
Baton Rouge, LA	3,509	3,612	2.9	413	10	-97.6	3,922	3,622	-7.6
Boise City, ID	6,923	7,570	9.3	1,994	3,062	53.6	8,917	10,632	19.2
Boston, MA	4,930	4,299	-12.8	9,253	10,789	16.6	14,183	15,088	6.4
Boulder, CO	899	742	-17.5	2,055	908	-55.8	2,954	1,650	-44.1
Cape Coral, FL	5,803	5,633	-2.9	3,918	3,472	-11.4	9,721	9,105	-6.3
Cedar Rapids, IA	490	509	3.9	469	305	-35.0	959	814	-15.1
Charleston, SC	4,787	4,758	-0.6	2,215	1,937	-12.6	7,002	6,695	-4.4
Charlotte, NC	16,407	16,253	-0.9	9,802	8,384	-14.5	26,209	24,637	-6.0
Chicago, IL	8,546	7,598	-11.1	9,135	10,487	14.8	17,681	18,085	2.3
Cincinnati, OH	4,282	4,488	4.8	1,794	1,535	-14.4	6,076	6,023	-0.9
Clarksville, TN	1,516	2,332	53.8	287	325	13.2	1,803	2,657	47.4
Cleveland, OH	2,733	2,584	-5.5	248	448	80.6	2,981	3,032	1.7
College Station, TX	1,023	1,091	6.6	833	389	-53.3	1,856	1,480	-20.3
Colorado Springs, CO	4,229	4,051	-4.2	1,505	1,457	-3.2	5,734	5,508	-3.9
Columbia, MO	555	633	14.1	2	166	8,200.0	557	799	43.4
Columbia, SC	4,478	4,209	-6.0	474	215	-54.6	4,952	4,424	-10.7
Columbus, OH	4,493	4,389	-2.3	4,947	3,701	-25.2	9,440	8,090	-14.3
Dallas, TX	36,832	34,939	-5.1	27,061	27,769	2.6	63,893	62,708	-1.9
Davenport, IA	490	533	8.8	69	268	288.4	559	801	43.3
Denver, CO	11,808	11,081	-6.2	9,921	8,227	-17.1	21,729	19,308	-11.1
Des Moines, IA	3,233	3,915	21.1	1,690	1,354	-19.9	4,923	5,269	7.0
Durham, NC	3,289	3,561	8.3	2,127	2,234	5.0	5,416	5,795	7.0
Edison, NJ	11,077	11,072	0.0	38,615	50,096	29.7	49,692	61,168	23.1
El Paso, TX	1,751	2,433	38.9	665	633	-4.8	2,416	3,066	26.9
Fargo, ND	1,080	939	-13.1	1,233	486	-60.6	2,313	1,425	-38.4
Fayetteville, NC	803	1,547	92.7	16	292	1,725.0	819	1,839	124.5
Fort Collins, CO	1,679	1,580	-5.9	1,265	910	-28.1	2,944	2,490	-15.4
Fort Wayne, IN	1,343	1,330	-1.0	541	626	15.7	1,884	1,956	3.8
Fort Worth, TX	36,832	34,939	-5.1	27,061	27,769	2.6	63,893	62,708	-1.9
Grand Rapids, MI	2,749	2,531	-7.9	1,105	1,624	47.0	3,854	4,155	7.8
Greeley, CO	3,194	3,335	4.4	913	1,052	15.2	4,107	4,387	6.8
Green Bay, WI	766	723	-5.6	435	407	-6.4	1,201	1,130	-5.9
Greensboro, NC	1,949	2,002	2.7	275	421	53.1	2,224	2,423	8.9
Honolulu, HI	983	912	-7.2	1,427	1,367	-4.2	2,410	2,279	-5.4
Houston, TX	40,321	39,507	-2.0	16,967	24,165	42.4	57,288	63,672	11.1
Huntsville, AL	2,870	3,399	18.4	71	167	135.2	2,941	3,566	21.3
Indianapolis, IN	7,291	7,120	-2.3	1,603	2,601	62.3	8,894	9,721	9.3
Jacksonville, FL	10,755	11,583	7.7	4,695	3,104	-33.9	15,450	14,687	-4.9
Kansas City, MO	5,608	4,811	-14.2	4,660	4,536	-2.7	10,268	9,347	-9.0
Lafayette, LA	1,657	1,632	-1.5	30	34	13.3	1,687	1,666	-1.2
Lakeland, FL	5,331	6,435	20.7	0	2,291	–	5,331	8,726	63.7
Las Vegas, NV	9,721	10,042	3.3	2,323	3,861	66.2	12,044	13,903	15.4
Lexington, KY	1,404	1,308	-6.8	1,368	938	-31.4	2,772	2,246	-19.0
Lincoln, NE	1,117	1,088	-2.6	687	1,010	47.0	1,804	2,098	16.3
Little Rock, AR	1,819	1,921	5.6	355	1,084	205.4	2,174	3,005	38.2
Los Angeles, CA	10,042	9,306	-7.3	19,482	21,248	9.1	29,524	30,554	3.5
Louisville, KY	3,104	3,122	0.6	2,409	2,644	9.8	5,513	5,766	4.6

Table continued on following page.

Metro Area	Single-Family			Multi-Family			Total		
	2018	2019	Pct. Chg.	2018	2019	Pct. Chg.	2018	2019	Pct. Chg.
Madison, WI	1,623	1,536	-5.4	2,029	1,807	-10.9	3,652	3,343	-8.5
Manchester, NH	709	691	-2.5	697	561	-19.5	1,406	1,252	-11.0
Memphis, TN	3,185	3,319	4.2	1,307	355	-72.8	4,492	3,674	-18.2
Miami, FL	7,022	7,241	3.1	12,531	13,447	7.3	19,553	20,688	5.8
Midland, TX	1,227	1,306	6.4	0	0	0.0	1,227	1,306	6.4
Milwaukee, WI	1,712	1,494	-12.7	2,057	925	-55.0	3,769	2,419	-35.8
Minneapolis, MN	8,985	9,610	7.0	9,221	12,804	38.9	18,206	22,414	23.1
Nashville, TN	13,470	14,460	7.3	5,689	8,242	44.9	19,159	22,702	18.5
New Haven, CT	406	399	-1.7	760	1,054	38.7	1,166	1,453	24.6
New Orleans, LA	3,046	3,241	6.4	818	785	-4.0	3,864	4,026	4.2
New York, NY	11,077	11,072	0.0	38,615	50,096	29.7	49,692	61,168	23.1
Oklahoma City, OK	5,430	5,924	9.1	300	633	111.0	5,730	6,557	14.4
Omaha, NE	2,791	2,633	-5.7	1,997	1,467	-26.5	4,788	4,100	-14.4
Orlando, FL	16,455	14,995	-8.9	12,427	9,475	-23.8	28,882	24,470	-15.3
Peoria, IL	228	218	-4.4	106	90	-15.1	334	308	-7.8
Philadelphia, PA	6,875	6,963	1.3	6,281	8,644	37.6	13,156	15,607	18.6
Phoenix, AZ	23,526	25,026	6.4	7,817	10,847	38.8	31,343	35,873	14.5
Pittsburgh, PA	2,977	2,830	-4.9	1,060	1,154	8.9	4,037	3,984	-1.3
Portland, OR	6,869	7,688	11.9	7,311	9,127	24.8	14,180	16,815	18.6
Providence, RI	1,553	1,592	2.5	410	456	11.2	1,963	2,048	4.3
Provo, UT	5,516	5,423	-1.7	1,325	1,524	15.0	6,841	6,947	1.5
Raleigh, NC	11,160	11,142	-0.2	4,790	2,178	-54.5	15,950	13,320	-16.5
Reno, NV	2,255	2,157	-4.3	2,195	3,106	41.5	4,450	5,263	18.3
Richmond, VA	4,498	4,481	-0.4	1,563	3,859	146.9	6,061	8,340	37.6
Riverside, CA	11,591	11,147	-3.8	3,218	3,452	7.3	14,809	14,599	-1.4
Rochester, MN	690	614	-11.0	1,126	497	-55.9	1,816	1,111	-38.8
Sacramento, CA	6,393	7,184	12.4	1,480	2,247	51.8	7,873	9,431	19.8
Salt Lake City, UT	5,391	4,760	-11.7	3,359	5,920	76.2	8,750	10,680	22.1
San Antonio, TX	8,013	9,103	13.6	3,484	6,792	94.9	11,497	15,895	38.3
San Diego, CA	3,489	3,019	-13.5	6,345	5,197	-18.1	9,834	8,216	-16.5
San Francisco, CA	4,048	4,076	0.7	13,373	9,805	-26.7	17,421	13,881	-20.3
San Jose, CA	2,466	2,603	5.6	6,278	3,627	-42.2	8,744	6,230	-28.8
Santa Rosa, CA	3,169	2,079	-34.4	110	350	218.2	3,279	2,429	-25.9
Savannah, GA	2,080	2,151	3.4	1,078	440	-59.2	3,158	2,591	-18.0
Seattle, WA	9,134	8,737	-4.3	19,052	17,862	-6.2	28,186	26,599	-5.6
Sioux Falls, SD	1,380	1,376	-0.3	1,008	743	-26.3	2,388	2,119	-11.3
Springfield, IL	193	149	-22.8	313	180	-42.5	506	329	-35.0
Tallahassee, FL	2,073	1,070	-48.4	1,128	1,275	13.0	3,201	2,345	-26.7
Tampa, FL	14,228	14,670	3.1	3,224	8,870	175.1	17,452	23,540	34.9
Tucson, AZ	3,240	3,490	7.7	1,164	823	-29.3	4,404	4,313	-2.1
Tulsa, OK	2,845	3,377	18.7	567	929	63.8	3,412	4,306	26.2
Tuscaloosa, AL	578	630	9.0	469	844	80.0	1,047	1,474	40.8
Virginia Beach, VA	4,168	4,345	4.2	1,436	1,563	8.8	5,604	5,908	5.4
Washington, DC	13,588	12,977	-4.5	12,169	13,827	13.6	25,757	26,804	4.1
Wichita, KS	1,223	1,389	13.6	735	737	0.3	1,958	2,126	8.6
Winston-Salem, NC	3,123	3,160	1.2	376	174	-53.7	3,499	3,334	-4.7
U.S.	855,300	862,100	0.7	473,500	523,900	10.6	1,328,800	1,386,000	4.3

Note: Figures cover the Metropolitan Statistical Area—see Appendix B for areas included; Figures represent new, privately-owned housing units authorized (unadjusted data); All permit data are based on estimates with imputation
Source: U.S. Census Bureau, Manufacturing, Mining, and Construction Statistics, Building Permits, 2018, 2019

Housing Vacancy Rates

Metro Area[1]	Gross Vacancy Rate[2] (%)			Year-Round Vacancy Rate[3] (%)			Rental Vacancy Rate[4] (%)			Homeowner Vacancy Rate[5] (%)		
	2018	2019	2020	2018	2019	2020	2018	2019	2020	2018	2019	2020
Albuquerque, NM	8.3	7.9	5.1	7.9	7.4	4.9	7.8	6.5	5.4	1.8	1.9	1.4
Allentown, PA	9.3	7.7	4.9	7.1	5.8	4.8	5.7	4.0	3.9	0.9	1.4	0.7
Anchorage, AK	n/a	n/a	n/a	n/a	n/a	n/a	n/a	n/a	n/a	n/a	n/a	n/a
Ann Arbor, MI	n/a	n/a	n/a	n/a	n/a	n/a	n/a	n/a	n/a	n/a	n/a	n/a
Athens, GA	n/a	n/a	n/a	n/a	n/a	n/a	n/a	n/a	n/a	n/a	n/a	n/a
Atlanta, GA	7.8	7.6	5.8	7.4	7.3	5.4	6.6	7.0	6.4	1.1	1.3	0.8
Austin, TX	9.7	10.7	7.0	8.7	10.3	6.8	7.0	8.2	6.6	1.2	1.8	2.0
Baton Rouge, LA	13.0	13.9	12.6	11.8	13.0	11.8	7.6	10.2	7.4	1.4	1.9	1.7
Boise City, ID	n/a	n/a	n/a	n/a	n/a	n/a	n/a	n/a	n/a	n/a	n/a	n/a
Boston, MA	7.5	7.1	6.8	6.5	6.2	5.6	3.8	3.6	4.7	1.0	0.8	0.4
Boulder, CO	n/a	n/a	n/a	n/a	n/a	n/a	n/a	n/a	n/a	n/a	n/a	n/a
Cape Coral, FL	41.5	40.0	35.1	16.6	17.9	15.8	5.8	8.5	15.5	3.0	2.3	1.9
Cedar Rapids, IA	n/a	n/a	n/a	n/a	n/a	n/a	n/a	n/a	n/a	n/a	n/a	n/a
Charleston, SC	16.0	18.4	18.1	14.5	16.6	16.5	17.0	16.7	27.7	3.4	2.2	2.3
Charlotte, NC	8.5	9.3	6.6	8.1	9.0	6.3	5.6	7.6	5.6	1.7	1.8	1.0
Chicago, IL	7.5	7.6	7.4	7.4	7.6	7.2	7.0	5.7	7.4	1.6	1.5	1.2
Cincinnati, OH	6.8	8.6	6.6	6.7	8.4	6.2	4.4	10.7	7.9	1.5	1.1	0.7
Clarksville, TN	n/a	n/a	n/a	n/a	n/a	n/a	n/a	n/a	n/a	n/a	n/a	n/a
Cleveland, OH	10.4	10.1	9.3	10.3	9.9	8.8	6.9	3.8	5.5	0.9	1.1	0.7
College Station, TX	n/a	n/a	n/a	n/a	n/a	n/a	n/a	n/a	n/a	n/a	n/a	n/a
Colorado Springs, CO	n/a	n/a	n/a	n/a	n/a	n/a	n/a	n/a	n/a	n/a	n/a	n/a
Columbia, MO	n/a	n/a	n/a	n/a	n/a	n/a	n/a	n/a	n/a	n/a	n/a	n/a
Columbia, SC	8.9	10.6	7.2	8.8	10.4	7.1	9.4	9.3	4.5	1.9	1.5	0.7
Columbus, OH	7.4	4.5	4.7	7.4	4.2	4.5	8.6	4.3	5.9	1.5	0.8	0.3
Dallas, TX	7.8	7.6	6.4	7.6	7.3	6.4	7.4	6.9	7.2	1.4	1.5	0.7
Davenport, IA	n/a	n/a	n/a	n/a	n/a	n/a	n/a	n/a	n/a	n/a	n/a	n/a
Denver, CO	8.0	7.5	5.8	7.4	7.0	5.1	3.8	4.7	4.8	0.9	1.0	0.5
Des Moines, IA	n/a	n/a	n/a	n/a	n/a	n/a	n/a	n/a	n/a	n/a	n/a	n/a
Durham, NC	n/a	n/a	n/a	n/a	n/a	n/a	n/a	n/a	n/a	n/a	n/a	n/a
Edison, NJ	10.3	9.2	9.1	9.1	7.8	7.8	4.5	4.3	4.5	1.6	1.4	1.3
El Paso, TX	n/a	n/a	n/a	n/a	n/a	n/a	n/a	n/a	n/a	n/a	n/a	n/a
Fargo, ND	n/a	n/a	n/a	n/a	n/a	n/a	n/a	n/a	n/a	n/a	n/a	n/a
Fayetteville, NC	n/a	n/a	n/a	n/a	n/a	n/a	n/a	n/a	n/a	n/a	n/a	n/a
Fort Collins, CO	n/a	n/a	n/a	n/a	n/a	n/a	n/a	n/a	n/a	n/a	n/a	n/a
Fort Wayne, IN	n/a	n/a	n/a	n/a	n/a	n/a	n/a	n/a	n/a	n/a	n/a	n/a
Fort Worth, TX	7.8	7.6	6.4	7.6	7.3	6.4	7.4	6.9	7.2	1.4	1.5	0.7
Grand Rapids, MI	8.9	7.4	7.1	6.8	5.1	4.7	6.8	4.5	4.6	0.3	0.5	1.1
Greeley, CO	n/a	n/a	n/a	n/a	n/a	n/a	n/a	n/a	n/a	n/a	n/a	n/a
Green Bay, WI	n/a	n/a	n/a	n/a	n/a	n/a	n/a	n/a	n/a	n/a	n/a	n/a
Greensboro, NC	11.6	9.9	8.3	11.5	9.5	8.2	11.4	8.1	7.2	1.0	0.7	0.7
Honolulu, HI	14.0	11.7	10.0	12.9	10.9	9.6	6.5	5.7	5.5	1.4	1.8	1.0
Houston, TX	8.8	9.8	6.8	8.2	9.1	6.3	8.8	11.4	9.7	2.0	1.9	1.1
Huntsville, AL	n/a	n/a	n/a	n/a	n/a	n/a	n/a	n/a	n/a	n/a	n/a	n/a
Indianapolis, IN	8.7	7.2	7.3	8.6	6.7	7.0	9.9	7.0	10.4	1.5	1.5	0.8
Jacksonville, FL	10.1	10.1	9.5	9.3	9.8	9.3	5.6	5.2	7.5	1.3	1.0	1.5
Kansas City, MO	7.8	8.9	9.1	7.7	8.7	9.1	7.9	10.0	9.4	1.2	1.4	0.7
Lafayette, LA	n/a	n/a	n/a	n/a	n/a	n/a	n/a	n/a	n/a	n/a	n/a	n/a
Lakeland, FL	n/a	n/a	n/a	n/a	n/a	n/a	n/a	n/a	n/a	n/a	n/a	n/a
Las Vegas, NV	11.4	10.2	7.8	10.4	9.5	7.1	6.8	5.5	5.0	0.9	2.0	1.1
Lexington, KY	n/a	n/a	n/a	n/a	n/a	n/a	n/a	n/a	n/a	n/a	n/a	n/a
Lincoln, NE	n/a	n/a	n/a	n/a	n/a	n/a	n/a	n/a	n/a	n/a	n/a	n/a
Little Rock, AR	10.5	9.9	9.4	10.2	9.6	9.1	10.9	11.4	9.1	1.8	1.7	1.3
Los Angeles, CA	6.6	6.3	5.5	6.2	5.8	4.8	4.0	4.0	3.6	1.2	1.1	0.6
Louisville, KY	7.6	7.9	6.9	7.4	7.8	6.9	7.7	10.6	6.4	1.4	0.7	1.4

Table continued on following page.

Metro Area[1]	Gross Vacancy Rate[2] (%)			Year-Round Vacancy Rate[3] (%)			Rental Vacancy Rate[4] (%)			Homeowner Vacancy Rate[5] (%)		
	2018	2019	2020	2018	2019	2020	2018	2019	2020	2018	2019	2020
Madison, WI	n/a	n/a	n/a	n/a	n/a	n/a	n/a	n/a	n/a	n/a	n/a	n/a
Manchester, NH	n/a	n/a	n/a	n/a	n/a	n/a	n/a	n/a	n/a	n/a	n/a	n/a
Memphis, TN	12.6	9.9	7.3	12.5	9.9	7.0	11.7	10.6	6.6	1.6	1.4	1.0
Miami, FL	14.9	14.1	12.6	7.9	7.4	6.8	7.4	7.0	5.4	1.9	1.8	1.4
Midland, TX	n/a	n/a	n/a	n/a	n/a	n/a	n/a	n/a	n/a	n/a	n/a	n/a
Milwaukee, WI	8.1	8.0	6.6	7.8	7.8	6.3	5.9	6.6	4.6	1.4	0.6	0.6
Minneapolis, MN	3.9	4.4	4.7	3.3	3.8	3.7	4.1	4.1	4.0	0.4	0.5	0.5
Nashville, TN	5.9	7.8	6.5	5.8	7.5	6.1	7.5	8.6	7.3	0.8	1.2	0.7
New Haven, CT	10.9	11.9	9.4	10.0	11.1	8.4	5.6	8.3	7.8	1.4	1.5	0.2
New Orleans, LA	11.9	12.9	10.7	11.8	12.8	9.8	9.7	9.4	6.1	1.7	1.8	1.3
New York, NY	10.3	9.2	9.1	9.1	7.8	7.8	4.5	4.3	4.5	1.6	1.4	1.3
Oklahoma City, OK	11.5	10.8	7.5	11.2	10.4	7.3	11.8	8.6	6.4	2.7	2.7	0.9
Omaha, NE	7.1	5.6	5.6	6.1	4.8	5.3	7.1	6.3	6.5	0.7	0.6	0.5
Orlando, FL	19.4	16.0	12.9	16.2	12.7	9.8	5.8	8.3	8.6	2.6	2.5	1.2
Peoria, IL	n/a	n/a	n/a	n/a	n/a	n/a	n/a	n/a	n/a	n/a	n/a	n/a
Philadelphia, PA	9.0	8.3	6.0	8.9	8.1	5.8	6.4	7.1	5.4	1.2	1.3	0.7
Phoenix, AZ	12.6	10.3	8.9	7.8	6.2	5.3	6.2	5.0	4.9	1.4	1.0	0.7
Pittsburgh, PA	10.2	10.6	11.5	9.9	10.3	11.3	6.3	7.3	9.3	2.2	1.2	1.0
Portland, OR	6.8	6.6	5.5	6.0	5.6	4.9	3.8	4.4	4.3	1.4	0.9	0.8
Providence, RI	10.3	9.8	8.7	8.5	8.2	6.6	5.0	4.2	3.5	1.1	0.9	0.8
Provo, UT	n/a	n/a	n/a	n/a	n/a	n/a	n/a	n/a	n/a	n/a	n/a	n/a
Raleigh, NC	6.7	6.6	4.6	6.6	6.5	4.5	6.4	7.0	2.3	0.9	0.8	0.4
Reno, NV	n/a	n/a	n/a	n/a	n/a	n/a	n/a	n/a	n/a	n/a	n/a	n/a
Richmond, VA	8.0	8.5	6.0	8.0	8.5	6.0	5.4	9.5	2.7	2.1	1.3	0.9
Riverside, CA	15.1	14.9	11.8	9.1	9.6	7.5	5.1	4.5	4.4	1.6	1.7	0.8
Rochester, MN	n/a	n/a	n/a	n/a	n/a	n/a	n/a	n/a	n/a	n/a	n/a	n/a
Sacramento, CA	8.6	7.8	6.1	7.9	7.1	5.8	5.1	4.2	4.2	1.5	0.8	1.0
Salt Lake City, UT	5.0	4.8	5.7	4.7	4.8	5.6	6.1	5.0	6.2	0.5	0.8	0.3
San Antonio, TX	6.7	9.0	7.4	5.8	8.2	6.7	7.4	10.1	7.2	0.6	2.0	1.0
San Diego, CA	7.6	7.5	6.0	7.4	7.3	5.6	4.5	5.8	3.9	0.7	0.8	0.8
San Francisco, CA	7.5	7.1	6.4	7.4	6.9	6.2	5.4	3.8	5.3	0.9	0.9	0.5
San Jose, CA	5.8	5.6	4.7	5.8	5.6	4.7	4.6	3.7	4.4	0.5	0.5	n/a
Santa Rosa, CA	n/a	n/a	n/a	n/a	n/a	n/a	n/a	n/a	n/a	n/a	n/a	n/a
Savannah, GA	n/a	n/a	n/a	n/a	n/a	n/a	n/a	n/a	n/a	n/a	n/a	n/a
Seattle, WA	5.9	5.5	4.7	5.4	5.2	4.5	4.8	4.4	3.6	0.8	1.0	0.6
Sioux Falls, SD	n/a	n/a	n/a	n/a	n/a	n/a	n/a	n/a	n/a	n/a	n/a	n/a
Springfield, IL	n/a	n/a	n/a	n/a	n/a	n/a	n/a	n/a	n/a	n/a	n/a	n/a
Tallahassee, FL	n/a	n/a	n/a	n/a	n/a	n/a	n/a	n/a	n/a	n/a	n/a	n/a
Tampa, FL	16.1	16.2	13.0	11.9	12.7	10.1	9.9	10.7	8.9	2.1	1.6	1.5
Tucson, AZ	12.5	14.8	12.1	8.1	9.2	7.7	4.4	7.3	8.6	1.8	1.5	0.5
Tulsa, OK	11.7	8.4	9.4	11.6	8.0	8.8	10.1	8.5	8.6	2.6	1.6	0.8
Tuscaloosa, AL	n/a	n/a	n/a	n/a	n/a	n/a	n/a	n/a	n/a	n/a	n/a	n/a
Virginia Beach, VA	8.9	10.4	7.9	7.6	9.3	7.0	7.1	7.1	5.5	1.2	2.2	0.6
Washington, DC	7.0	7.1	6.5	6.7	6.7	6.2	6.2	5.6	5.5	1.1	1.1	0.7
Wichita, KS	n/a	n/a	n/a	n/a	n/a	n/a	n/a	n/a	n/a	n/a	n/a	n/a
Winston-Salem, NC	n/a	n/a	n/a	n/a	n/a	n/a	n/a	n/a	n/a	n/a	n/a	n/a
U.S.	12.3	12.0	10.6	9.7	9.5	8.2	6.9	6.7	6.3	1.5	1.4	1.0

Note: (1) Metropolitan Statistical Area—see Appendix B for areas included; (2) The percentage of the total housing inventory that is vacant; (3) The percentage of the housing inventory (excluding seasonal units) that is year-round vacant; (4) The percentage of rental inventory that is vacant for rent; (5) The percentage of homeowner inventory that is vacant for sale; n/a not available
Source: U.S. Census Bureau, Housing Vacancies and Homeownership Annual Statistics: 2018, 2019, 2020

Bankruptcy Filings

City	Area Covered	Business Filings			Nonbusiness Filings		
		2019	2020	% Chg.	2019	2020	% Chg.
Albuquerque, NM	Bernalillo County	30	33	10.0	1,071	872	-18.6
Allentown, PA	Lehigh County	16	10	-37.5	599	433	-27.7
Anchorage, AK	Anchorage Borough	17	20	17.6	176	137	-22.2
Ann Arbor, MI	Washtenaw County	10	13	30.0	654	454	-30.6
Athens, GA	Clarke County	0	5	n/a	338	228	-32.5
Atlanta, GA	Fulton County	173	152	-12.1	4,013	2,591	-35.4
Austin, TX	Travis County	118	175	48.3	737	529	-28.2
Baton Rouge, LA	East Baton Rouge Parish	37	49	32.4	771	435	-43.6
Boise City, ID	Ada County	26	19	-26.9	878	589	-32.9
Boston, MA	Suffolk County	47	37	-21.3	530	279	-47.4
Boulder, CO	Boulder County	30	42	40.0	372	286	-23.1
Cape Coral, FL	Lee County	57	79	38.6	1,254	1,112	-11.3
Cedar Rapids, IA	Linn County	11	9	-18.2	365	285	-21.9
Charleston, SC	Charleston County	19	21	10.5	356	261	-26.7
Charlotte, NC	Mecklenburg County	64	45	-29.7	1,020	639	-37.4
Chicago, IL	Cook County	413	335	-18.9	27,789	16,384	-41.0
Cincinnati, OH	Hamilton County	48	25	-47.9	2,519	1,845	-26.8
Clarksville, TN	Montgomery County	11	6	-45.5	829	579	-30.2
Cleveland, OH	Cuyahoga County	69	96	39.1	6,013	4,189	-30.3
College Station, TX	Brazos County	7	6	-14.3	105	87	-17.1
Colorado Springs, CO	El Paso County	39	30	-23.1	1,525	1,154	-24.3
Columbia, MO	Boone County	6	8	33.3	375	263	-29.9
Columbia, SC	Richland County	11	12	9.1	837	520	-37.9
Columbus, OH	Franklin County	72	86	19.4	4,342	2,960	-31.8
Dallas, TX	Dallas County	355	568	60.0	3,572	2,452	-31.4
Davenport, IA	Scott County	10	7	-30.0	329	246	-25.2
Denver, CO	Denver County	68	91	33.8	1,338	1,029	-23.1
Des Moines, IA	Polk County	28	12	-57.1	962	782	-18.7
Durham, NC	Durham County	16	18	12.5	395	223	-43.5
Edison, NJ	Middlesex County	46	31	-32.6	1,718	1,097	-36.1
El Paso, TX	El Paso County	63	42	-33.3	2,079	1,290	-38.0
Fargo, ND	Cass County	4	5	25.0	198	183	-7.6
Fayetteville, NC	Cumberland County	8	8	0.0	795	506	-36.4
Fort Collins, CO	Larimer County	29	28	-3.4	558	404	-27.6
Fort Wayne, IN	Allen County	15	15	0.0	1,294	1,057	-18.3
Fort Worth, TX	Tarrant County	242	271	12.0	4,040	2,937	-27.3
Grand Rapids, MI	Kent County	35	47	34.3	935	613	-34.4
Greeley, CO	Weld County	20	21	5.0	691	509	-26.3
Green Bay, WI	Brown County	25	9	-64.0	599	418	-30.2
Greensboro, NC	Guilford County	25	21	-16.0	758	471	-37.9
Honolulu, HI	Honolulu County	35	46	31.4	1,225	1,106	-9.7
Houston, TX	Harris County	411	608	47.9	4,527	2,967	-34.5
Huntsville, AL	Madison County	20	42	110.0	1,463	1,024	-30.0
Indianapolis, IN	Marion County	100	39	-61.0	4,465	3,319	-25.7
Jacksonville, FL	Duval County	75	57	-24.0	2,349	1,604	-31.7
Kansas City, MO	Jackson County	36	26	-27.8	2,080	1,394	-33.0
Lafayette, LA	Lafayette Parish	44	22	-50.0	560	306	-45.4
Lakeland, FL	Polk County	31	53	71.0	1,466	1,168	-20.3
Las Vegas, NV	Clark County	228	204	-10.5	8,184	6,529	-20.2
Lexington, KY	Fayette County	56	54	-3.6	749	520	-30.6
Lincoln, NE	Lancaster County	16	11	-31.3	653	485	-25.7
Little Rock, AR	Pulaski County	233	30	-87.1	2,318	1,519	-34.5
Los Angeles, CA	Los Angeles County	882	857	-2.8	18,304	13,323	-27.2
Louisville, KY	Jefferson County	50	39	-22.0	2,893	2,174	-24.9
Madison, WI	Dane County	34	28	-17.6	773	527	-31.8

Table continued on following page.

City	Area Covered	Business Filings			Nonbusiness Filings		
		2019	2020	% Chg.	2019	2020	% Chg.
Manchester, NH	Hillsborough County	25	27	8.0	519	339	-34.7
Memphis, TN	Shelby County	72	41	-43.1	9,622	5,523	-42.6
Miami, FL	Miami-Dade County	215	322	49.8	8,490	7,108	-16.3
Midland, TX	Midland County	32	11	-65.6	72	48	-33.3
Milwaukee, WI	Milwaukee County	43	48	11.6	6,315	4,019	-36.4
Minneapolis, MN	Hennepin County	62	92	48.4	2,032	1,552	-23.6
Nashville, TN	Davidson County	53	60	13.2	2,051	1,330	-35.2
New Haven, CT	New Haven County	47	33	-29.8	1,884	1,258	-33.2
New Orleans, LA	Orleans Parish	36	21	-41.7	683	391	-42.8
New York, NY	Bronx County	44	24	-45.5	2,486	1,498	-39.7
New York, NY	Kings County	327	182	-44.3	2,743	1,710	-37.7
New York, NY	New York County	244	480	96.7	1,210	854	-29.4
New York, NY	Queens County	206	127	-38.3	3,708	1,990	-46.3
New York, NY	Richmond County	22	19	-13.6	835	459	-45.0
Oklahoma City, OK	Oklahoma County	89	139	56.2	2,147	1,679	-21.8
Omaha, NE	Douglas County	39	16	-59.0	1,283	1,064	-17.1
Orlando, FL	Orange County	154	167	8.4	2,956	2,477	-16.2
Peoria, IL	Peoria County	16	6	-62.5	548	391	-28.6
Philadelphia, PA	Philadelphia County	88	116	31.8	2,222	1,162	-47.7
Phoenix, AZ	Maricopa County	344	261	-24.1	11,095	8,954	-19.3
Pittsburgh, PA	Allegheny County	140	116	-17.1	2,280	1,700	-25.4
Portland, OR	Multnomah County	62	59	-4.8	1,394	1,147	-17.7
Providence, RI	Providence County	38	29	-23.7	1,246	887	-28.8
Provo, UT	Utah County	37	31	-16.2	1,408	1,151	-18.3
Raleigh, NC	Wake County	91	75	-17.6	1,314	882	-32.9
Reno, NV	Washoe County	34	44	29.4	960	765	-20.3
Richmond, VA	Richmond city	18	21	16.7	897	695	-22.5
Riverside, CA	Riverside County	165	145	-12.1	6,195	4,455	-28.1
Rochester, MN	Olmsted County	9	4	-55.6	151	138	-8.6
Sacramento, CA	Sacramento County	95	124	30.5	3,208	2,300	-28.3
Salt Lake City, UT	Salt Lake County	56	60	7.1	4,109	3,232	-21.3
San Antonio, TX	Bexar County	191	128	-33.0	2,173	1,445	-33.5
San Diego, CA	San Diego County	308	269	-12.7	7,366	5,848	-20.6
San Francisco, CA	San Francisco County	58	67	15.5	564	384	-31.9
San Jose, CA	Santa Clara County	94	86	-8.5	1,446	1,018	-29.6
Santa Rosa, CA	Sonoma County	32	29	-9.4	531	388	-26.9
Savannah, GA	Chatham County	18	13	-27.8	1,220	729	-40.2
Seattle, WA	King County	115	96	-16.5	2,174	1,516	-30.3
Sioux Falls, SD	Minnehaha County	18	11	-38.9	349	268	-23.2
Springfield, IL	Sangamon County	8	8	0.0	436	311	-28.7
Tallahassee, FL	Leon County	35	17	-51.4	446	288	-35.4
Tampa, FL	Hillsborough County	155	110	-29.0	3,356	2,538	-24.4
Tucson, AZ	Pima County	50	32	-36.0	2,438	1,727	-29.2
Tulsa, OK	Tulsa County	44	45	2.3	1,555	1,163	-25.2
Tuscaloosa, AL	Tuscaloosa County	9	10	11.1	1,246	799	-35.9
Virginia Beach, VA	Virginia Beach city	18	14	-22.2	1,606	1,206	-24.9
Washington, DC	District of Columbia	50	50	0.0	789	449	-43.1
Wichita, KS	Sedgwick County	30	15	-50.0	1,381	941	-31.9
Winston-Salem, NC	Forsyth County	17	15	-11.8	537	363	-32.4
U.S.	U.S.	22,780	21,655	-4.9	752,160	522,808	-30.5

Note: Business filings include Chapter 7, Chapter 9, Chapter 11, Chapter 12, Chapter 13, Chapter 15, and Section 304; Nonbusiness filings include Chapter 7, Chapter 11, and Chapter 13
Source: Administrative Office of the U.S. Courts, Business and Nonbusiness Bankruptcy, County Cases Commenced by Chapter of the Bankruptcy Code, During the 12-Month Period Ending December 31, 2019 and Business and Nonbusiness Bankruptcy, County Cases Commenced by Chapter of the Bankruptcy Code, During the 12-Month Period Ending December 31, 2020

Income: City

City	Per Capita ($)	Median Household ($)	Average Household ($)
Albuquerque, NM	30,403	52,911	72,265
Allentown, PA	20,792	41,167	56,842
Anchorage, AK	41,415	84,928	109,988
Ann Arbor, MI	42,674	65,745	96,906
Athens, GA	23,726	38,311	59,118
Atlanta, GA	47,424	59,948	106,300
Austin, TX	43,043	71,576	102,876
Baton Rouge, LA	28,491	44,470	70,902
Boise City, ID	34,636	60,035	82,424
Boston, MA	44,690	71,115	107,608
Boulder, CO	44,942	69,520	109,410
Cape Coral, FL	29,970	61,599	76,925
Cedar Rapids, IA	32,290	58,511	75,289
Charleston, SC	42,872	68,438	98,288
Charlotte, NC	38,000	62,817	94,516
Chicago, IL	37,103	58,247	90,713
Cincinnati, OH	30,531	40,640	65,213
Clarksville, TN	25,239	53,604	65,458
Cleveland, OH	21,223	30,907	46,137
College Station, TX	27,541	45,820	73,853
Colorado Springs, CO	34,076	64,712	84,708
Columbia, MO	30,244	51,276	74,727
Columbia, SC	30,461	47,286	76,118
Columbus, OH	29,322	53,745	69,315
Dallas, TX	34,479	52,580	86,393
Davenport, IA	28,645	51,029	68,559
Denver, CO	43,770	68,592	99,151
Des Moines, IA	28,554	53,525	69,074
Durham, NC	34,329	58,905	82,573
Edison, NJ	44,667	103,076	127,171
El Paso, TX	22,734	47,568	64,025
Fargo, ND	35,205	55,551	78,237
Fayetteville, NC	24,823	45,024	58,752
Fort Collins, CO	34,482	65,866	87,406
Fort Wayne, IN	26,970	49,411	65,377
Fort Worth, TX	29,531	62,187	82,977
Grand Rapids, MI	26,120	50,103	65,615
Greeley, CO	26,222	57,586	72,302
Green Bay, WI	26,618	49,251	64,595
Greensboro, NC	29,628	48,964	71,453
Honolulu, HI	37,834	71,465	97,456
Houston, TX	32,521	52,338	84,179
Huntsville, AL	35,634	55,305	80,877
Indianapolis, IN	28,363	47,873	68,367
Jacksonville, FL	30,064	54,701	74,873
Kansas City, MO	32,348	54,194	75,137
Lafayette, LA	32,998	51,264	78,055
Lakeland, FL	28,042	47,511	67,899
Las Vegas, NV	30,761	56,354	79,657
Lexington, KY	34,442	57,291	83,111
Lincoln, NE	31,301	57,746	76,763
Little Rock, AR	35,966	51,485	83,730
Los Angeles, CA	35,261	62,142	96,416
Louisville, KY	30,943	53,436	74,580
Madison, WI	38,285	65,332	87,055
Manchester, NH	31,951	60,711	75,665

Table continued on following page.

City	Per Capita ($)	Median Household ($)	Average Household ($)
Memphis, TN	25,605	41,228	62,588
Miami, FL	28,804	39,049	68,105
Midland, TX	40,252	79,329	112,701
Milwaukee, WI	23,462	41,838	57,332
Minneapolis, MN	38,808	62,583	89,282
Nashville, TN	35,243	59,828	83,348
New Haven, CT	26,429	42,222	65,362
New Orleans, LA	31,385	41,604	71,938
New York, NY	39,828	63,998	102,946
Oklahoma City, OK	30,567	55,557	77,896
Omaha, NE	33,401	60,092	82,945
Orlando, FL	32,085	51,757	75,669
Peoria, IL	31,497	51,771	74,900
Philadelphia, PA	27,924	45,927	68,379
Phoenix, AZ	29,343	57,459	80,631
Pittsburgh, PA	34,083	48,711	72,981
Portland, OR	41,310	71,005	95,998
Providence, RI	26,560	45,610	71,136
Provo, UT	20,792	48,888	69,265
Raleigh, NC	38,494	67,266	94,359
Reno, NV	34,475	58,790	81,700
Richmond, VA	33,549	47,250	76,182
Riverside, CA	26,028	69,045	85,486
Rochester, MN	39,518	73,106	96,015
Sacramento, CA	31,956	62,335	83,189
Salt Lake City, UT	36,779	60,676	88,127
San Antonio, TX	25,894	52,455	70,778
San Diego, CA	41,112	79,673	108,864
San Francisco, CA	68,883	112,449	160,396
San Jose, CA	46,599	109,593	142,635
Santa Rosa, CA	36,935	75,630	96,786
Savannah, GA	25,664	43,307	63,984
Seattle, WA	59,835	92,263	128,184
Sioux Falls, SD	33,065	59,912	79,847
Springfield, IL	34,607	54,648	77,473
Tallahassee, FL	27,677	45,734	66,889
Tampa, FL	36,169	53,833	87,818
Tucson, AZ	23,655	43,425	58,057
Tulsa, OK	30,970	47,650	73,816
Tuscaloosa, AL	26,437	45,268	68,837
Virginia Beach, VA	37,776	76,610	96,936
Washington, DC	56,147	86,420	127,890
Wichita, KS	28,806	52,620	71,335
Winston-Salem, NC	28,821	45,750	71,423
U.S.	34,103	62,843	88,607

Source: U.S. Census Bureau, 2015-2019 American Community Survey 5-Year Estimates

Income: Metro Area

Metro Area	Per Capita ($)	Median Household ($)	Average Household ($)
Albuquerque, NM	29,747	54,072	73,512
Allentown, PA	34,637	67,652	88,415
Anchorage, AK	38,725	83,048	105,968
Ann Arbor, MI	41,399	72,586	101,787
Athens, GA	27,653	47,214	70,940
Atlanta, GA	35,296	68,316	94,723
Austin, TX	39,827	76,844	104,847
Baton Rouge, LA	31,082	58,912	81,614
Boise City, ID	30,508	60,568	80,438
Boston, MA	47,604	90,333	122,399
Boulder, CO	46,826	83,019	115,966
Cape Coral, FL	33,543	57,832	82,544
Cedar Rapids, IA	34,039	64,687	82,498
Charleston, SC	35,011	63,649	88,023
Charlotte, NC	34,558	63,217	89,212
Chicago, IL	38,157	71,770	100,233
Cincinnati, OH	34,575	63,987	86,633
Clarksville, TN	25,931	53,027	67,368
Cleveland, OH	33,785	56,008	79,168
College Station, TX	27,698	50,240	73,129
Colorado Springs, CO	33,795	68,687	88,185
Columbia, MO	29,534	54,808	74,042
Columbia, SC	29,894	55,971	75,154
Columbus, OH	34,441	65,150	87,472
Dallas, TX	35,278	70,281	97,589
Davenport, IA	31,571	58,531	76,075
Denver, CO	41,988	79,664	106,322
Des Moines, IA	36,310	70,126	90,791
Durham, NC	36,322	62,289	90,054
Edison, NJ	43,409	78,773	116,604
El Paso, TX	21,644	46,795	62,663
Fargo, ND	35,812	64,666	85,794
Fayetteville, NC	24,228	48,459	61,989
Fort Collins, CO	37,363	71,881	93,301
Fort Wayne, IN	29,383	55,341	73,578
Fort Worth, TX	35,278	70,281	97,589
Grand Rapids, MI	31,388	63,302	83,235
Greeley, CO	31,793	74,150	89,427
Green Bay, WI	32,520	62,405	79,316
Greensboro, NC	28,787	50,891	71,256
Honolulu, HI	36,816	85,857	109,304
Houston, TX	34,400	67,516	97,410
Huntsville, AL	34,918	64,483	86,328
Indianapolis, IN	33,699	61,552	85,193
Jacksonville, FL	33,304	61,723	84,690
Kansas City, MO	35,761	66,632	89,308
Lafayette, LA	27,955	51,955	72,041
Lakeland, FL	24,864	50,584	66,810
Las Vegas, NV	30,704	59,340	80,762
Lexington, KY	33,153	58,685	82,094
Lincoln, NE	32,360	61,031	80,274
Little Rock, AR	30,599	54,746	76,145
Los Angeles, CA	35,916	72,998	104,698
Louisville, KY	32,630	59,158	80,682
Madison, WI	39,484	72,374	93,923
Manchester, NH	40,955	81,460	103,090

Table continued on following page.

Metro Area	Per Capita ($)	Median Household ($)	Average Household ($)
Memphis, TN	29,453	53,209	76,187
Miami, FL	32,522	56,775	86,518
Midland, TX	38,966	79,140	109,861
Milwaukee, WI	35,491	62,389	86,290
Minneapolis, MN	41,204	80,421	104,946
Nashville, TN	35,479	66,347	91,202
New Haven, CT	38,009	69,905	94,740
New Orleans, LA	31,072	53,084	76,818
New York, NY	43,409	78,773	116,604
Oklahoma City, OK	31,301	59,084	80,805
Omaha, NE	34,825	67,885	88,578
Orlando, FL	29,875	58,368	80,864
Peoria, IL	32,575	59,397	79,057
Philadelphia, PA	39,091	72,343	100,889
Phoenix, AZ	32,522	63,883	87,543
Pittsburgh, PA	36,208	60,535	82,754
Portland, OR	38,544	74,792	97,930
Providence, RI	35,991	67,818	89,281
Provo, UT	26,153	74,387	93,213
Raleigh, NC	38,370	75,851	100,551
Reno, NV	36,087	64,801	89,057
Richmond, VA	36,413	68,529	92,171
Riverside, CA	27,003	65,121	85,373
Rochester, MN	38,754	73,697	95,925
Sacramento, CA	35,563	72,280	96,023
Salt Lake City, UT	32,829	74,842	96,196
San Antonio, TX	29,071	60,327	81,852
San Diego, CA	38,073	78,980	106,600
San Francisco, CA	55,252	106,025	147,703
San Jose, CA	55,547	122,478	163,355
Santa Rosa, CA	42,178	81,018	108,169
Savannah, GA	32,088	59,459	82,125
Seattle, WA	45,750	86,856	115,653
Sioux Falls, SD	33,453	65,621	83,463
Springfield, IL	35,603	62,533	82,720
Tallahassee, FL	28,766	51,874	72,487
Tampa, FL	32,276	55,285	78,248
Tucson, AZ	29,707	53,379	73,554
Tulsa, OK	30,633	55,739	77,341
Tuscaloosa, AL	25,759	50,408	67,811
Virginia Beach, VA	33,907	66,759	86,062
Washington, DC	49,881	103,751	134,513
Wichita, KS	29,414	57,379	74,900
Winston-Salem, NC	28,986	50,774	71,206
U.S.	34,103	62,843	88,607

Note: Figures cover the Metropolitan Statistical Area (MSA)—see Appendix B for areas included
Source: U.S. Census Bureau, 2015-2019 American Community Survey 5-Year Estimates

Household Income Distribution: City

City	Percent of Households Earning							
	Under $15,000	$15,000 -$24,999	$25,000 -$34,999	$35,000 -$49,999	$50,000 -$74,999	$75,000 -$99,999	$100,000 -$149,999	$150,000 and up
Albuquerque, NM	13.1	10.8	10.4	13.1	17.7	12.0	13.3	9.4
Allentown, PA	15.9	13.8	13.0	15.2	19.3	10.2	8.0	4.5
Anchorage, AK	5.3	5.1	6.3	9.9	17.4	13.8	20.5	21.6
Ann Arbor, MI	14.5	7.3	7.6	9.3	15.8	11.4	14.5	19.7
Athens, GA	21.0	14.6	11.3	13.3	14.1	8.7	9.9	7.2
Atlanta, GA	15.4	9.6	8.0	10.6	14.8	10.3	12.8	18.5
Austin, TX	8.6	6.5	7.9	11.6	17.5	12.3	16.6	19.0
Baton Rouge, LA	18.2	13.1	11.0	12.0	15.5	9.1	11.4	9.7
Boise City, ID	10.2	9.7	9.3	13.2	18.2	12.3	14.8	12.3
Boston, MA	16.1	8.1	6.3	8.4	13.0	10.3	15.7	22.2
Boulder, CO	13.6	7.5	7.3	10.0	14.3	10.1	13.9	23.4
Cape Coral, FL	8.7	7.8	9.1	13.7	20.5	15.8	15.3	9.1
Cedar Rapids, IA	9.0	8.8	10.0	13.9	20.9	13.4	15.1	8.9
Charleston, SC	11.2	7.7	7.0	10.7	17.0	12.8	17.4	16.1
Charlotte, NC	8.6	7.9	9.7	13.3	17.9	12.5	14.6	15.5
Chicago, IL	14.0	10.3	8.9	11.0	15.1	11.2	13.8	15.7
Cincinnati, OH	21.1	12.6	11.2	12.3	15.6	9.1	9.4	8.7
Clarksville, TN	10.4	8.7	11.3	16.2	20.8	14.2	12.7	5.6
Cleveland, OH	27.1	15.1	12.9	13.7	14.2	7.9	5.7	3.4
College Station, TX	21.3	11.1	9.2	11.2	12.4	10.9	12.5	11.4
Colorado Springs, CO	8.8	8.3	8.5	12.5	19.0	13.8	16.2	12.8
Columbia, MO	14.8	10.6	9.8	13.8	15.2	11.2	13.6	11.0
Columbia, SC	17.9	11.5	10.8	11.7	15.6	10.9	10.4	11.2
Columbus, OH	12.1	9.7	10.2	14.4	19.5	13.3	13.4	7.3
Dallas, TX	11.8	10.4	10.7	14.7	17.9	10.6	10.8	13.1
Davenport, IA	12.5	11.4	10.6	14.6	19.1	12.3	12.1	7.4
Denver, CO	10.0	7.3	7.9	11.3	17.3	12.5	15.7	18.1
Des Moines, IA	12.0	10.6	10.2	14.2	19.9	13.7	12.4	7.1
Durham, NC	10.3	8.4	10.0	13.5	17.4	12.7	14.5	13.2
Edison, NJ	4.9	4.3	4.1	8.9	12.6	13.7	21.3	30.1
El Paso, TX	14.3	12.2	11.1	14.3	19.1	10.8	11.5	6.7
Fargo, ND	11.1	10.1	9.7	13.8	18.2	14.0	12.6	10.4
Fayetteville, NC	14.5	12.0	12.4	16.4	19.2	11.1	9.3	5.2
Fort Collins, CO	9.7	8.7	8.0	12.2	17.1	12.9	15.8	15.5
Fort Wayne, IN	11.5	11.3	11.9	15.8	19.4	12.6	10.8	6.6
Fort Worth, TX	10.2	8.3	9.5	12.0	18.8	13.4	15.5	12.3
Grand Rapids, MI	13.0	11.8	10.0	15.2	19.4	12.7	11.7	6.4
Greeley, CO	11.9	9.8	8.3	13.5	18.9	13.7	15.7	8.1
Green Bay, WI	11.9	10.9	11.8	16.2	19.6	12.6	11.4	5.5
Greensboro, NC	13.5	10.9	11.5	15.1	18.0	11.2	11.3	8.4
Honolulu, HI	10.1	6.9	6.8	11.8	16.8	12.8	17.0	17.6
Houston, TX	12.6	11.1	10.8	13.5	16.7	10.6	11.3	13.5
Huntsville, AL	13.7	10.7	10.0	11.8	15.2	10.9	13.9	13.8
Indianapolis, IN	13.5	11.1	11.8	15.3	17.9	11.3	11.0	8.0
Jacksonville, FL	11.3	9.4	10.1	14.6	19.4	13.2	12.9	9.2
Kansas City, MO	12.1	10.1	10.4	14.0	17.6	12.2	13.5	10.1
Lafayette, LA	15.8	11.1	10.1	12.0	17.1	10.2	11.1	12.7
Lakeland, FL	12.5	11.9	12.5	15.3	19.2	11.7	9.9	7.1
Las Vegas, NV	11.8	9.5	9.7	13.8	17.5	13.0	14.0	10.7
Lexington, KY	11.5	9.6	9.9	13.0	17.6	12.2	14.2	12.1
Lincoln, NE	9.6	9.2	10.5	13.9	19.3	13.0	14.7	9.9
Little Rock, AR	12.7	11.0	10.4	14.7	16.5	10.4	11.2	13.0
Los Angeles, CA	12.4	9.3	8.7	11.5	15.4	11.4	14.4	16.9
Louisville, KY	12.4	10.3	10.2	13.9	17.8	12.5	12.7	10.1

Table continued on following page.

City	Percent of Households Earning							
	Under $15,000	$15,000 -$24,999	$25,000 -$34,999	$35,000 -$49,999	$50,000 -$74,999	$75,000 -$99,999	$100,000 -$149,999	$150,000 and up
Madison, WI	10.3	7.6	8.8	12.1	17.7	13.3	16.4	13.6
Manchester, NH	10.1	8.6	9.9	12.5	19.8	13.3	16.3	9.3
Memphis, TN	18.3	13.5	11.8	14.6	16.5	9.4	8.8	7.0
Miami, FL	20.8	14.1	11.6	12.3	14.5	8.8	8.6	9.4
Midland, TX	6.7	6.7	6.9	9.8	17.3	13.7	18.0	20.8
Milwaukee, WI	17.8	13.1	11.7	15.1	17.2	10.6	9.6	4.8
Minneapolis, MN	13.0	8.7	8.2	11.6	16.0	12.3	14.6	15.5
Nashville, TN	9.8	8.5	9.3	14.1	18.9	13.6	14.3	11.8
New Haven, CT	20.2	11.9	11.1	12.5	15.8	9.6	9.7	9.4
New Orleans, LA	22.1	12.2	10.3	11.5	14.2	8.8	9.9	10.9
New York, NY	14.3	9.0	7.9	10.2	14.3	11.1	14.3	18.9
Oklahoma City, OK	11.3	9.5	10.0	14.0	18.6	12.6	13.3	10.7
Omaha, NE	10.5	8.8	8.8	13.5	18.5	13.4	14.4	12.1
Orlando, FL	12.5	10.4	11.1	14.2	19.8	10.9	10.8	10.3
Peoria, IL	16.8	11.0	8.8	12.0	17.3	11.6	11.8	10.7
Philadelphia, PA	19.1	11.2	10.2	12.7	15.8	10.5	11.0	9.4
Phoenix, AZ	10.4	9.3	9.5	14.3	18.5	12.6	13.6	11.9
Pittsburgh, PA	17.5	11.6	10.0	11.8	15.9	11.3	11.2	10.6
Portland, OR	10.6	7.2	7.8	10.4	16.4	13.0	16.9	17.7
Providence, RI	20.2	12.0	9.0	11.4	16.7	11.1	10.0	9.7
Provo, UT	12.2	12.9	12.3	13.5	18.9	11.8	10.6	7.8
Raleigh, NC	7.3	7.3	8.9	13.2	18.4	13.5	15.8	15.6
Reno, NV	9.2	9.5	9.5	14.5	18.6	12.7	14.5	11.5
Richmond, VA	17.6	11.0	10.1	13.3	16.2	10.2	10.5	11.0
Riverside, CA	9.0	7.6	8.3	11.4	17.8	14.8	17.6	13.6
Rochester, MN	8.2	7.0	7.1	11.6	17.6	14.1	17.8	16.6
Sacramento, CA	11.3	9.0	8.7	11.7	17.3	13.1	15.6	13.3
Salt Lake City, UT	12.0	8.5	9.1	12.4	17.6	12.5	14.3	13.7
San Antonio, TX	12.7	10.4	10.6	14.0	19.0	12.1	12.5	8.7
San Diego, CA	8.1	6.6	6.8	10.0	15.9	12.9	17.8	21.8
San Francisco, CA	9.7	5.8	4.9	6.2	9.8	9.0	15.6	38.9
San Jose, CA	6.2	4.8	4.9	7.2	12.0	10.7	18.0	36.2
Santa Rosa, CA	7.0	5.9	7.1	11.0	18.4	14.8	18.5	17.3
Savannah, GA	17.5	13.1	10.9	14.8	16.5	10.9	9.7	6.7
Seattle, WA	8.8	5.3	5.6	8.7	13.5	11.4	18.3	28.4
Sioux Falls, SD	8.8	8.3	10.7	13.2	19.0	14.4	15.2	10.5
Springfield, IL	13.7	10.7	9.6	12.1	17.2	13.0	12.9	10.9
Tallahassee, FL	16.8	10.9	11.7	13.8	17.3	10.2	10.4	8.8
Tampa, FL	14.6	10.3	9.9	12.2	15.8	10.7	12.0	14.6
Tucson, AZ	15.8	13.2	11.7	15.6	17.9	10.8	9.7	5.3
Tulsa, OK	14.2	11.6	11.2	15.2	17.4	10.3	10.1	10.0
Tuscaloosa, AL	19.4	11.0	11.0	12.3	16.5	9.4	10.2	10.2
Virginia Beach, VA	5.3	5.4	7.4	11.7	19.1	15.8	19.9	15.4
Washington, DC	12.9	6.0	5.9	7.7	12.2	10.6	16.4	28.2
Wichita, KS	12.3	10.5	10.5	14.6	18.7	12.0	12.8	8.7
Winston-Salem, NC	15.4	11.8	11.9	14.3	16.9	11.2	9.8	8.7
U.S.	10.3	8.9	8.9	12.3	17.2	12.7	15.1	14.5

Source: U.S. Census Bureau, 2015-2019 American Community Survey 5-Year Estimates

Household Income Distribution: Metro Area

Metro Area	Percent of Households Earning							
	Under $15,000	$15,000 -$24,999	$25,000 -$34,999	$35,000 -$49,999	$50,000 -$74,999	$75,000 -$99,999	$100,000 -$149,999	$150,000 and up
Albuquerque, NM	12.4	10.7	10.0	13.3	18.0	12.5	13.1	9.8
Allentown, PA	7.9	8.4	8.7	12.2	17.9	13.9	16.9	14.2
Anchorage, AK	6.1	5.6	6.5	9.9	17.2	13.7	20.5	20.5
Ann Arbor, MI	10.6	7.1	7.1	10.5	16.0	12.5	16.7	19.6
Athens, GA	16.4	12.1	10.3	13.5	15.2	10.2	12.6	9.6
Atlanta, GA	8.4	7.6	8.3	12.1	17.8	13.3	16.2	16.1
Austin, TX	7.3	6.0	7.3	11.1	17.3	13.3	18.1	19.8
Baton Rouge, LA	12.6	9.8	9.4	11.5	16.4	11.9	15.5	12.9
Boise City, ID	9.5	8.6	9.4	13.5	19.8	13.6	15.2	10.5
Boston, MA	8.8	6.2	5.8	8.3	13.5	11.8	18.5	27.1
Boulder, CO	8.5	6.0	6.6	10.2	14.5	12.4	17.2	24.5
Cape Coral, FL	9.4	9.1	10.3	13.9	19.6	13.2	13.3	11.3
Cedar Rapids, IA	7.7	7.9	9.1	13.3	19.3	14.4	16.9	11.4
Charleston, SC	10.0	8.4	8.5	12.1	18.4	13.5	15.6	13.6
Charlotte, NC	8.9	8.6	9.2	12.7	18.1	13.0	15.1	14.4
Chicago, IL	9.3	7.9	7.8	10.8	16.0	12.8	17.0	18.4
Cincinnati, OH	10.2	8.7	8.6	11.8	17.6	13.2	16.0	13.8
Clarksville, TN	11.4	9.1	10.8	16.0	19.7	13.7	12.4	6.8
Cleveland, OH	12.6	9.7	9.8	13.0	17.4	12.4	13.9	11.2
College Station, TX	16.3	11.0	9.8	12.7	15.8	11.5	12.8	10.2
Colorado Springs, CO	7.8	7.4	8.1	12.0	19.0	14.3	17.4	13.9
Columbia, MO	12.0	10.0	10.1	13.9	17.4	12.8	14.2	9.5
Columbia, SC	12.2	9.1	10.1	13.4	18.4	13.4	13.6	9.8
Columbus, OH	9.2	8.1	8.6	12.4	18.2	13.5	16.5	13.5
Dallas, TX	7.7	7.1	8.3	12.0	17.8	13.2	16.7	17.2
Davenport, IA	10.2	9.4	9.5	13.4	19.0	13.8	15.4	9.3
Denver, CO	6.7	5.8	6.7	10.8	17.1	13.7	18.9	20.2
Des Moines, IA	7.2	7.5	8.1	12.0	18.8	14.4	17.6	14.3
Durham, NC	10.0	8.6	9.3	12.7	16.8	12.6	14.7	15.3
Edison, NJ	10.5	7.5	7.0	9.3	13.9	11.4	16.4	24.1
El Paso, TX	14.6	12.2	11.4	14.5	19.0	10.8	11.2	6.3
Fargo, ND	9.4	8.6	8.2	12.1	18.3	15.3	15.7	12.4
Fayetteville, NC	13.8	11.1	11.2	15.5	18.9	12.5	11.5	5.6
Fort Collins, CO	7.9	7.9	7.3	11.6	17.2	14.1	17.9	16.1
Fort Wayne, IN	9.4	9.8	10.9	14.8	19.8	13.7	13.3	8.3
Fort Worth, TX	7.7	7.1	8.3	12.0	17.8	13.2	16.7	17.2
Grand Rapids, MI	7.6	9.0	8.8	13.5	19.8	14.4	15.9	11.0
Greeley, CO	7.7	6.9	7.2	11.0	17.7	16.3	19.3	13.9
Green Bay, WI	8.2	8.5	9.5	13.5	19.2	14.6	16.4	10.0
Greensboro, NC	12.4	10.8	11.3	14.7	18.2	12.2	11.9	8.6
Honolulu, HI	7.1	5.1	5.9	9.6	15.8	13.9	20.2	22.5
Houston, TX	8.8	8.3	8.7	11.7	16.8	12.3	15.8	17.7
Huntsville, AL	10.4	9.2	8.8	11.5	16.1	12.5	16.4	15.0
Indianapolis, IN	9.6	8.7	9.4	13.2	17.9	13.3	15.1	12.8
Jacksonville, FL	9.5	8.3	9.2	13.4	18.8	13.6	14.7	12.4
Kansas City, MO	8.4	7.8	8.7	12.6	17.8	13.9	16.8	14.1
Lafayette, LA	14.4	11.5	10.3	12.4	16.1	12.4	13.4	9.6
Lakeland, FL	11.1	11.2	11.2	16.0	19.9	12.6	11.3	6.8
Las Vegas, NV	10.2	8.8	9.7	13.9	18.6	13.5	14.5	11.0
Lexington, KY	10.9	9.4	9.7	13.1	17.5	13.1	14.7	11.5
Lincoln, NE	8.9	8.8	9.9	13.4	19.0	13.3	15.9	10.8
Little Rock, AR	12.0	10.0	10.4	13.7	18.1	11.9	14.1	9.8
Los Angeles, CA	9.6	7.7	7.6	10.6	15.6	12.4	16.5	20.1
Louisville, KY	10.2	9.3	9.4	13.6	18.4	13.4	14.4	11.4

Table continued on following page.

Metro Area	Percent of Households Earning							
	Under $15,000	$15,000 -$24,999	$25,000 -$34,999	$35,000 -$49,999	$50,000 -$74,999	$75,000 -$99,999	$100,000 -$149,999	$150,000 and up
Madison, WI	7.3	6.8	7.9	11.9	17.8	14.4	18.5	15.5
Manchester, NH	6.3	6.3	7.3	9.8	16.1	13.8	19.9	20.5
Memphis, TN	13.2	10.6	10.2	13.4	17.4	11.8	13.0	10.4
Miami, FL	11.8	9.9	9.8	13.0	17.2	11.7	13.3	13.4
Midland, TX	6.9	6.9	7.1	9.9	17.1	13.5	18.1	20.6
Milwaukee, WI	10.4	9.1	8.7	12.7	17.1	12.9	15.8	13.2
Minneapolis, MN	6.7	6.1	6.7	10.6	16.4	14.2	19.4	19.7
Nashville, TN	8.0	7.5	8.6	13.0	18.6	14.1	16.2	14.0
New Haven, CT	10.0	8.2	7.6	11.1	16.2	12.5	16.5	17.9
New Orleans, LA	14.8	10.9	9.6	12.2	16.4	11.6	13.0	11.5
New York, NY	10.5	7.5	7.0	9.3	13.9	11.4	16.4	24.1
Oklahoma City, OK	10.1	9.2	9.6	13.6	18.8	13.3	14.1	11.2
Omaha, NE	8.4	7.7	8.0	12.3	18.1	14.4	17.5	13.5
Orlando, FL	9.5	9.2	10.1	14.0	18.9	13.1	13.7	11.5
Peoria, IL	10.4	9.1	9.0	13.2	19.5	13.5	14.8	10.5
Philadelphia, PA	10.0	7.8	7.7	10.4	15.6	12.6	16.6	19.3
Phoenix, AZ	8.9	8.0	8.8	13.0	18.5	13.4	15.7	13.7
Pittsburgh, PA	10.6	9.7	9.3	12.3	17.4	12.9	15.5	12.3
Portland, OR	7.7	6.7	7.4	11.1	17.3	14.0	18.3	17.6
Providence, RI	11.0	8.8	7.9	10.8	15.9	13.2	17.0	15.4
Provo, UT	6.1	6.2	7.5	11.8	18.9	16.1	19.5	14.0
Raleigh, NC	6.5	6.6	7.6	11.7	17.1	13.7	18.2	18.6
Reno, NV	7.9	8.4	8.5	13.2	18.9	13.8	16.3	13.1
Richmond, VA	9.0	7.4	8.0	12.4	17.2	13.4	17.3	15.3
Riverside, CA	9.4	8.5	8.8	11.9	17.6	13.5	16.5	13.8
Rochester, MN	7.1	7.0	7.4	11.6	18.0	14.2	18.8	16.0
Sacramento, CA	9.1	7.6	7.7	10.6	16.6	13.1	17.4	17.9
Salt Lake City, UT	6.5	5.9	7.2	11.4	19.1	15.2	19.2	15.5
San Antonio, TX	10.3	8.9	9.4	12.8	18.7	13.2	14.8	11.9
San Diego, CA	7.6	6.7	7.1	10.3	16.1	13.0	18.0	21.1
San Francisco, CA	7.2	5.2	5.2	7.2	11.7	11.0	17.5	35.0
San Jose, CA	5.5	4.3	4.5	6.6	10.8	10.0	17.5	40.9
Santa Rosa, CA	6.7	6.0	6.8	10.0	16.6	14.2	18.5	21.1
Savannah, GA	10.6	9.5	9.2	13.0	17.8	13.8	14.6	11.4
Seattle, WA	6.7	5.4	5.9	9.5	15.7	13.3	19.5	23.9
Sioux Falls, SD	7.6	7.5	9.7	12.5	19.2	15.6	16.9	11.0
Springfield, IL	10.5	9.0	8.9	11.9	17.4	14.1	16.1	12.0
Tallahassee, FL	13.5	10.2	10.8	13.9	17.5	12.1	12.2	9.7
Tampa, FL	10.9	10.0	10.3	14.0	18.0	12.4	13.2	11.1
Tucson, AZ	12.0	10.6	10.2	14.3	18.2	12.3	12.7	9.6
Tulsa, OK	10.9	10.0	10.1	14.0	18.4	12.6	13.4	10.4
Tuscaloosa, AL	16.4	10.6	10.2	12.4	17.8	11.5	12.7	8.4
Virginia Beach, VA	8.7	7.7	8.2	12.3	18.8	14.4	17.1	12.7
Washington, DC	5.8	4.1	4.8	7.5	13.3	12.6	19.9	31.9
Wichita, KS	10.5	9.5	9.7	14.2	19.2	13.1	14.5	9.4
Winston-Salem, NC	12.1	11.3	11.0	14.8	18.0	12.8	11.6	8.3
U.S.	10.3	8.9	8.9	12.3	17.2	12.7	15.1	14.5

Note: Figures cover the Metropolitan Statistical Area (MSA)—see Appendix B for areas included
Source: Source: U.S. Census Bureau, 2015-2019 American Community Survey 5-Year Estimates

Poverty Rate: City

City	All Ages	Under 18 Years Old	18 to 64 Years Old	65 Years and Over
Albuquerque, NM	16.9	24.0	16.1	9.5
Allentown, PA	25.7	37.4	22.4	15.8
Anchorage, AK	9.0	13.1	8.1	5.5
Ann Arbor, MI	22.3	9.8	27.3	7.7
Athens, GA	29.9	33.7	32.2	9.4
Atlanta, GA	20.8	33.5	18.1	16.1
Austin, TX	13.2	18.0	12.3	9.4
Baton Rouge, LA	24.8	35.7	23.9	11.5
Boise City, ID	13.7	16.2	13.6	10.7
Boston, MA	18.9	27.7	16.5	20.9
Boulder, CO	20.4	6.3	25.2	6.9
Cape Coral, FL	10.4	13.1	10.3	8.6
Cedar Rapids, IA	12.5	17.0	12.2	7.0
Charleston, SC	13.2	14.7	13.8	8.8
Charlotte, NC	12.8	18.6	11.4	8.6
Chicago, IL	18.4	26.8	16.2	15.5
Cincinnati, OH	26.3	39.0	24.2	13.9
Clarksville, TN	14.5	18.5	13.5	9.0
Cleveland, OH	32.7	48.2	29.8	20.5
College Station, TX	29.6	12.3	35.9	7.9
Colorado Springs, CO	11.7	15.8	11.1	7.0
Columbia, MO	21.8	15.1	26.2	5.0
Columbia, SC	21.8	26.8	21.9	13.2
Columbus, OH	19.5	29.3	17.4	11.6
Dallas, TX	18.9	29.3	15.6	14.4
Davenport, IA	16.6	24.3	15.5	9.0
Denver, CO	12.9	18.2	11.6	10.9
Des Moines, IA	16.1	23.2	14.7	9.3
Durham, NC	15.9	24.5	14.3	8.4
Edison, NJ	5.7	6.8	5.1	6.8
El Paso, TX	19.1	27.1	15.9	17.6
Fargo, ND	13.2	12.8	14.3	7.6
Fayetteville, NC	19.3	28.0	17.4	11.6
Fort Collins, CO	16.3	10.3	19.3	7.7
Fort Wayne, IN	16.0	24.1	14.5	7.5
Fort Worth, TX	14.5	20.0	12.5	11.4
Grand Rapids, MI	20.4	28.9	19.4	10.1
Greeley, CO	16.2	19.6	16.1	9.3
Green Bay, WI	14.9	19.7	13.9	9.7
Greensboro, NC	18.5	26.7	17.1	11.5
Honolulu, HI	10.6	12.2	10.1	10.9
Houston, TX	20.1	31.2	16.6	14.2
Huntsville, AL	16.8	25.5	16.2	7.9
Indianapolis, IN	18.0	26.8	16.1	10.2
Jacksonville, FL	14.9	21.9	13.0	11.3
Kansas City, MO	16.1	24.3	14.5	9.6
Lafayette, LA	19.7	27.7	18.9	11.4
Lakeland, FL	16.4	23.5	15.5	12.3
Las Vegas, NV	15.3	21.3	14.1	10.6
Lexington, KY	16.8	20.4	17.5	7.4
Lincoln, NE	13.5	14.2	14.8	6.4
Little Rock, AR	16.6	23.8	15.2	10.9
Los Angeles, CA	18.0	25.7	16.0	15.6
Louisville, KY	15.9	24.0	14.6	9.4
Madison, WI	16.9	11.8	19.9	5.9

Table continued on following page.

City	All Ages	Under 18 Years Old	18 to 64 Years Old	65 Years and Over
Manchester, NH	14.1	19.8	13.2	10.1
Memphis, TN	25.1	40.8	21.1	13.6
Miami, FL	23.4	31.8	19.0	31.6
Midland, TX	9.2	11.5	7.7	11.8
Milwaukee, WI	25.4	36.7	22.7	13.6
Minneapolis, MN	19.1	25.5	18.2	13.2
Nashville, TN	15.1	24.2	13.2	9.2
New Haven, CT	26.5	36.2	24.7	16.3
New Orleans, LA	23.7	34.2	21.6	18.1
New York, NY	17.9	25.1	15.6	18.2
Oklahoma City, OK	16.1	23.7	14.2	9.0
Omaha, NE	13.4	18.7	12.3	8.5
Orlando, FL	17.2	24.4	15.4	14.8
Peoria, IL	19.7	24.6	20.1	10.1
Philadelphia, PA	24.3	34.8	22.2	17.6
Phoenix, AZ	18.0	26.6	15.6	10.8
Pittsburgh, PA	20.5	27.2	20.7	12.8
Portland, OR	13.7	15.5	13.9	10.4
Providence, RI	25.5	34.7	23.0	20.6
Provo, UT	26.3	19.6	30.2	7.9
Raleigh, NC	12.6	17.8	11.9	6.7
Reno, NV	13.5	15.8	14.0	8.2
Richmond, VA	23.2	37.0	21.5	13.2
Riverside, CA	13.9	17.9	13.0	10.5
Rochester, MN	10.1	12.8	10.0	5.7
Sacramento, CA	16.6	21.9	15.5	12.3
Salt Lake City, UT	16.6	20.4	16.4	10.9
San Antonio, TX	17.8	26.1	15.4	12.8
San Diego, CA	12.8	15.7	12.6	9.4
San Francisco, CA	10.3	10.0	9.7	13.6
San Jose, CA	8.7	9.3	8.4	9.5
Santa Rosa, CA	10.3	13.7	9.8	7.7
Savannah, GA	21.9	30.9	20.8	12.4
Seattle, WA	11.0	10.9	10.9	11.2
Sioux Falls, SD	10.4	12.9	9.9	8.0
Springfield, IL	18.6	29.8	17.5	8.4
Tallahassee, FL	26.4	24.3	29.3	9.9
Tampa, FL	18.6	26.5	16.2	17.6
Tucson, AZ	22.5	30.5	21.9	13.0
Tulsa, OK	19.4	29.7	17.7	8.8
Tuscaloosa, AL	24.0	24.2	26.6	10.3
Virginia Beach, VA	7.3	10.2	6.9	4.5
Washington, DC	16.2	24.0	14.5	14.5
Wichita, KS	15.9	22.0	15.0	8.8
Winston-Salem, NC	20.7	32.0	18.6	10.4
U.S.	13.4	18.5	12.6	9.3

Note: Figures are percentage of people whose income during the past 12 months was below the poverty level;
Source: U.S. Census Bureau, 2015-2019 American Community Survey 5-Year Estimates

Poverty Rate: Metro Area

Metro Area	All Ages	Under 18 Years Old	18 to 64 Years Old	65 Years and Over
Albuquerque, NM	16.2	22.6	15.5	10.1
Allentown, PA	10.4	16.3	9.3	6.8
Anchorage, AK	9.4	12.8	8.6	6.0
Ann Arbor, MI	14.0	12.0	16.1	6.7
Athens, GA	22.0	25.1	23.8	8.1
Atlanta, GA	12.1	17.4	10.7	8.6
Austin, TX	10.8	13.3	10.5	7.2
Baton Rouge, LA	15.9	21.8	14.9	10.0
Boise City, ID	11.9	13.5	11.8	9.1
Boston, MA	9.3	11.3	8.8	9.1
Boulder, CO	11.7	8.5	13.8	6.3
Cape Coral, FL	13.1	22.1	12.8	7.9
Cedar Rapids, IA	10.0	12.8	9.8	6.6
Charleston, SC	12.9	18.9	11.7	8.7
Charlotte, NC	11.7	16.5	10.7	8.2
Chicago, IL	11.8	16.5	10.7	9.1
Cincinnati, OH	12.2	16.8	11.5	7.8
Clarksville, TN	14.7	19.0	13.7	9.7
Cleveland, OH	14.3	20.7	13.6	9.0
College Station, TX	22.7	20.1	25.8	9.1
Colorado Springs, CO	10.0	13.1	9.6	6.3
Columbia, MO	17.2	15.0	20.1	6.5
Columbia, SC	15.0	20.2	14.3	9.5
Columbus, OH	13.2	18.5	12.2	7.9
Dallas, TX	11.7	16.6	10.1	8.5
Davenport, IA	12.5	18.8	11.5	7.5
Denver, CO	8.8	11.4	8.3	6.9
Des Moines, IA	9.3	11.6	9.0	6.3
Durham, NC	14.2	20.6	13.6	7.8
Edison, NJ	12.8	17.7	11.4	12.0
El Paso, TX	20.2	28.6	16.7	18.6
Fargo, ND	11.1	11.1	11.9	6.3
Fayetteville, NC	17.9	24.8	16.3	11.4
Fort Collins, CO	11.6	9.4	13.5	6.4
Fort Wayne, IN	13.0	19.4	11.7	6.5
Fort Worth, TX	11.7	16.6	10.1	8.5
Grand Rapids, MI	11.0	13.7	10.9	6.9
Greeley, CO	10.0	12.0	9.5	8.4
Green Bay, WI	9.6	12.5	9.0	7.3
Greensboro, NC	16.0	23.2	14.9	10.0
Honolulu, HI	8.3	10.1	7.8	7.8
Houston, TX	13.7	19.8	11.7	10.0
Huntsville, AL	12.7	18.5	11.8	7.7
Indianapolis, IN	12.4	17.5	11.4	7.4
Jacksonville, FL	12.6	17.7	11.6	8.9
Kansas City, MO	10.5	15.0	9.6	6.8
Lafayette, LA	19.1	26.4	17.4	13.7
Lakeland, FL	15.8	24.7	14.5	9.9
Las Vegas, NV	13.7	19.3	12.6	9.2
Lexington, KY	15.8	20.9	15.9	7.6
Lincoln, NE	12.2	12.5	13.5	5.8
Little Rock, AR	15.1	20.5	14.2	9.7
Los Angeles, CA	13.9	19.2	12.5	12.2
Louisville, KY	12.5	18.2	11.6	7.9
Madison, WI	10.3	8.7	11.8	5.6

Table continued on following page.

Metro Area	All Ages	Under 18 Years Old	18 to 64 Years Old	65 Years and Over
Manchester, NH	7.8	9.4	7.6	6.1
Memphis, TN	17.6	27.8	15.0	10.1
Miami, FL	14.6	20.2	12.6	15.1
Midland, TX	9.5	13.2	7.5	11.1
Milwaukee, WI	13.3	19.3	12.3	8.4
Minneapolis, MN	8.6	11.0	8.1	6.6
Nashville, TN	11.4	15.7	10.6	7.6
New Haven, CT	11.7	17.3	11.0	7.6
New Orleans, LA	17.3	25.2	15.7	12.5
New York, NY	12.8	17.7	11.4	12.0
Oklahoma City, OK	13.9	19.0	13.2	7.5
Omaha, NE	10.3	13.5	9.6	7.2
Orlando, FL	13.7	19.6	12.5	9.9
Peoria, IL	12.2	15.5	12.4	6.9
Philadelphia, PA	12.4	16.9	11.7	8.6
Phoenix, AZ	13.7	19.6	12.8	8.2
Pittsburgh, PA	11.2	14.9	11.0	8.0
Portland, OR	10.6	13.1	10.5	7.7
Providence, RI	12.0	16.9	11.1	9.6
Provo, UT	10.7	9.5	12.0	5.5
Raleigh, NC	9.8	13.4	9.1	6.3
Reno, NV	11.2	14.0	11.2	7.7
Richmond, VA	11.2	15.8	10.5	7.6
Riverside, CA	14.8	20.5	13.2	10.7
Rochester, MN	8.3	10.4	8.1	5.6
Sacramento, CA	13.4	16.8	13.2	8.9
Salt Lake City, UT	9.0	10.7	8.6	6.7
San Antonio, TX	14.4	20.6	12.7	10.4
San Diego, CA	11.6	14.7	11.1	8.9
San Francisco, CA	9.0	10.2	8.7	8.7
San Jose, CA	7.5	7.9	7.3	8.0
Santa Rosa, CA	9.2	10.7	9.4	7.0
Savannah, GA	13.7	18.4	13.1	8.7
Seattle, WA	9.0	10.8	8.6	7.8
Sioux Falls, SD	8.7	10.4	8.3	7.2
Springfield, IL	14.2	22.8	13.2	6.9
Tallahassee, FL	20.0	22.1	21.9	8.4
Tampa, FL	13.5	18.6	12.8	10.3
Tucson, AZ	16.8	23.9	16.9	8.8
Tulsa, OK	14.3	20.9	13.3	7.7
Tuscaloosa, AL	19.2	24.7	19.2	10.6
Virginia Beach, VA	11.3	17.1	10.2	6.9
Washington, DC	7.8	9.9	7.2	7.2
Wichita, KS	13.0	17.4	12.3	8.2
Winston-Salem, NC	16.0	24.8	14.6	9.0
U.S.	13.4	18.5	12.6	9.3

Note: Figures are percentage of people whose income during the past 12 months was below the poverty level;
Figures cover the Metropolitan Statistical Area—see Appendix B for areas included
Source: U.S. Census Bureau, 2015-2019 American Community Survey 5-Year Estimates

Employment by Industry

Metro Area[1]	(A)	(B)	(C)	(D)	(E)	(F)	(G)	(H)	(I)	(J)	(K)	(L)	(M)	(N)
Albuquerque, NM	6.8	n/a	17.3	4.9	20.9	1.3	8.7	3.8	n/a	2.8	16.5	10.9	2.8	2.9
Allentown, PA	3.5	n/a	20.8	3.6	10.5	1.2	7.7	10.5	n/a	3.4	12.8	10.8	10.9	3.8
Anchorage, AK	7.4	6.0	19.2	4.6	20.8	2.1	8.0	1.1	1.3	3.4	10.9	12.1	6.9	2.9
Ann Arbor, MI	2.2	n/a	13.3	3.0	38.3	2.8	4.6	6.3	n/a	2.5	14.0	7.3	2.2	3.0
Athens, GA	n/a	n/a	n/a	n/a	29.7	n/a	10.2	n/a	n/a	n/a	9.1	11.3	n/a	n/a
Atlanta, GA	4.7	4.6	13.1	6.6	12.0	3.5	8.8	6.0	<0.1	3.3	19.5	10.5	6.1	5.3
Austin, TX	6.4	n/a	11.2	6.2	16.9	3.6	9.5	5.8	n/a	3.8	18.6	10.0	2.6	4.9
Baton Rouge, LA	10.7	10.5	13.5	4.2	20.0	1.1	8.8	7.5	0.1	3.8	12.3	10.5	3.9	3.3
Boise City, ID	8.2	n/a	14.3	6.0	13.6	1.0	9.2	8.1	n/a	3.4	15.2	11.9	3.8	4.7
Boston, MA[4]	4.1	n/a	22.8	8.6	11.0	3.4	6.3	4.2	n/a	3.1	22.3	8.0	2.4	3.2
Boulder, CO	3.0	n/a	13.3	3.8	18.9	4.5	6.5	11.3	n/a	3.1	21.2	9.5	1.1	3.5
Cape Coral, FL	12.6	n/a	11.4	4.9	15.8	0.9	13.5	2.4	n/a	4.0	14.0	14.9	2.4	2.8
Cedar Rapids, IA	6.0	n/a	14.8	8.2	11.3	2.1	6.8	14.0	n/a	3.4	10.2	11.0	7.7	4.1
Charleston, SC	5.7	n/a	11.9	4.4	18.2	1.5	11.5	7.6	n/a	3.8	15.5	12.3	4.2	2.9
Charlotte, NC	5.6	n/a	10.1	9.1	12.8	1.9	9.4	8.5	n/a	3.5	17.4	10.6	6.1	4.6
Chicago, IL[2]	3.5	3.4	16.5	7.8	11.4	1.8	6.5	7.6	<0.1	4.1	19.1	9.6	6.4	5.1
Cincinnati, OH	4.2	n/a	15.8	6.9	11.8	1.2	8.9	10.5	n/a	3.4	15.7	10.1	5.7	5.2
Clarksville, TN	3.8	n/a	12.9	3.3	20.6	1.0	12.1	11.7	n/a	3.4	10.6	13.9	2.9	n/a
Cleveland, OH	3.7	n/a	19.4	6.5	12.8	1.2	8.3	11.2	n/a	3.3	15.0	9.7	3.6	4.8
College Station, TX	5.7	n/a	10.1	3.1	37.9	1.1	11.3	4.4	n/a	2.5	9.0	10.4	1.7	2.2
Colorado Springs, CO	6.3	n/a	14.7	6.5	18.4	1.8	9.5	4.0	n/a	5.9	16.6	11.6	2.2	2.0
Columbia, MO	n/a	n/a	n/a	n/a	29.2	n/a	n/a	n/a	n/a	n/a	n/a	10.9	n/a	n/a
Columbia, SC	4.4	n/a	12.2	8.1	21.7	1.2	8.9	7.9	n/a	3.8	12.4	10.8	4.4	3.6
Columbus, OH	4.1	n/a	14.5	8.0	16.4	1.3	7.6	6.7	n/a	3.6	16.4	9.3	7.9	3.7
Dallas, TX[2]	5.4	n/a	11.7	9.7	11.9	2.5	8.5	6.7	n/a	2.8	19.5	9.5	5.6	5.6
Davenport, IA	n/a	n/a	n/a	n/a	n/a	n/a	n/a	n/a	n/a	n/a	n/a	n/a	n/a	n/a
Denver, CO	7.5	n/a	12.8	7.7	13.5	3.4	7.3	4.7	n/a	3.7	18.8	9.7	5.5	5.0
Des Moines, IA	5.8	n/a	13.9	15.8	12.6	1.6	7.8	5.6	n/a	3.5	13.7	10.9	3.4	4.9
Durham, NC	2.9	n/a	22.1	5.1	19.9	1.7	6.2	10.4	n/a	3.3	15.3	7.4	2.5	2.6
Edison, NJ[2]	3.8	n/a	22.7	9.4	14.1	3.8	6.0	2.7	n/a	3.8	16.4	8.9	4.2	3.7
El Paso, TX	5.5	n/a	14.8	4.1	22.2	1.4	10.5	5.1	n/a	2.5	11.8	12.3	5.5	3.7
Fargo, ND	6.4	n/a	19.3	8.3	13.3	2.1	8.1	7.1	n/a	3.4	9.5	10.9	4.6	6.4
Fayetteville, NC	3.7	n/a	11.5	2.9	31.8	0.7	11.5	6.2	n/a	3.3	8.6	13.6	3.9	1.5
Fort Collins, CO	7.0	n/a	11.2	4.1	25.0	1.8	8.8	8.4	n/a	3.8	12.2	11.7	2.3	3.1
Fort Wayne, IN	5.3	n/a	19.1	5.5	8.8	0.9	8.4	16.5	n/a	4.7	9.9	11.3	4.6	4.6
Fort Worth, TX[2]	6.8	n/a	12.8	6.3	12.8	0.8	10.1	9.2	n/a	3.5	11.5	11.8	9.0	4.9
Grand Rapids, MI	4.7	n/a	17.6	5.0	9.0	1.0	5.8	20.4	n/a	3.7	13.6	9.2	3.5	5.9
Greeley, CO	14.9	n/a	9.8	4.2	15.9	0.4	8.1	13.1	n/a	3.4	10.7	10.5	4.6	4.0
Green Bay, WI	4.8	n/a	15.5	6.8	11.1	0.8	7.5	17.9	n/a	4.7	11.1	9.6	5.1	4.7
Greensboro, NC	4.5	n/a	14.3	5.2	12.1	1.2	8.5	14.5	n/a	3.3	13.0	11.1	6.4	5.3
Honolulu, HI	6.5	n/a	15.2	5.3	22.5	1.3	12.0	2.1	n/a	4.1	12.8	9.7	4.8	3.2
Houston, TX	8.9	6.7	13.2	5.4	14.0	0.9	9.5	6.9	2.2	3.5	16.1	10.1	5.7	5.2
Huntsville, AL	4.0	n/a	8.7	2.9	21.2	0.8	8.0	10.6	n/a	3.2	25.5	10.4	1.6	2.5
Indianapolis, IN	5.5	5.4	15.1	6.7	12.7	1.0	8.5	8.4	<0.1	3.5	15.9	9.8	7.9	4.4
Jacksonville, FL	6.6	6.5	15.4	9.6	10.8	1.2	10.4	4.4	<0.1	3.4	15.6	11.3	7.1	3.6
Kansas City, MO	4.9	n/a	14.6	7.4	13.7	1.3	8.1	7.4	n/a	3.8	17.7	10.3	5.7	4.6
Lafayette, LA	10.1	4.9	16.8	5.2	13.4	1.0	10.1	7.0	5.2	3.4	11.1	14.0	3.2	4.2
Lakeland, FL	6.3	n/a	14.6	5.8	11.7	0.7	8.7	7.2	n/a	2.5	13.9	13.5	10.0	4.5
Las Vegas, NV	7.0	6.9	11.4	5.8	11.2	1.0	21.4	2.6	<0.1	2.9	14.3	12.4	7.0	2.5
Lexington, KY	5.0	n/a	13.0	3.7	19.4	0.9	8.8	10.5	n/a	3.6	14.8	11.2	4.7	3.9
Lincoln, NE	5.1	n/a	16.6	6.8	21.9	1.7	7.6	7.0	n/a	3.6	11.4	9.8	5.9	2.3
Little Rock, AR	4.9	n/a	16.7	6.3	19.3	1.4	8.0	5.3	n/a	5.0	12.5	11.2	4.6	4.2
Los Angeles, CA[2]	3.5	3.5	20.1	5.1	13.4	4.3	8.5	7.4	<0.1	2.8	14.4	9.7	5.4	4.8
Louisville, KY	4.3	n/a	14.3	7.3	10.8	1.2	7.8	12.6	n/a	3.5	13.1	10.0	10.2	4.4
Madison, WI	4.6	n/a	12.6	5.9	21.5	4.5	6.4	9.1	n/a	5.2	13.5	10.3	2.4	3.6
Manchester, NH[3]	5.0	n/a	22.6	7.2	10.6	2.8	6.7	7.0	n/a	3.7	15.2	11.5	3.2	4.0

Table continued on following page.

Metro Area[1]	(A)	(B)	(C)	(D)	(E)	(F)	(G)	(H)	(I)	(J)	(K)	(L)	(M)	(N)
Memphis, TN	3.6	n/a	14.6	4.5	12.9	0.7	8.9	6.8	n/a	4.2	15.4	10.0	12.6	5.3
Miami, FL[2]	4.5	4.4	16.5	7.2	12.1	1.6	9.2	3.7	<0.1	3.9	15.9	12.0	7.1	6.0
Midland, TX	28.0	n/a	7.3	4.8	11.2	0.7	10.1	3.3	n/a	3.7	9.4	10.5	5.2	5.2
Milwaukee, WI	3.6	3.6	20.5	6.0	9.6	1.5	7.1	13.9	<0.1	5.4	14.3	9.4	3.6	4.5
Minneapolis, MN	4.3	n/a	17.7	8.7	12.9	1.6	5.3	10.2	n/a	3.6	16.6	9.8	4.0	4.7
Nashville, TN	4.8	n/a	14.8	6.9	11.8	2.4	9.2	7.9	n/a	3.8	17.3	10.0	6.5	4.0
New Haven, CT[3]	3.5	n/a	28.4	4.0	12.7	1.3	6.5	8.2	n/a	3.5	10.9	9.6	7.1	3.8
New Orleans, LA	5.6	4.9	19.1	5.2	13.5	1.0	11.9	5.6	0.7	4.0	13.2	11.5	5.2	3.8
New York, NY[2]	3.8	n/a	22.7	9.4	14.1	3.8	6.0	2.7	n/a	3.8	16.4	8.9	4.2	3.7
Oklahoma City, OK	6.0	4.8	15.4	5.4	20.2	0.9	10.4	5.2	1.2	4.3	12.8	10.7	4.8	3.4
Omaha, NE	6.2	n/a	16.0	9.2	13.2	1.9	8.5	6.8	n/a	3.5	14.3	10.9	5.5	3.4
Orlando, FL	7.0	7.0	13.1	6.5	10.6	2.0	15.1	4.0	<0.1	3.3	18.2	12.2	3.7	3.8
Peoria, IL	4.7	n/a	19.8	4.4	11.9	0.9	7.3	13.0	n/a	4.7	13.0	11.5	4.4	3.8
Philadelphia, PA[2]	2.6	n/a	32.1	6.3	14.4	1.9	6.0	3.5	n/a	3.7	14.7	7.7	4.1	2.4
Phoenix, AZ	6.2	6.1	15.9	9.4	11.1	1.6	8.9	6.1	0.1	3.0	16.8	11.3	5.3	3.7
Pittsburgh, PA	5.8	5.1	22.8	6.8	10.2	1.6	7.5	7.2	0.6	3.7	15.5	10.6	4.4	3.4
Portland, OR	6.4	6.3	15.8	6.2	12.4	2.1	6.3	10.6	0.1	3.2	16.4	10.4	4.8	4.8
Providence, RI[3]	4.5	4.5	21.4	6.6	13.2	1.0	8.6	8.7	<0.1	4.0	13.1	11.6	3.4	3.2
Provo, UT	9.5	n/a	18.7	4.3	11.9	4.7	8.2	7.3	n/a	2.1	15.2	13.2	1.7	2.6
Raleigh, NC	6.5	n/a	12.4	5.1	14.9	3.4	9.0	4.6	n/a	3.9	20.5	11.6	3.4	4.0
Reno, NV	7.4	7.2	11.5	4.5	12.4	1.2	12.3	10.3	0.2	2.3	14.4	9.9	9.3	3.9
Richmond, VA	6.1	n/a	14.7	8.0	16.4	0.9	7.9	4.6	n/a	4.2	17.2	10.3	5.3	3.8
Riverside, CA	7.3	7.2	16.6	2.8	16.2	0.5	8.3	6.0	<0.1	2.4	10.4	11.8	12.9	4.2
Rochester, MN	4.0	n/a	44.7	2.3	10.5	1.1	5.8	8.3	n/a	2.9	4.7	10.6	2.2	2.3
Sacramento, CA	7.5	7.5	16.4	5.3	24.0	1.0	8.0	3.6	<0.1	2.8	13.8	10.5	4.0	2.7
Salt Lake City, UT	6.6	n/a	11.6	8.3	14.1	2.7	7.5	7.8	n/a	2.7	17.5	10.4	5.9	4.4
San Antonio, TX	5.8	5.2	15.1	8.9	16.6	1.7	10.8	4.8	0.5	3.2	14.7	10.6	3.8	3.4
San Diego, CA	6.3	6.3	15.2	5.3	16.9	1.5	9.3	8.1	<0.1	2.9	18.2	10.4	2.6	2.8
San Francisco, CA[2]	3.9	3.9	13.5	7.9	11.9	10.3	6.5	3.4	<0.1	2.9	26.8	6.6	3.9	1.9
San Jose, CA	4.8	4.7	15.9	3.5	8.7	10.0	5.4	15.7	<0.1	1.9	22.3	7.2	1.6	2.6
Santa Rosa, CA	8.7	8.6	17.4	3.9	14.2	1.1	8.2	11.8	0.1	3.0	11.9	12.9	2.3	4.0
Savannah, GA	4.6	n/a	14.0	3.2	13.0	0.8	12.2	9.3	n/a	3.7	14.3	11.8	9.1	3.4
Seattle, WA[2]	6.3	6.2	13.1	5.2	12.2	8.1	6.2	8.6	<0.1	3.4	16.4	12.8	3.4	3.9
Sioux Falls, SD	5.5	n/a	22.2	9.9	9.4	1.5	7.8	9.0	n/a	3.7	9.4	12.0	3.6	5.4
Springfield, IL	3.3	n/a	20.4	6.0	25.9	1.7	6.6	2.8	n/a	5.7	10.5	11.7	2.0	2.7
Tallahassee, FL	4.5	n/a	13.7	4.2	32.8	1.7	9.4	1.9	n/a	5.0	12.8	10.0	1.3	2.0
Tampa, FL	6.2	6.1	15.5	9.2	11.2	1.7	9.9	4.9	<0.1	3.3	18.7	11.7	3.2	3.9
Tucson, AZ	5.3	4.8	18.1	4.6	19.8	1.3	9.3	7.1	0.5	3.3	12.2	11.3	5.4	1.8
Tulsa, OK	6.7	5.6	16.1	5.1	12.7	1.3	9.5	11.1	1.0	4.4	13.0	11.1	4.9	3.6
Tuscaloosa, AL	6.4	n/a	8.3	3.8	26.4	0.8	9.2	16.5	n/a	3.8	9.2	10.3	2.8	1.9
Virginia Beach, VA	5.2	n/a	14.2	5.0	20.5	1.2	10.0	7.4	n/a	4.1	14.8	11.2	3.6	2.3
Washington, DC[2]	5.0	n/a	12.8	4.5	22.8	2.3	7.3	1.4	n/a	6.4	24.5	8.0	2.6	1.8
Wichita, KS	5.8	n/a	16.3	4.1	14.3	1.2	10.3	15.5	n/a	3.5	11.8	10.6	3.3	2.8
Winston-Salem, NC	4.5	n/a	20.8	4.9	11.4	0.6	9.2	12.6	n/a	3.0	13.4	11.8	4.4	2.9
U.S.	5.5	5.1	16.3	6.1	15.2	1.9	9.0	8.5	0.4	3.8	14.4	10.9	4.6	3.9

*Note: All figures are percentages covering non-farm employment as of December 2020 and are not seasonally adjusted;
(1) Figures cover the Metropolitan Statistical Area (MSA) except where noted. See Appendix B for areas included; (2) Metropolitan
Division; (3) New England City and Town Area; (4) New England City and Town Area Division; (A) Construction, Mining, and Logging
(some areas report Construction separate from Mining and Logging); (B) Construction; (C) Education and Health Services; (D) Financial
Activities; (E) Government; (F) Information; (G) Leisure and Hospitality; (H) Manufacturing; (I) Mining and Logging; (J) Other Services;
(K) Professional and Business Services; (L) Retail Trade; (M) Transportation and Utilities; (N) Wholesale Trade; n/a not available
Source: Bureau of Labor Statistics, Current Employment Statistics, Employment, Hours, and Earnings, December 2020*

Labor Force, Employment and Job Growth: City

City	Civilian Labor Force			Workers Employed		
	Dec. 2019	Dec. 2020	% Chg.	Dec. 2019	Dec. 2020	% Chg.
Albuquerque, NM	284,609	280,764	-1.3	273,259	260,057	-4.8
Allentown, PA	56,275	55,559	-1.2	52,716	50,085	-4.9
Anchorage, AK	147,801	150,509	1.8	140,718	142,180	1.0
Ann Arbor, MI	66,802	63,917	-4.3	65,636	62,017	-5.5
Athens, GA	59,225	58,747	-0.8	57,596	55,706	-3.2
Atlanta, GA	264,779	266,767	0.7	256,964	248,040	-3.4
Austin, TX	601,055	606,519	0.9	587,607	576,501	-1.8
Baton Rouge, LA	111,969	112,989	0.9	106,514	104,304	-2.0
Boise City, ID	134,753	133,502	-0.9	131,600	127,739	-2.9
Boston, MA	399,841	382,754	-4.2	391,993	354,899	-9.4
Boulder, CO	66,229	64,864	-2.0	65,025	60,677	-6.6
Cape Coral, FL	93,172	90,468	-2.9	90,578	86,083	-4.9
Cedar Rapids, IA	73,629	67,681	-8.0	71,125	64,790	-8.9
Charleston, SC	75,308	72,571	-3.6	73,919	69,583	-5.8
Charlotte, NC	499,499	492,206	-1.4	483,932	461,278	-4.6
Chicago, IL	1,322,199	1,308,831	-1.0	1,281,869	1,177,846	-8.1
Cincinnati, OH	147,410	148,764	0.9	142,030	139,857	-1.5
Clarksville, TN	63,787	65,851	3.2	61,432	60,949	-0.7
Cleveland, OH	156,471	151,177	-3.3	149,465	137,384	-8.0
College Station, TX	62,425	62,445	0.0	60,916	59,698	-2.0
Colorado Springs, CO	238,705	245,635	2.9	232,124	223,547	-3.7
Columbia, MO	68,108	67,049	-1.5	66,459	64,199	-3.4
Columbia, SC	58,665	58,030	-1.0	57,222	55,091	-3.7
Columbus, OH	478,751	473,342	-1.1	463,416	448,688	-3.1
Dallas, TX	703,081	714,931	1.6	681,628	663,820	-2.6
Davenport, IA	51,918	47,841	-7.8	49,753	45,379	-8.7
Denver, CO	423,917	436,113	2.8	414,090	395,349	-4.5
Des Moines, IA	115,631	106,451	-7.9	111,652	101,736	-8.8
Durham, NC	150,280	147,613	-1.7	145,981	139,307	-4.5
Edison, NJ	55,345	54,084	-2.2	54,066	51,214	-5.2
El Paso, TX	305,478	303,471	-0.6	295,039	280,221	-5.0
Fargo, ND	69,702	73,397	5.3	68,423	71,067	3.8
Fayetteville, NC	76,883	75,832	-1.3	73,263	69,057	-5.7
Fort Collins, CO	103,931	102,364	-1.5	101,963	94,647	-7.1
Fort Wayne, IN	128,470	131,139	2.0	124,594	125,226	0.5
Fort Worth, TX	444,954	448,335	0.7	431,424	417,064	-3.3
Grand Rapids, MI	103,987	101,472	-2.4	100,701	95,669	-5.0
Greeley, CO	55,458	56,828	2.4	54,063	51,159	-5.3
Green Bay, WI	53,859	54,419	1.0	52,110	51,623	-0.9
Greensboro, NC	147,165	143,483	-2.5	141,957	132,895	-6.3
Honolulu, HI	452,859	447,861	-1.1	443,191	411,864	-7.0
Houston, TX	1,168,794	1,162,957	-0.5	1,128,145	1,071,532	-5.0
Huntsville, AL	99,396	97,639	-1.7	97,185	94,305	-2.9
Indianapolis, IN	446,151	467,925	4.8	433,373	443,878	2.4
Jacksonville, FL	469,934	463,646	-1.3	457,089	438,293	-4.1
Kansas City, MO	262,205	262,873	0.2	252,990	245,170	-3.0
Lafayette, LA	59,376	59,649	0.4	56,669	56,144	-0.9
Lakeland, FL	47,582	47,525	-0.1	46,092	44,428	-3.6
Las Vegas, NV	316,225	301,287	-4.7	305,003	270,332	-11.3
Lexington, KY	175,216	173,151	-1.1	170,118	164,394	-3.3
Lincoln, NE	160,552	162,129	0.9	156,783	157,418	0.4
Little Rock, AR	96,600	95,461	-1.1	93,594	90,677	-3.1
Los Angeles, CA	2,095,690	1,987,043	-5.1	2,011,531	1,777,290	-11.6
Louisville, KY	402,027	394,489	-1.8	388,284	371,824	-4.2
Madison, WI	157,534	157,457	0.0	154,347	151,326	-1.9

Table continued on following page.

City	Civilian Labor Force			Workers Employed		
	Dec. 2019	Dec. 2020	% Chg.	Dec. 2019	Dec. 2020	% Chg.
Manchester, NH	66,041	64,338	-2.5	64,553	61,492	-4.7
Memphis, TN	299,167	316,351	5.7	287,040	285,384	-0.5
Miami, FL	234,913	222,511	-5.2	231,476	205,346	-11.2
Midland, TX	88,858	84,069	-5.3	87,068	77,687	-10.7
Milwaukee, WI	271,222	276,192	1.8	260,380	253,283	-2.7
Minneapolis, MN	245,206	236,236	-3.6	238,869	224,977	-5.8
Nashville, TN	413,927	420,401	1.5	404,589	396,582	-1.9
New Haven, CT	65,459	65,774	0.4	63,121	59,553	-5.6
New Orleans, LA	179,138	182,736	2.0	170,426	162,218	-4.8
New York, NY	4,055,234	3,856,031	-4.9	3,932,458	3,408,146	-13.3
Oklahoma City, OK	322,420	325,821	1.0	313,116	308,959	-1.3
Omaha, NE	243,405	245,582	0.8	236,406	237,000	0.2
Orlando, FL	170,544	162,722	-4.5	166,541	149,954	-9.9
Peoria, IL	50,615	47,156	-6.8	47,924	43,020	-10.2
Philadelphia, PA	729,738	699,455	-4.1	690,247	634,633	-8.0
Phoenix, AZ	885,177	887,360	0.2	853,111	820,050	-3.8
Pittsburgh, PA	157,702	150,397	-4.6	151,169	140,388	-7.1
Portland, OR	376,061	380,047	1.0	366,666	355,132	-3.1
Providence, RI	86,891	84,686	-2.5	83,544	77,341	-7.4
Provo, UT	68,223	69,278	1.5	66,963	67,577	0.9
Raleigh, NC	260,153	256,088	-1.5	252,404	241,439	-4.3
Reno, NV	139,960	134,597	-3.8	136,175	127,830	-6.1
Richmond, VA	119,856	116,571	-2.7	116,483	108,936	-6.4
Riverside, CA	156,209	155,456	-0.4	151,257	142,354	-5.8
Rochester, MN	65,938	64,249	-2.5	64,352	61,741	-4.0
Sacramento, CA	237,846	239,336	0.6	230,186	217,425	-5.5
Salt Lake City, UT	117,922	119,415	1.2	115,531	115,159	-0.3
San Antonio, TX	740,486	738,883	-0.2	720,097	690,895	-4.0
San Diego, CA	724,077	722,739	-0.1	704,952	665,731	-5.5
San Francisco, CA	589,286	566,193	-3.9	578,146	529,919	-8.3
San Jose, CA	558,215	552,450	-1.0	545,337	515,386	-5.4
Santa Rosa, CA	90,456	87,703	-3.0	88,298	81,635	-7.5
Savannah, GA	66,855	68,668	2.7	64,804	63,654	-1.7
Seattle, WA	475,147	468,970	-1.3	464,721	440,258	-5.2
Sioux Falls, SD	106,508	105,414	-1.0	103,166	102,274	-0.8
Springfield, IL	56,539	55,105	-2.5	54,362	51,115	-5.9
Tallahassee, FL	102,369	97,422	-4.8	99,536	91,619	-7.9
Tampa, FL	205,639	203,778	-0.9	200,162	191,493	-4.3
Tucson, AZ	271,283	268,958	-0.8	259,611	246,980	-4.8
Tulsa, OK	196,335	194,348	-1.0	190,196	182,480	-4.0
Tuscaloosa, AL	48,708	47,374	-2.7	47,449	45,126	-4.9
Virginia Beach, VA	234,164	226,000	-3.4	228,643	216,261	-5.4
Washington, DC	416,329	413,158	-0.7	397,389	376,699	-5.2
Wichita, KS	189,743	189,451	-0.1	183,423	180,980	-1.3
Winston-Salem, NC	118,986	117,479	-1.2	114,945	109,601	-4.6
U.S.	164,007,000	160,017,000	-2.4	158,504,000	149,613,000	-5.6

Note: Data is not seasonally adjusted and covers workers 16 years of age and older
Source: Bureau of Labor Statistics, Local Area Unemployment Statistics

Labor Force, Employment and Job Growth: Metro Area

Metro Area[1]	Civilian Labor Force			Workers Employed		
	Dec. 2019	Dec. 2020	% Chg.	Dec. 2019	Dec. 2020	% Chg.
Albuquerque, NM	442,230	434,669	-1.7	423,884	402,897	-4.9
Allentown, PA	448,501	434,989	-3.0	428,188	408,208	-4.6
Anchorage, AK	195,036	197,957	1.5	184,796	186,758	1.0
Ann Arbor, MI	200,349	192,221	-4.0	196,082	185,271	-5.5
Athens, GA	99,032	97,723	-1.3	96,483	93,287	-3.3
Atlanta, GA	3,128,881	3,107,968	-0.6	3,045,413	2,939,513	-3.4
Austin, TX	1,255,200	1,267,150	0.9	1,224,993	1,202,103	-1.8
Baton Rouge, LA	417,880	416,461	-0.3	399,191	391,186	-2.0
Boise City, ID	381,230	377,479	-0.9	371,231	360,351	-2.9
Boston, MA[4]	1,694,809	1,609,639	-5.0	1,662,542	1,505,214	-9.4
Boulder, CO	197,746	194,238	-1.7	193,839	180,878	-6.6
Cape Coral, FL	353,248	344,421	-2.5	344,074	327,001	-4.9
Cedar Rapids, IA	148,694	136,358	-8.3	143,975	131,243	-8.8
Charleston, SC	395,683	381,666	-3.5	387,938	365,144	-5.8
Charlotte, NC	1,373,470	1,344,434	-2.1	1,331,441	1,267,112	-4.8
Chicago, IL[2]	3,687,479	3,541,085	-3.9	3,574,836	3,232,803	-9.5
Cincinnati, OH	1,128,063	1,122,791	-0.4	1,090,733	1,069,559	-1.9
Clarksville, TN	118,102	120,516	2.0	113,647	112,488	-1.0
Cleveland, OH	1,049,216	997,566	-4.9	1,009,725	921,287	-8.7
College Station, TX	137,059	137,930	0.6	133,696	130,968	-2.0
Colorado Springs, CO	356,603	365,426	2.4	346,681	333,941	-3.6
Columbia, MO	99,481	97,891	-1.6	97,069	93,768	-3.4
Columbia, SC	403,325	396,126	-1.7	394,519	379,089	-3.9
Columbus, OH	1,105,853	1,087,829	-1.6	1,070,103	1,037,232	-3.0
Dallas, TX[2]	2,719,675	2,742,810	0.8	2,640,356	2,571,653	-2.6
Davenport, IA	194,473	181,630	-6.6	185,909	172,320	-7.3
Denver, CO	1,688,220	1,720,681	1.9	1,650,053	1,575,283	-4.5
Des Moines, IA	366,728	336,296	-8.3	356,630	324,997	-8.8
Durham, NC	305,270	298,535	-2.2	296,522	283,058	-4.5
Edison, NJ[2]	7,008,087	6,694,644	-4.4	6,780,009	6,077,482	-10.3
El Paso, TX	367,648	366,204	-0.3	354,536	336,718	-5.0
Fargo, ND	138,402	143,685	3.8	135,435	139,201	2.7
Fayetteville, NC	148,437	145,648	-1.8	141,883	133,739	-5.7
Fort Collins, CO	209,156	205,612	-1.6	205,003	190,294	-7.1
Fort Wayne, IN	216,998	220,641	1.6	210,942	212,055	0.5
Fort Worth, TX[2]	1,311,941	1,316,316	0.3	1,273,454	1,230,725	-3.3
Grand Rapids, MI	575,885	557,316	-3.2	561,939	534,032	-4.9
Greeley, CO	172,545	174,099	0.9	168,655	159,598	-5.3
Green Bay, WI	172,794	173,847	0.6	167,575	165,813	-1.0
Greensboro, NC	371,920	360,292	-3.1	359,136	336,201	-6.3
Honolulu, HI	452,859	447,861	-1.1	443,191	411,864	-7.0
Houston, TX	3,462,635	3,445,575	-0.4	3,336,616	3,169,170	-5.0
Huntsville, AL	229,898	224,806	-2.2	225,028	218,441	-2.9
Indianapolis, IN	1,060,176	1,101,669	3.9	1,032,445	1,057,751	2.4
Jacksonville, FL	794,684	779,448	-1.9	774,172	742,219	-4.1
Kansas City, MO	1,145,405	1,145,812	0.0	1,109,920	1,089,310	-1.8
Lafayette, LA	210,923	212,283	0.6	200,667	199,150	-0.7
Lakeland, FL	308,057	308,560	0.1	298,597	287,817	-3.6
Las Vegas, NV	1,136,500	1,084,944	-4.5	1,096,609	971,954	-11.3
Lexington, KY	273,326	269,822	-1.2	265,044	256,418	-3.2
Lincoln, NE	186,998	188,745	0.9	182,613	183,294	0.3
Little Rock, AR	354,854	348,009	-1.9	343,794	333,024	-3.1
Los Angeles, CA[2]	5,171,306	4,867,991	-5.8	4,946,895	4,270,635	-13.6
Louisville, KY	674,729	662,325	-1.8	652,752	628,916	-3.6
Madison, WI	390,192	389,396	-0.2	381,370	373,552	-2.0

Table continued on following page.

Metro Area[1]	Civilian Labor Force			Workers Employed		
	Dec. 2019	Dec. 2020	% Chg.	Dec. 2019	Dec. 2020	% Chg.
Manchester, NH[3]	123,691	119,789	-3.1	121,082	115,342	-4.7
Memphis, TN	647,507	668,382	3.2	622,648	618,793	-0.6
Miami, FL[2]	1,377,214	1,301,119	-5.5	1,353,568	1,197,859	-11.5
Midland, TX	110,792	105,257	-5.0	108,522	96,833	-10.7
Milwaukee, WI	811,069	812,442	0.1	785,335	763,907	-2.7
Minneapolis, MN	2,037,880	1,953,111	-4.1	1,976,964	1,864,309	-5.7
Nashville, TN	1,102,127	1,112,635	0.9	1,076,372	1,054,820	-2.0
New Haven, CT[3]	331,537	326,637	-1.4	321,457	303,291	-5.6
New Orleans, LA	596,687	591,186	-0.9	570,042	542,565	-4.8
New York, NY[2]	7,008,087	6,694,644	-4.4	6,780,009	6,077,482	-10.3
Oklahoma City, OK	687,962	693,472	0.8	668,536	660,099	-1.2
Omaha, NE	496,578	495,217	-0.2	483,022	480,259	-0.5
Orlando, FL	1,372,173	1,294,626	-5.6	1,337,648	1,204,999	-9.9
Peoria, IL	173,154	158,961	-8.2	165,096	148,160	-10.2
Philadelphia, PA[2]	1,031,591	989,425	-4.0	980,295	906,853	-7.4
Phoenix, AZ	2,548,680	2,536,430	-0.4	2,456,125	2,361,237	-3.8
Pittsburgh, PA	1,217,975	1,157,008	-5.0	1,162,800	1,080,640	-7.0
Portland, OR	1,332,520	1,316,280	-1.2	1,294,803	1,235,940	-4.5
Providence, RI[3]	695,900	674,373	-3.0	673,941	622,895	-7.5
Provo, UT	319,576	325,243	1.7	313,261	316,139	0.9
Raleigh, NC	731,065	715,982	-2.0	709,901	678,982	-4.3
Reno, NV	261,692	251,522	-3.8	254,486	238,896	-6.1
Richmond, VA	692,884	665,116	-4.0	675,329	631,884	-6.4
Riverside, CA	2,087,383	2,086,402	0.0	2,014,602	1,896,009	-5.8
Rochester, MN	125,263	121,785	-2.7	121,567	117,057	-3.7
Sacramento, CA	1,104,616	1,096,884	-0.7	1,069,620	1,010,465	-5.5
Salt Lake City, UT	679,607	687,168	1.1	665,544	663,455	-0.3
San Antonio, TX	1,218,568	1,213,928	-0.3	1,184,374	1,136,070	-4.0
San Diego, CA	1,597,099	1,593,875	-0.2	1,552,857	1,466,461	-5.5
San Francisco, CA[2]	1,054,065	1,010,523	-4.1	1,034,791	948,543	-8.3
San Jose, CA	1,090,183	1,071,686	-1.7	1,065,627	1,007,069	-5.5
Santa Rosa, CA	259,689	250,632	-3.4	253,575	234,440	-7.5
Savannah, GA	187,692	190,082	1.2	182,609	179,365	-1.7
Seattle, WA[2]	1,724,567	1,722,800	-0.1	1,683,121	1,619,303	-3.7
Sioux Falls, SD	155,466	153,813	-1.0	150,743	149,521	-0.8
Springfield, IL	106,114	102,509	-3.4	102,129	96,019	-5.9
Tallahassee, FL	195,372	185,262	-5.1	190,212	175,456	-7.7
Tampa, FL	1,566,692	1,540,183	-1.6	1,525,133	1,459,839	-4.2
Tucson, AZ	504,172	497,081	-1.4	483,909	460,365	-4.8
Tulsa, OK	481,673	474,408	-1.5	466,612	447,916	-4.0
Tuscaloosa, AL	120,183	116,579	-3.0	117,420	111,848	-4.7
Virginia Beach, VA	858,173	834,317	-2.7	834,872	790,145	-5.3
Washington, DC[2]	2,779,621	2,686,651	-3.3	2,705,388	2,537,166	-6.2
Wichita, KS	315,547	315,051	-0.1	305,590	301,566	-1.3
Winston-Salem, NC	329,944	323,658	-1.9	319,404	304,539	-4.6
U.S.	164,007,000	160,017,000	-2.4	158,504,000	149,613,000	-5.6

Note: Data is not seasonally adjusted and covers workers 16 years of age and older; (1) Figures cover the Metropolitan Statistical Area (MSA) except where noted. See Appendix B for areas included; (2) Metropolitan Division; (3) New England City and Town Area; (4) New England City and Town Area Division
Source: Bureau of Labor Statistics, Local Area Unemployment Statistics

Unemployment Rate: City

City	2020											
	Jan.	Feb.	Mar.	Apr.	May	Jun.	Jul.	Aug.	Sep.	Oct.	Nov.	Dec.
Albuquerque, NM	4.4	4.4	5.5	12.8	9.4	9.1	13.2	11.2	9.5	7.5	6.3	7.4
Allentown, PA	6.6	6.6	8.2	20.1	18.3	19.8	19.0	16.9	12.9	12.1	10.7	9.9
Anchorage, AK	5.1	4.5	4.7	13.9	12.3	12.0	10.8	6.5	6.4	5.3	6.0	5.5
Ann Arbor, MI	2.0	1.8	1.9	12.4	11.6	8.9	6.6	5.7	5.0	3.3	2.8	3.0
Athens, GA	3.5	3.5	4.7	12.2	9.0	7.7	7.9	5.8	5.9	4.3	5.1	5.2
Atlanta, GA	3.6	3.7	5.4	13.4	11.9	11.0	10.6	8.6	8.4	6.1	7.4	7.0
Austin, TX	2.6	2.5	3.6	12.5	11.6	7.4	6.9	5.6	6.4	4.9	5.7	4.9
Baton Rouge, LA	5.7	4.1	6.2	14.7	15.0	11.6	11.3	9.1	8.8	10.1	9.2	7.7
Boise City, ID	2.8	2.4	2.3	12.6	9.6	5.9	5.2	4.0	5.8	5.3	4.8	4.3
Boston, MA	2.7	2.6	2.4	14.6	16.6	19.3	18.2	12.9	11.1	7.7	6.6	7.3
Boulder, CO	2.1	2.4	4.2	9.4	8.1	9.6	6.5	5.4	4.9	4.9	4.7	6.5
Cape Coral, FL	3.2	3.0	4.4	16.2	14.0	10.0	11.0	7.2	6.0	5.2	5.2	4.8
Cedar Rapids, IA	4.0	3.5	4.1	14.2	12.9	11.3	9.3	10.1	6.8	4.7	4.9	4.3
Charleston, SC	2.2	2.3	2.5	14.6	14.0	9.9	9.7	7.1	5.0	3.9	3.9	4.1
Charlotte, NC	3.8	3.5	4.0	13.0	13.9	8.8	10.2	8.0	8.1	6.8	6.7	6.3
Chicago, IL	3.7	3.5	5.0	18.7	17.2	18.6	15.2	15.5	14.4	10.5	8.6	10.0
Cincinnati, OH	4.7	4.3	4.7	15.1	13.7	12.7	11.1	11.2	10.0	7.5	6.4	6.0
Clarksville, TN	4.4	4.3	3.8	17.2	11.3	11.2	11.4	9.9	7.3	8.4	5.8	7.4
Cleveland, OH	5.9	6.4	9.0	26.1	21.9	19.4	17.3	15.9	15.3	10.3	9.0	9.1
College Station, TX	2.8	2.6	3.7	8.2	8.1	5.9	5.3	4.2	4.7	3.9	4.9	4.4
Colorado Springs, CO	3.3	3.4	6.1	13.0	10.0	10.7	7.1	6.4	6.1	6.1	6.2	9.0
Columbia, MO	3.1	2.4	2.5	6.6	6.7	5.8	5.2	5.2	3.0	2.7	2.9	4.3
Columbia, SC	3.1	3.1	3.1	8.9	10.2	9.1	9.1	6.9	5.1	4.4	4.6	5.1
Columbus, OH	4.1	3.7	4.1	14.6	12.4	11.3	9.8	9.8	8.8	6.5	5.7	5.2
Dallas, TX	3.4	3.3	4.8	13.0	12.8	8.9	8.4	7.1	8.4	6.9	8.0	7.1
Davenport, IA	4.9	4.2	4.7	15.4	15.0	12.1	10.3	9.6	7.0	5.2	5.3	5.1
Denver, CO	2.8	2.8	5.3	13.4	11.5	12.0	8.8	7.9	7.3	7.3	7.2	9.3
Des Moines, IA	4.6	4.0	4.4	14.6	14.0	12.2	9.5	9.1	6.6	4.6	4.5	4.4
Durham, NC	3.4	3.1	3.7	10.1	11.4	7.6	8.8	6.7	6.8	5.7	5.7	5.6
Edison, NJ	2.8	2.7	2.4	11.7	11.3	12.7	11.0	8.4	4.9	5.8	7.4	5.3
El Paso, TX	3.8	3.6	5.1	14.5	14.0	9.1	8.4	6.9	8.1	6.7	8.9	7.7
Fargo, ND	2.5	2.3	2.3	9.6	8.5	7.0	5.5	4.0	3.0	3.1	3.1	3.2
Fayetteville, NC	5.8	5.2	6.0	15.7	16.8	10.8	12.9	10.1	10.4	9.0	9.0	8.9
Fort Collins, CO	2.4	2.5	4.4	11.5	8.7	9.3	6.2	5.5	5.1	5.0	5.0	7.5
Fort Wayne, IN	3.6	3.5	3.2	20.6	14.9	12.9	9.6	7.7	6.8	6.0	5.6	4.5
Fort Worth, TX	3.5	3.3	5.0	13.5	13.1	8.9	8.3	7.1	8.1	6.7	7.9	7.0
Grand Rapids, MI	3.8	3.2	3.3	26.7	22.0	16.0	11.5	10.0	8.7	5.9	5.2	5.7
Greeley, CO	3.1	3.2	5.6	10.3	9.3	11.2	8.4	7.9	7.5	7.3	7.7	10.0
Green Bay, WI	4.2	3.8	3.2	14.6	14.4	10.2	8.1	7.0	5.1	5.7	4.9	5.1
Greensboro, NC	4.4	4.0	4.6	15.3	15.8	10.0	11.6	9.1	9.0	7.7	7.7	7.4
Honolulu, HI	2.8	2.5	2.1	20.5	20.8	12.2	11.5	11.0	13.6	12.4	9.1	8.0
Houston, TX	3.9	3.7	5.4	14.4	14.1	10.0	9.8	8.4	9.8	7.7	8.8	7.9
Huntsville, AL	2.8	2.4	2.6	11.8	8.6	7.5	7.8	5.6	6.4	5.3	3.8	3.4
Indianapolis, IN	3.4	3.2	3.1	14.0	11.3	12.6	9.9	8.4	7.7	7.0	6.4	5.1
Jacksonville, FL	3.3	3.1	4.6	11.5	11.0	8.4	9.7	6.4	5.5	5.6	5.7	5.5
Kansas City, MO	4.1	3.7	4.1	11.7	12.3	9.2	9.0	9.0	5.7	4.9	5.0	6.7
Lafayette, LA	5.4	4.0	6.1	13.5	12.8	9.3	9.1	7.2	7.0	7.9	7.0	5.9
Lakeland, FL	3.8	3.5	4.9	11.4	12.0	9.4	10.7	7.3	6.4	6.5	6.9	6.5
Las Vegas, NV	4.0	3.9	7.3	32.1	27.1	16.7	15.8	14.9	13.9	13.5	11.7	10.3
Lexington, KY	3.5	3.1	4.1	14.1	9.0	4.5	4.6	6.7	4.8	6.2	4.5	5.1
Lincoln, NE	2.8	2.7	3.7	9.6	5.3	5.9	5.2	3.9	3.3	2.7	2.7	2.9
Little Rock, AR	3.7	3.6	4.6	12.0	11.7	10.4	10.1	10.4	9.8	7.9	7.7	5.0
Los Angeles, CA	4.5	4.6	6.6	20.7	21.0	20.0	18.8	17.1	15.5	11.8	10.6	10.6
Louisville, KY	4.1	3.7	4.7	16.5	11.7	5.3	5.3	7.7	5.6	7.4	5.4	5.7
Madison, WI	2.7	2.3	1.9	10.4	9.7	7.8	6.2	5.4	3.9	4.3	3.7	3.9

Table continued on following page.

City	2020											
	Jan.	Feb.	Mar.	Apr.	May	Jun.	Jul.	Aug.	Sep.	Oct.	Nov.	Dec.
Manchester, NH	3.0	3.0	2.7	20.0	18.4	10.5	9.2	7.8	6.7	4.5	4.3	4.4
Memphis, TN	4.9	4.9	4.2	14.5	12.9	15.3	17.4	16.3	12.5	13.1	8.7	9.8
Miami, FL	1.4	1.4	3.7	12.4	12.8	12.5	15.4	8.6	13.6	9.3	8.4	7.7
Midland, TX	2.3	2.3	3.3	9.9	12.3	9.2	9.1	7.8	9.2	7.7	8.8	7.6
Milwaukee, WI	4.9	4.7	4.1	15.8	15.7	13.1	11.4	10.1	8.2	9.2	7.9	8.3
Minneapolis, MN	2.5	2.6	2.8	10.0	11.6	11.4	10.5	10.3	7.8	5.2	4.6	4.8
Nashville, TN	2.7	2.7	2.4	16.1	12.3	12.0	12.3	10.6	7.7	6.9	4.7	5.7
New Haven, CT	4.9	4.8	4.0	7.0	8.8	10.6	11.8	9.7	9.1	7.5	10.0	9.5
New Orleans, LA	5.5	4.2	6.3	22.2	20.7	15.9	15.1	12.6	12.4	15.1	13.6	11.2
New York, NY	3.8	3.8	4.2	15.5	20.2	18.7	18.8	14.9	14.7	11.7	11.7	11.6
Oklahoma City, OK	2.9	2.7	2.7	15.8	13.7	7.2	7.6	5.9	5.5	6.3	6.0	5.2
Omaha, NE	3.5	3.3	4.8	10.8	6.6	7.5	6.8	5.2	4.5	3.5	3.3	3.5
Orlando, FL	2.8	2.7	4.0	18.2	21.7	16.9	17.0	12.0	10.4	9.0	8.6	7.8
Peoria, IL	5.2	4.3	4.0	19.2	18.0	16.5	13.8	13.2	11.8	8.5	8.6	8.8
Philadelphia, PA	6.0	5.9	7.0	17.0	16.4	18.2	18.1	15.8	12.0	10.8	9.7	9.3
Phoenix, AZ	4.0	3.9	5.5	12.9	8.8	10.5	11.3	6.5	6.9	8.4	8.2	7.6
Pittsburgh, PA	4.7	4.6	5.6	15.2	13.6	13.8	14.6	12.2	8.9	7.7	6.9	6.7
Portland, OR	3.2	3.2	3.4	16.2	15.9	14.3	13.1	10.7	9.0	7.5	6.4	6.6
Providence, RI	4.7	4.7	5.9	19.5	18.7	15.2	14.9	16.7	13.3	8.5	8.5	8.7
Provo, UT	2.3	2.3	3.2	6.4	5.3	4.0	3.2	3.0	3.3	2.6	2.8	2.5
Raleigh, NC	3.6	3.3	3.9	12.4	13.2	8.2	9.1	6.9	6.9	5.9	5.9	5.7
Reno, NV	3.4	3.2	5.5	20.9	16.9	9.1	8.5	7.6	7.0	6.5	5.7	5.0
Richmond, VA	3.5	3.2	3.8	14.1	12.1	11.8	12.1	9.5	9.3	7.6	6.5	6.5
Riverside, CA	3.9	3.8	4.8	13.5	13.6	13.4	12.6	9.7	9.4	8.2	7.4	8.4
Rochester, MN	2.3	2.5	2.5	7.2	10.4	9.1	7.5	6.7	4.9	4.0	3.6	3.9
Sacramento, CA	4.0	3.8	4.9	14.5	14.5	14.0	13.1	10.4	10.2	8.7	8.0	9.2
Salt Lake City, UT	2.6	2.6	4.1	12.8	10.9	7.4	6.1	5.3	5.4	4.2	4.2	3.6
San Antonio, TX	3.2	3.1	4.5	13.8	13.0	8.5	8.3	6.9	7.9	6.3	7.4	6.5
San Diego, CA	3.2	3.1	4.0	14.7	14.9	13.7	12.2	9.3	8.7	7.1	6.3	7.9
San Francisco, CA	2.3	2.3	3.1	12.6	12.7	12.5	11.1	8.5	8.3	6.7	5.7	6.4
San Jose, CA	2.8	2.7	3.6	13.8	13.1	12.4	10.9	8.4	8.1	6.5	5.7	6.7
Santa Rosa, CA	3.0	2.9	3.8	14.9	13.6	12.2	10.4	8.0	7.7	6.7	6.1	6.9
Savannah, GA	3.7	3.7	5.1	18.5	13.7	11.3	11.0	8.8	8.8	6.3	7.5	7.3
Seattle, WA	2.4	2.2	5.3	13.7	13.2	9.0	7.9	6.8	6.5	4.2	3.9	6.1
Sioux Falls, SD	3.5	3.3	3.1	11.6	10.4	7.3	6.0	4.6	3.7	3.2	3.2	3.0
Springfield, IL	3.8	3.2	2.9	14.9	14.2	13.2	10.5	10.0	9.2	6.5	6.9	7.2
Tallahassee, FL	3.4	3.0	4.4	9.2	9.1	7.8	9.5	6.2	5.3	5.7	6.0	6.0
Tampa, FL	3.1	3.0	4.3	12.6	12.2	9.7	11.6	7.8	6.6	6.4	6.4	6.0
Tucson, AZ	4.7	4.4	6.3	13.8	9.2	10.9	11.7	6.6	7.1	8.7	8.6	8.2
Tulsa, OK	3.2	3.1	3.0	16.2	14.2	7.9	8.6	6.8	6.4	7.4	7.1	6.1
Tuscaloosa, AL	3.2	2.7	3.0	17.9	11.9	10.4	10.6	7.6	8.6	7.0	5.0	4.7
Virginia Beach, VA	2.9	2.6	3.1	12.2	9.4	8.2	7.7	6.0	5.9	4.6	4.2	4.3
Washington, DC	5.0	4.9	5.5	10.6	9.0	9.2	9.5	8.9	8.8	8.2	8.4	8.8
Wichita, KS	4.0	4.1	3.5	19.2	15.6	12.1	12.3	11.6	9.1	7.4	7.0	4.5
Winston-Salem, NC	4.2	3.7	4.3	12.9	13.9	8.8	10.3	8.0	8.2	6.9	6.8	6.7
U.S.	4.0	3.8	4.5	14.4	13.0	11.2	10.5	8.5	7.7	6.6	6.4	6.5

Note: Data is not seasonally adjusted and covers workers 16 years of age and older; All figures are percentages
Source: Bureau of Labor Statistics, Local Area Unemployment Statistics

Unemployment Rate: Metro Area

Metro Area[1]	2020											
	Jan.	Feb.	Mar.	Apr.	May	Jun.	Jul.	Aug.	Sep.	Oct.	Nov.	Dec.
Albuquerque, NM	4.6	4.6	5.7	12.3	9.1	9.0	13.1	11.1	9.5	7.5	6.4	7.3
Allentown, PA	5.0	5.0	5.7	16.2	13.8	14.1	12.8	10.6	7.5	6.9	6.5	6.2
Anchorage, AK	5.7	5.0	5.2	14.3	12.5	12.2	11.0	6.6	6.5	5.3	6.1	5.7
Ann Arbor, MI	2.5	2.2	2.3	14.8	13.9	10.7	8.0	6.9	6.1	4.0	3.4	3.6
Athens, GA	3.2	3.3	4.3	11.1	8.0	6.7	6.7	4.9	4.9	3.7	4.4	4.5
Atlanta, GA	3.2	3.3	4.4	12.7	9.9	8.6	8.6	6.4	6.6	4.6	5.6	5.4
Austin, TX	2.8	2.6	3.8	12.2	11.4	7.3	6.8	5.5	6.3	5.0	5.9	5.1
Baton Rouge, LA	5.1	3.8	5.6	13.0	12.6	9.6	9.2	7.2	7.0	8.0	7.2	6.1
Boise City, ID	3.2	2.7	2.6	12.3	9.2	5.8	5.2	4.1	6.0	5.4	4.9	4.5
Boston, MA[4]	2.7	2.6	2.4	14.2	15.3	16.9	15.5	10.7	9.3	6.7	5.9	6.5
Boulder, CO	2.4	2.4	4.4	9.7	8.3	9.6	6.7	5.8	5.3	5.2	5.1	6.9
Cape Coral, FL	3.1	3.0	4.3	14.6	13.0	9.6	10.7	7.1	5.9	5.4	5.4	5.1
Cedar Rapids, IA	3.8	3.4	3.9	12.5	11.1	9.6	7.9	8.3	5.6	3.8	4.1	3.8
Charleston, SC	2.4	2.5	2.6	12.1	12.2	9.0	9.2	6.9	5.0	4.0	4.0	4.3
Charlotte, NC	3.7	3.4	3.9	12.7	13.2	8.3	9.3	7.1	7.0	5.9	5.9	5.8
Chicago, IL[2]	3.8	3.7	3.9	16.4	15.8	15.7	13.3	13.0	12.2	8.8	8.9	8.7
Cincinnati, OH	4.3	4.0	4.4	14.1	11.2	9.0	7.6	7.9	6.8	5.6	4.8	4.7
Clarksville, TN	4.6	4.4	4.3	16.1	10.5	8.8	9.0	8.5	6.2	7.5	5.4	6.7
Cleveland, OH	5.0	5.4	6.2	21.8	17.3	12.7	9.2	8.1	8.8	7.2	7.1	7.6
College Station, TX	2.9	2.7	3.9	8.7	8.7	6.3	5.8	4.7	5.5	4.5	5.5	5.0
Colorado Springs, CO	3.3	3.4	6.2	12.6	9.7	10.5	6.9	6.2	5.9	6.0	6.0	8.6
Columbia, MO	3.2	2.5	2.6	6.5	6.5	5.7	5.1	5.1	2.9	2.6	2.8	4.2
Columbia, SC	2.7	2.8	2.8	8.5	9.3	7.8	7.8	6.0	4.4	3.7	3.8	4.3
Columbus, OH	4.2	3.8	4.2	13.7	11.0	9.9	8.3	8.3	7.4	5.5	4.9	4.7
Dallas, TX[2]	3.3	3.2	4.6	12.6	12.1	8.1	7.5	6.2	7.3	5.9	7.1	6.2
Davenport, IA	4.7	4.0	4.0	15.3	14.4	11.5	9.4	8.5	7.1	5.0	5.0	5.1
Denver, CO	2.7	2.8	5.2	12.3	10.5	11.1	7.9	7.0	6.5	6.5	6.4	8.5
Des Moines, IA	3.5	3.0	3.4	11.8	10.9	9.2	7.2	6.7	4.8	3.3	3.5	3.4
Durham, NC	3.5	3.1	3.7	9.6	10.6	6.9	7.9	5.9	6.0	5.2	5.2	5.2
Edison, NJ[2]	3.8	3.6	3.8	15.1	16.3	18.3	17.6	14.0	10.7	10.5	10.4	9.2
El Paso, TX	4.0	3.8	5.4	14.9	14.6	9.5	8.8	7.3	8.6	7.1	9.4	8.1
Fargo, ND	2.8	2.6	2.5	7.7	7.2	6.4	5.1	3.9	3.0	2.9	3.0	3.1
Fayetteville, NC	5.4	4.9	5.6	14.6	15.4	9.8	11.6	9.1	9.3	8.2	8.3	8.2
Fort Collins, CO	2.5	2.6	4.7	11.1	8.6	9.2	6.2	5.6	5.2	5.1	5.2	7.4
Fort Wayne, IN	3.4	3.3	3.0	19.4	13.5	11.2	8.2	6.5	5.7	5.1	4.8	3.9
Fort Worth, TX[2]	3.3	3.2	4.7	13.1	12.6	8.3	7.7	6.5	7.5	6.1	7.3	6.5
Grand Rapids, MI	2.9	2.5	2.6	21.5	17.1	12.0	8.4	7.2	6.3	4.2	3.7	4.2
Greeley, CO	2.7	2.9	5.1	9.9	8.6	10.1	7.3	6.6	6.3	6.2	6.4	8.3
Green Bay, WI	4.0	3.7	3.1	12.9	12.1	8.6	6.7	5.6	4.1	4.8	4.2	4.6
Greensboro, NC	4.3	3.9	4.5	14.8	14.5	9.0	10.2	7.8	7.9	6.9	6.9	6.7
Honolulu, HI	2.8	2.5	2.1	20.5	20.8	12.2	11.5	11.0	13.6	12.4	9.1	8.0
Houston, TX	4.1	3.9	5.5	14.3	13.9	9.7	9.5	8.1	9.6	7.7	8.9	8.0
Huntsville, AL	2.7	2.3	2.5	10.7	7.4	6.4	6.4	4.5	5.1	4.2	3.1	2.8
Indianapolis, IN	3.2	2.9	2.8	13.3	10.2	10.6	7.8	6.6	6.0	5.4	5.0	4.0
Jacksonville, FL	3.1	3.0	4.3	11.2	10.4	7.8	8.8	5.7	4.8	4.8	5.0	4.8
Kansas City, MO	3.7	3.4	3.5	11.3	10.8	7.8	7.6	7.3	5.0	4.4	4.4	4.9
Lafayette, LA	5.7	4.3	6.4	13.0	12.4	9.2	9.1	7.4	7.3	8.2	7.3	6.2
Lakeland, FL	3.7	3.5	4.9	14.0	17.6	13.6	13.2	9.2	7.9	7.1	7.0	6.7
Las Vegas, NV	3.9	3.9	7.2	34.0	28.8	17.8	16.6	15.6	14.6	13.7	11.8	10.4
Lexington, KY	3.7	3.3	4.2	15.2	9.1	4.4	4.5	6.5	4.7	6.1	4.4	5.0
Lincoln, NE	2.7	2.6	3.7	9.3	5.2	5.7	5.0	3.8	3.2	2.7	2.7	2.9
Little Rock, AR	3.7	3.6	4.6	10.9	10.2	9.0	8.3	8.4	7.8	6.4	6.4	4.3
Los Angeles, CA[2]	4.9	4.7	5.6	18.2	18.8	17.9	18.2	17.5	13.2	12.0	11.9	12.3
Louisville, KY	3.9	3.5	4.3	16.8	11.8	6.5	5.6	7.0	5.3	6.5	4.9	5.0
Madison, WI	3.1	2.8	2.3	11.1	9.7	7.5	6.0	5.1	3.7	4.2	3.7	4.1

Table continued on following page.

Metro Area[1]	2020											
	Jan.	Feb.	Mar.	Apr.	May	Jun.	Jul.	Aug.	Sep.	Oct.	Nov.	Dec.
Manchester, NH[3]	2.8	2.8	2.5	17.4	15.8	9.0	7.9	6.5	5.6	3.8	3.7	3.7
Memphis, TN	4.4	4.4	3.8	12.8	10.7	11.9	13.1	11.9	9.2	9.6	6.7	7.4
Miami, FL[2]	1.8	1.6	2.2	10.3	10.3	10.1	15.2	9.1	12.6	8.5	8.2	7.9
Midland, TX	2.4	2.3	3.4	10.1	12.6	9.5	9.5	8.1	9.5	8.0	9.3	8.0
Milwaukee, WI	4.0	3.8	3.2	13.6	12.9	10.2	8.6	7.5	5.9	6.6	5.7	6.0
Minneapolis, MN	3.1	3.1	3.1	9.2	10.1	9.2	8.2	7.8	5.9	4.2	4.0	4.5
Nashville, TN	2.8	2.8	2.5	15.2	11.1	10.2	10.0	8.4	6.1	6.1	4.2	5.2
New Haven, CT[3]	4.2	4.1	3.4	7.2	8.5	9.3	9.7	7.7	7.1	5.5	7.4	7.1
New Orleans, LA	5.2	3.9	5.9	19.0	17.4	12.8	11.9	9.7	9.4	11.2	10.0	8.2
New York, NY[2]	3.8	3.6	3.8	15.1	16.3	18.3	17.6	14.0	10.7	10.5	10.4	9.2
Oklahoma City, OK	2.9	2.7	2.7	14.8	12.9	6.9	7.1	5.6	5.1	5.9	5.6	4.8
Omaha, NE	3.2	3.1	4.3	10.0	6.4	6.9	6.0	4.6	3.9	3.0	2.9	3.0
Orlando, FL	3.0	2.9	4.2	16.8	21.1	16.1	15.4	10.8	9.2	7.8	7.4	6.9
Peoria, IL	5.0	4.2	3.8	17.7	15.4	13.5	10.8	9.8	8.6	6.1	6.3	6.8
Philadelphia, PA[2]	5.5	5.4	6.4	16.3	15.5	17.0	16.7	14.5	10.9	9.8	8.8	8.3
Phoenix, AZ	4.0	3.8	5.4	12.5	8.3	9.8	10.4	5.9	6.2	7.4	7.4	6.9
Pittsburgh, PA	5.2	5.2	6.1	16.4	13.6	12.9	13.1	10.9	7.9	6.9	6.3	6.6
Portland, OR	3.4	3.5	3.6	14.2	14.0	11.8	11.2	9.1	7.9	6.6	5.8	6.1
Providence, RI[3]	4.1	4.1	4.7	18.2	16.7	13.7	12.7	12.7	10.1	6.5	6.8	7.6
Provo, UT	2.5	2.5	3.6	7.9	6.2	4.4	3.6	3.4	3.8	3.1	3.3	2.8
Raleigh, NC	3.5	3.2	3.7	11.0	11.5	7.0	7.9	6.0	6.1	5.2	5.2	5.2
Reno, NV	3.4	3.2	5.6	20.4	16.0	8.7	8.2	7.3	6.7	6.3	5.6	5.0
Richmond, VA	3.1	2.8	3.4	11.2	9.4	8.9	8.8	6.9	6.8	5.5	4.9	5.0
Riverside, CA	4.1	4.0	5.2	14.7	15.1	14.3	13.4	10.5	10.2	8.7	7.9	9.1
Rochester, MN	3.1	3.1	3.1	6.9	9.3	8.1	6.6	5.8	4.2	3.5	3.4	3.9
Sacramento, CA	3.9	3.8	4.8	14.0	13.7	12.8	11.6	9.0	8.7	7.3	6.7	7.9
Salt Lake City, UT	2.6	2.7	4.0	11.2	9.4	6.4	5.3	4.7	5.2	4.1	4.2	3.5
San Antonio, TX	3.2	3.1	4.5	13.3	12.7	8.3	8.0	6.6	7.7	6.2	7.3	6.4
San Diego, CA	3.3	3.2	4.2	15.0	15.2	13.8	12.4	9.5	8.9	7.5	6.6	8.0
San Francisco, CA[2]	2.2	2.2	3.0	12.1	12.0	11.8	10.3	7.9	7.7	6.3	5.4	6.1
San Jose, CA	2.7	2.7	3.5	12.0	11.3	10.8	9.5	7.3	7.0	5.8	5.2	6.0
Santa Rosa, CA	2.9	2.8	3.7	14.5	13.0	11.6	10.0	7.5	7.2	6.0	5.5	6.5
Savannah, GA	3.3	3.3	4.4	15.3	10.8	8.6	8.5	6.5	6.7	4.7	5.6	5.6
Seattle, WA[2]	2.7	2.6	5.3	16.2	12.6	10.7	9.5	7.9	7.4	6.5	6.1	6.0
Sioux Falls, SD	3.4	3.2	3.0	10.5	9.4	6.7	5.6	4.3	3.4	3.0	3.0	2.8
Springfield, IL	3.9	3.2	2.9	14.2	13.1	11.7	9.2	8.7	7.8	5.5	5.9	6.3
Tallahassee, FL	3.2	2.9	4.2	8.3	8.1	7.0	8.4	5.5	4.7	5.0	5.4	5.3
Tampa, FL	3.1	3.0	4.3	13.2	12.2	9.0	10.2	6.7	5.7	5.4	5.5	5.2
Tucson, AZ	4.5	4.2	6.0	12.8	8.4	9.9	10.6	5.9	6.3	7.8	7.7	7.4
Tulsa, OK	3.2	3.0	3.0	15.1	12.9	7.1	7.6	6.1	5.7	6.6	6.4	5.6
Tuscaloosa, AL	2.9	2.5	2.8	16.6	10.8	9.0	9.1	6.3	7.1	6.0	4.4	4.1
Virginia Beach, VA	3.3	3.0	3.6	12.1	10.0	9.2	9.2	7.4	7.2	5.8	5.1	5.3
Washington, DC[2]	3.1	3.0	3.4	10.0	8.9	8.4	8.1	6.9	6.9	6.4	5.7	5.6
Wichita, KS	3.8	3.8	3.3	17.7	14.1	10.8	11.0	10.3	8.0	6.6	6.5	4.3
Winston-Salem, NC	3.9	3.5	4.1	12.7	12.7	7.7	8.8	6.6	6.8	5.9	6.0	5.9
U.S.	4.0	3.8	4.5	14.4	13.0	11.2	10.5	8.5	7.7	6.6	6.4	6.5

Note: Data is not seasonally adjusted and covers workers 16 years of age and older; All figures are percentages; (1) Figures cover the Metropolitan Statistical Area (MSA) except where noted. See Appendix B for areas included; (2) Metropolitan Division; (3) New England City and Town Area; (4) New England City and Town Area Division
Source: Bureau of Labor Statistics, Local Area Unemployment Statistics

Average Hourly Wages: Occupations A – C

Metro Area[1]	Accountants/ Auditors	Automotive Mechanics	Book-keepers	Carpenters	Cashiers	Computer Program-mers	Computer Systems Analysts
Albuquerque, NM	33.46	21.98	20.06	20.67	11.88	38.33	39.87
Allentown, PA	36.61	21.48	20.16	23.11	11.53	40.11	42.51
Anchorage, AK	39.02	22.66	23.63	33.12	14.55	44.08	41.47
Ann Arbor, MI	36.68	30.73	21.60	27.75	12.05	38.47	40.58
Athens, GA	31.72	20.47	17.40	19.07	10.70	32.83	43.69
Atlanta, GA	42.18	23.13	21.75	20.56	11.10	44.52	45.29
Austin, TX	37.28	26.39	20.95	19.33	12.25	42.42	41.18
Baton Rouge, LA	31.10	22.33	19.99	24.74	10.14	40.35	39.72
Boise City, ID	36.48	21.60	20.17	18.39	12.59	32.61	45.73
Boston, MA[2]	43.60	24.14	25.10	31.31	14.22	49.27	50.79
Boulder, CO	40.09	24.42	22.25	25.30	14.13	39.10	48.44
Cape Coral, FL	31.26	21.32	20.50	19.97	11.99	42.99	37.54
Cedar Rapids, IA	35.32	22.27	19.62	24.33	11.59	39.02	40.35
Charleston, SC	32.87	23.69	18.26	28.28	11.63	39.15	41.06
Charlotte, NC	42.38	23.40	20.71	19.73	10.98	48.79	48.01
Chicago, IL	37.81	24.87	22.39	34.74	12.61	49.84	45.00
Cincinnati, OH	36.81	22.26	20.71	24.06	11.71	44.99	47.80
Clarksville, TN	30.21	18.81	18.23	18.80	11.06	n/a	36.97
Cleveland, OH	36.64	22.16	20.46	25.76	12.11	39.60	40.53
College Station, TX	29.37	25.23	17.40	20.32	11.70	48.32	38.11
Colorado Springs, CO	36.33	25.52	19.93	24.48	13.94	34.84	49.76
Columbia, MO	29.02	20.93	17.87	24.13	11.10	30.68	38.55
Columbia, SC	29.39	21.06	17.97	23.15	10.58	43.48	37.52
Columbus, OH	36.98	21.18	21.79	24.76	11.99	44.57	44.18
Dallas, TX	40.31	23.53	21.33	19.85	11.39	53.87	49.58
Davenport, IA	32.27	20.88	19.51	25.19	11.12	42.62	44.10
Denver, CO	42.62	24.69	22.73	25.92	14.48	43.53	51.32
Des Moines, IA	37.04	24.11	21.99	22.21	11.87	35.53	42.70
Durham, NC	39.14	22.27	21.86	19.68	10.92	47.50	45.42
Edison, NJ	50.83	24.31	24.50	34.16	14.25	46.28	55.05
El Paso, TX	31.64	16.30	16.08	16.69	10.53	40.15	37.37
Fargo, ND	32.72	24.61	20.00	23.07	12.34	36.01	42.32
Fayetteville, NC	35.70	17.98	17.77	19.91	10.55	30.98	38.38
Fort Collins, CO	35.94	24.03	21.32	23.09	14.29	35.42	42.76
Fort Wayne, IN	34.36	18.77	19.67	20.21	11.30	25.61	37.13
Fort Worth, TX	40.31	23.53	21.33	19.85	11.39	53.87	49.58
Grand Rapids, MI	33.78	21.17	19.56	23.43	11.96	34.14	37.61
Greeley, CO	39.19	25.37	20.19	22.97	13.76	n/a	58.55
Green Bay, WI	33.64	20.09	20.68	26.03	11.26	37.56	39.08
Greensboro, NC	38.57	22.14	19.86	17.69	10.55	40.70	45.51
Honolulu, HI	31.74	25.73	21.44	39.88	13.68	39.65	38.51
Houston, TX	40.30	22.98	21.66	21.53	11.62	49.83	59.65
Huntsville, AL	35.97	23.40	20.47	20.55	10.97	41.94	49.70
Indianapolis, IN	37.22	21.50	20.88	24.11	11.33	45.99	40.06
Jacksonville, FL	32.52	20.49	20.33	19.12	11.34	38.38	37.87
Kansas City, MO	35.61	23.49	20.58	28.51	12.02	42.04	36.99
Lafayette, LA	31.83	18.68	18.14	19.37	9.98	35.29	39.77
Lakeland, FL	36.15	22.44	18.64	18.81	11.96	31.46	37.47
Las Vegas, NV	33.27	21.01	20.44	29.29	12.02	41.98	43.58
Lexington, KY	34.06	20.09	19.10	22.60	11.15	37.18	39.27
Lincoln, NE	33.35	22.34	19.37	19.78	11.87	36.02	36.79
Little Rock, AR	32.28	20.29	18.68	20.70	11.78	37.05	35.10
Los Angeles, CA	40.22	25.83	24.20	32.37	14.82	47.38	53.54
Louisville, KY	36.49	20.16	19.65	25.97	11.25	36.56	41.09
Madison, WI	35.56	23.85	21.38	27.06	12.20	51.95	44.21

Table continued on following page.

Metro Area[1]	Accountants/ Auditors	Automotive Mechanics	Book-keepers	Carpenters	Cashiers	Computer Programmers	Computer Systems Analysts
Manchester, NH[2]	36.21	23.60	20.53	22.51	11.60	33.07	45.34
Memphis, TN	34.52	25.99	21.21	21.37	10.80	41.07	39.88
Miami, FL	38.52	21.77	21.28	20.93	11.76	41.74	44.55
Midland, TX	49.58	30.42	23.19	20.45	13.31	57.40	n/a
Milwaukee, WI	36.97	21.67	21.43	27.70	11.60	40.27	40.47
Minneapolis, MN	37.42	23.75	22.79	27.95	13.27	43.22	49.04
Nashville, TN	34.65	21.80	21.53	22.23	11.54	45.25	40.00
New Haven, CT[2]	40.03	23.80	23.77	29.32	12.79	47.26	46.09
New Orleans, LA	33.52	19.89	18.98	22.06	10.47	49.80	46.68
New York, NY	50.83	24.31	24.50	34.16	14.25	46.28	55.05
Oklahoma City, OK	38.02	23.73	19.72	20.80	11.03	38.30	38.44
Omaha, NE	35.78	22.47	20.56	19.96	12.22	38.65	41.38
Orlando, FL	35.16	19.62	20.04	21.12	11.70	41.55	44.36
Peoria, IL	38.38	20.73	18.98	31.69	11.40	39.55	45.55
Philadelphia, PA	41.21	22.53	22.28	30.86	11.77	48.82	50.50
Phoenix, AZ	36.29	22.21	21.58	23.50	13.39	44.18	44.56
Pittsburgh, PA	35.65	20.59	19.36	28.43	11.02	41.89	41.16
Portland, OR	38.49	24.48	22.58	29.13	14.68	45.18	48.24
Providence, RI[2]	41.50	21.85	22.70	25.77	13.17	51.83	47.51
Provo, UT	30.23	23.85	19.47	21.85	12.14	42.53	40.09
Raleigh, NC	36.22	23.93	20.23	20.64	11.17	47.69	47.56
Reno, NV	31.29	25.37	21.43	25.23	12.11	44.10	43.87
Richmond, VA	39.89	24.49	21.27	22.33	11.07	45.10	47.11
Riverside, CA	36.22	24.02	22.43	26.58	14.92	43.59	43.34
Rochester, MN	33.90	21.22	20.99	26.07	12.84	29.59	41.46
Sacramento, CA	40.32	26.48	22.61	28.08	15.49	39.13	50.27
Salt Lake City, UT	33.91	21.58	20.00	22.62	12.06	41.48	37.30
San Antonio, TX	35.76	20.68	20.96	20.42	11.81	46.43	47.72
San Diego, CA	43.00	25.61	23.56	28.60	14.50	48.42	45.56
San Francisco, CA	48.60	31.07	26.61	36.44	16.58	60.30	60.27
San Jose, CA	49.48	30.53	27.26	31.80	17.29	54.58	64.41
Santa Rosa, CA	44.34	28.46	26.79	35.33	15.89	44.87	43.31
Savannah, GA	33.08	25.13	20.20	22.91	10.51	38.06	49.67
Seattle, WA	42.21	26.17	24.43	33.25	16.50	n/a	54.00
Sioux Falls, SD	34.97	20.87	17.77	18.73	12.24	28.31	37.94
Springfield, IL	34.50	21.31	20.55	29.86	11.24	47.45	45.09
Tallahassee, FL	27.29	21.76	19.47	20.05	11.07	31.03	29.13
Tampa, FL	37.28	21.62	20.88	19.31	11.46	38.78	42.77
Tucson, AZ	34.29	21.59	18.88	20.44	13.57	42.88	41.83
Tulsa, OK	36.62	19.11	21.11	24.67	11.12	40.37	45.55
Tuscaloosa, AL	34.36	20.19	17.36	19.72	10.43	30.43	43.48
Virginia Beach, VA	36.21	25.63	20.21	20.84	11.14	n/a	47.27
Washington, DC	47.13	27.27	24.81	24.98	13.22	50.51	56.09
Wichita, KS	33.82	18.41	17.96	18.76	11.17	39.71	36.62
Winston-Salem, NC	35.91	20.17	19.63	19.79	10.16	42.82	44.65

Notes: (1) Figures cover the Metropolitan Statistical Area (MSA) except where noted. See Appendix B for areas included; (2) New England City and Town Area; n/a not available
Source: Bureau of Labor Statistics, May 2020 Metro Area Occupational Employment and Wage Estimates

Average Hourly Wages: Occupations C – E

Metro Area	Comp. User Support Specialists	Construction Laborers	Cooks, Restaurant	Customer Service Reps.	Dentists	Electricians	Engineers, Electrical
Albuquerque, NM	21.74	16.94	12.77	16.16	77.97	23.25	58.20
Allentown, PA	27.07	21.92	13.74	17.59	66.64	27.36	50.31
Anchorage, AK	29.69	26.02	14.62	19.54	101.03	33.57	54.83
Ann Arbor, MI	23.79	22.53	15.59	18.78	71.19	33.74	42.05
Athens, GA	21.34	14.82	12.71	15.83	n/a	26.34	51.49
Atlanta, GA	28.15	16.51	13.35	17.73	77.08	27.77	47.62
Austin, TX	25.88	15.85	13.15	17.26	77.48	25.85	52.09
Baton Rouge, LA	24.19	17.93	12.04	16.40	91.40	26.16	53.11
Boise City, ID	24.03	16.83	12.67	16.30	105.24	24.69	48.27
Boston, MA[2]	33.22	28.35	16.99	22.68	100.75	34.07	55.65
Boulder, CO	30.99	18.47	15.58	20.26	107.71	26.35	52.75
Cape Coral, FL	23.30	16.84	15.40	16.51	83.47	21.88	53.83
Cedar Rapids, IA	20.83	19.76	11.87	19.74	55.16	29.19	51.76
Charleston, SC	26.66	16.83	13.15	18.77	70.75	22.35	47.79
Charlotte, NC	25.75	15.96	13.03	18.80	83.93	22.29	48.47
Chicago, IL	26.71	32.05	14.66	20.08	92.31	40.50	46.52
Cincinnati, OH	24.74	22.97	12.99	17.97	103.00	23.55	43.84
Clarksville, TN	20.86	15.26	10.88	16.79	n/a	23.71	42.56
Cleveland, OH	24.39	23.80	13.11	19.37	101.12	29.21	41.38
College Station, TX	21.68	15.89	11.24	14.68	n/a	24.78	19.71
Colorado Springs, CO	26.65	17.48	14.36	17.16	59.66	24.26	52.77
Columbia, MO	21.99	19.97	12.27	15.32	95.89	22.23	n/a
Columbia, SC	24.58	16.93	11.80	16.92	63.01	25.77	44.63
Columbus, OH	26.89	24.18	13.34	18.35	92.26	22.93	42.67
Dallas, TX	24.78	17.39	13.00	18.59	110.94	23.96	51.08
Davenport, IA	23.82	20.58	11.98	17.03	77.64	28.51	47.09
Denver, CO	30.27	19.27	15.39	19.75	99.20	26.85	47.84
Des Moines, IA	26.48	18.81	14.39	21.09	90.74	24.79	40.35
Durham, NC	30.19	15.67	14.28	19.11	109.88	24.99	48.84
Edison, NJ	31.34	29.45	17.33	21.93	81.29	40.48	54.54
El Paso, TX	20.29	13.74	11.29	12.83	92.58	18.18	41.46
Fargo, ND	22.59	21.54	15.48	18.69	83.78	28.94	47.67
Fayetteville, NC	23.78	15.30	11.83	16.47	92.25	21.06	41.81
Fort Collins, CO	28.31	18.20	14.74	17.04	84.69	30.01	52.44
Fort Wayne, IN	23.05	19.96	13.24	18.84	80.13	26.13	48.46
Fort Worth, TX	24.78	17.39	13.00	18.59	110.94	23.96	51.08
Grand Rapids, MI	25.00	17.99	13.49	18.78	115.44	23.51	39.99
Greeley, CO	28.57	18.27	15.14	16.42	80.53	27.27	51.35
Green Bay, WI	25.96	20.76	13.61	18.77	105.02	27.59	40.42
Greensboro, NC	24.49	15.45	12.56	18.30	72.13	23.33	49.13
Honolulu, HI	25.51	30.70	16.72	19.16	103.97	38.38	43.60
Houston, TX	24.90	17.92	12.03	17.51	69.53	25.57	54.61
Huntsville, AL	24.21	15.88	12.69	17.48	78.91	23.75	51.86
Indianapolis, IN	24.33	19.53	13.36	18.96	69.38	28.17	44.98
Jacksonville, FL	24.83	16.85	12.99	17.90	72.89	21.37	45.99
Kansas City, MO	26.35	22.20	13.89	18.68	82.22	29.28	43.98
Lafayette, LA	26.20	17.63	13.15	16.07	n/a	23.40	43.43
Lakeland, FL	26.15	16.45	12.88	15.53	97.38	19.94	43.16
Las Vegas, NV	24.94	17.98	15.83	17.00	98.54	33.90	40.75
Lexington, KY	25.92	18.55	13.47	16.56	n/a	23.98	41.54
Lincoln, NE	22.54	17.18	14.40	16.32	60.36	24.62	47.42
Little Rock, AR	23.55	14.24	11.97	17.45	95.92	19.85	44.73
Los Angeles, CA	29.62	23.18	15.95	20.32	65.87	37.25	58.88
Louisville, KY	24.98	18.87	13.45	17.72	61.30	28.14	42.60
Madison, WI	28.38	20.82	13.02	20.69	117.88	28.07	46.09

Table continued on following page.

Metro Area	Comp. User Support Specialists	Construction Laborers	Cooks, Restaurant	Customer Service Reps.	Dentists	Electricians	Engineers, Electrical
Manchester, NH[2]	27.45	19.30	15.58	20.34	111.95	26.41	52.51
Memphis, TN	23.06	15.86	12.46	18.07	71.03	24.89	46.46
Miami, FL	26.17	16.41	14.96	17.41	100.72	22.68	46.88
Midland, TX	24.74	17.43	13.11	17.41	n/a	28.94	52.80
Milwaukee, WI	25.85	23.25	13.14	20.22	98.32	33.98	44.41
Minneapolis, MN	28.26	28.53	16.38	21.32	105.18	35.78	50.53
Nashville, TN	24.09	17.16	13.19	18.01	75.33	25.45	45.40
New Haven, CT[2]	28.52	22.06	15.54	20.29	120.40	34.67	50.33
New Orleans, LA	24.41	16.66	12.31	16.48	74.68	27.52	54.15
New York, NY	31.34	29.45	17.33	21.93	81.29	40.48	54.54
Oklahoma City, OK	24.90	16.58	13.18	16.47	80.68	24.21	47.52
Omaha, NE	25.85	18.60	13.66	18.15	113.83	27.78	44.63
Orlando, FL	24.93	16.61	14.06	17.02	81.37	22.29	50.42
Peoria, IL	27.32	20.86	13.39	15.80	118.44	33.87	n/a
Philadelphia, PA	29.11	24.78	14.84	20.23	81.37	36.95	53.04
Phoenix, AZ	25.78	19.60	14.46	18.18	97.79	23.86	48.56
Pittsburgh, PA	24.98	21.30	13.04	18.03	71.78	31.54	47.12
Portland, OR	29.15	23.09	16.02	20.20	107.31	37.04	46.08
Providence, RI[2]	29.98	26.78	15.08	19.39	120.18	28.88	52.32
Provo, UT	26.06	16.78	13.93	16.82	n/a	22.38	35.78
Raleigh, NC	27.29	16.83	15.74	18.53	95.72	21.78	48.22
Reno, NV	24.94	20.58	14.82	17.38	99.87	26.92	43.83
Richmond, VA	26.74	15.20	12.97	17.99	79.04	26.98	47.93
Riverside, CA	29.70	24.28	15.12	19.74	84.77	26.51	48.20
Rochester, MN	27.37	23.17	14.87	17.51	93.21	30.42	48.07
Sacramento, CA	41.51	24.49	15.22	21.08	93.37	30.07	52.08
Salt Lake City, UT	26.07	18.26	13.09	18.57	60.05	26.94	47.95
San Antonio, TX	23.60	16.05	12.33	16.77	72.46	25.37	45.10
San Diego, CA	29.34	23.87	15.90	20.38	53.63	30.22	50.09
San Francisco, CA	37.82	28.43	19.21	24.01	85.30	51.29	58.99
San Jose, CA	34.93	27.64	17.22	22.94	94.63	41.61	72.35
Santa Rosa, CA	28.84	25.31	17.33	20.34	98.37	35.19	50.52
Savannah, GA	24.02	16.07	12.17	14.71	84.25	25.83	59.47
Seattle, WA	30.88	27.11	17.85	22.61	81.64	39.81	57.72
Sioux Falls, SD	20.11	16.27	13.58	17.26	78.71	24.23	46.65
Springfield, IL	29.20	26.62	11.66	17.52	86.11	34.16	45.48
Tallahassee, FL	21.83	14.26	13.54	16.05	78.74	21.70	44.42
Tampa, FL	24.82	15.90	13.00	17.32	71.77	22.08	46.52
Tucson, AZ	24.98	17.41	13.83	16.79	102.12	25.23	44.68
Tulsa, OK	24.46	16.60	12.51	16.05	n/a	23.73	49.81
Tuscaloosa, AL	29.04	15.01	10.38	16.06	73.08	25.65	43.67
Virginia Beach, VA	26.72	16.64	13.23	15.33	88.32	23.97	46.70
Washington, DC	32.03	18.44	15.40	21.22	105.63	31.72	62.57
Wichita, KS	22.03	16.12	12.82	16.56	77.90	25.06	43.33
Winston-Salem, NC	24.73	15.83	10.93	17.29	72.88	22.44	43.40

Notes: (1) Figures cover the Metropolitan Statistical Area (MSA) except where noted. See Appendix B for areas included;
(2) New England City and Town Area; n/a not available
Source: Bureau of Labor Statistics, May 2020 Metro Area Occupational Employment and Wage Estimates

Average Hourly Wages: Occupations F – H

Metro Area	Fast Food and Counter Workers	Financial Managers	First-Line Supervisors/ of Office Workers	General and Operations Managers	Hair-dressers/ Cosme-tologists	Home Health and Personal Care Aides	Janitors/ Cleaners
Albuquerque, NM	10.64	55.09	27.54	56.14	10.84	11.86	12.36
Allentown, PA	11.10	75.32	28.94	57.29	15.22	12.94	15.88
Anchorage, AK	12.54	54.93	32.38	58.03	14.27	16.10	16.48
Ann Arbor, MI	11.86	65.04	29.64	68.81	13.02	12.34	16.01
Athens, GA	9.77	52.35	24.64	45.41	10.25	12.00	12.46
Atlanta, GA	9.99	72.80	28.87	59.99	18.33	12.85	12.66
Austin, TX	11.34	72.96	31.36	57.34	15.92	11.06	14.50
Baton Rouge, LA	9.49	53.55	24.60	56.42	14.04	9.70	10.97
Boise City, ID	9.99	52.76	27.07	43.73	14.95	14.05	13.26
Boston, MA[2]	14.13	79.09	34.34	73.18	21.89	16.31	18.88
Boulder, CO	13.56	90.36	31.98	76.38	20.61	16.10	17.25
Cape Coral, FL	10.94	54.85	27.05	47.49	15.61	12.65	14.35
Cedar Rapids, IA	11.05	59.04	28.10	53.31	14.88	14.05	15.15
Charleston, SC	10.81	69.92	27.74	59.94	15.78	12.19	11.86
Charlotte, NC	10.65	83.71	28.74	64.43	15.60	11.20	12.26
Chicago, IL	11.94	75.24	32.97	66.06	15.60	13.73	15.85
Cincinnati, OH	11.06	67.69	29.76	59.57	14.55	12.32	15.23
Clarksville, TN	9.43	50.27	22.51	45.76	11.69	11.14	13.50
Cleveland, OH	11.12	73.35	29.66	63.12	15.00	11.54	14.61
College Station, TX	10.09	63.69	26.16	45.76	13.83	10.56	13.33
Colorado Springs, CO	12.80	71.91	28.53	62.51	19.89	14.62	14.95
Columbia, MO	12.41	57.39	26.61	41.33	15.87	12.15	14.70
Columbia, SC	9.32	58.42	27.64	54.33	17.75	11.20	12.24
Columbus, OH	10.98	68.77	29.82	58.25	17.11	12.26	14.37
Dallas, TX	10.98	77.10	30.67	62.23	12.81	10.68	14.25
Davenport, IA	10.58	53.76	26.30	48.05	13.57	13.27	14.93
Denver, CO	13.34	85.61	32.53	74.73	20.09	14.62	14.92
Des Moines, IA	11.04	66.80	31.26	53.18	15.31	14.13	13.43
Durham, NC	11.19	79.52	30.27	68.80	15.35	11.60	14.70
Edison, NJ	14.03	103.21	36.45	82.87	18.53	15.37	18.58
El Paso, TX	9.41	51.61	24.23	45.01	11.55	9.04	10.97
Fargo, ND	12.69	70.22	27.09	55.50	16.88	15.07	14.65
Fayetteville, NC	10.16	61.97	24.74	57.51	12.44	10.47	12.75
Fort Collins, CO	13.48	72.34	28.34	58.87	16.06	15.01	15.54
Fort Wayne, IN	10.87	57.58	28.51	55.31	13.03	12.24	11.86
Fort Worth, TX	10.98	77.10	30.67	62.23	12.81	10.68	14.25
Grand Rapids, MI	11.69	58.03	27.84	58.14	16.59	12.98	14.15
Greeley, CO	13.23	81.29	30.36	63.01	16.59	15.20	15.03
Green Bay, WI	10.40	60.24	30.04	66.79	14.46	12.75	14.61
Greensboro, NC	9.88	69.84	27.42	63.64	12.88	11.02	12.65
Honolulu, HI	13.15	60.38	29.59	58.24	18.80	14.07	16.41
Houston, TX	10.42	74.03	29.80	61.00	11.85	10.15	12.52
Huntsville, AL	9.32	65.66	26.99	71.84	11.25	9.93	12.52
Indianapolis, IN	10.96	68.18	30.65	59.89	15.32	12.21	13.87
Jacksonville, FL	10.31	63.49	28.46	52.07	16.47	12.37	12.06
Kansas City, MO	11.82	72.08	30.56	53.57	15.00	12.06	14.78
Lafayette, LA	9.61	49.98	24.38	59.04	11.41	9.98	11.01
Lakeland, FL	10.43	52.81	26.80	46.19	12.89	11.86	12.29
Las Vegas, NV	10.95	57.63	25.95	62.09	10.29	12.47	15.19
Lexington, KY	9.92	57.27	28.00	48.43	11.98	12.60	13.88
Lincoln, NE	11.43	58.67	26.69	50.22	13.35	13.55	13.37
Little Rock, AR	10.81	54.43	25.88	49.18	12.59	11.53	12.24
Los Angeles, CA	14.39	76.00	30.99	67.85	18.20	14.88	17.45
Louisville, KY	10.27	58.62	27.96	50.02	15.10	14.08	13.55

Table continued on following page.

Metro Area	Fast Food and Counter Workers	Financial Managers	First-Line Supervisors/ of Office Workers	General and Operations Managers	Hair-dressers/ Cosme-tologists	Home Health and Personal Care Aides	Janitors/ Cleaners
Madison, WI	11.02	71.61	31.88	65.89	13.94	13.95	15.37
Manchester, NH[2]	11.88	67.78	32.11	65.40	13.19	14.37	14.07
Memphis, TN	9.95	56.29	27.64	55.82	14.51	10.93	12.43
Miami, FL	10.90	72.93	30.04	55.19	13.80	12.10	12.75
Midland, TX	11.26	68.87	32.21	66.38	12.71	11.08	12.72
Milwaukee, WI	10.56	72.24	32.60	73.76	15.73	12.15	14.55
Minneapolis, MN	12.90	71.92	31.32	62.40	16.45	14.26	16.97
Nashville, TN	10.76	59.60	28.46	59.95	15.12	11.82	14.02
New Haven, CT[2]	13.15	67.42	33.60	71.07	15.79	14.00	17.93
New Orleans, LA	10.17	61.27	24.86	60.79	9.97	9.90	11.80
New York, NY	14.03	103.21	36.45	82.87	18.53	15.37	18.58
Oklahoma City, OK	10.46	56.40	26.50	53.95	13.21	11.30	12.31
Omaha, NE	11.57	60.81	27.79	51.20	17.22	12.78	14.62
Orlando, FL	10.44	67.64	27.02	50.37	14.70	12.02	12.97
Peoria, IL	10.98	60.22	28.72	50.68	14.84	12.88	12.80
Philadelphia, PA	11.82	82.22	33.44	74.57	16.17	12.96	15.31
Phoenix, AZ	13.06	64.55	29.32	58.07	16.74	13.34	14.73
Pittsburgh, PA	10.89	70.81	29.25	62.42	13.16	12.79	14.91
Portland, OR	13.97	65.29	30.19	61.17	16.58	15.31	16.47
Providence, RI[2]	13.21	78.87	33.57	71.70	16.31	15.37	15.75
Provo, UT	10.47	59.60	25.62	41.04	16.12	13.22	12.21
Raleigh, NC	10.01	68.49	28.13	70.88	14.20	11.45	12.29
Reno, NV	10.29	63.61	28.05	58.60	14.28	11.98	14.42
Richmond, VA	10.56	75.79	29.92	63.13	17.54	10.69	11.90
Riverside, CA	14.71	62.41	29.71	57.31	15.64	14.69	18.37
Rochester, MN	12.92	53.96	27.84	50.55	14.11	14.58	15.51
Sacramento, CA	14.18	65.80	31.37	59.57	16.75	14.17	17.86
Salt Lake City, UT	10.14	56.64	27.69	44.41	16.35	14.68	12.49
San Antonio, TX	11.01	67.11	26.77	61.53	12.89	10.91	12.76
San Diego, CA	14.44	74.59	31.30	69.74	18.23	14.88	17.57
San Francisco, CA	16.35	92.01	36.43	78.04	18.55	16.57	20.31
San Jose, CA	16.36	92.45	34.48	84.61	18.18	15.80	19.37
Santa Rosa, CA	14.43	69.07	31.18	61.63	17.02	16.21	17.54
Savannah, GA	10.40	49.27	26.00	50.31	11.68	11.70	12.39
Seattle, WA	16.04	76.28	37.04	73.17	22.82	16.24	21.21
Sioux Falls, SD	11.13	74.37	26.26	71.01	14.81	13.74	13.97
Springfield, IL	10.42	56.43	28.36	47.01	22.21	12.19	14.82
Tallahassee, FL	10.45	47.46	29.66	45.46	13.94	12.80	12.76
Tampa, FL	10.81	67.64	29.24	54.46	14.14	11.61	16.79
Tucson, AZ	12.90	53.26	25.41	46.52	16.70	13.18	14.72
Tulsa, OK	9.55	71.06	28.40	51.58	13.46	10.71	12.05
Tuscaloosa, AL	9.61	66.99	25.70	56.16	13.19	9.91	13.78
Virginia Beach, VA	10.94	66.75	28.75	53.58	12.55	10.52	12.31
Washington, DC	13.58	85.16	34.55	74.88	19.24	14.06	16.30
Wichita, KS	9.74	62.41	27.44	50.93	12.99	11.16	13.86
Winston-Salem, NC	10.40	73.56	26.29	59.21	12.93	11.42	11.67

Notes: (1) Figures cover the Metropolitan Statistical Area (MSA) except where noted. See Appendix B for areas included;
(2) New England City and Town Area; n/a not available
Source: Bureau of Labor Statistics, May 2020 Metro Area Occupational Employment and Wage Estimates

Average Hourly Wages: Occupations L – N

Metro Area	Landscapers	Lawyers	Maids/House-keepers	Main-tenance/Repairers	Marketing Managers	Network Admin.	Nurses, Licensed Practical
Albuquerque, NM	14.47	55.30	10.78	19.40	47.06	39.32	24.25
Allentown, PA	16.36	68.66	12.98	22.76	63.74	37.86	24.54
Anchorage, AK	17.23	55.18	15.11	24.45	49.02	39.64	33.65
Ann Arbor, MI	16.81	55.39	13.25	22.11	61.92	39.05	25.79
Athens, GA	16.07	37.80	10.10	17.26	61.63	32.23	21.52
Atlanta, GA	15.33	71.75	10.69	20.23	70.03	43.84	23.16
Austin, TX	15.64	69.36	11.26	18.11	74.00	41.06	23.83
Baton Rouge, LA	15.13	54.49	10.56	21.06	50.44	37.90	20.42
Boise City, ID	15.86	54.48	11.86	19.32	63.98	39.11	23.88
Boston, MA[2]	20.13	84.41	16.40	25.61	74.50	48.82	29.40
Boulder, CO	19.74	n/a	14.29	23.36	85.29	44.95	26.24
Cape Coral, FL	14.77	n/a	11.54	19.02	54.42	35.40	21.43
Cedar Rapids, IA	16.24	55.33	12.33	22.65	68.01	40.48	21.30
Charleston, SC	15.16	52.10	11.57	19.55	60.30	41.69	23.22
Charlotte, NC	15.09	69.55	11.69	21.36	72.17	40.33	22.77
Chicago, IL	16.89	76.45	14.09	23.38	68.69	43.67	28.45
Cincinnati, OH	14.62	67.43	12.24	21.32	66.12	38.88	23.84
Clarksville, TN	14.10	38.91	11.38	21.41	n/a	33.32	20.91
Cleveland, OH	17.07	71.56	12.07	21.06	66.16	42.80	23.78
College Station, TX	14.63	61.53	11.96	17.32	77.65	33.45	23.37
Colorado Springs, CO	15.28	57.73	13.68	20.63	80.71	39.94	27.45
Columbia, MO	14.70	43.61	11.43	15.89	54.36	34.22	21.46
Columbia, SC	13.75	57.84	11.26	19.16	57.61	38.25	21.20
Columbus, OH	15.69	54.42	12.55	21.51	73.13	41.93	22.50
Dallas, TX	16.49	72.23	12.05	21.14	74.99	43.23	25.11
Davenport, IA	16.09	70.60	11.68	20.79	61.19	37.00	21.77
Denver, CO	18.07	73.11	13.60	21.58	83.15	46.05	27.16
Des Moines, IA	17.08	63.08	12.53	21.27	64.28	41.04	23.35
Durham, NC	15.20	59.34	13.46	22.26	74.28	46.08	24.21
Edison, NJ	18.58	86.62	18.17	24.50	93.77	50.99	27.54
El Paso, TX	11.21	60.78	9.75	15.17	54.66	32.96	23.69
Fargo, ND	18.32	54.07	13.61	21.03	61.56	36.75	22.24
Fayetteville, NC	12.88	59.59	10.39	19.76	54.51	41.86	22.65
Fort Collins, CO	16.84	69.74	14.18	21.34	88.50	36.89	25.42
Fort Wayne, IN	14.26	59.12	11.29	21.47	60.08	32.57	22.79
Fort Worth, TX	16.49	72.23	12.05	21.14	74.99	43.23	25.11
Grand Rapids, MI	16.69	57.05	13.11	19.48	60.07	34.56	23.52
Greeley, CO	18.15	51.46	13.31	22.36	72.61	35.49	28.99
Green Bay, WI	16.03	51.55	12.13	22.68	60.63	33.41	20.81
Greensboro, NC	13.66	59.43	10.64	20.20	69.84	41.07	22.20
Honolulu, HI	19.34	56.12	19.89	24.13	52.09	40.41	26.08
Houston, TX	14.69	70.00	11.44	20.96	78.48	46.20	23.54
Huntsville, AL	15.69	56.43	10.54	17.99	72.22	40.01	19.99
Indianapolis, IN	16.30	60.41	12.05	20.39	61.76	40.98	23.39
Jacksonville, FL	14.63	61.24	12.55	19.96	68.66	37.71	22.65
Kansas City, MO	19.56	62.18	12.00	21.06	69.34	41.35	23.04
Lafayette, LA	15.41	45.40	9.86	17.55	43.77	34.54	19.08
Lakeland, FL	14.43	44.81	11.52	20.58	62.00	36.25	20.98
Las Vegas, NV	15.39	63.43	15.89	22.82	65.55	42.05	28.50
Lexington, KY	15.36	51.94	11.20	20.46	50.14	30.83	21.39
Lincoln, NE	14.29	56.03	13.51	21.24	43.46	35.90	22.16
Little Rock, AR	13.87	42.89	11.04	16.67	55.06	35.22	21.72
Los Angeles, CA	19.04	86.64	16.19	22.77	77.25	46.74	29.91
Louisville, KY	15.83	57.01	12.16	22.04	68.47	37.55	21.89
Madison, WI	17.69	57.68	14.08	21.18	64.29	37.64	23.27

Table continued on following page.

Metro Area	Landscapers	Lawyers	Maids/House-keepers	Main-tenance/Repairers	Marketing Managers	Network Admin.	Nurses, Licensed Practical
Manchester, NH[2]	16.72	66.91	12.82	23.16	75.31	41.64	27.45
Memphis, TN	13.86	51.22	11.39	19.63	47.56	36.25	21.46
Miami, FL	14.82	81.48	11.96	18.62	65.38	41.99	23.34
Midland, TX	16.68	79.48	12.97	19.94	81.11	44.09	25.03
Milwaukee, WI	17.16	67.17	13.05	22.36	65.22	36.67	25.10
Minneapolis, MN	18.17	65.42	15.37	24.86	74.13	42.76	25.10
Nashville, TN	14.16	62.16	12.20	20.31	59.03	37.49	21.95
New Haven, CT[2]	21.07	72.97	14.36	24.76	62.79	46.03	27.76
New Orleans, LA	13.11	59.17	11.03	19.02	48.62	34.09	21.91
New York, NY	18.58	86.62	18.17	24.50	93.77	50.99	27.54
Oklahoma City, OK	14.58	60.36	11.38	18.60	66.70	37.72	21.30
Omaha, NE	16.84	60.84	12.85	21.39	53.21	40.66	22.70
Orlando, FL	14.06	58.70	11.93	18.05	58.36	40.84	22.30
Peoria, IL	14.85	63.40	12.71	20.89	71.93	35.66	22.80
Philadelphia, PA	16.87	73.14	14.54	22.62	75.68	41.45	27.69
Phoenix, AZ	14.91	68.90	13.30	20.64	64.49	42.05	27.24
Pittsburgh, PA	15.16	60.20	12.74	21.02	67.26	38.22	21.99
Portland, OR	18.52	68.32	15.17	22.37	65.90	43.03	27.81
Providence, RI[2]	17.76	61.76	15.61	24.03	78.17	44.50	28.42
Provo, UT	16.13	73.52	12.41	20.26	54.83	39.72	22.86
Raleigh, NC	15.42	66.00	12.05	21.71	71.46	43.77	23.23
Reno, NV	15.83	59.64	13.96	23.28	55.19	41.53	30.36
Richmond, VA	15.83	67.92	12.10	21.90	74.21	43.79	23.80
Riverside, CA	16.79	79.37	15.65	22.90	62.78	43.26	29.90
Rochester, MN	17.47	56.23	13.55	20.95	55.51	38.82	24.74
Sacramento, CA	19.87	73.57	18.56	22.64	73.63	45.57	31.24
Salt Lake City, UT	16.86	72.69	12.37	20.90	62.53	39.60	25.62
San Antonio, TX	14.36	61.79	11.83	18.51	71.37	38.99	22.64
San Diego, CA	16.37	70.82	15.49	22.57	71.15	47.47	31.68
San Francisco, CA	21.71	97.08	21.46	27.95	94.36	51.30	35.83
San Jose, CA	22.59	111.35	19.47	26.36	101.54	64.55	36.51
Santa Rosa, CA	19.15	84.04	16.93	25.05	77.45	43.90	35.97
Savannah, GA	14.12	60.11	10.61	17.68	53.92	36.94	21.45
Seattle, WA	20.08	66.70	16.36	24.21	81.40	48.50	29.46
Sioux Falls, SD	16.01	62.19	11.67	19.64	66.03	32.40	19.44
Springfield, IL	16.70	50.23	12.27	21.57	51.93	37.76	21.99
Tallahassee, FL	13.54	48.96	10.81	17.35	47.03	31.12	20.87
Tampa, FL	14.01	57.69	11.21	18.38	70.07	40.32	22.60
Tucson, AZ	14.30	70.81	14.77	18.16	54.39	37.56	26.53
Tulsa, OK	14.93	68.67	11.08	18.93	66.79	35.66	21.60
Tuscaloosa, AL	14.92	54.99	10.48	16.55	46.18	36.95	19.30
Virginia Beach, VA	14.23	62.89	12.23	19.55	70.12	36.79	21.44
Washington, DC	17.19	89.46	15.44	24.33	84.55	49.25	26.79
Wichita, KS	13.64	47.07	11.59	18.91	59.34	35.01	21.14
Winston-Salem, NC	14.43	60.44	11.31	19.93	64.53	39.48	22.11

Notes: (1) Figures cover the Metropolitan Statistical Area (MSA) except where noted. See Appendix B for areas included;
(2) New England City and Town Area; n/a not available
Source: Bureau of Labor Statistics, May 2020 Metro Area Occupational Employment and Wage Estimates

Average Hourly Wages: Occupations N – P

Metro Area	Nurses, Registered	Nursing Assistants	Office Clerks	Physical Therapists	Physicians	Plumbers	Police Officers
Albuquerque, NM	36.89	14.68	13.26	42.37	93.46	22.34	27.77
Allentown, PA	34.19	16.29	18.15	42.47	n/a	33.01	34.49
Anchorage, AK	45.34	19.45	21.95	50.03	131.18	42.17	46.36
Ann Arbor, MI	39.09	17.55	16.78	42.90	92.84	35.65	33.41
Athens, GA	34.14	13.24	15.96	38.70	95.71	n/a	21.06
Atlanta, GA	36.53	16.57	17.83	42.77	127.01	26.53	24.70
Austin, TX	35.23	14.69	19.62	41.53	107.02	25.23	36.91
Baton Rouge, LA	31.33	12.25	13.85	43.09	104.38	29.38	21.21
Boise City, ID	35.63	14.84	17.45	39.54	115.74	24.22	30.14
Boston, MA[2]	47.79	18.34	21.18	41.62	86.54	40.46	37.76
Boulder, CO	39.80	17.23	22.67	44.97	132.80	25.79	40.27
Cape Coral, FL	34.06	15.25	17.14	41.34	125.98	21.62	26.01
Cedar Rapids, IA	29.59	14.88	18.09	37.39	120.60	29.06	31.16
Charleston, SC	33.46	14.93	15.18	37.56	134.84	26.03	24.33
Charlotte, NC	33.86	14.08	17.52	41.50	100.25	21.86	25.91
Chicago, IL	37.48	15.55	19.15	47.77	108.91	44.20	39.61
Cincinnati, OH	34.60	15.17	18.74	43.02	116.48	26.11	33.14
Clarksville, TN	31.25	13.32	15.39	43.19	113.83	24.00	22.17
Cleveland, OH	35.16	14.82	19.54	42.93	n/a	32.16	31.03
College Station, TX	33.67	12.92	15.42	40.64	n/a	20.44	31.50
Colorado Springs, CO	36.85	15.90	20.41	41.34	106.98	24.78	35.01
Columbia, MO	31.38	14.29	16.36	37.16	123.11	31.70	24.57
Columbia, SC	31.88	13.61	13.78	42.64	92.46	20.01	21.56
Columbus, OH	33.37	13.95	19.08	42.28	108.46	28.16	39.05
Dallas, TX	37.50	14.89	18.25	46.10	98.81	24.37	35.24
Davenport, IA	28.77	14.33	15.96	38.74	125.45	28.20	29.69
Denver, CO	38.12	17.19	22.26	42.29	119.46	29.30	41.15
Des Moines, IA	30.83	15.70	19.88	41.96	118.88	25.94	33.62
Durham, NC	34.04	14.98	18.39	37.70	60.22	23.42	25.52
Edison, NJ	45.63	19.48	19.03	47.81	99.88	35.78	41.48
El Paso, TX	35.14	13.03	15.07	46.19	113.76	18.19	30.62
Fargo, ND	35.67	16.56	20.46	39.52	n/a	26.34	32.53
Fayetteville, NC	36.31	12.73	15.84	41.85	125.79	21.51	22.19
Fort Collins, CO	37.00	16.20	20.49	38.37	114.80	26.03	40.60
Fort Wayne, IN	30.07	14.32	16.90	42.52	122.85	27.79	29.01
Fort Worth, TX	37.50	14.89	18.25	46.10	98.81	24.37	35.24
Grand Rapids, MI	33.54	14.54	18.46	40.21	103.72	25.17	30.97
Greeley, CO	34.49	15.51	21.15	43.71	117.71	25.41	36.09
Green Bay, WI	33.10	15.41	17.63	43.41	134.65	32.94	34.68
Greensboro, NC	33.75	13.32	16.51	43.44	133.51	24.87	24.42
Honolulu, HI	51.33	18.53	18.01	46.01	129.46	32.64	39.30
Houston, TX	40.85	14.11	20.18	40.55	97.14	26.71	32.55
Huntsville, AL	28.17	13.37	12.64	41.60	126.02	26.09	25.95
Indianapolis, IN	33.96	14.71	18.04	42.89	125.04	25.96	31.19
Jacksonville, FL	32.50	13.39	16.95	39.98	120.42	22.43	28.73
Kansas City, MO	33.77	14.40	17.65	42.64	77.69	32.53	27.86
Lafayette, LA	n/a	10.90	13.13	41.06	97.24	26.72	20.08
Lakeland, FL	31.77	13.41	16.98	45.93	111.82	21.29	28.08
Las Vegas, NV	44.58	16.81	18.26	54.41	112.43	29.48	38.04
Lexington, KY	30.92	14.26	16.76	41.60	117.61	30.48	23.72
Lincoln, NE	32.83	14.76	15.31	41.91	114.19	26.77	31.80
Little Rock, AR	33.20	13.43	17.00	37.99	90.23	22.80	24.32
Los Angeles, CA	54.38	18.28	19.87	50.77	111.66	29.04	53.23
Louisville, KY	31.94	14.54	17.26	41.20	119.15	28.33	25.33
Madison, WI	39.58	17.70	19.30	41.01	123.11	32.30	31.59

Table continued on following page.

Metro Area	Nurses, Registered	Nursing Assistants	Office Clerks	Physical Therapists	Physicians	Plumbers	Police Officers
Manchester, NH[2]	36.90	16.63	19.87	40.56	145.31	27.62	30.42
Memphis, TN	32.84	13.99	16.64	44.13	60.99	25.56	24.96
Miami, FL	34.76	13.66	17.51	39.20	103.07	22.66	35.19
Midland, TX	32.87	15.50	19.18	51.29	n/a	22.43	32.02
Milwaukee, WI	36.90	15.65	18.75	43.06	118.39	34.14	36.14
Minneapolis, MN	41.41	18.64	20.45	41.29	113.38	39.45	38.98
Nashville, TN	32.75	13.98	17.06	37.77	98.61	27.20	25.18
New Haven, CT[2]	41.58	17.50	19.49	48.99	109.62	37.97	36.22
New Orleans, LA	34.10	12.28	13.40	43.01	105.80	27.86	24.02
New York, NY	45.63	19.48	19.03	47.81	99.88	35.78	41.48
Oklahoma City, OK	32.94	13.44	15.49	43.27	98.08	27.58	27.64
Omaha, NE	33.90	15.61	17.67	40.54	113.21	33.69	32.51
Orlando, FL	32.37	13.57	17.28	41.78	87.69	21.20	28.75
Peoria, IL	32.97	14.10	18.03	42.48	108.82	38.03	26.30
Philadelphia, PA	38.45	15.82	19.59	45.60	110.75	33.19	36.66
Phoenix, AZ	39.13	16.56	20.25	44.20	117.44	25.87	34.93
Pittsburgh, PA	33.74	15.25	17.82	41.00	61.88	31.40	32.43
Portland, OR	47.45	18.03	19.73	44.08	84.07	37.75	39.52
Providence, RI[2]	39.75	16.41	19.47	41.73	101.63	29.94	31.88
Provo, UT	32.54	14.31	17.04	43.98	101.67	26.23	26.67
Raleigh, NC	33.71	14.25	17.60	40.47	131.23	21.78	25.39
Reno, NV	38.61	15.69	19.47	43.31	n/a	32.93	n/a
Richmond, VA	38.19	14.34	17.47	48.16	100.13	24.50	28.11
Riverside, CA	52.80	17.66	18.80	49.86	101.93	28.90	50.52
Rochester, MN	34.67	17.06	18.54	41.15	120.62	35.99	33.04
Sacramento, CA	64.59	20.17	19.88	53.64	125.17	30.79	48.23
Salt Lake City, UT	34.93	15.33	17.52	39.40	120.03	26.94	30.14
San Antonio, TX	36.11	13.97	17.09	41.28	104.54	21.49	29.60
San Diego, CA	53.66	19.08	19.89	47.32	115.36	30.73	44.39
San Francisco, CA	71.73	23.28	23.83	49.69	90.09	51.01	58.93
San Jose, CA	70.61	20.18	21.97	51.92	106.37	40.79	63.02
Santa Rosa, CA	60.02	18.91	21.01	52.11	110.94	36.11	55.62
Savannah, GA	31.19	12.86	17.14	42.25	79.65	25.97	22.03
Seattle, WA	45.73	18.20	21.98	44.19	121.55	39.45	41.70
Sioux Falls, SD	29.70	13.76	13.70	35.64	136.24	21.69	30.58
Springfield, IL	34.64	14.66	18.74	44.92	131.59	36.97	33.66
Tallahassee, FL	31.79	12.60	14.97	40.99	100.02	21.64	27.13
Tampa, FL	34.28	14.08	17.66	39.93	104.01	22.02	30.94
Tucson, AZ	36.86	15.70	19.72	42.86	96.12	24.44	31.18
Tulsa, OK	32.44	13.14	16.37	41.95	101.73	26.45	27.25
Tuscaloosa, AL	28.76	12.79	12.79	47.83	104.43	22.88	26.12
Virginia Beach, VA	35.27	14.43	15.93	43.59	103.50	23.91	27.28
Washington, DC	40.14	16.19	20.88	46.02	98.67	27.93	37.03
Wichita, KS	28.59	13.31	14.06	43.59	72.44	23.76	23.57
Winston-Salem, NC	33.96	13.84	16.40	47.63	59.26	21.42	21.49

Notes: (1) Figures cover the Metropolitan Statistical Area (MSA) except where noted. See Appendix B for areas included;
(2) New England City and Town Area; n/a not available
Source: Bureau of Labor Statistics, May 2020 Metro Area Occupational Employment and Wage Estimates

Average Hourly Wages: Occupations P – S

Metro Area	Postal Mail Carriers	R.E. Sales Agents	Retail Sales-persons	Sales Reps., Technical/ Scientific	Secretaries, Exc. Leg./ Med./Exec.	Security Guards	Surgeons
Albuquerque, NM	25.35	27.94	13.71	53.85	17.98	14.03	117.34
Allentown, PA	25.45	20.93	13.51	35.66	18.99	14.13	n/a
Anchorage, AK	25.19	35.74	16.71	41.68	21.33	21.46	n/a
Ann Arbor, MI	25.59	23.92	15.17	50.25	21.85	18.21	n/a
Athens, GA	24.88	27.22	12.23	22.13	15.66	15.56	121.05
Atlanta, GA	25.44	35.07	13.86	41.84	17.67	13.91	120.75
Austin, TX	25.90	32.45	13.91	51.09	18.80	16.12	123.62
Baton Rouge, LA	25.30	20.08	12.82	38.42	17.00	15.22	140.15
Boise City, ID	25.46	19.41	14.97	29.05	17.35	13.31	97.30
Boston, MA[2]	26.35	43.81	16.09	51.61	23.99	18.44	130.15
Boulder, CO	25.69	29.36	16.67	52.42	20.24	16.82	138.32
Cape Coral, FL	25.50	25.90	13.39	35.11	18.26	13.12	117.59
Cedar Rapids, IA	25.60	20.45	13.27	55.20	19.13	17.64	n/a
Charleston, SC	25.11	24.16	14.34	31.33	17.96	15.38	n/a
Charlotte, NC	25.80	26.82	14.40	45.84	19.39	15.19	n/a
Chicago, IL	25.88	21.35	14.74	43.30	20.83	16.67	126.47
Cincinnati, OH	26.01	22.97	14.27	54.66	18.99	17.36	136.71
Clarksville, TN	25.31	13.84	13.05	28.37	16.54	17.01	n/a
Cleveland, OH	25.57	25.39	13.80	44.45	18.72	15.88	n/a
College Station, TX	25.72	26.12	12.40	38.39	16.65	12.99	n/a
Colorado Springs, CO	25.33	36.06	15.75	51.66	17.72	16.33	138.49
Columbia, MO	24.78	15.74	16.35	37.54	17.90	15.12	n/a
Columbia, SC	25.03	21.37	13.33	35.54	19.69	15.89	n/a
Columbus, OH	25.57	24.24	14.13	43.53	19.06	17.50	130.76
Dallas, TX	25.84	32.44	14.22	42.11	19.17	15.96	96.15
Davenport, IA	25.05	35.10	16.04	41.15	17.40	16.63	n/a
Denver, CO	25.33	43.38	16.33	53.97	20.86	17.65	122.99
Des Moines, IA	25.38	24.89	13.93	48.46	21.68	16.81	n/a
Durham, NC	26.10	23.48	12.83	64.20	20.51	24.93	n/a
Edison, NJ	25.82	47.39	17.06	53.94	21.58	18.33	103.27
El Paso, TX	25.52	28.82	11.77	n/a	15.48	12.85	n/a
Fargo, ND	25.35	30.08	15.57	41.70	19.41	14.99	n/a
Fayetteville, NC	25.38	31.75	12.89	n/a	17.36	19.85	n/a
Fort Collins, CO	25.02	28.43	15.06	44.49	18.64	14.53	n/a
Fort Wayne, IN	25.01	23.92	13.59	39.15	18.02	17.34	102.77
Fort Worth, TX	25.84	32.44	14.22	42.11	19.17	15.96	96.15
Grand Rapids, MI	25.56	26.79	14.74	36.78	18.94	14.23	n/a
Greeley, CO	24.67	n/a	17.48	42.69	18.73	16.81	n/a
Green Bay, WI	25.05	27.21	15.84	45.73	18.17	14.03	n/a
Greensboro, NC	26.02	21.07	13.99	47.50	18.17	14.07	n/a
Honolulu, HI	26.27	34.78	16.86	41.95	22.13	16.81	125.38
Houston, TX	25.54	30.11	13.06	45.56	19.08	14.70	109.57
Huntsville, AL	25.08	n/a	14.19	40.45	17.89	15.08	n/a
Indianapolis, IN	25.51	24.10	15.14	58.59	18.14	15.06	83.72
Jacksonville, FL	26.36	32.81	12.90	55.76	18.29	12.98	n/a
Kansas City, MO	25.56	25.16	14.32	42.28	18.80	19.75	134.82
Lafayette, LA	25.61	20.02	13.19	41.34	15.02	11.63	n/a
Lakeland, FL	25.73	24.66	13.99	50.71	16.80	13.69	125.71
Las Vegas, NV	25.67	33.49	14.32	55.81	19.28	15.70	n/a
Lexington, KY	25.61	21.40	13.53	40.76	18.81	13.31	n/a
Lincoln, NE	25.26	26.16	13.66	39.84	18.52	17.86	142.38
Little Rock, AR	25.59	n/a	13.77	31.84	16.05	14.70	n/a
Los Angeles, CA	26.77	29.45	17.09	49.22	22.28	16.50	89.22
Louisville, KY	25.74	31.08	13.26	42.65	18.47	13.24	134.53
Madison, WI	24.45	22.36	15.01	38.52	20.01	18.11	n/a

Table continued on following page.

Metro Area	Postal Mail Carriers	R.E. Sales Agents	Retail Sales-persons	Sales Reps., Technical/ Scientific	Secretaries, Exc. Leg./ Med./Exec.	Security Guards	Surgeons
Manchester, NH[2]	25.30	23.78	14.27	48.55	18.80	17.13	n/a
Memphis, TN	25.90	28.54	14.05	42.81	18.28	13.18	n/a
Miami, FL	25.74	33.05	14.10	43.52	17.95	14.33	102.70
Midland, TX	24.14	43.87	15.66	47.47	18.67	17.54	n/a
Milwaukee, WI	25.52	24.22	15.05	42.81	19.69	15.28	n/a
Minneapolis, MN	25.48	22.43	15.67	43.88	21.10	18.83	n/a
Nashville, TN	25.66	22.88	14.62	38.86	20.08	14.59	87.98
New Haven, CT[2]	25.57	n/a	15.78	51.87	23.42	16.82	n/a
New Orleans, LA	25.18	n/a	12.85	32.30	17.67	14.16	n/a
New York, NY	25.82	47.39	17.06	53.94	21.58	18.33	103.27
Oklahoma City, OK	25.83	27.06	14.42	47.84	16.56	17.63	n/a
Omaha, NE	25.62	26.55	14.47	27.54	18.29	18.67	97.62
Orlando, FL	25.63	21.86	13.90	45.86	17.38	13.36	107.64
Peoria, IL	25.20	22.91	13.31	41.09	16.53	18.73	n/a
Philadelphia, PA	25.80	23.80	15.36	39.35	20.84	15.80	127.73
Phoenix, AZ	26.14	25.87	15.31	45.74	18.93	15.32	n/a
Pittsburgh, PA	25.28	35.64	14.07	41.12	18.26	14.45	n/a
Portland, OR	25.16	27.75	16.66	51.50	22.16	16.55	137.03
Providence, RI[2]	25.36	34.42	16.55	43.31	22.02	15.82	135.97
Provo, UT	25.17	19.82	14.08	35.28	17.09	18.95	n/a
Raleigh, NC	25.99	25.85	13.72	53.76	18.82	16.13	n/a
Reno, NV	25.58	18.91	16.30	50.40	20.94	18.12	n/a
Richmond, VA	25.32	31.14	14.11	52.19	19.17	13.71	129.69
Riverside, CA	26.10	n/a	16.16	47.48	21.05	16.42	116.37
Rochester, MN	24.97	25.68	15.36	44.55	18.15	15.79	n/a
Sacramento, CA	26.14	40.54	16.20	49.21	21.10	17.05	n/a
Salt Lake City, UT	25.55	n/a	15.78	45.08	19.50	17.37	120.78
San Antonio, TX	25.93	30.87	13.97	43.36	17.05	16.35	n/a
San Diego, CA	26.30	n/a	16.36	49.07	21.27	16.24	n/a
San Francisco, CA	26.61	35.07	18.15	57.04	25.23	20.24	120.47
San Jose, CA	26.28	48.70	20.75	69.16	24.97	21.24	124.63
Santa Rosa, CA	25.08	n/a	18.83	58.81	22.47	17.86	n/a
Savannah, GA	25.33	26.46	13.07	42.67	16.91	15.61	135.03
Seattle, WA	25.94	34.15	18.51	53.25	23.36	19.56	110.96
Sioux Falls, SD	25.69	n/a	16.24	59.28	14.98	14.66	135.63
Springfield, IL	25.77	19.54	14.55	41.97	17.85	23.01	137.30
Tallahassee, FL	25.24	26.87	14.02	38.03	17.26	13.85	n/a
Tampa, FL	25.84	27.84	14.16	38.88	17.85	16.60	99.80
Tucson, AZ	26.13	28.26	14.92	41.86	17.67	14.50	n/a
Tulsa, OK	25.76	43.74	13.54	39.78	16.99	15.16	n/a
Tuscaloosa, AL	24.94	29.55	14.23	n/a	17.36	13.60	n/a
Virginia Beach, VA	25.12	31.60	12.74	47.42	19.12	16.77	n/a
Washington, DC	25.68	32.62	15.08	60.70	23.83	22.34	128.61
Wichita, KS	25.19	34.94	16.50	48.42	17.11	15.40	n/a
Winston-Salem, NC	26.12	29.77	12.78	46.13	18.63	19.14	n/a

Notes: (1) Figures cover the Metropolitan Statistical Area (MSA) except where noted. See Appendix B for areas included; (2) New England City and Town Area; n/a not available
Source: Bureau of Labor Statistics, May 2020 Metro Area Occupational Employment and Wage Estimates

Average Hourly Wages: Occupations T – W

Metro Area	Teacher Assistants[3]	Teachers, Secondary School[3]	Telemarketers	Truck Drivers, Heavy	Truck Drivers, Light	Waiters/ Waitresses
Albuquerque, NM	10.86	25.68	n/a	20.15	18.42	10.00
Allentown, PA	14.41	34.29	13.77	23.61	17.65	13.50
Anchorage, AK	19.53	40.19	n/a	28.67	24.80	12.41
Ann Arbor, MI	14.25	30.94	n/a	23.07	20.97	12.42
Athens, GA	9.86	28.26	n/a	24.12	22.33	11.05
Atlanta, GA	11.99	30.58	13.88	24.03	19.17	11.09
Austin, TX	12.63	28.51	16.75	21.42	23.43	11.41
Baton Rouge, LA	10.61	25.88	13.65	20.24	16.72	9.75
Boise City, ID	13.33	24.81	13.26	22.95	18.28	12.34
Boston, MA[2]	18.17	39.93	18.30	25.04	22.25	16.02
Boulder, CO	16.60	33.44	n/a	21.44	21.14	15.29
Cape Coral, FL	14.99	31.83	13.57	21.06	18.21	12.55
Cedar Rapids, IA	12.78	25.85	12.92	18.16	16.81	10.61
Charleston, SC	12.41	28.34	9.27	20.05	17.41	9.82
Charlotte, NC	12.78	25.96	16.80	23.25	17.99	11.80
Chicago, IL	14.87	39.72	15.22	26.10	23.89	11.30
Cincinnati, OH	14.28	30.87	15.21	24.06	19.05	11.05
Clarksville, TN	13.56	33.45	n/a	19.83	19.57	10.91
Cleveland, OH	14.60	34.51	11.42	23.90	19.82	10.71
College Station, TX	9.90	23.45	n/a	18.16	17.70	9.94
Colorado Springs, CO	14.25	25.06	16.71	23.30	19.39	15.23
Columbia, MO	13.47	25.88	n/a	21.47	19.86	11.41
Columbia, SC	12.27	28.01	16.21	21.90	17.53	9.40
Columbus, OH	14.60	33.80	14.44	22.67	19.28	11.77
Dallas, TX	11.50	28.25	17.10	24.27	20.71	9.50
Davenport, IA	13.57	27.87	14.32	23.94	17.03	11.62
Denver, CO	15.53	29.76	18.67	26.50	20.37	15.26
Des Moines, IA	13.66	29.67	14.89	24.12	16.86	10.63
Durham, NC	12.80	26.34	12.24	19.82	20.75	12.65
Edison, NJ	17.07	43.94	18.00	27.38	21.27	18.12
El Paso, TX	13.05	30.31	10.36	23.37	17.27	9.93
Fargo, ND	16.34	31.20	n/a	24.48	20.00	12.90
Fayetteville, NC	11.91	22.89	n/a	17.95	17.42	9.29
Fort Collins, CO	14.31	n/a	n/a	22.10	18.76	16.23
Fort Wayne, IN	12.40	26.62	n/a	21.76	19.38	13.50
Fort Worth, TX	11.50	28.25	17.10	24.27	20.71	9.50
Grand Rapids, MI	14.25	29.14	12.06	22.41	20.39	14.47
Greeley, CO	14.61	25.80	n/a	25.81	20.06	12.56
Green Bay, WI	16.03	28.94	n/a	22.82	19.81	9.89
Greensboro, NC	12.38	24.19	n/a	24.63	17.87	10.40
Honolulu, HI	15.68	n/a	12.79	25.82	18.43	30.11
Houston, TX	10.92	29.18	14.80	23.21	20.42	11.44
Huntsville, AL	10.13	26.12	n/a	19.59	17.60	9.19
Indianapolis, IN	13.05	27.37	16.60	23.26	20.81	12.55
Jacksonville, FL	12.80	30.73	12.86	21.69	18.78	12.21
Kansas City, MO	13.33	26.10	15.91	24.16	18.51	11.20
Lafayette, LA	11.30	25.17	n/a	20.88	14.72	9.79
Lakeland, FL	11.20	24.22	12.40	22.02	22.47	11.43
Las Vegas, NV	15.75	28.05	12.82	23.35	17.59	13.15
Lexington, KY	15.32	28.71	n/a	25.24	22.54	10.77
Lincoln, NE	14.87	30.70	11.05	26.01	19.74	10.59
Little Rock, AR	11.35	26.77	12.43	24.40	14.91	10.92
Los Angeles, CA	18.25	41.94	15.89	24.13	21.40	16.07
Louisville, KY	15.06	27.29	n/a	25.60	20.42	11.01
Madison, WI	15.69	27.83	12.02	25.51	18.09	12.03

Table continued on following page.

Metro Area	Teacher Assistants[3]	Teachers, Secondary School[3]	Telemarketers	Truck Drivers, Heavy	Truck Drivers, Light	Waiters/ Waitresses
Manchester, NH[2]	15.12	28.80	n/a	24.56	18.27	13.46
Memphis, TN	12.21	26.97	15.50	22.93	19.09	9.84
Miami, FL	13.47	31.76	14.05	19.63	17.20	12.57
Midland, TX	10.43	28.63	n/a	24.50	21.89	9.28
Milwaukee, WI	16.15	29.89	16.04	24.97	17.36	11.33
Minneapolis, MN	16.69	31.99	18.31	25.51	21.47	15.04
Nashville, TN	13.09	25.02	18.69	25.40	17.83	9.89
New Haven, CT[2]	15.38	37.68	17.96	24.73	19.11	13.86
New Orleans, LA	12.38	26.55	17.07	22.70	18.90	9.90
New York, NY	17.07	43.94	18.00	27.38	21.27	18.12
Oklahoma City, OK	10.86	23.79	14.03	24.44	18.01	11.61
Omaha, NE	14.35	30.82	12.49	21.91	18.84	10.79
Orlando, FL	13.12	27.96	12.95	22.29	19.05	12.53
Peoria, IL	12.78	28.02	16.30	23.04	19.39	10.60
Philadelphia, PA	14.25	34.95	17.40	25.10	20.12	13.00
Phoenix, AZ	13.68	27.18	16.21	23.93	19.25	19.03
Pittsburgh, PA	14.11	34.46	12.75	26.03	17.58	13.55
Portland, OR	17.44	39.42	18.26	25.23	20.13	15.65
Providence, RI[2]	17.30	37.01	16.66	24.14	20.19	14.06
Provo, UT	13.67	38.46	14.13	20.44	18.31	12.13
Raleigh, NC	11.87	27.24	n/a	22.00	16.96	11.79
Reno, NV	10.42	25.59	14.61	25.19	21.37	11.35
Richmond, VA	12.74	n/a	14.96	23.73	21.33	12.03
Riverside, CA	17.96	41.62	15.27	25.57	22.32	14.16
Rochester, MN	15.75	30.87	n/a	23.53	16.41	15.44
Sacramento, CA	17.41	39.16	15.61	25.88	19.96	16.21
Salt Lake City, UT	13.35	29.93	12.47	24.57	20.04	10.55
San Antonio, TX	11.97	28.34	19.63	20.54	21.17	10.02
San Diego, CA	16.96	41.03	15.07	24.67	23.99	15.63
San Francisco, CA	19.29	44.41	n/a	27.78	25.20	19.64
San Jose, CA	19.75	44.47	16.69	27.47	24.95	17.28
Santa Rosa, CA	17.76	42.66	n/a	26.90	23.21	17.56
Savannah, GA	12.45	26.54	n/a	22.16	17.24	9.30
Seattle, WA	19.79	38.01	21.37	26.88	22.88	20.75
Sioux Falls, SD	12.32	23.01	n/a	22.48	18.48	10.59
Springfield, IL	12.03	27.07	n/a	24.22	18.96	10.05
Tallahassee, FL	13.00	24.52	14.79	20.09	17.87	12.10
Tampa, FL	14.49	30.07	13.79	20.31	17.75	14.24
Tucson, AZ	13.63	21.17	14.70	23.53	18.79	17.12
Tulsa, OK	11.41	26.46	12.45	27.46	18.88	9.11
Tuscaloosa, AL	9.49	24.81	n/a	20.28	18.27	9.02
Virginia Beach, VA	13.86	32.96	13.91	19.71	19.40	11.59
Washington, DC	17.52	41.57	14.54	24.43	22.49	15.99
Wichita, KS	13.20	27.00	12.02	22.85	17.72	9.40
Winston-Salem, NC	11.38	24.47	n/a	23.68	17.90	10.37

Notes: (1) Figures cover the Metropolitan Statistical Area (MSA) except where noted. See Appendix B for areas included;
(2) New England City and Town Area; (3) Hourly wages were calculated from annual wage data assuming a 40 hour work week;
n/a not available
Source: Bureau of Labor Statistics, May 2020 Metro Area Occupational Employment and Wage Estimates

Means of Transportation to Work: City

City	Car/Truck/Van		Public Transportation			Bicycle	Walked	Other Means	Worked at Home
	Drove Alone	Car-pooled	Bus	Subway	Railroad				
Albuquerque, NM	80.6	9.0	1.8	0.0	0.1	1.1	1.9	1.0	4.4
Allentown, PA	67.4	17.2	4.9	0.0	0.0	0.1	5.4	1.2	3.9
Anchorage, AK	76.3	11.8	1.5	0.0	0.0	1.3	2.9	2.3	4.0
Ann Arbor, MI	54.0	6.4	10.3	0.2	0.0	3.9	16.5	0.7	8.0
Athens, GA	72.5	10.0	4.6	0.0	0.0	1.4	4.4	1.5	5.6
Atlanta, GA	67.1	6.3	6.6	3.4	0.2	1.1	5.0	2.2	8.1
Austin, TX	73.7	9.1	3.2	0.1	0.1	1.3	2.4	1.3	8.7
Baton Rouge, LA	80.3	9.8	2.4	0.0	0.0	0.6	3.4	0.6	2.9
Boise City, ID	79.6	7.3	0.6	0.0	0.0	2.8	2.5	1.1	6.0
Boston, MA	38.3	5.9	13.5	17.8	1.1	2.3	15.1	2.6	3.4
Boulder, CO	50.8	5.5	7.3	0.0	0.0	9.9	11.1	1.1	14.5
Cape Coral, FL	81.7	9.0	0.1	0.0	0.0	0.2	0.8	1.2	7.0
Cedar Rapids, IA	84.0	8.2	0.8	0.0	0.0	0.5	1.7	1.1	3.6
Charleston, SC	76.4	7.0	0.8	0.0	0.0	2.4	5.0	1.7	6.8
Charlotte, NC	76.3	9.3	2.4	0.4	0.2	0.1	2.1	1.5	7.7
Chicago, IL	48.8	7.7	13.3	13.0	1.8	1.7	6.5	2.0	5.2
Cincinnati, OH	72.3	8.8	7.0	0.0	0.0	0.4	5.7	1.1	4.7
Clarksville, TN	85.9	7.8	0.9	0.0	0.0	0.0	1.3	1.3	2.7
Cleveland, OH	69.3	10.8	8.9	0.5	0.1	0.6	5.1	1.5	3.2
College Station, TX	78.2	9.3	2.8	0.0	0.0	2.1	2.7	1.0	3.8
Colorado Springs, CO	77.8	10.9	0.9	0.0	0.0	0.6	1.9	0.9	6.9
Columbia, MO	77.1	10.5	1.3	0.0	0.0	1.3	4.8	0.9	4.2
Columbia, SC	64.1	6.1	1.8	0.0	0.0	0.5	21.9	2.2	3.4
Columbus, OH	79.4	8.3	3.1	0.0	0.0	0.6	3.1	1.1	4.4
Dallas, TX	76.7	11.0	2.9	0.4	0.3	0.2	2.1	1.5	4.9
Davenport, IA	85.6	6.6	0.9	0.0	0.0	0.4	2.3	0.5	3.7
Denver, CO	69.1	7.7	4.4	0.9	0.5	2.2	4.7	1.9	8.5
Des Moines, IA	80.1	9.7	2.2	0.1	0.0	0.4	2.9	1.2	3.5
Durham, NC	76.9	9.3	3.6	0.0	0.0	0.6	2.4	1.3	5.8
Edison, NJ	69.4	9.0	0.5	0.5	12.6	0.3	1.7	1.2	4.8
El Paso, TX	81.1	10.6	1.6	0.0	0.0	0.2	1.4	1.9	3.2
Fargo, ND	82.8	8.3	0.9	0.0	0.0	0.6	3.7	0.8	2.9
Fayetteville, NC	77.2	9.4	0.6	0.0	0.0	0.2	7.8	1.7	3.1
Fort Collins, CO	71.9	7.2	2.2	0.0	0.0	5.4	4.2	1.0	8.0
Fort Wayne, IN	83.4	9.6	0.8	0.0	0.0	0.3	1.6	0.7	3.7
Fort Worth, TX	81.5	11.4	0.6	0.0	0.2	0.2	1.2	0.8	4.1
Grand Rapids, MI	75.3	11.1	3.6	0.1	0.0	1.1	4.1	1.0	3.8
Greeley, CO	79.5	11.3	0.6	0.0	0.0	0.7	2.8	1.2	3.9
Green Bay, WI	79.7	10.2	1.4	0.0	0.0	0.5	2.3	1.9	3.9
Greensboro, NC	81.9	7.6	1.9	0.0	0.0	0.2	1.9	0.9	5.6
Honolulu, HI	57.2	13.0	11.6	0.0	0.0	1.6	8.5	4.0	3.9
Houston, TX	77.7	10.4	3.5	0.1	0.0	0.4	2.0	2.0	4.0
Huntsville, AL	86.1	7.0	0.4	0.0	0.0	0.2	1.3	1.1	4.0
Indianapolis, IN	82.0	9.2	1.8	0.0	0.0	0.5	1.9	1.1	3.5
Jacksonville, FL	80.3	9.2	1.8	0.0	0.0	0.5	1.7	1.6	4.8
Kansas City, MO	81.5	7.8	2.5	0.0	0.0	0.2	2.0	1.2	4.9
Lafayette, LA	84.3	6.7	1.2	0.0	0.0	1.2	2.3	0.9	3.5
Lakeland, FL	80.5	10.5	0.8	0.0	0.0	0.3	1.6	1.8	4.6
Las Vegas, NV	78.0	9.8	3.4	0.0	0.0	0.2	1.5	2.8	4.2
Lexington, KY	78.5	9.3	1.9	0.0	0.0	0.6	3.7	1.5	4.4
Lincoln, NE	81.0	9.0	1.3	0.0	0.0	1.2	3.4	0.6	3.4
Little Rock, AR	81.6	9.8	0.9	0.0	0.0	0.1	1.8	1.5	4.2
Los Angeles, CA	69.6	8.8	7.8	0.9	0.2	1.0	3.4	2.0	6.3
Louisville, KY	79.6	8.9	3.1	0.0	0.0	0.4	2.0	1.8	4.3

Table continued on following page.

City	Car/Truck/Van		Public Transportation			Bicycle	Walked	Other Means	Worked at Home
	Drove Alone	Car-pooled	Bus	Subway	Railroad				
Madison, WI	64.3	7.0	9.1	0.0	0.1	4.5	9.1	1.3	4.7
Manchester, NH	79.1	11.0	0.7	0.0	0.1	0.3	3.2	1.3	4.2
Memphis, TN	82.0	10.5	1.4	0.0	0.0	0.2	1.6	1.3	2.9
Miami, FL	69.4	8.3	7.9	1.0	0.2	0.9	4.0	3.2	5.2
Midland, TX	85.1	10.1	0.2	0.0	0.0	0.1	0.6	1.0	2.8
Milwaukee, WI	72.8	10.2	7.2	0.0	0.1	0.8	4.6	0.8	3.5
Minneapolis, MN	60.5	7.4	11.2	1.1	0.2	4.0	7.4	2.3	5.8
Nashville, TN	77.7	10.0	2.0	0.0	0.1	0.2	2.4	1.2	6.4
New Haven, CT	58.7	9.1	10.5	0.1	1.1	3.1	11.4	1.2	4.7
New Orleans, LA	68.0	9.1	5.9	0.0	0.0	3.1	5.4	2.7	5.7
New York, NY	22.3	4.5	10.1	43.9	1.5	1.3	10.0	2.2	4.3
Oklahoma City, OK	82.6	10.5	0.5	0.0	0.0	0.1	1.5	1.1	3.6
Omaha, NE	81.7	9.1	1.4	0.0	0.0	0.3	2.3	1.3	4.0
Orlando, FL	79.0	8.0	3.4	0.1	0.0	0.6	1.8	1.9	5.3
Peoria, IL	80.1	9.5	2.4	0.0	0.0	0.3	2.7	1.1	3.7
Philadelphia, PA	50.3	8.2	16.0	5.6	2.8	2.1	8.5	2.3	4.2
Phoenix, AZ	74.6	12.6	2.7	0.1	0.1	0.6	1.6	1.9	5.9
Pittsburgh, PA	55.3	8.1	16.9	0.4	0.0	1.8	10.7	1.2	5.6
Portland, OR	57.3	8.3	9.9	0.9	0.3	6.0	5.8	3.0	8.5
Providence, RI	64.5	12.0	5.2	0.1	1.2	0.7	9.5	1.3	5.5
Provo, UT	62.0	11.8	2.6	0.2	1.1	2.4	13.0	1.6	5.3
Raleigh, NC	78.2	8.0	1.9	0.1	0.0	0.4	1.6	1.3	8.5
Reno, NV	75.2	12.6	2.3	0.0	0.0	0.8	3.6	1.1	4.4
Richmond, VA	71.1	9.5	5.5	0.1	0.1	2.1	5.2	1.8	4.6
Riverside, CA	76.4	12.6	1.7	0.0	0.7	0.7	2.6	1.1	4.2
Rochester, MN	70.6	12.5	6.2	0.0	0.0	1.0	4.3	0.9	4.4
Sacramento, CA	74.4	10.4	2.0	0.2	0.4	1.9	2.8	2.2	5.6
Salt Lake City, UT	67.8	10.5	4.8	0.4	0.8	2.5	5.1	2.7	5.5
San Antonio, TX	78.7	11.3	2.9	0.0	0.0	0.2	1.7	1.5	3.8
San Diego, CA	74.7	8.6	3.6	0.0	0.1	0.8	3.1	1.8	7.2
San Francisco, CA	32.1	6.9	22.0	8.8	1.7	4.0	11.8	6.1	6.6
San Jose, CA	75.8	11.7	2.6	0.3	1.2	0.8	1.8	1.6	4.2
Santa Rosa, CA	77.9	11.5	1.6	0.0	0.1	1.2	1.7	1.1	4.8
Savannah, GA	72.0	11.0	4.4	0.1	0.0	1.7	4.7	1.9	4.2
Seattle, WA	46.5	7.2	20.1	1.3	0.1	3.5	11.3	2.5	7.4
Sioux Falls, SD	84.3	8.5	0.8	0.0	0.0	0.5	2.0	0.6	3.4
Springfield, IL	81.8	7.9	2.2	0.1	0.0	0.7	2.1	1.3	3.9
Tallahassee, FL	78.5	8.7	2.4	0.0	0.0	0.8	3.3	1.5	4.8
Tampa, FL	77.1	8.8	2.1	0.0	0.0	1.0	2.4	1.5	6.9
Tucson, AZ	74.5	10.6	3.3	0.0	0.0	2.4	3.1	1.7	4.5
Tulsa, OK	80.2	10.7	0.9	0.0	0.0	0.3	1.8	2.1	4.0
Tuscaloosa, AL	84.2	8.1	0.8	0.1	0.0	0.5	1.8	0.6	3.9
Virginia Beach, VA	82.1	8.6	0.7	0.0	0.0	0.5	2.4	1.6	3.9
Washington, DC	33.5	5.2	13.2	21.1	0.3	4.5	13.4	2.3	6.6
Wichita, KS	83.5	9.5	0.7	0.0	0.0	0.3	1.5	1.3	3.2
Winston-Salem, NC	81.9	8.3	1.7	0.0	0.0	0.2	2.1	1.1	4.7
U.S.	76.3	9.0	2.4	1.9	0.6	0.5	2.7	1.4	5.2

Note: Figures are percentages and cover workers 16 years of age and older
Source: U.S. Census Bureau, 2015-2019 American Community Survey 5-Year Estimates

Means of Transportation to Work: Metro Area

Metro Area	Car/Truck/Van		Public Transportation			Bicycle	Walked	Other Means	Worked at Home
	Drove Alone	Car-pooled	Bus	Subway	Railroad				
Albuquerque, NM	80.6	9.6	1.3	0.0	0.2	0.8	1.7	1.1	4.8
Allentown, PA	81.7	8.4	1.5	0.1	0.1	0.2	2.4	1.1	4.6
Anchorage, AK	75.7	11.5	1.3	0.0	0.0	1.0	2.7	3.2	4.5
Ann Arbor, MI	71.8	7.9	5.1	0.1	0.0	1.6	7.0	0.6	5.9
Athens, GA	76.3	10.3	2.8	0.0	0.0	0.9	2.9	1.2	5.6
Atlanta, GA	77.3	9.2	2.0	0.8	0.1	0.2	1.3	1.6	7.4
Austin, TX	76.3	9.2	1.8	0.1	0.1	0.8	1.8	1.2	8.8
Baton Rouge, LA	84.8	8.7	0.8	0.0	0.0	0.3	1.5	0.9	3.1
Boise City, ID	79.9	8.9	0.3	0.0	0.0	1.2	1.7	1.1	6.8
Boston, MA	66.4	7.2	4.1	6.7	2.2	1.1	5.4	1.7	5.3
Boulder, CO	65.0	7.2	4.7	0.0	0.0	4.2	5.0	1.0	12.8
Cape Coral, FL	79.0	10.2	0.6	0.0	0.0	0.6	1.2	2.0	6.3
Cedar Rapids, IA	84.7	7.5	0.5	0.0	0.0	0.3	2.0	0.7	4.2
Charleston, SC	81.1	8.2	0.7	0.0	0.0	0.7	2.3	1.2	5.8
Charlotte, NC	80.4	8.9	1.1	0.2	0.1	0.1	1.4	1.2	6.6
Chicago, IL	70.0	7.7	4.4	4.4	3.3	0.7	3.0	1.4	5.2
Cincinnati, OH	82.3	8.0	1.7	0.0	0.0	0.2	2.0	0.8	5.0
Clarksville, TN	84.0	8.1	0.7	0.0	0.0	0.1	3.1	1.3	2.7
Cleveland, OH	81.4	7.7	2.7	0.2	0.1	0.3	2.2	1.1	4.4
College Station, TX	79.8	10.7	1.7	0.0	0.0	1.3	1.9	1.1	3.5
Colorado Springs, CO	77.0	10.4	0.6	0.0	0.0	0.4	3.4	1.0	7.0
Columbia, MO	78.9	10.7	0.8	0.0	0.0	0.8	3.3	0.9	4.5
Columbia, SC	80.7	8.6	0.6	0.0	0.0	0.1	4.4	1.9	3.6
Columbus, OH	82.2	7.6	1.6	0.0	0.0	0.4	2.2	1.0	5.0
Dallas, TX	80.6	9.7	0.9	0.2	0.2	0.1	1.2	1.2	5.8
Davenport, IA	85.6	6.8	0.9	0.0	0.0	0.2	2.0	0.9	3.6
Denver, CO	75.3	8.1	2.8	0.6	0.3	0.8	2.2	1.5	8.4
Des Moines, IA	83.6	7.8	1.1	0.0	0.0	0.2	1.8	0.8	4.6
Durham, NC	76.5	8.7	3.4	0.0	0.0	0.7	2.8	1.3	6.7
Edison, NJ	49.2	6.3	7.5	20.0	3.9	0.7	5.9	2.0	4.5
El Paso, TX	80.7	10.6	1.3	0.0	0.0	0.1	1.6	2.1	3.5
Fargo, ND	82.2	8.6	0.7	0.0	0.0	0.5	2.8	0.8	4.4
Fayetteville, NC	81.3	9.2	0.3	0.0	0.0	0.1	4.2	1.4	3.4
Fort Collins, CO	74.9	8.0	1.5	0.0	0.0	3.1	2.7	1.2	8.6
Fort Wayne, IN	83.9	9.0	0.6	0.0	0.0	0.3	1.4	0.7	4.2
Fort Worth, TX	80.6	9.7	0.9	0.2	0.2	0.1	1.2	1.2	5.8
Grand Rapids, MI	81.9	9.1	1.4	0.0	0.0	0.5	2.2	0.8	4.2
Greeley, CO	80.4	9.6	0.5	0.0	0.0	0.3	1.9	1.0	6.2
Green Bay, WI	83.8	7.9	0.7	0.0	0.0	0.2	1.8	0.9	4.7
Greensboro, NC	82.7	9.0	0.9	0.0	0.0	0.1	1.4	0.9	4.9
Honolulu, HI	64.7	14.2	8.0	0.0	0.0	0.9	5.5	2.7	4.0
Houston, TX	80.8	9.8	1.9	0.0	0.0	0.2	1.3	1.4	4.5
Huntsville, AL	88.0	6.2	0.2	0.0	0.0	0.1	0.8	1.0	3.7
Indianapolis, IN	83.2	8.3	0.8	0.0	0.0	0.3	1.5	0.9	4.9
Jacksonville, FL	80.9	8.2	1.2	0.0	0.0	0.5	1.5	1.7	6.0
Kansas City, MO	83.7	7.8	0.8	0.0	0.0	0.1	1.2	0.9	5.4
Lafayette, LA	84.8	8.2	0.5	0.0	0.0	0.4	1.9	1.1	3.0
Lakeland, FL	83.4	9.4	0.5	0.0	0.0	0.4	1.0	1.4	4.0
Las Vegas, NV	78.8	9.8	3.3	0.0	0.0	0.3	1.5	2.2	4.2
Lexington, KY	79.9	9.3	1.3	0.0	0.0	0.4	3.1	1.3	4.6
Lincoln, NE	81.3	8.9	1.1	0.0	0.0	1.1	3.3	0.6	3.7
Little Rock, AR	83.9	9.5	0.5	0.0	0.0	0.2	1.3	1.1	3.5
Los Angeles, CA	75.1	9.5	4.1	0.4	0.3	0.7	2.5	1.6	5.8
Louisville, KY	82.0	8.5	1.8	0.0	0.0	0.2	1.6	1.3	4.6

Table continued on following page.

Metro Area	Car/Truck/Van		Public Transportation			Bicycle	Walked	Other Means	Worked at Home
	Drove Alone	Car-pooled	Bus	Subway	Railroad				
Madison, WI	75.0	7.5	4.2	0.0	0.0	2.2	5.0	0.9	5.1
Manchester, NH	81.4	8.1	0.8	0.0	0.1	0.1	2.1	0.9	6.4
Memphis, TN	84.6	9.2	0.7	0.0	0.0	0.1	1.0	1.1	3.3
Miami, FL	77.9	9.1	2.8	0.3	0.2	0.6	1.6	1.8	5.7
Midland, TX	84.8	9.7	0.2	0.0	0.0	0.1	1.1	0.8	3.3
Milwaukee, WI	80.9	7.8	3.1	0.0	0.1	0.5	2.6	0.7	4.3
Minneapolis, MN	77.5	8.1	4.1	0.2	0.2	0.8	2.3	1.1	5.8
Nashville, TN	80.8	9.4	0.9	0.0	0.1	0.1	1.3	1.1	6.3
New Haven, CT	78.3	8.4	2.8	0.1	0.9	0.5	3.3	1.0	4.7
New Orleans, LA	78.1	9.8	2.3	0.0	0.0	1.1	2.5	1.7	4.5
New York, NY	49.2	6.3	7.5	20.0	3.9	0.7	5.9	2.0	4.5
Oklahoma City, OK	83.2	9.4	0.4	0.0	0.0	0.3	1.6	1.0	4.1
Omaha, NE	83.8	8.2	0.8	0.0	0.0	0.2	1.7	1.0	4.2
Orlando, FL	79.7	9.8	1.5	0.0	0.1	0.4	1.1	1.6	5.9
Peoria, IL	84.9	7.3	1.1	0.0	0.0	0.3	2.1	0.9	3.6
Philadelphia, PA	72.5	7.6	5.0	1.9	2.3	0.6	3.6	1.3	5.2
Phoenix, AZ	76.1	11.1	1.7	0.1	0.0	0.8	1.5	1.8	7.0
Pittsburgh, PA	76.6	8.3	5.1	0.2	0.0	0.3	3.4	1.1	5.0
Portland, OR	70.3	9.1	4.8	0.7	0.2	2.2	3.4	2.0	7.4
Providence, RI	80.7	8.6	1.5	0.2	1.0	0.2	3.1	0.8	3.9
Provo, UT	73.1	11.4	1.1	0.2	0.9	0.9	4.1	1.2	7.2
Raleigh, NC	79.7	8.3	0.8	0.0	0.0	0.2	1.1	0.9	8.9
Reno, NV	77.2	12.0	1.8	0.0	0.0	0.6	2.6	1.1	4.7
Richmond, VA	81.1	8.6	1.4	0.0	0.1	0.5	1.7	1.3	5.3
Riverside, CA	78.9	11.5	0.9	0.1	0.4	0.3	1.5	1.3	5.3
Rochester, MN	74.1	11.5	4.0	0.0	0.0	0.6	3.6	0.8	5.3
Sacramento, CA	76.8	9.4	1.6	0.2	0.2	1.4	1.8	1.5	7.1
Salt Lake City, UT	75.4	11.1	2.1	0.3	0.5	0.8	2.1	1.5	6.2
San Antonio, TX	79.5	10.7	1.9	0.0	0.0	0.2	1.7	1.3	4.7
San Diego, CA	76.2	8.6	2.5	0.0	0.2	0.6	2.9	1.9	7.0
San Francisco, CA	57.6	9.5	7.6	7.6	1.5	1.9	4.7	3.0	6.6
San Jose, CA	74.9	10.6	2.4	0.3	1.5	1.7	2.1	1.6	5.0
Santa Rosa, CA	74.6	11.3	1.6	0.0	0.2	1.0	2.7	1.3	7.4
Savannah, GA	79.5	9.7	1.8	0.1	0.0	0.8	2.4	1.6	4.2
Seattle, WA	67.5	10.0	8.7	0.4	0.5	1.1	4.0	1.5	6.2
Sioux Falls, SD	84.3	8.1	0.5	0.0	0.0	0.4	2.1	0.6	4.1
Springfield, IL	83.3	8.0	1.3	0.1	0.0	0.5	1.7	1.0	4.3
Tallahassee, FL	81.1	9.2	1.4	0.0	0.0	0.6	2.0	1.3	4.3
Tampa, FL	78.9	8.8	1.3	0.0	0.0	0.6	1.4	1.6	7.4
Tucson, AZ	76.8	10.0	2.2	0.0	0.0	1.5	2.3	1.8	5.4
Tulsa, OK	82.8	9.6	0.4	0.0	0.0	0.2	1.2	1.5	4.2
Tuscaloosa, AL	85.3	9.0	0.5	0.0	0.0	0.2	1.1	0.5	3.4
Virginia Beach, VA	81.3	8.3	1.4	0.0	0.0	0.4	3.3	1.4	3.8
Washington, DC	65.8	9.3	4.8	7.8	0.8	0.9	3.3	1.5	5.9
Wichita, KS	84.0	8.7	0.4	0.0	0.0	0.4	1.7	1.2	3.5
Winston-Salem, NC	83.6	8.9	0.7	0.0	0.0	0.1	1.3	0.9	4.5
U.S.	76.3	9.0	2.4	1.9	0.6	0.5	2.7	1.4	5.2

Note: Figures are percentages and cover workers 16 years of age and older; (1) Figures cover the Metropolitan Statistical Area—see Appendix B for areas included
Source: U.S. Census Bureau, 2015-2019 American Community Survey 5-Year Estimates

Travel Time to Work: City

City	Less Than 10 Minutes	10 to 19 Minutes	20 to 29 Minutes	30 to 44 Minutes	45 to 59 Minutes	60 to 89 Minutes	90 Minutes or More
Albuquerque, NM	11.1	35.8	28.1	17.7	3.1	2.8	1.4
Allentown, PA	11.5	34.8	28.6	14.6	4.2	4.1	2.2
Anchorage, AK	16.3	44.7	23.7	10.4	2.3	1.1	1.5
Ann Arbor, MI	12.9	45.5	19.9	13.3	5.3	2.4	0.7
Athens, GA	17.4	48.3	16.9	8.8	3.6	3.0	2.0
Atlanta, GA	6.8	28.7	26.4	22.2	7.6	5.2	3.1
Austin, TX	9.5	31.8	24.3	22.1	7.1	3.8	1.4
Baton Rouge, LA	11.9	39.3	25.5	15.1	3.6	2.8	1.9
Boise City, ID	13.7	46.2	25.8	10.4	1.5	1.3	1.1
Boston, MA	7.1	19.1	19.6	30.3	12.1	9.6	2.2
Boulder, CO	17.6	45.9	16.3	10.3	5.6	3.3	1.0
Cape Coral, FL	7.9	23.9	23.5	26.5	10.4	5.8	2.0
Cedar Rapids, IA	18.0	49.5	18.0	9.7	2.2	1.5	1.1
Charleston, SC	11.4	31.9	26.3	21.1	6.5	1.5	1.3
Charlotte, NC	8.2	28.3	26.6	24.4	7.1	3.5	2.0
Chicago, IL	4.5	16.0	17.4	30.6	15.3	12.8	3.5
Cincinnati, OH	11.0	33.2	27.0	19.2	4.5	3.2	1.9
Clarksville, TN	10.8	34.3	24.5	15.6	5.7	7.4	1.7
Cleveland, OH	9.4	33.3	27.0	19.5	5.0	3.7	2.0
College Station, TX	16.5	56.7	17.6	5.9	0.5	1.8	1.2
Colorado Springs, CO	11.6	35.9	28.5	15.2	3.5	3.0	2.3
Columbia, MO	20.2	55.0	11.8	8.2	2.8	0.8	1.2
Columbia, SC	31.3	36.6	17.6	9.7	1.8	1.8	1.2
Columbus, OH	10.0	34.5	29.8	18.8	3.7	2.1	1.1
Dallas, TX	7.9	26.6	23.0	26.5	8.0	5.9	2.0
Davenport, IA	17.0	47.8	20.8	9.0	3.1	1.2	1.0
Denver, CO	7.5	28.5	24.6	26.0	8.0	3.9	1.5
Des Moines, IA	13.0	43.8	27.2	11.9	1.9	1.1	1.0
Durham, NC	9.4	37.4	26.3	18.0	4.5	3.0	1.6
Edison, NJ	6.4	23.1	17.4	18.1	11.2	14.0	9.7
El Paso, TX	9.8	34.4	27.7	19.6	4.4	2.2	1.9
Fargo, ND	20.9	54.9	17.6	3.3	1.0	1.4	0.8
Fayetteville, NC	20.6	37.5	22.3	12.5	3.3	2.1	1.6
Fort Collins, CO	16.5	42.6	19.9	11.0	5.1	3.5	1.4
Fort Wayne, IN	12.2	40.5	27.4	12.5	3.1	2.4	1.9
Fort Worth, TX	8.4	28.3	22.5	23.9	8.7	6.2	2.0
Grand Rapids, MI	15.0	42.9	24.4	11.6	3.3	2.0	0.9
Greeley, CO	16.1	37.4	16.2	14.7	5.9	7.4	2.3
Green Bay, WI	18.1	48.8	19.4	7.7	3.1	1.8	1.1
Greensboro, NC	12.1	41.4	24.1	14.7	3.5	2.6	1.6
Honolulu, HI	7.9	35.3	23.7	22.0	5.5	4.3	1.4
Houston, TX	7.3	25.5	22.2	27.8	8.9	6.4	1.9
Huntsville, AL	12.8	41.7	26.3	15.2	2.3	0.7	0.9
Indianapolis, IN	9.7	30.0	29.9	22.1	4.3	2.5	1.5
Jacksonville, FL	8.3	27.7	27.5	25.6	6.5	2.9	1.6
Kansas City, MO	11.4	33.4	28.1	20.0	4.5	1.6	1.1
Lafayette, LA	16.4	42.1	20.4	12.5	2.5	2.8	3.3
Lakeland, FL	10.8	43.4	20.1	14.4	5.8	3.5	2.0
Las Vegas, NV	6.9	23.9	29.3	28.7	6.4	2.7	2.0
Lexington, KY	12.4	38.0	27.6	14.9	3.2	2.5	1.4
Lincoln, NE	17.2	44.8	23.1	9.3	2.5	2.1	1.1
Little Rock, AR	14.0	44.4	26.5	10.8	2.0	1.3	1.1
Los Angeles, CA	5.9	21.8	19.0	28.3	10.8	10.5	3.8
Louisville, KY	9.3	32.4	30.1	20.3	4.4	2.2	1.4
Madison, WI	14.4	40.7	24.1	15.3	2.9	1.9	0.8

Table continued on following page.

City	Less Than 10 Minutes	10 to 19 Minutes	20 to 29 Minutes	30 to 44 Minutes	45 to 59 Minutes	60 to 89 Minutes	90 Minutes or More
Manchester, NH	14.1	38.3	19.2	14.5	5.9	4.8	3.2
Memphis, TN	10.2	32.9	30.2	20.5	3.6	1.6	1.0
Miami, FL	4.9	21.3	22.7	31.7	10.2	7.4	1.8
Midland, TX	16.1	49.1	17.2	11.1	2.6	2.0	1.9
Milwaukee, WI	10.1	36.6	25.8	19.3	4.0	2.7	1.5
Minneapolis, MN	8.1	32.0	30.9	20.9	4.2	2.8	1.2
Nashville, TN	8.7	29.1	26.2	23.8	7.2	3.5	1.5
New Haven, CT	13.6	40.4	20.1	13.1	4.7	4.7	3.4
New Orleans, LA	9.9	33.9	25.4	19.7	4.5	4.2	2.3
New York, NY	3.8	12.1	13.4	27.1	16.4	19.5	7.7
Oklahoma City, OK	11.2	35.5	29.5	17.7	3.3	1.5	1.3
Omaha, NE	14.0	41.0	27.8	12.4	2.3	1.5	0.9
Orlando, FL	7.8	27.2	25.9	26.7	6.8	3.4	2.2
Peoria, IL	18.6	49.5	19.8	7.6	1.9	1.8	0.8
Philadelphia, PA	6.1	18.7	19.7	28.0	12.6	10.6	4.4
Phoenix, AZ	8.8	26.7	25.5	24.9	7.5	4.7	1.9
Pittsburgh, PA	9.4	31.5	25.8	22.9	5.1	3.7	1.6
Portland, OR	7.8	26.3	27.0	24.5	7.7	4.9	1.8
Providence, RI	12.2	39.9	20.8	14.3	5.6	4.1	3.1
Provo, UT	21.3	45.3	17.3	9.0	2.7	2.9	1.4
Raleigh, NC	9.8	33.0	25.8	21.0	5.7	3.1	1.7
Reno, NV	14.4	43.5	22.1	12.1	3.7	2.7	1.5
Richmond, VA	9.8	37.9	28.5	16.4	3.2	2.6	1.5
Riverside, CA	8.9	26.2	19.9	21.7	7.6	9.4	6.4
Rochester, MN	19.3	55.7	13.6	6.3	2.2	1.7	1.2
Sacramento, CA	8.0	31.2	25.1	22.5	5.9	4.0	3.3
Salt Lake City, UT	12.3	45.3	22.8	13.0	3.6	1.9	1.0
San Antonio, TX	8.5	30.8	27.2	22.1	6.1	3.3	2.0
San Diego, CA	7.6	32.1	27.6	21.7	5.7	3.4	1.8
San Francisco, CA	3.8	18.0	20.5	30.3	12.3	11.2	3.9
San Jose, CA	5.1	22.4	22.1	27.7	10.8	8.7	3.1
Santa Rosa, CA	13.8	39.2	21.7	13.6	3.9	4.6	3.2
Savannah, GA	16.0	40.0	22.3	12.8	4.4	3.2	1.4
Seattle, WA	6.7	23.4	24.4	28.6	10.5	5.0	1.5
Sioux Falls, SD	16.1	52.3	22.4	5.4	1.4	1.3	1.1
Springfield, IL	18.2	51.5	18.5	6.1	1.8	2.3	1.6
Tallahassee, FL	14.6	44.7	23.9	12.3	2.1	1.3	1.0
Tampa, FL	11.1	30.5	23.6	21.8	6.7	4.3	1.9
Tucson, AZ	11.9	34.4	25.0	19.7	4.8	2.5	1.6
Tulsa, OK	14.6	44.5	25.7	10.5	2.0	1.5	1.2
Tuscaloosa, AL	14.6	44.8	25.9	7.4	3.5	2.8	1.0
Virginia Beach, VA	10.7	29.8	28.1	22.3	5.1	2.7	1.4
Washington, DC	4.9	18.5	22.5	32.4	12.6	7.1	2.0
Wichita, KS	14.2	44.9	27.2	9.7	1.7	1.2	1.2
Winston-Salem, NC	13.6	40.8	23.8	13.7	4.2	2.1	1.8
U.S.	12.2	28.4	20.8	20.8	8.3	6.4	2.9

Note: Figures are percentages and include workers 16 years old and over
Source: U.S. Census Bureau, 2015-2019 American Community Survey 5-Year Estimates

Travel Time to Work: Metro Area

Metro Area	Less Than 10 Minutes	10 to 19 Minutes	20 to 29 Minutes	30 to 44 Minutes	45 to 59 Minutes	60 to 89 Minutes	90 Minutes or More
Albuquerque, NM	10.8	31.6	26.2	20.5	5.7	3.6	1.6
Allentown, PA	12.4	27.6	23.1	18.1	7.4	7.3	4.1
Anchorage, AK	15.7	41.0	21.8	10.8	4.3	4.0	2.5
Ann Arbor, MI	10.6	32.7	24.5	19.3	7.6	4.1	1.3
Athens, GA	14.1	41.1	21.4	12.9	4.7	3.5	2.2
Atlanta, GA	7.0	22.1	19.6	24.9	12.3	10.4	3.8
Austin, TX	9.6	27.1	22.3	23.1	10.0	6.1	1.8
Baton Rouge, LA	9.8	27.7	22.0	22.5	9.2	6.5	2.3
Boise City, ID	12.7	34.6	25.6	18.4	5.1	2.2	1.3
Boston, MA	9.0	22.0	17.9	24.4	12.1	11.0	3.7
Boulder, CO	13.7	34.4	21.4	17.6	7.0	4.6	1.3
Cape Coral, FL	8.7	25.3	23.1	25.6	10.2	5.1	2.0
Cedar Rapids, IA	17.4	40.6	21.6	13.1	3.9	2.0	1.3
Charleston, SC	8.7	25.6	24.3	26.0	9.3	4.4	1.7
Charlotte, NC	9.3	27.1	22.7	24.0	9.6	5.2	2.1
Chicago, IL	8.2	21.5	18.4	25.2	12.4	10.8	3.5
Cincinnati, OH	10.9	27.5	25.3	23.4	7.8	3.6	1.5
Clarksville, TN	15.2	32.1	21.1	17.4	6.1	6.0	2.1
Cleveland, OH	11.2	28.3	25.5	23.1	7.3	3.3	1.4
College Station, TX	15.6	49.4	19.1	10.1	2.3	2.1	1.5
Colorado Springs, CO	11.6	32.8	27.2	17.4	5.0	3.7	2.3
Columbia, MO	17.5	45.5	17.3	12.4	4.3	1.5	1.4
Columbia, SC	12.5	29.6	23.5	22.3	6.8	3.4	1.9
Columbus, OH	11.0	29.7	26.3	21.8	6.6	3.2	1.4
Dallas, TX	8.6	25.0	21.3	25.6	10.5	7.0	2.1
Davenport, IA	17.9	37.4	24.3	13.6	3.7	1.9	1.3
Denver, CO	8.0	24.9	23.0	26.3	10.2	5.8	1.8
Des Moines, IA	15.2	35.2	27.3	16.3	3.4	1.5	1.1
Durham, NC	9.8	31.6	24.8	21.2	6.8	4.2	1.5
Edison, NJ	6.7	18.2	16.1	23.9	12.7	15.3	7.1
El Paso, TX	10.7	32.6	26.8	20.6	4.9	2.4	2.0
Fargo, ND	18.5	50.6	19.3	7.0	2.0	1.6	1.1
Fayetteville, NC	14.4	29.4	23.3	20.1	6.6	4.1	2.1
Fort Collins, CO	14.5	34.6	22.0	15.6	6.4	5.1	1.9
Fort Wayne, IN	12.7	36.5	28.2	15.0	3.5	2.3	1.8
Fort Worth, TX	8.6	25.0	21.3	25.6	10.5	7.0	2.1
Grand Rapids, MI	14.8	35.3	24.9	16.1	5.0	2.5	1.5
Greeley, CO	11.9	27.1	19.2	22.3	9.5	7.5	2.5
Green Bay, WI	18.1	40.0	21.7	12.9	3.8	2.0	1.5
Greensboro, NC	12.2	34.8	25.3	18.4	5.0	2.6	1.7
Honolulu, HI	9.0	24.9	19.6	25.3	9.8	8.5	3.0
Houston, TX	7.7	23.3	19.4	26.5	11.8	8.9	2.5
Huntsville, AL	10.3	32.1	27.8	21.7	5.6	1.6	1.0
Indianapolis, IN	11.4	27.5	24.4	24.1	7.6	3.5	1.5
Jacksonville, FL	8.8	25.4	24.4	26.0	9.0	4.5	1.8
Kansas City, MO	12.2	30.7	25.2	21.7	6.6	2.6	1.1
Lafayette, LA	15.1	32.4	21.0	18.4	5.2	3.7	4.3
Lakeland, FL	8.4	30.0	21.7	21.0	9.9	6.3	2.7
Las Vegas, NV	7.4	27.5	29.0	26.1	5.4	2.7	1.9
Lexington, KY	14.3	34.6	25.1	17.7	4.5	2.5	1.3
Lincoln, NE	17.1	41.8	23.8	11.2	2.9	2.0	1.2
Little Rock, AR	12.6	33.0	23.4	19.9	7.0	2.8	1.3
Los Angeles, CA	6.9	24.4	19.5	25.4	10.2	9.8	3.7
Louisville, KY	9.7	29.9	27.3	22.6	6.4	2.6	1.5
Madison, WI	15.6	32.6	24.3	18.6	5.2	2.5	1.1

Table continued on following page.

Metro Area	Less Than 10 Minutes	10 to 19 Minutes	20 to 29 Minutes	30 to 44 Minutes	45 to 59 Minutes	60 to 89 Minutes	90 Minutes or More
Manchester, NH	11.1	29.7	19.7	19.8	8.6	7.2	3.9
Memphis, TN	10.2	28.3	26.7	24.1	6.8	2.7	1.2
Miami, FL	6.4	22.6	22.0	27.9	10.3	8.1	2.7
Midland, TX	15.8	46.2	17.9	12.5	3.1	2.6	1.8
Milwaukee, WI	11.9	31.6	25.8	21.3	5.5	2.5	1.4
Minneapolis, MN	10.2	27.3	25.1	23.7	8.1	4.3	1.4
Nashville, TN	9.2	26.5	21.7	23.4	10.6	6.6	2.0
New Haven, CT	11.5	31.8	22.9	19.5	6.6	4.8	2.9
New Orleans, LA	10.5	30.6	22.2	20.9	7.6	5.6	2.5
New York, NY	6.7	18.2	16.1	23.9	12.7	15.3	7.1
Oklahoma City, OK	12.3	32.0	25.7	20.3	5.7	2.4	1.5
Omaha, NE	13.9	36.4	27.5	15.8	3.7	1.7	1.0
Orlando, FL	7.1	22.9	22.9	28.1	11.1	5.6	2.3
Peoria, IL	18.6	34.8	23.6	15.1	4.4	2.1	1.4
Philadelphia, PA	9.2	23.6	20.3	24.0	11.1	8.5	3.3
Phoenix, AZ	9.9	26.2	23.7	23.7	9.0	5.7	1.9
Pittsburgh, PA	11.8	26.6	21.0	22.8	9.5	6.2	2.1
Portland, OR	10.2	26.9	22.6	23.1	9.3	5.8	2.1
Providence, RI	11.9	29.9	21.9	19.6	7.6	5.9	3.2
Provo, UT	18.0	35.3	20.1	15.5	5.6	3.9	1.6
Raleigh, NC	8.9	27.5	24.4	23.9	8.7	4.8	1.9
Reno, NV	12.1	37.7	25.0	16.6	4.2	2.7	1.7
Richmond, VA	8.7	29.1	27.4	23.2	6.3	3.1	2.0
Riverside, CA	9.4	26.2	18.6	19.7	8.5	10.4	7.2
Rochester, MN	18.9	41.6	18.4	12.8	3.9	2.7	1.7
Sacramento, CA	9.9	28.2	22.3	23.0	8.1	4.9	3.5
Salt Lake City, UT	10.5	33.4	27.0	19.6	5.6	2.8	1.1
San Antonio, TX	9.0	28.1	24.3	23.2	8.5	4.7	2.2
San Diego, CA	8.2	28.9	24.3	23.5	7.7	5.1	2.2
San Francisco, CA	6.4	22.0	17.4	23.7	12.5	12.9	5.1
San Jose, CA	6.6	25.0	22.6	25.1	9.6	7.8	3.2
Santa Rosa, CA	15.1	32.2	20.4	16.8	5.8	5.9	3.9
Savannah, GA	11.0	30.6	24.1	21.2	7.7	4.1	1.3
Seattle, WA	7.7	22.2	20.8	25.5	11.4	9.0	3.4
Sioux Falls, SD	16.5	44.0	24.6	10.0	2.4	1.4	1.2
Springfield, IL	15.6	42.6	23.6	11.5	2.7	2.3	1.7
Tallahassee, FL	11.0	34.3	24.8	20.4	5.6	2.4	1.5
Tampa, FL	9.6	26.9	21.6	23.0	10.1	6.5	2.3
Tucson, AZ	10.7	28.9	24.6	23.6	7.4	3.0	1.9
Tulsa, OK	13.3	33.9	26.5	18.1	4.5	2.2	1.4
Tuscaloosa, AL	11.3	32.4	26.5	16.5	6.6	5.0	1.7
Virginia Beach, VA	11.3	30.6	23.9	21.4	7.1	4.0	1.7
Washington, DC	5.9	18.9	17.7	25.7	14.2	13.1	4.6
Wichita, KS	16.3	37.5	26.5	14.3	2.8	1.4	1.3
Winston-Salem, NC	12.0	33.3	24.5	19.1	6.1	2.8	2.1
U.S.	12.2	28.4	20.8	20.8	8.3	6.4	2.9

Note: Figures are percentages and include workers 16 years old and over; Figures cover the Metropolitan Statistical Area—see Appendix B for areas included
Source: U.S. Census Bureau, 2015-2019 American Community Survey 5-Year Estimates

2020 Presidential Election Results

City	Area Covered	Biden	Trump	Jorgensen	Hawkins	Other
Albuquerque, NM	Bernalillo County	61.0	36.6	1.5	0.5	0.4
Allentown, PA	Lehigh County	53.1	45.5	1.2	0.1	0.2
Anchorage, AK	State of Alaska	42.8	52.8	2.5	0.0	1.9
Ann Arbor, MI	Washtenaw County	72.4	25.9	0.9	0.3	0.4
Athens, GA	Clarke County	70.1	28.1	1.6	0.1	0.1
Atlanta, GA	Fulton County	72.6	26.2	1.2	0.0	0.0
Austin, TX	Travis County	71.4	26.4	1.5	0.3	0.4
Baton Rouge, LA	East Baton Rouge Parish	55.5	42.5	1.2	0.0	0.8
Boise City, ID	Ada County	46.1	50.0	2.0	0.1	1.8
Boston, MA	Suffolk County	80.6	17.5	0.9	0.5	0.5
Boulder, CO	Boulder County	77.2	20.6	1.2	0.3	0.6
Cape Coral, FL	Lee County	39.9	59.1	0.5	0.1	0.3
Cedar Rapids, IA	Linn County	55.6	41.9	1.6	0.3	0.7
Charleston, SC	Charleston County	55.5	42.6	1.5	0.3	0.1
Charlotte, NC	Mecklenburg County	66.7	31.6	1.0	0.3	0.5
Chicago, IL	Cook County	74.2	24.0	0.8	0.5	0.5
Cincinnati, OH	Hamilton County	57.1	41.3	1.2	0.3	0.0
Clarksville, TN	Montgomery County	42.3	55.0	1.9	0.2	0.7
Cleveland, OH	Cuyahoga County	66.4	32.3	0.7	0.3	0.3
College Station, TX	Brazos County	41.6	55.9	2.1	0.3	0.1
Colorado Springs, CO	El Paso County	42.7	53.5	2.4	0.3	1.0
Columbia, MO	Boone County	54.8	42.3	2.2	0.3	0.4
Columbia, SC	Richland County	68.4	30.1	1.0	0.4	0.1
Columbus, OH	Franklin County	64.7	33.4	1.2	0.3	0.4
Dallas, TX	Dallas County	64.9	33.3	1.0	0.4	0.4
Davenport, IA	Scott County	50.7	47.2	1.2	0.2	0.7
Denver, CO	Denver County	79.6	18.2	1.2	0.3	0.7
Des Moines, IA	Polk County	56.5	41.3	1.3	0.2	0.7
Durham, NC	Durham County	80.4	18.0	0.8	0.3	0.4
Edison, NJ	Middlesex County	60.2	38.2	0.7	0.3	0.6
El Paso, TX	El Paso County	66.7	31.6	1.0	0.5	0.2
Fargo, ND	Cass County	46.8	49.5	2.9	0.0	0.7
Fayetteville, NC	Cumberland County	57.4	40.8	1.1	0.3	0.4
Fort Collins, CO	Larimer County	56.2	40.8	1.8	0.3	0.9
Fort Wayne, IN	Allen County	43.2	54.3	2.2	0.0	0.3
Fort Worth, TX	Tarrant County	49.3	49.1	1.2	0.3	0.0
Grand Rapids, MI	Kent County	51.9	45.8	1.5	0.3	0.5
Greeley, CO	Weld County	39.6	57.6	1.7	0.2	0.9
Green Bay, WI	Brown County	45.5	52.7	1.3	0.0	0.5
Greensboro, NC	Guilford County	60.8	37.7	0.8	0.2	0.4
Honolulu, HI	Honolulu County	62.5	35.7	0.9	0.6	0.4
Houston, TX	Harris County	56.0	42.7	1.0	0.3	0.0
Huntsville, AL	Madison County	44.8	52.8	1.9	0.0	0.5
Indianapolis, IN	Marion County	63.3	34.3	1.8	0.1	0.4
Jacksonville, FL	Duval County	51.1	47.3	1.0	0.2	0.5
Kansas City, MO	Jackson County	59.8	37.9	1.4	0.4	0.5
Lafayette, LA	Lafayette Parish	34.7	63.3	1.3	0.0	0.7
Lakeland, FL	Polk County	42.2	56.6	0.8	0.1	0.4
Las Vegas, NV	Clark County	53.7	44.3	0.9	0.0	1.1
Lexington, KY	Fayette County	59.2	38.5	1.6	0.1	0.6
Lincoln, NE	Lancaster County	52.3	44.6	2.4	0.0	0.7
Little Rock, AR	Pulaski County	60.0	37.5	1.0	0.3	1.3
Los Angeles, CA	Los Angeles County	71.0	26.9	0.8	0.5	0.8
Louisville, KY	Jefferson County	59.1	39.0	1.2	0.1	0.7
Madison, WI	Dane County	75.5	22.9	1.1	0.1	0.6
Manchester, NH	Hillsborough County	52.8	45.2	1.7	0.0	0.3

Table continued on following page.

City	Area Covered	Biden	Trump	Jorgensen	Hawkins	Other
Memphis, TN	Shelby County	64.4	34.0	0.6	0.2	0.8
Miami, FL	Miami-Dade County	53.3	46.0	0.3	0.1	0.3
Midland, TX	Midland County	20.9	77.3	1.3	0.2	0.2
Milwaukee, WI	Milwaukee County	69.1	29.3	0.9	0.0	0.7
Minneapolis, MN	Hennepin County	70.5	27.2	1.0	0.3	1.0
Nashville, TN	Davidson County	64.5	32.4	1.1	0.2	1.8
New Haven, CT	New Haven County	58.0	40.6	0.9	0.4	0.0
New Orleans, LA	Orleans Parish	83.1	15.0	0.9	0.0	1.0
New York, NY	Bronx County	83.3	15.9	0.2	0.3	0.3
New York, NY	Kings County	76.8	22.1	0.3	0.4	0.4
New York, NY	New York County	86.4	12.2	0.5	0.4	0.5
New York, NY	Queens County	72.0	26.9	0.3	0.4	0.4
New York, NY	Richmond County	42.0	56.9	0.4	0.3	0.4
Oklahoma City, OK	Oklahoma County	48.1	49.2	1.8	0.0	0.9
Omaha, NE	Douglas County	54.4	43.1	2.0	0.0	0.6
Orlando, FL	Orange County	60.9	37.8	0.7	0.2	0.4
Peoria, IL	Peoria County	51.9	45.6	1.6	0.6	0.4
Philadelphia, PA	Philadelphia County	81.2	17.9	0.7	0.1	0.2
Phoenix, AZ	Maricopa County	50.1	48.0	1.5	0.0	0.3
Pittsburgh, PA	Allegheny County	59.4	39.0	1.2	0.0	0.4
Portland, OR	Multnomah County	79.2	17.9	1.2	0.6	1.0
Providence, RI	Providence County	60.5	37.6	0.8	0.0	1.0
Provo, UT	Utah County	26.3	66.7	3.6	0.3	3.1
Raleigh, NC	Wake County	62.3	35.8	1.2	0.3	0.5
Reno, NV	Washoe County	50.8	46.3	1.4	0.0	1.5
Richmond, VA	Richmond City	82.9	14.9	1.5	0.0	0.6
Riverside, CA	Riverside County	53.0	45.0	1.0	0.3	0.6
Rochester, MN	Olmsted County	54.2	43.4	1.2	0.3	0.9
Sacramento, CA	Sacramento County	61.4	36.1	1.4	0.5	0.7
Salt Lake City, UT	Salt Lake County	53.0	42.1	2.2	0.4	2.2
San Antonio, TX	Bexar County	58.2	40.1	1.1	0.4	0.2
San Diego, CA	San Diego County	60.2	37.5	1.3	0.5	0.5
San Francisco, CA	San Francisco County	85.3	12.7	0.7	0.6	0.7
San Jose, CA	Santa Clara County	72.6	25.2	1.1	0.5	0.6
Santa Rosa, CA	Sonoma County	74.5	23.0	1.3	0.6	0.6
Savannah, GA	Chatham County	58.6	39.9	1.4	0.0	0.0
Seattle, WA	King County	75.0	22.2	1.5	0.5	0.8
Sioux Falls, SD	Minnehaha County	43.8	53.3	2.8	0.0	0.0
Springfield, IL	Sangamon County	46.7	51.1	1.4	0.6	0.3
Tallahassee, FL	Leon County	63.3	35.1	0.8	0.2	0.5
Tampa, FL	Hillsborough County	52.7	45.8	0.8	0.2	0.5
Tucson, AZ	Pima County	58.4	39.8	1.5	0.0	0.3
Tulsa, OK	Tulsa County	40.9	56.5	1.8	0.0	0.8
Tuscaloosa, AL	Tuscaloosa County	41.9	56.7	1.0	0.0	0.4
Virginia Beach, VA	Virginia Beach City	51.6	46.2	1.8	0.0	0.4
Washington, DC	District of Columbia	92.1	5.4	0.6	0.5	1.4
Wichita, KS	Sedgwick County	42.6	54.4	2.4	0.0	0.5
Winston-Salem, NC	Forsyth County	56.2	42.3	0.9	0.2	0.4
U.S.	U.S.	51.3	46.8	1.2	0.3	0.5

Note: Results are percentages and may not add to 100% due to rounding
Source: Dave Leip's Atlas of U.S. Presidential Elections

House Price Index (HPI)

Metro Area[1]	National Ranking[3]	Quarterly Change (%)	One-Year Change (%)	Five-Year Change (%)	Since 1991Q1 (%)
Albuquerque, NM	42	2.20	7.86	27.05	163.46
Allentown, PA	59	2.10	7.47	23.78	102.86
Anchorage, AK	205	1.39	4.88	9.73	184.56
Ann Arbor, MI	224	0.98	3.78	29.65	164.45
Athens, GA	66	1.41	7.40	43.79	181.78
Atlanta, GA	110	1.95	6.57	40.75	164.55
Austin, TX	30	3.27	8.26	41.08	401.86
Baton Rouge, LA	230	1.37	3.54	17.61	188.52
Boise City, ID	1	4.90	13.83	78.91	350.41
Boston, MA[2]	167	1.93	5.51	29.37	228.40
Boulder, CO	227	1.79	3.59	36.23	436.16
Cape Coral, FL	84	3.11	7.07	33.53	188.18
Cedar Rapids, IA	218	1.99	4.00	17.00	130.16
Charleston, SC	130	1.32	6.11	36.39	284.93
Charlotte, NC	60	2.55	7.46	41.48	183.15
Chicago, IL[2]	239	1.11	2.98	16.74	122.65
Cincinnati, OH	98	1.97	6.79	31.23	131.06
Clarksville, TN	n/a	n/a	n/a	n/a	n/a
Cleveland, OH	50	2.24	7.63	30.38	104.70
College Station, TX	n/a	n/a	n/a	n/a	n/a
Colorado Springs, CO	19	3.08	8.89	51.30	301.84
Columbia, MO	212	1.63	4.42	20.40	150.92
Columbia, SC	181	1.37	5.23	24.67	125.47
Columbus, OH	65	2.05	7.40	37.73	163.06
Dallas, TX[2]	206	2.07	4.81	38.75	203.48
Davenport, IA	225	0.97	3.73	15.46	153.27
Denver, CO	164	1.71	5.57	42.32	404.42
Des Moines, IA	237	1.39	3.15	20.11	154.39
Durham, NC	161	1.51	5.61	34.97	182.89
Edison, NJ[2]	220	1.50	3.91	23.15	199.59
El Paso, TX	158	1.05	5.68	18.03	118.41
Fargo, ND	240	0.70	2.82	16.07	201.82
Fayetteville, NC	n/a	n/a	n/a	n/a	n/a
Fort Collins, CO	217	1.38	4.19	38.15	365.72
Fort Wayne, IN	53	1.29	7.55	35.84	111.44
Fort Worth, TX[2]	191	2.39	5.13	42.54	191.04
Grand Rapids, MI	71	2.11	7.32	44.57	175.35
Greeley, CO	177	1.80	5.33	46.65	333.63
Green Bay, WI	169	2.46	5.48	28.92	157.42
Greensboro, NC	128	1.99	6.14	27.91	106.32
Honolulu, HI	250	1.23	0.53	16.08	154.83
Houston, TX	211	1.45	4.53	23.50	211.24
Huntsville, AL	9	3.60	9.98	30.56	124.28
Indianapolis, IN	46	2.17	7.74	36.43	135.15
Jacksonville, FL	136	2.34	6.06	43.85	224.14
Kansas City, MO	75	2.00	7.29	37.81	175.77
Lafayette, LA	221	0.62	3.89	8.70	180.99
Lakeland, FL	8	4.29	10.11	53.44	194.73
Las Vegas, NV	171	1.70	5.46	50.47	163.25
Lexington, KY	200	1.46	5.04	28.47	155.18
Lincoln, NE	198	2.22	5.09	30.00	177.71
Little Rock, AR	196	1.79	5.10	16.24	131.58
Los Angeles, CA[2]	193	1.98	5.13	31.04	214.04
Louisville, KY	111	2.46	6.56	29.08	178.89
Madison, WI	202	1.80	4.96	27.32	218.96

Table continued on following page.

Metro Area[1]	National Ranking[3]	Quarterly Change (%)	One-Year Change (%)	Five-Year Change (%)	Since 1991Q1 (%)
Manchester, NH	17	3.48	9.02	33.95	167.53
Memphis, TN	90	1.82	6.94	33.17	120.34
Miami, FL[2]	124	1.83	6.32	38.91	334.89
Midland, TX	n/a	n/a	n/a	n/a	n/a
Milwaukee, WI	172	1.59	5.45	26.53	171.34
Minneapolis, MN	157	1.56	5.70	30.96	210.96
Nashville, TN	88	1.88	6.96	45.40	266.19
New Haven, CT	99	2.80	6.78	15.33	80.58
New Orleans, LA	174	2.09	5.37	22.52	226.15
New York, NY[2]	220	1.50	3.91	23.15	199.59
Oklahoma City, OK	182	1.07	5.23	21.46	179.09
Omaha, NE	154	1.72	5.74	31.76	176.42
Orlando, FL	119	1.83	6.36	44.80	198.33
Peoria, IL	238	0.87	3.00	6.40	120.92
Philadelphia, PA[2]	145	1.50	5.90	33.20	191.57
Phoenix, AZ	7	3.44	10.26	47.39	283.82
Pittsburgh, PA	123	1.67	6.33	26.47	167.39
Portland, OR	127	2.22	6.27	37.96	381.42
Providence, RI	89	2.66	6.95	31.83	154.93
Provo, UT	23	3.08	8.61	46.91	339.23
Raleigh, NC	159	1.84	5.67	34.46	180.65
Reno, NV	96	2.61	6.81	48.07	229.64
Richmond, VA	134	2.05	6.10	28.56	172.25
Riverside, CA	86	2.74	7.03	34.65	169.25
Rochester, MN	116	1.70	6.45	32.58	175.69
Sacramento, CA	93	2.73	6.92	37.42	166.72
Salt Lake City, UT	15	3.24	9.07	50.25	408.84
San Antonio, TX	149	2.10	5.83	34.99	224.63
San Diego, CA	141	1.97	6.01	30.38	235.91
San Francisco, CA[2]	253	-3.20	-6.72	10.12	283.50
San Jose, CA	251	0.55	0.10	18.04	296.60
Santa Rosa, CA	246	1.59	2.15	26.52	225.13
Savannah, GA	214	0.50	4.40	33.56	221.18
Seattle, WA[2]	97	2.16	6.81	48.46	324.48
Sioux Falls, SD	139	2.09	6.03	29.70	212.39
Springfield, IL	248	0.83	1.79	8.16	85.25
Tallahassee, FL	186	1.55	5.20	30.45	154.52
Tampa, FL	33	2.36	8.17	52.43	254.29
Tucson, AZ	29	2.33	8.30	39.73	202.45
Tulsa, OK	179	1.98	5.26	22.61	153.16
Tuscaloosa, AL	n/a	n/a	n/a	n/a	n/a
Virginia Beach, VA	144	1.54	5.90	17.40	170.16
Washington, DC[2]	189	1.67	5.16	21.40	197.71
Wichita, KS	49	1.50	7.67	27.26	136.03
Winston-Salem, NC	94	2.58	6.92	28.40	118.04
U.S.[4]	–	3.81	10.77	38.99	205.12

Note: The HPI is a weighted repeat sales index. It measures average price changes in repeat sales or refinancings on the same properties. This information is obtained by reviewing repeat mortgage transactions on single-family properties whose mortgages have been purchased or securitized by Fannie Mae or Freddie Mac since January 1975; (1) figures cover the Metropolitan Statistical Area (MSA) unless noted otherwise—see Appendix B for areas included; (2) Metropolitan Division—see Appendix B for areas included; (3) Rankings are based on annual percentage change, for all MSAs containing at least 15,000 transactions over the last 10 years and ranges from 1 to 253; (4) figures based on a weighted division average; all figures are for the period ended December 31, 2020; n/a not available
Source: Federal Housing Finance Agency, Change in Metropolitan Area House Price Indexes, April 7, 2021

Home Value Distribution: City

Area	Under $50,000	$50,000 -$99,999	$100,000 -$149,999	$150,000 -$199,999	$200,000 -$299,999	$300,000 -$499,999	$500,000 -$999,999	$1,000,000 or more
Albuquerque, NM	4.5	4.4	16.9	25.1	29.5	15.9	3.3	0.5
Allentown, PA	4.5	22.0	35.2	24.0	8.7	4.1	1.1	0.4
Anchorage, AK	5.3	1.9	4.8	7.0	26.9	40.9	12.2	1.0
Ann Arbor, MI	1.3	3.6	6.0	8.2	25.2	37.6	15.7	2.4
Athens, GA	6.3	12.9	19.9	21.9	20.3	12.7	5.4	0.7
Atlanta, GA	4.5	10.1	9.6	10.6	16.6	19.7	20.2	8.8
Austin, TX	2.2	2.2	4.8	9.1	24.3	33.0	20.1	4.3
Baton Rouge, LA	5.6	17.7	15.6	19.4	21.4	12.9	5.8	1.6
Boise City, ID	3.9	1.9	8.6	17.4	31.6	26.6	9.0	1.0
Boston, MA	1.6	0.3	0.4	1.4	8.2	34.1	40.4	13.5
Boulder, CO	3.8	1.7	1.8	3.3	4.1	13.3	48.9	23.1
Cape Coral, FL	1.6	3.1	11.1	22.6	34.1	20.2	6.5	0.9
Cedar Rapids, IA	5.5	16.3	34.2	20.9	16.3	5.1	1.4	0.2
Charleston, SC	1.5	2.6	4.6	8.2	26.4	31.1	19.0	6.6
Charlotte, NC	2.1	8.2	17.3	17.6	21.0	19.5	10.9	3.4
Chicago, IL	2.7	7.0	11.1	15.0	23.8	24.1	12.5	3.9
Cincinnati, OH	6.9	25.4	22.2	11.9	14.7	11.5	6.2	1.3
Clarksville, TN	4.3	14.1	28.9	26.6	19.0	5.6	0.9	0.5
Cleveland, OH	28.8	44.0	14.0	5.9	3.6	2.1	1.2	0.4
College Station, TX	2.1	1.3	7.4	21.9	35.6	24.9	6.1	0.9
Colorado Springs, CO	3.0	2.1	6.5	14.5	33.6	30.4	8.6	1.2
Columbia, MO	3.4	7.4	19.0	22.8	25.7	17.2	4.2	0.3
Columbia, SC	4.5	15.3	19.7	16.0	15.6	16.5	10.9	1.6
Columbus, OH	5.9	19.5	23.8	20.7	19.8	7.9	2.0	0.3
Dallas, TX	6.7	19.2	15.4	10.7	12.6	17.6	13.2	4.6
Davenport, IA	6.3	24.6	28.4	16.1	15.6	7.4	1.1	0.4
Denver, CO	1.3	1.6	3.3	6.8	19.5	34.6	27.3	5.6
Des Moines, IA	5.9	21.6	33.1	20.5	12.1	4.8	1.8	0.2
Durham, NC	1.8	5.3	14.5	20.5	30.8	20.3	5.9	1.0
Edison, NJ	2.1	1.8	1.9	2.7	17.0	47.4	25.4	1.6
El Paso, TX	5.1	25.0	32.7	18.5	12.5	4.8	1.2	0.3
Fargo, ND	4.0	4.3	12.6	25.0	30.8	18.6	4.0	0.6
Fayetteville, NC	5.0	26.2	28.2	19.3	13.7	5.5	1.7	0.3
Fort Collins, CO	3.2	1.1	1.5	3.6	19.8	52.8	16.7	1.3
Fort Wayne, IN	10.6	30.1	28.9	16.1	9.6	3.7	0.9	0.1
Fort Worth, TX	6.2	17.3	17.6	19.3	22.9	11.9	4.0	0.8
Grand Rapids, MI	4.7	19.6	30.0	24.3	15.0	5.0	1.3	0.2
Greeley, CO	7.1	2.5	7.2	15.2	36.3	27.2	4.3	0.2
Green Bay, WI	3.3	20.8	35.3	20.4	12.8	5.7	1.5	0.3
Greensboro, NC	3.5	19.2	24.5	18.3	18.2	11.4	3.7	1.2
Honolulu, HI	0.8	0.8	0.8	1.4	7.2	22.6	42.5	24.0
Houston, TX	5.4	19.6	18.1	13.0	14.5	15.8	10.0	3.6
Huntsville, AL	5.3	17.9	15.0	16.6	22.8	16.6	4.6	1.1
Indianapolis, IN	7.1	22.9	27.0	18.8	12.5	8.0	3.1	0.7
Jacksonville, FL	7.4	15.2	17.4	19.0	24.0	11.9	3.9	1.2
Kansas City, MO	11.2	17.4	19.4	18.4	18.5	10.8	3.6	0.7
Lafayette, LA	5.5	8.2	14.9	23.2	23.8	16.0	6.5	1.9
Lakeland, FL	18.2	15.4	16.7	19.4	18.7	8.6	2.6	0.5
Las Vegas, NV	2.4	4.3	8.7	15.4	31.4	27.3	8.6	1.9
Lexington, KY	2.6	8.8	21.0	21.1	22.4	16.6	6.0	1.4
Lincoln, NE	3.5	9.8	25.5	23.9	23.3	11.2	2.4	0.5
Little Rock, AR	6.5	19.3	16.8	17.5	15.9	15.4	7.0	1.6
Los Angeles, CA	1.2	0.8	0.7	0.8	4.8	25.2	44.5	22.1
Louisville, KY	5.5	15.7	24.8	18.2	17.6	13.0	4.4	0.8
Madison, WI	1.6	2.6	8.5	18.5	35.6	25.7	6.7	0.8

Table continued on following page.

Area	Under $50,000	$50,000 -$99,999	$100,000 -$149,999	$150,000 -$199,999	$200,000 -$299,999	$300,000 -$499,999	$500,000 -$999,999	$1,000,000 or more
Manchester, NH	1.9	3.0	8.3	21.6	47.9	15.7	1.4	0.2
Memphis, TN	14.5	34.7	17.4	12.4	9.9	6.8	3.3	1.0
Miami, FL	2.2	4.6	6.0	9.8	24.1	29.6	16.1	7.5
Midland, TX	4.9	9.0	12.7	17.4	28.4	18.3	7.8	1.4
Milwaukee, WI	9.1	27.3	29.6	17.9	10.6	3.6	1.5	0.4
Minneapolis, MN	1.4	4.0	10.7	16.1	31.3	24.7	10.0	1.9
Nashville, TN	2.1	5.0	13.5	17.4	27.0	23.1	10.0	1.9
New Haven, CT	2.7	7.9	14.1	25.8	28.0	14.9	6.0	0.7
New Orleans, LA	2.8	7.9	13.8	18.6	19.9	20.5	13.0	3.7
New York, NY	2.9	1.3	1.9	2.4	6.6	23.7	41.4	19.9
Oklahoma City, OK	7.9	18.0	19.9	20.8	18.9	10.2	3.4	0.8
Omaha, NE	4.2	14.8	25.8	21.8	19.0	10.5	3.2	0.7
Orlando, FL	2.9	10.7	13.4	13.0	24.6	24.6	8.8	2.1
Peoria, IL	12.6	25.4	21.8	15.6	13.8	8.1	2.4	0.4
Philadelphia, PA	6.7	19.4	18.6	18.0	19.6	11.3	5.1	1.3
Phoenix, AZ	4.3	6.3	11.0	17.7	26.4	23.0	9.6	1.7
Pittsburgh, PA	11.8	27.6	18.0	12.8	12.4	10.6	5.7	1.0
Portland, OR	1.9	0.8	1.5	3.8	16.7	41.6	30.5	3.2
Providence, RI	2.1	5.3	16.9	25.7	23.9	15.6	8.6	1.9
Provo, UT	3.5	1.2	6.4	13.5	34.5	29.0	9.8	2.2
Raleigh, NC	2.0	2.7	11.4	19.4	27.1	24.8	10.8	1.8
Reno, NV	4.1	2.9	3.7	7.5	22.3	43.2	13.7	2.5
Richmond, VA	2.0	11.4	13.9	15.4	20.8	21.7	11.5	3.3
Riverside, CA	2.9	1.6	1.7	3.4	17.5	55.6	15.4	1.9
Rochester, MN	2.9	4.5	16.5	26.0	27.6	17.9	4.2	0.4
Sacramento, CA	2.5	2.0	3.5	7.2	26.0	39.6	17.2	2.0
Salt Lake City, UT	2.9	1.4	6.7	13.0	23.6	29.7	19.5	3.3
San Antonio, TX	6.8	24.5	20.0	18.4	17.9	9.4	2.5	0.6
San Diego, CA	1.6	1.0	0.8	1.1	5.3	27.4	47.6	15.3
San Francisco, CA	1.1	0.5	0.4	0.3	1.2	3.9	34.9	57.8
San Jose, CA	1.5	1.4	1.4	0.9	1.9	7.2	50.0	35.6
Santa Rosa, CA	2.7	2.0	1.7	1.5	5.2	30.6	50.0	6.2
Savannah, GA	6.1	20.2	20.4	19.5	18.7	9.4	4.6	1.1
Seattle, WA	0.6	0.4	0.4	1.0	5.0	22.3	52.5	17.8
Sioux Falls, SD	5.5	6.6	17.7	24.4	27.0	14.4	3.8	0.7
Springfield, IL	10.0	24.9	23.4	15.7	15.7	7.9	2.3	0.2
Tallahassee, FL	2.9	9.9	16.8	19.3	26.8	19.3	4.0	1.0
Tampa, FL	3.8	10.8	11.7	14.7	20.7	20.1	13.6	4.5
Tucson, AZ	10.6	13.5	22.6	24.6	19.6	6.8	1.9	0.3
Tulsa, OK	9.0	22.8	22.3	15.7	13.8	10.4	4.9	1.2
Tuscaloosa, AL	4.4	11.2	21.2	19.0	19.4	15.1	8.2	1.4
Virginia Beach, VA	2.2	1.5	6.1	12.6	33.7	30.5	11.1	2.3
Washington, DC	1.2	0.8	1.1	1.9	9.5	25.7	41.0	18.8
Wichita, KS	8.4	26.6	22.6	18.2	14.6	7.0	2.3	0.3
Winston-Salem, NC	6.6	19.7	24.8	20.8	13.4	8.8	5.2	0.8
U.S.	6.9	12.0	13.3	14.0	19.6	19.3	11.4	3.4

Note: Figures are percentages and cover owner-occupied housing units.
Source: U.S. Census Bureau, 2015-2019 American Community Survey 5-Year Estimates

Home Value Distribution: Metro Area

MSA[1]	Under $50,000	$50,000 -$99,999	$100,000 -$149,999	$150,000 -$199,999	$200,000 -$299,999	$300,000 -$499,999	$500,000 -$999,999	$1,000,000 or more
Albuquerque, NM	5.8	7.6	16.8	22.7	25.8	15.5	4.8	1.0
Allentown, PA	3.8	7.3	14.4	20.0	28.2	21.4	4.3	0.6
Anchorage, AK	4.9	2.6	5.2	9.3	29.6	37.3	10.3	0.9
Ann Arbor, MI	5.5	6.1	8.0	13.7	24.9	28.8	11.3	1.7
Athens, GA	8.8	12.2	17.4	17.3	21.0	16.1	6.2	1.0
Atlanta, GA	3.7	9.2	14.8	18.0	22.5	20.7	9.3	1.8
Austin, TX	3.3	3.9	6.9	12.7	27.8	28.3	13.9	3.2
Baton Rouge, LA	8.7	12.3	15.0	20.4	24.0	14.3	4.3	1.0
Boise City, ID	4.4	4.2	11.1	17.9	28.9	25.3	7.3	1.0
Boston, MA	1.6	1.0	1.6	3.6	14.5	38.5	31.8	7.4
Boulder, CO	2.9	1.1	1.3	2.9	10.6	31.6	38.3	11.3
Cape Coral, FL	6.2	8.9	11.8	16.4	24.5	20.2	9.2	2.8
Cedar Rapids, IA	6.5	13.7	27.1	19.7	20.8	9.2	2.4	0.6
Charleston, SC	6.0	7.5	11.6	15.3	23.1	21.1	11.7	3.7
Charlotte, NC	4.8	11.4	16.7	17.1	21.5	18.7	7.8	1.9
Chicago, IL	3.2	7.2	12.4	16.4	25.5	23.1	9.9	2.4
Cincinnati, OH	4.8	15.3	21.4	18.8	21.0	13.6	4.3	0.7
Clarksville, TN	6.6	17.3	23.7	21.4	19.5	9.0	1.8	0.7
Cleveland, OH	7.6	20.0	21.6	17.9	18.4	10.7	3.0	0.7
College Station, TX	10.0	13.0	13.2	18.1	23.3	16.1	5.3	1.0
Colorado Springs, CO	3.1	2.0	6.1	14.3	31.7	31.1	10.4	1.2
Columbia, MO	5.4	11.2	19.9	20.9	22.9	14.8	4.3	0.7
Columbia, SC	8.6	16.9	22.6	18.7	17.1	11.2	4.2	0.8
Columbus, OH	4.8	13.1	18.2	18.8	23.1	16.5	4.9	0.7
Dallas, TX	4.5	11.1	14.5	15.9	23.1	20.9	7.9	1.9
Davenport, IA	7.3	23.5	24.9	17.5	15.3	9.1	2.0	0.4
Denver, CO	2.2	1.3	2.3	5.3	19.2	42.7	23.3	3.5
Des Moines, IA	4.5	11.9	19.7	19.9	24.4	14.9	4.2	0.5
Durham, NC	5.0	7.8	14.2	16.4	23.6	22.0	9.7	1.4
Edison, NJ	2.0	1.4	2.4	3.9	13.2	35.1	32.1	9.9
El Paso, TX	7.7	26.8	31.4	17.2	11.2	4.3	1.1	0.2
Fargo, ND	3.7	5.3	13.1	23.0	30.1	19.4	4.8	0.7
Fayetteville, NC	8.8	21.8	23.2	20.1	18.1	6.2	1.5	0.4
Fort Collins, CO	3.9	1.4	1.6	4.7	20.7	46.4	19.1	2.2
Fort Wayne, IN	8.4	24.8	26.3	17.2	13.7	7.2	2.0	0.4
Fort Worth, TX	4.5	11.1	14.5	15.9	23.1	20.9	7.9	1.9
Grand Rapids, MI	6.7	11.6	20.2	21.8	22.4	13.0	3.6	0.7
Greeley, CO	4.6	2.7	4.6	9.7	28.6	36.6	12.0	1.1
Green Bay, WI	4.0	11.9	22.8	22.2	24.5	11.3	2.6	0.6
Greensboro, NC	7.0	19.7	23.7	17.7	17.2	10.7	3.4	0.7
Honolulu, HI	0.7	0.6	0.8	1.0	5.0	19.6	54.6	17.7
Houston, TX	5.3	12.1	16.7	17.8	22.0	16.9	6.9	2.3
Huntsville, AL	6.4	13.8	17.3	19.0	23.7	15.1	3.9	0.8
Indianapolis, IN	5.6	16.1	22.3	19.0	18.5	13.4	4.4	0.8
Jacksonville, FL	5.8	12.0	14.1	16.8	24.6	18.1	6.7	1.8
Kansas City, MO	6.2	12.8	17.6	18.7	22.7	16.1	5.0	0.9
Lafayette, LA	14.7	16.0	16.1	19.5	19.3	10.1	3.5	0.8
Lakeland, FL	14.7	18.2	16.8	18.6	20.6	8.3	2.2	0.6
Las Vegas, NV	3.5	4.3	8.0	14.1	31.6	28.6	8.2	1.7
Lexington, KY	3.5	9.9	22.0	20.7	21.4	15.4	5.9	1.3
Lincoln, NE	3.2	9.4	23.4	22.6	23.4	13.8	3.7	0.5
Little Rock, AR	7.9	17.6	22.4	19.5	18.4	10.1	3.2	0.9
Los Angeles, CA	1.9	1.4	0.9	1.2	4.9	25.2	47.5	17.0
Louisville, KY	4.8	13.7	22.6	18.9	20.8	13.6	4.5	0.9
Madison, WI	2.1	3.9	9.7	16.6	32.4	26.6	7.5	1.2

Table continued on following page.

MSA[1]	Under $50,000	$50,000 -$99,999	$100,000 -$149,999	$150,000 -$199,999	$200,000 -$299,999	$300,000 -$499,999	$500,000 -$999,999	$1,000,000 or more
Manchester, NH	1.9	2.5	5.9	12.0	37.5	32.8	6.7	0.7
Memphis, TN	9.1	21.8	18.2	16.5	18.6	11.2	3.6	0.9
Miami, FL	4.0	7.1	8.7	11.9	22.9	28.5	12.5	4.5
Midland, TX	8.7	10.4	11.9	15.9	26.2	17.9	7.5	1.3
Milwaukee, WI	3.7	8.8	15.1	18.2	27.1	20.0	6.0	1.1
Minneapolis, MN	2.7	2.7	7.9	16.7	32.8	27.1	8.8	1.4
Nashville, TN	2.9	6.1	13.1	16.5	25.6	23.0	10.5	2.3
New Haven, CT	2.0	4.9	10.6	17.0	29.8	26.8	7.6	1.2
New Orleans, LA	4.2	9.0	16.8	20.8	24.8	16.4	6.4	1.6
New York, NY	2.0	1.4	2.4	3.9	13.2	35.1	32.1	9.9
Oklahoma City, OK	7.5	17.7	21.3	19.6	18.4	10.9	3.7	1.0
Omaha, NE	3.9	12.1	23.4	21.0	22.0	13.5	3.4	0.7
Orlando, FL	6.1	8.5	11.7	17.0	28.6	20.3	6.2	1.7
Peoria, IL	8.6	25.9	23.0	17.4	15.3	7.6	1.9	0.4
Philadelphia, PA	3.4	7.3	10.2	14.8	26.3	26.2	10.1	1.7
Phoenix, AZ	5.5	5.2	8.7	15.2	28.2	25.2	9.8	2.2
Pittsburgh, PA	8.8	20.3	19.2	17.8	17.5	12.0	3.6	0.7
Portland, OR	3.2	1.3	2.1	4.9	21.0	42.8	22.1	2.6
Providence, RI	2.1	2.0	5.7	14.1	33.3	31.2	10.0	1.7
Provo, UT	2.4	0.9	3.6	10.1	32.2	37.0	12.1	1.7
Raleigh, NC	3.5	5.0	11.9	15.5	25.7	27.6	9.6	1.3
Reno, NV	4.0	2.8	4.2	7.5	23.6	38.4	15.4	4.1
Richmond, VA	2.4	5.3	11.7	18.2	29.4	23.7	8.2	1.2
Riverside, CA	4.9	3.4	4.1	6.8	21.0	40.8	17.0	2.0
Rochester, MN	4.6	6.8	16.1	22.2	24.5	19.3	5.5	1.0
Sacramento, CA	2.8	1.7	2.2	4.5	17.7	42.3	25.8	3.0
Salt Lake City, UT	2.9	1.2	5.2	11.5	29.6	34.2	13.7	1.7
San Antonio, TX	6.8	18.2	16.6	17.7	20.5	14.2	4.9	1.2
San Diego, CA	2.5	1.9	1.4	1.4	5.2	29.3	46.1	12.2
San Francisco, CA	1.2	0.9	0.8	0.8	2.8	13.2	43.9	36.2
San Jose, CA	1.3	1.0	1.2	0.9	1.8	6.4	40.1	47.3
Santa Rosa, CA	2.6	2.6	1.6	1.2	4.2	22.2	51.9	13.7
Savannah, GA	5.7	11.2	17.1	19.2	23.1	14.9	7.1	1.6
Seattle, WA	2.5	1.2	2.0	4.2	15.3	34.2	32.0	8.5
Sioux Falls, SD	5.6	7.7	16.6	22.7	26.5	15.7	4.4	0.8
Springfield, IL	8.2	23.3	22.4	17.8	18.2	8.0	1.9	0.2
Tallahassee, FL	8.3	15.3	16.5	16.9	22.4	15.2	4.6	0.8
Tampa, FL	8.8	13.0	13.5	16.7	23.7	16.4	6.4	1.6
Tucson, AZ	8.4	10.7	16.2	19.9	22.5	15.4	5.8	1.0
Tulsa, OK	9.4	18.7	21.7	19.4	17.3	9.4	3.4	0.8
Tuscaloosa, AL	13.0	14.9	17.5	20.5	19.7	9.8	3.9	0.7
Virginia Beach, VA	3.3	3.8	10.2	17.0	31.5	25.1	7.7	1.2
Washington, DC	1.5	1.0	2.1	4.7	17.1	35.8	31.2	6.7
Wichita, KS	8.3	24.2	22.6	19.1	15.6	7.8	2.0	0.4
Winston-Salem, NC	7.4	16.9	24.5	20.0	17.2	9.9	3.5	0.6
U.S.	6.9	12.0	13.3	14.0	19.6	19.3	11.4	3.4

Note: (1) Figures cover the Metropolitan Statistical Area (MSA)—see Appendix B for areas included; Figures are percentages and cover owner-occupied housing units.
Source: U.S. Census Bureau, 2015-2019 American Community Survey 5-Year Estimates

Homeownership Rate

Metro Area	2012	2013	2014	2015	2016	2017	2018	2019	2020
Albuquerque, NM	62.8	65.9	64.4	64.3	66.9	67.0	67.9	70.0	69.5
Allentown, PA	75.5	71.5	68.2	69.2	68.9	73.1	72.1	67.8	68.8
Anchorage, AK	n/a	n/a	n/a	n/a	n/a	n/a	n/a	n/a	n/a
Ann Arbor, MI	n/a	n/a	n/a	n/a	n/a	n/a	n/a	n/a	n/a
Athens, GA	n/a	n/a	n/a	n/a	n/a	n/a	n/a	n/a	n/a
Atlanta, GA	62.1	61.6	61.6	61.7	61.5	62.4	64.0	64.2	66.4
Austin, TX	60.1	59.6	61.1	57.5	56.5	55.6	56.1	59.0	65.4
Baton Rouge, LA	71.4	66.6	64.8	64.2	64.8	66.9	66.6	66.2	72.1
Boise City, ID	n/a	n/a	n/a	n/a	n/a	n/a	n/a	n/a	n/a
Boston, MA	66.0	66.3	62.8	59.3	58.9	58.8	61.0	60.9	61.2
Boulder, CO	n/a	n/a	n/a	n/a	n/a	n/a	n/a	n/a	n/a
Cape Coral, FL	n/a	n/a	n/a	62.9	66.5	65.5	75.1	72.0	77.4
Cedar Rapids, IA	n/a	n/a	n/a	n/a	n/a	n/a	n/a	n/a	n/a
Charleston, SC	n/a	n/a	n/a	65.8	62.1	67.7	68.8	70.7	75.5
Charlotte, NC	58.3	58.9	58.1	62.3	66.2	64.6	67.9	72.3	73.3
Chicago, IL	67.1	68.2	66.3	64.3	64.5	64.1	64.6	63.4	66.0
Cincinnati, OH	63.4	63.3	65.5	65.9	64.9	65.7	67.3	67.4	71.1
Clarksville, TN	n/a	n/a	n/a	n/a	n/a	n/a	n/a	n/a	n/a
Cleveland, OH	64.2	65.8	69.2	68.4	64.8	66.6	66.7	64.4	66.3
College Station, TX	n/a	n/a	n/a	n/a	n/a	n/a	n/a	n/a	n/a
Colorado Springs, CO	n/a	n/a	n/a	n/a	n/a	n/a	n/a	n/a	n/a
Columbia, MO	n/a	n/a	n/a	n/a	n/a	n/a	n/a	n/a	n/a
Columbia, SC	65.6	68.9	69.5	66.1	63.9	70.7	69.3	65.9	69.7
Columbus, OH	60.7	60.5	60.0	59.0	57.5	57.9	64.8	65.7	65.6
Dallas, TX	61.8	59.9	57.7	57.8	59.7	61.8	62.0	60.6	64.7
Davenport, IA	n/a	n/a	n/a	n/a	n/a	n/a	n/a	n/a	n/a
Denver, CO	61.8	61.0	61.9	61.6	61.6	59.3	60.1	63.5	62.9
Des Moines, IA	n/a	n/a	n/a	n/a	n/a	n/a	n/a	n/a	n/a
Durham, NC	n/a	n/a	n/a	n/a	n/a	n/a	n/a	n/a	n/a
Edison, NJ	51.5	50.6	50.7	49.9	50.4	49.9	49.7	50.4	50.9
El Paso, TX	n/a	n/a	n/a	n/a	n/a	n/a	n/a	n/a	n/a
Fargo, ND	n/a	n/a	n/a	n/a	n/a	n/a	n/a	n/a	n/a
Fayetteville, NC	n/a	n/a	n/a	n/a	n/a	n/a	n/a	n/a	n/a
Fort Collins, CO	n/a	n/a	n/a	n/a	n/a	n/a	n/a	n/a	n/a
Fort Wayne, IN	n/a	n/a	n/a	n/a	n/a	n/a	n/a	n/a	n/a
Fort Worth, TX	61.8	59.9	57.7	57.8	59.7	61.8	62.0	60.6	64.7
Grand Rapids, MI	76.9	73.7	71.6	75.8	76.2	71.7	73.0	75.2	71.8
Greeley, CO	n/a	n/a	n/a	n/a	n/a	n/a	n/a	n/a	n/a
Green Bay, WI	n/a	n/a	n/a	n/a	n/a	n/a	n/a	n/a	n/a
Greensboro, NC	64.9	67.9	68.1	65.4	62.9	61.9	63.2	61.7	65.8
Honolulu, HI	56.1	57.9	58.2	59.6	57.9	53.8	57.7	59.0	56.9
Houston, TX	62.1	60.5	60.4	60.3	59.0	58.9	60.1	61.3	65.3
Huntsville, AL	n/a	n/a	n/a	n/a	n/a	n/a	n/a	n/a	n/a
Indianapolis, IN	67.1	67.5	66.9	64.6	63.9	63.9	64.3	66.2	70.0
Jacksonville, FL	66.6	69.9	65.3	62.5	61.8	65.2	61.4	63.1	64.8
Kansas City, MO	65.1	65.6	66.1	65.0	62.4	62.4	64.3	65.0	66.7
Lafayette, LA	n/a	n/a	n/a	n/a	n/a	n/a	n/a	n/a	n/a
Lakeland, FL	n/a	n/a	n/a	n/a	n/a	n/a	n/a	n/a	n/a
Las Vegas, NV	52.6	52.8	53.2	52.1	51.3	54.4	58.1	56.0	57.3
Lexington, KY	n/a	n/a	n/a	n/a	n/a	n/a	n/a	n/a	n/a
Lincoln, NE	n/a	n/a	n/a	n/a	n/a	n/a	n/a	n/a	n/a
Little Rock, AR	n/a	n/a	n/a	65.8	64.9	61.0	62.2	65.0	67.7
Los Angeles, CA	49.9	48.7	49.0	49.1	47.1	49.1	49.5	48.2	48.5
Louisville, KY	63.3	64.5	68.9	67.7	67.6	71.7	67.9	64.9	69.3
Madison, WI	n/a	n/a	n/a	n/a	n/a	n/a	n/a	n/a	n/a
Manchester, NH	n/a	n/a	n/a	n/a	n/a	n/a	n/a	n/a	n/a

Table continued on following page.

Metro Area	2012	2013	2014	2015	2016	2017	2018	2019	2020
Memphis, TN	60.5	56.2	57.2	59.6	61.8	62.4	63.5	63.7	62.5
Miami, FL	61.8	60.1	58.8	58.6	58.4	57.9	59.9	60.4	60.6
Midland, TX	n/a	n/a	n/a	n/a	n/a	n/a	n/a	n/a	n/a
Milwaukee, WI	61.9	60.0	55.9	57.0	60.4	63.9	62.3	56.9	58.5
Minneapolis, MN	70.8	71.7	69.7	67.9	69.1	70.1	67.8	70.2	73.0
Nashville, TN	64.9	63.9	67.1	67.4	65.0	69.4	68.3	69.8	69.8
New Haven, CT	62.2	62.0	62.4	64.6	59.4	58.7	65.0	65.1	63.4
New Orleans, LA	62.4	61.4	60.6	62.8	59.3	61.7	62.6	61.1	66.3
New York, NY	51.5	50.6	50.7	49.9	50.4	49.9	49.7	50.4	50.9
Oklahoma City, OK	67.3	67.6	65.7	61.4	63.1	64.7	64.6	64.3	68.3
Omaha, NE	72.4	70.6	68.7	69.6	69.2	65.5	67.8	66.9	68.6
Orlando, FL	68.0	65.5	62.3	58.4	58.5	59.5	58.5	56.1	64.2
Peoria, IL	n/a	n/a	n/a	n/a	n/a	n/a	n/a	n/a	n/a
Philadelphia, PA	69.5	69.1	67.0	67.0	64.7	65.6	67.4	67.4	69.2
Phoenix, AZ	63.1	62.2	61.9	61.0	62.6	64.0	65.3	65.9	67.9
Pittsburgh, PA	67.9	68.3	69.1	71.0	72.2	72.7	71.7	71.5	69.8
Portland, OR	63.9	60.9	59.8	58.9	61.8	61.1	59.2	60.0	62.5
Providence, RI	61.7	60.1	61.6	60.0	57.5	58.6	61.3	63.5	64.8
Provo, UT	n/a	n/a	n/a	n/a	n/a	n/a	n/a	n/a	n/a
Raleigh, NC	67.7	65.5	65.5	67.4	65.9	68.2	64.9	63.0	68.2
Reno, NV	n/a	n/a	n/a	n/a	n/a	n/a	n/a	n/a	n/a
Richmond, VA	67.0	65.4	72.6	67.4	61.7	63.1	62.9	66.4	66.5
Riverside, CA	58.2	56.3	56.8	61.1	62.9	59.9	62.3	64.4	65.8
Rochester, MN	n/a	n/a	n/a	n/a	n/a	n/a	n/a	n/a	n/a
Sacramento, CA	58.6	60.4	60.1	60.8	60.5	60.1	64.1	61.6	63.4
Salt Lake City, UT	66.9	66.8	68.2	69.1	69.2	68.1	69.5	69.2	68.0
San Antonio, TX	67.5	70.1	70.2	66.0	61.6	62.5	64.4	62.6	64.2
San Diego, CA	55.4	55.0	57.4	51.8	53.3	56.0	56.1	56.7	57.8
San Francisco, CA	53.2	55.2	54.6	56.3	55.8	55.7	55.6	52.8	53.0
San Jose, CA	58.6	56.4	56.4	50.7	49.9	50.4	50.4	52.4	52.6
Santa Rosa, CA	n/a	n/a	n/a	n/a	n/a	n/a	n/a	n/a	n/a
Savannah, GA	n/a	n/a	n/a	n/a	n/a	n/a	n/a	n/a	n/a
Seattle, WA	60.4	61.0	61.3	59.5	57.7	59.5	62.5	61.5	59.4
Sioux Falls, SD	n/a	n/a	n/a	n/a	n/a	n/a	n/a	n/a	n/a
Springfield, IL	n/a	n/a	n/a	n/a	n/a	n/a	n/a	n/a	n/a
Tallahassee, FL	n/a	n/a	n/a	n/a	n/a	n/a	n/a	n/a	n/a
Tampa, FL	67.0	65.3	64.9	64.9	62.9	60.4	64.9	68.0	72.2
Tucson, AZ	64.9	66.1	66.7	61.4	56.0	60.1	63.8	60.1	67.1
Tulsa, OK	66.5	64.1	65.3	65.2	65.4	66.8	68.3	70.5	70.1
Tuscaloosa, AL	n/a	n/a	n/a	n/a	n/a	n/a	n/a	n/a	n/a
Virginia Beach, VA	62.0	63.3	64.1	59.4	59.6	65.3	62.8	63.0	65.8
Washington, DC	66.9	66.0	65.0	64.6	63.1	63.3	62.9	64.7	67.9
Wichita, KS	n/a	n/a	n/a	n/a	n/a	n/a	n/a	n/a	n/a
Winston-Salem, NC	n/a	n/a	n/a	n/a	n/a	n/a	n/a	n/a	n/a
U.S.	65.4	65.1	64.5	63.7	63.4	63.9	64.4	64.6	66.6

Note: Figures are percentages and cover the Metropolitan Statistical Area—see Appendix B for areas included; n/a not available
Source: U.S. Census Bureau, Housing Vacancies and Homeownership Annual Statistics: 2012-2020

Year Housing Structure Built: City

City	2010 or Later	2000 -2009	1990 -1999	1980 -1989	1970 -1979	1960 -1969	1950 -1959	1940 -1949	Before 1940	Median Year
Albuquerque, NM	4.3	16.3	15.3	15.5	19.6	10.3	11.5	4.4	2.8	1981
Allentown, PA	2.1	5.0	3.8	5.5	10.6	12.1	16.1	7.2	37.6	1953
Anchorage, AK	3.5	12.2	11.6	26.4	28.2	10.8	6.0	1.0	0.3	1981
Ann Arbor, MI	3.7	6.3	10.8	10.8	17.2	18.2	12.6	5.0	15.6	1969
Athens, GA	3.8	17.7	20.3	15.6	16.5	12.2	6.6	2.4	4.8	1985
Atlanta, GA	8.1	22.3	10.6	7.9	8.4	12.6	11.7	6.1	12.3	1979
Austin, TX	12.8	18.1	15.7	19.6	15.9	7.6	4.9	2.6	2.8	1988
Baton Rouge, LA	5.9	9.9	8.7	12.9	22.4	17.3	11.7	5.9	5.3	1974
Boise City, ID	6.5	11.9	22.5	15.0	19.2	7.1	7.1	4.4	6.2	1984
Boston, MA	5.0	6.5	4.2	5.9	7.9	7.8	7.3	5.8	49.6	1941
Boulder, CO	6.2	7.7	11.2	17.3	21.5	18.3	8.1	2.0	7.6	1976
Cape Coral, FL	3.8	37.8	17.8	22.9	11.9	4.7	0.8	0.2	0.1	1995
Cedar Rapids, IA	6.9	11.1	13.0	8.2	14.4	13.9	12.3	4.2	16.0	1972
Charleston, SC	12.3	20.3	12.8	13.8	10.2	8.3	6.1	4.1	12.2	1987
Charlotte, NC	8.9	23.1	19.4	15.1	12.0	9.5	6.6	2.6	2.8	1991
Chicago, IL	2.6	8.0	4.9	4.3	7.5	9.7	11.9	9.3	41.8	1949
Cincinnati, OH	2.3	3.7	4.2	5.3	9.9	13.0	12.2	8.1	41.2	1951
Clarksville, TN	13.0	22.8	20.9	13.2	12.4	8.6	4.7	2.5	2.0	1993
Cleveland, OH	1.7	3.8	3.2	2.4	5.4	7.1	12.5	11.3	52.6	<1940
College Station, TX	16.2	24.0	19.8	16.0	16.5	4.0	2.2	0.7	0.6	1995
Colorado Springs, CO	6.5	15.7	15.9	18.6	18.3	10.2	7.1	1.9	5.8	1984
Columbia, MO	12.6	21.5	17.9	12.0	12.5	10.7	5.1	2.2	5.5	1991
Columbia, SC	6.1	15.8	11.6	8.9	10.1	11.9	13.6	11.2	10.8	1972
Columbus, OH	5.9	11.4	15.4	13.0	15.0	12.0	10.8	5.0	11.6	1977
Dallas, TX	7.1	10.6	10.3	17.2	17.3	13.4	13.7	5.2	5.2	1977
Davenport, IA	3.4	8.6	7.9	5.9	15.7	13.3	11.2	5.6	28.5	1964
Denver, CO	9.0	11.3	6.6	7.4	14.2	10.9	15.0	6.6	18.9	1969
Des Moines, IA	3.2	7.3	6.5	6.4	13.4	10.5	15.2	8.2	29.3	1958
Durham, NC	11.6	21.0	16.3	15.4	10.5	8.8	6.6	3.8	6.1	1989
Edison, NJ	1.7	4.7	9.3	23.3	13.6	20.3	17.4	4.5	5.1	1972
El Paso, TX	9.8	15.2	13.4	14.0	16.5	10.8	11.5	4.1	4.6	1982
Fargo, ND	16.1	15.8	16.5	13.8	14.0	6.0	6.9	2.6	8.2	1989
Fayetteville, NC	6.9	11.9	18.1	16.9	21.6	13.2	6.6	2.9	1.8	1982
Fort Collins, CO	10.2	17.5	21.3	15.2	18.8	7.1	3.2	1.6	5.2	1989
Fort Wayne, IN	1.5	6.6	14.3	11.7	16.7	15.0	12.2	6.6	15.3	1970
Fort Worth, TX	9.9	24.5	11.5	13.2	9.8	8.2	11.3	5.3	6.3	1987
Grand Rapids, MI	2.5	4.2	6.1	7.0	8.5	10.3	15.7	8.9	36.8	1953
Greeley, CO	6.3	19.3	15.7	10.1	21.2	10.3	6.7	2.6	7.8	1982
Green Bay, WI	1.6	7.6	10.3	12.9	17.8	13.1	15.0	5.7	16.0	1970
Greensboro, NC	5.2	15.0	17.9	16.6	14.4	11.2	10.2	3.8	5.5	1983
Honolulu, HI	4.2	6.9	7.9	9.5	25.3	22.8	12.8	5.5	5.1	1971
Houston, TX	8.6	13.4	9.9	14.6	21.1	13.4	10.3	4.5	4.3	1978
Huntsville, AL	11.8	12.9	10.8	15.6	13.2	21.0	9.5	2.4	2.8	1981
Indianapolis, IN	3.4	9.2	13.2	12.1	13.5	13.1	12.7	6.1	16.8	1971
Jacksonville, FL	6.2	19.3	15.3	15.5	12.7	10.0	11.1	4.8	5.1	1984
Kansas City, MO	4.6	9.9	9.3	8.6	12.0	12.7	14.3	6.3	22.1	1966
Lafayette, LA	7.2	13.3	10.4	18.0	21.7	13.4	9.0	3.9	3.1	1979
Lakeland, FL	3.4	15.1	13.2	19.6	20.2	10.4	8.8	3.3	6.0	1981
Las Vegas, NV	5.2	23.0	32.0	16.6	9.9	7.4	4.2	1.3	0.5	1993
Lexington, KY	6.1	15.5	15.8	14.0	15.0	13.5	9.7	3.1	7.3	1981
Lincoln, NE	7.3	13.7	15.0	10.4	15.3	10.0	11.2	3.0	14.0	1978
Little Rock, AR	6.2	11.2	11.2	14.3	19.6	15.2	9.9	5.2	7.1	1976
Los Angeles, CA	3.2	5.6	5.7	10.2	13.7	14.1	17.4	9.8	20.3	1962
Louisville, KY	4.3	11.0	11.7	6.9	12.7	13.8	14.8	7.4	17.4	1968
Madison, WI	7.1	14.4	13.1	10.9	13.9	11.5	10.4	4.8	14.0	1977

Table continued on following page.

City	2010 or Later	2000 -2009	1990 -1999	1980 -1989	1970 -1979	1960 -1969	1950 -1959	1940 -1949	Before 1940	Median Year
Manchester, NH	1.9	6.7	8.1	15.9	10.4	7.9	10.3	6.1	32.6	1961
Memphis, TN	2.0	7.0	10.0	12.4	18.2	14.9	19.1	8.7	7.7	1970
Miami, FL	7.6	19.0	6.4	8.3	13.3	9.8	14.7	11.7	9.2	1973
Midland, TX	12.9	8.5	13.8	18.4	11.7	11.6	18.5	3.0	1.5	1982
Milwaukee, WI	1.5	3.3	2.9	3.9	8.7	11.1	20.2	9.8	38.6	1951
Minneapolis, MN	5.8	6.7	3.6	6.8	9.0	7.5	9.5	6.8	44.3	1948
Nashville, TN	9.3	14.6	12.4	15.3	14.8	12.2	10.6	4.5	6.2	1981
New Haven, CT	3.1	4.8	2.6	7.1	8.0	9.7	9.4	7.5	47.7	1943
New Orleans, LA	3.4	7.1	3.5	7.3	13.7	11.1	12.1	7.7	34.0	1957
New York, NY	2.8	5.6	3.7	4.8	7.1	12.5	13.0	9.9	40.6	1949
Oklahoma City, OK	9.4	13.1	9.5	14.9	16.1	12.6	10.6	5.5	8.4	1978
Omaha, NE	3.4	7.4	13.0	11.0	15.6	14.6	11.1	4.2	19.7	1970
Orlando, FL	9.6	21.6	16.3	16.9	13.9	7.2	8.6	2.9	3.0	1989
Peoria, IL	3.3	8.7	7.4	6.8	15.2	12.5	14.0	7.9	24.3	1963
Philadelphia, PA	2.7	3.0	3.2	3.7	7.1	10.7	16.3	11.6	41.7	1947
Phoenix, AZ	4.3	16.7	16.3	17.1	19.6	11.7	10.1	2.5	1.8	1983
Pittsburgh, PA	2.3	3.0	3.5	4.4	6.7	8.7	12.6	8.9	49.8	1940
Portland, OR	5.8	10.5	8.8	6.4	10.7	9.2	12.0	8.2	28.3	1962
Providence, RI	0.6	4.5	3.7	5.5	9.2	5.9	7.6	6.8	56.2	<1940
Provo, UT	4.6	11.8	21.1	14.3	17.7	10.4	7.6	5.1	7.3	1981
Raleigh, NC	10.7	25.0	19.0	17.3	10.6	7.7	4.5	2.1	3.1	1992
Reno, NV	6.2	19.7	19.2	13.9	18.3	9.5	7.2	3.0	3.0	1987
Richmond, VA	4.0	5.4	4.9	6.3	11.3	12.4	15.0	9.1	31.7	1956
Riverside, CA	2.8	11.5	10.6	16.4	18.4	12.1	16.0	5.0	7.2	1975
Rochester, MN	8.9	18.3	14.3	14.6	13.0	10.1	9.6	3.3	7.9	1984
Sacramento, CA	2.3	15.7	8.9	15.7	14.6	11.7	12.4	7.9	10.9	1975
Salt Lake City, UT	5.3	6.6	7.4	7.7	12.1	10.0	13.2	8.7	29.1	1959
San Antonio, TX	7.3	15.9	13.7	16.6	15.0	10.2	10.1	5.7	5.6	1982
San Diego, CA	3.9	10.3	11.4	17.7	21.2	12.5	12.1	4.3	6.7	1977
San Francisco, CA	3.7	6.6	4.3	5.3	7.6	8.2	8.4	9.1	46.8	1944
San Jose, CA	5.2	9.3	10.6	12.9	24.2	18.6	11.0	3.0	5.2	1975
Santa Rosa, CA	2.9	12.4	13.0	19.4	21.8	11.8	8.2	4.9	5.6	1979
Savannah, GA	6.3	11.3	7.4	9.8	12.7	12.6	15.0	8.1	16.7	1968
Seattle, WA	10.4	13.2	8.3	7.9	8.2	8.7	9.8	8.3	25.2	1968
Sioux Falls, SD	13.3	18.3	15.1	10.5	13.8	7.3	9.1	3.8	8.6	1987
Springfield, IL	2.3	8.8	12.6	9.6	16.5	12.7	11.3	7.0	19.2	1970
Tallahassee, FL	3.9	18.2	20.8	17.7	18.0	9.2	7.5	3.2	1.5	1986
Tampa, FL	7.8	17.9	12.4	11.8	11.9	10.0	14.4	5.2	8.7	1980
Tucson, AZ	2.6	12.6	13.4	16.2	21.4	11.5	14.8	3.9	3.7	1978
Tulsa, OK	3.6	6.1	9.5	13.3	21.0	14.4	16.8	6.4	9.0	1972
Tuscaloosa, AL	12.9	17.6	15.5	11.5	13.7	10.4	8.8	5.2	4.3	1987
Virginia Beach, VA	4.9	10.8	13.7	27.9	21.4	12.8	6.1	1.3	1.1	1983
Washington, DC	7.3	8.1	3.3	4.4	7.1	11.4	12.6	11.7	34.1	1953
Wichita, KS	4.2	10.2	12.9	12.5	12.8	9.3	20.0	7.4	10.7	1972
Winston-Salem, NC	4.7	14.0	12.1	14.3	16.7	13.6	11.8	5.4	7.4	1977
U.S.	5.2	14.0	13.9	13.4	15.2	10.6	10.3	4.9	12.6	1978

Note: Figures are percentages except for Median Year
Source: U.S. Census Bureau, 2015-2019 American Community Survey 5-Year Estimates

Year Housing Structure Built: Metro Area

Metro Area	2010 or Later	2000 -2009	1990 -1999	1980 -1989	1970 -1979	1960 -1969	1950 -1959	1940 -1949	Before 1940	Median Year
Albuquerque, NM	4.2	17.6	18.2	17.0	18.0	9.2	9.1	3.7	3.0	1984
Allentown, PA	3.0	11.5	10.6	11.1	12.0	9.7	11.2	5.3	25.5	1968
Anchorage, AK	4.5	17.2	13.0	25.7	24.4	9.0	5.0	0.9	0.4	1984
Ann Arbor, MI	3.7	13.2	17.0	11.5	16.1	12.6	10.1	4.2	11.8	1977
Athens, GA	5.0	18.1	21.7	17.4	15.3	10.1	5.5	2.0	5.0	1987
Atlanta, GA	6.2	24.3	21.5	17.7	13.0	7.6	4.8	1.9	2.9	1991
Austin, TX	16.4	25.1	18.1	16.4	11.6	4.9	3.3	1.8	2.3	1995
Baton Rouge, LA	9.4	19.8	14.6	15.0	17.4	10.2	6.9	2.9	3.9	1986
Boise City, ID	10.5	24.6	21.4	10.3	16.2	4.7	4.4	3.0	4.9	1993
Boston, MA	4.0	7.6	7.4	10.4	11.2	10.2	10.8	5.3	33.2	1961
Boulder, CO	6.5	12.1	19.3	17.2	20.8	11.6	4.6	1.5	6.4	1983
Cape Coral, FL	5.6	31.3	17.7	21.4	14.8	5.5	2.5	0.5	0.7	1993
Cedar Rapids, IA	6.8	14.2	14.6	7.5	13.4	12.3	9.9	3.6	17.7	1975
Charleston, SC	11.9	21.4	16.6	16.4	14.2	8.2	5.2	2.4	3.6	1990
Charlotte, NC	9.2	24.1	19.5	13.5	11.5	8.4	6.5	3.1	4.2	1991
Chicago, IL	2.4	11.5	11.1	9.0	14.2	11.6	13.0	6.1	21.0	1968
Cincinnati, OH	3.7	12.4	14.4	10.7	13.8	10.7	11.9	4.9	17.6	1974
Clarksville, TN	10.7	20.0	20.9	12.1	15.2	9.2	6.2	2.5	3.1	1991
Cleveland, OH	2.3	7.1	8.7	6.8	12.4	13.4	18.1	7.6	23.7	1960
College Station, TX	12.7	21.0	17.7	17.0	15.8	6.1	5.2	2.0	2.4	1991
Colorado Springs, CO	7.6	18.8	16.9	17.5	17.0	8.9	6.5	1.6	5.2	1986
Columbia, MO	9.5	19.4	18.0	12.8	15.4	10.1	5.3	2.5	7.2	1988
Columbia, SC	8.0	19.5	18.5	14.3	15.9	9.7	7.0	3.3	3.8	1987
Columbus, OH	5.8	14.2	16.5	11.7	14.4	11.1	10.2	4.1	12.2	1979
Dallas, TX	10.0	20.0	16.1	18.1	14.2	8.7	7.5	2.7	2.7	1988
Davenport, IA	3.6	7.5	8.3	6.4	16.6	13.4	11.9	7.1	25.2	1964
Denver, CO	7.4	16.4	15.2	14.2	18.6	9.3	9.2	2.8	6.8	1982
Des Moines, IA	10.4	16.7	12.6	8.7	13.6	8.6	9.1	4.2	16.1	1979
Durham, NC	9.3	19.7	18.7	15.8	12.4	9.2	6.4	3.0	5.6	1989
Edison, NJ	2.8	6.7	6.1	7.7	9.8	13.7	15.9	8.8	28.6	1958
El Paso, TX	11.0	16.5	14.6	14.5	15.7	9.7	10.1	3.6	4.2	1985
Fargo, ND	15.1	18.4	14.2	11.2	14.9	6.9	7.4	2.7	9.1	1988
Fayetteville, NC	9.3	17.9	21.7	14.5	16.4	9.6	5.6	2.4	2.5	1989
Fort Collins, CO	10.3	18.8	20.1	13.5	19.1	7.1	3.6	1.7	5.8	1989
Fort Wayne, IN	3.8	11.0	15.2	10.9	15.2	13.0	10.8	5.4	14.7	1974
Fort Worth, TX	10.0	20.0	16.1	18.1	14.2	8.7	7.5	2.7	2.7	1988
Grand Rapids, MI	4.7	12.4	16.3	12.1	14.0	9.5	10.4	5.0	15.7	1977
Greeley, CO	10.9	28.6	16.3	7.4	15.2	6.2	4.4	2.4	8.6	1994
Green Bay, WI	5.2	15.0	16.4	12.4	15.4	9.6	9.3	4.2	12.4	1979
Greensboro, NC	5.0	15.9	18.9	14.5	14.7	10.9	9.5	4.5	6.1	1983
Honolulu, HI	5.1	10.2	11.5	12.2	24.1	18.9	10.7	4.0	3.3	1975
Houston, TX	11.9	21.5	14.4	15.5	16.9	8.4	6.2	2.6	2.4	1989
Huntsville, AL	10.8	19.7	17.8	16.1	11.3	13.7	6.4	1.9	2.2	1989
Indianapolis, IN	6.5	15.5	16.7	10.6	12.5	10.6	10.3	4.4	12.8	1979
Jacksonville, FL	8.6	22.7	16.6	16.6	12.4	8.0	8.0	3.4	3.9	1989
Kansas City, MO	4.8	13.7	14.5	12.3	15.4	11.6	11.4	4.4	11.8	1977
Lafayette, LA	9.5	16.6	12.9	15.5	16.4	10.4	9.3	4.1	5.2	1983
Lakeland, FL	5.8	23.8	17.7	18.2	15.1	7.7	6.5	2.1	3.2	1989
Las Vegas, NV	7.2	30.1	29.1	14.6	10.6	5.1	2.2	0.7	0.4	1996
Lexington, KY	6.4	17.2	17.0	13.9	14.8	11.5	8.0	3.3	7.9	1983
Lincoln, NE	7.3	14.1	15.1	10.1	15.6	10.0	10.3	2.8	14.7	1978
Little Rock, AR	9.3	18.2	16.7	13.7	17.0	10.8	7.1	3.4	3.7	1986
Los Angeles, CA	2.9	6.1	7.6	12.3	16.1	15.9	18.7	8.4	11.9	1967
Louisville, KY	4.4	13.1	14.2	9.2	15.2	12.4	12.6	6.2	12.8	1974
Madison, WI	6.5	16.2	15.6	11.1	15.0	9.6	7.8	3.5	14.6	1980

Table continued on following page.

Metro Area	2010 or Later	2000 -2009	1990 -1999	1980 -1989	1970 -1979	1960 -1969	1950 -1959	1940 -1949	Before 1940	Median Year
Manchester, NH	3.0	10.1	10.3	20.9	15.3	9.6	7.1	3.7	19.9	1976
Memphis, TN	4.2	15.7	17.1	13.7	16.2	10.8	11.9	5.3	5.1	1980
Miami, FL	4.1	13.0	15.1	19.4	21.4	12.3	9.8	2.8	2.1	1981
Midland, TX	14.0	11.4	14.5	18.0	11.2	10.5	15.9	2.8	1.7	1984
Milwaukee, WI	2.7	8.2	10.8	8.0	13.0	11.5	16.3	6.8	22.9	1964
Minneapolis, MN	5.1	14.3	14.4	14.5	14.7	9.8	9.7	3.7	13.9	1979
Nashville, TN	10.7	19.7	17.8	14.3	13.6	9.2	6.9	3.1	4.7	1989
New Haven, CT	1.8	5.6	7.1	12.3	13.3	12.3	15.2	7.1	25.2	1962
New Orleans, LA	3.8	11.9	9.8	13.3	19.3	13.6	10.1	4.8	13.5	1974
New York, NY	2.8	6.7	6.1	7.7	9.8	13.7	15.9	8.8	28.6	1958
Oklahoma City, OK	9.3	15.0	11.1	14.8	17.2	12.0	9.6	4.8	6.2	1980
Omaha, NE	6.8	14.3	13.0	9.9	14.6	12.0	8.7	3.4	17.2	1976
Orlando, FL	8.8	23.8	20.6	20.2	12.8	5.9	5.2	1.2	1.5	1992
Peoria, IL	3.1	9.0	8.6	6.0	17.3	12.3	14.3	8.0	21.4	1965
Philadelphia, PA	3.1	7.8	9.6	10.0	12.1	11.9	15.7	7.5	22.2	1964
Phoenix, AZ	6.6	25.4	20.3	17.2	16.1	7.3	5.1	1.2	0.9	1991
Pittsburgh, PA	2.8	6.5	7.7	7.5	11.9	11.5	16.7	8.9	26.4	1959
Portland, OR	6.3	14.5	18.6	11.3	17.2	8.4	7.1	4.6	11.9	1981
Providence, RI	1.9	6.3	8.1	11.1	12.2	11.0	11.6	6.6	31.4	1960
Provo, UT	14.0	25.9	19.2	9.3	13.6	5.0	5.4	3.1	4.6	1995
Raleigh, NC	12.7	25.9	23.0	15.2	9.3	5.9	3.7	1.6	2.8	1995
Reno, NV	5.5	21.1	20.6	15.2	18.9	8.9	5.3	2.2	2.3	1988
Richmond, VA	5.9	14.9	15.3	16.1	15.1	9.7	9.4	4.3	9.2	1981
Riverside, CA	4.2	20.5	14.6	21.9	15.7	8.9	8.5	2.8	2.8	1985
Rochester, MN	7.0	18.0	14.3	12.1	13.5	9.0	8.0	3.4	14.6	1981
Sacramento, CA	3.5	17.6	15.1	16.6	18.3	10.9	10.0	3.7	4.2	1982
Salt Lake City, UT	8.9	15.5	15.5	12.6	18.4	8.8	8.7	3.6	8.0	1982
San Antonio, TX	11.4	20.2	14.5	15.4	13.5	8.4	7.7	4.2	4.6	1988
San Diego, CA	3.7	12.0	12.5	18.6	22.6	12.2	10.7	3.5	4.2	1979
San Francisco, CA	3.2	7.7	8.2	11.1	14.9	13.4	13.7	7.8	19.9	1966
San Jose, CA	5.6	9.0	10.6	12.6	21.6	18.0	13.9	3.6	5.1	1974
Santa Rosa, CA	2.5	10.6	13.6	18.6	21.0	11.6	8.5	5.0	8.4	1978
Savannah, GA	9.0	20.7	16.3	13.8	12.0	7.8	8.1	4.3	8.0	1987
Seattle, WA	7.7	15.2	15.5	14.4	14.2	11.0	7.4	4.4	10.1	1982
Sioux Falls, SD	11.9	18.7	15.3	9.5	14.0	6.8	8.1	3.7	12.1	1986
Springfield, IL	3.1	9.9	13.2	9.1	16.9	11.9	11.6	6.7	17.5	1971
Tallahassee, FL	4.0	18.7	22.6	19.2	16.2	8.3	6.6	2.6	1.7	1988
Tampa, FL	5.6	16.4	14.1	20.1	21.0	9.5	8.5	2.0	2.7	1983
Tucson, AZ	4.5	18.6	17.5	17.8	19.6	8.5	8.9	2.5	2.2	1985
Tulsa, OK	6.7	14.4	12.7	14.3	19.3	10.5	10.6	4.5	7.0	1979
Tuscaloosa, AL	9.2	18.7	18.7	14.2	14.6	9.7	7.1	4.0	3.9	1988
Virginia Beach, VA	6.0	12.7	15.2	18.9	15.8	11.8	9.7	4.2	5.7	1981
Washington, DC	6.7	14.5	14.4	15.8	14.0	12.0	9.4	4.9	8.3	1981
Wichita, KS	4.7	11.9	14.1	12.2	13.3	8.5	17.9	6.0	11.3	1975
Winston-Salem, NC	4.5	15.6	17.2	15.7	16.7	10.9	8.9	4.3	6.3	1982
U.S.	5.2	14.0	13.9	13.4	15.2	10.6	10.3	4.9	12.6	1978

Note: Figures are percentages except for Median Year; Figures cover the Metropolitan Statistical Area—see Appendix B for areas included
Source: U.S. Census Bureau, 2015-2019 American Community Survey 5-Year Estimates

Gross Monthly Rent: City

City	Under $500	$500 -$999	$1,000 -$1,499	$1,500 -$1,999	$2,000 -$2,499	$2,500 -$2,999	$3,000 and up	Median ($)
Albuquerque, NM	8.1	54.4	29.1	6.5	1.1	0.3	0.4	873
Allentown, PA	10.0	39.6	38.7	10.0	1.4	0.3	0.0	1,004
Anchorage, AK	4.0	21.8	36.9	19.9	11.7	4.1	1.4	1,320
Ann Arbor, MI	4.6	23.6	39.5	19.8	7.3	2.4	2.8	1,237
Athens, GA	7.9	59.5	24.2	6.6	1.4	0.2	0.1	856
Atlanta, GA	11.3	27.5	33.6	18.8	5.6	1.7	1.5	1,153
Austin, TX	3.1	18.1	45.2	22.4	7.1	2.3	1.8	1,280
Baton Rouge, LA	10.1	54.4	25.7	5.9	3.2	0.5	0.3	879
Boise City, ID	5.6	50.5	34.7	6.9	1.4	0.3	0.7	957
Boston, MA	16.5	11.4	16.6	22.7	15.3	8.2	9.3	1,620
Boulder, CO	2.8	9.4	35.1	25.4	14.8	5.5	6.9	1,554
Cape Coral, FL	0.9	22.4	46.8	22.5	5.0	1.0	1.4	1,244
Cedar Rapids, IA	15.8	61.0	20.2	1.5	0.6	0.3	0.7	767
Charleston, SC	6.4	20.8	40.8	22.1	5.9	1.8	2.2	1,257
Charlotte, NC	3.8	30.9	46.3	14.5	2.9	0.8	0.7	1,135
Chicago, IL	9.6	31.9	31.5	15.2	6.7	3.0	2.1	1,112
Cincinnati, OH	19.1	56.0	18.0	4.5	1.3	0.4	0.7	738
Clarksville, TN	5.8	48.7	35.6	7.8	1.8	0.1	0.1	961
Cleveland, OH	21.9	58.1	15.8	2.7	0.9	0.3	0.2	719
College Station, TX	3.2	48.7	27.6	14.1	5.0	1.0	0.5	983
Colorado Springs, CO	3.9	34.3	38.3	17.5	3.5	1.8	0.7	1,131
Columbia, MO	6.1	58.0	26.4	5.7	3.3	0.3	0.2	887
Columbia, SC	10.1	48.2	31.9	7.6	1.6	0.1	0.5	933
Columbus, OH	6.4	48.7	35.7	7.1	1.5	0.4	0.3	961
Dallas, TX	4.3	41.0	36.7	11.7	3.6	1.4	1.1	1,052
Davenport, IA	9.2	68.6	16.4	3.2	0.8	0.7	1.1	771
Denver, CO	8.2	18.4	35.8	23.2	9.6	3.2	1.6	1,311
Des Moines, IA	8.6	61.1	25.1	4.1	0.9	0.2	0.1	855
Durham, NC	7.4	36.4	42.6	10.3	2.0	0.5	0.8	1,058
Edison, NJ	2.8	5.8	39.4	35.3	13.2	2.6	0.9	1,528
El Paso, TX	15.2	53.4	25.4	4.9	0.5	0.3	0.2	837
Fargo, ND	7.0	65.6	20.7	5.3	1.1	0.2	0.1	823
Fayetteville, NC	5.6	51.7	36.6	5.2	0.7	0.2	0.1	947
Fort Collins, CO	2.9	20.0	39.7	26.3	9.1	1.4	0.7	1,346
Fort Wayne, IN	11.5	71.0	15.0	1.5	0.7	0.2	0.1	764
Fort Worth, TX	4.9	39.7	35.0	15.5	3.1	0.9	0.9	1,060
Grand Rapids, MI	10.2	48.9	31.0	6.5	2.8	0.5	0.1	925
Greeley, CO	9.2	40.3	32.2	14.0	3.2	0.6	0.5	1,007
Green Bay, WI	12.0	71.3	15.4	1.0	0.1	0.1	0.2	730
Greensboro, NC	6.8	61.7	26.0	3.4	1.2	0.4	0.5	877
Honolulu, HI	6.9	13.3	30.4	22.3	11.3	6.7	9.2	1,491
Houston, TX	3.8	42.7	34.6	12.8	3.3	1.4	1.4	1,041
Huntsville, AL	11.3	59.9	24.2	3.2	0.5	0.6	0.4	827
Indianapolis, IN	6.2	58.7	28.2	5.3	1.0	0.2	0.3	892
Jacksonville, FL	6.6	36.6	42.2	11.8	2.2	0.3	0.4	1,065
Kansas City, MO	8.7	48.0	33.8	7.2	1.5	0.5	0.4	941
Lafayette, LA	9.9	54.6	27.8	6.1	1.3	0.3	0.1	890
Lakeland, FL	5.6	44.6	39.6	7.9	1.4	0.6	0.3	999
Las Vegas, NV	4.7	35.4	41.8	13.8	2.9	0.8	0.6	1,102
Lexington, KY	8.1	52.5	30.6	5.8	2.2	0.4	0.3	896
Lincoln, NE	9.5	58.4	25.0	4.9	0.8	0.3	1.0	852
Little Rock, AR	9.9	54.3	29.0	4.8	0.8	0.6	0.6	872
Los Angeles, CA	5.3	15.7	32.0	22.6	12.4	6.1	5.9	1,450
Louisville, KY	13.7	54.1	25.9	4.9	0.7	0.4	0.3	846
Madison, WI	3.4	34.3	42.0	13.9	4.1	1.3	1.0	1,118

Table continued on following page.

City	Under $500	$500 -$999	$1,000 -$1,499	$1,500 -$1,999	$2,000 -$2,499	$2,500 -$2,999	$3,000 and up	Median ($)
Manchester, NH	7.4	28.2	45.1	15.4	2.5	0.7	0.6	1,135
Memphis, TN	8.1	54.6	31.2	4.7	0.9	0.2	0.2	901
Miami, FL	10.7	26.3	30.0	17.0	9.3	3.8	2.9	1,183
Midland, TX	1.7	26.0	41.3	19.5	7.5	2.9	1.2	1,262
Milwaukee, WI	9.1	60.2	24.2	4.7	1.2	0.4	0.2	858
Minneapolis, MN	12.8	35.3	30.2	14.4	4.7	1.4	1.1	1,027
Nashville, TN	8.7	31.5	39.8	14.1	4.0	1.1	0.8	1,100
New Haven, CT	13.3	18.7	41.2	19.5	5.1	1.5	0.8	1,196
New Orleans, LA	12.8	37.4	33.7	11.5	3.0	0.9	0.6	998
New York, NY	10.6	14.6	28.1	22.1	11.0	5.6	8.0	1,443
Oklahoma City, OK	8.1	57.1	27.0	6.0	1.2	0.4	0.4	871
Omaha, NE	7.7	51.6	31.4	7.0	1.3	0.3	0.7	923
Orlando, FL	3.7	24.7	48.8	17.6	4.0	0.8	0.4	1,196
Peoria, IL	15.6	58.0	20.6	3.7	1.0	0.3	0.9	806
Philadelphia, PA	11.0	35.4	34.7	11.6	4.4	1.5	1.3	1,042
Phoenix, AZ	4.5	40.2	40.2	11.5	2.4	0.6	0.5	1,053
Pittsburgh, PA	13.6	40.7	28.8	11.2	4.0	1.0	0.7	958
Portland, OR	6.5	22.1	38.1	20.9	8.1	2.7	1.6	1,248
Providence, RI	19.5	31.1	35.2	9.8	2.6	0.7	1.1	994
Provo, UT	12.8	49.7	24.3	10.2	2.3	0.5	0.2	877
Raleigh, NC	3.9	31.6	47.0	13.2	3.0	0.5	0.8	1,121
Reno, NV	5.6	42.2	33.7	14.3	3.2	0.5	0.6	1,029
Richmond, VA	12.6	35.0	37.0	11.7	2.7	0.3	0.6	1,025
Riverside, CA	3.4	16.0	39.3	28.9	9.9	1.8	0.7	1,378
Rochester, MN	9.1	43.7	30.2	13.0	1.7	0.9	1.3	974
Sacramento, CA	5.9	24.1	38.5	23.4	6.1	1.4	0.6	1,263
Salt Lake City, UT	8.9	42.8	31.8	12.5	3.1	0.6	0.4	985
San Antonio, TX	7.6	43.3	36.4	10.0	1.7	0.4	0.6	992
San Diego, CA	3.4	10.2	25.9	26.9	18.7	8.9	6.0	1,695
San Francisco, CA	9.3	13.0	15.6	15.3	13.6	11.7	21.4	1,895
San Jose, CA	4.5	6.9	13.6	20.9	19.2	16.2	18.7	2,107
Santa Rosa, CA	5.4	8.4	30.1	27.8	18.2	6.9	3.2	1,609
Savannah, GA	10.0	38.1	39.8	8.9	1.8	0.5	1.0	1,019
Seattle, WA	6.5	10.0	27.1	28.0	14.9	7.0	6.4	1,614
Sioux Falls, SD	8.5	65.9	19.8	4.0	0.6	0.5	0.8	827
Springfield, IL	12.4	62.3	19.5	3.4	1.1	1.1	0.2	805
Tallahassee, FL	5.3	42.2	39.8	8.5	3.2	0.6	0.3	1,023
Tampa, FL	8.1	30.2	37.6	16.0	4.8	1.9	1.5	1,131
Tucson, AZ	7.9	57.2	27.6	5.4	1.1	0.4	0.5	846
Tulsa, OK	10.9	59.4	24.1	3.6	1.0	0.5	0.6	829
Tuscaloosa, AL	13.1	57.0	22.2	4.6	1.9	0.3	1.0	844
Virginia Beach, VA	3.2	12.0	47.9	26.8	6.9	1.7	1.6	1,367
Washington, DC	10.4	13.2	24.7	21.1	13.6	8.2	8.9	1,541
Wichita, KS	11.6	61.3	22.4	3.3	0.6	0.2	0.7	809
Winston-Salem, NC	10.9	62.6	21.5	3.5	0.9	0.2	0.4	806
U.S.	9.4	36.2	30.0	14.0	5.6	2.4	2.4	1,062

Note: Figures are percentages except for Median; Gross rent is the contract rent plus the estimated average monthly cost of utilities (electricity, gas, and water and sewer) and fuels (oil, coal, kerosene, wood, etc.) if these are paid by the renter (or paid for the renter by someone else).

Source: U.S. Census Bureau, 2015-2019 American Community Survey 5-Year Estimates

Gross Monthly Rent: Metro Area

MSA[1]	Under $500	$500 -$999	$1,000 -$1,499	$1,500 -$1,999	$2,000 -$2,499	$2,500 -2,999	$3,000 and up	Median ($)
Albuquerque, NM	8.0	52.5	30.1	7.5	1.1	0.3	0.4	892
Allentown, PA	9.5	34.3	38.5	13.6	2.6	0.7	0.8	1,066
Anchorage, AK	4.2	23.2	37.1	19.7	10.8	3.7	1.3	1,288
Ann Arbor, MI	5.5	33.9	37.6	14.7	4.5	1.6	2.2	1,114
Athens, GA	8.4	59.5	23.6	6.2	1.5	0.5	0.2	853
Atlanta, GA	4.8	28.9	45.0	16.1	3.4	0.9	0.8	1,156
Austin, TX	3.1	19.4	44.5	22.7	6.7	2.1	1.6	1,273
Baton Rouge, LA	8.9	50.9	29.0	7.6	2.9	0.4	0.3	922
Boise City, ID	8.2	47.3	34.8	7.4	1.6	0.4	0.5	958
Boston, MA	12.4	13.4	25.6	23.5	13.2	6.1	5.8	1,475
Boulder, CO	4.0	11.7	34.6	27.2	13.3	5.0	4.2	1,495
Cape Coral, FL	4.2	29.8	43.3	14.3	4.8	1.6	2.0	1,154
Cedar Rapids, IA	16.9	60.9	18.9	1.9	0.5	0.3	0.7	753
Charleston, SC	6.1	29.6	40.2	17.0	4.2	1.5	1.4	1,156
Charlotte, NC	6.1	41.0	37.9	11.2	2.4	0.8	0.6	1,030
Chicago, IL	7.7	32.0	34.9	15.8	5.8	2.2	1.7	1,122
Cincinnati, OH	12.3	54.7	24.8	5.7	1.5	0.4	0.7	842
Clarksville, TN	8.7	49.9	32.7	7.3	1.3	0.2	0.0	919
Cleveland, OH	13.0	57.6	23.2	4.3	1.1	0.3	0.5	817
College Station, TX	6.3	51.7	26.5	10.6	3.6	0.8	0.5	935
Colorado Springs, CO	3.8	31.8	36.9	21.1	4.0	1.8	0.6	1,173
Columbia, MO	7.9	59.1	25.3	4.5	2.8	0.3	0.2	862
Columbia, SC	7.6	50.4	32.4	7.2	1.5	0.5	0.4	933
Columbus, OH	7.6	48.3	34.3	7.3	1.6	0.5	0.4	953
Dallas, TX	3.4	33.2	40.0	16.3	4.7	1.4	1.0	1,139
Davenport, IA	15.1	61.8	17.1	3.9	0.9	0.4	0.8	765
Denver, CO	5.1	16.7	37.2	26.2	10.2	2.9	1.7	1,380
Des Moines, IA	7.3	54.0	30.1	6.2	1.3	0.2	0.7	904
Durham, NC	7.9	38.7	39.1	10.0	2.5	0.6	1.1	1,033
Edison, NJ	9.4	13.9	30.7	23.1	11.0	5.3	6.7	1,439
El Paso, TX	15.0	53.4	25.4	5.2	0.5	0.3	0.2	837
Fargo, ND	8.0	62.0	21.3	6.7	1.4	0.4	0.3	837
Fayetteville, NC	7.3	50.9	33.4	7.2	1.1	0.1	0.1	932
Fort Collins, CO	4.1	23.2	37.4	25.2	7.7	1.7	0.7	1,297
Fort Wayne, IN	11.5	69.3	16.1	2.0	0.8	0.2	0.1	771
Fort Worth, TX	3.4	33.2	40.0	16.3	4.7	1.4	1.0	1,139
Grand Rapids, MI	8.8	56.1	26.7	5.7	1.9	0.3	0.3	884
Greeley, CO	7.7	36.4	33.4	16.3	4.0	1.0	1.2	1,085
Green Bay, WI	9.9	69.3	18.6	1.4	0.3	0.2	0.3	784
Greensboro, NC	9.6	63.4	22.4	2.9	1.0	0.3	0.5	834
Honolulu, HI	5.6	10.4	24.1	20.3	14.1	10.0	15.5	1,745
Houston, TX	3.8	37.0	37.0	15.6	4.0	1.4	1.2	1,101
Huntsville, AL	10.9	59.8	24.0	3.9	0.6	0.5	0.3	836
Indianapolis, IN	6.3	54.7	30.5	6.4	1.4	0.3	0.5	916
Jacksonville, FL	5.9	34.8	41.3	13.6	3.2	0.7	0.6	1,093
Kansas City, MO	8.2	46.4	34.4	8.0	2.0	0.5	0.6	961
Lafayette, LA	15.3	57.0	21.5	4.8	1.2	0.1	0.1	811
Lakeland, FL	6.7	45.8	33.6	11.3	1.8	0.5	0.3	978
Las Vegas, NV	2.8	34.4	42.1	15.9	3.5	0.8	0.6	1,132
Lexington, KY	9.6	55.1	28.1	4.9	1.7	0.3	0.3	867
Lincoln, NE	9.9	58.2	24.9	4.8	0.8	0.4	1.0	848
Little Rock, AR	10.1	58.9	25.0	4.7	0.6	0.4	0.3	845
Los Angeles, CA	4.2	12.7	30.8	25.7	14.0	6.7	5.9	1,545
Louisville, KY	13.1	54.3	26.6	4.6	0.8	0.4	0.3	854
Madison, WI	5.0	40.5	38.5	11.6	2.9	0.9	0.6	1,046

Table continued on following page.

MSA[1]	Under $500	$500-$999	$1,000-$1,499	$1,500-$1,999	$2,000-$2,499	$2,500-2,999	$3,000 and up	Median ($)
Manchester, NH	6.9	24.7	42.8	19.9	4.2	0.9	0.5	1,191
Memphis, TN	7.8	50.9	32.8	6.4	1.5	0.3	0.3	930
Miami, FL	5.2	17.0	37.9	24.5	9.5	3.4	2.4	1,363
Midland, TX	2.0	25.1	41.0	20.1	7.5	3.2	1.1	1,269
Milwaukee, WI	7.7	54.1	28.9	6.7	1.6	0.5	0.3	903
Minneapolis, MN	9.2	32.4	35.9	16.1	4.2	1.2	1.1	1,102
Nashville, TN	8.0	35.2	38.0	13.3	3.6	1.1	0.8	1,073
New Haven, CT	10.4	24.6	41.3	17.0	4.6	1.2	1.0	1,153
New Orleans, LA	9.3	41.9	35.6	10.0	2.2	0.6	0.5	991
New York, NY	9.4	13.9	30.7	23.1	11.0	5.3	6.7	1,439
Oklahoma City, OK	8.2	56.4	27.3	6.2	1.3	0.3	0.4	876
Omaha, NE	8.2	50.7	31.0	7.5	1.4	0.4	0.7	927
Orlando, FL	2.9	25.1	46.3	19.7	4.2	1.1	0.7	1,210
Peoria, IL	16.6	60.9	17.6	2.6	1.0	0.4	1.0	764
Philadelphia, PA	8.1	29.1	38.4	15.9	5.4	1.7	1.4	1,143
Phoenix, AZ	3.6	34.4	40.9	15.4	3.6	1.1	1.1	1,124
Pittsburgh, PA	15.6	51.9	23.2	6.0	1.9	0.6	0.8	831
Portland, OR	4.8	20.9	42.1	21.8	7.1	1.8	1.4	1,271
Providence, RI	16.0	37.6	31.8	10.3	2.8	0.6	0.7	968
Provo, UT	6.6	39.1	33.3	15.8	3.7	0.9	0.6	1,054
Raleigh, NC	4.9	32.8	43.7	13.4	3.4	0.8	1.0	1,113
Reno, NV	4.9	39.3	34.7	15.9	3.7	0.8	0.8	1,074
Richmond, VA	7.3	30.2	44.1	13.9	2.9	0.8	0.8	1,117
Riverside, CA	4.2	22.6	34.7	23.5	9.9	3.7	1.5	1,326
Rochester, MN	11.5	47.5	27.7	10.0	1.5	0.7	0.9	908
Sacramento, CA	4.6	22.7	37.5	23.2	8.1	2.4	1.4	1,290
Salt Lake City, UT	5.4	33.3	41.2	15.4	3.3	0.8	0.7	1,114
San Antonio, TX	7.0	40.8	36.6	11.8	2.3	0.7	0.8	1,024
San Diego, CA	3.5	9.9	28.1	27.2	17.0	8.2	6.2	1,658
San Francisco, CA	6.0	9.4	17.2	21.4	18.2	11.9	15.8	1,905
San Jose, CA	3.5	5.8	11.6	18.8	20.7	17.2	22.4	2,249
Santa Rosa, CA	5.2	10.6	27.7	27.0	17.3	7.6	4.5	1,621
Savannah, GA	7.3	33.4	43.3	12.0	2.8	0.4	0.8	1,086
Seattle, WA	5.1	14.0	31.4	27.7	12.8	5.0	4.0	1,492
Sioux Falls, SD	9.4	64.4	20.0	4.4	0.7	0.4	0.8	829
Springfield, IL	11.4	63.1	19.9	3.6	0.9	0.9	0.2	818
Tallahassee, FL	6.9	44.2	36.9	8.4	2.9	0.5	0.2	991
Tampa, FL	4.9	33.9	40.4	14.9	3.6	1.4	1.0	1,115
Tucson, AZ	7.2	51.4	30.9	7.5	1.6	0.7	0.8	907
Tulsa, OK	10.7	56.8	26.1	4.4	1.0	0.5	0.5	852
Tuscaloosa, AL	17.1	54.6	21.8	4.2	1.5	0.2	0.6	819
Virginia Beach, VA	7.0	26.2	41.2	18.4	4.9	1.3	1.0	1,180
Washington, DC	4.6	7.8	25.4	32.2	16.6	7.3	6.1	1,690
Wichita, KS	11.4	60.3	22.5	4.0	0.9	0.3	0.7	818
Winston-Salem, NC	12.9	63.9	18.9	3.1	0.7	0.2	0.2	773
U.S.	9.4	36.2	30.0	14.0	5.6	2.4	2.4	1,062

Note: (1) Figures cover the Metropolitan Statistical Area (MSA)—see Appendix B for areas included; Figures are percentages except for Median; Gross rent is the contract rent plus the estimated average monthly cost of utilities (electricity, gas, and water and sewer) and fuels (oil, coal, kerosene, wood, etc.) if these are paid by the renter (or paid for the renter by someone else).
Source: U.S. Census Bureau, 2015-2019 American Community Survey 5-Year Estimates

Highest Level of Education: City

City	Less than H.S.	H.S. Diploma	Some College, No Deg.	Associate Degree	Bachelors Degree	Masters Degree	Profess. School Degree	Doctorate Degree
Albuquerque, NM	10.3	22.5	23.4	8.5	19.4	10.6	2.7	2.5
Allentown, PA	21.0	38.0	18.3	7.4	9.6	3.9	1.0	0.8
Anchorage, AK	6.1	23.4	25.4	9.0	22.2	9.5	3.1	1.3
Ann Arbor, MI	2.7	7.1	10.0	4.2	30.2	26.9	7.1	11.7
Athens, GA	12.1	19.8	17.1	6.9	22.1	13.4	3.0	5.6
Atlanta, GA	9.1	18.9	15.3	4.9	28.9	15.1	5.3	2.5
Austin, TX	10.6	15.6	16.7	5.4	32.3	13.6	3.3	2.5
Baton Rouge, LA	12.0	27.8	22.5	4.5	19.3	8.8	2.6	2.5
Boise City, ID	4.9	21.4	23.1	9.1	26.8	10.1	2.7	1.9
Boston, MA	12.8	19.7	13.1	4.6	27.0	14.5	4.8	3.4
Boulder, CO	3.1	6.2	11.1	3.6	36.2	24.7	6.4	8.7
Cape Coral, FL	8.2	37.3	21.0	10.1	15.8	5.3	1.3	0.9
Cedar Rapids, IA	6.7	26.6	22.2	12.4	22.9	6.6	1.5	1.0
Charleston, SC	5.1	17.6	16.3	7.9	33.8	12.6	4.5	2.2
Charlotte, NC	10.9	17.1	20.0	7.7	28.9	11.7	2.6	1.1
Chicago, IL	14.9	22.5	17.3	5.8	23.3	11.3	3.3	1.6
Cincinnati, OH	11.9	24.4	19.1	7.4	21.4	10.4	3.1	2.1
Clarksville, TN	7.1	27.9	26.9	10.5	18.7	6.9	0.8	1.2
Cleveland, OH	19.2	32.7	23.2	7.4	10.9	4.5	1.4	0.7
College Station, TX	5.6	11.4	17.0	7.4	29.3	15.7	3.3	10.3
Colorado Springs, CO	6.1	20.0	23.4	10.6	24.3	12.0	2.0	1.5
Columbia, MO	4.8	18.1	18.7	6.2	27.4	14.9	4.6	5.3
Columbia, SC	10.6	20.1	18.6	6.9	24.4	12.8	3.9	2.7
Columbus, OH	10.2	25.5	20.6	7.2	23.8	9.4	1.9	1.5
Dallas, TX	22.5	21.7	17.8	4.6	21.0	8.3	2.9	1.1
Davenport, IA	9.5	32.5	21.8	10.7	17.0	6.3	1.5	0.8
Denver, CO	12.0	16.8	16.5	5.3	30.2	13.1	4.2	2.0
Des Moines, IA	13.7	29.5	21.2	8.9	18.6	5.5	1.7	0.9
Durham, NC	11.9	16.4	15.5	6.5	25.8	14.7	4.2	4.8
Edison, NJ	7.9	19.5	11.7	5.4	30.0	20.3	2.8	2.5
El Paso, TX	19.7	23.0	24.0	8.2	16.7	6.4	1.2	0.8
Fargo, ND	5.7	20.9	19.6	13.8	28.0	8.0	2.1	1.8
Fayetteville, NC	8.3	24.4	29.4	10.6	18.0	6.7	1.5	1.0
Fort Collins, CO	3.5	15.1	17.7	8.3	32.3	16.8	2.4	4.0
Fort Wayne, IN	11.5	28.2	22.1	10.3	18.3	7.1	1.4	1.0
Fort Worth, TX	17.8	24.9	20.8	6.9	20.0	7.1	1.5	1.1
Grand Rapids, MI	13.3	21.9	20.5	7.9	24.4	8.7	2.0	1.4
Greeley, CO	15.5	27.2	23.4	9.1	15.4	7.2	1.2	1.0
Green Bay, WI	12.5	31.4	20.1	11.2	17.9	5.1	1.1	0.7
Greensboro, NC	10.2	21.5	21.7	8.4	24.1	10.0	2.3	1.8
Honolulu, HI	11.0	23.5	18.3	10.1	23.7	8.3	3.2	2.0
Houston, TX	21.1	22.8	17.8	5.5	20.0	8.6	2.6	1.6
Huntsville, AL	9.0	18.7	20.3	7.9	26.4	13.8	1.8	2.2
Indianapolis, IN	14.2	27.9	19.4	7.6	20.0	7.6	2.1	1.1
Jacksonville, FL	10.5	28.4	22.3	10.1	19.1	7.0	1.7	0.8
Kansas City, MO	10.0	25.3	22.0	7.4	22.2	9.3	2.5	1.2
Lafayette, LA	10.5	27.0	20.0	4.3	25.6	8.5	2.7	1.4
Lakeland, FL	12.0	33.0	19.5	9.6	16.8	6.7	1.6	0.9
Las Vegas, NV	15.2	27.6	24.6	8.0	16.0	5.9	1.9	0.8
Lexington, KY	8.8	19.6	20.5	7.5	24.4	12.0	4.1	3.2
Lincoln, NE	6.7	21.3	21.2	11.2	24.8	9.8	2.2	2.8
Little Rock, AR	8.7	22.2	21.1	6.2	23.7	11.0	4.3	2.8
Los Angeles, CA	22.5	19.2	17.6	6.2	22.6	7.6	2.8	1.4
Louisville, KY	10.4	28.6	22.9	8.1	17.9	8.5	2.3	1.2
Madison, WI	4.5	14.2	15.3	8.0	32.1	16.2	4.2	5.3

Table continued on following page.

City	Less than H.S.	H.S. Diploma	Some College, No Deg.	Associate Degree	Bachelors Degree	Masters Degree	Profess. School Degree	Doctorate Degree
Manchester, NH	12.7	29.1	18.9	9.3	20.3	7.3	1.7	0.9
Memphis, TN	14.3	30.6	23.3	5.6	15.7	7.1	2.0	1.3
Miami, FL	22.0	28.4	12.5	7.4	17.9	7.1	3.6	1.1
Midland, TX	14.9	25.2	23.2	7.7	20.7	5.9	1.7	0.7
Milwaukee, WI	16.0	30.2	21.9	7.2	15.9	6.5	1.3	0.9
Minneapolis, MN	10.0	15.1	17.1	7.3	30.4	13.6	4.0	2.5
Nashville, TN	11.2	22.3	18.9	6.4	25.8	10.3	2.9	2.1
New Haven, CT	14.4	32.2	14.0	4.5	15.7	10.7	4.2	4.3
New Orleans, LA	13.5	22.8	21.5	4.7	21.2	9.9	4.4	2.0
New York, NY	17.8	24.0	13.7	6.3	22.2	11.2	3.2	1.5
Oklahoma City, OK	13.6	25.4	22.9	7.3	19.7	7.5	2.4	1.1
Omaha, NE	10.5	22.3	21.9	7.7	24.3	8.9	2.9	1.5
Orlando, FL	9.6	23.2	18.4	10.8	25.4	8.3	3.0	1.3
Peoria, IL	10.6	24.3	21.5	8.6	20.7	10.2	2.7	1.3
Philadelphia, PA	15.3	32.6	16.7	5.7	17.3	8.1	2.6	1.6
Phoenix, AZ	18.1	23.6	22.0	7.7	18.3	7.3	2.0	1.0
Pittsburgh, PA	7.1	25.5	15.1	7.9	23.2	13.1	4.3	3.9
Portland, OR	7.6	15.1	20.3	6.6	30.1	13.8	4.1	2.4
Providence, RI	18.4	31.4	15.2	5.0	16.1	8.6	2.9	2.5
Provo, UT	7.1	14.3	26.5	8.9	29.7	8.9	1.6	2.8
Raleigh, NC	8.2	15.6	17.8	7.5	32.4	13.1	3.1	2.3
Reno, NV	11.0	22.2	25.0	8.2	20.6	8.4	2.3	2.3
Richmond, VA	14.6	21.8	18.4	5.6	23.5	11.0	3.1	2.0
Riverside, CA	19.4	26.3	23.7	7.7	13.5	6.4	1.4	1.7
Rochester, MN	6.0	18.7	17.2	11.4	25.7	12.1	5.2	3.7
Sacramento, CA	14.7	21.3	22.4	8.5	21.2	7.7	2.9	1.3
Salt Lake City, UT	11.2	17.5	17.7	7.0	25.7	12.5	4.6	3.7
San Antonio, TX	17.6	26.3	22.4	7.7	16.6	6.7	1.7	1.0
San Diego, CA	11.9	15.1	19.7	7.4	27.0	12.2	3.7	3.0
San Francisco, CA	11.5	12.1	13.3	5.0	34.8	15.4	5.0	2.8
San Jose, CA	15.4	16.6	16.8	7.5	25.7	13.6	2.0	2.5
Santa Rosa, CA	13.8	19.3	24.5	9.8	20.1	8.0	2.9	1.5
Savannah, GA	12.4	26.8	25.9	6.7	17.8	7.6	1.6	1.2
Seattle, WA	5.2	9.6	15.0	6.2	36.7	18.1	5.3	3.9
Sioux Falls, SD	7.7	24.8	20.8	11.5	23.8	8.1	2.2	1.1
Springfield, IL	8.7	25.9	22.1	7.6	21.5	9.8	3.3	1.2
Tallahassee, FL	6.5	17.0	19.0	9.3	26.2	13.8	3.9	4.3
Tampa, FL	12.1	25.6	16.0	7.7	23.3	9.6	3.9	1.7
Tucson, AZ	15.0	23.6	25.6	8.4	16.5	7.8	1.4	1.6
Tulsa, OK	12.7	25.3	22.6	7.9	20.7	7.2	2.5	1.1
Tuscaloosa, AL	10.9	27.3	19.9	5.0	21.0	10.3	2.5	3.1
Virginia Beach, VA	6.5	21.0	25.7	10.9	22.6	10.2	2.1	1.1
Washington, DC	9.1	16.8	12.6	3.0	24.8	21.2	8.4	4.2
Wichita, KS	11.7	26.4	24.0	7.9	19.1	8.1	1.8	1.1
Winston-Salem, NC	11.8	24.9	21.5	7.4	20.8	8.9	3.0	1.9
U.S.	12.0	27.0	20.4	8.5	19.8	8.8	2.1	1.4

Note: Figures cover persons age 25 and over
Source: U.S. Census Bureau, 2015-2019 American Community Survey 5-Year Estimates

Highest Level of Education: Metro Area

Metro Area	Less than H.S.	H.S. Diploma	Some College, No Deg.	Associate Degree	Bachelors Degree	Masters Degree	Profess. School Degree	Doctorate Degree
Albuquerque, NM	11.4	24.6	23.3	8.5	17.9	9.8	2.3	2.2
Allentown, PA	10.0	34.2	17.1	9.3	18.3	8.4	1.6	1.2
Anchorage, AK	6.3	26.0	26.2	9.1	20.1	8.5	2.6	1.2
Ann Arbor, MI	4.7	14.6	17.6	7.1	26.3	18.8	4.7	6.0
Athens, GA	12.2	24.5	16.8	7.1	19.9	11.8	3.1	4.5
Atlanta, GA	10.4	23.9	19.5	7.6	24.0	10.6	2.5	1.5
Austin, TX	10.1	19.1	19.6	6.5	28.8	11.6	2.5	1.9
Baton Rouge, LA	12.6	32.2	21.4	6.2	18.0	6.6	1.7	1.3
Boise City, ID	8.2	25.8	24.8	9.4	21.3	7.4	1.7	1.3
Boston, MA	8.3	22.1	14.5	7.0	26.0	15.2	3.5	3.3
Boulder, CO	5.0	11.7	15.1	6.1	34.0	18.8	4.1	5.2
Cape Coral, FL	11.6	31.0	20.3	8.9	17.6	7.2	2.2	1.2
Cedar Rapids, IA	5.7	29.0	21.5	12.8	21.9	6.9	1.4	0.8
Charleston, SC	9.3	25.4	20.1	9.5	23.0	8.9	2.4	1.2
Charlotte, NC	11.0	23.5	21.1	9.2	23.5	9.0	1.8	0.9
Chicago, IL	11.3	23.9	19.5	7.2	23.0	10.9	2.6	1.4
Cincinnati, OH	9.0	29.7	19.2	8.4	21.0	9.3	2.0	1.4
Clarksville, TN	9.3	30.2	25.4	10.3	16.1	6.8	1.1	0.9
Cleveland, OH	9.4	28.9	21.8	8.7	18.9	8.7	2.4	1.2
College Station, TX	13.4	22.2	20.4	6.5	20.6	9.6	2.2	5.1
Colorado Springs, CO	5.6	20.5	24.0	11.3	23.5	11.8	1.8	1.4
Columbia, MO	6.4	23.7	19.8	7.4	24.5	11.3	3.2	3.7
Columbia, SC	10.1	26.9	21.2	9.0	20.1	9.2	1.8	1.5
Columbus, OH	8.5	27.7	19.6	7.5	23.4	9.7	2.2	1.4
Dallas, TX	14.4	22.3	21.1	7.0	23.0	9.2	1.9	1.1
Davenport, IA	9.0	30.5	23.0	10.5	17.2	7.3	1.5	0.8
Denver, CO	8.8	19.9	19.8	7.7	27.7	11.8	2.7	1.6
Des Moines, IA	7.5	25.6	20.2	10.3	25.4	7.7	2.2	1.1
Durham, NC	11.2	19.8	16.1	7.6	23.2	13.2	4.0	4.9
Edison, NJ	13.5	24.7	14.8	6.7	23.4	12.1	3.3	1.6
El Paso, TX	21.7	23.7	23.1	8.2	15.7	5.7	1.1	0.7
Fargo, ND	5.2	21.0	21.0	14.2	27.4	7.9	1.8	1.5
Fayetteville, NC	10.4	27.3	27.5	11.1	15.7	6.2	1.0	0.8
Fort Collins, CO	4.1	19.0	20.4	9.2	28.0	13.9	2.1	3.2
Fort Wayne, IN	10.4	29.2	21.7	10.9	18.4	6.9	1.5	0.9
Fort Worth, TX	14.4	22.3	21.1	7.0	23.0	9.2	1.9	1.1
Grand Rapids, MI	8.8	27.2	22.0	9.3	21.8	8.1	1.7	1.1
Greeley, CO	11.9	27.3	24.1	9.1	18.6	7.0	1.1	0.9
Green Bay, WI	8.0	32.1	19.7	12.4	19.6	6.0	1.5	0.7
Greensboro, NC	13.2	26.7	21.7	8.9	19.2	7.5	1.5	1.3
Honolulu, HI	8.1	25.9	20.3	10.7	22.9	8.1	2.5	1.5
Houston, TX	16.3	23.2	20.6	7.1	21.0	8.4	2.0	1.5
Huntsville, AL	9.8	22.7	20.2	8.1	24.2	11.9	1.4	1.7
Indianapolis, IN	10.3	27.9	19.3	7.9	22.4	8.8	2.2	1.3
Jacksonville, FL	9.1	27.7	21.8	10.0	20.6	7.9	1.9	1.1
Kansas City, MO	8.0	25.5	21.6	7.7	23.5	10.2	2.3	1.2
Lafayette, LA	15.9	36.4	18.6	5.7	16.4	5.0	1.3	0.7
Lakeland, FL	15.0	34.7	20.9	9.2	13.2	5.2	1.1	0.7
Las Vegas, NV	13.9	28.5	25.1	8.1	16.2	5.8	1.6	0.8
Lexington, KY	9.9	24.2	20.8	7.9	21.3	10.3	3.2	2.4
Lincoln, NE	6.3	21.9	21.2	11.7	24.5	9.7	2.2	2.6
Little Rock, AR	9.6	29.3	23.0	7.8	18.9	8.0	2.1	1.5
Los Angeles, CA	19.3	19.8	19.2	7.2	22.4	8.2	2.5	1.4
Louisville, KY	9.9	29.6	22.3	8.6	17.9	8.4	2.2	1.1
Madison, WI	4.7	21.0	17.9	10.3	27.7	12.1	3.0	3.2

Table continued on following page.

Metro Area	Less than H.S.	H.S. Diploma	Some College, No Deg.	Associate Degree	Bachelors Degree	Masters Degree	Profess. School Degree	Doctorate Degree
Manchester, NH	7.9	25.8	18.2	10.0	24.3	10.9	1.6	1.3
Memphis, TN	12.0	29.2	23.5	7.1	17.4	7.9	1.9	1.2
Miami, FL	14.5	26.5	17.4	9.3	20.2	7.9	2.9	1.2
Midland, TX	15.7	25.9	23.5	7.8	19.3	5.8	1.4	0.6
Milwaukee, WI	8.5	26.5	20.6	8.7	23.0	9.0	2.3	1.3
Minneapolis, MN	6.4	21.2	20.0	10.4	27.4	10.4	2.6	1.6
Nashville, TN	10.0	26.4	20.2	7.3	23.5	9.0	2.2	1.6
New Haven, CT	9.9	30.7	17.1	7.3	18.6	11.2	3.1	2.1
New Orleans, LA	13.1	28.2	22.5	5.8	19.0	7.3	2.8	1.2
New York, NY	13.5	24.7	14.8	6.7	23.4	12.1	3.3	1.6
Oklahoma City, OK	11.0	27.3	23.6	7.5	19.6	7.6	2.0	1.3
Omaha, NE	8.3	23.8	22.5	9.1	23.8	9.0	2.3	1.3
Orlando, FL	10.5	25.8	19.9	11.5	21.3	7.8	2.0	1.0
Peoria, IL	8.3	30.5	23.2	10.4	18.1	7.2	1.5	0.9
Philadelphia, PA	9.3	29.0	16.7	7.1	22.4	10.8	2.7	1.9
Phoenix, AZ	12.5	23.0	24.4	8.6	20.0	8.3	1.9	1.2
Pittsburgh, PA	6.1	32.4	16.4	10.2	21.3	9.8	2.3	1.7
Portland, OR	7.9	19.9	23.6	8.8	24.7	10.5	2.6	1.9
Providence, RI	12.3	28.8	18.0	8.6	19.6	9.2	1.9	1.5
Provo, UT	5.5	16.8	26.7	10.7	27.7	9.2	1.6	1.7
Raleigh, NC	8.3	17.7	18.2	9.0	29.6	12.6	2.4	2.2
Reno, NV	11.3	23.6	25.7	8.6	19.2	7.8	2.1	1.8
Richmond, VA	10.1	25.1	20.0	7.4	23.1	10.5	2.3	1.6
Riverside, CA	18.9	26.6	24.6	8.2	13.9	5.6	1.3	0.9
Rochester, MN	5.9	23.9	19.1	12.4	22.7	9.7	3.8	2.5
Sacramento, CA	10.7	21.2	24.7	9.9	21.8	7.8	2.6	1.4
Salt Lake City, UT	9.2	23.0	23.9	9.0	22.5	8.7	2.3	1.5
San Antonio, TX	14.9	26.3	22.6	8.0	18.0	7.5	1.7	1.0
San Diego, CA	12.6	18.2	22.3	8.1	23.8	10.0	2.9	2.1
San Francisco, CA	10.9	15.5	17.3	6.6	29.3	13.7	3.8	2.9
San Jose, CA	11.9	14.4	15.4	6.9	27.3	17.5	2.7	3.9
Santa Rosa, CA	11.2	18.7	25.0	9.6	22.2	8.6	3.1	1.6
Savannah, GA	10.2	26.3	24.2	7.9	19.5	8.4	2.2	1.3
Seattle, WA	7.4	19.4	21.0	9.3	26.6	11.7	2.7	2.0
Sioux Falls, SD	7.1	26.1	20.6	12.7	23.2	7.3	2.0	1.0
Springfield, IL	7.4	27.7	22.7	8.3	21.2	9.0	2.6	1.0
Tallahassee, FL	9.4	23.7	19.8	8.7	22.0	10.4	2.9	3.1
Tampa, FL	10.4	28.9	20.5	9.8	19.6	7.6	2.0	1.2
Tucson, AZ	11.6	22.2	25.1	8.7	18.7	9.4	2.3	2.0
Tulsa, OK	10.6	29.1	23.7	8.9	18.9	6.3	1.7	0.9
Tuscaloosa, AL	12.9	31.7	21.1	6.9	16.6	7.5	1.4	1.9
Virginia Beach, VA	8.6	24.9	24.7	9.9	19.5	9.3	1.8	1.2
Washington, DC	9.1	18.2	16.0	5.9	25.8	17.6	4.3	3.2
Wichita, KS	9.9	26.5	24.4	8.6	19.6	8.3	1.7	1.0
Winston-Salem, NC	13.0	29.4	21.6	9.3	17.4	6.5	1.6	1.2
U.S.	12.0	27.0	20.4	8.5	19.8	8.8	2.1	1.4

Note: Figures cover persons age 25 and over; Figures cover the Metropolitan Statistical Area—see Appendix B for areas included
Source: U.S. Census Bureau, 2015-2019 American Community Survey 5-Year Estimates

School Enrollment by Grade and Control: City

City	Preschool (%)		Kindergarten (%)		Grades 1 - 4 (%)		Grades 5 - 8 (%)		Grades 9 - 12 (%)	
	Public	Private	Public	Private	Public	Private	Public	Private	Public	Private
Albuquerque, NM	59.3	40.7	87.2	12.8	91.8	8.2	90.0	10.0	92.0	8.0
Allentown, PA	73.8	26.2	82.8	17.2	87.8	12.2	88.3	11.7	89.0	11.0
Anchorage, AK	56.6	43.4	94.0	6.0	92.3	7.7	92.5	7.5	95.1	4.9
Ann Arbor, MI	25.7	74.3	94.1	5.9	91.8	8.2	87.6	12.4	94.2	5.8
Athens, GA	67.9	32.1	92.6	7.4	91.9	8.1	88.8	11.2	88.5	11.5
Atlanta, GA	54.3	45.7	84.5	15.5	87.8	12.2	79.5	20.5	80.1	19.9
Austin, TX	51.0	49.0	86.9	13.1	89.3	10.7	88.9	11.1	91.0	9.0
Baton Rouge, LA	66.8	33.2	75.3	24.7	80.3	19.7	79.5	20.5	80.8	19.2
Boise City, ID	30.6	69.4	84.8	15.2	90.0	10.0	91.7	8.3	89.1	10.9
Boston, MA	50.7	49.3	84.9	15.1	85.7	14.3	86.8	13.2	87.8	12.2
Boulder, CO	44.0	56.0	84.5	15.5	92.5	7.5	93.4	6.6	92.2	7.8
Cape Coral, FL	84.8	15.2	94.8	5.2	92.0	8.0	93.0	7.0	91.8	8.2
Cedar Rapids, IA	67.5	32.5	86.4	13.6	88.9	11.1	93.0	7.0	90.0	10.0
Charleston, SC	41.2	58.9	78.8	21.2	83.4	16.6	78.9	21.1	78.9	21.1
Charlotte, NC	47.5	52.5	90.5	9.5	90.7	9.3	87.6	12.4	89.8	10.2
Chicago, IL	58.4	41.6	79.9	20.1	85.9	14.1	85.4	14.6	87.4	12.6
Cincinnati, OH	64.7	35.3	73.1	26.9	77.6	22.4	80.1	19.9	80.8	19.2
Clarksville, TN	57.3	42.7	90.6	9.4	93.7	6.3	92.5	7.5	92.4	7.6
Cleveland, OH	74.3	25.7	79.3	20.7	79.6	20.4	77.9	22.1	79.8	20.2
College Station, TX	46.9	53.1	85.1	14.9	86.5	13.5	93.5	6.5	92.7	7.3
Colorado Springs, CO	57.1	42.9	89.3	10.7	92.5	7.5	92.5	7.5	92.0	8.0
Columbia, MO	36.1	63.9	76.7	23.3	87.5	12.5	88.1	11.9	88.8	11.2
Columbia, SC	57.2	42.8	74.3	25.7	88.1	11.9	87.7	12.3	86.7	13.3
Columbus, OH	60.3	39.7	85.3	14.7	87.7	12.3	87.2	12.8	87.3	12.7
Dallas, TX	69.2	30.8	91.0	9.0	92.0	8.0	91.7	8.3	91.6	8.4
Davenport, IA	57.0	43.0	86.1	13.9	89.3	10.7	84.3	15.7	92.8	7.2
Denver, CO	64.4	35.6	86.3	13.7	91.4	8.6	91.0	9.0	91.4	8.6
Des Moines, IA	73.0	27.0	90.0	10.0	89.0	11.0	91.7	8.3	92.3	7.7
Durham, NC	52.1	47.9	91.9	8.1	88.8	11.2	87.3	12.7	89.7	10.3
Edison, NJ	30.2	69.8	67.7	32.3	90.1	9.9	90.0	10.0	91.6	8.4
El Paso, TX	78.5	21.5	93.3	6.7	95.0	5.0	94.6	5.4	96.2	3.8
Fargo, ND	53.4	46.6	94.7	5.3	90.4	9.6	89.3	10.7	93.7	6.3
Fayetteville, NC	63.5	36.5	88.7	11.3	87.2	12.8	87.4	12.6	89.7	10.3
Fort Collins, CO	41.9	58.1	91.7	8.3	94.5	5.5	95.1	4.9	94.6	5.4
Fort Wayne, IN	45.5	54.5	83.5	16.5	79.5	20.5	82.2	17.8	81.3	18.7
Fort Worth, TX	62.0	38.0	87.1	12.9	92.6	7.4	90.7	9.3	92.8	7.2
Grand Rapids, MI	60.4	39.6	74.5	25.5	83.4	16.6	83.4	16.6	84.9	15.1
Greeley, CO	69.6	30.4	83.6	16.4	91.5	8.5	92.6	7.4	95.3	4.7
Green Bay, WI	71.8	28.2	85.7	14.3	90.6	9.4	84.6	15.4	91.1	8.9
Greensboro, NC	53.2	46.8	89.5	10.5	93.4	6.6	90.2	9.8	91.6	8.4
Honolulu, HI	34.7	65.3	79.6	20.4	83.3	16.7	73.0	27.0	74.8	25.2
Houston, TX	66.9	33.1	90.8	9.2	94.2	5.8	92.7	7.3	93.5	6.5
Huntsville, AL	59.4	40.6	87.2	12.8	80.1	19.9	82.9	17.1	84.8	15.2
Indianapolis, IN	61.8	38.2	85.6	14.4	88.5	11.5	87.1	12.9	89.2	10.8
Jacksonville, FL	57.5	42.5	84.3	15.7	84.3	15.7	81.7	18.3	83.5	16.5
Kansas City, MO	57.7	42.3	85.3	14.7	90.1	9.9	88.3	11.7	85.4	14.6
Lafayette, LA	60.7	39.3	64.2	35.8	74.4	25.6	73.3	26.7	80.6	19.4
Lakeland, FL	61.7	38.3	85.0	15.0	83.6	16.4	83.7	16.3	88.0	12.0
Las Vegas, NV	65.7	34.3	88.6	11.4	91.3	8.7	91.7	8.3	93.0	7.0
Lexington, KY	44.2	55.8	86.4	13.6	87.2	12.8	86.6	13.4	86.1	13.9
Lincoln, NE	44.8	55.2	73.8	26.2	84.9	15.1	86.5	13.5	86.4	13.6
Little Rock, AR	60.3	39.7	82.3	17.7	82.7	17.3	82.0	18.0	79.8	20.2
Los Angeles, CA	60.2	39.8	88.1	11.9	89.0	11.0	88.6	11.4	88.8	11.2
Louisville, KY	51.1	48.9	80.2	19.8	83.4	16.6	79.9	20.1	79.3	20.7
Madison, WI	53.6	46.4	85.3	14.7	88.4	11.6	87.0	13.0	91.0	9.0

Table continued on following page.

City	Preschool (%)		Kindergarten (%)		Grades 1 - 4 (%)		Grades 5 - 8 (%)		Grades 9 - 12 (%)	
	Public	Private	Public	Private	Public	Private	Public	Private	Public	Private
Manchester, NH	52.6	47.4	86.1	13.9	89.9	10.1	93.1	6.9	89.5	10.5
Memphis, TN	67.2	32.8	87.3	12.7	87.9	12.1	87.2	12.8	85.5	14.5
Miami, FL	56.0	44.0	86.7	13.3	88.1	11.9	85.6	14.4	90.8	9.2
Midland, TX	64.4	35.6	89.1	10.9	86.0	14.0	88.3	11.7	89.9	10.1
Milwaukee, WI	73.5	26.5	79.4	20.6	77.1	22.9	75.8	24.2	81.4	18.6
Minneapolis, MN	53.4	46.6	85.1	14.9	88.2	11.8	88.9	11.1	87.7	12.3
Nashville, TN	50.7	49.3	87.4	12.6	85.6	14.4	83.4	16.6	82.0	18.0
New Haven, CT	83.6	16.4	94.0	6.0	94.8	5.2	93.8	6.2	92.2	7.8
New Orleans, LA	50.3	49.7	77.0	23.0	80.1	19.9	80.0	20.0	78.9	21.1
New York, NY	60.9	39.1	79.2	20.8	82.7	17.3	82.2	17.8	82.3	17.7
Oklahoma City, OK	73.4	26.6	91.7	8.3	91.8	8.2	91.0	9.0	90.2	9.8
Omaha, NE	53.5	46.5	82.0	18.0	83.5	16.5	85.3	14.7	83.2	16.8
Orlando, FL	62.2	37.8	86.4	13.6	91.2	8.8	85.0	15.0	93.3	6.7
Peoria, IL	60.1	39.9	70.0	30.0	83.9	16.1	83.4	16.6	88.7	11.3
Philadelphia, PA	56.8	43.2	79.1	20.9	79.1	20.9	80.6	19.4	80.1	19.9
Phoenix, AZ	62.7	37.3	90.0	10.0	92.9	7.1	92.4	7.6	93.1	6.9
Pittsburgh, PA	48.0	52.0	77.1	22.9	73.1	26.9	75.8	24.2	81.5	18.5
Portland, OR	39.4	60.6	84.8	15.2	88.0	12.0	87.1	12.9	85.1	14.9
Providence, RI	51.6	48.4	87.8	12.2	86.0	14.0	85.4	14.6	88.6	11.4
Provo, UT	53.8	46.2	95.7	4.3	93.9	6.1	95.8	4.2	88.5	11.5
Raleigh, NC	43.5	56.5	89.3	10.7	90.6	9.4	89.2	10.8	90.6	9.4
Reno, NV	60.7	39.3	86.1	13.9	94.1	5.9	93.2	6.8	94.0	6.0
Richmond, VA	58.6	41.4	91.1	8.9	87.8	12.2	80.8	19.2	87.1	12.9
Riverside, CA	66.0	34.0	90.5	9.5	94.0	6.0	93.6	6.4	95.0	5.0
Rochester, MN	50.9	49.1	80.4	19.6	86.9	13.1	87.1	12.9	91.4	8.6
Sacramento, CA	68.9	31.1	92.8	7.2	93.2	6.8	92.9	7.1	92.6	7.4
Salt Lake City, UT	47.7	52.3	88.2	11.8	91.2	8.8	91.0	9.0	92.8	7.2
San Antonio, TX	70.1	29.9	90.3	9.7	93.1	6.9	92.9	7.1	92.6	7.4
San Diego, CA	52.5	47.5	92.9	7.1	90.9	9.1	91.2	8.8	91.5	8.5
San Francisco, CA	37.5	62.5	73.1	26.9	72.2	27.8	68.1	31.9	75.0	25.0
San Jose, CA	41.9	58.1	81.2	18.8	87.0	13.0	87.0	13.0	86.8	13.2
Santa Rosa, CA	53.6	46.4	94.6	5.4	95.9	4.1	92.5	7.5	92.0	8.0
Savannah, GA	67.6	32.4	93.0	7.0	90.1	9.9	91.0	9.0	89.6	10.4
Seattle, WA	32.6	67.4	79.7	20.3	81.6	18.4	75.9	24.1	79.8	20.2
Sioux Falls, SD	51.1	48.9	87.3	12.7	88.2	11.8	87.5	12.5	84.2	15.8
Springfield, IL	65.7	34.3	80.4	19.6	81.9	18.1	83.9	16.1	85.6	14.4
Tallahassee, FL	48.6	51.4	86.3	13.7	85.9	14.1	83.3	16.7	87.4	12.6
Tampa, FL	49.9	50.1	83.4	16.6	89.5	10.5	85.7	14.3	84.5	15.5
Tucson, AZ	74.0	26.0	85.8	14.2	89.6	10.4	91.3	8.7	92.8	7.2
Tulsa, OK	67.6	32.4	87.1	12.9	88.3	11.7	85.8	14.2	85.2	14.8
Tuscaloosa, AL	62.5	37.5	91.8	8.2	86.2	13.8	92.2	7.8	85.1	14.9
Virginia Beach, VA	37.7	62.3	77.3	22.7	90.2	9.8	88.7	11.3	92.7	7.3
Washington, DC	77.1	22.9	92.3	7.7	87.6	12.4	82.7	17.3	82.6	17.4
Wichita, KS	62.5	37.5	83.7	16.3	85.4	14.6	84.7	15.3	84.2	15.8
Winston-Salem, NC	55.3	44.7	94.1	5.9	93.3	6.7	90.8	9.2	93.2	6.8
U.S.	59.1	40.9	87.6	12.4	89.5	10.5	89.4	10.6	90.1	9.9

Note: Figures shown cover persons 3 years old and over
Source: U.S. Census Bureau, 2015-2019 American Community Survey 5-Year Estimates

School Enrollment by Grade and Control: Metro Area

Metro Area	Preschool (%)		Kindergarten (%)		Grades 1 - 4 (%)		Grades 5 - 8 (%)		Grades 9 - 12 (%)	
	Public	Private	Public	Private	Public	Private	Public	Private	Public	Private
Albuquerque, NM	64.5	35.5	85.6	14.4	90.1	9.9	89.4	10.6	91.7	8.3
Allentown, PA	49.0	51.0	85.5	14.5	89.4	10.6	90.5	9.5	91.0	9.0
Anchorage, AK	58.3	41.7	92.4	7.6	90.7	9.3	90.5	9.5	92.8	7.2
Ann Arbor, MI	49.6	50.4	89.6	10.4	87.3	12.7	87.7	12.3	91.8	8.2
Athens, GA	67.9	32.1	90.9	9.1	90.1	9.9	86.0	14.0	86.7	13.3
Atlanta, GA	56.0	44.0	86.9	13.1	91.0	9.0	89.2	10.8	89.9	10.1
Austin, TX	51.5	48.5	88.1	11.9	90.7	9.3	90.7	9.3	92.4	7.6
Baton Rouge, LA	57.1	42.9	76.9	23.1	81.4	18.6	81.7	18.3	81.4	18.6
Boise City, ID	37.7	62.3	86.1	13.9	91.1	8.9	92.8	7.2	90.5	9.5
Boston, MA	45.7	54.3	87.7	12.3	91.2	8.8	89.8	10.2	86.9	13.1
Boulder, CO	50.7	49.3	84.7	15.3	90.8	9.2	90.8	9.2	93.9	6.1
Cape Coral, FL	65.5	34.5	89.7	10.3	92.6	7.4	91.5	8.5	90.8	9.2
Cedar Rapids, IA	69.1	30.9	87.8	12.2	89.0	11.0	92.3	7.7	92.3	7.7
Charleston, SC	51.2	48.8	86.2	13.8	89.8	10.2	89.3	10.7	90.4	9.6
Charlotte, NC	50.2	49.8	90.0	10.0	90.5	9.5	88.9	11.1	90.4	9.6
Chicago, IL	58.0	42.0	84.8	15.2	89.3	10.7	89.0	11.0	90.6	9.4
Cincinnati, OH	53.4	46.6	78.8	21.2	83.1	16.9	83.9	16.1	82.5	17.5
Clarksville, TN	62.9	37.1	92.1	7.9	88.8	11.2	89.5	10.5	89.0	11.0
Cleveland, OH	54.9	45.1	81.2	18.8	81.4	18.6	82.0	18.0	84.1	15.9
College Station, TX	60.1	39.9	86.1	13.9	88.9	11.1	92.4	7.6	93.3	6.7
Colorado Springs, CO	62.1	37.9	89.5	10.5	92.5	7.5	92.6	7.4	92.2	7.8
Columbia, MO	47.1	52.9	84.2	15.8	88.0	12.0	89.0	11.0	90.3	9.7
Columbia, SC	57.9	42.1	88.4	11.6	91.0	9.0	92.1	7.9	92.9	7.1
Columbus, OH	55.0	45.0	85.2	14.8	88.8	11.2	88.9	11.1	89.3	10.7
Dallas, TX	58.9	41.1	90.2	9.8	92.6	7.4	92.3	7.7	92.4	7.6
Davenport, IA	69.0	31.0	89.9	10.1	91.6	8.4	91.6	8.4	93.2	6.8
Denver, CO	59.6	40.4	90.1	9.9	92.5	7.5	92.0	8.0	91.9	8.1
Des Moines, IA	65.6	34.4	87.6	12.4	91.6	8.4	91.3	8.7	92.1	7.9
Durham, NC	49.5	50.5	88.6	11.4	89.6	10.4	88.8	11.2	90.8	9.2
Edison, NJ	54.8	45.2	82.3	17.7	85.6	14.4	85.7	14.3	85.1	14.9
El Paso, TX	81.0	19.0	93.9	6.1	95.1	4.9	94.8	5.2	96.4	3.6
Fargo, ND	58.8	41.2	93.6	6.4	89.5	10.5	89.3	10.7	93.8	6.2
Fayetteville, NC	63.5	36.5	88.7	11.3	87.7	12.3	88.9	11.1	89.4	10.6
Fort Collins, CO	52.2	47.8	91.0	9.0	92.3	7.7	91.9	8.1	91.4	8.6
Fort Wayne, IN	42.6	57.4	78.5	21.5	77.9	22.1	79.3	20.7	81.7	18.3
Fort Worth, TX	58.9	41.1	90.2	9.8	92.6	7.4	92.3	7.7	92.4	7.6
Grand Rapids, MI	62.5	37.5	82.2	17.8	84.8	15.2	86.2	13.8	86.1	13.9
Greeley, CO	69.7	30.3	89.1	10.9	91.9	8.1	94.0	6.0	93.9	6.1
Green Bay, WI	69.2	30.8	85.4	14.6	88.9	11.1	88.4	11.6	93.2	6.8
Greensboro, NC	50.5	49.5	89.4	10.6	90.3	9.7	89.1	10.9	90.3	9.7
Honolulu, HI	36.3	63.7	80.0	20.0	85.3	14.7	78.3	21.7	76.8	23.2
Houston, TX	58.1	41.9	90.2	9.8	93.1	6.9	93.0	7.0	93.3	6.7
Huntsville, AL	54.3	45.7	85.8	14.2	82.9	17.1	82.7	17.3	86.0	14.0
Indianapolis, IN	53.8	46.2	87.2	12.8	89.5	10.5	89.2	10.8	89.2	10.8
Jacksonville, FL	55.1	44.9	86.2	13.8	86.3	13.7	84.3	15.7	86.7	13.3
Kansas City, MO	58.1	41.9	88.5	11.5	89.6	10.4	89.2	10.8	89.4	10.6
Lafayette, LA	66.9	33.1	79.2	20.8	81.0	19.0	79.8	20.2	81.3	18.7
Lakeland, FL	69.5	30.5	85.9	14.1	89.0	11.0	86.1	13.9	90.5	9.5
Las Vegas, NV	61.7	38.3	89.8	10.2	92.5	7.5	92.9	7.1	93.4	6.6
Lexington, KY	47.1	52.9	83.9	16.1	88.1	11.9	86.9	13.1	86.8	13.2
Lincoln, NE	44.3	55.7	75.3	24.7	84.3	15.7	86.7	13.3	86.9	13.1
Little Rock, AR	63.2	36.8	87.1	12.9	88.9	11.1	88.9	11.1	87.4	12.6
Los Angeles, CA	58.5	41.5	88.4	11.6	90.8	9.2	91.0	9.0	91.4	8.6
Louisville, KY	49.2	50.8	82.9	17.1	84.2	15.8	81.4	18.6	81.3	18.7
Madison, WI	66.3	33.7	88.6	11.4	90.0	10.0	90.0	10.0	94.2	5.8

Table continued on following page.

Metro Area	Preschool (%)		Kindergarten (%)		Grades 1 - 4 (%)		Grades 5 - 8 (%)		Grades 9 - 12 (%)	
	Public	Private	Public	Private	Public	Private	Public	Private	Public	Private
Manchester, NH	42.4	57.6	83.7	16.3	87.1	12.9	89.9	10.1	88.9	11.1
Memphis, TN	61.4	38.6	86.2	13.8	86.6	13.4	86.3	13.7	84.7	15.3
Miami, FL	50.3	49.7	83.3	16.7	86.2	13.8	86.7	13.3	87.2	12.8
Midland, TX	64.3	35.7	89.1	10.9	86.9	13.1	90.0	10.0	90.3	9.7
Milwaukee, WI	56.6	43.4	80.0	20.0	80.5	19.5	79.7	20.3	85.2	14.8
Minneapolis, MN	59.4	40.6	88.5	11.5	89.4	10.6	90.1	9.9	91.6	8.4
Nashville, TN	47.3	52.7	86.2	13.8	87.1	12.9	86.3	13.7	84.4	15.6
New Haven, CT	65.1	34.9	90.7	9.3	92.2	7.8	90.5	9.5	89.3	10.7
New Orleans, LA	53.6	46.4	77.3	22.7	78.1	21.9	77.7	22.3	76.0	24.0
New York, NY	54.8	45.2	82.3	17.7	85.6	14.4	85.7	14.3	85.1	14.9
Oklahoma City, OK	72.1	27.9	90.7	9.3	91.2	8.8	90.8	9.2	90.7	9.3
Omaha, NE	57.3	42.7	85.4	14.6	85.7	14.3	87.2	12.8	85.9	14.1
Orlando, FL	55.2	44.8	81.0	19.0	86.3	13.7	85.6	14.4	89.6	10.4
Peoria, IL	61.4	38.6	82.9	17.1	89.1	10.9	89.1	10.9	91.0	9.0
Philadelphia, PA	46.0	54.0	81.8	18.2	84.9	15.1	84.9	15.1	83.3	16.7
Phoenix, AZ	60.3	39.7	89.4	10.6	92.0	8.0	92.5	7.5	92.9	7.1
Pittsburgh, PA	49.3	50.7	85.0	15.0	88.0	12.0	88.3	11.7	89.8	10.2
Portland, OR	42.8	57.2	86.2	13.8	89.0	11.0	89.5	10.5	90.3	9.7
Providence, RI	53.8	46.2	89.9	10.1	90.4	9.6	89.6	10.4	88.5	11.5
Provo, UT	53.3	46.7	91.6	8.4	92.9	7.1	94.4	5.6	94.4	5.6
Raleigh, NC	38.9	61.1	88.2	11.8	89.0	11.0	87.8	12.2	89.9	10.1
Reno, NV	58.2	41.8	85.6	14.4	92.7	7.3	92.9	7.1	93.2	6.8
Richmond, VA	41.9	58.1	89.0	11.0	89.8	10.2	88.6	11.4	90.3	9.7
Riverside, CA	68.6	31.4	91.8	8.2	94.4	5.6	94.2	5.8	94.9	5.1
Rochester, MN	62.6	37.4	85.5	14.5	87.3	12.7	89.1	10.9	92.1	7.9
Sacramento, CA	62.3	37.7	90.7	9.3	92.4	7.6	92.5	7.5	93.1	6.9
Salt Lake City, UT	54.5	45.5	88.8	11.2	92.6	7.4	93.4	6.6	93.7	6.3
San Antonio, TX	65.9	34.1	90.4	9.6	92.9	7.1	92.1	7.9	92.5	7.5
San Diego, CA	54.0	46.0	90.5	9.5	92.1	7.9	92.1	7.9	92.4	7.6
San Francisco, CA	41.3	58.7	84.2	15.8	86.3	13.7	85.8	14.2	87.2	12.8
San Jose, CA	36.2	63.8	81.2	18.8	85.7	14.3	85.4	14.6	86.2	13.8
Santa Rosa, CA	48.6	51.4	93.0	7.0	92.8	7.2	90.3	9.7	90.9	9.1
Savannah, GA	58.3	41.7	92.2	7.8	86.1	13.9	87.8	12.2	85.9	14.1
Seattle, WA	41.4	58.6	83.9	16.1	88.3	11.7	88.3	11.7	90.5	9.5
Sioux Falls, SD	53.6	46.4	88.3	11.7	88.4	11.6	89.2	10.8	86.8	13.2
Springfield, IL	66.2	33.8	86.4	13.6	87.2	12.8	88.6	11.4	90.1	9.9
Tallahassee, FL	49.6	50.4	86.3	13.7	86.0	14.0	81.7	18.3	86.2	13.8
Tampa, FL	57.1	42.9	84.8	15.2	86.9	13.1	87.1	12.9	88.3	11.7
Tucson, AZ	65.7	34.3	87.8	12.2	90.4	9.6	90.1	9.9	92.1	7.9
Tulsa, OK	69.4	30.6	88.7	11.3	88.9	11.1	88.2	11.8	87.7	12.3
Tuscaloosa, AL	66.5	33.5	89.8	10.2	87.4	12.6	90.3	9.7	86.1	13.9
Virginia Beach, VA	53.4	46.6	83.0	17.0	89.4	10.6	89.3	10.7	91.4	8.6
Washington, DC	44.9	55.1	86.1	13.9	88.7	11.3	87.9	12.1	88.3	11.7
Wichita, KS	63.1	36.9	83.3	16.7	86.3	13.7	87.3	12.7	86.6	13.4
Winston-Salem, NC	56.2	43.8	91.8	8.2	93.0	7.0	90.3	9.7	90.8	9.2
U.S.	59.1	40.9	87.6	12.4	89.5	10.5	89.4	10.6	90.1	9.9

Note: Figures shown cover persons 3 years old and over; Figures cover the Metropolitan Statistical Area—see Appendix B for areas included

Source: U.S. Census Bureau, 2015-2019 American Community Survey 5-Year Estimates

Educational Attainment by Race: City

City	High School Graduate or Higher (%)					Bachelor's Degree or Higher (%)				
	Total	White	Black	Asian	Hisp.[1]	Total	White	Black	Asian	Hisp.[1]
Albuquerque, NM	89.7	91.1	92.0	85.5	82.5	35.2	38.1	31.2	48.3	21.5
Allentown, PA	79.0	81.5	83.0	81.3	68.2	15.3	17.9	7.3	37.1	6.0
Anchorage, AK	93.9	96.5	93.6	84.0	85.3	36.1	43.2	19.6	25.2	22.3
Ann Arbor, MI	97.3	98.1	90.6	97.8	92.0	76.0	78.4	38.2	86.4	68.6
Athens, GA	87.9	90.9	81.5	94.5	57.0	44.0	54.8	18.6	73.2	19.8
Atlanta, GA	90.9	97.7	84.4	96.1	82.5	51.8	78.0	25.7	84.6	46.0
Austin, TX	89.4	91.2	89.6	93.9	72.3	51.7	55.1	28.8	77.0	25.8
Baton Rouge, LA	88.0	96.2	82.2	84.1	73.9	33.2	53.4	15.9	54.7	21.7
Boise City, ID	95.1	95.7	86.2	89.1	84.2	41.6	41.8	29.9	51.2	22.0
Boston, MA	87.2	93.0	83.8	78.9	70.0	49.7	65.7	21.8	53.2	23.7
Boulder, CO	96.9	97.5	92.2	96.1	76.4	76.0	76.9	39.9	80.4	42.1
Cape Coral, FL	91.8	92.3	89.3	88.5	86.9	23.3	23.7	19.8	24.7	18.7
Cedar Rapids, IA	93.3	94.7	83.4	83.8	75.8	32.1	32.7	15.0	51.2	21.0
Charleston, SC	94.9	97.4	86.9	93.5	91.4	53.1	61.0	22.3	67.3	45.6
Charlotte, NC	89.1	92.7	90.4	81.4	60.0	44.3	55.4	29.4	58.3	17.0
Chicago, IL	85.1	88.7	85.2	87.1	68.4	39.5	50.9	21.4	60.5	16.5
Cincinnati, OH	88.1	92.1	83.0	93.1	73.2	37.1	52.6	14.5	80.7	31.0
Clarksville, TN	92.9	93.5	92.6	85.2	87.2	27.6	28.1	24.7	41.9	18.2
Cleveland, OH	80.8	83.3	80.0	71.5	67.4	17.5	24.9	9.7	39.5	9.0
College Station, TX	94.4	95.1	87.8	95.2	85.6	58.6	58.8	29.4	80.9	45.8
Colorado Springs, CO	93.9	95.3	94.2	86.3	80.6	39.9	42.7	25.7	48.4	20.9
Columbia, MO	95.2	96.3	90.0	94.6	91.4	52.2	54.8	21.2	73.9	36.0
Columbia, SC	89.4	95.4	81.8	96.8	86.4	43.8	62.6	19.6	78.1	35.2
Columbus, OH	89.8	92.0	86.8	85.3	75.6	36.6	42.3	19.7	57.7	23.2
Dallas, TX	77.5	75.2	86.8	85.5	51.1	33.4	38.9	19.4	65.8	11.0
Davenport, IA	90.5	92.2	83.6	69.2	72.8	25.6	27.4	10.5	28.0	15.5
Denver, CO	88.0	90.3	86.9	83.4	64.7	49.4	54.5	24.7	53.9	15.9
Des Moines, IA	86.3	89.7	81.3	60.8	57.2	26.7	29.2	13.6	20.3	9.0
Durham, NC	88.1	90.1	87.6	90.5	49.4	49.6	60.1	34.2	73.9	13.6
Edison, NJ	92.1	92.8	94.7	93.0	82.0	55.5	37.2	35.0	77.0	24.1
El Paso, TX	80.3	81.1	95.7	90.1	76.4	25.1	25.7	30.5	54.0	20.7
Fargo, ND	94.3	96.1	81.9	71.8	92.0	40.0	41.7	20.2	46.6	21.2
Fayetteville, NC	91.7	93.7	90.6	86.3	88.5	27.2	31.3	22.9	43.0	21.7
Fort Collins, CO	96.5	96.9	97.0	93.4	84.3	55.5	55.8	40.2	72.3	34.2
Fort Wayne, IN	88.5	91.9	84.4	52.6	61.8	27.8	30.7	15.6	28.3	9.8
Fort Worth, TX	82.2	84.4	88.6	80.8	59.2	29.7	33.8	21.5	42.8	12.2
Grand Rapids, MI	86.7	90.8	83.2	72.3	50.3	36.4	43.1	17.4	43.9	11.9
Greeley, CO	84.5	86.2	79.2	80.0	65.6	24.8	25.9	16.6	43.4	8.4
Green Bay, WI	87.5	90.4	83.1	74.3	53.5	24.8	27.0	15.3	20.0	6.5
Greensboro, NC	89.8	93.4	88.5	75.2	64.2	38.2	49.1	24.5	41.9	18.2
Honolulu, HI	89.0	97.6	97.5	85.5	91.9	37.2	53.0	24.5	36.6	27.9
Houston, TX	78.9	78.0	88.8	86.9	58.5	32.9	37.4	22.6	58.9	13.6
Huntsville, AL	91.0	94.0	85.4	91.1	63.8	44.1	50.3	28.4	59.3	22.8
Indianapolis, IN	85.8	88.0	84.6	76.2	57.3	30.9	36.0	18.2	47.1	12.5
Jacksonville, FL	89.5	91.0	86.7	88.7	82.3	28.6	31.5	19.1	49.5	24.6
Kansas City, MO	90.0	93.2	86.5	80.3	70.2	35.2	43.5	16.6	47.2	18.6
Lafayette, LA	89.5	93.6	79.4	94.8	57.4	38.2	47.0	15.1	56.8	21.2
Lakeland, FL	88.0	89.3	83.3	81.6	78.8	25.9	27.5	15.7	51.0	19.5
Las Vegas, NV	84.8	87.5	89.2	91.1	63.5	24.6	26.9	18.2	40.7	9.9
Lexington, KY	91.2	93.4	85.4	91.1	61.0	43.6	47.7	19.5	68.5	19.2
Lincoln, NE	93.3	95.0	86.1	79.2	70.1	39.6	40.7	23.8	46.7	19.3
Little Rock, AR	91.3	93.8	88.2	95.3	61.3	41.8	54.6	22.6	70.2	10.2
Los Angeles, CA	77.5	80.9	88.7	90.3	56.3	34.4	39.8	26.5	54.9	12.3
Louisville, KY	89.6	90.7	86.9	81.4	80.2	29.9	32.9	17.8	49.0	25.8
Madison, WI	95.5	96.8	87.6	92.5	77.3	57.9	59.7	22.7	71.7	34.2

Table continued on following page.

City	High School Graduate or Higher (%)					Bachelor's Degree or Higher (%)				
	Total	White	Black	Asian	Hisp.[1]	Total	White	Black	Asian	Hisp.[1]
Manchester, NH	87.3	88.4	79.2	76.4	67.0	30.1	29.7	22.1	44.6	14.9
Memphis, TN	85.7	91.7	84.1	87.0	49.5	26.2	44.5	15.9	57.0	11.2
Miami, FL	78.0	78.7	74.2	90.4	75.3	29.6	32.2	14.8	63.5	25.9
Midland, TX	85.1	85.8	85.6	81.7	71.3	28.9	30.3	18.1	51.7	11.9
Milwaukee, WI	84.0	89.1	83.0	68.8	62.2	24.6	35.3	12.6	27.1	9.3
Minneapolis, MN	90.0	96.2	74.6	82.6	59.9	50.4	61.2	14.3	54.8	21.0
Nashville, TN	88.8	90.4	88.2	77.9	57.0	41.1	46.5	27.6	49.2	15.4
New Haven, CT	85.6	87.5	87.2	96.8	70.9	34.9	46.6	19.9	78.7	13.6
New Orleans, LA	86.5	95.7	81.0	75.8	80.9	37.6	63.9	19.7	40.4	35.9
New York, NY	82.2	88.7	83.5	76.1	68.9	38.1	51.0	24.4	42.4	18.6
Oklahoma City, OK	86.4	87.5	89.0	81.2	54.5	30.7	33.2	20.3	41.4	10.4
Omaha, NE	89.5	91.5	86.9	70.4	54.3	37.7	40.7	18.9	49.4	12.0
Orlando, FL	90.4	92.8	84.6	92.6	86.8	38.1	43.3	21.8	60.3	28.8
Peoria, IL	89.4	92.4	81.4	94.7	71.6	34.9	39.6	13.4	75.4	21.9
Philadelphia, PA	84.7	89.2	84.6	73.0	67.2	29.7	41.6	17.3	40.3	14.6
Phoenix, AZ	81.9	84.0	87.5	84.9	62.1	28.6	30.2	21.8	57.4	10.3
Pittsburgh, PA	92.9	94.5	88.6	90.9	87.1	44.6	50.2	18.4	78.3	48.4
Portland, OR	92.4	94.8	85.9	76.9	76.1	50.4	54.3	23.9	41.2	31.0
Providence, RI	81.6	86.4	84.4	79.3	71.9	30.1	38.0	19.1	48.1	10.4
Provo, UT	92.9	93.1	98.0	93.2	75.2	43.1	43.4	27.2	52.9	18.6
Raleigh, NC	91.8	95.9	89.7	86.8	61.2	50.9	61.8	31.0	60.0	21.9
Reno, NV	89.0	91.4	91.3	91.6	64.6	33.5	35.3	21.2	48.1	12.5
Richmond, VA	85.4	92.3	78.8	81.7	50.8	39.6	61.8	15.5	62.5	14.3
Riverside, CA	80.6	83.5	92.0	87.2	68.5	23.0	23.8	26.5	47.8	11.8
Rochester, MN	94.0	96.3	77.2	83.8	74.1	46.7	47.8	18.0	59.9	26.2
Sacramento, CA	85.3	89.2	90.1	79.7	73.0	33.1	39.6	21.0	37.4	17.7
Salt Lake City, UT	88.8	94.2	82.2	83.8	62.2	46.5	51.8	26.7	61.5	16.5
San Antonio, TX	82.4	82.4	91.1	87.2	74.8	26.0	26.0	23.9	53.1	16.4
San Diego, CA	88.1	89.2	91.3	88.7	69.1	45.9	48.1	25.8	53.8	20.4
San Francisco, CA	88.5	96.7	88.4	79.3	78.9	58.1	73.8	30.5	46.7	34.2
San Jose, CA	84.6	88.6	91.8	87.0	67.5	43.7	44.2	35.5	55.9	15.9
Santa Rosa, CA	86.2	91.3	87.6	87.1	62.8	32.6	37.4	30.2	40.2	12.1
Savannah, GA	87.6	93.0	83.3	85.8	79.4	28.2	42.9	15.5	46.7	27.1
Seattle, WA	94.8	97.8	86.8	88.4	83.5	64.0	69.8	29.5	61.5	43.0
Sioux Falls, SD	92.3	94.7	74.7	70.8	65.3	35.2	37.6	14.3	36.4	14.3
Springfield, IL	91.3	93.4	81.2	91.7	87.8	35.8	38.6	17.8	64.9	33.6
Tallahassee, FL	93.5	96.4	88.2	96.0	88.5	48.2	56.9	28.1	80.7	39.6
Tampa, FL	87.9	90.1	82.9	86.7	78.3	38.6	44.4	16.8	63.0	23.5
Tucson, AZ	85.0	88.0	84.3	86.7	72.7	27.4	30.1	21.3	48.0	14.0
Tulsa, OK	87.3	89.9	88.8	74.8	57.6	31.5	36.5	17.6	37.8	10.7
Tuscaloosa, AL	89.1	94.4	84.1	84.5	73.8	36.9	54.1	17.6	53.0	11.5
Virginia Beach, VA	93.5	95.3	91.1	88.2	84.5	36.0	38.8	26.4	40.6	25.5
Washington, DC	90.9	98.1	86.3	94.9	73.1	58.5	89.5	27.3	81.9	47.3
Wichita, KS	88.3	90.4	87.4	81.3	62.8	30.1	32.9	15.2	36.3	13.0
Winston-Salem, NC	88.2	89.9	87.8	87.7	58.1	34.5	41.8	21.0	65.7	13.5
U.S.	88.0	89.9	86.0	87.1	68.7	32.1	33.5	21.6	54.3	16.4

Note: Figures shown cover persons 25 years old and over; (1) People of Hispanic origin can be of any race
Source: U.S. Census Bureau, 2015-2019 American Community Survey 5-Year Estimates

Educational Attainment by Race: Metro Area

Metro Area	High School Graduate or Higher (%)					Bachelor's Degree or Higher (%)				
	Total	White	Black	Asian	Hisp.[1]	Total	White	Black	Asian	Hisp.[1]
Albuquerque, NM	88.6	90.4	91.0	87.3	81.1	32.2	35.0	30.4	47.8	19.1
Allentown, PA	90.0	91.1	88.0	87.5	74.9	29.5	30.1	19.5	54.6	13.2
Anchorage, AK	93.7	95.6	93.5	83.9	86.3	32.3	37.0	19.5	25.0	21.3
Ann Arbor, MI	95.3	96.3	89.2	96.6	85.5	55.9	57.7	27.4	83.0	42.9
Athens, GA	87.8	90.1	80.3	91.0	60.0	39.4	44.5	17.6	69.9	22.2
Atlanta, GA	89.6	91.0	90.5	87.5	64.9	38.6	42.6	30.2	58.1	20.6
Austin, TX	89.9	91.4	91.0	92.5	74.0	44.8	46.7	29.1	71.8	23.0
Baton Rouge, LA	87.4	90.5	82.8	86.1	67.5	27.6	31.9	18.5	53.2	16.4
Boise City, ID	91.8	93.4	88.7	86.6	67.8	31.7	32.5	27.9	46.7	11.4
Boston, MA	91.7	94.3	85.2	86.0	72.0	48.1	50.6	26.3	62.3	22.8
Boulder, CO	95.0	95.8	87.8	93.8	71.6	62.1	62.8	30.5	72.5	26.5
Cape Coral, FL	88.4	90.0	79.5	88.6	71.0	28.2	29.4	15.9	45.3	14.8
Cedar Rapids, IA	94.3	95.2	84.0	81.4	77.6	31.0	31.3	15.4	51.7	22.0
Charleston, SC	90.7	93.7	84.4	86.3	71.1	35.6	42.6	16.5	49.0	20.5
Charlotte, NC	89.0	90.8	88.4	84.9	63.1	35.1	37.7	25.9	58.1	17.7
Chicago, IL	88.7	91.4	87.8	90.7	68.0	38.0	41.6	22.7	64.7	14.8
Cincinnati, OH	91.0	91.9	86.6	88.9	74.1	33.6	34.8	19.2	65.9	24.6
Clarksville, TN	90.7	91.2	89.6	85.6	86.2	24.8	24.9	22.2	43.3	19.1
Cleveland, OH	90.6	92.3	85.2	86.8	74.6	31.2	34.5	15.1	61.5	15.8
College Station, TX	86.6	87.3	85.3	94.0	63.3	37.5	39.3	16.5	78.4	15.9
Colorado Springs, CO	94.4	95.5	94.5	87.4	82.7	38.5	40.5	27.2	44.8	20.9
Columbia, MO	93.6	94.3	89.3	93.9	86.8	42.7	43.8	18.8	71.2	34.4
Columbia, SC	89.9	91.7	87.9	90.5	65.1	32.7	37.3	23.2	58.9	20.0
Columbus, OH	91.5	92.7	87.4	88.5	76.6	36.7	38.3	21.5	63.7	25.6
Dallas, TX	85.6	85.9	91.0	88.8	60.3	35.2	35.8	27.4	62.0	14.0
Davenport, IA	91.0	92.6	79.5	80.4	72.9	26.9	27.6	13.8	46.8	15.6
Denver, CO	91.2	92.8	89.8	86.0	71.0	43.8	46.2	27.0	52.1	16.7
Des Moines, IA	92.5	94.2	84.6	74.1	62.8	36.5	37.6	19.8	38.7	13.6
Durham, NC	88.8	91.0	86.3	91.3	52.7	45.3	51.4	28.8	72.3	16.9
Edison, NJ	86.5	90.8	85.4	83.5	71.4	40.4	46.0	25.6	54.5	19.6
El Paso, TX	78.3	79.5	95.3	90.1	74.4	23.2	24.0	29.9	52.6	19.2
Fargo, ND	94.8	96.1	81.7	78.4	83.4	38.6	39.8	22.2	46.8	19.5
Fayetteville, NC	89.6	91.5	89.7	84.8	80.2	23.7	25.6	21.5	39.3	19.3
Fort Collins, CO	95.9	96.2	95.7	92.2	83.8	47.3	47.5	37.8	62.7	25.1
Fort Wayne, IN	89.6	91.9	85.2	57.5	63.5	27.8	29.4	15.8	33.7	10.4
Fort Worth, TX	85.6	85.9	91.0	88.8	60.3	35.2	35.8	27.4	62.0	14.0
Grand Rapids, MI	91.2	93.1	85.7	75.2	63.7	32.7	34.3	18.3	37.3	14.2
Greeley, CO	88.1	89.1	84.2	87.9	66.6	27.5	28.0	27.2	42.4	9.1
Green Bay, WI	92.0	93.5	83.2	83.1	57.0	27.8	28.5	17.3	44.2	9.2
Greensboro, NC	86.8	88.9	86.1	76.4	57.6	29.5	32.0	23.0	42.6	13.7
Honolulu, HI	91.9	97.3	97.0	88.8	93.4	35.0	48.3	29.9	36.1	25.2
Houston, TX	83.7	83.6	91.0	87.8	64.1	32.8	33.3	27.5	56.6	15.0
Huntsville, AL	90.2	91.6	86.8	92.7	66.6	39.2	40.9	31.4	61.9	24.3
Indianapolis, IN	89.7	91.3	85.9	82.6	63.7	34.7	36.7	20.7	56.2	17.6
Jacksonville, FL	90.9	92.2	87.2	89.4	84.3	31.4	33.8	19.7	49.7	27.0
Kansas City, MO	92.0	93.6	88.5	85.5	69.0	37.1	39.7	20.7	54.8	17.8
Lafayette, LA	84.1	87.0	76.3	73.1	63.9	23.4	26.4	13.0	34.9	12.3
Lakeland, FL	85.0	86.1	82.2	80.4	73.1	20.2	20.6	15.0	41.5	14.6
Las Vegas, NV	86.1	88.3	89.7	90.4	66.8	24.5	25.9	17.8	38.8	10.5
Lexington, KY	90.1	91.6	85.1	91.1	60.8	37.3	39.2	19.0	64.5	16.9
Lincoln, NE	93.7	95.2	86.1	78.9	70.4	39.0	39.8	23.9	46.3	19.7
Little Rock, AR	90.4	91.8	87.4	90.5	67.5	30.4	32.7	21.8	54.3	13.8
Los Angeles, CA	80.7	83.2	89.9	88.2	62.2	34.5	36.6	27.3	53.4	13.3
Louisville, KY	90.1	90.9	87.2	86.3	74.0	29.6	31.0	18.3	54.2	22.7
Madison, WI	95.3	96.2	88.8	90.9	76.4	46.1	46.2	23.9	68.0	26.7

Table continued on following page.

Metro Area	High School Graduate or Higher (%)					Bachelor's Degree or Higher (%)				
	Total	White	Black	Asian	Hisp.[1]	Total	White	Black	Asian	Hisp.[1]
Manchester, NH	92.1	92.6	83.7	88.3	71.7	38.1	37.4	24.0	64.8	19.4
Memphis, TN	88.0	91.9	85.2	87.9	57.7	28.3	35.7	19.1	58.2	14.8
Miami, FL	85.5	86.9	81.4	87.5	80.0	32.3	35.4	19.8	51.6	27.7
Midland, TX	84.3	84.9	85.7	83.4	69.6	27.1	28.3	18.3	54.5	10.6
Milwaukee, WI	91.5	94.4	83.8	83.5	68.7	35.6	39.9	14.3	51.0	14.5
Minneapolis, MN	93.6	96.3	82.6	81.2	68.5	42.0	44.3	22.0	45.3	20.1
Nashville, TN	90.0	90.9	88.5	84.0	62.9	36.2	37.5	28.2	51.5	17.3
New Haven, CT	90.1	91.8	87.6	90.1	74.4	35.0	37.4	20.2	65.3	15.6
New Orleans, LA	86.9	90.6	82.0	77.4	75.1	30.3	36.8	18.7	38.7	19.2
New York, NY	86.5	90.8	85.4	83.5	71.4	40.4	46.0	25.6	54.5	19.6
Oklahoma City, OK	89.0	89.9	90.0	84.3	60.6	30.5	32.0	21.3	46.0	13.2
Omaha, NE	91.7	93.1	88.0	76.7	61.2	36.3	37.7	21.5	49.7	14.8
Orlando, FL	89.5	91.1	85.8	88.8	83.6	32.2	33.9	22.8	52.3	23.2
Peoria, IL	91.7	92.9	80.3	92.4	75.4	27.7	28.1	12.8	69.8	20.9
Philadelphia, PA	90.7	93.2	87.5	84.6	70.1	37.9	42.1	21.4	57.1	17.8
Phoenix, AZ	87.5	89.1	90.1	88.6	68.5	31.5	32.3	25.7	58.9	13.1
Pittsburgh, PA	93.9	94.4	89.7	88.2	88.0	34.9	35.3	20.2	70.7	36.8
Portland, OR	92.1	93.5	88.2	86.7	68.7	39.8	40.3	28.0	52.1	19.5
Providence, RI	87.7	89.2	85.5	85.5	73.3	32.3	33.7	22.3	51.6	14.0
Provo, UT	94.5	94.9	97.4	94.6	75.3	40.3	40.6	35.4	58.9	20.2
Raleigh, NC	91.7	94.1	89.0	92.4	62.5	46.8	50.5	30.8	73.2	20.1
Reno, NV	88.7	91.0	90.3	91.8	63.3	30.8	32.5	21.7	45.4	11.0
Richmond, VA	89.9	92.8	85.0	88.8	67.3	37.4	43.4	21.8	64.0	21.3
Riverside, CA	81.1	83.7	89.6	90.4	67.4	21.7	22.0	23.8	48.6	10.7
Rochester, MN	94.1	95.5	78.3	84.4	71.3	38.7	38.7	18.1	58.0	23.1
Sacramento, CA	89.3	92.0	90.4	84.3	74.1	33.5	34.8	23.0	44.1	17.9
Salt Lake City, UT	90.8	94.0	85.4	86.8	69.0	35.0	37.2	25.1	51.4	14.3
San Antonio, TX	85.1	85.3	92.2	87.5	76.1	28.2	28.4	28.8	51.7	17.2
San Diego, CA	87.4	88.2	91.8	89.2	69.8	38.8	39.5	25.9	51.3	17.8
San Francisco, CA	89.1	93.6	90.7	87.3	71.5	49.7	56.1	28.8	55.4	21.7
San Jose, CA	88.1	90.4	92.0	90.8	69.3	51.5	49.4	38.2	65.5	17.6
Santa Rosa, CA	88.8	92.9	89.3	88.9	64.6	35.5	39.3	29.8	44.4	14.1
Savannah, GA	89.8	92.0	86.2	84.2	81.2	31.5	36.7	19.8	45.2	26.2
Seattle, WA	92.6	95.0	89.6	88.8	73.3	43.0	43.8	25.8	56.1	22.4
Sioux Falls, SD	92.9	94.5	75.5	72.1	66.9	33.5	35.0	14.4	37.1	15.6
Springfield, IL	92.6	93.9	81.6	92.7	87.0	33.9	35.2	17.4	64.0	31.5
Tallahassee, FL	90.6	93.9	83.5	96.3	82.1	38.4	44.1	23.0	79.3	30.2
Tampa, FL	89.6	90.8	87.0	85.4	80.2	30.4	30.9	22.4	51.7	22.6
Tucson, AZ	88.4	90.9	87.6	88.0	75.8	32.4	35.1	25.6	53.1	16.3
Tulsa, OK	89.4	90.9	89.5	77.7	63.4	27.7	29.8	19.2	37.0	12.4
Tuscaloosa, AL	87.1	89.9	82.8	81.1	70.1	27.4	33.4	16.2	51.8	11.5
Virginia Beach, VA	91.4	93.9	87.2	87.3	84.0	31.9	36.2	22.1	43.3	24.8
Washington, DC	90.9	94.1	91.5	91.1	68.0	50.9	59.2	34.8	65.1	25.7
Wichita, KS	90.1	91.7	87.1	81.9	65.8	30.6	32.3	17.2	36.9	15.3
Winston-Salem, NC	87.0	87.9	86.9	87.2	56.7	26.6	27.7	20.6	54.6	12.2
U.S.	88.0	89.9	86.0	87.1	68.7	32.1	33.5	21.6	54.3	16.4

Note: Figures shown cover persons 25 years old and over; Figures cover the Metropolitan Statistical Area—see Appendix B for areas included; (1) People of Hispanic origin can be of any race
Source: U.S. Census Bureau, 2015-2019 American Community Survey 5-Year Estimates

Cost of Living Index

Urban Area	Composite	Groceries	Housing	Utilities	Transp.	Health	Misc.
Albuquerque, NM	93.8	104.8	84.5	87.7	97.2	99.8	96.6
Allentown, PA	104.4	98.4	114.0	103.4	104.8	94.6	100.6
Anchorage, AK	124.5	132.6	140.0	124.0	114.8	144.2	109.7
Ann Arbor, MI	n/a	n/a	n/a	n/a	n/a	n/a	n/a
Athens, GA	n/a	n/a	n/a	n/a	n/a	n/a	n/a
Atlanta, GA	102.8	103.4	103.5	85.1	103.6	107.1	106.0
Austin, TX	99.7	91.2	105.5	95.2	90.7	105.8	101.4
Baton Rouge	99.4	102.6	92.3	85.4	100.5	104.5	106.5
Boise City, ID	98.7	94.5	97.5	81.9	108.5	103.0	102.8
Boston, MA	151.0	109.3	228.6	120.5	112.0	118.3	129.3
Boulder, CO	n/a	n/a	n/a	n/a	n/a	n/a	n/a
Cape Coral, FL	100.6	107.8	89.6	98.8	98.7	108.5	106.3
Cedar Rapids, IA	96.2	94.8	83.0	102.1	96.6	107.0	103.9
Charleston, SC	97.2	99.7	93.2	120.4	86.6	97.5	95.9
Charlotte, NC	98.2	101.7	88.8	95.6	90.7	105.1	106.0
Chicago, IL	120.6	101.9	155.7	92.4	125.9	100.0	109.4
Cincinnati, OH	99.7	91.2	105.5	95.2	90.7	105.8	101.4
Clarksville, TN	n/a	n/a	n/a	n/a	n/a	n/a	n/a
Cleveland, OH	96.9	106.0	83.3	96.1	99.4	104.4	102.6
College Station, TX	n/a	n/a	n/a	n/a	n/a	n/a	n/a
Colorado Springs, CO	101.1	95.9	101.3	97.2	97.7	108.6	104.1
Columbia, MO	91.8	95.5	75.0	100.0	92.0	102.6	99.8
Columbia, SC	93.5	103.1	72.7	126.2	87.1	79.9	100.5
Columbus, OH	92.6	98.6	81.2	89.1	95.5	88.5	99.7
Dallas, TX	108.2	100.2	118.8	106.8	96.7	105.4	106.7
Davenport, IA	92.0	99.7	76.9	98.9	105.8	105.3	93.7
Denver, CO	111.3	98.3	139.3	80.5	100.9	103.6	106.6
Des Moines, IA	89.9	95.2	80.2	90.1	99.1	95.4	92.3
Durham, NC	n/a	n/a	n/a	n/a	n/a	n/a	n/a
Edison, NJ[1]	120.6	108.7	149.3	105.8	107.8	102.5	112.4
El Paso, TX	87.7	102.3	73.7	85.7	99.0	99.3	89.0
Fargo, ND	98.6	111.5	77.6	90.5	100.4	120.1	108.9
Fayetteville, NC	n/a	n/a	n/a	n/a	n/a	n/a	n/a
Fort Collins, CO	n/a	n/a	n/a	n/a	n/a	n/a	n/a
Fort Wayne, IN	86.9	86.7	62.3	95.7	99.5	101.5	98.6
Fort Worth, TX	94.9	92.4	88.4	107.2	96.9	101.5	96.2
Grand Rapids, MI	94.1	92.8	87.4	98.5	104.1	92.3	96.3
Greeley, CO	n/a	n/a	n/a	n/a	n/a	n/a	n/a
Green Bay, WI	91.1	91.0	77.9	97.4	97.7	101.8	96.6
Greensboro, NC[2]	90.8	101.4	66.7	94.6	92.0	119.5	100.5
Honolulu, HI	192.9	165.0	332.6	172.3	138.2	118.8	124.2
Houston, TX	95.8	88.4	91.2	105.8	95.2	92.0	100.3
Huntsville, AL	91.3	95.1	66.6	99.0	97.3	96.4	104.7
Indianapolis, IN	92.4	94.1	78.4	105.4	97.9	90.6	98.0
Jacksonville, FL	91.7	98.4	88.0	97.7	86.0	83.7	92.7
Kansas City, MO	95.8	102.4	82.6	100.6	92.6	105.9	101.7
Lafayette, LA	88.9	101.8	72.0	88.0	104.7	88.0	93.3
Lakeland, FL	n/a	n/a	n/a	n/a	n/a	n/a	n/a
Las Vegas, NV	103.6	95.8	118.3	98.6	114.0	100.2	94.2
Lexington, KY	92.7	89.9	83.7	95.6	96.7	78.9	100.7
Lincoln, NE	93.0	95.6	78.7	90.2	93.4	105.8	102.2
Little Rock, AR	96.0	95.1	88.1	97.4	94.7	89.6	103.2
Los Angeles, CA	146.7	116.3	230.6	106.2	134.8	110.8	112.0
Louisville, KY	94.1	91.8	79.8	94.6	98.1	105.2	103.7
Madison, WI	107.0	107.6	108.6	99.8	104.4	124.0	106.0
Manchester, NH	108.9	102.2	109.6	117.9	104.1	116.0	108.9

Table continued on following page.

Urban Area	Composite	Groceries	Housing	Utilities	Transp.	Health	Misc.
Memphis, TN	99.7	91.2	105.5	95.2	90.7	105.8	101.4
Miami, FL	115.0	110.5	144.3	102.0	101.5	100.6	102.7
Midland, TX	102.1	93.6	91.5	106.6	104.1	96.5	112.6
Milwaukee, WI	96.7	93.4	100.5	94.8	99.8	115.9	92.4
Minneapolis, MN	106.6	103.6	102.9	97.5	104.4	105.6	113.9
Nashville, TN	98.9	99.5	98.5	97.0	97.9	92.4	100.4
New Haven, CT	122.3	111.0	128.5	136.7	110.6	115.8	121.9
New Orleans, LA	105.0	102.6	125.5	81.5	101.3	115.1	96.1
New York, NY[3]	181.6	128.4	339.0	121.4	113.7	107.1	123.1
Oklahoma City, OK	86.0	93.3	69.6	95.3	86.2	95.0	92.1
Omaha, NE	92.3	96.8	83.6	99.4	98.3	96.4	93.3
Orlando, FL	92.1	100.7	85.1	97.2	89.3	88.3	94.1
Peoria, IL	92.9	89.7	76.5	93.7	106.3	96.8	102.7
Philadelphia, PA	110.9	118.7	116.5	105.6	116.1	101.8	104.8
Phoenix, AZ	99.3	99.7	103.8	109.5	107.2	90.1	91.9
Pittsburgh, PA	103.1	111.9	105.7	116.1	114.0	93.1	92.6
Portland, OR	134.7	112.4	186.4	87.1	131.0	115.6	119.4
Providence, RI	119.2	106.7	132.8	126.4	112.1	109.3	114.6
Provo, UT	98.2	93.0	96.1	84.7	100.7	94.5	105.4
Raleigh, NC	95.4	92.7	89.0	98.3	90.9	103.8	100.9
Reno, NV	114.1	118.7	125.8	85.9	126.3	113.9	107.6
Richmond, VA	94.2	89.0	86.0	97.6	86.9	106.7	102.1
Riverside, CA	99.7	91.2	105.5	95.2	90.7	105.8	101.4
Rochester, MN	n/a	n/a	n/a	n/a	n/a	n/a	n/a
Sacramento, CA	118.4	120.2	134.2	102.9	139.0	113.6	104.8
Salt Lake City, UT	103.6	108.0	106.7	87.8	103.6	105.7	103.6
San Antonio, TX	89.5	88.0	82.2	87.6	89.1	87.2	96.5
San Diego, CA	142.1	116.1	216.3	123.2	129.2	107.3	107.3
San Francisco, CA	197.9	131.3	368.9	123.0	145.3	129.6	133.4
San Jose, CA	n/a	n/a	n/a	n/a	n/a	n/a	n/a
Santa Rosa, CA	n/a	n/a	n/a	n/a	n/a	n/a	n/a
Savannah, GA	89.5	95.7	66.2	96.0	94.9	106.1	100.0
Seattle, WA	157.5	129.1	227.6	108.0	137.8	128.6	136.2
Sioux Falls, SD	92.5	96.3	86.3	84.7	91.9	107.7	96.3
Springfield, IL	n/a	n/a	n/a	n/a	n/a	n/a	n/a
Tallahassee, FL	97.5	107.4	93.3	86.5	96.2	99.6	99.9
Tampa, FL	91.2	104.8	79.2	85.9	99.4	98.3	93.7
Tucson, AZ	97.5	100.5	87.9	99.9	101.1	98.7	102.0
Tulsa, OK	86.0	96.2	62.7	99.5	84.4	91.6	96.1
Tuscaloosa, AL	n/a	n/a	n/a	n/a	n/a	n/a	n/a
Virginia Beach, VA[4]	94.1	92.7	89.1	97.4	92.2	90.4	98.7
Washington, DC	159.9	116.0	277.1	117.9	110.6	95.8	118.1
Wichita, KS	91.1	94.3	69.6	99.3	95.3	96.1	102.5
Winston-Salem, NC	90.8	101.4	66.7	94.6	92.0	119.5	100.5
U.S.	100.0	100.0	100.0	100.0	100.0	100.0	100.0

Note: The Cost of Living Index measures regional differences in the cost of consumer goods and services, excluding taxes and non-consumer expenditures, for professional and managerial households in the top income quintile. It is based on more than 50,000 prices covering almost 60 different items for which prices are collected three times a year by chambers of commerce, economic development organizations or university applied economic centers in each participating urban area. The numbers shown should be read as a percentage above or below the national average of 100. For example, a value of 115.4 in the groceries column indicates that grocery prices are 15.4% higher than the national average. Small differences in the index numbers should not be interpreted as significant. In cases where data is not available for the city, data for the metro area or for a neighboring city has been provided and noted as follows: (1) Middlesex-Monmouth NJ; (2) Winston-Salem, NC; (3) Brooklyn, NY; (4) Hampton Roads-SE Virginia
Source: The Council for Community and Economic Research (formerly ACCRA), Cost of Living Index, 2020

Grocery Prices

Urban Area	T-Bone Steak ($/pound)	Frying Chicken ($/pound)	Whole Milk ($/half gal.)	Eggs ($/dozen)	Orange Juice ($/64 oz.)	Coffee ($/11.5 oz.)
Albuquerque, NM	11.18	1.16	2.10	1.41	3.96	4.63
Allentown, PA	13.52	1.36	2.09	1.36	3.47	3.73
Anchorage, AK	13.95	1.71	2.73	2.19	4.39	5.84
Ann Arbor, MI	n/a	n/a	n/a	n/a	n/a	n/a
Athens, GA	n/a	n/a	n/a	n/a	n/a	n/a
Atlanta, GA	14.32	1.30	1.99	1.25	3.76	4.92
Austin, TX	9.67	1.02	1.84	1.39	3.22	4.23
Baton Rouge	11.70	1.42	2.65	1.53	3.69	4.26
Boise City, ID	11.77	1.13	1.37	1.18	3.69	4.46
Boston, MA	13.53	1.64	2.27	2.00	3.73	4.41
Boulder, CO	n/a	n/a	n/a	n/a	n/a	n/a
Cape Coral, FL	11.21	1.92	2.40	1.51	3.36	3.34
Cedar Rapids, IA	10.99	1.68	2.49	1.24	3.31	4.86
Charleston, SC	12.80	1.27	2.25	1.26	3.53	4.42
Charlotte, NC	12.19	1.46	1.69	1.34	3.54	4.02
Chicago, IL	12.67	1.99	2.42	1.47	3.96	4.48
Cincinnati, OH	13.16	1.25	1.42	1.09	3.61	4.28
Clarksville, TN	n/a	n/a	n/a	n/a	n/a	n/a
Cleveland, OH	14.49	1.83	1.55	1.32	3.72	4.57
College Station, TX	n/a	n/a	n/a	n/a	n/a	n/a
Colorado Springs, CO	13.95	1.39	1.76	1.27	3.39	4.55
Columbia, MO	11.89	1.53	2.18	1.08	3.56	4.44
Columbia, SC	12.24	1.40	2.19	1.31	3.54	4.28
Columbus, OH	12.68	1.16	1.58	1.17	3.53	7.19
Dallas, TX	10.44	1.48	1.97	1.15	3.45	4.51
Davenport, IA	11.56	1.53	2.60	1.32	3.44	4.60
Denver, CO	12.57	1.48	1.76	1.46	3.36	4.17
Des Moines, IA	12.05	1.51	2.18	1.34	3.05	4.24
Durham, NC	n/a	n/a	n/a	n/a	n/a	n/a
Edison, NJ[1]	13.96	1.67	2.41	1.60	3.51	4.06
El Paso, TX	10.83	2.02	2.67	1.85	3.93	5.38
Fargo, ND	n/a	n/a	n/a	n/a	n/a	n/a
Fayetteville, NC	n/a	n/a	n/a	n/a	n/a	n/a
Fort Collins, CO	n/a	n/a	n/a	n/a	n/a	n/a
Fort Wayne, IN	11.87	1.07	1.31	0.74	3.13	3.47
Fort Worth, TX	9.35	1.87	1.92	1.26	3.55	4.49
Grand Rapids, MI	12.68	1.12	1.59	1.25	3.34	3.25
Greeley, CO	n/a	n/a	n/a	n/a	n/a	n/a
Green Bay, WI	11.37	1.10	1.93	1.51	3.64	4.47
Greensboro, NC[2]	11.86	1.27	1.55	1.45	3.94	4.03
Honolulu, HI	13.84	2.45	4.31	3.77	5.44	8.69
Houston, TX	11.29	1.13	1.58	1.42	3.50	3.84
Huntsville, AL	13.10	1.45	1.62	0.95	3.75	4.36
Indianapolis, IN	11.98	1.37	1.68	1.13	3.34	4.17
Jacksonville, FL	12.36	1.49	2.21	1.46	3.30	3.86
Kansas City, MO	11.83	1.92	1.87	1.17	3.22	3.44
Lafayette, LA	11.14	1.16	2.19	1.69	3.82	4.26
Lakeland, FL	n/a	n/a	n/a	n/a	n/a	n/a
Las Vegas, NV	10.89	1.35	2.46	2.07	3.99	4.69
Lexington, KY	10.82	1.11	1.64	1.16	3.18	3.69
Lincoln, NE	11.88	1.46	2.21	1.42	3.03	4.13
Little Rock, AR	10.99	1.16	1.78	1.43	3.23	3.89
Los Angeles, CA	12.32	1.72	2.19	2.88	4.09	4.90
Louisville, KY	12.70	1.09	1.15	1.02	3.13	4.01
Madison, WI	14.10	1.61	2.26	1.17	3.46	4.65

Table continued on following page.

Urban Area	T-Bone Steak ($/pound)	Frying Chicken ($/pound)	Whole Milk ($/half gal.)	Eggs ($/dozen)	Orange Juice ($/64 oz.)	Coffee ($/11.5 oz.)
Manchester, NH	13.66	1.19	2.79	1.52	3.41	3.66
Memphis, TN	9.64	0.98	1.79	1.27	3.09	4.05
Miami, FL	12.55	1.73	3.16	1.71	3.67	4.00
Midland, TX	10.05	1.16	1.51	1.47	3.37	4.14
Milwaukee, WI	12.91	1.22	1.98	1.11	3.38	4.14
Minneapolis, MN	13.63	2.10	2.60	1.81	3.71	4.67
Nashville, TN	13.20	1.42	1.96	1.05	3.65	4.37
New Haven, CT	10.42	1.51	2.52	1.73	3.32	4.03
New Orleans, LA	10.51	1.21	2.30	1.63	3.63	3.83
New York, NY[3]	15.20	2.36	2.82	2.78	4.36	4.74
Oklahoma City, OK	11.70	1.34	1.87	1.23	3.23	4.07
Omaha, NE	11.27	1.24	2.00	1.87	3.47	4.87
Orlando, FL	11.14	1.27	2.39	1.31	3.60	3.91
Peoria, IL	10.98	1.03	1.32	0.93	3.45	5.99
Philadelphia, PA	13.82	1.60	2.18	1.99	4.08	4.54
Phoenix, AZ	13.58	1.68	1.63	1.80	3.71	4.84
Pittsburgh, PA	13.64	1.61	2.03	1.35	3.36	4.62
Portland, OR	11.98	1.58	2.12	2.36	4.10	5.30
Providence, RI	12.73	1.75	2.52	2.17	3.57	4.42
Provo, UT	11.04	1.66	1.50	1.46	3.65	4.66
Raleigh, NC	10.15	0.97	1.61	1.19	3.79	3.83
Reno, NV	12.84	1.58	2.93	2.07	3.36	5.86
Richmond, VA	11.36	1.05	1.58	0.86	3.20	3.78
Riverside, CA	n/a	n/a	n/a	n/a	n/a	n/a
Rochester, MN	n/a	n/a	n/a	n/a	n/a	n/a
Sacramento, CA	10.84	1.31	2.66	2.50	4.16	5.46
Salt Lake City, UT	11.44	1.81	1.73	1.32	3.44	4.51
San Antonio, TX	9.89	1.01	1.63	1.66	3.14	3.93
San Diego, CA	12.27	1.72	2.19	2.88	4.09	5.21
San Francisco, CA	14.94	1.80	2.83	3.16	4.26	6.63
San Jose, CA	n/a	n/a	n/a	n/a	n/a	n/a
Santa Rosa, CA	n/a	n/a	n/a	n/a	n/a	n/a
Savannah, GA	11.65	1.51	1.76	1.50	3.22	3.92
Seattle, WA	12.88	2.15	2.50	2.13	4.05	6.00
Sioux Falls, SD	n/a	n/a	n/a	n/a	n/a	n/a
Springfield, IL	n/a	n/a	n/a	n/a	n/a	n/a
Tallahassee, FL	11.54	1.56	2.71	1.70	3.95	3.85
Tampa, FL	11.11	1.74	2.66	1.68	3.43	4.28
Tucson, AZ	13.61	1.65	1.59	1.89	3.70	5.03
Tulsa, OK	11.20	1.30	2.00	1.38	3.44	3.89
Tuscaloosa, AL	n/a	n/a	n/a	n/a	n/a	n/a
Virginia Beach, VA[4]	11.03	1.20	1.75	1.35	3.88	3.85
Washington, DC	13.57	1.80	2.46	1.80	3.91	4.77
Wichita, KS	11.94	1.23	1.75	0.94	3.70	4.17
Winston-Salem, NC	11.86	1.27	1.55	1.45	3.94	4.03
Average*	11.78	1.39	2.05	1.47	3.57	4.34
Minimum*	8.03	0.94	1.03	0.74	2.94	3.02
Maximum*	15.86	2.65	4.31	3.77	5.44	8.69

*Note: **T-Bone Steak** (price per pound); **Frying Chicken** (price per pound, whole fryer); **Whole Milk** (half gallon carton); **Eggs** (price per dozen, Grade A, large); **Orange Juice** (64 oz. Tropicana or Florida Natural); **Coffee** (11.5 oz. can, vacuum-packed, Maxwell House, Hills Bros, or Folgers); (*) Average, minimum, and maximum values for all 284 areas in the Cost of Living Index report; n/a not available; In cases where data is not available for the city, data for the metro area or for a neighboring city has been provided and noted as follows: (1) Middlesex-Monmouth NJ; (2) Winston-Salem, NC; (3) Brooklyn, NY; (4) Hampton Roads-SE Virginia Source: The Council for Community and Economic Research (formerly ACCRA), Cost of Living Index, 2020*

Housing and Utility Costs

Urban Area	New Home Price ($)	Apartment Rent ($/month)	All Electric ($/month)	Part Electric ($/month)	Other Energy ($/month)	Telephone ($/month)
Albuquerque, NM	329,645	874	-	114.55	40.75	183.90
Allentown, PA	397,306	1,488	-	100.14	86.52	189.10
Anchorage, AK	535,483	1,257	-	111.07	136.23	184.30
Ann Arbor, MI	n/a	n/a	n/a	n/a	n/a	n/a
Athens, GA	n/a	n/a	n/a	n/a	n/a	n/a
Atlanta, GA	380,418	1,245	-	87.42	33.41	185.10
Austin, TX	370,234	1,530	-	105.65	45.12	185.50
Baton Rouge	333,881	1,144	101.95	-	-	179.00
Boise City, ID	366,858	1,252	-	63.83	62.43	170.20
Boston, MA	744,522	3,157	-	72.47	161.39	181.10
Boulder, CO	n/a	n/a	n/a	n/a	n/a	n/a
Cape Coral, FL	328,513	1,061	158.56	-	-	187.80
Cedar Rapids, IA	322,911	831	-	139.90	48.93	180.80
Charleston, SC	325,960	1,372	228.13	-	-	187.30
Charlotte, NC	269,325	1,257	158.05	-	-	179.90
Chicago, IL	537,912	2,334	-	80.80	51.09	203.20
Cincinnati, OH	293,448	944	-	76.98	57.83	179.10
Clarksville, TN	n/a	n/a	n/a	n/a	n/a	n/a
Cleveland, OH	291,327	1,120	-	84.52	69.85	180.60
College Station, TX	n/a	n/a	n/a	n/a	n/a	n/a
Colorado Springs, CO	377,643	1,386	-	89.03	76.10	182.20
Columbia, MO	313,945	808	-	96.59	60.50	190.50
Columbia, SC	258,420	885	-	116.56	131.89	185.80
Columbus, OH	281,476	1,136	-	68.54	59.10	179.90
Dallas, TX	371,745	1,705	-	133.58	55.19	185.50
Davenport, IA	248,085	880	-	85.19	52.80	191.30
Denver, CO	530,852	1,545	-	59.31	46.19	186.50
Des Moines, IA	300,464	712	-	79.70	55.44	180.80
Durham, NC	n/a	n/a	n/a	n/a	n/a	n/a
Edison, NJ[1]	532,983	1,597	-	102.88	71.38	179.90
El Paso, TX	242,558	908	-	93.81	45.21	185.50
Fargo, ND	n/a	n/a	n/a	n/a	n/a	n/a
Fayetteville, NC	n/a	n/a	n/a	n/a	n/a	n/a
Fort Collins, CO	n/a	n/a	n/a	n/a	n/a	n/a
Fort Wayne, IN	204,729	859	-	93.81	50.38	184.30
Fort Worth, TX	258,331	1,164	-	133.52	54.42	184.70
Grand Rapids, MI	299,711	1,144	-	102.23	68.00	181.00
Greeley, CO	n/a	n/a	n/a	n/a	n/a	n/a
Green Bay, WI	304,129	813	-	82.41	78.05	179.40
Greensboro, NC[2]	248,204	1,242	158.18	-	-	169.60
Honolulu, HI	1,386,483	3,315	470.38	-	-	178.30
Houston, TX	297,296	1,119	-	161.68	38.31	184.00
Huntsville, AL	256,311	792	156.41	-	-	181.80
Indianapolis, IN	278,798	1,039	-	104.81	67.00	184.30
Jacksonville, FL	275,940	1,277	158.65	-	-	188.30
Kansas City, MO	299,164	1,207	-	96.98	60.15	189.70
Lafayette, LA	244,456	952	-	88.34	52.94	180.20
Lakeland, FL	n/a	n/a	n/a	n/a	n/a	n/a
Las Vegas, NV	412,949	1,205	-	120.44	50.07	175.30
Lexington, KY	309,955	976	-	79.97	77.60	206.50
Lincoln, NE	296,778	867	-	70.14	53.85	194.40
Little Rock, AR	371,333	740	-	85.47	57.54	197.30
Los Angeles, CA	841,834	2,775	-	122.73	62.94	189.50
Louisville, KY	273,187	1,038	-	80.02	77.60	180.80
Madison, WI	433,233	1,119	-	103.73	65.58	179.40

Table continued on following page.

Urban Area	New Home Price ($)	Apartment Rent ($/month)	All Electric ($/month)	Part Electric ($/month)	Other Energy ($/month)	Telephone ($/month)
Manchester, NH	362,551	1,625	-	117.62	88.11	180.00
Memphis, TN	273,404	903	-	90.75	43.22	185.00
Miami, FL	447,771	2,208	162.18	-	-	188.20
Midland, TX	301,432	1,078	-	125.29	39.71	184.40
Milwaukee, WI	358,549	1,315	-	102.30	56.96	178.70
Minneapolis, MN	386,294	1,204	-	95.03	65.60	181.00
Nashville, TN	339,380	1,130	-	88.87	55.47	185.00
New Haven, CT	393,588	1,995	-	170.80	131.69	178.60
New Orleans, LA	520,536	1,618	-	58.74	38.53	180.20
New York, NY[3]	1,278,996	3,486	-	95.03	78.96	189.50
Oklahoma City, OK	258,612	873	-	92.78	58.17	188.40
Omaha, NE	305,521	1,100	-	89.62	56.82	194.40
Orlando, FL	294,196	1,148	164.06	-	-	187.90
Peoria, IL	306,592	771	-	80.23	81.73	191.30
Philadelphia, PA	426,075	1,517	-	100.69	93.28	192.10
Phoenix, AZ	362,970	1,639	189.67	-	-	178.50
Pittsburgh, PA	378,703	1,232	-	108.94	101.72	190.60
Portland, OR	623,494	2,459	-	81.22	62.64	170.50
Providence, RI	430,197	1,800	-	125.74	114.83	189.00
Provo, UT	382,813	1,129	-	68.02	58.46	187.20
Raleigh, NC	308,897	1,309	-	103.82	58.98	179.90
Reno, NV	489,573	1,330	-	82.05	42.67	177.90
Richmond, VA	318,880	1,135	-	94.98	81.43	178.00
Riverside, CA	n/a	n/a	n/a	n/a	n/a	n/a
Rochester, MN	n/a	n/a	n/a	n/a	n/a	n/a
Sacramento, CA	484,470	1,948	-	145.58	46.79	186.50
Salt Lake City, UT	401,866	1,164	-	74.91	60.06	187.80
San Antonio, TX	271,143	1,396	-	96.33	37.17	184.30
San Diego, CA	797,634	2,351	-	183.35	64.21	176.00
San Francisco, CA	1,362,163	4,098	-	183.22	84.62	198.20
San Jose, CA	n/a	n/a	n/a	n/a	n/a	n/a
Santa Rosa, CA	n/a	n/a	n/a	n/a	n/a	n/a
Savannah, GA	218,111	905	155.12	-	-	182.20
Seattle, WA	854,748	2,680	186.95	-	-	194.20
Sioux Falls, SD	n/a	n/a	n/a	n/a	n/a	n/a
Springfield, IL	n/a	n/a	n/a	n/a	n/a	n/a
Tallahassee, FL	344,867	1,132	124.57	-	-	189.90
Tampa, FL	278,508	1,296	165.98	-	-	189.50
Tucson, AZ	372,120	955	-	121.08	48.38	185.50
Tulsa, OK	239,022	680	-	87.50	59.74	188.20
Tuscaloosa, AL	n/a	n/a	n/a	n/a	n/a	n/a
Virginia Beach, VA[4]	317,054	1,200	-	97.52	76.48	185.90
Washington, DC	1,020,885	3,033	-	135.39	69.36	184.50
Wichita, KS	254,831	771	-	100.11	56.39	188.70
Winston-Salem, NC	248,204	1,242	158.18	-	-	169.60
Average*	368,594	1,168	170.86	100.47	65.28	184.30
Minimum*	190,567	502	91.58	31.42	26.08	169.60
Maximum*	2,227,806	4,738	470.38	280.31	280.06	206.50

*Note: **New Home Price** (2,400 sf living area, 8,000 sf lot, in urban area with full utilities); **Apartment Rent** (950 sf 2 bedroom/1.5 or 2 bath, unfurnished, excluding all utilities except water); **All Electric** (average monthly cost for an all-electric home); **Part Electric** (average monthly cost for a part-electric home); **Other Energy** (average monthly cost for natural gas, fuel oil, coal, wood, and any other forms of energy except electricity); **Telephone** (price includes the base monthly rate plus taxes and fees for three lines of mobile phone service); (*) Average, minimum, and maximum values for all 284 areas in the Cost of Living Index report; n/a not available; In cases where data is not available for the city, data for the metro area or for a neighboring city has been provided and noted as follows: (1) Middlesex-Monmouth NJ; (2) Winston-Salem, NC; (3) Brooklyn, NY; (4) Hampton Roads-SE Virginia*
Source: The Council for Community and Economic Research (formerly ACCRA), Cost of Living Index, 2020

Health Care, Transportation, and Other Costs

Urban Area	Doctor ($/visit)	Dentist ($/visit)	Optometrist ($/visit)	Gasoline ($/gallon)	Beauty Salon ($/visit)	Men's Shirt ($)
Albuquerque, NM	106.93	98.97	108.12	1.85	39.81	30.50
Allentown, PA	75.54	110.86	106.13	2.54	43.55	25.80
Anchorage, AK	206.08	147.12	219.89	2.59	54.87	16.85
Ann Arbor, MI	n/a	n/a	n/a	n/a	n/a	n/a
Athens, GA	n/a	n/a	n/a	n/a	n/a	n/a
Atlanta, GA	119.80	105.78	110.27	2.23	47.13	27.27
Austin, TX	117.55	121.27	114.00	2.00	50.41	32.54
Baton Rouge	114.78	104.33	127.76	1.89	50.62	40.67
Boise City, ID	124.87	83.97	133.84	2.37	36.81	42.44
Boston, MA	194.00	108.27	102.75	2.19	64.17	44.46
Boulder, CO	n/a	n/a	n/a	n/a	n/a	n/a
Cape Coral, FL	123.46	110.14	85.53	2.45	33.41	25.30
Cedar Rapids, IA	122.25	115.00	102.58	2.15	37.59	28.78
Charleston, SC	131.23	102.76	81.87	2.06	57.83	27.44
Charlotte, NC	121.12	112.88	119.06	2.35	39.10	31.86
Chicago, IL	104.96	101.82	96.76	2.51	65.57	32.92
Cincinnati, OH	109.23	105.08	96.61	2.29	34.80	33.72
Clarksville, TN	n/a	n/a	n/a	n/a	n/a	n/a
Cleveland, OH	121.47	119.67	86.00	2.25	31.40	37.72
College Station, TX	n/a	n/a	n/a	n/a	n/a	n/a
Colorado Springs, CO	126.71	105.77	114.08	2.41	42.90	28.17
Columbia, MO	126.58	89.08	104.24	1.99	39.17	33.37
Columbia, SC	102.00	59.00	51.67	2.00	41.63	20.62
Columbus, OH	130.99	84.54	59.28	2.38	39.83	34.09
Dallas, TX	121.08	133.84	97.86	1.92	44.45	38.73
Davenport, IA	142.33	96.83	93.08	2.16	34.50	43.03
Denver, CO	111.77	105.51	104.86	2.49	44.29	30.30
Des Moines, IA	110.85	82.19	108.45	2.17	32.13	15.16
Durham, NC	n/a	n/a	n/a	n/a	n/a	n/a
Edison, NJ[1]	94.50	113.15	101.33	2.26	36.40	41.77
El Paso, TX	133.61	82.94	87.16	2.15	30.42	28.66
Fargo, ND	n/a	n/a	n/a	n/a	n/a	n/a
Fayetteville, NC	n/a	n/a	n/a	n/a	n/a	n/a
Fort Collins, CO	n/a	n/a	n/a	n/a	n/a	n/a
Fort Wayne, IN	129.50	94.17	89.56	2.30	33.00	33.48
Fort Worth, TX	91.05	108.33	92.25	1.83	53.57	39.58
Grand Rapids, MI	98.00	94.78	105.11	2.23	32.55	17.24
Greeley, CO	n/a	n/a	n/a	n/a	n/a	n/a
Green Bay, WI	176.50	81.33	74.00	1.71	22.70	30.51
Greensboro, NC[2]	124.74	139.81	109.70	2.12	35.48	39.18
Honolulu, HI	145.88	86.68	195.37	3.30	70.00	58.06
Houston, TX	88.11	111.03	119.84	1.92	61.37	33.46
Huntsville, AL	112.22	100.06	109.44	2.06	33.33	31.87
Indianapolis, IN	88.25	92.92	65.90	2.12	37.63	42.14
Jacksonville, FL	77.42	94.87	70.67	2.20	56.67	23.45
Kansas City, MO	108.18	107.03	106.75	2.02	38.27	33.28
Lafayette, LA	113.42	79.60	103.22	1.92	40.73	32.66
Lakeland, FL	n/a	n/a	n/a	n/a	n/a	n/a
Las Vegas, NV	106.13	96.98	105.92	2.36	46.67	29.07
Lexington, KY	82.39	76.80	74.07	2.08	37.90	38.67
Lincoln, NE	148.06	94.73	104.48	2.20	40.62	43.69
Little Rock, AR	125.22	69.23	101.50	1.89	42.83	35.86
Los Angeles, CA	125.00	110.78	125.58	3.31	76.50	32.87
Louisville, KY	133.98	82.89	71.56	2.28	49.58	32.27
Madison, WI	201.33	113.22	57.00	2.18	48.44	33.55

Table continued on following page.

Urban Area	Doctor ($/visit)	Dentist ($/visit)	Optometrist ($/visit)	Gasoline ($/gallon)	Beauty Salon ($/visit)	Men's Shirt ($)
Manchester, NH	152.49	121.64	101.89	2.00	41.18	34.23
Memphis, TN	84.25	77.68	74.47	1.94	36.63	25.89
Miami, FL	111.06	107.78	105.63	2.24	70.00	23.08
Midland, TX	98.67	109.17	103.22	2.03	33.61	25.58
Milwaukee, WI	175.40	101.10	60.00	2.01	41.93	22.41
Minneapolis, MN	147.85	86.94	89.59	2.06	34.39	34.39
Nashville, TN	94.18	107.94	91.08	2.05	35.67	32.97
New Haven, CT	130.27	107.76	112.13	2.30	47.72	35.60
New Orleans, LA	156.11	111.89	94.77	2.02	48.89	27.54
New York, NY[3]	116.89	116.47	100.16	2.32	70.14	49.22
Oklahoma City, OK	112.21	93.98	102.53	1.90	40.17	18.12
Omaha, NE	119.00	78.66	114.83	2.07	34.01	23.77
Orlando, FL	83.46	97.71	100.39	2.10	54.17	17.78
Peoria, IL	114.08	79.00	141.52	2.36	30.00	29.99
Philadelphia, PA	133.89	96.86	108.61	2.43	60.55	31.89
Phoenix, AZ	96.33	89.83	96.17	2.49	41.67	27.57
Pittsburgh, PA	93.55	102.37	90.39	2.55	34.18	22.73
Portland, OR	168.67	101.75	146.25	2.78	56.44	41.23
Providence, RI	157.87	92.75	131.39	2.15	48.53	38.26
Provo, UT	99.81	84.76	97.49	2.39	36.53	24.62
Raleigh, NC	145.22	99.00	98.89	2.27	48.42	30.33
Reno, NV	155.00	114.56	117.17	2.98	40.13	21.17
Richmond, VA	139.74	99.40	116.20	2.01	44.43	29.26
Riverside, CA	n/a	n/a	n/a	n/a	n/a	n/a
Rochester, MN	n/a	n/a	n/a	n/a	n/a	n/a
Sacramento, CA	194.75	94.80	148.50	3.24	62.28	24.56
Salt Lake City, UT	107.49	101.65	89.78	2.44	34.97	23.53
San Antonio, TX	86.07	87.61	97.83	1.90	45.96	31.37
San Diego, CA	125.00	107.18	117.65	3.24	64.57	32.48
San Francisco, CA	149.63	132.68	144.57	3.46	82.05	42.08
San Jose, CA	n/a	n/a	n/a	n/a	n/a	n/a
Santa Rosa, CA	n/a	n/a	n/a	n/a	n/a	n/a
Savannah, GA	109.21	127.37	93.79	2.10	35.80	25.61
Seattle, WA	136.39	143.77	158.73	3.19	50.33	36.89
Sioux Falls, SD	n/a	n/a	n/a	n/a	n/a	n/a
Springfield, IL	n/a	n/a	n/a	n/a	n/a	n/a
Tallahassee, FL	126.07	111.09	69.75	2.25	36.64	33.99
Tampa, FL	99.22	105.57	99.12	2.11	37.26	23.11
Tucson, AZ	138.05	91.20	96.00	2.14	51.51	49.50
Tulsa, OK	109.61	90.61	99.06	1.77	35.56	23.57
Tuscaloosa, AL	n/a	n/a	n/a	n/a	n/a	n/a
Virginia Beach, VA[4]	83.17	103.67	98.57	2.00	38.97	36.02
Washington, DC	109.41	94.31	79.25	2.31	66.76	37.74
Wichita, KS	100.20	86.82	148.22	2.03	39.58	43.51
Winston-Salem, NC	124.74	139.81	109.70	2.12	35.48	39.18
Average*	115.44	99.32	108.10	2.21	39.27	31.37
Minimum*	36.68	59.00	51.36	1.71	19.00	11.00
Maximum*	219.00	153.10	250.97	3.46	82.05	58.33

*Note: **Doctor** (general practitioners routine exam of an established patient); **Dentist** (adult teeth cleaning and periodic oral examination); **Optometrist** (full vision eye exam for established adult patient); **Gasoline** (one gallon regular unleaded, national brand, including all taxes, cash price at self-service pump if available); **Beauty Salon** (woman's shampoo, trim, and blow-dry); **Men's Shirt** (cotton/polyester dress shirt, pinpoint weave, long sleeves); (*) Average, minimum, and maximum values for all 284 areas in the Cost of Living Index report; n/a not available; In cases where data is not available for the city, data for the metro area or for a neighboring city has been provided and noted as follows: (1) Middlesex-Monmouth NJ; (2) Winston-Salem, NC; (3) Brooklyn, NY; (4) Hampton Roads-SE Virginia*
Source: The Council for Community and Economic Research (formerly ACCRA), Cost of Living Index, 2020

Number of Medical Professionals

City	Area Covered	MDs[1]	DOs[1,2]	Dentists	Podiatrists	Chiropractors	Optometrists
Albuquerque, NM	Bernalillo County	457.1	20.1	87.2	9.9	24.4	16.9
Allentown, PA	Lehigh County	347.8	83.3	88.3	12.2	29.5	20.0
Anchorage, AK	Anchorage Borough	360.0	46.1	128.5	4.9	63.2	31.3
Ann Arbor, MI	Washtenaw County	1,272.3	41.4	183.4	7.3	26.7	17.1
Athens, GA	Clarke County	313.5	14.9	53.8	4.7	21.0	16.4
Atlanta, GA	Fulton County	510.9	12.8	71.1	5.3	55.1	17.2
Austin, TX	Travis County	320.3	19.2	72.2	4.2	34.0	16.3
Baton Rouge, LA	East Baton Rouge Parish	388.4	7.2	75.9	4.5	12.5	13.9
Boise City, ID	Ada County	290.3	33.1	81.0	3.5	55.4	19.5
Boston, MA	Suffolk County	1,479.8	15.2	222.3	10.0	14.1	34.1
Boulder, CO	Boulder County	351.8	32.7	106.1	6.1	80.9	26.4
Cape Coral, FL	Lee County	190.7	29.8	49.8	8.3	27.4	12.6
Cedar Rapids, IA	Linn County	185.1	22.1	73.7	8.4	59.5	18.1
Charleston, SC	Charleston County	796.9	31.0	109.6	4.9	50.8	21.9
Charlotte, NC	Mecklenburg County	329.6	14.2	69.9	3.4	32.8	14.0
Chicago, IL	Cook County	432.8	23.4	94.5	12.4	28.7	20.8
Cincinnati, OH	Hamilton County	612.8	25.1	75.7	10.0	20.3	21.8
Clarksville, TN	Montgomery County	95.5	14.6	46.9	2.4	13.4	12.9
Cleveland, OH	Cuyahoga County	714.3	51.5	109.6	18.1	18.4	17.2
College Station, TX	Brazos County	258.7	19.0	52.4	3.1	17.5	15.7
Colorado Springs, CO	El Paso County	196.9	31.0	104.5	4.4	43.6	24.6
Columbia, MO	Boone County	815.9	59.8	69.8	5.5	35.5	27.2
Columbia, SC	Richland County	356.3	15.9	91.6	7.2	23.8	19.7
Columbus, OH	Franklin County	424.6	61.9	93.1	7.1	24.8	27.1
Dallas, TX	Dallas County	335.5	20.5	86.8	4.0	36.5	13.5
Davenport, IA	Scott County	233.2	52.1	79.2	4.6	182.7	16.8
Denver, CO	Denver County	595.6	32.7	76.3	6.6	36.2	16.9
Des Moines, IA	Polk County	213.2	96.7	73.9	10.8	55.3	21.0
Durham, NC	Durham County	1,131.3	15.8	75.0	4.0	19.3	14.6
Edison, NJ	Middlesex County	375.0	19.5	90.9	9.9	25.5	20.0
El Paso, TX	El Paso County	195.0	12.9	46.5	3.9	8.7	10.1
Fargo, ND	Cass County	392.7	19.4	79.7	4.4	73.1	31.3
Fayetteville, NC	Cumberland County	200.3	23.1	104.9	6.0	9.8	18.2
Fort Collins, CO	Larimer County	239.5	29.9	79.6	5.9	55.5	21.0
Fort Wayne, IN	Allen County	264.5	27.5	66.4	5.5	21.9	25.8
Fort Worth, TX	Tarrant County	183.1	34.4	60.4	4.4	27.0	15.9
Grand Rapids, MI	Kent County	343.8	69.5	74.6	4.7	37.0	25.1
Greeley, CO	Weld County	129.9	16.5	45.9	2.8	22.8	12.3
Green Bay, WI	Brown County	244.7	24.3	80.5	3.4	46.9	18.1
Greensboro, NC	Guilford County	252.9	14.1	57.0	5.0	14.1	10.2
Honolulu, HI	Honolulu County	351.0	17.3	101.1	3.4	19.6	24.3
Houston, TX	Harris County	333.5	11.5	70.7	4.7	22.3	20.4
Huntsville, AL	Madison County	275.5	12.0	56.6	3.8	23.3	19.0
Indianapolis, IN	Marion County	438.4	21.4	90.3	6.1	15.8	19.8
Jacksonville, FL	Duval County	351.1	22.9	83.3	8.4	25.0	16.2
Kansas City, MO	Jackson County	307.2	59.9	90.2	6.4	45.2	20.2
Lafayette, LA	Lafayette Parish	367.7	9.9	68.7	3.7	32.7	13.1
Lakeland, FL	Polk County	124.5	10.0	34.1	4.3	18.1	9.7
Las Vegas, NV	Clark County	177.4	34.8	63.7	4.3	19.6	13.1
Lexington, KY	Fayette County	728.8	36.6	148.5	7.4	22.6	23.2
Lincoln, NE	Lancaster County	218.3	12.6	101.5	5.3	45.1	21.6
Little Rock, AR	Pulaski County	737.4	14.3	77.6	4.6	22.5	21.4
Los Angeles, CA	Los Angeles County	302.4	13.5	89.6	6.4	30.1	18.7
Louisville, KY	Jefferson County	476.6	13.3	109.6	7.8	28.8	15.5
Madison, WI	Dane County	610.2	21.2	73.9	4.6	44.1	22.3
Manchester, NH	Hillsborough County	237.8	25.3	82.7	5.5	25.9	20.1

Table continued on following page.

City	Area Covered	MDs[1]	DOs[1,2]	Dentists	Podiatrists	Chiropractors	Optometrists
Memphis, TN	Shelby County	403.7	10.3	73.6	3.6	13.2	31.6
Miami, FL	Miami-Dade County	344.1	16.5	69.8	10.3	18.3	14.4
Midland, TX	Midland County	150.1	9.3	54.9	2.3	13.6	11.9
Milwaukee, WI	Milwaukee County	374.6	21.6	83.9	7.7	20.4	10.9
Minneapolis, MN	Hennepin County	524.3	22.3	99.8	5.2	73.2	21.5
Nashville, TN	Davidson County	647.2	12.2	81.1	4.3	25.6	16.9
New Haven, CT	New Haven County	556.7	10.7	79.9	10.1	26.9	17.3
New Orleans, LA	Orleans Parish	808.2	18.2	74.3	3.8	9.5	6.2
New York, NY	New York City	483.9	16.6	91.0	13.6	16.5	17.6
Oklahoma City, OK	Oklahoma County	410.1	41.7	105.6	5.3	27.3	18.3
Omaha, NE	Douglas County	540.6	27.5	97.0	5.3	41.1	20.5
Orlando, FL	Orange County	311.3	22.1	50.7	3.7	26.6	12.8
Peoria, IL	Peoria County	558.6	41.5	86.5	8.4	50.8	20.6
Philadelphia, PA	Philadelphia County	571.9	44.8	81.1	17.2	15.6	17.7
Phoenix, AZ	Maricopa County	245.6	31.3	68.2	6.6	33.2	15.5
Pittsburgh, PA	Allegheny County	642.7	43.9	98.1	10.9	44.7	20.9
Portland, OR	Multnomah County	634.2	31.0	99.8	5.3	74.7	22.4
Providence, RI	Providence County	496.3	18.1	60.6	9.9	20.3	20.7
Provo, UT	Utah County	116.3	19.0	61.0	4.6	25.5	11.0
Raleigh, NC	Wake County	276.9	11.4	71.6	3.5	26.5	16.6
Reno, NV	Washoe County	294.4	20.9	70.0	4.0	28.0	24.0
Richmond, VA	Richmond City	740.3	28.4	143.2	10.8	7.4	16.5
Riverside, CA	Riverside County	127.8	15.3	52.4	2.6	16.3	12.8
Rochester, MN	Olmsted County	2,492.4	48.6	126.3	6.3	41.1	24.0
Sacramento, CA	Sacramento County	315.5	15.7	78.3	4.6	22.0	18.1
Salt Lake City, UT	Salt Lake County	376.7	17.1	78.4	6.5	27.1	13.5
San Antonio, TX	Bexar County	324.7	18.6	89.2	5.3	16.3	18.1
San Diego, CA	San Diego County	325.9	18.3	90.9	4.3	34.4	19.1
San Francisco, CA	San Francisco County	814.1	13.6	156.7	10.4	39.6	29.4
San Jose, CA	Santa Clara County	421.9	10.9	118.4	6.8	42.7	27.5
Santa Rosa, CA	Sonoma County	279.6	18.2	93.7	6.7	40.9	18.2
Savannah, GA	Chatham County	352.0	18.0	69.8	6.9	19.0	13.5
Seattle, WA	King County	489.5	15.6	109.7	6.4	46.7	21.8
Sioux Falls, SD	Minnehaha County	362.3	25.7	55.4	6.2	58.0	19.2
Springfield, IL	Sangamon County	631.8	26.1	85.3	5.7	40.1	21.1
Tallahassee, FL	Leon County	304.5	14.1	49.0	3.4	23.8	18.7
Tampa, FL	Hillsborough County	344.9	26.1	58.9	5.6	26.4	14.2
Tucson, AZ	Pima County	361.9	24.6	65.1	5.4	19.1	15.9
Tulsa, OK	Tulsa County	269.3	122.0	69.7	4.0	38.8	23.5
Tuscaloosa, AL	Tuscaloosa County	228.0	9.1	49.7	5.3	20.5	15.8
Virginia Beach, VA	Virginia Beach City	252.3	13.3	77.3	7.6	27.3	16.9
Washington, DC	District of Columbia	779.6	16.7	123.0	8.9	9.4	14.5
Wichita, KS	Sedgwick County	258.0	35.2	65.9	2.5	42.6	28.1
Winston-Salem, NC	Forsyth County	660.3	29.3	62.3	5.8	16.5	17.8
U.S.	U.S.	282.9	22.7	71.2	6.2	28.1	16.9

Note: All figures are rates per 100,000 population; Data as of 2019 unless noted; (1) Data as of 2018 and includes all active, non-federal physicians; (2) Doctor of Osteopathic Medicine
Source: U.S. Department of Health and Human Services, Health Resources and Services Administration, Bureau of Health Professions, Area Resource File (ARF) 2019-2020

Health Insurance Coverage: City

City	With Health Insurance	With Private Health Insurance	With Public Health Insurance	Without Health Insurance	Population Under Age 19 Without Health Insurance
Albuquerque, NM	92.1	60.9	43.0	7.9	3.4
Allentown, PA	88.8	47.3	49.7	11.2	5.0
Anchorage, AK	88.8	70.3	30.4	11.2	8.2
Ann Arbor, MI	97.3	87.7	19.7	2.7	1.1
Athens, GA	86.5	68.5	26.9	13.5	7.3
Atlanta, GA	89.7	69.2	28.3	10.3	4.9
Austin, TX	86.4	73.3	20.2	13.6	8.9
Baton Rouge, LA	90.3	59.2	41.1	9.7	3.5
Boise City, ID	91.1	75.8	26.8	8.9	4.4
Boston, MA	96.5	67.2	36.7	3.5	1.3
Boulder, CO	95.9	84.0	20.1	4.1	1.2
Cape Coral, FL	87.4	65.9	36.8	12.6	8.6
Cedar Rapids, IA	95.5	74.3	34.3	4.5	2.7
Charleston, SC	91.9	78.0	25.5	8.1	3.3
Charlotte, NC	87.5	68.5	26.3	12.5	6.4
Chicago, IL	90.4	60.3	36.9	9.6	3.4
Cincinnati, OH	92.7	59.1	41.6	7.3	4.5
Clarksville, TN	91.6	71.5	33.7	8.4	3.4
Cleveland, OH	92.3	44.0	57.3	7.7	3.1
College Station, TX	92.0	85.0	13.7	8.0	4.9
Colorado Springs, CO	92.2	68.7	36.6	7.8	4.2
Columbia, MO	93.2	81.9	20.6	6.8	3.6
Columbia, SC	91.2	72.0	29.7	8.8	2.7
Columbus, OH	91.0	64.0	34.8	9.0	5.4
Dallas, TX	76.4	51.8	30.3	23.6	14.8
Davenport, IA	94.4	66.2	40.2	5.6	3.3
Denver, CO	90.7	65.5	33.0	9.3	4.2
Des Moines, IA	93.1	64.7	41.0	6.9	3.5
Durham, NC	87.5	68.8	28.3	12.5	7.3
Edison, NJ	94.6	81.1	22.8	5.4	1.3
El Paso, TX	80.9	54.7	33.8	19.1	9.1
Fargo, ND	93.5	80.6	24.3	6.5	4.1
Fayetteville, NC	90.0	65.3	40.4	10.0	3.3
Fort Collins, CO	94.0	78.7	24.3	6.0	5.0
Fort Wayne, IN	91.0	65.0	36.5	9.0	5.6
Fort Worth, TX	81.7	60.6	27.5	18.3	11.7
Grand Rapids, MI	91.4	62.1	39.6	8.6	3.9
Greeley, CO	91.5	63.7	38.4	8.5	4.3
Green Bay, WI	92.1	66.1	35.9	7.9	3.7
Greensboro, NC	89.7	65.9	34.1	10.3	4.5
Honolulu, HI	96.1	77.7	34.5	3.9	2.4
Houston, TX	76.9	51.9	30.8	23.1	13.1
Huntsville, AL	90.2	72.8	32.9	9.8	4.2
Indianapolis, IN	89.5	62.3	36.7	10.5	6.0
Jacksonville, FL	88.0	64.7	33.9	12.0	6.8
Kansas City, MO	88.2	68.6	29.1	11.8	6.6
Lafayette, LA	91.3	67.0	35.3	8.7	3.1
Lakeland, FL	90.0	62.2	41.4	10.0	5.2
Las Vegas, NV	87.7	61.6	36.0	12.3	7.2
Lexington, KY	93.2	71.6	32.5	6.8	4.3
Lincoln, NE	92.3	78.5	25.2	7.7	5.2
Little Rock, AR	91.6	65.6	37.6	8.4	4.8
Los Angeles, CA	88.6	54.4	40.5	11.4	4.2
Louisville, KY	94.6	67.1	40.3	5.4	2.7
Madison, WI	96.0	83.8	22.2	4.0	2.2

Table continued on following page.

City	With Health Insurance	With Private Health Insurance	With Public Health Insurance	Without Health Insurance	Population Under Age 19 Without Health Insurance
Manchester, NH	90.1	64.0	36.3	9.9	3.7
Memphis, TN	86.3	55.7	41.0	13.7	6.3
Miami, FL	80.2	46.7	36.7	19.8	8.6
Midland, TX	83.3	71.1	19.7	16.7	14.7
Milwaukee, WI	90.7	54.1	44.9	9.3	3.3
Minneapolis, MN	93.4	66.8	34.5	6.6	3.4
Nashville, TN	87.9	67.1	29.8	12.1	6.9
New Haven, CT	91.1	50.8	46.7	8.9	2.8
New Orleans, LA	90.8	56.3	42.9	9.2	3.4
New York, NY	92.5	58.3	43.0	7.5	2.4
Oklahoma City, OK	85.4	64.0	32.1	14.6	7.1
Omaha, NE	89.8	71.3	27.7	10.2	5.8
Orlando, FL	84.8	62.3	29.4	15.2	7.5
Peoria, IL	94.2	65.7	41.1	5.8	3.0
Philadelphia, PA	91.9	56.9	45.2	8.1	3.5
Phoenix, AZ	85.9	57.2	36.0	14.1	9.5
Pittsburgh, PA	94.7	73.5	33.4	5.3	3.3
Portland, OR	93.6	71.5	32.0	6.4	2.8
Providence, RI	92.5	53.2	46.4	7.5	3.1
Provo, UT	88.8	77.8	17.3	11.2	10.7
Raleigh, NC	89.8	74.2	24.5	10.2	5.4
Reno, NV	90.2	68.4	32.1	9.8	8.1
Richmond, VA	88.0	62.6	34.9	12.0	6.5
Riverside, CA	90.6	58.9	38.2	9.4	3.6
Rochester, MN	95.7	79.4	30.4	4.3	2.4
Sacramento, CA	94.2	62.2	42.1	5.8	2.2
Salt Lake City, UT	87.4	72.5	22.1	12.6	11.7
San Antonio, TX	83.3	60.1	32.7	16.7	8.6
San Diego, CA	92.2	69.7	31.6	7.8	3.6
San Francisco, CA	96.3	75.7	29.4	3.7	1.5
San Jose, CA	94.8	72.3	30.4	5.2	2.1
Santa Rosa, CA	92.4	67.6	37.9	7.6	4.9
Savannah, GA	83.0	57.3	34.5	17.0	7.7
Seattle, WA	95.8	80.6	24.0	4.2	1.4
Sioux Falls, SD	92.2	77.2	26.5	7.8	4.9
Springfield, IL	95.7	69.1	42.2	4.3	1.7
Tallahassee, FL	91.6	76.3	25.1	8.4	4.2
Tampa, FL	88.3	62.5	32.9	11.7	5.4
Tucson, AZ	88.5	56.5	42.8	11.5	8.1
Tulsa, OK	83.4	58.9	35.1	16.6	8.2
Tuscaloosa, AL	92.6	72.0	31.2	7.4	2.5
Virginia Beach, VA	92.4	80.7	25.8	7.6	3.8
Washington, DC	96.3	70.4	35.6	3.7	2.0
Wichita, KS	87.9	67.3	32.3	12.1	6.6
Winston-Salem, NC	87.6	62.4	36.3	12.4	4.9
U.S.	91.2	67.9	35.1	8.8	5.1

Note: Figures are percentages that cover the civilian noninstitutionalized population
Source: U.S. Census Bureau, 2015-2019 American Community Survey 5-Year Estimates

Health Insurance Coverage: Metro Area

Metro Area	With Health Insurance	With Private Health Insurance	With Public Health Insurance	Without Health Insurance	Population Under Age 19 Without Health Insurance
Albuquerque, NM	91.7	60.2	44.2	8.3	4.1
Allentown, PA	94.5	73.3	35.4	5.5	3.0
Anchorage, AK	87.8	68.3	31.3	12.2	9.4
Ann Arbor, MI	96.5	83.3	25.9	3.5	1.8
Athens, GA	87.6	69.5	28.5	12.4	6.7
Atlanta, GA	87.2	69.3	26.8	12.8	7.5
Austin, TX	87.5	74.5	21.7	12.5	8.1
Baton Rouge, LA	91.7	66.4	35.5	8.3	3.3
Boise City, ID	89.6	71.7	30.2	10.4	4.8
Boston, MA	97.1	76.7	32.7	2.9	1.3
Boulder, CO	95.4	79.5	25.6	4.6	2.1
Cape Coral, FL	86.7	62.4	43.6	13.3	9.3
Cedar Rapids, IA	96.5	77.1	33.1	3.5	2.0
Charleston, SC	89.5	71.1	31.4	10.5	5.7
Charlotte, NC	89.8	70.7	29.3	10.2	4.8
Chicago, IL	92.4	70.2	31.7	7.6	3.2
Cincinnati, OH	94.8	73.1	32.8	5.2	3.1
Clarksville, TN	91.8	69.1	37.2	8.2	5.3
Cleveland, OH	94.7	69.2	38.4	5.3	3.4
College Station, TX	87.4	73.5	23.1	12.6	8.4
Colorado Springs, CO	92.8	71.1	35.3	7.2	4.1
Columbia, MO	92.8	79.5	24.1	7.2	4.6
Columbia, SC	90.5	70.4	33.6	9.5	3.7
Columbus, OH	93.3	71.2	32.1	6.7	4.2
Dallas, TX	83.6	66.0	24.9	16.4	11.0
Davenport, IA	95.3	72.9	37.3	4.7	2.7
Denver, CO	92.6	72.6	29.2	7.4	4.0
Des Moines, IA	95.6	77.4	31.2	4.4	2.2
Durham, NC	89.7	71.7	29.7	10.3	6.1
Edison, NJ	92.8	67.2	36.0	7.2	2.9
El Paso, TX	79.7	52.6	33.9	20.3	9.8
Fargo, ND	94.6	82.1	24.4	5.4	4.2
Fayetteville, NC	89.3	64.6	38.7	10.7	3.6
Fort Collins, CO	94.1	76.0	29.1	5.9	4.7
Fort Wayne, IN	91.5	69.2	33.1	8.5	6.4
Fort Worth, TX	83.6	66.0	24.9	16.4	11.0
Grand Rapids, MI	94.6	75.5	31.5	5.4	3.1
Greeley, CO	92.1	70.1	32.2	7.9	4.6
Green Bay, WI	94.8	75.7	30.4	5.2	3.6
Greensboro, NC	89.6	65.5	35.2	10.4	4.7
Honolulu, HI	96.7	80.4	32.2	3.3	2.0
Houston, TX	81.9	62.1	26.6	18.1	11.1
Huntsville, AL	91.4	76.2	29.9	8.6	3.3
Indianapolis, IN	91.9	71.6	31.0	8.1	5.3
Jacksonville, FL	89.1	68.7	32.7	10.9	6.6
Kansas City, MO	91.1	75.3	27.2	8.9	5.2
Lafayette, LA	90.1	62.1	38.5	9.9	3.6
Lakeland, FL	87.3	59.0	41.4	12.7	7.2
Las Vegas, NV	88.3	64.2	33.7	11.7	7.4
Lexington, KY	93.7	70.8	34.5	6.3	4.0
Lincoln, NE	92.9	79.5	24.9	7.1	4.8
Little Rock, AR	92.4	67.0	38.9	7.6	4.4
Los Angeles, CA	90.9	60.6	37.4	9.1	3.8
Louisville, KY	94.6	71.4	36.4	5.4	3.3
Madison, WI	96.1	83.5	24.7	3.9	2.1

Table continued on following page.

Metro Area	With Health Insurance	With Private Health Insurance	With Public Health Insurance	Without Health Insurance	Population Under Age 19 Without Health Insurance
Manchester, NH	93.8	76.9	28.9	6.2	2.6
Memphis, TN	89.2	64.7	35.4	10.8	5.0
Miami, FL	84.9	58.9	33.6	15.1	7.8
Midland, TX	83.6	71.1	20.2	16.4	14.0
Milwaukee, WI	94.4	71.8	34.1	5.6	2.4
Minneapolis, MN	95.7	78.0	29.6	4.3	3.0
Nashville, TN	90.7	72.1	28.7	9.3	5.1
New Haven, CT	95.0	68.2	38.7	5.0	2.2
New Orleans, LA	90.3	60.4	40.1	9.7	3.7
New York, NY	92.8	67.2	36.0	7.2	2.9
Oklahoma City, OK	87.5	68.6	30.8	12.5	6.2
Omaha, NE	92.3	75.9	27.0	7.7	4.3
Orlando, FL	87.6	65.5	31.5	12.4	6.9
Peoria, IL	95.2	73.5	37.2	4.8	2.9
Philadelphia, PA	94.4	73.2	34.0	5.6	2.9
Phoenix, AZ	89.5	65.4	34.9	10.5	8.2
Pittsburgh, PA	96.2	77.0	35.8	3.8	1.7
Portland, OR	94.0	73.3	32.6	6.0	2.8
Providence, RI	96.1	70.9	38.8	3.9	2.1
Provo, UT	91.9	81.7	17.4	8.1	6.0
Raleigh, NC	91.0	75.9	24.8	9.0	4.6
Reno, NV	90.6	69.8	32.2	9.4	7.7
Richmond, VA	91.8	75.2	29.4	8.2	4.6
Riverside, CA	91.4	57.5	42.0	8.6	3.9
Rochester, MN	95.5	79.9	30.3	4.5	3.7
Sacramento, CA	94.9	69.3	38.2	5.1	2.5
Salt Lake City, UT	89.7	77.5	20.1	10.3	8.2
San Antonio, TX	85.3	65.1	31.0	14.7	8.1
San Diego, CA	92.2	68.4	33.8	7.8	3.8
San Francisco, CA	95.7	75.5	30.5	4.3	2.1
San Jose, CA	95.6	76.7	27.4	4.4	1.9
Santa Rosa, CA	93.9	71.6	36.7	6.1	3.2
Savannah, GA	87.0	67.6	30.1	13.0	6.2
Seattle, WA	94.4	75.9	29.2	5.6	2.5
Sioux Falls, SD	92.8	78.9	25.1	7.2	4.5
Springfield, IL	96.2	74.3	37.4	3.8	1.6
Tallahassee, FL	91.2	73.4	30.0	8.8	4.6
Tampa, FL	88.1	63.3	36.8	11.9	6.3
Tucson, AZ	90.8	62.2	42.6	9.2	7.1
Tulsa, OK	86.6	65.8	32.6	13.4	7.6
Tuscaloosa, AL	92.3	70.5	33.7	7.7	2.5
Virginia Beach, VA	91.6	75.2	30.5	8.4	4.6
Washington, DC	92.4	78.2	25.2	7.6	4.5
Wichita, KS	89.8	71.6	30.3	10.2	5.8
Winston-Salem, NC	89.1	66.0	35.7	10.9	4.9
U.S.	91.2	67.9	35.1	8.8	5.1

Note: Figures are percentages that cover the civilian noninstitutionalized population; Figures cover the Metropolitan Statistical Area (MSA)—see Appendix B for areas included
Source: U.S. Census Bureau, 2015-2019 American Community Survey 5-Year Estimates

Crime Rate: City

City	All Crimes	Violent Crimes				Property Crimes		
		Murder	Rape	Robbery	Aggrav. Assault	Burglary	Larceny -Theft	Motor Vehicle Theft
Albuquerque, NM	n/a	14.9	86.5	302.4	948.0	n/a	3,672.1	965.4
Allentown, PA	2,669.6	5.7	52.5	139.5	188.7	427.6	1,656.1	199.4
Anchorage, AK	5,505.8	11.1	187.7	215.8	829.9	588.0	3,141.1	532.1
Ann Arbor, MI	1,979.8	1.6	62.7	37.4	149.7	160.3	1,455.7	112.3
Athens, GA[2]	3,562.0	4.8	45.6	98.5	266.6	546.8	2,415.5	184.1
Atlanta, GA[1]	5,423.2	17.7	49.4	221.5	480.1	621.2	3,366.4	666.8
Austin, TX	4,111.4	3.2	54.2	98.5	245.0	440.5	2,962.9	307.1
Baton Rouge, LA	6,226.7	31.7	23.6	292.3	588.7	1,023.3	3,904.9	362.1
Boise City, ID	1,859.8	1.7	70.9	19.0	188.9	203.2	1,276.2	99.9
Boston, MA	n/a	6.0	33.1	148.7	419.5	243.7	1,515.1	n/a
Boulder, CO	3,282.4	0.9	37.8	34.1	183.4	373.2	2,421.7	231.3
Cape Coral, FL	1,237.0	2.6	8.2	18.5	87.0	141.1	895.5	83.9
Cedar Rapids, IA	3,593.1	1.5	20.1	61.9	173.9	624.6	2,438.7	272.4
Charleston, SC	2,632.8	5.8	36.9	68.7	261.8	211.2	1,688.9	359.5
Charlotte, NC	4,665.2	10.9	33.6	209.2	485.8	574.6	2,997.5	353.7
Chicago, IL	3,925.8	18.2	65.1	294.9	565.0	353.8	2,293.4	335.5
Cincinnati, OH	5,147.1	21.1	92.3	287.5	443.7	911.5	2,945.6	445.4
Clarksville, TN	3,370.7	8.8	64.4	72.5	433.1	339.4	2,160.7	291.9
Cleveland, OH	5,983.8	24.1	125.4	496.3	870.8	1,129.0	2,610.6	727.6
College Station, TX	1,948.1	0.8	40.3	36.1	111.5	327.9	1,282.2	149.3
Colorado Springs, CO	4,251.7	4.8	89.9	101.1	389.2	500.4	2,521.6	644.6
Columbia, MO	2,914.8	8.8	55.2	59.2	197.6	399.1	1,944.5	250.4
Columbia, SC	6,027.4	21.7	65.8	164.4	523.2	684.7	3,898.6	669.0
Columbus, OH	3,811.3	8.9	97.3	199.8	197.3	641.1	2,274.1	392.8
Dallas, TX	4,184.2	14.5	58.5	322.7	467.2	675.6	1,893.4	752.4
Davenport, IA	4,421.2	2.0	82.0	121.1	389.7	727.6	2,763.9	335.0
Denver, CO	4,492.4	9.2	97.8	165.3	476.6	544.2	2,473.0	726.3
Des Moines, IA	4,802.5	6.4	53.6	129.6	522.5	1,045.9	2,443.4	601.2
Durham, NC	4,537.6	13.2	43.2	223.3	450.3	703.6	2,833.6	270.4
Edison, NJ	1,450.9	1.0	9.0	18.9	54.8	137.6	1,139.8	89.7
El Paso, TX	1,863.7	5.8	45.1	49.2	252.5	152.6	1,234.6	123.9
Fargo, ND	3,572.4	3.9	87.1	61.2	298.2	651.4	2,163.7	306.9
Fayetteville, NC	4,401.4	11.4	55.8	134.1	674.1	651.2	2,691.1	183.7
Fort Collins, CO	2,389.9	0.6	24.0	21.1	171.5	204.8	1,834.5	133.4
Fort Wayne, IN	3,122.5	9.7	53.8	132.5	165.6	367.5	2,182.5	210.9
Fort Worth, TX	3,132.8	7.5	51.4	106.2	279.4	433.7	1,890.3	364.4
Grand Rapids, MI	2,545.1	4.0	71.4	135.8	426.2	294.8	1,364.7	248.3
Greeley, CO	2,680.0	1.8	65.0	61.3	225.2	309.4	1,737.2	280.1
Green Bay, WI	2,145.9	2.9	74.3	46.7	380.0	233.4	1,290.6	118.1
Greensboro, NC	4,507.7	14.4	37.9	208.4	558.0	743.2	2,614.5	331.2
Honolulu, HI	n/a	n/a	n/a	n/a	n/a	n/a	n/a	n/a
Houston, TX	5,391.7	11.7	53.0	388.3	619.2	723.3	3,040.2	556.0
Huntsville, AL[2]	5,635.0	11.3	88.1	184.5	621.0	731.7	3,462.6	535.9
Indianapolis, IN[1]	5,402.0	18.5	77.1	351.1	826.1	893.6	2,671.9	563.7
Jacksonville, FL	3,956.9	14.2	60.9	142.3	430.0	539.6	2,460.9	309.0
Kansas City, MO	5,287.3	30.2	70.0	290.9	1,040.2	619.0	2,470.5	766.4
Lafayette, LA	4,829.0	11.1	12.6	116.8	383.6	814.6	3,236.9	253.4
Lakeland, FL	3,189.7	6.2	56.1	86.4	163.0	390.2	2,306.7	180.9
Las Vegas, NV	3,302.8	5.0	86.3	127.1	312.8	638.7	1,694.3	438.6
Lexington, KY	3,294.7	8.0	53.7	111.0	123.9	471.4	2,248.9	277.9
Lincoln, NE	3,133.7	1.7	110.9	57.0	213.3	339.4	2,255.4	155.9
Little Rock, AR	7,638.8	19.2	105.4	197.1	1,195.2	887.2	4,696.0	538.9
Los Angeles, CA	3,115.5	6.4	56.6	240.4	428.7	343.9	1,649.9	389.5
Louisville, KY	4,578.4	13.9	29.8	149.2	494.0	638.9	2,670.2	582.4

Table continued on following page.

City	All Crimes	Violent Crimes				Property Crimes		
		Murder	Rape	Robbery	Aggrav. Assault	Burglary	Larceny -Theft	Motor Vehicle Theft
Madison, WI	2,833.9	1.5	41.0	83.1	234.2	400.4	1,865.1	208.6
Manchester, NH	2,972.7	5.3	54.9	117.8	422.5	264.8	1,970.9	136.4
Memphis, TN	8,029.9	29.2	72.0	373.9	1,426.3	1,204.3	4,302.1	622.1
Miami, FL	4,260.9	8.9	31.6	160.0	392.5	368.6	2,959.2	340.1
Midland, TX[1]	2,261.0	3.6	42.8	42.1	199.2	269.9	1,504.9	198.5
Milwaukee, WI	3,887.3	16.4	72.3	323.4	920.4	608.2	1,362.8	583.8
Minneapolis, MN	5,442.7	10.7	106.5	299.1	509.5	788.1	3,056.0	672.8
Nashville, TN	5,114.2	12.1	63.7	287.8	709.5	490.9	3,150.5	399.8
New Haven, CT	4,694.5	10.0	34.5	246.0	604.6	505.0	2,743.4	551.0
New Orleans, LA	6,437.3	30.7	196.2	256.8	661.1	543.2	4,001.3	748.0
New York, NY	2,030.3	3.8	33.1	159.9	374.0	117.5	1,276.2	65.9
Oklahoma City, OK	4,813.7	11.4	81.9	135.0	493.9	943.3	2,572.2	576.1
Omaha, NE	4,256.7	4.9	80.6	110.3	417.0	357.9	2,615.8	670.2
Orlando, FL	5,565.2	8.6	69.8	183.5	476.5	501.2	3,889.5	436.1
Peoria, IL	4,792.9	22.5	58.6	241.5	721.0	683.2	2,666.8	399.3
Philadelphia, PA[1]	4,005.6	22.1	69.0	331.6	486.0	409.4	2,329.5	357.9
Phoenix, AZ	4,013.5	7.8	67.4	189.3	434.4	560.8	2,334.7	419.0
Pittsburgh, PA[1]	3,594.8	18.8	40.0	230.0	289.9	443.2	2,331.9	241.0
Portland, OR	5,748.0	4.4	55.6	147.9	336.8	634.3	3,597.6	971.4
Providence, RI	3,507.4	7.2	59.0	134.1	295.9	397.7	2,349.8	263.7
Provo, UT	1,623.0	0.9	37.5	11.1	65.7	139.1	1,259.5	109.2
Raleigh, NC	2,038.8	1.0	34.3	67.4	153.0	251.1	1,375.4	156.5
Reno, NV	2,658.9	4.7	70.0	121.1	362.1	323.2	1,314.3	463.5
Richmond, VA	3,962.4	23.8	19.5	166.9	252.7	427.4	2,702.0	370.1
Riverside, CA	3,443.6	5.1	41.7	142.8	316.3	390.7	2,099.6	447.4
Rochester, MN	2,096.1	0.8	52.4	28.7	132.8	238.4	1,535.5	107.4
Sacramento, CA	3,809.2	6.6	24.7	202.2	393.6	582.4	2,071.1	528.7
Salt Lake City, UT	6,369.7	6.4	115.6	199.1	391.3	637.3	4,397.7	622.4
San Antonio, TX	5,032.7	6.7	104.5	126.0	471.1	524.1	3,301.1	499.0
San Diego, CA	2,244.2	3.5	38.9	93.4	226.0	245.7	1,278.0	358.7
San Francisco, CA	6,175.2	4.5	36.6	344.8	283.7	524.1	4,501.9	479.6
San Jose, CA	2,858.0	3.1	64.5	128.7	242.0	395.6	1,435.0	589.0
Santa Rosa, CA	2,097.4	1.7	82.1	70.8	327.2	273.2	1,167.6	174.8
Savannah, GA[1]	2,865.5	11.6	35.1	110.2	248.5	364.9	1,824.4	270.8
Seattle, WA	5,081.0	3.7	46.9	175.3	359.6	944.1	3,074.2	477.3
Sioux Falls, SD	3,528.6	2.2	62.5	36.6	381.9	374.4	2,316.5	354.5
Springfield, IL	5,218.0	7.9	94.4	181.8	493.0	908.3	3,300.9	231.7
Tallahassee, FL	4,675.5	10.3	101.0	129.2	456.2	608.4	3,022.5	348.0
Tampa, FL	2,033.7	7.7	30.0	71.2	296.1	255.2	1,242.9	130.6
Tucson, AZ	3,960.4	7.3	96.1	201.5	383.5	455.3	2,406.4	410.3
Tulsa, OK	6,298.2	13.7	84.9	178.7	709.5	1,206.4	3,350.0	755.0
Tuscaloosa, AL[1]	4,843.6	4.9	46.2	137.6	316.4	739.9	3,289.0	309.5
Virginia Beach, VA	1,890.0	6.7	17.6	43.6	61.5	118.0	1,513.7	128.9
Washington, DC	5,223.0	23.5	48.5	334.3	570.9	260.7	3,659.5	325.6
Wichita, KS	6,462.8	9.0	94.1	118.2	919.8	686.3	4,044.6	590.9
Winston-Salem, NC	n/a	n/a	n/a	n/a	n/a	n/a	n/a	n/a
U.S.	2,489.3	5.0	42.6	81.6	250.2	340.5	1,549.5	219.9

Note: Figures are crimes per 100,000 population in 2019 except where noted; n/a not available; (1) 2018 data; (2) 2017 data
Source: FBI Uniform Crime Reports, 2017, 2018, 2019

Crime Rate: Suburbs

Suburbs[1]	All Crimes	Violent Crimes				Property Crimes		
		Murder	Rape	Robbery	Aggrav. Assault	Burglary	Larceny -Theft	Motor Vehicle Theft
Albuquerque, NM	n/a	2.5	28.6	23.0	502.8	n/a	995.5	214.2
Allentown, PA	n/a	n/a	n/a	n/a	n/a	n/a	n/a	n/a
Anchorage, AK	5,634.3	10.9	32.6	92.4	277.1	787.8	3,955.4	478.1
Ann Arbor, MI	2,017.9	2.4	69.1	38.7	296.3	218.0	1,258.3	135.0
Athens, GA[3]	1,855.9	1.2	18.1	14.5	111.2	289.0	1,349.3	72.5
Atlanta, GA[2]	2,666.3	4.6	24.0	82.5	168.8	373.2	1,770.4	242.7
Austin, TX	1,564.4	1.9	43.6	23.6	126.5	212.3	1,059.4	97.1
Baton Rouge, LA	3,048.0	7.9	29.9	42.8	339.8	380.5	2,107.7	139.3
Boise City, ID	1,329.9	1.2	52.7	7.5	176.3	201.4	798.8	92.1
Boston, MA	n/a	1.4	30.1	41.9	212.4	126.0	804.5	n/a
Boulder, CO	2,439.7	0.9	83.1	20.9	175.3	269.8	1,686.5	203.0
Cape Coral, FL	1,476.1	3.1	40.1	61.0	201.4	186.4	880.9	103.2
Cedar Rapids, IA	911.9	0.0	21.6	5.0	95.2	183.1	523.4	83.6
Charleston, SC	3,168.8	9.6	42.3	61.1	290.1	419.0	2,025.9	320.8
Charlotte, NC	n/a	n/a	n/a	n/a	n/a	n/a	n/a	n/a
Chicago, IL	n/a	n/a	n/a	n/a	n/a	n/a	n/a	n/a
Cincinnati, OH	1,749.6	1.5	34.0	32.1	73.6	224.7	1,269.6	114.0
Clarksville, TN	1,876.6	4.7	31.4	23.3	124.1	401.6	1,146.8	144.8
Cleveland, OH	1,401.7	1.8	21.7	34.6	90.5	189.4	985.7	77.9
College Station, TX	2,466.8	2.7	79.5	46.6	193.9	419.9	1,565.3	158.9
Colorado Springs, CO	1,634.0	3.7	56.3	25.7	166.4	213.4	951.5	216.8
Columbia, MO	1,774.1	3.5	37.8	13.0	145.2	253.8	1,150.8	170.0
Columbia, SC	3,564.0	5.9	45.8	67.3	428.2	503.6	2,152.4	360.8
Columbus, OH	1,836.3	2.6	36.4	25.9	60.9	251.9	1,366.9	91.7
Dallas, TX	n/a	n/a	n/a	n/a	n/a	n/a	n/a	n/a
Davenport, IA	1,880.3	2.2	46.1	31.4	202.5	306.7	1,169.0	122.5
Denver, CO	n/a	n/a	n/a	n/a	n/a	n/a	n/a	n/a
Des Moines, IA	n/a	n/a	n/a	n/a	n/a	n/a	n/a	n/a
Durham, NC	1,853.6	2.7	22.5	32.4	157.6	332.5	1,221.8	84.0
Edison, NJ	n/a	n/a	n/a	n/a	n/a	n/a	n/a	n/a
El Paso, TX	1,251.9	0.6	37.2	15.8	195.1	156.6	746.2	100.4
Fargo, ND	1,642.9	0.0	34.9	22.4	76.5	277.5	1,087.8	143.8
Fayetteville, NC	n/a	n/a	n/a	n/a	n/a	n/a	n/a	n/a
Fort Collins, CO	1,855.9	1.1	44.9	14.6	189.3	184.4	1,296.7	124.9
Fort Wayne, IN	1,097.2	2.8	35.5	32.1	128.3	146.4	649.7	102.5
Fort Worth, TX	n/a	n/a	n/a	n/a	n/a	n/a	n/a	n/a
Grand Rapids, MI	n/a	1.8	81.2	19.6	146.3	n/a	933.5	85.2
Greeley, CO	1,419.9	1.4	41.0	12.3	90.5	171.1	940.9	162.6
Green Bay, WI	928.9	0.9	26.1	3.2	61.9	81.6	725.8	29.3
Greensboro, NC	2,421.7	6.7	29.9	53.7	258.8	475.5	1,421.1	175.9
Honolulu, HI	n/a	n/a	n/a	n/a	n/a	n/a	n/a	n/a
Houston, TX	n/a	n/a	n/a	n/a	n/a	n/a	n/a	n/a
Huntsville, AL[3]	2,220.1	4.2	32.4	31.2	227.3	432.2	1,337.1	155.6
Indianapolis, IN[2]	1,699.1	2.5	23.1	28.7	114.1	199.2	1,200.7	130.7
Jacksonville, FL	1,592.3	2.2	35.2	25.3	166.6	235.0	1,031.9	96.1
Kansas City, MO	n/a	n/a	n/a	n/a	n/a	n/a	n/a	n/a
Lafayette, LA	2,832.6	6.6	29.8	51.6	358.4	551.2	1,694.4	140.6
Lakeland, FL	1,687.2	2.6	17.0	33.6	217.9	249.4	1,045.5	121.2
Las Vegas, NV	2,501.4	4.6	36.8	114.4	354.9	390.7	1,310.3	289.7
Lexington, KY	2,369.2	0.5	30.9	28.3	60.2	318.5	1,748.7	182.1
Lincoln, NE	1,017.1	0.0	77.9	0.0	41.1	119.0	705.4	73.6
Little Rock, AR	n/a	6.8	60.7	54.6	393.0	n/a	n/a	278.3
Los Angeles, CA	2,574.0	4.1	31.4	148.3	263.3	400.2	1,366.0	360.7
Louisville, KY	1,847.8	1.9	21.7	30.8	98.0	230.7	1,263.0	201.7

Table continued on following page.

Suburbs[1]	All Crimes	Violent Crimes				Property Crimes		
		Murder	Rape	Robbery	Aggrav. Assault	Burglary	Larceny -Theft	Motor Vehicle Theft
Madison, WI	1,351.6	1.0	24.7	18.3	82.4	169.4	971.3	84.6
Manchester, NH	1,000.0	1.6	42.2	12.2	35.9	81.4	789.2	37.5
Memphis, TN	2,498.8	6.8	34.3	50.8	297.1	361.2	1,515.0	233.6
Miami, FL	3,417.0	6.9	35.0	125.5	289.7	268.7	2,428.8	262.4
Midland, TX[2]	2,400.0	11.5	25.9	31.7	368.8	299.6	1,293.6	368.8
Milwaukee, WI	1,671.2	1.4	20.7	24.3	79.0	124.4	1,348.6	72.7
Minneapolis, MN	2,224.5	1.6	36.4	48.6	98.2	238.6	1,611.4	189.7
Nashville, TN	1,872.5	2.8	29.2	26.7	236.4	201.0	1,238.9	137.5
New Haven, CT	1,934.6	2.2	24.3	47.9	77.5	206.4	1,361.4	214.9
New Orleans, LA	2,472.9	9.3	22.9	43.8	209.1	290.9	1,767.8	129.1
New York, NY	n/a	n/a	n/a	n/a	n/a	n/a	n/a	n/a
Oklahoma City, OK	2,410.6	4.4	46.1	32.5	150.0	447.5	1,495.7	234.3
Omaha, NE	1,880.3	2.3	43.8	23.0	147.2	232.1	1,212.2	219.7
Orlando, FL	2,485.9	4.1	42.0	75.9	269.2	341.2	1,573.1	180.5
Peoria, IL	1,462.2	1.7	46.0	15.2	161.7	265.2	890.0	82.4
Philadelphia, PA[2]	1,935.5	7.6	16.3	96.8	235.8	202.8	1,235.3	140.9
Phoenix, AZ	n/a	2.9	40.6	49.3	192.6	n/a	1,530.6	165.3
Pittsburgh, PA[2]	1,402.7	3.5	23.7	33.2	168.7	159.1	958.5	55.9
Portland, OR	2,077.6	1.6	48.3	37.5	128.0	233.0	1,381.8	247.4
Providence, RI	1,466.1	1.7	43.0	37.4	173.7	203.4	912.5	94.2
Provo, UT	1,312.0	1.1	30.2	7.2	46.1	131.5	1,018.1	77.8
Raleigh, NC	1,325.7	2.1	14.8	21.7	90.6	209.5	912.4	74.6
Reno, NV	1,965.3	1.4	55.1	47.4	262.9	331.5	1,041.2	225.8
Richmond, VA	2,045.4	4.9	28.3	37.0	106.2	170.5	1,580.8	117.6
Riverside, CA	2,643.4	5.8	29.0	111.1	273.8	441.1	1,367.7	414.9
Rochester, MN	653.1	1.0	9.7	2.9	67.2	122.6	407.8	41.9
Sacramento, CA	2,195.0	3.4	28.3	73.9	172.0	335.6	1,366.4	215.3
Salt Lake City, UT	3,178.0	2.3	62.6	48.1	186.0	349.3	2,211.9	317.8
San Antonio, TX	1,855.5	2.5	37.7	25.0	148.4	294.5	1,199.2	148.3
San Diego, CA	1,801.2	1.9	28.6	81.2	214.0	218.1	1,020.7	236.8
San Francisco, CA	2,534.2	1.3	42.6	87.1	128.4	294.1	1,778.4	202.3
San Jose, CA	2,582.6	1.5	27.9	54.6	118.4	291.8	1,875.3	213.0
Santa Rosa, CA	1,577.8	1.9	41.0	36.6	283.0	232.0	903.5	79.7
Savannah, GA[2]	3,497.3	5.3	37.2	67.1	245.2	497.1	2,366.1	279.1
Seattle, WA	n/a	n/a	n/a	n/a	n/a	n/a	n/a	n/a
Sioux Falls, SD	1,221.6	1.2	42.1	3.6	128.8	358.7	568.1	119.2
Springfield, IL	1,395.2	1.1	40.2	32.6	269.7	340.4	605.7	105.5
Tallahassee, FL	2,203.5	2.6	40.1	31.7	278.9	510.7	1,198.9	140.5
Tampa, FL	1,969.7	3.4	37.9	46.7	187.8	210.4	1,356.1	127.3
Tucson, AZ	2,634.2	3.2	25.3	38.5	115.5	349.9	1,905.9	195.9
Tulsa, OK	2,046.1	4.5	38.9	18.4	159.8	420.8	1,190.3	213.3
Tuscaloosa, AL[2]	2,503.0	3.3	28.5	41.7	249.6	518.3	1,449.1	212.5
Virginia Beach, VA	3,057.1	8.5	39.5	83.1	293.8	282.1	2,149.5	200.6
Washington, DC	n/a	n/a	26.7	61.2	96.5	98.4	1,055.9	126.4
Wichita, KS	n/a	1.6	42.3	14.5	156.8	271.8	n/a	129.8
Winston-Salem, NC	n/a	n/a	n/a	n/a	n/a	n/a	n/a	n/a
U.S.	2,489.3	5.0	42.6	81.6	250.2	340.5	1,549.5	219.9

Note: Figures are crimes per 100,000 population in 2019 except where noted; n/a not available; (1) All areas within the metro area that are located outside the city limits; (2) 2018 data; (3) 2017 data
Source: FBI Uniform Crime Reports, 2017, 2018, 2019

Crime Rate: Metro Area

Metro Area[1]	All Crimes	Violent Crimes				Property Crimes		
		Murder	Rape	Robbery	Aggrav. Assault	Burglary	Larceny -Theft	Motor Vehicle Theft
Albuquerque, NM	n/a	10.1	64.0	194.0	775.3	n/a	2,633.7	674.0
Allentown, PA	n/a	n/a	n/a	n/a	n/a	n/a	n/a	n/a
Anchorage, AK	5,513.6	11.1	178.4	208.4	796.7	600.1	3,190.1	528.8
Ann Arbor, MI	2,005.3	2.1	67.0	38.3	248.1	199.0	1,323.3	127.5
Athens, GA[4]	2,882.3	3.4	34.7	65.0	204.7	444.1	1,990.8	139.7
Atlanta, GA[3]	2,895.7	5.7	26.1	94.1	194.7	393.9	1,903.2	278.0
Austin, TX	2,697.1	2.5	48.3	56.9	179.2	313.8	1,905.9	190.5
Baton Rouge, LA	3,871.0	14.1	28.3	107.4	404.3	547.0	2,573.0	197.0
Boise City, ID	1,493.5	1.3	58.3	11.1	180.2	201.9	946.2	94.5
Boston, MA[2]	n/a	3.0	31.1	78.6	283.6	166.5	1,048.9	n/a
Boulder, CO	2,717.9	0.9	68.2	25.3	178.0	303.9	1,929.3	212.4
Cape Coral, FL	1,415.7	3.0	32.0	50.3	172.4	174.9	884.6	98.3
Cedar Rapids, IA	2,229.3	0.7	20.9	33.0	133.8	400.0	1,464.5	176.4
Charleston, SC	3,076.7	8.9	41.4	62.4	285.2	383.3	1,968.0	327.5
Charlotte, NC	n/a	n/a	n/a	n/a	n/a	n/a	n/a	n/a
Chicago, IL[2]	n/a	n/a	n/a	n/a	n/a	n/a	n/a	n/a
Cincinnati, OH	2,214.3	4.1	42.0	67.0	124.2	318.7	1,498.9	159.4
Clarksville, TN	2,648.0	6.8	48.4	48.7	283.6	369.5	1,670.2	220.7
Cleveland, OH	2,254.7	5.9	41.0	120.5	235.8	364.4	1,288.2	198.9
College Station, TX	2,233.6	1.9	61.8	41.9	156.8	378.5	1,438.0	154.6
Colorado Springs, CO	3,313.4	4.4	77.8	74.1	309.4	397.5	1,958.8	491.3
Columbia, MO	2,454.0	6.7	48.2	40.5	176.4	340.4	1,623.9	217.9
Columbia, SC	3,955.7	8.4	49.0	82.7	443.3	532.4	2,430.1	409.8
Columbus, OH	2,676.7	5.3	62.3	99.9	119.0	417.5	1,752.9	219.8
Dallas, TX[2]	n/a	n/a	n/a	n/a	n/a	n/a	n/a	n/a
Davenport, IA	2,565.2	2.1	55.8	55.5	253.0	420.1	1,598.8	179.8
Denver, CO	n/a	n/a	n/a	n/a	n/a	n/a	n/a	n/a
Des Moines, IA	n/a	n/a	n/a	n/a	n/a	n/a	n/a	n/a
Durham, NC	3,020.8	7.3	31.5	115.4	284.9	493.9	1,922.7	165.1
Edison, NJ[2]	n/a	n/a	n/a	n/a	n/a	n/a	n/a	n/a
El Paso, TX	1,749.1	4.9	43.7	42.9	241.7	153.3	1,143.1	119.5
Fargo, ND	2,635.2	2.0	61.8	42.4	190.5	469.8	1,641.1	227.6
Fayetteville, NC	n/a	n/a	n/a	n/a	n/a	n/a	n/a	n/a
Fort Collins, CO	2,112.3	0.8	34.8	17.7	180.7	194.2	1,555.0	129.0
Fort Wayne, IN	2,418.7	7.3	47.5	97.6	152.6	290.7	1,649.8	173.2
Fort Worth, TX[2]	n/a	n/a	n/a	n/a	n/a	n/a	n/a	n/a
Grand Rapids, MI	n/a	2.2	79.4	41.3	198.6	n/a	1,014.1	115.7
Greeley, CO	1,848.3	1.6	49.2	28.9	136.3	218.1	1,211.6	202.6
Green Bay, WI	1,324.3	1.5	41.8	17.3	165.3	130.9	909.3	58.2
Greensboro, NC	3,226.1	9.7	33.0	113.3	374.2	578.8	1,881.3	235.7
Honolulu, HI	n/a	n/a	n/a	n/a	n/a	n/a	n/a	n/a
Houston, TX	n/a	n/a	n/a	n/a	n/a	n/a	n/a	n/a
Huntsville, AL[4]	3,685.7	7.3	56.3	97.0	396.3	560.7	2,249.3	318.9
Indianapolis, IN[3]	3,285.3	9.3	46.3	166.8	419.1	496.7	1,830.9	316.2
Jacksonville, FL	2,980.1	9.2	50.3	94.0	321.2	413.8	1,870.6	221.0
Kansas City, MO	n/a	n/a	n/a	n/a	n/a	n/a	n/a	n/a
Lafayette, LA	3,349.4	7.8	25.3	68.5	365.0	619.4	2,093.7	169.8
Lakeland, FL	1,922.4	3.2	23.1	41.8	209.3	271.5	1,242.9	130.5
Las Vegas, NV	3,089.8	4.9	73.2	123.7	324.0	572.8	1,592.2	399.1
Lexington, KY	2,949.0	5.2	45.2	80.1	100.1	414.3	2,062.1	242.1
Lincoln, NE	2,843.7	1.5	106.4	49.2	189.7	309.2	2,043.0	144.7
Little Rock, AR	n/a	10.1	72.6	92.6	607.0	n/a	n/a	347.8
Los Angeles, CA[2]	2,790.2	5.1	41.5	185.0	329.4	377.7	1,479.4	372.2
Louisville, KY	3,300.8	8.3	26.0	93.8	308.7	447.9	2,011.8	404.3

Table continued on following page.

Metro Area[1]	All Crimes	Violent Crimes				Property Crimes		
		Murder	Rape	Robbery	Aggrav. Assault	Burglary	Larceny -Theft	Motor Vehicle Theft
Madison, WI	1,932.4	1.2	31.0	43.6	141.9	259.9	1,321.5	133.2
Manchester, NH	1,534.7	2.6	45.6	40.8	140.7	131.1	1,109.5	64.3
Memphis, TN	5,173.9	17.6	52.5	207.1	843.3	769.0	2,863.0	421.5
Miami, FL[2]	3,563.1	7.3	34.4	131.5	307.5	286.0	2,520.6	275.9
Midland, TX[3]	2,288.6	5.1	39.5	40.1	232.9	275.8	1,463.0	232.3
Milwaukee, WI	2,501.8	7.0	40.0	136.4	394.4	305.7	1,353.9	264.3
Minneapolis, MN	2,605.3	2.7	44.7	78.3	146.9	303.6	1,782.3	246.9
Nashville, TN	3,020.0	6.1	41.4	119.1	403.9	303.6	1,915.5	230.4
New Haven, CT	2,383.4	3.5	25.9	80.1	163.2	255.0	1,586.2	269.5
New Orleans, LA	3,701.4	15.9	76.6	109.8	349.1	369.1	2,459.9	320.9
New York, NY[2]	n/a	n/a	n/a	n/a	n/a	n/a	n/a	n/a
Oklahoma City, OK	3,530.9	7.7	62.8	80.3	310.3	678.7	1,997.6	393.6
Omaha, NE	3,059.7	3.6	62.0	66.4	281.1	294.5	1,908.8	443.3
Orlando, FL	2,829.9	4.6	45.1	87.9	292.4	359.1	1,831.9	209.0
Peoria, IL	2,386.5	7.5	49.5	78.0	316.9	381.2	1,383.1	170.3
Philadelphia, PA[2,3]	3,462.1	18.3	55.2	270.0	420.3	355.2	2,042.3	300.9
Phoenix, AZ	n/a	4.6	49.8	97.1	275.1	n/a	1,804.9	251.9
Pittsburgh, PA[3]	1,687.7	5.5	25.8	58.8	184.5	196.1	1,137.0	80.0
Portland, OR	3,049.5	2.4	50.2	66.7	183.3	339.3	1,968.5	439.1
Providence, RI	1,692.5	2.3	44.8	48.1	187.3	225.0	1,071.9	113.0
Provo, UT	1,368.4	1.1	31.6	7.9	49.6	132.9	1,061.8	83.5
Raleigh, NC	1,570.3	1.7	21.5	37.4	112.0	223.8	1,071.2	102.7
Reno, NV	2,336.2	3.2	63.1	86.8	315.9	327.1	1,187.2	352.9
Richmond, VA	2,388.9	8.3	26.7	60.3	132.4	216.6	1,781.7	162.9
Riverside, CA	2,700.9	5.7	29.9	113.4	276.9	437.5	1,420.4	417.2
Rochester, MN	1,425.3	0.9	32.6	16.7	102.3	184.6	1,011.3	76.9
Sacramento, CA	2,548.0	4.1	27.5	102.0	220.5	389.6	1,520.5	283.8
Salt Lake City, UT	3,700.3	3.0	71.3	72.8	219.5	396.4	2,569.6	367.6
San Antonio, TX	3,796.6	5.1	78.5	86.7	345.6	434.8	2,483.3	362.6
San Diego, CA	1,992.1	2.6	33.1	86.4	219.1	230.0	1,131.6	289.3
San Francisco, CA[2]	4,482.9	3.0	39.4	225.0	211.5	417.2	3,236.0	350.7
San Jose, CA	2,725.6	2.3	46.9	93.1	182.6	345.7	1,646.7	408.3
Santa Rosa, CA	1,763.5	1.8	55.7	48.8	298.8	246.8	997.9	113.7
Savannah, GA[3]	3,107.5	9.2	35.9	93.7	247.2	415.6	2,032.0	274.0
Seattle, WA[2]	n/a	n/a	n/a	n/a	n/a	n/a	n/a	n/a
Sioux Falls, SD	2,815.3	1.9	56.2	26.4	303.7	369.5	1,775.9	281.7
Springfield, IL	3,514.4	4.8	70.3	115.3	393.5	655.2	2,099.8	175.4
Tallahassee, FL	3,458.0	6.5	71.0	81.2	368.9	560.3	2,124.4	245.8
Tampa, FL	1,977.8	4.0	36.9	49.8	201.5	216.1	1,341.8	127.7
Tucson, AZ	3,328.8	5.3	62.4	123.9	255.9	405.1	2,168.0	308.2
Tulsa, OK	3,757.4	8.2	57.4	83.0	381.0	737.0	2,059.5	431.3
Tuscaloosa, AL[3]	3,445.1	4.0	35.6	80.3	276.5	607.5	2,189.7	251.6
Virginia Beach, VA	2,759.6	8.0	33.9	73.0	234.6	240.3	1,987.4	182.3
Washington, DC[2]	n/a	n/a	29.8	99.9	163.6	121.4	1,424.4	154.6
Wichita, KS	n/a	6.1	74.0	77.9	623.3	525.2	n/a	411.7
Winston-Salem, NC[3]	n/a	n/a	n/a	n/a	n/a	n/a	n/a	n/a
U.S.	2,489.3	5.0	42.6	81.6	250.2	340.5	1,549.5	219.9

Note: Figures are crimes per 100,000 population in 2019 except where noted; n/a not available; (1) Figures cover the Metropolitan Statistical Area except where noted; (2) Metropolitan Division (MD); (3) 2018 data; (4) 2017 data
Source: FBI Uniform Crime Reports, 2017, 2018, 2019

Temperature & Precipitation: Yearly Averages and Extremes

City	Extreme Low (°F)	Average Low (°F)	Average Temp. (°F)	Average High (°F)	Extreme High (°F)	Average Precip. (in.)	Average Snow (in.)
Albuquerque, NM	-17	43	57	70	105	8.5	11
Allentown, PA	-12	42	52	61	105	44.2	32
Anchorage, AK	-34	29	36	43	85	15.7	71
Ann Arbor, MI	-21	39	49	58	104	32.4	41
Athens, GA	-8	52	62	72	105	49.8	2
Atlanta, GA	-8	52	62	72	105	49.8	2
Austin, TX	-2	58	69	79	109	31.1	1
Baton Rouge, LA	8	57	68	78	103	58.5	Trace
Boise City, ID	-25	39	51	63	111	11.8	22
Boston, MA	-12	44	52	59	102	42.9	41
Boulder, CO	-25	37	51	64	103	15.5	63
Cape Coral, FL	26	65	75	84	103	53.9	0
Cedar Rapids, IA	-34	36	47	57	105	34.4	33
Charleston, SC	6	55	66	76	104	52.1	1
Charlotte, NC	-5	50	61	71	104	42.8	6
Chicago, IL	-27	40	49	59	104	35.4	39
Cincinnati, OH	-25	44	54	64	103	40.9	23
Clarksville, TN	-17	49	60	70	107	47.4	11
Cleveland, OH	-19	41	50	59	104	37.1	55
College Station, TX	-2	58	69	79	109	31.1	1
Colorado Springs, CO	-24	36	49	62	99	17.0	48
Columbia, MO	-20	44	54	64	111	40.6	25
Columbia, SC	-1	51	64	75	107	48.3	2
Columbus, OH	-19	42	52	62	104	37.9	28
Dallas, TX	-2	56	67	77	112	33.9	3
Davenport, IA	-24	40	50	60	108	31.8	33
Denver, CO	-25	37	51	64	103	15.5	63
Des Moines, IA	-24	40	50	60	108	31.8	33
Durham, NC	-9	48	60	71	105	42.0	8
Edison, NJ	-8	46	55	63	105	43.5	27
El Paso, TX	-8	50	64	78	114	8.6	6
Fargo, ND	-36	31	41	52	106	19.6	40
Fayetteville, NC	-9	48	60	71	105	42.0	8
Fort Collins, CO	-25	37	51	64	103	15.5	63
Fort Wayne, IN	-22	40	50	60	106	35.9	33
Fort Worth, TX	-1	55	66	76	113	32.3	3
Grand Rapids, MI	-22	38	48	57	102	34.7	73
Greeley, CO	-25	37	51	64	103	15.5	63
Green Bay, WI	-31	34	44	54	99	28.3	46
Greensboro, NC	-8	47	58	69	103	42.5	10
Honolulu, HI	52	70	77	84	94	22.4	0
Houston, TX	7	58	69	79	107	46.9	Trace
Huntsville, AL	-11	50	61	71	104	56.8	4
Indianapolis, IN	-23	42	53	62	104	40.2	25
Jacksonville, FL	7	58	69	79	103	52.0	0
Kansas City, MO	-23	44	54	64	109	38.1	21
Lafayette, LA	8	57	68	78	103	58.5	Trace
Lakeland, FL	18	63	73	82	99	46.7	Trace
Las Vegas, NV	8	53	67	80	116	4.0	1
Lexington, KY	-21	45	55	65	103	45.1	17
Lincoln, NE	-33	39	51	62	108	29.1	27
Little Rock, AR	-5	51	62	73	112	50.7	5
Los Angeles, CA	27	55	63	70	110	11.3	Trace
Louisville, KY	-20	46	57	67	105	43.9	17
Madison, WI	-37	35	46	57	104	31.1	42

Table continued on following page.

City	Extreme Low (°F)	Average Low (°F)	Average Temp. (°F)	Average High (°F)	Extreme High (°F)	Average Precip. (in.)	Average Snow (in.)
Manchester, NH	-33	34	46	57	102	36.9	63
Memphis, TN	0	52	65	77	107	54.8	1
Miami, FL	30	69	76	83	98	57.1	0
Midland, TX	-11	50	64	77	116	14.6	4
Milwaukee, WI	-26	38	47	55	103	32.0	49
Minneapolis, MN	-34	35	45	54	105	27.1	52
Nashville, TN	-17	49	60	70	107	47.4	11
New Haven, CT	-7	44	52	60	103	41.4	25
New Orleans, LA	11	59	69	78	102	60.6	Trace
New York, NY	-2	47	55	62	104	47.0	23
Oklahoma City, OK	-8	49	60	71	110	32.8	10
Omaha, NE	-23	40	51	62	110	30.1	29
Orlando, FL	19	62	72	82	100	47.7	Trace
Peoria, IL	-26	41	51	61	113	35.4	23
Philadelphia, PA	-7	45	55	64	104	41.4	22
Phoenix, AZ	17	59	72	86	122	7.3	Trace
Pittsburgh, PA	-18	41	51	60	103	37.1	43
Portland, OR	-3	45	54	62	107	37.5	7
Providence, RI	-13	42	51	60	104	45.3	35
Provo, UT	-22	40	52	64	107	15.6	63
Raleigh, NC	-9	48	60	71	105	42.0	8
Reno, NV	-16	33	50	67	105	7.2	24
Richmond, VA	-8	48	58	69	105	43.0	13
Riverside, CA	24	53	66	78	114	n/a	n/a
Rochester, MN	-40	34	44	54	102	29.4	47
Sacramento, CA	18	48	61	73	115	17.3	Trace
Salt Lake City, UT	-22	40	52	64	107	15.6	63
San Antonio, TX	0	58	69	80	108	29.6	1
San Diego, CA	29	57	64	71	111	9.5	Trace
San Francisco, CA	24	49	57	65	106	19.3	Trace
San Jose, CA	21	50	59	68	105	13.5	Trace
Santa Rosa, CA	23	42	57	71	109	29.0	n/a
Savannah, GA	3	56	67	77	105	50.3	Trace
Seattle, WA	0	44	52	59	99	38.4	13
Sioux Falls, SD	-36	35	46	57	110	24.6	38
Springfield, IL	-24	44	54	63	112	34.9	21
Tallahassee, FL	6	56	68	79	103	63.3	Trace
Tampa, FL	18	63	73	82	99	46.7	Trace
Tucson, AZ	16	55	69	82	117	11.6	2
Tulsa, OK	-8	50	61	71	112	38.9	10
Tuscaloosa, AL	-6	51	63	74	106	53.5	2
Virginia Beach, VA	-3	51	60	69	104	44.8	8
Washington, DC	-5	49	58	67	104	39.5	18
Wichita, KS	-21	45	57	68	113	29.3	17
Winston-Salem, NC	-8	47	58	69	103	42.5	10

Source: National Climatic Data Center, International Station Meteorological Climate Summary, 9/96

Weather Conditions

City	Temperature			Daytime Sky			Precipitation		
	10°F & below	32°F & below	90°F & above	Clear	Partly cloudy	Cloudy	0.01 inch or more precip.	1.0 inch or more snow/ice	Thunder-storms
Albuquerque, NM	4	114	65	140	161	64	60	9	38
Allentown, PA	n/a	123	15	77	148	140	123	20	31
Anchorage, AK	n/a	194	n/a	50	115	200	113	49	2
Ann Arbor, MI	n/a	136	12	74	134	157	135	38	32
Athens, GA	1	49	38	98	147	120	116	3	48
Atlanta, GA	1	49	38	98	147	120	116	3	48
Austin, TX	< 1	20	111	105	148	112	83	1	41
Baton Rouge, LA	< 1	21	86	99	150	116	113	< 1	73
Boise City, ID	n/a	124	45	106	133	126	91	22	14
Boston, MA	n/a	97	12	88	127	150	253	48	18
Boulder, CO	24	155	33	99	177	89	90	38	39
Cape Coral, FL	n/a	n/a	115	93	220	52	110	0	92
Cedar Rapids, IA	n/a	156	16	89	132	144	109	28	42
Charleston, SC	< 1	33	53	89	162	114	114	1	59
Charlotte, NC	1	65	44	98	142	125	113	3	41
Chicago, IL	n/a	132	17	83	136	146	125	31	38
Cincinnati, OH	14	107	23	80	126	159	127	25	39
Clarksville, TN	5	76	51	98	135	132	119	8	54
Cleveland, OH	n/a	123	12	63	127	175	157	48	34
College Station, TX	< 1	20	111	105	148	112	83	1	41
Colorado Springs, CO	21	161	18	108	157	100	98	33	49
Columbia, MO	17	108	36	99	127	139	110	17	52
Columbia, SC	< 1	58	77	97	149	119	110	1	53
Columbus, OH	n/a	118	19	72	137	156	136	29	40
Dallas, TX	1	34	102	108	160	97	78	2	49
Davenport, IA	n/a	137	26	99	129	137	106	25	46
Denver, CO	24	155	33	99	177	89	90	38	39
Des Moines, IA	n/a	137	26	99	129	137	106	25	46
Durham, NC	n/a	n/a	39	98	143	124	110	3	42
Edison, NJ	n/a	90	24	80	146	139	122	16	46
El Paso, TX	1	59	106	147	164	54	49	3	35
Fargo, ND	n/a	180	15	81	145	139	100	38	31
Fayetteville, NC	n/a	n/a	39	98	143	124	110	3	42
Fort Collins, CO	24	155	33	99	177	89	90	38	39
Fort Wayne, IN	n/a	131	16	75	140	150	131	31	39
Fort Worth, TX	1	40	100	123	136	106	79	3	47
Grand Rapids, MI	n/a	146	11	67	119	179	142	57	34
Greeley, CO	24	155	33	99	177	89	90	38	39
Green Bay, WI	n/a	163	7	86	125	154	120	40	33
Greensboro, NC	3	85	32	94	143	128	113	5	43
Honolulu, HI	n/a	n/a	23	25	286	54	98	0	7
Houston, TX	n/a	n/a	96	83	168	114	101	1	62
Huntsville, AL	2	66	49	70	118	177	116	2	54
Indianapolis, IN	19	119	19	83	128	154	127	24	43
Jacksonville, FL	< 1	16	83	86	181	98	114	1	65
Kansas City, MO	22	110	39	112	134	119	103	17	51
Lafayette, LA	< 1	21	86	99	150	116	113	< 1	73
Lakeland, FL	n/a	n/a	85	81	204	80	107	< 1	87
Las Vegas, NV	< 1	37	134	185	132	48	27	2	13
Lexington, KY	11	96	22	86	136	143	129	17	44
Lincoln, NE	n/a	145	40	108	135	122	94	19	46
Little Rock, AR	1	57	73	110	142	113	104	4	57
Los Angeles, CA	0	< 1	5	131	125	109	34	0	1
Louisville, KY	8	90	35	82	143	140	125	15	45

Table continued on following page.

City	Temperature			Daytime Sky			Precipitation		
	10°F & below	32°F & below	90°F & above	Clear	Partly cloudy	Cloudy	0.01 inch or more precip.	1.0 inch or more snow/ice	Thunder-storms
Madison, WI	n/a	161	14	88	119	158	118	38	40
Manchester, NH	n/a	171	12	87	131	147	125	32	19
Memphis, TN	1	53	86	101	152	112	104	2	59
Miami, FL	n/a	n/a	55	48	263	54	128	0	74
Midland, TX	1	62	102	144	138	83	52	3	38
Milwaukee, WI	n/a	141	10	90	118	157	126	38	35
Minneapolis, MN	n/a	156	16	93	125	147	113	41	37
Nashville, TN	5	76	51	98	135	132	119	8	54
New Haven, CT	n/a	n/a	7	80	146	139	118	17	22
New Orleans, LA	0	13	70	90	169	106	114	1	69
New York, NY	n/a	n/a	18	85	166	114	120	11	20
Oklahoma City, OK	5	79	70	124	131	110	80	8	50
Omaha, NE	n/a	139	35	100	142	123	97	20	46
Orlando, FL	n/a	n/a	90	76	208	81	115	0	80
Peoria, IL	n/a	127	27	89	127	149	115	22	49
Philadelphia, PA	5	94	23	81	146	138	117	14	27
Phoenix, AZ	0	10	167	186	125	54	37	< 1	23
Pittsburgh, PA	n/a	121	8	62	137	166	154	42	35
Portland, OR	n/a	37	11	67	116	182	152	4	7
Providence, RI	n/a	117	9	85	134	146	123	21	21
Provo, UT	n/a	128	56	94	152	119	92	38	38
Raleigh, NC	n/a	n/a	39	98	143	124	110	3	42
Reno, NV	14	178	50	143	139	83	50	17	14
Richmond, VA	3	79	41	90	147	128	115	7	43
Riverside, CA	0	4	82	124	178	63	n/a	n/a	5
Rochester, MN	n/a	165	9	87	126	152	114	40	41
Sacramento, CA	0	21	73	175	111	79	58	< 1	2
Salt Lake City, UT	n/a	128	56	94	152	119	92	38	38
San Antonio, TX	n/a	n/a	112	97	153	115	81	1	36
San Diego, CA	0	< 1	4	115	126	124	40	0	5
San Francisco, CA	0	6	4	136	130	99	63	< 1	5
San Jose, CA	0	5	5	106	180	79	57	< 1	6
Santa Rosa, CA	n/a	43	30	n/a	365	n/a	n/a	n/a	2
Savannah, GA	< 1	29	70	97	155	113	111	< 1	63
Seattle, WA	n/a	38	3	57	121	187	157	8	8
Sioux Falls, SD	n/a	n/a	n/a	95	136	134	n/a	n/a	n/a
Springfield, IL	19	111	34	96	126	143	111	18	49
Tallahassee, FL	< 1	31	86	93	175	97	114	1	83
Tampa, FL	n/a	n/a	85	81	204	80	107	< 1	87
Tucson, AZ	0	18	140	177	119	69	54	2	42
Tulsa, OK	6	78	74	117	141	107	88	8	50
Tuscaloosa, AL	1	57	59	91	161	113	119	1	57
Virginia Beach, VA	< 1	53	33	89	149	127	115	5	38
Washington, DC	2	71	34	84	144	137	112	9	30
Wichita, KS	13	110	63	117	132	116	87	13	54
Winston-Salem, NC	3	85	32	94	143	128	113	5	43

Note: Figures are average number of days per year
Source: National Climatic Data Center, International Station Meteorological Climate Summary, 9/96

Air Quality Index

MSA[1] (Days[2])	Percent of Days when Air Quality was...					AQI Statistics	
	Good	Moderate	Unhealthy for Sensitive Groups	Unhealthy	Very Unhealthy	Maximum	Median
Albuquerque, NM (365)	44.1	54.8	1.1	0.0	0.0	108	53
Allentown, PA (365)	75.3	23.6	1.1	0.0	0.0	119	42
Anchorage, AK (365)	71.8	24.9	2.2	1.1	0.0	160	31
Ann Arbor, MI (365)	80.5	19.5	0.0	0.0	0.0	88	39
Athens, GA (365)	67.1	32.9	0.0	0.0	0.0	87	44
Atlanta, GA (365)	44.4	50.4	4.9	0.3	0.0	172	52
Austin, TX (365)	68.2	31.2	0.5	0.0	0.0	115	44
Baton Rouge, LA (365)	61.4	36.2	2.5	0.0	0.0	119	45
Boise City, ID (365)	67.9	31.2	0.5	0.3	0.0	165	44
Boston, MA (365)	79.7	20.0	0.3	0.0	0.0	122	43
Boulder, CO (365)	62.2	36.4	1.4	0.0	0.0	119	47
Cape Coral, FL (365)	89.9	9.9	0.3	0.0	0.0	108	36
Cedar Rapids, IA (365)	78.6	21.4	0.0	0.0	0.0	84	39
Charleston, SC (357)	84.3	15.4	0.3	0.0	0.0	140	38
Charlotte, NC (365)	54.8	40.3	4.9	0.0	0.0	136	49
Chicago, IL (365)	33.2	62.2	4.4	0.3	0.0	174	55
Cincinnati, OH (365)	38.1	56.4	5.5	0.0	0.0	147	54
Clarksville, TN (365)	84.1	15.9	0.0	0.0	0.0	87	40
Cleveland, OH (365)	50.7	47.4	1.9	0.0	0.0	119	50
College Station, TX (352)	100.0	0.0	0.0	0.0	0.0	17	0
Colorado Springs, CO (365)	71.0	29.0	0.0	0.0	0.0	100	45
Columbia, MO (245)	97.6	2.4	0.0	0.0	0.0	71	38
Columbia, SC (365)	72.3	27.1	0.5	0.0	0.0	136	43
Columbus, OH (365)	64.9	34.8	0.3	0.0	0.0	101	46
Dallas, TX (365)	49.6	42.5	7.7	0.3	0.0	156	51
Davenport, IA (365)	59.5	39.7	0.8	0.0	0.0	115	46
Denver, CO (365)	24.9	69.0	5.5	0.5	0.0	154	58
Des Moines, IA (365)	83.8	16.2	0.0	0.0	0.0	100	39
Durham, NC (365)	75.3	24.7	0.0	0.0	0.0	92	44
Edison, NJ (365)	46.3	49.3	4.4	0.0	0.0	150	51
El Paso, TX (365)	40.3	56.2	3.0	0.5	0.0	157	53
Fargo, ND (363)	90.1	9.4	0.3	0.3	0.0	156	33
Fayetteville, NC (363)	77.7	22.3	0.0	0.0	0.0	84	41
Fort Collins, CO (365)	57.0	41.4	1.6	0.0	0.0	129	48
Fort Wayne, IN (365)	64.7	35.1	0.3	0.0	0.0	101	45
Fort Worth, TX (365)	49.6	42.5	7.7	0.3	0.0	156	51
Grand Rapids, MI (365)	81.6	18.4	0.0	0.0	0.0	100	38
Greeley, CO (365)	69.0	30.1	0.8	0.0	0.0	125	45
Green Bay, WI (365)	85.2	14.8	0.0	0.0	0.0	97	36
Greensboro, NC (365)	79.7	20.3	0.0	0.0	0.0	90	43
Honolulu, HI (365)	92.9	7.1	0.0	0.0	0.0	94	29
Houston, TX (365)	46.8	44.7	7.1	1.1	0.3	202	52
Huntsville, AL (361)	70.6	29.4	0.0	0.0	0.0	93	44
Indianapolis, IN (365)	40.5	58.1	1.4	0.0	0.0	119	54
Jacksonville, FL (365)	67.1	32.6	0.3	0.0	0.0	114	43
Kansas City, MO (365)	57.5	42.2	0.3	0.0	0.0	137	47
Lafayette, LA (365)	76.7	23.3	0.0	0.0	0.0	84	41
Lakeland, FL (365)	86.0	14.0	0.0	0.0	0.0	100	36
Las Vegas, NV (365)	42.2	56.4	1.4	0.0	0.0	122	54
Lexington, KY (365)	83.0	17.0	0.0	0.0	0.0	80	42
Lincoln, NE (360)	93.9	6.1	0.0	0.0	0.0	66	31
Little Rock, AR (365)	64.4	35.6	0.0	0.0	0.0	79	45
Los Angeles, CA (365)	18.1	57.0	17.0	7.7	0.3	201	72
Louisville, KY (365)	53.4	45.5	1.1	0.0	0.0	136	49

Table continued on following page.

MSA[1] (Days[2])	Percent of Days when Air Quality was...					AQI Statistics	
	Good	Moderate	Unhealthy for Sensitive Groups	Unhealthy	Very Unhealthy	Maximum	Median
Madison, WI (365)	78.1	21.9	0.0	0.0	0.0	93	39
Manchester, NH (365)	96.7	3.3	0.0	0.0	0.0	80	37
Memphis, TN (365)	60.5	38.1	1.4	0.0	0.0	148	45
Miami, FL (364)	78.3	21.2	0.5	0.0	0.0	146	41
Midland, TX (n/a)	n/a	n/a	n/a	n/a	n/a	n/a	n/a
Milwaukee, WI (365)	69.6	29.6	0.8	0.0	0.0	115	44
Minneapolis, MN (365)	58.6	40.5	0.5	0.3	0.0	200	46
Nashville, TN (365)	62.7	37.0	0.3	0.0	0.0	101	45
New Haven, CT (365)	76.7	19.5	3.3	0.5	0.0	159	41
New Orleans, LA (365)	62.7	36.7	0.5	0.0	0.0	112	45
New York, NY (365)	46.3	49.3	4.4	0.0	0.0	150	51
Oklahoma City, OK (365)	55.9	43.6	0.5	0.0	0.0	119	48
Omaha, NE (365)	77.5	22.5	0.0	0.0	0.0	97	40
Orlando, FL (365)	81.1	17.3	1.6	0.0	0.0	122	39
Peoria, IL (365)	78.1	21.4	0.5	0.0	0.0	101	41
Philadelphia, PA (365)	49.3	46.3	4.4	0.0	0.0	150	51
Phoenix, AZ (365)	13.7	71.5	11.5	0.5	0.8	886	74
Pittsburgh, PA (365)	35.3	60.3	3.3	1.1	0.0	161	56
Portland, OR (365)	78.1	21.1	0.8	0.0	0.0	128	38
Providence, RI (365)	79.2	20.3	0.5	0.0	0.0	126	44
Provo, UT (365)	69.3	30.4	0.3	0.0	0.0	107	46
Raleigh, NC (365)	65.5	34.5	0.0	0.0	0.0	93	46
Reno, NV (365)	66.8	33.2	0.0	0.0	0.0	97	46
Richmond, VA (365)	74.5	25.5	0.0	0.0	0.0	100	44
Riverside, CA (365)	11.5	48.8	21.6	15.9	2.2	213	89
Rochester, MN (364)	86.0	14.0	0.0	0.0	0.0	84	36
Sacramento, CA (365)	47.1	47.1	5.8	0.0	0.0	140	52
Salt Lake City, UT (365)	46.3	49.0	4.7	0.0	0.0	136	51
San Antonio, TX (365)	53.7	44.7	1.4	0.3	0.0	169	49
San Diego, CA (365)	23.8	69.3	6.3	0.5	0.0	169	64
San Francisco, CA (365)	69.6	27.9	2.5	0.0	0.0	150	43
San Jose, CA (365)	72.1	26.8	1.1	0.0	0.0	136	43
Santa Rosa, CA (365)	95.3	4.7	0.0	0.0	0.0	87	33
Savannah, GA (365)	80.8	19.2	0.0	0.0	0.0	87	39
Seattle, WA (365)	64.7	34.8	0.5	0.0	0.0	142	45
Sioux Falls, SD (365)	87.9	11.8	0.3	0.0	0.0	105	36
Springfield, IL (360)	79.7	20.3	0.0	0.0	0.0	87	40
Tallahassee, FL (365)	74.5	25.2	0.3	0.0	0.0	119	40
Tampa, FL (365)	73.2	25.2	1.6	0.0	0.0	132	43
Tucson, AZ (365)	61.6	37.8	0.5	0.0	0.0	103	47
Tulsa, OK (365)	68.2	31.2	0.5	0.0	0.0	105	45
Tuscaloosa, AL (264)	90.9	9.1	0.0	0.0	0.0	87	35
Virginia Beach, VA (365)	86.8	13.2	0.0	0.0	0.0	97	40
Washington, DC (365)	57.3	39.7	2.7	0.3	0.0	157	47
Wichita, KS (365)	82.5	17.5	0.0	0.0	0.0	97	40
Winston-Salem, NC (365)	61.6	38.4	0.0	0.0	0.0	97	45

Note: The Air Quality Index (AQI) is an index for reporting daily air quality. EPA calculates the AQI for five major air pollutants regulated by the Clean Air Act: ground-level ozone, particle pollution (also known as particulate matter), carbon monoxide, sulfur dioxide, and nitrogen dioxide. The AQI runs from 0 to 500. The higher the AQI value, the greater the level of air pollution and the greater the health concern. There are six AQI categories: "Good" The AQI is between 0 and 50. Air quality is considered satisfactory; "Moderate" The AQI is between 51 and 100. Air quality is acceptable; "Unhealthy for Sensitive Groups" When AQI values are between 101 and 150, members of sensitive groups may experience health effects; "Unhealthy" When AQI values are between 151 and 200 everyone may begin to experience health effects; "Very Unhealthy" AQI values between 201 and 300 trigger a health alert; "Hazardous" AQI values over 300 trigger health warnings of emergency conditions; Data covers the entire county unless noted otherwise; (1) Data covers the Metropolitan Statistical Area—see Appendix B for areas included; (2) Number of days with AQI data in 2019
Source: U.S. Environmental Protection Agency, Air Quality Index Report, 2019

Air Quality Index Pollutants

MSA[1] (Days[2])	Percent of Days when AQI Pollutant was...					
	Carbon Monoxide	Nitrogen Dioxide	Ozone	Sulfur Dioxide	Particulate Matter 2.5	Particulate Matter 10
Albuquerque, NM (365)	0.0	0.0	69.0	0.0	18.1	12.9
Allentown, PA (365)	0.0	3.6	61.4	0.0	35.1	0.0
Anchorage, AK (365)	1.4	0.0	0.0	0.0	69.9	28.8
Ann Arbor, MI (365)	0.0	0.0	66.6	0.0	33.4	0.0
Athens, GA (365)	0.0	0.0	37.3	0.0	62.7	0.0
Atlanta, GA (365)	0.0	2.5	46.8	0.0	50.7	0.0
Austin, TX (365)	0.0	1.9	48.8	0.0	49.3	0.0
Baton Rouge, LA (365)	0.0	1.6	47.9	0.3	50.1	0.0
Boise City, ID (365)	0.0	1.1	44.4	0.0	51.0	3.6
Boston, MA (365)	0.0	4.1	57.5	0.0	38.4	0.0
Boulder, CO (365)	0.0	0.0	73.7	0.0	26.3	0.0
Cape Coral, FL (365)	0.0	0.0	68.8	0.0	30.1	1.1
Cedar Rapids, IA (365)	0.0	0.0	47.9	1.1	51.0	0.0
Charleston, SC (357)	0.0	0.0	67.2	0.0	32.5	0.3
Charlotte, NC (365)	0.0	0.0	66.6	0.0	33.4	0.0
Chicago, IL (365)	0.0	5.5	24.1	4.9	62.5	3.0
Cincinnati, OH (365)	0.0	1.6	41.4	6.0	50.1	0.8
Clarksville, TN (365)	0.0	0.0	72.9	0.0	27.1	0.0
Cleveland, OH (365)	0.0	0.3	40.5	0.5	55.1	3.6
College Station, TX (352)	0.0	0.0	0.0	100.0	0.0	0.0
Colorado Springs, CO (365)	0.0	0.0	94.5	0.0	4.9	0.5
Columbia, MO (245)	0.0	0.0	100.0	0.0	0.0	0.0
Columbia, SC (365)	0.0	0.0	71.8	0.0	28.2	0.0
Columbus, OH (365)	0.0	1.4	49.0	0.0	49.3	0.3
Dallas, TX (365)	0.0	3.0	56.2	0.0	40.8	0.0
Davenport, IA (365)	0.0	0.0	37.8	0.0	41.9	20.3
Denver, CO (365)	0.0	16.4	57.8	0.3	17.3	8.2
Des Moines, IA (365)	0.0	0.8	67.4	0.0	31.8	0.0
Durham, NC (365)	0.0	0.0	56.7	1.6	41.6	0.0
Edison, NJ (365)	0.0	17.5	39.2	0.0	43.3	0.0
El Paso, TX (365)	0.0	5.8	55.9	0.0	37.5	0.8
Fargo, ND (363)	0.0	2.5	72.7	0.0	24.2	0.6
Fayetteville, NC (363)	0.0	0.0	56.7	0.0	42.1	1.1
Fort Collins, CO (365)	0.0	0.0	92.3	0.0	7.7	0.0
Fort Wayne, IN (365)	0.0	0.0	48.5	0.0	51.5	0.0
Fort Worth, TX (365)	0.0	3.0	56.2	0.0	40.8	0.0
Grand Rapids, MI (365)	0.0	2.5	69.9	0.0	26.3	1.4
Greeley, CO (365)	0.0	0.0	64.7	0.0	35.3	0.0
Green Bay, WI (365)	0.0	0.0	51.0	1.1	47.9	0.0
Greensboro, NC (365)	0.0	0.0	63.6	0.0	29.3	7.1
Honolulu, HI (365)	0.3	0.8	71.8	17.8	9.0	0.3
Houston, TX (365)	0.0	4.4	47.1	0.5	47.1	0.8
Huntsville, AL (361)	0.0	0.0	42.9	0.0	55.1	1.9
Indianapolis, IN (365)	0.0	0.0	34.2	1.1	64.7	0.0
Jacksonville, FL (365)	0.0	0.0	48.2	2.7	49.0	0.0
Kansas City, MO (365)	0.0	2.5	48.2	0.0	45.5	3.8
Lafayette, LA (365)	0.0	0.0	58.4	0.0	41.6	0.0
Lakeland, FL (365)	0.0	0.0	67.9	0.5	31.5	0.0
Las Vegas, NV (365)	0.3	5.5	69.0	0.0	23.0	2.2
Lexington, KY (365)	0.0	2.7	52.9	0.0	44.4	0.0
Lincoln, NE (360)	0.0	0.0	63.6	21.1	15.3	0.0
Little Rock, AR (365)	0.0	0.5	40.0	0.0	59.5	0.0
Los Angeles, CA (365)	0.0	9.0	56.2	0.0	32.3	2.5
Louisville, KY (365)	0.0	2.7	45.8	0.0	51.5	0.0

Table continued on following page.

MSA[1] (Days[2])	Carbon Monoxide	Nitrogen Dioxide	Ozone	Sulfur Dioxide	Particulate Matter 2.5	Particulate Matter 10
	Percent of Days when AQI Pollutant was...					
Madison, WI (365)	0.0	0.0	45.5	0.0	54.5	0.0
Manchester, NH (365)	0.0	0.0	97.5	0.0	2.5	0.0
Memphis, TN (365)	0.0	2.5	51.0	0.0	46.6	0.0
Miami, FL (364)	0.3	3.6	37.4	0.0	58.5	0.3
Midland, TX (n/a)	n/a	n/a	n/a	n/a	n/a	n/a
Milwaukee, WI (365)	0.0	2.7	51.8	0.0	43.3	2.2
Minneapolis, MN (365)	0.0	1.4	31.2	1.1	43.0	23.3
Nashville, TN (365)	0.0	6.8	40.5	0.0	52.6	0.0
New Haven, CT (365)	0.0	4.1	67.7	0.0	27.1	1.1
New Orleans, LA (365)	0.0	0.8	45.8	8.8	44.4	0.3
New York, NY (365)	0.0	17.5	39.2	0.0	43.3	0.0
Oklahoma City, OK (365)	0.0	1.1	52.9	0.0	45.8	0.3
Omaha, NE (365)	0.0	0.0	52.3	3.3	40.8	3.6
Orlando, FL (365)	0.0	0.0	80.5	0.0	19.5	0.0
Peoria, IL (365)	0.0	0.0	55.6	0.5	43.8	0.0
Philadelphia, PA (365)	0.0	3.6	50.1	0.0	46.3	0.0
Phoenix, AZ (365)	0.0	0.8	46.3	0.0	19.7	33.2
Pittsburgh, PA (365)	0.0	0.0	29.3	6.3	64.4	0.0
Portland, OR (365)	0.0	2.2	56.4	0.0	41.4	0.0
Providence, RI (365)	0.0	2.2	70.7	0.0	26.8	0.3
Provo, UT (365)	0.0	1.9	81.4	0.0	16.2	0.5
Raleigh, NC (365)	0.3	0.3	46.8	0.0	52.6	0.0
Reno, NV (365)	0.0	1.1	80.5	0.0	17.0	1.4
Richmond, VA (365)	0.0	4.4	67.4	0.0	28.2	0.0
Riverside, CA (365)	0.0	3.0	62.5	0.0	24.4	10.1
Rochester, MN (364)	0.0	0.0	53.6	0.0	46.4	0.0
Sacramento, CA (365)	0.0	0.3	71.0	0.0	27.1	1.6
Salt Lake City, UT (365)	0.0	8.8	67.1	0.0	22.7	1.4
San Antonio, TX (365)	0.0	0.8	44.1	0.0	54.8	0.3
San Diego, CA (365)	0.0	0.5	48.2	0.0	50.4	0.8
San Francisco, CA (365)	0.0	6.3	52.1	0.0	41.6	0.0
San Jose, CA (365)	0.0	0.5	64.7	0.0	33.7	1.1
Santa Rosa, CA (365)	0.0	0.8	70.7	0.0	25.8	2.7
Savannah, GA (365)	0.0	0.0	40.0	15.9	44.1	0.0
Seattle, WA (365)	0.0	8.5	43.3	0.0	48.2	0.0
Sioux Falls, SD (365)	0.0	2.5	84.1	0.0	12.9	0.5
Springfield, IL (360)	0.0	0.0	50.8	0.0	49.2	0.0
Tallahassee, FL (365)	0.0	0.0	47.7	0.0	52.3	0.0
Tampa, FL (365)	0.0	0.0	58.4	1.1	39.5	1.1
Tucson, AZ (365)	0.0	0.3	71.5	0.0	5.5	22.7
Tulsa, OK (365)	0.0	0.0	65.2	0.0	34.8	0.0
Tuscaloosa, AL (264)	0.0	0.0	71.2	0.0	28.8	0.0
Virginia Beach, VA (365)	0.0	12.1	61.9	0.0	26.0	0.0
Washington, DC (365)	0.0	6.8	61.9	0.0	31.2	0.0
Wichita, KS (365)	0.0	1.4	72.6	0.0	23.6	2.5
Winston-Salem, NC (365)	0.0	2.7	47.1	0.0	50.1	0.0

Note: The Air Quality Index (AQI) is an index for reporting daily air quality. EPA calculates the AQI for five major air pollutants regulated by the Clean Air Act: ground-level ozone, particle pollution (also known as particulate matter), carbon monoxide, sulfur dioxide, and nitrogen dioxide. The AQI runs from 0 to 500. The higher the AQI value, the greater the level of air pollution and the greater the health concern; (1) Data covers the Metropolitan Statistical Area—see Appendix B for areas included; (2) Number of days with AQI data in 2019
Source: U.S. Environmental Protection Agency, Air Quality Index Report, 2019

Air Quality Trends: Ozone

MSA[1]	1990	1995	2000	2005	2010	2015	2016	2017	2018	2019
Albuquerque, NM	0.072	0.070	0.072	0.073	0.066	0.066	0.065	0.069	0.074	0.067
Allentown, PA	0.093	0.091	0.091	0.086	0.080	0.070	0.073	0.067	0.067	0.064
Anchorage, AK	n/a	n/a	n/a	n/a	n/a	n/a	n/a	n/a	n/a	n/a
Ann Arbor, MI	n/a	n/a	n/a	n/a	n/a	n/a	n/a	n/a	n/a	n/a
Athens, GA	n/a	n/a	n/a	n/a	n/a	n/a	n/a	n/a	n/a	n/a
Atlanta, GA	0.104	0.103	0.101	0.087	0.076	0.070	0.073	0.068	0.068	0.071
Austin, TX	0.088	0.089	0.088	0.082	0.074	0.073	0.064	0.070	0.072	0.065
Baton Rouge, LA	0.105	0.091	0.090	0.090	0.075	0.069	0.066	0.069	0.069	0.066
Boise City, ID	n/a	n/a	n/a	n/a	n/a	n/a	n/a	n/a	n/a	n/a
Boston, MA	n/a	n/a	n/a	n/a	n/a	n/a	n/a	n/a	n/a	n/a
Boulder, CO	n/a	n/a	n/a	n/a	n/a	n/a	n/a	n/a	n/a	n/a
Cape Coral, FL	n/a	n/a	n/a	n/a	n/a	n/a	n/a	n/a	n/a	n/a
Cedar Rapids, IA	n/a	n/a	n/a	n/a	n/a	n/a	n/a	n/a	n/a	n/a
Charleston, SC	0.068	0.071	0.078	0.073	0.067	0.054	0.059	0.062	0.058	0.064
Charlotte, NC	n/a	n/a	n/a	n/a	n/a	n/a	n/a	n/a	n/a	n/a
Chicago, IL	0.074	0.094	0.073	0.084	0.070	0.066	0.074	0.071	0.073	0.069
Cincinnati, OH	0.091	0.091	0.081	0.085	0.075	0.068	0.071	0.067	0.074	0.067
Clarksville, TN	n/a	n/a	n/a	n/a	n/a	n/a	n/a	n/a	n/a	n/a
Cleveland, OH	0.085	0.092	0.076	0.083	0.077	0.071	0.072	0.070	0.074	0.070
College Station, TX	n/a	n/a	n/a	n/a	n/a	n/a	n/a	n/a	n/a	n/a
Colorado Springs, CO	n/a	n/a	n/a	n/a	n/a	n/a	n/a	n/a	n/a	n/a
Columbia, MO	n/a	n/a	n/a	n/a	n/a	n/a	n/a	n/a	n/a	n/a
Columbia, SC	0.093	0.079	0.096	0.082	0.070	0.056	0.065	0.059	0.060	0.066
Columbus, OH	0.090	0.091	0.085	0.084	0.073	0.066	0.069	0.065	0.062	0.060
Dallas, TX	0.095	0.105	0.096	0.097	0.080	0.077	0.070	0.073	0.078	0.071
Davenport, IA	n/a	n/a	n/a	n/a	n/a	n/a	n/a	n/a	n/a	n/a
Denver, CO	0.077	0.070	0.069	0.072	0.070	0.073	0.071	0.072	0.071	0.068
Des Moines, IA	n/a	n/a	n/a	n/a	n/a	n/a	n/a	n/a	n/a	n/a
Durham, NC	n/a	n/a	n/a	n/a	n/a	n/a	n/a	n/a	n/a	n/a
Edison, NJ	0.101	0.106	0.090	0.091	0.081	0.075	0.073	0.070	0.073	0.067
El Paso, TX	0.080	0.078	0.082	0.074	0.072	0.071	0.068	0.073	0.077	0.074
Fargo, ND	n/a	n/a	n/a	n/a	n/a	n/a	n/a	n/a	n/a	n/a
Fayetteville, NC	0.087	0.081	0.086	0.084	0.071	0.060	0.064	0.063	0.064	0.061
Fort Collins, CO	0.066	0.072	0.074	0.076	0.072	0.069	0.070	0.067	0.073	0.065
Fort Wayne, IN	0.086	0.094	0.086	0.081	0.067	0.061	0.068	0.063	0.071	0.063
Fort Worth, TX	0.095	0.105	0.096	0.097	0.080	0.077	0.070	0.073	0.078	0.071
Grand Rapids, MI	0.102	0.089	0.073	0.085	0.071	0.066	0.075	0.065	0.072	0.065
Greeley, CO	n/a	n/a	n/a	n/a	n/a	n/a	n/a	n/a	n/a	n/a
Green Bay, WI	n/a	n/a	n/a	n/a	n/a	n/a	n/a	n/a	n/a	n/a
Greensboro, NC	n/a	n/a	n/a	n/a	n/a	n/a	n/a	n/a	n/a	n/a
Honolulu, HI	0.034	0.049	0.044	0.042	0.046	0.048	0.047	0.046	0.046	0.053
Houston, TX	0.119	0.114	0.102	0.087	0.079	0.083	0.066	0.070	0.073	0.074
Huntsville, AL	0.079	0.080	0.088	0.075	0.071	0.063	0.066	0.063	0.065	0.063
Indianapolis, IN	0.084	0.094	0.081	0.080	0.069	0.064	0.070	0.067	0.073	0.067
Jacksonville, FL	0.080	0.068	0.072	0.076	0.068	0.060	0.057	0.059	0.060	0.062
Kansas City, MO	0.075	0.098	0.088	0.084	0.072	0.063	0.066	0.069	0.073	0.063
Lafayette, LA	n/a	n/a	n/a	n/a	n/a	n/a	n/a	n/a	n/a	n/a
Lakeland, FL	0.066	0.071	0.079	0.074	0.064	0.062	0.064	0.072	0.065	0.066
Las Vegas, NV	n/a	n/a	n/a	n/a	n/a	n/a	n/a	n/a	n/a	n/a
Lexington, KY	0.078	0.088	0.077	0.078	0.070	0.069	0.066	0.063	0.063	0.059
Lincoln, NE	0.057	0.060	0.057	0.056	0.050	0.061	0.058	0.062	0.062	0.056
Little Rock, AR	0.080	0.086	0.090	0.083	0.072	0.063	0.064	0.060	0.066	0.059
Los Angeles, CA	0.134	0.114	0.091	0.085	0.076	0.083	0.083	0.093	0.084	0.080
Louisville, KY	0.075	0.087	0.088	0.083	0.076	0.070	0.070	0.064	0.067	0.064
Madison, WI	0.077	0.084	0.072	0.079	0.062	0.064	0.068	0.064	0.066	0.059
Manchester, NH	n/a	n/a	n/a	n/a	n/a	n/a	n/a	n/a	n/a	n/a

Table continued on following page.

MSA[1]	1990	1995	2000	2005	2010	2015	2016	2017	2018	2019
Memphis, TN	0.088	0.095	0.092	0.086	0.076	0.065	0.069	0.063	0.069	0.065
Miami, FL	0.068	0.072	0.075	0.065	0.064	0.061	0.061	0.064	0.064	0.058
Midland, TX	n/a	n/a	n/a	n/a	n/a	n/a	n/a	n/a	n/a	n/a
Milwaukee, WI	0.095	0.106	0.082	0.092	0.079	0.069	0.074	0.072	0.073	0.066
Minneapolis, MN	0.068	0.084	0.065	0.074	0.066	0.061	0.061	0.062	0.065	0.059
Nashville, TN	0.089	0.092	0.084	0.078	0.073	0.065	0.067	0.063	0.068	0.064
New Haven, CT	n/a	n/a	n/a	n/a	n/a	n/a	n/a	n/a	n/a	n/a
New Orleans, LA	0.082	0.088	0.091	0.079	0.074	0.067	0.065	0.063	0.065	0.062
New York, NY	0.101	0.106	0.090	0.091	0.081	0.075	0.073	0.070	0.073	0.067
Oklahoma City, OK	0.078	0.086	0.082	0.077	0.071	0.067	0.066	0.070	0.072	0.067
Omaha, NE	0.054	0.075	0.063	0.069	0.058	0.055	0.063	0.061	0.063	0.050
Orlando, FL	0.081	0.075	0.080	0.083	0.069	0.060	0.064	0.067	0.062	0.062
Peoria, IL	0.071	0.082	0.072	0.075	0.064	0.062	0.067	0.066	0.070	0.063
Philadelphia, PA	0.102	0.109	0.099	0.091	0.083	0.074	0.075	0.073	0.075	0.067
Phoenix, AZ	0.080	0.087	0.082	0.077	0.076	0.072	0.071	0.075	0.074	0.071
Pittsburgh, PA	0.080	0.095	0.082	0.082	0.075	0.069	0.068	0.066	0.068	0.062
Portland, OR	0.081	0.065	0.059	0.059	0.056	0.064	0.057	0.073	0.062	0.058
Providence, RI	0.106	0.107	0.087	0.090	0.072	0.070	0.075	0.076	0.074	0.064
Provo, UT	0.070	0.068	0.083	0.078	0.070	0.073	0.072	0.073	0.073	0.073
Raleigh, NC	0.093	0.081	0.087	0.082	0.071	0.065	0.069	0.066	0.063	0.064
Reno, NV	0.074	0.069	0.067	0.069	0.068	0.071	0.070	0.068	0.077	0.063
Richmond, VA	0.083	0.089	0.080	0.082	0.079	0.062	0.065	0.063	0.062	0.061
Riverside, CA	0.146	0.129	0.104	0.102	0.093	0.094	0.096	0.099	0.097	0.091
Rochester, MN	n/a	n/a	n/a	n/a	n/a	n/a	n/a	n/a	n/a	n/a
Sacramento, CA	0.088	0.093	0.087	0.087	0.074	0.074	0.077	0.073	0.079	0.068
Salt Lake City, UT	n/a	n/a	n/a	n/a	n/a	n/a	n/a	n/a	n/a	n/a
San Antonio, TX	0.090	0.095	0.078	0.084	0.072	0.079	0.071	0.073	0.072	0.075
San Diego, CA	0.112	0.093	0.084	0.079	0.075	0.070	0.073	0.077	0.069	0.071
San Francisco, CA	0.058	0.074	0.057	0.057	0.061	0.062	0.059	0.060	0.053	0.060
San Jose, CA	0.079	0.085	0.070	0.065	0.073	0.067	0.063	0.065	0.061	0.062
Santa Rosa, CA	0.063	0.071	0.061	0.050	0.053	0.059	0.055	0.062	0.055	0.056
Savannah, GA	n/a	n/a	n/a	n/a	n/a	n/a	n/a	n/a	n/a	n/a
Seattle, WA	0.082	0.062	0.056	0.053	0.053	0.059	0.054	0.076	0.067	0.052
Sioux Falls, SD	n/a	n/a	n/a	n/a	n/a	n/a	n/a	n/a	n/a	n/a
Springfield, IL	n/a	n/a	n/a	n/a	n/a	n/a	n/a	n/a	n/a	n/a
Tallahassee, FL	n/a	n/a	n/a	n/a	n/a	n/a	n/a	n/a	n/a	n/a
Tampa, FL	0.080	0.075	0.081	0.075	0.067	0.062	0.064	0.064	0.065	0.065
Tucson, AZ	0.073	0.078	0.074	0.075	0.068	0.065	0.065	0.070	0.069	0.065
Tulsa, OK	0.086	0.091	0.081	0.072	0.069	0.061	0.064	0.065	0.067	0.062
Tuscaloosa, AL	n/a	n/a	n/a	n/a	n/a	n/a	n/a	n/a	n/a	n/a
Virginia Beach, VA	0.085	0.084	0.083	0.078	0.074	0.061	0.062	0.059	0.061	0.059
Washington, DC	0.088	0.093	0.082	0.081	0.077	0.067	0.069	0.065	0.066	0.061
Wichita, KS	0.077	0.069	0.080	0.074	0.075	0.064	0.062	0.063	0.064	0.062
Winston-Salem, NC	0.084	0.086	0.089	0.080	0.078	0.065	0.069	0.066	0.064	0.062
U.S.	0.088	0.089	0.082	0.080	0.073	0.068	0.069	0.068	0.069	0.065

Note: (1) Data covers the Metropolitan Statistical Area—see Appendix B for areas included; n/a not available. The values shown are the composite ozone concentration averages among trend sites based on the highest fourth daily maximum 8-hour concentration in parts per million. These trends are based on sites having an adequate record of monitoring data during the trend period. Data from exceptional events are included.
Source: U.S. Environmental Protection Agency, Air Quality Monitoring Information, "Air Quality Trends by City, 1990-2019"

Maximum Air Pollutant Concentrations: Particulate Matter, Ozone, CO and Lead

Metro Aea	PM 10 (ug/m³)	PM 2.5 Wtd AM (ug/m³)	PM 2.5 24-Hr (ug/m³)	Ozone (ppm)	Carbon Monoxide (ppm)	Lead (ug/m³)
Albuquerque, NM	141	7.7	20	0.069	1	n/a
Allentown, PA	31	8.5	26	0.065	n/a	0.04
Anchorage, AK	148	8.2	42	n/a	2	n/a
Ann Arbor, MI	n/a	8.5	22	0.060	n/a	n/a
Athens, GA	n/a	9.8	21	0.063	n/a	n/a
Atlanta, GA	40	10.8	24	0.075	2	n/a
Austin, TX	38	9.5	21	0.065	2	n/a
Baton Rouge, LA	51	9.2	23	0.070	1	0
Boise City, ID	83	6.9	25	0.057	1	n/a
Boston, MA	34	7.5	17	0.065	1	n/a
Boulder, CO	52	7.4	36	0.069	n/a	n/a
Cape Coral, FL	51	7.4	14	0.062	n/a	n/a
Cedar Rapids, IA	38	7.9	20	0.060	n/a	n/a
Charleston, SC	54	6.9	14	0.064	n/a	n/a
Charlotte, NC	36	9.5	18	0.074	1	n/a
Chicago, IL	73	10.8	26	0.071	2	0.19
Cincinnati, OH	108	11.9	26	0.072	2	n/a
Clarksville, TN	n/a	n/a	n/a	0.061	n/a	n/a
Cleveland, OH	79	10.8	26	0.071	2	0.01
College Station, TX	n/a	n/a	n/a	n/a	n/a	n/a
Colorado Springs, CO	32	5.0	13	0.065	2	n/a
Columbia, MO	n/a	n/a	n/a	0.058	n/a	n/a
Columbia, SC	35	7.2	15	0.067	1	n/a
Columbus, OH	39	9.7	22	0.068	1	n/a
Dallas, TX	40	9.0	19	0.076	1	0.23
Davenport, IA	129	8.6	22	0.066	1	n/a
Denver, CO	111	10.0	29	0.078	2	n/a
Des Moines, IA	39	7.0	19	0.064	1	n/a
Durham, NC	27	7.7	15	0.063	n/a	n/a
Edison, NJ	34	11.0	24	0.073	2	n/a
El Paso, TX	79	8.5	25	0.075	2	0.01
Fargo, ND	78	6.5	18	0.062	n/a	n/a
Fayetteville, NC	30	7.4	16	0.061	n/a	n/a
Fort Collins, CO	n/a	6.0	20	0.071	1	n/a
Fort Wayne, IN	n/a	9.0	22	0.063	n/a	n/a
Fort Worth, TX	40	9.0	19	0.076	1	0.23
Grand Rapids, MI	104	8.3	24	0.065	1	0.01
Greeley, CO	n/a	9.0	26	0.065	1	n/a
Green Bay, WI	n/a	7.3	19	0.061	n/a	n/a
Greensboro, NC	33	6.8	15	0.064	n/a	n/a
Honolulu, HI	32	3.9	8	0.053	1	n/a
Houston, TX	63	10.7	27	0.081	2	n/a
Huntsville, AL	34	7.4	14	0.063	n/a	n/a
Indianapolis, IN	57	12.6	27	0.067	2	n/a
Jacksonville, FL	57	8.6	20	0.065	1	n/a
Kansas City, MO	71	7.6	17	0.064	1	n/a
Lafayette, LA	52	7.9	17	0.063	n/a	n/a
Lakeland, FL	57	7.7	19	0.067	n/a	n/a
Las Vegas, NV	104	8.0	26	0.070	2	n/a
Lexington, KY	28	8.0	17	0.059	n/a	n/a
Lincoln, NE	n/a	6.5	17	0.056	n/a	n/a
Little Rock, AR	38	10.3	23	0.060	1	n/a
Los Angeles, CA	159	11.0	28	0.101	3	0.02
Louisville, KY	40	10.5	23	0.068	2	n/a
Madison, WI	35	8.0	21	0.059	n/a	n/a

Table continued on following page.

Metro Aea	PM 10 (ug/m^3)	PM 2.5 Wtd AM (ug/m^3)	PM 2.5 24-Hr (ug/m^3)	Ozone (ppm)	Carbon Monoxide (ppm)	Lead (ug/m^3)
Manchester, NH	n/a	3.0	10	0.057	0	n/a
Memphis, TN	54	8.8	19	0.070	1	n/a
Miami, FL	54	8.9	19	0.060	2	n/a
Midland, TX	n/a	n/a	n/a	n/a	n/a	n/a
Milwaukee, WI	58	9.3	24	0.068	1	n/a
Minneapolis, MN	98	8.0	23	0.062	1	0.07
Nashville, TN	32	9.2	18	0.066	1	n/a
New Haven, CT	67	7.7	18	0.084	1	n/a
New Orleans, LA	79	7.8	17	0.063	2	0.09
New York, NY	34	11.0	24	0.073	2	n/a
Oklahoma City, OK	63	10.0	21	0.066	1	n/a
Omaha, NE	50	7.8	22	0.062	2	0.06
Orlando, FL	49	6.9	16	0.072	1	n/a
Peoria, IL	n/a	8.0	19	0.064	n/a	n/a
Philadelphia, PA	49	9.8	26	0.072	2	0
Phoenix, AZ	990	10.9	30	0.076	2	0.05
Pittsburgh, PA	86	12.2	39	0.064	3	0
Portland, OR	32	7.0	25	0.065	1	n/a
Providence, RI	37	8.3	18	0.066	2	n/a
Provo, UT	53	6.1	21	0.066	1	n/a
Raleigh, NC	30	8.9	17	0.064	1	n/a
Reno, NV	78	6.0	16	0.066	2	n/a
Richmond, VA	27	8.4	20	0.064	1	n/a
Riverside, CA	243	12.8	36	0.106	1	0.01
Rochester, MN	n/a	n/a	n/a	0.054	n/a	n/a
Sacramento, CA	90	8.4	30	0.079	1	n/a
Salt Lake City, UT	67	9.0	31	0.073	1	n/a
San Antonio, TX	42	8.9	21	0.075	1	n/a
San Diego, CA	153	13.7	27	0.076	2	0.02
San Francisco, CA	34	9.4	19	0.072	2	n/a
San Jose, CA	75	9.1	21	0.064	2	0.07
Santa Rosa, CA	73	5.7	14	0.056	1	n/a
Savannah, GA	n/a	n/a	n/a	0.060	n/a	n/a
Seattle, WA	22	8.5	28	0.056	1	n/a
Sioux Falls, SD	37	3.9	16	0.065	1	n/a
Springfield, IL	n/a	8.2	18	0.062	n/a	n/a
Tallahassee, FL	n/a	7.7	20	0.063	1	n/a
Tampa, FL	64	7.7	17	0.070	1	0.09
Tucson, AZ	139	3.8	9	0.065	1	n/a
Tulsa, OK	36	8.7	22	0.066	1	0.01
Tuscaloosa, AL	n/a	7.9	15	0.060	n/a	n/a
Virginia Beach, VA	20	7.1	18	0.061	1	n/a
Washington, DC	46	9.1	25	0.075	2	n/a
Wichita, KS	64	7.5	18	0.062	n/a	n/a
Winston-Salem, NC	33	9.5	24	0.065	n/a	n/a
NAAQS[1]	150	15.0	35	0.075	9	0.15

Note: Data from exceptional events are included; Data covers the Metropolitan Statistical Area—see Appendix B for areas included; (1) National Ambient Air Quality Standards; ppm = parts per million; ug/m^3 = micrograms per cubic meter; n/a not available Concentrations: Particulate Matter 10 (coarse particulate)—highest second maximum 24-hour concentration; Particulate Matter 2.5 Wtd AM (fine particulate)—highest weighted annual mean concentration; Particulate Matter 2.5 24-Hour (fine particulate)—highest 98th percentile 24-hour concentration; Ozone—highest fourth daily maximum 8-hour concentration; Carbon Monoxide—highest second maximum non-overlapping 8-hour concentration; Lead—maximum running 3-month average Source: U.S. Environmental Protection Agency, Air Quality Monitoring Information, "Air Quality Statistics by City, 2019"

Maximum Air Pollutant Concentrations: Nitrogen Dioxide and Sulfur Dioxide

Metro Area	Nitrogen Dioxide AM (ppb)	Nitrogen Dioxide 1-Hr (ppb)	Sulfur Dioxide AM (ppb)	Sulfur Dioxide 1-Hr (ppb)	Sulfur Dioxide 24-Hr (ppb)
Albuquerque, NM	9	44	n/a	4	n/a
Allentown, PA	11	43	n/a	6	n/a
Anchorage, AK	n/a	n/a	n/a	n/a	n/a
Ann Arbor, MI	n/a	n/a	n/a	n/a	n/a
Athens, GA	n/a	n/a	n/a	n/a	n/a
Atlanta, GA	16	50	n/a	5	n/a
Austin, TX	12	32	n/a	2	n/a
Baton Rouge, LA	10	45	n/a	16	n/a
Boise City, ID	n/a	n/a	n/a	3	n/a
Boston, MA	14	49	n/a	10	n/a
Boulder, CO	n/a	n/a	n/a	n/a	n/a
Cape Coral, FL	n/a	n/a	n/a	n/a	n/a
Cedar Rapids, IA	n/a	n/a	n/a	25	n/a
Charleston, SC	n/a	n/a	n/a	14	n/a
Charlotte, NC	11	37	n/a	3	n/a
Chicago, IL	17	56	n/a	79	n/a
Cincinnati, OH	18	49	n/a	134	n/a
Clarksville, TN	n/a	n/a	n/a	n/a	n/a
Cleveland, OH	10	45	n/a	23	n/a
College Station, TX	n/a	n/a	n/a	8	n/a
Colorado Springs, CO	n/a	n/a	n/a	10	n/a
Columbia, MO	n/a	n/a	n/a	n/a	n/a
Columbia, SC	3	31	n/a	3	n/a
Columbus, OH	10	42	n/a	n/a	n/a
Dallas, TX	12	46	n/a	7	n/a
Davenport, IA	n/a	n/a	n/a	5	n/a
Denver, CO	27	69	n/a	7	n/a
Des Moines, IA	6	37	n/a	n/a	n/a
Durham, NC	n/a	n/a	n/a	41	n/a
Edison, NJ	21	66	n/a	11	n/a
El Paso, TX	14	n/a	n/a	n/a	n/a
Fargo, ND	4	39	n/a	3	n/a
Fayetteville, NC	n/a	n/a	n/a	n/a	n/a
Fort Collins, CO	n/a	n/a	n/a	n/a	n/a
Fort Wayne, IN	n/a	n/a	n/a	n/a	n/a
Fort Worth, TX	12	46	n/a	7	n/a
Grand Rapids, MI	6	36	n/a	14	n/a
Greeley, CO	n/a	n/a	n/a	n/a	n/a
Green Bay, WI	n/a	n/a	n/a	5	n/a
Greensboro, NC	n/a	n/a	n/a	n/a	n/a
Honolulu, HI	4	28	n/a	62	n/a
Houston, TX	17	56	n/a	14	n/a
Huntsville, AL	n/a	n/a	n/a	n/a	n/a
Indianapolis, IN	9	37	n/a	n/a	n/a
Jacksonville, FL	11	39	n/a	41	n/a
Kansas City, MO	11	47	n/a	7	n/a
Lafayette, LA	n/a	n/a	n/a	n/a	n/a
Lakeland, FL	n/a	n/a	n/a	26	n/a
Las Vegas, NV	24	58	n/a	5	n/a
Lexington, KY	6	42	n/a	4	n/a
Lincoln, NE	n/a	n/a	n/a	33	n/a
Little Rock, AR	8	38	n/a	13	n/a
Los Angeles, CA	23	78	n/a	8	n/a
Louisville, KY	15	49	n/a	15	n/a
Madison, WI	n/a	n/a	n/a	2	n/a

Table continued on following page.

Metro Area	Nitrogen Dioxide AM (ppb)	Nitrogen Dioxide 1-Hr (ppb)	Sulfur Dioxide AM (ppb)	Sulfur Dioxide 1-Hr (ppb)	Sulfur Dioxide 24-Hr (ppb)
Manchester, NH	n/a	n/a	n/a	1	n/a
Memphis, TN	10	40	n/a	2	n/a
Miami, FL	15	48	n/a	1	n/a
Midland, TX	n/a	n/a	n/a	n/a	n/a
Milwaukee, WI	13	47	n/a	4	n/a
Minneapolis, MN	8	41	n/a	10	n/a
Nashville, TN	14	51	n/a	n/a	n/a
New Haven, CT	12	46	n/a	2	n/a
New Orleans, LA	10	43	n/a	53	n/a
New York, NY	21	66	n/a	11	n/a
Oklahoma City, OK	12	n/a	n/a	1	n/a
Omaha, NE	n/a	n/a	n/a	38	n/a
Orlando, FL	4	30	n/a	3	n/a
Peoria, IL	n/a	n/a	n/a	17	n/a
Philadelphia, PA	13	52	n/a	17	n/a
Phoenix, AZ	25	52	n/a	5	n/a
Pittsburgh, PA	10	37	n/a	80	n/a
Portland, OR	11	33	n/a	3	n/a
Providence, RI	17	52	n/a	2	n/a
Provo, UT	9	42	n/a	n/a	n/a
Raleigh, NC	9	34	n/a	2	n/a
Reno, NV	11	46	n/a	3	n/a
Richmond, VA	12	43	n/a	14	n/a
Riverside, CA	29	74	n/a	7	n/a
Rochester, MN	n/a	n/a	n/a	n/a	n/a
Sacramento, CA	12	55	n/a	3	n/a
Salt Lake City, UT	18	55	n/a	13	n/a
San Antonio, TX	7	40	n/a	4	n/a
San Diego, CA	14	47	n/a	1	n/a
San Francisco, CA	15	48	n/a	15	n/a
San Jose, CA	14	52	n/a	2	n/a
Santa Rosa, CA	4	28	n/a	n/a	n/a
Savannah, GA	n/a	n/a	n/a	50	n/a
Seattle, WA	18	57	n/a	6	n/a
Sioux Falls, SD	5	31	n/a	2	n/a
Springfield, IL	n/a	n/a	n/a	n/a	n/a
Tallahassee, FL	n/a	n/a	n/a	n/a	n/a
Tampa, FL	10	37	n/a	11	n/a
Tucson, AZ	7	30	n/a	1	n/a
Tulsa, OK	7	n/a	n/a	6	n/a
Tuscaloosa, AL	n/a	n/a	n/a	n/a	n/a
Virginia Beach, VA	8	40	n/a	3	n/a
Washington, DC	16	49	n/a	5	n/a
Wichita, KS	6	21	n/a	3	n/a
Winston-Salem, NC	7	34	n/a	5	n/a
NAAQS[1]	53	100	30	75	140

Note: Data from exceptional events are included; Data covers the Metropolitan Statistical Area—see Appendix B for areas included; (1) National Ambient Air Quality Standards; ppb = parts per billion; n/a not available
Concentrations: Nitrogen Dioxide AM—highest arithmetic mean concentration; Nitrogen Dioxide 1-Hr—highest 98th percentile 1-hour daily maximum concentration; Sulfur Dioxide AM—highest annual mean concentration; Sulfur Dioxide 1-Hr—highest 99th per centile 1-hour daily maximum concentration; Sulfur Dioxide 24-Hr—highest second maximum 24-hour concentration
Source: U.S. Environmental Protection Agency, Air Quality Monitoring Information, "Air Quality Statistics by City, 2019"

Appendix B: Metropolitan Area Definitions

Metropolitan Statistical Areas (MSA), Metropolitan Divisions (MD), New England City and Town Areas (NECTA), and New England City and Town Area Divisions (NECTAD)

Note: In March 2020, the Office of Management and Budget (OMB) announced changes to metropolitan and micropolitan statistical area definitions. Both current and historical definitions (December 2009) are shown below. If the change only affected the name of the metro area, the counties included were not repeated.

Albuquerque, NM MSA
Bernalillo, Sandoval, Torrance, and Valencia Counties

Allentown-Bethlehem-Easton, PA-NJ MSA
Carbon, Lehigh, and Northampton Counties, PA; Warren County, NJ

Anchorage, AK MSA
Anchorage Municipality and Matanuska-Susitna Borough

Ann Arbor, MI MSA
Washtenaw County

Athens-Clarke County, GA MSA
Clarke, Madison, Oconee, and Oglethorpe Counties

Atlanta-Sandy Springs-Roswell, GA MSA
Barrow, Bartow, Butts, Carroll, Cherokee, Clayton, Cobb, Coweta, Dawson, DeKalb, Douglas, Fayette, Forsyth, Fulton, Gwinnett, Haralson, Heard, Henry, Jasper, Lamar, Meriwether, Morgan, Newton, Paulding, Pickens, Pike, Rockdale, Spalding, and Walton Counties
Previously Atlanta-Sandy Springs-Marietta, GA MSA
Barrow, Bartow, Butts, Carroll, Cherokee, Clayton, Cobb, Coweta, Dawson, DeKalb, Douglas, Fayette, Forsyth, Fulton, Gwinnett, Haralson, Heard, Henry, Jasper, Lamar, Meriwether, Newton, Paulding, Pickens, Pike, Rockdale, Spalding, and Walton Counties

Austin-Round Rock, TX MSA
Previously Austin-Round Rock-San Marcos, TX MSA
Bastrop, Caldwell, Hays, Travis, and Williamson Counties

Baton Rouge, LA MSA
Ascension, East Baton Rouge, East Feliciana, Iberville, Livingston, Pointe Coupee, St. Helena, West Baton Rouge, and West Feliciana Parishes
Previously Baton Rouge, LA MSA
Ascension, East Baton Rouge, Livingston, and West Baton Rouge Parishes

Boise City, ID MSA
Previously Boise City-Nampa, ID MSA
Ada, Boise, Canyon, Gem, and Owyhee Counties

Boston, MA

Boston-Cambridge-Newton, MA-NH MSA
Previously Boston-Cambridge-Quincy, MA-NH MSA
Essex, Middlesex, Norfolk, Plymouth, and Suffolk Counties, MA; Rockingham and Strafford Counties, NH

Boston, MA MD
Previously Boston-Quincy, MA MD
Norfolk, Plymouth, and Suffolk Counties

Boston-Cambridge-Nashua, MA-NH NECTA
Includes 157 cities and towns in Massachusetts and 34 cities and towns in New Hampshire
Previously Boston-Cambridge-Quincy, MA-NH NECTA
Includes 155 cities and towns in Massachusetts and 38 cities and towns in New Hampshire

Boston-Cambridge-Newton, MA NECTA Division
Includes 92 cities and towns in Massachusetts
Previously Boston-Cambridge-Quincy, MA NECTA Division
Includes 97 cities and towns in Massachusetts

Boulder, CO MSA
Boulder County

Cape Coral-Fort Myers, FL MSA
Lee County

Cedar Rapids, IA, MSA
Benton, Jones, and Linn Counties

Charleston-North Charleston, SC MSA
Previously Charleston-North Charleston- Summerville, SC MSA
Berkeley, Charleston, and Dorchester Counties

Charlotte-Concord-Gastonia, NC-SC MSA
Cabarrus, Gaston, Iredell, Lincoln, Mecklenburg, Rowan, and Union Counties, NC; Chester, Lancaster, and York Counties, SC
Previously Charlotte-Gastonia-Rock Hill, NC-SC MSA
Anson, Cabarrus, Gaston, Mecklenburg, and Union Counties, NC; York County, SC

Chicago, IL

Chicago-Naperville-Elgin, IL-IN-WI MSA
Previous name: Chicago-Joliet-Naperville, IL-IN-WI MSA
Cook, DeKalb, DuPage, Grundy, Kane, Kendall, Lake, McHenry, and Will Counties, IL; Jasper, Lake, Newton, and Porter Counties, IN; Kenosha County, WI

Chicago-Naperville-Arlington Heights, IL MD
Cook, DuPage, Grundy, Kendall, McHenry, and Will Counties
Previous name: Chicago-Joliet-Naperville, IL MD
Cook, DeKalb, DuPage, Grundy, Kane, Kendall, McHenry, and Will Counties

Elgin, IL MD
DeKalb and Kane Counties
Previously part of the Chicago-Joliet-Naperville, IL MD

Gary, IN MD
Jasper, Lake, Newton, and Porter Counties

Lake County-Kenosha County, IL-WI MD
Lake County, IL; Kenosha County, WI

Cincinnati, OH-KY-IN MSA
Brown, Butler, Clermont, Hamilton, and Warren Counties, OH; Boone, Bracken, Campbell, Gallatin, Grant, Kenton, and Pendleton County, KY; Dearborn, Franklin, Ohio, and Union Counties, IN
Previously Cincinnati-Middletown, OH-KY-IN MSA
Brown, Butler, Clermont, Hamilton, and Warren Counties, OH; Boone, Bracken, Campbell, Gallatin, Grant, Kenton, and Pendleton County, KY; Dearborn, Franklin, and Ohio Counties, IN

Clarksville, TN-KY MSA
Montgomery and Stewart Counties, TN; Christian and Trigg Counties, KY

Cleveland-Elyria-Mentor, OH MSA
Cuyahoga, Geauga, Lake, Lorain, and Medina Counties

College Station-Bryan, TX MSA
Brazos, Burleson and Robertson Counties

Colorado Springs, CO MSA
El Paso and Teller Counties

Columbia, MO MSA
Boone and Howard Counties

Columbia, SC MSA
Calhoun, Fairfield, Kershaw, Lexington, Richland and Saluda Counties

Columbus, OH MSA
Delaware, Fairfield, Franklin, Licking, Madison, Morrow, Pickaway, and Union Counties

Dallas, TX

Dallas-Fort Worth-Arlington, TX MSA
Collin, Dallas, Denton, Ellis, Hunt, Johnson, Kaufman, Parker, Rockwall, Tarrant, and Wise Counties

Dallas-Plano-Irving, TX MD
Collin, Dallas, Denton, Ellis, Hunt, Kaufman, and Rockwall Counties

Davenport-Moline-Rock Island, IA-IL MSA
Henry, Mercer, and Rock Island Counties, IA; Scott County

Denver-Aurora-Lakewood, CO MSA
Previously Denver-Aurora-Broomfield, CO MSA
Adams, Arapahoe, Broomfield, Clear Creek, Denver, Douglas, Elbert, Gilpin, Jefferson, and Park Counties

Des Moines-West Des Moines, IA MSA
Dallas, Guthrie, Madison, Polk, and Warren Counties

Durham-Chapel Hill, NC MSA
Chatham, Durham, Orange, and Person Counties

Edison, NJ
See New York, NY (New York-Jersey City-White Plains, NY-NJ MD)

El Paso, TX MSA
El Paso County

Fargo, ND-MN MSA
Cass County, ND; Clay County, MN

Fayetteville, NC MSA
Cumberland, and Hoke Counties

Fort Collins, CO MSA
Previously Fort Collins-Loveland, CO MSA
Larimer County

Fort Wayne, IN MSA
Allen, Wells, and Whitley Counties

Fort Worth, TX

Dallas-Fort Worth-Arlington, TX MSA
Collin, Dallas, Denton, Ellis, Hunt, Johnson, Kaufman, Parker, Rockwall, Tarrant, and Wise Counties

Fort Worth-Arlington, TX MD
Hood, Johnson, Parker, Somervell, Tarrant, and Wise Counties

Grand Rapids-Wyoming, MI MSA
Barry, Kent, Montcalm, and Ottawa Counties
Previously Grand Rapids-Wyoming, MI MSA
Barry, Ionia, Kent, and Newaygo Counties

Greeley, CO MSA
Weld County

Green Bay, WI MSA
Brown, Kewaunee, and Oconto Counties

Greensboro-High Point, NC MSA
Guilford, Randolph, and Rockingham Counties

Honolulu, HI MSA
Honolulu County

Houston-The Woodlands-Sugar Land-Baytown, TX MSA
Austin, Brazoria, Chambers, Fort Bend, Galveston, Harris, Liberty, Montgomery, and Waller Counties
Previously Houston-Sugar Land-Baytown, TX MSA
Austin, Brazoria, Chambers, Fort Bend, Galveston, Harris, Liberty, Montgomery, San Jacinto, and Waller Counties

Huntsville, AL MSA
Limestone and Madison Counties

Indianapolis-Carmel, IN MSA
Boone, Brown, Hamilton, Hancock, Hendricks, Johnson, Marion, Morgan, Putnam, and Shelby Counties

Jacksonville, FL MSA
Baker, Clay, Duval, Nassau, and St. Johns Counties

Kansas City, MO-KS MSA
Franklin, Johnson, Leavenworth, Linn, Miami, and Wyandotte Counties, KS; Bates, Caldwell, Cass, Clay, Clinton, Jackson, Lafayette, Platte, and Ray Counties, MO

Lafayette, LA MSA
Acadia, Iberia, Lafayette, St. Martin, and Vermilion Parishes

Lakeland-Winter Haven, FL MSA
Polk County

Las Vegas-Henderson-Paradise, NV MSA
Previously Las Vegas-Paradise, NV MSA
Clark County

Lexington-Fayette, KY MSA
Bourbon, Clark, Fayette, Jessamine, Scott, and Woodford Counties

Lincoln, NE MSA
Lancaster and Seward Counties

Little Rock-North Little Rock-Conway, AR MSA
Faulkner, Grant, Lonoke, Perry, Pulaski, and Saline Counties

Los Angeles, CA

Los Angeles-Long Beach-Anaheim, CA MSA
Previously Los Angeles-Long Beach-Santa Ana, CA MSA
Los Angeles and Orange Counties

Los Angeles-Long Beach-Glendale, CA MD
Los Angeles County

Anaheim-Santa Ana-Irvine, CA MD
Previously Santa Ana-Anaheim-Irvine, CA MD
Orange County

Louisville/Jefferson, KY-IN MSA
Clark, Floyd, Harrison, Scott, and Washington Counties, IN; Bullitt, Henry, Jefferson, Oldham, Shelby, Spencer, and Trimble Counties, KY

Madison, WI MSA
Columbia, Dane, and Iowa Counties

Manchester, NH

Manchester-Nashua, NH MSA
Hillsborough County

Manchester, NH NECTA
Includes 11 cities and towns in New Hampshire
Previously Manchester, NH NECTA
Includes 9 cities and towns in New Hampshire

Memphis, TN-AR-MS MSA
Fayette, Shelby and Tipton Counties, TN; Crittenden County, AR; DeSoto, Marshall, Tate and Tunica Counties, MS

Miami, FL

Miami-Fort Lauderdale-West Palm Beach, FL MSA
Previously Miami-Fort Lauderdale-Pompano Beach, FL MSA
Broward, Miami-Dade, and Palm Beach Counties

Miami-Miami Beach-Kendall, FL MD
Miami-Dade County

Midland, TX MSA
Martin, and Midland Counties

Milwaukee-Waukesha-West Allis, WI MSA
Milwaukee, Ozaukee, Washington, and Waukesha Counties

Minneapolis-St. Paul-Bloomington, MN-WI MSA
Anoka, Carver, Chisago, Dakota, Hennepin, Isanti, Le Sueur, Mille Lacs, Ramsey, Scott, Sherburne, Sibley, Washington, and Wright Counties, MN; Pierce and St. Croix Counties, WI

Nashville-Davidson-Murfreesboro-Franklin, TN MSA
Cannon, Cheatham, Davidson, Dickson, Hickman, Macon, Robertson, Rutherford, Smith, Sumner, Trousdale, Williamson, and Wilson Counties

New Haven-Milford, CT MSA
New Haven County

New Orleans-Metarie-Kenner, LA MSA
Jefferson, Orleans, Plaquemines, St. Bernard, St. Charles, St. James, St. John the Baptist, and St. Tammany Parish
Previously New Orleans-Metarie-Kenner, LA MSA
Jefferson, Orleans, Plaquemines, St. Bernard, St. Charles, St. John the Baptist, and St. Tammany Parish

New York, NY

New York-Newark-Jersey City, NY-NJ-PA MSA
Bergen, Essex, Hudson, Hunterdon, Middlesex, Monmouth, Morris, Ocean, Passaic, Somerset, Sussex, and Union Counties, NJ; Bronx, Dutchess, Kings, Nassau, New York, Orange, Putnam, Queens, Richmond, Rockland, Suffolk, and Westchester Counties, NY; Pike County, PA
Previous name: New York-Northern New Jersey-Long Island, NY-NJ-PA MSA
Bergen, Essex, Hudson, Hunterdon, Middlesex, Monmouth, Morris, Ocean, Passaic, Somerset, Sussex, and Union Counties, NJ; Bronx, Kings, Nassau, New York, Putnam, Queens, Richmond, Rockland, Suffolk, and Westchester Counties, NY; Pike County, PA

Dutchess County-Putnam County, NY MD
Dutchess and Putnam Counties
Dutchess County was previously part of the Poughkeepsie-Newburgh-Middletown, NY MSA. Putnam County was previously part of the New York-Wayne-White Plains, NY-NJ MD

Nassau-Suffolk, NY MD
Nassau and Suffolk Counties

New York-Jersey City-White Plains, NY-NJ MD
Bergen, Hudson, Middlesex, Monmouth, Ocean, and Passaic Counties, NJ; Bronx, Kings, New York, Orange, Queens, Richmond, Rockland, and Westchester Counties, NY
Previous name: New York-Wayne-White Plains, NY-NJ MD
Bergen, Hudson, and Passaic Counties, NJ; Bronx, Kings, New York, Putnam, Queens, Richmond, Rockland, and Westchester Counties, NY

Newark, NJ-PA MD
Essex, Hunterdon, Morris, Somerset, Sussex, and Union Counties, NJ; Pike County, PA
Previous name: Newark-Union, NJ-PA MD
Essex, Hunterdon, Morris, Sussex, and Union Counties, NJ; Pike County, PA

Oklahoma City, OK MSA
Canadian, Cleveland, Grady, Lincoln, Logan, McClain, and Oklahoma Counties

Omaha-Council Bluffs, NE-IA MSA
Harrison, Mills, and Pottawattamie Counties, IA; Cass, Douglas, Sarpy, Saunders, and Washington Counties, NE

Orlando-Kissimmee-Sanford, FL MSA
Lake, Orange, Osceola, and Seminole Counties

Peoria, IL MSA
Marshall, Peoria, Stark, Tazewell, and Woodford Counties

Philadelphia, PA

Philadelphia-Camden-Wilmington, PA-NJ-DE-MD MSA
New Castle County, DE; Cecil County, MD; Burlington, Camden, Gloucester, and Salem Counties, NJ; Bucks, Chester, Delaware, Montgomery, and Philadelphia Counties, PA

Camden, NJ MD
Burlington, Camden, and Gloucester Counties

Montgomery County-Bucks County-Chester County, PA MD
Bucks, Chester, and Montgomery Counties
Previously part of the Philadelphia, PA MD

Philadelphia, PA MD
Delaware and Philadelphia Counties
Previous name: Philadelphia, PA MD
Bucks, Chester, Delaware, Montgomery, and Philadelphia Counties

Wilmington, DE-MD-NJ MD
New Castle County, DE; Cecil County, MD; Salem County, NJ

Phoenix-Mesa-Scottsdale, AZ MSA
Previously Phoenix-Mesa-Glendale, AZ MSA
Maricopa and Pinal Counties

Pittsburgh, PA MSA
Allegheny, Armstrong, Beaver, Butler, Fayette, Washington, and Westmoreland Counties

Portland-Vancouver-Hillsboro, OR-WA MSA
Clackamas, Columbia, Multnomah, Washington, and Yamhill Counties, OR; Clark and Skamania Counties, WA

Providence, RI

Providence-New Bedford-Fall River, RI-MA MSA
Previously Providence-New Bedford-Fall River, RI-MA MSA
Bristol County, MA; Bristol, Kent, Newport, Providence, and
Washington Counties, RI

Providence-Warwick, RI-MA NECTA
Includes 12 cities and towns in Massachusetts and 36 cities and towns
in Rhode Island
Previously Providence-Fall River-Warwick, RI-MA NECTA
Includes 12 cities and towns in Massachusetts and 37 cities and towns
in Rhode Island

Provo-Orem, UT MSA
Juab and Utah Counties

Raleigh, NC MSA
Previously Raleigh-Cary, NC MSA
Franklin, Johnston, and Wake Counties

Reno, NV MSA
Previously Reno-Sparks, NV MSA
Storey and Washoe Counties

Richmond, VA MSA
Amelia, Caroline, Charles City, Chesterfield, Dinwiddie, Goochland,
Hanover, Henrico, King William, New Kent, Powhatan, Prince
George, and Sussex Counties; Colonial Heights, Hopewell,
Petersburg, and Richmond Cities

Riverside-San Bernardino-Ontario, CA MSA
Riverside and San Bernardino Counties

Rochester, MN MSA
Dodge, Fillmore, Olmsted, and Wabasha Counties

Sacramento—Roseville—Arden-Arcade, CA MSA
El Dorado, Placer, Sacramento, and Yolo Counties

Salt Lake City, UT MSA
Salt Lake and Tooele Counties

San Antonio-New Braunfels, TX MSA
Atascosa, Bandera, Bexar, Comal, Guadalupe, Kendall, Medina, and
Wilson Counties

San Diego-Carlsbad, CA MSA
Previously San Diego-Carlsbad-San Marcos, CA MSA
San Diego County

San Francisco, CA

San Francisco-Oakland-Hayward, CA MSA
Previously San Francisco-Oakland- Fremont, CA MSA
Alameda, Contra Costa, Marin, San Francisco, and San Mateo Counties

San Francisco-Redwood City-South San Francisco, CA MD
San Francisco and San Mateo Counties

Previously San Francisco-San Mateo-Redwood City, CA MD
Marin, San Francisco, and San Mateo Counties

San Jose-Sunnyvale-Santa Clara, CA MSA
San Benito and Santa Clara Counties

Santa Rosa, CA MSA
Previously Santa Rosa-Petaluma, CA MSA
Sonoma County

Savannah, GA MSA
Bryan, Chatham, and Effingham Counties

Seattle, WA

Seattle-Tacoma-Bellevue, WA MSA
King, Pierce, and Snohomish Counties

Seattle-Bellevue-Everett, WA MD
King and Snohomish Counties

Sioux Falls, SD MSA
Lincoln, McCook, Minnehaha, and Turner Counties

Springfield, IL MSA
Menard and Sangamon Counties

Tallahassee, FL MSA
Gadsden, Jefferson, Leon, and Wakulla Counties

Tampa-St. Petersburg-Clearwater, FL MSA
Hernando, Hillsborough, Pasco, and Pinellas Counties

Tucson, AZ MSA
Pima County

Tulsa, OK MSA
Creek, Okmulgee, Osage, Pawnee, Rogers, Tulsa, and Wagoner
Counties

Tuscaloosa, AL MSA
Hale, Pickens, and Tuscaloosa Counties

Virginia Beach-Norfolk-Newport News, VA-NC MSA
Currituck County, NC; Chesapeake, Hampton, Newport News,
Norfolk, Poquoson, Portsmouth, Suffolk, Virginia Beach and
Williamsburg cities, VA; Gloucester, Isle of Wight, James City,
Mathews, Surry, and York Counties, VA

Washington, DC

Washington-Arlington-Alexandria, DC-VA-MD-WV MSA
District of Columbia; Calvert, Charles, Frederick, Montgomery, and
Prince George's Counties, MD; Alexandria, Fairfax, Falls Church,
Fredericksburg, Manassas Park, and Manassas cities, VA; Arlington,
Clarke, Culpepper, Fairfax, Fauquier, Loudoun, Prince William,
Rappahannock, Spotsylvania, Stafford, and Warren Counties, VA;
Jefferson County, WV
Previously Washington-Arlington-Alexandria, DC-VA-MD-WV MSA
District of Columbia; Calvert, Charles, Frederick, Montgomery, and
Prince George's Counties, MD; Alexandria, Fairfax, Falls Church,
Fredericksburg, Manassas Park, and Manassas cities, VA; Arlington,
Clarke, Fairfax, Fauquier, Loudoun, Prince William, Spotsylvania,
Stafford, and Warren Counties, VA; Jefferson County, WV

Washington-Arlington-Alexandria, DC-VA-MD-WV MD
District of Columbia; Calvert, Charles, and Prince George's Counties,
MD; Alexandria, Fairfax, Falls Church, Fredericksburg, Manassas
Park, and Manassas cities, VA; Arlington, Clarke, Culpepper, Fairfax,
Fauquier, Loudoun, Prince William, Rappahannock, Spotsylvania,
Stafford, and Warren Counties, VA; Jefferson County, WV
Previously Washington-Arlington-Alexandria, DC-VA-MD-WV MD
District of Columbia; Calvert, Charles, and Prince George's Counties,
MD; Alexandria, Fairfax, Falls Church, Fredericksburg, Manassas
Park, and Manassas cities, VA; Arlington, Clarke, Fairfax, Fauquier,
Loudoun, Prince William, Spotsylvania, Stafford, and Warren
Counties, VA; Jefferson County, WV

Wichita, KS MSA
Butler, Harvey, Kingman, Sedgwick, and Sumner Counties

Winston-Salem, NC MSA
Davidson, Davie, Forsyth, Stokes, and Yadkin Counties

Appendix C: Government Type and Primary County

This appendix includes the government structure of each place included in this book. It also includes the county or county equivalent in which each place is located. If a place spans more than one county, the county in which the majority of the population resides is shown.

Albuquerque, NM
Government Type: City
County: Bernalillo

Allentown, PA
Government Type: City
County: Lehigh

Anchorage, AK
Government Type: Municipality
Borough: Anchorage

Ann Arbor, MI
Government Type: City
County: Washtenaw

Athens, GA
Government Type: Consolidated
city-county
County: Clarke

Atlanta, GA
Government Type: City
County: Fulton

Austin, TX
Government Type: City
County: Travis

Baton Rouge, LA
Government Type: Consolidated city-parish
Parish: East Baton Rouge

Boise City, ID
Government Type: City
County: Ada

Boston, MA
Government Type: City
County: Suffolk

Boulder, CO
Government Type: City
County: Boulder

Cape Coral, FL
Government Type: City
County: Lee

Cedar Rapids, IA
Government Type: City
County: Linn

Charleston, SC
Government Type: City
County: Charleston

Charlotte, NC
Government Type: City
County: Mecklenburg

Chicago, IL
Government Type: City
County: Cook

Cincinnati, OH
Government Type: City
County: Hamilton

Clarksville, TN
Government Type: City
County: Montgomery

Cleveland, OH
Government Type: City
County: Cuyahoga

College Station, TX
Government Type: City
County: Brazos

Colorado Springs, CO
Government Type: City
County: El Paso

Columbia, MO
Government Type: City
County: Boone

Columbia, SC
Government Type: City
County: Richland

Columbus, OH
Government Type: City
County: Franklin

Dallas, TX
Government Type: City
County: Dallas

Davenport, IA
Government Type: City
County: Scott

Denver, CO
Government Type: City
County: Denver

Des Moines, IA
Government Type: City
County: Polk

Durham, NC
Government Type: City
County: Durham

Edison, NJ
Government Type: Township
County: Middlesex

El Paso, TX
Government Type: City
County: El Paso

Fargo, ND
Government Type: City
County: Cass

Fayetteville, NC
Government Type: City
County: Cumberland

Fort Collins, CO
Government Type: City
County: Larimer

Fort Wayne, IN
Government Type: City
County: Allen

Fort Worth, TX
Government Type: City
County: Tarrant

Grand Rapids, MI
Government Type: City
County: Kent

Greeley, CO
Government Type: City
County: Weld

Green Bay, WI
Government Type: City
County: Brown

Greensboro, NC
Government Type: City
County: Guilford

Honolulu, HI
Government Type: Census Designated Place
(CDP)
County: Honolulu

Houston, TX
Government Type: City
County: Harris

Huntsville, AL
Government Type: City
County: Madison

Indianapolis, IN
Government Type: City
County: Marion

Jacksonville, FL
Government Type: City
County: Duval

Kansas City, MO
Government Type: City
County: Jackson

Lafayette, LA
Government Type: City
Parish: Lafayette

Lakeland, FL
Government Type: City
County: Polk

Las Vegas, NV
Government Type: City
County: Clark

Lexington, KY
Government Type: Consolidated city-county
County: Fayette

Lincoln, NE
Government Type: City
County: Lancaster

Little Rock, AR
Government Type: City
County: Pulaski

Los Angeles, CA
Government Type: City
County: Los Angeles

Louisville, KY
Government Type: Consolidated city-county
County: Jefferson

Madison, WI
Government Type: City
County: Dane

Manchester, NH
Government Type: City
County: Hillsborough

Memphis, TN
Government Type: City
County: Shelby

Miami, FL
Government Type: City
County: Miami-Dade

Midland, TX
Government Type: City
County: Midland

Milwaukee, WI
Government Type: City
County: Milwaukee

Minneapolis, MN
Government Type: City
County: Hennepin

Nashville, TN
Government Type: Consolidated city-county
County: Davidson

New Haven, CT
Government Type: City
County: New Haven

New Orleans, LA
Government Type: City
Parish: Orleans

New York, NY
Government Type: City
Counties: Bronx; Kings; New York; Queens;
   Staten Island

Oklahoma City, OK
Government Type: City
County: Oklahoma

Omaha, NE
Government Type: City
County: Douglas

Orlando, FL
Government Type: City
County: Orange

Peoria, IL
Government Type: City
County: Peoria

Philadelphia, PA
Government Type: City
County: Philadelphia

Phoenix, AZ
Government Type: City
County: Maricopa

Pittsburgh, PA
Government Type: City
County: Allegheny

Portland, OR
Government Type: City
County: Multnomah

Providence, RI
Government Type: City
County: Providence

Provo, UT
Government Type: City
County: Utah

Raleigh, NC
Government Type: City
County: Wake

Reno, NV
Government Type: City
County: Washoe

Richmond, VA
Government Type: Independent city
County: Richmond city

Riverside, CA
Government Type: City
County: Riverside

Rochester, MN
Government Type: City
County: Olmsted

Sacramento, CA
Government Type: City
County: Sacramento

Salt Lake City, UT
Government Type: City
County: Salt Lake

San Antonio, TX
Government Type: City
County: Bexar

San Diego, CA
Government Type: City
County: San Diego

San Francisco, CA
Government Type: City
County: San Francisco

San Jose, CA
Government Type: City
County: Santa Clara

Santa Rosa, CA
Government Type: City
County: Sonoma

Savannah, GA
Government Type: City
County: Chatham

Seattle, WA
Government Type: City
County: King

Sioux Falls, SD
Government Type: City
County: Minnehaha

Springfield, IL
Government Type: City
County: Sangamon

Tallahassee, FL
Government Type: City
County: Leon

Tampa, FL
Government Type: City
County: Hillsborough

Tucson, AZ
Government Type: City
County: Pima

Tulsa, OK
Government Type: City
County: Tulsa

Tuscaloosa, AL
Government Type: City
County: Tuscaloosa

Virginia Beach, VA
Government Type: Independent city
County: Virginia Beach city

Washington, DC
Government Type: City
County: District of Columbia

Wichita, KS
Government Type: City
County: Sedgwick

Winston-Salem, NC
Government Type: City
County: Forsyth

Appendix D: Chambers of Commerce

Albuquerque, NM
Albuquerque Chamber of Commerce
P.O. Box 25100
Albuquerque, NM 87125
Phone: (505) 764-3700
Fax: (505) 764-3714
http://www.abqchamber.com

Albuquerque Economic Development Dept
851 University Blvd SE, Suite 203
Albuquerque, NM 87106
Phone: (505) 246-6200
Fax: (505) 246-6219
http://www.cabq.gov/econdev

Allentown, PA
Greater Lehigh Valley Chamber of
Commerce
Allentown Office
840 Hamilton Street, Suite 205
Allentown, PA 18101
Phone: (610) 751-4929
Fax: (610) 437-4907
http://www.lehighvalleychamber.org

Anchorage, AK
Anchorage Chamber of Commerce
1016 W Sixth Avenue
Suite 303
Anchorage, AK 99501
Phone: (907) 272-2401
Fax: (907) 272-4117
http://www.anchoragechamber.org

Anchorage Economic Development
Department
900 W 5th Avenue
Suite 300
Anchorage, AK 99501
Phone: (907) 258-3700
Fax: (907) 258-6646
http://aedcweb.com

Ann Arbor, MI
Ann Arbor Area Chamber of Commerce
115 West Huron
3rd Floor
Ann Arbor, MI 48104
Phone: (734) 665-4433
Fax: (734) 665-4191
http://www.annarborchamber.org

Ann Arbor Economic Development
Department
201 S Division
Suite 430
Ann Arbor, MI 48104
Phone: (734) 761-9317
http://www.annarborspark.org

Athens, GA
Athens Area Chamber of Commerce
246 W Hancock Avenue
Athens, GA 30601
Phone: (706) 549-6800
Fax: (706) 549-5636
http://www.aacoc.org

Athens-Clarke County Economic
Development Department
246 W. Hancock Avenue
Athens, GA 30601
Phone: (706) 613-3233
Fax: (706) 613-3812
http://www.athensbusiness.org

Atlanta, GA
Metro Atlanta Chamber of Commerce
235 Andrew Young International Blvd NW
Atlanta, GA 30303
Phone: (404) 880-9000
Fax: (404) 586-8464
http://www.metroatlantachamber.com

Austin, TX
Greater Austin Chamber of Commerce
210 Barton Springs Road
Suite 400
Austin, TX 78704
Phone: (512) 478-9383
Fax: (512) 478-6389
http://www.austin-chamber.org

Baton Rouge, LA
Baton Rouge Area Chamber
451 Florida Street
Suite 1050
Baton Rouge, LA 70801
Phone (225) 381-7125
http://www.brac.org

Boise City, ID
Boise Metro Chamber of Commerce
250 S 5th Street
Suite 800
Boise City, ID 83701
Phone: (208) 472-5200
Fax: (208) 472-5201
http://www.boisechamber.org

Boston, MA
Greater Boston Chamber of Commerce
265 Franklin Street
12th Floor
Boston, MA 02110
Phone: (617) 227-4500
Fax: (617) 227-7505
http://www.bostonchamber.com

Boulder, CO
Boulder Chamber of Commerce
2440 Pearl Street
Boulder, CO 80302
Phone: (303) 442-1044
Fax: (303) 938-8837
http://www.boulderchamber.com

City of Boulder Economic Vitality Program
P.O. Box 791
Boulder, CO 80306
Phone: (303) 441-3090
http://www.bouldercolorado.gov

Cape Coral, FL
Chamber of Commerce of Cape Coral
2051 Cape Coral Parkway East
Cape Coral, FL 33904
Phone: (239) 549-6900
Fax: (239) 549-9609
http://www.capecoralchamber.com

Cedar Rapids, IA
Cedar Rapids Chamber of Commerce
424 First Avenue NE
Cedar Rapids, IA 52401
Phone: (319) 398-5317
Fax: (319) 398-5228
http://www.cedarrapids.org

Cedar Rapids Economic Development
50 Second Avenue Bridge
Sixth Floor
Cedar Rapids, IA 52401-1256
Phone: (319) 286-5041
Fax: (319) 286-5141
http://www.cedar-rapids.org

Charleston, SC
Charleston Metro Chamber of Commerce
P.O. Box 975
Charleston, SC 29402
Phone: (843) 577-2510
http://www.charlestonchamber.net

Charlotte, NC
Charlotte Chamber of Commerce
330 S Tryon Street
P.O. Box 32785
Charlotte, NC 28232
Phone: (704) 378-1300
Fax: (704) 374-1903
http://www.charlottechamber.com

Charlotte Regional Partnership
1001 Morehead Square Drive
Suite 200
Charlotte, NC 28203
Phone: (704) 347-8942
Fax: (704) 347-8981
http://www.charlotteusa.com

Chicago, IL
Chicagoland Chamber of Commerce
200 E Randolph Street
Suite 2200
Chicago, IL 60601-6436
Phone: (312) 494-6700
Fax: (312) 861-0660
http://www.chicagolandchamber.org

City of Chicago Department of Planning
and Development
City Hall, Room 1000
121 North La Salle Street
Chicago, IL 60602
Phone: (312) 744-4190
Fax: (312) 744-2271
https://www.cityofchicago.org/city/en/
depts/dcd.html

Cincinnati, OH
Cincinnati USA Regional Chamber
3 East 4th Street
Suite 200
Cincinnati, Ohio 45202
Phone: (513) 579-3111
https://www.cincinnatichamber.com

Clarksville, TN
Clarksville Area Chamber of Commerce
25 Jefferson Street
Suite 300
Clarksville, TN 37040
Phone: (931) 647-2331
http://www.clarksvillechamber.com

Cleveland, OH
Greater Cleveland Partnership
1240 Huron Rd. E
Suite 300
Cleveland, OH 44115
Phone: (216) 621-3300
https://www.gcpartnership.com

College Station, TX
Bryan-College Station Chamber of
Commerce
4001 East 29th St, Suite 175
Bryan, TX 77802
Phone: (979) 260-5200
http://www.bcschamber.org

Colorado Springs, CO
Colorado Springs Chamber and EDC
102 South Tejon Street
Suite 430
Colorado Springs, CO 80903
Phone: (719) 471-8183
https://coloradospringschamberedc.com

Columbia, MO
Columbia Chamber of Commerce
300 South Providence Rd.
P.O. Box 1016
Columbia, MO 65205-1016
Phone: (573) 874-1132
Fax: (573) 443-3986
http://www.columbiamochamber.com

Columbia, SC
The Columbia Chamber
930 Richland Street
Columbia, SC 29201
Phone: (803) 733-1110
Fax: (803) 733-1113
http://www.columbiachamber.com

Columbus, OH
Greater Columbus Chamber
37 North High Street
Columbus, OH 43215
Phone: (614) 221-1321
Fax: (614) 221-1408
http://www.columbus.org

Dallas, TX
City of Dallas Economic Development
Department
1500 Marilla Street
5C South
Dallas, TX 75201
Phone: (214) 670-1685
Fax: (214) 670-0158
http://www.dallas-edd.org

Greater Dallas Chamber of Commerce
700 North Pearl Street
Suite1200
Dallas, TX 75201
Phone: (214) 746-6600
Fax: (214) 746-6799
http://www.dallaschamber.org

Davenport, IA
Quad Cities Chamber
331 W. 3rd Street
Suite 100
Davenport, IA 52801
Phone: (563) 322-1706
https://quadcitieschamber.com

Denver, CO
Denver Metro Chamber of Commerce
1445 Market Street
Denver, CO 80202
Phone: (303) 534-8500
Fax: (303) 534-3200
http://www.denverchamber.org

Downtown Denver Partnership
511 16th Street
Suite 200
Denver, CO 80202
Phone: (303) 534-6161
Fax: (303) 534-2803
http://www.downtowndenver.com

Des Moines, IA
Des Moines Downtown Chamber
301 Grand Ave
Des Moines, IA 50309
Phone: (515) 309-3229
http://desmoinesdowntownchamber.com

Greater Des Moines Partnership
700 Locust Street
Suite 100
Des Moines, IA 50309
Phone: (515) 286-4950
Fax: (515) 286-4974
http://www.desmoinesmetro.com

Durham, NC
Durham Chamber of Commerce
P.O. Box 3829
Durham, NC 27702
Phone: (919) 682-2133
Fax: (919) 688-8351
http://www.durhamchamber.org

North Carolina Institute of Minority
Economic Development
114 W Parish Street
Durham, NC 27701
Phone: (919) 956-8889
Fax: (919) 688-7668
http://www.ncimed.com

Edison, NJ
Edison Chamber of Commerce
939 Amboy Avenue
Edison, NJ 08837
Phone: (732) 738-9482
http://www.edisonchamber.com

El Paso, TX
City of El Paso Department of Economic
Development
2 Civic Center Plaza
El Paso, TX 79901
Phone: (915) 541-4000
Fax: (915) 541-1316
http://www.elpasotexas.gov

Greater El Paso Chamber of Commerce
10 Civic Center Plaza
El Paso, TX 79901
Phone: (915) 534-0500
Fax: (915) 534-0510
http://www.elpaso.org

Southwest Indiana Chamber
318 Main Street
Suite 401
Evansville, IN 47708
Phone: (812) 425-8147
Fax: (812) 421-5883
https://swinchamber.com

Fargo, ND
Chamber of Commerce of Fargo Moorhead
202 First Avenue North
Fargo, ND 56560
Phone: (218) 233-1100
Fax: (218) 233-1200
http://www.fmchamber.com

Greater Fargo-Moorhead Economic
Development Corporation
51 Broadway, Suite 500
Fargo, ND 58102
Phone: (701) 364-1900
Fax: (701) 293-7819
http://www.gfmedc.com

Fayetteville, NC
Fayetteville Regional Chamber
1019 Hay Street
Fayetteville, NC 28305
Phone: (910) 483-8133
Fax: (910) 483-0263
http://www.fayettevillencchamber.org

Fort Collins, CO
Fort Collins Chamber of Commerce
225 South Meldrum
Fort Collins, CO 80521
Phone: (970) 482-3746
Fax: (970) 482-3774
https://fortcollinschamber.com

Fort Wayne, IN
City of Fort Wayne Economic Development
1 Main St
1 Main Street
Fort Wayne, IN 46802
Phone: (260) 427-1111
Fax: (260) 427-1375
http://www.cityoffortwayne.org

Greater Fort Wayne Chamber of Commerce
826 Ewing Street
Fort Wayne, IN 46802
Phone: (260) 424-1435
Fax: (260) 426-7232
http://www.fwchamber.org

Fort Worth, TX
City of Fort Worth Economic Development
City Hall
900 Monroe Street
Suite 301
Fort Worth, TX 76102
Phone: (817) 392-6103
Fax: (817) 392-2431
http://www.fortworthgov.org

Fort Worth Chamber of Commerce
777 Taylor Street
Suite 900
Fort Worth, TX 76102-4997
Phone: (817) 336-2491
Fax: (817) 877-4034
http://www.fortworthchamber.com

Grand Rapids, MI
Grands Rapids Area Chamber of Commerce
111 Pearl Street N.W.
Grand Rapids, MI 49503
Phone: (616) 771-0300
Fax: (616) 771-0318
http://www.grandrapids.org

Greeley, CO
Greeley Chamber of Commerce
902 7th Avenue
Greeley, CO 80631
Phone: (970) 352-3566
https://greeleychamber.com

Green Bay, WI
Economic Development
100 N Jefferson St
Room 202
Green Bay, WI 54301
Phone: (920) 448-3397
Fax: (920) 448-3063
http://www.ci.green-bay.wi.us

Green Bay Area Chamber of Commerce
300 N. Broadway
Suite 3A
Green Bay, WI 54305-1660
Phone: (920) 437-8704
Fax: (920) 593-3468
http://www.titletown.org

Greensboro, NC
Greensboro Area Chamber of Commerce
342 N. Elm Street
Greensboro, NC 27401
Phone: (336) 387-8301
Fax: (336) 275-9299
http://www.greensboro.org

Honolulu, HI
The Chamber of Commerce of Hawaii
1132 Bishop Street
Suite 402
Honolulu, HI 96813
Phone: (808) 545-4300
Fax: (808) 545-4369
http://www.cochawaii.com

Houston, TX
Greater Houston Partnership
1200 Smith Street
Suite 700
Houston, TX 77002-4400
Phone: (713) 844-3600
Fax: (713) 844-0200
http://www.houston.org

Huntsville, AL
Chamber of Commerce of
Huntsville/Madison County
225 Church Street
Huntsville, AL 35801
Phone: (256) 535-2000
Fax: (256) 535-2015
http://www.huntsvillealabamausa.com

Indianapolis, IN
Greater Indianapolis Chamber of Commerce
111 Monument Circle
Suite 1950
Indianapolis, IN 46204
Phone: (317) 464-2222
Fax: (317) 464-2217
http://www.indychamber.com

The Indy Partnership
111 Monument Circle
Suite 1800
Indianapolis, IN 46204
Phone: (317) 236-6262
Fax: (317) 236-6275
http://indypartnership.com

Jacksonville, FL
Jacksonville Chamber of Commerce
3 Independent Drive
Jacksonville, FL 32202
Phone: (904) 366-6600
Fax: (904) 632-0617
http://www.myjaxchamber.com

Kansas City, MO
Greater Kansas City Chamber of Commerce
2600 Commerce Tower
911 Main Street
Kansas City, MO 64105
Phone: (816) 221-2424
Fax: (816) 221-7440
http://www.kcchamber.com

Kansas City Area Development Council
2600 Commerce Tower
911 Main Street
Kansas City, MO 64105
Phone: (816) 221-2121
Fax: (816) 842-2865
http://www.thinkkc.com

Lafayette, LA
Greater Lafayette Chamber of Commerce
804 East Saint Mary Blvd.
Lafayette, LA 70503
Phone: (337) 233-2705
Fax: (337) 234-8671
http://www.lafchamber.org

Lakeland, FL
Lakeland Chamber of Commerce
35 Lake Morton Dr.
Lakeland, FL 33801
Phone: (863) 688-8551
https://www.lakelandchamber.com

Las Vegas, NV
Las Vegas Chamber of Commerce
6671 Las Vegas Blvd South
Suite 300
Las Vegas, NV 89119
Phone: (702) 735-1616
Fax: (702) 735-0406
http://www.lvchamber.org

Las Vegas Office of Business Development
400 Stewart Avenue
City Hall
Las Vegas, NV 89101
Phone: (702) 229-6011
Fax: (702) 385-3128
http://www.lasvegasnevada.gov

Lexington, KY
Greater Lexington Chamber of Commerce
330 East Main Street
Suite 100
Lexington, KY 40507
Phone: (859) 254-4447
Fax: (859) 233-3304
http://www.commercelexington.com

Lexington Downtown Development
Authority
101 East Vine Street
Suite 500
Lexington, KY 40507
Phone: (859) 425-2296
Fax: (859) 425-2292
http://www.lexingtondda.com

Lincoln, NE
Lincoln Chamber of Commerce
1135 M Street
Suite 200
Lincoln, NE 68508
Phone: (402) 436-2350
Fax: (402) 436-2360
http://www.lcoc.com

Little Rock, AR
Little Rock Regional Chamber
One Chamber Plaza
Little Rock, AR 72201
Phone: (501) 374-2001
Fax: (501) 374-6018
http://www.littlerockchamber.com

Los Angeles, CA
Los Angeles Area Chamber of Commerce
350 South Bixel Street
Los Angeles, CA 90017
Phone: (213) 580-7500
Fax: (213) 580-7511
http://www.lachamber.org

Los Angeles County Economic
Development Corporation
444 South Flower Street
34th Floor
Los Angeles, CA 90071
Phone: (213) 622-4300
Fax: (213) 622-7100
http://www.laedc.org

Louisville, KY
The Greater Louisville Chamber of
Commerce
614 West Main Street
Suite 6000
Louisville, KY 40202
Phone: (502) 625-0000
Fax: (502) 625-0010
http://www.greaterlouisville.com

Madison, WI
Greater Madison Chamber of Commerce
615 East Washington Avenue
P.O. Box 71
Madison, WI 53701-0071
Phone: (608) 256-8348
Fax: (608) 256-0333
http://www.greatermadisonchamber.com

Manchester, NH
Greater Manchester Chamber of Commerce
889 Elm Street
Manchester, NH 03101
Phone: (603) 666-6600
Fax: (603) 626-0910
http://www.manchester-chamber.org

Manchester Economic Development Office
One City Hall Plaza
Manchester, NH 03101
Phone: (603) 624-6505
Fax: (603) 624-6308
http://www.yourmanchesternh.com

Memphis, TN
Greater Memphis Chamber
22 North Front Street, Suite 200
Memphis, TN 38103-2100
Phone: (901) 543-3500
https://memphischamber.com

Miami, FL
Greater Miami Chamber of Commerce
1601 Biscayne Boulevard
Ballroom Level
Miami, FL 33132-1260
Phone: (305) 350-7700
Fax: (305) 374-6902
http://www.miamichamber.com

The Beacon Council
80 Southwest 8th Street
Suite 2400
Miami, FL 33130
Phone: (305) 579-1300
Fax: (305) 375-0271
http://www.beaconcouncil.com

Midland, TX
Midland Chamber of Commerce
109 N. Main
Midland, TX 79701
Phone: (432) 683-3381
Fax: (432) 686-3556
http://www.midlandtxchamber.com

Milwaukee, WI
Greater Milwaukee Chamber of Commerce
6815 W. Capitol Drive
Suite 300
Milwaukee, WI 53216
Phone: (414) 465-2422
http://www.gmcofc.org

Metropolitan Milwaukee Association of
Commerce
756 N. Milwaukee Street
Suite 400
Milwaukee, WI 53202
Phone: (414) 287-4100
Fax: (414) 271-7753
https://www.mmac.org

Minneapolis, MN
Minneapolis Community Development
Agency
Crown Roller Mill
105 5th Avenue South
Suite 200
Minneapolis, MN 55401
Phone: (612) 673-5095
Fax: (612) 673-5100
http://www.ci.minneapolis.mn.us

Minneapolis Regional Chamber
81 South Ninth Street
Suite 200
Minneapolis, MN 55402
Phone: (612) 370-9100
Fax: (612) 370-9195
http://www.minneapolischamber.org

Nashville, TN
Nashville Area Chamber of Commerce
211 Commerce Street
Suite 100
Nashville, TN 37201
Phone: (615) 743-3000
Fax: (615) 256-3074
http://www.nashvillechamber.com

Tennessee Valley Authority Economic
Development
400 West Summit Hill Drive
Knoxville TN 37902
Phone: (865) 632-2101
http://www.tvaed.com

New Haven, CT
Greater New Haven Chamber of Commerce
900 Chapel Street
10th Floor
New Haven, CT 06510
Phone: (203) 787-6735
https://www.gnhcc.com

New Orleans, LA
New Orleans Chamber of Commerce
1515 Poydras Street
Suite 1010
New Orleans, LA 70112
Phone: (504) 799-4260
Fax: (504) 799-4259
http://www.neworleanschamber.org

New York, NY
New York City Economic Development
Corporation
110 William Street
New York, NY 10038
Phone: (212) 619-5000
http://www.nycedc.com

The Partnership for New York City
One Battery Park Plaza
5th Floor
New York, NY 10004
Phone: (212) 493-7400
Fax: (212) 344-3344
http://www.pfnyc.org

Oklahoma City, OK
Greater Oklahoma City Chamber of
Commerce
123 Park Avenue
Oklahoma City, OK 73102
Phone: (405) 297-8900
Fax: (405) 297-8916
http://www.okcchamber.com

Omaha, NE
Omaha Chamber of Commerce
1301 Harney Street
Omaha, NE 68102
Phone: (402) 346-5000
Fax: (402) 346-7050
http://www.omahachamber.org

Orlando, FL
Metro Orlando Economic Development
Commission of Mid-Florida
301 East Pine Street
Suite 900
Orlando, FL 32801
Phone: (407) 422-7159
Fax: (407) 425.6428
http://www.orlandoedc.com

Orlando Regional Chamber of Commerce
75 South Ivanhoe Boulevard
P.O. Box 1234
Orlando, FL 32802
Phone: (407) 425-1234
Fax: (407) 839-5020
http://www.orlando.org

Peoria, IL
Peoria Area Chamber
100 SW Water Street
Peoria, IL 61602
Phone: (309) 495-5900
http://www.peoriachamber.org

Philadelphia, PA
Greater Philadelphia Chamber of
Commerce
200 South Broad Street
Suite 700
Philadelphia, PA 19102
Phone: (215) 545-1234
Fax: (215) 790-3600
http://www.greaterphilachamber.com

Phoenix, AZ
Greater Phoenix Chamber of Commerce
201 North Central Avenue
27th Floor
Phoenix, AZ 85073
Phone: (602) 495-2195
Fax: (602) 495-8913
http://www.phoenixchamber.com

Greater Phoenix Economic Council
2 North Central Avenue
Suite 2500
Phoenix, AZ 85004
Phone: (602) 256-7700
Fax: (602) 256-7744
http://www.gpec.org

Pittsburgh, PA
Allegheny County Industrial Development
Authority
425 6th Avenue
Suite 800
Pittsburgh, PA 15219
Phone: (412) 350-1067
Fax: (412) 642-2217
http://www.alleghenycounty.us

Greater Pittsburgh Chamber of Commerce
425 6th Avenue
12th Floor
Pittsburgh, PA 15219
Phone: (412) 392-4500
Fax: (412) 392-4520
http://www.alleghenyconference.org

Portland, OR
Portland Business Alliance
200 SW Market Street
Suite 1770
Portland, OR 97201
Phone: (503) 224-8684
Fax: (503) 323-9186
http://www.portlandalliance.com

Providence, RI
Greater Providence Chamber of Commerce
30 Exchange Terrace
Fourth Floor
Providence, RI 02903
Phone: (401) 521-5000
Fax: (401) 351-2090
http://www.provchamber.com

Rhode Island Economic Development
Corporation
Providence City Hall
25 Dorrance Street
Providence, RI 02903
Phone: (401) 421-7740
Fax: (401) 751-0203
http://www.providenceri.com

Provo, UT
Provo-Orem Chamber of Commerce
51 South University Avenue
Suite 215
Provo, UT 84601
Phone: (801) 851-2555
Fax: (801) 851-2557
http://www.thechamber.org

Raleigh, NC
Greater Raleigh Chamber of Commerce
800 South Salisbury Street
Raleigh, NC 27601-2978
Phone: (919) 664-7000
Fax: (919) 664-7099
http://www.raleighchamber.org

Reno, NV
Greater Reno-Sparks Chamber of
Commerce
1 East First Street
16th Floor
Reno, NV 89505
Phone: (775) 337-3030
Fax: (775) 337-3038
http://www.reno-sparkschamber.org

The Chamber Reno-Sparks-Northern
Nevada
449 S. Virginia St.
2nd Floor
Reno, NV 89501
Phone: (775) 636-9550
http://www.thechambernv.org

Richmond, VA
Greater Richmond Chamber
600 East Main Street
Suite 700
Richmond, VA 23219
Phone: (804) 648-1234
http://www.grcc.com

Greater Richmond Partnership
901 East Byrd Street
Suite 801
Richmond, VA 23219-4070
Phone: (804) 643-3227
Fax: (804) 343-7167
http://www.grpva.com

Riverside, CA
Greater Riverside Chambers of Commerce
3985 University Avenue
Riverside, CA 92501
Phone: (951) 683-7100
https://www.riverside-chamber.com

Rochester, MN
Rochester Area Chamber of Commerce
220 South Broadway
Suite 100
Rochester, MN 55904
Phone: (507) 288-1122
Fax: (507) 282-8960
http://www.rochestermnchamber.com

Sacramento, CA
Sacramento Metro Chamber
One Capitol Mall
Suite 700
Sacramento, CA 95814
Phone: (916) 552-6800
https://metrochamber.org

Salt Lake City, UT
Department of Economic Development
451 South State Street
Room 425
Salt Lake City, UT 84111
Phone: (801) 535-7240
Fax: (801) 535-6331
http://www.slcgov.com/economic-development

Salt Lake Chamber
175 E. University Blvd. (400 S)
Suite 600
Salt Lake City, UT 84111
Phone: (801) 364-3631
http://www.slchamber.com

San Antonio, TX
The Greater San Antonio Chamber of
Commerce
602 E. Commerce Street
San Antonio, TX 78205
Phone: (210) 229-2100
Fax: (210) 229-1600
http://www.sachamber.org

San Antonio Economic Development
Department
P.O. Box 839966
San Antonio, TX 78283-3966
Phone: (210) 207-8080
Fax: (210) 207-8151
http://www.sanantonio.gov/edd

San Diego, CA
San Diego Economic Development Corp.
401 B Street
Suite 1100
San Diego, CA 92101
Phone: (619) 234-8484
Fax: (619) 234-1935
http://www.sandiegobusiness.org

San Diego Regional Chamber of Commerce
402 West Broadway
Suite 1000
San Diego, CA 92101-3585
Phone: (619) 544-1300
Fax: (619) 744-7481
http://www.sdchamber.org

San Francisco, CA
San Francisco Chamber of Commerce
235 Montgomery Street
12th Floor
San Francisco, CA 94104
Phone: (415) 392-4520
Fax: (415) 392-0485
http://www.sfchamber.com

San Jose, CA
Office of Economic Development
60 South Market Street
Suite 470
San Jose, CA 95113
Phone: (408) 277-5880
Fax: (408) 277-3615
http://www.sba.gov

The Silicon Valley Organization
101 W Santa Clara Street
San Jose, CA 95113
Phone: (408) 291-5250
https://www.thesvo.com

Santa Rosa, CA
Santa Rosa Chamber of Commerce
1260 North Dutton Avenue
Suite 272
Santa Rosa, CA 95401
Phone: (707) 545-1414
http://www.santarosachamber.com

Savannah, GA
Economic Development Authority
131 Hutchinson Island Road
4th Floor
Savannah, GA 31421
Phone: (912) 447-8450
Fax: (912) 447-8455
http://www.seda.org

Savannah Chamber of Commerce
101 E. Bay Street
Savannah, GA 31402
Phone: (912) 644-6400
Fax: (912) 644-6499
http://www.savannahchamber.com

Seattle, WA
Greater Seattle Chamber of Commerce
1301 Fifth Avenue
Suite 2500
Seattle, WA 98101
Phone: (206) 389-7200
Fax: (206) 389-7288
http://www.seattlechamber.com

Sioux Falls, SD
Sioux Falls Area Chamber of Commerce
200 N. Phillips Avenue
Suite 102
Sioux Falls, SD 57104
Phone: (605) 336-1620
Fax: (605) 336-6499
http://www.siouxfallschamber.com

Springfield, IL
The Greater Springfield Chamber of
Commerce
1011 S. Second Street
Springfield, IL 62704
Phone: (217) 525-1173
Fax: (217) 525-8768
http://www.gscc.org

Tallahassee, FL
Greater Tallahassee Chamber of Commerce
300 E. Park Avenue
P.O. Box 1638
Tallahassee, FL 32301
Phone: (850) 224-8116
Fax: (850) 561-3860
http://www.talchamber.com

Tampa, FL
Greater Tampa Chamber of Commerce
P.O. Box 420
Tampa, FL 33601-0420
Phone: (813) 276-9401
Fax: (813) 229-7855
http://www.tampachamber.com

Tucson, AZ
Tucson Metro Chamber
212 E. Broadway Blvd
Tucson, AZ 85701
Phone: (520) 792-1212
https://tucsonchamber.org

Tulsa, OK
Tulsa Regional Chamber
One West Third Street
Suite 100
Tulsa, OK 74103
Phone: (918) 585-1201
https://www.tulsachamber.com

Tuscaloosa, AL
The Chamber of Commerce of West
Alabama
2201 Jack Warner Parkway
Building C
Tuscaloosa, AL 35401
Phone: (205) 758-7588
https://tuscaloosachamber.com

Virginia Beach, VA
Hampton Roads Chamber of Commerce
500 East Main Street
Suite 700
Virginia Beach, VA 23510
Phone: (757) 664-2531
http://www.hamptonroadschamber.com

Washington, DC
District of Columbia Chamber of
Commerce
1213 K Street NW
Washington, DC 20005
Phone: (202) 347-7201
Fax: (202) 638-6762
http://www.dcchamber.org

District of Columbia Office of Planning and
Economic Development
J.A. Wilson Building
1350 Pennsylvania Ave NW
Suite 317
Washington, DC 20004
Phone: (202) 727-6365
Fax: (202) 727-6703
http://www.dcbiz.dc.gov

Wichita, KS
Wichita Regional Chamber of Commerce
350 W Douglas Avennue
Wichita, KS 67202
Phone: (316) 265-7771
https://www.wichitachamber.org

Winston-Salem, NC
Winston-Salem Chamber of Commerce
411 West Fourth Street
Suite 211
Winston-Salem, NC 27101
Phone: (336) 728-9200
http://www.winstonsalem.com

Appendix E: State Departments of Labor

Alabama
Alabama Department of Labor
P.O. Box 303500
Montgomery, AL 36130-3500
Phone: (334) 242-3072
https://www.labor.alabama.gov

Alaska
Dept of Labor and Workforce Devel.
P.O. Box 11149
Juneau, AK 99822-2249
Phone: (907) 465-2700
http://www.labor.state.ak.us

Arizona
Industrial Commission or Arizona
800 West Washington Street
Phoenix, AZ 85007
Phone: (602) 542-4411
https://www.azica.gov

Arkansas
Department of Labor
10421 West Markham
Little Rock, AR 72205
Phone: (501) 682-4500
http://www.labor.ar.gov

California
Labor and Workforce Development
445 Golden Gate Ave., 10th Floor
San Francisco, CA 94102
Phone: (916) 263-1811
http://www.labor.ca.gov

Colorado
Dept of Labor and Employment
633 17th St., 2nd Floor
Denver, CO 80202-3660
Phone: (888) 390-7936
https://www.colorado.gov/CDLE

Connecticut
Department of Labor
200 Folly Brook Blvd.
Wethersfield, CT 06109-1114
Phone: (860) 263-6000
http://www.ctdol.state.ct.us

Delaware
Department of Labor
4425 N. Market St., 4th Floor
Wilmington, DE 19802
Phone: (302) 451-3423
http://dol.delaware.gov

District of Columbia
Department of Employment Services
614 New York Ave., NE, Suite 300
Washington, DC 20002
Phone: (202) 671-1900
http://does.dc.gov

Florida
Florida Department of Economic
Opportunity
The Caldwell Building
107 East Madison St. Suite 100
Tallahassee, FL 32399-4120
Phone: (800) 342-3450
http://www.floridajobs.org

Georgia
Department of Labor
Sussex Place, Room 600
148 Andrew Young Intl Blvd., NE
Atlanta, GA 30303
Phone: (404) 656-3011
http://dol.georgia.gov

Hawaii
Dept of Labor & Industrial Relations
830 Punchbowl Street
Honolulu, HI 96813
Phone: (808) 586-8842
http://labor.hawaii.gov

Idaho
Department of Labor
317 W. Main St.
Boise, ID 83735-0001
Phone: (208) 332-3579
http://www.labor.idaho.gov

Illinois
Department of Labor
160 N. LaSalle Street, 13th Floor
Suite C-1300
Chicago, IL 60601
Phone: (312) 793-2800
https://www.illinois.gov/idol

Indiana
Indiana Department of Labor
402 West Washington Street, Room W195
Indianapolis, IN 46204
Phone: (317) 232-2655
http://www.in.gov/dol

Iowa
Iowa Workforce Development
1000 East Grand Avenue
Des Moines, IA 50319-0209
Phone: (515) 242-5870
http://www.iowadivisionoflabor.gov

Kansas
Department of Labor
401 S.W. Topeka Blvd.
Topeka, KS 66603-3182
Phone: (785) 296-5000
http://www.dol.ks.gov

Kentucky
Department of Labor
1047 U.S. Hwy 127 South, Suite 4
Frankfort, KY 40601-4381
Phone: (502) 564-3070
http://www.labor.ky.gov

Louisiana
Louisiana Workforce Commission
1001 N. 23rd Street
Baton Rouge, LA 70804-9094
Phone: (225) 342-3111
http://www.laworks.net

Maine
Department of Labor
45 Commerce Street
Augusta, ME 04330
Phone: (207) 623-7900
http://www.state.me.us/labor

Maryland
Department of Labor, Licensing &
Regulation
500 N. Calvert Street
Suite 401
Baltimore, MD 21202
Phone: (410) 767-2357
http://www.dllr.state.md.us

Massachusetts
Dept of Labor & Workforce Development
One Ashburton Place
Room 2112
Boston, MA 02108
Phone: (617) 626-7100
http://www.mass.gov/lwd

Michigan
Department of Licensing and Regulatory
Affairs
611 W. Ottawa
P.O. Box 30004
Lansing, MI 48909
Phone: (517) 373-1820
http://www.michigan.gov/lara

Minnesota
Dept of Labor and Industry
443 Lafayette Road North
Saint Paul, MN 55155
Phone: (651) 284-5070
http://www.doli.state.mn.us

Mississippi
Dept of Employment Security
P.O. Box 1699
Jackson, MS 39215-1699
Phone: (601) 321-6000
http://www.mdes.ms.gov

Missouri
Labor and Industrial Relations
P.O. Box 599
3315 W. Truman Boulevard
Jefferson City, MO 65102-0599
Phone: (573) 751-7500
https://labor.mo.gov

Montana
Dept of Labor and Industry
P.O. Box 1728
Helena, MT 59624-1728
Phone: (406) 444-9091
http://www.dli.mt.gov

Nebraska
Department of Labor
550 S 16th Street
Lincoln, NE 68508
Phone: (402) 471-9000
https://dol.nebraska.gov

Nevada
Dept of Business and Industry
3300 W. Sahara Ave
Suite 425
Las Vegas, NV 89102
Phone: (702) 486-2750
http://business.nv.gov

New Hampshire
Department of Labor
State Office Park South
95 Pleasant Street
Concord, NH 03301
Phone: (603) 271-3176
https://www.nh.gov/labor

New Jersey
Department of Labor & Workforce
Development
John Fitch Plaza, 13th Floor
Suite D
Trenton, NJ 08625-0110
Phone: (609) 777-3200
http://lwd.dol.state.nj.us/labor

New Mexico
Department of Workforce Solutions
401 Broadway, NE
Albuquerque, NM 87103-1928
Phone: (505) 841-8450
https://www.dws.state.nm.us

New York
Department of Labor
State Office Bldg. # 12
W.A. Harriman Campus
Albany, NY 12240
Phone: (518) 457-9000
https://www.labor.ny.gov

North Carolina
Department of Labor
4 West Edenton Street
Raleigh, NC 27601-1092
Phone: (919) 733-7166
https://www.labor.nc.gov

North Dakota
North Dakota Department of Labor and
Human Rights
State Capitol Building
600 East Boulevard, Dept 406
Bismark, ND 58505-0340
Phone: (701) 328-2660
http://www.nd.gov/labor

Ohio
Department of Commerce
77 South High Street, 22nd Floor
Columbus, OH 43215
Phone: (614) 644-2239
http://www.com.state.oh.us

Oklahoma
Department of Labor
4001 N. Lincoln Blvd.
Oklahoma City, OK 73105-5212
Phone: (405) 528-1500
https://www.ok.gov/odol

Oregon
Bureau of Labor and Industries
800 NE Oregon St., #32
Portland, OR 97232
Phone: (971) 673-0761
http://www.oregon.gov/boli

Pennsylvania
Dept of Labor and Industry
1700 Labor and Industry Bldg
7th and Forster Streets
Harrisburg, PA 17120
Phone: (717) 787-5279
http://www.dli.pa.gov

Rhode Island
Department of Labor and Training
1511 Pontiac Avenue
Cranston, RI 02920
Phone: (401) 462-8000
http://www.dlt.state.ri.us

South Carolina
Dept of Labor, Licensing & Regulations
P.O. Box 11329
Columbia, SC 29211-1329
Phone: (803) 896-4300
http://www.llr.state.sc.us

South Dakota
Department of Labor & Regulation
700 Governors Drive
Pierre, SD 57501-2291
Phone: (605) 773-3682
http://dlr.sd.gov

Tennessee
Dept of Labor & Workforce Development
Andrew Johnson Tower
710 James Robertson Pkwy
Nashville, TN 37243-0655
Phone: (615) 741-6642
http://www.tn.gov/workforce

Texas
Texas Workforce Commission
101 East 15th St.
Austin, TX 78778
Phone: (512) 475-2670
http://www.twc.state.tx.us

Utah
Utah Labor Commission
160 East 300 South, 3rd Floor
Salt Lake City, UT 84114-6600
Phone: (801) 530-6800
https://laborcommission.utah.gov

Vermont
Department of Labor
5 Green Mountain Drive
P.O. Box 488
Montpelier, VT 05601-0488
Phone: (802) 828-4000
http://labor.vermont.gov

Virginia
Dept of Labor and Industry
Powers-Taylor Building
13 S. 13th Street
Richmond, VA 23219
Phone: (804) 371-2327
http://www.doli.virginia.gov

Washington
Dept of Labor and Industries
P.O. Box 44001
Olympia, WA 98504-4001
Phone: (360) 902-4200
http://www.lni.wa.gov

West Virginia
Division of Labor
749 B Building 6
Capitol Complex
Charleston, WV 25305
Phone: (304) 558-7890
https://labor.wv.gov

Wisconsin
Dept of Workforce Development
201 E. Washington Ave., #A400
P.O. Box 7946
Madison, WI 53707-7946
Phone: (608) 266-6861
http://dwd.wisconsin.gov

Wyoming
Department of Workforce Services
1510 East Pershing Blvd.
Cheyenne, WY 82002
Phone: (307) 777-7261
http://www.wyomingworkforce.org

2021 Title List

Visit www.GreyHouse.com for Product Information, Table of Contents, and Sample Pages.

Opinions Throughout History

Opinions Throughout History: The Death Penalty
Opinions Throughout History: Diseases & Epidemics
Opinions Throughout History: Drug Use & Abuse
Opinions Throughout History: The Environment
Opinions Throughout History: Gender: Roles & Rights
Opinions Throughout History: Globalization
Opinions Throughout History: Guns in America
Opinions Throughout History: Immigration
Opinions Throughout History: Law Enforcement in America
Opinions Throughout History: National Security vs. Civil &
    Privacy Rights
Opinions Throughout History: Presidential Authority
Opinions Throughout History: Robotics & Artificial Intelligence
Opinions Throughout History: Social Media Issues
Opinions Throughout History: Sports & Games
Opinions Throughout History: Voters' Rights

This is Who We Were

This is Who We Were: Colonial America (1492-1775)
This is Who We Were: 1880-1899
This is Who We Were: In the 1900s
This is Who We Were: In the 1910s
This is Who We Were: In the 1920s
This is Who We Were: A Companion to the 1940 Census
This is Who We Were: In the 1940s (1940-1949)
This is Who We Were: In the 1950s
This is Who We Were: In the 1960s
This is Who We Were: In the 1970s
This is Who We Were: In the 1980s
This is Who We Were: In the 1990s
This is Who We Were: In the 2000s
This is Who We Were: In the 2010s

Working Americans

Working Americans—Vol. 1: The Working Class
Working Americans—Vol. 2: The Middle Class
Working Americans—Vol. 3: The Upper Class
Working Americans—Vol. 4: Children
Working Americans—Vol. 5: At War
Working Americans—Vol. 6: Working Women
Working Americans—Vol. 7: Social Movements
Working Americans—Vol. 8: Immigrants
Working Americans—Vol. 9: Revolutionary War to the Civil War
Working Americans—Vol. 10: Sports & Recreation
Working Americans—Vol. 11: Inventors & Entrepreneurs
Working Americans—Vol. 12: Our History through Music
Working Americans—Vol. 13: Education & Educators
Working Americans—Vol. 14: African Americans
Working Americans—Vol. 15: Politics & Politicians
Working Americans—Vol. 16: Farming & Ranching
Working Americans—Vol. 17: Teens in America

Education

Complete Learning Disabilities Resource Guide
Educators Resource Guide
The Comparative Guide to Elem. & Secondary Schools
Charter School Movement
Special Education: A Reference Book for Policy & Curriculum
    Development

Grey House Health & Wellness Guides

Autoimmune Disorders Handbook & Resource Guide
Cancer Handbook & Resource Guide
Cardiovascular Disease Handbook & Resource Guide
Dementia Handbook & Resource Guide

Consumer Health

Autoimmune Disorders Handbook & Resource Guide
Cancer Handbook & Resource Guide
Cardiovascular Disease Handbook & Resource Guide
Comparative Guide to American Hospitals
Complete Mental Health Resource Guide
Complete Resource Guide for Pediatric Disorders
Complete Resource Guide for People with Chronic Illness
Complete Resource Guide for People with Disabilities
Older Americans Information Resource

General Reference

African Biographical Dictionary
American Environmental Leaders
America's College Museums
Constitutional Amendments
Encyclopedia of African-American Writing
Encyclopedia of Invasions & Conquests
Encyclopedia of Prisoners of War & Internment
Encyclopedia of Rural America
Encyclopedia of the Continental Congresses
Encyclopedia of the United States Cabinet
Encyclopedia of War Journalism
The Environmental Debate
The Evolution Wars: A Guide to the Debates
Financial Literacy Starter Kit
From Suffrage to the Senate
The Gun Debate: Gun Rights & Gun Control in the U.S.
History of Canada
Historical Warrior Peoples & Modern Fighting Groups
Human Rights and the United States
Political Corruption in America
Privacy Rights in the Digital Age
The Religious Right and American Politics
Speakers of the House of Representatives, 1789-2021
US Land & Natural Resources Policy
The Value of a Dollar 1600-1865 Colonial to Civil War
The Value of a Dollar 1860-2019
World Cultural Leaders of the 20th Century

Business Information

Business Information Resources
The Complete Broadcasting Industry Guide: Television, Radio,
    Cable & Streaming
Directory of Mail Order Catalogs
Environmental Resource Handbook
Food & Beverage Market Place
The Grey House Guide to Homeland Security Resources
The Grey House Performing Arts Industry Guide
Guide to Healthcare Group Purchasing Organizations
Guide to U.S. HMOs and PPOs
Guide to Venture Capital & Private Equity Firms
Hudson's Washington News Media Contacts Guide
New York State Directory
Sports Market Place

Grey House Publishing | Salem Press | H.W. Wilson | 4919 Route, 22 PO Box 56, Amenia NY 12501-0056

2021 Title List

Visit www.GreyHouse.com for Product Information, Table of Contents, and Sample Pages.

Statistics & Demographics

America's Top-Rated Cities
America's Top-Rated Smaller Cities
The Comparative Guide to American Suburbs
Profiles of America
Profiles of California
Profiles of Florida
Profiles of Illinois
Profiles of Indiana
Profiles of Massachusetts
Profiles of Michigan
Profiles of New Jersey
Profiles of New York
Profiles of North Carolina & South Carolina
Profiles of Ohio
Profiles of Pennsylvania
Profiles of Texas
Profiles of Virginia
Profiles of Wisconsin

Canadian Resources

Associations Canada
Canadian Almanac & Directory
Canadian Environmental Resource Guide
Canadian Parliamentary Guide
Canadian Venture Capital & Private Equity Firms
Canadian Who's Who
Cannabis Canada
Careers & Employment Canada
Financial Post: Directory of Directors
Financial Services Canada
FP Bonds: Corporate
FP Bonds: Government
FP Equities: Preferreds & Derivatives
FP Survey: Industrials
FP Survey: Mines & Energy
FP Survey: Predecessor & Defunct
Health Guide Canada
Libraries Canada
Major Canadian Cities: Compared & Ranked, First Edition

Weiss Financial Ratings

Financial Literacy Basics
Financial Literacy: How to Become an Investor
Financial Literacy: Planning for the Future
Weiss Ratings Consumer Guides
Weiss Ratings Guide to Banks
Weiss Ratings Guide to Credit Unions
Weiss Ratings Guide to Health Insurers
Weiss Ratings Guide to Life & Annuity Insurers
Weiss Ratings Guide to Property & Casualty Insurers
Weiss Ratings Investment Research Guide to Bond & Money
    Market Mutual Funds
Weiss Ratings Investment Research Guide to Exchange-Traded
    Funds
Weiss Ratings Investment Research Guide to Stock Mutual Funds
Weiss Ratings Investment Research Guide to Stocks

Books in Print Series

American Book Publishing Record® Annual
American Book Publishing Record® Monthly
Books In Print®
Books In Print® Supplement
Books Out Loud™
Bowker's Complete Video Directory™
Children's Books In Print®
El-Hi Textbooks & Serials In Print®
Forthcoming Books®
Law Books & Serials In Print™
Medical & Health Care Books In Print™
Publishers, Distributors & Wholesalers of the US™
Subject Guide to Books In Print®
Subject Guide to Children's Books In Print®

Grey House Publishing | Salem Press | H.W. Wilson | 4919 Route, 22 PO Box 56, Amenia NY 12501-0056

2021 Title List

Visit www.SalemPress.com for Product Information, Table of Contents, and Sample Pages.

LITERATURE

Critical Insights: Authors

Louisa May Alcott
Sherman Alexie
Isabel Allende
Maya Angelou
Isaac Asimov
Margaret Atwood
Jane Austen
James Baldwin
Saul Bellow
Roberto Bolano
Ray Bradbury
Gwendolyn Brooks
Albert Camus
Raymond Carver
Willa Cather
Geoffrey Chaucer
John Cheever
Joseph Conrad
Charles Dickens
Emily Dickinson
Frederick Douglass
T. S. Eliot
George Eliot
Harlan Ellison
Louise Erdrich
William Faulkner
F. Scott Fitzgerald
Gustave Flaubert
Horton Foote
Benjamin Franklin
Robert Frost
Neil Gaiman
Gabriel Garcia Marquez
Thomas Hardy
Nathaniel Hawthorne
Robert A. Heinlein
Lillian Hellman
Ernest Hemingway
Langston Hughes
Zora Neale Hurston
Henry James
Thomas Jefferson
James Joyce
Jamaica Kincaid
Stephen King
Martin Luther King, Jr.
Barbara Kingsolver
Abraham Lincoln
Mario Vargas Llosa
Jack London
James McBride
Cormac McCarthy
Herman Melville
Arthur Miller
Toni Morrison
Alice Munro
Tim O'Brien
Flannery O'Connor
Eugene O'Neill

George Orwell
Sylvia Plath
Philip Roth
Salman Rushdie
Mary Shelley
John Steinbeck
Amy Tan
Leo Tolstoy
Mark Twain
John Updike
Kurt Vonnegut
Alice Walker
David Foster Wallace
Edith Wharton
Walt Whitman
Oscar Wilde
Tennessee Williams
Richard Wright
Malcolm X

Critical Insights: Works

Absalom, Absalom!
Adventures of Huckleberry Finn
Aeneid
All Quiet on the Western Front
Animal Farm
Anna Karenina
The Awakening
The Bell Jar
Beloved
Billy Budd, Sailor
The Book Thief
Brave New World
The Canterbury Tales
Catch-22
The Catcher in the Rye
The Crucible
Death of a Salesman
The Diary of a Young Girl
Dracula
Fahrenheit 451
The Grapes of Wrath
Great Expectations
The Great Gatsby
Hamlet
The Handmaid's Tale
Harry Potter Series
Heart of Darkness
The Hobbit
The House on Mango Street
How the Garcia Girls Lost Their Accents
The Hunger Games Trilogy
I Know Why the Caged Bird Sings
In Cold Blood
The Inferno
Invisible Man
Jane Eyre
The Joy Luck Club
King Lear
The Kite Runner
Life of Pi
Little Women

Lolita
Lord of the Flies
Macbeth
The Metamorphosis
Midnight's Children
A Midsummer Night's Dream
Moby-Dick
Mrs. Dalloway
Nineteen Eighty-Four
The Odyssey
Of Mice and Men
One Flew Over the Cuckoo's Nest
One Hundred Years of Solitude
Othello
The Outsiders
Paradise Lost
The Pearl
The Poetry of Baudelaire
The Poetry of Edgar Allan Poe
A Portrait of the Artist as a Young Man
Pride and Prejudice
The Red Badge of Courage
Romeo and Juliet
The Scarlet Letter
Short Fiction of Flannery O'Connor
Slaughterhouse-Five
The Sound and the Fury
A Streetcar Named Desire
The Sun Also Rises
A Tale of Two Cities
The Tales of Edgar Allan Poe
Their Eyes Were Watching God
Things Fall Apart
To Kill a Mockingbird
War and Peace
The Woman Warrior

Critical Insights: Themes

The American Comic Book
American Creative Non-Fiction
The American Dream
American Multicultural Identity
American Road Literature
American Short Story
American Sports Fiction
The American Thriller
American Writers in Exile
Censored & Banned Literature
Civil Rights Literature, Past & Present
Coming of Age
Conspiracies
Contemporary Canadian Fiction
Contemporary Immigrant Short Fiction
Contemporary Latin American Fiction
Contemporary Speculative Fiction
Crime and Detective Fiction
Crisis of Faith
Cultural Encounters
Dystopia
Family
The Fantastic
Feminism

Grey House Publishing | Salem Press | H.W. Wilson | 4919 Route, 22 PO Box 56, Amenia NY 12501-0056

SALEM PRESS

2021 Title List

Visit www.SalemPress.com for Product Information, Table of Contents, and Sample Pages.

SALEM PRESS

Flash Fiction
Gender, Sex and Sexuality
Good & Evil
The Graphic Novel
Greed
Harlem Renaissance
The Hero's Quest
Historical Fiction
Holocaust Literature
The Immigrant Experience
Inequality
LGBTQ Literature
Literature in Times of Crisis
Literature of Protest
Magical Realism
Midwestern Literature
Modern Japanese Literature
Nature & the Environment
Paranoia, Fear & Alienation
Patriotism
Political Fiction
Postcolonial Literature
Pulp Fiction of the '20s and '30s
Rebellion
Russia's Golden Age
Satire
The Slave Narrative
Social Justice and American Literature
Southern Gothic Literature
Southwestern Literature
Survival
Technology & Humanity
Violence in Literature
Virginia Woolf & 20th Century Women Writers
War

Critical Insights: Film
Bonnie & Clyde
Casablanca
Alfred Hitchcock
Stanley Kubrick

Critical Approaches to Literature
Critical Approaches to Literature: Feminist
Critical Approaches to Literature: Moral
Critical Approaches to Literature: Multicultural
Critical Approaches to Literature: Psychological

Critical Surveys of Literature
Critical Survey of American Literature
Critical Survey of Drama
Critical Survey of Graphic Novels: Heroes & Superheroes
Critical Survey of Graphic Novels: History, Theme, and
    Technique
Critical Survey of Graphic Novels: Independents and
    Underground Classics
Critical Survey of Graphic Novels: Manga
Critical Survey of Long Fiction
Critical Survey of Mystery and Detective Fiction
Critical Survey of Mythology & Folklore: Gods & Goddesses
Critical Survey of Mythology & Folklore: Heroes and Heroines
Critical Survey of Mythology & Folklore: Love, Sexuality, and
    Desire
Critical Survey of Mythology & Folklore: World Mythology
Critical Survey of Poetry
Critical Survey of Poetry: Contemporary Poets
Critical Survey of Science Fiction & Fantasy Literature
Critical Survey of Shakespeare's Plays
Critical Survey of Shakespeare's Sonnets
Critical Survey of Short Fiction
Critical Survey of World Literature
Critical Survey of Young Adult Literature

Cyclopedia of Literary Characters & Places
Cyclopedia of Literary Characters
Cyclopedia of Literary Places

Introduction to Literary Context
American Poetry of the 20th Century
American Post-Modernist Novels
American Short Fiction
English Literature
Plays
World Literature

Magill's Literary Annual
Magill's Literary Annual, 2021
Magill's Literary Annual, 2020
Magill's Literary Annual, 2019

Masterplots
Masterplots, Fourth Edition
Masterplots, 2010-2018 Supplement

Notable Writers
Notable African American Writers
Notable American Women Writers
Notable Mystery & Detective Fiction Writers
Notable Native American Writers & Writers of the American West
Novels into Film: Adaptations & Interpretation
Recommended Reading: 600 Classics Reviewed

Grey House Publishing | Salem Press | H.W. Wilson | 4919 Route, 22 PO Box 56, Amenia NY 12501-0056